CARTRIDGES OF THE WORLD

A COMPLETE AND ILLUSTRATED REFERENCE FOR MORE THAN 1,500 CARTRIDGES

FRANK C. BARNES
Edited by RICHARD A. MANN

Published by

Gun Digest® Books, an imprint of F+W Media, Inc.
Krause Publications • 700 East State Street • Iola, WI 54990-0001
715-445-2214 • 888-457-2873
www.krausebooks.com

To order books or other products call toll-free 1-800-258-0929
or visit us online at www.gundigeststore.com

ISBN-13: 978-1-4402-3059-2
ISBN-10: 1-4402-3059-5

Edited by Richard A. Mann and Jennifer L.S. Pearsall
Cover Design by Al West
Designed by Al West

Printed in USA

About the Covers

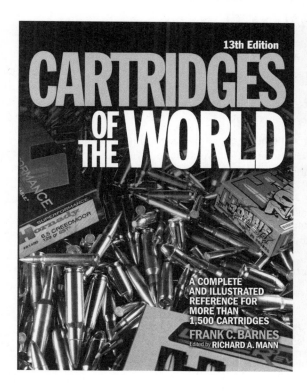

Hornady in the Spotlight

As has become traditiion, a number of Hornady's products grace the covers of this *Cartridges of the World 13th Edition*. This time we asked them to mix it up a little, focus on the products that truly speak the Hornady name, and that's just what the company did.

Topping the list is the LEVERevolution round, perhaps one of the most exciting creations to ever happen to lever-gun ammunition. The cleverly named round design brings you an innovation in ammunition performance that features patented, state of the industry, FTX (Flex Tip eXpanding) and MonoFlex bullets that are safe in tubular magazines. Before Hornady introduced this design, lever-gun/afficionados were limited to round-nose bullet profiles that wouldn't punch the primer of the round next in line in the tube magazine and set off a gun and body-part altering chain-fire reaction. But long-range and terminal performance of such rounds was limited. No longer. LEVERevolution's high ballistic coefficient delivers dramatically flatter trajectories and amazing bullet expansion at all ranges. It truly is an evolution in lever-gun ammunition!

See that really tiny cartridge in the mix? The shooting virtues of Hornady's .17 HMR (Hornady Magnum Rimfire) are now the stuff of legend—high velocity, flat trajectory, and long-range accuracy. The devastating V-MAX and XTP bullets deliver characteristics that takes the .17 HMR into the realm of the true hunting cartridge,and it's a great choice for small-game and varmint hunting.

Did you notice something different in the front cover? A dash of flourescent green? That's Hornady's ZOMBIE MAX ammunition and the proprietary PROVEN Z-MAX bullets. Honestly, it's been a long time since tongue-in-cheek marketing genius and a genuinely good product have gone so well together. This is the company that got the zombie craze started and these rounds are a force to be reckoned with, especially if you're a prairie dog ... or a member of the un-dead—have *you* seen a Zombie? See, PROVEN isn't just an adjective, it's part of the bullet name proper!

On a more serious note is Hornady's 6.5 Creedmoor with a pedigreed as storied as it is precise. Developed by Dave Emary, Hornady's Senior Ballistic Scientist, and Dennis DeMille, General Manager of Creedmoor Sports and two-time NRA National High Power champion, this cartridge was designed to allow any shooter to compete at the highest level with factory-loaded ammunition. Built for match rifles, including the Tubb 2000 and DPMS, its case is slightly shorter than the 260 Remington, eliminating any "cartridge overall length" issues when using .308 Winchester-length magazines.

Another round unique to the wizards at the Hornady laboratories became the .30 T/C (Thompson/Center). According to Horandy, many of today's so-called "short mags" are nothing more than an attempt to see how much powder can fit behind the bullet in a .308 Winchester-length magazine. Little thought is given to the crucial balance between case volume, bore volume, and the burn rates of different propellants. Well, Hornady and Thompson/Center give the short mags a run for their money with this highly individualized round. Specifically designed for T/C's Icon bolt-action rifle, the .30 T/C sports optimized case geometry, while advanced propellants deliver (or exceed!) .30-06 ballistic performance in a short-action case.

Finally, on our back cover is a glamour shot of Hornady's Critical Defense line of ammo. Law enforcement and tactical professionals now have a truly advanced handgun ammunition solution that delivers the most consistent and reliable urban barrier performance ever created! The proven Flex Tip design of the new FlexLock bullet eliminates clogging and aids bullet expansion. Its large, mechanical, jacket-to-core InterLock band works to keep the bullet and core from separating, resulting in maximum weight retention and proven terminal performance through all FBI test barriers.

Foreword

Sportsmen and firearms enthusiasts in general are fond of indulging in a timeless, endless discussion that usually begins something like this: "If you had the opportunity to hunt all over the world, but due to space-weight limitations could carry only one gun, what would it be?" This simple assumption is good for hours or even days of lively debate. Also, on occasion, a few fist fights. This is mentioned, not to engage in any phase of this classic argument, but because it is apropos to a summary of this book.

Let me put it this way, if you were traveling to Mars or some other planet by rocket ship, and because of space-weight limitations could carry only one book on cartridges, what would it be? We sincerely hope it would be this one, because it contains more usable information per pound than any other single book on the subject.

As of this writing, there is no record of any copies of *Cartridges of the World* having been carried to other worlds, although the effort did get off the ground here on earth. The many letters received by the author and editors indicate that we certainly followed the right path in our treatment of the many known cartridges. The word used most often in describing this book is "useful." We consider this a high compliment, because it describes our original objective—to publish a useful cartridge book. We sincerely believe the buyer of this edition will also find it so.—*Frank C. Barnes*

Dedications

To my parents, Clifford and Margaret Barnes, whose encouragement of my boyhood dreams and ambitions made all that came later possible, this book is wholeheartedly dedicated.—*F.C.B.*

This *13th Edition* is dedicated to my parents, who knew guns were not bad things, and to all my junior high and high school teachers who didn't freak out when I drew pictures of guns, cartridges, and bullets in my notebooks.—*Richard A. Mann*

Acknowledgments

For this and past editions of *Cartridges of the World*, we wish to give special thanks to the following people and organizations for their contributions toward the various improvements and additions:

Bill Ball, freelance journalist
Randy Brooks, CEO, Barnes Bullets
Steve Comus, Publications Director, Safari Club International
Michael Cyrus, Cross Outdoors / Lehigh Defense
Chris Ellis, Ellis Communications
Kevin Howard, President, Howard Communications
Hornady Manufacturing, Inc.
Tim Janzen, Chief Ballistician, Barnes Bullets
J.D. Jones, President, SSK Industries
Mike Jordan, Senior Account Executive, Howard Communications
Dave Kiff, Pacific Tool & Guage
Dr. Ken Oehler, Oehler Research, Inc.
Christer Larsson, Norma
Jeff Patterson, Swanson Russell Agency
Rick Patterson, SAAMI
Carroll Pilant, Ballistician, Sierra Bullets
Gary Reeder, Reeder Custom Guns

Contents

About the Covers: Hornady in the Spotlight 3

Introduction 6

About the Author and Editor 7

Preface 8

Chapter 1: Cartridge Nomenclature 9

Chapter 2: Current American Rifle Cartridges 13
Centerfire Sporting—Blackpowder and Smokeless

Chapter 3: Obsolete American Rifle Cartridges 106
Centerfire Sporting—Blackpowder and Smokeless

Chapter 4: Wildcat Cartridges 165
Rifle and Handgun

Chapter 5: Proprietary Cartridges 248
Rifle and Handgun

Chapter 6: Handgun Cartridges of the World 322
Current and Obsolete—Blackpowder and Smokeless

Chapter 7: Military Rifle Cartridges of the World 371
Current and Obsolete— Blackpowder and Smokeless

Chapter 8: British Sporting Rifle Cartridges 401
Current and Obsolete—Blackpowder and Smokeless

Features: AR-15 Cartridges—by J. Guthrie 433
SAAMI—by John Haviland 438
Wildcats—by Chub Eastman 448
Cartridge Identification—by Frank C. Barnes 453

Chapter 9: European Sporting Rifle Cartridges 457
Current and Obsolete—Blackpowder and Smokeless

Chapter 10: American Rimfire Cartridges 490
Current and Obsolete

Chapter 11: Shotgun Shells 509
Current and Obsolete—Blackpowder and Smokeless

Chapter 12: U.S. Military Ammunition 5.56 to 20mm 527
Description and Identification

Chapter 13: Cartridge Identification by Measurement 539

Introduction

The original philosophy worked out by myself and the late John T. Amber (the original editor) was to assemble a practical and useful book that would appeal to as broad a spectrum of the shooting fraternity as possible. The sales record of the book over the years indicates that this was the proper approach. The *11th Edition* carries on in the same tradition as the previous editions in offering both something new, as well as retaining old data that is either useful or of general interest. There is really not much that can be done in the area of, say, obsolete cartridges, because nothing changes except that occasionally one or two of the old-timers will be reintroduced. This requires moving such cartridges back into the chapter covering modern cartridges, or, on the other hand, some commercially loaded number will be discontinued and relegated to the obsolete designation. Such changes are updated in this next edition. We have retained the encyclopedic reference format and are continuing to present the information from a shooter's and hunter's point of view.

Included is information covering handgun, rifle, shotgun, obsolete blackpowder, European, British, military, wildcat, and proprietary cartridges, along with data on the guns that shoot these cartridges, something for everyone. The information was obtained from many sources, including textbooks, new and old catalogs, periodicals, and individuals. Amber supplied many out-of-print and rare cartridge catalogs from his extensive library. Much information is from the author's and editors' files, as well as other original sources, and will not be found elsewhere. Practical experience also weighs heavily in the balance. I had more than 50 years of hunting, shooting, reloading and collecting experience. Amber was a gun collector with extensive hunting experience in North America, Europe, and Africa. Ken Warner, successor to Amber and former editor of *Gun Digest*, is also a collector, hunter, and shooter with many years of experience. This collective experience is reflected in the pages of this book.

The book is divided into chapters based on each category of ammunition: Current American Rifle, Obsolete American Rifle, Handgun, Military, etc. Ballistics and basic loading data have been included with each cartridge listing if possible. Extensive dimensional charts and tables are found at the end of each chapter. Dimensional data is presented in this manner, rather than with the individual cartridges, in order to simplify the identification of unknown cartridges. Cartridges are listed in the order of increasing bullet diameter, or, if caliber is the same, by length or power. One of the more difficult facts to establish with certainty is the date of origin for older obsolete cartridges. This is a matter of some importance to historians and, occasionally, archaeologists digging into our recent past when they find spent cases or cartridges in graves or on old battlefields. It can be useful when attempting to determine the caliber of certain guns or the relationship between firearms, ammunition and historical events. Those who write western novels or make similar movies might be well served if they would peruse the pages of this book, so that they would not constantly be placing the wrong guns in the wrong time period. It might surprise them to discover that the U.S. Cavalry in the 1870s did not carry either Model 1892 or 1894 Winchester lever-action carbines. These guns were unavailable then, and none of the cartridges those rifles chambered were ever adopted by the military.

Many law-enforcement agencies and military organizations have found *Cartridges of the World* to be a worthwhile reference source. It is also used as a basic text in colleges and universities for firearms identification courses. Firearms identification involves working with cartridges as much as working with firearms. *Cartridges of the World* even made it into television when it showed up in one episode of the once-popular cop show, *Miami Vice*.

Under the heading "General Comments," an effort has been made to rate the various cartridges for hunting purposes. Admittedly, any such ratings are highly subjective, since there is no quantitative formula for determining what cartridge is suitable for what game. Evidence (or lack thereof), observations in the hunting field, and personal opinion inevitably enter this process. If the reader takes issue with the author or editor regarding the efficacy of a particular cartridge for some specific purpose, it doesn't necessarily follow that someone is wrong. Rather,

the problem is evaluated from different points of view. I remember reading several years ago about a fellow in Africa who fired a .22 Long Rifle at an elephant in an effort to scare it away from his garden. Unfortunately, he hit the poor beast and dropped it in its tracks with a single, misplaced round, and then really had a hell of a time getting it out. I hardly think that this qualifies the .22 Long Rifle as an elephant round, although some might think so. Also, many years ago, I ran into an old-time trapper in the Yukon Territory who had a much-used Savage Model 99 lever-action rifle chambered for the .303 Savage. He handloaded all his ammunition with hand-cast 190-grain bullets at a muzzle velocity of about 1950 fps, insisting this .30-30-class combination was more than adequate for moose, grizzly bear, or anything else—and with his experience as a woodsman, trapper, and hunter, it was. But not many present-day gun writers would agree. So ideas about what's good for what in the world of hunting cartridges depends a good deal on personal experience, skill, and opinion.

Finally we come to the subject of which cartridges should or should not be included within the pages of *Cartridges of the World*. Obviously, this book does not include every known cartridge in the world. If it did, it would have to be divided into many volumes. From time to time, certain readers write rather irate letters wondering why such-and-such a cartridge has not been included (or why we bothered to include certain cartridges). Admittedly, there must be hundreds of cartridges and variations that have been excluded. There are several reasons for this. First, editorial constraints on the number of pages don't leave sufficient room to include everything in one volume. The book has to be kept in balance to appeal to a general, rather than a specific, audience. Second, while most gun nuts are casual cartridge collectors, only a few shooters are avid cartridge collectors. There are already a large number of excellent books aimed specifically at the cartridge collector per se, such as those written by Charles Suydam, Herschel Logan, Fred Datig, and others. The criteria used in this book to determine what cartridges to include are based largely on what the author and editor perceive as being of greatest general interest, what has historical significance, or is of unusual interest. In this edition, we have expanded the proprietary and wildcat cartridge chapters, and others have new additions, as well. In fact, we included more than 50 new cartridges, easily identified with "NEW" and a schematic of dimensions. As we mentioned, though, we are always under a page contraint here, and if you add some, something has to give. To that end we relocated about 100 of the weirdest, most hard-to-come-by, and esoteric rounds from the paper pages to the CD included here. In all, the author and the editors have tried to please as many potential readers as possible, but remember, as in the biblical parable of the man and his donkey, it is impossible to please everybody.

—*Frank C. Barnes, with additional text by J.L.S.P.*

DISCLAIMER: Any and all loading data found in this book or previous editions is to be taken as reference material *only*. The publishers, editors, authors, contributors, and their entities bear no responsibility for the use by others of the data included in this book or the editions that came before it.

WARNING: For any modern firearm, it is essential that you adhere to the loading recommendations put forth in the reloading manuals of today's components manufacturers, as well as to the owners manual of the maker of your individual firearm (some of today's firearms are so specialized that they will chamber and function reliably only within a very narrow set of criteria in a given caliber range). The potential for things to go wrong is exacerbated in guns long out of production, those chambering obsolete cartridges, and those using cartridges containing blackpowder or cordite. As a seperate caution, you must *never* fire any cartridge in any gun just because it looks similar to, or has a similar designation to, the cartridge the gun is chambered for. This can be *extremely* dangerous. Almost is not good enough, so if you are at all uncertain about the proper cartridge, have a competent gunsmith check the bullet diameter and case dimensions and firearms chamber and headspace.

About the Author

It is not given to many of us in the bookish trades to create perennials, books that go on and on. A fellow named Webster did it with dictionaries, and a woman named Irma Rombauer hit a good lick with *Joy of Cooking* and Frank C. Barnes made the grade with this very book, *Cartridges of the World*.

Actually, Barnes was not, at the beginning, very deeply into bookish stuff. He was more of a doer. However, *COTW* caught him well and truly and held him, one edition after another, for decades.

Barnes died in 1992 and was sick awhile before that. It was during his illness that he handed over the job, sure that the book would go on for decades.

He was born in Chicago, June 25, 1918. He began collecting cartridge data about age 12, which would be about 1930.

Before he began to write of guns and ammunition, he made a living as a geologist-engineer and spent a lot of time in the field in the West and Southwest. He did not "go hunting," he said many times, because he was already there. This experience made Barnes a practical hunter/rifleman, entitled to his opinions on rifles and shotguns and their cartridges. Barnes came to the same sort of competence with handguns even earlier; his father was a police officer who let his son shoot his sidearms if he kept them clean. The net result was a practical sort of fellow, and his principal creation, *Cartridges of the World*, is a practical sort of book. He decided it should cover all the cartridges that count, that it should be a great guide to all of those and not get lost in the esoteric worlds of headstamps and variations. It proved a good plan.

Barnes was a pilot and raced sports cars and rode motorcycles. Eventually he received a Master's Degree in Justice and taught law enforcement matters at the college level.

And he designed cartridges, too, becoming a respected wildcatter. When he generated the 458 American by cutting ½-inch off the redoubtable .458 Winchester Magnum, Barnes put it into a practical rifle. His shortened big-bore fit very nicely into a short-actioned 722 Remington stocked to the muzzle.

Barnes' last project, his last wildcat, was another practical sort of thing. It involved a .416 on the .45-70 case fitted into the Marlin Model 1895 lever-action rifle. This one was not to be, though—he just didn't get it finished. He did finish enough in his 74 years, however. If he's remembered as long as this book lasts, that's a lot longer than the rest of us ever count on.

About the Editor

Richard A. Mann was born and raised in the West Virginia hills. He has chased coon hounds until daylight, waited out whitetails while perched high in an oak, canoed the New River, and hunted from the Montana Mountains to the Green Hills of Africa. During service in the Army, and later as a municipal police officer and Special Agent with the Railroad Police, Richard obtained numerous certifications in small arms instruction. He has trained military personnel, law enforcement officers, and civilians in the application of firearms for defensive, competitive, and recreational use. Richard won the West Virginia Governor's Twenty Award, the West Virginia National Guard State Pistol Competition, and earned his Distinguished Medal with pistol.

Badge and camo turned in, Richard is now a contributing editor for the National Rifle Association publications and several other magazines. He was the compiling author of the book, *Rifle Bullets for the Hunter* and conceptualized and contributed to the book *Selecting and Ordering a Custom Hunting Rifle.* Richard has patents on a rifle scope reticle and a revolutionary bullet testing media.

A self-proclaimed hillbilly at heart, Richard lives on Shadowland (his shooting range in West Virginia), with the most understanding wife in the world, their three kids, and a giant German shepherd.

Preface

The book you are holding in your hand is not just a reference manual. It is an ever-evolving historical document. I agreed to edit the *13th Edition of Cartridges of the World* very likely for many of the same reasons you are reading it. Shooters are very passionate about cartridges, often to almost a Frosty the Snowman level of hysteria. They think there "Must have been some magic in ..." this or that cartridge. I hate to be the bearer of bad news even before you start the first chapter, but there is no real magic.

In the absence of magic, we have passion, and passion can, in a way, be like magic—good or bad. I grew up in a hunting family and started early. I spent 51 weeks each year looking forward to the one week of deer season, when our extended family would gather at camp. I loved the atmosphere and the stories. More than anything, though, I loved the guns and the ammunition. I was fascinated by the sound of actions working, the shapes of cartridges and bullets, and the numbers and letters stamped on cases.

I had an uncle by marriage who could best be described as the rear end of a mule. We'll call him Jack. Every day we had to listen to him extol the virtues of his .30-06. For me, his personality imprinted itself on that cartridge to the point I disliked it as much as him. To this day, I've yet to hunt with a .30-06 and see no reason to mend my ways. That's bad magic.

On the other hand, when Dad bought his first deer rifle, he selected Winchester model 100 in .243 Winchester. I watched him use that open-sighted rifle through my youth to take groundhogs and deer. You can imagine the impression it made on me, and it should come as no surprise that the .243 Winchester is one of my favorites. When I hunt with a .243, I feel as though a little bit of Dad is with me. That's good magic.

Like others who are obsessed with the minutia of ballistics, I've also thought I could make my own cartridge, something better than I could buy off the shelf. "Wildcatting," as it's known, is the process of altering a current cartridge by changing its shape and/or the caliber bullet it fires. Most wildcat cartridges are never anything more than one person's 15 seconds of fame, but some like the .257 Roberts become greatest hits. Many do not understand the concept of wildcat cartridges, which is why I asked firearms oracle Chub Eastman to write about them for this *13th Edition.*

Wildcat cartridges live on the outskirts of reality, beyond the confines that commercial cartridges must operate in. These confines are established by the Sporting Arms and Ammunition Manufacturer's Institute (SAAMI). SAAMI is an organization most shooters are even less familiar with, but it exists as the reason for the ammo you purchase for your .30-06 actually working in your rifle and that it is safe. A book about cartridges with no information on SAAMI is like Snoopy without the Red Baron. In this Edition, John Haviland—the most knowledgeable handloader I know—addresses SAAMI and what it does.

Both of these chapters provide relevant information not contained in any previous edition of *Cartridges of the World,* a book that has become the preeminent reference for cartridges. Shooters reference *Cartridges of the World* for a variety of reasons. I think it's safe to say that *Cartridges of the World* readers represent a good cross section of shooters. Some want technical information, some historic information, and some are just plain curious. This diverse readership presents somewhat a challenge for an editor, because the content must provide a mix of all, without doting too much on a single aspect.

For example; my research found that about half the readers liked to see cartridge photographs and half enjoyed the schematics with dimensions. Not sure how to balance this, it was decided that all of the new cartridges for this Edition would be presented with a detailed drawing, while all previously covered cartridge entries would be supported by a photo.

As with any book of this magnitude, there will be some editing errors, but *Cartridges of the World* presents some more fascinating challenges. It is without question a treasure trove of information, the culmination of 47 years of research by eight different editors

and many others. Not only does it contain detailed and historical information on hundreds of cartridges, it is a reflection of each of those editor's opinions and experiences.

You'll see contradictions that are not supported by ballistic science. For example, a comment about the .22-250 says it, "... is not recommended for use on deer ..." but a comment about the .220 Swift says it, "... is considered adequate on all animals up to deer size." For all practical purposes, these cartridge are ballistic twins, so why this anomaly?

Several reasons. In 1965, when the first edition of Cartridges of the World was published, there were no .224-caliber bullets suitable for deer. Also at that time, there were a number of beliefs about cartridges and calibers that were considered rules of thumb, because they had not been challenged. And, finally, when it comes to a description of the proper application of cartridges, comments are based to a great extent on the real-world experiences of the persons writing about them.

Today, there is no question that many .224-caliber centerfire cartridges are capable deer cartridges. Newer bullets have, as they say, "Changed the game." I've used the .223 Remington extensively on deer, as have both my sons, and with complete satisfaction. To correct the misconception that .22-caliber rifles will not work on deer, you'll see a "13th Edition Update" on some of these cartridges and others that clarify this and similar things that have changed.

Why was the original text not just changed to reflect modern advances? *Cartridges of the World* is as much a historical document as it is a technical manual and user's guide. Some things that might be considered wrong with *Cartridges of the World* are, in fact, the things that make it the important book that it is. The times, notions, and reality change, and this book reflects those changes. Your experiences or mine, along with what is fact, does not alter history, it adds to it. So, as you absorb this book, consider that, while you may find things inconsistent with conventional wisdom, this book represents the evolution of conventional wisdom, and that is important, too.

Another example of this is the recent fascination with the AR 15-style rifle, which is currently the most popular rifle in the world. If there's any doubt, about 25 percent of the new cartridges included in the *13th Edition* were designed for or will work in an AR 15. Because of this, there is a chapter dedicated to cartridges for the AR 15 penned by J. Guthrie. Due to his starring role in the *Modern Sporting Rifle* television show, Guthrie has a tremendous level of experience with ARs and the cartridges they fire.

My goal as editor of the *13th Edition* was not to "fix" every technical inconsistency or to undo or discount the work of previous editors. It was only to make the book better. I'd like to think I've done that, and just so you'll know who to blame when you read something you consider good or bad magic—something that increases or diminishes your passion about a cartridge or caliber—you'll find my initials "R.A.M." after my contributions. This also dates the work new to this Edition.

In closing let me thank you for purchasing the most comprehensive, technical, and historical guide to cartridges ever assembled. Let me also suggest that, when you read about a particular cartridge, you also read the introduction to the chapter containing that cartridge. The chapter introductions set the framework for this book and will help you better understand the information presented on each cartridge. Every one of which, someone, somewhere, is or at one time was very passionate about.

— *Richard A. Mann*

Cartridge Nomenclature

It is difficult or impossible for the novice to follow the action without some knowledge of cartridge caliber designation. Even the individual experienced with standard American ammunition may be ignorant of British, European, or even obsolete American cartridge nomenclature. The subject, regrettably, is full of inconsistencies and confusion.

With the majority of American, British, or European (metric) cartridges, the caliber (indicating bore land diameter in $1/100$-inch) is the first figure given. However, there are exceptions that will be pointed out later. Caliber may be given in terms of bullet or bore diameter (land or groove), and is neither accurate nor consistent. For example, we have the .307 Winchester cartridge, which uses the same .308-inch diameter bullet as the .308 Winchester. Then there is the .458 Winchester Magnum and the .460 Weatherby Magnum, both of which are loaded with the same .458-inch diameter bullet. Similar examples abound. In the latter example, the Weatherby people didn't want anyone to get their round mixed up with the Winchester design, so they changed the figures a little. That is one reason some cartridges do not follow in normal caliber designation in the dimensional tables. There are others.

The second figure, if there is one, is usually some distinguishing feature such as case length or powder charge. Cartridges of European origin are, almost without exception, designated in metric units by caliber and case length. Obsolete American cartridges, or any that have a blackpowder origin, are designated by caliber and powder charge weight, or caliber-powder/charge-bullet weight (the last two in grain weight). Smokeless powder charges vary so widely with the powder type and grain structure that this system is no longer used. However, there are again such exceptions as the .30-30 Winchester and .30-40 Krag. Here, the second figure represents the original smokeless powder charge, although it no longer has anything to do with it. With blackpowder cartridges the designation .45-70 Springfield means a .45-caliber bullet with 70 grains of blackpowder; or .45-70-405 spells out the same cartridge, with a 405-grain bullet to distinguish it from such other bullet loadings as the .45-70-500. But then there was the .45-56-405 carbine load in the same case!

The truth of the matter is the American "system" of cartridge nomenclature really hasn't any system to it, and what there is can only be learned through reading and experience. Otherwise, you simply never know what is meant. For example, take the .30-06, a very popular military and sporting round. Here, the first figure shows the caliber, while the last two numbers are the date of origin. In other words, a .30-caliber cartridge—model of 1906. Or, again, the .250-3000 Savage (.25-3000 simply lacked that special "ring" the advertising folks wanted). This translates out as a .25-caliber cartridge firing a bullet at 3,000 fps muzzle velocity. The bullet diameter is actually .257-inch and muzzle velocity varies with bullet weight from 2,800 to over 3,000 fps. Some of the older blackpowder cartridges included the case length and type; thus the .44-90 Sharps $2\frac{5}{8}$-inch necked, or .45-120 Sharps $3\frac{1}{4}$-inch straight. As you can see, cartridge nomenclature isn't a system at all—it's a code.

The British, to a large extent, follow the same "system" as we do. However, they add to the general confusion with such cartridges as the .577/450 or .500/465. Here, the second figure gives the approximate bullet diameter in $1/1000$-inch, and what is meant is that the .577 case is necked to .450-caliber, while the

.500 case is necked to .465-caliber. The Britih may also add the case length. At this point, it is necessary to point out that some American wildcat (noncommercial) cartridges dreamed up by individual experimenters are designated by a similar though opposite system. Here, we have such cartridges as the 8mm-06, .30-338, and .25-06. These work out as an 8mm based on the .30-06 case, a .30-caliber based on the .338 Winchester case, and a .25-caliber based on the .30-06 case. Confusing indeed!

The Europeans have evolved the only real system of cartridge designation that is consistent and somewhat meaningful. Dimensions are in millimeters, including bore land diameter, case length, and type. The 7x57mm Mauser is a cartridge, for example, for use with a 7mm bore land size (7.21mm groove size), with a 57mm rimless case. The 9.3x74Rmm is a 9.3mm caliber with a 74mm rimmed case. The "R" denotes the rimmed type, while its absence indicates a rimless case. The name of the originator or manufacturer may follow. This is a relatively simple and straightforward system, but, unfortunately, it isn't perfect, either. The Germans used two rim types in some of their older cartridges, and this resulted in duplicate designations of cartridges that differ only in the rim (9.05x36.4R, 10.85x24.9R, etc.), and there must be at least three 9.3x72mm cartridges that differ only in case configuration. This is all something of a mess and probably too late to change. Mister Barnes, in an effort to straighten things out (or perhaps add to the confusion), developed two wildcat cartridges that he designated as the .308x1½-inch and .458x2-inch.

To further elucidate, the reader needs to know that there are two major classifications of cartridges—centerfire and rimfire. The former is fired by a primer located in the center of the case head, the latter by the priming compound distributed around the entire inside of the rim's outer diameter. The modern centerfire cartridge primer is removable and replaceable, so that the case can be reloaded after it is fired. It is possible, but not practical, to reload rimfire cases after they have been fired. Centerfire cartridges are subdivided into two types based on the primer, Berdan and Boxer. The Berdan-primed case has the anvil as a separate protrusion, or teat, in the bottom of the primer pocket. The Boxer primer is completely self-contained, and its anvil is a part of the primer. All American-made ammunition is normally Boxer-primed, whereas much British and European ammunition is Berdan-primed. Most foreign-made ammunition manufactured for the American market has the Boxer-type primer.

Rim Types

There are four common types of centerfire cartridge cases based on rim type. These are rimmed, rimless, semi-rimmed, and belted. The British equivalents are flanged, rimless, semi-flanged, and belted. There is a fifth type, not widely used, which is the rebated rimless, in which the rim is of smaller diameter than the base of the case. Examples would be the .284 Winchester and .30 Remington AR. The .41 Action Express pistol cartridge is also rebated. The purpose of the rebated rim is to allow the use of a standard diameter bolt with a larger diameter cartridge. In the past, there have been a few rimless cases without the usual extractor groove.

Both centerfire and rimfire cartridges may be of straight or necked type. Contrary to popular opinion, the necked case was *not* designed to provide greater velocity for smokeless powder cartridges. It evolved back in blackpowder days as a means of getting the same powder charge in a shorter case, thus allowing the repeating actions of the day to handle cartridges of the same power as the single-shots with their long, straight cartridges. Some of the very early rimfire cartridges were of the necked type.

The latest fad in cartridges is the caseless, or combustible type, an idea not really all that very new, as it acutally dates back to the early 1800s or before. The original design used a nitrated paper or cloth container for the powder charge, and sometimes, also, the bullet. The entire package was loaded into the gun, and the powder and its container were consumed in firing. During World War II, the Germans began an intense research and development program to perfect caseless ammunition and design weapons to shoot it. The principal motivating factor at the time was the severe shortage of brass and other metal for cartridge cases. The Germans are known to have had at least partial success with caseless cartridges, and some insist complete success. United States military ordnance facilities, as well as private industry, have been working on the problem of caseless ammunition for the past 50 years or more. There has been considerable success in developing caseless and partially caseless artillery rounds, but there are still many problems in the small arms field. Obturation is a big problem, as is ejecting a misfired round from the chamber of a repeating action. Modern caseless ammunition usually consists of compressed powder grains fastened to the base of the bullet, or the powder may be encased in a plastic case made of the same material as the propellant. Ignition may be percussion or electrical, and there is, in some types, a booster charge extending through the center of the powder charge.

Cartridge Collectors

Though this book is not a collectors' manual, it nonetheless includes considerable material of use and interest to collectors or any serious student of cartridges and related weapons. The tables of dimensions are organized to facilitate cartridge identification. The key to reading these tables lies in the bullet diameter and case type. The reader must understand that, in measuring cartridge dimensions, certain manufacturing tolerances must be allowed, and these can affect the last, or even the second, decimal figure. Dimensional tolerances can be rather considerable with old blackpowder cartridges and the modern bottlenecked numbers. Also, the true diameter of the obsolete paper-patched bullet should include the patch, not just the lead slug protruding from it. Minor variations in dimensions should not be mistaken for errors or the existence of an unknown caliber.

The dimensional tables can also be used to identify the caliber of a gun if the chamber dimensions are known. This can best be determined by a chamber casting. The means of doing this is explained in Chapter 3. If you own an obsolete or foreign gun for which ammunition is not available, the tables of dimensions will assist in determining whether ammunition can be made by reforming some similar existing case.

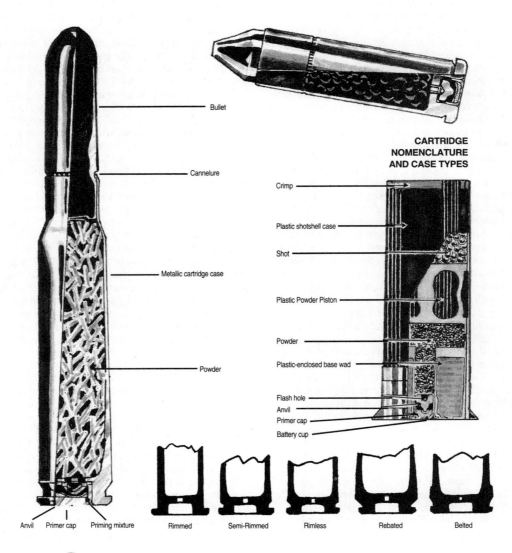

Bullet

Cannelure

Metallic cartridge case

Powder

Anvil   Primer cap   Priming mixture

CARTRIDGE NOMENCLATURE AND CASE TYPES

Crimp

Plastic shotshell case

Shot

Plastic Powder Piston

Powder

Plastic-enclosed base wad

Flash hole
Anvil
Primer cap
Battery cup

Rimmed   Semi-Rimmed   Rimless   Rebated   Belted

Metallic Cartridge Development

The self-contained metallic cartridge is a fairly modern development, one perfected only about 1850. The use of blackpowder as a propellant in guns in the Western world goes back something like 650 years, and the knowledge of gunpowder more than 700 years. The Chinese knew about gunpowder 500 or 600 years before it was introduced to Europeans, although they used it as fireworks and not as a propellant any earlier than the Europeans. The centerfire cartridge, a necessary prerequisite to our modern ammunition, evolved during the 1860s and '70s. Smokeless powder and high-velocity cartridges date back only to the 1890s. Improvements since the turn of the century have been more in the area of improved ignition, powder chemistry, and bullet construction, rather than cartridge design. Charles Newton designed cartridges back around 1910 that, had modern powders been available, would have equaled the performance of present-day high-velocity developments of similar caliber and type. Smokeless powder military cartridges designed between 1888 and 1915 were so good that improvement was possible only after more advanced powders became available, and many of these cartridges were still in use through World War II. As the result of this situation, many modern innovations in the gun and cartridge field turn out, after a little investigation, to be a reintroduction of something really quite old.

A few examples of the not-really-very-new among modern cartridges are worth pointing out. The .244 Remington (6mm) makes a good case to start with. Introduced in 1955, it is based on the .257 Roberts case necked down, which in turn is the 7x57mm Mauser slightly modified. Back in 1895, or thereabout, the Germans had a 6x57mm, made by necking down the 7x57mm Mauser. With the exception of a slight (insignificant) difference in the shoulder angle, the .244 Remington is a carbon copy of this much older cartridge.

The 7mm Remington Magnum is another brilliant "design" that is really just a modification of a much older cartridge. It is very similar to the .275 Holland & Holland Magnum introduced around 1912 or 1913. However, the H&H round didn't have a good American smokeless powder of later development to bring out its full potential. On the other hand, there are a number of wildcat 7mm short-belted magnums practically identical to the 7mm Remington Magnum that pre-date it by quite a few years and are identical in performance.

Yet another Remington innovation is the .280 Remington, a rimless cartridge based on the .30-06 case necked down. This is a dead ringer for the 7x64mm Brenneke, introduced in 1917. It is also practically identical to the wildcat 7mm-06 developed around 1928, so there is nothing very original here. However, none of these cartridges are interchangeable.

The commercial manufacturers are not alone in their design duplication. Many individuals have inadvertently done the same thing. One of the most popular wildcat cartridges anyone has thought up is the .35 Whelen, introduced about 1922 and adopted as a commercial standard by Remington, in 1987. This is simply the .30-06 case necked-up to .35-caliber and was originated by the late Col. Townsend Whelen. It is a very close copy of the German 9x63mm, which dates back to about 1905. As a matter of fact, a number of wildcat cartridges are nothing more than a duplication of some much older British or European designs. In fairness, it must be stated that the originator of the wildcat version probably was completely unaware of the existence of a parallel cartridge at the time.

Some companies and wildcatters go to considerable trouble to complete the circle, often coming up with something that duplicates a long-forgotten cartridge. If they were more familiar with the history of cartridge development, they could save a lot of time. The .444 Marlin, introduced during 1964, is a good case in point. To begin with, it is a poorly disguised copy of the wildcat .44 Van Houten Super that pre-dates it by at least three years. According to Parker Ackley, in his *Handbook for Shooters and Reloaders*, the .44 VHS is made by necking up the .30-40 Krag case, trimming it to two inches, and turning down the rim. When this is done, we end up with a near carbon copy of the 10.3x65Rmm Swiss cartridge (DWM 237A) that originated around 1900 or earlier. The only difference is in the fact that the 10.3mm case is .3-inch longer than the .44 VHS or .2-inch longer than the .444 Marlin. However, that's not all there is to the story, because the 10.3x65Rmm cartridge is based on the brass .410 shotgun shell loaded with a conical bullet and fired in a rifled barrel. It is possible to make the .444 Marlin from brass .410 cases, and the new originators could have done the same thing in the beginning.

Cartridges don't just happen—they evolve in response to some need or use requirement. Our Western frontier dictated American cartridge development for 50 years or more. Its influence is still an important factor in directing the imagination of the modern hunter. British rifle cartridges, in the main, were designed for conditions existing in other parts of the world, such as Africa and India, rather than the home island. European cartridges were developed on one hand because of hunting conditions and available game on the European continent, and on the other to compete with American and British innovations. Since the end of World War II, there has been considerable blending and standardization of the various worldwide cartridge designs. More British and European rifles and cartridges are used by American gun buffs than ever before, and they, in turn, have adopted many of our ideas.

Modern Ammunition

The most important factor influencing the ammunition available at any given time is economics. The ammunition manufacturers are willing to produce anything that will sell, but, obviously, are most reluctant to tool up and turn out something for which there is little or no demand. Military developments, as illustrated by the .30 Carbine, .30-06, 7.62mm NATO (.308 Winchester), 5.56mm (.223 Remington), .45 ACP, and that old standby, the .45-70, have almost always provided a good long-term sales record, when introduced in sporting version. For this reason, the ammunition companies have usually been quick to adopt these. They have not been quite so enthusiastic in their attitude toward cartridges developed by individuals or wildcatters. However, Remington has been the leader in introducing commercial versions of what were originally wildcat cartridges. They initiated the trend with the .257 Roberts back in 1934 and, since 1945, have added a number of others including the .17 Remington, .22-250 Remington, 6mm Remington, .25-06 Remington, 7mm-08, 7mm Remington Magnum, and the 8mm Remington Magnum, to name most of them. Actually, we must recognize that Winchester adopted the .22 Hornet (an original wildcat development), in 1930. Also, the .300 Winchester Magnum and possibly the .358 Winchester were around in wildcat versions before the company decided to develop something similar. The .444 Marlin is another cartridge based on an original wildcat innovation. Since most of these have had good sales records, it would not be surprising to see some of the other more popular wildcats introduced in commercial version as time goes on. This is a healthy trend, and we hope it will continue.

Nostalgia is another factor that is now exerting considerable influence on ammunition and firearms trends. Shooting muzzleloading and blackpowder cartridge guns of all types is a solidly established facet of the shooting game. Although there have always been a few muzzleloading clubs and a small core of blackpowder devotees, the current popularity of this sport has given birth to a whole new industry specializing in the manufacture of replica arms. Muzzleloading clubs with several hundred members are now common, and most states have special muzzleloading big-game hunting seasons. As an example of the magnitude of this development, Colt's once again sold its cap-and-ball revolvers, Harrington & Richardson offered replicas of the U.S. 1873 Trapdoor cavalry carbine, Shiloh Rifle Mfg. will sell you 1874 Sharps carbines and rifles, and one can buy any number of Hawken-type muzzleloading replicas. What is mentioned here is only a very small portion of what is available to blackpowder shooters. If you are interested in the full extent of the offerings in this field, I suggest you buy the latest edition of *Gun Digest* (from the same publishers that produce this book) and look in the manufacturer's web directory in the back of the book.

How does all this affect modern cartridges? The nostalgia syndrome is responsible for the reappearance of a number of long-obsolete cartridges, or at least new reloadable cases, although, admittedly, this is as yet on a rather limited or custom basis for most of the old-timers. Dixie Gun Works, for example, is offering new, reloadable cases in the old .50-70 Government caliber and has recently brought in the .41 Rimfire. The development of modern cartridges is a dynamic, rather than a static, process, although it does move in starts and stops, depending on the fads and trends of any given time. These, then, are the factors that shape our modern ammunition, and this includes some very exciting innovations (some old and some new) since the first edition of *Cartridges of the World*.

Cartridge Loading Data

Basic loading data has been furnished as part of the general information on each cartridge when available and if test rifles or cartridges were obtainable. Insofar as possible, the loads listed are for those powders that provide the most efficient velocity and energy for the caliber and bullet weight involved. With old blackpowder cartridges or obsolete smokeless powder numbers, the objective has been to supply data that more or less duplicates the original factory performance figures. The cartridge loading data has been gathered from various published sources and the extensive experience of the author and various editors. The data selected for inclusion in *COTW* provides a good starting point for the handloader, but there are many more good powders available for loading each cartridge than can possibly be presented here. It is therefore recommended that the serious reloader obtain one or more of the very fine reloading manuals published by Krause Publications, Lyman, Speer, Hornady, Hodgdon, Sierra, Nosler, P.O. Ackley, and others. Loading data listed here does not necessarily agree with that published elsewhere, regarding the velocity obtainable with a given charge of powder, because the test conditions and equipment are not the same. There is no such thing as absolute loading data, and all published loads reflect the conditions of test firing, which includes a number of important variables such as barrel length, chamber configuration, temperature, components used, test equipment, etc.

All loading data, wherever published, should be used with caution and common sense. If you are not sure or don't know what you are doing, *don't do it!* Since neither the author, editors, nor publisher has any control over the components, assembly of the ammunition, arms it is to be fired in, the degree of knowledge involved or how the resulting ammunition might be used, no responsibility, either implied or expressed, is assumed for the use of any of the cartridge loading data in this edition of *COTW*.

Cartridge Dimensional Data

The reader should understand that the cartridge schematics and the table of cartridge dimensional data at the end of this book are based either on actual cartridge measurements, SAAMI specs, or other drawings. In some instances, data is based on measurement of a single specimen. In others, it may be an average taken from several cartridges of different manufacture. The table is intended primarily to assist the reader in identifying cartridges, and its use for the purpose of chambering rifles is *not* recommended unless checked carefully against manufacturers' chamber dimensions. The reason? There are far greater differences in cartridge dimensions between makes and production lots than most people realize. There are differences in the third decimal place even within most 20-round boxes, in fact.

This brings up another point. From time to time the editors will receive letters from readers complaining that their measurement of some cartridge dimension does not agree with ours and, therefore, we must be wrong. We have, for example, two letters before us— one claiming a certain figure is too high, the other stating that the very same figure is too low. The differences are all in the third decimal place. This is not a matter of anyone being wrong, but rather variances in manufacturing tolerance.

As a more specific example of the tolerance factor, I acquired a box of 10mm pistol ammunition for the Bren 10 and other semi-autos and, in measuring several rounds, found some discrepancy in the rim diameters. Just to see what the minimum and maximum figures were, I measured the entire 20-round box. It turned out that the minimum rim diameter was .419-inch and the maximum was .426-inch, or a difference of .007-inch. Is that a sufficient range to cause the pistol to malfunction? I hardly think so.

All of this is just to get the subject of cartridge dimensions into proper perspective. In any event, if your measurements don't match someone else's by a few thousandths of an inch, don't get excited and don't get the idea you may have discovered a new and heretofore unknown cartridge. You may be dealing with maximum and the other guy with minimum dimensions.—*Frank C. Barnes*

CHAPTER
2

Current American Sporting Cartridges
(Centerfire Rifle)

The criterion used to determine which cartridges should be included in Chapter 2 is the requirement that the cartridge be currently manufactured and available to the American sportsman through local dealers, either on an over-the-counter basis, or by special order, since no gun store carries every single item of ammunition that is manufactured.

The cartridges listed here include not only the most modern developments, but also some that are ancient and obsolete by any standard. The characteristic they share is that they are manufactured on a commercial basis, still used, and rifles are available chambered for the round, although perhaps not made by the major American arms companies. Two of the oldest American centerfire cartridges included in this group are the .44-40 Winchester and the .45-70 Government, both of which originated in 1873 and have been in continuous use since. Several replica rifles are now chambered for the .44-40, and the .45-70 has staged a remarkable comeback. Both modern and replica rifles are being chambered for the .45-70. The popularity of this grand old military and sporting cartridge continues to increase.

One thing that can be said about many cartridges in Chapter 2 is that they have stood the test of time and include among their number the best and most useful designs available to the American shooter. Some of those that ended up in second place, often for good reasons, but sometimes for no reason anyone could reasonably understand or explain, will be found on the CD of obsolte cartrdges that accompanies this book. Interestingly, nostalgia is in the process of moving a few of these formerly obsolete rounds back into Chapter 2.

For many years, the new trend in cartridge and rifle design has been toward high velocity and flat trajectory, often at the expense of almost any other consideration. It appears to be the fashionable thing, in some circles, to show up on a big-game hunt with the largest caliber or most powerful rifle in the crowd. This odd psychosis is partly responsible for the success of the Weatherby line of rifles and cartridges, although prestige and owning a perceived superior product also enter into this. The major gun manufacturers in the United States were slow in recognizing this as a fact of life, but have since closed the gap. Modern high-velocity magnum cartridges can cancel out some small measure of poor judgment in estimating range or lead if the shooter can handle the added recoil and muzzle blast without flinching.

The editors, at various times, owned and shot most of the modern magnum rifles and handguns and have a very high regard for their capabilities, but also have reservations as to any real need for the larger calibers under normal North American hunting conditions. A great deal depends, of course, on what is to be hunted and under what conditions. Is there any actual advantage, for example, in owning a .300 Magnum if your hunting area is confined to, say, southern California? What game would one encounter there so large or so dangerous that would require all this extra power? Yes, I understand the magnum might provide an extra 100-yard sure-hit range. But, with a little practice in range estimation, wouldn't something like the .257 Roberts, .270 Winchester, or the .30-06 do just as well? Be that as it may, one should never disparage a man's wife, his automobile, or his favorite hunting rifle. Therefore, far be it for me to make enemies by casting aspersions on those who favor the magnum cartridges for whatever reason. My only point is that one doesn't need a magnum to kill a mouse, not that there is anything wrong with doing so. In any event, if you are looking for the latest and the most powerful, it will be found in Chapter 2.

The reader who is trying to determine which of the current American rifle cartridges best suits his hunting needs should first determine what game animals he intends to hunt. Second, he should decide which type of rifle action is preferred: bolt-, lever-, semi-auto, pump-, or single-shot. Next, sit down with a copy of *Gun Digest* or a variety of gun catalogs to see what calibers are available for the different actions. Finally, give some careful and realistic thought as to how the gun is to be used, type of cover, average range, and the variety of game animals to be legally hunted. Once you have all of these factors in hand, check through the cartridges listed in this chapter and pick the one that matches your particular needs and situation. Don't select the most powerful or the one with the highest velocity in the ballistics tables unless this actually offers some real advantage to you. Bear in mind that high velocity and flat trajectory offer no advantage if the bulk of your hunting is confined to brush or heavy timber with ranges that average only 50 yards or so. On the other hand, a big, heavy, slow bullet won't put meat in the freezer if you are shooting antelope at 300 yards and beyond. Always bear in mind that the 20 foot-pounds of recoil energy produced by cartridges in the .30-06 class is about all the average person can stand without flinching badly. In other words, use a little common sense and be realistic in your choice of hunting calibers. All the velocity, energy, and killing power in the world is of no value if you can't hit anything with the rifle.—*F.C.B.*

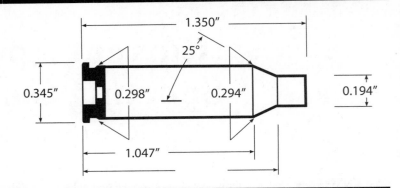

NEW
.17 Hornet

Historical Notes: With the introduction of the .17 HMR rimfire cartridge, in 2002, interest in .17-caliber cartridges has been rejuvenated. Hornady's .17 Hornet is the latest centerfire .17-caliber offering. The .17 Hornet uses the .22 Hornet as a parent case. The shoulder angle is increased from 5 to 25 degrees, and the shoulder diameter is increased, as well. The result is more powder capacity. Balistically, the .17 Hornet duplicates the performance of the 60-year-old .17 Ackley Hornet developed by P.O. Ackley. The major difference between the two is the 38-degree shoulder angle of the Ackley wildcat.

General Comments: Hornady wisely worked with Ruger to launch the .17 Hornet. Ruger's fine little 77/22 Hornet bolt-action rifle only needs a new barrel to be compatible with the .17 Hornet. Initially, Hornady will be offering a single load, a 20-grain V-Max with a muzzle velocity of 3650 fps. This is about 600 fps slower than the two other popular .17-caliber centerfire cartridges, the .17 Remington Fireball, or the .17 Remington. The .17 Hornet should show less barrel fouling and wear than either of these faster .17s. Out to about 400 yards, the trajectory of the .17 Hornet is very similar to a .223 Remington loaded with a 55-grain bullet. The .17 Hornet should prove to be a fine rifle for gophers or prairie dogs and even larger varmints inside 200 yards.—R.A.M.

.17 Hornet Loading Data and Factory Ballistics

Bullet (grains/type)	Powder	Grains	Velocity	Energy	Source
20 V-Max	AA 1680	10.7	3650	591	Hornady
20 V-Max	FL		3650	591	Hornady Factory Load

.17 Remington Fireball

Historical Notes: One of many wildcats dreamed up by P.O. Ackley through the years was the .17/221 Fireball, which is the .221 Remington Fireball case necked down for bullets measuring .172-inch in diameter. When Las Vegas gunsmith Vern O'Brien started building custom rifles around the small Sako L461 action, he obtained permission from Ackley to chamber them for the .17/221 but decided to rename it the .17 Mach IV. O'Brien offered the same chambering in custom single-shot pistols built on the XP-100 action, but called it the .17 Mach III, due to lower velocities from their shorter barrels. As is commonly seen in more than one wildcat, dimensions can vary slightly among makers of chamber reamers which means that even though at first glance the .17 Remington Fireball appears to be the old .17 Mach IV with a different name, a closer inspection may reveal minor dimensional differences. For this reason, Remington discourages the firing of .17 Fireball ammunition in rifles chambered to .17 Mach IV and vice versa.

General Comments: Even though case dimensions of the .17 Fireball can differ a bit from those of the .17 Mach IV, the two cartridges are virtually identical in powder capacity and for this reason their velocity potential is the same. Capable of accelerating a 20-grain bullet along at over 4000 fps, the trajectory of the .17 Fireball is quite flat, and mild recoil makes the little cartridge lots of fun to shoot. Contrary to what has been written about the .17 Mach IV in the past and will likely be written about the .17 Fireball in the future, neither cartridge is capable of matching the velocities of the .17 Remington which is on a modified version of the more capacious .223 Remington case. It has also been written that bullet jacket fouling builds up more rapidly in a rifle chambered for the .17 Remington, but the original auhor of this book found this to be untrue when the three cartridges are used in barrels having bores of equal quality and smoothness.

.17 Remington Fireball Loading Data and Factory Ballistics

Bullet (grains/type)	Powder	Grains	Velocity	Energy	Source
20 Hornady V-Max	H4198	17.3	4037	722	Hodgdon
20 Hornady V-Max	H335	20.5	4027	719	Hodgdon
25 Hornady HP	Benchmark	19.0	3745	778	Hodgdon
25 Hornady HP	IMR-4198	16.2	3692	756	Hodgdon
30 Berger HP	H322	18.0	3533	831	Hodgdon
30 Berger HP	Benchmark	18.7	3569	848	Hodgdon
20 AccuTip-V	FL		4250	802	Remington
25 HP	FL		3850	823	Remington

.17 Remington

Historical Notes: The .17 Remington was introduced, in 1971, as a new caliber for Remington's 700 series bolt-action rifles. It is the smallest caliber centerfire rifle cartridge offered on a commercial basis to date. The case is based on the .223 Remington necked-down to .17-caliber, with the shoulder moved back .087-inch to lengthen the neck while retaining the same shoulder angle. The .17 Remington is similar but not identical to the .17-223 wildcat developed about 1965. Experiments with .17-caliber rifles go back to 1944, when P.O. Ackley, the well-known gunsmith and experimenter, developed the .17 Ackley Bee based on necking down the Improved .218 Bee case. There are a number of other .17-caliber wildcat cartridges made by necking down .22-caliber centerfire cases, such as the .221 Remington Fireball, .222 Remington, etc. Remington, Ultra Light Arms, Wichita, and Sako offer rifles in this caliber.

General Comments: The .17 Remington has had a steady, though unspectacular, sales record since its introduction. Its greatest drawback is that it is a special-purpose cartridge suited almost exclusively for varmint shooting. For the sportsman who wants a rifle only for that purpose, this is not a disadvantage, but those requiring a rifle for both varmint and deer hunting would be better served with some other caliber.

With the 25-grain hollowpoint bullet loaded by Remington and similar bullets available for handloading by Hornady, the .17 Remington must be rated as a short-range varmint cartridge. On the other hand, it has certain advantages such as minimal recoil and ricochet probability, and a very flat trajectory due to the high initial velocity of over 4000 fps. Disadvantages include: rapid barrel fouling, extreme sensitivity to slight charge weight variation, and limited component availability. Factory loaded ammunition is available only from Remington. (New advances, such as moly-plated bullets and cleaner-burning powders, could eliminate the rapid fouling problem.)

.17 Remington Loading Data and Factory Ballistics

Bullet (grains/type)	Powder	Grains	Velocity	Energy	Source/Comments
25 HP	IMR-4064	22.5	3800	801	Hornady
25 HP	IMR-4320	24.7	4000	888	Hornady
25 HP	IMR-4895	23.8	3900	845	Hornady
25 HP	IMR-3031	21.6	3800	801	Hornady
25 HP	N135	22.8	4040	906	Vihtavuori
20 AccuTip	FL		4250	802	Remington factory load
25 HP	FL		4040	906	Remington factory load

Note: Remington cases and Remington No. 7½ primers used in all loads.

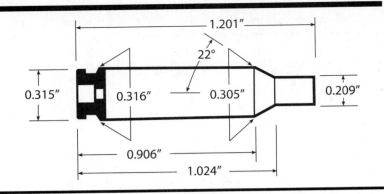

NEW
4.6x30 HK

Historical Notes: This cartridge was designed for the Heckler & Koch MP7 Personal Defense Weapon (PDW). The intent was to offer high volume fire in a lightweight, low recoiling firearm that was capable of defeating body armor. Typically, this cartridge is loaded with a steel core, brass-jacketed bullet. So loaded, this cartridge is capable of penetrating a 1.6mm titanium plate and 20 layers of Kevlar at 200 meters. Due to the limited availability of sporting bullets, as of now, this cartridge is almost entirely a military, law enforcement, or self-defense proposition.

General Comments: Due to the extreme small size of this cartridge, a solider or law enforcement officer can carry much more ammunition than he can if he was armed with a 5.56 NATO type weapon. Due to the lightweight bullet, recoil is minimal, and this offers fast follow-up shots or repetitive hits during automatic fire. While this cartridge does a tremendous job of defeating body armor, it does have limited wounding capacity due its small caliber bullet. Due to the cartridges limited application and the lack of adoption by any major military force, it looks to be headed to obsolescence in the near future.—R.A.M.

4.6 X 30 Factory Ballistics

Bullet (grains/type)	Powder	Grains	Velocity	Energy	Source/Comments
26 Steel AP	FL		2380	330	RUAG
31 Steel AP	FL		2272	351	RUAG
42 FMJ	FL		2000	401	RUAG

.204 Ruger

Historical Notes: Introduced in 2004 as a joint Hornady-Ruger project for varmint and target shooting, the .204 Ruger became the first .20-caliber cartridge to be produced on a large commercial scale. Remarkably, it also offers excellent barrel life. After shooting approximately 500 prairie dogs with the Ruger and Dakota rifles chambered for the .204 Ruger, a former contributing editor to this book found it to be an accurate, low-recoil round, superbly suited for long-range varminting. The .204 Ruger received the Academy of Excellence 2004 Cartridge of the Year Award.

General Comments: The .204 Ruger uses the 47mm-long .222 Remington Magnum as its parent case, necking it down to accept .204 bullets and changing the shoulder angle to 30 degrees. It performs best with 26-inch barrels using a 1:12 rifling twist. The cartridge is available in Ruger, Dakota, Remington, and Savage bolt-action rifles, Thompson/Center and SSK Industries Contender single-shot rifles, and AR-15 style rifles. Hornady, Remington, and Winchester offer loaded ammunition.

.204 Ruger Loading Data and Factory Ballistics

Bullet (grains/type)	Powder	Grains	Velocity	Energy	Source/Comments
32 V-Max	FL		4225	1268	Hornady
40 V-Max	FL		3900	1351	Hornady
32 V-Max	BL-C(2)	30.7	4081	1183	Hodgdon
32 V-Max	Benchmark	28.0	4047	1163	Hodgdon
40 V-Max	BL-C(2)	30.0	3774	1264	Hodgdon

.22 Hornet (5.6X36Rmm)

Historical Notes: The .22 Hornet, based on the blackpowder .22 WCF, was developed during the late 1920s by a group of experimenters at Springfield Armory, including Col. Townsend Whelen, Captain G. L. Wotkyns, and others. Winchester produced the first commercial ammunition, in 1930. Within a few years, the Hornet had been standardized by all American manufacturers. The original rifles were based on Springfield M1903 military and Martini single-shot actions. Winchester announced its Model 54 bolt action in .22 Hornet caliber in 1932, but rifles didn't actually reach the market until early 1933. Savage Model 23-D bolt-action rifles were available in .22 Hornet by August 1932. The Stevens single-shot Model 417 "Walnut Hill" target and 417½ sporting rifles were advertised in .22 Hornet caliber, in 1933. During World War II, military survival rifles were made for the Hornet. At present, Anschütz, Ruger, and Meacham chamber rifles for the Hornet, and Thompson/Center has the Contender in the caliber. In Europe, the Hornet is known by the metric designation 5.6x35Rmm.

General Comments: The .22 Hornet was the pioneer high-velocity smallbore cartridge marketed in the United States primarily for varmint and small-game shooting. It has never been commercially available in anything but bolt-action and single-shot rifles. For this reason, it quickly established a reputation for superb accuracy. No other cartridge of this type has ever caught on so fast or achieved such wide popularity.

Although not quite as powerful as the .218 Bee, it is a perfectly adequate small-game and varmint cartridge. It remains popular, but suffers in comparison with the .223 Remington and the .22-250. It remains a fine choice for economical shooting at ranges between 100 and 150 yards. Due to its reduced powder capacity, the Hornet won't do as well with heavier bullets of 50 or 55 grains, as will the .218 Bee. It is a good cartridge for use in settled areas, because of the light report and low incidence of ricochet. Early rifles had bores requiring bullets of .223-inch diameter. Sierra still offers such bullets. Later rifles had normal bores for .224-inch diameter bullets. Most bullet manufacturers offer special bullets for loading the Hornet. The Improved "K" Hornet is among the best-known wildcats based on the Hornet and the most common of all Improved chamberings. Loaded ammunition is available from Remington, Winchester, and Norma.

.22 Hornet Loading Data and Factory Ballistics

Bullet (grains/type)	Powder	Grains	Velocity	Energy	Source/Comments
35 V-Max	FL		3200	795	Hornady factory load
35 V-Max	H-110	11.2	3060	725	Hodgdon
40 SP	2400	10	2700	648	Sierra
40 SP	IMR 4227	11.4	2700	648	Speer, Sierra
45 SP	2400	9.2	2500	725	Hornady, Sierra
45 SP	IMR 4227	11	2600	678	Nosler, Hornady, Sierra
50 SP	2400	9	2400	640	Sierra, Hornady, Nosler
50 SP	IMR 4227	11	2550	694	Hornady, Nosler, Sierra
55 SP	IMR 4227	10.8	2400	704	Sierra, Hornady
55 SP	IMR 4198	12	2400	704	Sierra
45 SP	FL		2690	723	Factory load

.218 Bee

Historical Notes: The .218 Bee, introduced by Winchester, in 1938, was originally chambered in the Model 65 lever-action rifle, a modernized version of the Model 1892. Considerable enthusiasm greeted the announcement of this cartridge, and many magazine articles were devoted to comparing its superior killing power and range to the .22 Hornet. Although criticized as inaccurate, some Model 65s were capable of minute-of-angle accuracy. After WWII, Winchester brought out the Model 43 bolt-action rifle in .218 Bee. Mechanical troubles developed in some early models, and the rifle was discontinued. For a time, one or two European manufacturers, such as Sako and Krico, furnished small Mauser-type rifles in .218 Bee. The .218 Bee is based on the .32-20 case necked down to .22-caliber. Cases can be made by necking down .25-20 or .32-20 cases, then fire-forming.

General Comments: The .218 Bee has a larger case and somewhat greater powder capacity than the .22 Hornet. It provides higher velocity and a greater effective range than the Hornet, and, in a good single-shot or bolt-action rifle, is just as accurate. It is one of the most economical smal-game or varmint cartridges available. On small varmints, it can be counted on out to 200 yards, but on coyote, bobcat, or the like, it cannot be depended on for one-shot kills farther than 150 yards. On rabbits or other edible game, it is necessary to use full jacketed bullets or reduced loads, otherwise it ruins much of the meat.

The Bee is easy to reload, and one can duplicate anything from the .22 Short up to and exceeding the .22 Hornet. With modern powders, the factory performance can be improved safely. By using heavier bullets of 50 or 55 grains, its killing power and range can be increased.

Although still a fine cartridge and useful for many purposes, the .218 Bee has been largely displaced by the .223 Remington and .22-250 Remington. The .218 Bee, like the .22 Hornet, has a relatively mild report compared to the more powerful .22 centerfires and can be used under circumstances in which the larger cartridges would not be acceptable. It is a better performer than the .22 Hornet, and its lack of popularity has always been something of a mystery.

The Bee is the basis of several useful wildcats. Ackley's version approximately equals .222 Remington performance. The .17 Bee Improved offers impressive short-barrel performance. Factory loaded ammunition is available from Winchester.

.218 Bee Loading Data and Factory Ballistics

Bullet (grains/type)	Powder	Grains	Velocity	Energy	Source/Comments
40 HP	2400	12	2800	697	Sierra
40 HP	IMR-4227	11.7	2600	601	Hornady, Sierra
45 SP	2400	11.6	2700	729	Sierra
45 SP	IMR-4227	13	2800	784	Nosler, Sierra
50 SP	2400	10.5	2500	694	Sierra, Nosler
50 SP	IMR-4227	12	2700	810	Hornady, Sierra
55 SP	2400	10	2300	646	Sierra
55 SP	IMR-4198	14	2500	763	Sierra
55 SP	IMR-4227	12.5	2500	763	Sierra
46 SP	FL		2760	778	Winchester

.222 Remington

Historical Notes: The .222 Remington was introduced by Remington, in 1950, for the 722 bolt-action rifle, which was later superseded by the current 700 series. For a short time, the Remington Model 760 pump-action repeater was also available in this caliber. Much of the credit for the .222 is due to Mike Walker, a longtime Remington employee. The cartridge became very popular with benchrest competitors in the 1970s, and varmint hunters also found its performance excellent. But, by the early 1990s, the .222 Remington had lost much of its popularity to the .223 Remington.

General Comments: The .222 Remington is in about the same class as the older .219 Zipper, but is rimless and adapted to modern bolt-action rifles. It is not based on any older case necked down, but is of original design. It is a more or less scaled-down version of the 30-06 and fills the gap between the .218 Bee and the .220 Swift. It is well suited to the needs of the average person who desires a high-velocity .22. A great many benchrest matches have been won with the .222 Remington, and it has a reputation for superb accuracy. It is an excellent 200-yard cartridge for the full range of varmint and small-game animals up to, but not including, deer. It has been outlawed for big game in many of the 50 states because, like the .220 Swift, you can't always depend on it to kill large animals humanely. I have seen several deer and antelope killed very cleanly with the .222 handloaded with heavier-jacketed 55- and 60-grain bullets. Range was about 125 yards. This caliber is offered by all large domestic ammunition manufacturers and several foreign companies.

13th Edition Update: When Frank Barnes wrote the general comments on this cartridge, in 1965, it was considered foolish by most hunters to use a .22-caliber centerfire on deer or similarly sized game. Things have changed.

Nosler now offers a .224-caliber, 60-grain version of the famous Partition bullet, Barnes offers several different weight Triple Shock bullets, and Swift has the excellent 75-grain Sirocco bullet. Any of these bullets are totally adequate for use on animals that weigh up to 250 pounds or so, as long as impact velocities are high enough to ensure complete expansion, about 2300 fps or so. However, these bullets are often too long to work with standard twist rates common to the .222 Remington cartridge, so to find acceptable accuracy, a new barrel with a faster twist rate is often needed. Also, with regards to the statement "it has been outlawed for deer hunting in many of the 50 states," as of 2012, 38 states currently allow the hunting of deer with a centerfire .22-caliber round.—R.A.M.

.222 Remington Loading Data and Factory Ballistics

Bullet (grains/type)	Powder	Grains	Velocity	Energy	Source/Comments
35 V-Max	H4198	22.0	3591	1000	Hodgdon
40 HP	IMR 4198	20	3300	967	Speer, Sierra
40 HP	W748	26.3	3400	1027	Speer, Sierra
45 SP	H335	24.5	3100	960	Hornady, Speer
45 SP	IMR 4198	21	3300	1088	Hornady, Speer, Sierra, Nosler
50 SP	W748	25.8	3100	1067	Speer, Sierra, Hornady
50 SP	RE 7	20.9	3150	1102	Hornady, Speer, Sierra
50 SP	IMR 4198	20	3200	1132	Speer, Hornady, Sierra
55 SP	H335	24	3200	1174	Sierra, Speer, Hornady, Nosler
55 SP	IMR 4320	25	3000	1099	Hornady, Speer
55 SP	IMR 4895	24.5	3000	1099	Speer, Hornady, Sierra
55	Varget	25.0	2095	1170	Hodgdon
60 HP	IMR 4895	23	2900	1121	Nosler, Hornady, Speer
50 SP	FL		3140	1094	Factory load
55 FMJ	FL		3020	1114	Factory load

.223 Remington (5.56X45mm)

Historical Notes: The .223 Remington first appeared, in 1957, as an experimental military cartridge for the Armalite AR-15 assault rifle. In 1964, it was officially adopted by the U.S. Army as the 5.56mm ball cartridge M193. It is used in the selective-fire M16 rifle, which is based on the original AR-15 design. The cartridge was the work of Robert Hutton, who was technical editor of Guns & Ammo magazine and had a rifle range in Topanga Canyon, California. One of the requirements for the cartridge was that the projectile have a retained velocity in excess of the speed of sound (about 1080 fps at sea level) at 500 yards, something that could not be achieved with the .222 Remington. Working with Gene Stoner of Armalite, Bob Hutton designed a case slightly longer than the .222 and had Sierra make a 55-grain boat-tail bullet. This combination met the design requirements. All this was documented in the 1971 issue of the Guns & Ammo Annual.

Originally an alternative military cartridge, the .223 (5.56x45mm) is now the official U.S. and NATO military round; additional information will be found in Chapter 6 covering military cartridges. We should note here that NATO forces, including the United States, have standardized a new 5.56X45mm round with a heavy bullet, and the M193 is no longer standard.

Shortly after the military adopted this cartridge, Remington brought out the sporting version, which has largely replaced both the .222 Remington and Remington Magnum in popularity. Practically every manufacturer of bolt-action rifles has at least one model chambered for the .223. In addition, there are a large number of military-type semi-auto rifles available in this caliber. At one time, the Remington Model 760 pump-action was available in .223.

General Comments: The .223 Remington is nearly identical to the .222 Remington Magnum, the only difference being that the .223 has a slightly shorter case. The two are not interchangeable, although the .223 will chamber in a .222 Magnum rifle. The result, though, creates a gross headspace condition, and the .223 case can rupture if fired in the .222 Magnum chamber.

The .223 has proven to be an effective military cartridge for fighting in jungle or forested areas and for close-in fire support, and has been improved lately by NATO with heavier (SS109 designed by FN of Belgium) bullets fired through fast-twist (1:7) barrels. As a sporting round, it is just as accurate as any of the other long-range, centerfire .22s. Military brass cases are sometimes heavier than commercial cases, so maximum loads in military brass should be reduced by at least 10 percent and approached cautiously. That is because the reduced case capacity results in a higher loading density and increased pressure with the same powder charge. The .223 Remington can be classed as an excellent medium-range varmint cartridge at ranges out to 250 yards.

In 1979, SAAMI cautioned shooters that 5.56x45mm military chambers and throats differ from .223 Remington sporting rifle chambers. Therefore military ball ammo may produce high chamber pressures in sporting rifles.

13th Edition Update: In 1965, it was considered foolish by most hunters to use a .22-caliber centerfire on deer or similarly sized game. Things have changed. Nosler now offers a .224-caliber, 60-grain version of the famous Partition bullet, Barnes offers several different weight Triple Shock bullets, and Swift has the excellent 75-grain Sirocco bullet. Any of these bullets are totally adequate for use on animals that weigh up to 250 pounds or so, as long as impact velocities are high enough to insure complete expansion—about 2300 fps or so. However, these bullets are often too long to work with standard twist rates common with older .223 Remington rifles, so, to find acceptable accuracy, a new barrel with a faster twist rate or a more modern rifle with a faster twist rate is often needed.

There has also been a great deal of confusion on the interchangeability between the .223 Remington cartridge and 5.56x45mm NATO/Military ammunition. Dimensionally, these two cartridge cases are identical. However, 5.56 NATO ammo is generally loaded to a higher pressure than commercial .223 Remington ammunition. In a bolt-action rifle of quality manufacturer, this is a non-issue, but, in a semi-auto rifle, problems can be experienced. These can be as minor as reliability issues and as unsafe as blown primers and even firearm damage and shooter injury. The difference between these two cartridges is pressure and the difference in the rifles is the way the lead—the section of the chamber in front of the cartridge case is cut into the barrel; 5.56 NATO chambers have a longer lead. Maybe the simplest way to explain the difference is to say that the 5.56 NATO round is a +P version of the .223 Remington.—R.A.M.

.223 Remington Loading Data and Factory Ballistics

Bullet (grains/type)	Powder	Grains	Velocity	Energy	Source/Comments
40 SP	IMR 3031	25	3300	1140	Sierra, Speer
40 SP	IMR 4198	22	3200	995	Sierra, Speer
40 Nos BT	Varget	28.0	3674	1195	Hodgdon
45 SP	IMR 3031	25	3300	1162	Hornady, Sierra
45 SP	IMR 4198	22	3200	965	Hornady, Sierra, Speer
50 SP	IMR 3031	25.2	3250	1250	Sierra, Nosler, Hornady, Speer
50 SP	IMR 4198	21.5	3200	1155	Nosler, Hornady, Speer, Sierra
55 SP	IMR 3031	24.5	3200	1330	Hornady, Nosler, Sierra
55 SP	W748	25	3000	1110	Hornady, Nosler, Sierra
55	Varget	27.5	3384	1395	Hodgdon
60 HP	IMR 3031	24	3100	1130	Hornady, Sierra
80	Varget	25.0	2869	1460	Hodgdon
55 SP	FL		3240	1280	Factory load
55 FMJBT	FL		3250	1290	Military load
40 HP	FL		3650	1185	Federal factory load
62 Fusion	FL		3000	1239	Fusion Factory Load
60 Nosler Partition	FL		3160	1330	Federal Factory Load
75 BTHP	FL		2930	1429	Hornady Superformance

.22 PPC

Historical Notes: The .22 PPC was developed, in 1974, by Dr. Louis Palmisano and Ferris Pindell, primarily for use as a benchrest cartridge. Although originally a wildcat, Sako of Finland introduced commercial rifles and ammunition late in 1987. Norma followed suit, in 1993, with loaded ammunition. Since it is an American development, it is listed here as a current American rifle cartridge, rather than as a European cartridge. The cartridge is based on the .220 Russian case, which is a necked-down version of the 7.62X39mm Soviet military cartridge. The Wichita Engineering and Supply Co. made the first rifles for both the .22 and 6mm PPC cartridges. Many custom rifles have been turned out in this caliber. In 1993, Ruger announced its No. 1V and M77 varmint rifles in this caliber.

General Comments: The originators altered the .220 Russian case by giving it a 10-degree body taper and 30-degree shoulder angle, as well as expanding the neck to accept the standard .224-inch diameter bullet used in the U.S. The cartridge cases are made in Finland by Sako, or in Sweden by Norma, and use Small Rifle primers. Although the .22 PPC is a short, rather stubby case only 1.51 inches long, it nevertheless develops ballistics superior to some larger, longer cartridges such as the .222 and .223 Remington. The 52-grain bullet can be pushed out of the muzzle at over 3500 fps, and this definitely places the .22 PPC in the varmint and small-game class. A 1:14 twist has become pretty much standard for these rifles, although a 1:12 twist will sometimes be found.

.22 PPC Loading Data and Factory Ballistics

Bullet (grains/type)	Powder	Grains	Velocity	Energy	Source/Comments
40 Nos BT	Varget	29.5	3560	1125	Hodgdon
52 HP	BL-C2	28.3	3400	1335	Speer
52 HP	W748	28.0	3300	1258	Speer, Nosler, Hornady
55 SP	H-335	27.0	3200	1251	Speer, Nosler
55 SP	W748	28.0	3200	1251	Hornady, Nosler, Speer
52 HP	FL		3400	1335	Sako factory load

.225 Winchester

Historical Notes: The .225 Winchester was officially announced in June 1964. Both the standard and a heavier-barreled varmint version of the Model 70 bolt-action were offered for this round. The .225 replaced the older .220 Swift in the Winchester lineup. It is a semi-rimmed case with an unusually large rim for this type of cartridge. The .220 Swift never achieved great popularity, and neither did its replacement, the .225. The last Winchester catalog to list the cartridge as a caliber available for the Model 70 rifle was in 1972. No other manufacturer picked it up as a standard chambering, because the already popular .22-250 was standardized by Remington in 1965, and it was just common sense to adopt the .22-250 instead. Winchester still loads .225 ammunition, but this cartridge did not have a very long life, being semi-obsolete in only eight years.

General Comments: The .225 is a fine varmint cartridge with performance similar to the .224 Weatherby or the .22-250. But the .22-250 was already established as a popular wildcat with an outstanding reputation, and it was inevitable that it would dominate the field. Those who purchased .225 Winchester rifles have no need to feel bad or trade them off for anything else, because the .225 cartridge is just as accurate and will do anything that the more popular .22-250 will do. It simply turned out to be a design or idea whose time had not yet arrived. As a matter of fact, it might be well to hang on to your .225, because not a great many were sold and eventually some gun writer will rediscover it as the greatest .22 varmint cartridge conceived by the mind of man—and, at that point, all your shooting friends will wish they had one, too. The .225 has an edge over both the .222 and the .223 Remington for long-range varmint shooting, because of the increased muzzle velocity. At one time, Winchester was supposed to furnish a 50-grain loading at 3800 fps and a 60-grain at 3500 fps, along with the standard 55-grain at 3650 fps (now reduced to 3570 fps), but these loads never materialized. For handloaders, this cartridge is nothing more than a slightly modified .30-30. Neck down the .30-30 to .22-caliber, shorten the case slightly, turn the rim to '06 dimensions and slightly Improve, and you have the .225 Winchester.

Bullet (grains/type)	Powder	Grains	Velocity	Energy	Source/Comments
40 Speer SP	BL-C(2)	36.0	4020	1435	Hodgdon
40 HP	IMR 4064	31.5	3400	1027	Speer, Sierra
45 SP	IMR 4064	33	3600	1295	Hornady, Speer
50 SP	IMR 3031	31	3400	1284	Speer, Nosler, Hornady
50 SP	IMR 4895	33	3600	1439	Sierra
55 SP	IMR 4320	34.5	3700	1672	Hornady
60 HP	IMR 4064	31.8	3500	1632	Hornady
70 SP	IMR 4350	34.5	3000	1399	Speer
55 SP	FL		3570	1556	Winchester factory load

.224 Weatherby Magnum

Historical Notes: The Weatherby line of proprietary cartridges was somewhat incomplete for lack of an ultra-velocity .22. The previous .220 Weatherby Rocket was actually an Improved wildcat based on the .220 Swift case, and Weatherby never manufactured ammunition of this caliber. The .224 Varmintmaster was introduced in 1963, but according to the late Roy Weatherby, development work went back 10 years prior to that. Introduction of the cartridge was delayed because of lack of a suitable action. The caliber was offered in a reduced-size version of the Weatherby Mark V rifle, but is no longer available.

General Comments: The .224 Weatherby lies ballistically between the .223 Remington and the .220 Swift. It is a belted case with the advantages and disadvantages inherent in this type of construction. For the handloader, it mitigates certain headspace and case-stretch problems and should provide maximum case life. It is an excellent long-range varmint cartridge with performance similar to the .22-250 Remington. Its popularity was determined largely by economic factors. One could buy a Remington, Ruger or Winchester bolt-action in .22-250 caliber for much less than a .224 Weatherby. It was the smallest belted case manufactured commercially.

.224 Weatherby Magnum Loading Data and Factory Ballistics

Bullet (grains/type)	Powder	Grains	Velocity	Energy	Source/Comments
40 HP	IMR 4198	28.5	4100	1493	Sierra
45 SP	IMR 4198	28	3900	1520	Sierra
50 SP	IMR 4064	32.8	3800	1604	Hornady, Sierra
50 SP	IMR 4895	33	3800	1604	Hornady
53 HP	IMR 4064	32	3600	1526	Hornady, Sierra
55 SP	IMR 4064	32	3600	1583	Sierra, Hornady
55 SP	IMR 4895	32	3600	1583	Hornady
55 SP	FL		3650	1627	Factory load
60 HP	IMR 4895	31.5	3500	1632	Hornady

.22-250 Remington
(.22 Varminter, .22 Wotkyns Original Swift)

Historical Notes: The .22-250 Remington was adopted early in 1965, as one of the calibers for the Remington 700 series bolt-action rifles and also for the Model 40XB match rifle. Browning bolt-action rifles were offered in .22-250 two years earlier. This is not a factory design, but rather a popular wildcat that has been around for many years and made good. However, Remington's adoption of the round moved it into the commercial classification.

There is some confusion regarding date of origin of the .22-250, which is based on the .250-3000 Savage case necked to .22-caliber. Its moniker is derived from the caliber (.22) and the parent case name (.250). The parent cartridge was introduced in 1915, and a .22 version may have been made up experimentally shortly thereafter. Harvey Donaldson, Grosvenor Wotkyns, J.E. Gebby, J.B. Smith, and John Sweany all worked on versions of the .22-250 between 1934 and 1937. J.E. Gebby and J.B. Smith are usually credited with having developed the present configuration, in 1937. However, there are different versions of this cartridge, and much depends on which one is referred to. The Gebby version was named the .22 Varminter, and he obtained a copyright on the name. Other gunsmiths renamed it the .22-250. The Wotkyns version was the forerunner of the .220 Swift, although Winchester ended up using the 6mm Lee Navy case, rather than the .250 Savage.

At the present time, all of the major American and European rifle makers furnish bolt-action rifles in .22-250 chambering. In addition, the Ruger, Thompson/Center, and other single-shots are available in this caliber.

General Comments: The .22-250 is one of the best balanced and most flexible of the high-powered .22 centerfires. It is also the most popular of the long-range .22 varmint cartridges, effective to ranges of 400 yards or more. The .22-250 also has a reputation for outstanding accuracy and has been used with some success for benchrest shooting. Many individuals who have had experience with both the .22-250 and the .220 Swift report that the former gives significantly longer case life with full loads than the latter. The .22-250, as with most of the other high-powered .22s, is not recommended for use on deer or other medium game. The reason, of course, is that the light varmint bullets are made to expand quickly and will not offer sufficient penetration on a large animal. This is one of the best all-round, long-range .22 varmint cartridge available today.

In a 2000 press release, Remington announced the availability of electronic ignition .22-250 ammunition for use in its new (and now defunct) EtronX rifle. The initial loading used a 50-grain Hornady V-Max, polymer-tipped bullet. Owing to the unique primer, this ammunition will not work in a conventional rifle (just as conventional ammunition will not work in the EtronX rifle). Except for the primer, this ammunition uses conventional components.

13th Edition Update: When the .22-250 was introduced, in 1965, there were no .22-caliber bullets truly suitable for use on medium-sized game. Things have changed a great deal in the last 47 years. Nosler now offers a 60-grain version of the famous Partition bullet, Barnes offers several different weight Triple Shock bullets, and Swift has the excellent 75-grain Sirocco bullet. Any of these bullets are totally adequate for use on animals that weigh up to 250 pounds or so, as long as impact velocities are high enough to insure complete expansion—about 2300 fps or so. As a matter of fact, in Texas, the .22-250 and other .22-caliber centerfire rifles have become very popular for deer hunting.—R.A.M.

.22-250 Remington Loading Data and Factory Ballistics

Bullet (grains/type)	Powder	Grains	Velocity	Energy	Source/Comments
40 HP	IMR 4895	36	3900	1345	Speer, Sierra
40 HP	IMR 3031	35	3900	1345	Sierra, Speer
40	Varget	39.5	4135	1515	Hodgdon
45 SP	IMR 4064	37	3900	1520	Speer, Sierra
45 SP	IMR 3031	32	3500	1224	Hornady, Speer
50 SP	IMR 4064	36	3700	1520	Hornady, Speer, Sierra
50 SP	IMR 3031	34.5	3700	1520	Speer, Hornady, Sierra
55 SP	IMR 4064	35	3600	1580	Hornady, Speer, Sierra
55 SP	RL-7	29	3500	1496	Sierra
55 SP	IMR 4320	35	3500	1496	Nosler, Hornady, Sierra
60 HP	RL-7	28	3300	1451	Sierra
60 HP	IMR 4320	34	3500	1630	Hornady, Nosler, Sierra
70 SP	IMR 4064	33	3300	1690	Speer
70 SP	N205	41	3300	1690	NA
40 HP	FL		4000	1420	Federal factory load
55 SP	FL		3680	1655	Factory load

.220 Swift

Historical Notes:	The .220 Swift was developed by Winchester and introduced, in 1935, as a new caliber for the Model 54 bolt-action rifle. When the Model 70 Winchester bolt-action was first issued, in 1936, the .220 Swift was one of the standard calibers offered and continued to be until it was discontinued, in 1964. Now, the Savage Model 112V, the Ruger Model 77, and the Ruger No. 1V single-shot are offered in the .220 Swift chambering. The Model 70 Winchester is no longer made in this caliber. Norma of Sweden lists the .220 Swift with a 50-grain bullet at 4110 fps, and it also sells unprimed brass cases for reloading. Hornady/Frontier offer 55-grain SP and 60-grain HP loadings.
	The prototype for the .220 Swift was developed in 1934-'35 by Grosvenor Wotkyns, who necked down the .250-3000 Savage as a means of achieving very high velocities. However, the final commercial version developed by Winchester is based on the old 6mm Lee Navy cartridge necked down. It is a semi-rimmed case.
General Comments:	The .220 Swift was and still is the fastest commercial cartridge in the world. It is also one of the most accurate super-velocity .22 cartridges ever developed. Its popularity has been somewhat retarded by the fact that ammunition in this caliber is expensive. Swift barrels have never been noted for long life, but this factor has been negated to a large degree by development of modern, erosion-resistant barrel steels since World War II. Factory ammunition has always featured the 48-grain and 50-grain bullets, but the Swift will handle the 55-grain or heavier bullets quite well at slightly reduced maximum velocity. The .220 Swift is considered adequate on all animals up to deer size. There is certainly plenty of field evidence to demonstrate that, on occasion, it will give fantastic one-shot kills on deer and antelope. However, the .220 Swift tends to be erratic in its performance on large animals, and most states will not permit its use on big game of any kind. Properly constructed bullets would almost certainly solve this problem on animals to mule deer size. In any case, factory bullets are designed for quick expansion on light animals. Most varmint hunters agree that the .220 Swift is the best varmint cartridge made. It remains sufficiently popular that various manufacturers occasionally chamber it.
	In a 2000 press release, Remington announced the availability of electronic ignition 220 Swift ammunition for use in its new (and now defunct) EtronX rifle. The initial loading uses a 50-grain Hornady V-Max, polymer-tipped bullet. Owing to the unique primer, this ammunition will not work in a conventional rifle (just as conventional ammunition will not work in the EtronX rifle). Except for the primer, this ammunition uses conventional components.

.220 Swift Loading Data and Factory Ballistics

Bullet (grains/type)	Powder	Grains	Velocity	Energy	Source/Comments
40 HP	IMR 4064	39	4000	1421	Speer, Sierra
40	Varget	40.5	4113	1500	Hodgdon
45 HP	IMR 4350	41.5	3600	1295	Hornady, Speer, Sierra
45 SP	IMR 3031	37	4000	1599	Hornady, Speer, Sierra
45 SP	IMR 4895	38.5	3900	1520	Sierra
45 SP	H-380	43	3850	1481	Speer, Sierra
50 SP	IMR 4320	39	4400	1689	Sierra
50 SP	IMR 3031	37	4000	1777	Sierra
55 SP	IMR 4350	44	3800	1764	Speer, Hornady
55 SP	IMR 4320	40	3000	1955	Sierra
55 SP	H-380	42	3800	1764	Nosler, Sierra, Speer
60 HP	IMR 4895	33	3400	1541	Hornady, Sierra
*48 SP	FL		4110	1800	Factory Load
50 SP	FL		4110	1877	Norma factory load
55 SP	FL		3650	1627	Hornady/Frontier factory load
40 SP	FL		4250	1603	Federal
60 HP	FL		3600	1727	Hornady/Frontier factory load

* Discontinued loading.

.223 Winchester Super Short Magnum

Historical Notes: Announced in 2002, the .223 WSSM is intended to deliver a new level of long-range performance and accuracy to the .223 family of chamberings. Cartridge overall length is 2.36 inches, a half-inch shorter than the 2.8-inch length of existing short-action cartridges. The .223 WSSM will be chambered in super short rifle actions, which should improve receiver stiffness and accuracy. A new Browning bolt-action rifle, the Super Short Magnum A-Bolt, weights six pounds and uses a shorter action for the 2.36-inch cartridge. Winchester Firearms also plans a shorter-action rifle for this round, the Winchester Super Short Magnum Model 70.

General Comments: The .223 WSSM case does not employ a belt; it headspaces on the case shoulder. For efficient and consistent powder burning, it retains the short-fat cartridge case geometry of the Winchester Short Magnum line. Cartridges will be available in three bullet types: 55-grain Ballistic Silvertip and Pointed Soft Point, and 64-grain Power-Point. WSSM velocities are targeted at roughly 200 fps faster than the .22-250 Remington offerings. It is suitable for long-range varmint shooting and for light thin-skinned game, a good combination cartridge with light recoil.

13th Edition Update: Currently, Winchester is the only major ammunition manufacturer loading ammunition for the .223 WSSM. The cartridge and all its siblings became embroiled in a legal battle, and the end result was a less than enthusiastic appeal on the part of other manufacturers to offer rifles and/or ammunition for sale. The .223 WSSM is a fine cartridge, and the most accurate rifle I have ever fired was chambered for this cartridge. It looks, however, that all of the Super Short Winchester Magnum cartridges have peaked in terms of interest and availability.—R.A.M.

.223 Winchester Super Short Magnum Load Data/Factory Ballistics

Bullet (grains/type)	Powder	Grains	Velocity	Energy	Source
40 Nosler Ballistic Tip	H414	50.5	4301	1641	Hodgdon
45 Barnes X	IMR-4895	44.6	4194	1756	Hodgdon
50 Barnes XLC	BL-C(2)	46.0	4058	1826	Hodgdon
52 Speer HPBT	IMR-4064	43.3	3970	1818	Hodgdon
55 Hornady V-Max	H414	46.8	3886	1842	Hodgdon
60 Nosler Partition	IMR-4350	46.0	3707	1829	Hodgdon
69 Sierra HPBT	H4831	46.5	3489	1863	Hodgdon
77 Sierra HPBT	IMR-4831	44.8	3360	1928	Hodgdon
55 BST	FL		3850	1810	Winchester/Olin
55 PSP	FL		3850	1810	Winchester/Olin
64 PP	FL		3600	1841	Winchester/Olin

6mm PPC

Historical Notes: The 6mm PPC is an outgrowth of the .22 PPC and based on the same case configuration with the neck expanded to take 6mm (.243-inch) bullets. This cartridge was also developed by Dr. Louis Palmisano and Ferris Pindell and based on the .220 Russian case, which is a variation of the 7.62X39mm (M43) Soviet military cartridge. The original rifles were made by Wichita Engineering and Supply Co., in 1975. Many custom rifles have been made up in this caliber in both sporter and benchrest types. Although originally a benchrest wildcat, Sako of Finland began turning out commercial bolt-action rifles and supplying loaded ammunition late in 1987. In 1993, Ruger announced that its M77 Varmint and No. 1 Varmint rifles would be offered in this caliber, and, at the same time, Norma announced factory-loaded ammunition. The 6mm PPC is one of the top competitive benchrest cartridges. In addition to loaded ammunition and factory cases, many handloaders make their own cases by fireforming .220 Russian cases or necking-down and reforming 7.62X39mm brass.

General Comments: Chronograph tests by various individuals have demonstrated that the 6mm PPC gives very uniform velocity readings, which accounts for its fine accuracy. On the other hand, practically all rifles chambered for the cartridge are heavy-barrel accuracy jobs, and that must also be a factor. Rifles for match shooting usually have a 1:14 twist, although a few are turned out with a 1:12 twist. The 6mm PPC is not only an outstanding benchrest cartridge, but gives very good results on small game and varmints. It is only slightly less powerful than the .243 Winchester, despite the much smaller case. It should also do well on deer or antelope at moderate ranges. The velocity with the 90-grain bullet is only some 100 to 150 fps less than the .243 Winchester. Popularity of this caliber is growing beyond benchrest shooting, as varmint hunters are now also taking it up. Look for continued growth here.

6mm PPC Loading Data and Factory Ballistics

Bullet (grains/type)	Powder	Grains	Velocity	Energy	Source/Comments
60 Sierra HP	H-4895	29.0	3218	1375	Hodgdon
60 HP	H-322	28.4	3200	1365	Sierra
70 HP	H-335	29	3100	1494	Hornady, Sierra
75 HP	H-322	26.7	3100	1601	Hornady, Speer, Sierra
80 SP	W748	29	2800	1393	Speer
85 SP	H-335	28.0	3000	1699	Speer
90 SP	H-335	29	3000	1799	Speer
70 SP	FL		3140	1535	Sako factory load

6mm Norma BR

Historical Notes: In February 1996, Norma introduced this "new" cartridge. While case dimensions are identical to the 6mm BR Remington, chambering specifications differ. Remington perceived this cartridge as a traditional benchrest number. Therefore, it designed chambering specifications around bullets of about 70 grains. Conversely, with considerable prodding from the late Roger Johnston, Norma recognized the long-range target potential of this basic case. That company standardized a chambering specification appropriate for very low drag (VLD) bullets exceeding 100 grains. Therefore, the Norma chamber has a much longer neck. While there are no case differences, CIP (the European counterpart to SAAMI) requires a new designation for any cartridge or chambering differing in any way from any previous version. Therefore, Norma was required to apply a new name.

General Comments: While the 6mm BR Remington has failed to become a world-beater in traditional benchrest, with heavy VLD bullets, Norma's version has established itself as a force to be reckoned with in the long-range game. It is also a superior long-range varminting choice. Given a 28-inch barrel and loaded with any of the better 95- to 115-grain VLD moly-plated bullets, this cartridge can achieve sufficient velocity for 1,000-yard benchrest shooting. Owing to the high BCs of these bullets, 1,000-yard retained velocity is surprisingly high—often exceeding 1400 fps.

For cartridges of this genre, such loads generate unusually light recoil, which contributes to precise shooting. However, unless conditions are unusually good, those using larger-bored rifles usually fare better. While those rifles generate more recoil, which effectively reduces intrinsic accuracy, the longer bullets exhibit less wind drift and, therefore, reduce the error associated with imperfections in the shooter's ability to properly dope the wind.

6mm Norma BR Loading Data

Bullet (grains/type)	Powder	Grains	Velocity	Energy	Source/Comments
68 Berger Match	N202	32.0	3393	1735	Norma (26-inch Bbl)
80 Hornady	N203	32.1	3232	1855	Norma (26-inch Bbl)
95 Nosler	N203	30.1	2914	1790	Norma (26-inch Bbl)

6XC Tubb

Historical Notes: The 6XC is a development of well-known rifle competitor David Tubb. It is intended for the AR-10 rifle, as well as bolt-action rifles, such as the Tubb 2000, that utilize the AR-10 magazine. The .243 Winchester will also work in those rifles, but when extremely long bullets weighing over 100 grains are seated to an overall cartridge length compatible with the AR-180 magazine, the mouth of the case is, depending on the particular bullet, positioned over the ogive of the bullet rather than on its full-diameter shank. Using a shorter case with a gross capacity only seven grains less than the .243 Winchester case solved that problem. The 6XC case is in improved version of the 6mm International, a cartridge created during the early 1960s by avid benchrest shooter Mike Walker. Walker worked for Remington at the time, and the 40X target rifle built in the custom shop of that company has long been chambered for his cartridge. Whereas the 6mm International is the .250 Savage case necked down with no other change, the 6XC is the same case necked down and blown out to the Improved configuration with .015-inch of body taper and a 30-degree shoulder angle. Cases made by Norma are available from Superior Shooting Systems of Canadian, Texas, and they can also be made by fireforming .250 Savage or .22-250 cases in a rifle chambered for the 6XC. Loaded ammunition is also available from SSS.

General Comments: As this section was written, in late 2008, David Tubb has won 11 NRA National High Power Rifle championship titles at Camp Perry. He has also won close to 30 open, individual national championship titles in all four rifle categories of NRA Silhouette competition, along with seven Sportsmen's Team Challenge championships. In other words, if anyone is qualified to develop a cartridge for consistently winning matches at distances as great as 1,000 yards, it is David Tubb. When loaded with match-grade bullets of extremely high ballistic coefficients, such as the 105-grain Berger, 107-grain Sierra MatchKing, and 115-grain DETAC, the 6XC bucks wind as well as cartridges of larger caliber, but its lower level of recoil makes it easier to shoot accurately. Since it pretty much duplicates the velocity of the .243 Winchester with a case of less capacity, it is commonly loaded to slightly higher chamber pressures than that cartridge. Currently, only CorBon and Norma offer loaded ammunition for the 6XC Tubb.

6XC Loading Data and Factory Ballistics

Bullet (grains/type)	Powder	Grains	Velocity	Energy	Source
115 DETAC HPBT	H4350	39.5	2950	2220	David Tubb
115 DETAC HPBT	H4350	43.5	2950	2220	David Tubb
105 Berger DLBT	FL		3020	2124	Norma Precision

.243 Winchester

Historical Notes: The .243 Winchester was introduced by Winchester, in 1955, for its Model 70 bolt-action and Model 88 lever-action rifles. The .243 was quickly adopted by Savage for its Model 99 lever- and Model 110 bolt-action rifles. All the British and European manufacturers soon began chambering bolt-action rifles for this round. In fact, even Remington, which developed its own 6mm, had to recognize the popularity of the .243 and start chambering its rifles for it. The .243 (6mm) Winchester is nothing more than the .308 Winchester case necked down. Original development and publicity was due largely to the efforts of one gun writer, the late Warren Page, who, along with other wildcatters, worked out a similar version before Winchester. The .243 is probably chambered in more different rifles than any other cartridge, except possibly the .30-06 Springfield. All other manufacturers of rifles offer this caliber.

General Comments: The .243 Winchester represents a successful effort to develop a light deer rifle caliber that could hold its own with the high-velocity .22s for long-range use on small targets and still be adequate for larger animals. The .243 does this job well. It eliminates the need to own two different rifles for anything from small game and pests up to and including deer and antelope. The 80-grain bullet is intended primarily for varmint and small game and the 100-grain bullet for deer-size animals. The .257 Roberts and the .250-3000 Savage are supposed to cover the same range and certainly do. All major domestic and overseas manufacturers of commercial ammunition offer this caliber. Its popularity as a deer caliber has prevailed over its varmint capabilities.

(Editor's note: The .243 has garnered a reputation among ballisticians for erratic performance. Handloaders should keep this firmly in mind.)

In a 2000 press release, Remington announced the availability of electronic ignition .243 Winchester ammunition for use in its new (and now defunct) EtronX rifle. The initial loading uses a 90-grain Nosler Ballistic Tip bullet. Owing to the unique primer, this ammunition will not work in a conventional rifle (just as conventional ammunition will not work in the EtronX rifle). Except for the primer, this ammunition uses conventional components.

13th Edtion Update: The recent introduction of all-copper, mono-metal bullets like the Barnes Triple Shock and Tipped Triple Shock, the Hornady GMX, and Lapua Naturalis allow the .243 Winchester, as well as other 6mm cartridges that produce the same or higher velocities, to be very effective on big game while using a faster and lighter bullet. Additionally, Frank Barnes mentioned the erratic performance handloaders could expect when working with the .243 Winchester; while this has become an ever-presistant warning with this cartridge, I have been handloading the .243 Winchester for 20-plus years and find it as easy to work with as any other cartridge.—R.A.M.

.243 Winchester Loading Data and Factory Ballistics

Bullet (grains/type)	Powder	Grains	Velocity	Energy	Source/Comments
55 Nos BT	H4895	44.5	4058	2010	Hodgdon
75 HP	IMR 4064	40	3300	1814	Hornady, Speer
80 SP	IMR 4320	38	3000	1599	Speer, Hornady
85 SP	H-380	38.5	3100	1814	Sierra
90 SP	IMR 4831	44	3000	1799	Speer, Sierra
95 SP	IMR 3031	35	2900	1775	Nosler
100 SP	IMR 4350	42	2900	1868	Sierra, Hornady
80 SP	FL		3550	1993	Factory load
85 SP	FL		3320	2080	Factory load
100 SP	FL		2960	1945	Factory load
105 SP	FL		3100	2133	Factory load

.243 Winchester Super Short Magnum (.243 WSSM)

Historical Notes: Announced in 2002, the .243 WSSM is intended to deliver a new level of long-range performance and accuracy to the .243 family of chamberings. Cartridge overall length is 2.36 inches, a half-inch shorter than the 2.8-inch length of existing short-action cartridges. The .243 WSSM will be chambered in super-short rifle actions, which should improve receiver stiffness and accuracy. A new Browning bolt-action rifle, the Super Short Magnum A-Bolt, weighs six pounds and uses a shorter action for the 2.36 length cartridge. Winchester Firearms also plans a shorter-action rifle for this round, the Winchester Super Short Magnum Model 70. and accuracy. A new Browning bolt-action rifle, the Super Short Magnum A-Bolt, weighs six pounds and uses a shorter action for the 2.36-inch cartridge. Winchester Firearms also plans a shorter-action rifle for this round, the Winchester Super Short Magnum Model 70.

General Comments: The .243 WSSM case does not employ a belt; it headspaces on the case shoulder. For efficient and consistent powder burning, it retains the short-fat cartridge case geometry of the Winchester Short Magnum line. Cartridges will be available in three bullet types: 55-grain Ballistic Silvertip, 95-grain Ballistic Silvertip, and 100-grain Power Point. The .243 WSSM shares the same basic cartridge case with the .223 WSSM, also announced in 2002. Like its small-diameter brother, it is suitable for long-range varmint shooting and for light, thin-skinned game—a good combination cartridge with light recoil.

13th Edition Update: Currently, Winchester is the only major ammunition manufacturer loading ammunition for the .243 WSSM. The cartridge and all its siblings become embroiled in a legal battle and the end result was a less than enthusiastic appeal on the part of manufacturers to offer rifles and/or ammunition for sale. The .243 WSSM is a fine cartridge, but it appears that all of the Super Short Winchester Magnum cartridges have peaked in terms of interest and availability. —R.A.M.

.243 Winchester Super Short Magnum Load Data/Factory Ballistics

Bullet (grains/type)	Powder	Grains	Velocity	Energy	Source/Comments
58 Hornady V-Max	BL-C(2)	49.2	4068	2129	Hodgdon
70 Nosler Ballistic Tip	IMR-4320	45.0	3663	2083	Hodgdon
80 Sierra SBT	H414	48.0	3514	2191	Hodgdon
90 Swift Scirocco	IMR-7828	48.5	3280	2148	Hodgdon
100 Speer BTXP	Supreme 780	50.0	3117	2155	Hodgdon
55 BST	FL		4060	2013	Winchester/Olin
95 BST	FL		3250	2258	Winchester/Olin
100 PP	FL		3110	2147	Winchester/Olin

6mm Remington (.244 Remington)

Historical Notes: The 6mm Remington has exactly the same case dimensions as the .244 Remington. They differ only in the fact that the 6mm Remington is loaded with bullets of up to 100 grains, whereas the .244 Remington was never loaded with bullets of more than 90 grains. Ammunition marked .244 Remington can be fired in 6mm Remington chambers and vice versa. However, rifles marked .244 Remington will not always stabilize the 100-grain bullet. The difference in the two is that .244 rifles (if manufactured by Remington) have a 1:12 rifling twist, and rifles marked 6mm have a 1:9 twist. When Remington introduced the .244, in 1955, it selected the 1:12 twist as best suited to long-range accuracy with bullets of 75 to 90 grains. That was correct, except that most shooters wanted to be able to use bullets of 100 to 105 grains, in order to cover the range of game from varmints through deer with the same rifle. To correct this misjudgment, Remington renamed the cartridge 6mm Remington and changed to a 1:9 twist. To have retained the .244 designation and simply changed the twist would have brought on complaints from purchasers of the original .244s with the slower twist, when they tried to use the new 100-grain load. The change in cartridge nomenclature to 6mm and the faster twist occurred in 1963. The Remington 700 series and 788 bolt-action rifles, as well as the firm's autoloaders and the slide-actions, have been available in 6mm.

General Comments: The original 6mm Remington was loaded only with the 100-grain bullet. However, it is now available with 80-, 90-, and 100-grain bullets, which greatly extends its flexibility. Although the older .244 lost out to the .243 Winchester, the 6mm Remington with faster twist barrels is gradually picking up a following. It is an excellent choice for the varmint hunter who also wants to use his rifle for deer and antelope. Although the 6mm has a slightly larger powder capacity than the .243, the difference in performance is negligible as far as killing power is concerned. Nevertheless, this small advance in ballistics appeals to some people and so does the longer neck of the 6mm case, which many handloaders consider desirable. This caliber is commercially loaded by Federal and Winchester, as well as Remington.

6mm (.244) Remington Loading Data and Factory Ballistics

Bullet (grains/type)	Powder	Grains	Velocity	Energy	Source/Comments
55 Nos BT	H4895	45.5	4115	2065	Hodgdon
60 HP	H-335	42	3700	1824	Sierra
70 SP	IMR 4350	47	3400	1797	Sierra, Hornady
75 HP	IMR 4064	41	3500	2041	Speer, Nosler
75 HP	IMR 4350	47	3450	1983	Nosler, Speer, Sierra
80 SP	IMR 4350	45	3200	1820	Hornady
80 SP	IMR 4831	47	3200	1820	Hornady, Speer
90 HP	IMR 4350	45	3200	2047	Speer, Sierra
90 HP	IMR 4831	45	3100	1921	Speer, Sierra

6mm (.244) Remington Loading Data and Factory Ballistics

Bullet (grains/type)	Powder	Grains	Velocity	Energy	Source/Comments
100 SP	IMR 4350	42	2900	1868	Hornady, Speer, Sierra, Nosler
100 SP	IMR 4831	44	2900	1868	Speer, Sierra, Hornady
100	H1000	51.0	3111	2145	Hodgdon
105 SP	IMR 4350	42	2950	2030	Speer
105 SP	IMR 4064	37	2900	1961	Speer
80 SP	FL		3470	2139	Factory load
90 SP	FL		3190	2133	Factory load
100 SP	FL		3100	2133	Factory load

.240 Weatherby Magnum

Historical Notes: The .240 Weatherby was added to round out the Weatherby proprietary magnum line, in 1968. It differs from other 6mms in having a belted case with somewhat greater powder capacity. It is very similar to the .240 Belted Rimless Nitro-Express introduced by Holland & Holland around 1923. Thus far, it is available only in the Weatherby Mark V bolt-action rifle or through custom gunsmiths. It is an excellent cartridge and will push the 100-grain 6mm bullet with about 200 fps greater muzzle velocity than the 6mm Remington, and around 300 fps faster than the .243 Winchester. However, a considerable portion of this ballistic advantage results from increased barrel length and loading pressure. It is important to allow plenty of barrel cooling time with this and all high-intensity cartridges. The principal detraction regarding the .240 Weatherby Magnum is that ammunition is expensive and difficult to find. The .240 case has about the same capacity as the .30-06, and rim diameter is also the same.

General Comments: The .240 Weatherby is among the most powerful of the 6mm cartridges. It represents the maximum performance that one can squeeze through a 6mm tube with modern powders. The .244 H&H Belted Rimless Magnum, based on necking-down the .375 H&H Magnum case, will hold more powder, but doesn't produce any improvement in ballistics. The late Roy Weatherby built a successful proprietary gun business on the basis of a good product plus the all-important element of ballistic one-upmanship. The Weatherby magnum cartridges have traditionally offered higher velocity and energy than their standard factory counterpart. The .240 was born of this same tradition. Of course, Remington, Winchester, Norma, etc., have their own magnum lines in various calibers, and Winchester offered the .300 and .375 H&H Magnums before World War II. However, Roy Weatherby was the first to really popularize this British innovation in the United States, convincing the American shooters that it was something they truly needed.

.240 Weatherby Magnum Loading Data and Factory Ballistics

Bullet (grains/type)	Powder	Grains	Velocity	Energy	Source/Comments
60 HP	IMR 4350	53	3800	1924	Sierra
70 HP	IMR 4350	52	3700	2128	Hornady, Nosler
75 HP	IMR 4320	50.5	3800	2405	Hornady
80 SP	IMR 4831	52.5	3500	2177	Hornady, Speer
85 SP	IMR 4350	51	3450	2247	Nosler, Speer, Sierra
90 SP	IMR 4831	52	3400	2311	Speer, Hornady, Sierra
95 SP	IMR 4350	47	3050	1963	Nosler
100 SP	IMR 4831	52	3300	2419	Hornady
105 SP	IMR 4831	49.5	3150	2314	Speer
70 HP	FL		3850	2304	Weatherby factory load
87 SP	FL		3500	2366	Weatherby factory load
100 SP	FL		3395	2559	Weatherby factory load

.25-20 Winchester (.25-20 WCF)

Historical Notes: The .25-20 Winchester Center Fire was developed for the short action of the Winchester Model 1892 lever-action rifle. The case is based on the .32-20 necked down. There is a difference in opinion as to when it was actually introduced. Some authorities say 1893, others 1895. In any event, it was quickly adopted by a majority of the gun manufacturers and achieved considerable popularity. The Winchester lever-action 1892 and modernized Model 65, Remington pump-action Model 25, Marlin pump-action 27 and lever-action Model 94, and the Savage bolt-action repeater Model 23 were all available in .25-20 WCF. Marlin has reintroduced the .25-20 WCF in its Model 1894CL lever action. Winchester also loaded this same chambering with a slightly different bullet shape and headstamped it .25-20 Marlin.

General Comments: Prior to the .22 Hornet and the .218 Bee, the .25-20 WCF was one of the most popular small-game and varmint cartridges around. It was also advertised as being suitable for deer and similar animals. No doubt it has killed plenty of deer, but it is not a satisfactory big-game cartridge by any standard. Today, it is universally outlawed for big-game hunting. On smaller animals, the 60-grain bullet is quite effective for 100- to 150-yard varmint shooting. The 86-grain soft-point or lead bullet does a fine job on rabbit or turkey to 125 yards. A great many rifles were made in this caliber and are still in use by trappers, ranchers, and farmers. Under certain conditions, the .25-20 repeater is still a useful small-game number. It will probably be around for a good many more years. With the growing popularity of cowboy action shooting, the .25-20 is destined for renewed popularity.

The .25-20 is another old-timer the original author of this book played around with at various times. His ownership of a Winchester Model 1892 lever-action and later a Winchester Low Wall single-shot in this caliber allowed ample opportunity to test its potential for small game and varmint hunting. It will do the job, but has serious range limitations due in part to bullet design. The 60-grain high-velocity load achieves its maximum expansion at a range of between 50 and 70 yards. Beyond that, good bullet placement is essential for quick kills. At ranges out to 50 yards, bullet expansion will ruin most of the edible meat on small game. The 86-grain bullet is a better load for meat hunting, although the lower velocity requires good distance judgment at ranges much beyond 75 yards.

On the other hand, the .25-20 is one of those cartridges that can be improved to a satisfying degree by handloading. The 86-grain bullet can be loaded to deliver around 1700 fps, but the 60-grain bullet can't be improved much over the factory load. The .25-20 is also capable of very good accuracy when fired in a single-shot or bolt-action rifle. Both Winchester and Remington continue to offer this caliber only with the 86-grain bullet.

.25-20 Winchester (.25-20 WCF) Loading Data and Factory Ballistics

Bullet (grains/type)	Powder	Grains	Velocity	Energy	Source/Comments
60 Win OPE	680	13.0	2300	700	Hodgdon
60 SP	2400	9.6	2200	645	Hornady
60 SP	H-4227	11	2200	645	Hornady
60 SP	FL		2250	675	Factory load
86 SP	FL		1460	407	Factory load

.25-35 Winchester (.25-35 WCF)

Historical Notes: The .25-35 was developed by Winchester and introduced, in 1895, for the Model 94 lever-action rifle. Along with the .30-30, it was one of the first small-bore, smokeless powder sporting cartridges developed in the United States. Winchester, Marlin, and Savage all chambered repeating lever-action rifles for this cartridge. Quite a few single-shot rifles also chambered the .25-35 and, in Europe, it was used in combination-type arms. No American rifles have been made for the .25-35 since the end of World War II.

General Comments: The .25-35 is one of the most accurate cartridges available in the older lever-action rifles. In a good, solid-frame single-shot, it will shoot about as accurately as any .25 ever developed. It does not have sufficient velocity for long-range shooting. It has never been noted for great stopping power on deer or similar animals. In fact, it is illegal for this purpose in many states. There are still a large number of .25-35 rifles in use, but it is more or less obsolete. It is not nearly as effective as the .250-3000 Savage, .257 Roberts, or any of the more modern 6mm cartridges. However, it does have moderate recoil and will do a good job on small game and varmints at medium ranges. Modern powders would allow significant ballistic improvement if loads were at the same pressure as the current .30-30 factory ammunition. Loaded thusly, this cartridge might not appear to be quite so anemic and would be better suited to deer hunting. Ackley's improved version provides impressive performance. Winchester is the only remaining manufacturer of this ammunition.

.25-35 Winchester (.25-35 WCF) Loading Data and Factory Ballistics

Bullet (grains/type)	Powder	Grains	Velocity	Energy	Source/Comments
60 SP	IMR 4064	30.5	2800	1045	Hornady
60 SP	IMR 4320	32	2900	1120	Hornady
117 SP	IMR 3031	25.5	2300	1375	Hornady
117 SP	IMR 4320	27	2200	1258	Hornady
117 SP	FL		2230	1292	Winchester factory load

NEW
.25-45 Sharps

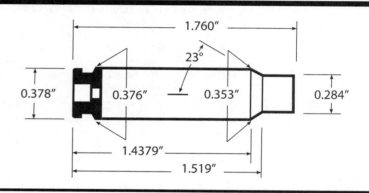

Historical Notes: The .25-45 Sharps cartridge was developed by Michael H. Blank of the Sharps Rifle Company (SRC). SRC is not to be confused with Shilo Rifles, which builds historically accurate, blackpowder Sharps rifles. The modern Sharps Rifle Company specializes in AR-15 styles of rifles, and that is the platform the .25-45 Sharps was developed for. The goal was to provide an optimum of ballistic performance from the .233 Remington (5.56 NATO) case. Blank felt the best all-around option was a .25-caliber bullet of 100 grains or less and ultimately settled on a .223 Remington case necked up to .25-caliber with a case length of 45mm and a shoulder angle of 23 degrees. The goal was to duplicate as closely as possible .250-3000 (.250 Savage) ballistics with an 87-grain bullet.

General Comments: An interesting side note to the .25-45 Sharps cartridge is the name. The .250 Sharps, .257 Sharps, and .25x45mm were considered. Ultimately, .25-45 Sharps was settled on, because it accurately depicted the caliber and case length. It should be noted that original Sharps cartridges were identified by two numbers as well, but, with those cartridges, the first number signified the caliber and the second the amount of blackpowder that was used in the load. The .25-45 Sharps continues this two-number naming tradition, but the second number now indicates case length. According to Blank, Federal will be manufacturing a factory load for the .25-45 Sharps, under the Sharps name. The cartridge does have merit, and not only in the AR-15 platform. Although velocities fall just a tad short of what can be obtained with a .250 Savage and an 87-grain bullet, the performance is close to that of the 6.5 Grendel with a similar weigh bullet, the main difference being that the Grendel requires a new bolt face and magazine for the AR-15, while the .25-45 Sharps can use both the existing magazine and bolt face for any AR-15 currently chambered for the .223 Remington/5.56 NATO. Those looking to up the performance of a lightweight .223 bolt-action, like the CZ 527 or Mossberg's new MVP Predator, will only need to install a new barrel. With modern, lightweight, mono-metal bullets, like the Barnes 80-grain Tipped TSX on the .25-45 Sharps should be a very effective deer and hog cartridge that offers very mild recoil from a bolt rifle or an AR-15.—R.A.M.

.25-45 Sharps Factory Ballistics

Bullet (grains/type)	Powder	Grains	Velocity	Energy	Source
87 Speer Hot Core	FL		2950	1671	Sharps Rifle Company

.250 Savage (.250-3000)

Historical Notes: Designed by Charles Newton, the .250 Savage was introduced by the Savage Arms Co. as a high-velocity round for the Model 99 lever-action rifle. The original loading used an 87-grain bullet at 3000 fps muzzle velocity, and Savage named it the .250-3000. One suspects the 87-grain bullet was chosen because it could be safely driven at 3000 fps with the powders then available. This allowed Savage to introduce it with the ever-so-sexy name .250-3000. Remember, in 1915, when this cartridge was introduced, riflemen were still marveling at cartridges achieving 2000 fps. About 1932, the 100-grain bullet load was marketed by Peters Cartridge Co., and later the velocity of the 87-grain bullet was slightly increased. Now it is simply called the .250 Savage. The Savage Model 20 and 40 bolt-action rifles also chambered the round, as did the Winchester Model 54 and 70 bolt-actions. Late in 1971, Savage announced that the Model 99 would again be available in this caliber. Others, such as Ruger and Remington, have made rifles in this caliber, also.

General Comments: Flat trajectory, outstanding accuracy, and good killing power on anything up to and including deer are established characteristics of the .250 Savage. It was, and is, excellent on varmints through deer. In the past few years, it has been edged out by the .257 Roberts and the new 6mm cartridges. It is far superior as a deer cartridge to the .30-30 or anything in that class, regardless of what some .30-30 addicts claim. Because of its light recoil, it is an excellent choice for youths and women. The .250-3000 is the basis of one of Ackley's best wildcats, the .250 Ackley Improved. Both Remington and Winchester continue to load this caliber. However, the 87-grain and 120-grain bullets are no longer factory loaded.

.250 Savage (.250-3000) Loading Data and Factory Ballistics

Bullet (grains/type)	Powder	Grains	Velocity	Energy	Source/Comments
60 Hdy SP	H4895	40.0	3667	1790	Hodgdon
60 SP	IMR 4064	39	3500	1632	Hornady
87 SP	IMR 4895	36.5	3200	1979	Sierra
87 SP	IMR 4064	35	3100	1857	Sierra
100 SP	IMR 4320	36	2800	1741	Nosler
117 SP	IMR 4064	32.5	2700	1894	Hornady
87 SP	FL		3030	1770	Factory load
100 SP	FL		2820	1765	Factory load
120 SP	FL		2645	1865	Factory load

.257 Roberts (.257 Roberts +P)

Historical Notes: The commercial version of the .257 Roberts was released by Remington, in 1934, chambered in its Model 30 bolt-action rifle. It was quickly picked up by Winchester for its Model 54 and the later Model 70. The Remington 722 bolt-action and the 760 pump-action models were also available in .257-caliber. In recent years, many American manufacturers have discontinued it, although Ruger continues to offer it in the Model 77 bolt-action. The original cartridge was designed by N.H. Roberts (a well-known experimenter and gun writer during the 1920s and '30s), and is based on the 7X57mm Mauser necked down. Remington changed the Roberts' shoulder angle from 15 to 20 degrees. The name of the cartridge was adopted to honor its original developer. Custom rifles in this caliber were made by the Niedner Rifle Co. as early as 1928.

General Comments: The .257 Roberts has often been referred to as the "most useful rifle cartridge ever developed." That is not very far wrong. It is suitable for a wide range of hunting under a variety of conditions. As a long-range varmint cartridge, it is as good as they come, being only slightly inferior to the newer 6mms. On deer, antelope, black bear, sheep, or goat, it is as good as any other cartridge available. Naturally, it is not as powerful as the .270 Winchester or .30-06, but it has ample power for the game mentioned at all practical ranges.

The .257 was underloaded by ammunition companies. However, in the late 1980s, higher pressure +P loads were introduced, which enabled factory-loaded .257 Roberts ammunition to reach full potential. With modern powders, the handloader can improve performance safely in all bullet weights. With 117- or 120-grain boat-tail bullets at velocities of around 2800 fps, the .257 can be used successfully on elk and caribou. It is at this end of the scale that it has an advantage over the 6mms. The original author of this book used it for many years, and it was one of his favorite calibers for Western hunting.

Ackley's Improved version of the .257 Roberts practically duplicates the ballistics of the longer .25-06. Winchester, Federal, and Remington all offer this cartridge. The 87- and 100-grain bullets are no longer factory loaded.

.257 Roberts (.257 Roberts +P) Loading Data and Factory Ballistics

Bullet (grains/type)	Powder	Grains	Velocity	Energy	Source/Comments
60 Hdy SP	H335	46.0	3885	2010	Hodgdon
60 SP	IMR 4064	44	3600	1727	Hornady
75 HP	IMR 4064	42	3300	1814	Sierra
75 Hdy HP	H4895	44.0	3561	2110	Hodgdon
87 SP	IMR 4320	37.5	3000	1739	Hornady
87 SP	H-380	46	3200	1979	Sierra, Hornady
100 SP*	IMR 4831	45.5	3100	2134	Nosler, Speer
100 SP	IMR 3031	34	2800	1741	Hornady, Sierra
117 SP	IMR 4320	36	2600	1757	Sierra
117 SP	IMR 4064	34.5	2600	1757	Hornady, Sierra
120 SP*	IMR 4831	42.5	2800	2091	Nosler
120 SP	IMR 4350	38.5	2600	1802	Hornady
87 SP	FL		3200	1980	+P factory load
100 SP	FL		3000	1998	+P factory load
117 SP	FL		2780	2009	+P factory load
120 SP	FL		2645	1865	Factory load

.25 Winchester Super Short Magnum

Historical Notes: Tailored for use in a shorter-action rifles, the .25 WSSM uses a short and fat cartridge case to equal .25-06 ballistics with 14-percent less powder and less perceived recoil. Winchester significantly redirected the shape of magnum cartridges through the year-2000 introduction of the Winchester short magnums and, later, the Winchester super short magnum families. Introduced in 2005, the .25 WSSM is intended as a versatile, dual purpose (varmint and medium game) hunting cartridge.

General Comments: The WSSM case is a half-inch shorter than the Winchester Short Magnum cases used for the .300, 7mm, and .270 WSM cartridges. The short and fat design improves interior ballistics of the .25 WSSM cartridge. Exposing more propellant surface area to the primer results in more consistent ignition. The beltless cartridge case headspaces off the shoulder to provide better centering of the bullet in the chamber. Winchester and Browning super-short rifle actions for this cartridge are stiffer, reducing accuracy inhibiting vibrations. Winchester offers .25 WSSM unprimed cartridge cases for reloaders.

13th Edition Update: Currently, Winchester is the only major ammunition manufacturer loading ammunition for the .25 WSSM. The cartridge and all its siblings become embroiled in a legal battle and the end result was a less than enthusiastic appeal on the part of manufacturers to offer rifles and/or ammunition for sale. The .25 WSSM is a fine cartridge, but it appears that all of the Super Short Winchester Magnum cartridges have peaked in terms of interest and availability. —R.A.M.

.25 Winchester Super Short Magnum Loading Data and Factory Ballistics

Bullet (grains/type)	Powder	Grains	Velocity	Energy	Source/Comments
85 BST	FL		3470	2273	Winchester
120 AccuBond	FL		3100	2347	Winchester
115 BST	FL		3060	2392	Winchester
120 PEP	FL		2990	2383	Winchester
75 V-Max	BL-C(2)	49.3	3775	2372	Hodgdon
85 Nos BT	BL-C(2)	47.5	3547	2374	Hodgdon
100 Spr BT	H4350	48.5C	3233	2320	Hodgdon
120 SP	H414	44.7	2985	2373	Hodgdon

.25-06 Remington

Historical Notes: The .25-06, originally a wildcat cartridge, was picked up by Remington and added to its commercial line, late in 1969. The wildcat version dates back to 1920, when it was introduced by A.O. Niedner. Remington has stuck to his original configuration of simply necking down the .30-06 case. The Remington Model 700 series bolt-action rifles were the first to be offered in the newly adopted caliber. At the present time, Remington, Interarms, Ruger, Savage, Winchester, Weatherby, Sako, and almost every other manufacturer of bolt-action rifles offer at least one version in .25-06. In addition, the Ruger single-shot is available in this caliber. This round became a very popular number, but that has waned recently.

General Comments: The .25-06 is a fine .25-caliber wildcat. Its emergence as a standardized factory load was welcomed by many. As a varmint cartridge with the 87-grain bullet, some have claimed it is unsurpassed. However, a comparison of factory ballistics and a little chronographing can be most informative. Comparing factory data, we see that as a varmint cartridge, both the 6mm Remington and .270 Winchester beat anything the .25-06 can offer in every category that matters. Amazingly, in spite of its much smaller case, the 6mm Remington 100-grain load is only marginally behind the .25-06 120-grain load in retained energy at long range. There really isn't any comparison between hunting loads in the .25-06 and the .270 Win. Chronograph results suggest that factory data is equally representative of what each can realistically do. So, just exactly what does the 2.5-06 offer? Evidently something, because many laud the .25-06 as among the best. Federal, Winchester, and Remington offer this cartridge in several bullet weights.

.25-06 Remington Loading Data and Factory Ballistics

Bullet (grains/type)	Powder	Grains	Velocity	Energy	Source/Comments
75 Hdy V-Max	H4350	62.0	3700	2275	Hodgdon
75 HP	IMR 4350	55	3500	2041	Hornady, Sierra
87 SP	IMR 4831	57	3500	2367	Hornady
100 SP	IMR 4831	54.5	3300	2419	Sierra, Speer
120 SP	IMR 4064	44	3000	2399	Hornady
120 SP	IMR 4831	50	3000	2399	Nosler, Speer
87 SP	FL		3500	2370	Factory load
90 SP	FL		3440	2364	Factory load
100 SP	FL		3230	2316	Factory load
117 SP	FL		2990	2320	Factory load
120 SP	FL		2940	2382	Factory load

.257 Weatherby Magnum

Historical Notes: This cartridge was designed by Roy Weatherby, in 1944, a year before he went into the commercial gun business. Like most other Weatherby cartridges, it is based on the necked-down and blown-out .300 H&H case. Commercial ammunition under the Weatherby name has been available since 1948. These have been based on Norma components since 1951. There are a number of wildcat versions of the .300 H&H Magnum necked down to .25-caliber, but the Weatherby cartridge has largely displaced these.

General Comments: The .257 Weatherby Maganum was one of the first modern, ultra-velocity, small-bore rifle cartridges to be produced on a commercial basis that developed and retained a degree of popularity. It is accurate and well-suited for long-range varmint shooting, but also delivers sufficient velocity and energy to take on almost any North American big game. A superb deer, antelope, sheep, goat, or black bear cartridge, it has also been used successfully on elk, moose, brown bear, lion, buffalo, and zebra. Many authorities insist that it is much too light for heavy game, but high-velocity advocates insist that, with proper bullets, it is adequate for anything except the largest game in close cover. However, like most of its ilk, this cartridge can be extremely hard on its barrel, especially if insufficient time is allowed between shots for the barrel to cool or if the barrel has not been cleaned adequately. And, like all high-intensity chamberings, it loses a great deal of velocity with barrels shorter than 26 inches. It is in its element for long-range plains or mountain hunting. The original author of this book used a custom Model 70 Winchester and, later, a Weatherby Mark V in this caliber, and it was dynamite on deer-size animals. For long-range varmint shooting, it can only be described as spectacular.

.257 Weatherby Magnum Loading Data and Factory Ballistics

Bullet (grains/type)	Powder	Grains	Velocity	Energy	Source/Comments
75 HP	IMR 4350	66.5	3800	2405	Hornady
87 SP	IMR 4831	71	3700	2645	Speer
100 SP	IMR 4831	66.5	3400	2568	Sierra, Speer, Nosler
117 SP	IMR 4831	61.5	3100	2497	Hornady, Sierra
120 SP	IMR 4350	59	3200	2729	Hornady
87 SP	FL		3825	2827	Weatherby factory load
100 SP	FL		3602	2882	Weatherby factory load
120 SP	FL		3305	2911	Weatherby factory load

.260 Remington/6.5-08 A-Square

Historical Notes: Inclusion of this cartridge presents us with a bit of a problem. Along about 1996, A-Square—a bona fide member of SAAMI—submitted drawings, chambering specifications, chambering reamers, sample cartridges, and all other necessary materials and data describing a new factory chambering to be adopted into the SAAMI fold. A-Square requested that the chambering be named "6.5-08 A-Square," as specified on the sample cartridge headstamp. Many months later, Remington submitted a memo to SAAMI, wherein it mentioned that it intended to eventually standardize a 6.5mm version of the .308 Winchester as the .260 Remington. Since SAAMI subsequently chose to christen this chambering as ".260 Remington," a disinterested observer would have to conclude that something was a bit rank somewhere.

General Comments: This cartridge has precisely two things to recommend it. First, it is a superior choice for long-range target shooting, particularly in the NRA High Power game, where reduced recoil with lighter bullets is valuable for the shorter-range events and where barrel life is an issue—a serious competitor can wear out several barrels each year. Second, for those who want or need a very light hunting rifle and are honest enough to admit that they cannot tolerate much recoil, this chambering is a superior choice.

Hunting load ballistics far exceed what the .243 Winchester can produce, but are not insurmountably far behind the 7mm-08 Remington. Nevertheless, this would seem to be a minimal chambering for use on any North American big game. Those intending to use this cartridge for elk hunting should consider only the best premium bullets, such as bonded core and partition designs and the 100-grain Barnes X.

.260 Remington Load Data/Factory Ballistics

Bullet (grains/type)	Powder	Grains	Velocity	Energy	Source/Comments
85 Sierra HP	RL-15	46.1	3500	2310	Sierra
100 Sierra HP	BigGame	46.2	3200	2271	Sierra
107 Sierra MatchKing	Varget	42.1	3100	2281	Sierra
120 Sierra MatchKing	V-N540	42.0	3000	2395	Sierra
140 Sierra MatchKing	RL-19	44.5	2700	2264	Sierra
120 Nosler BT	FL		2890	2226	Remington factory load
125 Nosler Partition	FL		2875	2294	Remington factory load
140 PSP Core-Lokt	FL		2750	2351	Remington factory load

6.5x55 Swedish Mauser

Historical Notes: Jointly developed by Norway and Sweden, this cartridge was adopted by both countries as an official military chambering, in 1894. Originally, both countries loaded and used essentially identical ammunition. Later, the Swedes modified dimensions and loaded to a higher pressure for use in their Mauser rifles, while the Norwegians kept the original version for use in the Krag rifle. In 1990, the National Rifle Associations of Denmark, Norway, and Sweden agreed on a standardized set of drawings and specifications, renaming the cartridge 6.5x55 SKAN. This cartridge remained in active Swedish military service until quite recently. It is quite popular throughout Scandinavia for hunting all types of game, including moose. It is also a popular choice for 300-meter target shooting and other forms of rifle competition.

Prior to World War II, the 6.5x55 Swedish was almost unknown in the United States. After the war, Canadian and U.S. sportsmen became acquainted with this chambering through the thousands of surplus Swedish Mauser rifles sold in North America. Many of these excellent rifles were sporterized in their original chambering. Canadian sportsmen were first off the mark to appreciate the virtues of this cartridge in the 1950s and 1960s. Later, U.S. sportsmen arrived at the same conclusions in the 1970s and 1980s. Other than imported rifles from Scandinavian countries, few sporting rifles in this chambering were available in the U.S. until the 1990s. This has now changed, as Winchester has offered its Featherweight M70 rifle and Ruger its M77 rifle in this chambering.

General Comments: The 6.5x55 is one of the few 6.5mm calibers ever to catch on in the United States. For many years, Norma of Sweden was the only manufacturer of this cartridge, until 1991-'92, when Federal Cartridge Co. added this cartridge to its Premium product line. This cartridge continues to gain popularity, as surplus Swedish Mauser rifles are still being imported. Two reasons for its growth in popularity are low recoil and superb accuracy. It is an excellent deer and antelope cartridge and is also suitable for bear and elk under good conditions at moderate ranges. Because of its flat trajectory, it is an outstanding choice in lightweight rifles for hunting sheep and goat in mountainous terrain.

Lack of suitable bullets and handload data handicapped the full potential of this cartridge for many years. This has changed, as good bullets and reloading data are now available from most component manufacturers. The 140-grain bullets are best for most types of hunting and are also the most accurate. The 6.5x55 Swedish Mauser case is not related to typical Mauser cartridge cases.

6.5x55mm Swedish Mauser Loading Data and Factory Ballistics

Bullet (grains/type)	Powder	Grains	Velocity	Energy	Source/Comments
85 Sierra HP	H4895	44.0	3370	2140	Hodgdon
85 HP	IMR 4320	47	3100	1814	Sierra
100 HP	H-380	43.5	3000	1999	Hornady
120 SP	H-4350	47	3000	2399	Nosler, Barnes
129 SP	H-380	43.5	2800	2246	Hornady
140 SP	IMR 4831	47	2600	2102	Speer, Barnes
140 Speer SP	H1000	51.5	2651	2185	Hodgdon
160 SP	H-4831	44	2600	2402	Speer
140 SP	FL		2550	2020	Federal factory load

6.5 Grendel

Historical Notes: The 6.5 Grendel cartridge underwent three years of development, before Bill Alexander (Alexander Arms) released it, in 2003, as a long-range cartridge specifically intended for the AR-15 family of rifles and carbines. The 6.5 Grendel transforms the military 7.62x39 parent case by necking it down to 6.5mm, blowing out the shoulder, and changing to a Small Rifle primer and flash hole. As a close relative of the benchrest-proven 6.5mm PPC, the 6.5 Grendel is the ideal length to seat long-ogive 120-grain and 130-grain bullets within the AR-15 magazine length constrictions.

General Comments: Accuracy in the 6.5 Grendel, in suitably barreled AR-15 rifles, readily attains sub-MOA, making it a great choice for long-range deer and varmint hunting. The 6.5 Grendel accommodates lightweight varmint bullets in the 90-grain class, which offer superb accuracy for competition and small-game shooting, mid-weight 108- or 120-grain competition bullets, and 130- or 140-grain game bullets for long shots on medium-sized game. Seventeen 6.5 Grendel cartridges will fit into an Alexander Arms-supplied magazine dimensioned to fit into the magazine well of an AR-15's lower receiver. The cartridge performs well in a 24-inch barrel using a 1:9 twist. Factory loads do not exceed 50,000 psi. Alexander Arms (www.alexanderarms.com) supplies rifles, magazines, ammunition, reloading dies, and brass.

13th Edition Update Alexander Arms has recently relinquished its trademark claim on the 6.5 Grendel, which has lead to recent SAAMI standardization of the cartridge. In fact, the approval by SAAMI was so recent, that we originally had this cartride and this 13th Edition Update slotted in the Wildcat Cartridge chapter, where it had been in the 12th Edition. SAAMI standardization happened during the proofing stages of this Edition, and Hornady is now factory loading this rounds, which places this cartridge in this chapter of American Centerfire Rifle Cartridges. We expect other manufacturers to join Hornady in factory loading this round.—R.A.M.

Bullet (grains/type)	Powder	Grains	Velocity	Energy	Source/Comments
90 Speer TNT	FL		3030		Alexander Arms
120 Nosler BT	FL		2580		Alexander Arms
123 Lapua Scenar	FL		2650		Alexander Arms
129 Hornady SST	FL		2450		Alexander Arms

6.5-284 Norma

Historical Notes: Hornady now produces cases and will produce ammunition (depending upon rifle manufacturing) for this long-popular wildcat chambering. Originally, this version of the .284 Winchester was designed to offer a shorter hunting cartridge that approximates 6.5-06 ballistics; the long-range accuracy potential was recognized much later. This chambering has been used extensively in NRA High Power and elsewhere, where accuracy and barrel life are important. Peak pressure specification for this thoroughly modern cartridge is comparatively high.

General Comments: A 28-inch barrel loaded with any of the better VLD (Very Low Drag) moly-plated bullets between 130 and 155 grains in this cartridge easily achieves sufficient velocities for accurate 1,000-yard benchrest shooting. These combinations generate much less recoil than any effective .30- or .33-caliber 1,000-yard match combination. This contributes to precise shooting. However, unless conditions are unusually good, those using larger-bored rifles usually fare better. While those rifles generate more recoil, which effectively reduces intrinsic accuracy, the longer bullets those bigger bores can accurately fire exhibit less wind drift and, therefore, reduce the error associated with imperfections in the shooter's ability to properly dope the wind.

Owing to a relatively high working pressure, ballistic potential is not too different from that of the .270 Winchester, making this a fine hunting cartridge and one that will function in medium-length actions. One only hopes that current gun writers treat the 6.5-284 Norma more fairly than their forebears did its progenitor.

6.5-284 Norma Loading Data

Bullet (grains/type)	Powder	Grains	Velocity	Energy	Source/Comments
100 Nosler Partition	H4350	55.0	3470	2671	Nosler
120 Nosler Ballistic Tip	RL-19	54.5	3175	2683	Nosler
120 Sierra/Nosler	RL-25	59.4	3217	2755	Norma (26-inch Bbl)
120 Sierra MatchKing	IMR-4350	44.8	2900*	2238	Sierra
125 Nosler Partition	RL-22	54.5	3137**	2728	Layne Simpson
130 Swift Scirocco	RL-22	54.0	3122**	2810	Layne Simpson
140 Match	RL-25	57.4	3028	2850	Norma (26-inch Bbl)
140 Nosler Partition	RL-22	52.5	2925	2657	Nosler
140 Sierra MatchKing	RL-22	47.5	2827*	2482	Layne Simpson
142 Sierra MatchKing	RL-22	47.5	2834*	2530	Layne Simpson
*Accuracy load					

**Favorite deer and pronghorn load

6.5 Creedmoor

Historical Notes: Cartridges of 6.5mm-caliber have never really caught on among American hunters, but some have gained a good bit of ground with long-range target shooters. The 6.5-284 Norma and .260 Remington are excellent examples. The .260 Remington has become popular not only among those who use bolt-action rifles, but among those who shoot AR-10 rifles. In that rifle, the .260 works fine with most hunting bullets, but when loaded with extremely long match bullets, such as the Sierra 140-grain MatchKing and Hornady 140-grain A-Max, they have to be seated quite deeply in the case in order to keep overall cartridge length compatible with its magazine. Engineers at Hornady solved that problem by developing a shorter cartridge called the 6.5 Creedmoor. Maximum length of the case is 1.915 inches, compared to 2.036 inches for the .260 Remington, but since the 6.5 Creedmoor case has a bit less body taper combined with a sharper shoulder angle, its gross capacity is only about five percent less.

General Comments: As competitors who shoot at great distances have proven, the .260 Remington is capable of delivering excellent accuracy and there is no reason to believe the same does not hold true for the 6.5 Creedmoor. The Remington cartridge will probably continue to be more popular among bolt-gun shooters, simply because its slightly greater powder capacity allows it to be loaded to slightly higher velocities. It also has the advantage of being easily formed by simply necking down the .308 Winchester case. Chances are good the 6.5 Creedmoor will crowd the .260 from the trough among those who shoot AR rifles in competition. As big-game cartridges, both are in the same class as the excellent 6.5x55mm Swedish.

6.5 Creedmoor Loading Data and Factory Ballistics

Bullet (grains/type)	Powder	Grains	Velocity	Energy	Source
120 A-MAX	FL		3050	2476	Hornady
140 A-MAX	FL		2820	2469	Hornady

.264 Winchester Magnum

Historical Notes: This cartridge was officially announced by Winchester, in 1958. The .264 Magnum is one of a series of cartridges based on the original Winchester .458 belted case, necked down. It is historically significant, as it is the first American 6.5mm cartridge since the long-defunct .256 Newton was announced back in 1913. It was originally available only in the Winchester bolt-action Model 70 Westerner with a 26-inch stainless steel barrel. For a time, the Remington 700 Series was offered in .264-caliber, as was the Ruger M77.

General Comments: The .264 Winchester is a fine, ultra-velocity cartridge with excellent long-range capabilities and ballistics superior to the time-tried .270 Winchester. Its development may well have been suggested by the .257 Weatherby Magnum, for the two are quite similar. The .264 is able to equal the .257 Weatherby Magnum, but with the added advantage of the heavier 140-grain bullet for larger species of big game. The 100-grain bullet is intended for animals in the deer and antelope class, the 140-grain for elk and above. The rifling twist used by Winchester is not quick enough to stabilize spitzer bullets of more than 140 grains. The handloader has a wide choice of bullets ranging from 87 to 160 grains.

All things considered, the .264 Magnum is adequate for any North American big game. It is a plains and mountain cartridge. Like most of its ilk, this cartridge can be extremely hard on its barrel, especially with either careless shooting, inadequate barrel cooling between shots, or inadequate cleaning. (Joyce Hornady said the company went through three barrels for this chambering just trying to work up the data for three bullets with a few powders each. They were tipped off to a problem, when the maximum charge for the 140-grain bullet turned out to be quite a bit higher than the maximum charge for the 120-grain bullet with the same powder.) Like all high-intensity chamberings, it loses a great deal of velocity with barrels shorter than 26 inches. To quantify this, the best-possible safe .264 Winchester Magnum loads from 22-inch barrels produce less energy than best-possible .270 Winchester loads from a 22-inch barrel, with equal-weight bullets. Both Remington and Winchester still offer this loading. However, only the 140-grain bullet is available.

.264 Winchester Magnum Loading Data and Factory Ballistics

Bullet (grains/type)	Powder	Grains	Velocity	Energy	Source/Comments
85 Sierra HP	H4831	78.0	3812	2740	Hodgdon
85 SP	IMR 4895	57	3700	2585	Sierra
100 SP	IMR 4831	65	3500	2721	Hornady
120 SP	IMR 4350	60	3200	2729	Nosler, Sierra
129 SP	IMR 4350	57	3100	2753	Hornady
140 SP	IMR 4831	61	3100	2988	Hornady
140 Nosler Part.	H870	73.0	3163	3110	Hodgdon
160 SP	IMR 4831	54.5	2700	2591	Hornady
140 SP	FL		3030	2854	Factory load

Loads shown are for the factory 26-inch barrel, using Winchester-Western cases.

6.8mm Special Purpose Cartridge (6.8 SPC)

Historical Notes: Anecdotal reports from U.S. forces involved in combat in Iraq and Afghanistan in recent years indicate the six decade-old 7.62X39 cartridge and AK47 rifle may be more effective in combat than the U.S. M4 carbines firing the 5.56X45 cartridge. In 2003, Steve Holland and Cris Murray, individuals associated with special forces and marksmanship units, developed a special-purpose cartridge to improve combat effectiveness in short-barreled (16.5-inch) M4 carbines used for special operations. The resulting 6.8 SPC (Special Purpose Cartridge) achieved favorable results in actual usage, but has not been officially adopted by the U.S. Army, as of 2005. The cartridge is under review by the U.S. Marine Corps and FBI.

General Comments: Intended to launch heavier bullets than the standard U.S. 5.56 round, the 6.8 SPC uses the 1906-vintage .30 Remington cartridge shortened and necked down to accept a .270-caliber (6.8mm) bullet. Holland and Murray selected the .30 Remington as a parent case for two reasons. First, bolts for the M-16 family of rifles and carbines can readily be manufactured to accept the .30 Remington's case head diameter (.420). Second, standard 20-round and 30-round M-16 magazines can accept the 6.8 SPC without change. After extensive test firings into ordnance gel blocks, and on military firing ranges with the .30 Remington cases sized for .30, 7mm, .270, 6.5mm, and 6mm bullets, .270-caliber bullets delivered the best balance of velocity, accuracy, and terminal performance. Hornady and Remington offer loaded 6.8 SPC ammunition. The cartridge is chambered by Barrett, DPMS, and PRI in AR15 rifles; by both SSK Industries and Thompson/Center in Contender, G2, and Encore single-shot actions; by Remington in bolt-action rifles; and by custom gunsmiths on CZ-527 bolt-actions. It is a good whitetail deer cartridge.

6.8mm Special Purpose Cartridge (6.8 SPC) Loading Data and Factory Ballistics

Bullet (grains/type)	Powder	Grains	Velocity	Energy	Source/Comments
110 V-Max	FL		2550	1588	Hornady
115 MC	FL		2800	2002	Remington
90 Spr HP	H4198	28.6C	3012	1812	Hodgdon
110 V-Max	Benchmark	27.0	2518	1548	Hodgdon
115 Sierra HPBT	H322	28.2C	2608	1736	Hodgdon

.270 Winchester

Historical Notes: Designed by Winchester, in 1925, for its Model 54 bolt-action rifle, the .270 caused quite a stir in shooting circles. It has remained somewhat controversial ever since. At the time of introduction, it offered better long-range performance than any big-game cartridge available on the American market. It has now been adopted by practically every manufacturer of standard bolt-action, high-powered sporting rifles in the world. The Remington pump-action and Remington and Browning semi-autos are also available in .270-caliber. The cartridge is based on the .30-06 case necked down to .277-inch. (It is just possible that Winchester chose a .277-inch bullet to avoid paralleling anything European or British, and they could possibly have been inspired by a Chinese cartridge that used a .277-inch bullet. We will likely never know.) The case neck is .050-inch longer but, except for the neck and headstamp, the .270 Winchester is otherwise identical to the .30-06. This cartridge was a long-time favorite of the late, well-known gun writer Jack O'Connor, who probably contributed more to popularizing the .270 than any other individual. Today, the .270 Winchester is one of the most popular calibers on the market.

General Comments: Along with the .30-06, this is one of the most accurate and effective all-round American big-game cartridges. Its reputation and popularity have increased steadily since its introduction. Although not intended as a varmint cartridge, the .270 will serve very well in that capacity when loaded with bullets of 90 to 110 grains. It is generally conceded to be a better long-range varmint cartridge than its parent, the .30-06. The 130-grain bullet at 3100 fps muzzle velocity is considered adequate by many experienced hunters for any North American big game. When first introduced, some deer hunters complained that the 130-grain bullet had such an explosive effect that it ruined too much meat. To satisfy the demand for a deer load, Winchester brought out a 150-grain bullet at a reduced velocity of 2675 fps. However, it was short-lived, because the people who demanded it wouldn't buy it. The present 150-grain bullet at 2860 fps is intended for maximum penetration on heavier animals such as elk, moose, or bear. Some disagree, but current evidence reinforces the conclusion that the .270 is adequate for any North American big game and some African plains game, as well. Assuming the hunter uses the proper bullet for the job at hand, the .270 will deliver reliable performance. In any comparison of the .270 with the .30-06, much depends on intended use and hunting conditions. For some reason, many individuals shoot better with the .270 than the .30-06. The .270 is flatter shooting than the .30-06 and, thus, makes a better varmint/big-game rifle where this is a consideration. The .30-06, with its 180-, 200-, and 220-grain bullets, must be conceded as a better heavy-game cartridge. In accuracy and general performance, there isn't a great deal to argue about. Anyone trying to make a big case for one against the other is beating a pretty dead horse. The .270 Winchester is commercially loaded by all large domestic and most foreign ammunition manufacturers.

.270 Winchester Loading Data and Factory Ballistics

Bullet (grains/type)	Powder	Grains	Velocity	Energy	Source/Comments
90 Sierra HP	H4350	62.0	3603	2590	Hodgdon
100 Speer SP	RL-19	64.0	3510	2735	Hodgdon
110 Hornady HP	H4350	57.0	3267	2605	Hodgdon
130 Speer SP	RL-19	60.0	3160	2880	Hodgdon
135 Sierra SPBT	H1000	63.0	3011	2715	Hodgdon
140 Swift SP	H1000	63.0	2979	2755	Hodgdon
150 SP	IMR 4831	54	2800	2612	Speer, Sierra, Hornady
150 Sierra SPBT	RL-22	58.5	3010	3020	Hodgdon
160 Nosler Part.	H1000	59.0	2765	2715	Hodgdon
180 Barnes JRN	RL-22	53.0	2762	3045	Barnes
100 SP	FL		3480	2612	Factory load
130 SP	FL		3060	2702	Factory load
150 SP	FL		2850	2705	Factory load

.270 Winchester Short Magnum (.270 WSM)

Historical Notes: Introduced in 2001 and intended for riflemen preferring the .270 family of cartridges, the .270 WSM is crafted from the instantly popular .300 WSM case, necked down to accept .277-inch diameter bullets. Compared to the long-popular .270 Winchester the late Jack O'Connor held in high esteem, the .270 WSM is a modern magnum upgrade, suitable for short-action rifles and offering higher performance—that approaching .270 Weatherby Magnum velocity levels with similar weight bullets. SSK Industries also re-barrels the AR-10 self-loading rifle for .270 WSM.

General Comments: For efficient and consistent powder burning, the .270 WSM continues the short-fat cartridge case geometry Winchester first popularized in the .300 WSM, a benchrest-proven concept for nearly three decades. Retaining the 35-degree shoulder of the parent .300 WSM case, the .270 WSM headspaces on the shoulder, which should provide for tighter headspacing tolerances and improved accuracy potential.

13th Edition Update: This cartridge and all its Winchester Short Magnum siblings became embroiled in a legal battle, and the end result was a less than enthusiastic appeal on the part of other manufacturers to offer rifles and/or ammunition for sale. However, unlike the Winchester Super Short Magnums that are collecting dust on the shelves or in shooters gun racks, the WSM line still enjoys moderate appeal, especially the .270 and .300 offerings.—R.A.M.

.270 Winchester Short Magnum Loading Data and Factory Ballistics

Bullet (grains/type)	Powder	Grains	Velocity	Energy	Source/Comments
130 BST	FL		3275	3096	Winchester
140 Fail Safe	FL		3175	3035	Winchester
150 XP3	FL		3120	3242	Winchester
140 Nosler Ballistic Tip	Magnum	71.0	3200	3182	Nosler
150 Nosler Ballistic Tip	Magpro	68.0	3187	3382	Nosler

.270 Weatherby Magnum

Historical Notes: Most shooting enthusiasts think that the .270 Weatherby was developed to satisfy a demand for this caliber after the popularity of the .300 Weatherby Magnum had been established. As a matter of fact, the .270 was the first of the line developed by Roy Weatherby on the necked-down .300 H&H case. This was in 1943, after experiments with an improved .220 Swift that Weatherby called the .220 Rocket. It was largely actual hunting experience with the .270 WM that started Weatherby on the high-velocity trail. This culminated in his starting a commercial gun business, in September 1945.

General Comments: The popularity of the .270 Winchester made it almost mandatory for Roy Weatherby to include this caliber in his line of commercial magnum rifle cartridges. The .270 Weatherby Magnum has been used extensively, and successfully, on all species of North American big game. It has also achieved notable success on African plains game. Those who have used it claim the .270 Weatherby provides flat trajectory, excellent long-range stopping power on all thin-skinned game, and noticeably less recoil than the famous .300 WM. As an added attraction, the .270 WM is not impractical for varmint shooting. The 100-grain bullet is excellent for this purpose, thus making the .270 WM a very versatile all-round caliber. However, it is important to allow plenty of barrel-cooling time with this and all high-intensity cartridges. The .270 WM is easy and economical to reload, and empty cases are available for it. Like the other large-capacity magnum cases, it does not lend itself to reduced loads and is at its best with full or nearly full charges. It is a very fine choice for the hunter who wants to include varmint hunting potential in a big-game rifle. It has been one of the most popular calibers that Weatherby offers.

.270 Weatherby Magnum Loading Data and Factory Ballistics

Bullet (grains/type)	Powder	Grains	Velocity	Energy	Source/Comments
90 HP	IMR 4350	73	3800	2886	Sierra
100 SP	IMR 4350	71	3600	2878	Speer
100 SP	H-4831	76.5	3500	2721	Hornady
130 SP	IMR 4350	68	3300	3144	Speer, Sierra, Nosler
130 SP	IMR 4831	70	3300	3144	Sierra, Speer
140 SP	IMR 4350	66.5	3100	2988	Nosler
150 SP	IMR 4350	66	3000	2998	Hornady, Speer
150 SP	IMR 4831	67	3000	2998	Nosler, Sierra
160 SP	IMR 4831	65	2900	2989	Nosler
100 SP	FL		3760	3139	Weatherby factory load
130 SP	FL		3375	3283	Weatherby factory load
150 SP	FL		3245	3501	Weatherby factory load

7-30 Waters

Historical Notes: The 7-30 Waters was introduced, in 1984, for the U.S. Repeating Arms Model 94XTR Angle Eject rifle and carbine. The cartridge was the work of Ken Waters, a well-known gun writer and ballistics expert. He began planning the cartridge, in 1976, as a high-velocity, flat-trajectory round for short, handy, lever-action carbines.

There are many problems to be overcome by those who would improve on the performance of the .30-30 cartridge class in lever-action rifles. Severe restrictions are imposed by tubular magazines, the length of the action, and permissible working pressures. However, by 1982, Ken had developed a cartridge that would push the 139-grain 7mm bullet at 2600 fps. At this point, U.S. Repeating Arms Co. became interested in the project and decided, in 1983, to produce Model 94 lever-action rifles in this new cartridge. Federal Cartridge Co. then completed the final version of the cartridge by making various dimensional changes and opting for a lighter 120-grain bullet to achieve higher velocity at less pressure. The current commercial loading uses a 120-grain Nosler Partition bullet that develops a muzzle velocity of 2700 fps when fired from a 24-inch barrel.

General Comments: The 7-30 Waters does offer improved performance for those who like lever-action carbines or rifles. This should make a good deer and black bear-class cartridge. However, the majority of .30-30 lever-action shooters prefer the short carbine, since most are woods hunters. The 7-30, with its light 120-grain bullet, is unlikely to best the .30-30, .32 Special, .38-55, etc., with shots at close range. Also, it is not going to be the answer for the long-range plains or mountain hunter. When fired from a 20-inch barrel, its performance is considerably reduced. So, anyone interested in this cartridge will be better served if they buy the rifle rather than the carbine. The light recoil of this cartridge makes it an excellent choice for a woman, boy, or anyone who is recoil sensitive. The 7-30 is at its best in broken country, with shots varying from patches of brush and trees to open areas with shots ranging from 75 to 175 yards.

7-30 Waters Loading Data and Factory Ballistics

Bullet (grains/type)	Powder	Grains	Velocity	Energy	Source/Comments
120 Nosler FP Part.	H414	42.0	2757	2025	Hodgdon
120 SP	H-335	28.5	2500	1666	Nosler
130 SP	H-335	33	2600	1952	Speer
139 Hornady FP	RL-15	34.7	2540	1990	Hodgdon
140 SP	W748	35	2500	1943	Hornady
140 SP	H-335	34	2600	2102	Hornady
145 SP	748	34	2400	1855	Speer
154 Hornady NR	H414	37.0	2347	1835	Hodgdon
120 SP	FL		2700	1940	Federal factory load

7mm Mauser (7x57mm)

Historical Notes: Developed by Mauser as a military cartridge, the 7x57mm was introduced in 1892. Shortly afterward, this caliber was adopted by the Spanish government and chambered in a limited quantity of Model 92 Mauser bolt-action rifles. In 1893, Spain adopted a new model Mauser rifle in this same cartridge. This rifle has been called the Spanish Mauser ever since, although it was also adopted by Mexico and a number of South American countries. Remington chambered its rolling block and Lee rifles for the 7mm about 1897, and later the Model 30. The Winchester Model 54 and 70 also chambered it. Recently, the Ruger Model 77 and Winchester Featherweight bolt-action, plus the Ruger No. 1 single-shot, offer the 7mm as standard. Also, most European-made bolt-action rifles and combination guns chamber the 7mm Mauser, as do many custom-made rifles each year.

General Comments: Although originally a military cartridge, the 7x57mm Mauser has proven to be one of the best all-round sporting rounds ever developed. It is particularly useful in lightweight rifles, because it

delivers good killing power with moderate recoil. It has been used successfully on every species of big game on earth. However, it is no dangerous-game cartridge in the true sense of the term. Its success in the field is due largely to the ability of the hunters who have used it. Ballistically, it is only slightly less powerful than the .270 Winchester or .280 Remington. It is adequate for most American big game, but is perhaps on the light side for large bear or moose. The 7mm Mauser was once discontinued by American gun manufacturers (about 1940) due to lack of popularity. Since the end of World War II, it has become increasingly common, due to the influx of surplus 7mm military rifles. The wide selection of 7mm bullets now available for handloading has also contributed to an increase in popularity. The 7x57mm Mauser is commercially loaded by all domestic and most foreign ammunition manufacturers.

7mm Mauser (7x57mm) Loading Data and Factory Ballistics

Bullet (grains/type)	Powder	Grains	Velocity	Energy	Source/Comments
100 HP	W748	52.6	3300	2419	Hornady
115 SP	IMR 3031	46	3000	2299	Speer
120 SP	IMR 4064	46	2900	2241	Hornady
130 SP	IMR 4350	52	2850	2345	Speer
139 SP	IMR 4064	45	2800	2420	Hornady
150 SP	IMR 4064	41.5	2700	2429	Sierra, Nosler, Hornady
160 Sierra SPBT	RL-22	50.0	2690	2570	Hodgdon
175 SP	IMR 4895	42	2500	2430	Hornady
175 SP	IMR 4064	39	2450	2333	Nosler, Sierra
140 SP	FL		2660	2199	Factory load
145 SP	FL		2690	2334	Factory load
154 SP	FL		2690	2475	Factory load
175 SP	FL		2440	2313	Factory load

7mm-08 Remington

Historical Notes: Remington introduced this medium-capacity rifle cartridge to the marketplace, in 1980. It is based on the .308 Winchester case necked down to 7mm and was loaded with a 140-grain bullet at 2860 fps. Remington advertised this cartridge as the "... first modern 7mm round designed for use in short-action rifles." This is an interesting claim, in view of the fact that the .284 Winchester, designed for the same purpose, arrived on the scene in 1963. Furthermore, the 7mm-08 is a direct copy of the 7mm/.308 wildcat dating back to 1958 and earlier. This is not meant to denigrate a fine cartridge, but to demonstrate that there really sometimes isn't much new under the sun, despite advertising claims. The 7mm-08 is chambered in exactly the same actions as the .284 Winchester, but cannot equal .284 ballistics.

Original rifles chambered for the 7mm-08 were the Remington Model 788 and 700BDL Varmint Special bolt actions. Current Remington catalogs list the 700 series and Model Seven bolt-actions as available in this chambering. Other makers have also chambered it.

Remington has hung its hat on the 7mm caliber, and with considerable success. It now offers six chamberings: 7mm BR, 7mm-08, 7x57mm Mauser, 7mm Express (.280 Remington), 7mm Remington Magnum, and 7 STW. The 7mm BR originated as something of a semi-wildcat based on the .308x1.5-inch necked down. Remington has contributed more than any other company to the belated recognition of the ballistic advantages of the 7mm caliber by U.S. shooters.

General Comments: Owing partly to a more pointed bullet shape, the 7mm-08 140-grain load surpasses the .308 Winchester 150-grain load downrange, according to Remington tests from a 24-inch barrel. This appears to be true. At 500 yards, the 7mm-08 bullet has an edge of 238 fps and 750 ft-lbs of energy over the .308 bullet. This would make quite some difference in potential killing power and also help in better bullet placement at unknown distances. There is not sufficient difference to cause owners of .308-caliber rifles to rush down and trade them off for 7mm-08s, but it does illustrate the ballistic advantages of the smaller caliber loaded with more streamlined bullets.

The 7mm-08 is a great favorite with many metallic silhouette shooters, and there are many glowing reports regarding its accuracy on the range, particularly with handloads. It is also building a good reputation as a long-range deer and antelope cartridge. When handloaded with bullets heavier than 140 grains, it is also suitable for heavier game, such as elk. Unfortunately, the two factory bullet weights do not make for a very flexible big-game cartridge. On the other hand, by handloading, this cartridge can be adapted to anything from varmint shooting through elk.

Case capacity of the 7mm-08 is slightly less than the 7x57mm Mauser, and performance with the heavier bullets of around 175 grains is about 100 to 150 fps less, which is not anything to get really excited about. The fact of the matter is that the 7mm-08 is adequate for most North American hunting, though handicapped by only two commercial bullet loadings. Remington has been joined by Federal in offering factory loaded ammunition in this caliber.

7mm-08 Remington Loading Data and Factory Ballistics

Bullet (grains/type)	Powder	Grains	Velocity	Energy	Source/Comments
100 HP	H-335	40.5	3000	1999	Hornady
120 SP	IMR 4320	41	2700	1943	Hornady, Sierra, Nosler
130 SP	IMR 4064	45	3000	2599	Speer
140 SP	IMR 4895	44	2900	2615	Sierra
150 SP	IMR 4320	38	2400	1919	Hornady, Sierra
160 SP	IMR 4350	44	2650	2496	Nosler, Sierra, Speer
175 SP	IMR 4350	44	2600	2627	Speer
120 SP	FL		3000	2398	Factory load
140 SP	FL		2860	2542	Factory load

.284 Winchester

Historical Notes: The .284 was introduced by Winchester, in 1963, for its Model 88 lever-action and Model 100 semi-auto rifles. Both have since been discontinued. This is the first American commercial cartridge to have a rebated, or undercut, rim of smaller diameter than the body of the case, though British and European designers used this type of case years ago. For a short time, the Savage Model 99 lever-action and Browning's BLR were available in .284. No major gun makers now offer this chambering.

General Comments: The .284 Winchester has the rim diameter of the .30-06 and the body diameter of the belted magnums. This provides increased case capacity in a relatively short case. The cartridge is designed for short actions and will increase the performance of these short, light rifles. Ballistics are practically identical to the .280 Remington. There is no difference in killing power, range, or capability between the two. (Except in some gun writers' imaginations!) The .284 Winchester should be a good long-range cartridge for any North American big game. It could also be adapted for varmint shooting. This cartridge has recently staged a well-deserved comeback and continues to prosper, particularly as a basis for short-action wildcats.

.284 Winchester Loading Data and Factory Ballistics

Bullet (grains/type)	Powder	Grains	Velocity	Energy	Source/Comments
100 HP	IMR 4350	60.5	3200	2274	Sierra
120 Hornady SP	RL-19	60.5	3265	2840	Hodgdon
130 SP	IMR 4350	58	3100	2775	Speer
140 SP	IMR 4350	55	3000	2799	Hornady
140 SP	IMR 4895	46	2800	2438	Sierra
145 Speer SP	RL-19	55.0	2940	2780	Hodgdon
150 SP	IMR 4350	53.5	2800	2612	Sierra

.284 Winchester Loading Data and Factory Ballistics

Bullet (grains/type)	Powder	Grains	Velocity	Energy	Source/Comments
160 Sierra SPBT	RL-19	54.0	2885	2955	Hodgdon
175 SP	IMR 4350	50	2600	2627	Hornady, Sierra, Speer
150 SP	FL		2860	2724	Winchester factory load

.280 Remington/ 7mm Express Remington

Historical Notes: The .280 Remington was introduced by that company, in 1957. Initially it was chambered in the Remington Model 740 autoloader, later in the 760 pump-action and the 721 and 725 bolt-actions. The Remington 700 series bolt-action rifles originally included the .280 chambering. In an effort to increase sales, from 1979 to 1980 Remington cataloged the .280 as the 7mm Express Remington. But too much confusion resulted, and Remington went back to the original .280 moniker. The .280 Remington, actually a 7mm with a bullet diameter of .284-inch, is based on the 30-06 case necked down. It is very similar to the wildcat 7mm-06, which has been around for a good many years. In 1979, Remington introduced a new 150-grain loading.

General Comments: This is a .30-06 case neckeddown and with the shoulder moved forward .050-inch to prevent it from being chambered in .270 Winchester rifles. Had this been possible, the oversized neck might not have had room to open enough to free the bullet, and the results could have been extremely dangerous—yet, by moving the shoulder forward, Remington created an even more dangerous situation. The .270 Winchester cartridge, which is visually almost indistinguishable from the .280, chambers effortlessly in .280 Remington rifles. Should the extractor catch the case during loading and then allow it to slip forward when the firing pin strikes the primer, or should the striker reach the primer of a load that was chambered ahead of the extractor, the results would be a .050-inch headspace problem with almost certain head separation and the resulting flood of 50,000-psi gas in one's face. Not a pretty thought. Remington could have solved the original problem and eliminated the one it created by simply enlarging the case at the shoulder or increasing the shoulder angle.

The .280 Remington is slightly more powerful than the .270 Winchester. It would be stretching a point to say that the .280 is better than the .270 Winchester, although it is probably a little more versatile, due to the wider variety of factory bullets available. If you are a handloader, any difference would be one of personal preference. The .280 is certainly adequate for any North American big game and would also lend itself for use on large varmints. It is another case of a good wildcat cartridge finally emerging in a commercial version. It has picked up a modest following among 7mm fans since its introduction. Loaded with the 120-grain or new 100-grain varmint bullets, the .280 becomes an excellent varmint cartridge. The 150-grain bullet at 2970 fps brings out some of the latent potential of this cartridge, which is truly an excellent long-range big-game cartridge. Both Remington and Winchester commercially load this cartridge.

.280 Remington Loading Data and Factory Ballistics

Bullet (grains/type)	Powder	Grains	Velocity	Energy	Source/Comments
100 Sierra HP	VarGet	51.3	3433	2615	Hodgdon
120 Barnes XFB	H4350	56.0	3114	2580	Hodgdon
130 SP	IMR 4350	57	3100	2775	Speer
140 Nosler Part.	H4831	58.5	2927	2660	Hodgdon
150 SP	IMR 4831	48	2900	2802	Sierra, Nosler
160 Sierra SPBT	RL-22	55.7	2795	2775	Hodgdon
175 SP	IMR 4350	52	2650	2730	Speer, Hornady
120 SP	FL		3150	2643	Factory load
150 SP	FL		2890	2781	Factory load
165 SP	FL		2820	2913	Factory load
140 SP	FL		3050	2799	Factory load

.280 Ackley Improved

Historical Notes: In addition to being a famous gunsmith, a barrel maker, and a college professor, P.O. Ackley absolutely ruled the roost when it came to creating wildcat and improved cartridges. One of his earliest was the 7mm-06 Improved, which was formed by necking down the .30-06 case and fire-forming it to less body taper and a 40-degree shoulder angle. Years later, and not long after the .280 Remington was introduced, reloading equipment maker Fred Huntington reformed its case to the Improved configuration with minimum body taper and a 35-degree shoulder angle and called it the .280 RCBS. Since cases for Huntington's cartridge could be formed by firing .280 Remington ammo in a rifle chambered for it, Ackley abandoned his 7mm-06 Improved and started chambering rifles for the .280 RCBS, but rather than staying with its 35-degree shoulder angle, he changed it to 40 degrees. And so was born a cartridge we know today as the .280 Ackley Improved. After close to a half-century of being something only handloaders could love, the .280 Ackley Improved became a factory number, when Nosler registered it with SAAMI, started loading the ammunition, and began chambering rifles for it, in 2007.

General Comments: We are tempted to say the .280 Ackley Improved is more accurate than the .280 Remington, but doing so would be unfair, since all of the rifles Frank Barnes tried it in were rather expensive custom jobs, while all he tested chambered for the standard .280 Remington were off-the-shelf factory rifles. The Ackley version is a fine old cartridge and, when loaded with the right bullet, is big enough medicine for game up to elk and moose. Even so, the .280 Ackley Improved is not as fast as the 7mm Remington Magnum, as a few of that cartridge's avid supporters would have us believe. All things including barrel length and the chamber pressure to which the two are loaded being equal, the .280 Ackley Improved is about 100 fps faster with all bullet weights than the standard .280 Remington. Cases are easily formed by firing .280 Remington factory ammo in a rifle properly chambered for the .280 Ackley Improved.

.280 Ackley Improved Loading Data and Factory Ballistics

Bullet (grains/type)	Powder	Grains	Velocity	Energy	Source
120 Nosler Ballistic Tip	H4831	65.0	3240	2794	Hodgdon
130 Sierra HPBT	IMR-4831	58.3	3128	2821	Hodgdon
140 Nosler Ballistic Tip	H4350	55.5	3012	2817	Hodgdon
150 Barnes TSX	IMR-4831	54.5	2881	2762	Hodgdon
160 Nosler AccuBond	IMR-4831	55.5	2847	2877	Hodgdon
175 Speer Grand Slam	IMR-4831	55.0	2702	2834	Hodgdon
140 Nosler AccuBond	FL	FL	3050	2889	Nosler

7mm Remington Magnum

Historical Notes: Introduced by Remington, during 1962, the 7mm Remington Magnum was brought out at the same time as the improved, bolt-action 700-series rifles, which replaced the earlier Models 721, 722, and 725. Most other manufacturers have since added this popular caliber to their lines. It took American firearms manufacturers nearly 40 years to realize that the .275 Holland & Holland (made long ago by Western Cartridge Co.) is a first-rate, medium-game, long-range cartridge. The long line of 7mm wildcats is much like the old .275 H&H, which came out in 1912. Remington chose to ignore the classic 7mm bullet—160-grain spitzer—in its 7mm Magnum loads.

General Comments: The 7mm Remington Magnum is a fine, long-range, big-game cartridge. There is a good selection of factory loaded 7mm bullets available, and the handloader could make it do just about anything. It has ample power for any North American big game and most thin-skinned African varieties. However, it is an open-country plains or mountain cartridge, rather than a woods or brush number. Many will compare it with the 7mm Weatherby Magnum or the 7x61mm Sharpe & Hart Super. Bitter arguments will ensue as to which is the best or most powerful. This will be akin to the ancient Greek pastime of discussing how many spirits can dance on the head of a pin. However, any difference in these cartridges will be strictly a matter of opinion or imagination. They all have nearly the same case capacity, and none will do anything the others can't duplicate. In fact, the 7mm Remington is hardly a new or brilliant design. It is largely a commercial version of several short-bellied wildcat 7mm magnums (Ackley, Luft, Mashburn, etc.). Its principal advantage lies in the fact that it is a standard factory product that is widely distributed and available in well-made, moderately priced rifles. Come to think of it, that's quite a bit to a lot of people. However, don't trade off your present 7mm Magnum with the idea that the Remington round is going to provide some mysterious extra margin of power or knockdown. The 7mm Rem. Mag. can be somewhat hard on barrels, especially with either careless shooting, inadequate barrel cooling between shots, or inadequate cleaning. And, like all similar chamberings, it loses significant velocity with barrels shorter than 24 inches. Actual ballistics may be closer to the 7mm Weatherby Magnum than factory data suggests. Ammunition in 7mm Remington Magnum caliber is available in a wide variety from all domestic and most foreign ammunition manufacturers.

7mm Remington Magnum Loading Data and Factory Ballistics

Bullet (grains/type)	Powder	Grains	Velocity	Energy	Source/Comments
100 HP	IMR 4831	71.5	3500	2721	Hornady
115 HP	IMR 4831	71	3400	2953	Speer
120 SP	IMR 4350	66	3350	2991	Sierra, Nosler
130 SP	IMR 4350	63	3200	2957	Speer
140 SP	IMR 4350	64	3100	2988	Nosler, Sierra, Hornady
150 SP	IMR 4831	62	3000	2998	Nosler, Sierra
160 SP	IMR 4831	62.5	3000	3198	Sierra, Nosler, Speer
175 SP	H-450	64.5	2900	3269	Sierra
140 SP	FL		3175	3133	Factory load
150 SP	FL		3110	3221	Factory load
160 SP	FL		2950	3090	Factory load
165 SP	FL		2900	3081	Factory load
175 SP	FL		2860	3178	Factory load

7mm Remington Short Action Ultra Mag

Historical Notes: In 2001, Remington introduced the 7mm Remington Short Action Ultra Mag cartridge as a competitor to Winchester's 7mm Winchester Short Magnum. Ballistic performance of the Remington and Winchester offerings is similar. The 7mm Remington Short Action Ultra Magnum easily exceeds or equals 7mm Remington Magnum performance, while fitting into easy-carrying, fast-handling rifles such as the short-action Remington Model 7.

General Comments: Based on a shortened .300 Ultra Magnum case, which is itself derived from a slightly modified .404 Jeffery cartridge of African fame, the 7mm Remington Short Action Ultra Magnum is slightly shorter and smaller in diameter than its Winchester counterpart. Short, fat cases burn powder very efficiently, since the primer's flash ignites a larger area of the packed gunpowder. The case is unbelted and headspaces on the shoulder for improved shoulder tolerances. Remington barrels for this cartridge use a twist rate of 1:9¼. Shooters are cautioned never to fire a 7mm Remington Short Action Ultra Magnum in a 7mm WSM-chambered rifle, as the headspace would be excessive, leading to possible injury or firearms damage.

7mm Remington Short Action Ultra Mag Loading Data and Factory Ballistics

Bullet (grains/type)	Powder	Grains	Velocity	Energy	Source/Comments
120 Nosler Ballistic Tip	H414	64.5	3424	3120	Nosler
140 Nosler Partition	RL-19	62.0	3147	3075	Nosler
Nosler 150 Partition	IMR-4350	58.5	3047	3089	Nosler
Nosler 160 AccuBond	RL-22	59.0	2942	3072	Nosler
Nosler 175 Partition	RL-22	59.0	2851	3155	Nosler
140 PSP	FL		3175	3133	Remington factory load
150 PSP	FL		3110	3221	Remington factory load
160 Nosler Partition	FL		2960	3112	Remington factory load

7mm Winchester Short Magnum (7mm WSM)

Historical Notes: Introduced in 2001 and intended for ranks of riflemen preferring 7mm calibers, the 7mm WSM is crafted from the instantly popular .300 WSM case, necked down to accept .284-inch diameter bullets. Also, the 7mm WSM shoulder was lengthened by .038-inch to prevent any possibility of chambering in a .270 WSM rifle. The 7mm WSM is the modern, short-action equivalent of the 7mm Remington Magnum, a cartridge that showed untold numbers of hunters just how effective a flat-shooting, highly efficient .284 cartridge could be for North American and large African plains game. SSK Industries also rebarrels the AR-10 self-loading rifle for 7mm WSM.

General Comments: For efficient and consistent powder burning, the 7mm WSM continues the short-fat cartridge case geometry Winchester first popularized in the .300 WSM, a benchrest-proven concept for nearly three decades. Omitting a belt on the case, the 7mm WSM headspaces on the shoulder, which should provide for tighter headspacing tolerances and bettered accuracy potential. Shooters are cautioned never to fire the slightly shorter, physically similar 7mm Remington Short Action Ultra Magnum in a .270 WSM- or 7mm WSM-chambered rifles, as the .270 bore is smaller and the headspace would be excessive, leading to possible injury or firearms damage.

13th Edition Update: This cartridge and all its Winchester Short Magnum siblings become embroiled in a legal battle, and the end result was a less than enthusiastic appeal on the part of other manufacturers to offer rifles and/or ammunition for sale. However, unlike the Winchester Super Short Magnums that are collecting dust on the shelves or in shooters gun racks, the WSM line still enjoys moderate appeal, especially the .270 and .300 offerings.—R.A.M.

7mm Winchester Short Magnum Loading Data and Factory Ballistics

Bullet (grains/type)	Powder	Grains	Velocity	Energy	Source/Comments
140 BST	FL		3225	3233	Winchester/Olin
150 P Pt	FL		3200	3410	Winchester/Olin
160 Fail Safe	FL		2990	3176	Winchester/Olin
140 BST	WXR	70.0	3200	3184	Winchester/Olin 61,500 psi
140 SP	WXR	66.5	3220	3224	Winchester/Olin 63,900 psi
150 SP	WXR	68.0	3145	3295	Winchester/Olin 61,600 psi
160 BST	WXR	60.5	2915	3020	Winchester/Olin 61,700 psi

7mm Weatherby Magnum

Historical Notes: The 7mm Weatherby Magnum was developed, in 1944, as one of a series of cartridges based on the necked-down .300 H&H case (it is the .270 WM necked up .007-inch, although it does use a longer overall cartridge length). There are several similar wildcat versions, but Weatherby's design is the most popular, due to the availability of commercial ammunition.

General Comments: The 7mm (or .284-caliber) has long been popular in the United States in various wildcat cartridges, yet the original 7mm Mauser never generated any great enthusiasm. The 7mm Weatherby Magnum, offered as a maximum-performance cartridge, is probably the best known and widely used of the current 7mm Magnums, with the single exception of the 7mm Remington Magnum. This is due in part to the availability of factory loaded ammunition having a good selection of bullet weights. The 7mm Weatherby has a slight edge over the .270 Weatherby on tough or dangerous game, because it can use heavier bullets and churns up greater energy. However, if long-range varmint shooting is on the agenda, the .270 is the better choice. The 7mm Weatherby Magnum is adequate for any North American big game and all thin-skinned African game. The 7mm Weatherby Magnum has, to a large extent, lost popularity to the 7mm Remington Magnum, because the Remington version is available in a wider variety of rifles that are generally less expensive than the Weatherbys. Like most high-intensity cartridges, the 7mm WM can be somewhat hard on its barrel, especially with either careless shooting, inadequate barrel cooling between shots, or inadequate barrel cleaning. And, like all similar chamberings, it loses significant velocity with barrels shorter than 24 inches. Ammunition in this caliber is now available from Remington and PMC, as well as Weatherby. For many years now, Norma has loaded Weatherby ammunition in all calibers under the Weatherby brand name. In 1992, Norma began offering Weatherby calibers under the Norma brand name. Norma ammunition is distributed in the United States by Dynamit Nobel.

7mm Weatherby Magnum Loading Data and Factory Ballistics

Bullet (grains/type)	Powder	Grains	Velocity	Energy	Source/Comments
100 HP	IMR 4350	73.5	3600	2878	Hornady
115 HP	IMR 4831	76	3600	3310	Speer
120 SP	IMR 4350	70	3400	3081	Sierra, Nosler, Hornady
130 SP	IMR 4320	63	3300	3144	Speer
139 SP	IMR 4350	68	3200	3161	Sierra, Nosler, Hornady
154 SP	IMR 4350	67	3100	3287	Hornady
160 SP	IMR 4350	65	3000	3198	Sierra, Speer
175 SP	IMR 4350	65	2800	3047	Speer, Hornady
195 SP	IMR 7828	61	2500	2707	Speer
139 SP	FL		3340	3443	Weatherby factory load
154 SP	FL		3260	3633	Weatherby factory load
175 SP	FL		3070	3662	Weatherby factory load

7mm Shooting Times Westerner (7mm STW)

Historical Notes: The 7mm Shooting Times Westerner (STW) was created around 1981 by firearms writer Layne Simpson and introduced in the May 1988 edition of Shooting Times magazine. Simpson initially called it the 7mm Remington Maximum, but later changed its name to 7mm Shooting Times Westerner as his way of dedicating it to his readers. It is simply the 8mm Remington Magnum case necked down, with no other change. Like other cartridges on the full-length Holland & Holland belted case, its length requires the use of a long-action rifle, such as the Remington Model 700, Winchester Model 70, and Weatherby Mark V. The first factory-built rifles chambered for the 7mm STW (actually while the round was still a wildcat), were Winchester Model 70s built by the U.S. Repeating Arms custom shop, and rifles built around the 1917 Enfield action by A-Square. The latter company was also first to offer the ammunition. In 1997, Remington registered the cartridge with SAAMI and began to load the ammunition and chamber Model 700 rifles for it. In a ceremony held during the 1997 NRA Annual Meetings, Simpson was presented with the very first production Model 700 built in 7mm STW, along with the first box of 140-grain Core-Lokt ammunition to come off the production line. Twelve months hence, Remington had sold just over 600,000 rounds of 7mm STW ammo.

General Comments: The hunting world was obviously ready for the 7mm STW, as few wildcats have been adopted by major ammunition and rifle manufacturers as quickly. Remington later introduced its own 7mm Ultra Mag., and while ballistics charts published by the company show it as being slightly faster, those who have compared the two in barrels of the same length know otherwise. The 7mm STW shoots extremely flat while delivering levels of energy adequate for taking game up to the size of elk and moose at long range, and yet its recoil is considerably milder than magnum cartridges of larger calibers. High performance comes at a price, and while barrel accuracy life is shorter than for a smaller cartridge such as the 7mm-08 Remington, a good barrel properly maintained and not heated excessively by a great deal of rapid-fire shooting should still be delivering long-range hunting accuracy at the 2,000-round mark and possibly beyond.

7mm Shooting Times Westerner (7mm STW) Loading Data and Factory Ballistics

Bullet (grains/type)	Powder	Grains	Velocity	Energy	Source
120 TSX/BT	RL-19	83.5	3625	3409	Barnes
140 TSX/BT	RL-22	82.0	3405	3600	Barnes
140 Nosler BT	RL-22	79.0	3410	3615	A-Square
150 SBT	IMR-7828	77.7	3300	3623	Sierra
160 SBT	RL-25	78.5	3250	3748	Sierra
175 SBT	H870	86.3	3100	3730	Sierra
140 Nosler BT	FL		3450	3700	A-Square
140 Swift S-Frame	FL		3325	3436	Remington
150 Nosler BT	FL		3180	3370	Federal
160 Nosler AccuBond	FL		3100	3415	Federal
160 Sierra SBT	FL		3250	3750	A-Square

7mm Remington Ultra Mag

Historical Notes: The 7mm Remington Ultra Mag draws upon a large-capacity case to become a serious contender for the title of flattest-shooting factory big-game cartridge on the planet. The performance-driven popularity of the .300 Remington Ultra Magnum cartridge, following its 1999 introduction, led Remington to offer a family of cartridges based on this beltless, magnum-sized case. Shooting flatter than the 7mm STW, the 7mm Ultra Mag. delivers a flatter trajectory with a 140-grain bullet than a .22-250 does with a 55-grain bullet. At 300 yards, it produces 24-percent more energy than the standard 7mm Remington Magnum, and 12-percent greater energy than the 7mm STW.

General Comments: In suitably equipped rifles, such as the Remington 700, and in the hands of a skillful hunter, the 7mm Ultra Magnum is a superb choice for long-range antelope, deer, and sheep. Except for bullet diameter, the technical details of this cartridge are identical to the .300 Remington Ultra Mag cartridges.

7 mm Remington Ultra Mag Load Data/Factory Ballistics

Bullet (grains/type)	Powder	Grains	Velocity	Energy	Source/Comments
120 Nosler Ballistic Tip	RL-25	95.5	3639	3525	Nosler
140 Nosler Partition	Retumbo	96.0	3485	3771	Nosler

150 Nosler Partition	Retumbo	94.0	3368	3774	Nosler
160 Nosler AccuBond	RL-25	88.0	3261	3774	Nosler
175 Nosler Partition	Retumbo	92.0	3164	3885	Nosler
140 PSP	FL		3425	3646	Remington factory load
140 Nosler Partition	FL		3425	3646	Remington factory load
160 Nosler Partition	FL		3200	3637	Remington factory load

.30 Carbine (.30 M1 Carbine)

Historical Notes: In 1940, the U.S. Ordnance Department concluded that a light carbine would have advantages over the .45-caliber pistol in many combat situations. Various designs were submitted by a number of private manufacturers and, in the end, Winchester's offering was selected. The semi-auto .30 M1 Carbine was officially adopted, in 1941. The cartridge, a modification of the .32 Winchester Self-Loading round of 1906, was hardly a revolutionary new design, but it served the purpose. About the same time, the Germans developed their StG 44 assault rifle and the 7.92mm Kurz cartridge. The M1 Carbine is not an assault rifle. The military insists it was designed to fulfill a different purpose.

For a few years, starting in 1966, the Marlin Model 62 Levermatic was available in .30 Carbine. Iver Johnson, Plainfield, and others manufactured several versions of the M1 Carbine for the sporting trade. Federal, Remington, and Winchester load soft-point sporting ammunition. One version of the Ruger Blackhawk single-action revolver is available in .30 Carbine.

General Comments: In mid-1963, the government began releasing .30-caliber M1 Carbines for sale to civilians through the National Rifle Association at the moderate price of around $20. Thousands of these guns are, as a result, used for sporting purposes. The .30 Carbine cartridge is in the same class as the .32-20 WCF. It is wholly a small-game and varmint number, despite contrary claims by those who love the short, light, handy M1 Carbine. The accuracy of the carbine, combined with the ballistics of the cartridge, limit the effective sporting accuracy range to about 150 yards maximum. This book's original author used an M1 Carbine to hunt small game and deer as early as 1943, before most people could get their hands on one, so he had a pretty good idea of the capability of the cartridge. Remember that the .32 Winchester Self-Loading round became obsolete, in 1920, because it was more or less useless for sporting purposes; the .30 Carbine was derived from it and shares the same shortcomings. Because of inadequate energy, the .30 Carbine is illegal for deer hunting in most states. It is, however, effective against the smaller deer species, when shots are at short range. It is ideal for hunting smaller game, such as peccary. Had the military chosen to adopt this round with a modern, full-pressure standard, performance would have been about 40-percent better, and we might have a different opinion.

.30 Carbine Loading Data and Factory Ballistics

Bullet (grains/type)	Powder	Grains	Velocity	Energy	Source/Comments
85 Sierra RN	H110	17.5	2458	1140	Hodgdon
100	H-110	14.5	1950	845	Speer
100	H-110	16.5	2200	1075	Hornady
110 SP	H-110	14	1900	882	Hornady, Speer
110 FMJ	FL		1900	882	Military load
110 SP	FL		1990	967	Factory load

.30-30 Winchester
(.30-30 WCF/.30 Winchester)

Historical Notes: The .30-30, or .30 WCF, was the first American small-bore, smokeless-powder sporting cartridge. It was designed by Winchester and first marketed, in early 1895, as one of the chamberings available for the Model 1894 lever-action rifle. The original loading used a 160-grain soft-point bullet and 30 grains of smokeless powder, thus the name .30-30 for a .30-caliber bullet and 30 grains of powder. This is really an older way of describing a caliber based on blackpowder usage. Muzzle velocity was 1970 fps.

It was adapted to the Winchester Model 54 bolt-action, as well as various versions of the original 1894 action, such as the Models 55 and 64. Marlin chambered it in the Model 1893 lever-action, the improved Model 36, and the Model 336. At one time, the Savage Model 99 lever-action was made in .30-30, and Savage also chambered the old Model 40 bolt-action for it, as well as Model 340. The Remington rolling block and Winchester single-shot were also at one time available in this caliber. In Europe, the .30-30 is known as the 7.62x51R and is popular in single-shot and combination guns. Modern factory loads in this caliber are assembled with 150- or 170-grain bullets. Despite the designation, .308-inch diameter bullets are used.

General Comments: The .30-30 has long been the standard American deer cartridge, and it is still the yardstick by which the performance of all others is compared. To say that a cartridge is in the .30-30 class means that it is suitable for game up to and including deer and black bear at moderate ranges. Its popularity is due to the fact that this cartridge has always been available in short, light rifles or carbines. It is extremely popular in Mexico and Latin America, so much so that, in many backcountry areas, the treinta-treinta, it is the only high-powered cartridge anyone knows or has heard of. It was, and to a large extent still is, the most popular small-bore sporting cartridge.

Despite this popularity, the .30-30 is no wonder cartridge, with regard to accuracy or killing power. For larger deer, the 170-grain bullet is a good choice, and the 170-grain Nosler Partition or the Barnes 150-grain XPF are the best choices for those who wish to tackle elk. For smaller species, 125- to 150-grain bullets give adequate penetration with reduced recoil. In no case is it suited for shots beyond about 200 yards. Although sometimes reloaded with bullets of 80 to 110 grains, it has neither the velocity nor the accuracy (in most rifles) to make a very good varmint round. Despite its faults, it is a perfectly adequate deer cartridge if properly used by a good shot. Frank Barnes' first modern high-powered rifle was a .30-30 Model 1894 Winchester carbine, and it served for many useful and game-filled years. All major domestic ammunition companies offer this cartridge.

13th Edition Update: Several attempts to increase the terminal performance and external ballistics of a lever gun in .30-30 Winchester have been attempted. Examples would be the 7x30 Waters, the .307 Winchester and the .308 Marlin Express. However, none have been as successful as Hornady's LEVERevoultion line of ammunition for the .30-30 Winchester. Using a special powder formulated by Hodgdon and high BC bullets with a soft rubber tip, this line of factory loaded ammunition has brought about the single largest advancement in lever-action rifles in more than a century.—R.A.M.

.30-30 Winchester Loading Data and Factory Ballistics

Bullet (grains/type)	Powder	Grains	Velocity	Energy	Source/Comments
100 SP	IMR 3031	33	2600	1394	Speer
110 Speer FP	H335	38.0	2684	1755	Hodgdon
125 Sierra JFP	RL-7	30.0	2630	1920	Hodgdon
150 Sierra JFP	RL-15	36.0	2450	1995	Hodgdon
170 Hornady JFP	RL-15	34.1	2330	2045	Hodgdon
150 SP	FL		2390	1902	Factory load
170 SP	FL		2200	1827	Factory load
55 Accelerator	FL		3400	1412	Remington Factory Load
140 Mono-Flex	FL		2465	1889	Hornady Factory Load

With the exception of Hornady FTX and Mono-Flex bullets, always use round- or flat-pointed bullets in tubular magazine rifles; sharp-pointed bullets might set off other cartridges in the magazine.

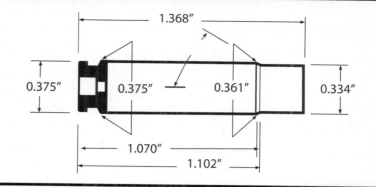

NEW
.300 AAC Blackout

Historical Notes:	The intent behind the .300 AAC Blackout was to offer a .30-caliber cartridge that would function in AR-15 rifles without a reduction in magazine capacity, that was also compatible with the standard bolt, and that would offer both supersonic and subsonic performance. The .300 AAC Blackout was developed by Advanced Armament Corporation (AAC), a subsidiary of the Freedom Group, and is almost identical to the .300 Whisper that was originally developed by J.D. Jones. Another way of looking at the .300 AAC Blackout is that as a standardization of the .300/.221 Wildcat cartridge. AAC standardized the case dimensions and submitted the cartridge to SAAMI, which has established the cartridge with a maximum average operating pressure of 55,000 psi.	
General Comments:	From a supersonic standpoint, the .300 AAC Blackout offers performance similar to the 7.62X39 Soviet cartridge. Hunters can expect performance on game to be similar to the 7.62X39 or the .30-30 Winchester. One thing hunters should recognize is that heavy match bullets at subsonic velocities will not expand in game animals. However, LeHigh Defense, working with J.D. Jones, has developed a subsonic bullet load that does offer expansion and good terminal performance at subsonic velocities.	

Much of the appeal of this cartridge is its subsonic performance, but there is some contention that optimum performance from an AR-15 is unattainable with either supersonic or subsonic suppressed loads. It is also arguable that a single twist rate offers optimal stabilization with both a 125-grain bullet at 2200 fps and a 220-grain bullet at 1050 fps. AAC suggests that a 1:8 twist be used, and most commercially offered rifles will come so equipped. DPMS and Bushmaster will offer AR-15 rifles in .300 AAC Blackout, and Remington will offer three factory loads. All three of these companies are sister companies to AAC under the Freedom Group banner. AAC is offering both Remington 700 .300 AAC Blackout replacement barrels and loading dies.—R.A.M.

300 AAC Blackout Loading Data and Factory Ballistics

Bullet (grains/type)	Powder	Grains	Velocity	Energy	Source/Comments
110 V-Max	IMR 4227	19.5C	2130	1107	Hodgdon
115 Berger TGT FB	H110	20.0	2348	1407	Hodgdon
125 Nosler BT	Lil'Gun	20.5	2393	1598	Hodgdon
135 Sierra HPBT	Lil'Gun	18.0	2127	1355	Hodgdon
220 Sierra HPBT	IMR 4198	11.5	1036	524	Hodgdon
220 Sierra HPBT	AA1680	11.2	1010	498	AAC
220 Sierra HPBT	W 296	9.9	1050	538	Hodgdon
125 Match	FL		2220	1367	Remington Factory Load
125 Accutip	FL		2230	1380	Remington Factory Load
220 OTM	FL		1010	498	Remington factory Load

.300 Savage

Historical Notes:	Developed and introduced by Savage Arms Co. for the Model 99 lever-action rifle, in 1920, the .300 Savage was later chambered in the Savage Models 20 and 40 bolt-actions. The .300 Savage was intended as a cartridge that would work through medium-length actions and deliver ballistics similar to the

.30-06. Remington chambered it in the Model 81 autoloader, 760 pump-action, and 722 bolt-action. The cartridge achieved considerable popularity, but has since lost out to the superior .308 Winchester.

General Comments: The .300 Savage provided lever-, pump-action, and semi-auto fans with performance close enough to the .30-06 to make rifles of this type useful for most American big game. The original factory load used a 150-grain bullet and matched the original .30-06 sporting load at 2700 fps. If loaded to original factory pressure levels with IMR-4064, it can significantly but safely exceed that velocity. It is not fully adequate for moose or brown bear, but it is a fine deer and elk cartridge; it is a better choice than the .30-30 for deer under any conditions. The .308 Winchester fulfills the same function as a short-action cartridge and has somewhat more power, so it has gradually replaced the .300 Savage. However, many thousands of .300 Savage-caliber rifles are still in use, so the cartridge will continue to be loaded for many more years. In a bolt-action rifle, it is as accurate as any other .30-caliber. All the major domestic ammunition companies offer this ammunition.

.300 Savage Loading Data and Factory Ballistics

Bullet (grains/type)	Powder	Grains	Velocity	Energy	Source/Comments
100 SP	IMR 4064	46	3000	1999	Speer
110 SP	IMR 4895	43	2800	1915	Speer, Sierra
110 SP	BL-C2	42	2800	1915	Hornady, Speer, Sierra
125 SP	IMR 4895	43.5	2800	2177	Sierra
130 SP	IMR 4064	43	2700	2105	Speer, Hornady
150 SP	IMR 4064	41.5	2600	2252	Sierra, Hornady, Speer
150 SP	IMR 4895	40.5	2600	2252	Sierra
150 SP	IMR 4064	44.0	2800	2610	Hornady
165 SP	IMR 3031	37.8	2500	2290	Hornady, Sierra
180 SP	IMR 4350	46	2400	2303	Hornady, Speer
180 SP	IMR 4895	39.5	2400	2303	Sierra
150 SP	FL		2630	2303	Factory load
180 SP	FL		2350	2207	Factory load

NEW

.30 Remington AR

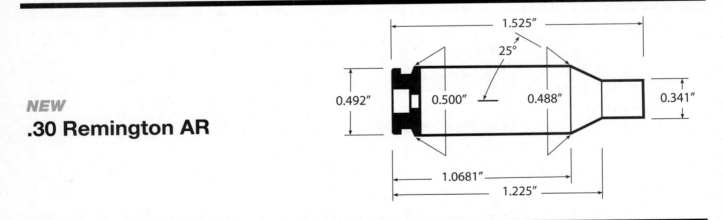

Historical Notes: The .30 Remington AR was designed by Remington as a big-game cartridge specifically for the company's R-15 rifle. It was introduced in 2009. Remington engineers started with the .450 Bushmaster case and went from there. A pointed .30-caliber bullet of reasonable weight is longer than a blunt-nosed .45-caliber bullet, so, to keep overall cartridge length compatible with the standard AR-15 magazine, the case was shortened to 1.525 inches from the original 1.7 inches of the Bushmaster design. Back at its base, the .30 AR case starts with a diameter of .500-inch, and from there it tapers to .488-inch at the juncture of the body and shoulder. Neck diameter is .341-inch, and the case has a shoulder angle of 25 degrees.

The AR-15 rifle in .450 Bushmaster utilizes the standard .223 Remington bolt, modified by increasing its bolt face diameter to a nominal .473-inch (same as the .308 Winchester). When this is done, the counter-bore wall or shroud of the bolt becomes rather thin. This is considered a safe modification for that cartridge, because it operates at a maximum chamber pressure level of 38,000 psi (same as the .30-30 Winchester). But, since the .30 AR is loaded to 55,000 psi, Remington opted for additional case rim support. This was accomplished by modifying the larger-diameter AR-10 bolt to fit the AR-15 upper. The face of that bolt is commonly sized for the .473-inch rim diameter of the .308 Winchester, but Remington went one step further by opening it up a bit and increasing the rim diameter of the .30 AR case to .492-inch. By the time the job was done, the only thing the .30 AR case had in common with the .450 Bushmaster case was a base diameter of .500-inch. Remington went with a case rim diameter larger than that for the .450 Bushmaster to prevent a bolt built for that cartridge from being used in an R-15 upper with a .30 AR barrel.

General Comments: With a length of .305-inch, the neck of the .30 Remington AR is capable of exerting plenty of tension on the bullet, a good thing to have on a cartridge designed to survive the rather violent trip it must take from the magazine to the chamber of an autoloading rifle. The short, fat case of rebated rim design has a gross capacity of 44 grains, about 10 grains less than for the .308 Winchester case, or approximately the same as for the .30-30 Winchester case. But, since the .30 AR is loaded to higher chamber pressures than the .30-30, it exceeds the maximum velocity of that cartridge. When the 125-grain Core-Lokt factory load is zeroed three inches high at 100 yards, it will strike about two inches above point of aim at 200 yards and approximately seven inches low at 300, where it is still packing upwards of 1000 ft-lbs of energy. The .30 AR comes close to duplicating the performance of the .300 Savage, when both are loaded with a 125-grain or 150 grain bullet.

The true allure of this cartridge is the fact that it turns the AR-15 platform into a true big-game rifle capable of terminal performance identical to that of the .300 Savage with bullets weighing 150 grains or less. It is suitable for deer, black bear, and similarly sized game out to around 300 yards. It is a true gem of a rifle in a compact bolt-action like the model 20 Short from New Ultra Light Arms, and it is suspected that wildcatters will soon neck the .30 Remington AR case up and down, further increasing the versatility of the AR 15 platform.—R.A.M.

.30 Remington AR Loading Data and Factory Ballistics

Bullet (grains/type)	Powder	Grains	Velocity	Energy	Source
123 Remington FMJ	FL		2800	2141	Remington
125 Remington Core-Lokt	FL		2800	2176	Remington
125 Remington Accutip	FL		2800	2176	Remington
150 Remington Core-Lokt	FL		2450	1998	Remington
110 Barnes Tipped Triple Shock	AA 2200	39.2	3115	2369	Accurate Powder
110 Hornady SP	Xterminator	41.7	3058	2283	Ramshot Powder
125 Nosler Ballistic Tip	H 335	40.0	2880	2301	Richard Mann
150 Nosler Accubond	AA 2200	35.2	2600	2251	Richard Mann

7.62X39mm
(7.62X39mm Soviet M43)

Historical Notes: This "assault rifle" cartridge was adopted by Russia, in 1943. It did not come into general use until after World War II, but the Russians now use it as their principal infantry small-arms cartridge. Original use was in the SKS semi-automatic carbine, later replaced by the AK-47 selective-fire assault rifle. The RPD light machine gun also uses the M43 cartridge. Finland, and those ex-satellite countries in the Soviet bloc, use the M43 cartridge in arms furnished by Russia or of their own design. This cartridge was adopted as the result of Russian military experience against German assault rifles chambered for the 7.92mm Kurz. Ruger introduced its Mini-30 semi-automatic rifle chambered for the 7.62x39mm, in 1987, and the bolt-action M77 Mark II rifle, in 1991. Most military ammunition has a steel case and corrosive Berdan primer, but reloadable cases are now readily available.

General Comments: The M43 is a ¼-inch longer than the German 7.92mm Kurz and will give substantially better performance with newer powders. This cartridge has been loaded commercially by Federal, Winchester, Remington, and Black Hills with Boxer-primed reloadable cases. Better handloads and factory ammunition using soft-point bullets up to about 150 grains place this cartridge far ahead of any reasonable .30-30 load, in terms of delivered energy beyond 100 yards.

13th Edition Update: This cartridge has become very popular, and is now well-known enough, used in enough sporting rifles, and loaded by enough American ammunition companies to warrant its inclusion in this chapter.

7.62X39mm Soviet Loading Data and Factory Ballistics

Bullet (grains/type)	Powder	Grains	Velocity	Energy	Source/Comments
110 SP	IMR 4727	42	2500	1527	Speer
125 SP	RL-7	26.5	2400	1599	Hornady, Sierra
125 Speer SP	H335	31.5	2408	1605	Hodgdon
135 SP	IMR 4227	22.5	2200	1451	Sierra
150 SP	IMR 4198	22	2100	1469	Hornady
150 Hornady SP	H322	28.5	2192	1600	Hodgdon
123 SP	FL		2300	1445	Federal factory load
123 SP	FL		2365	1527	Winchester factory load
125 SP	FL		2365	1552	Remington factory load
110 Sierra HP	AA 1680	27.5	2547	1580	Accurate Arms, Maximum load (.308")
125 Sierra SP	AA 1680	25.5	2368	1555	Accurate Arms, Maximum load (.311")
150 Sierra SP	AA 2015	26.0	2072	1430	Accurate Arms, Maximum load (.311")
122 Ball	ML		2329	1470	Military load
123 SP	FL		2300	1440	Black Hills factory load
150 SP	FL		2200	1610	Black Hills factory load

.30-40 Krag (.30 Army)

Historical Notes: The .30 U.S. Army, or .30-40 Krag—the first United States small-bore military cartridge—was adopted in 1892. (The first smokeless sporting cartridge, the .30-30, did not arrive until three years later, in 1895.)

The Winchester high-wall single-shot was the first commercial rifle in the United States produced for a small-bore, smokeless-powder cartridge. This happened when the .30-40 Krag was added to the available calibers, in 1893. The Remington-Lee bolt-action, Remington rolling block, and Winchester Model 95 lever-action and high-wall single-shot were the first commercial sporting rifles to offer this chambering. No commercial rifles used the cartridge from 1936 to 1973. From 1973 until 1977, the Ruger No. 3 single-shot was chambered for the .30-40 Krag, thus stimulating a renewed interest in the cartridge. A rimless version headstamped as .30 USA and loaded by United Metallic Cartridge was offered for use in the Blake rifle.

General Comments: The .30-40 Krag—.30-caliber/40 grains of the original smokeless powder load—holds the unusual distinction of being the cartridge used to take what was, until recently, the world's record Rocky Mountain elk, in 1899. This cartridge has retained its popularity, primarily because large numbers of fine sporting conversions of the Krag military rifles and carbines chambered for it are still in use. This speaks highly for both cartridge and gun.

Although not quite as powerful as either the .30-06 or the .308 Winchester, the .30-40 is well suited for use against North American big game. Just as with any cartridge, marksmanship and bullet choice are important, especially when going after the biggest and the meanest species on this continent. The Krag earned its reputation with the 220-grain loading, but it can be loaded to great advantage with lighter bullets for smaller species.

Interestingly, most authorities consider the 1895 Winchester chambering to be safe with loads at a somewhat higher pressure than the Krag rifle. However, both actions have limitations, and one should be particularly circumspect in this regard. Bountiful loading data can be found in current manuals. The .30-40 is the basis of an entire genre of powerful Ackley Improved chamberings particularly suited to strong single-shot rifles. Winchester is the only remaining manufacturer of this ammunition. Only the 180-grain bullet is still offered.

.30-40 Krag Loading Data and Factory Ballistics

Bullet (grains/type)	Powder	Grains	Velocity	Energy	Source/Comments
100 SP	H-322	45	3000	1999	Speer
110 SP	IMR 4320	47	2700	1781	Sierra, Speer
125 SP	IMR 4895	44.5	2600	1877	Sierra
130 SP	IMR 4064	45.5	2900	2428	Hornady, Speer
150 SP	IMR 4895	40	2400	1919	Nosler, Sierra
165 SP	IMR 4350	47	2500	2290	Hornady, Nosler, Sierra
180 SP	IMR 4350	46	2450	2400	Nosler, Sierra, Speer
180 SP	IMR 4895	39	2200	1935	Sierra
200 SP	IMR 3031	34	2100	1959	Nosler, Speer, Sierra
220 SP	IMR 4350	42	2100	2155	Hornady, Speer, Nosler
180 SP	FL		2430	2360	Factory load
220 SP	FL		2200	2360	Factory load

.307 Winchester

Historical Notes: The development of the rimmed .307 Winchester began in 1980, with the first public announcement in December 1982. However, the cartridge and the Model 94 XTR Angle Eject carbine chambered for it were not available until early 1983. The Marlin Model 336ER in .307 chambering introduced at the same time is no longer offered. The Angle Eject feature is a design modification of the beefed-up Model 94 XTR that ejects spent cartridge cases to the side, rather than straight up, the same as earlier Model 94 actions. This was accomplished by changing the position of the extractor and ejector and lowering the receiver's right sidewall.

The .307-caliber designation is to avoid confusing this cartridge with the other .30-calibers. It actually uses standard .308-inch bullets. The .307 Winchester is essentially a rimmed .308 Winchester, although there is a difference in the overall cartridge length. Original factory loadings had 150- and 180-grain bullets.

General Comments: The popular Model 1894 Winchester lever-action has always suffered from two major deficiencies. The design didn't allow center mounting of a scope sight, and the tubular magazine required the use of flat-point bullets to prevent one cartridge from setting off others in the magazine under recoil. These factors combined to relegate the Model 1894 to largely short-range use. The new XTR Angle Eject redesign eliminates the scope-mounting problem and modernizes an old but popular action.

The .307 Winchester will certainly enhance the range and power of lever-action rifles so chambered. It is, based on factory ballistic figures, faster than the .30-30 by some 375 fps in muzzle velocity. Although the .307 Winchester has the same general configuration as the rimless .308 Winchester, there are slight differences that prevent it from achieving the full power of the .308. For one thing, the bullet is seated slightly deeper, to maintain an overall length compatible with the length of the Model 1894 action. The result is that, for any given barrel length with the same bullet weight, the .308 will deliver approximately 60 to 110 fps more muzzle velocity. Also, with its pointed bullet, the .308 will lose velocity at a slower rate than the .307 flat-point.

It is possible to chamber and fire .308 cartridges in some .307 rifles. However, for various reasons, this is an unsafe practice that could result in damage to the rifle and possible injury to the shooter.

The .307 has slightly less velocity at 200 yards than the .30-30 has at 100 yards. If the .30-30 is an adequate 100-yard-plus deer cartridge, then the .307 is certainly a 200-yard deer cartridge. It is not likely to replace the .30-30 as America's favorite deer cartridge, but it is a more versatile cartridge and certainly takes the Model 94 carbine out of the woods, bush, and short-range class. Although it has been reported that the .307 Winchester has thicker case walls and, therefore, reduced internal volume, measurements do not verify this. Winchester is the only manufacturer of ammunition in this caliber. Only the 180-grain bullet is still offered.

.307 Winchester Loading Data and Factory Ballistics

Bullet (grains/type)	Powder	Grains	Velocity	Energy	Source/Comments
110 Sierra HP	H322	44.0	3000	2195	Hodgdon
130 Speer FP	H4895	43.0	2762	2200	Hodgdon
150 Hornady RN	H4895	42.0	2604	2255	Hodgdon
170 Hornady FP	BI-C (2)	44.0	2535	2425	Hodgdon
170 SP	IMR4064	41.0	2500	2360	Hornady
150 SP	FL		2760	2538	Factory load
180 SP	FL		2510	2519	Factory load

*In tubular magazine rifles, load only flat-point bullets.

.308 Marlin Express

Historical Notes: In 1982, Winchester introduced rimmed versions of the .308 Winchester and .358 Winchester and called them the .307 Winchester and .356 Winchester, respectively. They became available in a special version of the Winchester Model 94 lever-action rifle, with the receiver sidewalls reinforced to handle higher chamber pressures than are common for the .30-30 Winchester and other cartridges for which that rifle was originally designed. Two loadings of the .307 Winchester were available, a 150-grain deer load at 2760 fps and a 180-grain moose load at 2510 fps. Despite the fact that the new cartridge delivered the same level of energy at 200 yards as the .30-30 at 100 yards, it failed to win the hearts of America's deer hunters and was eventually dropped from the Model 94 rifle.

Many hunting seasons later, those clever chaps at Hornady developed a bullet with a pointed tip soft enough to make it safe to use in lever-action rifles with tubular magazines. Other cartridges such as the .30-30 Winchester, .35 Remington, and .444 Marlin were first to receive the new bullet design, but Hornady eventually got around to the .307 Winchester. In fact, I have a box of .307 Winchester ammunition loaded by Hornady with the new 160-grain Flex-Tip bullet. But all was not perfect with that particular idea. When both weigh the same, a pointed bullet is longer than one with a flat or round nose, and, when the 160-grain FTX bullet was loaded in the .307 Winchester to an overall cartridge length short enough to feed through lever actions such as the Marlin Model 336 and Winchester Model 94, the mouth of the case almost extended out onto the ogive of the bullet. This prompted Hornady technicians to come up with a shortened version of the .307 Winchester called the .308 Marlin Express. And, as its name implies, the new cartridge was introduced in the Marlin Model 336 rifle.

General Comments: Hunters who have used the .307 Winchester on deer, black bear, moose, and other game have often described it as the most effective cartridge to ever become available in the Winchester Model 94 and Marlin Model 336. The .308 Marlin Express is an even better cartridge—at the muzzle of a rifle, the .307 Winchester pretty much duplicates the performance of the fine old .300 Savage cartridge, but its flat-nosed bullet sheds velocity rather quickly and, by the time it reaches 100 yards, the .300 Savage is beginning to pull away in the race. Due to the more streamlined shape of its bullet, the .308 Marlin equals the performance of the .300 Savage at any distance. This is saying a lot, when you consider that there was a time long ago when many hunters considered the .300 Savage plenty of cartridge for use on any game animal in North America, including the grizzly bear. The .308 Marlin will never become as popular in lever-action rifles as the .30-30 Winchester, but, when we gaze into our crystal ball, we see it winning over far more hunters than the .307 Winchester ever did.

.308 Marlin Express Loading Data and Factory Ballistics

Bullet (grains/type)	Powder	Grains	Velocity	Energy	Source
125 Sierra HP/FN	Varget	42.3	2700	2021	Hodgdon
130 Speer FN	H335	41.5	2772	2216	Hodgdon
150 Hornady RN	H4895	40.5	2607	2262	Hodgdon

Bullet (grains/type)	Powder	Grains	Velocity	Energy	Source
170 Hornady FN	IMR-4064	39.3	2416	2201	Hodgdon
160 Hornady FTX	FL		2660	2511	Hornady
140 Hornady Mono-Flex	FL		2800	2437	Hornady

.30 TC (Thompson/Center)

Historical Notes: The .30 TC was developed by Hornady for Thompson/Center and introduced in that company's Icon rifle. Basically a shortened version of the .308 Winchester case with a sharper 30-degree shoulder angle, it has less powder capacity than that cartridge and yet, due to the utilization of Light Magnum technology previously developed by Hornady for other cartridges, it exceeds in performance standard loadings of the .308 Winchester and equals the performance of the .30-06 Springfield when the three cartridges are loaded with a 150-grain bullet. As this is written, in early 2009, only the T/C Icon rifle is chambered for the .30 TC and only Hornady loads the ammunition.

General Comments: Despite impressive velocities for its size, the .30 TC is rather an odd duck, to say the least, and this has raised questions about its existence among hunters and shooters. The Icon rifle was introduced with a short action, and had the action been too short to handle the .308 Winchester, the .30 TC would have made sense—but this was not the case. Not only is the short version of the Icon action long enough to handle the .308 Winchester, it was one of the first chamberings offered in the Icon rifle. And, while it is true that, in its factory loading, the .30 TC delivers higher velocity than standard loadings of the .308 Winchester, it is also true that Light Magnum loadings of the .308 Winchester from Hornady are just as fast. When both are handloaded with bullets of the same weight and to the same chamber pressure, velocity will be a bit lower with the .30 TC, due to the smaller capacity of its case.

.30 Thompson/Center Data and Factory Ballistics

Bullet (grains/type)	Powder	Grains	Velocity	Energy	Source
135 Sierra HPBT	H335	47.0	3127	2928	Hodgdon
150 Hornady IB	IMR-3031	42.5	2856	2714	Hodgdon
165 Barnes TSX	W748	46.0	2748	2764	Hodgdon
180 Hornady SP	H335	42.0	2580	2658	Hodgdon
150 Hornady SST	FL		3000	2994	Hornady

.308 Winchester (7.62x51mm NATO)

Historical Notes: Introduced by Winchester as a new sporting cartridge, in 1952, the .308 is nothing more than the NATO 7.62x51mm military round. This was a very smart move, to tack the Winchester name onto what was sure to become a popular sporting number. Practically every manufacturer of high-powered sporting rifles chambers the .308, since it will work through medium- or standard-length actions. The Model 70 bolt-action and 88 lever-action Winchesters were the first American sporting rifles so chambered. It was adopted as the official U.S. military rifle cartridge, in 1954, although guns for it were not ready until 1957.

General Comments: In power, the .308 Winchester is superior to the .300 Savage and almost equal to the .30-06. It delivers about 100 fps less muzzle velocity than the larger .30-06 with any given bullet weight. Most authorities consider the .308 suitable for most North American big game, although it's on the light side for moose or brown bear. This chambering is a favorite of target shooters and has a reputation for excellent accuracy. It is the basis for a number of wildcat cartridges that have been adopted as factory chamberings: .243 Winchester, 6.5-08, 7mm-08 Remington, .358 Winchester, and the rimmed versions of the .307 Winchester and .356 Winchester. All major domestic and foreign ammunition companies offer this cartridge.

Bullet (grains/type)	Powder	Grains	Velocity	Energy	Source/Comments
110 SP	IMR 4064	50	3200	2502	Sierra
110 SP	IMR 4895	48	3200	2502	Hornady, Sierra
125 SP	W748	51.5	3100	2668	Sierra, Nosler
150 SP	IMR 4064	46	2800	2612	Nosler, Sierra, Speer
150 SP	IMR 4895	44	2700	2429	Nosler, Speer, Sierra
165 SP	IMR 4064	43	2600	2477	Sierra, Speer, Nosler, Hornady
180 SP	IMR 3031	41	2500	2499	Nosler
180 SP	IMR 4064	41.5	2500	2499	Nosler, Sierra, Hornady
190 SP	IMR 4064	41.5	2500	2637	Hornady, Speer, Sierra
200 SP	IMR 4064	41.5	2400	2559	Sierra
150 SP	FL		2820	2648	Factory load
168 HPBT	FL		2600	2180	Factory load
180 SP	FL		2620	2743	Factory load

.30-06 Springfield (7.62Z63mm/.30 Government M'06)

Historical Notes: The .30-06 Springfield is a United States military cartridge adapted from the .30-03 by employing a lighter, streamlined bullet and making other minor changes. In this it parallels other military cartridge developments of the era, with French and German developments leading the way. It was adopted, in 1906, for the Model 1903 Springfield service rifle, which was based on the Mauser bolt-action system. The Winchester Model 1895 lever-action appears to have been the first sporting rifle chambered for the .30-06. The cartridge was added to the line in 1908. The Remington bolt-action Model 30, introduced in 1921, and the Winchester bolt-action Model 54, brought out in 1925, both offered the .30-06, among other chamberings. The Savage bolt-action Model 40 and 45 Super-Sporter rifles were also so chambered, when introduced in 1928. At present, in addition to the many bolt-action rifles, the Remington Model 7600 pump-action and 7400 semi-auto, as well as the Browning semi-auto, include the ,30-06 as standard chamberings. The Ruger No. 1 single-shot rifle is also offered in .30-06. A number of British and European side-by-side or over/under double rifles can be ordered in this chambering, and so can some European rifle-shotgun combination guns.

General Comments: The .30-06 is undoubtedly the most flexible, useful, all-round big-game cartridge available to the American hunter. For many years, it has been the standard by which all other big-game cartridges have been measured. To say that a cartridge is in the .30-06 class means it is suitable for any game in North America. The secret to success, when using this cartridge, is to select the right bullet for the game and hunting conditions at hand. Lighter bullets of 100 to 130 grains should be used only for varmint and small-game hunting. While these bullets can be driven at impressive velocities (well over 3000 fps), they are designed to expand rapidly on small game and will not penetrate properly on large game. For deer, antelope, goats, sheep, or black or brown bear under most hunting conditions, the 150- or 165-grain bullet is proper and a good compromise for those seeking one load for medium to heavy game. For heavier game, such as elk, moose, or large brown bear, the 165-, 180-, 200-, or 220-grain bullets are the best choice. The '06 performs impressively with handloads using 250-grain bullets. Many experienced hunters consider the 180-grain bullet the most satisfactory all-round loading for the .30-06, because it can be used effectively on anything from deer to the heaviest game under almost any hunting conditions. As a matter of fact, the .30-06 will give a good account on all but the heaviest or most dangerous African or Asiatic species, under average hunting conditions. The 220-grain bullet is generally recommended for African game, although the 180-grain also has a good reputation. With the proper bullet, this cartridge can be adapted to any game or hunting situation in North or South America, whether in the mountains, plains, woods, or jungles. Few other cartridges can claim equal versatility.

.30-06 Springfield Loading Data and Factory Ballistics

Bullet (grains/type)	Powder	Grains	Velocity	Energy	Source/Comments
100 SP	IMR 4064	59	3400	2568	Speer
110 SP	IMR 4064	54.5	3300	2660	Sierra, Hornady
110 SP	H-380	56	3300	2660	Sierra
125 SP	IMR 3031	50	3100	2668	Sierra
130 SP	IMR 4350	58	3000	2599	Hornady, Speer
150 SP	IMR 4350	59	3000	2998	Nosler, Speer, Sierra, Hornady
150 SP	IMR 4895	51	2900	2802	Nosler
165 SP	IMR 4320	50.5	2800	2873	Sierra
180 SP	IMR 4320	48.5	2700	2910	Sierra, Nosler
180 SP	IMR 4831	57	2750	3023	Speer, Nosler, Sierra
190 SP	IMR 4350	54	2700	3076	Hornady, Speer, Sierra
200 SP	IMR 4320	47	2400	2559	Nosler, Sierra
220 SP	IMR 4350	50.5	2400	2854	Hornady, Sierra, Barnes
220 SP	IMR 4831	54	2500	3054	Hornady, Sierra
250 SP	IMR 4831	47	2100	2499	Barnes
55 SP	FL (Accelerator)		4080	2033	Remington factory load
125 SP	FL		3140	2736	Factory load
150 SP	FL		2920	2839	Factory load
165 SP	FL		2800	2873	Factory load
168 HPBT	FL		2700	2720	Factory load
180 SP	FL		2700	2913	Factory load
220 SP	FL		2410	2837	Factory load

.300 Holland & Holland Magnum (.300 H&H Super)

Historical Notes: The .300 H&H Magnum was introduced, in 1925, by the British firm of Holland & Holland as "Holland's Super 30." The Western Cartridge Co., the first American company to load this round commercially, offered it here, in 1925. No American-made commercial rifles were chambered for the .300 H&H until 12 years after its introduction. However, Griffin & Howe and other custom rifle makers turned out rifles for it almost as soon as the British. In 1935, Ben Comfort won the 1,000-yard Wimbledon Cup Match with this cartridge and, overnight, it became a sensation. The Model 70 Winchester was chambered for the .300 H&H in 1937, and the Model 721 and succeeding Model 700 Remingtons were also available in this chambering. Most European bolt-action rifles chambered it as standard.

General Comments: Since 1935, the .300 H&H has enjoyed a limited popularity in the United States. Many shooters consider it the best all-round .30-caliber available to the American hunter. Others insist it is hardly better than the .30-06. Regardless of which side one favors, this is an accurate cartridge and adequate for any North American big game. Its most useful range is for elk on up, but it is also a very fine long-range cartridge for antelope, sheep, or goats. It is popular in Africa as an all-round caliber for plains game. Lately, its popularity has suffered considerably from competition with the .300 Weatherby and .300 Winchester Magnums. It is no longer used for match competition. Derived from the earlier .375 H&H, the .300 H&H is the direct progenitor of an entire family of belted magnums. With modern powders and best handloads, the .300 H&H is very close ballistically to even the biggest .300 Magnums. Winchester, Remington, and Federal all load this cartridge.

Bullet (grains/type)	Powder	Grains	Velocity	Energy	Source/Comments
110 HP	IMR 4350	76	3600	3166	Sierra, Hornady
130 SP	IMR 4320	64	3400	3338	Hornady
150 SP	IMR 4831	73	3300	3628	Nosler, Sierra, Speer
165 SP	IMR 4350	69	3100	3522	Sierra, Speer, Hornady
180 SP	IMR 4831	68	2900	3362	Sierra, Speer
190 SP	H-380	65.5	3000	3798	Hornady
200 SP	IMR 4831	67.5	2800	3483	Sierra, Speer
220 SP	IMR 4350	63	2700	3562	Hornady, Sierra
150	FL		3190	3390	Factory load
180	FL		2880	3315	Factory load
220	FL		2620	3350	Factory load

.300 Remington Short Action Ultra Mag (SAUM)

Historical Notes:	In 2001, Remington introduced the .300 Remington Short Action Ultra Mag cartridge as a competitor to Winchester's .300 Winchester Short Magnum. Ballistic performance of the Remington and Winchester offerings is similar.
General Comments:	Based on a shortened .300 Ultra Mag case, which is itself derived from a slightly modified .404 Jeffery cartridge of African fame, the .300 Remington Short Action Ultra Mag is slightly shorter and smaller in diameter than its Winchester counterpart. Short, fat cases burn powder very efficiently, since the primer's flash ignites a larger area of the packed gunpowder. The case is unbelted and headspaces on the shoulder for improved shoulder tolerances. Remington barrels for this cartridge use a twist rate of 1:10. Shooters are cautioned never to fire a .300 Remington Short Action Ultra Magnum in a .300 WSM-chambered rifle, as the headspace would be excessive, leading to possible injury or firearms damage.

.300 Remington Short Action Ultra Mag Loading Data and Factory Ballistics

Bullet (grains/type)	Powder	Grains	Velocity	Energy	Source/Comments
150 PSP	FL		3200	3410	Remington factory load
165 PSP	FL		3075	3464	Remington factory load
180 Nosler Partition	FL		2960	3501	Remington factory load
180 Scirocco	FL		3250	4221	Remington factory load

.300 Winchester Short Magnum (.300 WSM)

Historical Notes:	At the start of the twenty-first century, cartridge designs diverged. One direction was longer, fatter cartridges chambered in long-action rifles. Winchester took another path, with new, chubby, stubby cartridges sized to fit the more rigid short-action rifles. Introduced in 2000 and chambered in short, light Browning and Winchester rifles, the .300 Winchester Short Magnum demonstrated a remarkably accurate ability to duplicate .300 Winchester Magnum velocities, while consuming about 10-percent less powder. SSK Industries also re-barrels the AR-10 self-loading rifle for .300 WSM.

General Comments: The .300 WSM, an original Winchester cartridge case design, fits handily into bolt-actions sized for a cartridge length of 2.860 inches. Officially a rimless cartridge, the case rim is slightly rebated by .02-inch, and the case rim is sized to fit existing magnum bolt face dimensions. For highly efficient and consistent powder burning, the .300 WSM employs a short-fat powder column geometry, a concept revered by accuracy obsessed benchrest shooters for nearly three decades. Eschewing a belt on the case, the .300 WSM headspaces on the 35-degree shoulder, which should provide tighter headspacing tolerances and improved accuracy potential. Shooters are cautioned never to fire the slightly shorter, physically similar .300 Remington Short Action Ultra Magnum in a .300 WSM-chambered rifle, as the headspace would be excessive, leading to possible injury or firearms damage.

13th Edition Update: This cartridge and all its Winchester Short Magnum siblings became embroiled in a legal battle and the end result was a less than enthusiastic appeal on the part of other manufacturers to offer rifles and/or ammunition for sale. However, unlike the Winchester Super Short Magnums that are collecting dust on the shelves or in shooters gun racks, the WSM line still enjoys moderate appeal, especially the .270 and .300 offerings—R.A.M.

.300 Winchester Short Magnum Loading Data and Factory Ballistics

Bullet (grains/type)	Powder	Grains	Velocity	Energy	Source/Comments
150 BST	FL		3300	3628	Winchester/Olin factory load
180 Fail Safe	FL		2970	3526	Winchester/Olin factory load
180 P Pt	FL		2970	3526	Winchester/Olin factory load
110 Hornady V-Max	Big Game	71.8	3600	3162	Hornady
130 Hornady SP	W760	71.4	3400	3333	Hornady
150 Hornady IB	H4350	70.9	3250	3514	Hornady
150 BST	WW760	71.0	3250	3519	Winchester/Olin 60,000 psi
165 Fail Safe	WW760	68.5	3130	3590	Winchester/Olin 63,300 psi
165 Hornady IB	W760	69.1	3150	3631	Hornady
168 BST	WW760	69.8	3090	3563	Winchester/Olin 60,300 psi
180 Hornady SST	V-N560	71.3	3000	3593	Hornady
180 SP	WW760	66.9	2960	3503	Winchester/Olin 60,500 psi
180 Fail Safe	WW760	68.0	2940	3456	Winchester/Olin 60,200 psi

.300 Ruger Compact Magnum (.300 RCM)

Historical Notes: The tail end of the twentieth century will go down in shooting history as the era of short, fat cartridges of true magnum performance. First out of the starting gate from the major ammunition manufacturers was Winchester's .300 WSM and other calibers on the same case. As rumor had it, Remington actually had the first in its family of Short Action Ultra Mag cartridges ready for launching sometime before Winchester was ready to unveil its WSM family, but chose to introduce the .300 Ultra Mag first, with plans to introduce the .300 Short Action Ultra Mag the following year. That allowed Winchester to beat Remington to the punch and, as everyone knows, when it comes to introducing cartridges of the same caliber and similar performance, the first one to exit the starting gate usually wins the popularity race among hunters and shooters. The .300 WSM went on to become at least mildly popular, while the .300 SAUM has been a commercial failure. Whereas the Winchester and Remington cartridges are basically shortened and necked-down versions of the old .404 Jeffrey case, the .300 Ruger Compact Magnum is basically a shortened and necked-down version of the .375 Ruger case. And, while the length of the .300 RCM case is the same as that of the .300 WSM, body diameter is a bit smaller. For this reason, its powder capacity is less. According to my measurements, gross capacity of the .300 RCM case is eight-percent less than that of the .300 WSM and about one-percent greater than that of the .300 SAUM.

General Comments: In its factory loading, the .300 RCM pretty much duplicates the performance of the .300 SAUM. Unless the Light Magnum loading technology used by Hornady in loading this cartridge eventually becomes available to handloaders, those who load their own will be unable to greatly exceed .30-06 velocities with 180-grain bullets. Some claim short, fat cartridges are inherently more accurate than long, slim cartridges, but they have yet to come up with proof in rifles light enough to use for hunting. Most benchrest shooters will tell you that, when it comes to match-winning accuracy, a short, fat cartridge (with the 6mm PPC being a classic example), is the way to go. While this might be true in the world of benchrest competition where, in order to win, a rifle must be capable of consistently shooting five bullets inside .250-inch at 100 yards, the new breed of short magnums have proven to be no more accurate than longer and slimmer cartridges when all are fired in big-game rifles. In other words, if a gunsmith who specializes in building super-accurate hunting rifles were to build five in the .300 WSM, .300 SAUM, .300 RCM, .300 Winchester Magnum, .300 H&H Magnum, and .300 Weatherby Magnum, their accuracy would likely be the same. The one advantage a short cartridge has over a long cartridge is that it works in a short action weighing a few ounces less than a long action, and this is important to those who are in need of the lightest rifle possible.

.300 RCM Loading Data and Factory Ballistics

Bullet (grains/type)	Powder	Grains	Velocity	Energy	Source
150 Hornady IB	IMR-4895	56.0	3081	3158	Hodgdon
165 Barnes TSX	H414	59.5	2958	3202	Hodgdon
180 Hornady SP	H414	58.2	2813	3159	Hodgdon
150 Hornady SST	FL		3200	3410	Hornady
165 Hornady SST	FL		3140	3612	Hornady
180 Hornady SST	FL		3000	3597	Hornady

.300 Winchester Magnum

Historical Notes: This cartridge was introduced, in 1963, for the Winchester Model 70 bolt-action rifle. Rifles chambered for the .300 Winchester Magnum have since been introduced by most domestic and European manufacturers.

General Comments: Arrival of the .300 Winchester Magnum was rather anti-climatic, because everyone had been predicting it from the day the .338 Winchester Magnum was brought out, in 1958. The .30-338 wildcat quickly followed. The newer .300 Winchester Magnum has a slightly longer body (by about .12-inch), and a shorter neck than its predecessors. This short neck is considered a poor feature, as it means the heavy bullets have to seat back into the powder space quite a bit. The .308 Norma Magnum, introduced in 1960, is nearly identical to the .338 Winchester Magnum necked down. If that chambering had not been offered before Winchester was ready to produce its own .30-caliber magnum, it is possible the company would simply have necked the .338 to 30-caliber. In any event, the .300 Winchester Magnum is a fine long-range, big-game cartridge in the same class as the .300 Weatherby and suitable for any North American species. Actual factory-load ballistics may be closer to .300 Weatherby Magnum ballistics than published data suggests. With cartridges in this class and above, recoil becomes a factor for many shooters. It is loaded by all domestic and many foreign ammunition manufacturers.

.300 Winchester Magnum Loading Data and Factory Ballistics

Bullet (grains/type)	Powder	Grains	Velocity	Energy	Source/Comments
110 HP	IMR 4350	80	3600	3166	Hornady, Sierra
125 SP	IMR 4350	77	3400	3209	Sierra
130 SP	IMR 4064	66	3300	3144	Speer, Hornady
150 SP	IMR 4350	76	3300	3628	Sierra
150 SP	IMR 4895	62	3150	3306	Speer, Sierra
150 SP	IMR 4350	76	3200	3412	Speer, Sierra
165 SP	IMR 4831	76	3200	3753	Speer, Sierra
180 SP	IMR 4350	71	3000	3598	Sierra
190 SP	IMR 4831	74	3150	4187	Speer
200 SP	IMR 4350	68	2950	3866	Nosler
220 SP	IMR 4350	60	2500	3054	Hornady, Sierra
150 SP	FL		3290	3605	Factory load
180 SP	FL		2960	3501	Factory load
200 SP	FL		2825	3544	Factory load
220 SP	FL		2680	3508	Factory load

.300 Weatherby Magnum

Historical Notes: The .300 Weatherby Magnum is the most popular and well-known cartridge of the Weatherby line. At the same time, it is one of the most controversial. It was developed in 1944. Commercial ammunition has been available since 1948, under the Weatherby label. Weatherby brand ammunition is loaded by Norma of Sweden. The Weatherbys were the only U.S. rifles chambered for this round on a commercial basis, but it is a popular caliber among custom rifle makers. In 1989, Remington offered the Model 700 Classic in .300 Weatherby, and other makers have since followed suit. Recently, several ammo manufacturers have begun offering ammunition in this caliber.

General Comments: Until the advent of the .30-378 Weatherby, the .300 Weatherby Magnum was the biggest of the commercial .300 belted magnums. Barrel life can be short, some might classify recoil as severe, and ballistics suffer greatly when shorter barrels are tried. None of these limitations matter to many who use it strictly for big-game hunting and seldom fire the round more than a few dozen times a year. It can be adapted to long-range varmint shooting, if one can develop an accurate enough load, but it is not very flexible in that regard. For the hunter who wants one rifle suitable for any species of non-dangerous big game worldwide, the .300 Weatherby Magnum is an excellent choice. However, because of caliber restrictions, local game laws may prohibit its use, even against non-dangerous species. This is another case of archaic regulations, where the law might allow one to use an entirely inappropriate loading from a much less powerful big-bore, when, given the right choice of bullets, the .300 WM would be much more effective and humane.

.300 Weatherby Magnum Loading Data and Factory Ballistics

Bullet (grains/type)	Powder	Grains	Velocity	Energy	Source/Comments
110 HP	IMR 4064	79.5	3800	3528	Hornady, Sierra
125 SP	IMR 4831	87.5	3500	3401	Sierra
150 SP	H-380	77	3300	3628	Sierra
150 SP	IMR 4350	80.5	3200	3412	Hornady, Speer
165 SP	IMR 4831	82	3200	3753	Speer, Sierra

.300 Weatherby Magnum Loading Data and Factory Ballistics

Bullet (grains/type)	Powder	Grains	Velocity	Energy	Source/Comments
180 SP	IMR 4350	76.5	3000	3598	Hornady, Speer, Nosler, Sierra
180 SP	MRP	84	3100	3842	Speer
200 SP	IMR 4350	75	2900	3736	Speer, Sierra
220 SP	H-450	77	2800	3831	Hornady
250 SP	IMR 7828	69	2350	3066	Barnes
150 SP	FL		3600	4316	Factory load
165 SPBT	FL		3450	4360	Factory load
180 SP	FL		3300	4352	Factory load
190 SPBT	FL		3030	3873	Factory load
220 SP	FL		2905	4122	Factory load

.300 Remington Ultra Mag

Historical Notes: When it debuted the .300 Remington Ultra Mag cartridge, in 1999, Remington joined an increasingly popular trend toward big, beltless rounds. Popular from the onset, the .300 Remington Ultra Mag launched a whole family of non-belted, high-performance magnums, which includes the 7mm, .338, and .375 Remington Ultra Mags. When tested by Remington at 200 yards, the .300 Ultra Mag delivered nearly 18-percent greater retained energy than the .300 Weatherby Mag. and almost 27-percent greater retained energy than the .300 Winchester Magnum.

General Comments: The velocity and energy performance of Remington Ultra Mag cartridges comes from an innovative case design. Modifying the .404 Jeffery case with a rebated rim to fit Model 700 rifle bolt faces (for magnum cartridges), increased body taper, and .30-caliber-sized neck, Remington's resulting case allows about 13-percent more internal capacity than the .300 Weatherby. It offers a similarly sized ballistic advantage. The result is a "non-belted magnum" with a larger case diameter, which allows for dramatically increased powder capacity. Headspacing on the shoulder of the case, rather than the use of a belt, promotes better accuracy, due to precise bore alignment.

.300 Remington Ultra Mag Load Data/Factory Ballistics

Bullet (grains/type)	Powder	Grains	Velocity	Energy	Source/Comments
150 Sierra SBT	RL-25	99.3	3500	4076	Sierra
165 Sierra SBT	Magnum	100.8	3450	4356	Sierra
180 Sierra SBT	Retumbo	97.3	3250	4217	Sierra
190 Sierra MatchKing	RL-25	93.1	3200	4315	Sierra
150 Scirocco	FL		3450	3964	Remington factory load
180 PSP	FL		3250	4221	Remington factory load
180 Nosler Partition	FL		3250	4221	Remington factory load
180 Scirocco	FL		3250	4221	Remington factory load
200 Nosler Partition	FL		3025	4063	Remington factory load

.30-378 Weatherby

Historical Notes: The .30-378 Weatherby Magnum is the .378 Weatherby Magnum case necked to .30-caliber. It was created by Roy Weatherby, during the 1950s, upon request by the U.S. Government for determination of the resistance of various types of armor plating to penetration by high-speed projectiles. Using special lightweight bullets made by Speer Bullet Company, Weatherby managed to exceed a muzzle velocity of 6000 fps during his tests. Years later, while still a wildcat, the .30-378 became popular among members of the Original 1,000-Yard Rifle Club, in Pennsylvania, where it was used to shoot the world's record group at that distance. After several years of coaxing by firearms writer Layne Simpson, Roy's son, Ed Weatherby, decided to add the cartridge to the Weatherby lineup, in 1996. During that year, Norma started loading the ammunition for Weatherby, and Weatherby began to offer its Mark V rifle in that chambering. The first rifle was auctioned off with the proceeds going to Ed Weatherby's favorite charity, while the second rifle was presented to Layne Simpson. Much to the surprise of everyone (except Simpson), the .30-378 went on to become the best-selling cartridge in the Mark V rifle for several years and continues to sell at a steady pace.

General Comments: The .30-378 case can hold more than 120 grains of powder, compared to about 90 grains for the .300 Weatherby. With the advent of new slower-burning powders, increased capacity promises a useful advantage to the handloader. (Recent availability of 250-grain match-grade bullets served to increase potential benefit and demand for a chambering with increased powder capacity.) The .30-378 Weatherby certainly delivers on this promise. It is a simple matter to load 250-grain Sierra MatchKing bullets to produce almost 3000 fps muzzle velocity, without exceeding .30-06 pressure levels—from a 26-inch barrel! Lighter bullets can be driven faster, but with those this chambering offer less advantage over standard .300 Magnum chamberings. When bullets lighter than 200 grains are fired from a 26-inch barrel, this cartridge is only marginally superior to the .300 Weatherby. Recently, tests have demonstrated that lighter bullet (150- to 180-grain) ballistics are markedly improved by use of slower rifling twist (1:13 to 1:15 works well), compared to the factory 1:10 twist. However, with 30-inch barrels installed, ballistic difference is significant with all bullet weights. Those looking for the ultimate long-range hunting rifle for smaller species might give this chambering a hard look. A single-shot rifle equipped with a 30-inch tube offers reasonable handling ease and, if chambered for this cartridge, would deliver huge doses of energy to a distant target with the flattest trajectory available. Accurate Arms data shows the 250-grain MatchKing generating the same muzzle energy as the .458 Winchester Magnum, when loaded to about the same pressure! So long as a good barrel is properly cleaned and not subjected to excessive rapid-fire shooting, its accuracy can remain good enough up to 2,000 rounds for long-range target shooting, and perhaps 2,500 to 3,000 rounds for big-game hunting.

.30-378 Weatherby Loading Data/Factory Ballistics (26-inch barrel)

Bullet (grains/type)	Powder	Grains	Velocity	Energy	Source/Comments
180 Barnes-X	AA 8700	118.0	3283	4310	Accurate
200 Nosler Partition	AA 8700	117.0	3208	4570	Accurate
200 Sierra HPBT	AA 8700	117.0	3163	4440	Accurate
220 Sierra HPBT	AA 8700	115.0	3050	4545	Accurate
250 Sierra HPBT	AA 8700	111.0	2954	4840	Accurate
165 Ballistic Tip	FL		3500	4483	Weatherby
180-gr. AccuBond	FL		3400	4619	Weatherby
200-gr. Partition	FL		3160	4434	Weatherby

.303 British

Historical Notes: The .303 British was the official military rifle cartridge of England and the British Empire from its adoption, in 1888, until the 7.62 NATO came along, in the 1950s. The original loading was a 215-grain bullet and a compressed charge of blackpowder—cordite became the propellant in 1892. Manufacture in the United States began about 1897. Remington chambered its Lee bolt-action magazine rifle for this cartridge, and Winchester did likewise in its Model 95 lever-action. No American rifle has chambered the .303 British since 1936. However, Winchester, Federal, and Remington continue to load this popular cartridge.

General Comments: The .303 British has always been popular in Canada and other parts of the British Empire. In the United States, it has not been as widely used, because of its performance similarity to the .30-40 Krag. However, since the end of World War II, the importation of large numbers of British Lee-Enfield military rifles has altered this situation. At the present time, the .303 is more popular than the .30-40 Krag. Norma imports 130- and 180-grain loads that greatly increase the flexibility and usefulness of this cartridge for the American hunter. The 215-grain bullet has always had a good reputation for deep penetration and is a favorite for moose and caribou in the Canadian backwoods. The .303 is suitable for anything the .30-40 Krag is in the way of game. In Australia, a number of popular sporting cartridges are based on necking down and/or reforming the .303 case.

Note: Although often classed with the .30-40 Krag, this cartridge is loaded to higher pressures and delivers superior ballistics. Foreign factory loads place it very close ballistically to the .308 Winchester and measurably above any factory .30-40 load, though handloads for the .30-40 in the Model 95 Winchester can match the .303 British.

.303 British Loading Data and Factory Ballistics

Bullet (grains/type)	Powder	Grains	Velocity	Energy	Source/Comments
123 Hornady SP	RL-15	49.8	3015	2480	Hodgdon
150 SP	IMR 4064	43	2600	2252	Speer, Hornady
150 SP	IMR 4895	42	2400	1919	Sierra, Speer
150 SP	IMR 4064	43	2600	2252	Speer, Sierra
150 Speer SP	RL-15	46.2	2755	2525	Hodgdon
180 SP	IMR 4895	42	2400	2303	Sierra
180 SP	IMR 4350	46	2400	2303	Speer, Hornady
180 Sako SP	N140	41.7	2540	2575	VihtaVuori
130 SP	FL		2789	2246	Factory load
150 SP	FL		2690	2400	Factory load
180 SP	FL		2460	2420	Factory load
215 SP	FL		2180	2270	Factory load

.32-20 Winchester (.32-20 WCF)

Historical Notes: Introduced by Winchester, in 1882, for the Model 73 lever-action rifle, the .32-20 quickly attained considerable popularity as a medium-power cartridge in both rifle and revolver. Practically all American makers have chambered rifles for the .32-20 in lever-, pump-, or bolt-action, and most single-shot rifles have also chambered it. Colt's, Smith & Wesson, and Bayard made revolvers in this caliber. Marlin reintroduced it for its Model 94CL lever action, in 1988. Winchester once offered a lighter 100-grain bullet blackpowder load for the .32 Colt Lightning magazine rifle, headstamped .32 C.L.M.R. A similar 100-grain loading specifically for Marlin rifles was headstamped .32-20. Both Remington and Winchester still offer factory-loaded ammunition.

General Comments: Although recently semi-obsolete, the .32-20 still enjoys modest popularity with farmers, ranchers, trappers and pot hunters. It can be reloaded easily and at moderate cost. In addition, it delivers good killing power on small and medium game at ranges out to 100 yards, without destroying all the edible meat.

Winchester once advertised it as a combination small-game and deer cartridge. However, it is much too underpowered for deer-size animals. It is, nonetheless, a useful small-game and varmint cartridge at short ranges, and it is quite accurate in a bolt-action or solid-frame single-shot.

Frank Barnes had considerable personal experience with the old .32-20, having owned and hunted with several rifles of this caliber. These included (in chronological order) a Winchester Model 1892 lever-action, Savage Model 23C bolt-action, Remington Model 25A slide-action, and a rechambered Greener single-shot Cadet rifle. The Savage bolt-action with a scope sight would shoot very consistently into 1 to 1¼ inches at 100 yards. This was a very nice little varmint and small-game combination at ranges of 100 to 125 yards. Frank used this in the immediate post-World War II era, when nothing else was available, and it worked out very well within its range limitations. Frank also used the .25-20, but always considered the .32-20 a better all-around cartridge in this class. It's a better killer on just about anything at practical ranges.

In a strong single-action revolver, the .32-20 can be loaded to 1050 to 1100 fps from a six-inch barrel, which makes a very effective field gun. Trouble is, the cartridge is too long for most modern revolver cylinders. The .32 H&R Magnum is shorter and will serve to fill the requirement for a high-performance .32-caliber handgun round. The .357 Magnum revolver cartridge chambering in a rifle will out-perform the .32-20 by a substantial margin. The advent of cowboy action shooting has given this round a new lease on life. The .32-20 is the basis for the .25-20 and the .218 Bee.

.32-20 Winchester Loading Data and Factory Ballistics

Bullet (grains/type)	Powder	Grains	Velocity	Energy	Source/Comments
85 SP	2400	12.5	2100	833	Rifle only — Hornady
85 SP	IMR 4227	17	2300	999	Rifle only — Hornady
85 SP	H-110	14	2100	833	Rifle only — Hornady
110 SP	IMR 4227	15	2000	977	Rifle only — Hornady
110 SP	H-110	15.5	2100	1077	Rifle only — Hornady
110 SP	2400	10.5	1700	706	Rifle only — Hornady
80 SP	FL		2100	780	Factory load
100 SP	FL		1210	325	Factory load

WARNING: Do not use rifle loads in revolvers; pressures develop beyond what the average handgun is designed to withstand.

.32 Winchester Special (.32 WS)

Historical Notes: Introduced, in 1902, for the Winchester Model 1894 lever-action, the .32 Winchester Special was an original smokeless powder design. Because it is a rimmed shell, it has never been used in anything but lever-action and single-shot rifles. Remington brought out a rimless version to function in its bolt and semi-auto rifles. Winchester and Marlin were the principal American companies to chamber the .32 Special. Federal, Remington, and Winchester continued to offer factory loaded ammunition until quite recently.

General Comments: In the 1916 catalog, Winchester had this to say about the 32 Special: "The .32 Winchester Special, which we have perfected, is offered to meet the demands of many sportsmen for a smokeless powder cartridge of larger caliber than the .30 Winchester and yet not so powerful as the .30 Army." It goes on to explain that the .32 Special meets these requirements, and the 1916 ballistics chart shows it generating 10.6-percent more energy than the .30-30 at the muzzle, retaining an edge to any reasonable hunting range.

Today, it is still loaded to higher velocity and, if loaded to equal pressure, it easily beats the .30-30 by over 100 fps. However, bullet selection is limited. Speer's 170-grain flat-point, the most streamlined available, actually has a higher ballistic coefficient than most 170-grain .30-30 bullets. For those whose .32 Special rifle has a truly shot-out barrel, Hornady's 170-grain round-nose .323-inch bullet works wonderfully.

There has been a mountain of bunk written about the .32 Special answering the demand of handloaders who wanted to use blackpowder. Since the same rifle was originally chambered for the .32-40 at about one-half the price of the nickel-steel .32 Special version, this seems highly unrealistic. Those writers would have us believe that the man wanting to save money on ammunition would for no reason spend the price of two rifles for the privilege. The fact that blackpowder can be used successfully in the .32 Special, and the fact that Winchester once provided a blackpowder-height rear sight for the rifle, certainly do not prove that the cartridge was invented to allow folks to do what they could already do with the much cheaper .32-40 Model 94.

Much ink has also been spilled, claiming the .32 Special just wouldn't shoot straight after the barrel got a bit of wear. Frank Barnes experimented with two .32 Special carbines, a very early Winchester and a 1936 Marlin. With bullets that fit, both shot inside three inches at 100 yards with open sights. The Winchester had been so abused that its rifling hardly showed until it was thoroughly cleaned it. The bore was pitted but it shot just fine.

.32 Winchester Special Loading Data and Factory Ballistics

Bullet (grains/type)	Powder	Grains	Velocity	Energy	Source/Comments
170 SP	RL7	31.0	2283	1965	Lyman
170 SP	W748	36.2	2240	1890	Winchester
170 SP	FL		2250	1910	Factory load
165	FL		2410	2128	Hornady Factory Load

8mm Mauser (7.92mm Mauser/ 8x57mmJ/8x57mmI/8x57mmS/ 8x57JS)

Historical Notes: The 8mm or 7.92 Mauser was the German military rifle cartridge through both World Wars. It was officially adopted, in 1888, with a bullet diameter of .318-inch. In 1905, the bullet diameter was increased to .323-inch. In Europe, the 8mm Mauser and several other 8mm cartridges are available in both sizes. The larger size is always designated as "S" or "JS" bore. In the United States, ammunition companies load only the .323-inch diameter or "S" bullet. The 8mm Mauser is widely chambered in European sporting rifles, but American gunmakers have not adopted it as a standard sporting caliber. The "J" or "I" in the name denotes infantry ammunition. The German capital "I" was mistaken for a capital "J" by U.S. military interpreters after World War I, and the "J" misnomer came into common use here and even in Europe thereafter!

General Comments: The 8mm Mauser had not been very popular in the United States prior to World War II. However, the large number of obsolete, surplus 8mm military rifles sold here since the end of the war has increased its use substantially. American cartridge companies only put out one loading, the 170-grain bullet at 2360 fps or so. As loaded by Norma and by other European companies, such as RWS, it is in the same class as our .30-06. It is adequate for any North American big game if the proper bullets and full loadings are used. A large variety of good .323-inch bullets is now available for the individual handloader, and this has increased the usefulness of the 8mm Mauser for the American shooter.

8mm Mauser (8x57mm JS) Loading Data and Factory Ballistics

Bullet (grains/type)	Powder	Grains	Velocity	Energy	Source/Comments
125 SP	H-4198	44	3100	2668	Hornady
125 SP	IMR 3031	49	3100	2668	Hornady
150 SP	IMR 4320	53.5	2900	2802	Hornady
150 SP	IMR 3031	49	2750	2519	Speer
175 SP	IMR 3031	45.5	2600	2627	Sierra
200 SP	IMR 4831	54	2400	2559	Speer
220 SP	IMR 4831		2200	2365	Hornady
159 SP	FL		2723	2618	European factory load
170 SP	FL		2360	2100	U.S. factory load
196 SP	FL		2526	2778	European factory load
198 SP	FL		2625	3031	European factory load
200 SP	FL		2320	2390	European factory load
227 SP	FL		2330	2737	European factory load

WARNING! Many J-bore (.318-inch) rifles still exist and will fire S-bore (.323-inch) cartridges, creating dangerous pressures. When in doubt, check bore diameter CAREFULLY!

.325 Winchester Short Magnum (.325 WSM)

Historical Notes: After introducing its Short Magnum family of cartridges in the year 2000, Winchester recognized the need for another cartridge capable of launching 200-grain bullets (and heavier) with high inherent accuracy, energy capable of stopping the largest North American game, and lower perceived recoil. After considering different calibers, Winchester engineers determined the .325-caliber provided the best performance using the Short Magnum case. Released in 2005, the new .325 WSM cartridge delivers similar energies as the .338 Winchester Magnum, while using a smaller case.

General Comments: In addition to delivering excellent ballistics, the .325 WSM also exhibits exceptional accuracy. Initially, Winchester fielded three loads for the .325 WSM, a 200-grain Nosler Accubond CT, a Winchester 220-grain Power-Point bullet, and a 180-gain Ballistic Silvertip. Hunters can expect delayed, controlled expansion and deep penetration through thick, tough skin and heavy muscle tissue and bone, with ballistic coefficients ranging up to .477 for the 200-grain Nosler bullet. The .325 WSM is well suited for elk, bear, moose, or other large and dangerous game, where a lightweight short magnum rifle is desired.

.325 Winchester Short Magnum Load Data/Factory Ballistics

Bullet (grains/type)	Powder	Grains	Velocity	Energy	Source/Comments
150 Hornady SP	H414	70.0	3200	3407	Hornady
180 Barnes TSX	W760	69.0	3119	3884	Barnes
195 Hornady SP	RL-19	70.6	2850	3513	Hornady
200 Barnes TSX	W760	67.0	2951	3863	Barnes
200 Nosler Partition	RL-19	69.0	2964	3897	Nosler
180 BST	FL		3060	3743	Winchester
200 Nos AccuBond	FL		2950	3866	Winchester
220 Win PP	FL		2840	3941	Winchester

8mm Remington Magnum

Historical Notes: This cartridge was a Remington development, announced in 1978, for the Model 700 BDL bolt-action rifle. The 8mm Magnum is something of a departure from the usual belted, short magnum configuration favored by Remington in the past (a design that will work through the standard-length bolt-action). The 8mm Magnum is based on the full-length .375 H&H case blown out, thus requiring a .375-inch longer bolt travel than the standard 3.0-06.

Again, this is not an entirely original design, since it was preceded by similar developments in years past. The 8x68mm (S) Magnum, for example, originated in Germany around 1940, and a number of 8mm wildcat magnums such as the 8mm Ernst, 8x62 Durham, .323 Hollis, 8mm PMM, etc., date back to the late 1950s and early 1960s. However, this is the first commercial 8mm magnum cartridge introduced by an American company. Remington originally offered two loadings, a 185-grain bullet at a muzzle velocity of 3080 fps, and a 220-grain at 2830 fps. The 220-grain load has since been dropped. There is a good selection of 8mm (.323-inch diameter) bullets available for handloading this cartridge.

General Comments: Comparing either handloaded or factory ballistics for the .338 Winchester Magnum and the 8mm Remington Magnum, one can easily see why the latter failed to garner any great following. Any minuscule ballistic advantage it might have just didn't justify the increased cartridge length and recoil resulting from a heavier powder charge. Add to that a more limited bullet selection, and the 8mm Remington Magnum dims even further. With lighter recoil and potentially flatter trajectories, the various .300 Magnums have it beaten on that side, and, with heavier bullets shooting almost as flat and delivering more energy, the .338 Winchester Magnum and the .340 Weatherby Magnum have it beaten on the other. This is a classic example of a cartridge that fails to fill any useful niche. Due to its large powder capacity, this cartridge is another that is particularly sensitive to barrel length.

Bullet (grains/type)	Powder	Grains	Velocity	Energy	Source/Comments
125 SP	IMR 4064/76		3600	3598	Hornady
150 SP	IMR 4350/	79.5	3300	3628	Speer, Hornady, Sierra
175 SP	IMR 4831	80	3100	3735	Speer, Sierra, Hornady
200 SP	IMR 4831	78	3050	4132	Nosler, Speer
220 SP	IMR 4831	76	2800	3831	Sierra, Hornady
250 SP	IMR 7828	72	2550	3611	Barnes
185 SP	FL		3080	3896	Remington factory load
220 SP	FL		2830	3912	Remington factory load

.338 Marlin Express

Historical Notes: In 1982, Winchester introduced rimmed versions of the .308 Winchester and .358 Winchester cartridges and called them the .307 Winchester and 356 Winchester. They became available in a special version of the Winchester Model 94 lever-action rifle, with its receiver sidewalls reinforced to handle higher chamber pressures than is common for the .30-30 Winchester and other cartridges for which that rifle was originally designed. Two loadings of the .356 Winchester were available, a 200-grain deer load at 2460 fps, and a 250-grain moose load at 2160 fps. Despite the fact that the new cartridge delivered the same level of energy at 200 yards as the .30-30 at 100 yards, it failed to win the hearts of America's deer hunters and was eventually dropped from the Model 94 rifle. Marlin also built a few Model 336 rifles in .356 Winchester.

Many hunting seasons later, those clever chaps at Hornady developed the Flex-Tip bullet with a pointed tip soft enough to make it safe to use in lever-action rifles with tubular magazines. Other cartridges such as the .30-30 Winchester, .35 Remington, 444 Marlin, and .45-70 Government were first to receive the new bullet design, but Hornady eventually got around to a couple of new rimmed cartridges called .308 Marlin Express and .338 Marlin Express. As their names imply, they were introduced in the Marlin Model 336 rifle. Whereas Winchester had previously simply necked up the .307 Winchester case to produce the .356 Winchester cartridge, Hornady came up with a case of greater capacity for the new .338-caliber cartridge than it had for the .308 Marlin Express. The rim of the case is a rather odd diameter, a bit smaller than the rim of the .45-70 Government cases and considerably smaller than the rim of the .30-30 Winchester case. As rim diameters of various rifle cartridges of American design go, the closest we could find to it is a long-obsolete cartridge called the .40-63 Ballard.

General Comments: A past editor's favorite lever-action rifle had long been the old Winchester Model 71 in .348 Winchester, the only cartridge it was chambered for on a production basis. Even though the .348 Winchester case is longer than the .338 Marlin case, the Hornady factory load equals its velocity when both cartridges are loaded with a 200-grain bullet. But, since the Hornady Flex-Tip bullet is pointed, it sheds velocity more slowly, giving it a slightly flatter trajectory and allowing it to deliver more energy to a target downrange. When digging a wounded bear out of an alder thicket, the availability of 250-grain bullets that can be handloaded in the .348 Winchester gives an edge in effectiveness, although the 200-grain bullet of the .338 Marlin Express should be plenty of medicine for broadside, behind-the-shoulder shots on game as large as elk and moose.

.338 Marlin Express Loading Data and Factory Ballistics

Bullet (grains/type)	Powder	Grains	Velocity	Energy	Source
200 Hornady FTX	FL		2565	2919	Hornady

.338 Federal

Historical Notes: In collaboration with Sako Rifles, Federal Cartridge's engineers and ballisticians have developed the .338 Federal, which necks up the proven .308 Winchester case to accept a .338-caliber bullet. This design, which is the first to bear the name "Federal" on the headstamp, is intended to provide big-bore wallop with moderate recoil for today's lightweight, short, bolt-action rifles. The .338 Federal was slated to be available in 2006, in Federal's Premium line of ammunition.

General Comments: The .338 Federal bears more than a passing resemblance to the .358 Winchester cartridge, which was introduced in 1955. Like the .358 Winchester, the .338 Federal offers excellent performance on big game without magnum recoil. Its muzzle energy exceeds the .30-06 with a similar weight bullet, equaling the muzzle energy of the 7mm Remington Magnum. Its muzzle velocity ranges to approximately 200 fps greater than its parent .308 Winchester with similar weight bullets. Leaving nothing to chance, Federal offers three loads for the .338 Federal, each tipped with a premium-grade bullet proven to deliver devastating results on game ranging from deer to elk to bear.

The .358 Winchester, having been introduced in a time when ever-higher velocities were the craze, now languishes in obscurity. Given the current interest in lightweight rifles and efficient cartridge designs, one hopes that the .338 Federal will fare better with the shooting public.

.338 Federal Load Data/Factory Ballistics

Bullet (grains/type)	Powder	Grains	Velocity	Energy	Source/Comments
180 Nosler AccuBond	Varget	48.0	2706	2923	Nosler
185 Barnes TSX	Benchmark	45.5	2709	3011	Barnes
200 Nosler AccuBond	W748	47.0	2529	2837	Nosler
210 Barnes TSX	AA-2230	46.0	2570	3076	Barnes
225 Barnes TSX	Benchmark	41.5	2360	2780	Barnes
180 Nos AccuBond	FL		2830	3200	Federal
185 Barnes TSX	FL		2750	3106	Federal
210 Nos Part	FL		2630	3225	Federal

.338 Ruger Compact Magnum (.338 RCM)

Historical Notes: The tail end of the twentieth century will go down in shooting history as the era of short, fat cartridges of true magnum performance. First out of the starting gate from the major ammunition manufacturers was Winchester's .300 WSM, and other calibers such as .323 (8mm), .270, and 7mm on the same case. As rumor had it, Remington actually had the first in its family of Short Action Ultra Mag cartridges ready for launching sometime before Winchester was ready to unveil its WSM family, but chose to introduce the .300 Ultra Mag first with plans to introduce the .300 Short Action Ultra Mag the following year. That allowed Winchester to beat Remington to the punch and, as everyone knows, when it comes to introducing cartridges of the same caliber and similar performance, the first one to exit the starting gate is usually the winner. The .300 WSM went on to become at least mildly popular, while the .300 SAUM has been a commercial failure. Whereas the Winchester and Remington cartridges are basically shortened and necked-down versions of the old .404 Jeffery case, the .338 Ruger Compact Magnum is basically a shortened and necked-down version of the .375 Ruger case. As short and fat magnums go, the .338 RCM is similar in performance to the .325 WSM. And while the length of the .338 RCM case is the same as that of the .325 WSM case, body diameter is a bit smaller. For this reason, its powder capacity is less. According to our measurements, gross capacity of the .338 RCM case is eight-percent less than that of the .325 WSM.

General Comments: Performance of the .338 RCM falls somewhere between the .338-06 A-Square on the slower side and the .338 Winchester Magnum on the faster side. It makes a lot more sense than the .325 WSM, simply because cartridges of .338-caliber are at least mildly popular among big-game American hunters, whereas those of 8mm caliber (which is what the .325 WSM is), have never been and probably never will be. Its biggest shortcoming as this is written in early 2009 is availability only in rifles built by Ruger, plus the fact that only Hornady loads it. Nothing wrong with either Ruger rifles or Hornady ammunition, but everyone does not hunt with Ruger rifles and not every gun shop stocks Hornady ammo. If other rifle manufacturers start chambering for the .338 RCM, and if other ammunition manufacturers start offering the ammo, it will surely become more successful than the .325 WSM, which has yet to find a place in the hearts of American hunters.

.338 RCM Loading Data and Factory Ballistics

Bullet (grains/type)	Powder	Grains	Velocity	Energy	Source
185 Barnes TSX	W748	59.5	2937	3540	Hodgdon
200 Hornady SP	BL-C(2)	61.0	2870	3654	Hodgdon
210 Swift Scirocco	BL-C(2)	57.0	2739	3494	Hodgdon
225 Hornady IB	W748	56.0	2654	3515	Hodgdon
200 Hornady SST	FL		2950	3865	Hornady
225 Hornady SST	FL		2775	3847	Hornady

.338-06 A-Square/.338-06

Historical Notes: During 1945 to 1946, Charles O'Neil, Elmer Keith, and Don Hopkins developed a cartridge they named the .333 OKH, which was based on the .30-06 case necked up to .333-caliber. It was a very good big-game cartridge, but today it suffers from the lack of good, readily available .333-inch diameter bullets. When the .338 Winchester Magnum was introduced, in 1958, it was followed immediately by a variety of commercial .338-inch diameter bullets. Shortly thereafter, several individuals at different places conceived the idea of either altering the .333 OKH or necking up the .30-06 to accept .338-inch diameter bullets. Any difference in performance between the .333 OKH and the .338-06 is purely academic and almost invisible. The latter uses a commercial bullet of standard diameter, which has the advantage of being readily available through handloading supply dealers. The two cartridges are so nearly alike that one can use loading data from the .333 OKH in the .338-06 with virtually the same results. A-Square standardized the .338-06 as a factory round, in 1998, and, about 2001, Weatherby began chambering rifles in .338-06. With typical Weatherby honesty, their catalogs list the cartridge as the .338-06 A-Square.

General Comments: The .30-06 case is necked up to accept .338-diameter bullets, and retains the original 17.5-degree shoulder. The .338-06 delivers about 85 percent of the performance of the .338-caliber magnum cartridges, but without the recoil, cigar-sized cases, or magnum-length actions. Most .30-06 bolt-action rifles can be rebarreled to the .338-06, and the wide range of available bullets makes the .338-06 a flexible hunting alternative to its ballistic near-twin, the .35 Whelen. Weatherby uses Norma brass and powders, matching them with bullets well suited for the intended purpose. The Weatherby catalog lists just one bullet for the .338-06, the Nosler Partition. Weatherby offers Mark V Super Big Game Master and Ultra Lightweight rifles in .338-06 A-Square, both well suited for North American game.

.338-06 A-Square Loading Data and Factory Ballistics

Bullet (grains/type)	Powder	Grains	Velocity	Energy	Source/Comments
200 SP	IMR 3031	48.0	2465	2700	NA
200 SP	IMR 4320	54.0	2610	3020	NA
250 SP	IMR 4064	56.0	2585	3730	NA
250 SP	IMR 3031	47.0	2370	3130	NA
275 SP	IMR 4350	55.0	2305	3250	NA
275 SP	IMR 4895	50.0	2275	3165	NA
210 Nosler Partition	FL		2750	3527	Weatherby factory load

.338 Winchester Magnum

Historical Notes: Announced in 1958, the .338 is another of the series based on the .458 Winchester necked down. Initially available only in the Winchester Model 70 Alaskan bolt-action rifle, Remington adopted it for the 700 Series bolt-action. Some of the European rifle makers also chamber it, as does Ruger for the Model 77 and No. 1 rifles, as well as many custom and semi-custom rifles. Browning's autoloader, lever-, and pump-action rifles also chamber it.

General Comments: With proper bullets, the .338 Winchester Magnum shoots almost as flat across 500 yards as similar loads in the various .30-caliber magnums—the difference amounts to only a few inches more drop. Designed to handle the heaviest North American big game, the .338 has also done well in Africa on the larger varieties of plains game. Although slightly less powerful than the .375 H&H Magnum, the .338 is better suited for North American hunting conditions and game. It is a well-balanced cartridge for anything from elk through moose and grizzly bear, under almost any situation. It could also serve very well for deer or antelope, even though it is overly powerful for this class. Like the .300 WM, the .338 Winchester would make an excellent one-gun cartridge for the worldwide hunter who has to travel light, though the .338 is automatically barred in some African countries in which the .375 is the minimum caliber. Lately, the .338 has enjoyed a renewed and well-deserved popularity. Winchester, Remington, and Federal all load this ammunition.

.338 Winchester Magnum Loading Data and Factory Ballistics

Bullet (grains/type)	Powder	Grains	Velocity	Energy	Source/Comments
175 SP	IMR 4895	67.5	3200	3980	Barnes
180 Nosler BT	H4350	74.5	3157	3980	Hodgdon
200 SP	IMR 4350	71.5	2900	4048	Speer, Hornady
210 SP	IMR 4350	73	2900	3923	Nosler
225 Hornady SP	RL-19	75.3	2865	4100	Hodgdon
250 SP	IMR 4831	71	2700	4048	Speer, Sierra
250 SP	IMR 4350	70	2700	4048	Sierra
275 SP	IMR 4831	68	2500	3817	Speer
275 SP	IMR 4064	58	2400	3518	Speer
300 SP	IMR 7828	70	2500	4164	Barnes
200 SP	FL		2960	3890	Factory load
225 SP	FL		2760	3860	Factory load
250 SP	FL		2660	3921	Factory load

.340 Weatherby Magnum

Historical Notes: The growing popularity of the .338 Winchester Magnum for elk and larger game undoubtedly influenced the development of the .340 Weatherby. First announcement of the new caliber came in 1962. John Amber had one of the first .340 Weatherby Magnum rifles and reported 100-yard groups of two inches or less— quite good for such a heavy-caliber hunting rifle of that era.

General Comments: With its larger case, the .340 Weatherby develops higher velocities with any given bullet weight than does the .338 Winchester. Velocities of 3260 fps with the 200-grain bullet and 2980 with the 250-grain are impressive; this means around 4700 ft-lbs of energy with either bullet. This should be quite effective on African game. A 210-grain Nosler bullet loading is also available with a muzzle velocity of 3250 fps (all from 26-inch barrels). The cartridge is suitable for all North American big game and most African species, as well. Weatherby ammunition is loaded by Norma of Sweden.

Handloaders will find that case life with older Weatherby (Norma) cases is very limited with top handloads, because of soft case heads. This problem can be eliminated by reforming 8mm Remington Magnum cases, but these require a significant reduction in charge because of the resulting much-reduced capacity. Nevertheless, such loads can surpass any safe load in older Norma cases, because Remington cases can safely withstand somewhat higher pressures and because the lost powder space wasn't necessary anyway. Ballistics are greatly handicapped if shorter barrels are used.

.340 Weatherby Magnum Loading Data and Factory Ballistics

Bullet (grains/type)	Powder	Grains	Velocity	Energy	Source/Comments
175 SP	IMR 4350	85.5	3250	4105	Barnes
200 SP	IMR 4350	82	3000	3998	Speer, Hornady
200 SP	IMR 4350	84	3200	4549	Hornady
210 SP	IMR 4350	83.5	3200	4776	Nosler
225 SP	IMR 4831	83	3000	4498	Hornady
250 SP	IMR 4350	77	2800	4353	Sierra, Speer, Hornady
250 SP	IMR 4831	80	2800	4353	Sierra, Hornady, Speer
275 SP	IMR 4350	76	2600	4129	Speer
275 SP	IMR 7828	88	2750	4619	Speer
300 SP	IMR 7828	77.5	2550	4333	Barnes
200 SP	FL		3260	4719	Weatherby factory load
210 SP	FL		3250	4924	Weatherby factory load
250 SP	FL		2980	4931	Weatherby factory load

Federal 215 primers used in all cases.

.338 Remington Ultra Mag

Historical Notes: The .338 Remington Ultra Mag is one of the most powerful .338-caliber rounds available, delivering 25-percent greater muzzle energy than the .338 Winchester Magnum and retaining a flatter trajectory all the way out to 500 yards. Remington introduced this cartridge, in 2002, as a member of the Ultra Mag family of cartridges.

General Comments: In suitably equipped rifles, such as the Remington 700, and in the hands of a skillful hunter, the .338 Ultra Mag is an excellent choice for bear, elk, and moose. Except for bullet diameter and a slightly shorter case length, technical details of this cartridge are identical to the .300 Remington Ultra Mag.

.338 Remington Ultra Mag Factory Ballistics

Bullet (grains/type)	Powder	Grains	Velocity	Energy	Source/Comments
250 PSP	FL		2860	4540	Remington
250 Swift A-Frame	FL		2860	4540	Remington

.338 Lapua Magnum 8.58x71mm (Finland)

Historical Notes: In 1983, Research Armament Co., in the U.S., began development of a new, long-range sniper cartridge capable of firing a 250-grain, .338-inch diameter bullet at 3000 fps. After preliminary experiments, a .416 Rigby case necked down to .338-inch was selected. Brass Extrusion Labs Ltd. (then of Bensenville, Illinois), made the cases, Hornady produced bullets, and Research Armament built the gun under contract for the U.S. Navy. Subsequently, Lapua and Norma have put this cartridge into production. It is now a CIP standard chambering; since CIP and SAAMI have reciprocal agreements in place (at least in theory), that makes this a standard SAAMI chambering, as well.

General Comments: You have to burn a lot of powder to launch a 250-grain bullet at 3000 fps. The .338 Lapua Magnum, as it is known commercially, or the 8.58x71mm, does just that. The full metal jacket, boat-tail military bullet is reportedly very effective at 1500 meters. The commercial soft-point bullet is intended for hunting very heavy game. Cartridge cases are brass with Boxer primers. Guns for this cartridge are bolt-actions, but at least one gas-operated M-16-style rifle has been developed (RND Manufacturing, 14399 Mead Street, Longmont, CO 80504; 970-535-4458).

.338 Lapua Magnum Factory Ballistics

Bullet (grains/type)	Powder	Grains	Velocity	Energy	Source/Comments
250 FMJ-BT Ball	FL		2950	4830	Military load
250 SP			2855	4525	Factory load

.338-378 Weatherby

Historical Notes: In response to special requests from close friends, Roy Weatherby chambered a few rifles for a cartridge in which the case was formed by necking down his .378 Magnum case to .338 caliber. This took place as early as the 1970s, but it wasn't added to the Weatherby lineup of loaded cartridges and rifle chamberings until 1999. The .338-378 Weatherby Magnum is sometimes confused with the earlier .338-378 Keith-Thompson wildcat, but since the K-T version is on the shortened .378 Magnum case, loading data are not interchangeable between the two.

General Comments: The .338-378 Weatherby Magnum is in the same performance league as the .338 Remington Ultra Mag and .338 Lapua, and, from a practical point of view, that's not saying a whole lot. The smaller .340 Weatherby Magnum generates considerably less recoil, and yet Weatherby rates it only 100 fps slower than the .338-378 Magnum and at about the same speed as the .338 Remington Ultra Mag., when the three cartridges are loaded with 250-grain bullets.

.338-378 Weatherby Load Data/Factory Ballistics

Bullet (grains/type)	Powder	Grains	Velocity	Energy	Source
180 Barnes TSX	RL-25	113.0	3373	4542	Barnes
210 Barnes TSX	RL-25	108.5	3183	4719	Barnes
225 Barnes TSX	RL-25	105.0	3066	4691	Barnes
250 Barnes TSX	RL-25	102.5	2906	4683	Barnes
200 Nosler AccuBond	FL		3380	5075	Weatherby
225 Barnes TSX	FL		3180	5052	Weatherby
250 Nosler Partition	FL		3060	5197	Weatherby

.348 Winchester

Historical Notes: The .348 was developed by Winchester for the Model 71 lever-action rifle and introduced in 1936. No other rifle has ever been commercially available for this cartridge, and the Model 71 was discontinued in 1958. In 1987, Browning marketed a limited number of reproduction Model 71s that were made in Japan. At this writing, only Winchester still loads the .348, and the 200-grain bullet load is the lone survivor. The Model 71 was the smoothest lever-action ever built.

General Comments: One of the more powerful rimmed cartridges available for the lever-action rifle, the .348 was supposedly made obsolete by the newer .358 Winchester and the more modern Model 88 lever-action rifle (now also discontinued). The .348 is an excellent cartridge for any North American big game at close range. Due to the flat-point bullets required for use in the tubular magazine of the Model 71 rifle, it is not a particularly good long-range cartridge. The 150-grain bullet has very poor ballistic properties, due to its short, flat shape, and the 200- or 250-grain bullets are preferred for anything beyond 100 yards. Winchester dropped the 150-grain and 250-grain loads, in 1962, but still offers the 200-grain loading. Remington no longer loads the round. The .348 is the basis for an entire list of Improved cartridges. Perhaps the best of these, a somewhat Improved .45-caliber version—which is very close to .458 Winchester Magnum performance—is still prized as among the best combination ever invented for use in Alaska, against heavy game in close quarters.

.348 Winchester Reloading Data and Factory Ballistics

Bullet (grains/type)	Powder	Grains	Velocity	Energy	Source/Comments
200 SP	H-4895	53	2500	2776	Hornady
200 SP	IMR 4350	60.5	2500	2776	Hornady
200 SP	IMR 4064	51	2400	2559	Hornady
250 SP	IMR 4350	55	2300	2937	Barnes
150 SP	FL		2890	2780	Factory load
200 SP	FL		2520	2820	Winchester factory load
250 SP	FL		2350	3060	Factory load

.35 Remington

Historical Notes: Introduced with the Remington Model 8 semi-automatic rifle, in 1906, the .35 Remington was later also chambered in the Remington Models 14 and 141 pump-actions, the Model 81 semi-auto, Model 30 bolt-action, and, for a short time, in the Winchester bolt-action Model 70. At one time, the Marlin 336 lever-, Mossberg 479 lever-, and Savage 170 pump-action rifles were offered in .35 Remington. Currently, only the Marlin 336 rifle is still available; Remington's XP-100 was and Thompson/Center's handgun is still chambered for the .35 Remington.

General Comments: The .35 Remington is the only one of the Remington rimless line of medium-powered cartridges still alive. It has proven itself over the years as a reliable short-range woods cartridge on deer or black bear. It has far better knockdown power than the .30-30 under any conditions and at any range. The velocity and energy figures are not very different from the .30-30, but the larger, heavier bullet has greater shock and makes a more severe wound. The .35 Remington, with its moderate recoil, is a good cartridge for light rifles or carbines at short ranges (150 yards or less). It was originally the Remington counter to the much more powerful .35 Winchester. Remington, Winchester, Hornady, and Federal offer this ammunition.

13th Edition Update: Hornady now offers a LEVERevolution load with improved external ballistics, with about a 200 fps velocity advantage over standard factory loads. Buffalo Bore also offers a "heavy" .35 Remington load utilizing the excellent 220-grain Speer FP. Several bolt-action rifles have been chambered for the .35 Remington. My first custom bolt-action rifle was a .35 Remington built by Melvin Forbes' New Ultra Light Arms. Factory .35 Remington ammunition is held to a maximum average pressure of 33,500 psi, but, in a modern bol-action, these is no reason this cartridge cannot be loaded to pressures (that's pressures, not velocities) similar to that of the more modern .358 Winchester. When chambered in a strong bolt-action like the Remington model 7 available from the Remington custom shop as the model 7 MS, a handloaded .35 Remington can push a 200-grain bullet to 2400 fps with ease. Additionally, Indiana hunters looking for a cartridge that meets the new .35-caliber and 1.8-inch case restriction would be wise to consider trimming a .35 Remington case by .12-inch.—R.A.M.

.35 Remington Loading Data and Factory Ballistics

Bullet (grains/type)	Powder	Grains	Velocity	Energy	Source/Comments
200 Remington PSP	AA 2015	43.5	2400	2557	Richard Mann
125 SP	W680	32	2400	1599	Speer
140 HP	RL-7	40	2500	1943	Speer
158 SP	IMR 3031	37	2200	1698	Hornady, Speer
180 Speer FP	H4895	39.0	2232	1990	Hodgdon
200 Hornady RN	VarGet	39.5	2139	2030	Hodgdon
220 Speer FP	H4895	36.3	2010	1970	Hodgdon
150 SP	FL		2300	1762	Factory load
200 SP	FL		2080	1921	Factory load
220 Speer FP	FL		2200	2364	Buffalo Bore Factory Load

For light loads for small-game or varmint shooting at short range, use any 150- to160-grain lead, gascheck, or half-jacketed .38 revolver bullet and 15 grains of 2400. Muzzle velocity will be about 2200 fps.

.356 Winchester

Historical Notes: The .356 Winchester is a rimmed cartridge developed concurrently with the .307 Winchester for the Winchester Model 94 XTR Angle Eject lever-action carbine. Development of both cartridges began in 1980. Guns and ammunition were sold early in 1983. Marlin introduced the lever-action Model 336ER in .356-caliber about the same time the Winchester hit the market. The Winchester Model 94 XTR is a beefed-up version of the original Model 94 lever-action to allow the use of higher-pressure cartridges. The angle-eject feature is an additional modification to eject spent cartridge cases to the side instead of straight up. This feature allows center mounting of a scope sight, something not possible with the original 1894 action. This was accomplished by repositioning the extractor and ejector and lowering the right sidewall of the receiver slightly.

The .356-caliber designation was used to avoid confusion with the rimless .358 Winchester. In fact, the .356 is little more than a rimmed .358 and uses the same diameter bullets. The .356 and the .358 are not identical, since the. 356 not only has a rim, but also the bullet is seated deeper to reduce overall length. It's possible to chamber .358 cartridges in .356 rifles, but firing them is an unsafe practice that could damage the gun and cause serious injury to the shooter.

General Comments: The ballistics of the .356 are slightly below the older rimless .358. Although it has been reported that the .356 Winchester and .307 have thicker case walls than the corresponding rimless .308 and .358 cartridges (and therefore reduced internal volume), measurements do not verify this. However, the .356 delivers performance superior to the .35 Remington by a significant margin. Factory published ballistics data show that the .35 Remington 200-grain bullet has a muzzle velocity of 2080 fps, whereas the .356 Winchester delivers 2460 fps with the same bullet weight, both from a 24-inch barrel.

While the .35 Remington is largely a short-range cartridge for deer or black bear, the .356 Winchester would be adequate for larger game up to elk at longer ranges. One should consider, though, that both the Winchester and Marlin lever-action carbines, with their short 20-inch barrels, are intended primarily as light, handy guns for use in heavy cover. A hunter armed with one of the .356 carbines could probably take on just about anything likely to be encountered in the continental United States at short to moderate ranges. The .358 Winchester never achieved great popularity, and the .356 does not appear to be doing much better. Winchester is the only commercial manufacturer of this cartridge.

Bullet (grains/type)	Powder	Grains	Velocity	Energy	Source/Comments
158 SP	H-322	49	2600	2372	Speer
180 SP	H-322	48	2600	2703	Speer
180 Speer FP	H4198	43.0	2600	2700	Hodgdon
220 SP	IMR 4064	46	2300	2585	Speer
250 Hornady RN	BL-C(2)	48.0	2163	2595	Hodgdon
200 SP	FL		2460	2688	Factory load
250 SP	FL		2160	2591	Factory load

In tubular-magazine rifles, load only flat-point bullets.

.358 Winchester

Historical Notes: Introduced in 1955 by Winchester for its Model 70 Lightweight bolt-action and Model 88 lever-action rifles, the .358 Winchester is based on the .308 Winchester case necked-up. It is known in Europe as the 8.8x51mm. Many European rifle makers chamber the round. In the United States, only the Browning BLR lever-action is currently chambered for this cartridge. The Model 99 Savage was also once available in .358.

General Comments: The .358 Winchester is one of the best commercial (non-magnum) .35-caliber cartridges turned out by any American manufacturer. It is a big improvement over the .35 Remington, slightly more powerful than the old .35 Winchester, and more useful than the .348 Winchester. As the 308 Winchester is a shortened version of the .30-06, by the same token the .358 is a shortened .35 Whelen. With its spitzer-pointed bullets, the .358 is a good medium- to long-range cartridge with capabilities out to 250 yards on big game. Although a good woods number, it is definitely beyond the short-range, deer-only class. In fact, the .358 is adequate for any North American big game. With the 250-grain bullet, it is better than the .30-06 on heavy game at close ranges. The .358 in a bolt-action rifle with a good scope is as accurate as any hunting cartridge available. Performance can be improved by handloading. Winchester is the only remaining manufacturer of this ammunition.

.358 Winchester Loading Data and Factory Ballistics

Bullet (grains/type)	Powder	Grains	Velocity	Energy	Source/Comments
158 SP	RL-7	48	2850	2850	Speer
180 SP	IMR 3031	51	2700	2914	Speer
200 SP	IMR 4320	50.5	2500	2776	Hornady, Sierra
200 SP	H-4198	40.5	2500	2776	Hornady
220 SP	BL-C2	49	2500	3054	Speer
250 SP	IMR 3031	41.5	2200	2687	Hornady, Speer
250 SP	IMR 4064	44	2250	2811	Speer
300 SP	IMR 4895	43	2200	3225	Barnes
200 SP	FL		2490	2753	Factory load
250 SP	FL		2250	2810	Factory load

.35 Whelen

Historical Notes: Facts uncovered in recent research suggest that Col. Townsend Whelen may, after all, have been intimately involved in the creation of this cartridge, which has generally been heretofore attributed to James Howe of Griffin & Howe, of whom it was said developed and named it after the famous writer, hunter, and gun authority. The .35 Whelen is simply the .30-06 case necked up without any other change. Ackley championed an Improved version, which features less body taper and a sharper shoulder. The Improved version has two significant advantages. First it has about 10-percent more usable capacity, providing a similar increase in ballistics. The second is the more distinct shoulder, which completely solves the poor headspacing problem, resulting from a too narrow, steeply sloping shoulder, that .35 Whelen rifles have. One is hard pressed to explain why Remington chose to standardize the inferior version, when it adopted the .35 Whelen as a factory chambering in 1987.

General Comments: Remington has been active in adding popular wildcats to its line of commercial cartridges. The .35 Whelen is just one example. Previous editors for this book have had considerable past experience with the .35 Whelen, and it is an excellent cartridge for any North American big game, and most African species, as well. A pump-action rifle chambered for .35 Whelen makes a good combination. The .35 Whelen is one of the best balanced and most flexible medium bores for North American big game. There is a large variety of .35-caliber bullets available to the handloader, ranging from 110 to 300 grains in weight. The popularity of this round has waxed and waned over the years, reaching a peak during the 1920s and again shortly after World War II. Only Remington manufactures this ammunition.

.35 Whelen Loading Data and Factory Ballistics

Bullet (grains/type)	Powder	Grains	Velocity	Energy	Source/Comments
180 SP	IMR 4895	59	2700	2914	Hornady
180 SP	IMR 4320	56	2700	2914	Nosler
200 SP	IMR 4064	58.5	2600	3003	Hornady
225 SP	IMR 4320	56	2500	3123	Sierra
250 SP	IMR 4895	52.5	2500	3470	Hornady
250 SP	IMR 4064	54.5	2400	3198	Hornady
250 SP	RL-15	55	2400	3198	Hornady
200 SP	FL		2675	3177	Remington factory load
250 SP	FL		2400	3197	Remington factory load

.350 Remington Magnum

Historical Notes: Remington reintroduced the .350 Remington Magnum, in 2002, chambered in its new Model 673 bolt-action rifle. The cartridge first appeared in the 1965 Remington catalog, concurrently with the Model 600 Magnum bolt-action carbine that chambered it. The original carbine had an 18-inch barrel, but, in 1968, this was lengthened to 20 inches in the Model 660 Magnum carbine. By 1971, the Model 600 and 660 Magnum carbines had been discontinued, but the .350 Magnum was continued as a standard chambering for the Model 700 bolt-action rifle until 1974. For a short time, the Ruger Model 77 bolt-action rifle was available in .350 Magnum. Currently, Remington offers the .350 Remington Magnum in the Model 673 Guide Rifle, which is a near lookalike M600 and based on the Model Seven action. The cartridge is unique in having a somewhat short, fat, belted case with somewhat more capacity than the .30-06. This allows for its use in short-action rifles that can be made a bit lighter and handier than those based on the standard-length bolt action.

General Comments: With bullets of moderate weight, the .350 Remington Magnum can nearly duplicate .35 Whelen ballistics in a much shorter barrel, and it can be chambered in short bolt-action rifles. This is a significant advantage for those preferring a light, handy rifle with plenty of punch. Also, many find the short-throw bolt to be much easier to use and master. For those preferring heavier bullets, the round-nose design doesn't take up so much of the powder space and, therefore, can safely develop better muzzle energy. For use where shots will not be long, these may be the best choice. For those with .350 Remington Magnum rifles in full-length actions, heavy spitzers can sometimes safely be seated to exceed the nominal 2.80-inch length for the cartridge, and increased muzzle energy can be achieved. Here, though, it is hard to see much advantage over the .35 Whelen, which generally feeds more smoothly from a magazine holding two additional cartridges. The .350 Remington Magnum is adequate for any North American big game at short to medium ranges.

.350 Remington Magnum Loading Data and Factory Ballistics

Bullet (grains/type)	Powder	Grains	Velocity	Energy	Source/Comments
125 HP	IMR 4895	60	2850	2255	Speer
158 SP	IMR 3031	58	2850	2850	Speer
180 SP	IMR 4064	62	2900	3362	Speer
200 SP	IMR 4320	60	2700	3238	Hornady, Sierra
220 SP	IMR 4895	60	2650	3431	Speer
250 SP	IMR 4895	53	2350	3066	Speer, Nosler
300 SP	IMR 4064	52	2300	3525	Barnes
200 SP	FL		2710	3261	Factory load

9.3x62mm Mauser

Historical Notes: Developed about 1905, by Otto Bock, a well-known Berlin gunmaker, this chambering was introduced to give the farmers and hunters in the German colonies of Africa an adequate cartridge. The story goes that, when many African countries were in the process of adopting restrictive laws specifying minimum chamberings for dangerous game hunting, most ruled for a minimum bore size of .40-caliber. Almost universally, the 9.3x62mm Mauser was exempted from the banned classification. It was soon used in Europe on wild boar and red deer. Mauser sporters were sold in the United States in this chambering until 1940. It is listed in late RWS and Norma catalogs. Browning and other rifles are available in Europe for this cartridge, and Steyr-Mannlicher rifles are currently so chambered.

General Comments: The 9.3x62mm is a powerful big-game cartridge, with a good reputation in Africa and Asia. It is sufficiently powerful for any North American big game and would be a good number for Alaskan bear. At one time, it was one of the most widely used, general-purpose medium bores in Africa. This was due partly to good performance, and partly to the fine, moderately priced bolt-action rifles that chambered it. A-Square and Norma produce ammunition and offer components, while Speer also makes appropriate bullets. A previous editor of this book used the listed 232-grain Norma Oryx load (bonded-core bullet) to dispatch his first moose. Bullet performance was flawless; at the shot, the bull dropped in his tracks and never so much as wiggled. This type of performance is the basis of the superior reputation this cartridge has earned worldwide.

13th Edition Update: In the last several years, due in part to the work of gun writers like John Barsness, many American hunters are staring to warm up to this cartridge. It is starting to be chambered in factory new American rifles and several ammunition companies are now loading ammo for it. Previously listed in Chapter 9 ("European Sporting Cartridges"), this newfound American appreciation of the 9.3x62mm cartridge warrants its movement to this chapter.

9.3x62mm Mauser Loading Data and Factory Ballistics

Bullet (grains/type)	Powder	Grains	Velocity	Energy	Source/Comments
250 SP	IMR 4350	63.0	2606	3754	Barnes (optimistic)
270 SP	IMR 4350	64.0	2550	3899	Speer (optimistic)
286 SP	H414	57.0	2500	3970	Barnes (optimistic)
232 Oryx	FL		2624	3548	Norma factory load

9.3x62mm Mauser Loading Data and Factory Ballistics

Bullet (grains/type)	Powder	Grains	Velocity	Energy	Source/Comments
256 SP	FL		2560	3726	RWS factory load (optimistic)
286 SP	FL		2360	3544	Norma factory load
293 SP	FL		2430	3842	RWS factory load (optimistic)

.370 Sako Magnum
9.3x66mm Sako Magnum

Historical Notes: Few hunters who own rifles built by the Finnish firm of Sako realize the company started manufacturing ammunition during World War II, several years prior to building its first rifle. Sako rifles were introduced to the United States market during the early 1950s, but, with the exception of the .22 PPC and 6mm PPC, the ammunition has never been readily available here. Sako also makes big-game bullets of its own design, but also imports bullets from Sierra, Nosler, and Barnes for some cartridge loadings.

Around 2002, Sako introduced a new cartridge to the European market called the 9.3x66mm Sako. Lengthen the .30-06 case by three millimeters, expand its neck to accept a bullet of 9.3mm (or .366-inch) diameter and you've got it. Sako factory ammunition loaded with 250- and 286-grain bullets is rated at 2750 and 2550 fps, respectively. Worldwide, Sako exports more sporting rifles to the United States than any other country, and, since the 9.3x66mm Sako cartridge had quickly gained acceptance among Scandinavian hunters, the company decided to offer it to American hunters, as well. However, it saw a big, fat fly swimming around in that particular bowl of soup: historically, American hunters have pretty much ignored to death any cartridge with a metric designation. So, in an effort to make the cartridge more appealing to American hunters, its name was changed to .370 Sako Magnum. Since Sako doesn't import ammunition to the United States, the company chose Federal to make the ammo. This, by the way, was the second time those two companies have collaborated to bring us a new cartridge (the .338 Federal was first).

General Comments: While its slightly greater powder capacity allows the 9.3x66mm Sako Magnum to push all bullet weights about 100 fps faster than the considerably older 9.3x62mm Mauser, the two cartridge are still in the same performance class. When all are loaded with 250-grain bullets, the .35 Whelen also belongs here, although the slightly larger diameter of 9.3mm bullets, along with the fact that they are available in heavier weights, may give the two metric cartridges a bit of an edge, when used on the larger game animals. One of the biggest things the 9.3 Sako Magnum has going for it is any rifle chambered for any member of the .30-06 family of cartridges can be converted to it with rebarreling, and that being the only modification necessary. As factory cartridges of its caliber go, only the 9.3x64mm Brenneke is more powerful, and not by a lot at that.

13th Edition Update: Quality Cartridge (www.qual-cart.com) currently lists brass for this round.

.370 Sako Magnum Loading Data and Factory Ballistics

Bullet (grains/type)	Powder	Grains	Velocity	Energy	Source
286 Nosler Partition	FL		2550	4125	Federal
286 Barnes TSX/FB	FL		2550	4125	Federal

9.3x66mm Sako Magnum Factory Ballistics

Bullet (grains/type)	Powder	Grains	Velocity	Energy	Source/Comments
250 Nosler BT	FL		2756	4210	Sako factory load
286 RN Hammerhead	FL		2559	4147	Sako factory load
286 Barnes X-Bullet	FL		2543	4093	Sako factory load
286 Barnes Solid	FL		2559	4147	Sako factory load

.375 Ruger

Historical Notes: The actions of popular rifles such as the Remington Model 700, Weatherby Mark V, and Winchester Model 70 are long enough to handle full-length belted magnums such as the .300 Weatherby Magnum and .375 Holland & Holland Magnum, but, with the exception of the rather expensive "Magnum" variation of the Ruger Model 77, the actions of Ruger bolt-action rifles are too short to handle them. So, rather than creating a more affordable version of the Magnum action, Ruger officials made the decision to team up with Hornady and introduce a magnum-performance chambering short enough for the company's standard action.

Maximum overall length of the .375 Ruger is 3.340 inches, which is the same as for medium-length belted cartridges such as the 7mm Remington Magnum and .300 Winchester Magnum. Rim diameter of the case is also the same as for those cartridges, but its powder capacity is greater, due to a body diameter close to that of the .375 Remington Ultra Mag.

General Comments: With a case capacity slightly greater than that of the .375 H&H Magnum, the .375 Ruger is about 100 fps faster than that cartridge, pretty much duplicating the performance of the .375 Dakota and treading closely on the heels of the .375 Weatherby Magnum. As any big-game hunter of experience knows, that puts it in very good company. As readily available factory cartridges of the same caliber go, only the .378 Weatherby Magnum and the .375 Remington Ultra Mag. are faster. Capable of pushing a 300-grain bullet along at 2600 fps, the .375 Ruger is plenty of cartridge for use on any game animal anywhere in the world, with the possible exception of the really big stuff, such as African elephant. Also in its favor is the fact that many excellent bullets of .375-caliber in both solid and expanding styles are available. Only time will tell if companies other than Hornady offer the ammunition.

.375 Ruger Loading Data and Factory Ballistics

Bullet (grains/type)	Powder	Grains	Velocity	Energy	Source
235 Barnes TSX/FB	H380	79.5	2907	4405	Hodgdon
260 Nosler Partition	RL-15	76.0	2883	4493	Nosler
300 Barnes TSX/FB	W760	78.5	2642	4645	Barnes
300 Nosler Partition	RL-15	72.0	2619	4564	Nosler
300 Hornady RN	H414	79.5	2642	4645	Hodgdon
300 Hornady DGX	FL		2660	4708	Hornady

.375 Winchester

Historical Notes: Developed by Winchester, the .375 was announced, in 1978, as a new cartridge for the Model 94 Big Bore lever-action carbine. The gun is a strengthened version of the standard Model 94 action and can be distinguished by the beefed-up rear quarter of the receiver, as opposed to the flat sides of the regular Model 94. The cartridge is based on a shortened (about 1/10-inch) .38-55 case, although .375 Winchester cases are heavier and stronger than those of the .38-55. Two carbines were initially available in this caliber, the Winchester Model 94 Big Bore and the Ruger No. 3 single-shot. This is a rimmed case and not well-suited to Mauser-type bolt-actions. Two bullet weights are offered, a 200-grain at 2200 fps muzzle velocity, and a 250-grain at 1900 fps, as advertised by Winchester.

General Comments: The .375 Winchester fills a gap in the line of cartridges available for the popular Winchester Model 1894 lever-action series. Many hunters who hunt in heavy cover prefer large- or medium-caliber rifles firing heavy bullets as the best combination for their particular hunting environment. Such a combination was not available for the Winchester Model 1894. The .375 offers competition to lever-actions chambered for the .35 Remington and the .444 Marlin. Comparisons will be made between this .375 and the other popular woods cartridges, such as the .35 Remington, .44 Magnum, .444 Marlin, and the .45-70. Ballistically, the .444 Marlin, with its 240-grain bullet and 2400 fps muzzle velocity, has the edge on all the others in the group. However, all these cartridges have one common failing: They are used in lever-action rifles with tubular magazines. This requires a flat-pointed bullet so that, under recoil, one cartridge won't set off the one ahead of it in the magazine. These blunt bullets offer high air resistance. No matter what the initial velocity, they all slow down quite rapidly. The result is that, at 200 yards or less, they all end up with about the same energy, which varies from 1000 to 1100 ft-lbs. All these brush cartridges, then, are at their best at ranges of 150 yards or less.

Certainly the .375 Winchester is a fine deer or black bear cartridge and would probably also do well on heavier game such as moose or brown bear. Within its range limitations, it would also serve as a good meat-getter on thin-skinned African species. The .375 cartridge can be chambered in .38-55 rifles, but must never be fired in any rifle except those specifically marked for it, because it develops much higher pressure than the older .38-55. To fire it in any of the old blackpowder rifles would almost certainly result in a wrecked gun and serious injury to the shooter. Winchester is the only commercial manufacturer of this ammunition.

.375 Winchester Loading Data and Factory Ballistics

Bullet (grains/type)	Powder	Grains	Velocity	Energy	Source/Comments
200 Sierra JFP	H4198	38.0	2480	2730	Hodgdon
220 Hornady JFP	RL-7	36.0	2260	2495	Hodgdon
220 SP	RL-7	38	2200	2365	Hornady
235 SP	IMR 4198	32	2000	2088	Speer
235 SP	RL-7	35	1950	1985	Speer
255 SP	IMR 3031	36	1900	2045	Barnes
200 SP	FL		2200	2150	Winchester factory load
250 SP	FL		1900	2005	Winchester factory load

.376 Steyr

Historical Notes: Hornady and Steyr announced this chambering at the 2000 SHOT Show. Jeff Cooper has long heralded the "Scout Rifle" concept. Basically, this is a short, lightweight, bolt-action rifle that is essentially designed to be equipped with a forward-mounted, compact, long eye relief scope of low magnification. Hence, the Scout Rifle is a package deal. Cooper wanted a chambering for his creation that would do in a pinch for stopping practically any game on earth. The specific critter of his actual concern was the Cape buffalo, long noted for bad temper, tenacity, and terminally effective retaliation. From this backdrop grew the .376 Steyr. Using bullets up to 300-grains and easily generating as much as 4000 ft-lbs of muzzle energy, it would seem that the .376 Steyr should fulfill Jeff's wishes.

General Comments: This case, while an essentially new design, shares characteristics with several earlier numbers. Base diameter, at .500-inch, is just about the same as the .284 Winchester (nominally .496-inch) or the 9.3x64mm Brenneke (nominally .504-inch). The rim, at .494-inch, is sufficiently smaller than the case body, so as to qualify this as a (slightly) rebated rim design. Shoulder angle is quite shallow, to facilitate smooth feeding from the magazine. Case and cartridge length (2.35-inch and 3.075, respectively), are both intermediate between traditional short-action and long-action numbers. Capacity and maximum pressure specification are sufficient to accommodate substantial performance. With the ready availability of a wide selection of bullets of various quality levels and weights, this should be a very versatile chambering. We predict that it will also form the basis of an entire genre of new wildcat cartridges. To establish precedence, one of the former editor's of this book took the opportunity to declare his intentions to adjust neck diameter and length on the .376 Steyr case to produce cartridges appropriate to both 2.8-inch and 3.2-inch actions in every feasible bore size from 6mm to .41-caliber.

For those who prefer the style, the Scout Rifle is a very fine design for hunting dangerous game. However, with the proposed Steyr rifle weighing in at far under eight pounds—making it significantly heavier would seem to defeat Mr. Cooper's design intent—recoil is no small matter.

13th Edition Update: The .376 Steyr drew a moderate amount of attention, when it was introduced. This was probably due to the fact it was available in the Steyr Scout Rifle. However, the cartridge has failed to catch on, very likely becasue no American firearms manufacturer offers rifles chambered for this cartridge. Some also predicted the case would become the basis for a wide range of wildcat cartridges. These, if any at all have been created, are getting no attention. However, it could be argued that the .30 Remington AR is loosely based on the .376 Steyr case.—R.A.M.

Bullet (grains/type)	Powder	Grains	Velocity	Energy	Source/Comments
225 Hornady SP	FL		2560	3325	Hornady, Steyr Specified Loading
270 Hornady SP	FL		2560	3990	Hornady
250 Sierra SP	H 4895	65.0	2732	4142	Hodgdon
300 Swift SP	Varget	62.5C	2560	3325	Hodgdon
225 Hornady SP	FL		2560	3325	Hornady Factory Load
270 Hornady SP	FL		2560	3990	Hornady Factory Load

.375 Holland & Holland Magnum (.375 H&H Magnum)

Historical Notes: Originated by the British firm Holland & Holland, in 1912, this is one of the original belted, rimless, magnum-type cartridges. It has been used as the basis for numerous wildcats and most of the Weatherby cartridges. H&H furnished it in a magnum Mauser action, and Griffin & Howe chambered rifles for it, beginning about 1926. The Western Cartridge Co. first offered it in 1925. At present, Federal, Remington, and Winchester load the .375. The first commercial rifle of American make to chamber the round was the Model 70 Winchester, in 1937. Weatherby rifles were at one time available in .375 H&H, as was the Remington Model 725 Kodiak. At present, several American manufacturers list the .375 H&H as standard including Ruger, Winchester, and Remington.

General Comments: Long considered the best all-round African caliber, the .375 H&H is overpowered for North American big game. However, many Alaskan hunters and guides prefer it for moose and grizzly bear. It isn't a very flexible cartridge for the American hunter, unless one expects to hunt the heaviest species and spend time in Africa or Asia. John Taylor, in his 1948 book African Rifles and Cartridges, rates the .375 as the best of the medium bores for African hunting. It is his candidate for the most effective all-round cartridge. This cartridge was the basis for H&H's latter .300 H&H Magnum and is therefore the great-grandfather of almost all modern belted magnum chamberings. It can certainly be said that it inspired the entire genre.

.375 Holland & Holland Magnum Loading Data and Factory Ballistics

Bullet (grains/type)	Powder	Grains	Velocity	Energy	Source/Comments
200 SP	IMR 4064	80	3200	4549	Sierra
220 SP	SR4759	42	2300	2585	Hornady
235 SP	IMR 4064	77	3000	4697	Speer
270 SP	RL-15	74	2700	4372	Hornady
270 SP	IMR 4064	70	2600	4054	Hornady
285 SP	IMR 4831	85	2700	4615	Speer
300 SP	IMR 4064	68	2500	4164	Hornady
300 SP	IMR 4350	77	2600	4504	Sierra, Hornady
350 SP	IMR 4320	65.5	2400	4478	Barnes
270 SP	FL		2690	4340	Factory load
300 SP	FL		2530	4265	Factory load

.375 Weatherby Magnum

Historical Notes: The .375 Weatherby Magnum was developed by the late Roy Weatherby, between 1944 and 1945, and was chambered only in Weatherby rifles. There are several similar wildcat versions, such as the .375 Ackley Improved Magnum, but the .375 Weatherby had the advantage of commercial ammunition loaded by Weatherby using Norma cases. Its popularity lasted until the more powerful, harder-recoiling .378 Weatherby displaced it, about 1953, but returned to the Weatherby line when many hunters demanded something that recoiled less than the .378 Weatherby, but had more power than the .375 H&H.

General Comments: The .375 WM is a full-length, blown-out, and Improved cartridge based on the .375 H&H case. It holds more powder and delivers higher velocities with the same bullets, compared to the parent cartridge. It is really overpowered for North American big game. On African game, it will qualify for just about anything and is considered a fine all-round cartridge, particularly for dangerous game. The 270-grain bullet approximates .30-06 trajectories and is a fine long-range load for large North American game and for thin-skinned African animals. Commercial chambers are free-bored in the Weatherby tradition, and this increases the charge required to achieve any given pressure and velocity.

Out of production for several decades, the .375 Weatherby was reintroduced in 2001 and is available in Weatherby's Mark V Dangerous Game Rifle and Fibermark composite rifles. Some factory .375 H&H rifles can be rechambered to the .375 Weatherby.

.375 Weatherby Magnum Loading Data and Factory Ballistics

Bullet (grains/type)	Powder	Grains	Velocity	Energy	Source/Comments
235 SP	IMR 4064	84.0	3015	4745	Ackley
270 SP	IMR 4064	80.0	2795	4685	Ackley
300 SP	IMR 4350	86.0	2675	4770	Ackley
270 SP	FL		2940	5181	Weatherby factory load
300 SP	FL		2800	5223	Weatherby factory load
300 Nosler Partition	FL		2800	5224	Weatherby factory load

.375 Remington Ultra Mag

Historical Notes: With the flat trajectory of a 150-grain .270 Winchester load, the .375 Remington Ultra Mag is one of the hardest-hitting .375 chamberings available. Introduced in 2002 and based on Remington's Ultra Mag cartridge family, the .375 Ultra Mag has 23-percent more energy at the muzzle than the .375 H&H and delivers more energy at 200 yards than does the .375 H&H at 100 yards.

General Comments: In suitably equipped rifles, such as the Remington 700, and in the hands of a skillful hunter, the .375 Ultra Magnum is an excellent choice for African and Alaskan game noted for their fangs, teeth, claws, and attitude. Except for bullet diameter, technical details of this cartridge are identical to the .300 Remington Ultra Magnum. (See separate listing.)

.375 Remington Ultra Magnum Load Data/Factory Ballistics

Bullet (grains/type)	Powder	Grains	Velocity	Energy	Source/Comments
Bullet (grains/type)	Powder	Grains	Velocity	Energy	Source
235 Barnes TSX	RL-19	107.0	3191	5307	Barnes
260 Nosler Partition	IMR-4350	96.0	3026	5280	Nosler

Bullet (grains/type)	Powder	Grains	Velocity	Energy	Source/Comments
270 Barnes TSX	RL-19	102.5	3019	5458	Barnes
300 Nosler Partition	IMR-7828	96.0	3026	6093	Nosler
270 SP	FL		2900	5041	Remington factory load
300 Swift A-Frame	FL		2760	5073	Remington factory load

.378 Weatherby Magnum

Historical Notes: Another development by the late Roy Weatherby, this one dating back to 1953, this is an original design not based on any existing cartridge, although it is hard to miss the similarity in all critical dimensions to the .416 Rigby. It was first field-tested in the spring of 1953 by Weatherby, who downed an elephant with one shot. The Federal Cartridge Co.'s No. 215 Magnum Large Rifle primer was originally developed for this cartridge, as existing primers did not properly ignite the large quantity of powder used. Only the Weatherby line of rifles is commercially chambered for this round.

General Comments: According to the Weatherby catalog, the .378 WM was designed for deep penetration on heavy, thick-skinned game. It is also intended to furnish an extra margin of insurance when facing dangerous game such as rhino, Cape buffalo, elephant, or lion in thick cover. Field reports indicate that it lives up to these expectations. However, for proper performance at the velocities developed, it is necessary to use bullets with a very heavy jacket. Although considerably overpowered for any North American big game, it is nonetheless a fine cartridge for the hunter who requires optimum stopping power. Recoil of these cartridges is extremely heavy, so one should be sure such power is really needed before selecting anything in this class.

.378 Weatherby Magnum Loading Data and Factory Ballistics

Bullet (grains/type)	Powder	Grains	Velocity	Energy	Source/Comments
235 SP	H-4831	115	3200	5345	Barnes
250 SP	H-4831	113	3050	5165	Barnes
270 SP	IMR 4350	108	3100	5763	Hornady
300 SP	H-4831	112	2900	5604	Sierra, Nosler
350 SP	H-4831	102	2650	5459	Barnes
270 SP	FL		3180	6062	Weatherby factory load
300 SP	FL		2925	5701	Weatherby factory load

.38-55 Winchester (.38-55 Ballard)

Historical Notes: Like the smaller .32-40, the .38-55 was originally a Ballard-developed target cartridge. The present commercial version was introduced, in 1884, as one of the cartridges for the Ballard Perfection No. 4, which was originally chambered for the .38-50 Everlasting. According to Satterlee, in his Catalog of Firearms, 2nd Ed. (Detroit, 1939), the Union Hill Nos. 8 and 9 were also chambered for the .38-55 Ballard, in 1884. The external dimensions of the .38-55 Everlasting and the .38-55 Winchester & Ballard are nearly identical, but the heavier, thicker Everlasting version was a handloading proposition. The implication in Saterlee's book is that the original Everlasting case was introduced when Marlin Fire Arms Co. took over Ballard, in 1881. The .38-55 Everlasting is nothing more than a 1/10-inch longer case than the .38-50 that Ballard introduced in 1876.

The Marlin Model 93 and Winchester 94 lever-action repeaters were available in .38-55, as was the Remington-Lee bolt-action, Colt's New Lightning pump-action, Stevens, Remington, and Winchester single-shot rifles, and also the Savage Model 99. No commercial rifles were available after Winchester dropped the .38-55 from the Model 94 list of calibers, in 1940. However, Winchester has reintroduced the cartridge in several versions of the Model 94 in recent years, and it also has been offered in the H&R Handi-Rifle and others. The .225 Winchester, .22 Savage High Power, .25-35 Winchester, .32-40 Winchester, .30-30 Winchester, .32 Winchester Special, .375 Winchester, and a host of wildcat cartridges are based on this case.

General Comments: The .38-55 built up a reputation for fine accuracy at ranges out to 200 yards, and the growing popularity of cowboy action shooting has breathed new life into this fine old cartridge. It also developed a modest popularity with deer and black bear hunters. It gave good knockdown on deer-size animals with the 255-grain bullet at velocities of over 1500 fps. At one time, factory-loaded cartridges were available with the 255-grain bullet at a muzzle velocity of 1700 fps. At these higher velocities, it is a better deer cartridge than the .30-30. Present factory loadings more or less duplicate blackpowder ballistics. In old Ballard and Stevens single-shot rifles, it is not safe to use loads developing velocities over 1500 fps. Discontinued in 1970, the .38-55 is again listed in Winchester ammunition catalogs. Proper bullet diameter for cast bullets is .379-inch.

.38-55 Winchester & Ballard Loading Data and Factory Ballistics

Bullet (grains/type)	Powder	Grains	Velocity	Energy	Source/Comments
200 FN	XMP5744	25.5	1853	1525	Accurate Arms
220 SP	RL-7	31	1600	1257	Hornady
220 SP	IMR 3031	33	1600	1251	Hornady
220 SP	IMR 3031	34.5	1700	1412	Hornady
220 SP	IMR 4198	26	1600	1251	Hornady
220 SP	RL-7	29.5	1400	958	Hornady
240 Lead	XMP5744	22.0	1601	1365	Accurate
222 FN	XMP5744	23.5	1648	1325	Accurate
255 SP	H-4895	35	1700	1637	Barnes
255 SP	FL		1320	987	Winchester factory load
255 JFN	FL		1980	2153	Buffalo Bore Factory Load

.38-40 Winchester (.38-40 WCF)

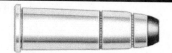

Historical Notes: The .38-40 was developed by Winchester as a companion cartridge to its .44-40 and introduced in 1874. It is based on the .44-40 case necked down to what is actually .40-caliber (.401-inch). It was originally a blackpowder cartridge chambered in the Winchester Model 73 lever-action. About 1878, Colt's began chambering revolvers for it. It was later offered in the Remington Model 14½ pump-action, Winchester 92 and Marlin 94 lever-actions, plus a number of single-shot rifles. No rifles have been chambered for the .38-40 since 1937. Winchester loaded a slightly different version especially for the Colt Lightning Magazine Rifle, headstamped .38 C.L.M.R. Another version was loaded with the same 180-grain bullet as the .38 Winchester, but with 40 grains of blackpowder instead of Winchester's standard load of 38 grains and was headstamped .38-40 instead of .38 W.C.F. This raises the intriguing possibility that the name we now use, .38-40, came from 38 grains of blackpowder and a .40-caliber bore.

General Comments: The .38-40 was, at one time, a popular medium-power cartridge. Winchester used to load a high-velocity rifle version with a 180-grain bullet at 1775 fps. This was considered a pretty good short-range deer number, but was not intended for old blackpowder rifles or revolvers. It was discontinued because it caused a lot of trouble for people who never read labels. The present factory loading is strictly for revolvers, and it is necessary to handload in order to realize the full potential in a rifle. With proper load and bullets, the .38-40 can be used on small game, varmints, medium-size game, or even deer at short range. Rifle loads should not be used in revolvers, as these loads develop pressures beyond safe limits.

Frank Barne's experience with the .38-40 was limited to one Remington Model 14½R pump-action carbine that was used for several years before being traded off for something more useful. Although it was a nice, handy little rifle, he was not particularly impressed with the cartridge. The .38-40 is a bit much for most varmint and small-game shooting and really not adequate for deer-size animals. In any event, it is quite limited in its effective range on whatever you happen to be using it for. This lack of enthusiasm notwithstanding, the .38-40 enjoyed a certain popularity from its inception until about 1920, after which it declined in sales volume. It was finally discontinued, in 1937. Actually, there is no great difference in performance between the .38-40 and the .44-40, although some considered the .38-40 a better cartridge for a woman or young boy, because it had less recoil. Honestly, neither one has any great recoil, and Frank could never tell much difference between the two in that regard.

The .38-40 made a better revolver cartridge than it did a rifle cartridge. The present factory load with the 180-grain bullet at 1160 fps (Winchester) cannot be considered adequate for deer, and only by handloading can one achieve acceptable performance for much of anything except self-defense, for which it is formidable.

.38-40 Winchester Loading Data and Factory Ballistics

Bullet (grains/type)	Powder	Grains	Velocity	Energy	Source/Comments
155 SP	2400	15	1200	496	Hornady
155 SP	IMR 4227	19.5	1200	496	Hornady
180 HP	2400	14.5	1100	484	Hornady
180 HP	Unique	9	1100	484	Hornady
180 HP	IMR 4227	18.5	1100	484	Hornady
200 HP	Unique	8.4	1000	444	Hornady
200 HP	2400	13.5	1050	490	Hornady
180 SP	FL		1160	538	Winchester factory load

.416 Ruger

Historical Notes: The actions of popular rifles such as the Remington Model 700, Weatherby Mark V, and Winchester Model 70 are long enough to handle full-length belted magnums such as the .375 Holland & Holland Magnum and .416 Remington Magnum, but with the exception of the rather expensive "Magnum" variation of the Ruger Model 77, the actions of Ruger bolt-action rifles are too short to handle them. So, rather than coming up with a more affordable version of the Magnum action, Ruger officials made the decision to team up with Hornady and introduce a magnum-performance chambering short enough for the company's standard action. Maximum overall length of the .416 Ruger is 3.240 inches, which is the same as for medium-length belted cartridges such as the 7mm Remington Magnum and .300 Winchester Magnum. Rim diameter of the case is also the same as for those cartridges, but its powder capacity is greater, due to a body a diameter close to that of the .375 Remington Ultra Mag.

General Comments: With a case capacity only slightly less than that of the .416 Remington Magnum, the .416 Ruger comes close to duplicating the performance of that cartridge, and it exceeds standard loadings of the .416 Rigby. As any big-game hunter who has used the Remington and Rigby cartridges on game knows, this puts the Ruger cartridge in very good company. As readily available factory cartridges of the same caliber go, only the .416 Weatherby Magnum is faster. Capable of easily pushing a 400-grain bullet along at 2400 to 2500 fps, the .416 Ruger is plenty of cartridge for use on any game animal anywhere in the world, when loaded with the proper bullets. Also in its favor is the fact that many excellent bullets of .416-caliber in both solid and expanding styles are available.

.416 Ruger Loading Data and Factory Ballistics

Bullet (grains/type)	Powder	Grains	Velocity	Energy	Source
400 Hornady DGX	FL		2500	5545	Hornady

.416 Remington Magnum

Historical Notes: Officially announced in November of 1988, the .416 Remington Magnum was the first American cartridge designed for use on African game to be introduced since the .458 Winchester Magnum in 1956, and the .460 Weatherby Magnum back in 1958. The .416 is based on the 8mm Remington Magnum necked-up to .416-caliber. It was initially available with either a 400-grain pointed soft-point or a 400-grain solid bullet loaded to a muzzle velocity of 2400 fps and a muzzle energy of 5115 ft-lbs. The company says that the 400-grain solid is exactly that, turned from solid brass and not a lead core with a heavy jacket. The cartridge was available in the Remington Model 700 Safari bolt-action rifle. Other rifle manufacturers have picked up the .416 Remington. It is available in a variety of bolt-action and single-shot rifles, including those from Ruger. It has proven to be a fairly popular cartridge.

General Comments: There has been a persistent call, by those who hunt dangerous game, for a cartridge to fill the gap between the .375 Holland & Holland Magnum and the .458 Winchester Magnum. The .416 Rigby accomplished this rather well, but both rifles and ammunition became increasingly difficult to obtain, until Federal began offering that cartridge in the late 1980s. This problem was then solved, to some extent, by a number of wildcat cartridges such as the .416 Taylor, .416 Hoffman, and the .425 Express. These cartridges all more or less duplicated the performance of the .416 Rigby, and the .416 Remington does pretty much the same thing. However, the Remington version has one great advantage in that it is available as a commercial loading in a proven commercial rifle. The combination will be much easier and less expensive to come by than a custom rifle for wildcat or proprietary cartridges.

Although the .416 bullet is 100 grains lighter than that of the .458 Winchester, it starts out with an almost 300 fps higher velocity. That, combined with better sectional density and a superior aerodynamic shape, gives it certain ballistic advantages. It not only has a higher initial velocity, it also increases its retained velocity over the .458 as the range increases. According to the factory figures, it has an 11-percent advantage in muzzle energy, and this increases to 18-percent at 100 yards and 30-percent at 200 yards.

The .416 Remington should be ideal for dangerous game, including Cape buffalo, elephant, lion, and brown bear. It would also do well on moose and elk. The .416 Remington has a trajectory very similar to the .375 H&H and is a better long-range cartridge than the .458 Winchester for use against thin-skinned game. For the man who has to travel light, the .416 would be a good one-gun cartridge choice for use in Africa. To date, only Remington loads ammunition in this caliber.

.416 Remington Magnum Loading Data and Factory Ballistics

Bullet (grains/type)	Powder	Grains	Velocity	Energy	Source/Comments
300 SP	H-4895	78	2850	5412	Barnes
350 SP	H-4895	80	2700	5667	Barnes
400 SP	IMR 4064	78	2400	5117	Hornady
400 SP	IMR 4895	76.5	2400	5117	Hornady
300 SP	FL		2530	4262	Remington factory load
350 SP	FL		2520	4935	Remington factory load
400 SP	FL		2400	5115	Remington factory load

.416 Weatherby Magnum

Historical Notes: There has been a moderate, but persistent, interest in .40-caliber dangerous-game cartridges for a good many years. The demand has been filled by several wildcat cartridges, but the call for a factory .40-caliber intensified in the 1980s. Remington was the first to exploit this potential market with its .416 Remington Magnum, in 1988. This was followed by the .416 Weatherby Magnum (which is based on the .378 Weatherby Magnum), in 1989. In the game of cartridge one-upmanship, the Weatherby version was bound to be somewhat more powerful than an "ordinary" .416.

General Comments: The .416 Weatherby Magnum offers 300 fps more initial velocity than the .416 Remington Magnum with the same bullet weight. How useful this will be in the field is difficult to assess, because both cartridges are adequate for the intended purpose, which is to dispatch large and/or dangerous game with a minimum of fuss. On the other hand, Weatherby rifles carry a certain prestige, and there is nothing wrong with having a little extra power when the crucial moment arrives. The choice between the two will probably be a matter of personal preference. However, recoil is rather brisk with any such chambering, and more powder pushing the same bullet faster translates into more recoil.

.416 Weatherby Loading Data and Factory Ballistics

Bullet (grains/type)	Powder	Grains	Velocity	Energy	Source/Comments
300 SP	IMR 4831	115	3000	5997	Barnes
350 SP	IMR 4831	110	2800	6095	Barnes
400 SP	IMR 4831	110.5	2700	6477	Hornady
400 SP	H-450	119	2700	6477	Hornady
400 SP	IMR 7828	117	2600	6006	Hornady
400 SP	FL		2700	6474	Weatherby factory load

.416 Rigby

Historical Notes: Introduced by John Rigby of London, the .416 Rigby is a good example of a sound design that refuses to die. Until quite recently, less than 10,000 rifles in this caliber had been made. However, most of the older rifles in that chambering are still in use. In 1992, Ruger added this cartridge to its rifle product line. Ruger thus increased the total number of guns in this chambering by 10 percent in one year. The company continues to produce it. In 1989, Federal Cartridge Co. added the .416 Rigby to its Premium product line. In so doing, Federal became the first major American manufacturer to offer this classic African cartridge. By their actions, both Ruger and Federal took away much of the momentum from the new .416 Remington Magnum cartridge. Their efforts in reintroducing the .416 Rigby have been successful, and sales remain brisk. This only goes to show that not all new product success stories use totally new products.

General Comments: The .416 Rigby is today a great favorite of African game wardens and professional hunters alike. It is an excellent choice for the hunter who wishes to take only one rifle to Africa. Federal ballistics are identical to previous British loads, so the point of impact with express sights will be the same. Breech pressures of the .416 are only about 40,000 CUP, in order to avoid sticky extraction exhibited by high pressures on very hot days. This is strictly good sense, based on many years of African experience. Remington has chosen to load the .416 Remington Magnum to pressure levels of 50,000 CUP, which makes one wonder if extraction at very high temperatures has been adequately tested, and handloaders should resist the urge to improve the .416 Rigby ballistics for this reason. Bullets and brass for handloading are available from Huntington (www.huntingtonsports.com).

.416 Rigby Loading Data and Factory Ballistics

Bullet (grains/type)	Powder	Grains	Velocity	Energy	Source/Comments
300 Barnes XFB	RL-22	103.0	2590	4470	Hodgdon
350 Barnes XFB	H4350	102.0	2518	4925	Hodgdon
400 Hornady FMJNR	H4831	106.0	2422	5210	Hodgdon
410 SP/FMJ	FL		2370	5115	Federal factory load

.44-40 Winchester
(.44 WCF, .44 Winchester)

Historical Notes: This was the original cartridge of the famous Winchester Model 1873 lever-action repeating rifle. By 1878, Colt's began offering revolvers in .44-40-caliber. At one time or another, just about every American arms manufacturer has offered some kind of gun chambered for this cartridge. The Colt-Burgess lever-action rifle of 1883 was made for the .44-40, and so was the 1885 Colt Lightning pump-action rifle. The Remington Model 14½ pump-action used it, as did the Winchester 92 and Marlin 94, both lever-action repeaters. Most of the single-shot rifles made in the United States had a .44-40 model at one time or another. In Spain, there was a copy of the Winchester Model 92 in .44-40 caliber manufactured for police and civil guard use. No American-made rifles have chambered the round since 1937, but Colt's revolvers retained it until 1942. Several foreign-made replicas of the Henry Carbine and the Winchester Model 66 and 73 are currently available in .44-40, as are new revolvers.

Winchester once loaded a 217-grain bullet in two separate headstamps: .44 C.L.M.R. for the Colt Lightning Magazine Rifle, and .44-40 for Marlin rifles. It also offered a 34-grain blackpowder load behind a 115-grain bullet for the Marble Game Getter rifle, which was headstamped .44 G.G.

General Comments: The .44-40 is one of the all-time great American cartridges. It is said that it has killed more game, large and small, good and bad, than any other commercial cartridge ever developed. In its original blackpowder loading, it was the first effective combination cartridge that could be used interchangeably in rifle or revolver, and was a great favorite in the early days of the American West.

With proper handloads used in strong rifles, the .44-40 can safely propel the 200-grain jacketed bullet at 1800 fps. Compared to the standard .30-30 load with a 170-grain bullet at about 2100 fps, this is a superior combination against deer at short range. It was once offered in a high-velocity loading specifically designed to take advantage of the Model 92 Winchester's strength. As with many other high-velocity loadings of yesteryear, it had to be discontinued, because certain folks just insisted on chambering anything that would fit in whatever gun was at hand. The .44-40 became obsolete in the revolver with the advent of the .357 and .44 Magnums, and in the rifle by the .30-30 and similar cartridges that have a flatter trajectory at ranges beyond 100 yards. Present factory loads by Remington and Winchester are intended for revolvers, and it is necessary to handload in order to get top performance from the rifle. Many .44-40 rifles have been rebarreled for the .44 Magnum. The rise of cowboy action shooting has rekindled the .44-40's popularity.

.44-40 Winchester Loading Data and Factory Ballistics

Bullet (grains/type)	Powder	Grains	Velocity	Energy	Source/Comments
180 SP	2400	18	1250	625	Hornady
180 SP	SR4756	11	1150	529	Hornady
180 SP	2400	16.5	1000	400	Hornady
180 SP	Unique	10.4	1150	529	Hornady
200 SP	IMR 4227	20	1100	537	Hornady
200 SP	2400	15.3	1000	444	Hornady
200 SP	Unique	9.5	1050	490	Hornady
200 SP	FL		1190	629	Factory load

.444 Marlin

Historical Notes: News and data on the .444 Marlin round was released to the public in June 1964. The cartridge was designed for the Marlin Model 336 lever-action rifle. Initially, the rifle was manufactured with a 24-inch Micro-Groove barrel, two-thirds length magazine, and recoil pad. The straight-grip stock had a Monte Carlo cheekpiece. Original ammunition was made by Remington.

The .444 Marlin is somewhat similar to the .44 Van Houten Super. The .44 VH was developed by E.B. Van Houten and "Lucky" Wade of Phoenix, Arizona. It was made by necking up .30-40 Krag brass, trimming it to two inches, and turning down the rims slightly. It was designed for the 336 Marlin or 94 Winchester actions. It pre-dates the Marlin round by at least three years. Ballistics of the two rounds are nearly identical.

General Comments: The .44 Magnum revolver cartridge achieved popularity as a rifle round. However, anyone using it discovers quite quickly that it has a rainbow-like trajectory, and its killing power on heavier game such as elk and moose is adequate only at close range. Consequently, there was need for a somewhat more powerful option. The .444 Marlin extends both the effective range and killing power inherent in the .44 Magnum. This round fires the same 240-grain soft-point bullet at 2330 fps, as compared to 1850 fps for the average .44 Magnum rifle. The .444 Marlin is substantially more powerful than the old .30-30 or the .35 Remington at short ranges. It develops about the same energy as the .348 Winchester and slightly more than the later .358 Winchester. However, with its larger diameter bullet, it should provide better knockdown power. It is a short- to medium-range cartridge and should be adequate for any North American big game. It would also be effective on most thin-skinned African game, except the dangerous varieties. Its advantage over the above-named cartridges is at ranges out to 150 yards. Beyond that, due to better bullet shape and sectional density, those all catch up to and finally surpass the .444 in retained velocity and energy. The .444 Marlin was formerly available as a superb all-round hunting load with a 265-grain bullet. Remington, Hornady, and Buffalo Bore now offer ammunition, with the latter firm offering several superior-performance, heavy-bullet loads.

.444 Marlin Loading Data and Factory Ballistics

Bullet (grains/type)	Powder	Grains	Velocity	Energy	Source/Comments
180 HP	IMR 4198	51	2500	2499	Sierra
220 SP	IMR 4198	49	2350	2698	Sierra
240 HP	IMR 4198	46.5	2300	2820	Hornady, Sierra
240 HP	H-322	53	2300	2820	Hornady, Sierra
250 SP	IMR 4198	47	2250	2811	Sierra
265 Hornady JFP	H-4198	47.0	2273	3040	Hodgdon
275 SP	RL-7	47	2250	3092	Barnes
280 Swift HP	H322	49.5	2120	2790	Hodgdon
300 SP	RL-7	46	2150	3080	Barnes
300 Swift HP	H4198	42.5	2082	2885	Hodgdon
240 SP	FL		2330	2942	Remington factory load

.45-70 Government
(.45-70-330/.45-70-350/
.45-70-405/.45-70-500)

Historical Notes: Adopted by the U.S. military, in 1873, with the single-shot "Trapdoor" Springfield rifle, this continued as the official service cartridge for 19 years. It was replaced, in 1892, by the .30-40 Krag. The .45-70 Government was also a popular cartridge for sporting use, and many repeating and single-shot rifles were chambered for it, icluding the Remington rolling block, Remington-Keene, Remington-Lee, Marlin Model 81, Winchester Model 86, and Hotchkiss, plus many others. Though the Krag officially replaced the .45-70, in 1892, all volunteer Spanish-American War regiments—with the reported sole exception being Teddy Roosevelt's Rough Riders—were equipped with the Trapdoor .45-70. Many state militias were armed with the .45-70 Springfields well beyond the year 1900. American companies dropped the .45-70 as a rifle chambering in the early 1930s. However, it has staged a major comeback in popularity, and currently Marlin, Ruger, and Browning chamber rifles for the .45-70. Winchester once loaded many versions of the basic .45-70 case with different bullet weights, shapes, and blackpowder charges. It also loaded one variant of the .45-70-405 Winchester load expressly for the Marlin 1881 lever-action rifle. That load featured a differently shaped 405-grain bullet and was headstamped .45-70 Mar.

General Comments: "Old soldiers never die," and apparently neither do old military cartridges. The .45-70 has been with us for more than 125 years and is still very much alive. As a short-range cartridge for anything from deer to grizzly bear, the .45-70 will hold its own with most of our more modern developments. Its greatest fault is the curved trajectory that makes it difficult to place shots beyond 150 yards with any certainty. Unfortunately, the U.S. Springfield and most of the other blackpowder rifles won't stand pressures over 25,000 psi or so. This prevents using heavy loads of smokeless powder. In late-Model 86 Winchesters or other smokeless powder rifles, the .45-70 can be loaded to deliver very impressive performance on the heaviest species of big game. Winchester, Remington, Federal, CorBon, and Buffalo Bore offer .45-70 ammunition.

.45-70 U.S. Government Loading Data and Factory Ballistics

Bullet (grains/type)	Powder	Grains	Velocity	Energy	Source/Comments
300 HP	IMR 4198	34	1400	1306	Hornady, Sierra
300 HP	IMR 4227	29	1400	1306	Hornady, Sierra
300 HP	IMR 3031	43	1400	1306	Hornady
300 HP	SR 4759	27	1400	1306	Hornady

Loads for Modern Smokeless Powder Rifles Only

Bullet (grains/type)	Powder	Grains	Velocity	Energy	Source/Comments
300 HP	IMR 4198	46	2000	2665	Hornady
300 HP	IMR 4227	43	2100	2938	Sierra
350 Hornady JFP	H4198	54.0	2191	3730	Hodgdon
400 SP	H4198	50.5	2002	3555	Hodgdon
400 SP	IMR 3031	54	1800	2878	Speer
300 SP	FL		1880	2355	Factory load
405 SP	FL		1330	1590	Factory load
350 JFN	FL		2100	3427	Buffalo Bore Factory Load
325 FTX	FL		2050	3032	Hornady Factory Load

.450 Bushmaster

Historical Notes: The .450 Bushmaster (parent cartridge is the .45 Professional) rifle/cartridge conversion, was developed by Tim LeGendre, of LeMag Firearms LLC, and licensed to Bushmaster Firearms International for production and distribution. LeGendre still retains ownership. The .450 Bushmaster is designed to be used in the standard M-16/AR-15 platform, using five-round magazines.

Bushmaster asked Hornady to produce the .45 Professional ammunition for this project, and Hornady agreed. Hornady wanted the .45 Professional shortened to accommodate its 250-grain pointed SST bullet. Hornady asked Bushmaster for the change (1.771-inch to the now standard 1.7-inch), and Bushmaster asked LeGendre to sign off on that change. He did. Bushmaster eventually wanted a name change, and LeGendre agreed to that, too, and that is what has now become the popular .450 Bushmaster.

Based on a concept by Col. Jeff Cooper ("Thumper"), the goal was to provide guaranteed one-shot kills on big game animals at 250 yards, with a large-bore semi-auto (.44-caliber or larger). Colonel Cooper, upon being presented with the early .45 Professional, stated, "This is Thumper Senior … . I can now own an AR-15." A .45 Pro was indeed built for Col. Cooper, which was remarkable, considering his disdain for the AR-15 in 5.56 NATO. Hornady, with its extreme expertise, busted the Cooper 250-yard limit. The result is the .450 Bushmaster, a semi-auto rifle/cartridge combination that absolutely provides more than enough stopping power to adequately kill all big game in North America.

General Comments: While the two cartridges have nothing in common dimensionally, the appearance of the .450 Bushmaster is remindful of the old .401 Winchester, which was designed for another autoloading rifle, the Winchester Model 1910. The .401 Winchester is capable of pushing a .40-caliber 250-grain bullet along at 1900 fps, while the .450 Bushmaster pushes a .45-caliber bullet of the same weight along at 2200 fps. But, due to its higher velocity, along with the more streamlined shape of the Hornady FTX bullet, the newer cartridge delivers a deadlier blow downrange. Out to about 225 yards, it retains a sufficient level of energy to handle game as large as moose and elk.

.450 Bushmaster Loading Data and Factory Ballistics

Bullet (grains/type)	Powder	Grains	Velocity	Energy	Source
250 Hornady FTX	FL		2200	2686	Hornady

.450 Marlin

Historical Notes:	Hornady and Marlin announced the .450 Marlin at the 2000 SHOT Show. This is the first new chambering from Marlin since the introduction of the .444 Marlin, in mid-1964. The motivation for this cartridge is simple. Handloaders have been souping up .45-70 loads for use in Marlin's modern 1895 since the day that gun was introduced. Owing to the many weaker .45-70 rifles still in use, Marlin could not condone this practice, nor could it stop it. Something had to give. Some have asked why Marlin didn't simply lengthen the .45-70 case and standardize a new higher-pressure cartridge. That alternative wasn't tenable, because such a cartridge would have chambered in older (potentially weaker) rifles designed for the .45-90, .45-110, etc.
General Comments:	When one considers a simple approach that could have been taken, this cartridge design is a poor, second-best choice for chambering in the new M-1895 Marlin. The simple adoption of an "Ackley Improved" version of the .45-70 would have provided a superior case design with a cartridge that would function better through the Marlin rifle and would not chamber in any older factory rifle. In any case, the .450 Marlin offers lever-action fans a factory chambering with significant ballistic potential. Shooters in this country have a long history of fascination with large-bore lever-action rifles. Except for caliber, Marlin's new number is quite reminiscent of Winchester's circa-1903 .50-110 Winchester High Velocity load, which originated for the same reason; muzzle energy is essentially identical. This cartridge and rifle make a fine and versatile combination for those who hunt dangerous game under the worst possible conditions. Given correct bullet choice and shot placement, this is a capable performer for any task.
	Interstingly, Lewis Potter, proprietor of Potter & Walker (Evasham, Worcestershire, UK), reports that, around the time the .450 Marlin was being introduced, he—quite coincidentally—successfully shortened and reformed .375 H&H Magnum cases to something quite similar to the new Marlin number, for use in a client's modified Ruger No. 1. Potter's wildcat, the performance of which fell somewhere between that of a high-end .45-70 and the .450 Marlin, was playfully christened the .45-70 Nitro Express.

.450 Marlin Load Data and Factory Ballistics

Bullet (grains/type)	Powder	Grains	Velocity	Energy	Source/Comments
250 Barnes TSX/FN	H4198	54.0	2493	3446	Barnes
300 Nosler PPP	H335	67.0	2282	3465	Nosler
350 Hornady FP	RL-7	51.5	2000	3105	Hornady
400 Speer JFP	H335	55.0	1953	3383	Hodgdon
350 Hornady FP	FL		2100	3427	Hornady factory load

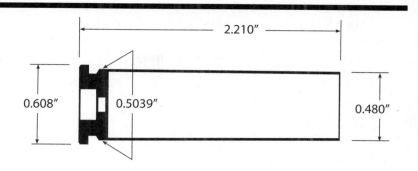

NEW
.457 WWG

Historical Notes: Wild West Guns out of Alaska, and now Las Vegas, Nevada, has been building custom lever guns for a long time. Many are chambered for the .47-70 and will endure potent high-pressure loads not available in standard SAAMI-spec ammunition. CorBon has been supplying Wild West Guns with hot-loaded .45-70 ammo for these exquisite lever guns, but the concern always existed that someone would stuff one of these high pressure loads in an older and not so strong rifle. This led Jim West, the man behind Wild West Guns, to develop his own hot-rod .45-caliber lever gun cartridge that he calls the .457 WWG. Originally a proprietary design on its own unique case, the cartridge has been chambered in many Wild West Guns. As of the publication of the 13th Edition of Cartridges of the World, the .457 WWWG has been submitted to SAAMI and is pending approval. One of the most unique things about lever guns chambered for this cartridge is that they can still function and fire .45-70 ammunition. The .457 WWG has an operating pressure of 43,500 psi, as compared to 28,000 psi for the .45-70.

General Comments: The most popular rifle available from Wild West Guns is its Co-Pilot model, which is a compact, take-down lever gun designed to offer bush pilots or anyone else existing in big bear country a compact rifle capable of stopping any critter that might decide to do them harm. Pushing a 405-grain bullet to almost 2000 fps, this cartridge lives up to that claim. It is suspected that, once it's SAAMI approved, you will see firearms from other manufacturers offered in this chambering, as well as ammunition from CorBon, The Hunting Shack, and maybe even other ammo manufacturers.—R.A.M.

.457 WWG Loading Data and Factory Ballistics

Bullet (grains/type)	Powder	Grains	Velocity	Energy	Source/Comments
350 A Frame	FL		2300	4112	Cor-Bon Factory Load
405 Hard Cast	FL		1950	3420	Cor-Bon Factory Load

.458 Winchester Magnum

Historical Notes: The .458 Winchester Magnum was introduced, in 1956, for a dressed-up version of the Model 70 rifle called the "African." The Remington 700 Safari is available in .458, and so are many other American- and European-made rifles, such as the A-Square, Dakota 76, BRNO, and the Ruger 77. The .458 has become a world standard, and many factories and individual makers provide hunting arms for it. Ruger also chambers the .458 in its No. 1 single-shot rifle.

General Comments: With an increasing number of American sportsmen making the trek to Africa, and with the Weatherby Magnum line of cartridges selling rather well, Winchester decided to get into the act. The result is the fine .458, a cartridge suitable for any of the most dangerous game in the world. This cartridge has been tested thoroughly in Africa and has proven itself adequate for the toughest game found there. It is as powerful as most of the oversized English big-bore elephant cartridges. Although overpowered for North American big game, it has nonetheless found favor with many hunters as a woods and brush cartridge, when reloaded with lighter-than-standard factory bullets. With the 300-, 350-, or 405-grain bullets, it can be loaded to duplicate the .45-70 at any level and to cover a wide range of game and hunting conditions. As a factory load, it isn't good for anything but the biggest and toughest. But, then, that is what it was intended for. Federal, Winchester, and Remington offer ammunition.

.458 Winchester Loading Data and Factory Ballistics

Bullet (grains/type)	Powder	Grains	Velocity	Energy	Source/Comments
300 SP	RL-7	58	2100	2938	Hornady
300 SP	IMR 4198	49	2100	2938	Hornady, Sierra
350 SP	IMR 4198	70.5	2500	4859	Hornady
400 SP	IMR 4198	64	2250	4498	Speer
400 SP	IMR 4320	77	2200	4300	Speer
500 SP	IMR 3031	70	2100	4897	Hornady
350 SP	FL		2470	4740	Factory load
400 SP	FL		2380	5031	Factory load
500 FMJ	FL		2040	4620	Factory load
510 SP	FL		2040	4712	Factory load

.458 Lott

Historical Notes: When a twice-shot African buffalo energetically squashed Jack Lott, dissatisfaction with his .458 Winchester's performance led to the creation, in 1971, of a more capable .458 cartridge, the .458 Lott. By using a case 2.8 inches long, the .458 Lott was able to achieve 2150 fps with a 500-grain bullet. The genius of the late Lott's design is that .458 Lott rifles also chambered and fired .458 Winchester Magnum ammo. On the downside, the wildcat .458 Lott was strictly a handloading and custom rifle proposition. Then, in 2002, Hornady decided to produce factory ammunition, and Ruger chambered its Model 77 MKII in .458 Lott.

General Comments: The .458 Winchester is advertised as developing 2040 fps with the 500-grain bullet when fired from a 24-inch barrel. In reality, poorly constructed factory loads often produce little more than 1900 fps in 22-inch barreled rifles. The .458 Lott will do an honest 2,300-plus fps from a 22-inch barrel. It has been field-tested in Africa, and it has chalked up an impressive number of one-shot kills on elephants and buffalo. It is similar to the .450 Watts, which is also based on the full-length .375 H&H case expanded to .458-caliber, but is shorter. Rifles chambered for the .458 Lott will also safely shoot .458 Winchester ammo. Since Hornady has adopted this cartridge as a factory loading, availability of ammo and brass should improve markedly. Numerous bullet makers make bullets suitable for the .458 Lott, with weights ranging from 350 grains to 600 grains. With factory ammo and production rifles now readily available, the .458 Lott continues to be a superb choice for virtually any dangerous game worldwide.

.458 Lott Loading Data and Factory Ballistics

Bullet (grains/type)	Powder	Grains	Velocity	Energy	Source/Comments
500 SP	IMR 4320	85.0	2330	6020	NA
500 SP	IMR 4064	79.0	2230	5520	NA
500 RN	FL		2300	5873	Factory load

.460 Weatherby Magnum

Historical Notes: This big, potent caliber was brought out, in 1958, for the avowed purpose of providing the world's most powerful commercial rifle cartridge. It was developed by necking the .378 Weatherby case up to .45-caliber. Rifles and ammunition are available only through Weatherby on a commercial basis, but custom-made rifles based on Mauser-type bolt actions are occasionally chambered for this round.

General Comments: Until the advent of the .700 Nitro Express, which is just barely in the ranks of commercial cartridges, the .460 Weatherby Magnum was among the most powerful available. Recent factory ballistics have been toned down a bit, but it still delivers better than 7500 ft-lbs of muzzle energy, which far exceeds most dangerous game loads. The big .460 is overly powerful for any North American big game, but it does provide that ultimate bit of insurance against the dangerous African or Asiatic varieties under adverse conditions—it would, of course, be preferable to be caught slightly overgunned than to be eaten by a lion or trampled by an elephant. Two wildcat cartridges, the .450 and .475 Ackley, are in the same class as the .460 Weatherby insofar as energy is concerned. The .475 A&M Magnum reportedly develops a muzzle energy of some 10,000 ft-lbs. However, none of these are commercial cartridges. Recently, many new A-Square and proprietary numbers have exceeded the .460 Weatherby.

.460 Weatherby Magnum Loading Data and Factory Ballistics

Bullet (grains/type)	Powder	Grains	Velocity	Energy	Source/Comments
300 SP	IMR 4320	112	3000	5997	Barnes
350 SP	IMR 4064	111	2900	6538	Hornady
500 SP	IMR 4350	123.5	2650	7799	Hornady
500 SP	IMR 4320	108	2550	7221	Hornady
500 SP	IMR 3031	99	2500	6941	Hornady
500 SP	H-4831	125	2650	7799	Barnes
500 SP/FMJ	FL		2600	7507	Weatherby factory load

.470 Nitro Express (.470 NE)

Historical Notes: Since its introduction, in 1907, the .470 Nitro Express has proven to be one of the most popular and long lived of the British Nitro Express cartridges. Guns in this chambering are not excessively heavy, and recoil, while stout, is acceptable. This makes a good combination for the hunter who wants to use one cartridge for all African game, without fear of being under-gunned. For this reason, most guns in this cartridge are the tried-and-true double rifles, such as the English-made H&H, Purdey, J. Rigby & Co., Westley Richards, Powell, and a few others. Production of such rifles is also abundant in Europe, with Beretta of Italy, Francotte of Belgium, and Heym of Germany offering models priced from $10,000 on up. The 5130 ft-lbs of muzzle energy generated by the 500-grain, steel-jacketed solid bullet is the stuff from which myths are made in the hot-stove league.

General Comments: In 1989, Federal Cartridge Co. added this caliber to its Premium product line, making it the first British Nitro Express caliber offered by a major American manufacturer. The .470 is generally too powerful for most North American game, but works well on medium to large game worldwide. Many .470 shooters reload the cartridge, because of the high cost of factory ammo. Federal's factory loads can provide cases, and Barnes offers bullets.

.470 Nitro Express Loading Data and Factory Ballistics

Bullet (grains/type)	Powder	Grains	Velocity	Energy	Source/Comments
500 Barnes SP	H4831	119.0	2159	5175	Hodgdon
600 Barnes SP	H4831	105.0	1941	5020	Hodgdon
500 SP/FMJ	FL		2150	5130	Federal factory load

.50 Browning Machine Gun (.50 BMG)

Historical Notes: The .50 BMG was invented by its namesake and adopted into United States military service, in 1918, for John M. Browning's famous heavy machine gun. Browning's attentions in this area were prompted by a battlefield need recognized during World War I. There have been other developments, and at least once the Pentagon considered dropping the .50 BMG in favor of more modern and generally bigger chamberings. However, the .50 BMG has remained. The advent of saboted loads generating 4500 fps muzzle velocities and having devastating armor-penetration capabilities, and its performance in the Gulf War have seemed to cement its continued existence as a stable part of NATO's arsenal.

Battlefield use is against light-armored vehicles to ranges of a mile or more, and used against the unprotected, it is effective to several times that range.

General Comments: There has long been interest in the .50 BMG as a quasi-sporting round. Today, the most significant sporting use for this chambering is long-range accuracy shooting, with some competitions exceeding one mile. The 1,000-yard .50-caliber record, as of this writing, is a five-shot group of just under three inches on centers. Several bolt-action rifles are currently available for the Big 50. The .50 BMG easily launches the 750-grain bullets available for it at 2700 fps. The lighter 647-grain bullets available can be launched at 3000 fps. For obvious reasons, sporting rifles chambered for the Big 50 uniformly feature muzzlebrakes and weigh 20 pounds or more. Recoil is a bit harsh until the rifle's weight approaches 30 pounds.

Commercial ammunition is available for the .50 BMG from PMC and Hornady, among others that are loading both once-fired and new brass and calling their offerings "factory new." Components and specialized tools and equipment to handload this cartridge are available to the advanced reloader.

.50 Browning Machine Gun Loading Data and Factory Ballistics

Bullet (grains/type)	Powder	Grains	Velocity	Energy	Source/Comments
750	H870	225.0	2769	12,775	Barnes
800	AA8700	215.0	2675	12,720	Barnes
660	FL		3080	13,910	PMC factory load

Cartridge	Case	Bullet Dia.	Neck Dia.	Shoulder Dia.	Base Dia.	Rim Dia.	Rim Thick.	Case Length	Ctge. Length	Primer	Page
.17 Hornet	A	.172	.194	.294	.298	.345	.050	1.350	1.72	S	14
.17 Remington Fireball	C	.172	.204	.3655	.3759	.332	.045	1.410	1.83	S	14
.17 Remington	C	.172	.198	.355	.374	.377	.041	1.79	1.86	S	15
4.6x30 HK	C	.183	.209	.305	.316	.315	.043	1.201	1.516	S	16
.204 Ruger	C	.204	.229	.360	.373	.375	.045	1.850	2.260	S	16
.22 Hornet	A	.223	.242	.274	.294	.345	.060	1.40	1.72	S	17
.218 Bee	A	.224	.241	.331	.349	.408	.060	1.35	1.68	S	17
.222 Remington	C	.224	.253	.355	.375	.375	.041	1.70	2.15	S	18
.223 Remington	C	.224	.249	.349	.373	.375	.041	1.76	2.10	S	19
.22 PPC	C	.224	.245	.430	.440	.441	.050	1.52	1.96	S	21
.225 Winchester	A	.224	.260	.406	.422	.473	.045	1.93	2.50	L	21
.224 Weatherby Magnum	E	.224	.247	.405	.413	.425	.045	1.92	2.44	L	22
.22-250 Remington	C	.224	.254	.412	.466	.470	.045	1.91	2.33	L	22
.220 Swift	G	.224	.260	.402	.443	.472	.045	2.20	2.68	L	24
.223 WSSM	C	.224	.254	.544	.555	.535	.040	1.670	2.360	L	25
6mm PPC	C	.243	.260	.430	.441	.442	.050	1.50	2.12	S	25
6mm Norma BR	C	.243	.271	.458	.469	.470	.051	1.56	2.44	S	26
6XC Tubb	C	.243	.271	.450	.466	.468	.049	1.898	2.808	L	27
.243 Winchester	C	.243	.276	.454	.470	.470	.049	2.05	2.71	L	27
.243 WSSM	I	.243	.287	.544	.555	.535	.054	1.67	2.06 (2.36)	L	28
6mm Remington/.244 Remington	C	.243	.276	.454	.470	.472	.045	2.23	2.91	L	29
.240 Weatherby Magnum	E	.243	.271	.432	.453	.473	.045	2.50	3.06	L	30
.25-20 Winchester (WCF)	A	.257	.274	.329	.349	.405	.060	1.33	1.60	S	31
.25-35 Winchester (WCF)	A	.257	.280	.355	.420	.500 (.506)	.059	2.04	2.53	L	31
.25-45 Sharps	C	.257	.284	.353	.376	.378	.045	1.760	2.135	S	32
.250 Savage (.250-3000)	C	.257	.286	.413	.468	.470	.045	1.91	2.52 (2.515)	L	33
.257 Roberts (257 Roberts +P)	C	.257	.290	.430	.468	.473	.045	2.23	2.74	L	34
.25 WSSM	C	.257	.299	.544	.555	.535	.040	1.670	3.260	L	35
.25-06 Remington	C	.257	.287	.441	.470	.471	.045	2.49	3.00	L	35
.257 Weatherby Magnum	E	.257	.285	.490	.511	.530	.048	2.55	3.25	L	36
.260 Remington/6.5-08 A-Square	C	.264	.294	.452	.468	.467	.045	.025	2.80	L	37
6.5x55 Swedish Mauser	C	.264	.297	.435	.480 (.477)	.480 (.479)	.050	2.16	3.15	L	37
6.5 Grendel	C	.264	.293	.428	.439	.441	.059	1.526		SR	38
6.5-284 Norma	I	.264	.297	.475	.500	.470	.051	2.17	3.23	S	39
6.5 Creedmoor	C	.264	.297	.458	.467	.468	.054	1.915	2.720	L	39
.264 (6.5mm) Win. Magnum	E	.264	.289	.490	.515 (.5127)	.532	.047	2.52	3.29	L	40
6.8 Special Purpose Cartridge (SPC)	C	.277	.306	.401	.421	.417	.049	1.686	2.260	L	41
.270 Winchester	C	.277	.307	.440	.468	.470	.045	2.54	3.28	L	41
.270 WSM	A	.277	.314	.5381	.555	.535	.054	2.10	2.86	L	42
.270 Weatherby Magnum	E	.277	.305	.490	.511	.530	.048	2.55	3.25	L	43
7-30 Waters	A	.284	.306	.399	.422 (.4215)	.506	.058	2.04	2.52	L	44
7mm Mauser (7x57mm)	C	.284	.320	.420 (.4294)	.470	.474	.046	2.24 (2.235)	3.06	L	44
7mm-08 Remington	C	.284	.315	.454	.470	.473	.050	2.04 (2.035)	2.80	L	45
.284 Winchester	I	.284	.320	.465 (.4748)	.495 (.500)	.470	.049	2.17	2.75	L	46
.280 Remington (7mm Express Remington)	C	.284	.315	.441	.470	.472	.045	2.54	3.33	L	47
.280 Ackley Improved	C	.284	.311	.454	.470	.472	.049	2.525	3.330	L	48
7mm Remington Magnum	E	.284	.315	.490	.511	.525	.047	2.50	3.24	L	48
7mm Remington SAUM	I	.284	.320	.534	.550	.534	.050	2.035	2.45 (2.86)	L	49
7mm WSM	I	.284	.321	.538	.555	.535	.054	2.10	2.56 (2.86)	L	50

Dimensional Data (SAAMI Maximum Cartridge Data)

Cartridge	Case	Bullet Dia.	Neck Dia.	Shoulder Dia.	Base Dia.	Rim Dia.	Rim Thick.	Case Length	Ctge. Length	Primer	Page
7mm Weatherby Magnum	E	.284	.312	.490	.511	.530	.048	2.55	3.25	L	51
7mm STW	E	.284	.316	.487	.513	.532	.048	2.85	3.65	L	51
7mm Remingtom Ultra Mag	I	.284	.322	.525	.550	.534	.050	2.85	3.45 (3.60)	L	52
.30 Carbine	D	.308	.335	.355	.360	.046	1.29	1.65	16		53
.30-30 Winchester	A	.308	.328	.402	.422 (.4215)	.502	.058	2.03 (2.039)	2.53	L	54
.300 AAC Blackout	C	.308	.334	.361	.375	.375	.045	1.368	1.78	S	55
.300 Savage	C	.308	.339	.443 (.4466)	.470	.470	.045	1.87	2.62	L	55
.30 Remington AR	I	.308	.341	.488	.500	.492	.054	1.525	2.260	S	56
7.62x39mm Soviet	C	.311	.340 (.337)	.344 (.396)	.438 (.433)	.440	.053	1.52 (1.528)	2.20	S	57
.30-40 Krag	A	.308	.338	.415 (.419)	.457 (.4577)	.540	.059	2.31	3.10 (3.089)	L	58
.307 Winchester	G	.308	.344	.454	.470	.506	.059	2.02 (2.015)	2.60 (2.56)	L	59
.308 Marlin Express	A	.308	.344	.448	.463	.502	.049	1.910	2.585	L	60
.30 TC	C	.308	.343	.464	.470	.473	.054	1.920	2.645	L	61
.308 Winchester	C	.308	.344	.454	.470	.470	.049	2.01 (2.015)	2.75	L	61
.30-06 Springfield	C	.308	.340	.441	.470	.473	.045	2.49	3.34	L	62
.300 H&H Magnum	E	.308	.338	.447	.513	.530	.048	2.85	3.60	L	63
.300 Remington SAUM	I	.308	.344	.534	.550	.534	.050	2.015	2.450 (2.825)	L	64
.300 WSM	I	.308	.344	.538	.555	.535	.054 (2.860)	2.10	2.560	L	64
.300 Ruger Compact Magnum	C	.308	.344	.515	.532	.532	.040	2.100	2.825	L	65
.300 Winchester Magnum	E	.308	.334	.4891	.5126	.530	.046	2.60 (2.62)	3.30	L	66
.300 Weatherby Magnum	E	.308	.337	.495	.513 (.5117)	.530	.048	2.82 (2.825)	3.56	L	67
.300 Remington Ultra Mag	I	.308	.344	.525	.550	.532	.050	2.845	3.60	L	68
.30-378 Weatherby Magnum	K	.308	.330	.560	.589	.603/.5803	.060	2.90	3.865	L	69
.303 British	A	.311	.338	.401	.458	.530	.062	2.21 (2.222)	3.05 (3.075)	L	69
.32-20 Winchester	A	.312	.326	.338 (.3424)	.353	.405	.058	1.32 (1.315)	1 59	S	70
.32 Winchester Special	A	.321	.343	.396 (.4014)	.422 (.4219)	.506	.058	2.04	2.55 (2.565)	L	71
8X57 Mauser	C/A	.323	.350	.435	.470	.473/.526	.043/.048	2.24/2.25	3.17/3.55	5603/366D1	72
.325 WSM	C	.323	.358	.538	.555	.535	.054	2.10	2.560	L	73
8mm Remington Magnum	E	.323	.351 (.3541)	.485 (.4868)	.509 (.5126)	.530	.047	2.85	3.57 (3.600)	L	73
.338 Marlin Express	A	.338	.370	.493	.506	.553	.055	1.890	2.585	L	74
.338 Federal	C	.338	.369	.454	.470	.473	.049	.201	2.75	L	75
.338 Ruger Compact Magnum	C	.338	.370	.515	.532	.532	.040	2.100	2.825	L	75
.338-06 A-Square	C	.338	.370	.441	.470	.473	.049	2.494	3.24 (3.44)	L	76
.338 Winchester Magnum	E	.338	.369	.480 (.491)	.515 (.5127)	.530	.047	2.49 (2.50)	3.30 (3.34)	L	77
.340 Weatherby Magnum	E	.338	.366	.495	.513	.530	.048	2.82	3.60	L	77
.338 Remington Ultra Mag	I	.338	.371	.526	.550	.532	.050	2.76	3.60	L	78
.338 Lapua Magnum	C	.338	.370	.540	.590	.590	.060	2.72	3.60		8
.338-378 Weatherby Magnum	E	.338	.369	.561	.581	.579	.063	2.193	3.638	L	79
.348 Winchester	A	.348	.379 (.3757)	.485	.553	.610	.062	2.26 (2.255)	2.80 (2.795)	L	79
.35 Remington	C	.358	.384	.419 (.4259)	.458 (.4574)	.460	.046	1.92	2.52	L	80
.356 Winchester	G	.358	.388	.454	.4703	.508	.058	2.02 (2.015)	2.56	L	81

Dimensional Data (SAAMI Maximum Cartridge Data)

Cartridge	Case	Bullet Dia.	Neck Dia.	Shoulder Dia.	Base Dia.	Rim Dia.	Rim Thick.	Case Length	Ctge. Length	Primer	Page
.358 Winchester	C	.358	.388	.454	.4703	.473	.048	2.01 (2.015)	2.78	L	82
.35 Whelen	C	.358	.388	.441	.470	.473	.045	2.50 (2.494)	3.34	L	83
.350 Remington Magnum	E	.358	.388	.495	.5126	.532	.046	2.17	2.8	L	83
9.3x62mm Mauser	C	.365	.388	.447	.473	.470	.044	2.42	3.29	5603/474	84
.370 Sako Magnum/9.3x66 Sako	C	.366	.405	.450	.477	.470	.047	2.598	3.346	L	85
.375 Ruger	C	.375	.405	.515	.532	.532	.050	2.580	3.340	L	86
.375 Winchester	B	.375	.400	.415 (.4198)	.502	.046	.063	2.56	12	L	86
.376 Steyr	I	.375	.398	.472	.501	.494	.048	2.35	3.075	L	87
.375 H&H Magnum	E	.375	.402	.440 (.4478)	.521	.530	.046	2.85	3.60	L	88
.375 Weatherby Magnum	E	.375	.402	.492	.512	.531	.051	2.85	3.54 (3.80)	L	89
.375 Remington Ultra Mag	I	.375	.405	.525	.550	.534	.050	2.85	3.54 (3.60)	L	89
.378 Weatherby Magnum	E	.375	.399	.560	.582	.579	.063	2.913	3.65	L	90
.38-55 Winchester (.38-55 Ballard)	B	.379	.392	.3938	.422	.506	.058	2.12 (2.085)	2.51	L	90
.38-40 Winchester (WCF)	A	.401	.416	.438 (.4543)	.465	.520	.058	1.30	1.59	L	91
.416 Ruger	C	.416	.445	.515	.532	.532	.050	2.580	3.240	L	92
.416 Remington Magnum	E	.416	.447	.487	.509	.530	.046	2.85	3.60	L	93
.416 Weatherby Magnum	K	.416	.444	.561	.584	.603/.580∂	.062	2.915	3.75	L	93
.416 Rigby	C	.416	.445 (.4461)	.539 (.5402)	.589	.586	.058	2.90	3.75	L	94
.44-40 Winchester (WCF)	A	.427/ .429	.443	.4568	.471	.525	.058	1.31	1.92	LP	95
.444 Marlin	B	.429	.453	.4549	.469	.514	.058	2.16 (2.225)	2.57	L	95
.45-70 Government	B	.458	.475 (.480)	.4813	.500	.600 (.608)	.065	2.105	2.55	L	96
.450 Bushmaster	J	.458	.480	–	.500	.473	.050	1.700	2.260	L	97
.450 Marlin	F	.458	.480	.511	.532	.47	.047	2.55	2.2	L	98
.457 WWG	B	.458	.480	-	.5039	.605	.07	2.21	2.49	L	99
.458 Winchester Magnum	F	.458	.478 (.4811)	.4825	.513	.532	.046	2.50	3.34	L	99
.458 Lott	F	.458	.481		.513	.532	.048	2.80	3.60	L	100
.460 Weatherby Magnum	K	.458	.485	.560	.584	.603/.580∂	.062	2.91	3.75	L	100
.470 Nitro Express	A	.475	.504	.528 (.5322)	.5728	.655	.037	3.25	3.98	L	101
.50 BMG	C	.510/ .511	.560	.714	.804	.804	.080	3.91	5.545	50 BMG	102

Case Type: A = Rimmed, bottleneck. B = Rimmed, straight. C = Rimless, bottleneck. D = Rimless, straight. E = Belted, bottleneck. F = Belted, straight. G = Semi-rimmed, bottleneck. H = Semi-rimmed, straight. I = Rebated, bottleneck. J = Rebated, straight. K = Rebated, belted bottleneck. L = Rebated, belted straight.

Primer Type: S = Small rifle (0.175"). SP = Small pistol (0.175"). L = Large rifle (0.210"). LP = Large pistol (0.210"). 50 BMG = CCI-35/VihtaVuori-110/RWS-8212. B-1 = Berdan #1. B-2 = Berdan #2.

Other codes: Belt/Rim Diameter. Unless otherwise noted, all dimensions in inches. Twist (factory) is given as inches of barrel length per complete revolution, e.g., 12 = 1 turn in 12", etc. Unless otherwise noted, all dimensions are in inches. Data in parenthesis represents SAAMI maximum specifications. Bullet upset performance of the 264 Winchester Magnum 140 gr. Power Point at ranges of 100, 200, 300, 400 and 500 yards.

Obsolete American Rifle Cartridges
(Centerfire Sporting – Blackpowder and Smokeless)

Chapter 3 covers obsolete rifle cartridges, those no longer loaded by American ammunition manufacturers or those no longer chambered in commercially available rifles. Sometimes such ammunition is still available out of dealers' old stocks. Both smokeless powder and blackpowder cartridges are included in this section. The total number of old blackpowder sporting cartridge types is quite large. Many of those are now collectors' items.

Some authorities are bound to disagree with a few of the cartridges placed in the obsolete category. For example, wildcat experimenters have kept the Newton cartridge line alive over the years, and it might be argued that those belong in that classification. A wildcat cartridge is usually defined as one that is not loaded, chambered, or available on a commercial basis. Strictly speaking, this would make wildcats of almost all the cartridges listed in this chapter. However, these have one common, differentiating characteristic—all were, at one time, available as true commercial cartridges. Furthermore, used rifles and ammunition out of old stock are sometimes still available for the majority of smokeless powder types. These are also listed in old catalogs and ballistics tables, and it might create confusion to call these wildcats.

The cartridges in Chapter 3 can be considered as commercial innovations that have not stood the test of time. This is as true of the Newton cartridges as the others, but ,in addition, the Newton designs must be recognized as too advanced for their day. If Charles Newton were alive and his cartridges were introduced today, they would be hailed as brilliant and modern in every respect. Unfortunately, modern powders and entirely suitable actions were not available back around 1910, nor was the sporting world quite ready to accept high-intensity cartridges. The general big-game hunting conditions at that time made the benefits of this development of doubtful value. The trouble with being ahead of the times is that people do not appreciate your genius during your lifetime. Posthumous recognition must be of precious little comfort to the individual involved. The late Roy Weatherby, on the other hand, arrived on the scene at the right time. He was also a far better promoter and businessman than Charles Newton. Result? Ultra-velocity Weatherby rifles are a commercial success and Weatherby's ideas are accepted the world over by all but a few die-hards.

The principal importance of obsolete commercial cartridges to today's sportsman is that rifles for many of these are still floating around, particularly the smokeless powder types. It is well to be aware of its existence and disadvantages before some sharpy unloads an obsolete rifle on you. Obtaining ammunition for any of these chamberings is going to be an ever-increasing problem. Of course, certain handloaders like to play around with obsolete cartridges just to be different or to try to improve performance. If you belong to this group, well and good, you probably know what you are doing. However, cartridges in Chapter 2 will serve the average sportsman better.

Up to this point, we have aimed most of these remarks toward obsolete smokeless powder cartridges. The true blackpowder types are a different story. Many of the old blackpowder rifles are now quite valuable, and we find a considerable and growing trend toward use of these old rifles for target shooting, hunting, and cowboy action shooting.

Cartridge Development

Blackpowder cartridges discussed in this chapter cover arms development from about 1868 to 1895. Ideas and experiments of this interval were a necessary prerequisite to perfection of modern, high-powered rifles and ammunition. This was also one of the most romantic periods of American history, that being the consolidation and settling of the western frontier.

The first successful, self-contained metallic cartridge produced on a commercial basis in the United States was the .22 Short rimfire, introduced by Smith & Wesson for its small, tip-up revolver, in 1857. Commercial cartridge production from then until after the close of the Civil War was mostly in the rimfire field. Patents issued to George W. Morse, in 1856 and 1858, covered the essential features of the modern centerfire cartridge. His design incorporated an anvil, formed out of a wire, soldered inside the case. A perforated rubber disc held at the base of the case by this wire supported the primer (or cap, as was the common name at that time).

American Col. Hiram Berdan perfected his priming system, with the anvil formed in the bottom of the primer pocket, during 1866. British Col. Edward Boxer developed his self-contained primer and anvil, in 1867. (Oddly, European manufacturers use the Berdan type extensively, while American manufacturers use the Boxer primer almost exclusively.) Frankford Arsenal initiated experiments to develop a satisfactory centerfire system as early as 1858. The Union Metallic Cartridge Co. (now Remington), began manufacturing Berdan centerfire cartridges in 1868, about a year after formation of the company. The first of the American outside-primed, Berdan-type cartridges were probably the .50-70 Govt. and .50 Remington Navy rounds.

After 1870, development and introduction of improved centerfire cartridges was quite rapid. In 1885, the French chemist Paul Marie Eugène Vieille developed the first practical smokeless powder, and, in 1886, the French adapted this to the new 8mm Lebel military cartridge. The United States military adopted its first smokeless powder small-bore cartridge, in 1892, for the Krag bolt-action rifle. Winchester developed the first smokeless powder sporting round, the .30 Winchester Center Fire (now known as the .30-30 Winchester), during 1895. Popularity of blackpowder cartridges did not begin a serious decline in the United States until after about 1910. Both Remington and Winchester were still loading blackpowder in some of the old cartridges as late as 1936 or 1937. Many blackpowder centerfire cartridges, such as the .32-20, .32-40, .38-55, .38-40, .44-40, .45 Colt, and .45-70 survived the change to smokeless powder. Several manufacturers load one or more of these, but now with smokeless powder. (CorBon offers a limited production of blackpowder Cowboy Action loads in .45

Colt and .45-70.) We cover those early rounds still produced in other chapters, as appropriate.

Cartridge Designation Confusion

Two great sources of confusion with blackpowder sporting cartridges are the method of nomenclature and the manufacturer's habit of sticking its name on any cartridge it manufactured or for which that company chambered guns. Two or three numbers were normally used to designate a particular cartridge and loading, e.g., .45-70 Gov't. or the .45-70-500 Gov't. The first numeral represents the caliber (approximate bullet diameter in hundredths of an inch); the second numeral signifies the blackpowder charge (in grains); the third numeral specifies bullet weight (in grains). The manufacturer often tacked on its name after the final numeral. Worse, sometimes, a manufacturer would offer several interchangeable cartridges, but with differing and distinct names. For example, Winchester offered two essentially identical .45-70 loadings, one called .45-70-350 WCF, the other, offered for Marlin rifles, was called .45-70-300 Marlin. As a matter of confusing fact, the Sharps Rifle Co. designated this same .45-70 Govt. round as the .45/2.1-inch Sharps. Winchester introduced the tapered-case .40-65 WCF, while, for its rifle, Marlin loaded the same case with 60 grains of blackpowder and called the resulting round the .40-60 Marlin. Despite the distinct names, these two cartridges are nearly identical and are fully interchangeable. However, Winchester also introduced its own .40-60 WCF, a shorter and entirely different case than the "so-called" .40-60 Marlin. Then consider the following trio: .50-100, .50-105, and .50-110 Winchester. Some references have listed these as different cartridges, but these are, in reality, just different loadings of the same case, which Winchester originally offered as the .50-110-300 WCF. Confusing!

To add a bit more difficulty to this mess, consider the Everlasting, a heavy, reloadable-type case that was popular for many years. Often, these cases were so thick and heavy that the original powder charge would not fit. Manufacturers solved this problem by making the case slightly longer than standard. This practice gave rise to all manner of different cartridges, which are simply a slightly lengthened version of something else. Trying to tie the standard original and the longer reloadable version together is often difficult. We have attempted to unravel this confusion as much as possible.

Most cartridge-book authors list bullet diameter based upon that portion of the projectile protruding from the case mouth. This is okay for identification purposes, but not much help to the handloader. Bullet diameter, as given here, is that recommended for loading and shooting and is based upon average groove diameter. We obtained this by measuring bullets removed from factory ammunition or from old Ideal catalogs or manufacturers' specifications. Ideal catalogs had a reference table listing various cartridges and the loading tool and standard bullet furnished. This is a good index for bullet diameter in any given cartridge, but old rifle bores exhibited considerable variation. It is a good idea to measure bore diameter before you order a mould, just to be on the safe side.

If you cannot figure out the chambering of your rifle, have it checked by a gunsmith or make a chamber cast and measure it. A comparison of chamber dimensions with the cartridge dimensions in Chapter 13 should allow you to determine chambering of almost any rifle. These cartridge dimensions will also assist in making up ammunition for the old-timers or determining the proper name of unmarked cases.

Chamber Casting

In making chamber castings, one can use sulphur, a low melting point bismuth alloy, or paraffin wax. Lead alloy can also be used, but it is not recommended.

Flowers of sulphur (obtainable on www.Amazon.com, pretty much like anything else these days), is satisfactory. However, sulphur casts are extremely brittle and prone to breakage during removal from the chamber or during later handling. The tinker must heat a sulphur solution (four ounces of sulphur, a pinch of lampblack, and about a teaspoon of camphor), very slowly, with continuous stirring. As soon as this becomes fully molten, it is ready for pouring into the chamber. It should be poured quickly and allowed to cool thoroughly before attempting to remove the cast. The chamber must be thoroughly cleaned and lightly oiled before pouring. The bore should be plugged just forward of the chamber, thus also giving you a cast of the bore for measurement. A good method is to drive a piece of wire through a bore-fitting cork and leave this wire extending from the breech. A finger loop on the end of this wire mandrel aids in removing the cast.

For a less precise, but nonetheless perfectly useful, casting, simply prepare the chamber the same way, then plug the bore with a paper wad or other similar device and fill the chamber with molten paraffin. After thorough cooling, this casting will easily come free from the chamber. This provides a very good casting, but will always shrink a few thousandths of an inch in every dimension. Nevertheless, this will usually be adequate to distinguish correct chambering designation.

The most satisfactory and durable chamber casts are accomplished with chamber cast metal available from gunsmith supply houses (such as Brownells, 800-741-0015; www.brownells.com). These are bismuth alloys. The user can repeatedly re-melt and reuse casts made from this material. Lightly oil the chamber and throat as above. One of the typical bismuth alloys used for chamber castings is Cerrosafe. This alloy has a pouring temperature of 190-degrees Fahrenheit, significantly below the boiling point of water. You should be cautious to avoid overheating this material, as doing so will destroy its reusability. Cerrosafe shrinks slightly for a few minutes after it hardens, which simplifies removal of large or long castings. Measurements made approximately one hour after removal give truest dimensions. Surfaces of bismuth alloy casts are very smooth, unlike those of lead alloy, which often wrinkle badly.

Blackpowder Loads and Shooting

Although considerable differences in terminal performance exist among blackpowder sporting cartridges, little variation in effective range exists. Stories abound about market-era buffalo hunters killing game at ranges of a half-mile or more, and, no doubt, this sometimes happened. Competitors used some of the big-bore match cartridges for 1,000- and even 1,400-yard target shooting. Buffalo hunters were generally professionals who had spent years in the field and must have developed a keen ability for estimating distances. On the target range, distance was known and the rifle sighted-in before the match started. Many people cannot tell 100 feet from 100 yards in the field, and that is why blackpowder rifles, with their rainbow-like trajectories, are restricted to an effective game range of not much beyond 150 yards. An experienced hunter, someone with an accurate rangefinder, or anyone who has practiced with his rifle and knows how to judge distance with reasonable accuracy can, of course, do better. Blackpowder cartridges below about .38-caliber are mostly for small or medium game. Larger calibers include many good short- to medium-range deer and black bear cartridges. The big and long .45- to .50-caliber numbers would knock the stuffing out of the largest moose or grizzly bear that ever lived. All you have to do is place the shot correctly.

Loading ammunition for blackpowder rifles requires caution, if you intend to use smokeless powder. As a matter of safety, velocity and pressure must be kept at the original level in most rifles. Jacketed bullets and high velocity are out of the question, unless you have a modern action and a steel barrel designed for use with smokeless powder loads. While a few of the old actions are strong enough to be re-barreled to modern chamberings, most are not. Among the strongest are the Peabody-Martini, Remington rolling blocks and Hepburns, Sharps-Borchardt, Stevens 44½, and the Winchester single-shot. Late models of these are as strong as many modern actions, but early models do not have the improved "smokeless powder steel," and caution is advisable. The weakest of the lot are the U.S. 1866 and 1873 Springfields, Kennedys, Whitneys, and Winchester Models 1873s and 1876s. In these, use blackpowder or very light smokeless powder loads.

Also, do not use a smokeless powder charge given for one bullet weight with a heavier bullet, as this will raise pressures, perhaps beyond safe limits. Old cartridge cases are often of the folded-head (balloon) type, which are not particularly strong. Furthermore, since blackpowder residue is corrosive to brass, inspect your cases very carefully. It is safer to use modern-made cases in original or reformed sizes, when possible. Non-corrosive primers do not leave chloride salts in the bore, hence, they reduce that corrosion. However, these can also raise pressures—a fact to bear in mind when working up loads. Shooting blackpowder rifles and cartridges is lots of fun, and it can be just as safe as shooting modern rifles. On the other hand, it requires common sense and education. If in doubt, don't do it! Ask a good gunsmith and follow his advice—in the end, that practice will be cheaper.

Shooting old blackpowder rifles has become such a popular pastime that furnishing ammunition for these obsolete guns is a growing business. As a further aid in obtaining ammunition, get a copy of the book *Cartridge Conversions* by the late Maj. George C. Nonte, Jr. This will tell you how to make, via re-forming, most of the non-existent blackpowder cartridges. An article by Nonte in the 1962 16th Edition of *Gun Digest* introduces this subject. The *Lyman Reloaders Handbook* and the *NRA's Illustrated Reloading Handbook* (out of print) also have much valuable information on making and loading obsolete cartridges.

It is not surprising to find reproductions (identical in every important way to the originals), and replicas (dimensionally and functionally similar to the originals), of some of the more popular blackpowder cartridge rifles being manufactured. This follows the success of percussion replica arms. Many supplies for loading both these rifles and the origials can be obtained from Huntington's (www.huntingtonsports.com) or The Old Western Scrounger (www.ows-ammo.com).— *F.C.B.*

13th Edition Update

As we mentioned briefly in the introductory portion of this book, space constraints and the addition of more than 50 new cartridges and their schematic drawings to this 13th Edition have forced us to be creative with the vast amounts of cartridges and information inherent to this kind of reference volume. To that end you'll find a CD on the back inside cover of this book that contains more than 100 cartridges that we removed from these pages to make room for the new stuff. Removal to the CD was based loosely and mostly on the scarcity of the round (i.e., if we came across a passage of text that said a round was hard to find even in collections, onto the CD it went), scarcity or nonexistence of brass or suitable bullets for reloading, and sometimes just on the unique oddball nature of the round itself.

This paring down became something of a problem when it came to this chapter, which contains nothing *but* obsolete cartridges. We didn't want to just chop the whole chapter out and put it on the CD, so we went as judiciously by the cull method described as we could. But, perhaps more importantly than what we cut is what we left in these pages.

While you'll certainly still find a solid collection of obsolete and probably hard to find American Rifle Cartridges in the following pages of this chapter, they are, by majority, those less obscure than the ones on the CD. We also chose to leave here those cartridges that, while still rare, could possibly be confused with more modern cartridges, or even among their obsolete brethren. By the very nature of the often confusing nomenclature that is the naming of the world's cartridges, there is an inherently dangerous proposition in place for anyone attempting to fire a round in a gun similarly, but not specifically, chambered for it. The potential danger is amplified in old and antique guns that feature indistinct and unfamiliar markings, in addition to what may be their overall poor quality after more than a century in existence. What this boils down to is an admonishment that any book like this should have, and that is be safe. If you're not sure a cartridge will work in your gun (or that your gun is or isn't in a fireable condition), don't fire it. Same goes for the loading and measurements listed here. Follow the rule "measure twice and cut once," and always, *always* consult a full reloading manual for accurate recipes before attempting to load any round for any gun.

Cartridges removed from this chapter relocated to the CD include the following: .25-15-60 Stevens; .22 Extra Long Centerfire (Maynard); .228 Weatherby Magnum; .350 Griffin & Howe Magnum; .38-45 Stevens; .38-45 Bullard; .38-70 Winchester; .40-60 Colt; .40-65 Ballard Everlasting; .40-70 Peabody "What Cheer"; .44-100 Remington "Creedmoor"/.44-90 Remington Straight; .44-85 Wesson; .45-100 Remington (Necked); .45-125 Winchester (.45 Express); .55-100 Maynard; .70-150 Winchester.

—*Jennifer L.S. Pearsall, Editor Gun Digest Books*

.219 Zipper

Historical Notes:	The .219 Zipper was brought out, in 1937, by Winchester for its Model 64 lever-action rifle, which was a modernization of the Model 94. This combination (as with the .218 Bee in the Model 65), did not prove sufficiently accurate for long-range shooting on small targets and, in addition, did not allow the proper mounting of telescopic sights. Winchester discontinued the Model 64 after World War II. The last commercial rifle chambered for this cartridge was Marlin's Model 336 lever-action, discontinued in this chambering in 1961. A number of custom-made single-shot and Krag-Jorgensen rifles have been made for the .219 Zipper. It is not and never has been very popular. It is based on the necked-down .25-35 WCF case. Winchester dropped the .219 Zipper in 1962, and Remington followed shortly thereafter.
General Comments:	In a good, solid-frame single-shot or bolt-action rifle, the .219 Zipper is just as accurate as any other high-velocity .22 in its class. Since it was designed for tubular magazines, all factory-loaded

ammunition is furnished with flat- or round-nosed bullets, and this causes rapid velocity loss. Although overshadowed by the .222 Remington, it is still an entirely satisfactory small-game, varmint, or target cartridge. Given carefully prepared ammunition in a carefully prepared lever-action, performance of this cartridge and rifle combination is limited more by the necessary use of blunt bullets, than by intrinsic accuracy constraints. Such a combination is certainly capable of 200-yard shots on vermin, which is stretching what most shooters can do with iron sights anyway; beyond that range, velocity drops off so fast that trajectory limits usefulness, even given a telescopic sight. This is one of the few American cartridges that functions well through the British Lee-Enfield action. Some of these rifles have been rebarreled and altered to handle the Zipper. Anecdotal information from several serious shooters who have bothered to wring out the cartridge's accuracy in the Model 64 suggests that Winchester should have spent more effort on ammunition quality.

.219 Zipper Loading Data and Factory Ballistics

Bullet (grains/type)	Powder	Grains	Velocity	Energy	Source/Comments
45 SP	IMR 4320	30.0	3600	1295	Hornady
45 SP	BL-C	27.0	3400	1152	Hornady
45 SP	H380	30.5	3500	1224	Sierra
50 SP	IMR 3031	26.0	3400	1284	Sierra
50 SP	H380	31.0	3500	1360	Sierra, Hornady
55 SP	IMR 4320	29.0	3300	1330	Hornady, Sierra
55 SP	H380	30.0	3300	1330	Hornady, Sierra
55 SP	IMR 4320	27.0	3300	1330	Sierra
60 SP	IMR 4064	28.0	3300	1451	Hornady
60 SP	H380	31.0	3300	1451	Hornady
55 SP	FL		3110	1200	Factory load

.222 Remington Magnum

Historical Notes: The .222 Remington Magnum was originally developed as an experimental military cartridge in a cooperative effort between Remington and Springfield Arsenal. Since it was never adopted by the military, Remington introduced it as a sporting round, in 1958, as one of the calibers for its Model 722 bolt-action rifle, and also, for a time, in the later 700 series bolt-action rifles. At present, no Remington rifles are available in this caliber. None of the other major American sporting arms manufacturing companies currently offer the .222 Remington Magnum.

General Comments: In comparison to the standard .222 Remington, the Magnum version has about 20-percent greater case capacity and consequently delivers 100 or so fps higher muzzle velocity and an effective range of between 50 and 75 yards greater than the .222. Though its case capacity is four- to five-percent greater than the .223 Remington, the performance of these two is indistinguishable because the .222 Remington Magnum is factory loaded to a lower maximum pressure. The .222 Magnum is nearly 1/10-inch longer than the .223 in overall case length, and it is also slightly longer in body length. As a result, the two are not interchangeable, and though the .223 can be chambered and fired in a .222 Magnum rifle, a dangerous headspace condition exists and case rupture is almost certain to occur when the round is fired. The .222 Remington Magnum is probably every bit as accurate as the standard .222 or the .223 and is certainly adequate for anything up to, but not including, deer. It never achieved the popularity of the standard .222 and has been largely superseded by the .223 Remington. It is, nevertheless, a very fine long-range varmint cartridge.

.222 Remington Magnum Loading Data and Factory Ballistics

Bullet (grains/type)	Powder	Grains	Velocity	Energy	Source/Comments
40 Sierra SP	BL-C(2)	30.0	3818	1290	Hodgdon
45 SP	H-380	29.5	3400	1125	Hornady

Bullet (grains/type)	Powder	Grains	Velocity	Energy	Source/Comments
45 SP	BL-C2	27	3400	1236	Hornady, Sierra
45 SP	IMR 4895	27	3400	1082	Speer, Hornady
50 SP	H-380	30	3400	1180	Hornady
50 SP	BL-C2	26	3300	1190	Nosler, Hornady, Speer
50 SP	IMR 3031	26	3300	1204	Speer
55 SP	H-380	29	3200	1234	Hornady
55 SP	RL-7	22	3200	1170	Sierra
55 SP	IMR 3031	26	3300	1332	Speer
55 SP	IMR 4064	26	3300	1340	Hornady
60 HP	IMR 4895	25	3000	1242	Nosler, Hornady
55 SP	FL		3240	1282	Remington factory load

.22 Winchester Centerfire (.22 WCF)

Historical Notes: The .22 WCF was introduced, in 1885, as one of the original cartridges for the famous Winchester single-shot rifle, first manufactured that year. It was also chambered in the Remington No. 7 rolling block rifle, in 1904. It was actually too long for most of the short repeating actions of the day, although Winchester once cataloged it for the Model 1873, so its use was confined mostly to single-shot rifles. It is the predecessor of the .22 Hornet.

General Comments: The .22 WCF enjoyed considerable popularity as a target, small-game, and varmint cartridge, until 1925. Winchester advertised it as a 200-yard cartridge, but, with its mid-range trajectory of some 13.5 inches, it was more of a 100- to 125-yard number. Although originally a blackpowder cartridge, it was loaded in a smokeless powder version with identical ballistics. In Europe, it was stepped up to about 1700 to 1800 fps and used in drillings or other combination guns. The .22 WCF was discontinued in 1936.

.22 Winchester Centerfire Loading Data and Factory Ballistics

Bullet (grains/type)	Powder	Grains	Velocity	Energy	Source/Comments
45 SP	Unique	4.0	1500	226	
45 SP	2400	6.0	1650	273	
45 Cast	blackpowder (FFg)	13.0	1560	244	Lyman No. 228151
45 Lead	blackpowder (FFFg)	13.0	1540	240	Factory load

.22 Savage High-Power
(.22 High-Power/.22 Imp)
5.6x52Rmm

Historical Notes: Designed by Charles Newton, this cartridge was introduced as a commercial cartridge by the Savage Arms Co., in its Model 99 lever-action rifle, about 1912. The cartridge was first called the "Imp." In the United States, only Savage produced a commercial rifle in this chambering, although a great many custom rifles were chambered for it. In England, the BSA Martini single-shot was chambered for it, about 1912. In Europe, it is known as the 5.6x52Rmm and has been chambered in various drillings or combination rifle and shotgun arms. The .22 Savage is based on the .25-35 case necked down. It has been obsolete in the U.S. since the 1930s. Norma still manufactures this ammunition.

General Comments: The .22 Savage High-Power enjoyed considerable popularity through the early 1900s. However, accuracy was often marginal for small game and the bullets sometimes failed to penetrate adequately on larger game. No doubt, considering the general quality of jacketed bullets of that era, the Imp was greatly handicapped by poor bullet quality. Nonetheless, the .22 Savage was used in Africa and Asia on such unlikely beasts as lion and tiger, with some glowing reports on its effectiveness. It is a perfectly adequate small-game and varmint cartridge, but no big-game number by any standard. It has been rendered obsolete by new and much improved modern cartridges, such as the .222 Remington. For single-shot rifles, most modern shooters prefer the .225 Winchester, because of the availability of ammunition and cases, plus the fact that the .225 uses standard .224-inch diameter bullets, as opposed to the .228-inch bullets of the .22 Savage High-Power.

.22 Savage High-Power Loading Data and Factory Ballistics

Bullet (grains/type)	Powder	Grains	Velocity	Energy	Source/Comments
55 SP	IMR 4895	27.0	2870	1106	
55 SP	IMR 3031	30.0	3260	1291	
55 SP	H380	29.0	3200	1249	
70 SP	RI-7	23.0	2900	1308	Hornady
70 SP	IMR 4198	23.0	3000	1399	Hornady
70 SP	IMR 3031	27.0	3100	1494	Hornady
71 SP	FL		2790	1228	Norma factory load

6mm Bench Rest Remington
(6mm BR Remington)

Historical Notes: The 6mm BR Remington is one of eight cartridges based on the .308x1½-inch case necked either up or down. It is impossible to determine who first came up with the 6mm version, because a number of individuals claim the honor, dating back to 1962 and 1963, shortly after the original author of this book introduced the .308x1½-inch. However, Mike Walker, of Remington Arms, deserves credit for standardizing dimensions and the configuration, in 1978. This allowed the cartridge to be adopted as a standard commercial cartridge. In late 1988, Remington announced that the 6mm BR would be produced as loaded factory ammunition. Prior to that, it was a sort of factory wildcat. Cases had to be formed from Remington BR brass, which is actually a modified .308 Winchester with a Small Rifle primer pocket, comparatively thin walls, and annealing to facilitate reforming. The factory load has a 100-grain bullet with a muzzle velocity of 2550 fps and muzzle energy of 1444 ft-lbs. The 6mm BR was intended primarily as a benchrest cartridge, but it also makes a good varmint number. It was available as one of the chamberings for the Remington XP-100 single-shot pistol. (Editor's note: Since the 6mm BR was in use before it was a factory round, there will be some chamber confusion. The original chambers were mostly intended for cases with turned necks.)

General Comments: The 6mm BR is similar to the 6mm PPC, except that the case is of larger diameter and has about 10-percent greater capacity. The 6mm PPC is loaded somewhat hotter than the 6mm BR, with some loading manuals listing the 90-grain bullet around 3000 fps. There is no reason why the 6mm BR can't do anything the 6mm PPC can, and the availability of factory ammunition should increase its popularity. This will also help overcome one of the problems with the 6mm PPC—the matter of obtaining suitable brass on an over-the-counter basis and at a reasonable price. Remington was the only manufacturer to take up commercial production of this caliber, and that briefly.

6mm BR Remington Loading Data and Factory Ballistics

Bullet (grains/type)	Powder	Grains	Velocity	Energy	Source/Comments
60 Sierra HP	H322	32.0	3481	1610	Hodgdon
70 SP	W748	32	3200	1592	Hornady
75 HP	W748	33	3200	1706	Hornady
80 SP	W748	31.5	3100	1708	Hornady
80 SP	RL-7	24	2900	1494	Hornady
80	Varget	32.5	3159	1740	Hodgdon
87 SP	W748	31	3000	1739	Hornady
87 SP	H-322	25.5	2800	1515	Hornady
100 SP	FL		2550	1444	Remington factory load

.244 Remington (.243 Rockchucker)

Historical Notes: The .244 Remington was introduced by Remington, in 1955, in its Model 722 bolt-action rifle. The cartridge is based on the .257 Roberts necked down to 6mm. It was actually originated as a wildcat by Fred Huntington of Oroville, California. The wildcat version preceded the factory design by several years and was called the .243 Rockchucker. Only Remington chambered the .244 among American manufacturers, but several European-made bolt-action rifles were available in this chambering.

General Comments: The .244 Remington is ballistically almost identical to the .243 Winchester. The only notable difference is that Remington made its 6mm rifles with a 1:12 twist, whereas Winchester adopted a 1:10 twist for its 6mm. The faster twist rate of the Winchester enabled use of 100-grain spitzer bullets, whereas the slower twist of the Remington did not. The net result is that the .244 Remington will not stabilize spitzer bullets heavier than about 90 grains in weight, while the .243 Winchester does very well with all 100- and even 105-grain bullets. Remington looked on the 6mm as largely a varmint and small-game development and concluded that anything beyond the 90-grain bullet was unnecessary. Winchester, on the other hand, decided the 6mm was very much a big-game cartridge and, therefore, heavier bullets would be highly desirable. Who was right? It appears as if something like 10 .243 Winchester-chambered rifles were sold for each .244 Remington-chambered gun. Remington changed to a 1:9 twist at the last, but too late to rescue the .244 from oblivion. What Remington did to extricate themselves from this dilemma was to change the name of the 2.44 to the 6mm Remington and make all such rifles with a 1:9 twist. (Since, with lighter bullets, the 6mm Remington is interchangeable with the .244 Remington, then, strictly speaking, only the headstamp is obsolete.)

.244 Remington Loading Data and Factory Ballistics

Bullet (grains/type)	Powder	Grains	Velocity	Energy	Source/Comments
75 HP	IMR 4831	48.0	3300	1814	Speer, Hornady
75 HP	IMR 4350	47.0	3400	1926	Nosler, Sierra
75 HP	H380	42.0	3150	1653	Hornady
90 SP	IMR 4831	47.0	3200	2047	Speer, Sierra, Hornady
90 SP	IMR 4350	44.5	3100	1921	Sierra, Speer, Hornady
90 SP	H380	39.0	3000	1799	Sierra, Speer
90 SP	IMR 3031	36.6	3000	1799	Sierra
75 SP	FL		3500	2040	Remington factory load
90 SP	FL		3200	2050	Remington factory load

6mm Lee Navy
(.236 Navy)

Historical Notes: The 6mm Lee cartridge (also known as the .236 Navy) was used in the 1895 Lee Straight Pull bolt-action military rifle manufactured by Winchester for the United States Navy. About 15,000 of these rifles were made and used by the Navy on a trial basis. Winchester, Remington, and Blake also chambered sporting rifles for this cartridge. No factory-loaded ammunition has been available since 1935.

General Comments: The .244-caliber, or 6mm, was revived in two cartridges introduced by Remington and Winchester in 1955, the .244 (now the 6mm Remington) and the .243, respectively. The 6mm Lee cartridge died out mainly because it was too far ahead of its time. The powders available in 1895 were not suitable to a caliber this small. A few shooters who have old rifles for this round reload and use it for hunting. It is a good varmint, medium-game, deer, black bear, and antelope cartridge at moderate ranges. It is not as powerful as the 6mm Remington or the .243 Winchester. By increasing the rim to fit the standard Mauser bolt face and necking the case to accept .224-inch bullets, Winchester created the .220 Swift.

6mm Lee Navy Loading Data and Factory Ballistics

Bullet (grains/type)	Powder	Grains	Velocity	Energy	Source/Comments
75 SP	IMR 3031	37.0	3300	1809	Ackley
95 Cast	Unique	5.0	1200	305	Lyman No. 244203
100 SP	IMR 4895	34.0	2680	1595	
112 SP	IMR 3031	30.0	2650	1895	Ackley
112 SP	IMR 4895	34.0	2670	1946	
112 SP	FL		2560	1635	Factory load

.25-20 Single Shot

Historical Notes: Designed by J. Francis Rabbeth—a gun writer at the turn of the century who used the pen name of J. Francis—the .25-20 Single Shot first appeared about 1882 and was one of the first .25-caliber centerfire wildcats. The first commercial cartridges were loaded by Remington (UMC) and, shortly thereafter, Maynard, Remington, Stevens, and Winchester chambered single-shot rifles for the round. No commercial rifles have been available in this chambering since the late 1920s, and manufacturers stopped loading this number in the mid '30s. Buffalo Arms (www.buffaloarms.com) shows this as an available cartridge in its vast lineup of antique and obsolete loadings.

General Comments: The .25-20 Single Shot was too long to work through the action of the Winchester Model 1892, so Winchester designed the .25-20 WCF, or Repeater, version with a shorter, more bottlenecked case. The .25-20 SS is quite accurate and was used almost entirely in single-shot rifles. As a varmint or small-game cartridge, it is in the same class as the .25-20 WCF. At one time there was a good deal of leftover ammunition on dealer shelves, but, as this cartridge is the base for forming the once-popular 2R Lovell wildcat, most of this was bought up by 2R fans. Most rifles for this cartridge have been rechambered for the still-available .25-20 WCF.

.25-20 Single Shot Loading Data and Factory Ballistics

Bullet (grains/type)	Powder	Grains	Velocity	Energy	Source/Comments
60 SP	2400	8.0	1535	310	Ackley
65 Cast	2400	8.0	1620	380	Lyman No. 257420
86 SP	IMR 4227	8.5	1400	370	Ackley
86 SP	FL		1410	380	Factory load

.25-20 Marlin

Historical Notes: This cartridge was loaded for the Marlin repeating rifle Model 1894. Winchester loaded the .25-20 Marlin, beginning at the turn of the century and until about World War I. It is nothing more than a special version of the .25-20 Winchester, except perhaps for the bullet nose shape, seating depth, and the .25-20 Marlin headstamp. It is otherwise identical to the current .25-20 Winchester. In 1916, Winchester offered five versions of this cartridge: lead, blackpowder (86 grains, 17 grains); soft-point, smokeless powder; full-patch, smokeless powder; high-velocity, soft-point; and high-velocity, full-patch.

General Comments: Sales of Marlin's Model 1894 rifles evidently generated sufficient demand for special-cartridge versions of the rifle's typical chamberings or, perhaps, cartridges with slightly different bullet shapes or loading lengths were found to function better in it. There must have been some good reason, for Winchester's 1916 catalog shows separate cartridge loadings with the following names: .25-20 Marlin, .32-20 Marlin, .38-40 Marlin, and .44-40 Marlin. It is possible the .25-20 Marlin was somehow unique from the .25-20 Winchester, because the catalog does not specify adaptation to Winchester rifles, as it does with the others. In addition, Winchester showed the same blackpowder load and bullet weight for both the .25-20 Winchester and the .25-20 Marlin. The .32-20, .38-40, and .44-40 were unique loadings.

.25-21 Stevens

Historical Notes: The .25-21 Stevens was developed, about 1897, as a shortened version of the slightly older .25-25. First introduced for the Stevens 44 rifles and later available in the 44½ series, it was designed by Capt. W.L. Carpenter of the 9th U.S. Infantry, the man who also designed the .25-25 Stevens. The Remington-Hepburn was available in various models for the .25-21, and it was a popular target and small-game number. Many shooters of the period disliked the bottlenecked case, and the .25-21 was intended as a straight-case version of the .25-20 SS.

General Comments: The .25-21 was noted as a very accurate cartridge, reportedly capable of ½-inch, 100-yard groups. It gave about the same performance as the .25-20 SS, but was much too long for the standard repeating actions. It is easy to reload and quite pleasant to shoot. Use Lyman No. 25720 flat-point or No. 25727 hollowpoint cast bullets. The former weighs 86 grains, the latter 75 grains. Twenty to 23 grains of FFFg blackpowder or the light smokeless powder loads listed below can be used.

.25-21 Stevens Loading Data

Bullet (grains/type)	Powder	Grains	Velocity	Energy	Source/Comments
86 Lead	2400	9.0	1610	498	NA
86 Lead	Unique	5.0	1500	434	NA
88 Cast	Unique	5.5	1440	406	Lyman No. 257231

.25-25 Stevens

Historical Notes: The .25-25 was the first straight case manufactured for Stevens. Designed by Capt. Carpenter, in 1895, Stevens introduced it for its Model 44 single-shot rifles and for the 44½ series after this action was marketed, in 1903. It was also a standard chambering for some of the Remington-Hepburn target rifles. It was somewhat popular, but the shorter .25-21 developed practically the same performance and was a little cleaner shooting.

General Comments: A very freakish-appearing cartridge, with its excessive length-to-diameter ratio, it is the .25-21 with about a half-inch added to its overall length. The late Phil Sharpe wrote (The Rifle in America, 1938)

that the .25-25 caused much extraction trouble, and that is why the shorter .25-21 was developed. However, modern users say this is not so, although the .25-25 fouls the bore a little more than the .25-21. It is highly probable the .25-21 was developed because it was found that 20 or 21 grains of powder gave practically the same ballistics as the extra four grains or so. You can use any cast .257-inch diameter bullet of 60- to 86-grain weight; the gascheck type is preferable with smokeless powder.

.25-25 Stevens Loading Data and Factory Ballistics

Bullet (grains/type)	Powder	Grains	Velocity	Energy	Source/Comments
86 Lead	Unique	5.5	1525	448	NA
86 Lead	IMR 4198	10.2	1520	446	NA
86 Lead	FL		1500	434	Factory load

.25-36 Marlin

Historical Notes: This cartridge, adopted by Marlin, in 1895, for its lever-action Model 93 rifle, was designed by William V. Lowe a year or so prior and originally called the .25-37. It was probably inspired by the .25-35 Winchester. The two are very similar, but not interchangeable, although the .25-35 can be fired in the slightly longer .25-36 chamber. The .25-36 Marlin was loaded in a smokeless powder version and survived until the early 1920s.

General Comments: The .25-36 and the .25-35 WCF are similar; however, many rifles for the Marlin cartridge were not strong enough to withstand maximum loads safely. In general, one should not exceed 2000 fps velocity with the .25-36. It is not an adequate deer cartridge, and its use should be confined to small or medium game. It did not acquire a reputation for outstanding accuracy.

.25-36 Marlin Loading Data and Factory Ballistics

Bullet (grains/type)	Powder	Grains	Velocity	Energy	Source/Comments
87 SP	IMR 3031	20.0	2010	770	NA
117 SP	IMR 3031	20.0	1800	845	NA
117 SP	FL		1855	893	Factory load

.256 Winchester Magnum

Historical Notes: The .256 Winchester Magnum was announced, in 1960, as a new handgun cartridge. However, the only handgun that chambered it was the single-shot, enclosed-breech Ruger Hawkeye, introduced in late 1961. The .256 Winchester Magnum is listed as a rifle cartridge, because Marlin produced its Model 62 lever-action rifle in this chambering, and Universal Firearms made the semi-auto Ferret on the M-1 Carbine action. The Marlin rifle was available about a year after the Ruger Hawkeye, and both were discontinued after a relatively short production life. The Thompson/Center Contender, a single-shot pistol, was also available for this round. The cartridge is based on the necked-down .357 Magnum revolver case.

General Comments: As a rifle cartridge, the .256 is considerably more potent than the .25-20 and several jumps ahead of the .22 Hornet or the .218 Bee. The factory-loaded 60-grain bullet develops over 2760 fps muzzle velocity when fired from a 24-inch rifle barrel. This offers 1015 ft-lbs of muzzle energy, which is well above the Hornet or Bee. The .256 Magnum is an effective varmint cartridge out to ranges of 200 yards. It can be handloaded with heavier 75- or 87-grain bullets to velocities of 2500 and 2230 fps, respectively. Although a good varmint and small-game chambering, it is not an adequate deer cartridge, and most states will not allow its use for this purpose. Winchester was the only commercial manufacturer to offer the .256 Winchester Magnum. It was discontinued in the early 1990s.

.256 Winchester Magnum Loading Data and Factory Ballistics

Bullet (grains/type)	Powder	Grains	Velocity	Energy	Source/Comments
60 SP	H4227	14.0	2500	833	Hornady
60 SP	H4227	16.0	2800	1045	Hornady
60 SP	2400	14.0	2600	901	Hornady
75 HP	H4227	14.0	2400	958	Hornady
75 HP	IMR 4227	15.5	2500	1041	Sierra
87 SP	IMR 4227	14.0	2200	935	Sierra
87 SP	H4227	14.0	2200	935	Hornady
60 SP	FL		2760	1015	Winchester factory load

.25 Remington

Historical Notes: The .25 Remington is one of a series of rimless cartridges developed for the Remington Model 8 Autoloading rifle and later used in other Remington rifles. It was introduced in 1906. The Remington Model 14 pump-action and Model 30 bolt-action and the Stevens Model 425 lever-action also used the .25 Remington. No rifles have chambered this cartridge since 1942, and the ammunition companies stopped loading it about 1950.

General Comments: The .25 Remington is nothing more than a rimless version of the .25-35, but it differs slightly in shape. The two are not interchangeable. Since the Remington line of rifles, particularly the Model 30 bolt-action, would stand higher pressures than the lever-action, it is possible to get slightly better performance out of the .25 Remington. However, the difference is not sufficient to make the rimless version anything but a barely adequate deer cartridge. It will do for varmints and small to medium game quite well, and deer in a pinch, provided the hunter is a good shot. The .30-30 is a better cartridge for anything, and the .25 Remington is hardly in the same class as the .250 Savage or the .257 Roberts.

.25 Remington Loading Data and Factory Ballistics

Bullet (grains/type)	Powder	Grains	Velocity	Energy	Source/Comments
60 SP	H4895	31.0	2900	1121	Hornady
60 SP	IMR 4320	32.0	2900	1121	Hornady
117 SP	H4895	26.5	2200	1258	Hornady
117 SP	IMR 3031	25.5	2300	1375	Hornady
100 SP	FL		2330	1216	Factory load
117 SP	FL		2125	1175	Factory load

.256 Newton

Historical Notes: One of several high-velocity rimless cartridges designed by Charles Newton for his bolt-action rifles, the .256 Newton was introduced, in 1913, by the Western Cartridge Co. Until the .264 Winchester Magnum came along, in 1958, this was the only American-designed 6.5mm to be offered on a commercial basis. The last of the Newton rifle companies failed in the early 1920s, and Western quit loading Newton cartridges in 1938. The .256 Newton is based on the .30-06 case necked down.

General Comments: The .256 Newton has hung on as a wildcat cartridge and, occasionally, custom rifles are made for it. Cases can be made by necking down, reforming, and shortening .30-06 brass. This is a good cartridge and adequate for practically all North American big game, but it is not as effective as the .270 Winchester. With modern, slow-burning powders, its performance can be improved over original factory ballistics.

.256 Newton Loading Data and Factory Ballistics

Bullet (grains/type)	Powder	Grains	Velocity	Energy	Source/Comments
120 SP	IMR 4350	55.0	2980	2362	NA
130 SP	IMR 4895	46.0	2900	2425	NA
140 SP	IMR 4831	57.0	2890	2598	NA
129 SP	FL		2760	2180	Western factory load

6.5mm Remington Magnum

Historical Notes: The 6.5mm is a Remington innovation, introduced in 1966 for its Model 600 carbine. The 6.5mm Remington Magnum is based on the .350 Remington Magnum case necked down to 6.5mm (.264-inch). The Remington Model 600 carbine had an 18½-inch barrel, and the later 660 carbine a 20-inch barrel. Neither of these carbines allowed the cartridge to develop its full velocity potential and both were discontinued. By 1971, only the Remington Model 700 and 40-XB target rifle with 24-inch barrels were cataloged as available in 6.5mm Magnum chambering. For a short time, the Ruger Model 77 was offered in this chambering. All of the rifles referred to are bolt-actions. Currently, no one offers rifles chambered for the 6.5mm Remington Magnum.

General Comments: The 6.5mm Remington Magnum has greater case capacity and develops higher velocities than any of the European military 6.5s. It is an excellent cartridge for North American big game and can double as a varmint cartridge by handloading the lighter bullets. Probably one reason it never achieved great popularity was that the chambering's rifles had short magazines, which required deep seating of heavier bullets, with a consequent loss in powder capacity and performance. Combined with the short barrels of the Remington Model 600 and 660 carbines, this added up to ballistics well below the .30-06 class of cartridges. In a standard long action that will allow seating heavier bullets farther out, one can approach the performance of the .270 Winchester. With the proper bullet, the 6.5mm Magnum is adequate for North American big game at moderate ranges under normal hunting conditions. Unfortunately, this is another case of a good cartridge that did not catch on. At one time, Remington offered two bullet weights, a 100-grain bullet at an advertised muzzle velocity of 3450 fps, and a 120-grain bullet at 3220 fps. The older 6.5mm cartridges gained its reputation with heavier bullets of 140 to 160 grains; the lack of such a factory load is very likely another reason for the demise of the Remington version. Early factory-advertised ballistics were based on a longer-than-standard barrel and were, therefore, unrealistic.

6.5mm Remington Magnum Loading Data and Factory Ballistics

Bullet (grains/type)	Powder	Grains	Velocity	Energy	Source/Comments
85 SP	IMR 4350	57.0	3100	1814	Sierra
100 SP	H4831	56.2	3200	2274	Hornady
100 SP	H380	51.5	3100	2134	Sierra
120 SP	IMR 4831	55.0	3000	2399	Speer
129 SP	H4831	54.0	3000	2579	Hornady
140 SP	IMR 4831	52.0	2750	2352	Speer
160 SP	H4831	54.5	2800	2786	Hornady
120 SP	FL		3210	2745	Remington factory load

.275 Holland & Holland Magnum (.275 H&H Magnum)

Historical Notes: First loaded in Great Britain about 1912, this cartridge was introduced in the United States by Western Cartridge Co., in 1926. Western Cartridge loaded this cartridge with only the 175-grain bullet, until production was discontinued, in 1939.

General Comments: The .275 H&H was never particularly popular in this country. It resembled the .280 Ross, but did not give the velocity of the Ross. Its chief advantage over other 7mm cartridges was its ability to handle a 175-grain bullet at increased velocity. The Western Cartridge loading, with a 175-grain soft-point boat-tail bullet, gave a muzzle velocity of 2690 fps, a muzzle energy of 2810 ft-lbs, and a mid-range (iron-sight) trajectory at 100 yards of .7-inch. Impressive performance, considering the powders then available. See Chapter 8 for additional information.

.275 H&H Magnum Loading Data

Bullet (grains/type)	Powder	Grains	Velocity	Energy	Source/Comments
140	IMR 4064	48.0	2810	2455	Ackley
160	IMR 4350	59.0	3050	3305	Ackley
180	IMR 4350	58.0	2850	3245	Ackley
195	IMR 4350	52.0	2671	3090	Ackley

7x61mm Sharpe & Hart Super (7x61mm S&H Super)

Historical Notes: The 7x61mm was developed in the United States by Philip B. Sharpe and Richard F. Hart. Its design was originally based on a rimless, experimental French 7mm semi-auto military cartridge. It was copyrighted and made available on a commercial basis in the Schultz & Larsen rifle, in 1953. Ammunition was loaded and imported by Norma. The final version had a belted case with "Super" added to its name. Ammunition loaded with a 154-grain bullet (instead of the original 160-grain), was recently offered by Norma.

General Comments: The 7x61mm Sharpe & Hart (now listed as the S&H Super), is very similar to the .275 H&H Magnum, a belted case cartridge that was chambered and loaded in England. It is in the short 7mm magnum class, and its performance is the same as a number of other wildcat cartridges based on the blown out and shortened .300 H&H Magnum case. However, the Sharpe & Hart case has a slightly larger base diameter than the .300 H&H. This cartridge is quite popular in Canada, but its popularity in the United States was limited by competition from the 7mm Weatherby Magnum, the 7mm Remington Magnum, and various wildcats. The 7mm S&H is, nonetheless, a fine cartridge for any North American game and most African plains game.

Like any of this ilk, this number can be somewhat hard on its barrel, especially with careless shooting, not allowing plenty of time between shots for barrel cooling, or inadequate cleaning. Moreover, like all similar chamberings, it loses significant velocity with barrels shorter than 24 inches. Actual ballistics may be closer to the 7mm Weatherby than factory data suggests.

7x61mm Sharpe & Hart Super Loading Data and Factory Ballistics

Bullet (grains/type)	Powder	Grains	Velocity	Energy	Source/Comments
120 SP	IMR 4350	64.0	3300	2902	Sierra
140 SP	IMR 4831	63.0	3100	2988	Sierra
140 SP	IMR 4350	62.5	3200	3184	Hornady, Sierra
150 SP	IMR 4831	64.5	3100	3202	Sierra

160 SP	IMR 4350	58.0	2900	2989	Hornady, Sierra
175 SP	IMR 4350	60.5	2900	3269	Hornady
154 SP	FL		3060	3200	Norma factory load (latest)
160 SP	FL		3100	3410	Norma factory load (original)

.28-30-120 Stevens

Historical Notes: The .28-30-120 was probably the first American-designed, commercial 7mm cartridge. Introduced by the J. Stevens Arms & Tool Co., in 1900, it was designed by Charles H. Herrick of Winchester, Massachusetts. Both 44 and 44½ Stevens rifles were chambered for the round. It was an early favorite of Harry M. Pope, who made and fitted barrels to a variety of single-shot actions in this chambering. As a match cartridge, it established a reputation for exceptional accuracy.

General Comments: Remington made the first factory loads for the .28-30, and these used the 120-grain bullet and 30 grains of Fg blackpowder. By 1918, it was no longer listed in the Remington catalog. Some match shooters who used the .28-30 considered it superior to the .32-40 out to 300 yards. It makes a good 150-yard small-game or varmint cartridge. Lyman No. 285222 or 285228 is the proper cast bullet, but one can use any standard cast 7mm bullet up to 180 grains. Do not use jacketed bullets in the old blackpowder barrels, as they will wear the bore excessively and the fine accuracy may be destroyed within a few hundred rounds. Gas-checked bullets are okay.

.28-30-120 Loading Data and Factory Ballistics

Bullet (grains/type)	Powder	Grains	Velocity	Energy	Source/Comments
135 Lead	blackpowder (Fg)	28.0	1410	602	
135 Lead	IMR 4198	17.0	1500	605	
120 Lead	FL		1500	605	Factory load

.30-30 Wesson

Historical Notes: The .30-30 Wesson was used in rifles designed and marketed by Frank Wesson, of Worcester, Massachusetts, who operated from the 1860s into the late 1880s. During the Civil War, the government purchased about 150 Wesson military carbines in caliber .44 rimfire. Some of the state militias also purchased Wesson carbines. His sporting rifles were marketed, in rimfire types, as early as 1861. As near as can be determined, the .30-30 Wesson was probably developed sometime around 1880. Frank Wesson was a brother of Daniel B. Wesson, co-founder of Smith & Wesson. Both Remington and Winchester made bullets and cases for this cartridge, and U.S. Cartridge Co. catalogs listed it. Usable cases can probably be fabricated from .357 Maximum cases.

General Comments: The most common Wesson rifle was a single-shot with a double trigger arrangement. The forward trigger unlatched the breech, allowing the barrel to be tipped up for loading and unloading. Several models were marketed, including sporting and target types. There were, in addition, under-lever falling-block solid-frame types that are quite scarce, as are the Wesson cartridges themselves. The .30-30 Wesson is not the same as the .30-30 Winchester, and there is nothing to indicate that it had any influence on the design of the .30-30. Smokeless powder loads would not be advisable in this rifle.

.30-30 Wesson Loading Data and Factory Ballistics

Bullet (grains/type)	Powder	Grains	Velocity	Energy	Source/Comments
165 Lead	blackpowder (Fg)	30.0	1250	1010	Factory load

.30 Remington

Historical Notes:	A rimless version of the .30-30 Winchester, the .30 Remington was introduced by Remington, in 1906, for its Model 8 autoloader. When the Model 14 pump-action came out, in 1912, it was also chambered for the .30 Remington, as was the Model 30 bolt-action, introduced in 1921. The Stevens lever-action Model 425 and the Standard gas-operated rifle also used the .30 Remington. No new rifles have chambered this round since immediately after World War II. Some domestic ammunition companies continued to load it, until recently. There are a large number of rifles for this caliber still in use. The original rifles were marked ".30-30 Remington."
	Editor's note: Imagine the confusion that must have arisen when Remington originally called this cartridge the ".30-30 Remington." One wonders how many hunters found themselves in the wilderness with a box of Remington-brand .30-30 Winchester ammunition and a Model 8 rifle the rounds would not fit into. The simple request to "Give me a box of Remington .30-30s" was bound to lead to this problem.
General Comments:	Identical to the .30-30 Winchester in performance, the .30 Remington is strictly in the small-, medium-, and deer-size game class. Its advantages are in the nature of the guns that chambered it. It is possible to use spitzer bullets in most .30 Remington rifles, which help retain velocity at longer ranges. The .30 Remington can be reloaded to better performance than the .30-30 Winchester. Interestingly, handloading data has seldom, if ever, reflected this possibility. Similarly, factory ammunition has uniformly downplayed the Remington rimless series, with loads rated a full 100 fps slower than their rimmed counterparts. However, the difference is not great enough to take the .30 Remington out of the .30-30 class. Note: The nominal bullet diameter is given as .307-inch.

.30 Remington Loading Data and Factory Ballistics

Bullet (grains/type)	Powder	Grains	Velocity	Energy	Source/Comments
150 SP	IMR 4895	35.5	2350	1840	Lyman
150 SP	IMR 4320	36.0	2320	1794	Lyman
170 SP	IMR 3031	30.0	2115	1690	Lyman
170 SP	IMR 4895	33.0	2145	1735	Lyman
170 SP	FL		2120	1696	Remington factory load

.30 USA/.30-40 Rimless

Historical Notes:	We have little information on this cartridge. It was used in the Blake rifle, and ammunition was produced by United Metallic Cartridge for a time. No doubt, considerable confusion ensued in that era of rapid development and the nascent exposure of U.S. shooters to rimless chamberings. We include this number here to demonstrate that Europeans were not the only ones to muddy up the water with rimless and rimmed versions of otherwise identical or nearly identical cartridges.

.30-03 Springfield/
.30-03 Government

Historical Notes:	In 1903, the U.S. Government adopted a new military loading to replace the .30 Army (.30-40 Krag), which had been adopted in 1892. Like the .30-40 Krag, this new (.30-Caliber, Model of 1903) cartridge featured a 220-grain round-nosed, full metal jacket bullet. However, the '03 increased muzzle velocity by about 100 fps, even though the M1903 rifle featured a significantly shorter barrel. The

rimless cartridge design, generously borrowed from Mauser, was also an improvement, as it featured superior feeding from a box magazine. Nevertheless, as seems to have been typical in that era, the U.S. Army was slow to the task of modernizing. As the .30-03 was standardized, all other world powers were in the process of adopting spitzer-bullet military loadings; the brand new .30-03 became instantly obsolete. A crash program was instituted and, in 1906, a modified version of this basic cartridge was adopted as the .30 Caliber, Model of 1906. That loading featured a lighter spitzer bullet and a shorter case neck. The spitzer bullets had a much shorter bearing surface, so the existing rifles were modified by turning back the barrels two threads and recutting the chambers.

General Comments: Despite its short life, this cartridge, like the .30-06, found application in John M. Browning's Winchester Model 1895. Considering the ambitious pressure levels common in the early days of these chamberings, that was perhaps not such a good idea. For the handloader, case life could be extremely limited, owing to case stretching because of the rear lockup on those rifles. Compared to the .30-06, the .30-03 offers no advantage as a sporting round. Ammunition was available at least until World War I. By today's standards, that is remarkable, for there were very few sporting rifles chambered for this cartridge and, very soon after 1906, virtually all 1903 Springfields had been converted to .30-06.

.30 Newton
.30 Adolph Express

Historical Notes: The .30 Newton was originally designed for Fred Adolph and was called the "Adolph Express," when introduced in 1913. It was not until several years later that Charles Newton produced rifles for his own brainchild and the cartridge received the gun inventor's name. The Western Cartridge Co. produced the .30 Newton cartridge. No commercial rifle other than the Newton ever chambered it. Production of rifles ceased in the early 1920s, and Western dropped the cartridge, about 1938.

General Comments: The .30 Newton is a rimless, magnum-type cartridge similar to the .30-06, but larger in diameter. Neither ammunition nor cases are readily available, since it has been obsolete for more than 50 years. However, brass can be readily formed from RWS 8x68mm. A limited quantity of new cases was manufactured right after World War II, by Richard Speer. The .30 Newton is powerful enough for any North American big game. The .300 H&H Magnum and .300 Weatherby Magnum outperform it, although its performance can be improved by handloading with modern powders.

.30 Newton Loading Data and Factory Ballistics

Bullet (grains/type)	Powder	Grains	Velocity	Energy	Source/Comments
150 SP	IMR 4320	67.0	3175	3361	NA
150 SP	IMR 4831	76.0	3100	3206	NA
180 SP	IMR 4320	62.0	2840	3235	NA
180 SP	IMR 4831	73.0	2890	3350	NA
200 SP	IMR 4350	66.0	2730	3318	NA
180 SP	FL		2860	3270	Western factory load

.32-40 Remington/
.32-40-150 (2¹/₈-inch)
Remington

Historical Notes: The .32-40-150 (21/8-inch) Remington was one of the cartridges for the single-shot, rolling block Sporting Rifle No. 1, introduced in 1870. This cartridge appears to have been introduced shortly after the rifle, about 1871 to '72. The .32-40 Remington was also one of the cartridges for the No. 3 Hepburn and some of the Farrow single-shot rifles. Other than this, no one else seems to have adopted it. Remington quit loading it, in 1910.

General Comments: This is a very odd-looking cartridge, with a long tapered shoulder that merges imperceptibly with an elongated neck. It is usually listed as a straight case, but it is not straight and is not exactly necked. It might best be described as a taper-necked case. On the dimensional chart, it is shown as type "A," or rimmed, bottleneck, but this is not totally correct, either. The shoulder diameter is arbitrary, since it is difficult to decide just where the shoulder begins. Although called a .32-caliber, true bullet diameter is .308- or .309-inch; hence, it is really a .30-caliber. It was both a hunting and target round of limited popularity. It lost out to the .32-40 Ballard, which was available in both single-shot and repeating rifles. It was a small- to medium-game cartridge, but was probably also used to some extent for hunting deer-size animals. Usable cases might be formed from either .30-40 Krag or .303 British cases.

.32-40 Remington Loading Data and Factory Ballistics

Bullet (grains/type)	Powder	Grains	Velocity	Energy	Source/Comments
150 Lead	IMR 4198	14.5	1350	607	Lyman No. 308156
150 Lead	FL125		1350	607	Factory load

.303 Savage
.301 Savage

Historical Notes: Originally developed as a potential military cartridge, in 1895, the .303 Savage was later introduced commercially as one of several chamberings for the popular Savage Model 1899 lever-action. Savage discontinued this chambering, when rifle production was resumed after World War II. In England, it is known as the .301 Savage. No new rifles are chambered for this round at present.

General Comments: Dogma holds that the .303 Savage is not a true .303 but, instead, uses standard .308-inch bullets. However, current SAAMI specifications call for a bullet of .311-inch. Measurements of bullets on three lots of each of two makes of World War II-era factory loads yielded mixed results. Some were .308-inch-plus, others .310-inch-plus. The .303 is similar to the .30-30 in size, shape, and performance, but the two are not interchangeable. With its 190-grain bullet, many old woods hunters swore by it. With the relatively heavy bullet at moderate velocity, it gave good penetration on deer-size animals. However, it is ballistically no more powerful than the .30-30, so its use should be restricted to deer at short ranges. Unfortunately, Savage never took advantage of the fact that the 99 rifle is particularly suited to the use of spitzer bullets. Proper loadings of 150-grain spitzers in the .303 could have moved it completely out of the .30-30 class and might have gone a long way toward increasing its popularity. As it has always been loaded, it is effective only at close range. This need not have been the case. Many handloaders still use the .303 Savage with 150-grain spitzer bullets loaded to about 2500 fps. It is still no long-range wonder, but such a load gives it a decided edge over any other .30-30-class chambering.

.303 Savage Loading Data and Factory Ballistics

Bullet (grains/type)	Powder	Grains	Velocity	Energy	Source/Comments
150 SP	IMR 4064	36	2400	1919	Lyman
170 SP	IMR 3031	31	2170	1778	Lyman
180 SP	FL		2140	1830	Factory load
190 SP	FL		1890	1507	Winchester factory load

.32-20 Marlin
.32-20-100 Marlin Safety

Historical Notes: This cartridge was loaded for the Marlin 1894 repeating rifle. Winchester loaded this cartridge, beginning around the turn of the century and until about World War I. It is nothing more than a special version of the .32 WCF (.32-20 Winchester). Compared to the Winchester round, it was loaded with a lighter bullet of 100 grains versus 117 grains. With the exceptions of perhaps bullet nose shape, seating depth, and headstamp, this loading appears to have been otherwise identical to the .32-20 Winchester. In 1916, Winchester offered three versions of this cartridge: lead and blackpowder (100 grains, 20 grains); soft-point (117 grains) and smokeless powder; and full-patch (117 grains) and smokeless powder. High-velocity loadings were not offered.

General Comments: Evidently, sales of Marlin's Model 1894 rifle generated sufficient demand for special versions of the cartridges for which that rifle was nominally chambered. Perhaps cartridges with slightly different bullet shapes or loading lengths were found to function better in it. Whatever the reason, the 1916 catalog shows separate cartridge loadings with these names: .25-20 Marlin, .32-30 Marlin, .38-40 Marlin, and .44-40 Marlin. Winchester says this cartridge was adapted to both Winchester and Marlin rifles, as were the .38-40 and .44-40 Marlin cartridges.

.32-30 Remington

Historical Notes: This bottleneck cartridge, similar to the .32-20 WCF, was one of the chamberings available for the Remington-Hepburn No. 3 series single-shot rifle, introduced in 1880. The cartridge was first made in November of 1884. Not a true .32, bullet diameter is .312-inch.

General Comments: The Remington-Hepburn was billed as a "long-range hunting and target rifle," but the .32-30 is hardly a long-range cartridge. It is only a notch or so above the .32-20 WCF. It was not a popular cartridge and died out in 1912. Like most other single-shot cartridges, this one was too long for the short repeating actions, such as the Model 92 Winchester. These were, in addition, too small for the larger actions. This in-between position eliminated these, as the repeater gained popularity. Rifles for the .32-30 are comparatively rare today. Ammunition can be made by reforming .357 Magnum or .357 Maximum cases.

.32-30 Remington Loading Data and Factory Ballistics

Bullet (grains/type)	Powder	Grains	Velocity	Energy	Source/Comments
111 Lead	IMR 4198	14.0	1650	676	Lyman No. 311316
115 Lead	blackpowder (FFg)	35.0	1430	528	NA
125 Lead	FL		1380	535	Factory load

.32-35 Stevens & Maynard

Historical Notes: A match cartridge, introduced by J. Stevens Arms & Tool Co. in the mid-1880s, this was one of the chamberings available for the New Model Range Rifle Nos. 9 and 10, which first appeared in 1886. These were on a tip-up, single-shot action, and some of the earlier models of this type might have chambered the .32-35. Later rifles based on the 44 and 44½ under-lever single-shot actions were available in .32-35.

General Comments: This was one of the most accurate of the Stevens target cartridges, and many records were established with it. The .32-40 was responsible for the .32-35's gradual obsolescence. Best accuracy usually was obtained by seating the bullet in the chamber 1/16-inch or so ahead of the case; the case, full of powder and with a wad to prevent powder spillage, was then inserted in the chamber behind the bullet. Lyman's No. 3117 bullet of 153 grains was popular with many riflemen. The correct charge of blackpowder was 35 grains of Fg or FFg.

.32-35 Stevens & Maynard Loading Data and Factory Ballistics

Bullet (grains/type)	Powder	Grains	Velocity	Energy	Source/Comments
153 Lead	IMR 4198	14.0	1410	683	NA
165 Lead	IMR 4227	11.0	1380	696	NA
165 Lead	FL		1400	683	Factory load

.32-40 Bullard

Historical Notes: This is the smallest cartridge of a series designed for the Bullard single-shot and repeating rifles. Bullard patents were granted in 1881, and manufacture of its rifles is believed to have started during 1882 or 1883. Exact date of introduction of the individual cartridges is difficult to establish, but all were available by 1887.

General Comments: The Bullard lever-action repeating rifle resembled the Winchester, but employed a different rack-and-pinion mechanism. The loading port in the magazine was located on the bottom, unlike the Winchester's side port. The single-shot was of the under-lever type and quite strong. Although Bullard rifles and cartridges were as good as any of contemporary manufacture, they did not endure beyond 1900. Some Bullard cartridges were made by Remington and Winchester. Performance of the .32-40 Bullard is the same as the .32-40 Winchester and Marlin. Both are scarce items. Usable cases can be easily formed from .357 Remington Maximum cases.

.32-40 Bullard Loading Data and Factory Ballistics

Bullet (grains/type)	Powder	Grains	Velocity	Energy	Source/Comments
150 Lead	IMR 4198	15.0	1470	719	Lyman No. 311241
155 Lead	2400	13.0	1400	674	NA
150 Lead	FL		1492	750	Factory load

.32 Long (Center Fire)

Historical Notes: This centerfire, reloadable version of the .32 Long rimfire with an outside-lubricated bullet was introduced, in 1875, in a variety of light-frame single-shot rifles and the Marlin Models of 1891 and 1892. Some of these were constructed so that both rimfire and centerfire ammunition could be used by changing the firing pin or hammer.

General Comments: The .32 Long was not a satisfactory or effective cartridge. A longer case called the "Extra Long" was soon employed, in order to increase range and killing power on small game. Eventually the .32 Long was replaced by such numbers as the .32-20 WCF, .32 Ideal, and the .32-35 Stevens. It is very similar to the .32 Colt revolver cartridge. The standard load consisted of 13 grains of FFFg blackpowder and an 80- to 85-grain bullet. Muzzle velocity was only about 800 to 900 fps, depending on load and barrel length. The .32 S&W Long or .32 Long Colt will work in most old rifles in this chambering. These cartridges are now collector's items.

.32 Long (CF) Loading Data and Factory Ballistics

Bullet (grains/type)	Powder	Grains	Velocity	Energy	Source/Comments
85 Lead	FL		850	136	Factory load

.32 Ballard Extra Long

Historical Notes: The .32 Extra Long is an elongated version of the .32 Long centerfire, the latter being one of the chamberings available for the J.M. Marlin 1876 Ballard No. 2 Sporting Rifle. The .32 Extra Long cartridge appeared in 1879. This was after Marlin Fire Arms Co. began manufacturing Ballard rifles. Marlin introduced (or continued) the Sporting Rifle No. 2, in 1881. Stevens, Remington, Wurfflein, and other single-shot rifles were also available in this chambering. It was popular, but lost out to the .32-20 WCF. Most companies stopped loading it by 1920. Rifles chambered for this cartridge will usually chamber and fire both the .32 S&W Long and .32 Long Colt.

General Comments: This is essentially a centerfire version of the .32 Extra Long rimfire, and ballistics are practically identical. It was used as a target and small-game cartridge throughout the late 1800s. It is very similar in performance to the blackpowder loading of the .32-20 WCF. Most of the old rifles for this cartridge will not safely withstand heavy loads of modern smokeless powder. An outside-lubricated bullet of the same diameter as the case neck was first used.

.32 Ballard Extra Long Loading Data and Factory Ballistics

Bullet (grains/type)	Powder	Grains	Velocity	Energy	Source/Comments
115 Lead	IMR 4198	9.0	1360	473	NA
115 Lead	blackpowder (FFg)	20.0	1200	372	Factory load

.32 Winchester Self-Loading (.32 WSL)

Historical Notes: This is the second of two cartridges developed for the Winchester Model '05 self-loading rifle, which was introduced in 1905-1906. It became obsolete, when the rifle was discontinued in 1920. The case is of the semi-rimmed type similar to the 35 SL, which was the original cartridge for the Model '05 rifle. The .32 Winchester SL was probably the prototype of the .30 U.S. Carbine cartridge. The two are very similar, except for bullet diameter and the fact that the .30 Carbine cartridge is rimless.

General Comments: The .32 Winchester SL cartridge is in the same class as the .32-20 Winchester, strictly a small- to medium-game number at close range. However, it is not nearly as flexible as the .32-20, because of the semi-automatic rifle in which it was used. This was never a very popular cartridge. Not only was the cost of ammunition relatively high, the cartridge is not well-suited to reloading, even if you could find the empty cases after being ejected from the action. Some might consider this cartridge the best candidate for the title, "World's Most Useless Centerfire Rifle Cartridge."

.32 Winchester Self-Loading Loading Data and Factory Ballistics

Bullet (grains/type)	Powder	Grains	Velocity	Energy	Source/Comments
155 Cast	2400	9.5	1270	556	Lyman No. 321298
165 SP	2400	12.0	1450	775	NA
165 SP	IMR 4227	12.5	1440	760	NA
165 SP	FL		1400	760	Winchester factory load

.32-40 (.32-40 Ballard/ .32-40 Winchester)

Historical Notes: Originally developed as a blackpowder match or target cartridge for the single-shot Ballard Union Hill Rifle Nos. 8 and 9, the .32-40 was introduced, in 1884, loaded with a 165-grain lead bullet in front of 40 grains of Fg blackpowder. It established a reputation for fine accuracy, and Winchester and Marlin added it to their lines of lever-action repeating and single-shot rifles late in 1886. The late Harry Pope's favorite cartridges were the .32-40 and his own variant, the .33-40. Ammunition has been discontinued by major companies. However, in the early 1980s, Winchester loaded this cartridge to boost sales of its John Wayne Commemorative rifle.

General Comments: In a good, solid-frame rifle, the .32-40 will shoot as well as any modern high-powered match cartridge out to 200 or 300 yards. It was a popular hunting cartridge for medium game and deer and, while it has certainly killed its share of deer, the factory loading barely qualifies in that class. However, in a strong action, it can be handloaded to equal the .30-30. For small to medium game or varmints, it will do very well at moderate ranges. Do not use high-velocity loadings in the old Ballard or Stevens 44 rifles. A number of modern copies of old Sharps single-shot rifles and a special commemorative M1894 Winchester have been chambered for the .32-40 in recent years. Usable cases can easily be formed from .30-30, .32 Special, or .38-55 cases.

.32-40 Loading Data and Factory Ballistics

Bullet (grains/type)	Powder	Grains	Velocity	Energy	Source/Comments
155 Lead	2400	13.0	1460	786	
165 Lead	H4895	16.0	1410	729	OK for old rifles – Hodgdon
165 Lead	H4198	14.0	1340	658	OK for old rifles – Hodgdon
165 Lead	H4895	22.0	1865	1275	Not for old rifles – Hodgdon
165 Lead	H335	23.0	1890	1309	Not for old rifles – Hodgdon
170 Lead	AA 5744	20.0	1802	1226	Accurate Arms
165 SP	FL		1440	760	Winchester factory load
165 SP	FL		1752	1125	Winchester factory load high velocity

.32 Remington

Historical Notes: Another of the Remington rimless line of medium high-power rifle cartridges, this one is a rimless version of the .32 Winchester Special. Introduced in 1906, it was originally chambered in the Model 8 autoloader and later available in Remington pump-action and bolt-action rifles. The ammunition companies discontinued it many years ago.

General Comments: Remington felt some need to counter the popular series of rimmed cartridges chambered in Winchester's Model 94 lever-action. The incentive was great enough to persuade Remington to invent substitutions for Winchester's rimmed .25-, .30-, and .32-caliber cartridges. It could be argued that the .35 Remington was an answer to Winchester's .38-55., but a bit of reflection suggests the folks at Remington were confused. It was not the cartridges that made Browning's invention successful, it was Browning's invention that made the cartridges successful. The .32 Remington is, nonetheless, perfectly adequate for any task to which the .30-30 or .32 Special are suited.

.32 Remington Loading Data and Factory Ballistics

Bullet (grains/type)	Powder	Grains	Velocity	Energy	Source/Comments
170 SP	IMR 4895	33.0	2070	1578	Lyman
170 SP	IMR 3031	30.0	2020	1546	NA
170 SP	IMR 4198	26.0	1992	1718	NA
170 SP	FL		2220	1860	Remington factory load

.32 Ideal/.32-25-100

Historical Notes: One of the chamberings available for the single-shot Stevens 44 and 44½ rifles, as well as for other single-shot rifles, this cartridge was introduced in 1903 and was quite popular for 20 years or so.

General Comments: The .32 Ideal is an improvement over the older .32 Extra Long Ballard in having inside lubrication and better performance. It is cleaner to handle and easier to reload. It was also quite accurate and an adequate 150-yard small- or medium-game number. Use of bullets lighter than standard provides room for more powder and gives higher velocity. Sometimes called the .32-25-150, the .32 Ideal uses a bullet diameter of .323-inch and, as pointed out in early Ideal handbooks, it offered new life, via reboring and re-rifling, to "thousands of .32-caliber, Short, Long and Extra Long, Rim and Center Fire rifles that have been shot out or rusted … ."

.32 Ideal Loading Data and Factory Ballistics

Bullet (grains/type)	Powder	Grains	Velocity	Energy	Source/Comments
115 Lead	blackpowder (FFg)	38.0	1425	524	Lyman No. 32359
150 Lead	blackpowder (Fg)	25.0	1250	526	Lyman No. 32360
150 Lead	IMR 4198	12.0	1330	596	NA
150 Lead	blackpowder (FFg)	25.0	1250	526	Factory load

.33 Winchester

Historical Notes: Introduced in 1902 for the Winchester Model 86 lever-action rifle and discontinued, along with the rifle, in 1936, it was replaced by the .348 Winchester developed for an updated version of its '86, the Model 71 rifle. It was also chambered in Marlin's Model 95 lever-action and in the Winchester Model of 1885 single-shot. This round was dropped in 1940.

General Comments: The .33 Winchester earned a good reputation as a deer, black bear, and elk cartridge, when used in the woods at moderate ranges. Its paper ballistics are no better than the .35 Remington rimless, but it uses a smaller diameter bullet with better sectional density than the 200-grain .35-caliber. It gave good penetration and satisfactory killing power, when properly used. It is still a good cartridge for anything up to and including elk, and it can be improved safely with modern powders. In any case, it is not quite as powerful as the .348 Winchester, and early Model 86 actions are not quite as strong as the Model 71's. Cases can be formed from .45-70 brass.

.33 Winchester Loading Data and Factory Ballistics

Bullet (grains/type)	Powder	Grains	Velocity	Energy	Source/Comments
200 SP	H4895	45.0	2200	2150	Hornady
200 SP	IMR 3031	40.0	2100	1959	Hornady
200 SP			2200	2150	Winchester factory load

.35 Winchester Self-Loading (.35 WSL)

Historical Notes: The .35 SL was the original cartridge for the Winchester Model '05 semi-auto rifle, introduced in 1905. The Model '05 was the only rifle that ever chambered it, and the cartridge was such a poor one that it was discontinued by 1920.

General Comments: The .35 SL cartridge was unsuitable for anything but small to medium game at very close ranges. However, it was too expensive for such shooting. It is too underpowered for deer and ranks right along with the .32 SL as a rather useless cartridge. It is semi-rimless and can be fired in the .38 Special or .357 Magnum revolver if reloaded with .357-inch diameter lead bullets. Just what value this might have is difficult to imagine, but it is an interesting fact.

Bullet (grains/type)	Powder	Grains	Velocity	Energy	Source/Comments
180 SP	IMR 4227	13.5	1440	834	NA
180 SP	2400	13.0	1430	823	NA
165 Lead	2400	8.0	920	312	NA
180 SP	FL		1452	842	Winchester factory load

.351 Winchester Self-Loading (.351 WSL)

Historical Notes: Introduced in 1907 to replace the underpowered .35 SL, the .351 Self-Loading is a more powerful round for the improved Model 1907 Winchester autoloading rifle. This cartridge was used to a very limited extent by the French, in both World War I and II, as a military cartridge. The rifle was discontinued in 1957.

General Comments: The .351 SL does not have much to offer, although it is an improvement over the older .35. It does not qualify as a suitable deer cartridge, although it has been used for that purpose. It is a good medium-game cartridge for coyote, mountain lion, or other animals in that class, but is too powerful for small game; it is expensive, not accurate enough, and too limited in range for varmint shooting. Nevertheless, it far surpasses even the best .357 Magnum rifle loads and comes very close to duplicating the .357 Remington Maximum. It has been popular for Latin American jungle hunting because, at the short ranges involved, it has sufficient power for the game encountered there. Here in the United States, the .351 WSL and the handy Model 1907 semi-automatic rifle in which it was introduced were used extensively by prison guards. The rifle is notorious for being one of the guns used in the killings of Bonnie and Clyde, and it has been used from low-flying light aircraft, in the western United States, for pest control. Like the .35, the .351 SL is semi-rimmed. The principal differences are a .24-inch longer case used in the .351 and higher loading pressures. Winchester was the last company to offer ammunition.

.351 Winchester Self-Loading Loading Data and Factory Ballistics

Bullet (grains/type)	Powder	Grains	Velocity	Energy	Source/Comments
177 Cast	IMR 4227	16.0	1550	947	Lyman No. 351319
180	2400	19.0	1793	1280	Medium game only; Lyman
180	IMR 4227	19.5	1751	1225	NA
180	FL		1850	1370	Factory load

.35 Winchester

Historical Notes: Developed by Winchester for its Model 1895 lever-action rifle, the .35 Winchester was introduced in 1903. The Remington-Lee bolt-action rifle also chambered this round. It was discontinued in 1936, along with the Model 95 rifle. It was listed in the 1962 British Kynoch ammunition catalogs.

General Comments: The .35 Winchester is a more powerful cartridge than the .33 Winchester, but is not as potent as the .348 or the .358 Winchester. It had a good reputation as a short-range number for elk, moose, or brown bear. It is certainly powerful enough for any North American big game, but has little to offer when compared to more modern cartridges. It can be improved by using modern powders, but pressures in the old 1895 lever-action should be kept to about 45,000 psi. This cartridge, like the .405 Winchester, is based on the same basic case as the .30-40 Krag. Here, by moving headspace control to the case shoulder, it is feasible to form perfectly useful cases from .30-40 Krag cases. The case neck will be somewhat shorter than with original cases, but this poses no problem, because it is not necessary to crimp the case mouth in cartridges used in the M-95.

.35 Winchester Loading Data and Factory Ballistics

Bullet (grains/type)	Powder	Grains	Velocity	Energy	Source/Comments
200 SP	IMR 4895	52.0	2480	2738	NA
200 SP	IMR 4064	45.0	2220	2182	NA
204	IMR 4227	18.0	1550	1091	Lyman No. 358315
250 SP	IMR 4895	50.0	2290	2920	NA
250 SP	IMR 4320	48.0	2190	2670	NA
250 SP	FL		2195	2670	Winchester factory load

.35 Newton

Historical Notes: The .35 Newton was listed in the 1915 Newton Rifle Co. catalog, which presumably was the year it was introduced. It is the .30 Newton case necked up to .35-caliber. The Western Cartridge Co. listed it until 1936, but no commercial rifles other than the Newtons chambered this round.

General Comments: The .35 Newton is more powerful, in some loadings, than the .375 H&H Magnum. The factory load listed below was the last one offered by the Western Cartridge Co. but, at one time, other loads were available. This cartridge is somewhat overpowered for most North American big game. It has been used in Africa with considerable success, although the Newton rifle was much too light and poorly stocked for such a powerful cartridge. Cases can be readily formed from RWS 8x68mm brass or by necking up the .30 Newton, itself a scarce item. Performance is similar to the later .358 Norma Magnum, which would be a far better choice, because ammunition has been recently offered and handloading is easier through a simple conversion of readily available cases.

.35 Newton Loading Data and Factory Ballistics

Bullet (grains/type)	Powder	Grains	Velocity	Energy	Source/Comments
200 SP	IMR 3031	78.0	3030	4100	NA
250 SP	IMR 4064	70.0	2650	3918	NA
250 SP	IMR 4320	75.0	2815	4410	NA
250 SP	FL		2660	3930	Western factory load
250 SP	FL		2975	4925	Western factory load

.35-30 Maynard (1882)

Historical Notes: The .35-30 was one of a series of cartridges designed for and introduced with the Model 1882 Maynard single-shot rifle. The Improved Hunters Rifle Nos. 7 and 9, along with the Target & Hunting No. 10 and Improved Target No. 16, were available in this chambering.

General Comments: Maynard rifles were used during the Civil War. After the war, the company manufactured sporting rifles. The Maynard rifle used a tip-up breech linked to an under-lever. These were smooth operating, safe, and possessed excellent accuracy. Ammunition for the .35-30 can be made from .38-55 cases. Nominal .358-inch case bullets can usually be used as cast (without sizing). Lyman's 165-grain No. 358429 bullet usually works well. A version with an unusually wide rim was also made. Such cases are available from Ballard Rifle & Cartridge Co. (307-587-4914; www.ballardrifles.com).

.35-30 Maynard 1882 Loading Data and Factory Ballistics

Bullet (grains/type)	Powder	Grains	Velocity	Energy	Source/Comments
165 Lead	IMR 4198	16.0	1320	645	Lyman No. 350293
165 Lead	2400	13.0	1450	787	Lyman No. 350293
250 Lead	FL		1280	918	Factory load

.35-40 Maynard (1882)

Historical Notes: This an elongated version of the .35-30 and used in the Model 1882 Maynard rifles.

General Comments: The .35-40 provides greater powder capacity than the shorter .35-30. The case dimensions are not identical, but cases can be made from .38-55 cases, just as with the .35-30. The long case is probably superior for hunting, but, since both are strictly small- to medium-game numbers, any advantage would be a matter of opinion. Any cast .358-inch rifle or revolver bullet can be sized to work. The Lyman No. 358429 (165 grains) would be a good choice.

.35-40 Maynard Loading Data and Factory Ballistics

Bullet (grains/type)	Powder	Grains	Velocity	Energy	Source/Comments
165 Lead	IMR 4198	18.0	1400	725	Lyman No. 358429
250 Lead	FL		1355	1018	Factory load

.35-30 Maynard (1865)

Historical Notes: This unusual, externally ignited "cartridge" was chambered in the Model of 1865 Maynard rifle. This was a forerunner to all centerfire cartridges, because it featured a central flash hole in the base of the case. This was also forerunner to the .35-30 Maynard cartridge used in Model 1873 and 1882 rifles. While Maynard rifles saw Civil War usage, this particular combination came along quite late in that conflict.

General Comments: This rifle combines what appears to be a more-or-less conventional cartridge case with external priming. The base of the case has a centered, small-diameter flash hole. This hole carries the flash from a conventional cap into the charge. Conceptually, it is a very small step from this design to one combining the cap and the case into one unit.

One could argue that this "cartridge" falls outside the purview of this book, because it does not incorporate a self-contained primer and is, therefore, not a complete cartridge in the modern sense. It is, however, much closer to the modern cartridge than its forerunners, the paper-cased "cartridge." Therefore, since this rifle and cartridge represent a significant step toward perfection of the self-contained cartridge, we feel that this number is worthy of mention here. Fully functional .35-30 Maynard pinfire cases are available from Ballard Rifle & Cartridge Co. (307-587-4914; www.ballardrifle.com).

.38-40 Remington-Hepburn

Historical Notes: Although listed as the .38-40 Remington-Hepburn, this cartridge was available in the No. 1 Sporting Model rolling block rifle that preceded the Hepburn action by 10 years. The No. 1 rifle was also chambered for the .38-40 WCF shortly after Winchester introduced it, during 1873 and 1874. It is likely this cartridge was intended as a straight-case version of the bottlenecked Winchester round. The .38-40 Remington-Hepburn appeared about 1875.

General Comments: Rifle and ammunition manufacturers went all out to please every segment of the trade, during the 1800s. Some riflemen didn't cotton to bottlenecked cases, so all kinds of straight, tapered, and bottleneck designs appeared in the same calibers and with the same powder charge. This may have provided a great lift to the men using these, but it is very confusing. The .38-40 Remington and .38-40 Winchester are a case in point. Neither could do anything the other would not, but the Winchester round won out in company with the repeating rifle. The Remington cartridge is a good target or small- to medium-game number. The original bullet is slightly heavier than the .38 WCF, but loading data for one will give similar results in the other. It is possible to convert .30-40 Krag cases to load this cartridge.

.38-40 Remington-Hepburn Loading Data and Factory Ballistics

Bullet (grains/type)	Powder	Grains	Velocity	Energy	Source/Comments
190 Lead	IMR 4198	16.0	1427	865	Lyman No. 373164
250 Lead	2400	15.0	1300	937	NA
245 Lead			1200	790	Remington factory load

.38 Long, Centerfire (.38 Long, CF)

Historical Notes: The .38 Long, Centerfire is another old-timer designed to replace a similar rimfire cartridge. It was introduced in 1875-'76 and used in a number of single-shot rifles, including the Ballard, Stevens, Remington, and others. It was obsolete by 1900. Oddly, the original rimfire version outlived the centerfire.

General Comments: The .38 Long, Centerfire, like the .32 and .44, was not very effective and had a short life. It was an alternative to the rimfire, and many of the old rifles could, by a simple adjustment, fire either. The .38 Long Colt or .38 S&W Special can be used to make ammunition. The standard load was 20 to 25 grains of blackpowder and a 140- to 150-grain bullet.

.38 Long, Centerfire Loading Data and Factory Ballistics

Bullet (grains/type)	Powder	Grains	Velocity	Energy	Source/Comments
145 Lead	FL		950	291	Factory load

.38 Ballard Extra Long

Historical Notes: This centerfire version of the .38 Ballard Extra Long rimfire was introduced in 1885-'86 as one of the chamberings for the Ballard No. 2 Sporting Model. It also was used by many other companies. It had the old No. 1 primer that now has not been made for many years. Some of these rifles were furnished with a changeable firing pin or hammer arrangement, so they could fire the rimfire or centerfire version with only a minor adjustment.

General Comments: The .38 Ballard Extra Long was designed to furnish a reloadable case to those who favored the .38 Extra Long rimfire ballistics. It was a nice little plinking, small game, or target cartridge for those who wanted economy. Any .358-inch bullet of suitable weight can be used. Using Lyman No. 358161 (145 grains) and 31 grains of FFg blackpowder will work fine. The .357 Remington Maximum case can be converted to work in the .38 Ballard Extra Long chamber.

.38 Ballard Extra Long Loading Data and Factory Ballistics

Bullet (grains/type)	Powder	Grains	Velocity	Energy	Source/Comments
150 Lead	Unique	6.0	1160	450	Lyman No. 358160
146 Lead	FL		1275	533	Factory load

.38-35 Stevens

Historical Notes: Introduced, in 1875, for the Stevens tip-up single-shot rifles, this was one of the special Stevens "Everlasting" cartridges. It was not very popular, so it was dropped after a few years. In its original form, it is occasionally referred to as the .38-33.

General Comments: Stevens "Everlasting" shells were sold as separate components; the older, less popular numbers are seldom encountered as loaded rounds. These cases, intended to give very long reloading life, were necessarily thick and heavy. About six of these special chamberings survived. Loadings were not standard, and they may be found with a variety of bullet weights in both grooved and paper-patched form. A load of 35 grains or so of Fg blackpowder and any bullet of 180 to 255 grains can be used in this cartridge. It should be possible to chamber and safely shoot either .41 Short Colt or the .41 Long Colt lead bullet loads in these rifles. The softer oversize bullet will safely swage down to bore diameter.

.38-35 Stevens Loading Data and Factory Ballistics

Bullet (grains/type)	Powder	Grains	Velocity	Energy	Source/Comments
180 Lead	blackpowder (Fg)	35.0	1350*	729	NA
215 Lead	blackpowder (Fg)	35.0	1255	758	Factory load
* Estimated					

.38-50 Maynard (1882)

Historical Notes: The .38-50 Maynard is practically identical to the .38-55 Ballard and Winchester and uses a bullet of similar diameter. It was not popular, because it was so similar to the Winchester number.

General Comments: To reload the .38-50, one can make cases by resizing and trimming .38-55 cases and loading .38-caliber cast rifle bullets sized to correct diameter. The .38-55 would only hold 48 to 50 grains of blackpowder, after the ammunition companies began using heavier, solid-head cases. For all practical purposes, there is no performance difference between the .38-50 Maynard and the .38-55.

.38-50 Maynard Loading Data and Factory Ballistics

Bullet (grains/type)	Powder	Grains	Velocity	Energy	Source/Comments
149 Lead	IMR 4198	10.0	1100	420	Lyman No. 37583
250 Lead	IMR 4198	16.0	1320	974	Lyman No. 375248
255 Lead	FL		1325	990	Factory load

.38-50 Ballard Everlasting

Historical Notes: This cartridge was the forerunner of the .38-55. It was introduced, in 1876, for the Ballard Perfection No. 4 and Pacific No. 5 rifles, but was also available in other models. It is an Everlasting-type case, heavier than the standard .38-55 and 3/16-inch shorter. It was replaced by the .38-55, when that cartridge was introduced in 1884.

General Comments: Standard bullet diameter for most .38-caliber rifles was .375-inch, but many had a groove diameter of .379-inch, requiring a larger bullet. It is wise to measure the bore diameter before ordering a bullet mould for these old rifles. Lyman moulds are available in a variety of .38 rifle bullets, from 150 grains to more than 300 grains. Modern .38-55 cases can be used in .38-50 rifles by shortening the case to the proper length. Performance and usefulness are on a par with the .38-55.

The so-called "Everlasting," or reloadable case, was popular with hunters and target shooters during the 1880-'90 period. These heavy cases could be reused repeatedly. In fact, they were made so heavy that powder capacity was often reduced by five or 10 grains. To get around this, the Everlasting case was often made longer than the standard.

.38-50 Ballard Loading Data and Factory Ballistics

Bullet (grains/type)	Powder	Grains	Velocity	Energy	Source/Comments
145 Lead	IMR 4198	14.0	1300	550	Lyman No. 37583
250 Lead	IMR 4198	17.0	1350	1020	Lyman No. 375248
255 Lead	FL		1321	989	Factory load

.38-50 Remington-Hepburn

Historical Notes: Introduced, in 1883, as one of the chamberings for the Remington-Hepburn match rifles, this was too similar to the popular .38-55 to gain much of a following and was discontinued after a few years.

General Comments: Loading data for the .38-55 Winchester and Marlin can be applied to this cartridge. There is no difference in usefulness or performance. It should be possible to convert .303 British or .30-40 Krag cases to work in these rifles.

.38-50 Remington-Hepburn Loading Data and Factory Ballistics

Bullet (grains/type)	Powder	Grains	Velocity	Energy	Source/Comments
255 Lead	IMR 4198	23.0	1580	1421	NA
250 Lead	Unique	10.0	1200	797	NA
255 Lead	FL		1320	989	Factory load

.38-56 Winchester

Historical Notes: Introduced, in 1887, for the Model 1886 Winchester repeater, this cartridge was also used in the single-shot and the 1895 Marlin. The .38-56 made the transition into the smokeless powder era and was loaded until about 1936. The Colt New Lightning pump-action magazine rifles also used this cartridge.

General Comments: Design of this cartridge was intended to develop increased velocity without lengthening the case. It is a sort of super .38-55 in conception, but not in fact. With smokeless powder and within allowable pressures, there isn't any real performance difference. It is a bottlenecked case and will not interchange with others of similar designation. Although advertised as a powerful big-game number, it is little more than a deer or black bear cartridge. With maximum handloads, it might do okay for elk at short range. Cases can be made from .45-70 cases.

.38-56 Winchester Loading Data and Factory Ballistics

Bullet (grains/type)	Powder	Grains	Velocity	Energy	Source/Comments
255 Lead	IMR 3031	36.0	1830	1908	NA
265 Lead	IMR 4198	25.0	1600	1512	Lyman No. 375296 gas checked
255 SP	FL		1395	1105	Factory load

.38-90 Winchester Express Single Shot (.38 Express)

Historical Notes: Introduced, in 1886, as one of many chamberings for the successful Winchester Model 1885 single-shot, this was not a popular cartridge and, by 1904, it had been discontinued.

General Comments: This is a long, bottlenecked case with a light bullet for cartridges in this class. Since it is designated an "Express" cartridge, it was probably intended to develop superior velocity for a .38-caliber rifle. Old Ideal catalogs list bullet No. 375248 as standard with the No. 3 loading tool for this cartridge, but any of the lighter .38-55 bullets can be used. A charge of 90 grains of Fg blackpowder was the original factory loading.

.38-90 Winchester Express Loading Data and Factory Ballistics

Bullet (grains/type)	Powder	Grains	Velocity	Energy	Source/Comments
218 Lead	IMR 4198	21.0	1350	886	Lyman No. 37584
218 Lead	IMR 4198	23.0	1470	1045	Lyman No. 37584
217 Lead	FL		1595	1227	Winchester factory load

.38-72 Winchester

Historical Notes: This round was designed for and introduced with the Model 1895 Winchester lever-action box magazine repeater. Both gun and cartridge were obsolete by 1936. The .38-72 was only moderately popular.

General Comments: This is a nearly straight case with a very slight neck. Some cases have a pronounced groove around the neck to prevent the bullet from receding under recoil. This tends to obscure the slight neck. This is another .38-caliber cartridge touted as being very powerful when, in fact, it is nearly the same as the .38-55. The .38-72 case has the same basic body as the .30-40 Krag, but, because headspacing is on the rim, it may not be possible to safely use that case to make the .38-72, except for very low-pressure loads.

.38-72 Winchester Loading Data and Factory Ballistics

Bullet (grains/type)	Powder	Grains	Velocity	Energy	Source/Comments
255 Lead	IMR 3031	33.0	1735	1715	NA
275 Lead	IMR 4198	27.0	1350	1120	Lyman No. 375167
275 Cast	blackpowder (Fg)	72.0			Lyman No. 357167
275 SP	FL		1475	1330	Winchester factory load

.40-50 Sharps (Straight)
.40-1⁷/₈-inch Sharps

Historical Notes: Introduced in 1879, this is the smallest of the Sharps cartridges. There is a similar necked version. In addition to Sharps rifles, the Winchester single-shot was available in this chambering, as was the Remington rolling block. This is also known as the .40-17/8-inch Sharps.

General Comments: Although listed as the .40-50, this cartridge was actually loaded with 40 or 45 grains of powder and was identical in performance to the .40-40 Maynard and other similar rounds. Standard diameter of most .40-caliber rifle bullets is .403-inch, and almost any bullet of that diameter can be used. These chambers were cut to use bore-diameter paper-patch bullets; groove diameter is typically .408-inch to .411-inch. It should be possible to convert the .30-40 Krag case to work in these rifles. However, the rim is .010-inch too thin, so only very light loads should be used. Better to get the correct case from Buffalo Arms Co. (208-263-6953; www.buffaloarms.com).

.40-50 Sharps (Straight) Loading Data and Factory Ballistics

Bullet (grains/type)	Powder	Grains	Velocity	Energy	Source/Comments
260 Lead	IMR 4198	21.0	1450	1220	Lyman No. 403169
265 Lead	FL		1410	1168	Factory load

.40-50 Sharps (Necked)
.40-1¹¹/₁₆-inch Sharps

Historical Notes: Also known as the .40-111/16-inch, this cartridge was introduced, in 1869, for that model of Sharps Sporting rifle. It was available with several bullet weights, including 265, 285, and 296 grains. The Remington rolling block and other single-shot rifles also chambered this cartridge.

General Comments: The .40-50 bottlenecked cartridge is shorter than the straight version, but there is little difference in ballistics. The .40-50 Sharps (Straight) and .40-50 Sharps (Necked) are not interchangeable. Proper bullet diameter is .403-inch, and several Lyman bullet moulds are available in this size. These chambers were cut to use bore-diameter paper-patch bullets; groove diameter is typically .408-inch to .411-inch. This is largely a medium-game, deer, or intermediate-range target cartridge. It should be possible to convert .45-70 cases to work in these rifles.

.40-50 Sharps (Necked) Loading Data and Factory Ballistics

Bullet (grains/type)	Powder	Grains	Velocity	Energy	Source/Comments
260 Lead	IMR 4198	21.0	1500	1308	Lyman No. 403169
265 Lead	FL		1460	1262	Factory load

.40-60 Marlin

Historical Notes: The .40-60 is one of the chamberings for Marlin 1881 and 1895 lever-action repeaters. The 1895 uses the same basic system as the 1893 and 1894 models, but is larger and longer. This appears to be the same case as the .40-65 Winchester, but with a slightly different loading. The pump-action Colt New Lightning rifles also used the Marlin loading of this cartridge.

General Comments: During the late 1800s, the same cartridge often went under various names, depending on who loaded it or whose rifle it was used in. It was also common practice to change the name if you furnished more than one load or bullet in the same case; that is what happened here. The .40-60 Marlin and the .40-65 Winchester are interchangeable and either can be used in the same gun. However, the old Ideal catalog states the .40-60 Marlin "must not be confused with the .40-60 Winchester, as they are not the same." This, of course, is true. If the reader is not thoroughly confused by now, he should be. Go ahead. Read it through a few more times and it will clear up. Converting .45-70 cases into .40-60 Marlin cases is easily done. Marlin .40-caliber rifles often have significantly oversize bores. Groove diameters as large as .414-inch are noted.

.40-60 Marlin Loading Data and Factory Ballistics

Bullet (grains/type)	Powder	Grains	Velocity	Energy	Source/Comments
260 Lead	IMR 4198	23.0	1500	1308	Lyman No. 403170
260 Lead	IMR 3031	35.0	1480	1263	NA
260 Lead	FL		1385	1115	Factory load

.40-63 Ballard Everlasting
.40-70 Ballard Everlasting

Historical Notes: These two cartridges have identical length and outside dimensions, so are listed together. The .40-63 is actually just a heavier-cased version of the .40-70 factory cartridge. Both are, in turn, an outgrowth of the original .40-65 Ballard Everlasting case, which had to be handloaded. The .40-63 and .40-70 were first listed for the Ballard Perfection No. 4 and Pacific No. 5, after the Marlin Fire Arms Co. took over manufacture of these rifles, in 1881.

General Comments: This was a popular cartridge among Ballard rifle fans and was as good as similar cartridges offered by Winchester and others. However, cartridges designed for repeating rifles tended to survive longer than those intended for single-shots. These were used more as match cartridges than anything else, but these also made good deer, black bear, or elk numbers. Their performance is identical to the .40-70 Sharps Straight or the .40-72 Winchester. The .444 Marlin case should work in these rifles. However, the rim is generally too small to properly engage the extractor. These chambers were cut to use bore-diameter (.403-inch), paper-patch bullets; groove diameter is typically .408-inch to .411-inch.

The so-called "Everlasting," or reloadable case, was popular with hunters and target shooters during the 1880-'90 period. These heavy cases could be reused repeatedly. In fact, they were made so heavy that powder capacity was often reduced by five or 10 grains. To get around this, the Everlasting case was often made longer than the standard.

.40-63 Ballard Everalsting/.40-70 Ballard Everlasting Loading Data and Factory Ballistics

Bullet (grains/type)	Powder	Grains	Velocity	Energy	Source/Comments
330 Lead	IMR 4198	22.0	1310	1260	Lyman No. 403149 — 1/20 or 1/30 tin-lead
330 Lead	FL		1335	1318	Factory load

.40-70 Sharps (Straight)
.40-65 Sharps (1876)

Historical Notes: This is the .40-2½-inch straight case, introduced in 1876. It is sometimes referred to as the .40-65, because, with heavy, reloadable cases, that is all the powder it would hold, unless a lighter bullet was used. Remington and Winchester single-shots also chambered this round.

General Comments: This is another cartridge with ballistics similar to a half-dozen others of different make or origin. There are actually more than a dozen .40-caliber cartridges with powder charges of around 40 to 70 grains, but none offer any stupendous advantage over the others. Like other .40 Sharps numbers, this one used a .403-inch bullet weighing 330 or 370 grains. These chambers were cut to use bore-diameter bullets (often paper-patched). Groove diameter is typically .408-inch to .411-inch. A number of Lyman bullet moulds are available in this size. Although longer, this case has the same basic body as the .30-40 Krag. However, because headspacing is on the rim, it may not be possible to safely use that case to make the .40-70, except for very low-pressure loads.

.40-70 Sharps (Straight) Loading Data and Factory Ballistics

Bullet (grains/type)	Powder	Grains	Velocity	Energy	Source/Comments
330 Lead	IMR 4198	23.0	1250	1150	Lyman No. 403149
330 Lead	FL		1258	1160	Factory load

.40-70 Sharps (Necked)

Historical Notes: This is the .40-2¼-inch bottlenecked Sharps that was brought out, in 1871, for the Model 1871 Sporting rifle. It was used in other single-shot rifles, also.

General Comments: The .40-70 necked cartridge had a reputation for fine accuracy and was popular as a match cartridge, as much as for hunting. While many people regard the Sharps rifles as strictly buffalo guns, Sharps also made match rifles that gained worldwide respect on the range—hence the name "Sharps-shooter." The best marksmen were given Sharps rifles in a special squad, and its notoriety grew until the single word "sharpshooter" was synonymous with accurate rifle fire.

It should be possible to convert the .45-70 case to work in these rifles, but the neck would be very short. The .45 Basic will make perfect cases. These rifles have chambers that were cut to use a bore-diameter (.403-inch), paper-patched bullet. Groove diameter is typically .408-inch to .411-inch.

.40-70 Sharps (Necked) Loading Data and Factory Ballistics

Bullet (grains/type)	Powder	Grains	Velocity	Energy	Source/Comments
330 Lead	IMR 4759	26.0	1510	1671	NA
330 Lead	IMR 4198	27.0	1450	1542	Lyman No. 403139
330 Lead	FL		1420	1482	Factory load

.40-85 Ballard Everlasting
.40-90 Ballard Everlasting

Historical Notes: The .40-85 and the .40-90 Ballard Everlastings are the same case with different loadings. L.D. Satterlee lists the .40-90 Everlasting with the J.M. Marlin Ballard Pacific No. 5 and Sporting No. 4½ (introduced in 1878). He shows the .40-85 chambering for the Pacific No. 5, after the Marlin Fire Arms Co. took over manufacture, in 1881.

General Comments: The 4.0-90 Ballard Everlasting case is heavier and about an 1/8-inch longer than the regular .40-90 or .40-85 case. Many of the .40-90 Everlasting cases were nickel-plated. This is a hunting cartridge very similar to the .40-90 Sharps (Straight). The same loading data can be used for both, though they are not interchangeable. Although the case of the .40-85 Ballard Everlasting is longer, it has the same basic body as the .444 Marlin case. It should be possible to make usable, albeit shorter, cases from those. These rifles had chambers designed to use a .403-inch (bore-diameter), paper-patched bullet. Groove diameter typically ran .408-inch to .411-inch.

The so-called "Everlasting," or reloadable case, was popular with hunters and target shooters during the 1880-'90 period. These heavy cases could be reused repeatedly. In fact, they were made so heavy that powder capacity was often reduced by five or 10 grains. To get around this, the Everlasting case was often made longer than the standard.

.40-85/.40-90 Ballard Loading Data and Factory Ballistics

Bullet (grains/type)	Powder	Grains	Velocity	Energy	Source/Comments
370 Lead	IMR 4198	28.0	1400	1615	Lyman No. 40395
370 Lead	FL		1427	1672	Factory load

.40-90 Sharps (Straight)

Historical Notes: Sharps catalogs do not list this cartridge, although Sharps rifles and others chambered for it are known. It was introduced about 1885. The Remington-Hepburn No. 3 single-shot was advertised in this chambering, and UMC and Winchester manufactured cases and ammunition.

General Comments: The so-called "Everlasting," or reloadable, case was popular with hunters and target shooters during the 1880-'90 period. These heavy cases could be reused repeatedly. In fact, they were made so heavy that powder capacity was often reduced by five or 10 grains. To get around this, the Everlasting case was often made longer than the standard. UMC cases of the .40-3¼-inch are usually of very heavy, reloadable construction.

The reason for mentioning this is that it might have a bearing on the origin of this cartridge. Physical measurements of the so-called .40-90 Sharps Straight are practically identical to the .40-90 Ballard Everlasting, except for the length. It is possible that the design of the.40-90 Sharps Straight is based on lengthening the Ballard cartridge to create an "Everlasting" version with the same capacity and ballistics. Anyway, the idea would probably occur to anyone who compared the two. Although longer, this case has the same basic body as the .444 Marlin. It should be possible to make usable, albeit much shorter, cases from those. These rifles had a chamber cut to use a bore-diameter (.403-inch), paper-patched bullet; groove diameter was .408-inch to .411-inch.

.40-90 Sharps (Straight) Loading Data and Factory Ballistics

Bullet (grains/type)	Powder	Grains	Velocity	Energy	Source/Comments
370 Lead	IMR 4198	30.0	1400	1612	Lyman No. 403171
370 Lead	FL		1387	1582	Factory load

.40-90 Sharps (Necked)
.40-100 Sharps (Necked)

Historical Notes: The .40-90 Sharps was introduced, in 1873, for the Sharps side-hammer model rifles. There was also another loading, referred to as the .40-100 Sharps, which used a 190-grain hollowpoint bullet on the same 25/8-inch long case.

General Comments: This became one of the more popular Sharps cartridges. The hollowpoint Express bullets made by Sharps were designed to accept a .22 rimfire blank, which was supposed to provide explosive expansion and better knockdown power. The original author of this book experimented with bullets of this type, and they did not work as they were intended to. An ordinary hollowpoint or a properly constructed soft-point will do as much damage. Perfect cases can be made from the .45 Basic case.

.40-90 Sharps (Necked) Loading Data and Factory Ballistics

Bullet (grains/type)	Powder	Grains	Velocity	Energy	Source/Comments
370 Lead	IMR 4198	28.0	1450	1735	Lyman No. 403171
370 Lead	FL		1475	1800	Factory load

.40-110 Winchester Express (.40 Express)

Historical Notes: Designed for the Winchester single-shot rifle and introduced in 1886, the .40-110 was intended to compete with the big Sharps cartridges.

General Comments: In its original form, the .40-110 used a copper-tubed bullet. The Ideal catalog lists bullet No. 403169 (260 grains) as proper for reloading. The .50 Basic will make perfect cases.

.40-110 Winchester Express Loading Data and Factory Ballistics

Bullet (grains/type)	Powder	Grains	Velocity	Energy	Source/Comments
260 Lead	FG	110.0	1617	1509	NA
260 Lead	IMR 4198	32.0	1650	1580	Lyman No. 403169
260 SP	FL		1617	1509	Winchester factory load

.40-60 Winchester

Historical Notes: The .40-60 Winchester is a sharply tapered, slightly necked cartridge made for the Model 1876 Winchester rifle, which is a heavier version of the lever-action Model 1873 and designed to handle more powerful cartridges. Rifle and cartridge were marketed from 1876 until 1897. This was a popular cartridge, and Winchester continued to load it up to 1934.

General Comments: The big, powerful cartridges available for the Sharps and other single-shot rifles forced Winchester to bring out a more potent line of rounds for its repeaters. The cartridges for the Centennial Model marked the beginning of such a trend. This is not the same as the .40-60 Marlin. It is a better hunting choice than the old .44-40 WCF. The .45-70 case can be easily converted to make .40-60 Winchester cases.

Bullet (grains/type)	Powder	Grains	Velocity	Energy	Source/Comments
210 Lead	IMR 4198	21.0	1520	1083	Lyman No. 403168
210 Lead	FL		1562	1138	Winchester factory load

.40-70 Winchester

Historical Notes: This cartridge was developed for the Model 1886 Winchester repeater and was used in the Winchester single-shot. It was introduced in 1894, but never became popular or widely used. The Marlin Model 1895 repeating rifle was also available in this chambering.

General Comments: This is a bottlenecked case generally similar to the .38-70 Winchester. It provides a larger, heavier bullet in a cartridge suitable to the same action as the .38-caliber. This case is not the same as that of the .40-72 Winchester. However, the ballistics are nearly identical. It should be possible to convert .45-70 cases to work in these rifles, but the neck would be short. The .45 Basic will make perfect cases. Although groove diameter was typically .408-inch, original bullets were .406-inch diameter.

.40-70 Winchester Loading Data and Factory Ballistics

Bullet (grains/type)	Powder	Grains	Velocity	Energy	Source/Comments
330 Lead	IMR 4759	26.0	1540	1738	
330 Lead	IMR 4198	25.0	1380	1050	Lyman No. 406150
330 Lead	FL		1383	1333	Factory load

.40-70 Remington

Historical Notes: Although listed as the .40-70 Remington, this cartridge is really Remington's version of the .40-70 Sharps necked. The Remington rolling block No. 1 Sporting Model chambered it, and so did the Hepburn No. 3. It was added to the Remington line, in 1880.

General Comments: Two versions of this cartridge were available, one with a regular brass case, the other with a special reloading case having a brass body and steel head. The steel head fastened to the brass body with an inside screw, which served as a primer anvil and had a flash hole drilled through it. Steel head cases—in 1880! There really is nothing new under the sun. The .40-70 was used more for match shooting than for hunting. It should be possible to convert .45-70 cases to work in these rifles, but the neck would be very short. The .45 Basic will make perfect cases.

.40-70 Remington Loading Data and Factory Ballistics

Bullet (grains/type)	Powder	Grains	Velocity	Energy	Source/Comments
330 Lead	IMR 4198	27.0	1450	1542	Lyman No. 403139
330 Lead	FL		1420	1482	Remington factory load

.40-65 Winchester
.40-65 Winchester & Marlin

Historical Notes: The .40-65 Winchester (also known as the .40-65 Winchester & Marlin) was introduced, in 1887, for the Model 1886 Winchester rifle. The Winchester single-shot also chambered it, as did the Marlin Model 1895. The .40-65 Winchester was loaded in both blackpowder and smokeless powder versions, and Winchester catalogs listed it to 1935.

General Comments: The .40-65 was a further effort to put more steam in the repeating rifles' cartridges so they would be competitive with similar single-shot cartridges. This one, reasonably popular, continued for almost 50 years. Rifles in this chambering are common and ammunition can be made by reforming .45-70 cases. Although groove diameter was typically .408-inch, original load bullets were .406-inch diameter.

.40-65 Winchester Loading Data and Factory Ballistics

Bullet (grains/type)	Powder	Grains	Velocity	Energy	Source/Comments
260 Lead	IMR 4198	23.0	1500	1308	Lyman No. 403169
260 Lead	IMR 3031	44.0	1720	1708	NA
260 Lead	AA 5744	26.0	1651	1573	Accurate Arms
300 Lead	AA 5744	24.0	1515	1528	Accurate Arms
260 Lead	FL		1420	1165	Factory load

.40-72 Winchester

Historical Notes: Introduced for and with the Winchester Model 1895 lever-action box-magazine repeater, the .40-72 was not very popular, but was loaded until 1936.

General Comments: This cartridge uses a smaller diameter but heavier 30-grain bullet, compared to the much more powerful .405 Winchester. The latter was preferred by most purchasers of the Model 1895. Blackpowder cartridges of the 1890s suffered from competition with the newly introduced smokeless powder cartridges of that era. Most blackpowder cartridges introduced at that time had no chance to establish any degree of popularity. Although longer, this case has the same basic body as the .30-40 Krag. Because headspacing is on the rim, it may not be possible to safely use that case to make the .40-72, except for very low-pressure loads.

.40-72 Winchester Loading Data and Factory Ballistics

Bullet (grains/type)	Powder	Grains	Velocity	Energy	Source/Comments
330 Lead	IMR 3031	40.0	1435	1510	Lyman No. 406150
300 Lead	FL		1425	1350	Winchester factory load
330 Lead	FL		1407	1451	Winchester factory load

.40-82 Winchester (WCF)

Historical Notes: Introduced, in 1885, for the Winchester single-shot and also available for the Model 1886 lever-action repeater, this cartridge was popular enough to make the transition into the smokeless powder era. It was loaded up to 1935.

General Comments: The .40-82 WCF gained a favorable reputation on elk and heavy game. It developed a higher muzzle velocity than many other blackpowder cartridges, which made it easier to make contact with over unknown distances. Despite the relative popularity, rifles in this chambering are seldom encountered. Most of the original single-shots and Model 1886s have been rebarreled to some more modern chambering. It should be possible to convert the .45-70 case to work in these rifles, but the neck would be very short. The .45 Basic will make perfect cases. Although groove diameter was typically .408-inch, bullets used in original loads were only .406-inch diameter.

.40-82 Winchester Loading Data and Factory Ballistics

Bullet (grains/type)	Powder	Grains	Velocity	Energy	Source/Comments
260 Lead	IMR 4198	28.0	1425	1180	Lyman No. 403169
260 Lead	FL		1490	1285	Winchester factory load

.401 Winchester Self-Loading (.401 WSL)

Historical Notes: The .401 was introduced by Winchester, in 1910, for its new Model 10 Autoloading rifle, which was a minor modification of the Model 1907. Both the cartridge and the rifle were discontinued in 1936, but the ammunition was loaded by most ammunition companies until after World War II. It is another obsolete "Self-Loading" cartridge.

General Comments: The .401 is the most powerful of the Winchester Autoloading line and the only one suitable for deer. The .401 found favor with many hunters as a quick, short-range number for hunting deer and black bear. Velocity is too low and the trajectory too high for this to be a useful cartridge beyond about 150 yards. It can be reloaded but, like all cartridges used in semi-auto guns, it is necessary to stick to the factory ballistics or the rifle action may not function properly. Proper bullet diameter is .406-inch, but .410-inch revolver bullets can sometimes be used safely—verify chamber clearance. With a bit of lathe work, .35 Remington cases can be converted to work perfectly in .401 WSL chambered rifles.

.401 Winchester Loading Data and Factory Ballistics

Bullet (grains/type)	Powder	Grains	Velocity	Energy	Source/Comments
200 SP	2400	24.7	1915	1625	Lyman
212 Lead	IMR 4227	29.0	2074	2025	Lyman
240 Lead	IMR 4227	27.5	1968	2150	Lyman
200 SP	FL		2135	2020	Winchester factory load
250 SP	FL		1870	1940	Winchester factory load

.40-90 Peabody "What Cheer"

Historical Notes: This unusually shaped cartridge was for the Peabody-Martini Rifle No. 3, introduced in 1877-'78. This rifle was a fancy model similar to the No. 2 "Creedmoor," but was designated the "What Cheer." This was in line with the Peabody policy of naming its rifles after famous target ranges of the day, in this case the What Cheer Range of Greenwood, Rhode Island, which was originally opened in 1875.

General Comments: The .40-90 Peabody "What Cheer" is a bottlenecked case similar to other "What Cheer" cartridges. This was a popular match cartridge, until the early 1900s. Proper bullet diameter is .408-inch. Cast bullets intended for the .405 Winchester can be sized down and used in this round. No one lists a mould for a 500-grain bullet for this cartridge. For these low-pressure loads, .348 Winchester cases could be converted to work in this chamber.

Bullet (grains/type)	Powder	Grains	Velocity	Energy	Source/Comments
330 Lead	IMR 4198	27.0	1450	1550	Lyman No. 406150
500 Lead	FL		1250	1735	Factory load

.405 Winchester

Historical Notes: The .405 is another of the rimmed cartridges developed for the Winchester Model 1895 lever-action rifle. Introduced in 1904, the rifle became obsolete in 1936, but has been reproduced recently in limited runs; most were chambered for cartridges that are somewhat more modern, but one run was promised in .405. The Winchester single-shot also chambered the .405, and a number of double rifles were turned out in this chambering in England and Europe. The Remington-Lee bolt-action rifle was available in .405-caliber, between 1904 and 1906. The old Eley-Kynoch catalog lists the .405 Winchester with a 300-grain soft-point bullet at the standard factory load velocity.

General Comments: The .405 Winchester is the most powerful rimmed cartridge ever developed for the lever-action rifle. It is adequate for any North American big game at short to medium ranges and has been used successfully in Africa on all species. In the old Model 1895 Winchester, with its curved buttplate and poorly-designed stock, it had a reputation for punishing recoil. Theodore Roosevelt used the .405 in Africa and thought very highly of it as a lion cartridge. However, John Taylor, in his excellent book, African Rifles and Cartridges, rates it as a poor choice compared to other available chamberings for African use. The short, fat, 300-grain round-nosed bullet loses velocity rapidly and lacks the sectional density necessary for deep penetration of heavy game. Nevertheless, it is quite adequate for any North American animals at ranges of 100 to 150 yards. Although longer, this case has the same basic body as the .30-40 Krag. However, because headspacing is on the rim, it is not possible to safely use that case to make .405s, except for very low-pressure loads (which the original author of this book did). With modern jacketed pistol bullets, one can thus make perfectly adequate short-range deer loads. A-Square (www.a-square.com) has recently reintroduced .405 ammunition. Buffalo Arms (208-263-6953; www.buffaloarms.com) offers modified .30-40 cases that are the correct length and have a modified rim to give the correct headspace.

.405 Winchester Loading Data and Factory Ballistics

Bullet (grains/type)	Powder	Grains	Velocity	Energy	Source/Comments
290 Cast	IMR 3031	40.0	1500	1449	Lyman No. 412263
300 SP	IMR 4895	56.0	2230	3321	NA
300 SP	IMR 3031	57.0	2250	3380	NA
300 SP	FL		2200	3220	Winchester factory load

.40-75 Bullard

Historical Notes: Introduced, in 1887, for the Bullard lever-action repeating rifle and available for the single-shot, the .40-75 was the same case with a different bullet weight and powder charge as the .40-60 Bullard.

General Comments: This is a big-game cartridge similar in performance to the .40-60 Marlin or the .40-65 Winchester. Winchester's cartridge achieved the greatest popularity of these three. Proper diameter for a cast bullet is .413-inch, which is significantly larger than many of the other .40-caliber cartridges, which used a bullet of .403-inch diameter. The old Bullard catalog states that the .40-60 Marlin can be fired in guns of the above chambering. If so, then the .40-65 WCF could also be used, as it is the same case as the Marlin round. It should be possible to convert .45-70 cases to work in these rifles.

.40-75 Bullard Loading Data and Factory Ballistics

Bullet (grains/type)	Powder	Grains	Velocity	Energy	Source/Comments
260 Lead	blackpowder (Fg)	75.0	1513	1315	Lyman No. 412174
260 Lead	IMR 4198	20.0	1500	1302	Lyman No. 412174
258 Lead	FL		1513	1315	Factory load

.40-90 Bullard

Historical Notes: This rather odd, bottlenecked cartridge was developed for the Bullard single-shot and repeating rifles, introduced in 1886-'87. Both Winchester and Remington manufactured this round for a number of years.

General Comments: This is a rather large, fat cartridge with ballistics similar to other .40-caliber cartridges of the period, such as the .40-82 Winchester. There was not a lot to choose from, regarding performance between any of these. Cartridges designed by the big manufacturers for their rifles were more widely advertised and distributed and, consequently, won the popularity race. Cartridges like the Bullard line gradually faded into the background. The .40-90 Bullard was undoubtedly an effective big-game cartridge, particularly if the now-rare 400-grain loading was used. Considering the low-pressure loads used, it should be possible to convert .50-90 Sharps cases for safe use in rifles so chambered.

.40-90 Bullard Loading Data and Factory Ballistics

Bullet (grains/type)	Powder	Grains	Velocity	Energy	Source/Comments
300 Lead	blackpowder (Fg)	90.0	1569	1648	Lyman No. 415175
300 Lead	IMR 4198	29.0	1450	1405	Lyman No. 415175
300 Lead	FL		1569	1648	Factory load

.40-40 Maynard (1882)

Historical Notes: A cartridge for the Maynard 1882 rifle, Improved Hunting or Target No. 9, and the Mid Range Target or Hunting No. 10, it was advertised as a combination hunting and target cartridge.

General Comments: In performance, the .40-40 is similar to the .44-40 WCF. Maynard made only two bullet weights in .40-caliber; the 330-grain was intended for the longer .40-60, but was sometimes used in the .40-40. Bullet diameter of these cartridges is not the same as the .403-inch of most Sharps and Winchester cartridges. The Maynard Co. sold moulds or factory-made bullets for its rifles. The .40-caliber Maynard bore is usually .415- to .417-inch diameter. It should be possible to convert .303 British cases to work in these rifles.

.40-40 Maynard 1882 Loading Data and Factory Ballistics

Bullet (grains/type)	Powder	Grains	Velocity	Energy	Source/Comments
260 Lead	IMR 4198	24.0	1400	1140	Lyman No. 413174
270 Lead	FL		1425	1222	Factory load
330 Lead	FL		1260	1168	Factory load

.40-60 Maynard (1882)

Historical Notes: This is an intermediate-range match cartridge for the 1882 Maynard Models 10, 12, and 13 Hunting and the Models 15-16 Target rifles. It does not use the same case as the longer .40-70 Maynard.

General Comments: The .40-60 Maynard is an elongated version of the .40-40 and differs mainly in the longer case length. Unfortunately, it duplicated the performance of similar Marlin, Sharps, and Winchester cartridges and, for that reason, it did not become popular or widely used. It should be possible to convert .303 British cases to work in these rifles.

.40-60 Maynard 1882 Loading Data and Factory Ballistics

Bullet (grains/type)	Powder	Grains	Velocity	Energy	Source/Comments
300 Lead	IMR 4198	26.0	1370	1248	Lyman No. 413175
330 Lead	FL		1370	1380	Factory load

.40-70 Maynard (1882)

Historical Notes: This has the longest case of the three .40-caliber cartridges chambered in the 1882-type Maynard single-shot rifle, which was available in both Target and Hunting models.

General Comments: Some publications show the .40-70 Maynard to be the same as the .40-60, but with a different load. Others indicate that it is identical except for length. Actually, it has a little longer case (.21-inch), with a slightly larger rim and base diameter. The .40-60 can be fired in a .40-70 chamber, but the reverse is not true. In overall length, this is the shorter of the two cartridges, because of the lighter bullet seated farther down in the case. This is more of a hunting cartridge, although it was also available in the target rifle models. It should be possible to convert .303 British cases to work in these rifles.

.40-70 Maynard (1882) Loading Data and Factory Ballistics

Bullet (grains/type)	Powder	Grains	Velocity	Energy	Source/Comments
260 Lead	IMR 4198	27.0	1450	1211	Lyman No. 413174
270 Lead	FL		1645	1620	Factory load

.44 Evans Short

Historical Notes: This is the cartridge for the various Old Model Evans rifles, introduced in 1875. Winchester loaded the ammunition until the early 1920s.

General Comments: The Evans rifle was designed for military use, but, when it was turned down by the U.S. Ordnance Department, it was manufactured as a sporting number. The Evans had a magazine capacity of 34 cartridges held in the four-column tubular magazine located in the butt. This was an odd-looking lever-action rifle. Evans rifles were once somewhat common items, and box lots of ammunition could be purchased until 1940-'41. This is not a particularly strong action, so only use blackpowder loads. A load of 28 grains of Fg or FFg was used in the original round. Cases can be made by cutting off .303 Savage cases and perhaps thinning the rim, as required. (As in similar rim-thinning situations, pistol primers may have to be used, but those work well in most blackpowder or blackpowder pressure loads anyway.) Also, either the case mouth must be thinned or an undersized bullet must be used to provide adequate case-neck to chamber-wall clearance.

.44 Evans Short Factory Ballistics

Bullet (grains/type)	Powder	Grains	Velocity	Energy	Source/Comments
215 Lead	FL		850	350	Winchester factory load

.44 Evans Long
.44-40 Straight
.44-40-300

Historical Notes: The .44 Evans Long was developed for the 1877 New Model Evans sporting rifle. It is sometimes referred to as the .44-40 Straight or the .44-40-300, because of its different loadings.

General Comments: The New Model Evans rifle was similar to the Old Model, except for the change to a longer, more powerful cartridge. The magazine capacity was only (!) 26 rounds, compared to 34 for the Old Model. Again, this is not a strong action, so it is advisable to use only blackpowder loads. The cartridge was loaded with 275- to 300-grain bullets and 40 to 43 grains of blackpowder. Although this case is somewhat larger in diameter, usable cases might be made by cutting off .303 Savage cases, as with the Henry Center Fire Flat. As with all similar numbers, it is best to load only with blackpowder or Pyrodex. Also, either the case mouth must be thinned or an undersized bullet must be used, to provide adequate case-neck to chamber-wall clearance.

.44 Evans Long Factory Ballistics

Bullet (grains/type)	Powder	Grains	Velocity	Energy	Source/Comments
280 Lead	FL		200	903	Factory load

.44 Henry Center Fire Flat

Historical Notes: This is a centerfire version of the rimfire .44 Henry Flat. In 1891, 1,020 M1866 Winchester rifles were chambered for this cartridge and shipped to Brazil.

General Comments: Rifles for this cartridge are extremely rare. The 1866 Henry rifle was not very strong. Those who want to shoot one of these should stick to blackpowder. The proper charge is 26 or 28 grains of FFg or FFFg. Cast bullets for the .44-40 WCF can be used. Cases can be made by cutting off .303 Savage cases and perhaps thinning the rim, as required. (As in similar rim-thinning situations, pistol primers may have to be used, but these are preferable in almost every blackpowder or blackpowder pressure load anyway.)

.44 Henry Center Fire Flat Factory Ballistics

Bullet (grains/type)	Powder	Grains	Velocity	Energy	Source/Comments
200 Lead	FL		1150	594	Factory load
227 Lead	FL		1200	725	Factory load

.44 Game Getter
.44-40 Marlin
.44 Colt Lightning

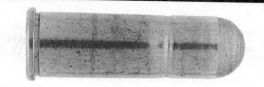

Historical Notes: In 1908, Marble Arms Corp. introduced its Game Getter, a double-barrel, over/under pistol with a removable skeleton buttstock. The upper barrel was rifled and chambered for the .22 rimfire cartridge; the lower barrel was smoothbore and chambered for the .44 shot cartridge. The introduction of this pistol bolstered the popularity of the several varieties of .44 shot cartridges.

The Stevens Model 101 Featherweight rifle (1914-'16) was chambered for this cartridge, as well as the .44 XL and .44 WCF shot cartridges. The .44 WCF shot cartridge was a crimped case with cardboard wadding; others were loaded with a wood or paper "bullet" that enclosed the shot. The Marble catalog of 1914 stated, "Shot cartridges with paper or wooden ends are especially adapted to rifled barrels. However, they can be used in the Game Getter, but give uncertain results." UMC loaded a .44 round ball cartridge before the introduction of the Game Getter, using 34 grains of blackpowder and a 115-grain round lead ball. This combination of gun and cartridge became very popular and Winchester and U.S. Ammunition Co. began to offer it, calling it the .44 Game Getter.

General Comments: The .44-40 is, of course, still loaded today, but, during its life span as a blackpowder cartridge (and the early smokeless powder days), it was available in a variety of loads that are now obsolete.

The standard load of 40 grains of blackpowder and a 200-grain bullet of the .44 WCF was altered slightly (a 217-grain bullet was used), and the resulting cartridge was called the .44-40 Marlin or the .44 Colt Lightning Magazine Rifle. All are nothing more than load variations on the standard .44-40 Winchester—some rifles may require shorter overall cartridge lengths.

Also obsolete today are the high-velocity smokeless powder loads that were offered for rifles with stronger actions.

.44-40 Extra Long

General Comments: The .44-40 Extra Long is listed in various publications, and sample rounds are common. It has a longer body and neck than the standard .44-40 WCF. The original author of this book was unable to find any record indicating the gun for which this cartridge was designed. It is listed so the reader will not confuse it with the straight Ballard or Wesson Extra Long .44 cartridges. Some believe this is the .44-40 shot case with a conical bullet. According to William R. Small, of Ojo Caliente, New Mexico, the Stevens Model 101 Featherweight rifle (1914-'16) chambered this round, as well as the .44 XL and .44 WCF shot cartridges. Cases can be made by shortening and necking .444 Marlin cases.

.44 Long Center Fire (Ballard)

Historical Notes: The .44 Long Center Fire (Ballard) was introduced, in 1875-'76, as one of the chamberings for the J.M. Marlin Ballard Sporting Rifle No. 2. It was also used in a number of other single-shot rifles, including those of Frank Wesson. It was replaced by the .44 Extra Long CF, and then both were phased out by the more popular .44-40 WCF. It is the centerfire equivalent of the .44 Long rimfire.

General Comments: This is a more-or-less transitional cartridge from the rimfire to the better centerfires. Most early breech-loading rifles were developed for rimfire cartridges, and it was a simple matter to bring out a similar centerfire for the same basic rifle. This allowed the shooter to reload. However, most of these cartridges were no more effective than the rimfire they replaced and, so, did not last long. The original load used 35 grains of blackpowder and a 227-grain bullet. Muzzle velocity was low—only about 1100 to 1200 fps. As with the .44 Evans Long, Short, or Henry Flat Center Fire, cases can be made by cutting off .303 Savage cases, but stick to blackpowder and cast bullets.

.44 Extra Long/
.44 Extra Long Center Fire (Ballard)

Historical Notes: This cartridge is sometimes listed simply as the .44 Extra Long. It is a straight case and is the centerfire version of the .44 Rimfire Extra Long. As near as can be determined, it was introduced, in 1876, for the J.M. Marlin Ballard Sporting Rifle No. 2. It was only available for a few years, before being replaced in the Ballard rifles by the .44-40 WCF. Rifles in this chambering are rare today.

General Comments: The .44 Extra Long was not a popular Ballard number, because there were too many better .44-caliber cartridges available. The .44-40 WCF was already popular by the time the Ballard round hit the market, and the 44 Extra Long was available only in the single-shot. It did, however, provide a reloadable case for those used to the .44 EL rimfire, and quite a few of the old rimfire rifles were probably converted to use the centerfire type. Remington loaded this with 50 grains of blackpowder and a 265-grain bullet. Cases can be made by cutting off .303 Savage cases as mentioned in the discussion about the .44 Henry Flat Center Fire.

.44 Extra Long (Ballard) Factory Ballistics

Bullet (grains/type)	Powder	Grains	Velocity	Energy	Source/Comments
265 Lead	FL		1320	1030	Remington factory load

.44 Wesson Extra Long

Historical Notes: Made for the Frank Wesson tip-up rifles, this cartridge appears to be identical to the .44 Extra Long Ballard except for the shape of the bullet. The Wesson bullet shows two grease grooves when loaded in the case, while the Ballard shows only one.

General Comments: Many of the Wesson tip-up rifles were furnished with a patented adjustable hammer, permitting the use of both rim- and centerfire cartridges. Lyman No. 419182 (240-grain) or 424100 (170-grain) bullets can be adapted to this cartridge. Original loads used 48 to 50 grains of blackpowder. Wesson rifles in this chambering are very rare. As discussed with the .44 Henry Flat Center Fire, cases can be made by cutting off .303 Savage cases.

.44 Wesson Extra Long Factory Ballistics

Bullet (grains/type)	Powder	Grains	Velocity	Energy	Source/Comments
250-257 Lead	FL		1340	1010	Factory load

.44-90 Remington Special
(Necked)

Historical Notes: The .44-90 Remington Special looks like the .44-90 Sharps but, on closer inspection, it has a shorter case with a slightly larger body diameter—these are not interchangeable. The .40-90 was introduced as a match cartridge for the Remington rolling block Creedmoor series, in 1873. Remington catalogs listed empty cases and bullets for this cartridge as late as 1910.

General Comments: The .44-77 Sharps had a 2¼-inch case, the .44-90 Sharps a 25/8-inch case. The .44-90 Remington Special case was 27/16-inch, or 2.44-inch long. The Remington cartridge was regularly loaded with a 550-grain patched or lubricated lead bullet, which is heavier than the normal bullet used in Sharps cartridges. Remington probably designed its .44-90 so that a heavy bullet and 90 grains of powder could be used without increasing the overall length of the cartridge. The loaded length is actually less than the similar Sharps cartridges. This is primarily a match cartridge, but would also be effective on almost any big game. Lighter bullets and more powder could be used to increase blackpowder ballistics for hunting. The only safe source of cases (those that have been extensively modified from .348 Winchester size) is Buffalo Arms (208-263-6953; www.buffaloarms.com).

.44-90 Remington Special Loading Data and Factory Ballistics

Bullet (grains/type)	Powder	Grains	Velocity	Energy	Source/Comments
470 Lead	IMR 4198	30.0	1270	1688	Lyman No. 446187
470 Lead PP	blackpowder (Fg)	90.0			Factory load, early paper patch
550 Lead	blackpowder (Fg)	90.0	1250	1812	Remington factory load

.44-95 Peabody "What Cheer"
.44-100 Peabody "What Cheer"

Historical Notes:	The .44-95 Peabody also had a 100-grain loading and was occasionally referred to as the .44-100 Peabody. It is the largest of the Peabody "What Cheer" cartridges. It was the original chambering for the Peabody-Martini Long-Range Creedmoor Rifle. The straight stock version was the No. 3 "What Cheer," and, eventually, the cartridge was given this name. Some authorities say it was introduced in 1877, but it may have made its debut as early as 1875. It was popular primarily as a target round.
General Comments:	Peabody and Peabody-Martini rifles were manufactured by the Providence Tool Co. of Providence, Rhode Island. The action was patented by H.L. Peabody, of Boston, Massachusetts, in 1862. Peabody-Martini military rifles were manufactured for the Turkish government, during 1873, and something like 600,000 were delivered. The original Peabody pivoting block action had a side-hammer, but the Swiss Martini modification did away with this, instead employing an internal lock. The British Martini-Henry rifle is based on this modified American design. This is one of the strongest of the old single-shot actions.
	Adding the phrase "What Cheer" was in line with the Peabody policy of naming its rifles after famous target ranges of the day, in this case the What Cheer Range, of Greenwood, Rhode Island, which was originally opened in 1875.

.44-95 Peabody "What Cheer" Loading Data and Factory Ballistics

Bullet (grains/type)	Powder	Grains	Velocity	Energy	Source/Comments
470 Lead	blackpowder (Fg)	100.0	1380	1990	Lyman No. 446187
470 Lead	IMR 4759	21.0	1380	1990	Lyman No. 446187
550 Lead	FL		1310	2100	Factory load

.44-70 Maynard (1882)

Historical Notes:	Introduced for the 1882-type Maynard single-shot rifle, the .44-70 was also available for the Hunters Model No. 11 and the Creedmoor No. 14 match rifle.
General Comments:	The .44-70 Maynard is a .44-caliber version of the popular .45-70 Government military round. Many riflemen of the late 1880s preferred the .44-caliber over the larger .45 bore, although there is little difference in bore dimensions. The Maynard company furnished a 430-grain bullet for hunting and general shooting and a 520-grain for target work. Although somewhat too short, .45-70 cases will work in these rifles.

Bullet (grains/type)	Powder	Grains	Velocity	Energy	Source/Comments
470 Lead	IMR 4198	26.0	1300	1768	Lyman No. 446187
430 Lead	FL		1310	1640	Factory load

.44-75 Ballard Everlasting

Historical Notes: The .44-75 is one of the rarer Ballard cases. Seldom found in collections and not mentioned in most cartridge books, L.D. Satterlee* lists it as available for the J.M. Marlin Ballard Perfection No. 4, Pacific No. 5 and Schuetzen No. 6, all introduced in 1876. He gives case length as 2¼-inch.† This chambering is not listed in the Marlin Fire Arms Co. after Marlin began making Ballard rifles, in 1881. James J. Grant ** says this was one of the special Marlin Everlasting cases using the shallow Berdan-type No. 2 primer similar to the .40-65. He also has specimens using Large Rifle primers.

General Comments: The 44-75-2½-inch can be made by trimming and sizing Sharps .45-29/10-inch cases. This must have been intended as both a target and hunting cartridge, since it was available in rifles of both types. Marlin and Ballard catalogs listed a patched 405-grain, .44-caliber bullet, which was probably one of the weights used in the .44-75. Bullets for .44-caliber Sharps cartridges of .446-inch diameter can be adapted to the .44-75 Ballard. No factory ballistics are available, so it is probable that only empty cases and bullets were furnished.

The so-called "Everlasting," or reloadable case, was popular with hunters and target shooters during the 1880-'90 period. These heavy cases could be reused repeatedly. In fact, they were made so heavy that powder capacity was often reduced by five or 10 grains. To get around this, the Everlasting case was often made longer than the standard.

* op. cit.

** More Single Shot Rifles (New York, 1959).

† John T. Amber, the first editor of this book, owned a fine No. 7 Ballard in .44-75 chambering, complete in case with hunting and target sights, etc., and including a score or more of cases. All were 2½ inches long, not 2¼ inches, and were Berdan-primed Everlasting type.

.44-100 Ballard

Historical Notes: The .44-100 Ballard Everlasting was one of the chamberings introduced with the various J.M. Marlin Ballard rifles. It is first listed for the 1876 Model Pacific No. 5 and Long Range No. 7A. It was discontinued about 1880 and does not appear as a standard chambering in later Marlin Fire Arms Co. catalogs. However, the 1888 Marlin & Ballard catalog again lists brass shells under obsolete sizes at 12 cents each. The .45-100 Ballard, which came out later, is based on this same case with the neck reamed out to accept the larger-diameter bullet.

General Comments: This is another rare Ballard cartridge. It was an accurate target number and had considerable knockdown power for big game. Ballard rifles were manufactured by several companies. The best known of these were made by the Marlin Fire Arms Co., after it was incorporated, in 1881. Most of its models and cartridges are not particularly scarce. John M. Marlin organized the Marlin Fire Arms Co. but, prior to that, he turned out Ballard rifles under the name of J.M. Marlin (1875-1881). The first Ballard arms were for rimfire cartridges, and these were introduced by Ball & Williams, in 1861, and continued until 1866 under its brand. From 1866 to 1869, these were made by Merrimack Arms & Manufacturing Co. and, from 1869 to 1873, by Brown Manufacturing Co. Some of these early models and cartridges are rare and valuable. Although the .44-100 Ballard is larger and somewhat longer in diameter, it might be possible to form .45-70 cases to work in these rifles. Basic .45s could be cut to the proper length. In either case, one might have to turn down the rim to fit the chamber.

.44-100 Ballard Loading Data and Factory Ballistics

Bullet (grains/type)	Powder	Grains	Velocity	Energy	Source/Comments
365 Lead	blackpowder (Fg)	110.0	1500	1830	Lyman No. 446109
365 Lead	IMR 4198	26.0	1350	1480	Lyman No. 446109
535 Lead	FL		1400	2328	Factory load

.44-100 Wesson

Historical Notes: As with the .44-85 Wesson, this one was found on a U.S. Cartridge Co. advertising sheet printed in 1881-'82. This is also a straight case, with the length listed as 33/8 inches. The bullet is seated deeply so the total length of the loaded cartridge is 39/10 inches. The load is given as 100 or 120 grains of blackpowder with a 550-grain, paper-patched bullet.

General Comments: What date and what rifle? There is no information given on this. As previously stated, all .44-caliber Sharps cartridges are necked and, perhaps, this is intended as the straight case counter to the necked .44-100 or 105 (25/8-inch) Sharps. This is speculation, but many shooters of this period did prefer the straight case. The .44-100 Wesson is not listed in any previous cartridge book, and now that its existence has been brought to the attention of collectors, additional information may be forthcoming. Muzzle velocity of this combination would be approximately 1350 to 1400 fps, depending on charge, barrel length, etc.

.44-77 Sharps & Remington

Historical Notes: This is the 2¼-inch Sharps bottlenecked case introduced, in 1869, for the Model 1869 Sharps breech-loading sporting rifle. It was also one of the chamberings available for the Remington-Hepburn or No. 3. It was a popular target round, used more for this purpose than hunting. The design of the .44-77 is said to have been based on a combination of the .42 Russian and the .43 Spanish military cartridges.

General Comments: A variety of factory loadings were turned out for the .44-77, with bullet weights from 300 grains to 470 grains. It is sometimes listed as the .44-70 or .44-75, depending on the powder charge used. Remington made an unusual two-piece reloadable case with a steel head and brass body.

.44-77 Sharps & Remington Loading Data and Factory Ballistics

Bullet (grains/type)	Powder	Grains	Velocity	Energy	Source/Comments
365 Lead	IMR 4198	28.0	1480	1782	Lyman No. 446109
470 Lead PP	blackpowder (Fg)	77.0	UNK	UNK	Factory load, early paper patch
365 Lead	FL		1460	1730	Factory load

.44-90 Sharps Necked (.44-100 Sharps 2⁵/₈-inch/ .44-105 Sharp Necked)

Historical Notes: This is the .44-90 Sharps 25/8-inch case of larger capacity than the .44-77 Sharps. It was the chambering for the Sharps 1873 Creedmoor rifle made by the old Sharps Rifle Manufacturing Co. before its reorganization, in 1875-'76, and was chambered in later side-hammer models. Advertisements list it as early as June of 1873. Sharps rifles of .44-caliber were discontinued, during 1878, in favor of the more popular .45-caliber.

General Comments: These are just different loadings and bullet weights. Ammunition was available with bullets weighing 277, 450, 470, 500, and 520 grains. It was not as popular for hunting as some of the other Sharps chamberings, but was used for 1,000-yard match shooting. A version with a .19-inch shorter case also existed. Both are listed in the 1910 Winchester catalog. The only safe source of cases is Buffalo Arms; they extensively modify .348 Winchester cases to properly fit these chambers (208-263-6953; www.buffaloarms.com).

.44-90 Sharps (Necked) Loading Data and Factory Ballistics

Bullet (grains/type)	Powder	Grains	Velocity	Energy	Source/Comments
470 Lead	IMR 4198	28.0	1300	1630	Lyman No. 446187
520 Lead	FL		1270	1860	Factory load

.44-60 Sharps & Remington (Necked)

Historical Notes: This 17/8-inch .44 case was loaded by Remington and Winchester. It was introduced, in 1869, for the 1869 Sporting Rifle and used in Sharps, Winchester, and Remington single-shot rifles.

General Comments: This was a general purpose cartridge for hunting or target shooting. It was listed by Remington and labeled as one of its "Creedmore" types (note the spelling), which has caused some confusion identifying the round. Sharps match rifles for long-range shooting were named after the famous range at Creedmoor, Long Island. Other rifle makers also used this name. Remington applied the name to cartridges not originally chambered in the Sharps Creedmoor line. It is interesting to compare this cartridge with the .42 Russian Berdan Carbine round. Except for bullet diameter, the two are practically identical. This suggests the possibility that the .44-60 was developed by expanding the neck of the Russian Carbine cartridge, much as some modern wildcats are made. The .44-60 necked Peabody, Winchester, Remington, etc., appear to be the same as the .44-60 (17/8-inch) Sharps cartridge.

.44-60 Sharps (Necked) Loading Data and Factory Ballistics

Bullet (grains/type)	Powder	Grains	Velocity	Energy	Source/Comments
315 Lead	IMR 4198	24.0	1300	1188	Lyman No. 446110
396 Lead	FL		1250	1375	Factory load

.45-50 Peabody (Sporting)

Historical Notes: A sporting cartridge for the Peabody-Martini single-shot rifle, the .45-50 was introduced in 1873-'74, shortly after the Martini modification of the Peabody action was adopted.

General Comments: The .45-50 bears a close resemblance to the Peabody .45-55 Turkish carbine cartridge. It is probable that it is a modification of the Turkish military round, adapted to sporting use. Physical measurements of the two are not identical, but very close. This is a rare cartridge, and rifles in this chambering are seldom encountered. Almost any .45-caliber rifle bullet can be sized down to .454-inch diameter and used; the Lyman No. 456191 (300-grain) will work fine. Powder charge can be varied from 50 to 55 grains of Fg blackpowder, depending on bullet weight and seating depth. For smokeless powder loads, use 22 to 23 grains of Du Pont (IMR) 4198. This will more or less duplicate original blackpowder ballistics. It could be possible to cut and form .45-70 cases to work in these rifles. This is one of the few Peabody designs close enough to common current chamberings to offer hope of conveniently shooting the rifle chambered for it.

.45-50 Peabody (Sporting) Loading Data and Factory Ballistics

Bullet (grains/type)	Powder	Grains	Velocity	Energy	Source/Comments
255 Lead	IMR 4198	25.0	1350	1080	Lyman No. 454190
300 Lead	blackpowder (Fg)	50.0	1285	1080	Lyman No. 456191
290 Lead	FL		1295	1085	Factory load

.44-60 Winchester
.44-60 Peabody "Creedmoor"

Historical Notes: This cartridge is for the Peabody-Martini "Creedmoor" rifle, introduced in 1877-'78. It is not a well-known cartridge and apparently was of limited popularity. Winchester loaded this round under its own name, which it introduced in 1874-'75. This is the same as the Sharps .44-60-17/8-inch-inch necked cartridge.

General Comments: Examination of these cartridges in comparison with the .42 Russian Carbine indicates they are identical except for neck and bullet diameter. The .44-60 was likely developed by expanding the neck of the Russian cartridge, very much as some of our modern wildcats are made. The Russian Carbine cartridge is a shortened version of the .42 Berdan.

.44-60 Peabody "Creedmoor" Loading Data and Factory Ballistics

Bullet (grains/type)	Powder	Grains	Velocity	Energy	Source/Comments
365 Lead	blackpowder (Fg)	65.0	1280	1410	Lyman No. 446109
395 Lead	FL		1250	1375	Winchester factory load

.45-60 Winchester

Historical Notes: The .45-60 is one of several cartridges designed for the Winchester 1876 Centennial Model rifle. The .45-60 cartridge was introduced in 1879. Winchester continued production of this cartridge until 1935, although the rifle was discontinued in 1897. The Kennedy lever-action repeating rifle used this cartridge, as did the Colt Lightning pump-action repeater.

General Comments: The .45-60 was brought out, with others of the Model 1876 cartridge line, to provide greater power than the .44-40 and other short cartridges used in the Model 1873 Winchester. The .45-60 design was probably influenced by the .45-70 Government round. The Model 1876 rifle had a medium-length action that would not handle the long cartridges used in the single-shots of the period. The .45-60 would be a better deer cartridge than the .44 WCF, but would not be suitable for larger game. Rifles for this cartridge are not strong, so one should not attempt to exceed original ballistics. It should be easy to form .45-70 cases to work in these rifles.

.45-60 Winchester Loading Data and Factory Ballistics

Bullet (grains/type)	Powder	Grains	Velocity	Energy	Source/Comments
300 Lead	IMR 4198	25.0	1450	1410	Lyman No. 456191
300 Lead	FL		1315	1152	Winchester factory load

.45-75 Winchester (Centennial)

Historical Notes: The .45-75 Winchester was the original chambering for the Model 1876 Centennial rifle. Other chamberings were added later. The Kennedy repeating rifle also used this round. Winchester continued to produce this cartridge until 1935. The Canadian Northwest Mounted Police adopted the Model 76 Winchester in the .45-75 chambering and used it for 27 years.

General Comments: To compete with the big Sharps and other single-shot cartridges, Winchester needed a longer repeating action. The Model 76 was designed to fill that need. However, as produced, it wasn't long enough to handle cartridges with an overall length exceeding 2¼ inches. The .45-75 gives performance equal to, or slightly better than, the .45-70 Government by use of a shorter, fatter, bottlenecked case. The Model 76 action is not noted for great strength, and heavy smokeless powder charges should be avoided. The .45-75 would be a good short-range deer or black bear cartridge, by modern standards. It was favored by Theodore Roosevelt for grizzly bear. Usable cases can be made from .348 Winchester cases.

.45-75 Winchester Loading Data and Factory Ballistics

Bullet (grains/type)	Powder	Grains	Velocity	Energy	Source/Comments
350 Lead	IMR 4198	24.0	1380	1480	Lyman No. 456192
350 Lead	FL		1383	1485	Factory load

.45-100 Ballard

Historical Notes: Satterlee* indicates that this cartridge was introduced, in 1878, with the Ballard Sporting No. 4½ rifle. However, Grant first shows it with the 1882 (Marlin Fire Arms Co.) Pacific No. 5. Manufacture of Ballard single-shot rifles, discontinued between 1888 and 1890. The .45-100 cartridge was still listed as a standard chambering in the 1888 Marlin & Ballard catalog. This was the last catalog that advertised the Ballard, according to some authorities.

General Comments: The .45-100 is not a common cartridge, although it was available up to the time Ballard rifles were discontinued. It is the same case as the .44-100 Ballard, but the inside of the neck was reamed, to accommodate the larger .45-caliber bullet. Almost any .45-caliber lead rifle bullet can be sized to fit this case. The company offered .45-caliber bullets in 285, 405, 420, and 550 grains for loading this and other cartridges. Lighter bullets left room for up to 120 grains of blackpowder. This was used as both a target and hunting round and was equal in power to some of the big Sharps and Winchester cartridges of similar capacity. The old Ballard action is not particularly strong, and caution is advised when using smokeless powder. Although the base is a bit smaller than the .45-70, one suspects usable cases could be made from .45-70 cases. If so, Basic .45 cases could be cut to the proper length to duplicate this cartridge, which is very similar to the .45-90 Winchester, only longer.

*op. cit.

.45-100 Ballard Loading Data and Factory Ballistics

Bullet (grains/type)	Powder	Grains	Velocity	Energy	Source/Comments
500 Lead	blackpowder (Fg)	100.0	1400	2180	Lyman No. 457125
500 Lead	IMR 4198	22.0	1250	1740	Lyman No. 457125
550 Lead	FL		1370	2300	Factory load

.45-70 Van Choate

Historical Notes: This cartridge was originally designed for the experimental Van Choate military bolt-action rifle made by the Brown Manufacturing Co., in 1872. It is similar to the .45-70 Government, but has a case length of 2¼ inches instead of 21/10 inches. It was used in other rifles as well, because it was listed in Remington and Winchester catalogs as late as 1910-'12. The paper patched bullet weighed 420 grains.

General Comments: There are a number of variations of the basic .45-70 Government cartridge. Most of these vary by bullet weight, but a few use a different case length. One of these was the .45-78-475 Wolcott with a 2.31-inch case. There was also a .45-80 Sharpshooter cartridge that was used in special target rifles. This had a 24/10-inch case that was very similar, if not identical, to the Sharps 24/10-inch case. Although these cartridges are identical in all dimensions except length, a rifle would have to be chambered to accept the extra-long case, so these would not be interchangeable. Just what the originators hoped to gain from these variations is hard to imagine. It was probably done to allow a full or increased powder charge with a heavier or longer-than-standard bullet. Most of these variations have an odd-shaped bullet. For any of these, one can use the same bullets and loading data given with the .45-70. Standard .45-70 cases chamber in these rifles. To duplicate the original case, trim Basic .45s to the proper length.

.45-75 Sharps (Straight)
.45-70 Sharps 2¹/₁₀-inch

Historical Notes: This cartridge is identical to the .45-70 Government. It represents another instance of a manufacturer adding his name to a cartridge when chambered for his rifles. Also known as the .45-70 Sharps, it was added to the company product line early to mid-1875. It was one of the loadings designated as the Sharps .45-21/10-inch case.

General Comments: Use the same loading data as that given for the .45-70 Government. Most original Sharps rifles have blackpowder steel barrels, so it is advisable to stick to lead bullets to reduce wear on the bore. Any load safe for the 1873 "Trapdoor" Springfield will be okay in Sharps rifles of any vintage.

.45-75 Sharps (Straight) Factory Ballistics

Bullet (grains/type)	Powder	Grains	Velocity	Energy	Source/Comments
400 Lead	FL		1330	1580	Factory load

.45-82 Winchester
.45-85 Winchester
.45-90 Winchester
.45-90 Winchester High Velocity

Historical Notes: These designations are often listed separately, giving different case dimensions. However, these are nothing more than different loads and bullet weights in the same basic .45-90 case. All loads were for the Winchester Model 1886 repeater or the 1885 single-shot. The .45-90 was introduced in 1886. The other loads followed. The Marlin Model 1895 was also chambered for the group. The smokeless powder .45-90 came out in 1895 and was discontinued about 1936.

General Comments: For many decades after its introduction, the .45-90 was a popular sporting cartridge. Once offered in a high-velocity loading with its standard 300-grain bullet at nearly 2000 fps and generating over 2,900 ft-lbs of energy, it was no doubt a good killer. With a 200 fps advantage over the high-velocity .45-70-300 load, it would shoot a bit flatter and give, perhaps, 50 yards more usable range.

The .45-90 case is practically identical to the .45-70, only longer. It is common practice to fire the .45-70 in these rifles, when the proper ammunition is not available. The .45-90 is adequate for any North American big game at moderate ranges. Use standard .458-inch diameter bullets for loading. For handloading, use only lead bullets, to avoid excessive barrel wear.

.45-82, .45-85, .45-90 Winchester Loading Data and Factory Ballistics

Bullet (grains/type)	Powder	Grains	Velocity	Energy	Source/Comments
300 Lead	IMR 4198	38.0	1530	1565	NA
405 Lead	IMR 4198	32.0	1410	1790	Lyman No. 457483 gas checked
405 Cast	IMR 3031	40.0	1500	2023	Lyman No. 457124
300 Lead	FL		1554	1609	Factory load
350 Lead	FL		1510	1775	Factory load
405 Lead	FL		1468	1938	Factory load

.45-90 Sharps (Straight)
.45-100 Sharps (Straight)
.45-110 Sharps (Straight)
.45 Sharps Special

Historical Notes: When the Sharps company adopted the .45-caliber, it developed a variety of loads and case lengths. The first of these was introduced in mid-1876 (27/8 inches), and different case lengths were added late in 1876 (26/10 inches), and mid-1877 (24/10 inches). The principal difference in these cartridges was in bullet weight, powder charge, and case length. Other dimensions are the same. Some are heavy reloadable cases that had to be lengthened slightly to hold the same charge as the originals.

General Comments: The .45-100 (24/10 inches), .45-100 (26/10 inches), .45-90 (23/4 inches), .45-100 (27/8 inches) and the .45-110 (27/8 inches), all appear to be identical except for loading and/or case length. The .45-23/4-inch case, listed in the 1876 catalog, is otherwise unknown. There is no point listing all of these separately because of slight differences. However, the reader should know that each exists, as these are encountered in literature referring to Sharps rifles or loading data for them. The .45-90 Winchester case can be fired in any of the above chambered rifles by seating the bullet well out of the case. With cast bullets, .45-70 cartridges can be fired in these rifles. These cases can be made from Basic .45 cases, and many custom bullet moulds are currently available.

Bullet (grains/type)	Powder	Grains	Velocity	Energy	Source/Comments
485 Lead	IMR 4198	24.0	1300	1822	Lyman No. 451112
550 Lead	FL		1360	2240	Factory load

.45-120 (3¼-inch) Sharps (Straight)
.45-125 (3¼-inch) Sharps (Straight)

Historical Notes: The .45-caliber 3¼-inch case is the largest Sharps cartridge of this caliber. Because of differences in case thickness, it usually came in two versions, the .45-120 and the .45-125. It was introduced, in 1878-'79, for the Sharps-Borchardt rifles, although there is no documentary evidence that the Sharps factory produced rifles in this chambering or any of the 3¼-inch cases, either .40, .45, or. 50. Original rifles in this chambering and original ammunition are collector's items. The Sharps Rifle Co. failed in 1881, so the big 3¼-inch case did not have a particularly long life, although other single-shot rifles could be (and were) chambered for it. In 1991-'92, Eldorado Cartridge made a run of cases and loaded this ammunition.

General Comments: The .45-120 Sharps is a very powerful blackpowder cartridge adequate for any North American big game. It is usually considered one of the big buffalo cartridges, but it could not have participated in the slaughter of these animals to any great extent, because it arrived on the scene very late. Western buffalo hunting reached its peak in 1875-'76 and, by 1880, was on the wane. The last of the great herds was destroyed in 1884, and the need for the big, powerful buffalo rifles and cartridges passed with the last of these animals. The repeating rifle and the small-bore, high-velocity cartridge would, within a decade, give them the final shove into obsolescence. Most of the Sharps-Borchardt single-shot rifles in this and other chamberings have been rebarreled and made into modern small-bore varmint rifles.

Bullet (grains/type)	Powder	Grains	Velocity	Energy	Source/Comments
485 Lead	IMR 4198	26.0	1360	2000	Lyman No. 451112
500 Cast	Blackpowder (FFg)	85.0	1299	1873	Lyman No. 457125
500 Lead	FL		1520	2561	Factory load

.50-90 Sharps
.50-100 Sharps
.50-110 Sharps

Historical Notes: The 2½-inch .50-caliber Sharps was introduced in the 1872 Sharps catalog, which also listed the .50-70, among others. This period was the heyday of buffalo hunting. There was a strong demand for more potent loads in all game chamberings. The .50-90 offered more power. When western writers refer to the "Big 50" Sharps buffalo rifle and cartridge, this is the cartridge they mean, whether they know it or not. The longer Sharps (3¼-inch) .50-caliber cartridge did not arrive on the scene until after the buffalo were finished.

General Comments: Soon after its introduction, it was the "Big 50" or "Poison Slinger." The .50-90 is also called the .50-100 or .50-110, depending on what bullet weight and powder charge was used. Sharps discontinued its .40- and .50-caliber cartridges, except on special order, when it adopted the .45-caliber. Correct bullet diameter is .509-inch; several Lyman moulds in this size are available. One should not confuse various loadings of this cartridge with the .50-110 Winchester. Cases are readily available from several sources.

Bullet (grains/type)	Powder	Grains	Velocity	Energy	Source/Comments
365 Lead	AA 5744	37.0	1652	2210	Accurate Arms
422 Cast	IMR 4198	25.5	1129	1194	Lyman No. 515141
440 Lead	AA 5744	33.0	1418	1965	Accurate Arms
465 Lead	IMR 4198	30.0	1320	1804	Lyman No. 509133
550 Lead	AA 5744	30.0	1275	1985	Accurate Arms
335 Lead	FL		1475	1630	Factory load
473 Lead	FL		1350	1920	Factory load

.50-140 (3¼-inch) Sharps
.50-140 Winchester Express

Historical Notes: This is another special-order Sharps cartridge. It was introduced in 1880, but specific reference is lacking. Dimensions, except for length, are the same as the .50-90 Sharps. Some authorities believe rifles were made by rechambering .50-90s. None of the Sharps catalogs lists this cartridge or chambering.

General Comments: Winchester loaded the .50-140 with a 473-grain bullet, but many handloaders used the 700-grain paper-patched type, which could be purchased on a commercial basis. UMC also offered empty cases. Rifles chambered for this round are rare, and cartridges are collector's items. This was the most powerful of the Sharps "buffalo" cartridges, but it was introduced after most of the great herds were long gone. By 1880, buffalo hunting had almost ended, though it continued sporadically until 1884, when the last remaining herd was destroyed. Buffalo hunting for scattered individuals or small groups was not economically feasible. Sharps rifles used .509-inch diameter bullets, while Winchester used .512-inch diameter. The Basic .50 duplicates this case.

.50-140 Sharps, .50-140 Winchester Express Loading Data and Factory Ballistics

Bullet (grains/type)	Powder	Grains	Velocity	Energy	Source/Comments
422 Cast	IMR 4198	39.0	1386	1780	Lyman No. 515141
440 Lead	AA 5744	55.0	1978	3820	Accurate Arms
550 Lead	AA 5744	50.0	1736	3680	Accurate Arms
465 Lead	IMR 4198	33.0	1450	2190	Lyman No. 509133
700 Lead	AA 5744	48.0	1529	3635	Accurate Arms
473 Lead	FL		1580	2520	Winchester factory load
700 Lead	FL		1355	2850	Factory load

.50-115 Bullard

Historical Notes: This, the largest of the Bullard cartridges, was introduced in 1886. It is unique in being both the first semi-rimmed and solid-head cartridge produced in the United States. It was chambered in the repeating Bullard rifles and possibly the single-shot. No other rifle makers used it.

General Comments: The .50-115 Bullard has a slight shoulder. With its larger body diameter, it is shorter than similar .50-caliber cartridges. It delivers the same performance as the longer .50-110 Winchester. It is another rare cartridge and would be difficult to duplicate out of some other case because of the semi-rim construction, although one could turn down the rim on the .470 Nitro Express to make usable cases.

.50-115 Bullard Loading Data and Factory Ballistics

Bullet (grains/type)	Powder	Grains	Velocity	Energy	Source/Comments
290 Lead	blackpowder (Fg)	115.0	1539	1580	Lyman No. 512139
290 Lead	IMR 4198	32.0	1570	1647	Lyman No. 512139
300 Lead	FL		1539	1583	Factory load

.50-100 Winchester
.50-105 Winchester
.50-110 Winchester
.50-110 Winchester High Velocity

Historical Notes: Here we have another example of different loadings in the same case causing confusion, as if they had been used in differently chambered guns. These are all variations of the original .50-110 Winchester, introduced in or before 1916 for the Model 1886 repeating rifle. The original .50-110 was cataloged in November 1887, the .50-100-450 version was offered in August 1895, and the High Velocity version came along sometime after 1910, but is shown in the 1916 catalog. This chambering was also available for the single-shot. Winchester listed cartridges until 1935.

General Comments: Originally a blackpowder number, both a standard- and high-velocity smokeless powder version also were developed. The high-velocity load pushed the 300-grain bullet at 2225 fps and developed 3298 ft-lbs of energy at the muzzle. This was quite a potent number, being comparable to some of the British-designed African cartridges. For loading, use the Lyman No. 512139 (290-grain) hollowpoint, No. 512138 (450-grain), or one of those bullets listed with the loading data. In spite of being a bit shorter, straightened .348 Winchester cases should work in most rifles.

.50-100, .50-105, .50-110 Winchester Loading Data and Factory Ballistics

Bullet (grains/type)	Powder	Grains	Velocity	Energy	Source/Comments
285 Lead	blackpowder (Fg)	110.0	1600	1710	Lyman No. 518144
285 Lead	IMR 4198	39.0	1750	2045	Lyman No. 518144
450 Lead	blackpowder (Fg)	100.0	1475	2190	Lyman No. 515141
300 Lead	FL		1605	1720	Winchester factory load, standard
300 Lead	FL		2225	3298	Winchester factory load, high velocity

.50-50 Maynard (1882)

Historical Notes: This is the Maynard version of the .50 U.S. Carbine cartridge. It was used in the 1882 Model Maynard single-shot rifle.

General Comments: Some of the .50-50 Maynard cartridges have a smaller base diameter than that listed, but this is more a matter of manufacturing tolerance than design difference. Ammunition for old rifles of this chambering can be made by trimming .50-70 cases to the correct length. Powder charge is 50 to 60 grains of blackpowder, depending on bullet weight and type. Lyman No. 518144 (285-grain) or 518145 (350-grain) make good cast bullets for these old rifles. By shortening and possibly thinning the rim, .348 Winchester cases can be used in these rifles.

.50-50 Maynard Factory Ballistics

Bullet (grains/type)	Powder	Grains	Velocity	Energy	Source/Comments
350 Lead	FL		1270	1260	Factory load
400 Lead	FL		1210	1305	Factory load

.50-95 Winchester
.50-95 Winchester Express

Historical Notes: The .50-95 is another of the short-necked cartridges developed for the Winchester 1876 Centennial Model repeater. This is the big bore of the group and was introduced in 1879. It was not as popular as some of the others and had a relatively short production life. The Colt New Lightning pump-action rifle was also available in this chambering.

General Comments: The .50-70 Government cartridge gained a certain following among buffalo hunters of the period, and the .50-95 is essentially an improved, repeating rifle version of that cartridge. Lyman hollowpoint bullets No. 512137 (350 grains) or 512139 (290 grains) can be used for loading. It is advisable to stick to blackpowder or low-pressure smokeless powder loads for the Model 76 Winchester; it is not a strong action, although entirely adequate for any blackpowder load. Shortened .348 Winchester cases should work in most rifles, with very light loads. Cases from the .50-90 Sharps can be converted into perfectly fitting .50-95 WCF cases.

.50-95 Winchester Loading Data and Factory Ballistics

Bullet (grains/type)	Powder	Grains	Velocity	Energy	Source/Comments
285 Lead	IMR 4198	26.0	1420	1302	Lyman No. 518144
350 Lead	IMR 4198	23.0	1350	1420	Lyman No. 518145
300 Lead	FL		1557	1615	Winchester factory load

.50 U.S. Carbine (.50 Carbine)

Historical Notes: Introduced as a carbine loading for the 1870 Trapdoor Springfield single-shot rifle or carbine, this is a centerfire modification of similar rimfire types developed during and immediately after the Civil War.

General Comments: The .50 Carbine round is a short-case variation of the standard .50-70 military cartridge. It can be fired in the rifle, but the standard .50-70 case is too long to fit in carbines. The carbine load consisted of a 400-grain bullet and 45 to 50 grains of Fg blackpowder. Lyman No. 518144 (285 grains) is a good bullet for loading these old shells. If your gun will not take the regular .50-70, just trim the case to the proper length. The 1870 Springfield has a weak action, so do not try any hot smokeless powder loads. Cases can be converted from .50-90 Sharps cases.

.50 U.S. Carbine Loading Data and Factory Ballistics

Bullet (grains/type)	Powder	Grains	Velocity	Energy	Source/Comments
400 Lead	IMR 4198	22.0	1200	1285	NA
400 Lead	FL		1200	1285	Factory load

.58 Carbine (Berdan)

Historical Notes: This is the carbine version of the .58 Berdan Musket cartridge, introduced in 1869. The two differ only in case length and powder charge. The carbine case is 1½ inches long, whereas the musket case is 1¾ inches long. There is no other difference except the powder charge.

General Comments: Rifles for .58 Berdan cartridges are scarce items. Proper load for the carbine version is 40 to 45 grains of Fg blackpowder. Use Lyman No. 585213 (476-grain) bullet. For a good smokeless powder load, try 22 grains of Du Pont (IMR) 4198.

.58 Berdan Carbine Factory Ballistics

Bullet (grains/type)	Powder	Grains	Velocity	Energy	Source/Comments
530 Lead	FL		925	1012	Factory load

.58 U.S. Musket (Berdan)

Historical Notes: Introduced, in 1869, for use in the Berdan breech-loading conversion of the Springfield rifled musket, this cartridge was produced in both a rifle version (listed here) and a carbine version (listed above). Bullet weight is the same in both cartridges. This cartridge was never officially adopted by the United States armed forces, but was used experimentally. The centerfire cartridge evolved from earlier rimfire and inside-primed types. The Springfield muzzle-loading musket used a 500-grain bullet and 60 grains of powder for 950 to 1000 fps, before conversion to breech loading.

General Comments: Colonel Hiram Berdan, noted chiefly for his part in organizing and leading Berdan's Sharpshooters during the Civil War, was also a firearms designer of considerable importance in the post-war period. The breech-loading conversion system he designed was not used by the United States, but was adopted by Spain, Russia, and other European powers. His Berdan I (hinged cam-lock) and Berdan II (bolt-action) single-shot rifles were both officially adopted and used by Russia for a number of years. In 1895, his widow was awarded a judgment for patent infringement in a suit filed against the U.S. Government; the 1866 Springfield rifle used a breech system that copied essential features of the Berdan design.

In 1870, Col. Berdan developed the priming form that bears his name, the Berdan system that is used almost universally outside the United States. Evidently, Berdan was truly unappreciated by his homeland. The Boxer primer used here was invented by an Englishman who seems to have been equally unappreciated by his homeland. The .58 Musket cartridge is common, but arms in this chambering are scarce.

.58 U.S. Musket (Berdan) Loading Data and Factory Ballistics

Bullet (grains/type)	Powder	Grains	Velocity	Energy	Source/Comments
476 Lead	blackpowder (Fg)	80-85	1230	1608	Lyman No. 585213
476 Lead	IMR 4198	25.0	1230	1608	Lyman No. 585213
530 Lead	blackpowder (Fg)	80-85	1100	1420	Factory load

Dimensional Data

Cartridge	Case	Bullet Dia.	Neck Dia.	Shoulder Dia.	Base Dia.	Rim Dia.	Rim Thick.	Case Length	Ctge. Length	Primer	Page
.219 Zipper	A	.224	.252	.364	.421	.497	.058	1.94	2.26	L	108
.222 Remington Magnum	C	.224	.253	.355	.375	.375	.041	1.85	2.21	S	109
.22 Winchester Center Fire (WCF)	A	.228	.241	.278	.295	.342	.058	1.39	1.61	S	110
.22 Savage High Power	A	.228	.252	.360	.416	.500	.056	2.05	2.51	L	111
6mm Bench Rest Remington	C	.243	.263	.457	.466	.468	.045	1.52	2.19	S	111
.244 Remington (.236 Navy)	C	.243	.276	.429	.470	.472	.045	2.23	2.90	L	112
6mm Lee Navy	C	.244	.278	.402	.445	.448	UNK/NA	2.35	3.11	L	113
.25-20 Single Shot	A	.257	.275	.296	.315	.378	UNK/NA	1.63	1.90	S	113
.25-20 Marlin	A	.257	.274	.329	.349	.405	UNK/NA	1.33	UNK/NA	S	114
.25-21 Stevens	B	.257	.280	UNK/NA	.300	.376	UNK/NA	2.05	2.30	S	114
.25-25 Stevens	B	.257	.282	UNK/NA	.323	.376	UNK/NA	2.37	2.63	S	114
.25-36 Marlin	A	.257	.281	.358	.416	.499	.056	2.12	2.50	S	115
.256 Winchester Magnum	A	.257	.283	.370	.378	.440	.055	1.30	1.53	S	115
.25 Remington	C	.257	.280	.355	.420	.421	.045	2.04	2.54	L	116
.256 Newton	C	.264	.290	.430	.469	.473	.045	2.44	3.40	L	116
6.5mm Remington Magnum	E	.264	.300	.490	.512	.532	.047	2.17	2.80	L	117
.275 H&H Magnum	E	.284	.375	.375	.513	.532	.048	2.50	3.30	L	118
7x61mm Sharpe & Hart Super	E	.284	.320	.478	.515	.532	.048	2.40	3.27	L	118
.28-30-120 Stevens	B	.285	.309	UNK/NA	.357	.412	UNK/NA	2.51	2.82	L	119
.30-30 Wesson	A	.308	.329	.330	.380	.440	UNK/NA	1.66	2.50	L	119
.30 Remington	C	.307	.328	.402	.420	.421	.045	2.03	2.525	L	120
.30 USA/.30-40 Rimless	C	.308	.333	.417	.454	.456	.054	2.31	3.10	L	120
.30-03 Springfield/Gov't.	C	.308	.340	.441	.470	.473	.045	2.54	3.34	L	120
.30 Newton/.30 Adolph Express	C	.308	.340	.491	.523	.525	UNK/NA	2.52	3.35	L	121
.32-40 Remington	A	.309	.330	.358	.453	.535	UNK/NA	2.13	3.25	S	121
.303 Savage/.301 Savage	A	.308/ .311	.334 (.3322)	.408 (.4135)	.439	.501	.058	2.00 (2.015)	2.52	L	122
.32-20 Marlin	A	.312	.326	.338	.353	.405	UNK/NA	1.32	UNK/NA	S	122
.32-30 Remington	A	.312	.332	.357	.378	.437	UNK/NA	1.64	2.01	S	123
.32-35 Stevens & Maynard	B	.312	.339	UNK/NA	.402	.503	UNK/NA	1.88	2.29	S	123
.32-40 Bullard	A	.315	.332	.413	.453	.510	UNK/NA	1.85	2.26	S	124
.32 Long, CF*	B	.317	.318	UNK/NA	.321	.369	UNK/NA	0.82	1.35	S	124
.32 Ballard Extra Long*	B	.317	.318	UNK/NA	.321	.369	UNK/NA	1.24	1.80	S	124
.32 Winchester SL (WSL)	H	.320	.343	UNK/NA	.346	.388	UNK/NA	1.28	1.88	S	125
.32-40 Ballard & Winchester	B	.320	.338	UNK/NA	.424	.506	.058	2.13	2.59	L	125
.32 Remington	C	.320	.344	.396	.420	.421	.045	2.04	2.57	L	126
.32 Ideal	B	.323	.344	UNK/NA	.348	.411	UNK/NA	1.77	2.25	S	126
.33 Winchester	A	.333	.365	.443	.508	.610	.065	2.11	2.80	L	127
.35 Winchester SL (WSL)	H	.351	.374	UNK/NA	.378	.405	.045	1.14	1.64	S	127
.351 Winchester SL (WSL)	H	.351	.374	.378	.407	1.38	.045	1.91	UNK/NA	S	128
.35 Winchester	A	.358	.378	.412	.457	.539	UNK/NA	2.41	3.16	L	128
.35 Newton	C	.358	.383	.498	.523	.525	2.52	3.35	12		129
.35-30 Maynard (1882)	B	.359	.395	UNK/NA	.400	.494	UNK/NA	1.63	2.03	S	129
.35-40 Maynard (1882)	B	.360	.390	UNK/NA	.400	.492	UNK/NA	2.06	2.53	S	130
.35-30 Maynard (1865)	B	.370	.397	UNK/NA	.408	.771/ 1.076	.037	1.53	1.98	ext. primed	130
.38-40 Remington-Hepburn	B	.372	.395	UNK/NA	.454	.537	UNK/NA	1.77	2.32	S	131
.38 Long, CF*	B	.375	.378	UNK/NA	.379	.441	UNK/NA	1.03	1.45	S	131
.38 Ballard Extra Long*	B	.375	.378	UNK/NA	.379	.441	UNK/NA	1.63	2.06	S	131
.38-35 Stevens	B	.375	.402	UNK/NA	.403	.492	UNK/NA	1.62	2.43	S	132
.38-50 Maynard (1882)	B	.375	.415	UNK/NA	.421	.500	.069	1.97	2.38	S	132
.38-50 Ballard Everlasting	B	.376	.395	UNK/NA	.425	.502	UNK/NA	2.00	2.72	S	133
.38-50 Remington-Hepburn	B	.376	.392	UNK/NA	.454	.535	UNK/NA	2.23	3.07	S	133
.38-56 Winchester	A	.376	.403	.447	.506	.606	.065	2.10	2.50	L	133
.38-90 Winchester Express	A	.376	.395	.470	.477	.558	UNK/NA	3.25	3.70	L	134
.38-72 Winchester	A	.378	.397	.427	.461	.519	UNK/NA	2.58	3.16	L	134

Dimensional Data

Cartridge	Case	Bullet Dia.	Neck Dia.	Shoulder Dia.	Base Dia.	Rim Dia.	Rim Thick.	Case Length	Ctge. Length	Primer	Page
.40-50 Sharps (Straight)	B	.403	.421	UNK/NA	.454	.554	.078	1 88	2.63	B-1	135
.40-50 Sharps (Necked)	A	.403	.424	.489	.501	.580	UNK/NA	1.72	2.37	B-1	135
.40-60 Marlin	B	.403	.425	UNK/NA	.504	.604	UNK/NA	2.11	2.55	S	136
.40-63/.40-70 Ballard Everlasting	B	.403	.430	UNK/NA	.471	.555	UNK/NA	2.38	2.55	S	136
.40-70 Sharps (Straight)	B	.403	.420	UNK/NA	.453	.533	.078	2.50	3.18	L	137
.40-70 Sharps (Necked)	A	.403	.426	.500	.503	.595	UNK/NA	2.25	3.02	L	137
.40-85/.40-90 Ballard Everlasting	B	.403	.425	UNK/NA	.477	.545	UNK/NA	2.94	3.81	S	138
.40-90 Sharps (Straight)	B	.403	.425	UNK/NA	.477	.546	UNK/NA	3.25	4.06	B-1	138
.40-90/.40-100 Sharps (Necked)	A	.403	.435	.500	.506	.602	UNK/NA	2.63	3.44	B-1	139
.40-110 Winchester Express	A	.403	.428	.485	.565	.651	UNK/NA	3.25	3.63	L	139
.40-60 Winchester	A	.404	.425	.445	.506	.630	UNK/NA	1.87	2.10	S	139
.40-70 Winchester	A	.405	.430	.496	.504	.604	UNK/NA	2.40	2.85	L	140
.40-70 Remington	A	.405	.434	.500	.503	.595	UNK/NA	2.25	3.00	L	140
.40-65 Winchester	B	.406	.423	UNK/NA	.504	.604	UNK/NA	2.10	2.48	L	141
.40-72 Winchester	B	.406	.431	UNK/NA	.460	.518	UNK/NA	2.60	3.15	L	141
.40-82 Winchester (WCF)	A	.406	.428	.448	.502	.604	.060	2.40	2.77	L	141
.401 Winchester (WSL)	H	.406	.428	UNK/NA	.429	.457	.055	1.50	2.00	L	142
.40-90 Peabody "What Cheer"	A	.408	.433	.546	.586	.659	UNK/NA	2.00	3.37	B-1	142
.405 Winchester	B	.412	.436	UNK/NA	.461	.543	.075	2.58	3.18	L	143
.40-75 Bullard	B	.413	.432	UNK/NA	.505	.606	UNK/NA	2.09	2.54	S	143
.40-90 Bullard	A	.413	.430	.551	.569	.622	UNK/NA	2.04	2.55	L	144
.40-40 Maynard (1882)	B	.415	.450	UNK/NA	.456	.532	UNK/NA	1.78	2.32	S	144
.40-60 Maynard (1882)	B	.417	.448	UNK/NA	.454	.533	UNK/NA	2.20	2.75	S	145
.40-70 Maynard (1882)	B	.417	.450	UNK/NA	.451	.535	UNK/NA	2.42	2.88	B-1	145
.44 Evans Short	B	.419	.439	UNK/NA	.440	.513	UNK/NA	0.99	1.44	S	145
.44 Evans Long/.440-40 Straight	B	.419	.434	UNK/NA	.449	.509	UNK/NA	1.54	2.00	L	146
.44 Henry Center Fire Flat	B	.423	.443	UNK/NA	.445	.523	UNK/NA	0.88	1.36	S	146
.44 Game Getter/.44-40 Marlin/.44 Colt Lightning	A	.427	.443	.458	.471	.520	.065	1.31	Varies	L	147
.44-40 Extra Long	A	.428	.442	.463	.468	.515	UNK/NA	1.58	1.96	S	147
.44 Long Center Fire (Ballard)*	B	.439	.440	UNK/NA	.441	.506	UNK/NA	1.09	1.65	S	147
.44 Extra Long Center Fire (Ballard)*	B	.439	.441	UNK/NA	.441	.506	UNK/NA	1.63	2.10	S	148
.44 Wesson Extra Long*	B	.440	.441	UNK/NA	.441	.510	UNK/NA	1.63	2.19	S	148
.44-90 Rem. Special (Necked)	A	.442	.466	.504	.520	.628	.075	2.44	3.08	L	148
.44-95/.44-100 Peabody "What Cheer"	A	.443	.465	.550	.580	.670	UNK/NA	2.31	3.32	B-1	149
.44-70 Maynard (1882)	B	.445	.466	UNK/NA	.499	.601	UNK/NA	2.21	2.87	B-1	149
.44-75 Ballard Everlasting	B	.445	.487	UNK/NA	.497	.603	UNK/NA	2.50	3.00	B-2	150
.44-100 Ballard	B	.445	.485	UNK/NA	.498	.605	.080	2.81	3.25	L	150
.44-100 Wesson	B	.445	UNK/NA	UNK/NA	.515-.520	.605-.610	UNK/NA	3.38	3.85	L	151
.44-77 Sharps & Remington	A	.446	.467	.502	.516	.625	UNK/NA	2.25	3.05	L-B1	151
.44-90 Sharps (Necked)	A	.446	.468	.504	.517	.625	.065	2.63	3.30	B-1	152
.44-60 Sharps & Remington (Necked)	A	.447	.464	.502	.515	.630	UNK/NA	1.88	2.55	L-B1	152
.45-50 Peabody (Sporting)	A	.454	.478	.508	.516	.634	2.08	2.08	2.08	UNK/NA	152
.44-60 Winchester/ Peabody "Creedmoor"	A	.447	.464	.502	.518	.628	UNK/NA	1.89	2.56	B-1	153
.45-60 Winchester	B	.454	.479	UNK/NA	.508	.629	UNK/NA	1.89	2.15(?)	L	153
.45-75 Winchester (Centennial)	A	.454	.478	.547	.559	.616	UNK/NA	1.89	2.25	L	154
.45-100 Ballard	B	.454	.487	UNK/NA	.498	.597	UNK/NA	2.81	3.25	L	154
.45-70 Van Choate	B	.457	UNK/NA	Same as 45-70, see chapter 2	UNK/NA	UNK/NA	UNK/NA	2.25	2.91	L	155
.45-75/.45-70 Sharps 2¹/₁₀-inch (Straight)	B	.457	UNK/NA	Same as 45-70, see chapter 2	UNK/NA	UNK/NA	UNK/NA	2.10	2.90	L	155
.45-82/.45-85/.45-90 Winchester & .45-90 Winchester High Velocity	B	.457	.477	UNK/NA	.501	.597	.065	2.40	2.88	L	156

Dimensional Data

Cartridge	Case	Bullet Dia.	Neck Dia.	Shoulder Dia.	Base Dia.	Rim Dia.	Rim Thick.	Case Length	Ctge. Length	Primer	Page
.45-90/.45-100/.45-110 Sharps (2⁴/₁₀, 2⁶/₁₀, 2¾, 2⁷/₈-inch) Straight	B	.458	.489	.500	.597	.065	2.40, 2.60, 2.75, 2.87	2.85, 3.00	18-20	B-1	156
.45-120/.45-125 (3¼-inch) Sharps	B	.458	.490	UNK/NA	.506	.597	.065	3.25	4.16	L	157
.50-90/.50-100/.50-110 Sharps	B	.509	.528	UNK/NA	.565	.663	.060	2.50	3.20	L	157
.50-140 (3¼") Sharps & Winchester	B	.509/ .512	.528	UNK/NA	.565	.665	.060	3.25	3.94	L	158
.50-115 Bullard	G	.512	.547	.577	.585	.619	UNK/NA	2.19	2.56	L	158
.50-100/50-105/.50-110 Winchester/.50-110 Winchester High Velocity	B	.512	.534	UNK/NA	.551	.607	.063	2.40	2.75	L	159
.50-50 Maynard (1882)	B	.513	.535	UNK/NA	.563	.661	UNK/NA	1.37	1.91	L	159
.50-95 Winchester/Win. Express	A	.513	.533	.553	.562	.627	UNK/NA	1.94	2.26	L	160
.50 U.S. Carbine	B	.515	.535	UNK/NA	.560	.660	UNK/NA	UNK/NA	UNK/NA	B-1	160
.58 Carbine (Berdan)	B	.589	.625	UNK/NA	.640	.740	UNK/NA	UNK/NA	UNK/NA	B-2	161
.58 U.S. Musket (Berdan)	B	.589	.625	UNK/NA	.646	.740	.062	1.75	2.15	B-1	161

Case Type: A = Rimmed, bottleneck. B = Rimmed, straight. C = Rimless, bottleneck. D = Rimless, straight. E = Belted, bottleneck. F = Belted, straight. G = Semi-rimmed, bottleneck. H = Semi-rimmed, straight. I = Rebated, bottleneck. J = Rebated, straight. K = Rebated, belted bottleneck. L = Rebated, belted straight.

Primer Type: S = Small rifle (.175"). SP = Small pistol (.175"). L = Large rifle (.210"). LP = Large pistol (.210"). 50 BMG = CCI-35/VihtaVuori-110/RWS-8212. B-1 = Berdan #1. B-2 = Berdan #2.

Other codes: V = OAL depends upon bullet used. V = Rifling twist varies, depending upon bullet and application. Belt/Rim Diameter. Unless otherwise noted, all dimensions in inches. UNK/NA = Unknown/Not Applicable

* Cartridges so marked used an outside lubricated bullet when originally introduced, and this was of a diameter about the same as the neck or shell mouth. Later, inside lubricated loadings used a much smaller diameter bullet than listed, usually with a long, hollow base. Before the recent advent of effective wax-type lubricants, outside lubricated bullets were never very popular or effective. The inside lubricated hollow-base bullets were cleaner to handle and use and the hollow base was intended to expand the bullet to fit the larger barrel. This never worked very well and accuracy suffered.

** Original 22-10-45 Maynard case length was 1.25".

*** This is a blackpowder primer smaller than the small rifle or pistol size. It has not been made for many years.

Note on blackpowder primers: Not all companies used the same primer type or size in the same cartridge or length case. For example, the 45-70 or its equivalent was usually loaded with the large rifle size primer. However, the Marlin version had the small rifle size and Sharps Co. ammunition had Berdan primers. Primer type and size listed is what appears to have been the most general size and type used. Unless otherwise noted, all dimensions are in inches. So-called 44-caliber blackpowder rifles had groove diameters varying from about .446-inch to about .460-inch. Most use bullets of about .448-inch to .452-inch diameter.

Wildcat Cartridges
(Rifle & Handgun)

Wildcat cartridges have been around for a long time, at least 100 years. Originally, wildcats were developed by some gunsmith or individual experimenter attempting to improve on the ballistics of a commercial cartridge, in order to fulfill a personal or special requirement, and possibly to increase the effective range for varmint shooting or the knockdown power on big game. I do not know who coined the term "wildcat" to describe these efforts, but, for our purposes, we will define wildcat cartridges as cartridge designs and loads not available from major manufacturers as over-the-counter ammunition, or cartridges not generally available even in custom loadings. To shoot wildcat cartridges, you have to load these yourself or contract that loading with a custom handloader or ammunition producer.

A great proliferation of wildcat cartridge designs has occurred in the past 30 years or so, some of those quite good and some not. In some instances, the wildcat filled, or was perceived to fill, some niche not accommodated by commercially available ammunition. Good examples include the .35 Whelen and the .45 Alaskan. The former lingered in wildcat limbo for a generation before being commercially adopted. The latter, though certainly useful, will likely never achieve commercialization, chiefly because the only rifle appropriate for it was long ago discontinued (as an aside, Ruger offered its short-barreled Super Redhawk Alaskan in .45 Alaskan for a while, but the 2012 website no longer shows this revolver offered in this cartridge). In other instances, the only basis for a wildcat was to offer ballistics previously unavailable in a certain type of firearm, such as the entire genre of current Thompson/Center custom chamberings. Benchresters have long experimented with wildcats, creating designs in which the only criterion was potential inherent accuracy. These wildcats are built to precisely fit a single firearm and, though these are nominally of the same specifications, cannot be interchanged in other so-chambered firearms with impunity.

Several new entries describe recent developments, while others describe Australian wildcats from the post-World War II era that are almost unknown in the United States. Still others describe wildcats of historical importance that have not previously appeared here. Some older wildcats of historical or developmental interest are retained because many younger or new shooters do not know that these exist. Such ignorance is probably one reason for the development of wildcats that are just a variation on a theme and do not offer anything new.

It is quite impossible to include every known wildcat cartridge, because so many exist. Previous editions claimed the number to be in excess of 300. Your current editor suspects the number is now well into the thousands, which seems to be substantiated by Dave Kiff of Pacific Precision reamer manufacturing company, who holds drawings for more than 6,000 distinctly named wildcats!

Wildcat cartridges tend to be regional in nature—what is popular in one area may be completely unknown in the rest of the country—so some viable numbers will never find representation in these pages. Even those wildcats that have been written up and published in gun magazines may have only a limited following. Probably the best indicator of the popularity of a cartridge is the number of loading die sets sold in that particular type. RCBS in Oroville, California, is the world's largest manufacturer of wildcat loading and case-forming dies. They make up special-order die sets to customer specifications at relatively modest prices. Quite a few wildcat cartridges have retained sufficient popularity over the years to warrant RCBS carrying those as standard stocked items. Less popular numbers are available on special order, subject to minor delays in delivery.

For many years, the trend in wildcat cartridge development has been toward increased case capacity and higher velocity. Currently, wildcat cartridge design and chambering simply for the sake of improved performance has declined from enthusiastic to almost nonexistent. One explanation for this is a maturity among shooters. We have grown into the realization that there really are no magic cartridges. Within safe pressure parameters, no wildcat chambering in any standard case chambered in any standard gun is going to deliver ballistics significantly different from what is already available in commercial form. Of course, some will disagree, and one must admit that exceptions always exist. However, it is safe to say that the vast majority of recent wildcatting has been directed toward filling target-shooting and gun-type chambering niches, e.g., the aforementioned Thompson/Center chamberings.

Wildcat cartridges are made in a number of ways, from the simple to the more complex. Wildcats can be grouped into basic categories: those with increased case capacity, created by modifying an existing cartridge; those with unusual case capacity for bore diameter, made by necking up or down a case that is larger or smaller than any common commercial example; those with unusual bullet sizes, created by necking an existing case to accept a different size bullet; and those with unusually close cartridge-to-chamber tolerances, building the rifle and loading dies to match the custom handloaded ammunition. Most recently, we have seen entire new lines of unusually short cases, based upon an unusually large diameter case, which, for any given capacity, provides a shorter cartridge and powder column, and possibly superior accuracy.

Let us look at some examples. A very early wildcat became the .22 Hornet. In this instance, no change in the case was required, since the cartridge was based on the .22 WCF blackpowder cartridge and simply loaded with smokeless powder and jacketed 45-grain bullets designed for the 5.5mm Velo Dog revolver cartridge. Early wildcats were rather simple and are good examples of simply necking a standard commercial cartridge case either up or down. The .35 Whelen is an example of the former, the .25-06 the latter, both being based on the standard .30-06 case. Improved cartridges are examples of increasing performance in the original case in an uncomplicated manner. Here, the standard cartridge is fired in the Improved chamber, from which it emerges with less body taper and a sharper shoulder. This increases powder capacity and general reloading of the Improved case provides improved performance over the standard-case load. The Ackley Improved .250 Savage and .257 Roberts chamberings, along with the various improved versions of the .300 H&H Magnum, are good examples of improved wildcats that result in a noticeable, but still modest, ballistic enhancement over the original cartridge. The same cannot be said of some of the others.

One advantage of Improved chambers is that these will also chamber and fire factory cartridges designed for the original chambering. This is very handy if you happen to run out of Improved reloads in some place far from home. This practice will, of course, result in a slight velocity reduction. Another potentially significant advantage, such as in the .35 Whelen, is improved headspace control.

Several wildcat cartridges are rather complicated to make. These can require extensive reforming and trimming, lathe-turning of the rim or neck, and even swaging a belt on the base of the case. Such cartridges are, generally, impractical for the average shooter. If a wildcat is to achieve any degree of popularity, cases must be relatively simple and easy to form, otherwise its use will be confined to a handful of serious tinkerers—something to keep in mind, if you happen to be working on a wildcat project you hope will one day become a commercial success.

Some readers might think that someone who develops a popular wildcat eventually adopted by one of the big commercial ammunition companies will make a lot of money. Not true. He will be lucky if he even gets credit as the originator. No major company is going to adopt a wildcat cartridge until it has a long-term, proven record. By that time, it will have been around so long it will fall into the category of general public knowledge, and no one will have any claim to it. It is also futile to patent a cartridge design, because any slight variation becomes a new cartridge. I mention this because occasionally we hear from someone who thinks developing a "new" cartridge is the road to fame and fortune.

A good number of commercial cartridges originated as wildcats. Some prime examples are: .17 Remington, .22 Hornet, .22-250 Remington, .243 Winchester, .244 Remington, .257 Roberts, .25-06 Remington, .280 Remington, 7mm-08 Remington, 7-30 Waters, and the .35 Whelen. Moreover, a large number of commercial cartridges are simply variations of what were originally wildcats themselves. These include practically all of the American 7mm and .30-caliber factory magnum cartridges. Remington has been the leader in adopting wildcat designs, and this has been very beneficial to the shooting sports. The .300 Whisper / AAC Blackout is a perfect example.

Working with wildcat cartridges is very instructive. Those of us who have done so have learned a great deal about the relationship between case size and configuration, bore diameter, and powder combustion. One of the areas that has provided some real surprises is in working with short rifle cartridges (case lengths of around 1½ inches). This is a trend begun by the Germans, during World War II, with the 7.92x33mm assault rifle cartridge, which uses a 1.3-inch long case. The Russians recognized a good idea when they saw one and so developed the 7.62x39mm (M43) cartridge, with a case 1.52 inches long.

As a group, wildcatters tend to be advanced handloaders and true devotees of the shooting sports. Wildcat rifles and cartridges are also a good topic of conversation around the hunting campfire, and, if you happen to have a rifle so chambered, it sort of sets you apart as someone who is at least a little above average in gun knowledge. However, one should never enter lightly into the wildcat arena, because this usually entails a custom-built rifle, plus the investment in forming and loading dies. Rifles chambered for wildcat cartridges are much more difficult to trade or sell in the event you decide that what you have is not exactly what you want. Nevertheless, individuals who have developed wildcat cartridges have spurred major advances to our knowledge of internal ballistics and have spawned a number of very fine cartridges that eventually entered the commercial line. Large companies such as Federal, Remington, and Winchester are, by nature, rather conservative and disinclined to market something that will not sell. It is in the area of innovation that the wildcatters make their major contributions, and we have not seen the end yet. No telling what great ideas will come to fruition over the next decade or so.

— *F.C.B., with additional text by Stan Skinner*

Pocket Manual for Shooters and Reloaders by Parker O. Ackley. Salt Lake City, 1964.
Practical Dope on the .22 by F.C. Ness. New York and Harrisburg, PA, 1947.
Small Game and Varmint Rifles by Henry F. Stebbins. New York City, 1950.
Twenty-Two Caliber Varmint Rifles by Charles S. Landis. Plantersville, SC, 1947.
Why Not Load Your Own? by Col. Townsend Whelen. Washington, DC, 1949 and later eds.
Wildcat Cartridges by Richard F. Simmons. New York City, 1947.
Woodchucks and Woodchuck Rifles by C.S. Landis. New York City, 1951. 10 Eichelberger Long Rifle

13th Edition Update

Readers should keep in mind that the proliferation of any of the wildcat cartridges listed in this chapter will vary considerably. While some may be in wide use all over the world, others are more regional in popularity. This is especially true in Indiana, where new hunting laws now permit the use of a rifle cartridge as long as the cartridge case is 1.8 inches or less in length and the caliber is .357 or larger. We are seeing a variety of wildcat cartridges designed to meet these specific regulations. While these cartridges may be appealing to other shooters and hunters for various reasons, there is little practicality in choosing one unless you intend to deer hunt with a rifle in Indiana.

Other wildcat cartridges may not really have a following at all. This could be because they are brand new or possibly because no one really knows about them. This does not mean they are a bad idea or that they have no practical application. They have been included in this edition, because I felt they had merit for one reason or the other.

Another thing to keep in mind is that most who design a wildcat cartridge become very emotionally attached to it, treating it almost like an offspring, as opposed to a material object. As a result, as far as the designer is concerned, their cartridge is the best in every way. Past editors and I have tried to limit the hype associated with the wildcat cartridges listed by offering the facts and ballistics. Sure, it's likely you will see some praise dished out here and there based on nothing more than the breadth of experience and personal bias of all of the editors of this book. Cartridges, after all, are something we feel passionate about or we would be reading something else.—*R.A.M.*

It may seem surprising, but we did select a few of the wildcat cartridges from this chapter for inclusion in the CD paired with this book. But there were a handful that were so obscure, had been made in such limited quantities, or that had, say, such a unique facet to them that components were nearly impossible to find, that their removal from the paper pages here was at least somewhat warranted. Those removed and relocated to the CD include: R-2 Lovell; .220 Weatherby Rocket; .22 Newton; .30 American; ..333 OKH; .334 OKH; .475 A&M Magnum.—*J.L.S.P.*

.10 Eichelberger Long Rifle

Historical Notes: The .10 Eichelberger Long Rifle is the smallest wildcat cartridge known to exist at this time. Pioneering sub-caliber experimenter Bill Eichelberger created this wildcat, in 1999, by necking down .22 Long Rifle cases to accept a bullet measuring .103-inch. Over the years, Eichelberger crafted more than 10,000 cartridge cases for the .10 Eichelberger Long Rifle and its bigger siblings in .12-, .14-, and .17-caliber. As a rimfire cartridge, each .10 Eichelberger Long Rifle case, after forming, loading, and bullet seating, can be fired only one time.

General Comments: The .10 Eichelberger Long Rifle cartridge uses Winchester .22 Long Rifle brass as the parent case. Since this cartridge is a rimfire, careful and safe reloading practices are needed to remove the bullet from the internally primed .22 Long Rifle case. Using a series of case forming dies, the live (primed) brass is necked down to .10-caliber and given a 25-degree shoulder—resulting in a diminutive bottleneck shape. After many repetitions of necking down and annealing, the case is trimmed to the final overall length dimension. To avoid excess pressure, extreme care is appropriate in measuring the tiny powder charge. The cartridge works well with 21-inch barrels having a rifling twist of 1:7. Suitable actions to rebarrel and chamber for the .10 Eichelberger Long Rifle include modern .22 LR bolt-actions and single-shots, such as the Thompson/Center Contender and G2. SSK Industries (www.sskindustries.com) can supply Contender barrels and .10-caliber bullets for this cartridge on a special-order basis.

.10 Eichelberger LR Loading Data

Bullet (grains)	Powder	Grains	Velocity	Energy	Source/Comments
7.2	AA9	1.8	2160	74	Bill Eichelberger

.10 Eichelberger Pup

Historical Notes: In the diminutive world of experimenter Bill Eichelberger, no cartridge case seems too small to transform into a sub-caliber wildcat. The .10 Eichelberger Pup, built on the less common Cooper CCM brass around 1999, can drive .10-caliber bullets weighing 7.2 grains at velocities over 3600 fps. The .10 Eichelberger Pup is intended for small game at ranges approaching 75 to 100 yards. With quality barrels, bullets, and shooting techniques, it is capable of MOA or better performance.

General Comments: The .10 Eichelberger Pup uses .22 Cooper CCM brass as its parent case. The brass is necked down in a series of dies to accept .103-inch diameter bullets and given a 30-degree shoulder. After many repetitions of necking down and annealing, the case is trimmed to the final overall length dimension. The cartridge uses Federal No. 205 primers. To avoid excess pressure, extreme care is required in measuring the tiny powder charge. The cartridge works well with 21-inch barrels having a rifling twist of 1:7. Suitable actions for the .10 Eichelberger Pup include the Thompson/Center Contender and G2. SSK Industries (www.sskindustries.com) can supply Contender barrels and .10-caliber bullets for this cartridge on a special-order basis.

.10 Eichelberger Pup Loading Data

Bullet (grains)	Powder	Grains	Velocity	Energy	Source/Comments
7.2	AA9	3.5	3230	160	Bill Eichelberger
7.2	2400	3.9	3615	208	Bill Eichelberger
10	AA1680	3.9	3134	218	Bill Eichelberger

.10 Eichelberger Squirrel

Historical Notes: In a decades-long quest to explore sub-calibers in small cases, Bill Eichelberger found ways to transform brass cases most folks would consider small into tiny powerhouses. His pre-1999 era .10 Squirrel comes very close to breaking the 4000 fps threshold with 7.2-grain, .103-inch diameter bullets. The .10 Squirrel is the fastest .10-caliber cartridge created by Eichelberger. It is suitable for small game at ranges up to 100 yards. Eichelberger also designed .12-caliber and .14-caliber versions of this cartridge.

General Comments: The .10 Squirrel uses rimmed Remington .22 Hornet brass as its parent case. The brass is necked down in a series of steps to accept .103-inch diameter bullets and given a 30-degree shoulder. After many repetitions of necking down and annealing, the case is trimmed to the final overall length dimension. The cartridge uses Federal No. 205 primers. To avoid excess pressure, extreme care is required in measuring the tiny powder charge. The cartridge works well with 21-inch barrels having a rifling twist of 1:7. Suitable actions for the .10 Squirrel include the Thompson/Center Contender and G2. SSK Industries (www.sskindustries.com) can supply Contender barrels and 10-caliber bullets for this cartridge on a special-order basis.

.10 Squirrel Loading Data

Bullet (grains)	Powder	Grains	Velocity	Energy	Source/Comments
7.2	Win 748	6.5	3924	246	Bill Eichelberger
10	H380	6.4	3290	240	Bill Eichelberger

.12 Eichelberger LR

Historical Notes: In a 21-inch barrel, the .12 Eichelberger Long Rifle can zip a 10-grain .12-caliber bullet to over 2800 fps—blistering performance, compared to an ordinary .22 Long Rifle cartridge. Another of Bill Eichelberger's sub-caliber wildcat cartridges dating back to 1982, the .12 Eichelberger Long Rifle was designed for short- to mid-range small game and target shooting. Eichelberger also designed .10-caliber and .14-caliber versions of this cartridge.

General Comments: The .12 Eichelberger Long Rifle cartridge uses Winchester .22 Long Rifle brass as the parent case. Since this cartridge is a rimfire, careful and safe reloading practices are needed to remove the bullet from the internally primed .22 Long Rifle case. Using a series of case forming dies, the live (primed) brass is necked down to accept .123-inch diameter bullets and given a 25-degree shoulder, resulting in a diminutive bottleneck shape. After multiple cycles of necking down and annealing, the case is trimmed to the final overall length dimension. To avoid excess pressure, extreme care is appropriate in measuring the tiny powder charge. The cartridge works well with 22-inch barrels having a rifling twist of 1:5½. Suitable actions to rebarrel and chamber for the .12 Eichelberger Long Rifle include modern .22 LR bolt actions, and single shots such as the Thompson/Center Contender and G2. SSK Industries (www.sskindustries.com) can supply Contender barrels and .12-caliber bullets for this cartridge on a special-order basis.

.12 Eichelberger LR Loading Data

Bullet (grains)	Powder	Grains	Velocity	Energy	Source/Comments
10	Accurate Arms 9	2.6	2810	175	Bill Eichelberger

.12 Eichelberger Winchester Rimfire Magnum

Historical Notes: Strictly a one-shot proposition, the .12 Eichelberger WRM wildcat cartridge rockets an 11.5-grain, .123-inch diameter bullet to almost 3500 fps—stellar performance from a rimfire case. During testing, in 1982, of his family of wildcats based on rimfire cartridge cases, designer Bill Eichelberger necked down more than 10,000 rimfire cases (both Long Rifle and WRM), without one of the internally primed cases discharging. This cartridge is tailored for short- to mid-range varmint and informal target shooting. Eichelberger also designed a .14-caliber version of this cartridge.

General Comments: The .12 Eichelberger WRM cartridge uses Winchester .22 WRM brass as the parent case. Since this cartridge is a rimfire, careful and safe reloading practices are needed to remove the bullet from the internally primed case. Using a series of case forming dies, the live (primed) brass is necked down to accept .123-inch diameter bullets and given a 25-degree shoulder, resulting in a diminutive bottleneck shape. After multiple repetitions of necking down and annealing, the case is trimmed to the final overall length dimension. To avoid excess pressure, extreme care is appropriate in measuring the tiny powder charge. The cartridge works well with 21-inch barrels having a rifling twist of 1:5½. Suitable actions to rebarrel and chamber for the .12 Eichelberger WRM include modern .22 WRM bolt actions, and single-shots such as the Thompson/Center Contender and G2. SSK Industries (www.sskindustries.com) can supply Contender barrels and .12-caliber bullets for this cartridge on a special-order basis.

.12 Eichelberger Winchester Rimfire Magnum Loading Data

Bullet (grains)	Powder	Grains	Velocity	Energy	Source/Comments
7.2	Win 748	6.5	3924	246	Bill Eichelberger
10	H380	6.4	3290	240	Bill Eichelberger

.12 Cooper (CCM)

Historical Notes: The .12 Cooper, as designed by Bill Eichelberger, in 1996, is a rimmed, sub-caliber wildcat cartridge capable of driving 10-grain, .12-caliber bullets to velocities of almost 3800 fps. It is suitable for small-game hunting and target shooting.

General Comments: The .12 Cooper uses rimmed Cooper CCM brass as its parent case. The brass is necked down in a series of dies to accept .123-inch diameter bullets and given a 32-degree shoulder. After multiple repetitions of necking down and annealing, the case is trimmed to the final overall length dimension. The cartridge uses Federal No. 205 primers. To avoid excess pressure, extreme care is required in measuring the tiny powder charge. The cartridge works well with 15-inch barrels having a rifling twist of 1:5½. Suitable actions for the .12 Cooper include the Thompson/Center Contender and G2. SSK Industries (www.sskindustries.com) can supply Contender barrels and .12-caliber bullets for this cartridge on a special-order basis.

.12 Cooper (CCM) Loading Data

Bullet (grains)	Powder	Grains	Velocity	Energy	Source/Comments
10	Win 680	6.6	3770	315	Bill Eichelberger
11.5	Win 680	6.1	3500	312	Bill Eichelberger

.12 Eichelberger Carbine

Historical Notes: The original designers of the .30 Carbine cartridge would be amazed to learn sub-caliber experimenter Bill Eichelberger used their military brass to drive knitting needle-sized bullets to .220 Swift and higher velocities. Conceived in 1997, the .12 Eichelberger Carbine is the fastest wildcat .12-caliber cartridge known to exist. For small-game hunting and shooting, it can drive 10-grain bullets to almost 4400 fps. Eichelberger also designed a .14-caliber version of this cartridge.

General Comments: The .12 Eichelberger Carbine uses Winchester .30 Carbine brass as its parent case. The brass is necked down in a series of dies to accept .123-inch diameter bullets and given a 25-degree shoulder. After multiple repetitions of necking down and annealing, the case is trimmed to the final overall length dimension. The cartridge uses Federal No. 205 primers. To avoid excess pressure, extreme care is required in measuring the tiny powder charge. The cartridge works well with 15-inch barrels having a rifling twist of 1:5½. Suitable actions for the .12 Eichelberger Carbine include the Thompson/Center Contender and G2. SSK Industries (www.sskindustries.com) can supply Contender barrels and .12-caliber bullets for this cartridge on a special-order basis.

.12 Eichelberger Carbine Loading Data

Bullet (grains)	Powder	Grains	Velocity	Energy	Source/Comments
10	H335	13.8	4390	427	Bill Eichelberger
11.5	H335	13.5	4145	438	Bill Eichelberger

.14 Eichelberger Dart

Historical Notes: Essentially similar to its smaller .10- and 12-caliber siblings, the .14 Eichelberger Dart turns the .25 ACP pistol case, holding a precisely measured powder charge, into a velocity powerhouse for 10-grain and 13-grain bullets measuring .144-inch in diameter. About 1983, wildcatter Bill Eichelberger designed the .14 Eichelberger Dart to push these micro-sized bullets in the 2330 to 2960 fps range,, creating a sub-caliber cartridge for small game and paper punching.

General Comments: The .14 Eichelberger Dart uses Winchester .25 ACP brass as its parent case. The brass is necked down in a series of dies to accept .144-inch diameter bullets and given a 30-degree shoulder. After several repetitions of necking down and annealing, the case is trimmed to the final overall length dimension. The cartridge uses Federal No. 205 primers. To avoid excess pressure, extreme care is required in measuring the tiny powder charge. The cartridge works well with 15-inch barrels having a rifling twist of 1:9. Suitable actions for the .14 Eichelberger Dart include the Thompson/Center Contender and G2. SSK Industries (www.sskindustries.com) can supply Contender barrels and .14-caliber bullets for this cartridge on a special-order basis.

.14 Eichelberger Dart

Bullet (grains)	Powder	Grains	Velocity	Energy	Source/Comments
10	Accurate Arms 9	3.5	2967	195	Bill Eichelberger
12.7	H110	3.2	2614	192	Bill Eichelberger
13	H110	3.3	2692	209	Bill Eichelberger

.14 Eichelberger Bee

Historical Notes: The .218 Bee cartridge, introduced by Winchester, in 1938, never achieved great popularity, even though it offered greater case capacity than the contemporary .22 Hornet round. In 1980, Bill Eichelberger exploited the case capacity of the .218 Bee, when he modified the brass to accept .144-inch diameter bullets in a cartridge named the .13 Eichelberger Bee. It is capable of driving 15-grain bullets about 150 fps faster than Eichelberger's Hornet-based wildcat, and can speed the heavier 18-grain bullets to more than 3600 fps. The .14 Eichelberger Bee fits into the small-game and target-shooting niches and falls within the 100-yard limitation of the sub-caliber wildcats.

General Comments: The .14 Eichelberger Bee uses .218 Bee brass as the parent case. The brass is necked down in a series of bushings to accept .144-inch diameter bullets and given a 30-degree shoulder. After several cycles of necking down and annealing, the case is trimmed to the final overall length dimension. The cartridge uses Remington No, 7½ primers. To avoid excess pressure, extreme care is required in measuring the tiny powder charge. The cartridge works well with 21-inch barrels having a rifling twist of 1:10. Suitable actions for the .14 Eichelberger Bee include the Thompson/Center Contender and G2. SSK Industries (www.sskindustries.com) can supply Contender barrels and .14-caliber bullets for this cartridge on a special-order basis.

.14 Eichelberger Bee Loading Data

Bullet (grains)	Powder	Grains	Velocity	Energy	Source/Comments
13	H335	14.6	4124	490	Bill Eichelberger
15	Accurate Arms 2460	14.6	3910	509	Bill Eichelberger
18	Accurate Arms 2495	14.2	3634	527	Bill Eichelberger

.14 Cooper (CCM)

Historical Notes: The .14 Cooper, as designed by Bill Eichelberger, in 1993, is a rimmed, sub-caliber wildcat cartridge capable of driving 10-grain, .14-caliber bullets to velocities of almost 3900 fps. It is suitable for small-game hunting and target shooting.

General Comments: The .14 Cooper uses rimmed Cooper CCM brass as its parent case. The brass is necked-down in a series of dies to accept .144-inch diameter bullets, and given a 32-degree shoulder. After several repetitions of necking-down and annealing, the case is trimmed to the final overall length dimension. To avoid excess pressure, extreme care is required in measuring the tiny powder charge. The cartridge works well with 21-inch barrels having a rifling twist of 1:8¾. Suitable actions for the .14 Cooper include the Thompson/Center Contender and G2. SSK Industries (www.sskindustries.com) can supply Contender barrels and .14-caliber bullets for this cartridge on a special-order basis.

.14 Cooper (CCM) Loading Data

Bullet (grains)	Powder	Grains	Velocity	Energy	Source/Comments
10	H110	7.4	3895	336	Bill Eichelberger
12	H110	7.1	3491	343	Bill Eichelberger
13	H110	7.0	3443	342	Bill Eichelberger
15	H110	7.5	3487	404	Bill Eichelberger

.14 Walker Hornet

Historical Notes: As designed by David Walker, the .14 Walker Hornet combines a straight body, sharp shoulder angle, and long neck to drive 10-grain bullets to almost 4200 fps. It was one of the first .14-caliber wildcats and served as the basis for the .14 Eichelberger Hornet, which achieves greater case volume and resulting higher velocities. Like all the .14-caliber wildcats, the .14 Walker Hornet is a short-range, small-game cartridge.

General Comments: The .14 Walker Hornet uses Remington .22 Hornet brass as its parent case. The brass is necked down in a series of dies to accept .144-inch diameter bullets and given a 30-degree shoulder. After several cycles of necking down and annealing, the case is trimmed to the final overall length dimension. The cartridge uses Remington No. 7½ primers. To avoid excess pressure, extreme care is required in measuring the tiny powder charge. The cartridge works well with 21-inch barrels having a rifling twist of 1:8¾. Suitable actions for the .14 Walker Hornet include the Thompson/Center Contender and G2. SSK Industries (www.sskindustries.com) can supply Contender barrels and .14-caliber bullets for this cartridge on a special-order basis.

.14 Walker Hornet Loading Data

Bullet (grains)	Powder	Grains	Velocity	Energy	Source/Comments
10	Accurate Arms	10.3	4198	391	Bill Eichelberger
13	Accurate Arms	9.9	3757	407	Bill Eichelberger
15	Win 748	11.2	3737	469	Bill Eichelberger

.14 Jet Junior

Historical Notes: The almost forgotten, 1961-vintage .22 Remington Jet cartridge inspired the .14 Jet Junior. Originally intended as a small-game hunting cartridge, the .22 Remington Jet had a long shoulder tapering gently from case body to the neck. It originally pushed a 40-grain bullet to about 2460 fps and was a solid, but not spectacular, cartridge. Sometime before 1998, the late Bud Pylinski transformed it into the .14 Jet Junior, which sends 10-grain bullets screaming downrange at almost twice the velocity of the .22 Remington Jet—4570 fps! In addition, the .14 Jet Junior can handle relatively heavy (for a .14-caliber) bullets weighing 18 grains. Across the full range of bullets, though, the .14 Jet Junior is best suited for target shooting and small game at ranges up to 100 yards.

General Comments: The .14 Jet Junior uses .22 Remington Jet brass as the parent case. The brass is necked down in a series of bushings to accept .144-inch diameter bullets, and given a 10-degree shoulder. After several repetitions of necking down and annealing, the case is trimmed to the final overall length dimension. The cartridge uses Remington No. 7½ primers. To avoid excess pressure, extreme care is required in measuring the tiny powder charge. The cartridge works well with 21-inch barrels having a rifling twist of 1:8¾. Suitable actions for the .14 Jet Junior include the Thompson/Center Contender and G2. SSK Industries (www.sskindustries.com) can supply Contender barrels and .14-caliber bullets for this cartridge on a special-order basis.

.14 Jet Junior Loading Data

Bullet (grains)	Powder	Grains	Velocity	Energy	Source/Comments
10	Win 748	14.8	4570	463	Bill Eichelberger
13	Win 748	13.8	4087	482	Bill Eichelberger
15	Win 748	14.3	3925	513	Bill Eichelberger
18	H380	13.3	3479	483	Bill Eichelberger

.14-222

Historical Notes: In the decade following World War II, there was considerable interest and experimentation with sub-caliber cartridges of .14- and even .12-caliber. Although interest subsided, it never completely died out, and a small but persistent group continued to work with the .14-caliber. The .14-222 is among these cartridges. It was originated by Helmut W. Sakschek, about 1985. It is based on the .222 Remington case necked down to .14-caliber. Information covering the cartridge was published in the 1988 issue (20th Edition) of Guns Illustrated (DBI Books, Inc., edited by Harold A. Murtz). Mild report and practically zero recoil are characteristics of these small-caliber rifles. With initial velocities of over 4000 fps, these are quite deadly on smaller species of vermin.

General Comments: An 11-grain bullet starting out at 4465 fps develops 505 ft-lbs of energy, which doesn't sound very impressive. However, anything moving at such velocity imparts a sizable portion of that velocity to the molecular structure of whatever it impacts, with devastating results. On the other hand, once remaining velocity drops below about 3500 fps, the effectiveness of these small, lightweight bullets diminishes rapidly, so these are not really all that good for long-range shooting. There are also many problems in working with such small projectiles. For example, metal fouling can be a serious problem, and such cartridges generally exhibit extreme sensitivity to charge variations. Wind drift with such light projectiles is also a frequent complaint. Some older .14-caliber cartridges used bullets of 20 to 25 grains, which are easier to handle and load but cannot be pushed at quite the velocity of the lighter projectiles. In any event, the sub-calibers are extremely interesting and represent an area that may see additional development. Bullet-making equipment is available through Corbin Inc. (www.corbins.com). The advent of cleaner powders, such as those now available from Ramshot, and moly-plated bullets (NECO process) can significantly mitigate bore fouling.

.14-222 Loading Data

Bullet (grains/type)	Powder	Grains	Velocity	Energy	Source/Comments
11.4 HP	IMR 4198	20.0	4200	445	NA
11.4 HP	IMR 3031	21.0	4465	505	NA

.14/222
Eichelberger Magnum

Historical Notes: The .14/222 Eichelberger Magnum is the big brother to the .14/221 Eichelberger. As conceived in 1978, Bill Eichelberger adapted the .222 Remington Magnum case, an unsuccessful contender for the small-bore U.S. M16 rifle, as the dynamo for this sub-caliber wildcat. The 47mm-long case allows for greater powder capacity, enabling heavier bullets to be driven over 3900 fps, and lighter ones to over 4300 fps. The .14/222 Eichelberger Magnum is the ultimate .14-caliber wildcat now available to the serious, curious, and dedicated shooter with considerable time and money to invest.

General Comments: The .14/222 Eichelberger uses .222 Remington Magnum brass as the parent case. The brass is necked down in a series of bushings to accept .144-inch diameter bullets and given a 23-degree shoulder with a short neck. After several repetitions of necking down and annealing, the case is trimmed to the final overall length dimension. The cartridge uses Remington No. 7½ primers. To avoid excess pressure, extreme care is required in measuring the tiny powder charge. The cartridge works well with 21-inch barrels having a rifling twist of 1:8¾. Suitable actions for the .14/222 Eichelberger Magnum include the Thompson/Center Contender and G2. SSK Industries (www.sskindustries.com) can supply Contender barrels and .14-caliber bullets for this cartridge on a special-order basis.

.14/222 Eichelberger Magnum Loading Data

Bullet (grains)	Powder	Grains	Velocity	Energy	Source/Comments
13	H380	24.5	4368	550	Bill Eichelberger
15	Win 780	24.3	4155	574	Bill Eichelberger
18	Accurate Arms 3100	24.4	3959	626	Bill Eichelberger

NEW
.17-32 Magnum

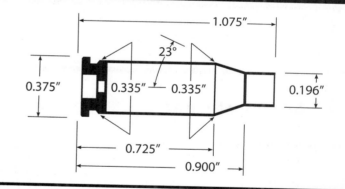

Historical Notes: The .17-32 Magnum was developed by Carroll Pilant, a long time employee of Sierra Bullets. Carroll was trying to figure out what to do with the more than 1,000 .32 H&R Magnum cases he had on hand, in 1994. Carroll says he woke up in the middle of the night with the idea to neck the case down to .17-caliber. The first rifle was built on a Ruger single shot No. 3 action and, according to Carroll, was very accurate.

General Comments: The .17-32 Magnum offers ballistics that fall between the rimfire .17 HMR and the newer Hornady .17 Hornet. From a practicality standpoint, it offers no advantage over either cartridge, unless you have a large store of .32 H&R Magnum brass on hand. For those looking for more performance, a wildcat similar to this cartridge but built on the newer .327 Federal Magnum case would offer more capacity and a much higher velocity. Either would be a good option in a rifle set up for use with a rimmed cartridge.—R.A.M.

.17 - 32 Magnum Loading Data

Bullet (grains/type)	Powder	Grains	Velocity	Energy	Source/Comments
25 Hornady HP	AA 1680	7.4	3250	418	Carroll Pilant
20 V-Max	N 130	7.4	3320	489	Carroll Pilant

.17 VHA
(Varmint Hunter Association)

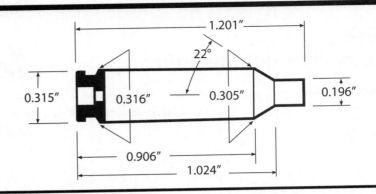

Historical Notes: The .17 VHA was developed by the John Anderson who is the editor of the Varmint Hunter Association's magazine. Anderson used the 4.6x40 HK submachine gun round as the parent case for this wildcat and simply necked it down to .17 caliber. By working with M.L. McPherson, a previous editor of Cartridges of the World (Editions 8 and 9), Anderson developed the load data for the .17 VHA. Ballistically, the .17 VHA offers similar velocities to the .17 Hornet, which is a rimmed cartridge. It is capable of pushing a 20-grain bullet to 3700 fps. According to John Anderson, because of the diminutive size of this case, it is necessary to use Small Pistol primers, as opposed to Small Rifle primers. Rifle primers are a bit potent for this small-sized case, and accuracy will be better with the pistol primers.

General Comments: Anderson's intent with the .17 VHA was to provide a low-recoil, small-caliber cartridge suitable for ground squirrels and prairie dogs. This cartridge offers some advantages over the rimfire .17 HMR and the .17 Hornet. For starters it is reloadable and the .17 HMR is not. It is also rimless, which means feeding is not an issue. The case walls on the .17 VHA are also thicker than those of the Hornet, which should extend case life. Reamers are available from Pacific Tool & Gauge (www.pacifictoolandgauge.com), and dies are available on a custom basis from Redding (www.redding-reloading.com).—R.A.M.

.17 VHA Loading Data

Bullet (grains/type)	Powder	Grains	Velocity	Energy	Source/Comments
20 V-Max	AA 1690	10.9	3562	563	John Anderson
20 V-Max	Lil' Gun	8.7	3577	568	John Anderson
25 V-Max	AA 1680	10.0	3263	590	John Anderson

.17 Ackley Hornet

Historical Notes: The .17 Ackley Hornet is simply the .22 Hornet Improved necked down to .17-caliber. It was originated by P.O. Ackley, in the early 1950s, and he describes this cartridge as one of the most balanced of the .17-caliber cartridges. Although small, it delivers ballistics equal to some of the larger .17-caliber cartridges. It is an effective 200-yard varmint cartridge and is quite accurate. It is normally used in single-shot rifles, although the small Sako bolt-action was favored by many, because it was made to handle rimmed cartridges such as the .22 Hornet or .218 Bee.

General Comments: The .17 Hornet is a good cartridge for use in settled areas where mild report and minimum ricochet are desirable characteristics. It is one of the most accurate of the .17-calibers. Its use should be confined to varmint shooting. The standard twist is 1:10, the same as most other .17-caliber rifles. Reportedly, IMR 4198 gives the most uniform results, although Ball BL-C2, as well as several of the newer powders, should work well. Berger Bullets (www.bergerbullets.com) has recently offered .17-caliber bullets of various styles and weights. This significantly improves the versatility of all .17-caliber cartridges.

.17 Ackley Hornet Loading Data

Bullet (grains/type)	Powder	Grains	Velocity	Energy	Source/Comments
25 HP	BL-C2	15.0	3040	510	NA
25 HP	IMR 4198	11.0	3300	600	Ackley
25 HP	IMR 4198	12.0	3585	710	Ackley
25 HP	H4227	11.5	3570	705	Ackley

.17 Ackley Improved Bee

Historical Notes: The .17 Ackley Bee is a step up from the .17 Hornet, as it is based on the .218 Improved Bee case, which has significantly larger powder capacity. This cartridge was developed by P.O. Ackley, back in the 1950s, and he considered it the ideal small case for a .17-caliber cartridge. There is relatively little gain in ballistic performance by using cartridge cases larger than the .17 Bee. In fact, cases of very much larger capacity often produce erratic results and poor accuracy.

General Comments: The .17 Bee, like the .17 Hornet, is chambered mostly in single-shot rifles, usually of the under-lever type. Bolt-actions are sometimes used, but will not always handle the rimmed case well, when feeding from the magazine. The small Sako bolt-action was favored, when available. Like most of the smaller .17-caliber cartridges, the .17 Bee is noted for its mild report and low recoil. This is a good 200- to 225-yard varmint cartridge for use in settled areas. P.O. Ackley recommended IMR 4198 or H4198 as the propellants that produce the most uniform results, and several new choices now available should work, as well. Bullets are available from Hornady (www.hornady.com). Berger Bullets (www.bergerbullets.com) has recently offered .17-caliber bullets of various styles and weights. This significantly improves the versatility of all .17-caliber cartridges.

.17 Ackley Bee Loading Data

Bullet (grains/type)	Powder	Grains	Velocity	Energy	Source/Comments
20	H4227	11.0	3845	655	Ackley
25 HP	BL-C2	16.5	3190	565	NA
25 HP	H335	17.0	3285	595	NA
25 HP	IMR 4198	13.0	3180	555	NA

.17 Mach IV
.17 Mach III

Historical Notes: The .17/221 was created by P.O. Ackley, who gave permission to Vern O'Brien, owner of O'Brien Rifle Company, of Las Vegas, Nevada, to rename it .17 Mach IV, when building custom rifles for it on the small Sako action. O'Brien also offered it in custom single-shot pistols built on the XP-100 action, in which case he called it the .17 Mach III, due to lower velocities in a short barrel. It succeeded on both counts, but could not compete against a factory chambering, i.e., the .17 Remington.

General Comments: This short cartridge can be used in short rifle actions. Efficiency is much better than in the various full-power .17s available. This diminutive chambering can produce more than 3850 fps with 25-grain bullets and is fully capable of delivering good varmint accuracy to about 250 yards, perhaps a bit further on a calm day. Muzzle blast is in a different league from larger .17s and the various high-performance .22s. While by no means "quiet," the .17 Mach IV generates so much less report, the difference is significant. Use of the faster powders listed, while necessitating a slight velocity sacrifice, results in much quieter loads. Since it uses significantly less powder than the .17 Remington, the 17 Mach IV generally produces much less barrel fouling, an important consideration in this diminutive bore size. Berger Bullets has recently offered .17-caliber bullets of various styles and weights. This significantly improves the versatility of all .17-caliber cartridges.

.17 Mach IV, .17 Mach III Loading Data

Bullet (grains/type)	Powder	Grains	Velocity	Energy	Source/Comments
25	2400	13.1	3600	720	Hornady
25	H4227	14.6	3700	760	Hornady

25	H4198	15.6	3700	760	Hornady
25	2015	18.5	3850	820	Accurate
25	2230	20.3	3861	825	Accurate
25	2460	20.5	3883	835	Accurate (Compressed)
25	2520	20.5	3768	785	Accurate (Compressed)

.17/222

Historical Notes: The .17/222 is simply the .222 Remington case necked-down to .17-caliber. There are several versions of this cartridge, but the one listed here is the most popular. The .17/222 dates back to about 1957, possibly earlier. Many shooters considered the .17/222 more accurate and less sensitive to load variations than the wildcat .17/223, which was the forerunner of the later .17 Remington. P.O. Ackley considered the .222 Remington case about maximum capacity for the .17-caliber and states in his book Handbook for Shooters and Reloaders that larger cases tend to be inflexible. Those who have experimented with larger cases have usually found him to be right.

General Comments: The .17/222 did not achieve great popularity, but was well liked by those who worked with it. Performance is practically the same as the .17 Remington, which has a larger case. Best accuracy is usually with IMR 4198 powder and the 25-grain bullet. Recommended twist is 1:10. Cases are simple and easy to form by necking-down .222 Remington cases with no other modification. There has been some renewed interest in this cartridge during the past couple years.

.19 Badger

Historical Notes: In one shooting day, in 2001, Jim Harrison, and Jim Leahy of James Calhoon Mfg., shot seven Montana badgers with a .19-caliber cartridge based on the .30 Carbine case. The results from this small-caliber (4.85mm) cartridge effectively ended the search for a reliable, 300-yard, flat-shooting varmint cartridge with low recoil, noise, fouling, and barrel heating characteristics, and its makers gave the cartridge its name, the .19 Badger. Harrison, the cartridge designer, previously tested many .19-caliber and parent case combinations, but found most exceeded the "too large and too fast" threshold.

General Comments: The .30 Carbine parent case, when necked to .19-caliber with a 30-degree shoulder, creates a short powder column with thick case walls at the case neck. Both features contribute to varmint-grade accuracy. Suitable for any firearm capable of accommodating the Hornet case, the .19 Badger works well in 24-inch barrels using a 1:13 twist. Incidentally, the .19 Badger holds about 25-percent more powder than the .19 Calhoon cartridge (which uses the .22 Hornet as its parent case). James Calhoon (www.jamescalhoon.com) offers rifles, barrel kits, loaded ammunition, reloading supplies, and components for the .19 Badger cartridge. Cooper Firearms (www.cooperfirearms.com) also chambers single-shot rifles for this cartridge on special order.

.19 Badger Loading Data and Factory Ballistics

Bullet (grains/type)	Powder	Grains	Velocity	Energy	Source/Comments
27 Calhoon DBL HP	Accurate Arms 1680	16.3	3775	854	James Calhoon
32 Calhoon DBL HP	FL		3550	895	James Calhoon

.19 Calhoon

Historical Notes: Around 1997, Jim Leahy (James Calhoon Mfg.) decided to adapt a military cartridge development, the 4.85mm (.19-caliber), to varmint cartridges. His decision reflected two consideration: (1) ballistic superiority over the .22-calibers, and (2) consistency and ease of loading over .17-calibers. One of his resulting .19-caliber cartridge offerings, the .19 Calhoon, is the most powerful proprietary cartridge based on the .22 Hornet case.

General Comments: Occasionally described as a Hornet on steroids, the .19 Calhoon adds an additional 100-yards range over the factory .22 Hornet and easily drives a 32-grain bullet as fast as the wildcat .17 Hornet cartridge can drive a 25-grain bullet. This performance translates into a significant range—best at 250 yards and effective to 350 yards—and killing power advantage. Using the parent Hornet case blown out and given a 30-degree shoulder, it can be chambered in any firearm suitable for the Hornet case, such as the CZ 527 and Ruger 77. The chambering works well with 24 inch barrels using a 1:13 twist. The .19 Calhoon delivers performance similar to the .17 Mach IV (.17-221) in a compact and reliable cartridge. James Calhoon (www.jamescalhoon.com) offers rifles, barrel kits, loaded ammunition, reloading supplies, and components. Cooper Firearms (www.cooperfirearms.com) also chambers single-shot rifles for this cartridge.

.19 Calhoon Loading Data and Factory Ballistics

Bullet (grains/type)	Powder	Grains	Velocity	Energy	Source/Comments
27 Calhoon DBL HP	Accurate Arms 1680	14.7	3610	781	James Calhoon
32 Calhoon DBL HP	FL		3400	821	James Calhoon
36 Calhoon DBL HP	Accurate Arms 2200	15.0	3165	800	James Calhoon
40 Calhoon DBL HP	Accurate Arms 2200	14.5	3060	831	James Calhoon

.19-223 Calhoon

Historical Notes: During 1970 NATO trials intended to identify a superior infantry cartridge, the 4.85mm Experimental provided exceptional performance to 500-plus meters, outperforming other competitors. Essentially a .222 Magnum case adapted to a .19-caliber bullet, the 4.85mm Experimental led to the creation of the .19-223 Calhoon by James Leahy, in 1997. Leahy's cartridge, however, used the readily available .223 Remington for its parent case. It offers less recoil and a flatter trajectory than the .223 Remington, and is a superb long-range, flat-shooting varmint cartridge with abundant terminal energy.

General Comments: This cartridge offers significant bullet weight versatility, ranging from 32 grains for pelt hunting to 44 grains for improved long-range shooting. The .19-223 Calhoon drives heavier (better ballistic coefficient) bullets than the .17 Remington at similar velocities. The .223 parent case is necked down to .19-caliber in one pass through a forming die, and the case shape is subsequently formed by fire-forming. With a 30-degree shoulder, the fire-formed case attains the powder capacity of the .222 Remington Magnum and delivers velocities normally associated with the .220 Swift. The .19-223 Calhoon can be accommodated in firearms suitable for the .223 Remington-length cases. It works well with 26-inch barrels using a 1:13 twist. James Calhoon Mfg. offers rifles, barrel kits, loaded ammunition, reloading supplies, and components. Cooper Firearms also chambers single-shot rifles for this cartridge.

.19-223 Calhoon Loading Data and Factory Ballistics

Bullet (grains/type)	Powder	Grains	Velocity	Energy	Source/Comments
32 Calhoon DBL HP	BLC-2	27.0	4025	1151	James Calhoon
36 Calhoon DBL HP	Accurate Arms 2015 BR	24.5	3840	1178	James Calhoon

40 Calhoon DBL HP	FL		3750	1248	James Calhoon
44 Calhoon DBL HP	VV N550	27.0	3670	1315	James Calhoon

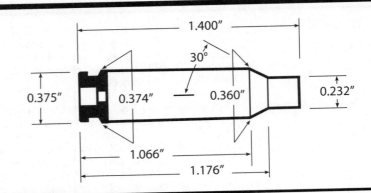

NEW
.20 Vartarg

Historical Notes: The .20 Vartarg (varmint/target) is a very efficient .20-caliber cartridge based on the .221 Fireball case. Like the PPC cartridges, it has a very good bore-to-powder capacity ratio and is popular with varmint hunters, because it uses very little power compared to other .20-caliber cartridges. It was developed by Todd Kindler, who is also responsible for the .20 Tactical wildcat cartridge. However, the .20 Vartarg is a bit easier to work with; just run a .221 Fireball case through a .20 Vartarg sizing die, load, and shoot.

General Comments: Of all the .20-caliber factory and wildcat cartridges, the .20 Vartarg probably has the best reputation for accuracy. It is a great cartridge for high-volume varmint shooting out to around 300 yards, due to its high velocity, accuracy, and minimal recoil, this last of which will allow the shooter to observe bullet impact through the rifle scope.—R.A.M.

.22 Vartarg Loading Data and Ballistics

Bullet (grains/type)	Powder	Grains	Velocity	Energy	Source/Comments
32 Sierra	X-Terminator	20.4	3556	898	Ramshot
40 V-Max	X-Terminator	18.8	3356	1000	Ramshot

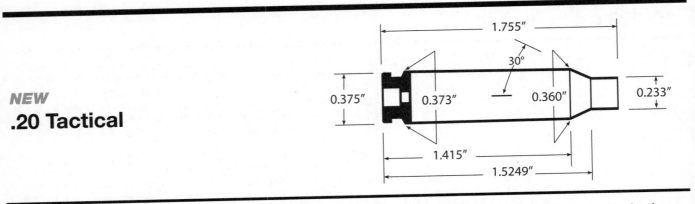

NEW
.20 Tactical

Historical Notes: This cartridge might be considered the forerunner to the .204 Ruger. It is a wildcat cartridge developed by Todd Kindler well before the .204 Ruger became a factory loaded cartridge. The .20 Tactical is based on the .223 Remington case, but is, of course, necked down to .20-caliber. It also has a steeper, 30-degree shoulder. Brass for the .20 Tactical is made by pushing a full-length and sized .223 Remington case into a .20 Tactical forming die and then into a .20 Tactical sizing die. For all practical ballistic purposes, the .20 Tactical is identical to the .204 Ruger.

General Comments: The .20 Tactical does use a slightly shorter case than the .204 Ruger. This can be beneficial when working with certain long or heavy-for-caliber bullets, where maximum overall cartridge length might require they be seated into the case mouth past the ogive. This, of course, will depend on the configuration of the rifles chamber and magazine box, as well. Cooper and Dakota both offer .20 Tactical rifles, something that can also be built by any good custom gunsmith. Lapua is now offering .20 Tactical brass, which eliminates the need for forming cases with dies followed by fire forming in chambers. This cartridge has a reputation for fine accuracy, and it is surprising that it has not caught on faster with AR-15 shooters.—R.A.M.

.20 Tactical Loading Data and Ballistics

Bullet (grains/type)	Powder	Grains	Velocity	Energy	Source/Comments
33 V-Max	H 335	26.7	3917	1124	Hodgdon
36 Berger HP	H 4895	26.5C	3746	1121	Hodgdon

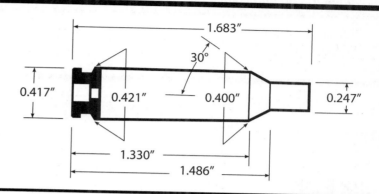

NEW
.20 PDK

Historical Notes: This cartridge was designed to shoot varmints and targets with 40-, 45-, and 50-grain .20-caliber bullets. It was conceptualized by Illinois wildcatter Roy Winnett, in collaboration with Dave Kiff at Pacific Tool & Gauge and benchrest shooter John Hutchins. The parent case for the .20 PDK (Prairie Dog Killer) is the 6.8 Remington SPC. The .20 PDK will work well in either a bolt rifle or AR-15.

General Comments: Both Roy Winnett and John Hutchins are avid long-range shooters and have conducted extensive testing with the .20 PDK on both paper and prairie dogs. They have found a 1:9 twist best for stabilization of 40- to 50-grain bullets. A re-barreled Savage rifle chambered for the .20 PDK was tested by this editor and was found to deliver both excellent accuracy and velocities on par with those shown below. Cartridge cases and handloading dies are available directly from Roy Winnett, 309-367-4867; www.pdk20.com.—R.A.M.

.20 PDK Loading Data

Bullet (grains/type)	Powder	Grains	Velocity	Energy	Source
40 V-Max	10 X	27.5	4077	1476	Roy Winnett
50 Berger	Benchmark	25.5	3603	1441	Roy Winnett

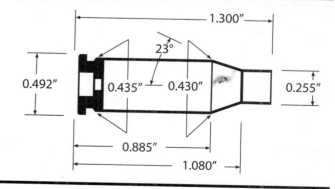

NEW
.22 Fawn

Historical Notes: Carroll Pilant is an employee of Sierra Bullets and has been the face of the company for many years. Carroll is an avid shooter and reloader. When Carroll's son Hunter was young, he wanted to design his own wildcat cartridge and was continually putting drawings in front of his father, who would repeatedly tell him, "It's already been done." That changed, in October of 1992, when Hunter showed Carroll a .41 Magnum case necked down to .22-caliber. Hunter had named it after his sister, Fawn. Carroll then worked with Clymer Reamers and Bullberry Barrel Works and had a Thompson/Center single-shot rifle built for his son for Christmas. The only change Carroll made to his son's drawing and design was to open the primer pocket to accept Large Rifle primers. Carroll later found out that, in 1969, Dennis Hrusosky had developed a similar cartridge with a 30-degree shoulder that he called the .224 Rimmed Critter Gitter.

General Comments: The .22 Fawn is capable of driving a 50-grain bullet faster than 3200 fps. This cartridge offers similar ballistics to the .222 Remington Magnum, the .22 PPC, and the .223 Remington, but in a much shorter configuration. The .22 Fawn is a rimmed cartridge that is well-suited to single-shot rifles and pistols like the Thompson/Center Contender. Aside from the rimmed case, the .22 Fawn offers little advantage over these other cartridges, unless you have a large stash of .41 Magnum cases lying around and nothing else to use them for. It is mostly unique in that it was conceived by a young man, as opposed to a seasoned wildcatter.—R.A.M.

.22 Fawn Loading Data

Bullet (grains/type)	Powder	Grains	Velocity	Energy	Source/Comments
50 Sierra SPT	AA 2015	22.0	3250	1172	Carroll Pilant

NEW

.22 PDK

Dimensions: 1.750", 30°, 0.417", 0.421", 0.400", 0.256", 1.330", 1.486"

Historical Notes: The intent of the .22 PDK was to offer a high-velocity .22-caliber cartridge that consumed less powder than a .22-250 or .220 Swift. It was conceptualized by Illinois wildcatter Roy Winnett, in collaboration with benchrest shooter John Hutchins. The parent case was the .20 PDK (Prairie Dog Killer), which is based on the 6.8 Remington SPC case. The .22 PDK will work well in either a bolt rifle or AR-15. It has a 30-degree shoulder and a case capacity of 36 grains of water.

General Comments: The .22 PDK may be especially appealing to AR-15 shooters looking for a higher velocity option to the .223 Remington for shooting targets or varmints at long range. This cartridge is also capable of driving premium, heavy-for-caliber bullets suitable for medium-sized game like deer to much higher velocities than the .223 Remington. While the cartridge does not offer a substantial advantage over the .22-250 in a bolt-action rifle, it is indeed a lightning rod in an AR-15. A twist rate of 1:9 or 1:10 is ideal for this cartridge. Cartridge cases are available from Silver State Armory, and handloading dies and cases are available directly from Roy Winnett, 309-367-4867; www.pdk20.com.—R.A.M.

.22 PDK Loading Data

Bullet (grains/type)	Powder	Grains	Velocity	Energy	Source/Comments
50 Nosler BT	H 4895	31.0	3880	1672	Roy Winnett
55 V-Max	W 748	31.5	3770	1735	Roy Winnett
60 Berger	AA 2230	31.0	3580	1707	Roy Winnett
65 JLK	H4895	31.0	3520	1788	Roy Winnett
80 JLK VLD	VV 540	29.5	3230	1852	Roy Winnett

.22 Taranah Hornet

Historical Notes: The Taranah Hornet was developed by Andy Montgomery, assistant technical editor of Guns and Game magazine, in Australia. An article on that cartridge appeared in issue No. 27, July-September 2000, of that magazine. The .22 Taranah Hornet is essentially a .22 K-Hornet shortened by .15-inch. The reason for the shorter length is to allow the long-for-weight 40-grain Nosler Ballistic Tip projectile to be used, without running into overall-length problems. The cartridge was specifically designed to operate through the ZKW 465 and CZ 527 Hornet detachable magazines. Montgomery reports velocities in excess of the standard Hornet, and only marginally behind the conventional K-Hornet. The original rifle was chambered by Sprinter Arms of South Australia, using one of its 1:10 twist barrels.

General Comments: The Taranah Hornet is an ideal small-game cartridge that utilizes ballistically efficient bullets to gain better down-range performance. It not only produces higher velocities than the original Hornet, but, when 40-grain Nosler Ballistic Tip bullets are used, it also shoots flatter. It is a very efficient cartridge, has a mild report, and is economical to shoot. Montgomery has found good case life and excellent accuracy from the cartridge. It would be suitable for most small game and varmints, and it extends the effective range of the standard Hornet a little. The cartridge can be fed through the magazine of popular bolt-action rifles.

.22 Taranah Hornet Loading Data

Bullet (grains/type)	Powder	Grains	Velocity	Energy	Source/Comments
40 Nosler BT	Win 680	11.5	2831	712	Andy Montgomery
40 Nosler BT	2400	10.5	2827	710	Andy Montgomery
50 Speer SP	2400	10.0	2489	688	Andy Montgomery
50 Sierra SP	Win 680	11.5	2571	734	Andy Montgomery

.22 K-Hornet

Historical Notes: Originated by Lysle Kilbourn, in 1940, this was one of the first of the so-called "Improved" cartridges. It is based on the fire-formed and blown-out .22 Hornet case, with a straight body, sharp shoulder, and short neck. There are other versions, but this is the most popular and is representative of the lot. It has been used for a good many years and is still popular in varmint-shooting circles. Extensive experience with this cartridge in the Thompson Contender shows substantial improvements over the .22 Hornet.

General Comments: The popularity of the .22 K-Hornet was based on increased performance, plus the fact that any regular factory-loaded ammunition could also be fired in the same chamber. In addition, the conversion is quite cheap, and any Hornet rifle can be re-chambered. Ammunition is no problem, because the round is based on easily obtainable factory ammunition. It brings the .22 Hornet into the same class as the .218 Bee, with the added advantage that the .22 Hornet was chambered in several good bolt-action rifles. It is suitable for the same range of varmints and small game as the .218 Bee. Those lucky enough to find an original Kimber rifle chambered for the .22 K-Hornet can pride themselves in owning a superb rifle. The very similar Harvey Kay-Chuck was developed by Jim Harvey, about 1956. In that round, loading length was kept short enough so that the ammunition would chamber in modified S&W K-22 revolvers.

.22 K-Hornet Loading Data

Bullet (grains/type)	Powder	Grains	Velocity	Energy	Source/Comments
45 SP	IMR 4227	12.5	2875	825	Ackley
45 SP	2400	11.5	2900	840	Ackley
45	IMR 4198	14.5	2800	780	Ackley
50 SP	2400	11.0	2700	810	Ackley

.218 Mashburn Bee

Historical Notes: The .218 Mashburn Bee is an Improved version of the factory .218 Bee. Cases are made by firing factory ammunition in the Mashburn chamber, so no special case-forming dies are required. The cartridge was the work of A.E. Mashburn, of the Mashburn Arms Co., in Oklahoma City, Oklahoma. As near as can be determined, the cartridge originated in or about 1940. The Improved case produced better ballistics than the original Bee and offered longer case life. There are other Improved versions of the .218 Bee, but all are rather similar. The Mashburn Bee will deliver about the same velocity with the 55-grain bullet as the factory Bee does with the 45-grain bullet.

General Comments: The Mashburn Bee was popular until the advent of the .222 Remington. It was, and still is, a very accurate varmint cartridge. The recommended powders for loading these small cartridges are similar to IMR 4198 and IMR 4227.

.218 Mashburn Bee Loading Data

Bullet (grains/type)	Powder	Grains	Velocity	Energy	Source/Comments
40 HP	IMR 4227	16.5	3300	960	NA
45 SP	IMR 4227	16.3	3319	1100	Ackley
50 SP	IMR 4198	17.3	3300	1210	Ackley

.22 Reed Express

Historical Notes: In 2004, Fred Zeglin and Ron Reed began working on a high-velocity .22-caliber pistol for varminting and self-defense. As the foundation for their idea, they selected the inexpensive CZ-52 pistol, a quality military pistol currently available from surplus firearm dealers and chambered in the 1930s-vintage 7.62x25 Tokarev cartridge. This cartridge was widely used by the former Soviet Union and its allies, before Soviet Bloc countries switched to the 9.x18 Makarov cartridge, after WWII. Zeglin and Reed necked the 7.62x25 round to .22-caliber and loaded it with bullets ranging from 30 to 50 grains to create a high-velocity round. Interestingly, the .22 Reed Express achieves velocities with 50-grain bullets that rival those of the FN 5.7x28 cartridge with 26-grain bullets.

General Comments: The .22 Reed uses 7.62x25 brass as the parent case. The brass is necked-down to accept .224-inch bullets and the shoulder angle changed. With heavier bullets, the powder charge must be reduced to allow the longer bullets to fit into the CZ-52 pistol magazine. Barrels in .22 Reed Express chambering are also available for the Thompson/Center Contender. Reed's Ammunition & Research (www.reedsammo.com) offers barrels, reloading components, and ammunition.

.22 Reed Express Loading Data

Bullet (grains/type)	Powder	Grains	Velocity	Energy	Source/Comments
30 Berger	H110	12.7	2782	515	Fred Zeglin
35 V-Max	H110	12.6	2721	575	Fred Zeglin
50	Accurate Arms 9	10.0	2401	639	Fred Zeglin

.22 Waldog

Historical Notes: The .22 Waldog was originated by Dan Dowling of Accuracy Gunsmithing, in Arvada, Colorado, in 1980. He named it after a friend, Waldo G. Woodside, thus the Waldog, or Waldo-G. The cartridge is made by running .220 Russian cases through a shortened .22-250 die and trimming the case to a length of 1.375 inches. It is, in effect, a shortened .22 PPC. The idea was to create a more efficient case than the .22 PPC by reducing volumetric capacity to approximately that of the .222 Remington. This cartridge was originally used exclusively in heavy benchrest rifles. Several 100-yard benchrest world records have been broken by the .22 Waldog.

General Comments: The .22 Waldog is another effort to develop a super-accurate benchrest cartridge. The current trend is toward smaller, more efficient cases, and the Waldog has proven to be a very accurate cartridge. Best accuracy has been obtained with 52-grain match bullets and 24 grains of H322 powder, but any powder that works well in the .222 Remington should give comparable results in the Waldog. Although not as widely used as the .22 PPC, the Waldog has found a significant following among benchrest shooters. It is reminiscent of the 308x1.5-inch necked down to .22-caliber, also known as the .22 Remington BR, as the two have similar case capacities. However, the .22 Remington BR case is larger in diameter and length is about .12-inch longer.

.219 Donaldson Wasp

Historical Notes:	This cartridge originated in 1937, shortly after Winchester introduced the .219 Zipper. It is made by shortening, re-necking, and blowing-out .219 Zipper cases. The Donaldson Wasp became the most popular version of such adaptations, and more or less the standard. Many benchrest matches have been won with the .219 Wasp, and it has a well-deserved reputation for excellent accuracy. It has been used mostly in custom-made single-shot rifles, because of the rimmed case.
General Comments:	The .219 Wasp is another .22 wildcat that achieved notable, continued popularity. This is one of the better wildcat numbers, but like most of the other offbeat .22s, it was overshadowed by the .222 Remington. The .219 Improved Zipper, developed by P.O. Ackley, in 1938, is a more practical cartridge, because it is made by simply fire-forming standard .219 Zipper cases in the Improved chamber. The Improved version offers velocities similar to the standard Wasp, but with significantly lower pressures. Cases for these wildcats can also be made from .25-35 and .30-30 cases. It was claimed, by some authorities, that breech pressures developed by popular loads in the Wasp ran as high as 55,000 to 60,000 psi, which, in a strong action, is of no consequence.

.219 Donaldson Wasp Loading Data

Bullet (grains/type)	Powder	Grains	Velocity	Energy	Source/Comments
45 SP	IMR 3031	30.0	3780	1425	Ackley
45 SP	H380	33.0	3510	1215	NA
50 SP	IMR 4064	32.0	3605	1440	Ackley
50 SP	H380	32.0	3370	1255	NA

.22 BR Remington

Historical Notes:	The .22 BR Remington is based on the .308x1.5-inch Barnes case necked down to .22-caliber and lengthened by .02-inch, with the shoulder angle increased to 30 degrees. It is difficult to determine who originated the .22 version of the necked-down 308x1½, because there are a number of versions dating back to about 1963. J. Stekl is credited with having developed the Remington rendition. In any event, Remington standardized the dimensions, in 1978, as its .22 BR. It is one of a series of BR cartridges, including the 6mm and 7mm, all based on the same case. The .22 BR is a factory wildcat, because loaded ammunition is not available. Cases must be made from special Remington or necked BR cases, which have a Small Rifle primer pocket, or from full-size Remington 6mm or 7mm BR cases. The .22 BR has won many honors in benchrest competition and has great accuracy potential.
General Comments:	The .22 BR is similar to the .22 PPC, but has a case of larger base diameter and slightly greater powder capacity with the same case length. Anything one can do, the other can duplicate. Both can push a 55-grain bullet at over 3000 fps and duplicate the performance of the .223 Remington. Both are extremely accurate and make excellent varmint cartridges, as well as competitive benchrest numbers.

.22 BR Remington Loading Data

Bullet (grains/type)	Powder	Grains	Velocity	Energy	Source/Comments
53 HP Hornady	2460	32.8	3653	1570	Accurate, 26-inch barrel
55 BT Nosler	2460	32.5	3605	1585	Accurate, 26-inch barrel
60 HP Hornady	2460	31.7	3455	1590	Accurate, 26-inch barrel

.224 Clark

Historical Notes: Every few years, someone will neck down the 6mm Remington case to .22-caliber, fire-form it to the Improved configuration, and proclaim it to be the greatest invention since the round wheel. Occasionally, one of those cartridge development "pioneers" will manage to sell his story to a young and innocent magazine editor, who is unaware that the idea is far from new. No one knows for certain who was first to try it, but the one who received the most attention was varmint shooter and gunsmith Kenneth Clark, of Madera, California. Back in 1962, he necked down the .257 Roberts case to .22-caliber, blew it out to less body taper and a 30-degree shoulder angle, and called it the .224 Clark. And, since the 6mm Remington case is nothing more than the .257 Roberts case necked down with a minor change made to its shoulder angle, the .22-6mm Remington Improved and the .224 Clark are performance peas of the same pod. An avid shooter of California ground squirrels at extreme ranges, Clark wanted something capable of bucking wind better than the .22-250 and .220 Swift did, so he talked friend Joyce Hornady into making .224-inch 80-grain bullets for his cartridge. That may be the only time in history a major company has made bullets specifically for a wildcat cartridge on a production basis. Kenneth Clark was also a deer hunter, so he designed an 85-grain bullet for his cartridge and made it in his shop. Like the Hornady 80-grain varmint bullet, it was a hollowpoint, but his early design was of double-jacket construction for expansion control.

General Comments: When building rifles for his cartridge, Clark used barrels with a rifling twist rate of 1:9, in order to stabilize the extremely long 80- and 85-grain bullets in flight. Since those bullets weren't as long as match bullets of the same weight now being made (Sierra 80-grain MatchKing being an example), anyone building a rifle in .224 Clark today would be wise to go with a twist rate of 1:8. Even after 6mm Remington cases became available, Clark stayed with Winchester .257 Roberts brass for forming his cartridge because, in his opinion, it handled higher pressures. Whether or not this is true today is debatable and, in reality, a moot argument, since .257 Roberts cases are as easy to come by as 6mm Remington cases.

.224 Clark Loading Data and Factory Ballistics

Bullet (grains/type)	Powder	Grains	Velocity	Energy	Source
80 Clark HP	H4831	50.0	3500	2174	Ken Clark
85 Clark HP	H870	59.0	3518	2333	Ken Clark

Warning: These powder charges are maximum and must be reduced by 10 percent for starting loads.

.224 Texas Trophy Hunter

Historical Notes: Every year, Texas hunters take an incredible number of whitetail deer, and more than a few take whitetails with hot .22s. The .224 Texas Trophy Hunter, conceived by gun writer Ralph Lermayer, in 1998, uses the greater capacity of the 6mm Remington case to deliver more power than the .22-250 and .220 Swift.

General Comments: Following extensive experiments with the .220 Swift, .22-250, and .240 Weatherby cases, Lermayer settled on the 6mm Remington case as the best balance of case taper, shoulder angle, length, and capacity. Necking the 6mm Remington case down to .224 (with the factory's 26-degree shoulder angle), the designer created a cartridge that would deliver heavier, well-constructed, 70- to 80-grain .224 bullets accurately at relatively high velocities. The 6mm case provides optimum capacity for the .224 bore, brass is readily available, and standard actions and magazines require no modification other than a new barrel. Proper rifling twist for the .224 Texas Trophy Hunter is 1:8 or 1:9. Bullet construction is the key to success; it takes a stout, thick jacket solid or bonded core bullet to hold up to the velocity potential. Stoutly constructed bullets can be driven in excess of 3500 fps. Dies are available from Redding (www.redding-reloading.com). Nosler recently endorsed its .22-caliber 60-grain Partition bullet for whitetail deer hunting.

.224 Texas Trophy Hunter Loading Data

Bullet (grains/type)	Powder	Grains	Velocity	Energy	Source/Comments
55 Trophy Bonded	H4831	46.5	3840	1800	Ralph Lermayer
60 Nosler Partition	H4831	46.0	3780	1903	Ralph Lermayer
75 Hornady A-Max	Win Mag Rifle	47.0	3780	2379	Ralph Lermayer
79 Lost River	VV N165	45.0	3520	2173	Ralph Lermayer

.220 Wotkyns-Wilson Arrow

Historical Notes: The .220 Wotkyns-Wilson Arrow was the work of Grosvenor Wotkyns and L.E. Wilson and is the .220 Swift with the shoulder angle increased from 21 degrees to 30 degrees. It dates back to the 1940s. Cases are made by reforming unfired .220 Swift cases in full-length sizing dies. Because of the longer neck, standard Swift ammunition will not fully enter the Arrow chamber and cases cannot be made by fire-forming.

General Comments: The .220 Wotkyns-Wilson Arrow represented an effort to remedy a problem by making a minor change in cartridge configuration. Factory Swift cases had the reputation of lengthening after only a few firings, thus requiring frequent trimming. Changing to a steeper shoulder angle improved headspacing and made for longer case life. The Arrow was a popular benchrest cartridge and a true long-range varmint number. It delivers ballistics comparable to the .220 Swift.

.220 Wotkyns-Wilson Arrow Loading Data

Bullet (grains/type)	Powder	Grains	Velocity	Energy	Source/Comments
45 SP	H450	47.0	3985	1580	NA
50 SP	H450	46.0	3850	1640	NA
50 SP	IMR 4064	40.0	3915	1695	NA
55 SP	H380	39.0	3510	1500	NA

.22 CHeetah

Historical Notes: The .22 CHeetah was developed by Jim Carmichael, Shooting Editor of Outdoor Life magazine, and Fred Huntington, of RCBS fame, thus the capital "C" and "H" for each of their surname initials. It appears to have originated in the late 1970s. The cartridge is essentially a full-length Remington .308 BR case—with the Small Rifle primer pocket—necked down to .22-caliber, but with the shoulder moved forward. What you end up with is a variation of the .308 Winchester necked down to .22, but using a special match case. This is not exactly new, because there are in existence several slightly different versions made by necking the .243 Winchester case down (such as the .243 Middlestead, which used a 30-degree shoulder angle), and these date back to the early 1960s. However, the .22 CHeetah is an original, with regard to the .308 BR case and its Small Rifle primer pocket.

General Comments: The major differences between the .22 CHeetah and its predecessors are the use of the lighter, more uniform BR case, blown-out 40-degree shoulder angle, and short neck. In other words, the case has been designed to benchrest specifications. It also has greater powder capacity than any of the older versions. There are actually two case types, the MKI, with the 40-degree shoulder angle, and the MKII, with the original 28-degree shoulder. The .22 CHeetah is somewhat more powerful than the .220 Swift, but ballistics were measured from a 27-inch barrel. The cartridge has proven to be superbly accurate and a very effective 300-yard varmint cartridge.

.22 CHeetah Loading Data (MKI)

Bullet (grains/type)	Powder	Grains	Velocity	Energy	Source/Comments
50 SP	IMR 4064	46.0	4285	2040	NA
52 HP	IMR 4064	44.0	4135	1970	NA
55 SP	IMR 4350	49.0	4090	1990	NA

.228 Ackley Magnum

Historical Notes: The .228 Ackley Magnum dates back to about 1938, and although it has been around for a number of years, it developed only a limited popularity. Like the .22 Newton, it was designed as a combination varmint and big-game cartridge. Ammunition is made by necking-down and shortening .30-06 or .308 Winchester cases. There are several versions of this cartridge, but Ackley's design is the most popular.

General Comments: Rifles for .228-inch diameter, heavy-jacketed bullets designed for big game have been used very successfully all over the world. Bullets of this type were made in weights from 70 to more than 100 grains by Fred Barnes, but are now difficult to obtain. Rifles in this class have proven rather conclusively that the difficulties encountered with the .220 Swift and other high-velocity .22s have been mostly a result of improper bullet design. Factory .22-caliber centerfire loads are all made for varmint shooting and do not hold together or penetrate deeply enough on big game—most of the time. Sometimes these do and the results are spectacular, but mostly these blow up on contact and inflict a massive, but not immediately fatal, wound. Consequently, hunting deer with any .22-caliber centerfire rifle is illegal in most states. Bear this matter of bullet construction in mind next time you get in an argument over the effectiveness of small-caliber rifles on big game.

.228 Ackley Magnum Loading Data

Bullet (grains/type)	Powder	Grains	Velocity	Energy	Source/Comments
70 SP	IMR 4350	46.0	3650	2070	Ackley
90 SP	IMR 4350	43.0	3480	2420	Ackley

6x45mm (6mm-223 Remington)

Historical Notes: The 6mm-223 Remington, also known as the 6x45mm, came into being in late 1965, shortly after Remington introduced the .223 Remington as a sporting round. Various experimenters built rifles for the cartridge (in order to take advantage of the reduced wind drift offered by the 6mm, as opposed to the original .22-caliber bullet), for benchrest or varmint shooting. Jim Stekl, then-manager of Remington's custom shop, set an IBS 200-yard Sporter aggregate record of .3069 MOA, in 1973, using the 6x45mm. For a time, some owners of AR-15 rifles rebarreled their rifles to this chambering for use in NRA National Match Course competition. However, the 6x45mm cannot compete successfully with the 7.62x51mm NATO (.308 Winchester) round at ranges beyond 300 yards. After its brief flurry as a benchrest and match cartridge, the 6x45mm has now been relegated to designation primarily as a varmint cartridge used by those who want more power than the .223 with the added advantage of being able to utilize inexpensive military cases. Reloading dies are available from RCBS, and chambering reamers from Clymer (www.clymertool.com).

General Comments: The 6x45mm is one of a series of 6mm benchrest cartridges based on necking up .223 Remington and .222 Remington Magnum cases. None have any great advantage over the other and all are capable of extremely fine accuracy. Probably the only advantage of the 6x45mm is that it is based on the 5.56mm (.223 Remington) military case, which assures a good supply of cases. On the other hand, its shorter case permits the use of bullets of up to 100 grains to be seated to an overall length that will feed through magazine rifles such as the Colt AR-15, Ruger Mini-14, or Remington 788. In power, the 6x45mm is between the old .25-35 and the .250 Savage, which would make it rather marginal as a deer cartridge, except under ideal conditions. It is, however, close to ideal as a varmint and small-game cartridge out to 300 yards. This cartridge has become very popular in the Thompson/Center Contender and Remington XP-100 handguns. Bob Milek, the late field editor of Guns & Ammo and Petersen's Hunting magazines, shot a custom XP-100 in 6x45mm for a number of years. Rifles chambered for cartridges in this group are pleasant to shoot, have a relatively low report, and are noted for long barrel life.

6x45mm (6mm-223 Remington) Loading Data

Bullet (grains/type)	Powder	Grains	Velocity	Energy	Source/Comments
70 HP	W748	27.5	2890	1295	NA
75 HP	H335	27.0	2900	1400	NA
80 HP	W748	27.0	2780	1370	NA

6mm Dasher

Historical Notes: Early in 1998, this cartridge, based upon the .22 Dasher, was announced in a Precision Shooting magazine article that was co-authored by Al Ashton and Dan Dowling. The .22 Dasher was developed as a means of approximating .22-250 ballistics in a shorter case, but using cases with the same base diameter. Thinner case walls and the modern Ackley case shape make it possible for the significantly shorter BR case to achieve that goal. This 6mm version is simply the .22-caliber Dasher necked up to accept 6mm bullets with no other changes.

General Comments: Lighter 6mm varminting bullets can come very close to matching the trajectory of best .22 Dasher loads; heavier 6mm varmint bullets can exhibit significantly less wind drift. This cartridge will push Nosler's excellent 55-grain BT 150 fps faster than the .22 Dasher will push the same weight bullet. Perhaps a more important advantage is that, since the 6mm version is much easier on the barrel, one can expect double the barrel life. Moreover, it is much harder to overheat the barrel during an extended shooting string. The latter fact is a significant consideration to all serious varmint hunters. Concerns over undue barrel heating prompt many varminters to carry several rifles, so they can switch between guns during any extended period of shooting. For this reason alone, the 6mm Dasher is a superior high-performance varminting choice. This cartridge, like the 6mm Norma BR, is finding application in 1,000-yard benchrest events, where it can excel on calm days.

6mm-250 (6mm International) Loading Data

Bullet (grains/type)	Powder	Grains	Velocity	Energy	Source/Comments
55 Nosler BT	H335	39.0	4000	1955	Al Aston (2.175-inch OAL)
70 Nosler BT	H335	36.8	3650	2070	Al Aston (2.175-inch OAL)

6mm-250 (6mm International) Walker Version

Historical Notes: Prior to World War II, the 6mm (.243-caliber) was nearly an exclusive British and European development, with some cartridges dating back to the early 1900s. Immediately after World War II, American wildcatters began to work with this caliber. The simple process of necking the .250 Savage case down to take .243 bullets probably occurred to several individuals, but was obscured by other 6mm developments. Several versions exist, and two of these have become popular with benchrest and match shooters. The Donaldson 6mm International was developed by Harvey Donaldson, of Fultonville, New York, the man known as the father of modern benchrest shooting. The Remington 6mm International originated with Mike Walker, of the Remington Arms Co.

General Comments: Cartridges of 6mm based on the .250 Savage case are all similar, but vary slightly in length and shoulder angle. Original design was the .250 case necked down with no other change. Donaldson's version used a ¼-inch shortened case with the shoulder pushed back; on that version, shoulder angle is 30 degrees. The Walker 6mm retains the standard length, but pushes the shoulder back, creating a long neck. Body taper and shoulder angle are the same as the .250. The Remington 40X match rifle has been chambered on special order for the Walker cartridge. Robert Hutton, long-time experimenter and gun writer, has worked with these cartridges, and his results were presented in the 1962 (16th edition) of Gun Digest. The late John T. Amber reported 5/8-inch averages for five-shot, 100-yard groups with the Walker cartridge in the Remington 40X target rifle, impressive performance for that era.

6mm-250 (6mm International) Loading Data

Bullet (grains/type)	Powder	Grains	Velocity	Energy	Source/Comments
60 HP	IMR 3031	32.0	3450	1630	NA
75 HP	IMR 3031	32.0	3390	1910	NA
90 SP	IMR 3031	30.0	3160	2000	NA
100 SP	IMR 3031	28.0	2900	1870	NA

6mm CHeetah

Historical Notes: The 6mm CHeetah, designed by Outdoor Life's shooting editor Jim Carmichael, is a highly accurate, long-range varmint cartridge. It is best described as a variation of Jim's earlier (and racy) .22 CHeetah cartridge necked up to accommodate 6mm bullets. Based on a modified .243 Winchester parent case, the cartridge employs both fire-forming and neck-turning techniques and requires knowledge of advanced reloading practices.

General Comments: The principle advantage of the 6mm CHeetah is accuracy. This performance results from a combination of precise cartridge case preparation steps (especially neck turning to a diameter of .267-inch to achieve precision bullet alignment), and chambering in high-quality rifles with target-grade barrels and expert gunsmithing. The case design is not a true Improved cartridge, and factory .243 Winchester ammunition can not safely be fired in the 6mm CHeetah. Loading data for the .243 AI cartridge can be used for the 6mm CHeetah. The fire-forming load uses 46.5-grains of Reloader 19 and a Sierra 85-grain bullet seated for an overall loaded cartridge length of 2.747 inches. Rifles using the Remington 40X or modern benchrest-type actions provide the best platform for the 6mm CHeetah. Reamers are available from JGS Precision Tool Mfg (www.jgstools.com); rifles for the 6mm CHeetah can be supplied by gunsmiths specializing in high precision firearms.

6mm CHeetah Loading Data

Bullet (grains/type)	Powder	Grains	Velocity	Energy	Source/Comments
55 Nosler Ballistic Tip	H4350	51.0	3627	1606	Jim Carmichael
70 Speer TNT	H4350	47.5	3525	1931	Jim Carmichael
100 Sierra Boat-tail	H4350	45.0	3074	2098	Jim Carmichael

Spitzer 6mm-06

Historical Notes: The earliest 6mm cartridge of American design was the 6mm Lee Navy, with its 112-grain bullet at around 2600 fps. No one knows for certain when wildcatters begin to take a serous look at bullets measuring .243-inch in diameter, but it probably didn't happen in great numbers until the 1940s. The Canadians had their 6mm-303 Epps on the .303 British case, while Americans necked down about everything they could get their hands on. Three of the more popular were the .240 Cobra (on the .220 Swift case); Fred Huntington's .243 Rockchucker, which eventually became known as the .244 Remington; and Warren Page's .240 Page Pooper, which was eventually produced commercially as the .243 Winchester. Wildcats on the .30-06 case went by various names, but the most popular were probably the plain-vanilla 6mm-06 and the .240 Super Varminter, the latter created by Jerry Gebby, who also popularized the .22-250. With its minimum body taper, stubby neck length, and extremely sharp shoulder angle, another wildcat called the .240 Gibbs was basically an Improved version of the Super Varminter. Others of similar powder capacities that came along later are the 6mm-284, on the .284 Winchester case, and the 6mm-350, on the .350 Remington Magnum case.

General Comments: The 6mm-06 case is easily formed by necking down the .30-06 case in two steps, first with a 6.5-06 or .25-06 full-length resizing die, and then with a 6mm-06 die, all available from RCBS (www.rcbs.com) and Redding (www.redding-reloading.com). An intermediate sizing die is not required when necking down .270 Winchester or .25-06 cases. Regardless of the case used, neck diameter with a bullet seated must be held to .290-inch or smaller, and should a batch of formed cases exceed that dimension, their neck walls will need to be thinned by the necessary amount by reaming or outside turning. Maximum case length of 2.494 inches is the same as for the .30-06, so cases formed from .270 Winchester brass will require trimming back by a slight amount. While pressure-tested load data are not available for the 6mm-06, its powder capacity is quite close to those of the .240 Weatherby Magnum and the 6mm-284, so starting loads published for them in various reloading manuals can be used. The chamber of the Weatherby Mark V in .240 Magnum is not freebored, as is the case for that same rifle chambered for other Weatherby cartridges, but its throat is a bit longer than is commonly seen in rifles chambered for other 6mm cartridges, so, to be on the safe side, starting loads published for the .240 Magnum should be reduced by five percent when used in the 6mm-06. Continuing on with a note of caution, starting loads found in the Hornady manual for the 6mm-284 should also be reduced by the same amount when used in the 6mm-06.

A gross-capacity comparison of 6mm-06 cases formed from Remington .25-06 cases, .240 Magnum cases, and 6mm-284 cases formed from Winchester .284 brass reveals that the 6mm-06 averages a half grain greater capacity than the .240 Magnum, and 2.3 grains less than the 6mm-284. This gives the 6mm-284 a slight edge over the other two, but only when it is used in a rifle with an action long enough to allow seating the heavier bullets out of its powder space. More often, that cartridge is used in a short-action rifle in which deep seating of bullets is required, and this reduces its net powder capacity to about the same as for the .240 Magnum and the 6mm-06.

Like the .240 Weatherby Magnum, the 6mm-06 has an extremely flat trajectory, making it an excellent choice for hunting deer and pronghorn antelope in open country. When the Swift 90-grain Scirocco exits a 26-inch barrel at 3425 fps and is zeroed three inches high at 100 yards, it strikes about four inches high at 200 yards, dead on at 300, and low by about half the body depth of a whitetail deer at 400 yards, where it is still packing close to 1200 ft-lbs of punch.

Spitzer 6mm-06 Loading Data and Factory Ballistics

Bullet (grains/type)	Powder	Grains	Velocity	Energy	Source
55 Nosler Ballistic Tip	H414	52.0	3817	1777	Layne Simpson
75 Sierra HP	V-N160	53.0	3644	2209	Layne Simpson
80 Sierra HP	Magnum	55.0	3382	2030	Layne Simpson
85 Barnes XBT	IMR-4350	49.0	3479	2282	Layne Simpson
90 Swift Scirocco	H4831	53.0	3428	2346	Layne Simpson
100 Nosler Partition	IMR-7828	52.0	3272	2375	Layne Simpson
105 Speer SP	RL-22	51.0	3210	2400	Layne Simpson

Warning: All powder charges are maximum and should be reduced by 15 percent for starting loads. Cases were formed by necking down Remington .25-06 brass.

6mm/30-30 Ackley Improved

Historical Notes: There are actually two common versions of the 6mm/30-30, one based on the .30-30 Winchester case necked down without any other change, and the other using the Improved configuration. The

Improved version was the most popular and the one recommended. The 6mm/30-30 has the same dimensions as the .22/30-30, except for a larger .243-inch neck diameter. The cartridge dates back to the 1940s or earlier, and the version referred to here is the Ackley Improved, although there may be others. One of the original purposes of the 6mm/30-30 was for use in re-bored and re-chambered .22 Hi-Power Model 99 Savage lever-actions. This chambering has also been used in single-shot actions. Cases can be formed from .30-30 or .32 Special cases, which might require a set of forming dies plus a final fire-forming. More recent versions use a shortened case for application to single-shot pistols.

General Comments: The 6mm/30-30, when used in a strong action, can be loaded to almost equal the .243 Winchester. It is a good varmint-through-deer cartridge, but its current usefulness is primarily as a chambering for single-shot actions.

6mm/30-30 Improved Loading Data

Bullet (grains/type)	Powder	Grains	Velocity	Energy	Source/Comments
75 HP	IMR 3031	37.0	3450	1980	Ackley
75 HP	IMR 4895	36.0	3265	1770	Ackley
*85 HP	IMR 4895	37.0	3300	2060	Ackley
90 SP	IMR 4320	38.0	3065	1880	Ackley

*Ackley, op cit.

6x47mm

Historical Notes: Simply the .222 Remington Magnum case necked up for .243-inch bullets, the 6x47mm is thought to be a brainchild of Mike Walker who, in addition to working for Remington at the time, was an avid benchrest competitor. Introduced to the sport during the early 1960s, it and the .222 Remington absolutely dominated benchrest shooting, until the 6mm PPC came along. The popularity of the 6x47mm prompted Federal to start making nickel-plated cases during the 1970s, but they are long out of production.

General Comments: While most often thought of as a competition cartridge, the 6x47mm is a fine varmint cartridge when loaded with relatively light bullets for its caliber. As for bigger game, there are better deer cartridges, but a good marksman who desires a lightweight rifle with very little recoil could get by with it by handloading the Nosler 85-grain Partition to a velocity of 2800 fps and restricting shots to no farther than 200 yards. Benchrest shooters customarily stick with relatively light bullets in various 6mm cartridges, and the 1:14 twist rate in barrels they choose are too slow to stabilize bullets much heavier than 75 grains. When the 6x47mm is used for applications where heavier bullets are needed, the twist should be quicker with 1:10 or even 1:9, recommended for hunting bullets up to 100 grains. A good bolt-action rifle chambered for any member of the .222 Remington family of cartridges can be converted to 6x47mm by simply rebarreling it. True to its benchrest competition heritage, the 6x47mm can be incredibly accurate in a good barrel, although some competitors consider it to be more finicky than the 6mm PPC that replaced it.

6x47mm Loading Data and Factory Ballistics

Bullet (grains/type)	Powder	Grains	Velocity	Energy	Source
58 Hornady V-Max	A-2230	28.8	3500	1576	Hornady
65 Hornady V-Max	IMR-3031	27.8	3300	1570	Hornady
70 Hornady SP	BL-C(2)	30.7	3200	1590	Hornady
75 Hornady HP	H322	25.9	3000	1497	Hornady
85 Nosler Partition*	H335	27.5	2810	1489	Layne Simpson

*Excellent 200-yard deer and pronghorn load

WARNING: All powder charges are maximum and must be reduced by 10 percent for starting loads.

6mm-284

Historical Notes: It is anybody's guess who might have been first to size Winchester's rebated-rim .284 down to 6mm. The conversion is good for those interested in achieving maximum velocity with this bullet size. This cartridge can be chambered in medium-length actions.

General Comments: The 6mm-284 has practically the same capacity as the .240 Weatherby Magnum and the 6mm-06. If loaded to similar chamber pressures, it will produce similar velocity. Therefore, ballistics are indistinguishable. However, it has advantages over the Weatherby offering; cases are easier to come by and non-belted. The 6mm-284 can also be chambered in medium-length actions.

Just like the 6mm-06 and .240 Weatherby, when loaded with 100-grain bullets, the 6mm-284 produces only about 100 fps more velocity than the 6mm Remington, when loaded to the same peak pressures and fired from equal-length barrels. Likely, with heavier-than-standard bullets, this difference could reach 150 fps. As to whether such an advantage might justify conversion of a .243 Winchester or 6mm Remington rifle to 6mm-284, consider that this performance difference exceeds the performance difference between the .280 Remington and 7mm Remington Magnum!

6mm-284 Loading Data (26-inch barrel)

Bullet (grains)	Powder	Grains	Velocity	Energy	Source/Comments
70	IMR 4320	45.0	3600	2015	Hornady
70	IMR 4350	49.5	3600	2015	Hornady
70	H4831	52.5	3600	2015	Hornady
75	H4831	54.1	3600	2155	Hornady
87	H4831	51.7	3400	2230	Hornady
100	IMR 4350	49.0	3200	2275	Hornady
100	H4831	51.4	3200	2275	Hornady

.240 Hawk

Historical Notes: Unlike other members of the Hawk cartridge family, the Fred Zeglin-designed .240 Hawk is an over-bored, velocity-addicted varmint cartridge. It is capable of shooting groups as small as .300-inch at 100 yards and offers one of the flattest trajectories available in 6mm varmint cartridges. Performance comes at a price, however, and .240 Hawk barrel life may be shorter than other 6mm varmint cartridges using lighter powder charges. Devout long-range varmint shooters may decide the trade-off is okay.

General Comments: All Hawk cartridges fit into standard .30-06 length actions and use a .473-inch bolt-face. The .240 Hawk uses .280 Remington brass as its parent case. The brass is necked down in a sizing die and fire-formed in a .240 Hawk chamber. The .240 Hawk is designed for lighter weight 6mm varmint bullets. Reloading data for the .240 Weatherby can be used as a starting point, as the .240 Hawk enjoys a four-percent greater case capacity advantage. However, barrel life will be less than other 6mm varmint cartridges that use lighter powder charges. It is best suited for bolt-action rifles with 28-inch barrels with a 1:14 twist. Z-Hat Custom (www.z-hat.com) offers rifles, dies, and reloading information. Use caution with the listed loads, as Z-Hat has not conducted pressure tests on them.

.240 Hawk Loading Data

Bullet (grains/type)	Powder	Grains	Velocity	Energy	Source/Comments
60 Sierra HP	VV N150	53.0	3968	2097	Z-Hat Custom

75 Speer HP	H4064	49.0	3652	2220	Z-Hat Custom
80 Remington HP	RL-15	53.0	4055	2920	Z-Hat Custom
87 Hornady SPT	Win 748	51.0	3954	3019	Z-Hat Custom

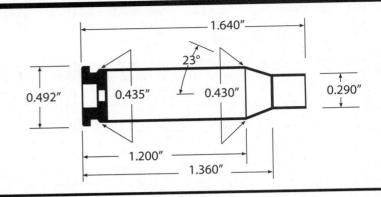

NEW
.25 Hunter

Historical Notes: In 1994, Elgin Gates designed the .414 Super Mag. cartridge and was having it chambered in Dan Wesson and Thomson/Center handguns. Gates passed away before he could see his project come to fruition, but a few years later, Starline made brass for the .414 Super Mag. and Carroll Pliant worked with the cartridge to develop data for the Sierra loading manual. Carroll necked this case down to .25-caliber, reamed the primer pocket deeper to accept Large Rifle primers, and named the wildcat the .25 Hunter after his son, who is now Media Relation/Tech at Starline Brass (www.starlinebrass.com). This is a good hunting cartridge with mild recoil that offers performance just shy of the .250-3000 Savage. It works well in single-shot break-open rifles like the Thomson/Center, and single-shot bolt-action rifles, as well.

General Comments: For all practical purposes the .25 Hunter duplicates .250 Savage performance, but in a rimmed case that is more suited to single-shot rifles and pistols. Current brass availability is questionable, so, while this cartridge does have a practical application, it is unlikely it will receive much attention. It is the third in a line of wildcat cartridges developed by Carroll Pilant from pistol cartridges that were primarily designed for use in a rifle, and the project does illustrate the usefulness of this type conversion.—R.A.M.

.25 Hunter Loading Data

Bullet (grains/type)	Powder	Grains	Velocity	Energy	Source/Comments
75 Sierra HP	AA 2015	30.0	3253	1762	Carroll Pilant
87 Sierra SPT	AA 2520	26.5	2950	1680	Carroll Pilant

.25-222 Copperhead

Historical Notes: The .25-222 Copperhead was created, during the early 1970s, by firearms writer John Wootters in his search for a varmint cartridge with more punch than the .222 Remington and yet small enough to work in a lightweight rifle built on the Sako L-461 action. The custom rifle he ended up with had a barrel measuring 18 3/8 inches long with a rifling twist rate of 1:14. The rifle wore a Mannlicher-style stock, and a clamp on its scope allowed easy attachment of a spotlight for calling coyotes and bobcats at night. Wootters also developed several reduced-velocity loads with the Lyman 257463 cast bullet for use on Rio Grande turkeys, which were and still are abundant in his home state of Texas. The case is formed by necking up the .222 Remington case to .25-caliber with no other change.

General Comments: The .25-222 Copperhead is in the same performance class as the 6x45mm and 6x47mm wildcats, and choosing between them boils down to a preference in .24- or .25-caliber.

.25-222 Copperhead Loading Data and Factory Ballistics

Bullet (grains/type)	Powder	Grains	Velocity	Energy	Source
60 Hornady FP	H4227	19.5	2955	1162	John Wootters
72 Lyman 257463	IMR-4198	16.0	2070	684	John Wootters
75 Hornady HP	IMR-4198	21.0	2765	1272	John Wootters
87 Sierra SP	IMR-4198	20.5	2590	1294	John Wootters

.25 Ackley Krag Short
.25 Ackley Krag

Historical Notes: Ackley offered at least two versions of this cartridge. The .25 Ackley Krag Short holds about 50 grains of IMR-type powder, compared to the full-length .25 Ackley Krag, which holds about 55 grains. The shorter version seems to have been Ackley's favorite, and he preferred it for chambering in P14 Enfields and various single-shot actions. In the heyday of Ackley's developments, the slowest powders available limited performance gains with case capacity increases much beyond this level in the quarter-bore. This fact explains the similar performance he reported for the two versions.

General Comments: The Short version of the .25 Ackley Krag offers very impressive performance, when properly loaded in a strong modern action, but it is now overshadowed by the full-length version of the .25 Ackley Krag and other larger-capacity cases, such as the .25-06. Nevertheless, either of these cartridges are fully capable as big-game cartridges for smaller North American species. These can be highly recommended for single-shot rifle conversions. Very similarly performing .25-caliber versions of the .303 British were championed in Canada and other former British-ruled lands for use in the British SMLE (Enfield) or the much stronger P14 Enfield or Martini single-shot action.

.25 Ackley Krag Short Loading Data

Bullet (grains/type)	Powder	Grains	Velocity	Energy	Source/Comments
87	H380	49.0	3460	2310	Ackley
100	IMR 4064	43.0	3265	2365	Ackley
100	H380	49.0	3412	2585	Ackley
100	IMR 4350	50.0	3300	2415	Ackley
117	H4831	50.0	3285	2855	Ackley

.25 Ackley Krag (full-length .30-40 conversion) Loading Data

Bullet (grains/type)	Powder	Grains	Velocity	Energy	Source/Comments
87	IMR 4064	48.0	3360	2180	Ackley
100	IMR 4350	50.0	3090	2120	Ackley
100	IMR 4895	49.0	3414	2585	Ackley
125	IMR 4350	50.0	3000	2495	Ackley

.250/3000 Ackley Improved

Historical Notes: The .250/3000 Improved was originated by P.O. Ackley in the late 1940s and, although one of the best of the Ackley "Improved" line of cartridges, has never achieved great popularity. This statement about it being the best is based upon the observation that it offers the greatest percentage velocity increase of any of the Improved line of wildcats. Increased shoulder angle affects performance chiefly because it increases case capacity. However, it also improves headspacing and decreases case stretching. There are no significant internal ballistic effects related to any particular shoulder design. There are several versions of the .250 Improved, but the Ackley configuration is the best known. The Savage Model 99 lever-action has recently been offered chambered for the .250/3000, and tens of thousands of these fine rifles are in the hands of hunters. Handloading owners of these rifles should be interested in this excellent conversion, which improves extraction, extends case life, and increases performance markedly.

General Comments: The .250/3000 Improved offers performance equal to or better than the .257 Roberts. It will, for example, push the 100-grain bullet at a muzzle velocity of 3200 fps, compared to the factory .257 loading of the same bullet that is listed at 2900 fps. The commercial .250/3000 loading of the 100-grain bullet, incidentally, is rated at 2820 fps.

.250/3000 Ackley Improved Loading Data

Bullet (grains/type)	Powder	Grains	Velocity	Energy	Source/Comments
87 SP	IMR 4350	42.0	3310	2110	Ackley
100 SP	IMR 4350	41.0	3045	2060	Ackley
100 SP	IMR 4350	42.0	3200	2275	Ackley
120 SP	IMR 4350	40.0	2650	1870	Ackley
120 SP	IMR 4350	41.0	2750	2020	Ackley

.257 Ackley Improved

Historical Notes: A number of "Improved" versions of the .257 Roberts exist. Most were developed in the late 1940s and early 1950s. The .257 Ackley Improved is one of the best and certainly the most popular of the crop. This cartridge has rather straight, blown-out case walls with very little taper and a 40-degree shoulder angle. As with the other Ackley Improved cartridges, cases are made by firing factory ammunition in the Improved chamber. The .257 Improved has about the ideal case capacity for the .25-caliber and is quite efficient in the velocity it produces with a given charge of powder. The gains achieved by Improved cartridges are a matter of increasing case capacity by changing shoulder angle and sometimes moving the shoulder forward to lengthen the body and, at the same time, reducing body taper. Shoulder angle affects performance chiefly because it increases case capacity. It also improves headspacing and decreases case stretching. However, there are no significant internal ballistic effects related to any particular shoulder design. The .257 Improved will develop from 100 to 300 fps more velocity than the standard .257 Roberts, depending on bullet weight. In fact, velocities are only slightly below those developed by the .25-06 with the same weight bullets (capacities of these two are quite similar).

General Comments: The .257 Improved has proven to be an excellent cartridge for long-range varmint shooting and for big game such as deer, antelope, black bear, big horn sheep, etc. This is one of the best of the Improved cartridge line, in terms of useful velocity and energy gain.

.257 Improved (Ackley) Loading Data

Bullet (grains/type)	Powder	Grains	Velocity	Energy	Source/Comments
75 HP	IMR 4895	44.0	3570	2365	Ackley
87 SP	IMR 4895	43.0	3352	2160	Ackley
100 SP	IMR 4831	51.0	3200	2280	Ackley
100 SP	IMR 4350	49.0	3160	2220	Ackley
117 SP	IMR 4831	47.0	2850	2112	Ackley
120 SP	IMR 4831	46.0	2875	2210	Ackley

.257 Kimber

Historical Notes: When Jack Warne and his son, Greg, founded the original Kimber of Oregon, the rifle they introduced to American hunters and shooters was the Model 82 in .22 Long Rifle. Rifles in .22 Hornet, .218 Bee, and .25-20 Winchester were also built on that same action, but, when the time came to add the .223 Remington to the lineup, a new Model 84 with front locking lugs on its bolt was developed. In addition to eventually being chambered for a number of other factory cartridges, such as the .17 Remington, .221 Remington Fire Ball, and .222 Remington Magnum, a limited number of Model 82 rifles were built in various wildcat chamberings, one being the .257 Kimber, introduced in 1987. It was also offered in the Kimber Predator, a single-shot handgun built on the Model 84 action. Developed by Mike Hill, the .257 Kimber case is formed by necking up the .222 Remington Magnum case and fire-forming it to the Improved configuration with minimum body tape and a 40-degree shoulder angle. Hill received the first rifle built in this caliber.

General Comments: As combination varmint/deer cartridges go, the .257 Roberts is a better choice for rifles with actions large enough to handle it, but it is too long for the Kimber Model 84 action, thereby explaining the reasoning behind the .257 Kimber. Since the little cartridge pretty much duplicates the performance of the .250 Savage, it has to be considered the best deer cartridge to be offered by Kimber in its Model 84 rifle. Reloading dies are available from Redding. When fire-forming the .257 Kimber case, the shoulder of the .222 Magnum case is moved forward for a considerable increase in the headspace dimension. This requires seating of bullets out of the case for hard contact with the rifling in preparation for fire-forming. Doing so holds the head of the case firmly in contact with the face of the bolt, thus preventing case stretching and separation in the web area. Failure to follow this procedure can result in case separation, with possible damage to rifle and shooter.

.257 Kimber Loading Data and Factory Ballistics

Bullet (grains/type)	Powder	Grains	Velocity	Energy	Source
75 Sierra HP	H335	31.5	3195	1698	Hodgdon
87 Sierra SP	H4895	31.0	3056	1802	Hodgdon
87 Sierra SP	IMR-3031	30.0	3040	1783	Hodgdon
100 Sierra SP	H4895	28.0	2760	1690	Hodgdon
117 Sierra SP	H4895	24.0	2223	1282	Hodgdon

.25-284

Historical Notes: It is anybody's guess who might have been the first to size the .284 Winchester down to the quarter-bore. This conversion is a good one, offering usable capacity practically identical to the .25-06 in a cartridge that can be chambered in medium-length actions.

General Comments: The .25-284 is ballistically indistinguishable from the .25-06, but offers several advantages. First, the sharper case shoulder of the shorter case reduces case stretching and extends case life, compared to the .25-06. Second, the shorter powder column promises superior accuracy potential. Finally, this more compact cartridge is easier to handle. Nevertheless, the .25-06 was easier to make, because .30-06 cases have long been plentiful. Further, the .25-06 enjoyed decades of wildcat history. For these reasons, it is not surprising that the .25-06 was the round chosen to achieve factory chambering. This is too bad, because the .25-06 offers no ballistic advantages over the .25-284, and the aforementioned facts would tend to suggest the .25-284 as a better all-around choice.

.25-284 Loading Data

Capacity and chamber pressure are essentially identical to the .25-06, and that data can be used, providing a prudent reduction in starting loads and adherence to standard loading practices to ensure against inadvertent use of too-hot loads.

.257 STW (Shooting Times Westerner)

Historical Notes: The .257 STW is the third member of the Shooting Times Westerner family of wildcats developed by firearms writer Layne Simpson (the 7mm STW and .358 STA were the first and second). It was introduced in the June 1998 issue of Shooting Times magazine. Custom rifle builder Lex Webernick built the first rifle in .257 STW for Simpson, and the first game taken by the writer with it was a Coues deer, in Old Mexico. The .257 STW case is formed by necking down the 7mm STW case to .25-caliber with no other change. Reloading dies are available from Redding (www.redding-reloading.com) and RCBS (www.rcbs.com).

General Comments: The .257 STW is capable of accelerating a 100-grain bullet to a muzzle velocity of 3700 fps, making it one of the flattest-shooting big-game cartridges in existence. When a 100-grain bullet of high-ballistic coefficiency is zeroed three inches high at 100 yards, it strikes about an inch high at 300 yards and six inches low at 400 yards, where it is still moving along at close to 2600 fps. Due to the extremely high velocities of this cartridge, lightly constructed bullets may blow up before penetrating to the vitals of big game and, for this reason, only those of extreme controlled-expansion design should be used.

A cartridge capable of burning such a heavy powder charge in a relatively small bore can be finicky to work with, making the .257 STW a cartridge for experienced handloaders only. Those of less experience should stick with the time-proven .257 Weatherby Magnum, which is not a bad deal, since it is only about 200 fps slower with bullets of various weights, not to mention that factory ammunition is available.

.257 STW Loading Data and Factory Ballistics

Bullet (grains/type)	Powder	Grains	Velocity	Energy	Source
75 Sierra HP	RL-22	85.0	4036	2710	Shooting Times
85 Nosler Ballistic Tip	RL-22	83.0	3914	2888	Shooting Times
100 Nosler Partition	H1000	86.0	3709	3051	Shooting Times
100 Swift A-Frame	RL-25	82.0	3712	3056	Shooting Times
120 Nosler Partition	H1000	82.0	3466	3197	Shooting Times
120 Swift A-Frame	RL-25	78.0	3419	3111	Shooting Times
120 Swift A-Frame	H50BMG	88.0	3410	3095	Shooting Times

WARNING: All powder charges are maximum and must be reduced by 10 percent for starting loads.

.25 Gibbs

Historical Notes: The .25 Gibbs was designed, in the 1950s, by firearms experimenter R.E. "Rocky" Gibbs. It was a natural follow-up to Gibbs' original .270 Gibbs, which he developed while seeking the optimum case capacity for the .270 bore size in combination with a 150-grain bullet.

General Comments: The .25 Gibbs is a blown-out .30-06 (or .270 Winchester) case with a steep shoulder and short neck. The shoulder is pushed forward about .196-inch, compared to the standard .270 case, and the case holds about six grains more IMR4350 powder than a standard .270 Winchester. Although Gibbs used this and his other wildcats as front ignition cartridges, the following is a "standard" loading, without the front ignition tube.

.25 Gibbs Loading Data

Bullet (grain/type)	Powder	Grains	Velocity	Energy	Source/Comments
87 Sierra SP	IMR4350	62.0	3617	2527	R.E. Gibbs

6.5 STW
(Shooting Times Westerner)

Historical Notes: The 6.5 STW is the fourth member of the Shooting Times Westerner family of wildcats developed by firearms writer Layne Simpson (the 7mm STW, .358 STA, and .257 STW came first, in that order). He introduced it in the September 1999 issue of Shooting Times magazine, soon after taking a huge Vancouver Island black bear with the new cartridge. Simpson's first rifle in this caliber was built by the Canadian firm of Prairie Gun Works (www.pgwdti.com). The 6.5 STW case is formed by necking down the 7mm STW case for bullets of .264-inch diameter with no other change. Reloading dies are available from Redding (www.redding-reloading.com) and RCBS (www.rcbs.com).

General Comments: The 6.5 STW is capable of accelerating a 140-grain bullet to a muzzle velocity of 3300 fps, making it an extremely flat-shooting big-game cartridge capable of handling anything up to the size of elk and moose. When a 140-grain bullet of high-ballistic coefficient is zeroed three inches high at 100 yards, it strikes about an inch high at 300 yards and only seven inches low at 400 yards, where it is still packing close to 2000 ft-lbs of energy. Due to the extremely high velocities of this cartridge, lightly constructed bullets may blow up before penetrating to the vitals of big game and, for this reason, only those of extreme controlled expansion design should be used. A good 140-grain bullet is hard to beat for elk and such, but the Swift 120-grain A-Frame, Nosler 125-grain Partition, or Swift 130-grain Scirocco are tough to beat on deer and pronghorn antelope at long range. A cartridge capable of burning such a heavy powder charge in a relatively small bore can be finicky to work with, making the 6.5 STW a cartridge for experienced handloaders only.

6.5 STW (Shooting Times Westerner) Loading Data and Factory Ballistics

Bullet (grains/type)	Powder	Grains	Velocity	Energy	Source
85 Sierra HP	IMR-7828	85.0	4016	3041	Shooting Times
100 Nosler Partition	H1000	88.0	3863	3310	Shooting Times
120 Swift A-Frame	H1000	83.0	3511	3281	Shooting Times
125 Nosler Partition	H1000	83.0	3460	3319	Shooting Times
130 Swift Scirocco	H50BMG	88.0	3461	3454	Shooting Times
140 Nosler Partition	A-8700	90.0	3316	3414	Shooting Times
140 Swift A-Frame	H870	88.0	3312	3406	Shooting Times

WARNING: All powder charges are maximum and must be reduced by 10 percent for starting loads.

6.5x52mm American

Historical Notes: The 6.5x52mm American was created by firearms writer Layne Simpson, in response to requests from his readers for a cartridge short enough to work in a short-action rifle and capable of duplicating the performance of the 6.5x55mm Swedish. It was introduced in the August 1994 issue of Shooting Times, about three years before the .260 Remington was introduced commercially. The case was originally formed by necking down the 7mm-08 Remington case and fire-forming it to the Improved shape with minimum body taper and a 40-degree shoulder angle. It can also be formed from the .260 Remington and .308 Winchester cases. With the exception of its neck diameter, the case is identical to Simpson's earlier 7mm SGLC. The first rifle chambered for the cartridge was a custom job on the Remington Model Seven action with a Lilja 21-inch barrel and a McMillan fiberglass stock.

General Comments: When the three cartridges are loaded to the same chamber pressure and fired in barrels of the same length, the 6.5x62mm American is a bit faster than the 6.5x55mm Swedish and .260 Remington. The velocities published for it were from a 21-inch barrel, and about 100 fps can be added for a 24-inch barrel. Like the other two cartridges, it is an excellent choice for hunting deer-sized game and, when loaded with the Sierra 85-grain bullet, it is not a bad choice for varminting. Best bullets for open-country hunting of deer are those weighing from 120 to 130 grains, with the Swift 130-grain Scirocco a great choice for use on everything from whitetail deer and pronghorn antelope to caribou and black bear. Clymer (www.clymertool.com) offers the chamber reamer, and reloading dies are available from Redding (www.redding-reloading.com).

6.5x52mm American Loading Data and Factory Ballistics (21-inch barrel)

Bullet (grains/type)	Powder	Grains	Velocity	Energy	Source
85 Sierra HP	H414	51.0	3381	2155	Layne Simpson
100 Nosler Partition	W760	49.0	3054	2345	Layne Simpson
120 Swift A-Frame	H4350	48.0	2968	2354	Layne Simpson
125 Nosler Partition	N-204	47.0	2914	2448	Layne Simpson
130 Swift Scirocco	A-4350	46.0	2829	2398	Layne Simpson
140 Swift A-Frame	H414	45.0	2731	2316	Layne Simpson
140 Sierra MatchKing	W760	45.0	2712	2284	Layne Simpson

WARNING: All powder charges are maximum and must be reduced by 15 percent for starting loads.

EABCO 6.5mm Bench Rest Magnum (6.5 BRM)

Historical Notes: In 1996, Eben Brown lengthened the .219 Donaldson Wasp benchrest cartridge by a ¼-inch and opened the neck to 6.5mm to create the 6.5 Bench Rest Magnum cartridge. This cartridge was developed to give big-game hunting performance from small-frame single-shot rifles and pistols, such as the Thompson/Center Contenders and Encores, BF pistols, Ruger No. 1 rifles, and EABCO model 97D rifles.

General Comments: Brass is mechanically formed from virgin .30-30 Winchester cases and given a longer body with a slight taper, sharp 30-degree shoulder, and 6.5mm neck. A long, skinny cartridge body keeps bolt thrust manageable for small-frame firearms. In suitable single-shot firearms, the 6.5mm BRM works well with barrel lengths of 24 inches and 1:8 rifling. The sectional density of 140-grain 6.5mm bullets is similar to 190-grain bullets in .30-caliber cartridges. For large game, such as moose or elk, suitable bonded core or partition bullets should be loaded. EABCO (www.eabco.com) provides rifles, barrels, loaded ammunition, and reloading supplies for the 6.5 BRM cartridge. In addition, it offers a family of cartridges in .224, 6mm, 7mm, and .300 BRM chamberings. All loads listed use EABCO custom-formed brass and CCI BR Large Rifle primers.

EABCO 6.5mm Bench Rest Magnum (6.5 BRM) Loading Data and Factory Ballistics

Bullet (grains/type)	Powder	Grains	Velocity	Energy	Source/Comments
100 Sierra	VV N150	38.0	2877	1837	EABCO
140 Sierra GameKing	FL		2400	1790	EABCO
140 Sierra GameKing	VV N160	38.0	2496	1936	EABCO
140 Hornady A-Max	H4831SC	39.5	2401	1791	EABCO

NEW
.264 LBC-AR

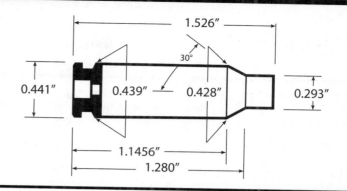

Historical Notes: The .264 LBC-AR cartridge is, for all practical purposes, a 6.5 Grendel. Alexander Arms has held the trademark on the name 6.5 Grendel since that cartridge was introduced. Les Bear started offering rifles for the 6.5 Grendel, but, apparently, there was some contention between the two companies. Les Baer Custom subsequently introduced a new cartridge called the ".264 LBC-AR." As best as can be determined, the cartridge is identical to the 6.5 Grendel, but the chambers in rifles are cut slightly different. However, .264 LBC-AR and 6.5 Grendel ammunition and rifles are interchangeable.

General Comments: This is an example of what can happen when a wildcatter holds his creation as proprietary. Another company can produce a very similar and even compatible cartridge, call it by another name, put marketing dollars behind it, and a cartridge war begins. Currently, and according to Les Baer Custom, Black Hills is offering .264 LBC-AR factory ammunition. Hornady and Wolf both offer 6.5 Grendel ammo. However, just recently, Alexander Arms released its trademark on the 6.5 Grendel cartridge. This will lead to SAAMI standardization in November 2011, which, in turn, will most probably lead to the availability of 6.5 Grendel firearms from other manufacturers, as well as an assortment of factory ammunition. Ultimately, one can speculate that now the 6.5 Grendel will regain its title as the most prolific 6.5mm AR-15 cartridge extant.—R.A.M.

.264 LBC-AR Factory Ammunition and Ballistics

Bullet (grains/type)	Powder	Grains	Velocity	Energy	Source
123 Sierra Matchking	FL		2650	1917	Les Baer Custom

.264 Hawk

Historical Notes: Designed by Wyoming gunmaker Fred Zeglin, in 1998, the .264 Hawk, one of the proprietary Hawk cartridge family, is a flat-shooting, open-country hunting cartridge. For antelope, mule deer, and similarly sized game, the .264 Hawk can speed 6.5mm bullets to impressive velocities.

General Comments: All Hawk cartridges fit into standard .30-06 length actions and use a .473-inch bolt face. The .264 Hawk uses .280 Remington brass as its parent case. The brass is necked-down in a sizing die and fire-formed in a .264 Hawk chamber. The .264 Hawk can accommodate bullet weights ranging from light 6.5mm varmint bullets up to 140-grain big-game hunting bullets. It is best suited for bolt-action rifles with 26-inch barrels having a 1:14 rifling twist. Z-Hat Custom (www.z-hat.com) offers rifles, dies, and reloading information.

.264 Hawk Loading Data

Bullet (grains/type)	Powder	Grains	Velocity	Energy	Source/Comments
85 Sierra HP	H4895	51.0	3575	2411	Z-Hat Custom
120 Nosler BP	VV N160	57.0	3440	3152	Z-Hat Custom
129 Hornady SP	H4831	56.0	2970	2526	Z-Hat Custom
140 Nosler	IMR 7828	54.0	2955	2714	Z-Hat Custom

6.5 Gibbs

Historical Notes: The 6.5 Gibbs was designed in the 1950s by firearms experimenter R.E. "Rocky" Gibbs. It was a natural follow-on to Gibbs' original .270 Gibbs, which he developed while seeking the optimum case capacity for the .270 bore size in combination with a 150-grain bullet.

General Comments: The 6.5 Gibbs is a blown-out .30-06 (or .270) case with a steep shoulder and short neck. The shoulder is pushed forward about .196-inch compared to the standard .270 case, and the case holds about six grains more IMR4350 powder than a standard .270 Winchester. Although Gibbs used this and his other wildcats as front-ignition cartridges, the following is a "standard" loading without a front ignition tube.

6.5 Gibbs Loading Data

Bullet (grains/type)	Powder	Grains	Velocity	Energy	Source/Comments
120 SP	IMR4350	60.0	3325	2995	R.E. Gibbs
140 Speer	H4831	62.0	2967	2736	R.E. Gibbs

6.5mm-06 Ackley Improved

Historical Notes: This cartridge was a natural outgrowth from the 6.5-06. After World War II, many military rifles of 6.5mm were surplused by various countries. Most found their way to the shores of the United States, as a means of bringing much needed cash to countries that would have otherwise simply scrapped these guns. Since ammunition for these chamberings was difficult or impossible to obtain, it was natural for gunsmiths to consider re-chambering them to 6.5-06, since abundant, inexpensive .30-06 cases are easily necked-down to 6.5 and the conversion offered the promise of more power than the original chambering. Similarly, bullet manufacturers responded to the availability of 6.5mm guns by offering component bullets for handloading. This later served only to increase demand for wildcat conversions. It was only reasonable for customers to want to chamber for the Improved version of the 6.5mm-06, because this added nothing to the cost of the conversion and promised a ballistic benefit and increased case life. With the powders then available, the latter was delivered; the former was not.

General Comments: Ackley's experiences with this chambering are most interesting. He first chambered a 6.5mm barrel to 6.5mm-06 and worked up load data. Then, he re-chambered the same barrel to the Improved version and again worked up data. We can only assume that he used the same pressure criteria and the same components for both studies, but, perhaps, this is an erroneous assumption. The reason for doubt stems from the fact that Ackley reported higher velocities with the standard 6.5-06 than with the Improved version. It must be noted that he was limited to powders no slower burning than H4831. Using the slower powders now available, he might have found the Improved version to have the ballistic edge. In any case, the difference in ballistics is marginal. It should be noted that the .25-06 and the 6.5mm-06 Improved have almost exactly the same relative case capacity. Therefore, considering bullet availability, including light varmint-style bullets and hunting bullets that are much heavier than anything available in .257-inch, the 6.5mm-06 Improved is everything the .25-06 will ever be, and more.

6.5mm-06 Ackley Improved Loading Data

Bullet (grains/type)	Powder	Grains	Velocity	Energy	Source/Comments
120	IMR 4350	53.0	3100	2560	Ackley
140	IMR 4350	51.0	2920	2650	Ackley
140	H4831	53.0	2950	2705	Ackley
150	IMR 4350	49.0	2780	2575	Ackley
150	H4831	51.0	2760	2535	Ackley
165	IMR 4350	46.0	2550	2090	Ackley
165	H4831	48.0	2550	2090	Ackley

6.5mm Leopard

Historical Notes: In 2001, Outdoor Life's shooting editor Jim Carmichael designed a 6.5mm long-range hunting and target cartridge, based on newly available Winchester Short Magnum brass. The resulting cartridge, the 6.5 Leopard, proved successful in long-range competitive shooting and offers a highly competitive alternative to the 6.5x284 cartridges used by some shooters. At top-end loadings, the 6.5 Leopard is capable of pushing a Sierra 142-grain Match King bullet to velocities exceeding 3200 fps.

General Comments: Following initial experimentation with .300 WSM cases, the 6.5 Leopard case construction became a simple, one-step necking down operation, once .270 WSM cases became available. No other case changes are needed, because the .270 WSM case length, shoulder diameter, and shoulder angle are optimal. The 6.5 Leopard works well in 26-inch barrels with a 1:9 twist. The cartridge is suitable for short-action rifles, such as the Remington 700. Reamers are available from JGS Precision Tool (www.jgstools.com), and Redding (www.redding-reloading.com) offers reloading dies. Rifles for the 6.5 Leopard can be supplied by Borden Rifles (www.bordenrifles.com) and other gunsmiths specializing in high precision firearms. Listed loads are starting loads.

6.5 Leopard Loading Data

Bullet (grains/type)	Powder	Grains	Velocity	Energy	Source/Comments
107	IMR 4831	62.0	3404	2752	Jim Carmichael
120	RETUMBO	65.0	3203	2733	Jim Carmichael
140	RETUMBO	60.0	3036	2865	Jim Carmichael

.270 REN

Historical Notes: Designed in 1985 by Charles Rensing and Jim Rock, this cartridge was developed in response to NRA Hunter Pistol Silhouette competition rules. This category only allows use of straight-walled cartridges. This diminutive number fulfills that requirement while producing minimal recoil, as intended by the inventors.

General Comments: The .270 REN is based on the .22 Hornet simply necked straight to accept .270 bullets. Recoil is very mild in typical guns, and this little chambering can propel the excellent 90-, 100-, and 110-grain bullets available to considerable velocity with modest powder charges. Guns chambered for the .270 REN are currently available from several manufacturers, including RPM, Thompson/Center, and Merrill.

.270 REN Loading Data (10-inch barrel)

Bullet (grains/type)	Powder	Grains	Velocity	Energy	Source/Comments
90	AA No. 7	8.2	1650	540	Accurate
90	AA No. 9	11.1	1888	710	Accurate
90	A1680	14.5	1811	655	Accurate
100 Hornady	H110	10.2	1600	565	Hornady
100 Hornady	AA 5744	10.4	1600	565	Hornady
100 Hornady	W296	11.0	1600	565	Hornady
100 Hornady	AA No. 7	8.2	1566	540	Accurate
100 Hornady	AA No. 9	10.8	1799	715	Accurate
100 Hornady	A1680	14.5	1815	730	Accurate
110 Sierra	AA No. 7	8.0	1474	530	Accurate
110 Sierra	AA No. 9	10.2	1666	675	Accurate
110 Sierra	A1680	14.0	1675	685	Accurate

.270 Hawk

Historical Notes: Like the .270 Ackley Improved, the .270 Hawk delivers about 50 fps more velocity than the factory .270 Winchester cartridge with identical bullets. Fred Zeglin designed the .270 Hawk as a member of his proprietary Hawk cartridge family, about 1998. The .270 Hawk is an excellent deer and antelope cartridge.

General Comments: All Hawk cartridges fit into standard 30-06 length actions and use a .473-inch bolt face. The .270 Hawk uses .280 Remington brass as its parent case. The brass is necked up to .30-caliber, full length sized, and fire-formed in a .270 Hawk chamber. The .270 Hawk works well in bolt-action rifles with 24- to 26-inch barrels and a 1:10 rifling twist. Quality Cartridge (www.qual-cart.com) supplies ammunition and correctly headstamped brass. Z-Hat Custom (www.z-hat.com) offers rifles, dies, and reloading information.

.270 Hawk Loading Data

Bullet (grains/type)	Powder	Grains	Velocity	Energy	Source/Comments
130 gr.	H4350	61.0	3295	3133	Z-Hat Custom
140 gr.	H4350	58.0	3161	3105	Z-Hat Custom
150 gr.	H4350	57.0	3051	3100	Z-Hat Custom

.270 Gibbs

Historical Notes: The .270 Gibbs was designed in the 1950s by firearms experimenter R.E. "Rocky" Gibbs. It was developed while seeking the optimum case capacity for the .270 bore size in combination with a 150-grain bullet. Gibbs wanted a case with more capacity than a .270 Ackley, but believed the capacity of "short magnum" .270 cases to be excessive. He wanted to seat a heavy (150-grain) bullet to "normal depth" and leave very little air space to produce high loading-density maximum loads.

General Comments: The .270 Gibbs is a blown-out .30-06 (or .270) case with a steep shoulder and short neck. The shoulder is pushed forward about .196-inch, compared to the standard .270 case, and the case holds about six grains more of IMR4350 powder than a standard .270 Winchester. Although Gibbs used this and his other wildcats as front-ignition cartridges, the following is a "standard" loading without a front ignition tube.

.270 Gibbs Loading Data

Bullet (grains/type)	Powder	Grains	Velocity	Energy	Source/Comments
150 SPBT	H4831	63.0	3175	3357	R.E. Gibbs

.270 IHMSA

Historical Notes: Just one of an entire series of cartridges designed by Elgin Gates, the .270 IHMSA (International Handgun Metallic Silhouette Association) is among the more popular of the group, which ranges from .25- through .35-caliber. All are similar and are designed specifically for chambering in single-shot handguns. The intention was to offer competitors a choice of easy-to-make chamberings that could deliver the desired momentum to distant targets. In this endeavor, Gates appears to have been notably successful. Other IHMSA numbers include 7mm and .30-caliber versions.

General Comments: The .270 IHMSA is based on the .300 Savage case. Cases are formed by simply necking the case down to accept .270 bullets. The sizing die also drives the inside of the shoulder back to achieve a 38-degree shoulder angle, providing superior headspace control and a longer case neck. The same treatment is utilized for all cases in the IHMSA line.

.270 IHMSA Loading Data (14-inch barrel)

Bullet (grains)	Powder	Grains	Velocity	Energy	Source/Comments
90	H414	45.0	2691	1445	Hodgdon
90	BL-C(2)	40.0	2719	1475	Hodgdon
100	H414	45.0	2654	1560	Hodgdon
100	H4895	38.0	2654	1560	Hodgdon
110	H414	44.0	2626	1680	Hodgdon
110	H4895	37.0	2590	1635	Hodgdon
130	H414	41.0	2442	1720	Hodgdon
130	H450	44.0	2423	1695	Hodgdon
140	H4831	43.0	2449	1860	Hodgdon
140	H4350	41.0	2394	1780	Hodgdon
150	H4350	40.0	2291	1745	Hodgdon
150	H4895	33.0	2274	1720	Hodgdon

.270 Savage
.270 Ackley Improved Savage

Historical Notes: The .270 Savage was, in its day, a very good cartridge for the Model 99 Savage, and it remains so today. With the standard 130-grain bullet, it delivers performance reasonably close to factory .270 Winchester loads. Heavier bullets intrude much of the available powder space and, therefore, do not perform as well. The Ackley Improved version comes very close to .270 Winchester ballistics and is a much better Model 99 chambering option in all respects (see discussion at .250-300 Ackley Improved).

General Comments: While the .250 Savage is a fine deer cartridge, the .270 version offers the potential to use heavier bullets at about the same velocity. Therefore, this chambering (particularly the Ackley version), is a much better big-game hunting option. With properly constructed bullets, this is also a much better elk cartridge.

.270 Savage Loading Data

Bullet (grains/type)	Powder	Grains	Velocity	Energy	Source/Comments
100 SP	IMR 4064	42.0	3107	2140	Ackley
100 SP	IMR 3031	39.0	2950	1930	Ackley
130 SP	IMR 4064	39.0	2763	2200	Ackley
150 SP	IMR 4350	43.0	2574	2205	Ackley

7mm TCU
7mmX223

Historical Notes: The 7mm TCU is another of the series of cartridges developed by Wes Ugalde for Thompson/Center and offered as a standard chambering in the single-shot Contender pistol. All are based on the .223 Remington case necked up, this one to 7mm (.284-inch). The 7mm TCU dates back to about 1980 and has become quite popular for metallic silhouette pistol shooting. It is also known as the 7mmx223. Other TCU numbers include 6mm, .25-caliber, and 6.5mm versions of this same basic case.

General Comments: The 7mm TCU has a reputation for exceptional accuracy and makes a good varmint cartridge in the T/C Contender pistol, particularly with the 14-inch barrel, which provides an extra couple hundred feet per second over the 10-inch barrel. It is on the marginal side for deer or other medium game. The originators recommend that only commercial .223 Remington cases be used for forming cases. Do not use military cases. Cases are easy to make and can be formed in one operation once the dies are properly adjusted. Proper case length is 1.740 inches.

7mm TCU Loading Data

Bullet (grains/type)	Powder	Grains	Velocity	Energy	Source/Comments
100 SP	BL-C2	28.0	2100	980	14-inch barrel
115 SP	IMR 4198	23.0	2185	1220	14-inch barrel
130 SP	IMR 4198	22.0	2050	1215	14-inch barrel
140 SP	H4895	24.0	1880	1100	14-inch barrel
150 SP	BL-C2	25.0	1910	1220	14-inch barrel

.280 Hawk

Historical Notes: In 1997, Wyoming gunmaker Fred Zeglin designed the Hawk family of proprietary hunting cartridges suitable for varminting through dangerous game. Fred's .280 Hawk offers a modest ballistic advantage over factory .280 Remington ammunition. Using the same bullets and barrel length, the .280 Hawk produces about 50 fps more velocity. The cartridge is well suited for most North American big game, except for the Alaskan and Canadian grizzly and brown bears.

General Comments: All Hawk cartridges use standard length actions with a .473-inch bolt face. The .280 Hawk uses .280 Remington brass as the parent case. The brass is necked up to .30-caliber, sized in a .280 Hawk die to set the headspace, and fire-formed in a .280 Hawk chamber. The cartridge is well suited for bolt-action and modern single-shot rifles. Barrel lengths of 24 to 26 inches with a 1:10 twist are recommended. Loaded ammunition and correctly headstamped brass are available from Quality Cartridge (www.qual-cart.com). Z-Hat Custom (www.z-hat.com) offers rifles, dies, and reloading information.

.280 Hawk Loading Data

Bullet (grains)	Powder	Grains	Velocity	Energy	Source/Comments
140	H4831	60.0	3015	2825	Z-Hat Custom
154	RL-22	59.0	2827	2732	Z-Hat Custom
160	RL-22	60.0	2845	2875	Z-Hat Custom

7mm JRS

Historical Notes: The 7mm JRS was designed by Jon R. Sundra. It is based on the .280/7mm Express Remington case, but is more than an Improved .280 in that it cannot be made by fire-forming .280 Remington ammo in a 7mm JRS chamber. Attempting to do so is dangerous, because the 7mm JRS pushes a 35-degree shoulder more than .05-inch forward of where it would be on the .280 Improved. Therefore, headspace is increased commensurately.

To give some idea of relative case capacities, the .280 Remington/7mm Express holds about 63 grains of water to the base of the neck; the .280 RCBS holds about 66 grains; the 7mm JRS about 70.5 grains (Norma cases). The 7mm Remington Magnum holds about 82 grains.

General Comments: Chamber reamers for the 7mm JRS are made by Clymer Mfg. (www.clymertool.com), while reloading dies are made by Hornady. Sundra found that very little load development work was necessary with this cartridge. Norma MRP and Reloader 22 are the best powders, with H4831, IMR 4831, and IMR 7828 coming in as close seconds. Other slow burners like IMR 4831 and H450 also do well. Depending on the individual rifle and case (Remington, Norma, or Winchester), maximum loads range between 60.5 to 63.5 grains of Rl-22 with a 150-grain Nosler. Velocity has ranged from 3060 to 3120 fps in various barrels of 23½ to 24 inches.

The 7mm JRS is chambered by E.R. Shaw (www.ershawbarrels.com). Standard length actions like the Ruger 77 and Mauser (commercial or military) can be used. To take full advantage of case capacity, these loads assume bullet bases seated no deeper than the shoulder (overall length of 3 7/16-inch with a 154-grain Hornady, 3 3/8-inch with a 150-grain Nosler). Sundra recommends that chambers be throated so a dummy round with either of the above bullets will have a 1/16-inch leade. To accommodate cartridges of this length, you will need a Model 70, Remington 700, or long Sako action. Grayback Wildcats (541-882-3492), offers fire-formed (once-fired) cases for the 7mm JRS. Similar "pushed shoulder '06-based" Improved cartridges exist in .30-, .338-, .35-, and .375-caliber. All are very good, but those in otherwise factory chamberings (.280, .30-06, and, now, the .35 Whelen) create serious safety concerns. Any rifle thus chambered will chamber the factory cartridge of the proper bore diameter, which will then have enough headspace to separate and destroy the gun, and perhaps even the shooter and bystanders.

7mm JRS Loading Data

Bullet (grains/type)	Powder	Grains	Velocity	Energy	Source/Comments
145 SP	Rl-22	63.0	3130	3155	Jon Sundra
154 SP	Rl-22	61.5	3020	3120	Jon Sundra

7mm Gibbs

Historical Notes: The 7mm Gibbs was designed, in the 1950s, by firearms experimenter R.E. "Rocky" Gibbs. It was a natural follow-up to Gibbs' original .270 Gibbs, which he developed while seeking the optimum case capacity for the .270 bore size in combination with a 150-grain bullet.

General Comments: The 7mm Gibbs is a blown-out .30-06 (or .270) case with a steep shoulder and short neck. The shoulder is pushed forward about .196-inch, compared to the standard .270 case, and the case holds about six grains more of IMR4350 powder than a standard .270 Winchester. Although Gibbs used this and his other wildcats as front ignition cartridges, the following is a "standard" loading without a front ignition tube.

7mm Gibbs Loading Data

Bullet (grains/type)	Powder	Grains	Velocity	Energy	Source/Comments
140 Sierra	H4831	67.0	3293	3370	R.E. Gibbs
160 Speer	H4831	67.0	3173	3574	R.E. Gibbs

7mm SGLC (Simpson's Good Little Cartridge)

Historical Notes: Back in the 1970s, determined to have a rifle that hung light on the shoulder at an affordable price, firearms writer Layne Simpson decided to convert a 6½-pound Weatherby Varmintmaster from .22-250 to a flat-shooting cartridge powerful enough for handling most mountain game. The wildcat cartridge he came up with is the .308 Winchester case necked down to 7mm and blown out to the Improved shape with minimum body taper and a 40-degree shoulder angle. Gunsmith Wally Strutz, of Eagle River, Wisconsin, re-barreled the Weatherby rifle and modified its magazine to handle the cartridge. The first animal taken by Simpson with the outfit was a Shiras moose, and shortly thereafter, on a hunt in Rhodesia (now Zimbabwe), he used the rifle to take 12 animals ranging from impala to greater kudu with a total of 14 cartridges. The story of that hunt was published in the March-April 1979 issue of Rifle magazine.

Simpson eventually made a switch-barrel rifle of his Varmintmaster with a barrel in 250 Savage Improved added to his collection. Years later, Roy Weatherby's son, Ed, who was running the company by that time, found a copy of the Rifle magazine article in his father's files. Ed liked the idea and decided to offer the Varmintmaster in a .250 Savage version called the "Whitetail Deluxe." A page in the 1993 Weatherby catalog was devoted to the new rifle, and a couple of those rifles were on display at the SHOT show that year. Unfortunately, not many people buy rifles in .250 Savage any more, so Ed Weatherby wisely took Simpson's idea a step further by increasing the length of the Varmintmaster action by about an inch, introducing it in 1997 as the standard Mark V. This made the action long enough to handle not only short cartridges, such as the .22-250, .243 Winchester, and .308 Winchester, but longer best-sellers such as the .30-06 and .270 Winchester, as well. And it was all started by a wildcat cartridge and a firearms writer who had a hankering for a light big-game rifle.

General Comments: Simpson is quick to admit today that, if the 7mm-08 Remington had been available during the mid-1970s, he probably would have chosen it for his Varmintmaster conversion, since factory ammo is available. A bit older now, he also says that, if he were developing the cartridge today, he wouldn't give it such a "silly, tongue-twisting name." The 7mm SGLC case can be formed the original way by necking down and fire-forming the .308 Winchester case, or by firing 7mm-08 Remington factory ammunition in a rifle properly chambered for the 7mm SGLC. Simpson's favorite bullet, and the one he's used to take most of the game bagged with this cartridge, is the Nosler 140-grain Partition, but he also likes the performance of the Speer 130-grain spitzer on whitetail deer and pronghorn antelope. Excellent choices of powders for handloads with all bullet weights are H414, W760, and Reloader 19.

7mm SGLC Loading Data and Factory Ballistics (24-inch barrel)

Bullet (grains/type)	Powder	Grains	Velocity	Energy	Source
120 Hornady HP	W760	53.0	3210	2743	Layne Simpson
130 Speer SP	H414	52.0	3177	2910	L. Simpson
140 Nosler Partition	H414	49.0	3010	2813	L. Simpson
150 Nosler Partition	RL19	52.0	2968	2931	L. Simpson
160 Nosler Partition	RL19	51.0	2902	2989	L. Simpson
175 Nosler Partition	RL19	49.0	2738	2910	L. Simpson

WARNING: All powder charges are maximum and must be reduced by 10 percent for starting loads.

7mm Shooting Times Easterner (7mm STE)

Historical Notes: The 7mm Shooting Times Easterner (7mm STE) was designed, in 1987, by gun writer Layne Simpson for Marlin 336 and Winchester Model 94 lever-action rifles. This cartridge is the .307 Winchester case necked down and fire-formed to the Improved configuration with minimum body taper and a 40-degree shoulder. The .307 Winchester is actually a rimmed version of the .308 Winchester, thus providing the 7mm STE with more powder capacity than either the .30-30 Winchester or the 7-30 Waters. Load data for the 7mm STE was developed with the Nosler 120-grain and Hornady 139-grain flat-nosed bullet, as these are compatible with the tubular magazines of the lever guns. Maximum velocities for these bullets in a 22-inch barrel are 2900 fps and 2700 fps, respectively.

General Comments: This cartridge has enjoyed fair success on whitetails, mule deer, pronghorns, black bear, caribou, and wild hogs. Performance of the Nosler bullet on all of these has been nothing less than outstanding. A favorite open-country "single-shot" recipe for loading directly into the chamber (i.e., not for use in a tubular magazine), is the Nosler 140-grain Ballistic Tip loaded to 2700 fps. Chamber pressures generated by the 7mm STE are comparable to those developed by the .307 Winchester. Consequently, only Model 336 and 94 rifles of recent manufacture and in excellent condition should be considered for this conversion. Those rifles in .30-30 Winchester, .307 Winchester, .356 Winchester, and .444 Marlin are easily converted to the 7mm STE by rebarreling with no other modifications necessary.

7mm Shooting Times Easterner (STE) Loading Data

Bullet (grains/type)	Powder	Grains	Velocity	Energy	Source/Comments
120 SP	H414	47.0	2915	2265	Layne Simpson
120 SP	H4895	41.0	2910	2250	Layne Simpson
139 SP	W760	45.0	2710	2265	Layne Simpson
139 SP	RI-22	50.0	2710	2265	Layne Simpson

.285 OKH
7mm-06 Mashburn
7mm-06

Historical Notes: These cartridges are lumped together, because all are practically identical and, except for headspace specification, are very similar to the .280 Remington. The .285 OKH is another O'Neil-Keith-Hopkins development that originally used a duplex loading consisting of different powders with different burning rates loaded one on top of the other. It also employed a long flash tube that ignited the powder at the front of the case instead of the rear. This was supposed to improve ballistics and apparently did so, but was a lot of trouble, proving rather impractical for the average handloader. All of these cartridges originated in the late 1940s and early 1950s.

General Comments: Because these cartridges hold about two grains of powder less than the .280 Remington, maximum .280 Remington loads are not recommended. The various 7mms based on the .30-06 case are worthy of mention, because these were the wildcat forerunners of the commercial .280.

.285 OKH Loading Data

Bullet (grains/type)	Powder	Grains	Velocity	Energy	Source/Comments
100 SP	IMR 3031	45.0	3110	2150	NA
125 SP	IMR 4350	57.0	3195	2840	NA
150 SP	IMR 4895	48.0	2890	2780	NA
165 SP	IMR 4350	52.0	2820	2920	NA
175 SP	IMR 4350	55.0	2720	2880	NA

.30 Kurz

Historical Notes: The .30 Kurz is made by shortening the .30-06 or .308 Winchester to 1.290 inches. This produces a short cartridge very similar to the German 7.92 Kurz assault rifle cartridge of World War II. The idea originated in the 1960s, and there are other versions of this cartridge. It is intended for use in modified M1 carbines and is the same length as the .30 Carbine case.

General Comments: The .30 Carbine cartridge is not very flexible and is not a particularly good choice for hunting. Because of this, many efforts have been made to improve the performance of the handy little M1 Carbine through wildcat cartridge designs. The .30 Kurz is one of these. The problem is that the cartridge has capabilities beyond the ability of the M1 Carbine. When loaded within the pressure limits of the gun, it does not provide much of an improvement. It is, however, an interesting development as one of the shortest of the short .30-calibers. It is usually loaded with a 110-grain bullet.

.308x1.5-inch Barnes

Historical Notes: The .308x1.5-inch was developed by the original author of this book, Frank C. Barnes, in March 1961. It is based on the .308 Winchester case shortened from the original 2.01 inches to a length of 1.50 inches. The only other difference is in shoulder diameter, which is .003-inch larger than the original cartridge. Two rifles were made up for the developmental work, one on a Swedish Model 96 short military bolt-action (1:12 twist) by Les Corbett, the other on a Remington rolling block single-shot action (1:10-inch twist) by P.O. Ackley. Both rifles proved to be extremely accurate, although the 1:12 twist appears to be the one that has become more or less standard for this cartridge. The .308x1.5 inch is similar to the Russian 7.62x39mm (M43) military round, but is larger in base diameter and has a greater powder capacity. Consequently, it can be loaded to produce higher velocity with any given bullet weight. At the time this cartridge was introduced, several gun designers, working on assault rifle designs they hoped to sell to the government, chambered guns to handle the .308x1.5 inch. However, nothing came of these efforts, and the cartridge has never been seriously considered as a military round.

A number of individual experimenters have worked with variations of the original .308x1.5-inch case configuration by lengthening it to 1.6 inches, 1.7 inches, etc., and it has been necked down to .22, 6mm, and 7mm, and necked up to .375-inch. Case capacity of the .308x1.5 inch is close to that of the .223 Remington and, if necked down to .22-caliber, it delivers approximately the same ballistics. The original case-forming and loading dies were made up by RCBS (www.rcbs.com), and these can still be ordered as a regular stock item.

General Comments: As originally conceived, the .308x1.5-inch was envisioned as a varmint-through-deer sporting cartridge that could be chambered in very lightweight, short-action rifles for hunting under conditions in which reduced bulk and heft would be important. As a secondary possibility, it could provide a very efficient .30-caliber match or even a benchrest cartridge. However, it has emerged as more of a special-purpose handgun cartridge for use in custom single-shot pistols for silhouette shooting. Many custom barrels have been made for the popular Thompson/Center Contender single-shot pistol in .308x1.5-inch chambering and, in addition, the Wichita Silhouette Pistol, made by Wichita Arms (www.wichitaarms.com), offers it as a standard chambering. In addition, a number of custom pistolsmiths who make up single-shot pistols based on the Remington XP-100 bolt-action offer it as a chambering choice.

As a rifle cartridge, the .308x1.5-inch delivers initial velocities in excess of the factory-loaded .30-30 Winchester (a true 2530 to 2540 fps with the 150-grain bullet, as opposed to the advertised 2410 fps of the commercial .30-30). Actually, as demonstrated through chronograph tests, the factory 150-grain loading of the .30-30 develops only about 2250 fps from a 22-inch barrel, and most of the .30-30s sold have 20-inch barrels. Since the .308x1.5-inch is used exclusively in bolt- or single-shot actions, this allows the use of spitzer bullets, which means that the retained velocity at the longer ranges will also be greater than the flat-pointed .30-30 bullet. Frank Barnes had great success with this little cartridge in hunting deer, feral pigs, and feral goats. Properly loaded, it has good killing power on animals up to deer-size at ranges out to about 150 yards or so.

Small cartridges such as the .308x1.5-inch are very efficient and deliver performance out of all proportion to their size. However this is only achieved at relatively high pressure levels. When loading the .308x1.5-inch or any similar cartridges to maximum performance levels, adding only a few tenths of a grain of powder can run the pressure up to unsafe levels. Also, if military cases are used, all maximum charges must be reduced, because those cases are generally heavier, which reduces capacity and increases loading density, again thereby increasing pressure. A number of shooters have been using the .308x1.5-inch for shooting cast bullets. Lou Delgado of Thousand Oaks, California, experimented with cast bullets and various twists from 1:12 through 1:16.

Editor's note: This cartridge would be a good choice for the "Hunter Benchrest" game, but is not allowed, owing to insufficient case capacity to satisfy the rule requiring that the case must have at least as much capacity as the .30-30 case. Since .308x1.5-inch performance far outclasses any factory .30-30 loading, some might question the common sense of such a rule.

Bullet (grains)	Powder	Grains	Velocity	Energy	Source/Comments
80	IMR 4198	28.0	2875	1468	NA
80	IMR 4198	29.0	2938	1533	NA
93	IMR 4198	28.5	2835	1659	NA
100	IMR 4198	28.5	2810	1755	NA
125	H380	30.0	2015	1125	NA
125	H380	30.0	2015	1126	NA
125	IMR 3031	29.0	2352	1548	NA
125	IMR 4198	27.0	2557	1814	NA
125	IMR 3031	29.0	2350	1535	NA
125	IMR 4198	28.0	2640	1935	NA
150	IMR 4198	27.0	2530	2130	NA
150	H380	23.0	1589	850	NA
150	IMR 4064	27.0	2032	1375	NA
150	IMR 4198	21.0	2027	1368	NA
150	IMR 4198	26.0	2456	2008	NA
150	IMR 3031	28.0	2370	1870	NA
170	IMR 3031	27.5	2112	1653	NA
170	IMR 4198	24.5	2233	1882	NA
180	IMR 4198	24.0	2180	1900	NA
180	IMR 3031	26.0	2035	1655	NA

.30 Herrett

Historical Notes: The .30 Herrett was developed as a handgun hunting cartridge by grip-maker Steve Herrett and the late noted gun writer Bob Milek. It was intended for use in the Thompson/Center single-shot pistol, and the first barrels were made up in 1972, although Thompson/Center did not offer it as a standard chambering until 1973. The cartridge is based on a shortened and reformed .30-30 Winchester case reduced to 1.6 inches, as compared to the original length of 2.04 inches. The case is longer and has greater powder capacity than the .30 Carbine and, when fired in the 10-inch barrel of the Thompson/Center pistol, delivers a rather impressive performance. Muzzle velocities of more than 2000 fps are possible with the 125- or 130-grain bullet.

General Comments: Conceived as a superior handgun hunting cartridge, the .30 Herrett has been used successfully on everything from varmints to deer. However, as loaded and used in the Thompson/Center pistol, it develops less velocity and energy than the standard .30-30 rifle and must be considered on the marginal side as a medium-game cartridge in the hands of the average hunter. Much of its success has been due in no small part to the skill of the people who have used it. On the other hand, it offers greater power than the .357 Magnum cartridge, which some consider adequate for big game in the hands of a skilled hunter. As with all big-game hunting with a handgun, it boils down to the question of who is doing the hunting. What Bob Milek or someone in that class can do and what the average person can do are two different things. In any event, the .30 Herrett is an outstanding long-range handgun varmint cartridge, particularly with 110-, 125-, or 130-grain bullets. It has also been used with success for silhouette shooting, although most shooters prefer the .357 Herrett for that sport. The .30 Herrett is a good example of a wildcat cartridge designed for a specific purpose not really covered by anything in commercial lines, and one that fulfills its design purpose extremely well.

.30 Herrett Loading Data

Bullet (grains/type)	Powder	Grains	Velocity	Energy	Source/Comments
100 SP	2400	19.0	2210	1090	NA
110 HP	2400	20.0	2270	1260	NA
125 SP	IMR 4227	23.0	2205	1350	NA
130 SP	2400	19.0	2000	1160	NA
150 SP	Norma 200	27.0	2100	1470	NA

.30-30 Ackley Improved

Historical Notes: The .30-30 Winchester is one of the most popular sporting cartridges ever produced. It is the standard American deer cartridge, but its popularity is due more to the light, handy carbines that chamber it than to its ballistics. Many hunters have wished that the .30-30 had a little more oomph. The .30-30 Improved does just that by providing an additional 200 to 300 fps within the working pressure limits of the standard Model 94 Winchester action. There are various versions of the .30-30 Improved, but the Ackley version is the most popular. The exact date of introduction is not known, but was probably sometime in the early 1950s or, perhaps, even earlier.

General Comments: Basically, the .30-30 Improved requires only a simple re-chambering job. Cases are made by firing standard .30-30 Winchester ammunition in the Improved chamber, then reloading the fire-formed cases. However, anyone who favors the Model 94 Winchester or Marlin 336 and wants more power than the standard .30-30 can simply buy one in .307 Winchester. This would seem to make the Improved .30-30 obsolete for new rifles, but it is still a good modification for older Model 94s and Marlins.

Editor's note: Since the .307 Winchester appears on its way to obsolescence, perhaps one should not be so hasty in condemning Ackley's solution.

.30-30 Ackley Improved Loading Data

Bullet (grains/type)	Powder	Grains	Velocity	Energy	Source/Comments
100 SP	RI-7	36.0	2750	1680	NA
110 HP	RI-7	35.0	2610	1660	NA
130 SP	W748	36.0	2385	1645	NA
150 SP	RI-7	30.0	2270	1720	NA
150 SP	IMR 3031	37.0	2617	2280	Ackley
170 SP	IMR 3031	35.0	2310	2020	NA

.30-06 Ackley Improved

Historical Notes: The .30-06 Ackley Improved is made by firing the standard .30-06 in the Improved chamber. Headspace is the same, but the Improved case has a more abrupt shoulder, less body taper, and a larger shoulder diameter. The most popular version was developed by P.O. Ackley, in 1944, but there are other versions as experiments going back to 1940 and earlier. This has always been a controversial cartridge, with its detractors claiming it was not as good as the standard '06, and its defenders claiming it was better than the .300 H&H Magnum. Actual chronograph tests have proven it definitely superior to the standard .30-06 cartridge with slow-burning powders. However, it could never match the various magnums, since usable case capacity is significantly less.

General Comments: The advantage of owning a wildcat-chambered rifle that will also shoot standard factory ammunition is obvious. The various Improved cartridges from .22- through .35-caliber are all designed to do exactly that. The idea is to provide superior performance by handloading the Improved case, without preventing use of the standard factory round when an ammunition shortage or other occasion demands.

The .30-06 Ackley Improved is one of the most popular and widely used of the Improved breed. With the proper powder, it will add a little over 100 fps muzzle velocity to any bullet weight, as compared to the standard factory-loaded cartridge. This does make it equal to the original factory-loaded .300 H&H Magnum with 150-, 180-, and 220-grain bullets, but, of course, the .300 Magnum can also be handloaded to exceed anything possible in the Improved '06. Best results are obtained with slow-burning powders such as IMR 4350 or Hodgdon 4831. The .30-06 Improved would be adequate for any North American game. As is typical of Ackley's improved series of cartridges, this design exhibits reduced case stretching and easier extraction, compared to the more tapered standard version.

.30-06 Ackley Improved Loading Data

Bullet (grains/type)	Powder	Grains	Velocity	Energy	Source/Comments
130 SP	IMR 4895	54.0	3150	2860	Ackley
150 SP	IMR 4350	59.0	3070	3150	Ackley
165 SP	IMR 4350	58.0	2940	3180	Ackley
180 SP	IMR 4350	56.0	2825	3200	Ackley
200 SP	H4831	59.0	2760	3180	Ackley
200 SP	IMR 4350	54.0	2675	3190	Ackley
220 SP	IMR 4350	54.0	2620	3365	Ackley

.30 Gibbs

Historical Notes: The .30 Gibbs was designed, in the 1950s, by firearms experimenter R.E. "Rocky" Gibbs. He called it "The world's most powerful .30-06." It was a natural follow-up to Gibbs's original .270 Gibbs, which he developed while seeking the optimum case capacity for the .270 bore size in combination with a 150-grain bullet.

General Comments: The .30 Gibbs is a blown-out .30-06 case with a steep shoulder and short neck. The shoulder is pushed forward about .196-inch, compared to the standard .30-06 case, and the case holds about seven grains more of IMR4350 powder than a standard .30-06 Winchester. Although Gibbs used this and his other wildcats as front ignition cartridges, the following is a "standard" loading without a front ignition tube.

.30 Gibbs Loading Data

Bullet (grains/type)	Powder	Grains	Velocity	Energy	Source/Comments
150 Hornady	IMR4064	60.0	3285	3593	R.E. Gibbs
180 Barnes	IMR4350	65.0	3139	3937	R.E. Gibbs

.30-338 Winchester Magnum

Historical Notes: This cartridge was developed specifically for use in 1,000-yard benchrest competition and is now popular in NRA High Power competition for the long-range events. It was created by simply necking the .338 Winchester Magnum to .30-caliber and almost exactly duplicates the .308 Norma Magnum. (Norma's commercial offering has slightly less case taper and is slightly longer.)

General Comments: The .30-338 Winchester Magnum fills a void in Winchester's Magnum line, created when Winchester introduced the .300 Magnum. The .264, .338, and .458 Magnum all share a 2½-inch case length. Evidently to avoid direct competition with the existing .308 Norma Magnum and to better compete with the well-established and substantially longer .300 Weatherby Magnum, Winchester opted to increase case length and push the shoulder forward on its new .30-caliber magnum (actual usable capacity increase was marginal). The Wildcat .30-338 is likely exactly what Winchester would have offered had Norma not offered it first. Ballistics are very similar to the .300 Winchester Magnum, despite the slight reduction in powder capacity. Compared to that commercial chambering, a slightly longer case neck provides superior purchase for longer bullets. Remington and other mainstream manufacturers have offered rifles chambered for this round as a cataloged item.

.30-338 Winchester Magnum Loading Data (26-inch barrel)

Bullet (grains/type)	Powder	Grains	Velocity	Energy	Source/Comments
150 PSP-CL (Rem)	A4350	71.5	3203	3415	Accurate
150 PSP-CL (Rem)	A3100	76.0	3145	3295	Accurate
168 Sierra MK	A3100	68.5	3047	3460	Accurate
168 Sierra MK	A4350	73.5	3076	3530	Accurate
180 Sierra MK	A3100	72.5	2964	3510	Accurate
180 Sierra MK	A4350	66.0	2929	3430	Accurate
190 Sierra MK	A3100	72.3	3006	3810	Accurate
190 Sierra MK	A4350	65.0	2888	3520	Accurate
200 Sierra MK	A3100	71.0	2921	3790	Accurate
200 Sierra MK	A4350	64.0	2811	3510	Accurate
220 Sierra MK	A3100	70.0	2735	3655	Accurate
220 Sierra MK	A4350	63.0	2646	3420	Accurate
220 Sierra MK	AA 8700	80.0	2528	3120	Accurate

NEW

.327 Martin Meteor

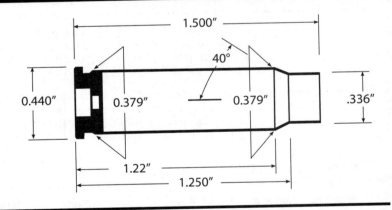

Historical Notes: The .327 Martin Meteor was developed, in December of 2008, to provide terminal performance that far exceeded that of the new .327 Federal in a revolver. It was engineered by Lee Martin, of Arlington, Virginia, and is based off the .357 Maximum cartridge case. Cases are formed by running virgin .357 Maximum brass through a full-length .327 Martin Meteor sizing die, and they are then are lathe-turned to a length of 1.52. Final length adjustment is completed on a case trimmer so that cases measure 1.50 inches. This is a bottleneck pistol cartridge developed to work in converted Ruger Blackhawk revolvers.

General Comments: Eight-inch barrels are preferred for this cartridge, in order to extract maximum performance. Custom cylinders made from 416 stainless provide the necessary strength. With an extremely flat trajectory and incredibly high velocities, this cartridge should work well on smallish big game like hogs and deer. Be careful with bullet selection; few .312-caliber bullets are engineered to withstand the high velocity impacts this cartridge can deliver. Speer's 110- and 115-grain Gold Dots and Hornady's 100-grain XTP bullets should be excellent choices. Do not try to duplicate these loads in a .327 Federal Magnum; you will ruin your revolver and possible some of your body parts.—R.A.M.

327 Martin Meteor Loading Data and Ballistics

Bullet (grains/type)	Powder	Grains	Velocity	Energy	Source/Comments
85 Hornady XTP	H 110	26.0	2203	915	Lee Martin
100 Hornady XTP	Lil' Gun	24	2108	986	Lee Martin

8mm-06

Historical Notes: Immediately after World War II, many shooters found themselves in possession of 8mm Mauser military rifles for which they could not obtain suitable ammunition. What could have been more natural than to re-chamber those rifles for the .30-06 case, with the neck expanded to take .323-inch bullets? Presto! The 8mm-06 was born. It is impossible to state positively who first accomplished this, as it probably happened at several places about the same time.

General Comments: The 8mm-06 in standard or Improved form is one of the better wildcat developments. It is similar to the German 8x64mm(S) Brenneke in both dimensions and performance. Using European nomenclature, this would be the 8x63mm(S). With the 125-grain bullet, it makes a very good varmint cartridge, while the 200- to 250-grain bullets are adequate for any North American big game. For those who do not like the performance of the standard 8mm cartridge, the 8mm-06 provides an inexpensive means of altering Mauser military rifles to a more powerful cartridge. However, the conversion eliminates the use of cheap, surplus military ammunition and requires use of handloads. Ballistics of the standard version well exceed .30-06 performance, while the Improved version adds another 100 fps and suggests serious big-game hunting performance potential.

8mm-06 Loading Data

Bullet (grains/type)	Powder	Grains	Velocity	Energy	Source/Comments
150	IMR 4895	59.0	3026	3050	Ackley
170 SP	IMR 4064	57.0	2930	3240	Ackley
200 SP	IMR 4350	61.0	2700	3260	
225 SP	IMR 4350	58.0	2515	3165	
250 SP	IMR 4831	62.0	2380	3145	Ackley

.33-08

Historical Notes: There was a time when, immediately after the introduction of a new cartridge, wildcatters would scream out with glee and neck its case up and down to various calibers. They had a field day, in 1952, when the .308 Winchester arrived on the scene. Winchester quickly covered two bases with its .243 Winchester and .358 Winchester cartridges, and, many years later, Remington took a couple wildcats under its wing and called them the .260 Remington and 7mm-08 Remington. One that got away for an even longer period of time was the .33-08 which, as its name implies, is the .308 case necked up for bullets of .338 caliber. One of the first reports on this one was filed by Roy Smith, in Rifle magazine. A fan of the Winchester Model 88 lever-action rifle, Smith had one of those rifles rebarreled to .33-08. Federal adopted the cartridge, in 2006, and renamed it the .338 Federal.

General Comments: When it comes to performance on game, the .33-08 and the .358 Winchester are in the same league, but the .33-caliber cartridge has the advantage of a better selection of bullets for handloading. Same goes for factory ammunition. Only one loading of the .358 is available from Winchester, while Federal offers seven .338 Federal loadings as this volume goes to print. Like the .338 Federal, this cartridge is seen at its best on big game, when loaded with bullets weighing from 200 to 225 grains, with the Nosler 210-grain Partition an old favorite. Starting loads published by various reloading component manufacturers for the .338 Federal can be used in this cartridge as well.

.338-223 Straight

Historical Notes: The .338-223 Straight originated, in 1972, with Max Atchisson of Atlanta, Georgia. It was intended as the cartridge for a blow-back semi-auto rifle he'd designed. It also had a secondary purpose as a possible cartridge for use in re-barreled Model 1907 Winchester self-loading rifles chambered for the .351 Winchester SL. At that time, .351 WSL ammunition was no longer manufactured and difficult to obtain in quantity. Winchester eventually reintroduced .351 WSL ammunition and eliminated that problem.

Although strictly an experimental development, the .338-223 is interesting, because it is the ultimate possibility in necking up the .223 Remington or similar cases. There are two versions of the cartridge, one made by necking up the full-length .223 case, the other based on cutting off the .223 case at the shoulder and trimming it to 1.412 inches. The full-length version presented two problems. First it was difficult to make without splitting the case neck. Second, with an overall length of 2.54 inches, it was too long to function through the action of re-barreled Model 1907 Winchester rifles. The short case, on the other hand, is almost the same length as the .351 Winchester SL and can be made to work in the Model 1907 rifle.

General Comments: The .351 Winchester SL is loaded with a 180-grain bullet at a muzzle velocity of 1850 fps. The .338-223 has a 200-grain bullet at 1820 fps, so the two are ballistically almost identical. Both cartridges are considered marginal for deer, but do very well on coyotes, bobcats, mountain lions, or similar predators at close range. The .338-223 project was eventually dropped, because the reappearance of .351 Winchester ammunition made such a cartridge non-viable. One problem with the .338-223 is that it is a rimless case, which must headspace on the case mouth. This works well with short pistol cartridges, but not as well with high-powered rifle cartridges. Finally, there seems to be no real need for such a cartridge.

.338-223 Loading Data

Bullet (grains/type)	Powder	Grains	Velocity	Energy	Source/Comments
200 SP	2400	18.3	1820	1880	NA
200 SP	IMR 4227	19.0	1750	1370	NA

Loading data for the short case only.

.338/50 Talbot

Historical Notes: The .338/50 is the work of Skip Talbot, of Talbot's Custom Equipment, in Fallon, Nevada. Skip began development of the cartridge, in 1984, as an outgrowth of working with the .50-caliber Browning Machine Gun cartridge. The .338/50 is the .50 BMG necked-down to .33-caliber and with the shoulder angle increased to 35 degrees. The primary purpose of the .338/50 is long-range target shooting at ranges out to 3,000 yards. Forming dies are made by RCBS (www.rcbs.com).

General Comments: The .338/50 is a highly specialized cartridge and not intended for hunting. It is, of course, adequate for any big game. Owing to the unusually large capacity, severe throat erosion occurred within 250 rounds. Talbot also tried a shortened version of the cartridge, about one inch shorter than the full-length case, in order to increase loading density. In the full-length version, a maximum load of 170 grains of Accurate Arms 8700 powder occupied only about 77 percent of the volumetric capacity. However, the short version was unsuccessful, because muzzle velocity was reduced about 500 fps. The full-length case developed a muzzle velocity of 3700 fps with the 250-grain bullet when fired from a 44-inch barrel. By comparison, the .340 Weatherby Magnum pushes the 250-grain bullet at an initial velocity of 2850 fps from a 26-inch barrel, so the .338/50 develops an additional 850 fps with the same bullet. The internal ballistic predictor program, QuickLOAD, shows that 581 fps of this difference results solely from the longer barrel. Equally, given a 44-inch barrel and loaded to similar pressures, the .340 Weatherby would produce 3350 fps. Therefore, these ballistics are not so impressive. However, with a much slower powder and bullets of 300 grains or heavier, the results might be spectacular. It is an interesting cartridge, but not very practical for most purposes until ceramic barrel liners come into vogue.

Bullet (grains/type)	Powder	Grains	Velocity	Energy	Source/Comments
250 SP	AA 8700	170.0	3700	7625	NA

9mm Action Express

Historical Notes: This is a 1988 innovation by Evan Whildin, who was Vice President of Action Arms, Ltd. at that time. The 9mm Action Express (9mm AE) is the .41 Action Express case necked-down to 9mm. It retains the .41 AE rebated rim, which is the same diameter as the standard 9mm Luger. The advantage of this in the 9mm AE is that the cartridge offers a larger case that can be used in firearms originally designed for the 9mm Luger without the necessity of changing the bolt or breech face. This will allow a number of .41 AE semi-auto pistols and carbines to be changed to the 9mm version through the installation of kits made available for specific guns.

General Comments: The 9mm AE has been tested in the Uzi semi-auto pistol and in specially altered 1911 Colt pistols. As a commercial round, it appeared chambered in the Action Arms TZ-75S88. It is a sort of super 9mm and, as such, is more powerful than the .38 Colt Super Auto. It has an advantage over the 9mm Winchester Magnum, since it is shorter and most 9mm pistols can be adapted to it. Tests in a 10-inch pressure barrel gave muzzle velocities with a 95-grain bullet of 1880 fps at 31,760 CUP, and 1903 fps with a 100-grain bullet at 34,880 CUP. These pressures are a bit on the high side for some semi-auto pistols. On the other hand, these are top loads and can be reduced and still maintain impressive velocities. A 124-grain bullet was measured at 1590 fps and 28,550 CUP, a load that could be digested by most 9mm autos. The 9mm AE is a potentially good self-defense and field cartridge. Of course, converted auto pistols are not likely to have 10-inch barrels, five inches being more normal. However, safe loads of around 1500 fps with the 124-grain bullet have been tested in converted Colt 1911 autos with five-inch barrels. This beats the .38 Colt Super Automatic and its 130-grain bullet at 1275 fps. Currently, this cartridge is not being commercially manufactured.

9mm Action Express Loading Data

Bullet (grains/type)	Powder	Grains	Velocity	Energy	Source/Comments
115 JHP	AA No. 9	16.1	1825	850	Action Arms
124 JHP	IMR 4227	13.3	1225	415	Action Arms
124 JHP	H110	16.5	1530	645	Action Arms

9x25mm Dillon

Historical Notes: Final design of the 9x25mm was completed in 1988, but the cartridge languished until top IPSC competitor Rob Leatham began testing, in 1991. This cartridge was developed by a group of people at Dillon, but was chiefly Randy Shelly's concept, and he is primarily responsible for the design. Randy's intention was to create a 9mm cartridge that would function through standard pistols and still produce IPSC Major Power Factor without requiring excessive pressures. In an effort to achieve Major Power Factor ratings with light bullets, which reduce recoil, many IPSC competitors have routinely used .38 Super loads generating rifle-type peak pressures! The 9x25mm is based on the 10mm Automatic case necked to 9mm. Its increased capacity allows loads to achieve the Major level with more reasonable pressure.

General Comments: The 9x25 Dillon is formed by necking the 10mm Automatic case to 9mm with a sharp shoulder and a short neck. This creates a relatively high-capacity pistol cartridge, which is based on a high-pressure case. With the proper bullet and powder, the 9x25mm Dillon can generate significant muzzle energy and easily achieves IPSC Major-Power levels. VihtaVuori has recently designed a powder (called Vit N105) specifically for this and similar cartridges. Appropriate 9mm bullets are readily available. The future is bright for this cartridge, and McNett's Double Tap Ammunition (www.doubletapammo. com) is currently offering 10 loads for this round. Springfield Armory offers guns in this chambering, and several custom barrel makers chamber tubes for this round. Representing an increasingly unique example of the breed, the 9x25mm Dillon meets a recognized need. For more information on the 9x25mm and Randy's more recent development, the 9x30mm, contact him at Dillon Precision (www. dillonprecision.com).

9x25mm Dillon Loading Data (8-inch barrel)

Bullet (grains/type)	Powder	Grains	Velocity	Energy	Source/Comments
100 FMJ RN	AA No. 9	15.3	1751	680	Lyman
100 FMJ RN	W296	17.2	1769	690	Lyman
115 JHP	Her-2400	13.0	1587	640	Lyman
115 JHP	W296	15.0	1566	625	Lyman
124 FMJ FP	W296	14.4	1529	640	Lyman
130 Cast	W296	13.5	1479	630	Lyman (No. 356634)

.357 Auto Mag

Historical Notes: The .357 Auto Mag is an outgrowth of the .44 Auto Mag and is based on the .44 Auto Mag case necked-down to .35-caliber. The .44 Auto Mag, in turn, is made by cutting off .30-06 or .308 Winchester case to a length of 1.298 inches and inside reaming to accept a .429-inch diameter bullet. The first Auto Mag pistols were announced in 1970 and delivered in late 1971. These were, of course, in .44-caliber. The .357 Auto Mag did not appear until 1973. One could purchase both the .357 and .44 barrel and slide assembly units to convert the pistol to handle either cartridge with a relatively easy parts change. Auto Mag ammunition was made in Mexico for a time, and by Norma in Sweden. Conversion of .44 Auto Mag cases to a smaller caliber is routine. Auto Mag semi-auto pistols are no longer in production.

General Comments: The .357 and .44 Auto Mag pistols were made of stainless steel, had a 6½-inch barrel, an overall length of 11½ inches and weighed 3.4 pounds. In other words, these were quite large and heavy, much like the Desert Eagle pistols currently available from Magnum Research. The .357 Auto Mag pushed the 158-grain jacketed bullet at a muzzle velocity of 1600 fps, and the 110-grain bullet at over 1900 fps, when loaded to maximum performance levels. This is certainly well in excess of anything feasible from a .357 Magnum revolver. Auto Mag pistols in .357 have been used with success on everything from varmints to deer. Like many of the more powerful handgun cartridges, ballistics of the .357 Auto Mag are marginal for big game, but, like the others, it can do the job in the hands of a good shot and accomplished hunter. As a self-defense gun, the Auto Mag pistols are a bit unwieldy and overpowered. These are strictly for sporting use.

.357 Auto Mag Loading Data

Bullet (grains/type)	Powder	Grains	Velocity	Energy	Source/Comments
110 JHP	BlueDot	19.0	1935	920	NA
125 JHP	BlueDot	18.0	1810	915	NA
140 JHP	BlueDot	17.0	1725	930	NA
158 JSP	BlueDot	16.0	1500	795	NA
158 JSP	H110	22.0	1635	940	NA

.357 Herrett

Historical Notes: Although the .30 Herrett proved a good handgun hunting cartridge when used in the 10- or 14-inch barrel of the Thompson/Center Contender single-shot pistol, it needed to be improved for hunting heavy game. One solution was to neck it up to .35-caliber, to take advantage of larger diameter, heavier bullets. This was done in the initial development. However, it appeared desirable to increase the powder capacity of the original .30 Herrett case, and, so, the final design used a case length of 1.75 inches, which is .15-inch longer than the .30 Herrett case. The development of the .357 Herrett was the work of Steve Herrett and gun writer Bob Milek. It was introduced as a standard chambering for the Thompson/Center pistol, in 1974. Cases are made by reforming, shortening, and necking up .30-30 or .32 Winchester Special cases. The case has a 30-degree shoulder angle. After forming, the cases are fire-formed to the final configuration.

General Comments: The .357 Herrett is another example of a wildcat cartridge developed for a specific firearm and purpose, filling a gap in the commercial line of ammunition. It was intended primarily as a hunting cartridge for the heavier varieties of medium game, although it also has become quite popular among silhouette shooters. It serves both purposes well, but one must bear in mind that, as a hunting cartridge, it delivers ballistics inferior to the .35 Remington fired from a rifle. While it is perfectly capable of handling large animals under average conditions, much depends on the skill of the user, something that is true of all handguns and handgun cartridges when used for hunting. The .357 Herrett is, nevertheless, one of the best of the handgun cartridges for field use on medium or small game and varmints.

.357 Herrett Loading Data

Bullet (grains/type)	Powder	Grains	Velocity	Energy	Source/Comments
110 JHP	2400	28.0	2600	1650	NA
110 JHP	IMR 4227	33.0	2685	1710	NA
125 JHP	IMR 4227	31.0	2565	1820	NA
150 JHP	IMR 4227	30.0	2380	1910	NA
158 JSP	IMR 4227	29.0	2310	1870	NA
180 JSP	IMR 4227	27.0	2130	1820	NA
180 JSP	Norma 200	32.0	2125	1810	NA

These loads are for the Thompson/Center Pistol with 14-inch barrel.

.35-30/30 (.35-30)

Historical Notes: Although not widely known, the .35-30/30 is one of our oldest wildcats, having originated around the turn of the century. Its original purpose was to salvage worn-out .32-40 and .32 Winchester Special barrels by reboring these to .35-caliber. The idea was also applied to improve the performance of Winchester Model 1894 rifles and carbines, while staying within the cartridge length and pressure limitations of that action. While the .35-30/30 cartridge is based on necking up .30-30 or .32 Winchester Special cases without any other change, a few rifles have been made up to accept the somewhat superior Ackley Improved version. Recently, there has been a rebirth of interest in this cartridge by silhouette shooters who like to use cast bullets. In 1976, Arizona gunsmith Paul Marquart built several .35-30/30 silhouette rifles based on the Remington 788 action, and these quickly established a reputation as being both accurate and effective for the intended sport. Information on these rifles was published in The Fouling Shot, published by the Cast Bullet Association (www.castbulletassoc.org), and other shooters found it promising as a target and hunting cartridge. The .35-30/30 can be loaded to about equal the ballistics of the .35 Remington, and, in fact, if Remington had not introduced its rimless .35, in 1908, it is highly possible that the necked-up .30-30 would have become much more popular than it did. In any event, it has gained a new but modest following.

General Comments: With jacketed bullets there is little, if any, difference between the ballistics and killing power of the .35-30/30 and the .35 Remington. On paper, the .35 Remington appears to have an edge over the .35-30/30, because it has about a 14-percent greater powder capacity, but the factory 200-grain bullet loading rarely attains 2000 fps, except in a 24-inch test barrel, chiefly because of rather anemic loading pressures. As a cast bullet cartridge, the .35-30/30, with its longer neck, permits use of cast bullets as heavy as 270 grains seated to a depth that will feed through magazine rifles designed for the .30-30. This is not possible with the .35 Remington and its short neck. In a strong action, the .35-30/30 can be loaded to deliver performance approaching the .375 Winchester. However, in a strong action, the .35 Remington can be stepped up quite a bit, too. It is possible to attain 1800 fps with a 300-grain bullet in a strong action chambered for the .35-30/30, which would make it suitable for elk or moose at short range. It is a good cartridge for upping the performance of .30-30 rifles or for salvaging worn-out .32 Special barrels. For a wildcat, it is rather a special-purpose cartridge, but one that may fill the needs of a number of shooters. Dies are available from RCBS (www.rcbs.com) and chambering reamers from Clymer (www.clymertool.com).

.35/30-30 Loading Data

Bullet (grains/type)	Powder	Grains	Velocity	Energy	Source/Comments
200 JSP	IMR 4198	25.0	1925	1650	NA
208 Lead	IMR 4198	25.0	1895	1660	NA
210 Lead	W630	15.0	1520	1080	Lyman 35875
245 Lead	H335	30.0	1770	1710	Lyman 358318
282 Lead	H335	28.0	1700	1810	Lyman 3589
292 Lead	W748	33.5	1620	1580	NA

NEW
.358 BFG (1.625 Inch)

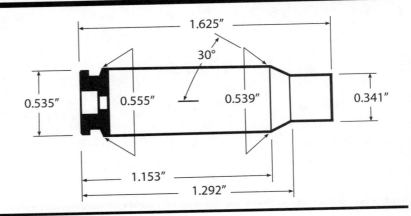

Historical Notes: In 2007, the Indiana Natural Resources Commission made a significant change to the State's deer hunting regulations, making it legal to hunt deer with a rifle as long as the cartridge case used measured no longer than 1.625 inches in length and fired a bullet that was no less than .35-caliber (.358-inch in diameter). Immediately, wildcat rifle cartridges that met these restrictions started appearing. The .358 BFG (1.625 inches) cartridge was designed by Bryan Farrington, from Clinton, Indiana, and utilizes the .25 WSSM cartridge case necked up to .358-caliber. It should be noted that, as with many wildcats based on new cartridge cases, this particular .35/.25 WSSM is not the only version of this conversion being used. However, the .358 BFG (1.625 Inch) cartridge does fall within the guidelines of a legal Indiana rifle cartridge for deer hunting.

Note: On September 20, 2011, the Indiana Natural Resources Commission made a significant change to the State's deer hunting regulations. The allowable length of a centerfire rifle case was increased from 1.625 inches—made legal in 2007—to 1.80 inches. The previous restriction had been in place to limit hunters to using rifles chambered for pistol caliber cartridges, and the increase in case length was, it is thought, to allow the use of the .460 Smith & Wesson. The regulation also specifies a minimum cartridge caliber of .358.

General Comments: This cartridge closely duplicates the ballistics of the .358 Winchester, which has long been considered a sublime deer cartridge. I discovered this, in 2005, when I worked with Charlie Sisk of Sisk Rifles and Dave Kiff of Pacific Tool & Gauge to produce an almost identical version of this wildcat. Bryan Farrington indicates that necks will need to be trim turned for his cartridge, and I had the same experiences when I worked with my version of the .35/.25 WSSM. It is also necessary to neck up from .25 to .35 in at least a two-stage process, going from .25- to .30-caliber and then to .35 using a tapered expander ball. As noted, various versions of this cartridge exist, and neck diameter and free-bore vary a great deal from one chamber to another, so approach with caution. It is strongly suggested that you utilize one source for a rifle and dies to eliminate this issue.—R.A.M.

.358 BFG (1.625 Inch) Loading Data and Ballistics

Bullet (grains/type)	Powder	Grains	Velocity	Energy	Source
180 Hornady SP/SSP	Reloader 10X	48.0	2700	2913	Bryan Farrington
200 Hornady SP	Reloader 10X	46.0	2550	2887	Bryan Farrington

NEW

.35 Indiana

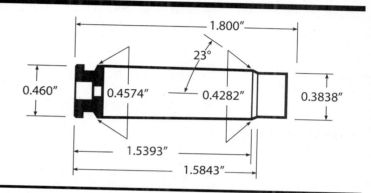

Historical Notes: While working on the 13th Edition of Cartridges of the World, I used my Empty Cases blog (www. gunwriter.wordpress.com), to gain feedback for the book and to uncover new wildcat cartridges. A reader from Indiana by the name of Scott Jones contacted me about wildcats that would meet the .35-caliber/1.8-inch case length requirements for deer hunting in Indiana with a rifle. (On September 20, 2011, the Indiana Natural Resources Commission made a significant change to the State's deer hunting regulations. The allowable length of a centerfire rifle case was increased from 1.625 inches—made legal in 2007—to 1.80 inches. The previous restriction had been to limit hunters to using rifles chambered for pistol-caliber cartridges, and the increase in case length was, it is thought, to allow the use of the .460 Smith & Wesson. The regulation also specifies a minimum cartridge caliber of .358.) Scott and I decided that the simplest solution was to just shorten a .35 Remington case from 1.92 to 1.8 inches. Factory .35 Remington dies can still be used. Additionally, since Jones intended to chamber this new wildcat in a bolt-action rifle, the cartridge could be loaded to pressures well in excess of factory .35 Remington ammunition.

General Comments: Another factoid not realized by many is that even though the .35 Remington has a rim diameter that is 0.013 smaller than cartridges based on the common .308 rim diameter of 0.473, it will still function perfectly in Remington 700 rifles originally set up for a cartridge with a 0.473 rim. No alterations to the Remington 700 magazine box are required, either. The .35 Indiana can drive a 180-grain bullet to 2450 fps from a 22-inch barrel. This is more than sufficient for deer hunting out to 250 yards or so.—R.A.M.

.35 Indiana Loading Data & Ballistics

Bullet (grains/type)	Powder	Grains	Velocity	Energy	Source
180 Barnes Tipped TSX	AA 2015	25.5	2455	2408	Richard Mann
200 Core-Lokt PSP	AA 2015	43.5	2400	2557	Richard Mann

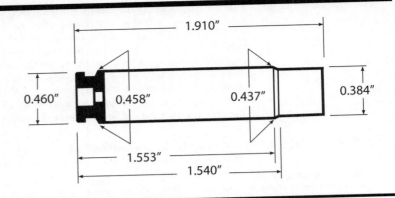

NEW
.35 SuperMann

Historical Notes: The .35 SuperMann is nothing more than an Improved version of the classic .35 Remington cartridge intended for use in bolt-action rifles only. The cartridge was developed by gun writer Richard Mann and custom rifle builder Charlie Sisk (www.siskguns.com) by blowing out or increasing the shoulder diameter of the .35 Remington case to from .419 to .437. Mann is a fan of the .358 Winchester cartridge, but factory ammunition is sometimes hard to come by, and necking up .308 Winchester cases can be time consuming. He wanted a .35-caliber cartridge that offered .358 Winchester power, but liked the idea of being able to use the less expensive factory .35 Remington ammunition for practice or as low-recoil hunting loads. The difference in the two cartridges is twofold; diameter of the shoulder, and pressure. This very slightly increases powder capacity, but, more importantly, it prevents the hotter loaded cartridge from being chambered in weak actions intended for .35 Remington operating pressures. Dies and reamers are available on a custom basis from Pacific Tool & Gauge (www.pacific-toolandgauge.com).

General Comments: A rifle in .35 SuperMann is easy to assemble. All that is needed is a short-action Remington 700 with a .473 bolt face—one in .308 Winchester is perfect—and a new barrel. Even though the .35 Remington has a slightly smaller rim diameter of .460, it will still function fine with a Remington 700 bolt sized for a .308 case. Loaded to a maximum average pressure of 58,000 psi, the .35 SuperMann delivers some impressive ballistics from a 16¼-inch barrel; a 200-grain bullet can be pushed to 2400 fps. A bolt-action rifle in .35 SuperMann will function perfectly with and accurately shoot factory .35 Remington ammunition. For the handloader, this makes for a versatile eastern woods rifle for deer, bear, or hogs that can also be used with factory ammunition for practice or recoil-sensitive hunters.—R.A.M.

.35 SuperMann Loading Data

Bullet (grains/type)	Powder	Grains	Velocity	Energy	Source
158 Hornady XTP (.357 Pistol)	AA 2015	43.5	2480	2157	Richard Mann / Sisk Rifles
150 LeHigh Brass HP	AA 2015	44.5	2520	2114	Richard Mann / Sisk Rifles
180 Hornady SP	AA 2015	44.0	2456	2410	Richard Mann / Sisk Rifles
200 Remington Whelen PSP	AA 2015	43.5	2410	2578	Richard Mann / Sisk Rifles
200 Barnes TSX	AA 2015	44.0	2420	2600	Richard Mann / Sisk Rifles
200 Remington PSP	AA 1680	36.5	2359	2470	Richard Mann / Sisk Rifles
225 Nosler Partition	AA 2015	41.5	2261	2553	Richard Mann / Sisk Rifles

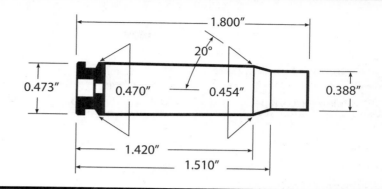

NEW
.358 Hoosier

Historical Notes: On September 20, 2011, the Indiana Natural Resources Commission made a significant change to the State's deer hunting regulations. The allowable length of a centerfire rifle case was increased from 1.625 inches—made legal in 2007—to 1.80 inches. The previous restriction had been in place to limit hunters to using rifles chambered for pistol caliber cartridges, and the increase in case length was, it is thought, to allow the use of the .460 Smith & Wesson. The regulation also specifies a minimum cartridge caliber of .358. For several years, wildcatters have been building rifles chambered for .35-caliber bullets on a short 1.625-inch case. The recent allowance of the longer case increases the allowable powder capacity and potential performance. Indiana rifleman, hunter, and wildcatter Bill Herring saw the potential for shortening the .358 Winchester case for use as a legal deer cartridge in his state. The first incarnation of this cartridge had a 1.625-inch case. More recently, Herring lengthened the case to 1.80 inches, and the result is what he calls the .358 Hoosier.

General Comments: The .358 Hoosier case is formed by cutting off the .358 Winchester case to 1.8 inches and then running it through a .358 Hoosier die one time. After this single pass through the die, the case will need to be trimmed back to 1.8 inches, but no other modifications are necessary. Pacific Tool and Guage (www.pacifictoolandgauge.com) can supply chamber reamers, and dies are available from Hornady on a custom basis. The resulting cartridge performs best with 180- and 200-grain bullets and will deliver muzzle velocities of 2600 and 2500 fps, respectively, from a 22-inch barrel. The .358 Hoosier comes close to matching standard .358 Winchester velocities and greatly enhances the power that an Indiana deer hunter can apply to a whitetail deer. At the same time, when compared to the pistol caliber cartridges this regulation was intended to encompass, an Indiana deer hunter now has a firearm with a much longer effective range. It is questionable if any major manufacturer will adopt this cartridge, since the potential for sales is mostly limited to one state. However, that does not take anything away from the .358 Hoosier, which would be just as effective for deer or larger game anywhere else on earth.—R.A.M.

.358 Hoosier Loading Data and Ballistics

Bullet (grains/type)	Powder	Grains	Velocity	Energy	Source
180 Hornady SP/SSP	Reloader 7	42.6	2690		Bill Herring
180 Barnes TTSX	Reloader 10X	43.0	2640		Bill Herring
200 Hornady PSP	Reloader 10X	43.0	2550		Bill Herring

.35 Sambar

Historical Notes: Breil Jackson, Editor of Australia's Guns and Game magazine, developed the .35 Sambar. David Stendell built the first rifle on a Model 70 Classic .300 WSM action. The .35 Whelen is a popular sambar deer cartridge in southeast Australia, and Jackson was trying to improve upon its performance, while allowing for the use of a short-action compact rifle for hunting in thick brush. The project was launched in 2001, and development of the .35 Sambar was featured in a series of articles in Guns and Game magazine throughout 2002.

General Comments: The .35 Sambar is the .300 WSM case necked up to .35-caliber with no other changes. Using 250-grain bullets of good construction, it is a very powerful cartridge in a short-action rifle, suitable for most big game. Velocities of 2700 fps can be achieved with 250-grain bullets from a 23-inch barrel. Lighter bullets can also be used for smaller game and longer range, especially the Nosler Ballistic Tip bullets.

.35 Sambar Loading Data

Bullet (grain/type)	Powder	Grains	Velocity	Energy	Source/Comments
200 Hornady SP	Varget	65.0	2771	3410	Breil Jackson
200 Hornady SP	Varget	68.0	2920	3787	Breil Jackson
225 Nosler BT	Varget	65.0	2755	3793	Breil Jackson
225 Nosler BT	H4350	75.0	2843	4039	Breil Jackson
250 Speer GS	H4350	72.0	2700	4048	Breil Jackson

NEW

.358 Gremlin

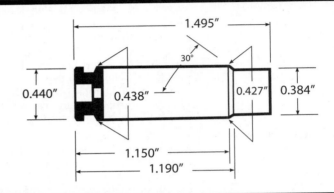

Historical Notes: The .358 Gremlin is a wildcat based on the 6.5 Grendel cartridge, which uses the 7.62X39 cartridge case as a base. It was developed, in 2008, by Bryan Farrington, from Clinton, Indiana, to meet the requirements established in 2007 by the Indiana Natural Resources Commission (INRC). In that year, the INRC made it legal to hunt deer with a rifle with any cartridge using a case that measured no longer than 1.625 inches and fired a bullet that no less than .35-caliber (.358-inch in diameter.) Immediately, wildcat rifle cartridges that met these restrictions started appearing. The .358 lure of the .358 Gremlin is that it was designed to utilize the AR-15 platform. Conversion to the .358 Gremlin is easy with any AR-15 that is set up for the 7.62X39 or 6.5 Grendel cartridge.

Note: On September 20, 2011, the Indiana Natural Resources Commission made a significant change to the State's deer hunting regulations. The allowable length of a centerfire rifle case was increased from 1.625 inches—made legal in 2007—to 1.80 inches. The previous restriction had been in place to limit hunters to using rifles chambered for pistol caliber cartridges, and the increase in case length was, it is thought, to allow the use of the .460 Smith & Wesson. The regulation also specifies a minimum cartridge caliber of .358.

General Comments: This cartridge closely duplicates the ballistics of the .35 Remington, a cartridge with a stellar track record in the deer woods. Although conceived for the AR-15 platform, in Indiana, it has become a popular conversion for bolt-action rifles like the Ruger 77 and CZ 527 that started life out as 7.62X39mm. Hunters are also chambering this cartridge in Thompson G2/Encore rifles. Though conceived as a one-state answer to newly passed hunting laws, the cartridge has great merit in a rifle specifically designed for young hunters or those who maybe intolerant of excessive recoil. Additionally, anyone looking for a cartridge for an AR-15 that offers more punch than a .223 Remington for hunting wild hogs might want to consider the .358 Gremlin.—R.A.M.

.358 Gremlin Loading Data and Ballistics

Bullet (grains/type)	Powder	Grains	Velocity	Energy	Source
140 Hornady XTP	Lil Gun	25.5	2460	1880	Bryan Farrington
180 Hornady SS/SP	Lil Gun	25.5	2350	2206	Bryan Farrington
200 Hornady SP	H 4227	25.0	2025	1820	Bryan Farrington

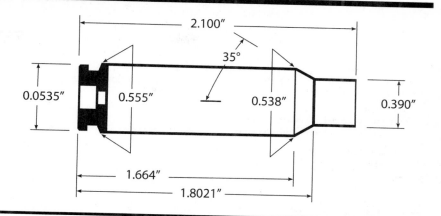

NEW
.358/300 WSM

Historical Notes: As soon as wildcatters heard about Winchester's new .300 WSM cartridge, their brains started turning. This short fat case with a large powder capacity and a rebated rim has been necked up and down. Winchester did the same necking it down to both .277- and .284-caliber for its .270 and 7mm WSM cartridges. Necking the case up to .358-caliber was an obvious choice. Almost every factory .30-caliber cartridge has had the same treatment; consider the .358 Winchester, which is based on the .308 Winchester case, and the .35 Whelen, which is based on the .30-06 case. The .358-300 WSM caries on this tradition, and though a number of wildcatters have made this conversion, not all of them followed the same design criteria. You can find several versions of this wildcat chambering where the dimensions differ slightly. Anyone looking to work with this cartridge should take care in assuring that their handloading dies match the chamber dimensions of their rifle.

General Comments: Gun writer Bryce Towsley took the most logical approach, as have several others. He simply necked the .300 WSM case up to .358-caliber, but did not alter the shoulder diameter, datum line, base-to-shoulder, or base-to-neck dimensions. This method of wildcatting is the common-sense approach, when necking up to a larger caliber. However, when necking down, especially by one caliber, care should be taken to slightly alter these dimensions so that the larger caliber cartridge cannot chamber in the smaller caliber cartridge firearm.

The .358-300 WSM is a powerful medium-bore cartridge suitable for any game in North America, and all but the most dangerous game anywhere else. It will push a 225-grain Nosler Accubond in excess of 2800 fps. This is a clear 150 fps advantage over the .35 Whelen, which requires a longer action, and at least a 300 fps velocity advantage when compared to the .358 Winchester.—R.A.M.

.358 / 300 WSM Loading Data and Ballistics

Bullet (grains/type)	Powder	Grains	Velocity	Energy	Source
220 Speer FP	Reloader 17	76.0	2929	4190	Bryce Towsley
225 Nosler Accubond		75.0	2816	3961	Bryce Towsley

.358 UMT (Ultra Mag Towsley)

Historical Notes: A 1999 idea of gun writer Bryce Towsley, the .358 Ultra Mag Towsley puts zip back into the family of .35-caliber cartridges. The 358 UMT shoots flatter than the 7mm Remington Magnum or the .300 Winchester Magnum. The cartridge is intended for elk, big bears, moose, and larger African plains game. Towsley tested the cartridge in Africa, taking kudu, zebra, nyala, gemsbok, and waterbuck at ranges varying from 10 to 450 yards. If Remington ever decided to extend the Ultra Mag series to .35-caliber, odds are the new cartridge would be a spitting image of the .358 UMT.

General Comments: Based on necking up the available and affordable .300 Remington Ultra Mag parent case, the .358 UMT maintains the same body taper, 30-degree shoulder, and headspacing datum line. Only the larger neck and resulting shorter shoulder distinguish the .358 UMT from its non-belted parent case and, naturally, Remington 700 actions are well-suited for this cartridge. The high velocities possible with this wildcat demand premium bullets, such as the Barnes X-bullet, Nosler Partition, or Swift A-Frame. Many .35-caliber bullets are designed for lower velocity cartridges and may not perform well in the .358 UMT. Loads listed below were tested in the Barnes Ballistic Lab.

.358 Ultra Mag Towsley Loading Data

Bullet (grains/type)	Powder	Grains	Velocity	Energy	Source/Comments
180 X-Bullet	MRP	101.5	3408	4641	Barnes/59,000 psi
225 XLC	IMR7828	95.0	3039	4613	Barnes/59,100 psi
250 X-Bullet	RL-25	90.0	2965	4879	Barnes/58,000 psi
250 Nosler Partition	H-1000	102.0	3029	5092	Barnes/61,400 psi
250 Nosler BT	H-1000	104.0	3011	5032	Barnes/57,300 psi

NEW
9.3 Sisk

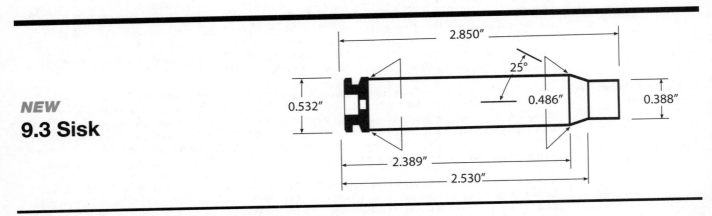

Historical Notes: Charlie Sisk of Sisk Rifles (www.siskguns.com) in Dayton, Texas, has an affinity for cartridges that shoot a .366 (9.3mm) bullet and so has developed several wildcats in this caliber. The one he has used and sold the most is the 9.3 Sisk, which is an 8mm Remington Magnum case necked up to .366. This is indeed a powerful cartridge that will drive a 286-grain Nosler Partition in excess of 2800 fps, besting the time-honored 9.3X62mm cartridge by at least 300 fps.

General Comments: Initially, Sisk has used his 9.3 Sisk cartridge on a variety of large game in America and Africa, with very fine results. An awakened interest in the 9.3X62mm in the states has brought about an interest in 9.3-caliber rifle cartridges in general, and the 9.3 Sisk is one of the most powerful of the lot. Matched with a 250-grain Barnes Triple Shock or 286-grain Nosler Partition, it is capable of cleanly taking any game animal on the planet.—R.A.M.

9.3 Sisk Loading Data and Ballistics

Bullet (grains/type)	Powder	Grains	Velocity	Energy	Source/Comments
250 Barnes Triple Shock	H 4350	88.0	2920	4732	Sisk Rifles
286 Nosler Partition	H 4350	84.0	2820	5049	Sisk Rifles

NEW
9.3 BS

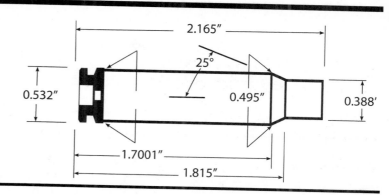

Historical Notes: Developed partially as a joke—hence the "BS"—that pokes fun at the notion the world needs another wildcat cartridge, but also to take advantage of some modern 9.3-caliber big-game bullets and a shorter-actioned rifle than will work with the famous 9.3X62 mm, the 9.3 BS is the brainchild of gun writer John Barsness (B) and custom rifle builder Charlie Sisk (S). The 9.3 BS is based off the .350 Remington Magnum case, which is simply necked up to 9.3-caliber.

General Comments: Initially, Charlie Sisk (www.siskguns.com) made two rifles chambered for this cartridge, one for Barsness and the other for himself. After an article in Handloader magazine and some savvy Internet promotion, several other custom rifles were built by those who recognized the virtues of the cartridge or by those who were readers and fans of Barsness' writings. Even though the cartridge was initially conceived as sort of a joke, it is a viable big-game cartridge suitable for use anywhere in the world. Both Barsness and Sisk have taken several animals to include Asian water buffalo and grizzly. Brass with the 9.3 BS head stamp is available from Sisk Rifles, reamers are available from Pacific Tool & Gauge (www.pacifictoolandgauge.com), and custom dies can be obtained from Redding (www. redding-reloading.com). The 9.3 BS will do anything the much older 9.3X62 mm will do.—R.A.M.

9.3 BS Loading Data

Bullet (grains/type)	Powder	Grains	Velocity	Energy	Source/Comments
250 Barnes Triple Shock	TAC	58.0	2610	3780	Sisk Rifles
286 Nosler Partition	H 4895	54.0	2460	3842	Sisk Rifles

.366 DGW

Historical Notes: A high performance, medium-bore wildcat cartridge crafted by Maine gunsmith Judson Stewart Bailey, the .366 DGW is identified with the initials of its creator, David G. Walker. Walker's idea was to achieve optimum performance from the .416 Rigby parent case, directly necking it down to accept .366 (9.3mm) bullets. With a 24-inch barrel propelling high sectional density and ballistic coefficient bullets at relatively low pressures, Bailey believes the .366 DGW will shoot flatter and out-penetrate the Remington Ultra Magnums, the .338 Lapua, and the .338/378 Weatherby. In 2001, Bailey successfully hunted with the cartridge in South Africa, taking zebra, kudu, warthog, wildebeest, nyala, blesbok, and gemsbok.

General Comments: Strictly a custom rifle proposition, the .366 DBW cartridge has been chambered in Ruger No. 1 single-shot and converted Enfield P14 bolt-action rifles. The Beretta/SAKO TRG-s and longer BRNO ZKK 602 and CZ actions would also be suitable for this .416 Rigby-based cartridge. Reloading dies are available from RCBS (www.rcbs.com). Suitably dimensioned bullets are available from various manufacturers, including Nosler, Woodleigh, Swift, Barnes, and Speer.

.366 DGW Loading Data

Bullet (grains/type)	Powder	Grains	Velocity	Energy	Source/Comments
250 Nosler BT	IMR4350	98.0	3253	5875	Judson Bailey
286 Nosler Partition	IMR7828	103.0	3020	5775	Judson Bailey
300 Swift A-Frame	H4831	97.0	2911	5607	Judson Bailey

.375 Whelen (.375-06)
.375 Ackley Improved

Historical Notes: The .375 Whelen, also known as the .375-06, was not developed by the late Col. Townsend Whelen, but was named in his honor. The cartridge was actually the work of the late gunsmith and writer L.R. "Bob" Wallack, in 1951, and is based on the .30-06 case necked up. There are two versions, one based on the standard case and retaining the original 17-degree, 30-minute shoulder angle, the other the Improved case with a 40-degree shoulder angle. The Improved case holds slightly more powder and provides vastly superior headspace control, so it is the more popular version. An increment of .375-inch is about as far as one can go in expanding the .30-06 case without running into headspace problems, due to lack of a distinct shoulder. Experiments with larger diameter bullets have invariably led to headspacing problems. An example of this was the .400 Whelen, which never became popular and is no longer chambered.

General Comments: The .375 Whelen is not as powerful as the .375 H&H Magnum, but is, nevertheless, a good medium bore for application against most dangerous game. It is certainly adequate for any North American big game. It uses bullets from 200 to 300 grains and, because it is strictly a handloading proposition, can be quite flexible. It can be loaded down with 200- or 250-grain bullets for deer hunting, as well as loaded to full power for larger animals. This is one advantage of wildcat cartridges; these must be handloaded and, so, can be tailored to fit different game and hunting situations. As with the .338 and .35 versions of the '06, Ackley's Improved design is superior. In this instance, it is mandatory to ensure adequate headspace control.

.375 Ackley Improved Loading Data

Bullet (grains/type)	Powder	Grains	Velocity	Energy	Source/Comments
200 SP	IMR 4895	58.0	2450	2265	
235 SP	IMR 4064	60.0	2475	3205	
270 SP	IMR 4064	57.0	2380	3400	
300 SP	IMR 4064	52.0	2110	2975	

.400 Whelen

Historical Notes: Of the various cartridges named after the late Col. Townsend Whelen, recent research indicates that he actually developed both the .35 and the .400 rounds that bear his name. According to Phil Sharpe,[*] Col. Whelen developed this cartridge while he was commanding officer at Frankford Arsenal, during the early 1920s. The .400 Whelen is based on the .30-06 case necked up with no other changes.

General Comments: The .400 Whelen was not a successful development, because expansion of the .30-06 case neck to this size leaves only a very slight shoulder. This can give rise to serious headspace problems—particularly with incautious handloading and sloppy chambering practices. Nonetheless, properly built custom rifles in this chambering were used successfully in the United States, Canada, and Africa on big game. The .37-caliber bore size is the maximum for the .30-06 case without creating a potential for headspace problems. The combination of careful chambering and ammunition production can evidently mitigate this potential, because G&H rifles in .400 Whelen were used extensively, with no known complaints. J.D. Jones, at SSK Industries (www.sskindustries.com), now offers a .416-06 Improved using a 60-degree shoulder and a body taper similar to Ackley's design. The .400 Whelen works perfectly with no headspace complaints to date. Had Whelen utilized an Improved design, perhaps his .400 would have fared better. Good evidence also suggests that one reason for its short popularity was that most shooters considered it both unnecessarily powerful for North American hunting and only marginally powerful for the most serious of African applications.

*Sharpe, Phillip B., Complete Guide to Handloading, Funk & Wagnalls Co., 1941, p. 398.

Bullet (grains/type)	Powder	Grains	Velocity	Energy	Source/Comments
300 JSP	IMR 3031	60.0	2265	3415	
350 JSP	IMR 3031	57.0	2100	3430	

.41 Special

Historical Notes: It would be impossible to guess who might have been the first to think of this cartridge as a wildcat chambering. Almost certainly, the first gun was completed within a few years of introduction of the .41 Magnum (1964). Basically, the .41 Special is nothing more than the .41 Magnum case shortened to 1.16-inch, which matches case length for both .38 and .44 Special, hence the "Special" moniker. Typically, gunsmiths fit and re-chamber a .38 or .357 cylinder to a .41 Magnum gun or install a converted cylinder and new barrel into some other large-frame revolver. Ruger's Flattop and Old Model (three-screw frame) and Smith & Wesson's 586 and 686 are some of the better revolvers for this conversion.

General Comments: In 1932, Colt's pursued development of a .41 Special cartridge for police use. At least three versions were tested. These differed only in case length (and ballistics). That .41 Special used a .385-inch bullet and, except for the name, had no relationship whatsoever to this wildcat. Commercial production was not pursued.

Compared to the longer-cased .41 Magnum, this cartridge gives better ballistic uniformity with so-called mid-range loads—200- to 220-grain bullets launched at about 1000 fps—which is a fine self-defense combination. Top loads can approach the ballistics of .41 Magnum factory levels, but that defeats the intended purpose of providing sufficient energy and velocity for serious self-defense use, or for hunting of smaller big-game species up to deer. This is a very good cartridge and deserves more attention than it has heretofore received. Note that bullets as light as 135 grains are offered for .40-caliber pistols. This would suggest that 140-grain, .41-caliber JHP bullets should be workable. Supposing revolvers of essentially the same weight with loads generating about 500 ft-lbs of energy, the lighter bullet would generate 15-percent less recoil energy. This is a significant difference and would reduce recovery time and make the gun easier for shooters to manage and master.

.41 Special Ballistic Data

Bullet (grains/type)	Powder	Grains	Velocity	Energy	Source/Comments
200 Speer JHP	H4227	14.5	1035	475	John Taffin
200 Speer JHP	Unique	7.0	1043	480	John Taffin
200 Speer JHP	2400	12.5	1082	520	John Taffin
215 Cast SWC	Unique	7.0	1027	500	John Taffin
215 Cast SWC	2400	12.5	1063	385	John Taffin
215 Cast SWC	H4227	14.5	1037	500	John Taffin

.416 Barnes

Historical Notes: The .416 Barnes was the last cartridge design of the late Frank Barnes, the original author of this book. In the late 1980s, Barnes began to think about various .40-caliber rifle cartridges. He realized that, though there were many available, most were designed for use in Africa. Barnes felt there would be strong interest in a .416 designed for American game and hunting conditions, rather than the dangerous African species. Additionally, he felt it would be advantageous if it could be adapted to several different rifle actions, rather than being limited to a single type. After studying the old .40-caliber cartridges, which are too long for today's actions, Barnes settled on the final version, which uses the .45-70 Government cartridge as its base. By using the .45-70, a number of current actions become available, which make for easy conversions to the .416 Barnes. Readily available and very reasonably priced in particular is Marlin's M-1895 lever-action. Unfortunately, few commercial bullets in .416 are available in the weight range intended and appropriate for use in tubular-magazine rifles.

General Comments: The .416 Barnes would be an excellent cartridge for North American big game. Loading data for this cartridge is limited. Barnes recommended using 37 grains of Rl-7 to push a 400-grain bullet at 1625 fps. IMR 3031 is another good, general-purpose powder for the .416 Barnes in a lever-action rifle. Barnes found an accurate load of 50 grains of IMR 3031 behind a 330-grain bullet. It gave him a velocity of 2045 fps. This cartridge really comes into its own when used with 270- and 330-grain bullets. Though it provides no real advantage for the deer hunter, it would prove to be an excellent elk, moose, or brown bear cartridge.

.416 Barnes Loading Data

Bullet (grains/type)	Powder	Grains	Velocity	Energy	Source/Comments
300 SP	IMR 4198	52.0	2355	3695	NA
300 SP	Rl-7	54.0	2270	3435	NA
330 Lead	IMR 3031	50.0	2045	3065	NA
400 SP	IMR 4198	44.0	1920	3275	NA
400 SP	IMR 4064	58.0	2140	4070	NA
400 SP	H335	59.0	2155	4125	NA
400 Lead	IMR 4198	39.0	1830	2975	NA

.416 Aagaard

Historical Notes: Named as a tribute to the late African professional hunter and writer Finn Aagaard, the .416 Aagaard delivers .404 Jeffery ballistics in a compact cartridge suitable for a medium-length action. Fred Zeglin designed this cartridge, in 2002, for Frank Selman, a friend and hunting partner of Aagaard's.

General Comments: The .416 Aagaard uses Hornady's .376 Steyr brass as the parent case. The modern Hornady brass is necked up to .416 and sized to create a new shoulder before fire-forming in a .416 Aagaard chamber. The cartridge is well suited for bolt-action rifles using a 24-inch barrel and a 1:14 rifling twist. Note that the .376 Steyr case requires a special bolt face diameter. Z-Hat Custom (www.z-hat.com) offers rifles, dies, and reloading information. Hornady sells .376 Steyr brass. Ballistics data cited below was measured in a 21-inch barrel.

.416 Aagaard Loading Data

Bullet (grains/type)	Powder	Grains	Velocity	Energy	Source/Comments
350 Speer	VV N133	62.0	2239	3895	Z-Hat Custom
350 Speer	H4895	65.0	2316	4168	Z-Hat Custom
400 Hawk	RL-15	64.0	2160	4143	Z-Hat Custom

NEW
.416 SM²
(.416/300 WSM)

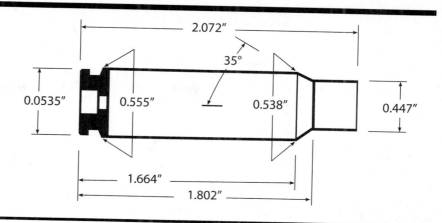

Historical Notes: Designed by Charlie Sisk of Sisk Rifles and gun writer Richard Mann, the .416 SM² was intended as a dangerous-game cartridge that would work in a standard length short-action rifle. The SM² designation stands for Sisk/Mann and Short/Magnum. Essentially, this cartridge slightly betters the performance of the great .404 Jeffery and another wildcat cartridge, the .416 Aagaard designed by Fred Zeglin of Z-hat Custom. This wildcat has been conceptualized by several other wildcatters, but no standardized SAAMI measurements exist. It is nothing more than a .300 WSM necked up to .416-caliber.

General Comments: This cartridge was developed by Sisk and Mann for an African buffalo hunt that never materialized. It is indeed a very powerful cartridge for a short-action rifle and, when loaded with proper bullets, is suitable for use on any dangerous game animal. Interest in short magnum cartridges has somewhat waned in recent years, and rifles with a proper bolt face are not as readily available as one may have thought just a few years back. Still, there are quite a few .300 WSM rifles around, and all one needs to do to convert to a .416 SM² or .416/300 WSM is chamber and install a new barrel. Handloading dies are available from Redding (www.redding-reloading.com)on a custom basis, and chamber reamers can be supplied by Pacific Tool & Gauge (www.pacifictoolandgauge.com).—R.A.M.

.416 SM² Loading Data

Bullet (grains/type)	Powder	Grains	Velocity	Energy	Source
350 Barnes TSX	Ramshot TAC	67.5.0	2450	4664	Sisk Rifles
400 Barnes TSX	AA 2495	60.0	2300	4697	Sisk Rifles

NEW
.416 UMT
(Ultra Mag Towsley)

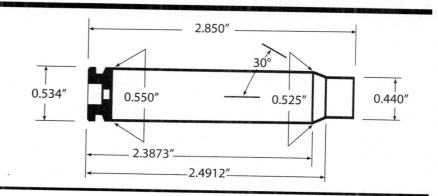

Historical Notes: The .416 UMT, (the "UMT" stands for Ultra Mag Towsley) was the second of a pair of cartridges gun writer Bryce M. Towsley designed and based on the Remington Ultra Mag case. Towsley worked with custom gunmaker Mark Basner (www.basnersrifles.com) to build the rifles. Like the .358 UMT, the .416 UMT is not a complicated wildcat. It is simply a .375 Remington Ultra Mag case necked up to take a .416 bullet. The shoulder angle, base-to-shoulder length, and datum line are all the same as the .375 RUM. The case holds 120.2 grains of water. By comparison, the .416 Remington holds 103.4 grains of water, and the .416 Rigby 129.6 grains. The Ultra Mag class of cartridges were all designed to operate at a maximum average pressure of 65,000 psi, which is the same as the .416 Remington, but much higher than the Rigby. The .416 UMT generates more muzzle energy than either the .458 Winchester or the mighty .470 Nitro Express. It's actually in the same class as the .500 Nitro Express and very close to the .458 Lott, which is enough power to handle anything on earth, in any circumstance.

General Comments: Towsley first tested his .416 UMT rifle in Tanzania, on Cape buffalo and several smaller species. It was also used by his son, Nathan, a few months later to take a moose in their home state of Vermont. While it's designed for African dangerous game up to and including elephant, the .416 UMT is also an excellent choice in North America for big animals like moose or brown bear. It shoots much flatter than the .458 or .500 cartridges, which are in the same power range, and is a better choice for moderate long-range work.—R.A.M.

.416 UMT Loading Data and Ballistics

Bullet (grains/type)	Powder	Grains	Velocity	Energy	Source
400 Swift A Frame	Reloader 15	85.4	2525	5662	Bryce Towsley
400 Barnes Solid	IMR 4350	94.0	2486	5488	Bryce Towsley

.445 Super Magnum

Historical Notes: Knocking down metallic silhouettes at 200 meters with a handgun bullet requires delivery of a relatively large dose of momentum. In the mid-1970s, handgun silhouette shooter Elgin Gates began developing a line of powerful magnum revolver cartridges for the purpose of IHMSA handgun silhouette shooting competitions. His work on the .357 Super Mag led to that cartridge's adoption by Remington as the .357 Maximum. The .445 Super Mag is Elgin's .429- (.44) caliber entry into the long-range revolver competition shooting and hunting arena. Work on this cartridge had just begun, when Gates died, in 1988. It is essentially a lengthened version .44 Remington Magnum case and that round's most potent descendant. It is superior to the .44 Magnum, especially when heavier bullets are used. As is the case with the .44 Magnum, the name is somewhat misleading, as it uses bullets of .429-inch diameter. The .445 Super Mag, however, can drive the same bullets nearly 300 fps faster than the .44 Magnum. Dan Wesson Arms Co. was the only company that manufactured a production gun for this cartridge. Starline (www.starlinebrass.com) is the only company that produced cases. Custom loaded ammunition is available from various custom loading companies.

General Comments: Due to the pressures involved and overall cartridge length, guns chambered for this cartridge tend to be somewhat large and heavy. This has proven to be a very accurate cartridge and a fine performer with bullets weighing up to 300 grains. There is a price to pay for such performance, and it comes in the form of considerable muzzle blast and recoil. The barrel compensator on some of the Wesson firearms has tamed this cartridge considerably, reducing its recoil to that of a .44 Magnum. For those willing to put up with the recoil and muzzle blast, this cartridge could prove to be an excellent choice for competition silhouette shooting or handgun hunting of large game. With more and more bullet manufacturers producing jacketed, .44-caliber bullets of 300 grains and heavier, this cartridge can really come into its own. A note of caution may be advised here. With this cartridge, different guns reach maximum loads at different rates. While some work comfortably at the maximum loads listed in loading manuals, others peak out well before this. As with any load, work up to maximum loads with care.

13th Edition Update: Gates developed a full line of Super Mag revolver cartridges covering calibers from 7mm to .61. The three most popular were the .357, .414, and .445. The .357 Super Mag become the .357 Maximum, and the .414 and .445 were offered in limited numbers by Dan Wesson, but Dan Wesson is now owned by CZ-USA and is no longer manufacturing revolvers. Though all of these cartridges have mostly faded into the obscure category, they retain a limited but cult-like following by some who enjoy shooting at excessive long ranges with revolvers. However, it is doubtful that the .445 will ever see resurgence. For the hunter or handgun silhouette shooter looking to score at long range, the .445 is an excellent cartridge if the shooter can handle the intense recoil.—R.A.M.

.445 Super Mag Loading Data

Bullet (grains/type)	Powder	Grains	Velocity	Energy	Source/Comments
240 JHP	H110	31.7	1400	1045	Hornady
240 JHP	W680	35.2	1500	1200	Hornady
300 SP	H110	28.2	1300	1125	Hornady
300 SP	AA 1680	33.6	1350	1215	Hornady
240 Sierra JHC	AA 1680	38.9	1600	1364	Sierra
300 Sierra JSP	W 296	30.4	1350	1213	Sierra

.458x1.5-inch Barnes

Historical Notes: The .458x1.5-inch, which was never intended to be anything except an abstract experiment, has surfaced in a number of roles, including a military one (see Chapter 7). It all goes back to 1962, when the original author of this book was playing around with the .458 Winchester Magnum and cutting it off to various lengths. That work culminated in the .458x2-inch. All this was reported in the June 1963 issue of Guns & Ammo magazine. Nothing noteworthy developed with this very short version as a sporting round until the metallic silhouette game came into bloom, at which point several individuals built up special silhouette pistols based on the Remington XP-100 action and chambered for the .458x1.5-inch. One of these was Larry Stevens of Carson City, Nevada, who won a number of matches in the Unlimited class with this combination. He reports that recoil with bullets over 300 grains is rather heavy.

General Comments: The 458x1.5-inch will certainly knock down the metallic pigs and rams, when fired from either a pistol or a rifle. Also, a 300-grain bullet exiting the muzzle at 1500 to 1800 fps is a potent field load and could be effective for anything from small game and varmints on up to deer-size animals. Cases are easy to make by cutting off a standard magnum case to 1.50 inches. No one makes loading dies for the cartridge, but one can improvise by using .45 Colt or other .45 pistol dies.

.458x1.5-inch Barnes Loading Data

Bullet (grains/type)	Powder	Grains	Velocity	Energy	Source/Comments
300 JSP	IMR 4198	40.0	1805	2180	24-inch barrel
300 JSP	IMR 4198	40.0	1680	1885	15-inch barrel
*350 JSP	2400	23.0	1376	1470	12-inch barrel
*350 JSP	2400	24.0	1435	1602	12-inch barrel
*430 Lead	IMR 4227	26.0	1348	1740	12-inch barrel

*Loading data furnished by Larry Stevens

.45 Silhouette

Historical Notes: The .45 Silhouette is an approach to a big-bore silhouette cartridge using the full-length .45-70 Government case, which is inefficient when used in 10- or 12-inch barrels. Initial development was carried out by Frank Barnes (not the original author of this book) and Dick Smith of the Washoe County Crime Laboratory, during 1984. The idea resulted from earlier experience with the 458x1.5-inch cartridge, which is based on the .458 Winchester Magnum shortened to 1½ inches. The .45 Silhouette is made by cutting back the .45-70 case from 2.1 inches to 1½ inches. Performance of these two is similar, although the .45 Silhouette is a rimmed case, while the 458x1½-inch is a belted case. The rimmed case is better suited to break-open type actions, such as the Thompson/Center Contender, and might even be used in a revolver. Original testing was in a Siamese Mauser bolt-action rifle with a 20-inch barrel.

The idea is neither brilliant nor highly original. The result is very similar to the old .45-50 Peabody sporting cartridge or the 11.75Rmm Montenegrin revolver cartridge, both of blackpowder vintage. In any event, those wanting to work with the .45 Silhouette can obtain a set of trim and loading dies from RCBS (www.rcbs.com).

General Comments: The .45 Silhouette is intended primarily to shoot a 300-grain bullet of .457- or .458-inch diameter. Lighter or heavier bullets can be used, but this detracts somewhat from the original purpose, which is to provide a .45-caliber handgun cartridge that shoots a 300-grain bullet. We think the late Elmer Keith would have approved of this. Although developed as a silhouette cartridge, this would obviously also make a pretty good hunting number for anything from small game on up through deer and black bear, at least when fired from a 20-inch or longer rifle barrel. After all, a 300-grain bullet with a muzzle velocity of over 1800 fps and 2100 ft-lbs of energy outperforms a number of popular deer-class cartridges. Loading data listed below was developed in a Siamese Mauser bolt-action rifle with 20-inch barrel, and a custom-barreled and modified Thompson/Center Contender pistol with a 10-inch barrel. A twist of 1:16 or 1:18 is recommended with a ¼-inch of freebore.
Note: One could argue that this was the intellectual forerunner of the .475 Linebaugh.

.45 Silhouette Loading Data

Bullet (grains/type)	Powder	Grains	Velocity	Energy	Source/Comments
200 Lead	Unique	12.0	1325	785	10" barrel
300 Lead	SR 4759	23.0	1420	1350	10" barrel
300 JHP	IMR 4198	34.0	1240	1030	10" barrel
300 Lead	IMR 4198	36.0	1610	1732	Lyman 456191 20" barrel
300 Lead	Blackpowder	44.0 (FFg)	1170	930	Lyman 456191 20" barrel
300 JHP	IMR 4198	35.0	1485	1470	20" barrel
300 JHP	IMR 4198	38.0	1670	1860	20" barrel
300 JHP	IMR 4198	40.0*	1810	2180	20" barrel

*Compressed charge

.45 Wildey Magnum

Historical Notes: In 1997, the .45 Wildey Magnum became the first big-bore bottleneck magnum cartridge chambered for a production autoloading pistol. Wildey Moore designed the cartridge for a gas-operated, autoloading pistol featuring a three-lug rotary bolt and interchangeable barrel assemblies. Revising the armament planned for the movie Death Wish III, actor Charles Bronson replaced the original .45 Wildey Magnum pistol with its bigger brother, the .475 Wildey Magnum, to maximize the power effect of Wildey's big-bore magnums on the audience.

General Comments: Wildey recommends this cartridge for hunting and target shooting, but not for self-defense purposes, due to the potential for damage or injury to bystanders. The cartridge is suited for barrel lengths of eight to 18 inches and a 1:16 rifling twist. A 10-inch barrel offers the best blend of performance and carrying convenience. The .45 Wildey Magnum uses readily available .451-inch diameter pistol bullets. Wildey Guns (www.wildeyguns.com) offers pistols, carbines, barrel assemblies, reloading data, and dies for the .45 Wildey Magnum.

.45 Wildey Magnum Loading Data and Factory Ballistics

Bullet (grains/type)	Powder	Grains	Velocity	Energy	Source/Comments
230	Blue Dot	22.0	Not Given	UNK	Wildey/FA
250	FL		1829	1856	Wildey/FA
260	Blue Dot	19.5	Not Given	UNK	Wildey/FA

.458x2-inch American

Historical Notes: This belted cartridge was designed by the original author of this book, Frank C. Barnes, in mid-1962. It uses the .458 Winchester Magnum case, shortened from 2½ inches to two inches. It is designed as a medium-power, big-bore cartridge for North American hunting conditions and game. It is short enough to work through either standard- or medium-length rifle actions. The original rifle was made up on the short Remington Model 722 action, as a lightweight carbine with 21-inch barrel. This provides an extremely powerful rifle for its size and weight of 7¼ pounds. The cartridge also works very well in re-barreled Winchester Model 94 Big Bore rifles.

General Comments: The standard .458 Winchester Magnum and the .460 Weatherby Magnum are overpowered for North American big game. Both have very heavy recoil and require heavy, expensive rifles. Efforts have been made by various designers to provide a medium-power, big-bore cartridge more suited to American needs. The .450-348 and .450 Alaskan are examples of this, but these are rimmed cases suitable only for lever-action or single-shot rifles. The .458x2-inch fills the need for a bolt-action round of modern design tailored to game found on the North American continent. The .458x2-inch American is intended for 300- to 405-grain bullets. It gives good performance with these and is adequate for the heaviest North American game at short to medium ranges. It would also be quite handy for use against any but the more dangerous varieties of African game in close cover. Case dimensions and capacity are similar to the .45-70, but modern rifles permit heavier loads. This cartridge is, in effect, a belted .45-70, rather than just a shortened .458 Magnum. Ammunition can easily be made from .458 Magnum or most other belted Magnum cases. Dies are available from RCBS (www.rcbs.com). Early in 2000, Marlin began shipping Model 1895 rifles chambered for its version of this cartridge, the .450 Marlin. That case features a different belt and is slightly longer; the 458x2-inch is definitely not safe for use in .450 Marlin-chambered rifles.

.458x2-inch Cast Bullet Loading Data

Bullet (grains/type)	Powder	Grains	Velocity	Energy	Source/Comments
210	IMR 4198	23.0	1285	778	Lyman No. 457127 Light plinking load
250	IMR 4198	28.0	1828	1860	Lyman No. 454485 gas checked sized .457-inch
300	IMR 4198	25.0	1370	1257	Lyman No. 457191
405	IMR 3031	45.0	1535	2120	Lyman No. 457483 gas checked

These loads are economical, accurate, and pleasant to shoot. The heavier bullet loads are adequate for deer out to 150 yards.

.458x2-inch Jacketed Bullet Loading Data

Bullet (grains/type)	Powder	Grains	Velocity	Energy	Source/Comments
300 H SJ	IMR 4198	36.0	1650	1820	
300 H JHP	IMR 4198	40.0	1825	2223	Very accurate deer load
300 Barnes SP	IMR 4198	55.0	2412	3900	
405 Win SP	IMR 4198	51.0	2110	4005	

Jacketed bullet loads are intended for big game.

Note: All loads fired from 24-inch barrel, average temperature 78 degrees F. Winchester .458 Magnum cases and Federal No. 215 primers used for all loads. Velocity measured with Avtron Model T333 electronic chronograph.

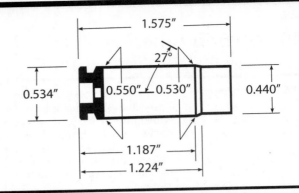

NEW
.460 Alliance

Historical Notes: The .460 Alliance was developed by Michael A. Wayne of Alliance Armament LLC, in 2010, specifically for use in the AK-47 platform. It was intended as a short-range hunting/tactical cartridge. It is based on the Remington Short Action Ultra Mag case.

General Comments: This cartridge substantially changes the bark of the AK-47 by allowing it to fire a .458-caliber bullet to velocities of that of the .44 Magnum and duplicate those of most factory .45-70 loads. It should be a great cartridge for short-range wild hog and deer hunting, and it has tactical applications, as well. Factory loaded ammunition is available from Alliance Armament (www.alliancearmament.com).—R.A.M.

.460 Alliance Loading Data and Factory Ballistics

Bullet (grains/type)	Powder	Grains	Velocity	Energy	Source
300 JHP	FL		2000	2665	Alliance Factory Load
405 JSP	FL		1650	2448	Alliance Factory Load
405 JFP	Lil' Gun	29.0	1650	2448	Alliance Armament

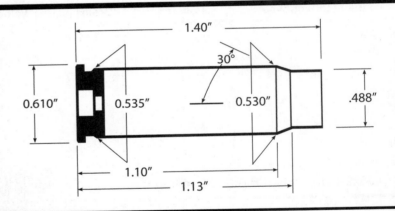

NEW
.450 Bonecrusher

Historical Notes: The .450 Bonecrusher was developed by Lee Martin, of Arlington, Virginia, in 2002, as a lower pressure alternative to another .45-caliber wildcat he had been working with. Cases are made by full-length sizing a .500 Linebaugh case in a .450 Bonecrusher die. Subsequent fire-forming extends the shoulder to 30 degrees with minimal body taper. The operating pressure of the .450 Bonecrusher is set at 40,000 psi. The .450 Bonecrusher is capable of pushing a 405-grain bullet to over 1400 fps from an 8.5-inch-barreled revolver.

General Comments: The .450 Bonecrusher is indeed a specialty round and is not intended for everyone. While it might have some nostalgic and entertainment appeal, due to its sheer power, the real draw of this cartridge is its ability to turn an 8.5-inch barreled Ruger Super Blackhawk Revolver into a .45-70. This would make a great short-range revolver hunting cartridge for large game—for anyone who can withstand the recoil.—R.A.M.

.450 Bonecrusher Loading Data and Ballistics

Bullet (grains/type)	Powder	Grains	Velocity	Energy	Source/Comments
300 Hornady	H 110	42.0	1783	2117	Lee Martin
350 Hornady	H 110	38.0	1705	2259	Lee Martin

.450 Alaskan
(.45-348 Winchester Improved)

Historical Notes: The .450 Alaskan was designed by Harold Johnson, a resident of Cooper's Landing, Alaska. This cartridge was designed to meet the demands of hunters who wanted a lever-action rifle that could deliver substantial energy and bullet mass for use against the largest and most dangerous of Alaskan game. Winchester Model 71s converted to this chambering are among the most prized rifles in Alaska. Belted Magnum bolt-action rifles are legion on used gun racks in Alaska at certain times of the year, but Alaskan-chambered Model 71s are never seen for sale at any price! This is ample testimony to the power, dependability, accuracy, and ruggedness this combination delivers.

General Comments: Ackley might have been the first to open the hole through the barrel and Improve the chamber of a Model 71 Winchester. However, by Ackley's own testimony, Johnson's version of the .45-caliber .348 Improved is a better choice. The .450 Alaskan will function through the Model 71's action with little or no alteration to the feeding mechanism, while Ackley's version will not. Ackley's version has slightly less body taper and holds slightly more powder, but ballistics are very similar. The .450 Fuller is essentially identical to the .450 Alaskan, except for a different shoulder angle. Conversion to any of these cartridges produces a Model 71 lever-action rifle capable of delivering ballistics practically duplicating the .458 Winchester Magnum. Any such conversion necessitates special attachment measures, to prevent the magazine and fore-end from being separated from the receiver under the stresses of the substantial recoil these cartridges generate. The data shown below is based on Ackley's recommendation of reducing .450-348 Ackley Improved data five percent for use in the .450 Alaskan chambering (velocities are estimates only).

.450 Alaskan Loading Data (26-inch barrel)

Bullet (grains/type)	Powder	Grains	Velocity	Energy	Source/Comments
350	IMR 3031	67.0	2415	4535	Adapted .450-348 Ackley data, see text
400	IMR 4064	67.0	2095	3900	Adapted .450-348 Ackley data, see text
400	IMR 3031	67.0	2215	4360	Adapted .450-348 Ackley data, see text
500	IMR 4064	66.0	2005	4465	Adapted .450-348 Ackley data, see text

.450 Howell

Historical Notes: The .450 Howell is one of three cartridges designed by Ken Howell. Howell's idea was to design a series of cartridges capable of taking African game and that would fit in a standard-length bolt-action. Ken began his design sometime in the mid 1970s, when magnum-length Mauser actions were prohibitively expensive and relatively rare. The cartridge cases of the .375 H&H Magnum and .416 Rigby were much longer than needed for efficient use with modern smokeless powders. The original version, the .375 Howell, was designed for approximately the optimum smokeless powder capacity for its bore size. All cartridges are based on the .404 Jeffery case, which measures .540-inch in diameter at the base, versus the .532-inch diameter of the H&H base, thus offering substantial powder capacity in a short case. The .450 Howell is actually based on Ken's .416 Howell, which was the first of the three he designed; the .450 was just a necked-up version. The design of these non-belted magnums is exceptional, but, unfortunately, was never picked up by any of the commercial cartridge companies, although similar numbers are now offered by Dakota Arms and others.

General Comments: With about a 10-percent increase in capacity over the .458 Winchester Magnum, this cartridge can generate fully 100 fps more velocity at the same pressure and with the same cartridge length. It has the further significant advantage of superior accuracy potential, because it headspaces on the shoulder, rather than a belt and, therefore, can be aligned better in the chamber.

.450 Watts Magnum

Historical Notes: The .450 Watts Magnum is made by necking up .375 H&H Magnum cases to accept .458-inch diameter bullets. According to P.O. Ackley*, it was originated by Watts and Anderson of Yakima, Washington. It dates back to the 1950s or earlier. The case is .35-inch longer than the .458 Winchester Magnum. Because it holds more powder, it can be loaded to slightly higher velocities than the .458 Winchester Magnum.

General Comments: The .450 Watts is a powerful cartridge that can push a 500-grain bullet a couple hundred feet per second faster than the .458 Winchester. This makes the .450 Watts a fine choice for the handloader. Arizona Ammunition (www.arizonaammunition.net), now offers factory-loaded custom ammunition for this and practically any other chambering. Guns so chambered safely shoot .458 Winchester Magnum loads.

*op cit, p. 501

.450 Watts Magnum Loading Data*

Bullet (grains/type)	Powder	Grains	Velocity	Energy	Source/Comments
400 SP	IMR 4198	85.0	2670	6320	Ackley
500 SP	IMR 4320	98.0	2500	6920	Ackley
*P.O. Ackley, p. 501					

.450 KNR

Historical Notes: Developed, in 1992, by Kase Reeder for an African safari, the proprietary .450 KNR readily fits into the classic family of big, cigar-sized dangerous-game cartridges. Kase, the son of Arizona gunmaker Gary Reeder, successfully dropped all of Africa's Big Five game animals with the .450 KNR. A few hardy souls purchased Thompson/Center Encore pistols in this chambering, but the general consensus suggests the cartridge is too much of a bone-crusher to be shot from a handgun.

General Comments: The .450 KNR, essentially a .470 Nitro Express necked down to accept industry-standard .458-caliber bullets, works very well in heavy-barreled Ruger No. 1 rifles. Gary Reeder Custom Guns (www.reedercustomguns.com) offers dies, barrels, firearms, reloading components, and information. When using Reeder's reloading information for lighter loads, a kapok or facial tissue filler is advisable, in order to hold the powder closer to the primer to prevent misfires.

.450 KNR Loading Data

Bullet (grains/type)	Powder	Grains	Velocity	Energy	Source/Comments
500 Hornady	H414	105.0	2300	5872	Gary Reeder
510 Hornady	IMR 4350	100.0	2300	5990	Gary Reeder

.460 G&A Special

Historical Notes: On a 1971 Uganda safari, then Guns and Ammo magazine publisher and wildcatter Tom Siatos designed the .460 G&A Special to provide the optimum velocity—2350 fps with 500-grain soft-point or solid bullets—for hunting dangerous game. Considered more efficient and effective than the .458 Winchester Magnum, the .460 G&A compiled a most successful track record on African Cape buffalo and rhino, and on water buffalo in Brazil and Australia. Professional hunters have used the .460 G&A extensively in elephant culling operations. Firearms authority Jeff Cooper considers it suitable medicine for crumpling irritated Cape buffalo at ping-pong table distances, should a hunter step into an unwise circumstance.

General Comments: Testing 500-grain solids against hard pine boards, the .460 G&A cartridge reliably penetrates to a depth of 48 inches before stopping. The .460 G&A uses the beltless .404 Jeffery parent case with the shoulder moved forward, neck expanded to accept .458 bullets, and fire-formed in a .460 G&A chamber. Barrels of 23 to 24 inches with a 1:14 twist work well with the .460 G&A cartridge. The cartridge adapts readily to magnum Mauser bolt-action rifles and accepts .458-inch diameter bullets. For tough, nasty, and otherwise dangerous game, premium hunting bullets should be the responsible hunter's first consideration.

.460 G&A Special Loading Data

Bullet (grains/type)	Powder	Grains	Velocity	Energy	Source/Comments
500 Hornady SP	IMR 4064	88.0	2370	6235	J. P. Lott & Bob Forker
500 Hornady FMJ	IMR 4064	88.0	2375	6261	J. P. Lott & Bob Forker

NEW
.475 Lehigh

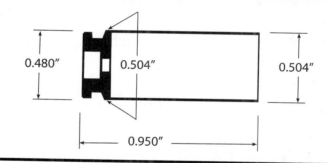

Historical Notes: This wildcat handgun cartridge was developed in September 2011, by Michael Cyrus of Cross Outdoors for Lehigh Defense. It is based on the .480 Ruger case, but the rim is turned down to match that of the .45 Auto, and an extractor groove is cut into the base of the cartridge case. The result is a rebated rimmed cartridge that is basically the same length as a .45 Auto cartridge, but for .475-caliber bullets. The intent was to offer a larger caliber option to .45 Auto handguns for hunting and personal protection and that would only require a barrel swap to complete the conversion.

General Comments: The .475 Lehigh offers performance very close to that of the 10mm Auto, but with a larger caliber bullet. Converting about any double-stacked magazine .45 Auto generally only requires a barrel swap, and barrels and brass are available form Lehigh Defense. Most currently available .475-caliber pistol bullets were developed for the higher velocities achievable from a .480 Ruger and, therefore, will not expand reliably at .475 Lehigh velocities. However, Lehigh Defense (www.lehighdefense.com) is offering its penetrator and controlled-fracturing hollowpoint bullet in .47-caliber, and both perform admirably from this cartridge.—R.A.M.

.475 Lehigh Loading Data

Bullet (grains/type)	Powder	Grains	Velocity	Energy	Source
200 Lehigh CFHP/penetrator	AA No. 7	14.3	1250	693	Lehigh Defense
275 Speer Deep Curl	True Blue	8.0	800	390	Lehigh Defense

.475 Wildey Magnum

Historical Notes: The .475 Wildey is the brainchild of Wildey J. Moore. This cartridge was designed to be used in a big-bore, gas-operated, semi-automatic handgun, which was also designed by Wildey. The original pistol was chambered for the .45 Winchester Magnum. In order to build the gun, Moore decided to sell stock in his company to raise capital for production. In time, some of the investors wanted to take active roles in production and marketing of this particular handgun. Unfortunately, many of these were not shooters or people knowledgeable about firearms. Moore's share in the Wildey company was diluted to 25 percent and, without his knowledge, other shareholders in the company formed a separate investment company to gain control of Wildey, Inc. In January 1983, Moore was fired from his own company, but the new management ended up in bankruptcy less than a year later.

It took a few years for Moore to get back on his feet. Using this time to advantage, he designed an entirely new pistol, with improved ballistics and a new cartridge, the .475 Wildey Magnum. The .475 Wildey is based on the .284 Winchester cartridge shortened to 1.395 inches, then neck reamed to handle .475-inch bullets. The cartridge is the same length as the .45 Winchester Magnum, but of greater diameter. Case forming dies for this cartridge are available from RCBS (www.rcbs.com). Bullets for the 475 Wildey are available from Barnes Bullets (www.barnesbullets.com). Several designs are available, in both soft-points and solids.

General Comments: The Wildey is a very heavy handgun, designed to handle breech pressures exceeding 48,000 psi. Due to its size and weight, usefulness will most likely be limited to hunting and some sport shooting. Accuracy has proven to be outstanding. Five-shot, 25-yard groups consistently average less than one inch. Ballistics are also impressive, with 100-yard remaining energies exceeding .44 Magnum muzzle energy. Load data from Wildey indicates that 18 grains of BlueDot powder should be used with a 300-grain jacketed bullet. With that load, a 300-grain Barnes JSP gives an impressive muzzle velocity of 1610 fps with a muzzle energy of 1727 ft-lbs.

.475 Wildey Magnum Loading Data

Bullet (grains/type)	Powder	Grains	Velocity	Energy	Source/Comments
250 SP	BlueDot	21.0	1850	1900	Wildey Inc.
300 SP	BlueDot	18.0	1610	1727	Wildey Inc.

.475 Ackley Magnum
.475 OKH Magnum

Historical Notes: These two cartridges are listed together, because they are virtually identical. Both are formed by necking up .375 H&H cases without any other change. The Ackley .475 Magnum originated in the middle 1950s. The bullet used is the Barnes 600-grain soft-point or solid at a muzzle velocity of 2250 fps. The cartridge is normally chambered in bolt-action rifles.

General Comments: A 600-grain bullet at 2250 fps develops 6752 ft-lbs of energy, making for a very powerful cartridge, adequate for any dangerous African game. However, for those who like lots of energy and power, the .475 Ackley/OKH is not as powerful as either the .460 Weatherby or the .475 A&M Magnum. In actual practice, this probably wouldn't make much difference, because any of these cartridges is capable of dispatching an elephant or Cape buffalo with one shot. Of course, this has also been done with smaller numbers developing less energy. Therefore, in the final analysis, a great deal depends on the hunter and his skill. This cartridge is overpowered for North American big game.

.475 Ackley Magnum Loading Data

Bullet (grains/type)	Powder	Grains	Velocity	Energy	Source/Comments
600*	IMR 4320	90.0	2250	6750	Ackley

*Ackley, op. cit.

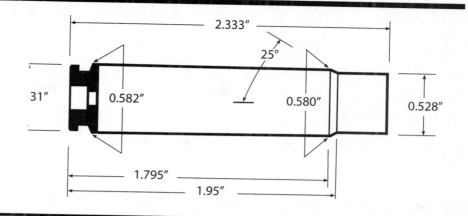

NEW
.500 Cyrus

Historical Notes: This true .500-caliber rifle cartridge was developed by wildcatter Michael Cyrus, of Cross Outdoors, Prichard, West Virginia. The idea was to provide big-bore enthusiasts with a short-action—3.00 inches or less—rifle capable of matching .470 Nitro performances. Cyrus also wanted to take advantage of the new wave of .500-caliber handgun bullets that were becoming available. The parent case for the .500 Cyrus is a straight-wall .416 Rigby case that has had the rim turned down from 0.586 to 0.531. Then the case is shortened and necked to .500-caliber.

General Comments: The .500 Cyrus may represent the most power that can be harnessed in a short, three-inch action. It will drive a 500-grain bullet at almost 2300 fps. The problem with the concept is a lack of .500-caliber bullets capable of handling impact velocities this high. To solve this, Cyrus turned to Lehigh Defense and had special .500-caliber all-copper or -brass bullets machined. These bullets expand and then the petals break off, creating additional wound channels inside game animals. I used the .500 Cyrus to take two eland and a wildebeest in Africa with as many shots using somewhat reduced loads. Cross Outdoors currently offers custom .500 Cyrus rifles, ammunition, bullets, and dies. A neat aspect of this cartridge is that it can be downloaded to fire .500-caliber pistol bullets and even saboted muzzleloading bullets, making it a very versatile choice for hunting any big-game animals anywhere.—R.A.M.

.500 Cyrus Loading Data

Bullet (grains/type)	Powder	Grains	Velocity	Energy	Source
325 Barnes XPB	Benchmark	92.0C	2720	5338	Hodgdon
400 Lead w/ Gas Check	Trail Boss	30.0C	1388	1710	Hodgdon
500 Hornady	H 4895	87.0C	2291	5826	Hodgdon

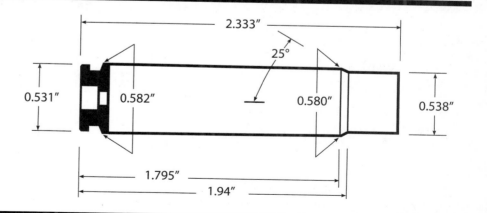

NEW
.50 TAC

Historical Notes: Developed from the .500 Cyrus cartridge, in 2008, the .50 TAC is a .510-caliber version of the .500 Cyrus. It was developed to provide a tactical rifle that would work off a long-action, but that would be capable of firing .510-caliber (.50 BMG bullets). The parent case for the .50 TAC is the .500 Cyrus or a straight-wall .416 Rigby case that has had the rim turned down from 0.586 to 0.531. Then the case is shortened and necked to .510-caliber.

General Comments: The .50 TAC is a good alternative to the .50 BMG for tactical teams that need the penetration power of the big Browning round, but who do not want to deal with the heavy rifles and intense recoil of that cartridge. The .50 TAC offers about 70 percent of the .50 BMG's capabilities, but in a much more portable rifle. This cartridge is also conducive to subsonic loading and is one of the few .50-caliber cartridges that can be said about. Cross Outdoors in Prichard, West Virginia, currently offers custom .50 TAC rifles, ammunition, bullets, and dies.—R.A.M.

.50 TAC Loading Data

Bullet (grains/type)	Powder	Grains	Velocity	Energy	Source
645 Lehigh	H 4895	70.0	2050	6018	Cross Outdoors
606 Lehigh	H 5744	30.0	1050	1438	Cross Outdoors

.500 Belted Magnum

Historical Notes: Gunsmiths Frederick Teal and James C. Tucker designed this medium-length cartridge, in mid-1998. It uses the .460 Weatherby belted case, opened and trimmed to 2½ inches with a maximum cartridge length of 3¼ inches. It was designed to provide a cartridge for dangerous game hunting that does not require the use of a magnum-length action. The original rifle was made up on a P14 Enfield with a 26-inch barrel. This provided an extremely powerful rifle weighing in at 11 pounds. Reloading dies are available from RCBS (www.rcbs.com), chamber reamers from JGS (www.jgstools.com), and jacketed bullets from Barnes and Woodleigh.

General Comments: The .500-bore cartridges and the rifles chambered for them are very expensive and generate excessive recoil. Also, quality loaded ammunition and cases can be problematic. The .500 Belted Magnum offers a practical alternative. This cartridge is, in effect, a .500 Nitro-Express in a .30-06-length case, designed for use in common, low cost, Mauser 98-pattern bolt-action rifles. Classic Nitro Express performance is achieved using Weatherby cases and updated, improved magnum powders. A 535-grain bullet with a charge of up to 80 grains generates the required velocity and muzzle energy to stop dangerous game. Recoil is acceptable with all heavy loads. Working chamber pressures are kept to moderate levels, so as to ensure positive extraction in the tropics. For more information on this interesting development, contact James C. Tucker, custom stockmaker, at P. O. Box 366, Medford, Oregon 97501.

.500 Belted Magnum Load Data

Bullet (grains/type.)	Powder	Grains	Velocity	Energy	Source/Comments
440 SP	RL -7	67	2135	4452	Woodleigh BPE SP
500 Cast	SR4759	36	1515	2545	Cast Lee 515-500-F
450 FN	IMR4198	66	2163	4675	Barnes Flat Nose
535 SP	IMR3031	78	2150	5489	Woodleigh SP
535 FMJ	H.335	78	2174	5612	Woodleigh FMJ
535 BS	H.4895	80	2178	5633	Barnes Jeffrey BS (Banded Solid)
570 BS	Varget	80	2131	5745	

.510 Nitro Express

Historical Notes: The .510 Nitro Express is the brainchild of Bob Schneidmiller and custom gun maker D'Arcy Echols. Schneidmiller grew up in the West and, from early childhood, developed a passion for buffalo hunting. He read virtually everything he could get his hands on and dreamed of owning a .50 Sharps. As he grew up, his interests broadened to include the Dark Continent. On his first trip to Africa, Schneidmiller carried a .50-90 Sharps, with which he took a Cape buffalo, but the performance of the .50-90 left much to be desired. After his return, he met D'arcy Echols, and thoughts of building a bigger, more powerful rifle were discussed. Schneidmiller had hoped to build a .500 Nitro, but case supplies for that particular cartridge was drying up fast. He had a good supply of Sharps .50-140 3¼-inch cases, but D'arcy was not keen about building a custom rifle for an obsolete cartridge. So, instead, they used the same basic case design as the .50-140-3¼ Sharps with modern bullets and powders to achieve or better .500 Nitro Express ballistics. Schneidmiller suggested they call the new cartridge the .510 Echols Express, but Echols didn't favor the idea. They finally settled on the .510 Nitro Express. The rifle was built on a Martin Hagn falling-block action and proved superbly accurate. Originally, the rifle was built without a muzzle brake. However, recoil was so heavy that the forearm was torn off with the first shot. The barrel was then so equipped, and Schneidmiller claims it is now a pussycat. Some might disagree.

General Comments: The .510 Nitro Express is a superb cartridge for anyone desiring a single-shot rifle for dangerous game. This cartridge and rifle combination can offer plenty of power, without the expense of a double rifle. Though many hunters shy away from the thought of a single-shot rifle for dangerous game, there is still a strong following for the single-shot. For those not wishing to spend the time and money for a custom rifle, the Ruger No. 1 action would probably be an excellent choice for this cartridge.

.510 Nitro Express Loading Data

Bullet (grains/type)	Powder	Grains	Velocity	Energy	Source/Comments
500 SP/FMJ	IMR 4895	90.0	2337	6062	Bob Schneidmiller
550 SP	IMR 4895	88.0	2172	5762	Bob Schneidmiller
600 SP	IMR 4831	102.0	2053	5614	Bob Schneidmiller
700 SP	IMR 4350	85.0	1942	5860	Bob Schneidmiller

.50 McMurdo

Historical Notes: Developed by Fifty Caliber Shooter Association member, and later president, Lynn McMurdo, in 1995, the .50 McMurdo (12.7x92mm) is a long-range sporting cartridge successfully used for 1,000-yard shooting competition. It proved to be a worthy contender in the art of extreme long-range accuracy shooting with .50-caliber rifles. The .50 McMurdo enjoyed wide use by five-time world champion .50-caliber shooter Scott Nye, the late Skip Talbot, and other long-range competitive shooters in Fifty Caliber Shooter Association matches.

General Comments: The .50 McMurdo is an accurate competition cartridge. The .50 McMurdo is strictly a handloading proposition for custom rifles—the .50 BMG parent case is shortened by seven millimeters and given a 30-degree shoulder. The resulting case was designed to provide optimum loading densities for the 800-grain bullets. The .50 McMurdo uses the McMurdo "Ironhand" solid brass projectile.

.50 McMurdo Loading Data

Bullet (grains/type)	Powder	Grains	Velocity	Energy	Source/Comments
800 McMurdo Ironhand	VV N29	238.0	2650	12473	Lynn McMurdo

.50 McMillan FatMac

Historical Notes:	The late Gale McMillan and his son, Rock, developed this cartridge, in 1996. Their primary goal was to create a modern (short, fat) case like those now used in benchrest competitive events, but designed to launch .50-caliber match bullets for use in 1,000-yard (or longer-range) Fifty Caliber Shooters Association (FCSA) matches. This case was derived by significantly shortening the bottlenecked 20mm cannon case. The primer pocket has been modified to accept a steel insert. This bushing insert sizes the primer pocket to accept a .50 BMG primer and doubles as a flash tube. The latter carries the primer blast to near the front of the powder charge, which provides significant internal ballistic benefits, including improved shot-to-shot uniformity and increased muzzle velocity.
General Comments:	Case capacity exceeds 415 grains of water, which is probably more than is necessary for the intended application (this is comparatively similar to a .30-caliber case of 150-grain capacity). Barrel length in .50-caliber match rifles is commonly quite long, up to about 42 inches. Chronographing showed that this cartridge easily launches 750-grain match bullets in excess of 3400 fps (using 330 grains of powder), without placing any undue stress on the case. The .50 BMG manages only about 2700 fps (using about 225 grains of powder).
	It seems likely that anyone seriously interested in pushing the envelope of .50-caliber performance might do well to consider an even shorter version of this case (perhaps about 350 grains of water capacity). The forward ignition feature is probably a worthwhile addition; this system is routinely used in artillery, where it is more feasible than in small arms. Generally, forward ignition adds measurably to ballistic efficiency (performance) and ballistic uniformity (accuracy). Since McMillan conceived this number strictly as a benchrest cartridge, he used a very short case neck. This could allow one to partially seat a bullet into a case that has been sized to provide very modest neck tension. Then, during chambering, the ogive would come to rest against the rifling before the bolt was fully closed. As the bolt was locked, the short, loose case neck would allow the bullet to seat more deeply. As that occurred, the bullet could center and align to the chamber and bore—all are good features for such a cartridge. Shoulder angle is 30 degrees. The rifle uses a custom receiver built by Rock McMillan's McMillan Machine Company and a stock built by Kelly McMillan's McMillan Fiberglass Stocks (both at www.mcmfamily.com).

.50 McMillan FatMac Ballistic Data

Bullet (grains/type)	Powder	Grains	Velocity	Energy	Source/Comments
750 Hornady A-Max			3425	19,545	McMillan (4.666-inch OAL)

.505/530 Woodleigh

Historical Notes:	The .505/530 Woodleigh was developed by Geoff McDonald, of Woodleigh Bullets, for an African elephant hunter. Several of these rifles have been built on Enfield P14 actions, which handle the large case head of the .505. BRNO 602 or CZ550 Magnum actions would also be suitable. The rifles are fitted with Ashley ghost ring peep sights and custom-built mercury recoil reducers and weigh 13½ pounds. The .505/530 Woodleigh was preceded by the .530 Woodleigh Magnum created, in 1982, by necking up the .460 Weatherby case to fit .530-inch, 750-grain bullets. Its maximum muzzle velocity, with acceptable pressures, is 2150 fps.
General Comments:	The .505/530 Woodleigh is the .505 Gibbs case necked up to take .530-inch bullets. With a muzzle velocity of up to 2350 fps (9200 ft-lbs), it is quite a handful. Having a groove and bullet diameter of .530-inch and firing 750-grain FMJ and soft-nose bullets, it is suitable, and more than adequate, for all dangerous game. Field-testing in Zimbabwe, in 2001, delivered excellent results on elephant, hippo, and buffalo. Woodleigh Bullets of Australia (www.wooodleighbullets.com.au/), makes .530-inch bullets.

505/530 Woodleigh Factory Ballistics and Loading Data

Bullet (grains/type)	Powder	Grains	Velocity	Energy	Source/Comments
750 Soft Nose or FMJ	H4350	130.0	2100	7346	Geoff McDonald
750 Soft Nose or FMJ	H4350	136.0	2200	8062	Working load
750 Soft Nose or FMJ	H4350	146.0	2352	9215	Geoff McDonald

Use only Federal No. 215 Magnum Primer.

.585 Nyati

Historical Notes: With available muzzle energy exceeding 10,000 ft-lbs, the .585 Nyati deserves mention as very likely the world's most powerful shoulder-gun cartridge. The .50 Browning Machine Gun cartridge is used for sporting purposes, generating vastly more power than the .585 as it launches bullets of the same weight 300 to 400 fps faster. However, the .50 BMG is not, by any stretch of the imagination, a shoulder firearm cartridge. The .585 is.

This cartridge was created by Ross Seyfried, who modified .577 Nitro cases. Besides case forming, the rim has to be turned down to fit the bolt face. Either standard belted magnum or .416 Rigby rim size is used, as the bolt requires. Length allows chambering in "magnum-length" Mauser actions with minimal modifications. Modified magazine capacity is three cartridges. Seyfried reports very satisfactory accuracy, no doubt a result of careful chambering and quality workmanship throughout the rifle and load. Nyati (en-YAH-tee) means "Cape buffalo" in several African languages, and this is certainly a good name for a cartridge delivering so much bullet and energy.

General Comments: The .585 gives those who really want power a much more affordable option than the big British double rifles, which can often cost tens of thousands of dollars. However, one must mention recoil. It is an open question as to how many among us can tolerate the kind of recoil this cartridge will generate with full-power loads. In a 10-pound rifle with a good muzzle brake, top loads will generate more than 150 ft-lbs of recoil energy. Compare this to a .30-06 generating a mere 20 ft-lbs. Perhaps a better understanding of what this means is this: Imagine having this 10-pound rifle dropped off a 32-foot cliff and catching it with your shoulder. The originator suggests maximum loads defeat the design purpose. He recommends loads in the 2200 fps range. Sound advice. A quality muzzle brake can significantly mitigate recoil and is almost certainly necessary on such a rifle. Bullets for the .585 are available from Barnes, Woodleigh, and numerous custom manufacturers. This cartridge also performs superbly with pure-lead cast bullets.

.585 Nyati Loading Data

Bullet (grains/type)	Powder	Grains	Velocity	Energy	Recoil Energy*	**	***
650 Barnes TC Solid	IMR 4350	160.0	2402	8325	130	80	65
750 Barnes	IMR 4350	130.0	1925	6175	105	65	58
750 Barnes	IMR 4350	140.0	2040	6935	130	80	65
750 Woodleigh	IMR 4350	140.0	2196	8035	140	90	70
750 Barnes Solid	IMR 4350	140.0	2210	8135	145	92	68
750 Barnes	IMR 4350	150.0	2287	8715	150	95	75
750 Barnes	IMR 4350	160.0	2487	10,300	180	115	90
750 Barnes	RI-15	120.0	2070	7140	115	70	58
750 Barnes	RI-15	130.0	2235	8320	135	85	68
750 Barnes	RI-15	140.0	2420	9755	155	100	78

750 Barnes	RI-15	Max (147.0)	2525	10,620	175	110	88
545 Lead Patched	IMR 4198	72.0	1641	3255	35	25	18
650 Lead Patched	IMR 4198	73.0	1660	3975	55	35	28

All recoil data for vented barrel. *10-pound rifle,**14-pound rifle,***18-pound rifle

.729 Jongmans

Historical Notes: About 1990, Clive Downie, of Ripplebrook, in Victoria, Australia, began experimenting with parallel-sided Browning .50-caliber machine gun cases, with the idea of producing a huge-caliber rifle. He gave the project to John Jongmans, a riflemaker with experience with .50-caliber arms, and Jongmans perfected the design by putting a slight shoulder on the case and using a .727-inch bullet. John Jongmans gave it the .729 designation. The rifle was built on a Jongmans action with a 30½-inch barrel and a huge, homemade muzzle brake produced by Downie. The gun weighs 21 pounds, bare.

General Comments: The .729 Jongmans is needlessly over-powerful for any game on earth and is, perhaps, as large a bullet as one could reliably get to work in a Browning .50 case. Loads were worked up with an 896-grain solid-copper turned bullet and then, later, with a 1,048-grain turned copper bullet. Up to 340 grains of powder is used, and recoil is brutal. Downie suggests that 15 shots maximum in any session is all a seasoned shooter could handle. He estimated the Taylor Knock-Out scale figure is about 250.

.729 Jongmans Loading Data

Bullet (grain/type)	Powder	Grains	Velocity	Energy	Source/Comments
895 solid copper	H50BMG	270	1847	6781	Clive Downie
895 solid copper	H50BMG	300	2210	9700	Clive Downie
895 solid copper	H50BMG	340	2367	11137	Clive Downie
1,048 solid copper	H50BMG	280	1955	8890	Clive Downie
1,048 solid copper	H50BMG	310	2205	11317	Clive Downie
1,048 solid copper	H50BMG	330	2265	11941	Clive Downie

Dimensional Data

Cartridge	Case	Bullet Dia.	Neck Dia.	Shoulder Dia.	Base Dia.	Rim Dia.	Rim Thick.	Case Length	Ctge. Length	Primer	Page
.10 Eichelberger LR	A	.103	.122	.223	.225	.275	.043	.568	UNK	RF	167
.10 Eichelberger Pup	A	.103	.122	.247	249	.308	.050	.767	UNK	S	167
.10 Eichelberger Squirrel	A	.103	.122	.291	.294	.350	.065	.613	UNK	S	168
.12 Eichelberger LR	A	.123	.140	.224	.225	.275	.043	.568	UNK	RF	168
.12 Eichelberger WRM	A	.123	.140	.238	.241	.293	.050	1.064	UNK	RF	169
.12 Cooper	A	.123	.145	.247	.249	.308	.050	1.106	UNK	S	169
.12 Eichelberger Carbine	C	.123	.147	.356	.356	.360	.050	1.240	UNK	S	169
.14 Eichelberger Dart	A	.144	.164	.274	.278	.301	.043	.640	UNK	S	170
.14 Eichelberger Bee	A	.144	.162	.329	.349.	.408	.065	1.310	UNK	S	170
.14 Cooper	A	.144	.166	.247	.249	.3085	.051	1.104	UNK	S	171
.14 Walker Hornet	A	.144	.170	.285	.294	.350	.065	1.350	UNK	S	171
.14 Jet Junior	A	.144	.177	.366	.378	.440	.059	1.260	UNK	SP	172
.14-222	C	.144	.165	.356	.375	.375	.041	1.70	1.92	S	172
.14/222 Eichelberger Magnum	C	.144	.170	.356	.376	.378	.045	1.850	UNK	UNK	173
.17-32 Magnum	A	.172	.196	.335	.335	.375	.055	.900	1.450	S	173
.17 VHA (Varmint Hunters Assn.)	C	.172	.196	.305	.316	.315	.043	1.201	1.60	S	174
.17 Ackley Hornet	A	.172	.195	.290	.295	.345	.060	1.39	1.47	S	174
.17 Ackley Improved Bee	A	.172	.201	.341	.350	.408	.060	1.35	1.78	S	175
.17 Mach IV/Mach III	C	.172	.199	.361	.375	.378	.041	1.40	UNK	S	175
.17/222	C	.172	.199	.355	.375	.375	.041	1.69	1.82	S	176
.19 Badger	C	.198	UNK	UNK	UNK	UNK	UNK	UNK	1.3	S	176
.19 Calhoon	A	.198	.215	.286	.294	.350	.063	1.39	1.47	S	177
.19-223 Calhoon	C	.198	.224	.364	.373	.373	.041	1.76	2.	S	177
.20 Vartarg	C	.204	.232	.360	.374	.375	.048	1.40	1.90	S	178
.20 Tactical	C	.204	.233	.360	.373	.375	.041	1.755	2.1	S	178
.20 PDK	C	.204	.247	.400	.421	.417	.049	1.683	2.236	S	179
.22 Fawn	A	.224	.255	.430	.435	.492	.060	1.30	1.90	S	179
.22 PDK	C	.224	.256	.400	.421	.417	.049	1.750	2.25	S	180
.22 Taranah Hornet	A	.224	UNK	UNK	.294	.350	.063	UNK	UNK	UNK	180
.22 K-Hornet	A	.224	.242	.286	.294	.345	.060	1.39	1.70	S	181
.218 Mashburn Bee	A	.224	.241	.340	.349	.408	.060	1.34	1.75	S	181
.22 Reed Express	C	.224	UNK	UNK	UNK	UNK	UNK	UNK	UNK	UNK	182
.22 Waldog	C	.224	.245	.431	.440	.441	.053	1.375	1.820	S	182
.219 Donaldson Wasp	A	.224	.251	.402	.418	.497	.058	1.71	2.10	L	183
.22 BR Remington	C	.224	.245	.450	.466	.468	.045	1.502	2.00	S	183
.224 Clark	C	.224	.255	.455	.471	.473	.049	2.235	3.075	L	184
.224 Texas Trophy Hunter	C	.224	UNK	UNK	.470	.472	.045	UNK	UNK	UNK	184
.220 Wotkyns-Wilson Arrow	G	.224	.261	.402	.443	.472	.045	2.205	2.70	L	185
.22 CHeetah	C	.224	.250	.451	.466	.470	.048	2.00	2.36	S	185
.228 Ackley Magnum	C	.228	.265	.445	.470	.473	.045	2.25	2.55	L	186
6x45mm (6-223 Rem)	C	.243	.266	.354	.376	.378	.041	1.76	2.26	S	186
6mm Dasher	C	.224	.271	.462	.470	.470	.050	1.54	V	S	187
6mm-250 Walker	C	.243	.274	.420	.468	.470	.045	1.91	2.21	L	187
6mm CHeetah	C	.243	.260	.456	.470	.473	.049	2.00	UNK	L	188
Spitzer 6mm-06	C	.243	.276	.441	.470	.473	.049	2.494	3.350	L	188
6mm/30-30 Ackley Improved	A	.243	.275	.392	.422	.502	.058	2.03	2.55	L	189
6x47mm	C	.243	.266	.357	.375	.378	.045	1.850	2.485	S	190
6mm-284	I	.243	.276	.475	.500	.473	.049	2.165	2.80	L	191
.240 Hawk	C	.243	.276	.454	.471	.473	.049	2.485	UNK	L	191
.25 Hunter	A	.257	.293	.430	.435	.492	.046	1.625	2.30	L	192
.25-222 Copperhead	C	.224	.285	.357	.375	.378	.045	1.695	2.130	S	192
.25 Ackley Krag	A	.257	.293	.415	.457	.540	.059	2.24-2.31	V	L	193
.25 Ackley Krag Short	A	.257	.293	.442	.457	.540	.059	2.31	UNK	L	193
.250/3000 Ackley Improved	C	.257	.284	.445	.467	.473	.045	1.91	2.52	L	193
.257 Ackley Improved	C	.257	.288	.457	.471	.474	.045	2.23	2.78	L	194

Cartridge	Case	Bullet Dia.	Neck Dia.	Shoulder Dia.	Base Dia.	Rim Dia.	Rim Thick.	Case Length	Ctge. Length	Primer	Page
.257 Kimber	C	.257	.279	.365	.376	.373	.041	1.82	2.985	UNK	195
.25-284	I	.257	.285	.495	.500	.473	.049	2.17	2.80	L	195
.257 STW	E	.257	.285	.487	.511	.532	.050	2.850	3.600	L	196
.25 Gibbs	C	.257	UNK	UNK	.440	.468	.045	UNK	UNK	UNK	196
6.5 STW	E	.264	.298	.487	.511	.532	.050	2.850	3.600	L	197
6.5x52mm American	C	.264	.297	.465	.470	.473	.054	2.024	2.735	L	197
EABCO 6.5mm BRM	A	.264	UNK	UNK	.422	.502	.058	UNK	UNK	UNK	198
.264 LBC-AR	C	.264	.293	.428	.439	.441	.059	1.526	2.20	S	199
.264 Hawk	C	.264	.296	.454	.471	.473	.049	2.485	UNK	L	199
6.5 Gibbs	C	.264	UNK	UNK	.440	.468	.045	UNK	UNK	UNK	200
6.5mm-06 Ackley Improved	C	.264	.300	.455	.471	.473	.045	2.50	3.30	L	200
6.5mm Leopard	C	.264	.295	.539	.551	.533	.049	2.093	UNK	L	201
.270 REN	B	.277	.295	UNK	.298	.350	.060	1.29	UNK	S	201
.270 Hawk	C	.277	.308	.453	.471	.473	.049	2.485	UNK	L	202
.270 Gibbs	C	.277	UNK	UNK	.440	.468	.045	UNK	UNK	UNK	202
.270 IHMSA	C	.277	.305	.448	.471	.473	.045	1.866	2.60	L	202
.270 Savage	C	.277	.308	.413	.470	.470	.045	1.88	2.62	L	203
.270 Ackley Improved Savage	C	.277	.308	.450	.470	.470	.045	1.88	2.62	L	203
7mm TCU (7mmx223)	C	.284	.302	.350	.373	.375	.041	1.74	2.28	S	203
.280 Hawk	C	.284	.315	.454	.471	.473	.049	2.485	UNK	L	204
7mm JRS	C	.284	.312	.454	.470	.467	.045	2.525	3.455	L	204
7mm Gibbs	C	.284	UNK	UNK	.440	.468	.045	UNK	UNK	UNK	205
7mm SGLC	C	.284	.315	.465	.470	.473	.054	2.024	2.735	L	205
7mm STE	A	.284	.315	.454	.467	.502	.059	2.1	2.54	L	206
.285 OKH/7mm-06	C	.284	.315	.442	.470	.472	.045	2.55	3.35	L	207
.30 Kurz	C	.308	.334	.443	.470	.473	.045	1.29	1.65	L	207
.308x1.5-Inch Barnes	C	.308	.338	.450	.466	.470	.048	1.50	2.05	L	208
.30 Herrett	A	.308	.329	.405	.421	.505	.058	1.61	2.01	L	209
.30-30 Ackley Improved	A	.308	.328	.405	.422	.502	.058	2.04	2.54	L	210
.30-06 Ackley Improved	C	.308	.340	.454	.470	.473	.045	2.49	3.35	L	210
.30 Gibbs	C	.308	UNK	UNK	.440	.468	.045	UNK	UNK	UNK	211
.30-338 Winchester Magnum	E	.308	.340	.491	.513	.532	.048	2.50	UNK	L	211
.327 Martin Meteor	A	.312	.336	.379	.379	.440	.060	1.50	1.77	S	212
8mm-06	C	.323	.351	.441	.470	.473	.045	2.47	3.25	L	213
.33-08	C	.338	.369	.454	.470	.470	.049	2.015	2.820	L	213
.338-223 Straight	D	.338	.362	UNK	.376	.378	.041	1.41	2.25	S	214
.338/50 Talbot	C	.338	.380	.748	.774	.782	.080	3.76	4.25	.50 BMG	214
9mm Action Express	I	.355	.390	.433	.435	.394	.045	.866	1.152	S	215
9x25 Dillon	C	.355	.382	.423	.423	.424	.050	0.99	1.26	SP	215
.357 Auto Magnum	C	.357	.382	.461	.470	.473	.048	1.298	1.60	LP	216
.357 Herrett	A	.358	.375	.405	.420	.505	.058	1.75	2.10	L	217
.35-30/30	A	.358	.378	.401	.422	.506	.058	2.04	2.55	L	217
.358 BFG	I	.358	.382	.539	.555	.535	.054	1.625	2.370	L	218
.35 Indiana	C	.358	.384	.437	.458	.460	.046	1.80	2.780	L	219
.35 SuperMann	C	.358	.384	.437	.458	.460	.046	1.91	2.780	L	220
.358 Hoosier	C	.358	.388	.454	.470	.473	.048	1.80	2.70	L	221
.35 Sambar	I	.358	UNK	.538	.555	.535	.054	2.10	2.86	UNK	221
.358 Gremlin	C	.358	.384	.427	.438	.440	.059	1.495	2.250	S	222
.358/300 WSM	I	.358	.390	.538	.555	.535	.054	2.10	2.560	L	223
.358 UMT (Ultra Mag Towsley)	E	.358	.390	.525	.550	.534	.054	2.85	3.5	UNK	223
9.3 Sisk	C	.366	.388	.486	.512	.532	.047	2.85	3.57	L	224
9.3 BS	E	.366	.390	.495	.5126	.532	.046	2.165	2.80	L	225
.366 DGW	C	.366	UNK	UNK	.589	.586	.058	UNK	UNK	UNK	225
.375 Whelen & Ackley Imp. Whelen	C	.375	.403	.442/.455	.470	.473	.045	2.50	3.42	L	226
.400 Whelen	C	.405	.436	.462	.470	.473	.048	2.49	3.10	L	226

Dimensional Data

Cartridge	Case	Bullet Dia.	Neck Dia.	Shoulder Dia.	Base Dia.	Rim Dia.	Rim Thick.	Case Length	Ctge. Length	Primer	Page
.41 Special	B	.410	.432	UNK	.433	.488	.056	1.16	1.60	LP	227
.416 Barnes	A	.416	.432	.484	.505	.608	.065	2.112	2.95	L	227
.416 Aagaard	C	.416	.441	.492	.506	.496	.049	2.35	UNK	L	228
.416 SM2	B	.416	.447	.538	.555	.535	.054	2.072	3.75	L	229
.416 UMT	C	.416	.440	.525	.550	.534	.050	2.850	3.540	L	229
.445 Super Mag	B	.432	.456	UNK	.457	.514	.055	1.60	1.985	LP	230
.458x1.5-inch Barnes	F	.458	.481	UNK	.513	.532	.048	V	UNK	L	231
.45 Silhouette	B	.458	.477	UNK	.501	.600	.065	1.51	1.97	L	231
.45 Wildey Magnum	C	.45	UNK	UNK	.500	.473	.048	1.295	1.580	L	232
.458x2-inch American	F	.458	.478	UNK	.508	.532	.048	2.00	2.60	L	233
.460 Alliance	I	.458	.485	.530	.550	.534	.045	1.575	2.015	L	234
.450 Bonecrusher	A	.458	.488	.530	.535	.610	.060	1.40	1.77	L	234
.450 Alaskan	A	.458	.480	.515	.547	.605	.062	2.25	2.79	L	235
.450 Howell	C	.458	.480	.515	.545	.534	.045	2.50	3.25	L	235
.450 Watts Magnum	F	.458	.481	UNK	.513	.530	.048	2.85	3.65	L	236
.450 KNR	A	.458	UNK	UNK	UNK	UNK	UNK	UNK	UNK	UNK	236
.460 G&A Special	C	.458	.480	.530	.545	.545	.049	2.86	UNK	L	237
.475 Lehigh	J	.475	.504	UNK	.504	.480	.044	.950	1.17	LP	237
.475 Wildey Magnum	I	.475	.497	UNK	.500	.473	.048	1.295	1.58	L	238
.475 Ackley/OKH Magnum	F	.474	.496	UNK	.508	.528	.048	2.739	3.518	L	238
.500 Cyrus	L	.500	.528	.580	.582	.531	.058	2.333	2.90	L	239
.50 TAC	I	.510	.538	.580	.582	.531	.058	2.333	3.75	L	239
.500 Belted Magnum	L	.510	.540	N/A	.584	.603/.580	.062	2.50	3.25	L	240
.510 Nitro Express	B	.510	.535	UNK	.565	.665	UNK	3.245	4.185	L	241
.50 McMurdo	C	.510	.554	.725	.800	.802	.078	3.700	5.722	.50 BMG	241
.50 McMillan FatMac	C	.510	.550	1.111	1.152	1.158	.090	2.645	V	.50 BMG	242
.505/530 Woodleigh	C	.530	UNK	UNK	UNK	UNK	UNK	UNK	UNK	UNK	242
.585 Nyati	I	.585	.605	.650	.660	.532/.586	UNK	2.79	3.525	L	243
.729 Jongmans	C	.727	UNK	UNK	.804	.804	.080	UNK	UNK	UNK	244

Case Type: A = Rimmed, bottleneck. B = Rimmed, straight. C = Rimless, bottleneck. D = Rimless, straight. E = Belted, bottleneck. F = Belted, straight. G = Semi-rimmed, bottleneck. H = Semi-rimmed, straight. I = Rebated, bottleneck. J = Rebated, straight. K = Rebated, belted bottleneck. L = Rebated, belted straight.

Primer Type: S = Small rifle (.175"). SP = Small pistol (.175"). L = Large rifle (.210"). LP = Large pistol (.210"). 50 BMG = CCI-35/VihtaVuori-110/RWS-8212. B-1 = Berdan #1. B-2 = Berdan #2.

Other codes: V = OAL depends upon bullet used. V = Rifling twist varies, depending upon bullet and application. Belt/Rim Diameter. Unless otherwise noted, all dimensions in inches.

Proprietary Cartridges
(Rifle & Handgun)

These proprietary cartridges and guns so chambered are special. These developments represent the culmination of efforts of serious gunsmiths to provide guns and ammunition that are a cut above the ordinary. All represent a level of hand fitting and precision that is simply not feasible in run-of-the-mill offerings. For those shooters willing and able to pay a premium price, these rifles offer the option of a factory gun that is, in many instances, equal to the best of the fully-custom numbers in both fit and function. The cartridges used in these guns represent an effort toward ballistic perfection. Some are more successful than others.

The concept of the proprietary cartridge was well developed in Great Britain, beginning in the late 1800s. That tradition continued until quite recently, when unfortunate and thoroughly nonsensical political developments probably destroyed the practice forever. Under our current definition, many of the reasonably well-known cartridges associated with such firms as Holland & Holland were originally strictly proprietary. Those cartridges were designed to fulfill some specific need in the best possible way. For a fuller understanding of this relationship, one should review the introductory text and cartridge write-ups in Chapter 8, British Sporting Rifle Cartridges.

A good example is the belted .375 H&H Magnum. That case was designed to provide solid headspace control, while facilitating reliable functioning under extreme and adverse conditions in a bolt-action rifle. Considerations included functionality under extremely hot conditions, and when either the ammunition or the rifle chamber might not be perfectly clean. The belt provided for solid headspacing, despite a comparatively loose fit of the case body in the chamber of the rifle. Caliber, capacity, bullet design, and loading pressure (case capacity) were also chosen with consideration of the intended applications—in this instance, chiefly short- to medium-range shots on smaller species of dangerous African game.

Similarly, Sharps and many other stateside manufacturers followed the same route during the era of Buffalo exploitation and development of long-range target shooting competitive events. Most of those cartridge developments are long obsolete, but others moved into the mainstream and are still with us. An example of the former is the .44-50 Peabody, while the .38-55 Ballard (now known as the .38-55 Winchester), exemplifies the latter group.

In many instances, cartridges we now think of as standard items were once essentially proprietary. A good example is the .348 Winchester. Here was a cartridge designed by Winchester, which was commercially chambered only by Winchester (in its Model 71 rifle). For many years, Winchester was the only source of .348 ammunition. Similarly, the .444 Marlin was designed for use in only one rifle (Marlin's .444) and, until the advent of Buffalo Bore ammunition's new offerings, was never commercially loaded by anyone other than Remington. While these are SAAMI standard chamberings, both are, in some manner, proprietary. Other examples abound. In some sense, practically every factory chambering that did not originate as a military cartridge was once proprietary. Nevertheless, we will maintain an arbitrary and perhaps unfair distinction between offerings from mainstream manufacturers and those from smaller producers.

Regarding the wildcat connection, consider the .35 Whelen. While this fine cartridge might seem to fit the proprietary bill, really it does not. For many decades it was a widely chambered wildcat cartridge, but was not commercially loaded. Now it is commercially loaded and chambered as a mainstream offering. Even before that, it was too widely known and chambered for inclusion in this chapter.

While many cartridges discussed in this chapter had antecedents in the wildcat arena (or among European developments), they have not yet achieved standard commercial status. The distinction seems significant. It would be convenient if all proprietary cartridges were unique developments and if no wildcat cartridges fit into this category. However, that is not the situation. Gray areas of overlap are noteworthy and somewhat abundant.

Most proprietary offerings detailed in this chapter followed a developmental path similar to the aforementioned historical British proprietary cartridges. Some custom gun manufacturer noted a void in the offerings from major arms manufacturers. That manufacturer then designed a cartridge to fill that void in the best way possible —according to his likes and based upon what basic case types were available for improvement. Here, we might consider the history of the major commercial cartridge offerings with which, in many instances, these proprietary chamberings compete.

Big-bore (.50-caliber and up) rifles convey almost romantic images and historic links to the great dangerous game hunters of years past. However, the years between then and now have seen the introduction of legal restrictions on the ownership of these firearms. When proprietary cartridges contain a projectile larger than a half-inch in diameter, they may be considered as destructive devices, according to the United States' Code of Federal Regulations, Title 27, Volume 1. The statutory authority granted to the BATFE allows the director to determine that the device, among other things, is a rifle that the owner intends to use solely for sporting purposes. Certain combinations of firearms actions, barrel lengths, and bore diameter may not meet the criteria of "being a rifle that the owner intends to use solely for sporting purposes" and would otherwise constitute a destructive device. Possession of an unauthorized destructive device may subject the possessor to criminal or civil penalties. For shooters interested in purchasing or possessing one of the ,50-caliber or larger cartridges documented in this chapter, it is important to confirm that the manufacturer of the rifle and cartridge combination has an exemption from the BATFE for its manufacture.

13th Edition Update

Although several custom cartridge designers continue to develop wildcat cartridges and keep them in the proprietary arena, in most cases, it is not the best path to follow, if someone wants to see their design become a commercial success. As an example, let's look at the .300 Whisper, which was developed as a proprietary cartridge by J.D. Jones. AAC, in conjunction with Remington, standardized this wildcat as a SAAMI cartridge, and sales immediately exploded, at least for Remington and AAC. It is indeed understandable that ballistic engineers, regardless of their notoriety or training, want to protect their creations. However, this protection often does little more than prevent very good cartridges from going mainstream. Some of the most notable proprietary cartridges come from J.D. Jones, Gary Reeder, Lazzeroni, A-Square, and Dakota.—*R.A.M.*

.222 Remington Rimmed

Historical Notes: During the 1950s and 1960s, thousands of rifles built on the small Martini action and chambered for a rimmed cartridge called the .310 Cadet (also known as the .310 Greener) were sold on the military surplus market. Manufactured from 1910 to 1940 by Birmingham Small Arms (BSA), Greener, Webley & Scott, and other English firms, they were used as training rifles by military cadets in Great Britain and Australia. Once those rifles became available on the surplus market, many custom rifles were built on the action and, since its extractor was designed for a rimmed cartridge, some of the more common cartridges chosen were the .22 Hornet, .218 Bee, .22 Jet, .256 Winchester, and Improved versions of same. The action became popular enough in Australia to prompt the Super Cartridge Company of that country to manufacture a rimmed version of the .222 Remington specifically for it. Since the action was also quite popular among custom rifle builders in America, the Williams Gun Sight Company (www.williamsgunsight.com) imported the cases. Think of the .222 Remington case with the rim diameter of the .38 Special pistol cartridge, and you have the .222 Remington Rimmed.

General Comments: Not much can be said about the .222 Rimmed that has not already been said many times about the .222 Remington, except that, for a time, it was a way to give a wonderful little military surplus rifle a second useful life. In the United States, the cartridge became unnecessary, after Michigan gunsmith Robert Snapp started making rimless extractors that allowed the standard .222 Remington cartridge compatible with the Martini Cadet action. Reloading data for the two cartridges are interchangeable.

.222 Remington Rimmed Loading Data and Factory Ballistics

Bullet (grains/type)	Powder	Grains	Velocity	Energy	Source
40 Sierra BlitzKing	RL-7	22.0	3358	1000	Layne Simpson
50 Nosler Ballistic Tip	RL-7	21.0	3316	1219	Layne Simpson
52 Sierra MatchKing	RL-7	21.0	3334	1282	Layne Simpson
55 Sierra BlitzKing	RL-7	20.5	3118	1186	Layne Simpson

.226 JDJ

Historical Notes: Designed by J.D. Jones, in 1979, this cartridge is the .225 Winchester, Improved. It provides a reduction in chamber pressure, which improves Contender functioning; factory .225 Winchester ammunition sometimes gave extraction difficulties in Contender barrels. This design solved that problem. Factory .225 Winchester ammunition can be used.

General Comments: As is typical of the JDJ line, this chambering offers ½ MOA accuracy potential with proper handloads. New barrels feature a 1:9 twist for use with heavier bullets, which are gaining popularity in the .22-caliber bore. Typical loads with the 40-grain bullet easily exceed 3600 fps from a 16-inch barrel. The Barnes 45-grain XBT is an effective choice for peccary-size game species. However, use of this bullet requires special handloading techniques (deeper bullet seating and a reduction in powder charge). Further, those bullets work best when a minimum-friction coating (such as moly-plating) is used. For this reason, SSK does not support the use of X-style bullets in its guns. While no bullet substitution is benign, never substitute any X-style bullet in any load—begin with data specifically created for that bullet. For information on components, loading data, barrels, and guns designed for this cartridge, contact SSK Inudstries, 720-264-0176; www.sskindustries.com.

.226 JDJ Loading Data

Bullet (grains/type)	Powder	Grains	Velocity	Energy	Source/Comments
50 Hornady	IMR 3031	32.0	2864	905	SSK/maximum load, SSK barrel only
55	IMR 4064	33.0	2808	960	SSK/maximum load, SSK barrel only

55 Hornady SX	BL-C(2)	32.0	2637	849	SSK/maximum load, SSK barrel only
60 Hornady SP	H414	35.0	2732	995	SSK/maximum load, SSK barrel only
63 Sierra	H4831	38.5	2831	1115	SSK/maximum load, SSK barrel only

6 Whisper

Historical Notes: Created by J.D. Jones, the 6 Whisper uses a modified .221 Fireball case necked up to 6mm to propel heavy bullets at subsonic velocities and lighter bullets at higher velocities. In a 10-inch-barreled Contender pistol, the 6 Whisper can propel 115-grain bullets to 1054 fps, and lighter 55-grain bullets to over 3000 fps.

General Comments: This cartridge is well-suited for Thompson/Center Contenders, bolt-action rifles, and AR15-type rifles. At subsonic velocities, it functions quietly and accurately in suppressed firearms. For information on components, loading data, barrels, and guns designed for this cartridge, contact SSK Inudstries, 720-264-0176; www.sskindustries.com.

6mm JDJ

Historical Notes: This cartridge was designed and developed by noted gun writer and experimenter J.D. Jones, hence the "JDJ" designation. Jones began development of his series of cartridges around 1978, and they are generally fired in barrels furnished by his company, SSK Industries. The purpose of this cartridge is to give added range and power to the Thompson/Center Contender pistol for the primary purpose of hunting varmints and small game. Some of his cartridges have proven to be excellent metallic silhouette numbers, as well. The JDJ series of cases is easy to make. All JDJ cartridges are proprietary, and SSK neither sells reamers nor permits the reamer maker to duplicate any of SSK's reamers.

General Comments: Based on the .225 Winchester case, itself a modified .30-30 case, this improved chambering provides ample capacity to deliver maximum 6mm velocity from handgun-length barrels (14 to 16 inches). Best applications are in handgun varminting and hunting of the smallest big-game species. With the proper 70- to 75-grain bullet, this chambering can deliver 300-yard varmint accuracy and trajectory. Heavier, well-constructed bullets can deliver adequate performance for smaller big-game out to perhaps 100 yards. The Barnes 75-grain and 85-grain X bullets offer serious hunting performance. However, use of these bullets requires special handloading techniques (deeper bullet seating and a reduction in powder charge). Further, those bullets work best when a minimum-friction coating (such as moly-plating) is used. For this reason, SSK does not support the use of X-style bullets in its guns. While no bullet substitution is benign, never substitute any X-style bullet in any load—begin with data specifically created for that bullet. For information on components, loading data, barrels, and guns designed for this cartridge, contact SSK Inudstries, 720-264-0176; www.sskindustries.com.

6 JDJ No. 2 Loading Data

Bullet (grains/type)	Powder	Grains	Velocity	Energy	Source/Comments
70 HP	Rl-7	29.0	2845	1260	SSK/maximum load, SSK barrel only
*70 HP	AA 2700	35.0	2540	1000	SSK/maximum load, SSK barrel only
80 HP	Rl-19	37.0	2370	1000	SSK/maximum load, SSK barrel only

Note: These loads for use only in SSK barrels

6.17 Spitfire

Historical Notes: Lazzeroni Arms designed this cartridge, in 1997. While somewhat related to an older case, for all practical purposes, this is a new case design. This cartridge was created in response to requests for a high-performance cartridge that would work in a 2.8-inch action and yet deliver the ballistics of a full-length belted magnum. Case diameter is similar to conventional belted case rim diameter, so adaptation to a standard action is quite simple.

General Comments: Bullet diameter is .243-inch (Lazzeroni bases its designations on bullet diameter, instead of bore diameter, which is the common practice). Ballistics are quite impressive for such a short cartridge. The Spitfire comes very close to top .240 Weatherby ballistics. Case design is typical of the Lazzeroni line: moderate body taper, 30-degree shoulder, sufficiently long neck, and thick rim of approximate case-body diameter. In other words, this is a well-designed case. For more information on Lazzeroni custom guns, ammunition, and reloading data, contact 888-492--7247; www.lazzeroni.com.

6.17 Spitfire Factory Ballistics (24-inch barrel)

Bullet (grains)	Powder	Grains	Velocity	Energy	Source/Comments
70			3750	2186	Lazzeroni factory load
85			3550	2379	Lazzeroni factory load
100			3350	2493	Lazzeroni factory load

6.17 Flash

Historical Notes: Lazzeroni Arms designed this cartridge, in 1996. While somewhat related to an older case, for all practical purposes, this is a new case design. John Lazzeroni believes that those hunters who will take the time to become competent marksmen can legitimately take game at ranges out to about 500 yards, given a gun with the requisite accuracy and a bullet that will perform properly. This cartridge was created to provide sufficient velocity that would enable medium-weight hunting bullets with dependable expansion at maximum ranges. Adaptation to standard actions is quite simple. Lazzeroni has recently discontinued this as a standard chambering, but still offers it on a special-order basis.

General Comments: Bullet diameter is .243-inch (Lazzeroni bases its designations on bullet diameter, instead of bore diameter, which is the common practice). Flash ballistics surpass any other current 6mm cartridge. Case design is typical of the Lazzeroni line: moderate body taper, 30-degree shoulder, sufficiently long neck, and thick rim of approximate case-body diameter. In other words, this is a well-designed case. Designed specifically for hunting, with limited barrel life (no more than 500 rounds), this cartridge is not recommended for any other use. While 27-inch barrels are standard, all the smaller-caliber, full-length Lazzeroni numbers would benefit significantly from even longer barrels. Most of Lazzeroni's full-length cartridge loadings use specially lubricated (proprietary process) premium bullets from Nosler, Barnes, or Swift. This is a superior performer for those who only hunt the smaller species of big game and who will not abuse the barrel via incautious shooting. The 85-grain Nosler Partition works extremely well. For more information on Lazzeroni custom guns, ammunition, and reloading data, contact 888-492--7247; www.lazzeroni.com.

6.17 Flash Factory Ballistics (27-inch barrel)

Bullet (grains/type)	Powder	Grains	Velocity	Energy	Source/Comments
70			4150	2678	Lazzeroni factory load
85			3900	2871	Lazzeroni factory load
100			3700	3041	Lazzeroni factory load

NEW
.255 Banshee

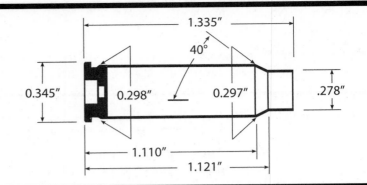

Historical Notes: Gary Reeder's Banshee series of cartridges is based on the .22 K Hornet case. Gary wanted a pistol cartridge that was capable of pushing a 65- to 75-gain bullet to 2000 fps from a 12-inch barrel. The Banshee will even work in a revolver.

General Comments: According to Gary Reeder, the .255 Banshee will work well with bullets as heavy as 87 grains and performs admirably on smaller-bodied deer. He takes the .22 K Hornet cases, which are necked up and then fire formed with loads reduced by 10 percent. This is a fun cartridge to shoot from a revolver and should be great fun for snooping around grown-up pastures holding groundhogs, badgers, and such. Information on custom guns, ammunitin, and reloading data can be obtained by contacting Gary Reeder Custom Guns, 928-527-4100; www.reedercustomguns.com.—R.A.M.

.255 Banshee Loading Data and Ballistics

Bullet (grains/type)	Powder	Grains	Velocity	Energy	Source/Comments
60 Hornady FP	H 110	12.0	2178	631	Gary Reeder
75 Hornady HP	AA # 9	10.0	1960	639	Gary Reeder
85 Nosler Ballistic Tip	H 110	10.0	1810	618	Gary Reeder

NEW
.257 Raptor

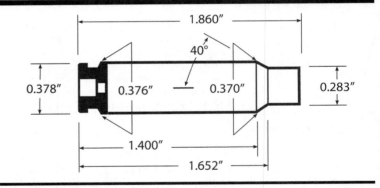

Historical Notes: Becoming less and less enthralled with powerful, hard-kicking cartridges, Gary Reeder decided to put together a couple very practical wildcat cartridges based on the .204 Ruger case. The 257 Raptor was one of three Raptor cartridges he developed. Reeder's first .257 Raptor was put together on a Thompson/Center Encore, with the help of Dave Manson, who supplied the reamers.

General Comments: Balistically, the .257 Raptor is in the same class as the old .25-35 Winchester, which is the cartridge my son used to take his first whitetail deer. However, the .257 Raptor comes in a much smaller package and, since it's a rimless cartridge, can work in a wider range of rifles including AR-15s. Reeder has used the .257 Raptor to take a bunch of whitetail deer, as well as several wild hogs and assorted exotic game animals. For more information on custom guns, ammunition, and reloading data, contact Reeder Custom Guns, 928-527-4100; www.reedercustomguns.com.—R.A.M.

.257 Raptor Loading Data and Ballistics

Bullet (grains/type)	Powder	Grains	Velocity	Energy	Source/Comments
75 HP	H 335	29.0	2608	1132	Gary Reeder
85 Nosler Ballistic Tip	IMR 3031	27.0	2539	1216	Gary Reeder

.257 JDJ

Historical Notes: This is another cartridge designed and developed by J.D. Jones, hence the JDJ designation. Jones began development of his cartridges around 1978, and they are generally fired in barrels furnished by his company, SSK Industries. The purpose of these cartridges is to give added range and power to the Thompson/Center Contender pistol. Some of Jones' cartridges have also proven to be excellent metallic silhouette numbers. JDJ cartridges are relatively easy to make. All JDJ cartridges are proprietary, and SSK neither sells reamers nor has permitted the reamer maker to duplicate any of the reamers for the series.

General Comments: Based on the .225 Winchester case, itself a modified .30-30 case, this Improved chambering provides ample capacity to deliver near-maximum quarter-bore velocity from handgun-length barrels (14 to 16 inches). Best applications are in handgun varminting and hunting of smaller big-game species. A preferred bullet for the latter application is Nosler's 85-grain Ballistic Tip. This cartridge can launch this bullet to about 2900 fps with top loads from a 14-inch barrel. This combination is said to provide good terminal performance to 300 yards. One can use heavier bullets to deliver more energy. However, reduced velocity limits expansion; trajectory errors increase. Therefore, hunters should limit use of such bullets to shorter ranges. For information on components, loading data, barrels, and guns designed for this cartridge, contact SSK Inudstries, 720-264-0176; www.sskindustries.com.

.257 JDJ Loading Data

Bullet (grains/type)	Powder	Grains	Velocity	Energy	Source/Comments
75 HP	H322	30.0	2310	890	SSK/maximum load, SSK barrels only
75 HP	W748	37.0	2645	1165	SSK/maximum load, SSK barrels only
100 SP	W748	34.0	1405	1285	SSK/maximum load, SSK barrels only
117 SP	IMR 4350	35.0	2195	1250	SSK/maximum load, SSK barrels only

.25/06 JDJ

Historical Notes: Virtually identical to the 6.5/270 JDJ, the .25/06 JDJ uses a modified .270 Winchester case, necked down to handle .25-caliber bullets. Other changes include shortening the neck, reducing case taper to maximize powder capacity, and forming a 60-degree shoulder to achieve ballistics normally associated with belted magnum cartridges in similar length (15-inch) Encore barrels.

General Comments: The .25/06 JDJ is well-suited for Thompson/Center Encore firearms, Ruger No. 1 rifles, or appropriate bolt-action rifles. This cartridge provides long case life, consumes less powder than belted magnum cartridges, and uses relatively inexpensive cases. For information on components, loading data, barrels, and guns designed for this cartridge, contact SSK Inudstries, 720-264-0176; www.sskindustries.com.

.257 Mini Dreadnaught

Historical Notes: This cartridge was designed by J.D. Jones, at SSK Industries. Application is to Thompson/Center Encore or Contender single-shot pistols fitted with a custom SSK barrel. Typical barrel length is 15 inches. Cases are fire formed from empty .220 Swift cases. Neck length is minimal, which is acceptable for a cartridge used in a single-shot gun. Shoulder angle is 60 degrees, which seems to work just fine. Body taper is minimal. Therefore, this is a maximized .25-caliber version of the .220 Swift case. Capacity is similar to the .257 Roberts (about 57 grains) and working pressure is higher (about 60,000 psi), so ballistics are quite similar, despite the significant deficit in barrel length.

General Comments: Since the Swift case has a rim, it is possible to fire-form necked-up Swift cases to fit this chamber. For this purpose, use loads that are near the maximum level. Jones recommends 100- to 120-grain bullets for big-game hunting applications on smaller species. Nosler's Ballistic Tip and Partition bullets have demonstrated superior performance. However, it would appear this cartridge is capable of driving 120-grain bullets fast enough to give dependable expansion. While one could use the lightest Barnes X bullets, which can offer impressive terminal performance, the handloader must use X-bullet-specific loading data and special handloading techniques (e.g., the bullet ogive must be seated a minimum of .050-inch from the rifling). Further, those bullets work best when a minimum-friction coating (such as moly-plating) is used. For this reason, SSK does not support the use of X-style bullets in its guns. While no bullet substitution is benign, never substitute any X-style bullet in any load—begin with data specifically created for that bullet. For information on components, loading data, barrels, and guns designed for this cartridge, contact SSK Inudstries, 720-264-0176; www.sskindustries.com.

.257 Mini Dreadnaught Loading Data

Bullet (grains/type)	Powder	Grains	Velocity	Energy	Source/Comments
100 Nosler BT	AA 4350	48.7	3008	2005	SSK/maximum load, SSK barrels only

6.53 Scramjet

Historical Notes: Lazzeroni Arms designed this cartridge, in 1996. While somewhat related to an older case, for all practical purposes this is a new case design. John Lazzeroni believes that those hunters who will take the time to become competent marksmen can legitimately take game at ranges out to about 500 yards, given a gun with the requisite accuracy and a bullet that will perform properly. This cartridge was created to launch lightweight hunting bullets with sufficient velocity to provide dependable expansion at maximum ranges. Adaptation to standard actions is quite simple. While this case does not sell well, Lazzeroni will continue to handle it, owing to the founder's love for this bore size.

General Comments: Bullet diameter is .257-inch (Lazzeroni bases its designations on bullet diameter, instead of bore diameter, which is the common practice.). Scramjet ballistics exceed any other current .25-caliber cartridge. Case design is typical of the Lazzeroni line: moderate body taper, 30-degree shoulder, sufficiently long neck, and thick rim of approximate case-body diameter. In other words, this is a well-designed case. Designed specifically for hunting, and with limited barrel life, this cartridge is not recommended for any other use. While 27-inch barrels are standard, all the smaller-caliber, full-length Lazzeroni numbers would benefit significantly from even longer barrels. Most of Lazzeroni's full-length cartridge loadings use specially lubricated (proprietary process) premium bullets from Nosler, Barnes, or Swift. For hunting, John prefers the 100-grain Nosler Partition and the 90-grain Barnes XBT, while the 85-grain Nosler BT is especially accurate and makes a superb long-range varminting choice. A significant portion of the accuracy and ballistic potential of these cartridges results from the unusually effective reduced-friction coating used. For more information on Lazzeroni custom guns, ammunition, and reloading data, contact 888-492--7247; www.lazzeroni.com.

6.53 Scramjet Factory Ballistics (27-inch barrel)

Bullet (grains/type)	Powder	Grains	Velocity	Energy	Source/Comments
85	FL		4000	3021	Lazzeroni factory load
100	FL		3750	3123	Lazzeroni factory load
120	FL		3550	3219	Lazzeroni factory load

6.5mm Whisper

Historical Notes: Designed by J.D. Jones, in the early 1990s, this cartridge was intended for use in sound-suppressed M-15s, bolt-action rifles, and T/C Contenders. As with most of Jones' line, this cartridge was designed at SSK Industries. This cartridge is based upon the .221 Remington case.

General Comments: When combined with a very quick rifling twist, this chambering will deliver 155-grain very low drag (VLD) bullets from SSK Contender barrels with ½ MOA accuracy at subsonic velocities (1040 fps). Lighter bullets can achieve a more typical muzzle velocity, but such applications sacrifice the design purpose of this chambering. The 6.5mm Whisper performs well as a short-range deer cartridge. For information on components, loading data, barrels, and guns designed for this cartridge, contact SSK Inudstries, 720-264-0176; www.sskindustries.com.

6.5mm Whisper Loading Data

Bullet (grains/type)	Powder	Grains	Velocity	Energy	Source/Comments
100 Hornady	H110	19.0	2300	1170	Maximum load, SSK barrel only (10")
120 Nosler BT	A-1680	19.0	2150	1230	Maximum load, SSK barrel only (10")
155	H110	8.3	970	320	SSK/M-16 (gas port open)
155	H110	8.3	1051	375	SSK/M-16 (gas port blocked)
155	AA No. 9	8.4	1050	375	SSK/M-16 (gas port open)
155	AA No. 9	8.4	1074	395	SSK/M-16 (gas port blocked)

NEW
6.5x25 CBJ

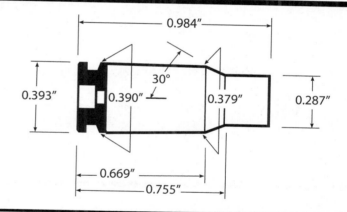

Historical Notes: The 6.5X25 CBJ was developed by CBJ Tech AB in Sweden, which was founded, in 1997, by C. Bertil Johansson, who is also the inventor of the cartridge. The purpose of the cartridge is to increase the performance of pistols and shoulder weapons chambered for 9x19 Parabellum cartridge, in terms of range, penetration, and wounding effect.

General Comments: The geometry of this case—up to the shoulder, as well as overall cartridge length—is identical to the 9X19 Luger (Parabellum) cartridge and it generates the same level of impulse (pressure). This means that most weapons currently chambered for the 9mm Luger can be converted to the 6.5X25 CBJ by only changing the barrel. The cartridge has several different proprietary projectiles, all of which can be used interchangeably to meet different requirements. The main variant is the 6.5x25 CBJ Ball, which has a sub-caliber projectile consisting of a 4mm tungsten core encased in a discarding plastic sabot. When shot from an eight-inch barrel—when zeroed at 100 meters—it will have a maximum trajectory height of ¾-inch. It is also capable of defeating an 8mm hardened armor plate at 100 yards. CBJ Tech AB is currently working with several countries and major military units worldwide who are interested in this cartridge. The 6.5X25 CBJ is a high-velocity pistol/sub-machine pistol cartridge with subsonic capability. Both subsonic and supersonic cartridges function with the same reliability. At this time, CBJ Tech AB has no plans for commercial sales.—R.A.M.

6.5x25 CBJ Factory Ballistics

Bullet (grains/type)	Powder	Grains	Velocity	Energy	Source/Comments
30.9 Sub-caliber AP	FL		2788	533	CBJ Tech AB
38.6 Frangible	FL		2788	666	CBJ Tech AB
123.5 MC (Subsonic)	Fl		1049	302	CBJ Tech AB t

6.5mm JDJ

Historical Notes: Designed by J.D. Jones, at SSK Industries, this is the .225 Winchester case Improved and necked up to 6mm. The purpose was to provide a Contender hunting cartridge for smaller big-game species.

General Comments: Excellent bullets are available and, with proper loads and in the hands of a good shot, this chambering is capable of 300-yard shots on smaller big-game species. Jones considers this cartridge one of the premier small-bore hunting choices. For information on components, loading data, barrels, and guns designed for this cartridge, contact SSK Inudstries, 720-264-0176; www.sskindustries.com.

6.5mm JDJ Loading Data

Bullet (grains/type)	Powder	Grains	Velocity	Energy	Source/Comments
85 Sierra	IMR 4320	35.0	2644	1315	SSK/maximum load, SSK barrel only (14")
100 Sierra HP	H322	35.0	2714	1635	SSK/maximum load, SSK barrel only (14")
120 Speer	IMR 4350	38.5	2467	1620	SSK/maximum load, SSK barrel only (14")
125 Nosler Part	IMR 4320	33.0	2410	1610	SSK/maximum load, SSK barrel only (14")
129 Hornady	IMR 4320	32.0	2342	1570	SSK/maximum load, SSK barrel only (14")
140 Speer	IMR 4350	34.0	2097	1365	SSK/maximum load, SSK barrel only (14")

6.5mm JDJX30

Historical Notes: This J.D. Jones cartridge is the 7-30 Waters necked down to 6.5mm and Improved. Its purpose is to meet customer demand for improved performance with readily obtained cases. Since the 7-30 is based on the .30-30 Winchester, one can easily use those abundant cases to form this round. Other than rim diameter and a slight increase in case length, this is essentially identical to the 6.5mm JDJ.

General Comments: Excellent bullets are available and, with proper loads and in the hands of a good shot, this chambering is capable of 300-yard shots on the smaller species. Jones considers this one of the premier small-bore hunting choices. For information on components, loading data, barrels, and guns designed for this cartridge, contact SSK Inudstries, 720-264-0176; www.sskindustries.com.

6.5mm JDJ x30 Loading Data

Bullet (grains/type)	Powder	Grains	Velocity	Energy	Source/Comments
85 Sierra	W760	42.0	2710	1385	SSK/maximum load, SSK barrel only (14")
120 Speer	W760	40.0	2477	1635	SSK/maximum load, SSK barrel only (14")
120 Nosler BT	IMR 4064	37.5	2580	1770	SSK/maximum load, SSK barrel only (14")
129 Hornady	IMR 4350	40.7	2481	1760	SSK/maximum load, SSK barrel only (14")
140 Sierra	IMR 4350	40.7	2376	1755	SSK/maximum load, SSK barrel only (14")

6.5 Mini Dreadnaught

Historical Notes: This cartridge was designed by J.D. Jones, at SSK Industries. Application is to Thompson/Center Encore or Contender single-shot pistols fitted with a custom SSK barrel. Typical barrel length is 15 inches. Cases are formed from empty .220 Swift cases. Neck length is minimal, which is acceptable for a cartridge used in a single-shot gun. Shoulder angle is 60 degrees, which seems to work just fine. Body taper is minimal, similar to the Ackley Improved designs. Therefore, this is a maximized, 6.5mm version of the .220 Swift case. Capacity is similar to the .257 Roberts (about 56 grains) and with a larger bore and higher working pressure (about 60,000 psi), ballistics easily duplicate the Roberts, despite the significant deficit in barrel length.

General Comments: Since the Swift case has a rim, it is possible to fire-form necked-up Swift cases to fit this chamber. For this purpose, use loads that are near the maximum level. Jones recommends 120- to 140-grain bullets for big-game hunting applications on smaller species. Nosler's Ballistic Tip and Partition bullets have demonstrated superior performance. However, it would appear that this cartridge is capable of driving 155-grain bullets fast enough to give dependable expansion. While one could use 100-grain Barnes X bullets, which can offer impressive terminal performance, the handloader must use X bullet-specific loading data and special handloading techniques (e.g., the bullet ogive must be seated a minimum of .050-inch from the rifling). Further, those bullets work best when a reduced-friction coating (such as moly-plating) is used. For this reason, SSK does not support use of X-style bullets in its guns. While no bullet substitution is benign, never substitute any X-style bullet in any load—begin with data specifically created for that bullet. This cartridge has a significantly shorter case body than the .257 Mini Dreadnaught, so it fails to exceed the ballistic potential of its smaller-bored sibling. For information on components, loading data, barrels, and guns designed for this cartridge, contact SSK Inudstries, 720-264-0176; www.sskindustries.com.

6.5 Mini Dreadnaught Load Data

Bullet (grains/type)	Powder	Grains	Velocity	Energy	Source/Comments
120 Sierra	Vit N560	52.0	2852	2165	SSK/maximum load, SSK barrels only
120 Sierra	AA 2700	49.5	2775	2050	SSK/maximum load, SSK barrels only
140 Remington	Vit N560	52.0	2736	2325	SSK/maximum load, SSK barrels only
140 Hornady	AA 2700	48.2	2618	2130	SSK/maximum load, SSK barrels only

6.5mm JDJ No. 2

Historical Notes: This J.D. Jones cartridge is the .307 Winchester necked down to 6.5mm and Improved. It provides a 6.5mm chambering based upon the .307 Winchester case.

General Comments: Excellent bullets are available and, with proper loads and in the hands of a good shot, this chambering is fine for 300-yard shots on smaller species. In handgun-length barrels, ballistics are not significantly superior to the smaller 6.5mm JDJ cartridges and so do not justify the existence of this chambering. For information on components, loading data, barrels, and guns designed for this cartridge, contact SSK Inudstries, 720-264-0176; www.sskindustries.com.

6.5mm JDJ No. 2 Loading Data

Bullet (grains)	Powder	Grains	Velocity	Energy	Source/Comments
120	IMR 4350	43.0	NA	NA	SSK/maximum load, SSK barrel only
129	IMR 4350	42.0	NA	NA	SSK/maximum load, SSK barrel only
140	IMR 4350	41.0	NA	NA	SSK/maximum load, SSK barrel only

6.5/270 JDJ

Historical Notes: If anyone produced more successful cartridge designs than J.D. Jones, of SSK Industries, they're not widely recognized. In creating the 6.5/270 JDJ, Jones used a modified .270 Winchester case, necking it down to handle 6.5mm bullets, shortening the neck, reducing case taper, and forming a 60-degree shoulder to achieve ballistics normally associated with belted magnum cartridges in similar length (15-inch) Encore barrels.

General Comments: The 6.5/270 JDJ is well suited for Thompson/Center Encore firearms, Ruger No. 1 rifles, or appropriate bolt-action rifles. This cartridge provides long case life, consumes less powder than belted magnum cartridges, and uses relatively inexpensive cases. For information on components, loading data, barrels, and guns designed for this cartridge, contact SSK Inudstries, 720-264-0176; www.sskindustries.com.

6.71 Phantom

Historical Notes: Lazzeroni Arms designed this cartridge, in 1997. While somewhat related to an older case, for all practical purposes, this is a new case design. This cartridge was created in response to requests for a high-performance cartridge that would work in a 2.8-inch action and yet deliver the ballistics of a full-length belted magnum. Case diameter is similar to rim diameter of the conventional belted case, so adaptation to a standard action is quite simple.

General Comments: Bullet diameter is .264-inch (Lazzeroni bases its designations on bullet diameter, instead of bore diameter, which is the common practice). Ballistics are quite impressive for such a short cartridge. The Phantom essentially duplicates 24-inch barrel .264 Winchester Magnum ballistics. Case design is typical of the Lazzeroni line: moderate body taper, 30-degree shoulder, sufficiently long neck, and thick rim of approximate case-body diameter. In other words, this is a well-designed case. For more information on Lazzeroni custom guns, ammunition, and reloading data, contact 888-492--7247; www.lazzeroni.com.

6.71 Phantom Factory Ballistics (24-inch barrel)

Bullet (grains)	Powder	Grains	Velocity	Energy	Source/Comments
100	FL		3450	2643	Lazzeroni factory load
120	FL		3250	2815	Lazzeroni factory load
140	FL		3050	2892	Lazzeroni factory load

6.71 Blackbird

Historical Notes: Lazzeroni Arms designed this cartridge, in 1996. Lazzeroni no longer routinely chambers this number, but will still do so on a special-order basis. While somewhat related to an older case, for all practical purposes, this is an original case design. John Lazzeroni believes that those hunters who will take the time to become competent marksmen can legitimately take game at ranges out to about 500 yards, given a gun with the requisite accuracy and a bullet that will perform properly. This cartridge was created to provide sufficient velocity to medium-weight hunting bullets so as to enable dependable expansion at maximum ranges. Adaptation to standard actions is quite simple.

General Comments: Bullet diameter is .264-inch (Lazzeroni bases its designations on bullet diameter, instead of bore diameter, which is the common practice). Ballistics exceed any other current 6.5mm cartridge. Case design is typical of the Lazzeroni line: moderate body taper, 30-degree shoulder, sufficiently long neck, and thick rim of approximate case-body diameter. In other words, this is a well-designed case. Intended specifically for hunting, and with limited barrel life (typically between 700 and 1,000 rounds, when the rifle is not overheated and is properly cleaned), this cartridge is not recommended for any other use. While 27-inch barrels are standard, all the smaller-caliber, full-length Lazzeroni numbers would benefit significantly from even longer barrels. This is a superior performer for those who only hunt smaller species of big game and who will not abuse the barrel via incautious shooting. The 125-grain Nosler Partitions and 100-grain Barnes Xs work extremely well. For more information on Lazzeroni custom guns, ammunition, and reloading data, contact 888-492--7247; www.lazzeroni.com.

6.71 Blackbird Factory Ballistics (27-inch barrel)

Bullet (grains)	Powder	Grains	Velocity	Energy	Source/Comments
100	FL		4000	3021	Lazzeroni factory load
120	FL		3750	3123	Lazzeroni factory load
140	FL		3550	3219	Lazzeroni factory load

.270 JDJ

Historical Notes: This is another cartridge designed and developed by J.D. Jones, around 1978. It is generally fired in barrels furnished by his company, SSK Industries. The purpose of these cartridges is to give added range and power to the Thompson/Center Contender pistol for hunting medium game. All of the JDJ cartridges are proprietary, and SSK neither sells reamers nor has permitted the reamer maker to duplicate any of the reamers for this series.

General Comments: Based on the .225 Winchester case (itself a modified .30-30 case) this Improved chambering provides ample capacity to deliver impressive velocity from handgun-length barrels, now commonly 14 to 16 inches. Best applications are in handgun varminting and hunting of smaller big-game species through mule deer-size. For varminting, best performance is probably achieved with bullets of 100 grains. Either Hornady's or Sierra's 110-grain bullets would be good choices for pronghorn hunting. For hunting deer and similar-sized game, the best bullet weight is 130 grains. Heavier bullets can deliver more energy, but expansion is unreliable. This chambering has seen considerable use in various types of handgun competition. This is ample testimony to the potential accuracy of this chambering and the quality of gunsmithing involved in such alterations. For information on components, loading data, barrels, and guns designed for this cartridge, contact SSK Inudstries, 720-264-0176; www.sskindustries.com.

.270 JDJ Loading Data

Bullet (grains/type)	Powder	Grains	Velocity	Energy	Source/Comments
100 SP	RI-7	34.0	2795	1735	SSK/maximum load
110 SP	IMR 4320	36.0	2520	1555	SSK/maximum load
130 SP	RI-7	30.7	2370	1625	SSK/maximum load
130 SP	IMR 3031	35.0	2470	1765	SSK/maximum load (SSK barrels only)

.270 JDJ No. 2

Historical Notes: Another creation of J. D. Jones, the .270 JDJ No. 2 uses a modified .30-06 family of cases with a shortened neck, reduced case taper, and 60-degree shoulder to achieve ballistics normally associated with belted magnum cartridges in similar length barrels. In a short-barreled Encore pistol, the .270 JDJ No. 2 can propel 130-grain bullets to 2487 fps. The cartridge can accommodate a range of .270 bullet weights ranging from 90 grains to 150 grains, including some fine hunting bullets. For information on components, loading data, barrels, and guns designed for this cartridge, contact SSK Inudstries, 720-264-0176; www.sskindustries.com.

General Comments: The .270 JDJ No. 2 is well suited for Thompson/Center Encore firearms or appropriate bolt-action rifles. Capable of sub-MOA accuracy, this cartridge provides long case life, consumes less powder than belted magnum cartridges, and uses relatively inexpensive cases. For information on components, loading data, barrels, and guns designed for this cartridge, contact SSK Inudstries, 720-264-0176; www.sskindustries.com.

7mm Whisper

Historical Notes: Designed by J.D. Jones in the early 1990s, this cartridge was designed for use in sound-suppressed M-15s, bolt-action rifles, and T/C Contenders. As with most of the JDJ line, this cartridge was designed at SSK Industries. The 7mm Whisper is based upon the .221 Remington case.

General Comments: When combined with a very quick rifling twist, this chambering will deliver heavy 7mm bullets from SSK Contender barrels, with ½ MOA accuracy at subsonic velocities (1040 fps). Lighter bullets can achieve velocities that are more typical, but they sacrifice the design purpose of this chambering. For information on components, loading data, barrels, and guns designed for this cartridge, contact SSK Inudstries, 720-264-0176; www.sskindustries.com.

7mm Whisper Loading Data

Bullet (grains/type)	Powder	Grains	Velocity	Energy	Source/Comments
120	AA 1680	20.0	2250	1345	SSK/maximum load, 16½" brl.
140 Nosler BT	AA 1680	18.5	2060	1315	SSK/maximum load, 16½" brl.
168	AA 1680	9.5	1056	415	SSK/subsonic
168	Vit N540	12.6	1064	420	SSK/subsonic

7mm JDJ

Historical Notes: This is another cartridge designed and developed by J.D. Jones. Its purpose is to give added range and power to the Thompson/Center Contender pistol for the primary purpose of hunting medium game. This cartridge has also proved to be an excellent choice for metallic silhouette competition. All JDJ cartridges are relatively easy to make. These are proprietary, and SSK neither sells reamers nor has permitted the reamer maker to duplicate any of the reamers for the series.

General Comments: Based on the .225 Winchester case (itself a modified .30-30 case), this Improved chambering provides ample capacity to deliver impressive velocity, especially with longer handgun-length barrels (14 to 16 inches). Best applications are in handgun hunting of smaller big-game species through mule deer-size. Best hunting performance is probably achieved with bullets of 120 to 140 grains. Experts have tallied many kills at ranges exceeding 200 yards. Heavier bullets can deliver more energy, but expansion is not reliable. Heavier bullets have proven effective in the handgun silhouette game; bullets of about 150 grains are noted for their effectiveness in toppling the ram target. This is ample testimony to the potential accuracy of this chambering and the quality of gunsmithing involved in such alterations. For information on components, loading data, barrels, and guns designed for this cartridge, contact SSK Inudstries, 720-264-0176; www.sskindustries.com.

7mm JDJ Loading Data

Bullet (grains/type)	Powder	Grains	Velocity	Energy	Source/Comments
120 SP	H4895	34.0	2480	1640	SSK/maximum load,
139-140 SP	IMR 4320	34.0	2145	1420	SSK/maximum load, SSK barrels only
150-154 SP	IMR 4320	34.0	2110	1520	SSK/maximum load,

7mm-30 JDJ

Historical Notes: This JDJ cartridge is the 7-30 Waters, Improved. The purpose is to meet customer demand for improved performance with readily obtained cases. Since the 7-30 is based on the .30-30 Winchester, one can easily use those abundant cases to form this round. Other than rim diameter and a slight increase in length, this chambering is essentially similar to the 7mm JDJ.

General Comments: Excellent bullets are available. With proper loads and in the hands of a marksman, this chambering is capable of 300-yard shots on smaller game species. Significantly, it delivers substantially more energy than the 6.5mm JDJ offerings. Despite a shorter barrel, this Improved cartridge will drive a 140-grain bullet at about the same velocity as the 7-30 Waters will drive the 120-grain bullet. For information on components, loading data, barrels, and guns designed for this cartridge, contact SSK Inudstries, 720-264-0176; www.sskindustries.com.

7mm JDJ No. 2

Historical Notes: This JDJ cartridge is the .307 Winchester necked down to 7mm and Improved. The purpose was to provide a 7mm chambering based upon the .307 Winchester case.

General Comments: Excellent bullets are available for this cartridge. With proper loads and in the hands of a good shot, this chambering is capable of 300-yard shots on smaller big-game species. In handgun-length barrels, ballistics are not significantly superior to the smaller 7mm JDJ offerings to justify the existence of this chambering. For information on components, loading data, barrels, and guns designed for this cartridge, contact SSK Inudstries, 720-264-0176; www.sskindustries.com.

7mm JDJ No. 2 Loading Data

Bullet (grains/type)	Powder	Grains	Velocity	Energy	Source/Comments
100 Hornady	W760	47.0	2532	1420	SSK, maximum load, 14" barrel
115 Speer	W760	46.0	2453	1535	SSK, maximum load, 14" barrel
139 Hornady	H4350	45.0	2369	1730	SSK, maximum load, 14" barrel
140 Nosler SB	H414	43.0	2257	1580	SSK, maximum load, 14" barrel
140 Nosler SB	W760	44.0	2303	1645	SSK, maximum load, 14" barrel

NEW
.280 GNR

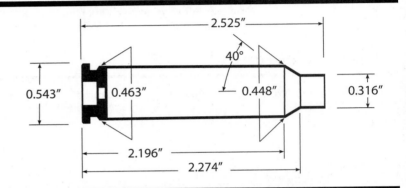

Historical Notes: Gary Reeder is one of the most experienced cartridge wildcatters of all time. He makes not just any wildcat cartridges, rather, he typically designs a group of wildcats based on a particular case. The .280 GNR is a perfect example. After developing the .310 and 8mm GNR rounds, Reeder decided he wanted to make a 7mm (.284). He put the entire project together in the six weeks leading up to an African safari. This is a spin-off on the .405 Winchester case, which is simply necked down to 7mm with a 40-degree shoulder. One reason Reeder chose the .450 case is because it has about 18-percent more capacity than the .30-06 case, which is the parent case for the .280 Remington. Without the time available to get dies in hand, Reeder necked the .405 case down to .308-caliber using his .310 GNR dies. Then he took the cases to 7mm with a set of 7mm-08 Improved dies, and, with nothing but load workup left, he was ready for Africa.

General Comments: The .280 GNR was specifically developed for medium to large deer-sized game at long range. It will drive a 140-grain bullet in excess of 2950 fps out of a single-shot pistol with a 15-inch barrel. This is very similar to 7mm Remington Magnum performance, but from a rimmed cartridge that works great in single-shot rifles or handguns. Information on custom guns, ammunitin, and reloading data can be obtained by contacting Gary Reeder Custom Guns, 928-527-4100; www.reedercustomguns. com.—R.A.M.

.280 GNR Loading Data and Ballistics

Bullet (grains/type)	Powder	Grains	Velocity	Energy	Source/Comments
139 Hornady BTSP	H 4350	56	2965	2713	Gary Reeder

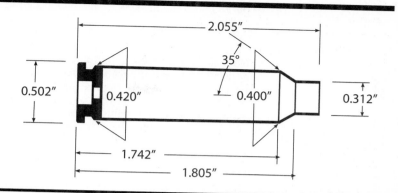

NEW
7mm GNR

Historical Notes: One of the most experienced cartridge wildcatters of all time, Gary Reeder is, as you would expect, an avid shooter and hunter. The 7mm GNR was developed as a handgun hunting round for a single-shot pistol like the Thompson/Center Contender. The 7mm GNR is a very close ballistic performer to the 7-30 Waters, but a serious ballistic comparison will show it is capable of velocities about 300 to 350 fps faster. The 7mm GNR, when fired from a 14-inch barrel, will duplicate the external ballistics of a 7-30 Waters out of a 24-inch barrel. Originally based on the .30-30 Winchester case, due to the compatibility of its rim with single-shot actions, Reeder later switched to the .375 Winchester case, but found pressures were too high. Reeder switched back to .30-30 brass, but with the availability of factory new 7-30 Waters brass, that became the go-to choice for making brass for the 7mm GNR.

General Comments: Though it must be handloaded, and even though cases must be fire-formed from .30-30 Winchester or 7-30 Waters brass, the 7mm GNR is a great cartridge for deer- or antelope-sized game, particularly if you are a lover of single-shot, break-action pistols like the Contender. Gary Reeder has no qualms about designing a niche cartridge that has a specific, if narrow, use, and the 7mm GNR is a perfect example of his skill at wildcatting. Like with all the cartridges developed by Reeder, Gary figures out the ballistics he wants from a specific platform and for a specific purpose and then builds a cartridge accordingly. Information on custom guns, ammunitin, and reloading data can be obtained by contacting Gary Reeder Custom Guns, 928-527-4100; www.reedercustomguns.com.—R.A.M.

7mm GNR Loading Data and Ballistics (14 inch barrel TC Contender)

Bullet (grains/type)	Powder	Grains	Velocity	Energy	Source/Comments
120 gr.	H-322	32	2300	1409	Gary Reeder (Fire-form Load)
120 gr.	H-4895	38	2650	1871	Gary Reeder
130 gr.	AA 2520	38	2625	1988	Gary Reeder
139 Hornady BTSP	H 4350	36	2475	1890	Gary Reeder

.280 JDJ

Historical Notes: This cartridge was designed by J.D. Jones, at SSK Industries. Application is to Thompson/Center Encore single-shot pistols fitted with a custom SSK barrel. Typical barrel length is 15 inches. Cases are formed from empty .280 Remington cases by special means and cannot be fire-formed from any other case. Neck length is minimal, which is acceptable for a cartridge used in a single-shot gun. Shoulder angle is 60 degrees, which seems to work just fine. Body taper is minimal, similar to Ackley's Improved designs. Therefore, this is a maximized, .28-caliber version of the .280 case. Case capacity is a whopping 76 grains of water, which is only 10 grains less than the 7mm Remington Magnum. Working pressure is about 60,000 psi, so ballistics are quite impressive. Best handloads in SSK barrels come close to duplicating .280 (rifle) ballistics.

General Comments: Since this case has no rim, it is not generally safe to directly fire-form it in the conventional manner. However, owing to the captive extractor system used in the Encore, it is possible to use a special technique in those guns, to wit: In a standard .280 case (sized), seat a jacketed bullet hard against the rifling so that the gun will just close. The correct powder charge is about five-percent below the maximum SSK-recommended load. Jones recommends 140-grain bullets for big-game hunting applications on smaller species and bullets up to 175 grains on larger species. With the velocity potential of this chambering, premium bullets are probably a superior choice for hunting applications. While one could use 120-grain Barnes X bullets, which can offer impressive terminal performance, the handloader must use X bullet-specific loading data and special handloading techniques (e.g., the bullet ogive must be seated a minimum of .050-inch from the rifling). Further, those bullets work best when a friction-reducing application (such as moly-plating) is used. For this reason, SSK does not support use of X-style bullets in its guns. While no bullet substitution is benign, never substitute any X-style bullet in any load—begin with data specifically created for that bullet. Speer's 110-grain TNT should provide impressive varminting performance. For information on components, loading data, barrels, and guns designed for this cartridge, contact SSK Inudstries, 720-264-0176; www.sskindustries.com. .

.280 JDJ

Bullet (grains/type)	Powder	Grains	Velocity	Energy	Source/Comments
120 Nosler BT	IMR 4831	70.0	3119	2590	SSK/maximum load, SSK barrels only
140 Nosler BT	IMR 4831	67.5	2975	2750	SSK/maximum load, SSK barrels only
150 Nosler Part	Rl-22	68.4	2775	2565	SSK/maximum load, SSK barrels only
175 Remington	IMR 4831	64.3	2670	2770	SSK/maximum load, SSK barrels only

7.21 Tomahawk

Historical Notes: Lazzeroni Arms designed this cartridge, in 1997. While somewhat related to an older case, for all practical purposes, this is a new case design. This cartridge was created in response to requests for a high-performance cartridge that would work in a 2.8-inch action and yet deliver the ballistics of a full-length belted magnum. Adaptation to a standard action is feasible, but is not recommended.

General Comments: Bullet diameter is .284-inch (Lazzeroni bases its designations on bullet diameter, instead of bore diameter, which is the common practice). Ballistics are impressive for such a short cartridge. Given equal-length barrels, the Tomahawk essentially duplicates top 7mm Weatherby Magnum ballistics, coming very close to the 7mm STW. Case design is typical of the Lazzeroni line: moderate body taper, 30-degree shoulder, sufficiently long neck, and thick rim of approximate case-body diameter. In other words, this is a well-designed case. For more information on Lazzeroni custom guns, ammunition, and reloading data, contact 888-492--7247; www.lazzeroni.com.

7.21 Tomahawk Factory Ballistics (24-inch barrel)

Bullet (grains)	Powder	Grains	Velocity	Energy	Source/Comments
120	FL		3525	3310	Lazzeroni factory load
140	FL		3300	3386	Lazzeroni factory load
150	FL		3200	3412	Lazzeroni factory load
160	FL		3100	3415	Lazzeroni factory load

7mm Dakota

Historical Notes:
The 7mm Dakota is based on the .404 Jeffery case. This case is long enough to create standard- or magnum-length cartridges. In any given cartridge length, use of the non-belted .404 Jeffery case offers about 15-percent more case capacity, compared to the standard belted magnum case. Because maximum case diameter is slightly larger than the standard belted magnum, re-chambering to 7mm Dakota often reduces magazine capacity by one cartridge, unless a slight deepening of the magazine well is accomplished.

General Comments:
This cartridge functions properly through standard-length (3.35-inch) actions. Guns chambered for the 7mm Remington Magnum are easily converted to 7mm Dakota with only re-chambering and slight bolt-face alterations. This chambering offers capacity similar to the much longer 7mm STW (3.65 inches). If loaded to similar pressures with appropriate powders, the 7mm Dakota offers a useful velocity advantage over the 7mm Remington Magnum; with the heaviest bullets, this advantage might be significant. For those interested in getting all the performance possible from the 7mm bore, the 7mm Dakota is worth considering. The 7mm STW has a slight capacity advantage, but the ballistic difference is marginal and the STW requires a longer action. Finally, because this cartridge headspaces between the case shoulder and bolt face, it's easier to get it to line up properly in the rifle's chamber. This can lead to superior accuracy. It is worth noting that there are no disadvantages to the rimless bottleneck design for most applications. Contact Dakota Arms for more information, 605-347-4686; www.dakotaarms.com.

7mm Dakota Loading Data

Bullet (grains)	Powder	Grains	Velocity	Energy	Source/Comments
140	IMR 4831	73.0	3355	3495	Dakota/maximum load
140	H4831	76.0	3295	3375	Dakota/maximum load
140	RI-22	77.0	3365	3515	Dakota/maximum load
140	IMR 7828	80.0	3421	3645	Dakota/maximum load
160	IMR 4831	68.0	3064	3335	Dakota/maximum load
160	H4831	74.0	3156	3535	Dakota/maximum load
160	RI-22	74.5	3212	3660	Dakota/maximum load
160	IMR 7828	75.0	3171	3570	Dakota/maximum load
140	FL		3400	3593	Dakota factory load
160	FL		3200	3637	Dakota factory load

7mm Canadian Magnum

Historical Notes:
This cartridge was developed, about 1989, by North American Shooting Systems (NASS) and is similar to the 7mm Imperial Magnum. This design features a slightly rebated, rimless bottleneck case. Design intent was to provide maximum powder capacity available in a standard action with minimal gunsmithing. (Without deepening the magazine well slightly, magazine capacity is usually reduced by one round.) Bolt face alteration is not necessary. Cartridge feeding and headspacing characteristics are improved.

General Comments:
The Canadian Magnum series is similar to the Dakota cartridge family in both design and purpose. However, Canadian Magnums all take advantage of the entire 3.65-inch magazine length of the long-action Remington M700 and similar rifles. On these cartridges, body diameter is significantly larger than the standard belted magnum (.544-inch versus .513-inch at the base). Re-chambering of nominal belted magnums with the same bore diameter is generally quite simple, requiring no other rifle alterations. For any given case length, capacity is fully 15-percent greater than can be achieved with the belted version. Body taper is minimal, and the shoulder is comparatively sharp. However, neck length is sufficiently generous to provide good bullet purchase for hunting ammunition. Performance is commensurate with the generous capacity and pressures used in these loadings. We must note that one should expect this chambering to be rather hard on barrels.

Bullet (grains)	Powder	Grains	Velocity	Energy	Source/Comments
140	H4831	82.0	3426	3645	NASS/maximum load
140	RI-22	85.0	3523	3855	NASS/maximum load
140	IMR 7828	86.5	3480	3760	NASS/maximum load
160	RI-22	82.0	3264	3780	NASS/maximum load
160	IMR 7828	83.5	3257	3765	NASS/maximum load
160	H1000	87.0	3288	3835	NASS/maximum load
175	IMR 7828	79.0	3018	3540	NASS/maximum load
175	H1000	83.0	3098	3725	NASS/maximum load
175	H870	93.0	3109	3750	NASS/maximum load
140	FL		3525	3860	NASS factory load

7.21 Firehawk

Historical Notes: Lazzeroni Arms designed this cartridge, in 1996. It was discontinued from standard chambering in 1999, but is still available as a special-order item. It was replaced by the 7.21 Firebird. While somewhat related to an older case, for all practical purposes, this is a new case design. John Lazzeroni believes that those hunters who will take the time to become competent marksmen can legitimately take game at ranges out to about 500 yards, given a gun with the requisite accuracy and a bullet that will perform properly. This cartridge was created to provide sufficient velocity to medium-weight hunting bullets so as to enable dependable expansion at maximum ranges. Adaptation to standard actions is quite simple.

General Comments: Bullet diameter is .284-inch (Lazzeroni bases its designations on bullet diameter, instead of bore diameter, which is the common practice). Until the introduction of the 7.21 Firebird (also from Lazzeroni), ballistics exceeded any other current 7mm cartridge. Case design is typical of the Lazzeroni line: moderate body taper, 30-degree shoulder, sufficiently long neck, and thick rim of approximate case-body diameter. In other words, this is a well-designed case. Designed specifically for hunting and with limited barrel life, this cartridge is not recommended for any other use. While 27-inch barrels are standard, all smaller-caliber, full-length Lazzeroni numbers would benefit significantly from even longer barrels. Most of Lazzeroni's full-length cartridge loadings use specially lubricated (proprietary process) premium bullets from Nosler, Barnes, or Swift. These are the only bullets providing the necessary accuracy and terminal performance to meet Lazzeroni's strict requirements. A significant portion of the accuracy and ballistic potential of these cartridges results from the unusually effective, reduced-friction coating used. For more information on Lazzeroni custom guns, ammunition, and reloading data, contact 888-492--7247; www.lazzeroni.com.

7.21 Firehawk Factory Ballistics (27-inch barrel)

Bullet (grains)	Powder	Grains	Velocity	Energy	Source/Comments
120	FL		3800	3848	Lazzeroni factory load
140	FL		3600	4030	Lazzeroni factory load
150	FL		3500	4081	Lazzeroni factory load
160	FL		3400	4108	Lazzeroni factory load

7.21 Firebird

Historical Notes: Lazzeroni Arms designed this cartridge, in 1998, by necking down the 7.82 Warbird. John Lazzeroni believes that hunters who will take the time to become competent marksmen can legitimately take game at ranges out to about 500 yards, given a gun with the requisite accuracy and a bullet that will perform properly. This cartridge was created to eliminate the intermediate Lazzeroni case size and stay one step ahead of the competition. Lazzeroni believes that 7mm is the ideal bore size for North American hunting needs and that there is no such thing as too much velocity. This cartridge can provide sufficient velocity to medium-weight hunting bullets for dependable expansion at maximum ranges. Adaptation to standard actions is not recommended.

General Comments: Bullet diameter is .284-inch (Lazzeroni bases its designations on bullet diameter, instead of bore diameter, which is the common practice). Ballistics exceed any other current 7mm cartridge. Case design is typical of the Lazzeroni line: moderate body taper, 30-degree shoulder, sufficiently long neck, and thick rim of approximate case-body diameter, making this a well-designed case. Designed specifically for hunting and with limited barrel life, this cartridge is not recommended for any other use. While a 27-inch barrel is standard, this number would benefit significantly from use of a longer barrel. Only the best premium bullets provide the necessary accuracy and terminal performance. Factory loads use specially lubricated (proprietary process) premium bullets from Nosler, Barnes, or Swift. A 27- or 28-inch barrel with specially prepared Lazzeroni/Barnes 120-grain XBT bullets produces the flattest shooting (shortest time of flight to 1,000 yards) combination of any commercially available hunting or target rifle. One would be hard-pressed to do better with any wildcat. For more information on Lazzeroni custom guns, ammunition, and reloading data, contact 888-492--7247; www.lazzeroni.com.

7.21 Firebird Factory Ballistics (27-inch barrel)

Bullet (grains)	Powder	Grains	Velocity	Energy	Source/Comments
120	FL		3950	4155	Lazzeroni factory load
140	FL		3750	4370	Lazzeroni factory load
150	FL		3650	4435	Lazzeroni factory load
160	FL		3550	4475	Lazzeroni factory load
175	FL		3400	4490	Lazzeroni factory load

7.62 Micro-Whisper

Historical Notes: Designed by J.D. Jones at SSK Industries, in the early 1990s, this is simply the .30 Luger case adapted to use .30-caliber rifle bullets. Case dimensions are identical, but chambering specifications are different. The design intent was for an extremely quiet, sound-suppressed load that would shoot 180-grain bullets to about 1040 fps.

General Comments: This cartridge provides much better subsonic performance than the .308 Winchester. Civilian applications are limited. Nevertheless, performance is startling. For those looking for minimal recoil and noise for short-range use, this is an interesting choice. For information on components, loading data, barrels, and guns designed for this cartridge, contact SSK Inudstries, 720-264-0176; www.sskindustries.com. .

7.62 Micro-Whisper Loading Data

Bullet (grains/type)	Powder	Grains	Velocity	Energy	Source/Comments
93 Norma SP	AA No. 9	11.5	1762	640	SSK/maximum load, 8¾" barrel
150 Hornady FMJ	H110	7.0	1018	345	SSK/subsonic, 8¾" barrel

150 Hornady FMJ	AA No. 9	8.0	1259	525	SSK/subsonic, 8¾" barrel
168 Hornady Match	AA No. 9	7.1	1056	445	SSK/subsonic, 8¾" barrel
180 Speer	H110	7.0	1025	420	SSK/subsonic, 8¾" barrel
180 Speer	H110	8.0	1161	535	SSK/subsonic, 8¾" barrel

7.63 Mini-Whisper

Historical Notes: Designed by J.D. Jones at SSK Industries, in the early 1990s, this is simply the .30 Mauser case adapted to use .30-caliber rifle bullets. Case dimensions are identical, but chambering specifications are different. The design intent was for an extremely quiet, sound-suppressed load that would shoot 200-grain bullets to about 1040 fps.

General Comments: This cartridge provides much better subsonic performance than the .308 Winchester. Civilian applications are limited. Nevertheless, performance is startling. For those looking for minimal recoil and noise for short-range use, this is an interesting choice. For information on components, loading data, barrels, and guns designed for this cartridge, contact SSK Inudstries, 720-264-0176; www.sskindustries.com.

7.63 Mini-Whisper Loading Data

Bullet (grains/type)	Powder	Grains	Velocity	Energy	Source/Comments
93 Norma	Clays	7.5	1727	615	SSK/maximum load, 7" barrel
110 Speer Carb	Clays	7.5	1588	615	SSK/maximum load, 7" barrel (1.415" OAL)
110 Speer Carb	AA No. 7	11.4	1742	740	SSK/maximum load, 7" barrel (1.415" OAL)
150 Hornady FMJ	AA No. 2	4.5	1025	350	SSK/subsonic, 7" barrel
150 Hornady FMJ	AA No. 9	10.5	1445	695	SSK/maximum load, 7" barrel
168 Hornady Match	AA No. 2	5.2	1031	395	SSK/subsonic, 7" barrel
168 Hornady Match	HP-38	5.7	1035	395	SSK/subsonic, 7" barrel

.300 Whisper
(See also .300 AAC Blackout)

Historical Notes: The .300 Whisper is a new concept in the development of small case-capacity, highly efficient cartridges combined with bullets of extreme ballistic efficiency. This is a special-purpose design, by J.D. Jones of SSK Industries, based on a .221 Remington case necked up to .308-caliber. It is intended to fire extremely heavy, accurate, ballistically efficient bullets at subsonic velocities in suppressed guns. It delivers more energy more accurately than any other subsonic round at 200 yards. In addition, it has interesting supersonic capabilities above 1160 fps, thus offering greater versatility than any other cartridge capable of performing in these vastly differing arenas. Because powder charges are very small, suppressor size is proportionately smaller.

General Comments: Bullet weights from 100 to 240 grains can be used. Best accuracy is obtained with heavier bullets. For silhouette shooting, 220- to 240-grain bullets are best. With 125- or 150-grain projectiles, this cartridge is outstanding for deer and other medium game, offering better performance than the .30-30 Winchester in the T/C Contender pistol and with less than half the felt recoil. In suppressed guns, noise can be reduced to less than that of a .177-caliber spring-air rifle.For information on components, loading data, barrels, and guns designed for this cartridge, contact SSK Inudstries, 720-264-0176; www. sskindustries.com.

.300 Whisper Loading Data

Bullet (grains/type)	Powder	Grains	Velocity	Energy	Source/Comments
125 Nosler BT	H110	20.6	2283	1445	SSK/maximum rifle load, AR-15
150 Nosler BT	H110	18.0	2073	1430	SSK/maximum rifle load
165	AA 1680	10.3	1013	375	SSK/subsonic, AR-15
125 Nosler BT	H110	20.6	2283	1445	SSK/maximum load, AR-15
125 Nosler BT	H110	18.0	2014	1350	SSK/maximum load, AR-15
165	AA 2015	12.6	1046	400	SSK/subsonic, AR-15
168	AA 1680	20.2	1906	1355	SSK/maximum load, rifle
200	AA 2015	12.0	1007	450	NA
220	AA No. 9	8.5	1013	500	SSK/subsonic, AR-15
250	H110	8.6	980	530	SSK/subsonic, AR-15

NEW
.307 GNR

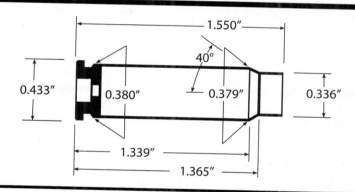

Historical Notes: Custom gun builder and cartridge designer Garry Reeder will tell you that, while he has taken most of the game he has hunted with T/C Contenders and Encores, he is really a revolver man at heart. Reeder wanted a cartridge that would duplicate .300 GNR and .30 Herret ballistics from a revolver, and the .307 GNR was his answer. The case is formed by necking a .357 Maximum case down to .308-caliber with one pass through a sizing die.

General Comments: I have not hunted with the .307 GNR, but have spent some time on the range with it. The cartridge requires a revolver with a longer than normal frame; one sized for the .357 Maximum like Ruger's .357 Maximum Blackhawk is what is needed. Recoil is tolerable, considering this cartridge generates a good bit of power from a revolver. With proper bullets, the .307 GNR should be sufficient for hunting all medium-sized, non-dangerous game. Information on custom guns, ammunitin, and reloading data can be obtained by contacting Gary Reeder Custom Guns, 928-527-4100; www.reedercustom-guns.com.—R.A.M.

.307 GNR Loading Data & Ballistics

Bullet (grains/type)	Powder	Grains	Velocity	Energy	Source
110 FP	H 110	21.0	2303	1295	Gary Reeder
125 FP	IMR 4227	20.0	2084	1205	Gary Reeder

.309 JDJ

Historical Notes: This cartridge was designed and developed by J.D. Jones, about 1978. It is generally fired in barrels furnished by SSK Industries. Its purpose is to give added power and range to the T/C Contender pistol for hunting medium game. The JDJ series of cartridges are easy to make. All JDJ designs are proprietary rounds, and SSK neither sells reamers nor allows the reamer maker to duplicate the reamers for sale. Should you desire to chamber a JDJ cartridge, contact SSK Industries (www.sskindustries.com).

General Comments: The .309 JDJ is based on a .444 Marlin case necked down to .30-caliber in a .308 full-length sizing die, and then fire-formed to obtain the sharp shoulder. This cartridge offers about 2600 fps with a 125-grain bullet, 2450 fps with a 150-grain bullet, and 160-grainers can be driven at 2400 fps. For general use, 165-grain bullets are an excellent choice. Jones has taken large plains game in Africa with this round. In a pinch, it would do for elk with 180-grain bullets. The .309 is easy to shoot and can be extremely versatile. With the proper load and bullet sighted to shoot about three inches high at 100 yards, it will be dead on at about 225 to 250 yards. It can be very effective on moderate-sized game to that range, with the right bullet and a shooter possessing adequate skills. For information on components, loading data, barrels, and guns designed for this cartridge, contact SSK Inudstries, 720-264-0176; www.sskindustries.com.

.309 JDJ Loading Data

Bullet (grains/type)	Powder	Grains	Velocity	Energy	Source/Comments
150 SP	IMR 4320	41.0	2010	1360	SSK/maximum load, SSK barrels only
150 SP	IMR 4350	43.0	2370	1875	SSK/maximum load, SSK barrels only
165 SP	IMR 4350	52.0	2430	1775	SSK/maximum load, SSK barrels only
180 SP	IMR 4350	49.0	2135	1825	SSK/maximum load, SSK barrels only

.30-06 JDJ

Historical Notes: This cartridge was designed by J.D. Jones, at SSK Industries. Application is to Thompson/Center Encore single-shot pistols fitted with a custom SSK barrel. Typical barrel length is 15 inches. Cases are formed from empty Remington .30-06 cases by special means and cannot be fire-formed from any other case. Neck length is minimal, which is acceptable for a cartridge used in a single-shot gun. Shoulder angle is 60 degrees, which works fine. Body taper is minimal, similar to Ackley's Improved designs. Therefore, this is a maximized version of the .30-06 case. Capacity is a whopping 75 grains of water, which is significantly greater than the .30-06 (about 70). Working pressure is about 60,000 psi, so ballistics are quite impressive. Best handloads in SSK barrels come very close to duplicating .30-06 (rifle) ballistics.

General Comments: Since this case has no rim, it is not generally safe to directly fire-form it in the conventional manner. However, owing to the captive extractor system used in the Encore, it is possible to use a special technique in those guns, to wit: To fire-form, use a standard .30-06 case (sized), seat a jacketed bullet hard against the rifling so that the gun will just close. Correct powder charge is about five-percent below the maximum SSK-recommended load. Jones recommends 150-grain bullets for big-game hunting applications on smaller species, and bullets up to 200 grains on larger species. With the velocity potential of this chambering, premium bullets are probably a superior choice for hunting applications. While one could use 140-grain Barnes X bullets, which can offer impressive terminal performance, the handloader must use X bullet-specific loading data and special handloading techniques (i.e., the bullet ogive must be seated a minimum of .05-inch from the rifling). For this reason, SSK does not support use of the X-stle bullets in its guns. Further those bullets work best when a reduced-friction coating (such as moly-plating) is used. While no bullet substitution is benign, never substitue any X-style bullet in any load, rather begin with data specifically created for that bullet. For information on components, loading data, barrels, and guns designed for this cartridge, contact SSK Inudstries, 720-264-0176; www.sskindustries.com.

30-06 JDJ Loading Data

Bullet (grains/type)	Powder	Grains	Velocity	Energy	Source/Comments
125	IMR 4064	62.0	3167	2785	SSK/maximum load, SSK barrels only
150	IMR 4064	60.0	2930	2860	SSK/maximum load, SSK barrels only
165 Hornady	RI-15	58.3	2790	2850	SSK/maximum load, SSK barrels only
180 Speer	RI-19	66.2	2666	2840	SSK/maximum load, SSK barrels only
200 Speer	Vit N560	63.4	2504	2785	SSK/maximum load, SSK barrels only

.308 CorBon

Historical Notes: This cartridge was designed by CorBon and announced at the 1999 Shooting, Hunting, Outdoor Trade (SHOT) Show. The purpose was to achieve the greatest feasible performance from an action designed to handle 2.8-inch cartridges, but without the necessity of any significant magazine or action modifications. In a crowded market, Peter Pi (CEO at CorBon) seems to have found a combination that fills a useful niche. Ballistics approximate those of the conventional .30-caliber belted magnum, which is designed to work in a 3.3-inch (or longer) action.

General Comments: A significant trend in the wildcat and proprietary arena is toward shorter cartridges. This design promises advantages in both rifle and ballistics. This shorter case chambers in a shorter, lighter, more rigid action that is faster and easier to manipulate. This cartridge might also have intrinsic accuracy advantages; the big push in accuracy competition is toward shorter and fatter cases. Evidently, such a design might promote earlier and more consistent ignition of individual powder granules. Contact CorBon for more information, 800-626-7266; www.shopcorbon.com.

.308 CorBon Factory Ballistics

Bullet (grains/type)	Powder	Grains	Velocity	Energy	Source/Comments
165 SPBT	FL		3100	3520	CorBon factory load
180 SPBT	FL		3000	3600	CorBon factory load

7.82 Patriot

Historical Notes: Lazzeroni Arms designed this cartridge, in 1997. While somewhat related to an older case, for all practical purposes, this is a new case design. This cartridge was created in response to requests for a high-performance cartridge that would work in a 2.8-inch action, yet deliver the ballistics of a full-length belted magnum. While feasible, adaptation to a standard action (3.35-inch) is not recommended.

General Comments: Bullet diameter is .308-inch (Lazzeroni bases its designations on bullet diameter, instead of bore diameter, which is the common practice). Ballistics are quite impressive for such a short cartridge. Given equal-length barrels, the Patriot essentially duplicates .300 Winchester Magnum ballistics. Case design is typical of the Lazzeroni line: moderate body taper, 30-degree shoulder, sufficiently long neck, and thick rim of approximate case-body diameter. In other words, this is a well-designed case. This cartridge has already become quite popular and successful in the various 1,000-yard target-shooting games. Dick Davis, of Lazzeroni Arms, is doing quite well with it. This case is the basis for several wildcat and target chamberings (6mm Thermos Bottle, 6mm LBFM, 6.5 LBFM, 7mm LBFM, and .30-LBFM.) For more information on Lazzeroni custom guns, ammunition, and reloading data, contact 888-492--7247; www.lazzeroni.com.

7.82 Patriot Factory Ballistics (24-inch barrel)

Bullet (grains)	Powder	Grains	Velocity	Energy	Source/Comments
130	FL		3550	3635	Lazzeroni factory load
150	FL		3300	3628	Lazzeroni factory load
180	FL		3100	3842	Lazzeroni factory load
200	FL		2950	3866	Lazzeroni factory load

.300 Dakota

Historical Notes: The .300 Dakota is based upon the .404 Jeffery case. In this application, the case is shortened to create a cartridge of .30-06 length (3.34 inches). The rim of the .300 Dakota is slightly larger than the rim on a standard belted-magnum case, so, besides re-chambering, the gunsmith must also perform a minor bolt-face alteration. In any given-length cartridge, use of the non-belted .404 Jeffery case provides about a 15-percent increase in usable case capacity, compared to the standard belted case. Because maximum case diameter is slightly larger (.544-inch versus .532-inch), magazine capacity is usually reduced by one round. However, minor gunsmithing alterations will usually remedy that situation.

General Comments: The .300 Dakota functions properly through standard-length actions (3.35 inches). This cartridge provides a significant capacity advantage over the .300 Winchester Magnum and comes close to duplicating capacity and performance of the much longer .300 Weatherby Magnum. Re-chambering to .300 Dakota is possible in most rifles originally chambered for any standard belted .300 Magnum. One thereby gains the improved feeding and accuracy advantages offered by this non-belted case. If loaded to similar pressures using appropriate powders, the .300 Dakota offers a worthwhile velocity advantage over the .300 Winchester Magnum. For those interested in an all-around .30-caliber hunting cartridge, the .300 Dakota is worth considering. The .300 Weatherby does have a slight capacity advantage, but the ballistic difference is marginal, and Weatherby's cartridge requires a longer action. Contact Dakota Arms for more information, 605-347-4686; www.dakotaarms.com.

.300 Dakota Loading Data and Factory Ballistics

Bullet (grains)	Powder	Grains	Velocity	Energy	Source/Comments
165	IMR 4350	77.0	3247	3860	Dakota/maximum load
165	H4831	82.0	3283	3945	Dakota/maximum load
165	RI-22	83.0	3307	4000	Dakota/maximum load
165	IMR 7828	85.0	3277	3930	Dakota/maximum load
180	H4831	77.5	3114	3875	Dakota/maximum load
180	RI-22	81.0	3249	4215	Dakota/maximum load
180	IMR 7828	82.0	3221	4140	Dakota/maximum load
200	H4831	77.5	2965	3900	Dakota/maximum load
200	RI-22	78.0	3052	4130	Dakota/maximum load
200	IMR 7828	80.5	3026	4060	Dakota/maximum load
200	H1000	82.5	2986	3955	Dakota/maximum load
150	FL		3300	3626	Dakota factory load
180	FL		3100	3840	Dakota factory load

.300 Canadian Magnum

Historical Notes: This cartridge was developed, about 1989, by North American Shooting Systems (NASS) and is somewhat similar to the .300 Imperial Magnum. This design features a slightly rebated, rimless bottleneck case. Design intent was to provide maximum powder capacity available in a standard action with minimal gunsmithing. (Without deepening the magazine well slightly, magazine capacity is usually reduced by one round.) Bolt face alteration is unnecessary. Cartridge feeding and headspacing characteristics are improved.

General Comments: The Canadian Magnum series are similar to those in the Dakota cartridge family in both design and purpose. However, this cartridge takes advantage of the entire 3.65-inch magazine length of the long-action Remington M700 and similar rifles. On the Canadian Magnums, body diameter is significantly larger than the standard belted magnum (.544-inch versus .513-inch at the base). Re-chambering of nominal belted magnums with the same bore diameter is generally quite simple, requiring no other rifle alterations. For any given case length, capacity is about 15-percent greater than can be achieved with the standard belted magnum case. Body taper is minimal and the shoulder is comparatively sharp. However, neck length is sufficiently generous to provide good bullet purchase for hunting ammunition. Performance is commensurate with the generous capacity and pressures used in these loadings. Barrel life is a consideration—there are no free lunches.

Editor's note: This cartridge is similar to Remington's Ultra round.

.300 Canadian Magnum Loading Data and Factory Ballistics

Bullet (grains)	Powder	Grains	Velocity	Energy	Source/Comments
165	H4831	86.0	3231	3820	NASS/maximum load
165	RI-22	87.0	3434	4315	NASS/maximum load
165	IMR 7828	89.5	3466	4395	NASS/maximum load
180	RI-22	83.0	3354	4490	NASS/maximum load
180	IMR 7828	87.5	3367	4525	NASS/maximum load
180	H1000	92.0	3163	3995	NASS/maximum load
200	RI-22	79.0	3053	4135	NASS/maximum load
200	IMR 7828	82.0	3093	4245	NASS/maximum load
200	H870	95.0	3070	4180	NASS/maximum load
180	FL		3425	4685	NASS factory load

.300 Pegasus

Historical Notes: This 1994 chambering is based upon an entirely original case that features a .580-inch head size. The rim is essentially identical to the .378 Weatherby case, but the design has no belt. Therefore, case capacity is substantially greater for any given cartridge length. This standard rimless bottleneck design also facilitates proper chambering, with tight tolerances. Design intent was the acceleration of 180-grain hunting bullets to a velocity in excess of 3500 fps from a 26-inch barrel, without exceeding about 62,000 psi (piezo transducer pressure units)—a typical modern cartridge pressure limit. The .300 Pegasus easily achieves this goal.

General Comments: This cartridge seems a good choice for those who feel they need a flat-shooting round that can deliver substantial energy to targets at long range. Rifles originally chambered for the .378 and .460 Weatherby numbers can be rebarreled to accept this cartridge. The slowest handloader powders now available offer the best velocity potential. In a typical rifle, recoil would have to be classed as a bit heavy, and barrel life is quite limited.

.300 Pegasus Loading Data and Factory Ballistics

Bullet (grains/type)	Powder	Grains	Velocity	Energy	Source/Comments
150 Nosler BT	IMR 7828		3642	4420	A-Square/maximum load
150 Nosler BT	RI-22		3675	4495	A-Square/maximum load
150 Nosler BT	AA 8700		3703	4565	A-Square/maximum load
180 Nosler BT	RI-22		3371	4540	A-Square/maximum load
180 Nosler BT	IMR 7828		3413	4655	A-Square/maximum load
180 Nosler BT	AA 8700		3456	4775	A-Square/maximum load
180 Nosler BT	H870		3505	4910	A-Square/maximum load
150 Nosler BT	FL		3780	4760	A-Square Factory load
180 Nosler BT	FL		3523	4960	A-Square Factory load

7.82 Warbird

Historical Notes: Lazzeroni Arms designed this cartridge, in 1995. While somewhat related to an older case, for all practical purposes this is a new case design. John Lazzeroni believes that those hunters who will take the time to become competent marksmen can legitimately take game at ranges out to about 500 yards, given a gun with the requisite accuracy and a bullet that will perform properly. This cartridge was created to provide sufficient velocity for medium-weight hunting bullets to provide dependable expansion at maximum ranges and to have sufficient energy for taking larger species at longer ranges. Adaptation to standard actions is feasible, but is not recommended.

General Comments: Bullet diameter is .308-inch. (Lazzeroni bases its designations on bullet diameter, instead of bore diameter, which is the common practice.) Ballistics equal or exceed any other factory .30-caliber cartridge. Case design is typical of the Lazzeroni line: moderate body taper, 30-degree shoulder, sufficiently long neck, and thick rim of approximate case-body diameter. In other words, this is a well-designed case. Designed specifically for hunting, and with limited barrel life, this cartridge is not recommended for any other use. While 27-inch barrels are standard, all the smaller-caliber, full-length Lazzeroni numbers would benefit significantly from even longer barrels. Most of Lazzeroni's full-length cartridge loadings use specially lubricated (proprietary process) premium bullets from Nosler, Barnes, or Swift. These are the only bullets providing the necessary accuracy and terminal performance to meet Lazzeroni's strict requirements. One could argue that this is a superior all-around choice for lighter species. The premium 130-grain bullet will handle most species in North America, while a 200-grain bullet is adequate for most critters anywhere in the world. For more information on Lazzeroni custom guns, ammunition, and reloading data, contact 888-492--7247; www.lazzeroni.com.

7.82 Warbird Factory Ballistics (27-inch barrel)

Bullet (grains)	Powder	Grains	Velocity	Energy	Source/Comments
130	FL		4000	4620	Lazzeroni factory load
150	FL		3800	4810	Lazzeroni factory load
165	FL		3600	4750	Lazzeroni factory load
180	FL		3550	5040	Lazzeroni factory load
200	FL		3350	4985	Lazzeroni factory load

8mm JDJ

Historical Notes: Designed by J.D. Jones of SSK Industries, about 1980, this cartridge uses the .444 Marlin case necked down to 8mm with a sharp shoulder. Design intent was a Thompson/Center chambering that would surpass .35 Remington rifle ballistics.

General Comments: With a 200-grain Nosler Partition loaded to top handgun velocity (2100 fps), this chambering can deliver substantial energy within the useful range. The Barnes 180-grain X bullets can deliver superior terminal performance, but its use requires special handloading techniques (deeper bullet seating and a reduction in powder charge). Effectiveness on the lightest of species is improved with Hornady's 150-grain bullet at 2400 fps muzzle velocity.For information on components, loading data, barrels, and guns designed for this cartridge, contact SSK Inudstries, 720-264-0176; www.sskindustries.com.

8mm JDJ Loading Data

Bullet (grains/type)	Powder	Grains	Velocity	Energy	Source/Comments
150 Hornady	IMR 4320	47.5	2286	1740	SSK/maximum load,
150 Hornady	H322	47.5	2420	1950	SSK/maximum load, SSK barrel only (14")
170 Hornady	IMR 4320	47.5	2254	1915	SSK/maximum load, SSK barrel only (14")
170 Hornady	AA 2520	49.5	2373	2125	SSK/maximum load, SSK barrel only (14")
200 Speer	H4350	52.0	2192	2130	SSK/maximum load, SSK barrel only (14")
225	H4350	51.5	2131	2265	SSK/maximum load, SSK barrel only (14")

.338 Whisper

Historical Notes: Designed by J.D. Jones of SSK Industries, in the early 1990s, this chambering is the 7mm BR opened up to accept .338-inch bullets with no other changes. JDJ's intention was the delivery of significant long-range energy from a low-noise rifle. This combination certainly succeeded in attaining that goal.

General Comments: Usually this cartridge is chambered in rebarreled .308 Winchester rifles. With a quick rifling twist, 300-grain Sierra MatchKings will deliver superb accuracy past 600 yards. Long-range penetration and energy are surprising. For information on components, loading data, barrels, and guns designed for this cartridge, contact SSK Inudstries, 720-264-0176; www.sskindustries.com.

.338 Whisper Loading Data

Bullet (grains/type)	Powder	Grains	Velocity	Energy	Source/Comments
200 Nosler BT	H4227	11.5	1075	510	SSK/Subsonic, 12" barrel
200 Nosler BT	HP-38	8.8	1077	515	SSK/Subsonic, 12" barrel
250 Nosler BT	HP-38	9.6	1029	585	SSK/Subsonic, 12" barrel
250 Nosler BT	Vit N350	10.8	1040	600	SSK/Subsonic, 12" barrel
300 Nosler BT	Vit N350	12.3	1040	720	SSK/Subsonic, 12" barrel
300 Nosler BT	HP-38	10.8	1050	735	SSK/Subsonic, 12" barrel

NEW
.338 Spectre

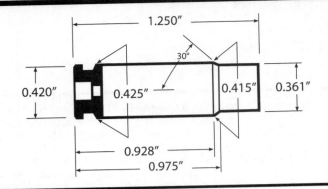

Historical Notes: The .338 Spectre was developed by Marty ter Weeme, founder of Teppo Jutsu LLC. He was also the developer of the .458 SOCOM. The Spectre is the result of improvements to the earlier .358 CQB cartridge, which came about during the design of the .458 SOCOM. The concept behind the .338 Spectre was to offer a cartridge with broad-spectrum application, but one that was primarily designed to deliver a heavy, subsonic bullet with a very high ballistic coefficient at extended distances. The designer boasts that the .338 Spectre is capable of MOA accuracy out to 500 yards. Like the .300 AAC Blackout, the .338 Spectre was developed to also provide supersonic and subsonic loads from the same weapon system. The cartridge is based on a shortened 6.8 SPC case that has been necked up to .338-caliber. All of the dimensions in the accompanying drawing—with the exception of the shoulder angle and case length from the base to the shoulder—were provided by Marty ter Weeme, who told me he hopes to "... avoid having non-licensed folks copying the reamer ... ." These unknown dimensions were estimated by measuring.

General Comments: The ballistics of the .338 Spectre cartridge are similar to that of a .357 Magnum. However, it should be noted that commercial .338-caliber bullets are not designed to expand at such low velocities. Still, the cartridge is quite versatile and does have some tactical applications. Subsonic loads will work through and can be suppressed by a 9mm-caliber suppressor. And, with an overall cartridge length similar to that of the .223 Remington, 7.62X39, and 6.8 SPC, it will work from the AR-15 platform. Handloading dies can be obtained from CH Tool & Die or the Hornady Custom Shop. Loaded ammunition is available from Southern Ballistics Research , 912-264-5822; www.sbr-usa.com.—R.A.M.

.338 Spectre Loading Data and Factory Ballistics

Bullet (grains/type)	Powder	Grains	Velocity	Energy	Source/Comments
	H 4350	57	2710	2935	Gary Reeder
250 Hornady	AA 1680	17.0	1300	938	SBR
300 Sierra BTHP	IMR 4227	9.5	985	646	SBR
250 Hornady	FL		1450	1166	SBR Factory Load
300 Sierra HPBT	FL		990	652	SBR Factory Load

NEW
.338 Lehigh

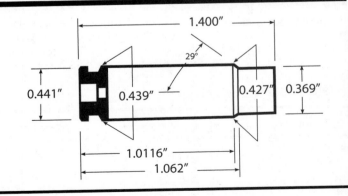

Historical Notes: Developed to offer a larger caliber, harder hitting option for hunters and tactical operatives using the AR-15 platform, the .338 Lehigh is based on the 6.5 Grendel cartridge from Alexander Arms. Both the 338 Lehigh and the 6.5 Grendel are based on the old Russian 7.62X39mm cartridge. The development of the .338 Lehigh comes on the heels of the introduction of the .300 AAC Blackout cartridge and fills the same niche, that being a larger caliber AR-15 cartridge capable of both subsonic and supersonic performance. From a subsonic standpoint, the .338 Lehigh is similar to the .338 Spectre, but, due to the Lehigh's larger case capacity, it well out-performs the Spectre when loaded to supersonic velocities.

General Comments: Conversions for .338 Lehigh AR-15s are simple with rifles that have a 0.441 bolt face, like the .65 Grendel and the 7.62X39mm, i.e., a new barrel is all that is needed. Bolt guns chambered for the 7.62X39mm can be converted to the .338 Lehigh just as easily. The .338 Lehigh offers superior supersonic ballistics, when compared to both the .300 AAC Blackout and the .338 Spectre. It can drive a 145-grain bullet in excess of 2400 fps. This would make a great multi-purpose tactical cartridge and would be great for hunting big game at close to moderate ranges. Ammunition, dies, brass, and bullets for both subsonic and supersonic applications are available from Lehigh Defense, 267-217-3539; www.lehighdefense.com.— R.A.M.

.338 Lehigh Loading Data

Bullet (grains/type)	Powder	Grains	Velocity	Energy	Source
145 Lehigh CFHP	AA 1680	24	2410	1869	Lehigh Defense Factory Load
240 Lehigh Subsonic	AA No. 2	9.0	1050	489	Lehigh Defense Factory Load

.338 JDJ

Historical Notes: Like several other chamberings based upon the same basic case (.444 Marlin), this cartridge was designed and developed by J.D. Jones, about 1978. Barrels in this chambering are furnished by SSK Industries. The purpose is to provide increased power and range for T/C Contender and other single-shot hunting handguns. Like most of the JDJ line, these cases are easily formed from the parent case. Chambering dimensions are proprietary.

General Comments: Based on the .444 Marlin necked down, this chambering provides ample capacity and bullet area to produce impressive muzzle energy, especially with longer handgun-length barrels (14 to 16 inches). With bullets of only slightly lighter weight, the .338 JDJ offers muzzle velocities similar to the .375 Winchester when fired from a rifle. Since this cartridge uses spitzer bullets, performance at normal hunting ranges is significantly superior to the parent ,444 Marlin's rifle ballistics. Conventional bullets of 180 to 220 grains are good choices. However, the Barnes 160-grain X bullet can deliver superior terminal performance, reduced recoil, and a flatter trajectory, but requires special handloading techniques (e.g., deeper bullet seating and a reduction in powder charge). With proper hunting bullets loaded to maximum velocity (necessary to assure proper terminal performance), recoil can be rather stiff. For information on components, loading data, barrels, and guns designed for this cartridge, contact SSK Inudstries, 720-264-0176; www.sskindustries.com.

.338 JDJ Loading Data and Ballistics

Bullet (grains)	Powder	Grains	Velocity	Energy	Source/Comments
225	Win 760	42.5	1561	1217	SSK 12" barrel
250	Win 760	42.5	1488	1228	SSK 12" barrel
275	IMR 4831	945.5	1609	1580	SSK 12" barrel

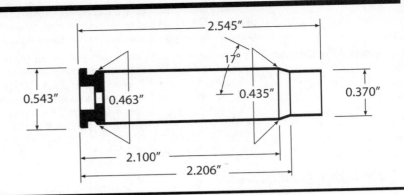

NEW
.338 GNR

Historical Notes: Developed in early 1985 by Gary Reeder, the .338 GNR was specifically designed for an African Safari. Reeder wanted an extra-long-range cartridge for a Thompson/Center Contender, one that still had plenty of power for 650- to 750-pound animals. The .338 GNR is based on the .405 Winchester case.

General Comments: Gary Reeder has used the .338 GNR on a number of big-game hunts, with great success. It does best with bullets in the 180- to 225-grain weight range. Due to the large amounts of powder this cartridge consumes, Contender barrels in the 15- to 16-inch range work best. Gary Reeder also recommends a muzzle brake to prolong scope life, as the recoil is quite intense.Information on custom guns, ammunitin, and reloading data can be obtained by contacting Gary Reeder Custom Guns, 928-527-4100; www.reedercustomguns.com.—R.A.M.

.338 GNR Loading Data and Ballistics

Bullet (grains/type)	Powder	Grains	Velocity	Energy	Source
180 SP	H 4350	57	2710	2935	Gary Reeder
225 SP	Reloader 15	50	2510	3147	Gary Reeder

.338-06 JDJ

Historical Notes: This cartridge was designed by J.D. Jones of SSK Industries. Application is to Thompson/Center Encore single-shot pistols fitted with a custom SSK barrel. Typical barrel length is 15 inches. Cases are formed from .30-06 or .35 Whelen cases by special means and cannot be fire-formed from any other case. Neck length is minimal, which is acceptable for a cartridge used in a single-shot gun. Shoulder angle is 60 degrees, which seems to work just fine. Body taper is minimal, similar to Ackley's Improved designs. Therefore, this is a maximized .338-06 case. Capacity is a whopping 76 grains of water, which is significantly greater than the .338-06 (about 71). Working pressure is about 60,000 psi, so ballistics are quite impressive. Best handloads in SSK barrels can approach .338-08 A-Square (rifle) ballistics.

General Comments: Since this case has no rim, it is not generally safe to directly fire-form it in the conventional manner. However, owing to the captive extractor system used in the Encore, it is possible to use a special technique in those guns, to wit: Resize and neck-expand a .30-06 case, then seat a .338-inch jacketed bullet hard against the rifling so that the gun will just close. Correct powder charge is about five-percent below the maximum SSK-recommended load. Jones recommends 180-grain bullets for big-game hunting applications on smaller species, and bullets up to 250 grains on larger species. This cartridge generates sufficient energy for hunting on any continent. Not all shooters have equal abilities and tolerances—while Jones' nine-year old grandson proved capable of handling this combination, recoil may exceed what some adult shooters can handle. For information on components, loading data, barrels, and guns designed for this cartridge, contact SSK Inudstries, 720-264-0176; www.sskindustries.com.

.338-06 JDJ Loading Data

Bullet (grains/type)	Powder	Grains	Velocity	Energy	Source/Comments
175 Barnes X	IMR 4064	62.5	2863	3185	SSK/max. load, SSK barrels only
180 Nosler BT	IMR 4064	62.5	2850	3245	SSK/max. load, SSK barrels only
200 Hornady	IMR 4064	61.5	2693	3220	SSK/max. load, SSK barrels only
225 Speer BT	IMR 4064	60.5	2643	3490	SSK/max. load, SSK barrels only
250 Speer GS	IMR 4064	58.0	2481	3415	SSK/max. load, SSK barrels only

8.59 Galaxy

Historical Notes: Lazzeroni Arms designed this cartridge, in 1997. While somewhat related to an older case, for all practical purposes, this is a new case design. This cartridge was created in response to requests for a high-performance cartridge that would work in a 2.8-inch action, yet deliver the ballistics of a full-length belted magnum. Adaptation to a standard action is feasible, but is not recommended.

General Comments: Bullet diameter is .338-inch (Lazzeroni bases its designations on bullet diameter, instead of bore diameter, which is the common practice.) Ballistics are quite impressive for such a short cartridge. Given equal-length barrels, the Galaxy easily exceeds the .338 Winchester Magnum. Case design is typical of the Lazzeroni line: moderate body taper, 30-degree shoulder, sufficiently long neck, and thick rim of approximate case-body diameter. In other words, this is a well-designed case. For more information on Lazzeroni custom guns, ammunition, and reloading data, contact 888-492--7247; www.lazzeroni.com.

8.59 Galaxy Factory Ballistics (24-inch barrel)

Bullet (grains)	Powder	Grains	Velocity	Energy	Source/Comments
200	FL		3100	4269	Lazzeroni factory load
225	FL		2950	4349	Lazzeroni factory load
250	FL		2750	4199	Lazzeroni factory load

.330 Dakota

Historical Notes: The .330 Dakota is based upon a shortened version of the rimless bottleneck .404 Jeffery case. The .330 Dakota is dimensioned to function through a standard-length action (3.35 inches). Design intent was to offer a factory alternative to the .338 Winchester Magnum, with .340 Weatherby performance. This also offers .338 Winchester Magnum rifle owners a simple conversion to improve ballistics and cartridge-feeding characteristics.

General Comments: Like the 7mm and .300 Dakota cartridges, the .330 Dakota functions properly through .30-06 length (3.35-inch) actions. This cartridge provides a significant case capacity advantage over the .338 Winchester Magnum (about 15 percent) and comes very close to duplicating capacity and performance of the much longer .340 Weatherby Magnum. Most rifles chambered for the .338 Winchester Magnum are easily converted to .330 Dakota. This conversion offers advantages in function, accuracy, and ballistics, because of the non-belted case. If loaded to similar pressures with appropriate powders, the .330 Dakota should produce five-percent more velocity (10-percent more energy) than Winchester's .338 Magnum. With the heaviest bullets, the advantage is more significant. For those interested in a hunting cartridge geared to larger big game, the .330 Dakota is a serious contender. Combined with the right bullets, this flat-shooting cartridge can deliver more energy to targets a quarter-mile away than factory .270 ammunition produces at the muzzle! The .340 Weatherby does have a slight capacity advantage, but the ballistic difference is marginal, and Weatherby's cartridge requires the use of a longer action. For hunters who want maximum performance from the .338-inch bore, the Canadian Magnum, A-Square, and Lazzeroni offerings are better choices. Contact Dakota Arms for more information, 605-347-4686; www.dakotaarms.com.

.330 Dakota Loading Data and Factory Ballistics

Bullet (grains)	Powder	Grains	Velocity	Energy	Source/Comments
200	IMR 4350	80.0	3082	4215	Dakota/maximum load
200	RI-22	86.5	3146	4390	Dakota/maximum load
200	H4831	88.0	3200	4545	Dakota/maximum load
200	IMR 7828	88.0	3100	4265	Dakota/maximum load
250	IMR 4350	76.0	2853	4515	Dakota/maximum load
250	RI-22	80.5	2849	4500	Dakota/maximum load
250	H4831	81.5	2878	4595	Dakota/maximum load
250	IMR 7828	82.0	2829	4440	Dakota/maximum load
210	FL		3200	4480	Dakota factory load
250	FL		2900	4668	Dakota factory load

.338 Canadian Magnum

Historical Notes: This cartridge was developed, about 1989, by North American Shooting Systems (NASS) and is somewhat similar to the .338 Imperial Magnum. This design features a slightly rebated rimless bottleneck case. Design intent was to provide maximum powder capacity available in a standard action with minimal gunsmithing. (Without deepening the magazine well slightly, magazine capacity is usually reduced by one round.) Bolt face alteration is not necessary. Cartridge feeding and headspacing characteristics are improved.

General Comments: The Canadian Magnum series is similar to the Dakota cartridge family in both design and purpose. However, this cartridge takes advantage of the entire 3.65-inch magazine length of the long-action Remington M700 and similar rifles. On the Canadian Magnums, body diameter is significantly larger than the standard belted magnum (.544-inch versus .513-inch at the base). Re-chambering of nominal belted magnums with the same bore diameter is generally quite simple, requiring no other rifle alterations. For any given case length, capacity is about 15-percent greater than can be achieved with the standard belted-magnum case. Body taper is minimal, and the case shoulder is comparatively sharp. However, neck length is sufficiently generous to provide good bullet purchase for hunting ammunition. Performance is commensurate with the capacity and pressures used in these loadings. As with the .300 Canadian Magnum, one is impressed with the similarity to Remington's Ultra cartridge in the same bore size.

.338 Canadian Magnum Loading Data and Factory Ballistics

Bullet (grains)	Powder	Grains	Velocity	Energy	Source/Comments
225	IMR 4831	88.0	3083	4745	NASS/maximum load
225	H4831	91.0	3047	4635	NASS/maximum load
250	IMR 4831	88.0	2924	4740	NASS/maximum load
250	RI-19	89.0	2977	4915	NASS/maximum load
250	H4831	91.0	2951	4830	NASS/maximum load
225	FL		3110	4830	NASS factory load

.338 Woodswalker

Historical Notes: Created during the late 1990s, by J.D. Jones of SSK Industries, the .338 Woodswalker was designed specifically for use in the T/C Contender pistol with a 10-inch barrel. The case is formed by necking up and fire-forming the European-designed 8.15x46R case for .338-inch bullets. At the time of this cartridge's development, those cases were being imported by RWS.

General Comments: One of very few to write about the .338 Woodswalker was Layne Simpson, who used it to take several whitetail deer and wild boar. When fired in a 10-inch barrel, it is not far behind the velocity of the old .33 Winchester and, for this reason, the 200-grain flat-nose bullet made by Hornady for that cartridge is the best choice for deer. Unfortunately, it has been discontinued, and other bullets of its caliber are constructed for much higher velocities. The Nosler 180-grain AccuBond and 200-grain Ballistic Tip work satisfactorily on deer out to about 150 yards, but expansion decreases rapidly as the range is increased beyond that. For information on components, loading data, barrels, and guns designed for this cartridge, contact SSK Inudstries, 720-264-0176; www.sskindustries.com.

.338 Woodswalker Loading Data and Factory Ballistics

Bullet (grains/type)	Powder	Grains	Velocity	Energy	Source
180 Nosler AccuBond	H335	41.0	2044	1668	Layne Simpson
200 Nosler Ballistic Tip	H335	39.5	1927	1647	Layne Simpson
200 Nosler Ballistic Tip	H4198	33.0	2009	1790	Layne Simpson
200 Hornady FP	H335	39.5	1910	1618	Layne Simpson
200 Hornady FP	RL-7	32.0	1852	1522	Layne Simpson
200 Hornady FP	H4198	33.0	1979	1737	Layne Simpson
200 Hornady FP	BL-C(2)	40.0	1908	1615	Layne Simpson
200 Hornady FP	W748	39.0	1867	1546	Layne Simpson
210 Nosler Partition	BL-C(2)	37.0	1909	1697	Layne Simpson

WARNING: All powder charges are maximum and must be reduced by 10 percent for starting loads.

.338 A-Square

Historical Notes: This 1978 design is a somewhat modified .378 Weatherby Magnum necked down to accept .338-inch bullets. The intention was to provide a flat-shooting cartridge capable of delivering substantial energy to medium-sized game animals at normal hunting ranges. With minor modifications, most nominal 3.65-inch bolt-action magazines will handle this cartridge.

General Comments: Ballistics are very close to A-Square's .338 Excaliber, but this cartridge will not feed from a magazine as smoothly as that beltless design. The basic design incorporates a sharp shoulder for good headspace control, but features a comparatively generous body taper. Ballistics are impressive. This cartridge can deliver massive doses of energy to long-range targets. For more informationon A-square custom rifles and ammunition, contact 605-234-0500 (South Dakota) or 307-436-5677 (Wyoming); www.a-squareco.com.

.338 A-Square Loading Data and Factory Ballistics

Bullet (grains/type)	Powder	Grains	Velocity	Energy	Source/Comments
200 Nosler BT	H4831	104.0	3259	4715	A-Square/maximum load
200 Nosler BT	IMR 7828	106.0	3353	4990	A-Square/maximum load

Bullet (grains/type)	Powder	Grains	Velocity	Energy	Source/Comments
200 Nosler BT	RI-22	104.0	3355	4995	A-Square/maximum load
250 Sierra SBT	IMR 7828	95.0	2879	4600	A-Square/maximum load
250 Sierra SBT	RI-22	95.0	2965	4880	A-Square/maximum load
250 Sierra SBT	H870	118.0	3094	5310	A-Square/maximum load
250 Sierra SBT	AA 8700	120.0	3100	5330	A-Square/maximum load
200 Nosler BT	FL		3500	5435	A-Square factory load
250 Sierra SBT	FL		3120	5400	A-Square factory load
250 Triad	FL		3120	5400	A-Square factory load

.338 Excaliber

Historical Notes: This 1994 chambering is based upon an entirely new case that features a .580-inch head size. The rim is sentially identical to the .378 Weatherby case, but there is no useless belt. Therefore, case capacity is substantially greater for any given cartridge length. This standard rimless bottleneck design also facilitates proper chambering with tight tolerances. Design intent was acceleration of a 200-grain hunting bullet in excess of 3500 fps without exceeding about 62,000 psi (piezo transducer pressure units)—a typical pressure for modern cartridges. The .338 Excaliber accomplishes this goal.

General Comments: This cartridge is a superior choice for those who feel they need a flat-shooting cartridge that can deliver substantial energy to medium-sized game targets at long-range. Rifles originally chambered for the .378 and .460 can be re-barreled to accept this cartridge. The slowest handloader powders now available offer the best velocity potential. In a typical rifle, recoil would have to be classed as heavy, especially when shooting heavier bullets. As is normal with .338-inch chamberings, trajectories are essentially indistinguishable from the similar .30-caliber counterpart, but with the delivery of a heavier bullet carrying more energy.

.338 Excaliber Loading Data

Bullet (grains/type)	Powder	Grains	Velocity	Energy	Source/Comments
200 Nosler BT	RI-22	113.0	3434	5240	A-Square/maximum load
200 Nosler BT	H870	138.0	3480	5380	A-Square/maximum load
200 Nosler BT	AA 8700	140.0	3493	5415	A-Square/maximum load
200 Nosler BT	IMR 7828	116.0	3497	5430	A-Square/maximum load
250 Sierra SBT	IMR 7827	105.0	2966	4885	A-Square/maximum load
250 Sierra SBT	H5010	128.0	3109	5365	A-Square/maximum load
250 Sierra SBT	RI-22	110.0	3192	5655	A-Square/maximum load
250 Sierra SBT	H870	128.0	3200	5685	A-Square/maximum load
250 Sierra SBT	AA 8700	130.0	3202	5690	A-Square/maximum load

8.59 Titan

Historical Notes: Lazzeroni Arms designed this cartridge, in 1994, based upon an earlier 1992 design. This was the first Lazzeroni cartridge. While somewhat related to an older case, for practical purposes, this is a new case design. John Lazzeroni believes that those hunters who will take the time to become competent marksmen can legitimately take game at longer ranges. This cartridge was created to launch medium- to heavy-weight hunting bullets with sufficient velocity to provide dependable expansion at longer ranges and to have sufficient energy for taking the largest species. Adaptation to standard actions is feasible, but is not recommended.

General Comments: Bullet diameter is .338-inch (Lazzeroni bases its designations on bullet diameter, instead of bore diameter, which is the common practice). Ballistics equal or exceed any factory .33-caliber cartridge. Case design is typical of the Lazzeroni line: moderate body taper, 30-degree shoulder, sufficiently long neck, and thick rim of approximate case-body diameter. In other words, this is a well-designed case. While designed specifically for hunting, this cartridge does have application to long-range target shooting. Standard barrel length is 27 inches, which provides a good measure of the ballistic potential of this cartridge. Most of Lazzeroni's full-length cartridge loadings use specially lubricated (proprietary process) premium bullets from Nosler, Barnes, or Swift. These are the only bullets providing the necessary accuracy and terminal performance to meet Lazzeroni's strict requirements. He designed this as the ultimate North American hunting cartridge for the hunter who is interested primarily in elk. His experience with a .33-caliber magnum that would not deliver the accuracy necessary to take an elk cleanly at somewhat beyond 350 yards prompted this development and the entire subsequent Lazzeroni line. For more information on Lazzeroni custom guns, ammunition, and reloading data, contact 888-492--7247; www.lazzeroni.com.

8.59 Titan Factory Ballistics (27-inch barrel)

Bullet (grains)	Powder	Grains	Velocity	Energy	Source/Comments
200	FL		3450	5287	Lazzeroni factory load *
225	FL		3300	5442	Lazzeroni factory load *
250	FL		3150	5510	Lazzeroni factory load *

*RI-25 will produce superior velocity, but accuracy has so far been dismal. RI-19 is the preferred powder for this cartridge.

.38 Casull

Historical Notes: Repeatedly proven for nearly a century, the story of the endurance and reliability of John Browning's 1911 pistol approaches the status of legend. Not well known, however, is the adaptability of the 1911 design to different cartridges. Casull Arms used improved steels and technologies to update its 1911-design pistol to accommodate a new short cartridge, the .38 Casull. Created by Dick Casull, in 1998, its case capacity equals or exceeds the .357 Magnum, while fitting in a .45 ACP magazine.

General Comments: The cartridge is for long-range target and hunting uses, or for when self-defense needs call for a more powerful cartridge than its parent case, the .45 ACP. (It is also said to be similar to the wildcat .38-45 Clerke, developed around 1963 by Bo Clerke, a New Mexico gunsmith, but the .38 Casull has thicker case walls.) The .38 Casull uses a longer case neck and rebated rim for more reliable feeding. For handgun hunters, the .38 Casull demonstrates high accuracy and flat trajectories at 100 yards. The barrel is five inches long, with 1:18 rifling. Shooters are advised that only Casull Arms pistols are designed and constructed for this cartridge; chambering in other firearms is strongly discouraged. Loaded ammunition wis available from Casull Arms, and initial chronograph testing indicates the factory ammo does attain the specified velocities.

13th Edition Update: This round was previously categorized in the Handgun Cartridges chapter, but would, in fact, have been a proprietary loading of Casull Arms. That company was formed by Dick Casull after he parted ways with Wayne Baker and Freedom Arms, the company they'd founded together, but Casull Arms doesn't seem to be in existence at this point. There's little to no information on the availability of brass or bullets for this round, let alone more than just a handful of guns chambered for it out there, so for all intents and purposes, this round seems to be obsolete. For these reasons, it seems we had a toss-up between slotting it in the proprietary or wildcat cartridges, but, given its history, we have opted for the proprietary designation is being most appropriate at this time.

.38 Casull Loading Data and Factory Ballistics

Bullet (grains/type)	Powder	Grains	Velocity	Energy	Source/Comments
124 Hornady	FL		1800		Casull Arms
147 Hornady	FL		1600		Casull Arms

NEW
.356 GNR

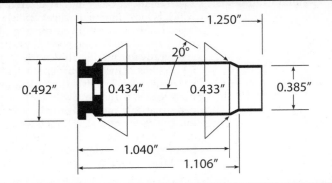

1.250"
20°
0.492" | 0.434" | 0.433" | 0.385"
1.040"
1.106"

Historical Notes: One of Gary Reeder's favorite Thompson/Center Contender cartridges has been the .357/44 B&D. Gary wanted to chamber that cartridge in a revolver, but had problems making the combination work; the case constantly set back and pulled crimp, locking up the cylinder. In the mid-1990s, Reeder decided to give it another go, but this time he took a .41 Magnum case and necked it down to .357. He made the case walls straight and put in a sharp shoulder with a short neck—and it worked perfectly. The .356 GNR was originally developed for bullets ranging in weight from 125 to 140 grains, and it has worked very well as a deer cartridge.

General Comments: Additional experimentation has also shown the .356 GNR to work very well with 180-grain cast LBT bullets. This discovery proved that the .356 GNR was suitable not just for deer, but would work for big game, as well. Reeder has chambered the .356 GNR in many T/C Contender barrels, but he feels it is best at home in a six-shot revolver like the Ruger Blackhawk and Redhawk and the S&W Models 27 and 28. Those looking for a .357-caliber alternative to a .357 Magnum that has more punch and will still work in revolvers with cylinders shorter than those used for the .357 Maximum should find the .356 GNR to their liking. Information on custom guns, ammunitin, and reloading data can be obtained by contacting Gary Reeder Custom Guns, 928-527-4100; www.reedercustomguns.com.—R.A.M..

.356 GNR Loading Data and Ballistics

Bullet (grains/type)	Powder	Grains	Velocity	Energy	Source
125 JHP	H 110	24.0	2000	1110	Gary Reeder
140 JHP	W 296	24.0	1870	1086	Gary Reeder
180 Cast LBT	H 110	24	1700	1154	Gary Reeder

.358 JDJ

Historical Notes: This is another cartridge designed and developed by J.D. Jones. Jones began development of his cartridges, around 1978, to give added range and power to the Thompson/Center Contender pistol. Some of his cartridges have also proven to be excellent metallic silhouette numbers. JDJ cartridges are relatively easy to make. All JDJ cartridges are proprietary and SSK does not sell reamers, nor has it permitted the reamer maker to sell them. Should you desire a JDJ cartridge, contact SSK Industries (www.sskindusries.com).

General Comments: The first version of this cartridge used the .303 British case, but was later changed to the .444 Marlin necked down. This chambering provides ample capacity and bullet area to produce impressive muzzle energy, especially with longer handgun-length barrels (14 to 16 inches). Any .357 Magnum, .35 Remington, or .35 Herrett Thompson/Center Contender barrel is easily re-chambered to use this cartridge. The .358 JDJ offers muzzle velocities similar to the .375 Winchester (rifle loads) with bullets of equal weight. Since this chambering uses spitzer bullets, delivered energy at normal hunting range is significantly higher than with the the parent .444 Marlin, even when the latter is fired from a rifle. Bullets of 180 to 225 grains are good choices. Top loads in this chambering generate significant recoil. An effective muzzle brake (which increases the already significant muzzle blast effect) is essential. Recoil of top loads compares to top .44 Magnum revolver loads, a recoil level many shooters cannot learn to tolerate. When bullets of proper hunting weight are driven at full velocity (necessary to assure proper terminal performance), even the seasoned handgunner would describe the recoil generated as rather brisk. For information on components, loading data, barrels, and guns designed for this cartridge, contact SSK Inudstries, 720-264-0176; www.sskindustries.com.

.358 JDJ Loading Data

Bullet (grains/type)	Powder	Grains	Velocity	Energy	Source/Comments
180 JSP	RI-7	49.0	2295	2105	SSK/max. load, SSK barrels only
200 SP	RI-7	48.0	2275	2295	SSK/max. load, SSK barrels only
225 SP	RI-15	52.5	2145	2300	SSK/max. load, SSK barrels only
250 SP	AA 2520	50.0	2100	2205	SSK/max. load, SSK barrels only

.35-06 JDJ

Historical Notes: This cartridge was designed by J.D. Jones, of SSK Industries. Application is to Thompson/Center Encore single-shot pistols fitted with a custom SSK barrel. Typical barrel length is 15 inches. Cases are formed from empty .30-06 or .35 Whelen cases by special means and cannot be fire-formed from any other case. Neck length is minimal, which is acceptable for a cartridge used in a single-shot gun. Shoulder angle is 60 degrees, which seems to work just fine. Body taper is minimal, similar to Ackley's Improved designs, therefore, this is equivalent to a maximized .35 Whelen. Capacity is a whopping 76 grains of water, which is significantly greater than the .35 Whelen (about 72). Working pressure is about 60,000 psi, so ballistics are quite impressive. Best handloads in SSK barrels can approach .35 Whelen (rifle) ballistics.

General Comments: Since this case has no rim, it is not generally safe to directly fire-form it in the conventional manner. However, owing to the captive extractor system used in the Encore, it is possible to use a special technique in those gun, to wit: Resize a .35 Whelen case, and then seat a .358-inch jacketed bullet hard against the rifling so that the gun will just close. Correct powder charge is about five-percent below the maximum SSK-recommended load. Jones recommends 200-grain bullets for big-game hunting applications on smaller species, and bullets up to 250 grains on larger species. This cartridge generates sufficient energy for hunting on any continent. SSK has not yet fully developed optimal loading data for this number. Recoil may exceed what some shooters can learn to handle. For information on components, loading data, barrels, and guns designed for this cartridge, contact SSK Inudstries, 720-264-0176; www.sskindustries.com.

.35-06 JDJ Loading Data

Bullet (grains)	Powder	Grains	Velocity	Energy	Source/Comments
180	H335	67.0	2742	3005	SSK/max. load, SSK barrels only
220	IMR 4064	62.8	2584	3260	SSK/max. load, SSK barrels only
225	IMR 4064	62.8	2614	3415	SSK/max. load, SSK barrels only
250	RI-15	61.8	2415	3235	SSK/max. load, SSK barrels only

9.09 Eagle

Historical Notes: Lazzeroni Arms designed this cartridge, in 1998. While somewhat related to an older case, for all practical purposes, this is a new case design. This cartridge was created in response to requests for a high-performance cartridge that would work in a 2.8-inch action and yet deliver the ballistics of a full-length belted magnum. Adaptation to a standard action is feasible, but is not recommended. Although standardized, this is essentially a wildcat chambering using Lazzeroni's Patriot case. Lazzeroni does offer dies and reamer specifications, but does not normally chamber for this cartridge or provide properly headstamped cases.

General Comments: Bullet diameter is .358-inch (Lazzeroni bases its designations on bullet diameter, instead of bore diameter, which is the common practice). Ballistics are quite impressive for such a short cartridge. Given equal-length barrels, the Eagle essentially duplicates .358 Norma Magnum ballistics. Case design is typical of the Lazzeroni line: moderate body taper, 30-degree shoulder, sufficiently long neck, and thick rim of approximate case-body diameter. In other words, this is a well-designed case. For more information on Lazzeroni custom guns, ammunition, and reloading data, contact 888-492--7247; www.lazzeroni.com.

9.09 Eagle Factory Ballistics (24-inch barrel)

Bullet (grains)	Powder	Grains	Velocity	Energy	Source/Comments
250	FL		2850	4510	Lazzeroni factory load

.358 Shooting Times Alaskan (.358 STA)

Historical Notes: The .358 STA was the second cartridge developed by firearms writer Layne Simpson on the 8mm Remington Magnum case, and it is second in popularity to the 7mm STW, which came first. It has been reported that the first version of the .358 STA was formed by necking up the 8mm Remington Magnum with no other change, but this is not true. It is true for the 7mm STW, because the 8mm Magnum case holds all the powder that can be burned in a bore of that size at an acceptable level of efficiency. But, more powder can be burned in a .35-caliber bore and, right from the start, Simpson chose to reform the case to the Improved configuration with minimum body taper and a 35-degree shoulder angle. The case is formed by necking up the 8mm Remington Magnum case and loading it with a reduced powder charge with 80 grains of H4350 behind a 250-grain bullet for a popular fireforming load. The first rifle chambered for this cartridge was built by gunsmith Kenny Jarrett, and the first commercial rifles chambered for it were built by A-Square. That company was also first to offer loaded ammunition. Layne Simpson introduced the cartridge in the September 1992 issue of Shooting Times, soon after using it to bag an Alaskan brown bear.

General Comments: Powerful enough to handle any big-game animal in North America, the .358 STA shoots as flat as a .300 Magnum and delivers more energy to the target than the .375 H&H Magnum. When loaded with a 250-grain bullet, it is about 200 fps faster than the .358 Norma Magnum and duplicates the performance of a cartridge of the 1920s called the .350 Griffin & Howe Magnum. For more informationon A-square custom rifles and ammunition, contact 605-234-0500 (South Dakota) or 307-436-5677 (Wyoming); www.a-squareco.com.

.358 STA Loading Data and Factory Ballistics

Bullet (grains/type)	Powder	Grains	Velocity	Energy	Source
180 Barnes XFB	RL-19	95.0	3357	4501	Barnes
200 Barnes XFB	IMR-4831	90.0	3217	4591	Barnes
225 Nosler Partition	H4350	87.0	3182	5053	Hodgdon
225 Barnes XFB	IMR-4831	87.0	312883	4883	Barnes

.358 STA Loading Data and Factory Ballistics

Bullet (grains/type)	Powder	Grains	Velocity	Energy	Source
250 Barnes XFB	IMR-4831	86.0	2995	4974	Barnes
250 Nosler Partition	H4350	89.0	2981	4928	Layne Simpson
275 A-Square LL	H4831	90.0	2857	4979	A-Square
300 Barnes SN	RL-19	84.0	2714	4901	Layne Simpson
300 Barnes SN	H4831	86.0	2719	4919	Layne Simpson
275 A-Square Lion Load	FL		2850	4954	A-Square
275 A-Square Dead Tough	FL		2850	4954	A-Square

WARNING: All powder charges are maximum and must be reduced by 10 percent for starting loads.

9.3mm JDJ

Historical Notes: Designed by J.D. Jones, of SSK Industries, this chambering is the .444 Marlin case necked down to 9.3mm with no other changes. Design intent was a Thompson/Center chambering that would surpass .35 Remington rifle ballistics and use the newly available U.S.-manufactured 9.3mm bullets.

General Comments: Any ballistic difference between this chambering and the .358 JDJ would be very hard to demonstrate. This chambering is reported to deliver impressive performance against deer and black bear-sized game when heavy bullets are used. The primary market is European, where the 9.3mm bore is quite popular. This chambering generates significant recoil. An effective muzzle brake (which increases the already significant muzzle-blast effect), is essential. Recoil of top loads compares to top .44 Magnum revolver loads, a recoil level many shooters cannot learn to tolerate. When bullets of proper hunting weight are driven at full velocity (necessary to assure proper terminal performance), even the seasoned handgunner would describe the recoil as very brisk. For information on components, loading data, barrels, and guns designed for this cartridge, contact SSK Inudstries, 720-264-0176; www.sskindustries.com.

9.3mm JDJ Loading Data

Bullet (grains/type)	Powder	Grains	Velocity	Energy	Source/Comments
270 Speer	H322	44.0	1906	2175	SSK/max. load, SSK barrel only (14")
270 Speer	H414	57.3	1924	2240	SSK/max. load, SSK barrel only (14")
270 Speer	IMR 4064	52.0	1974	2335	SSK/max. load, SSK barrel only (14")
270 Norma	RI-15	53.0	2027	2465	SSK/max. load, SSK barrel only (14")
270 Speer	RI-15	54.0	2077	2585	SSK/max. load, SSK barrel only (14")

.375 Whisper

Historical Notes: Created by J.D. Jones, the .375 Whisper, like all other Whisper cartridges, must be capable of subsonic extreme accuracy with very heavy bullets, while maintaining excellent accuracy with light bullets at moderate to high velocity..

General Comments: Using a 7mm Bench Rest Remington case necked up to .375-caliber, the .375 Whisper launches a 300-grain Hornady projectile at just under sub-sonic speeds (1050 fps). It can propel 250-grain bullets to 2250 fps. The .375 Whisper can be chambered in suitably barreled Thompson/Center Contender firearms, as well as other single-shot and many bolt-action firearms. For information on components, loading data, barrels, and guns designed for this cartridge, contact SSK Inudstries, 720-264-0176; www.sskindustries.com.

.375/454 JDJ Woodswalker

Historical Notes: Another big-bore, short-range hunting round from SSK Industries, the .375/454 JDJ Woodswalker is based on necking the powerful .454 Casull cartridge to .375-caliber. Barrels, dies, and cases for the 375/454 JDJ are available from SSK Industries (www.sskindustries.com).

General Comments: Using a .375-caliber, 200-grain Sierra projectile in modified .454 Casull cases and 15-inch SSK barrels, the .375/454 JDJ achieves about 2375 fps. With 270-grain Hornady Spire Points, it can achieve velocities exceeding 1900 fps. It is suitable for the Thompson/Center Encore.

.375 JDJ

Historical Notes: This is another cartridge designed and developed by J.D. Jones, hence the JDJ designation. Development of his cartridges began around 1978, and these are generally fired in barrels furnished by his company, SSK Industries. The purpose of these cartridges is to give added range and power to the Thompson/Center Contender pistol for hunting. Some of Jones' cartridges have also proven to be excellent metallic silhouette numbers. JDJ cartridges are relatively easy to make. All JDJ cartridges are proprietary, and SSK neither sells reamers nor allows the reamer maker to sell them.

General Comments: Based on the .444 Marlin necked down, this chambering provides ample capacity and bullet area to produce muzzle energy similar to what .30-06-chambered rifles deliver, especially with longer handgun-length barrels (14 to 16 inches). The .375 JDJ loaded to top velocity with 250-grain bullets is fully capable of taking elk-sized game with proper shot placement. However, the Barnes 210-grain X bullet can deliver superior terminal performance, reduced recoil, and a flatter trajectory, but does require special handloading techniques (deeper bullet seating and a reduction in powder charge). With heavier bullets of proper construction, this chambering is adequate for species to the one-ton class. Jones himself has repeatedly proven this fact. An excellent selection of good bullets that work well when loaded to top .375 JDJ velocities is available.

This chambering generates significant recoil. An effective muzzle brake (which increases the already significant muzzle-blast effect), is essential. Top loads generally produce more recoil than top .44 Magnum revolver loads, a recoil level many shooters cannot learn to tolerate. When bullets of proper hunting weight are driven at full velocity (necessary to assure proper terminal performance), even the seasoned handgunner would describe the recoil as very brisk.For information on components, loading data, barrels, and guns designed for this cartridge, contact SSK Inudstries, 720-264-0176; www.sskindustries.com.

.375 JDJ Loading Data

Bullet (grains/type)	Powder	Grains	Velocity	Energy	Source/Comments
220 SP	H4895	51.0	2350	2365	SSK/max. load, *12-14" SSK barrels only
270 SP	IMR 4064	48.0	2100	2165	SSK/max. load, *12-14" SSK barrels only
270 SP	IMR 4064	49.2	2100	2400	SSK/max. load, *12-14" SSK barrels only
300 SP	W748	50.8	1950	2405	SSK/max. load, *12-14" SSK barrels only

.375-06 JDJ

Historical Notes: This cartridge was designed by J.D. Jones, of SSK Industries. Application is to Thompson/Center Encore single-shot pistols fitted with a custom SSK barrel. Typical barrel length is 15 inches. Cases are best formed from empty .30-06 or .35 Whelen cases by special means. Neck length is minimal, which is acceptable for a cartridge used in a single-shot gun. Shoulder angle is 60 degrees, which seems to work just fine and is probably necessary to maintain headspace against the firing pin blow and primer blast. Body taper is minimal, similar to Ackley's Improved designs. Therefore, this is equivalent to a maximized .375 Whelen. Capacity is a whopping 77 grains of water, which is significantly greater than the .375 Whelen (about 73). Working pressure is about 60,000 psi, so ballistics are quite impressive. Best handloads in SSK barrels easily exceed the energy of top factory .35 Whelen (rifle) loads.

General Comments: Since this case has no rim, it is not generally safe to directly fire-form it in the conventional manner. However, owing to the captive extractor system used in the Encore, it is possible to use a special technique in those guns, to wit: Resize and neck expand a .35 Whelen case, then seat a .375-inch jacketed bullet hard against the rifling so that the gun will just close. Correct powder charge is about five-percent below the maximum SSK-recommended load. Jones recommends 220-grain bullets at reduced velocity for big-game hunting applications on smaller species and bullets up to 300 grains for the largest species. While one could use 210- and 235-grain Barnes X bullets, which can offer impressive terminal performance, handloaders must use X bullet-specific loading data and special handloading techniques (e.g., bullet ogive must be seated a minimum of .050-inch from rifling). Further, those bullets work best when a reduced-friction coating (such as moly-plating) is used. For this reason, SSK does not support use of X-style bullets in its guns. While no bullet substitution is benign, never substitute any X-style bullet in any load—begin with data specifically created for that bullet. This cartridge generates sufficient energy for hunting on any continent. SSK has not fully developed optimal loading data for this number at this time. With heavy bullets and top loads, recoil may exceed what even seasoned shooters want to experience. For information on components, loading data, barrels, and guns designed for this cartridge, contact SSK Inudstries, 720-264-0176; www.sskindustries.com.

.375-06 JDJ Loading Data

Bullet (grains)	Powder	Grains	Velocity	Energy	Source/Comments
220	AA 4350	55.6	1825	1625	SSK/max. load, SSK barrels only
220	VarGet	67.3	2601	3305	SSK/max. load, SSK barrels only
270	Vit N140	65.2	2421	3515	SSK/max. load, SSK barrels only
300	IMR 4320	63.4	2330	3615	SSK/max. load, SSK barrels only

9.53 Hellcat

Historical Notes: Lazzeroni Arms designed this cartridge, in 1997. While somewhat related to an older case, for all practical purposes, this is a new case design. The Hellcat was created in response to requests for a high-performance cartridge that would work in a 2.8-inch action and yet deliver the ballistics of a full-length belted magnum. Adaptation to a standard action is feasible, but is not recommended.

General Comments: Bullet diameter is .375-inch (Lazzeroni bases its designations on bullet diameter, instead of bore diameter, which is the common practice.) Ballistics are quite impressive for such a short cartridge. Given equal-length barrels, the Hellcat essentially duplicates the ballistics of the legendary .375 H&H Magnum. Case design is typical of the Lazzeroni line: moderate body taper, 30-degree shoulder, sufficiently long neck, and thick rim of approximate case-body diameter. In other words, this is a well-designed case.

Bill George owns the first Hellcat rifle ever built. With very modest assistance from a former editor of this book, George assembled some extremely accurate handloads (well under 1 MOA accuracy) using the 300-grain Nosler Partition. He took those to Africa and proceeded to kill everything he shot at, using exactly one round for each animal in almost every instance. This Hellcat load dropped George's Cape buffalo in its tracks, a feat that left his guide practically in shock. The quote was, "Never seen that happen before in my life!" Shot placement and bullet performance count. For more information on Lazzeroni custom guns, ammunition, and reloading data, contact 888-492--7247; www.lazzeroni.com.

9.53 Hellcat Factory Ballistics (24-inch barrel)

Bullet (grains)	Powder	Grains	Velocity	Energy	Source/Comments
300	FL		2600	4500	Lazzeroni factory load

.375 JRS Magnum

General Comments: The .375 JRS was designed by noted gun writer Jon R. Sundra. It is based on the 8mm Remington Magnum case necked up to .375 with no other changes. It can be made by fire-forming .375 H&H factory ammunition; by necking up the 8mm Rem. Mag. using tapered expanders of .358-inch, then .375-inch; or by fire-forming, using blank loads in 8mm Rem. Mag. cases. Of these options, Sundra recommends the latter, because only the neck is worked. The procedure for making the blanks requires a load of 35 grains of IMR SR 4756, a small over-powder wad of tissue, then filling the remainder of the case to the base of the neck with Cream of Wheat cereal (uncooked, of course). Seal off the case mouth with a plug of soap by pushing the case neck into a soap bar. The resultant blank will expand the neck perfectly in a .375 JRS chamber. As of 1990, A-Square Co. began offering .375 JRS unprimed cases, as well as loaded ammunition with its headstamp. In1992, U.S. Repeating Arms began chambering the Winchester Model 70 Super Grade (the pre-'64 action with controlled round feeding) for the .375 JRS. E.R. Shaw and the H-S Precision company also chamber for the .375 JRS. This cartridge ballistically duplicates the .375 Weatherby Magnum and a host of older wildcats of the same general design. Hornady and RCBS make reloading dies.

General Comments: Case capacity of the .375 JRS is about eight-percent greater than that of the .375 H&H. The best powder for 270- to 330-grain bullets is IMR 4350. Velocity in 24-inch barrels for a 300-grain bullet will average between 2700 and 2750 fps. Any max load listed for the .375 H&H can be used for a starting load in the .375 JRS.

.375 JRS Loading Data

Bullet (grains/type)	Powder	Grains	Velocity	Energy	Source/Comments
270 SP	IMR 4350	85.0	2750	4535	Jon Sundra
300 SP	IMR 4350	83.0	2700	4855	Jon Sundra

.375 Dakota

Historical Notes: The .375 Dakota is a shortened and necked-down version of the basic, rebated rimless .404 Jeffery case, but the rim is enlarged slightly to eliminate the rebated feature. Design purpose was to create a cartridge that would duplicate .375 H&H performance from a .30-06-length action (3.35 inches). The case features a rim that is slightly larger than the standard belted-magnum cases; using this cartridge in a rifle with a standard belted-magnum bolt face will require a slight bolt alteration. Despite its similar capacity, maximum case diameter of this much shorter case is only slightly larger than the .375 H&H Magnum. Typically, magazine capacity is reduced by one cartridge. This is perhaps a significant consideration for a dangerous-game rifle, but a minor magazine alteration will remedy the problem.

General Comments: The .375 Dakota, just like the 7mm, .300, and .330 Dakota cartridges, functions properly through standard-length (3.35-inch) actions. Usable case capacity is nearly identical to the .375 H&H Magnum and, if loaded to equal pressures, ballistics are the same. This cartridge provides superior feeding and a potential accuracy advantage over the .375 H&H. Geared toward larger species, this should be a good choice for those who feel lesser calibers are inadequate for the task at hand. Combined with some of the superior bullets now available, this cartridge can rival the long-range trajectory of the best .270 Winchester loads. When loaded with proper dangerous-game bullets and in the hands of an expert, this cartridge would suffice for any game worldwide. Contact Dakota Arms for more information, 605-347-4686; www.dakotaarms.com.

.375 Dakota Loading Data and Factory Ballistics

Bullet (grains)	Powder	Grains	Velocity	Energ	Source/Comments
270	RI-15	75.0	2829	4795	Dakota/maximum load
270	IMR 4350	85.0	2895	5020	Dakota/maximum load
270	H4350	85.0	2883	4980	Dakota/maximum load
300	IMR 4350	78.0	2660	4710	Dakota/maximum load
300	H4350	78.0	2648	4670	Dakota/maximum load
300	IMR 4831	79.0	2641	4640	Dakota/maximum load
300	RI-19	83.5	2662	4720	Dakota/maximum load
270	FL		2800	4680	Dakota factory load
300	FL		2600	4502	Dakota factory load

.375 Canadian Magnum

Historical Notes: This cartridge was developed, about 1994, by North American Shooting Systems (NASS), and is simply a .375-caliber version of the .338 Canadian Magnum. This design features a slightly rebated, rimless bottleneck case. Design intent was to provide the maximum feasible powder capacity in a standard action with minimal gunsmithing (without deepening the magazine well slightly, magazine capacity is usually reduced by one round). Bolt face alteration is unnecessary. Cartridge feeding and headspacing characteristics are improved.

General Comments: The Canadian Magnum series is similar to Dakota's cartridge family in both design and purpose. However, this cartridge (like the entire Canadian line) takes advantage of the full 3.65-inch magazine length of the long-action Remington M700 and similar rifles. On the Canadian Magnums, body diameter is significantly larger than the standard belted magnum (.544-inch versus .513-inch at the base). Re-chambering of nominal belted magnums with the same bore diameter is generally quite simple, requiring no other alterations to the gun. For any given case length, case capacity is about 15-percent greater than can be achieved with the belted version. Body taper is minimal and the shoulder is comparatively sharp. However, neck length is sufficiently generous to provide good bullet purchase for hunting ammunition. Performance is commensurate with the capacity and pressures used in these loadings. Actual performance of this number is very close to the vaunted .378 Weatherby Magnum.

.375 Canadian Magnum Loading Data and Factory Ballistics

Bullet (grains)	Powder	Grains	Velocity	Energy	Source/Comments
270	H4831	103.0	3010	5430	NASS/maximum load
270	FL		3000	5395	NASS factory load

.375 A-Square

Historical Notes: This is a somewhat modified .378 Weatherby Magnum, designed in 1975. The changes were intended to allow duplication of .378 Weatherby Magnum performance in a .375 H&H magazine length (3.65 inches).

General Comments: Ballistics duplicate the parent .378 Weatherby Magnum, and chambering is easily achieved in any of the many .375 H&H-chambered magazine rifles. Cases are easily converted from .378 Weatherby Magnum cases. This chambering is a viable choice for a light rifle in Africa. The heavier solids offered are certainly capable of use against the heaviest of game, with proper shot placement. Recoil is distinctly less than recoil with any of the .40-caliber and larger dangerous-game chamberings. For more informationon A-square custom rifles and ammunition, contact 605-234-0500 (South Dakota) or 307-436-5677 (Wyoming); www.a-squareco.com.

.375 A-Square Loading Data and Factory Ballistics

Bullet (grains/type)	Powder	Grains	Velocity	Energy	Source/Comments
250 Sierra SBT	IMR 4831	106.0	3184	5625	A-Square/maximum load
250 Sierra SBT	H4831	114.5	3186	5630	A-Square/maximum load
250 Sierra SBT	RI-22	113.0	3217	5740	A-Square/maximum load
300 Monolithic Solid	RI-22	105.0	2839	5370	A-Square/maximum load
300 Monolithic Solid	IMR 4831	101.0	2911	5640	A-Square/maximum load
300 Monolithic Solid	H4831	110.0	2974	5890	A-Square/maximum load
300 Sierra & TRIAD	FL		2920	5675	A-Square factory load (3 A-Square bullet types)

9.53 Saturn

Historical Notes: Lazzeroni Arms designed this cartridge, in 1996. While somewhat related to an older case, for all practical purposes, this is a new case design. John Lazzeroni believes that those hunters who will take the time to become competent marksmen can legitimately take game at longer ranges. This cartridge was created to provide sufficient velocity for medium-weight or heavyweight hunting bullets to enable dependable expansion at longer ranges, and to have sufficient energy for taking the largest species. Adaptation to standard actions is feasible, but is not recommended.

General Comments: Bullet diameter is .375-inch (Lazzeroni bases its designations on bullet diameter, instead of bore diameter, which is the common practice). Ballistics equal or exceed any factory .37-caliber cartridge. Case design is typical of the Lazzeroni line: moderate body taper, 30-degree shoulder, sufficiently long neck, and thick rim of approximate case-body diameter. In other words, this is a well-designed case. Although designed specifically for hunting, this cartridge does have application to long-range target shooting. While a 27-inch barrel was originally standard, Lazzeroni has recently changed to a 24-inch barrel for this number, there is no significant sacrifice in performance. Lazzeroni's cartridge loadings use premium bullets from Nosler, Barnes, or Swift. These are the only bullets providing the necessary accuracy and terminal performance to meet Lazzeroni's strict requirements. For more information on Lazzeroni custom guns, ammunition, and reloading data, contact 888-492--7247; www.lazzeroni.com.

9.53 Saturn Factory Ballistics (24-inch barrel)

Bullet (grains/type)	Powder	Grains	Velocity	Energy	Source/Comments
300	FL		3010	6035	Lazzeroni factory load *

* Lazzeroni has used loads exceeding 3100 fps, but that is pressing the issue rather hard. RI-19 is a preferred powder for this number.

.400 CorBon

Historical Notes: Peter Pi, CEO of CorBon, designed this cartridge, in 1995, by simply necking down the .45 Automatic to .40-caliber with a 25-degree shoulder. Unlike some earlier necked-down .45 Automatic designs, this case has a reasonably long neck. With the advent of plentiful .40-caliber pistol bullets, this was an obvious high-performance cartridge choice.

This design offers several advantages. First, in most pistols, conversion is completed by a simple barrel replacement. Second, the feed ramp in the chamber can easily be shortened or eliminated, thus allowing safe use of loads generating significantly higher pressure. Third, owing to the bottleneck design, this case can function better with a wider variety of bullet shapes and is generally more forgiving toward machining, fit, and finish tolerances. Finally, for any given energy level, the .400 CorBon produces significantly less recoil than the .45 Automatic (lighter bullets, launched faster).

General Comments: This is a very fine cartridge for those who do not like excessive recoil. Factory loads offer significant self-defense ballistics in a package that most shooters can easily learn to handle. Those who are satisfied with the .45 Automatic will probably find little appeal with the .400 CorBon. On the other hand, those who are dissatisfied with 9mm and .40 S&W ballistics might find this a viable option. Cases are easily converted from the ubiquitous .45 Automatic, but Starline (www.starlinebrass.com) offers these as a component. Owing to increased case capacity, ballistics of the .400 CorBon approach those of the 10mm Automatic, but with significantly less pressure. For more information on CorBon ammunition, contact 800-626-7266; www.shopcorbon.com

.400 CorBon Loading Data and Factory Ballistics

Bullet (grains/type)	Powder	Grains	Velocity	Energy	Source/Comments
135 JHP	Vit N340	9.7	1400	585	Cor-Bon
155 JHP	WAP	10.5	1310	590	Cor-Bon
165 JHP	Vit N105	10.5	1250	570	Cor-Bon
180 Cast	Unique	7.0	1100	480	Cor-Bon
135 JHP	FL		1450	625	Cor-Bon factory load
155 JHP	FL		1350	625	Cor-Bon factory load
165 JHP	FL		1300	615	Cor-Bon factory load

.40-44 Woodswalker

Historical Notes: This cartridge was designed by J.D. Jones, of SSK Industries. Application is to Thompson/Center Encore or Contender single-shot pistols fitted with a custom SSK barrel. Typical barrel length is 10 inches. Cases are formed from empty .44 Magnum cases by simply running the case into a full-length sizing die. Neck length is rather short, which is acceptable for a cartridge used in a single-shot gun. Shoulder angle is 30 degrees.

General Comments: This is very reminiscent of the .357 Bain & Davis. The only advantage of such a conversion is the ability to launch lighter bullets at higher velocities (compared to the parent cartridge). Working pressure is about 60,000 psi. Energy of top loads approachs that for .454 Casull revolver loads. It is an open question as to whether any readily available JHP bullet will function properly when used at twice the designed velocity. However, broadside lung shots on smaller game species (and some not so small) have resulted in spectacular kills, when using 180-grain and heavier bullets For information on components, loading data, barrels, and guns designed for this cartridge, contact SSK Inudstries, 720-264-0176; www.sskindustries.com. .

.40-44 Woodswalker Loading Data

Bullet (grains/type)	Powder	Grains	Velocity	Energy	Source/Comments
150 Sierra	AA No. 9	30.7	2404	1925	SSK/max. load, SSK barrels only
165 Speer	Vit N110	25.2	2122	1650	SSK/max. load, SSK barrels only
170 Sierra	H110	31.4	2213	1845	SSK/max. load, SSK barrels only
190 Speer	AA No. 9	27.5	2116	1885	SSK/max. load, SSK barrels only

.40-454 JDJ

Historical Notes: This cartridge was designed by J.D. Jones, of SSK Industries. Application is to Thompson/Center Encore and Contender single-shot pistols fitted with a custom SSK barrel. Typical barrel length is 12 inches. Cases are formed from empty .454 Casull cases by simply running the case into the full-length sizing die. Neck length is rather short, which is acceptable for a cartridge used in a single-shot gun. Shoulder angle is 30 degrees.

General Comments: This is very reminiscent of the .357 Bain & Davis (the .44 Magnum necked to .35-caliber). The only advantage of such a conversion is the ability to launch lighter bullets at higher velocity (compared to the parent cartridge). Working pressure is about 60,000 psi. Muzzle energy of top loads can exceed any feasible .454 Casull revolver load. It is an open question as to whether any readily available JHP bullet will function properly, when used at almost three times the designed velocity. Use on smaller game species with broadside lung shots has resulted in spectacular kills, when using 180-grain and heavier bullets. For information on components, loading data, barrels, and guns designed for this cartridge, contact SSK Inudstries, 720-264-0176; www.sskindustries.com.

.40-454 JDJ Loading Data

Bullet (grains/type)	Powder	Grains	Velocity	Energy	Source/Comments
165 Speer	AA No. 9	36.6	2825	2925	SSK/maximum load
190 Speer	AA No. 9	34.5	2525	2690	SSK/maximum load

.408 CheyTac

Historical Notes: The .408 CheyTac may just be the ultimate long-range sniper and anti-material cartridge. Designed, in 2001, by Dr. John Taylor and his technical team to fill a gap between the .50 BMG and .338 Lapua, the .408 CheyTac can drive a 419-grain bullet to a supersonic range exceeding 2,200 yards. After 400 yards, the retained energy of the .408 CheyTac exceeds that of .50 BMG ball ammunition. With high kinetic energy retention, the .408 can defeat any material that the .50 BMG can defeat, unless an explosive projectile is required. In test firings, the cartridge delivered sub-MOA accuracy at ranges beyond 2,500 yards. Doppler radar testing at the U.S. Army Proving Ground in Yuma, Arizona, confirmed the .408's ballistics. The .408 CheyTac advantages over the .50 BMG include less weight, a more compact cartridge, improved velocity and accuracy, and lower recoil, along with shorter time for the bullet to reach the target. Special operations soldiers tested .408 CheyTac rifles and cartridges in Iraq and Afghanistan (2004). Informal reports of a first-shot hit at ranges exceeding 2,300 yards have circulated within the military community.

General Comments: Using new, high-quality brass, the .408 CheyTac is based on a redesigned and strengthened .505 Gibbs case with a modified web area. The cartridge works well with 25- to 29-inch barrels using a 1:13 rifling twist. The 305-grain and 419-grain bullets for the .408 are CNC-turned bullets from copper-nickel alloy and encompass a patented "balanced flight" design. A tungsten carbide penetrator (armor-piercing) bullet is also available. CheyTac LLC (www.cheytac.com) offers bolt-action and self-loading rifles, ballistic computers, ammunition, and cases.

.408 CheyTac Factory Ballistics

Bullet (grains/type)	Powder	Grains	Velocity	Energy	Source/Comments
305 Solid	FL		3500		CheyTac
419 Solid	FL		3000		CheyTac

NEW
.41 GNR

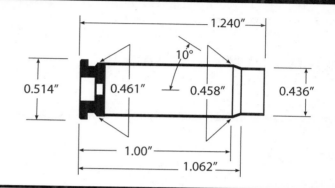

Historical Notes: Gary Reeder has been a long-time fan of the .41 Auto Mag cartridge, which is simply a .44 Auto Mag necked down to .41-caliber. Gary desired to run this cartridge in a revolver, but its rimless design made that difficult. Gary found a simple solution by necking a .44 Remington Magnum case down to .41-caliber.

General Comments: The .41 GNR was an early success and continues to be one of the most popular cartridges Gary Reeder offers. It is frequently chambered in Thompson/Center Contender barrels, custom revolvers, and even Marlin lever-action rifles. It will drive a 170-grain bullet to 1980 fps from a 10-inch Contender barrel, and, from a 20-inch lever gun, velocities are well in excess of 2000 fps. Using the 170-grain Sierra jacketed hollow point bullet, this cartridge has taken everything from coyotes to caribou with one shot.Information on custom guns, ammunitin, and reloading data can be obtained by contacting Gary Reeder Custom Guns, 928-527-4100; www.reedercustomguns.com.—R.A.M..

.41 GNR Loading Data and Ballistics

Bullet (grains/type)	Powder	Grains	Velocity	Energy	Source
170 JHP	W 296	29.5	1980	1479	Gary Reeder
210 JHP	W 296	28.0	1900	1683	Gary Reeder
250 Cast LBT	W 296	28	1810	1818	Gary Reeder

NEW
.410 GNR

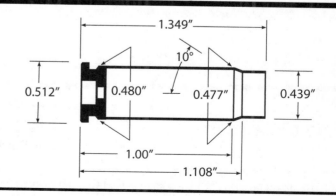

Historical Notes: The .410 GNR was an effort by Gary Reeder to develop another .41-caliber revolver cartridge. It was developed in 2001. Out of a six-inch revolver, the .410 GNR will almost match .41 GNR performance when fired from a 10-inch Contender. It is based on the .454 Casull case, which is necked down to .41-caliber. Due to the high pressures generated by this cartridge, Reeder only offers it in Contender barrels and in revolvers with a five-shot cylinder.

General Comments: This is a very powerful revolver cartridge suitable for taking any game animal on earth. Within two months of the release of the .410 GNR, it was used to take seven buffalo (some African, some Asian), some American bison, and one Australian water buffalo. All but two were taken with one shot each. A 250-grain bullet moving at 1645 fps out of a six-inch revolver is not something to be taken lightly, regardless of which end of the gun you are on. Information on custom guns, ammunitin, and reloading data can be obtained by contacting Gary Reeder Custom Guns, 928-527-4100; www.reedercustom-guns.com.—R.A.M..

.410 GNR Loading Data and Ballistics

Bullet (grains/type)	Powder	Grains	Velocity	Energy	Source
170 Sierra JHP	W 296	33.0	1900	1362	Gary Reeder
210 Hornady JHP	Accurate # 9	32.0	1795	1502	Gary Reeder
250 Cast LBT	W 296	30.0	1645	1502	Gary Reeder

.411 JDJ

Historical Notes: Based upon the .444 Marlin case, this cartridge is designed to take advantage of the plentiful .41-caliber pistol and revolver bullets now on the market. With cast rifle bullets sized properly, it provides more versatility than the .416-inch bore. J.D. Jones designed this at SSK Industries.

General Comments: Various pistol and revolver bullets can be loaded to achieve as high as 2400 fps from a 14-inch Contender barrel. Special cast bullets in the 400-grain range are easily loaded to achieve 1800 fps in the same guns. This approaches top .45-70 modern rifle ballistics. Even with the best Pachmayr Decelerator grips and the most effective muzzle brake possible, this combination will generate massive recoil. Many otherwise competent shooters simply cannot learn to master such a chambering in a handgun. The Barnes 300-grain X bullet offers reduced recoil with potentially superior terminal performance and a flatter trajectory, but requires special handloading techniques (deeper bullet seating and a reduction in powder charge). With the proper bullets, those who can handle the recoil will find this a serious handgun chambering for use against any species in the world. For information on components, loading data, barrels, and guns designed for this cartridge, contact SSK Inudstries, 720-264-0176; www.sskindustries.com.

.411 JDJ Loading Data

Bullet (grains/type)	Powder	Grains	Velocity	Energy	Source/Comments
210 Sierra	H4198	45.0	1878	1640	SSK/maximum load
275 Harrison	H4227	38.0	1990	2415	SSK/maximum load
295 Cast	H322	45.0	1683	1855	SSK/maximum load
330 Harrison	RI-7	46.0	2000	2930	SSK/maximum load
385 Cast	RI-7	46.0	1711	2500	SSK/maximum load

.411 Express

Historical Notes: Created by Z-Hat Custom owner Fred Zeglin, in 2002, the .411 Express is the longest version of the .30-06 case that will function in a standard-length action. The .411 Express uses the largest diameter bullet that will fit into the .30-06 case. With good shooting and good bullets, the cartridge is capable

RUSH!
NEW SUBSCRIBER SAVINGS!

BUSINESS REPLY MAIL
FIRST-CLASS MAIL   PERMIT NO. 31   BOONE IA

POSTAGE WILL BE PAID BY ADDRESSEE

RIFLESHOOTER

PO BOX 37539
BOONE IA 50037-2539

of and succeeded in taking North American elk at ranges exceeding 300 yards. The .411 Express is a powerful, large-bore cartridge with stout, but manageable, recoil.

General Comments: This cartridge fits into standard-length actions with a .473-inch bolt face. The .411 Express uses .30-06 cylindrical brass as the parent case. Since the case manufacturer does not neck down cylindrical brass, only experienced handloaders should attempt to form the .411 Express case. The parent brass is necked to .411-inch and then fire-formed in a .411 Express chamber. This Z-Hat offering is best suited for bolt-action rifles using 24-inch barrels with a 1:18 or 1:20 rifling twist. Loaded ammunition and correctly headstamped brass are available from Quality Cartridge (www.qual-cart.com). Z-Hat Custom (www.z-hat.com) offers rifles, dies and reloading information.

.411 Express Loading Data

Bullet (grains)	Powder	Grains	Velocity	Energy	Source/Comments
300	H4895	66.0	2561	4368	Z-Hat Custom
360	Accurate Arms 2230	60.0	2296	4212	Z-Hat Custom
400	RL-15	59.0	2160	4361	Z-Hat Custom

.411 Hawk

Historical Notes: The .411 Hawk is the most popular member in the Hawk family of hunting cartridges. Building on an idea of Bob Fulton's, in 1997, Fred Zeglin created the .411 Hawk to accept the largest diameter bullets that can be loaded into the .30-06 case. With the right bullets, the .411 Hawk can produce more than 4000 ft-lbs of energy from a .30-06 case! This is a premier big-game cartridge, suitable for anything on the North American continent and most game in Africa.

General Comments: All Hawk cartridges fit into standard-length actions with a .473-inch bolt face. The .411 Hawk uses .30-06 cylindrical brass or .35 Whelen brass as the parent case. Since the case manufacturer does not neck down cylindrical brass, only experienced handloaders should attempt to form the .411 Express case from .30-06 cylindrical brass. The cylindrical brass is necked down in a cold forming step and then fire-formed in a .411 Hawk chamber. As an alternative, .35 Whelen brass can be expanded using a .430 tapered expander, then sized in a full length die and fire-formed in a .411 Hawk chamber. While the .411 Hawk shoulder appears minimal, extensive testing confirmed the shoulder area was ample to safely headspace this powerful cartridge. This Hawk cartridge is suited for bolt-action, single-shot, and lever-action rifles (such as the Browning/Winchester 1895 and BLR) using 24- to 26-inch barrels with a 1:20 rifling twist. Hunters who plan to shoot only 400-grain bullets can use 1:24 twist rifling. Loaded ammunition and correctly headstamped brass are available from Quality Cartridge (www.qual-cart.com). Z-Hat Custom (www.z-hat.com) offers rifles, dies, and reloading information.

.411 Hawk Loading Data

Bullet (grains/type)	Powder	Grains	Velocity	Energy	Source/Comments
300 Hawk	H4895	64.0	2553	4341	Z-Hat Custom
325 North Fork	H4895	64.0	2479	4434	Z-Hat Custom
350 A-Frame	IMR 4064	61.0	2366	4350	Z-Hat Custom
360 North Fork	Accurate Arms 2230	57.0	2281	4158	Z-Hat Custom
400 Hawk	RL-15	57.0	2159	4139	Z-Hat Custom

.416 JDJ

Historical Notes: Based upon the .444 Marlin case, this cartridge is designed to take advantage of the plentiful .416-caliber rifle bullets now on the market. With cast rifle bullets sized properly, it provides some versatility, but is only intended for big-game hunting. J.D. Jones designed this at SSK Industries, after the advent of .416 handloader bullets.

General Comments: Rifle bullets in the 400-grain range are easily loaded to achieve 1800 fps from a 14-inch Contender barrel. This approaches top .45-70 ballistics from a modern rifle. Even with the best Pachmayr Decelerator grips and the most effective muzzle brake possible, this combination will generate massive recoil. Many otherwise competent shooters simply cannot learn to master such a chambering in a handgun. The Barnes 300-grain X bullet offers reduced recoil with potentially superior terminal performance and a flatter trajectory, but requires special handloading techniques (deeper bullet seating and a reduction in powder charge). With the proper bullets, those who can handle the recoil will find this a serious handgun chambering for use against any species in the world. For information on components, loading data, barrels, and guns designed for this cartridge, contact SSK Inudstries, 720-264-0176; www.sskindustries.com.

.416 JDJ Loading Data

Bullet (grains/type)	Powder	Grains	Velocity	Energy	Source/Comments
300 Hawk	Rl-7	51.0	2016	2705	SSK/maximum load
350 CB	AA 2230	56.0	1908	2830	SSK/maximum load
400 Hornady	Rl-15	53.5	1727	2650	SSK/maximum load
400 Hawk	Rl-15	56.5	1810	2910	SSK/maximum load

.416-06 JDJ

Historical Notes: This cartridge was designed by J.D. Jones, of SSK Industries. Application is to Thompson/Center Encore single-shot pistols fitted with a custom SSK barrel. Typical barrel length is 15 inches. Cases are formed from empty .35 Whelen cases by special means. Neck length is minimal, which is acceptable for a cartridge used in a single-shot gun. Shoulder angle is 60 degrees, which seems to work just fine. An unusually sharp case shoulder is certainly necessary to maintain headspace against firing pin impact and primer blast. Body taper is minimal, similar to Ackley'sImproved designs. Therefore, this is equivalent to a maximized, .41-caliber .30-06 case. Capacity is a whopping 78 grains of water, compared to about 100 grains for the .416 Rem. Mag. Working pressure is about 60,000 psi, so ballistics are, nevertheless, quite impressive. Best handloads in SSK barrels far surpass any normal .35 Whelen loads.

General Comments: Since this case has no rim, it is not generally safe to directly fire-form it in the conventional manner. However, owing to the captive extractor system used in the Encore, it is possible to use a special technique in those guns, to wit: Resize and neck-expand a .35 Whelen case, then seat a jacketed .416-inch bullet hard against the rifling so that the gun will just close. Correct powder charge is about five-percent below the maximum SSK-recommended load. Jones recommends 300-grain bullets for big-game hunting applications on medium species, and bullets up to 400 grains for the largest species. Never substitute any bullet without beginning with specific loading data developed for that bullet. Achieving sufficient velocity to assure bullet expansion is an issue. Lightly constructed bullets would seem to be in order here. On the other hand, velocity is adequate with the 400-grain solid to make this a thoroughly acceptable cartridge for hunting any species on this planet. SSK has not fully developed optimal loading data for this number at this time. With heavy bullets and top loads, recoil probably exceeds what most shooters want to experience or could ever learn to handle. Whether this cartridge has sufficient headspace control seems to be an open question. Do not anneal the case, as doing so will almost certainly allow excessive case stretching. For information on components, loading data, barrels, and guns designed for this cartridge, contact SSK Inudstries, 720-264-0176; www.sskindustries.com.

Bullet (grains)	Powder	Grains	Velocity	Energy	Source/Comments
300	AA 2015	62.3	2229	3310	SSK/max. load, SSK barrels only
400	AA 2015	60.0	2065	3785	SSK/max. load, SSK barrels only

.416 Taylor

Historical Notes:	The .416 Taylor was developed by Robert Chatfield-Taylor, in 1972. It is based on the .458 Winchester Magnum case necked-down to .416-caliber. However, it can also be made by necking up .338 Winchester Magnum cases. The late Chatfield-Taylor was a writer and hunter of note, and he used the cartridge in Africa and reported very favorably on it. It was also checked out on Cape buffalo, elephant, and lion by several others with success, including John Wootters. At one time, there were rumors that the cartridge would be commercialized by Remington or Winchester, but it remained for A-Square to do that. The .416 Taylor is ballistically similar to the .416 Rigby and is adequate for the same range of game, including the tough, dangerous, African varieties. It is overpowered for most North American big game, but would be good backup against brown bears.
General Comments:	The .416 Taylor came about partly because .416 Rigby cartridges and cases were difficult to obtain, and partly because the .416-caliber represents a gap in the lineup of American commercial cartridges. The .416 Taylor can also be used in a standard-length action. This gap has now been filled by Remington with its .416 Remington Magnum based on the 8mm Remington Magnum case, and by Weatherby with its new .416. In 1988, Federal introduced .416 Rigby ammunition, thus ending the shortage of .416 Rigby ammunition.
	The .416 Taylor can be considered something of a forerunner to the Remington .416, because it proved the feasibility and effectiveness of a new .416-caliber to replace the venerable .416 Rigby. The cases are easy to make, and RCBS (www.rcbs.com) can furnish loading dies. Originally, the problem was the availability of good .416-inch bullets. However, that deficiency has been eliminated by Barnes and Hornady. A-Square (www.a-squareco.com) currently furnishes rifles, cases, bullets, and loaded ammunition in .416 Taylor, so it has become a proprietary cartridge.

.416 Taylor Loading Data and Factory Ballistics

Bullet (grains/type)	Powder	Grains	Velocity	Energy	Source/Comments
400 SP	IMR 4320	70.0	2270	4595	NA
400 SP	IMR 4320	71.0	2305	4700	NA
400	FL		2350	4905	A-Square factory load

10.57 Maverick

Historical Notes:	Lazzeroni Arms designed this cartridge, in 1998. While somewhat related to an older case, for all practical purposes, this is a new case design. This cartridge was created in response to requests for a high-performance cartridge that would work in a 2.8-inch action and yet deliver the ballistics of a full-length belted magnum. Adaptation to a standard action is feasible, but is not recommended.
General Comments:	Bullet diameter is .416-inch (Lazzeroni bases its designations on bullet diameter, instead of bore diameter, which is the common practice.) Ballistics are quite impressive for such a short cartridge. Given equal-length barrels, the Maverick easily duplicates .416 Remington Magnum ballistics, although in a short-action rifle. Case design is typical of the Lazzeroni line: moderate body taper, 30-degree shoulder, sufficiently long neck, and thick rim of approximate case-body diameter. In other words, this is a

well-designed case. For those who feel .37-caliber rifles are a bit on the light side for dangerous-game hunting, this is a fine choice. For more information on Lazzeroni custom guns, ammunition, and reloading data, contact 888-492--7247; www.lazzeroni.com.

10.57 Maverick Factory Ballistics (24-inch barrel)

Bullet (grains)	Powder	Grains	Velocity	Energy	Source/Comments
400	FL		2400	5117	Lazzeroni factory load

.416 Hoffman

Historical Notes: The .416 Hoffman is another of the wildcat cartridges adopted by A-Square Co., with bullets and loaded ammunition currently available there. It originated with George L. Hoffman, of Sonora, Texas, in the late 1970s and is based on the necked-up and Improved .375 H&H Magnum case. Ballistically it duplicates the .416 Rigby and the .416 Taylor, except that the case is about 3/10-inch longer than the Taylor case and holds more powder. The cartridge case is of smaller base diameter than the Rigby, which allows an extra round to be carried in a magazine of equal size. A-Square can also furnish rifles of this caliber (www.a-squareco.com).

General Comments: The .416 Hoffman is the most practical of the .416 wildcats, because one can obtain all the components without the necessity of reworking .375 H&H cases. With its 400-grain bullet at 2400 fps, it is relatively flat shooting out to 200 yards and extremely accurate. It would be a good candidate for a one-gun cartridge to use on whatever Africa has to offer. Although overpowered for most North American big game, it would nevertheless do very well on moose or grizzly bear and could be loaded down for use on some of the smaller species. It is a very good cartridge for those who need or favor the .416-bore. Being very similar, Remington's .416 seems a superior option. For more informationon A-square custom rifles and ammunition, contact 605-234-0500 (South Dakota) or 307-436-5677 (Wyoming); www.a-squareco.com.

.416 Hoffman Loading Data and Factory Ballistics

Bullet (grains/type)	Powder	Grains	Velocity	Energy	Source/Comments
400 SP	IMR 4064	77.0	2400	5125	NA
400 SP	IMR 4895	74.0	2350	4910	NA
400 SP	IMR 4895	77.0	2425	5230	NA
400 SP	IMR 4320	77.0	2400	5125	NA
400 SP	IMR 4350	88.0	2375	5040	NA
400	FL		2400	5125	A-Square factory load

.416 Rimmed

Historical Notes: This cartridge was designed by A-Square, about 1991, at the behest of several Continental rifle makers. This is essentially a lengthened and rimmed .416 Rigby. Cartridge length (capacity) was chosen to allow 400-grain bullets to reach 2400 fps, with pressures that are acceptable in double rifles (about 40,000 psi). The basic design is quite good. For the first time, the hunter who prefers a double rifle in .41-caliber can achieve the vaunted ballistics of typical .41-caliber bolt-action rifle/cartridge combinations. Older .41-caliber double-rifle numbers fall short of this mark by several hundred feet per second.

General Comments: A-Square (www.a-squareco.com) specializes in cartridges and bullets intended for dangerous game applications. This new number is an interesting mix of old and new. Professional dangerous game hunters have long recognized that a muzzle velocity of about 2400 fps seems to be about ideal for these applications. Equally, the .41-caliber bore size launching 400-grain bullets has long been recognized as a fine combination. In guns of reasonable weight, recoil is manageable, while both delivered energy and penetration potential are significant. For more informationon A-square custom rifles and ammunition, contact 605-234-0500 (South Dakota) or 307-436-5677 (Wyoming); www.a-squareco.com.

.416 Rimmed Loading Data and Factory Ballistics

Bullet (grains/type)	Powder	Grains	Velocity	Energy	Source/Comments
400 Lion	IMR 7828	112	2437	5275	A-Square
400 Lion	RI-22	108	2402	5125	A-Square
400	FL		2400	5115	A-Square factory load

.416 BGA

Historical Notes: A large-bore, high performance cartridge, the .416 BGA was designed, in 2003, by Raymond Oelrich, publisher of Big Game Adventures magazine, as one of a family of proprietary BGA cartridges. The .416 BGA uses standard-length actions, bolt faces, and magazines. It is a competent peer to other .416 magnum cartridges. The cartridge should do well on elk, moose, bear, and large North American and African game, where reach and good retained energy are needed.

General Comments: The .416 BGA parent case is the European 9.3x64 manufactured to BGA proprietary specifications. The BGA cartridges are not offered for handloaders. Proprietary ammunition is available from two custom loading ammunition companies, A-Square (www.a-squareco.com) and Superior Ammo (www.superiorammo.com).

.416 BGA Factory Ballistics

Bullet (grains)	Powder	Grains	Velocity	Energy	Source/Comments
350	FL		2350	4291	Raymond Oelrich
400	FL		2200	4298	Raymond Oelrich

.416 Dakota

Historical Notes: The .416 Dakota uses a modified full-length .404 Jeffery case, which features a rim that is only slightly larger than the standard belted-magnum rim. In any given-length cartridge, use of the non-belted .404 Jeffery case offers about 15-percent more case capacity than the standard belted magnum. Because maximum case diameter is only slightly larger, one can retain full magazine capacity through minor magazine well modifications. Dakota designed its .416 to offer maximum .416-bore ballistics in a standard-size action.

General Comments: With about 15-percent more usable capacity, the .416 Dakota offers ballistic performance substantially superior to the .416 Remington Magnum. Lacking the belt, this cartridge also feeds better from the magazine and offers potentially superior accuracy. This cartridge requires use of a so-called magnum-length action (3.65 inches). Gunsmiths can easily rechamber most .416 Remington Magnum rifles to .416 Dakota. Restrictive laws often prohibit taking of dangerous game with cartridges of lesser caliber (although often there is no restriction on bullet weight, type, or velocity!), so the various .416s present themselves as a minimum-caliber alternative in some African countries. Many find the reduction in recoil, compared to larger bores shooting heavier bullets, a worthwhile advantage. When loaded with proper spitzer bullets, the .416 Dakota offers a trajectory similar to the .270 Winchester and can deliver energy levels at extended ranges that rival the muzzle energies of many magnum cartridges. However, even with an effective muzzle brake, recoil becomes a bit stiff in typical rifles. Contact Dakota Arms for more information, 605-347-4686; www.dakotaarms.com.

Bullet (grains)	Powder	Grains	Velocity	Energy	Source/Comments
400	IMR 4350	90.0	2489	5500	Dakota/maximum load
400	IMR 4831	95.0	2527	5670	Dakota/maximum load
400	RI-19	100.0	2558	5810	Dakota/maximum load
400	H4831	100.0	2556	5800	Dakota/maximum load
400	FL		2450	5330	Dakota factory load

10.57 Meteor

Historical Notes: Lazzeroni Arms designed this cartridge, in 1997. While somewhat related to an older case, for all practical purposes, this is a new case design. This cartridge was created to provide sufficient velocity for heavyweight hunting bullets to provide dependable expansion at intermediate ranges and to have sufficient energy for taking the largest species. Adaptation to standard actions is feasible, but is not recommended.

General Comments: Bullet diameter is .416-inch (Lazzeroni bases its designations on bullet diameter, instead of bore diameter, which is the common practice.) Ballistics equal or exceed any factory .41-caliber cartridge. Case design is typical of the Lazzeroni line: moderate body taper, 30-degree shoulder, sufficiently long neck, and thick rim of approximate case-body diameter. In other words, this is a well-designed case. Designed specifically for dangerous-game hunting, this cartridge is not recommended for any other use. A 24-inch barrel is standard. A longer barrel will not significantly improve ballistics. Muzzle energy approaches 7000 ft-lbs. Lazzeroni's full-length cartridge loadings use premium bullets from Nosler, Barnes, or Swift. These are the only bullets providing the necessary accuracy and terminal performance to meet Lazzeroni's strict requirements. For more information on Lazzeroni custom guns, ammunition, and reloading data, contact 888-492--7247; www.lazzeroni.com.

10.57 Meteor Factory Ballistics (24-inch barrel)

Bullet (grains/type)	Powder	Grains	Velocity	Energy	Source/Comments
300 Barnes X	FL		3100	6400	Lazzeroni factory load
400	FL		2750	6719	Lazzeroni factory load

.416 Barrett

Historical Notes: The .416 Barrett was developed by Pete Forrest, of Barrett Firearms, a well-known Tennessee manufacturer of bolt-action and semiautomatic rifles chambered for the .50 Browning Machine Gun cartridge. A number of rifles built by Barrett have been used successfully by American troops deployed in Iraq and Afghanistan. The .416 Barrett is the .50 BMG case shortened to a length of 3.273 inches and necked down to accept bullets of .416-inch diameter, the same diameter as bullets loaded in the .416 Remington Magnum and .416 Rigby. Shoulder angle of the case is 25 degrees. It was initially loaded with a solid bronze bullet of Very Low Drag (VLD) form weighing 395 grains. As of early 2009, Barrett, McMillan, and EDM Arms offer rifles chambered to .416 Barrett.

General Comments: How the performance of the .416 Barrett stacks up against the .50 BMG in performance depends on which loading of the .50 the .416 Barrett is compared. The Barrett cartridge is more accurate than standard military loadings of the Big Fifty, but, since that cartridge has proven to be capable of sub-minute-of-angle accuracy out to 1,000 yards when loaded with a match bullet such as the Hornady 750-grain V-Max, the accuracy potential of the two cartridges is probably about the same. Ballistic coefficient of the Barrett bullet is .730, lower than the 1.050 of the Hornady bullet. That, along with the additional weight of the latter, gives the larger caliber a considerable edge in downrange energy delivery. When the 395-grain VLD bullet of the .416 Barrett exits the muzzle at 3290 fps, its residual energy at 1,000 yards is 3710 ft-lbs. When the Hornady .50-caliber, 750-grain V-Max starts out at 2850 fps, it is packing 6900 ft-lbs at 1,000 yards. Bullet drop and wind deflection are also less for the .50 BMG. In the favor of the .416 Barrett is a lower level of recoil and less ammo weight, both important characteristics in a combat cartridge designed to be used in shoulder-fired weapons. Contact Barrett at 615-896-2938; www.barrett.net/.

.416 Barrett Loading Data and Factory Ballistics

Bullet (grains/type)	Powder	Grains	Velocity	Energy	Source
395 Solid VLD	FL		3290	9517	Barrett

.425 Express

Historical Notes: The .425 Express was developed as a joint effort between Cameron Hopkins and Whit Collins, with John French building the prototype rifle. The entire story was published in the May 1988 issue of Guns magazine. The cartridge is based on the .300 Winchester Magnum case shortened from 2.620 inches to 2.550 inches, then fire-formed in the .425 chamber. Loading dies are available from Redding Reloading Equipment (www.redding-reloading.com). The prototype rifle was built on a Ruger Model 77 action.

General Comments: The .425 Express fills a gap in the medium-bore cartridge lineup between the 3.75 Holland & Holland Magnum and the .458 Winchester Magnum. This cartridge fits standard-length bolt actions, such as the Winchester Model 70, 1917 Enfield, Mauser 98, or other similar-length actions. This cartridge uses either a 350-grain or a 400-grain bullet and has proven very effective on heavy African game. It is overpowered for most North American hunting, but would provide a margin of safety if going after brown bears in the far North. Colonel Charles Askins used the .425 Express very successfully on buffalo in Australia. A-Square (www.a-squareco.com) now loads .425 Express ammunition.

.425 Express Loading Data

Bullet (grains/type)	Powder	Grains	Velocity	Energy	Source/Comments
350 SP	IMR 4064	79.0	2535	5000	Cameron Hopkins
350 SP	H4895	77.0	2490	4825	Cameron Hopkins
350 SP	W760	77.0	2210	3795	Cameron Hopkins
400 SP	H4895	73.0	2420	5210	Cameron Hopkins
400 SP	IMR 4064	76.0	2370	4995	Cameron Hopkins
400 SP	W760	76.0	2155	4120	Cameron Hopkins

.440 CorBon

Historical Notes: CorBon designed this cartridge, in 1997, by the simple expedient of necking down the .50 Action Express to .44-caliber (actually, a .429-inch bullet). This case has a reasonably long neck. With the advent of the .50 AE and the existence of plentiful .44-caliber pistol bullets, this was an obvious choice for a high-performance hunting chambering geared toward those who prefer a semi-automatic handgun.

Compared to the parent case, this design offers several advantages. First, conversion of the gun is completed by a simple barrel replacement. Second, owing to the bottleneck, this cartridge can give better functioning with a wider variety of bullet shapes and is generally more forgiving toward machining, fit, and finish tolerances. Finally, for any given energy level, the .440 CorBon produces significantly less recoil than the .50 AE and shoots flatter (lighter bullets, launched faster). However, with top loads, the .440 cannot match the energy of the .50 AE.

General Comments: This is a very fine cartridge for those who do not like excessive recoil. Factory loads offer significant hunting handgun ballistics in a package that most shooters can easily learn to handle (providing only that they have large enough hands to properly hold the gun). Except for a flatter trajectory with the .440 CorBon, those who are satisfied with the .50 AE will probably find little appeal to this conversion. On the other hand, those who are dissatisfied with the .44 Magnum and who can handle the big AE pistol might find this a viable option. Cases are easily converted from .50 AE cases. This chambering offers the handloader a wide selection of bullets, which is not the case with the .50 AE. Ballistics of the .440 CorBon are essentially those of the .454 Casull. For more information on CorBon ammunition, contact 800-626-7266; www.shopcorbon.com

.440 CorBon Loading Data and Factory Ballistics

Bullet (grains)	Powder	Grains	Velocity	Energy	Source/Comments
240	H110 | W296	30.0	1800	1725	Cor-Bon
260	IMR 4227	27.5	1700	1665	Cor-Bon
240	FL		1900	1920	Cor-Bon factory load
260	FL		1700	1665	Cor-Bon factory load
305	FL		1600	1730	Cor-Bon factory load

.44/454 JDJ Woodswalker

Historical Notes: A big-bore, short-range hunting round from SSK Industries, the .44/454 JDJ Woodswalker is based on necking the powerful 454 Casull cartridge to 44-caliber. Barrels, dies, and cases for the 44/454 JDJ are available from SSK Industries (www.sskindustries.com).

General Comments: Using a .44-caliber, 300-grain Nosler projectile in modified .454 Casull cases and 15-inch SSK barrels, the .44/454 JDJ achieves about 2100 fps. With the Hornady 240-grain XTP bullet, it can reach 2300 fps. It is suitable for the Thompson/Center Encore.

.458 SOCOM

Historical Notes: After a bloody 1993 battle in Mogadishu, Somalia, several individuals addressed the opportunity to increase single-hit stopping power from the U.S. military's M-16 and M-4 family of rifles and carbines. Maarten ter Weeme (Teppo Jutsu LLC) developed the .458 SOCOM cartridge to provide the equivalent of .45-70 firepower from M-16 rifles. The .458 SOCOM hurls big chunks of metal at substantial velocity from unaltered lower receivers and magazines—in full auto and suppressed, if desired. During testing, the cartridge defeated Level IIIa protective vests.

General Comments: The .458 SOCOM uses the .50 AE as the parent case, lengthened to 1.575 inches (40mm) and necked to accept .458-inch bullets. It features a rebated .473-inch rim. It accepts readily available .458-caliber bullets ranging from 250 grains to 600 grains and in a wide variety of bullet styles and construction. Using standard M-16 lower receivers and unmodified magazines, 10 .458 SOCOM rounds will fit into a military 30-round M-16 magazine; the 20-round magazine will hold seven rounds. In 16-inch barreled rifles, the 600-grain subsonic load works well with a 1:14 rifling twist. The 300-grain bullets do better with a 1:18 twist. CorBon supplies loaded .458 SOCOM ammunition (www.shopcorbon.com); Starline offers new brass cases (ww.starlinebrass.com), CH4D lists reloading dies (www.ch4d.com); and Teppo Jutsu LLC provides reloading data (www.teppojutsu.com).

.458 SOCOM Factory Ballistics

Bullet (grains)	Powder	Grains	Velocity	Energy	Source/Comments
300	FL		2000		Teppo Jutsu LLC
500	FL		1300		Teppo Jutsu LLC

.458 Whisper

Historical Notes: Designed by J.D. Jones of SSK Industries, in 1993, this chambering uses a shortened .458 Winchester Magnum case. With custom 600-grain very low drag (VLD) bullets, this cartridge will function through standard-length magazines. The design intent was to create a hard-hitting subsonic round with superior penetration potential.

General Comments: This is a rather esoteric chambering. For proper use, it requires very expensive custom bullets. Nevertheless, ballistic consistency and accuracy are impressive. When launched at subsonic velocities (1040 fps is typical for the .458 Whisper), the long and heavy VLD bullet loses velocity so slowly that crosswinds have little effect. It also retains much of its muzzle energy beyond one mile! For information on components, loading data, barrels, and guns designed for this cartridge, contact SSK Inudstries, 720-264-0176; www.sskindustries.com.

.458 Whisper Loading Data

Bullet (grains/type)	Powder	Grains	Velocity	Energy	Source/Comments
500 H.T.	W231	15.6	1021	1155	SSK/Subsonic
560 H.T.	BlueDot	18.0	1101	1505	SSK/Subsonic
600 H.T.	AA 2015	27.0	1044	1450	SSK/Subsonic

.450 Assegai

Historical Notes: This cartridge was designed by A-Square, at the behest of several professional African hunters. The .450 Assegai case is similar to a lengthened, rimmed .416 Rigby case. This makes it suitable for application to double rifles. Cartridge length (capacity) was chosen to allow 500-grain bullets to reach 2400 fps with acceptable double rifle pressures (about 40,000 psi). The basic design is quite good. The hunter who prefers a double rifle in .45-caliber can achieve the vaunted ballistics of the best .45-caliber bolt-action rifle/cartridge combinations, with a case of reasonable capacity. Older .45-caliber double rifle numbers cannot achieve this velocity with acceptable pressures. The Assegai (pronounced, approximately, as AS-sa-guy) is the ancient stabbing spear of the Zulu, which makes this an interesting moniker for this thoroughly modern cartridge.

General Comments: This new number is an interesting mix of old and new. Professional dangerous-game hunters have long recognized that a muzzle velocity of about 2400 fps seems to be about ideal for these applications. Some prefer more bullet weight than smaller calibers can manage. Compared to the .41-caliber with a 400-grain bullet, the .45-caliber launching a 500-grain bullet has long been recognized as a fine combination for those who can handle the heavier rifle and increased recoil. A-Square (www.a-sqaureco.com) can supply brass. For more informationon A-square custom rifles and ammunition, contact 605-234-0500 (South Dakota) or 307-436-5677 (Wyoming); www.a-squareco.com.

Bullet (grains/type)	Powder	Grains	Velocity	Energy	Source/Comments
500 Lion	H4831	125	2480	6830	A-Square
500 Lion	IMR 4831	117	2379	6285	A-Square
500 Lion	RI-22	120	2378	6280	A-Square
500	FL		2400	6400	A-Square factory load

.450 Ackley Magnum

Historical Notes: The late, great gunsmith and master experimenter Parker Ackley designed this cartridge, about 1960. Ackley describes the genesis of the .458 Ackley as an effort to achieve maximum feasible case capacity using the full-length (2.85-inch) H&H belted magnum case necked to .45-caliber. Obviously, this required elimination of most of the case body taper and incorporation of a sharp case shoulder with a comparatively short neck. Ackley recognized that several others had designed very similar cartridges with the same goals and essentially identical results. A-Square (www.a-squareco.com), which now offers factory ammunition, adopted this chambering, about 1995.

General Comments: Compared to the tapered-case .458 Watts, this Ackley-designed number does achieve the same velocity with somewhat less pressure. Conversely, this cartridge does provide for slightly more muzzle velocity when loaded to any given peak chamber pressure. Ackley noted that any difference is essentially academic. All similar numbers can deliver similarly large doses of energy and recoil in guns of reasonable weight. According to Ackley, an advantage the .458 Watts has over this chambering is that one can safely fire .458 Winchester Magnum ammunition in the Watts chamber. Field testing has confirmed this. Further, Ackley reported that some users complained of limited case life with this number. Evidently, the modest case shoulder can allow excessive brass working during the firing and resizing cycle.

.450 Ackley Magnum Loading Data and Factory Ballistics

Bullet (grains/type)	Powder	Grains	Velocity	Energy	Source/Comments
465 Solid	H4895	86.0	2422	6055	A-Square
465 Solid	IMR 4064	86.0	2376	5830	A-Square
465 Solid	RI-12	88.0	2395	5925	A-Square
465 Solid	FL		2400	5950	A-Square factory load

.458 Canadian Magnum

Historical Notes: North American Shooting Systems (NASS) developed this cartridge, about 1994. This cartridge features a slightly rebated, rimless bottleneck case. Design intent was provision of maximum powder capacity in a standard action with minimal gunsmithing. (Without deepening the magazine well slightly, use of this cartridge usually reduces magazine capacity by one round.) Bolt face alteration is unnecessary. Cartridge feeding and headspacing characteristics are improved. This particular cartridge is factory loaded to modest pressures to provide proper functioning in the hottest climes—a worthwhile consideration.

General Comments: This cartridge takes advantage of the entire 3.65-inch magazine length of the long-action Remington M700 and similar rifles. This represents the maximum feasible bullet size for use in this beltless case—headspace control, while adequate, is marginal with such a narrow case shoulder (one would be well advised to avoid magnum-strength striker springs). Body diameter is significantly larger than the standard belted magnum (.544-inch versus .513-inch at the base). Re-chambering of nominal belted magnums with the same bore diameter is generally quite simple, requiring no other rifle alterations. For any given case length, capacity is about 15-percent greater than can be achieved with the belted version. Body taper is minimal and the case shoulder is comparatively sharp. However, neck length is sufficiently generous to provide good bullet purchase for hunting ammunition.

Bullet (grains)	Powder	Grains	Velocity	Energy	Source/Comments
500	IMR 4064	89.0	2360	6180	NASS/maximum
350	FL		2575	5150	NASS factory load

.450 Dakota

Historical Notes: Formerly, Dakota had based its entire cartridge line on the .404 Jeffery case. With the introduction of the .450 Dakota, that changed. Dakota's latest addition, the .450 Dakota, uses an Improved .416 Rigby case. Design purpose was to provide a cartridge capable of driving a 500-grain bullet at about 2400 fps with moderate chamber pressures.

General Comments: Since the .450 Dakota uses an Improved full-length .416 Rigby case, capacity is substantially identical to the .460 Weatherby Magnum. Obviously, if loaded to similar pressures, these two will produce similar ballistics. However, Dakota does not advocate loading this cartridge to full Weatherby pressures. The logic: By slightly reducing peak pressure, one can ease the effort of extracting a fired case. This approach also helps to minimize pressure excursions related to use under extreme tropical heat. Since that is what this cartridge was designed for, such an approach seems reasonable. When loaded to similar peak pressures, the .450 Dakota can propel a 500-grain bullet about 350 fps faster than the .458 Winchester Magnum. The nominal .450 Dakota loading gives up only about 150 fps to full-power .460 Weatherby loads. If one follows Dakota's advice, one ends up with a load propelling a 500-grain bullet at about 2450 fps. Most dangerous-game experts agree that 2450 fps is nearly the perfect muzzle velocity for maximizing terminal performance with solids. Because of its non-belted design, this cartridge offers superior functioning from a box magazine and can deliver superior accuracy. However, most would agree that recoil is a bit heavy for a day of shooting holes in paper targets. Contact Dakota Arms for more information, 605-347-4686; www.dakotaarms.com.

.450 Dakota Loading Data and Factory Ballistics

Bullet (grains)	Powder	Grains	Velocity	Energy	Source/Comments
400	RI-15	105.0	2732	6625	Dakota/maximum load
400	IMR 4064	105.0	2763	6775	Dakota/maximum load
400	IMR 4350	115.0	2650	6235	Dakota/maximum load
500	H4350	110.0	2460	6715	Dakota/maximum load
500	IMR 4350	110.0	2470	6770	Dakota/maximum load
500	IMR 4831	112.0	2444	6630	Dakota/maximum load
500	FL		2450	6663	Dakota factory load

.460 A-Square Short

Historical Notes: The A-Square series of cartridges was designed, in 1974, by Col. Arthur Alphin, in response to a hunting incident involving a Cape buffalo and a hunter equipped with a .458 Winchester Magnum. (Alphin first designed the .500 A-Square, with the purpose of providing maximum stopping power.) In order to gain more powder capacity and more power, all original A-Square cartridges were based upon the .460 Weatherby case.

General Comments: The .460 A-Square Short provides better ballistics than the .458 Winchester, but with the same length cartridge. It would be an excellent choice for re-chambering a .458 Winchester. Aside from re-chambering, this would require work on the magazine well and feed ramp, as well as opening up the bolt face. This cartridge can easily push a 500-grain bullet at velocities of 2400 fps or more. The .460 Short is an efficient cartridge, as well as a very accurate one. Groups tighter than one inch at 100 yards have been reported on numerous occasions. For more informationon A-square custom rifles and ammunition, contact 605-234-0500 (South Dakota) or 307-436-5677 (Wyoming); www.a-squareco.com.

Bullet (grains/type)	Powder	Grains	Velocity	Energy	Source/Comments
500 SP	IMR 4064	88.0	2385	6315	A-Square
500 SP	IMR 4895	91.0	2450	6670	A-Square
500 SP	IMR 4320	91.0	2435	6580	A-Square
500 SP	IMR 4320	91.0	2435	6580	A-Square

.475 Linebaugh

Historical Notes: The .475 Linebaugh is the creation of John Linebaugh, of Maryville, Missouri. It is a current favorite in the contest to develop the world's most powerful revolver cartridge, a role it fills rather well. The cartridge is based on the .45-70 government case cut off at 1½ inches and loaded with .475-inch diameter bullets weighing from 320 to 440 grains. The gun used is a modified, large-frame Ruger Bisley revolver fitted with a five-shot cylinder and 5½-inch barrel. Longer barrels are available if so desired. Freedom Arms (www.freedomearms.com) now chambers this round.

Cutting .45-70 cases to a length of 1½ inches is not a new idea—the original author of this book did this, back in 1984, to make the .45 Silhouette. However, adapting the 1½-inch rimmed case to handle .47-caliber bullets is definitely an innovative move.

The .475 Linebaugh was first announced in an article written by Ross Seyfried, in the May 1988 issue of Guns & Ammo magazine. Loading dies are available from RCBS (www.rcbs.com) and Redding (www.redding-reloading.com).

General Comments: The .475 Linebaugh, like all other super-magnum handgun cartridges, is intended primarily for hunting big game or as a backup when confronting dangerous animals. A 370-grain bullet starting out at 1495 fps develops 1840 ft-lbs of energy, and a 440-grain bullet at 1360 fps develops 1800 ft-lbs. This is 108 ft-lbs greater than top .454 Casull loadings, so we can accept the claim that the .475 Linebaugh is one of the world's most powerful revolver cartridge. However, other factors would probably make it even more effective, because the top energy load for the .454 Casull is a 260-grain bullet at 1723 fps muzzle velocity. If we compare the 300-grain .454 bullet at 1353 fps and 1220 ft-lbs, with the 370-grain .475 bullet at 1495 fps and 1840 ft-lbs, the difference is even more pronounced in favor of the .475. In fact, this works out to be 620 ft-lbs more energy on the side of the .475 Linebaugh. On the other hand, if we are talking about handgun cartridges in general, a number of silhouette cartridges fired in single-shot pistols produce more energy than the .475. In any event, the .475 Linebaugh should make a very fine big-game revolver cartridge for those who insist on the biggest or the most. Buffalo Bore (www.buffalobore.com) now offers factory loaded ammunition.

.475 Linebaugh Loading Data and Factory Ballistics

Bullet (grains/type)	Powder	Grains	Velocity	Energy	Source/Comments
370 SP	W296	25.0	1000	825	John Linebaugh
370 SP	H110	29.0	1285	1360	John Linebaugh
370 SP	H110	33.0	1495	1840	John Linebaugh
440 SP	W296	27.0	1280	1605	John Linebaugh
440 SP	W296	29.0	1360	1800	John Linebaugh
420 LFN	FL		950	840	Buffalo Bore factory load
420 LFN	FL		1350	1695	Buffalo Bore factory load
420 WFN	FL		1350	1695	Buffalo Bore factory load
440 ExWN	FL		1300	1650	Buffalo Bore factory load
350 JHP	FL		1500	1745	Buffalo Bore factory load
400 JFN	FL		1400	1740	Buffalo Bore factory load

.470 Capstick

Historical Notes: This cartridge was designed by Col. Arthur B. Alphin and is named after the famous author and African big-game hunter, Peter Capstick. It delivers the maximum possible power from the .375 H&H Magnum case size while retaining the greater magazine capacity of the H&H over the Weatherby or Rigby cartridges. The .475-inch diameter bullets deliver much more shock than the .458-caliber cartridges. The .470 Capstick is designed for heavy game out to 200 yards, and dangerous game at close ranges. Trajectory is flat enough to allow taking medium-size game at ranges up to 250 yards.

General Comments: The .470 Capstick was designed to deliver 500-grain bullets at a muzzle velocity of approximately 2400 fps. It offers a muzzle energy of 6394 ft-lbs and retains well over 5200 ft-lbs of energy at 100 yards. The .470 Capstick is nearly identical in dimensions to the .475 Ackley Magnum, designed quite a few years prior. Probably the most notable difference is the use of a 500-grain bullet in the .470 Capstick (as opposed to a 600-grain bullet), in order to obtain a flatter trajectory. Capstick was a legend in his own time and did much to promote African hunting. He certainly deserves to have a cartridge with his name on it.

.470 Capstick Loading Data and Factory Ballistics

Bullet (grains/type)	Powder	Grains	Velocity	Energy	Source/Comments
500 Solid	H4895	85.0	2387	6325	A-Square/maximum load
500 Solid	RI-12	89.5	2410	6450	A-Square/maximum load
500 Solid	IMR 4064	88.0	2404	6420	A-Square/maximum load
500 Solid	RI-15	91.0	2385	6315	A-Square/maximum load
500	FL		2400	6400	A-Square factory load

.475 JDJ

Historical Notes: This cartridge was designed and developed by J.D. Jones, hence the JDJ designation. Jones began development of his series of cartridges, in 1978. They are generally fired in barrels furnished by his company, SSK Industries. The purpose of these cartridges is to give added range and power to the Thompson/Center Contender pistol for the primary purpose of hunting. Some of Jones' cartridges have proven to be excellent metallic silhouette cartridges. The JDJ series is relatively simple and easy to make. All of the JDJ cartridges are proprietary, and SSK neither sells reamers nor permits the reamer maker to sell them. If you desire a JDJ cartridge, contact SSK Industries (www.sskindustries.com).

General Comments: The .475 JDJ is the first .475-caliber handgun cartridge. It is made by straightening out the tapered .45-70 Government case to a straight-wall configuration. This is easily done by expanding the neck and firing a .475-inch bullet. Cast bullets work very well in this cartridge, and many good designs are available. Standard .475-inch rifle bullets will not expand reliably. However, a .475-inch diameter 500-grain bullet pushed at 1650 fps does expand—big animals fall down quickly. Jones has taken several buffalo with the .475. When properly loaded, it is very impressive on animals in the 2,000-pound category. It is noticeably more effective than the .45-70 Government, when loaded correctly. Recoil exceeds what most shooters can tolerate. On deer, 400-grain Horrnady pistol bullets deliver excellent results. For information on components, loading data, barrels, and guns designed for this cartridge, contact SSK Inudstries, 720-264-0176; www.sskindustries.com.

Bullet (grains/type)	Powder	Grains	Velocity	Energy	Source/Comments
298 Cast	H322	54.0	Fire-forming	N/A	SSK Industries, Inc.
400 Hornady	2015BR	53.0	Not Specified	N/A	SSK Industries, Inc.
440	H322	54.0	1727	N/A	SSK Industries, Inc.
500 Cast	IMR 3031	48.5	1338	N/A	SSK Industries, Inc.
500 Woodleigh	IMR 3031	48.5	1140	N/A	SSK Industries, Inc.

12.04 Bibamufu

Historical Notes: Lazzeroni Arms designed this cartridge, in 1999, at the request of world hunter and famed gun writer Col. Craig Boddington. While somewhat related to an older case, for all practical purposes, this is a new case design. This cartridge was created to provide sufficient velocity for heavyweight hunting bullets to deliver significant doses of energy to the world's biggest and most dangerous game. Adaptation to standard actions is feasible, but is not recommended.

General Comments: Bullet diameter is .475-inch (Lazzeroni bases its designation on bullet diameter, instead of bore diameter, which is the common practice). Ballistics are impressive. Case design is typical of the Lazzeroni line: moderate body taper, 30-degree shoulder, sufficiently long neck, and thick rim of approximate case-body diameter. As produced, the case shoulder is sufficiently hard and thick to provide adequate headspace control. However, the margin of strength is small enough to suggest that one should not anneal these cases. Designed specifically for dangerous-game hunting, this cartridge makes no sense for any other purpose. Recoil is significant by any measure. A 24-inch barrel is standard, and adding a few inches of barrel length will not significantly improve ballistics. Muzzle energy exceeds 7505 ft-lbs. Ammunition is offered only as a special-order item and can be equipped with any bullet the customer desires. For more information on Lazzeroni custom guns, ammunition, and reloading data, contact 888-492--7247; www.lazzeroni.com.

12.04 Bibamufu Factory Ballistics (24-inch barrel)

Bullet (grains)	Powder	Grains	Velocity	Energy	Source/Comments
500	FL		2600	7505	Lazzeroni factory load

.500 Wyoming Express

Historical Notes: This large-capacity revolver cartridge was introduced, in 2005, by Freedom Arms to be chambered in the FA Model 83 single-action revolver. The 1.370-inch case is belted to provide reliable headspacing in the Model 83 revolver. Freedom Arms designed the case to minimize forcing cone erosion by matching powder column length, volume, and bullet diameter with bullet weights, pressure levels, and velocity ranges.

General Comments: Case shortening and slight belt expansion is normal with maximum loads. Tests show as much as .002-inch expansion on the first firing, with much less expansion on subsequent firings, for a total expansion of about .003-inch after 10 firings with the case still usable. More than .004-inch expansion may render the case unusable, because of interference between the belt and chamber headspace area. This cartridge was designed to use bullets weighing from 350 to 450 grains. Freedom Arms does not recommend using bullets outside this weight range. Maximum loads should not be exceeded, because small increases in the powder charge can cause a dramatic increase in chamber pressure. Powder charges in reduced loads should not be below 90 percent of case capacity. The .500 WE is designed to use a Large Rifle primer for reliable and consistent ignition. Freedom Arms can be contacted at 307-883-2468; www.freedomarms.com.

.500 Wyoming Express Loading Data

Bullet (grains/type)	Powder	Grains	Velocity	Energy	Source/Comments
350 XTP	TrailBoss	10.0	831	537	Freedom Arms
370WFNGC	Li'lGun	31.0	1528	1918	Freedom Arms
370WFNGC	H4227	34.0	1535	1936	Freedom Arms
370WFNGC	H110	36.0	1607	2122	Freedom Arms
400WFNGC	Li'lGun	31.0	1565	2175	Freedom Arms
400WFNGC	H4227	33.0	1509	2022	Freedom Arms
400FWNGC	H110	34.5	1589	2242	Freedom Arms
440WFNGC	Li'lGun	28.0	1450	2054	Freedom Arms
440WFNGC	H4227	30.0	1413	1951	Freedom Arms
440FWNGC	H110	29.5	1415	1956	Freedom Arms

.510 GNR

Historical Notes: The 510 GNR is the largest caliber proprietary handgun cartridge designed by Gary Reeder, who chambers it in specially prepared Ruger Blackhawk and Super Blackhawk revolvers. In 2002, Reeder designed this cartridge to accommodate a loading range varying from the 50 Special to the 500 Linebaugh. At the top end loading, recoil is somewhat less than the 500 Linebaugh. Hunters have used the 510 GNR to take large Alaskan bear and African dangerous game.

General Comments: The 510 GNR uses 500 Linebaugh brass as the parent case shortened by .100-inch – about the same length as a 44 Magnum case. The 510 GNR works well in heavy-duty single-action revolvers with five-shot cylinders and five-inch barrels. Custom loaded ammunition (varying from mild to hot) is available from Cartridge Performance Engineering. Correctly headstamped brass, dies, firearms, reloading components and information are available from Reeder Custom Guns. Ballistic data was recorded in a five-inch custom revolver barrel. Note: H4227 loads are based on crimping the LBT bullet at the first lube groove to increase internal powder capacity.

510 GNR Loading Data

Bullet (grains/type)	Powder	Grains	Velocity	Energy	Source/Comments
350-gr LBT	Win 296	30.0	1250		Gary Reeder
350-gr LBT	H4227	34.0	1320		Gary Reeder
435-gr LBT	H4227	32.0	1200		Gary Reeder

.50 Beowulf

Historical Notes: In 1999, Bill Alexander (Alexander Arms) designed the .50 Beowulf to be the biggest possible cartridge that could be chambered in the AR-15 family of rifles and carbines. No contemporary cartridges existed at the time Bill re-worked the .50 AE parent cartridge case, extended it slightly and rebating the rim to fit an AR-15 bolt face. For close range and brush hunting, the .50 Beowulf is superbly suited for wild hogs and even larger game.

General Comments: The .50 Beowulf delivers exceptional stopping power at short to medium ranges using ½-inch diameter bullets ranging in weight from 325 grains to 400 grains at velocities from 1900 to 2050 fps. The .50

Beowulf shares the .445-inch case rim dimension with the military 7.63x39 cartridge case. Seven cartridges will fit into an Alexander Arms-supplied magazine dimensioned to fit into the magazine well of an AR15's lower. The cartridge performs well in a 16-inch barrel using a 1:19 twist. Factory loads do not exceed 33,000 psi. Alexander Arms (www.alexanderarms.com) supplies rifles, magazines, ammunition, reloading dies, and brass.

.50 Beowulf Factory Ballistics

Bullet (grains/type)	Powder	Grains	Velocity	Energy	Source/Comments
300r Gold Dot	FL		1900	2404	Alexander Arms
325 Unicor	FL		1950	2743	Alexander Arms
334 HP	FL		1900	2677	Alexander Arms
334 FMJ	FL		1900	2677	Alexander Arms
400 SP	FL		1800	2877	Alexander Arms

.50 GI

Historical Notes: Frustrated by laws that banned .50-caliber handguns in his native Denmark, Alex Zimmerman created the proprietary .50 GI cartridge, in 2002, Zimmerman having moved to the United States a decade earlier. First seen publicly at the 2004 SHOT Show, the .50 GI cartridge is not a magnum cartridge. Zimmerman engineered a 1911-style pistol and .50 GI cartridge combination to achieve highly controllable knock-down power for self-defense and IPSC shooting.

General Comments: One .50 GI factory load drives a 300-grain bullet at 700 to 725 fps (translating into a 210 power factor), with felt recoil comparable to a 230-grain .45 ACP hardball round. For serious stopping power, a second factory load drives a 275-grain bullet at 875 fps, with felt recoil similar to a 10mm. With hotter loads, the .50 GI is suitable for feral hog and deer hunting at moderate ranges. To fit 1911 frames and slides, the .50 GI cartridge features a .45 ACP base and rim on a proprietary cartridge case manufactured by Starline (www.starlinebrass.com). This feature allows the use of a standard .45 breech face, extractor, and ejector on 1911-style pistols. Changing a Guncrafters Industries (www.guncraftersindustries.com) .50 GI-chambered pistol to .45 ACP requires only a different barrel and magazine. A firm taper crimp must be applied when reloading the .50 GI, and finished cartridges should measure .5235/.5240-inch at the case mouth. Guncrafter Industries offers 1911-type pistols, ammo, empty cases, reloading dies and magazines for the 50 GI cartridge. Hornady (www.hornady.com) and Lee Precision (www.leeprecision.com) sell reloading dies.

.50 GI Loading Data

Bullet (grains/type)	Powder	Grains	Velocity	Energy	Source/Comments
275 GI HP (copper clad)	Herco	8.0	875	467	Factory Load
300 GI FP (copper clad)	Titegroup	5.1	700	326	Factory Load
300 IMI JHP	Titegroup	5.9	800	426	OAL 1.220 "
240 Lead SWC	VV N310	4.4	750	299	OAL 1.230 "
300 Speer TMJ	Herco	8.0	875	509	OAL 1.220 "

.500 Phantom

Historical Notes: In 2005, Maarten ter Weeme (Teppo Jetsu, LLC) and Garber Supply Co. jointly created the .500 Phantom, specifically for AR-10 firearms. The .500 Phantom is the largest cartridge case that will function through

the AR-10 action. The case design accommodates a wide range of .50-caliber bullet weights, including match-grade projectiles and smaller calibers in sabots. It produces velocity levels varying from 2000 fps to subsonic. The .500 Phantom is intended for law enforcement and special operations applications.

General Comments: The .500 Phantom cartridge uses a special .50-caliber non-belted short magnum brass case manufactured by Garber Supply Company, with a rebated head and strengthened web for the higher operating pressures. Factory bolt faces for WSM or RSAUM cases readily accept the .500 Phantom cartridge case. Remarkably, unmodified .308 Winchester magazines can accept eight .500 Phantom rounds, and AR-10 lower receivers require no modification. Suitable firearms for the .500 Phantom include the AR-10 and DPMS LR-308 rifles. Teppo Jutsu LLC (www.teppojutsu.com) offers AR-10 upper receivers and information on the .500 Phantom. Both Quality Cartridge (www.qual-cart.com) and Reed's Ammunition & Research (www.reedsammo.com) sell loaded ammunition. New brass and loading data are available from Garber Supply Co (gsc.feistyrooster.com).

.500 Phantom Factory Ballistics

Bullet (grains/type)	Powder	Grains	Velocity	Energy	Source/Comments
525 Barnes RN	FL		2,000	4,664	Teppo Jutsu LLC
750 HornadyA-Max	FL		1040	1802	Teppo Jutsu LLC

.500 Whisper

Historical Notes: Designed by J.D. Jones, in 1993, at SSK Industries, this chambering is based upon a shortened .460 Weatherby Magnum case. Custom very low drag (VLD) bullets up to 900 grains have been tested. Design intent was to create a very hard-hitting subsonic round with superior penetration potential for use against lightly armored vehicles.

General Comments: This is a very esoteric chambering. For proper use, it requires expensive custom bullets. Nevertheless, ballistic consistency and accuracy are impressive when launched at subsonic velocities (1040 fps is typical for the .500 Whisper). Typical heavy VLD bullets lose velocity so slowly that crosswinds have little effect, and retained energy exceeds one-half of muzzle energy well beyond one mile. Yes, such bullets will travel that far with exceedingly good accuracy! For information on components, loading data, barrels, and guns designed for this cartridge, contact SSK Inudstries, 720-264-0176; www.sskindustries.com.

.500 Whisper Loading Data

Bullet (grains)	Powder	Grains	Velocity	Energy	Source/Comments
650 to 750	Vit N110	36.6	1050	1590/1835	SSK/Load must be tuned to individual gun

.500 Linebaugh

Historical Notes: The .500 Linebaugh is the design creation of John Linebaugh, of Maryville, Missouri. Linebaugh started out by converting a .45 Colt revolver from six-shot to five-shot, thus offering more strength in the cylinder. It was a successful venture, but he continued to search for a more powerful handgun. The result is the .500 Linebaugh. The .500 Linebaugh is based on the .348 Winchester cartridge, which is cut down to 1½ inches and reamed to .50-caliber. He uses a large-frame Ruger Bisley revolver, as he has found the Ruger frame is the only one that can withstand the severe recoil of this cartridge. He replaces the Ruger barrel with one of .50-caliber, usually 5½ inches long. However, he will cut a barrel of any length the customer desires.

The .500 proved to be a very successful round, pushing 500-grain bullets at more than 1200 fps. Accuracy is outstanding, but recoil can only be described as severe. Not long after Linebaugh designed this cartridge, the supply of .348 Winchester cases began to dry up, which is why he designed the .475 Linebaugh based on the readily available .45-70 Government case. Not long after the .475 was designed, Browning reintroduced its Model 1871 rifle in .348 Winchester, and so those cases are again readily available.

General Comments: There are more powerful pistol cartridges, but primarily for single-shot handguns, such as the T/C Contender. When it comes to the revolver, this is close to the ultimate in power. Generally, in these revolvers, the .475 Linebaugh can safely be loaded to higher pressure and, therefore, can deliver more energy. Due to its accuracy and easy handling, this cartridge could prove to be an excellent heavy-game handgun cartridge and possibly a revolver cartridge suitable for taking African game. Specialized bullets are made by Bear Ammunition (www.dkgtrading.com). The jackets for these bullets are turned on a screw machine, and a lead core is swaged in. These bullets have been found to be excellent performers in terms of both accuracy and penetration. The .500 Linebaugh should find a strong following in the wilds of Alaska or the plains of Africa, where it could be used as a primary hunting gun or a backup. Buffalo Bore (www.buffalobore.com) offers factory-loaded ammunition.

.500 Linebaugh Loading Data and Factory Ballistics

Bullet (grains/type)	Powder	Grains	Velocity	Energy	Source/Comments
400 Cast	H110	27.0	1200	1280	John Linebaugh
410 SP	H110	29.0	1250	1425	John Linebaugh
410 SP	H110	31.0	1320	1590	John Linebaugh
500 SP	FL		1200	1599	John Linebaugh
435 LFN	FL		950	870	Buffalo Bore factory load
435 LFN	FL		1300	1630	Buffalo Bore factory load
440 WFN	FL		1300	1650	Buffalo Bore factory load
400 JHP	FL		1400	1740	Buffalo Bore factory load

.495 A-Square

Historical Notes: The A-Square series of cartridges was designed, in 1974, by Col. Arthur Alphin, as a result of a hunting incident with Cape buffalo using the .458 Winchester Magnum. Alphin first designed the .500 A-Square to provide maximum stopping power. In order to gain more powder capacity and more power, all original A-Square cartridges were based on the .460 Weatherby case. A-Square (www.a-squareco.com) offers cases and loaded ammunition for each of the A-Square cartridges.

General Comments: The .495 A-Square was designed to push 600-grain, .510-inch bullets from a cartridge that could be used in .375 Magnum-length actions. Though the .495 A-Square may not have as much energy as the .460 Weatherby, it does have the advantage of a larger diameter bullet. For a .50-caliber cartridge, recoil is reported as relatively low. It has also been reported that this cartridge does well with cast bullets. For more informationon A-square custom rifles and ammunition, contact 605-234-0500 (South Dakota) or 307-436-5677 (Wyoming); www.a-squareco.com.

.495 A-Square Loading Data

Bullet (grains/type)	Powder	Grains	Velocity	Energy	Source/Comments
600 SP	IMR 4895	100.0	2275	6890	A-Square
600 SP	IMR 4320	103.0	2280	6925	A-Square

.500 A-Square

Historical Notes: The A-Square series of cartridges was designed, in 1974, by Col. Arthur Alphin, after a hunting incident with Cape buffalo using the .458 Winchester Magnum. Alphin first designed the .500 A-Square to provide maximum stopping power. In order to gain more powder capacity and more power, all original A-Square cartridges were based on the .460 Weatherby case. A-Square Co. (www.a-squareco. com) offers cases and loaded ammunition for each of the A-Square cartridges.

General Comments: The .500 A-Square requires a long magazine (3.77 inches, same as a .416 Rigby and .460 Weatherby). This cartridge delivers high energy and stopping power from a bolt-action rifle. This was Alphin's first design and is based on the .460 Weatherby cartridge necked up and blown out. Alphin reports that this cartridge is the backbone and main reason for the formation of the A-Square Co., in 1979. In addition to custom rifles made for this caliber, A-Square makes its own rifles so chambered. The .500 A-Square is an excellent choice for a backup rifle and has stopping power about equal to the .577 Nitro Express. Naturally, recoil from this dangerous-game cartridge can be extremely heavy. For more information on A-square custom rifles and ammunition, contact 605-234-0500 (South Dakota) or 307-436-5677 (Wyoming); www.a-squareco.com.

.500 A-Square Loading Data

Bullet (grains/type)	Powder	Grains	Velocity	Energy	Source/Comments
600 SP	IMR 4320	116.5	2475	8155	A-Square

.50 Peacekeeper

Historical Notes: This cartridge was designed by J.D. Jones, of SSK Industries, in 1999. This is simply the .460 Weatherby Magnum necked up to .50-caliber with no other changes. Therefore, this is nothing new—this case is essentially identical to the .500 A-Square. What is unique about the .50 Peacekeeper are the loads used and the intended purpose. This combination is specifically designed to launch heavy, long-range match bullets from highly accurate rifles of moderate weight. It is intended to compete directly with the various 30-pound class of .50 BMG-chambered rifles. Fired from a rifle of about half that weight, recoil energy is similar—bullets are launched at somewhat less velocity, but using much less powder.

General Comments: Muzzle ballistics are sufficient to suggest that this number is worth considering for those who believe they need a .50 BMG-class rifle. Several rifles will easily handle this cartridge in single-shot mode: Ruger M-77 Magnum, Sako large action, Weatherby large action, Ed Brown action, and Prairie Gun Works' new action (which will also feed this round from the magazine). The .50 Peacekeeper can be chambered in the large Sako action. For information on components, loading data, barrels, and guns designed for this cartridge, contact SSK Inudstries, 720-264-0176; www.sskindustries.com.

.50 Peacekeeper Loading Data (23-inch barrel)

Bullet (grains/type)	Powder	Grains	Velocity	Energy	Source/Comments
650 Ball	H335	108	2350	7975	SSK/maximum load
700 AP	AA 2700	117	2200	7525	SSK/maximum load
750 A-Max	AA 2520	105	2205	8100	SSK/maximum load

.510 Whisper

Historical Notes: Created by J. D. Jones, the .510 Whisper, like all other Whisper cartridges, must be capable of subsonic extreme accuracy with very heavy bullets, while maintaining excellent accuracy with light bullets at moderate to high velocities. Barrels, dies, and cases for the .510 Whisper are available from SSK Industries (www.sskindustries.com).

General Comments: Using a .338 Lapua case shortened to 1.875 inches and necked up to .50-caliber, the .510 Whisper launches a 750-grain Hornady A-Max projectile at just under 1050 fps. The case neck is turned for accuracy and to create a shoulder for headspacing. SSK testing in suppressed, re-barreled, SAKO TRG-S rifles achieved MOA accuracy at 600 yards, with occasional groups of ½ MOA. For information on components, loading data, barrels, and guns designed for this cartridge, contact SSK Inudstries, 720-264-0176; www.sskindustries.com.

.50 American Eagle

Historical Notes: SSK Industries designed the .50 American Eagle for a single-shot M-16 rifle in suppressed applications. Barrels, dies, and cases for the .50 American Eagle are available from SSK Industries (www.sskindustries.com).

General Comments: Using a .50-caliber 650-grain projectile in Speer .50 AE cases opened to accept .510-inch bullets, the .50 American Eagle achieves about 1000 fps. Case heads are reduced in diameter to fit 7.62x39-sized bolt faces in the M-16. It is suitable for the Thompson/Center Encore, AR-15, bolt-action firearms, and Ruger No. 1 rifles.

.577 Tyrannosaur

Historical Notes: This entirely new cartridge was designed, in 1993, in response to the demands of two professional African hunting guides who'd had bad experiences with lesser chamberings as backup guns when clients were hunting dangerous species. There is no secret to the design: This is the longest, largest-diameter case that will properly function through a standard-size, bolt-action rifle. Bullet diameter is limited by the necessity of a sufficient case shoulder to control headspace. Design pressure assures proper functioning in even the hottest climes and will not overstress the action.

General Comments: Case capacity is on par with the .600 Nitro Express. When loaded to .30-30 Winchester pressure levels, this cartridge can develop 10,000 ft-lbs of muzzle energy. When chambered in a 13-pound rifle with a properly designed stock containing three mercury recoil suppressers, recoil of the .577 Tyrannosaur is claimed to be less punishing than Weatherby's Mark V chambered for the much less powerful .460 WM. Nevertheless, by no means should one call this a "mildly recoiling" combination. For those looking for the ultimate in affordable, repeating rifle firepower, the .577 is the factory option of choice. Compared to purchasing a typical top-quality, big-bore British double rifle, one could buy several .577 Tyrannosaurs, a lifetime supply of .577 ammunition, and a new 4x4 pickup to haul the lot around in—with considerable leftover change!

.577 Tyrannosaur Loading Data and Factory Ballistics

Bullet (grains/type)	Powder	Grains	Velocity	Energy	Source/Comments
750 Monolithic Solid	RI-19	177.5	2473	10,180	A-Square/max. load
750 Monolithic Solid	FL		2400	9590	A-Square factory load

14.5 JDJ

Historical Notes: The 14.5 JDJ, the latest in an amazing series of big-bore boomers from J.D. Jones, uses the .50 BMG case with the neck expanded and case fire-formed to launch .585-inch diameter bullets at high velocities. Using a quality McMillan bolt-action built into an SSK rifle, the 14.5 JDJ is capable of achieving sub-MOA groups at 1,000 yards using SSK Industries CNC-machined bronze bullets. A 2005 offering from SSK Industries (www.sskindustries.com), the 14.5 JDJ cartridge should be considered as the very top end of proprietary cartridges based on the .50 BMG parent case. It can accommodate bullet weights ranging from 750 grains to 1,200 grains and works well with powders suitable for .50 BMG.

General Comments: Rifles for the 14.5 JDJ are strictly custom creations and can use only those actions suitable for the .50 BMG cartridge. The 14.5 JDJ can be quite expensive to own and shoot. A typical 14.5 JDJ rifle will weigh about 42 pounds with the recommended 36-inch barrel and muzzle brake. SSK possesses a BATFE destructive device exemption for the 14.5 JDJ cartridge, which enables the company to manufacture this cartridge and rifles chambered for it. Interestingly, the Barnes 750-grain bullet can be driven faster than 3000 fps. Listed reloading data are the fireforming loads. SSK Industries (www.sskindustries.com) offers rifles, reloading dies, bullets, and loading data.

14.5 JDJ Loading Data and Factory Ballistics

Bullet (grains/type)	Powder	Grains	Velocity	Energy	Source/Comments
750 Barnes	FL		3000	14986	SSK Industries
750 Barnes	5010	250.0	2900	14004	SSK Industries
1,173 SSK Bronze	5010	235.0	2600	17605	SSK Industries

.600/577 JDJ

Historical Notes: Long considered the epitome of big-bore elephant cartridges, the .577 Nitro Express was chambered by premier English gun-makers in top-end double rifles. The .600/577 JDJ, as crafted by SSK Industries, expands the .577 Nitro case to a straight taper to accept .620-inch diameter bullets.

General Comments: The .600/577 JDJ fires a 900-grain bullet at approximately 1800 fps. Muzzle brakes and hydraulic counter-coil recoil-reducing devices are highly recommended in this caliber. It can be chambered in suitably converted Ruger No. 1 rifles. The BATFE does not classify this cartridge as a destructive device. For information on components, loading data, barrels, and guns designed for this cartridge, contact SSK Inudstries, 720-264-0176; www.sskindustries.com.

.700 JDJ

Historical Notes: Prolific cartridge designer J.D. Jones created the .700 JDJ, in 1995. Using a .50-caliber BMG case necked up to .70-caliber, the .700 JDJ launches an 1100-grain projectile at about 2200 fps.

General Comments: The .700 JDJ is still in production and can be chambered in any action suitable for the .50 BMG cartridge. SSK Industries uses special-order Krieger barrels for the .700 JDJ. The BATFE does not classify this cartridge as a destructive device. For information on components, loading data, barrels, and guns designed for this cartridge, contact SSK Inudstries, 720-264-0176; www.sskindustries.com.

.950 JDJ

Historical Notes: At .95-caliber, this cartridge defines the upper limit of rifle cartridges. As its creator, J.D. Jones described that the .950 JDJ it is not for the faint of heart, nor the financially-challenged shooter. The cartridge is based on the 20mm Vulcan case fired in rotary barrel cannon on U.S. Air Force fighter aircraft. Using a shortened, bottlenecked 20mm case, the .950 JDJ launches a 3,600-grain projectile at approximately 2200 fps.

General Comments: Developed in 1996, the .950 JDJ is no longer in production. SSK Industries developed a few custom rifles in the chambering, using super-sized McMillan single-shot rifles and Krieger special-order barrels. When completed, these bolt-action rifles looked like .50-caliber rifles on steroids, weighing between 100 and 110 pounds. The muzzle brake alone weighed about 18 pounds, but, even so, recoil was brisk. The BATFE does not classify this cartridge as a destructive device. For information on components, loading data, barrels, and guns designed for this cartridge, contact SSK Inudstries, 720-264-0176; www.sskindustries.com.

Cartridge	Case	Bullet Dia.	Neck Dia.	Shoulder Dia.	Base Dia.	Rim Dia.	Rim Thick.	Case Length	Ctge. Length	Primer	Page
.222 Remington Rimmed	A	.224	.253	.357	.375	.440	.049	1.700	2.130	S	249
.226 JDJ	A	.224	.256	.410	.419	.467	.045	1.93	V	L	249
6 Whisper	C	.243	UNK	UNK	.370	.375	.040	UNK	UNK	UNK	250
6mm JDJ	A	.243	.272	.415	.421	.470	.045	1.905	2.65	L	250
6.17 Spitfire	C	.243	.275	.510	.530	.530	.050	2.05	2.8	L	251
6.17 Flash	C	.243	.275	.510	.530	.530	.050	2.80	3.55	L	251
.255 Banshee	A	.257	.278	.297	.298	.345	.050	1.335	1.80	S	252
.257 Raptor	C	.257	.283	.370	.376	.378	.045	1.860	2.135	S	252
.257 JDJ	A	.257	.288	.415	.421	.473	.045	1.905	2.81	L	253
.25-06 JDJ	C	.257	UNK	UNK	.440	.468	.045	UNK	UNK	UNK	253
.257 Mini Dreadnaught	G	.257	.290	.425	.445	.467	.045	2.145	V	L	253
6.53 Scramjet	C	.257	.289	.510	.530	.530	.055	2.80	3.575	L	254
6.5mm Whisper	C	.264	.286	.357	.372	.375	.041	1.36	V	S	254
6.5X25 CBJ	C	.264	.287	.379	.390	.393	.049	.984	1.169	S	255
6.5mm JDJ	A	.264	.293	.410	.419	.467	.045	1.93	V	L	256
6.5mm JDJx30	A	.264	.285	.409	.419	.497	.058	2.03	V	L	256
6.5 Mini Dreadnaught	G	.263	.296	.425	.445	.467	.045	2.150	V	L	257
6.5mm JDJ No. 2	A	.264	.292	.450	.466	.502	.059	2.00	V	L	258
6.5/270 JDJ	C	.264	UNK	UNK	.440	.468	.045	UNK	UNK	UNK	258
6.71 Phantom	C	.264	.297	.510	.530	.530	.055	2.05	2.8	L	258
6.71 Blackbird	C	.264	.297	.524	.544	.544	.055	2.80	3.575	L	259
.270 JDJ	A	.277	.305	.415	.419	.467	.045	1.905	2.875	L	259
.270 JDJ No. 2	C	.277	UNK	UNK	.440	.468	.045	UNK	UNK	UNK	260
7mm Whisper	C	.284	.306	.357	.372	.375	.041	1.36	V	S	260
7mm JDJ	A	.284	.312	.415	.421	.473	.045	1.905	V	L	261
7mm-30 JDJ	A	.284	.306	.409	.419	.497	.058	2.03	V	L	261
7mm JDJ No. 2	A	.284	.313	.450	.466	.502	.059	2.00	V	L	261
.280 GNR	A	.284	.316	.448	.463	.543	.075	2.525	3.0	L	262
7mm GNR	A	.284	.312	.400	.420	.502	.058	2.055	2.65	L	263
.280 JDJ	C	.284	.312	.455	.470	.467	.045	2.505	V	L	263
7.21 Tomahawk	C	.284	.318	.557	.577	.577	.060	2.05	2.80	L	264
7mm Dakota	C	.284	.314	.531	.544	.544	.042	2.50	3.33	L	265
7mm Canadian Magnum	I	.284	.322	.530	.544	.532	.046	2.83	3.60	L	265
7.21 Firehawk	C	.284	.318	.524	.544	.544	.055	2.80	3.55	L	266
7.21 Firebird	C	.284	.318	.557	.577	.577	.060	2.80	3.6	L	267
7.62 Micro-Whisper	C	.308	.328	.382	.389	.392	.045	.846	V	SP/S	267
7.63 Mini-Whisper	C	.308	.329	.375	.381	.385	.045	.985	V	SP/S	268
.300 Whisper	C	.308	.330	.369	.375	.375	.041	1.50	2.575	S	268
.307 GNR	A	.308	.336	.379	.380	.433	.055	1.55	2.00	S	269
.309 JDJ	A	.308	.335	.453	.470	.514	.058	2.20	3.16	L	270
.30-06 JDJ	C	.308	.335	.455	.470	.467	.045	2.455	V	L	270
.308 CorBon	C	.308	.333	.532	.545	.532	.050	2.08	2.80	L	271
7.82 Patriot	C	.308	.340	.557	.577	.577	.060	2.05	2.8	L	271
.300 Dakota	C	.308	.338	.531	.544	.544	.046	2.55	3.33	L	272
.300 Canadian Magnum	I	.308	.342	.530	.544	.532	.046	2.83	3.60	L	273
.300 Pegasus	C	.308	.339	.566	.580	.580	.058	2.99	3.75	L	273
7.82 Warbird	C	.308	.340	.557	.577	.577	.060	2.80	3.60	L	274
8mm JDJ	A	.323	.356	.455	.470	.514	.058	2.22	V	L	275
.338 Whisper	C	.338	.360	.457	.463	.466	.048	1.47	V	S	275
.338 Spectre	C	.338	.361	.415	.425	.420	.049	1.25	2.10	L	276
.338 Lehigh	C	.338	.369	.4268	.439	.441	.053	1.40	2.26	S	276
.338 JDJ	A	.338	.365	.453	.470	.514	.058	2.20	V	L	277
.338 GNR	A	.338	.370	.435	.463	.543	.075	2.545	3.20	L	278
.338-06 JDJ	C	.338	.370	.455	.470	.467	.045	2.465	V	L	278
8.59 Galaxy	C	.338	.368	.557	.577	.577	.060	2.05	2.80	L	279

Dimensional Data

Cartridge	Case	Bullet Dia.	Neck Dia.	Shoulder Dia.	Base Dia.	Rim Dia.	Rim Thick.	Case Length	Ctge. Length	Primer	Page
.330 Dakota	C	.338	.371	.530	.544	.544	.045	2.57	3.32	L	279
.338 Canadian Magnum	I	.338	.369	.530	.544	.532	.046	2.83	3.60	L	280
.338 Woodswalker	A	.338	.360	.410	.420	.482	.060	1.860	2.510	L	281
.338 A-Square	K	.338	.367	.553	.582	.603/.580∂	.060	2.85	3.67	L	281
.338 Excaliber	C	.338	.371	.566	.580	.580	.058	2.99	3.75	L	282
8.59 Titan	C	.338	.369	.557	.577	.577	.060	2.80	3.60	L	282
.38 Casull	C	.357	UNK	UNK	.476	.476	.044	UNK	1.170	UNK	283
.356 GNR	A	.358	.360	.433	.434	.498	.054	1.250	UNK	UNK	284
.358 JDJ	A	.358	.362	.453	.470	.514	.058	.220	3.065	L	284
.35-06 JDJ	C	.358	.385	.455	.470	.467	.045	2.445	V	L	285
9.09 Eagle	C	.358	.387	.557	.577	.577	.060	2.05	2.80	L	286
.358 Shooting Times Alaskan (STA)	E	.358	.386	.502	.513	.532	.048	2.85	3.65	L	286
9.3mm JDJ	A	.366	.389	.455	.465	.506	.058	2.22	V	L	287
.375 Whisper	C	.375	UNK	UNK	.466	.468	.045	UNK	UNK	UNK	287
.375/454 JDJ Woodswalker	B	.375	UNK	UNK	.480	.515	.055	UNK	UNK	UNK	288
.375 JDJ	A	.375	.396	.453	.470	.514	.058	2.20	3.13	L	288
.375-06 JDJ	C	.375	.405	.457	.470	.467	.045	2.435	V	L	289
9.53 Hellcat	C	.375	.404	.557	.577	.577	.060	2.05	2.80	L	289
.375 JRS Magnum	E	.375	.498	.485	.535	?	.048	2.84	3.69	L	290
.375 Dakota	C	.375	.402	.529	.544	.544	.046	2.57	3.32	L	290
.375 Canadian Magnum	I	.375	.402	.530	.544	.532	.046	2.83	3.60	L	291
.375 A-Square	K	.375	.405	.551	.582	.603/.580∂	.060	2.85	3.65	L	292
9.53 Saturn	C	.375	.404	.557	.577	.577	.060	2.80	3.60	L	292
.400 CorBon	C	.401	.423	.469	.470	.471	.050	.898	1.20	LP	293
.40-44 Woodswalker	A	.401	.428	.455	.455	.510	.055	1.295	V	LP	293
.40-454 JDJ	A	.401	.428	.470	.470	.510	.055	1.395	V	LP	294
.408 CheyTac	C	.408	.438	.601	.637	.640	.065	3.04	4.307	L	294
.41 GNR	A	.410	.436	.458	.461	.514	.055	1.240	1.60	L	295
.410 GNR	A	.410	.439	.477	.480	.512	.055	1.349	1.69	L	295
.411 JDJ	A	.411	.425	.455	.465	.506	.058	2.235	V	L	296
.411 Express	C	.411	UNK	UNK	.440	.468	.045	UNK	UNK	UNK	296
.411 Hawk	C	.411	UNK	UNK	.440	.468	.045	UNK	UNK	UNK	297
.416 JDJ	A	.416	.430	.455	.465	.506	.058	2.22	V	L	298
.416-06 JDJ	C	.416	.443	.455	.470	.467	.045	2.415	V	L	298
.416 Taylor	E	.416	.447	.491	.513	.532	.048	2.50	3.34	L	299
10.57 Maverick	C	.416	.445	.557	.577	.577	.060	2.05	2.80	L	299
.416 Hoffman	E	.416	.447	.491	.513	.532	.048	2.85	3.60	L	300
.416 Rimmed	A	.416	.446	.549	.573	.665	.060	3.300	4.100	L	300
.416 BGA	C	.416	UNK	UNK	.504	.492	UNK	UNK	UNK	UNK	301
.416 Dakota	C	.416	.441	.527	.544	.544	.042	2.85	3.645	L	301
10.57 Meteor	C	.416	.445	.557	.577	.577	.060	2.80	3.62	L	302
.416 Barrett	C	.416	.460	.730	.803	.804	.083	3.273	4.563	Bx	302
.425 Express	E	.423	.429	.490	.513	.532	.048	2.552	3.34	L	303
.440 CorBon	I	.429	.461	.529	.538	.510	.055	1.280	1.59	LP	303
.44/454 JDJ Woodswalker	B	.429	UNK	UNK	.480	.515	.055	UNK	UNK	UNK	304
.458 SOCOM	I	.458	.452	.530	.538	.473	.048	1.575	2.015	UNK	304
.458 Whisper	F	.458	.485		.506	.525	.048	1.75	V	L	305
.450 Assegai	A	.458	.487	.549	.573	.665	.060	3.300	4.100	L	305
.450 Ackley Magnum	E	.458	.487	.503	.512	.532	.048	2.85	3.65	L	306
.458 Canadian Magnum	I	.458	.485	.530	.544	.532	.046	2.83	3.60	L	306
.450 Dakota	C	.458	.485	.560	.582	.580	.058	2.90	3.74	L	307
.460 A-Square Short	K	.458	.484	.560	.582	.603/.580∂	.060	2.50	3.50	L	307
.475 Linebaugh	B	.475	.495		.501	.600	.065	1.50	1.77	L	308
.470 Capstick	F	.475	.499		.513	.532	.048	2.85	3.65	L	309
.475 JDJ	B	.475	.497	UNK	.502	.604	.065	2.10	V	L	309

Dimensional Data

Cartridge	Case	Bullet Dia.	Neck Dia.	Shoulder Dia.	Base Dia.	Rim Dia.	Rim Thick.	Case Length	Ctge. Length	Primer	Page
12.04 Bibamufu	C	.475	.500	.557	.577	.577	.060	2.80	3.62	L	310
.500 Wyoming Express	F	.500	UNK	UNK	UNK	UNK	UNK	1.370	1.765	LR	310
.510 GNR	B	.500	.514	.548	.550	.614	.070	1.190	UNK	UNK	311
.50 Beowulf	J	.500	.525	N/A	.535	.445	.055	1.650	2.125	UNK	311
.50 GI	J	.500	.526	N/A	.526	.480	.048	.899	1.221	UNK	312
.500 Phantom	I	.500	.535	UNK	.620	.532	UNK	1.525	2.280	UNK	312
.500 Whisper	K	.510	.549	.563	.580	.603/.580∂	.060	2.90	V	L	313
.500 Linebaugh	B	.510	.540	UNK	.553	.610	.062	1.405	1.755	L	313
.495 A-Square	L	.510	.542	UNK	.582	.603/.580∂	.060	2.80	3.60	L	314
.500 A-Square	K	.510	.536	.568	.582	.603/.580∂	.060	2.90	3.74	L	315
.50 Peacekeeper	K	.510	.538	.565	.586	.603/.580∂	.058	2.882	V	L	315
.510 Whisper	C	.510	UNK	UNK	.590	.590	.060	1.875	UNK	UNK	316
.50 American Eagle	I	.510	.560	.714	.804	.440	.053	UNK	UNK	UNK	316
.577 Tyrannosaur	C	.585	.614	.673	.688	.688	.060	2.99	3.71	L	316
14.5 JDJ	C	.585	UNK	UNK	.804	.804	.080	UNK	UNK	UNK	317
.600/577 JDJ	B	.620	UNK	UNK	.660	.748	.052	UNK	UNK	UNK	317
.700 JDJ	C	.727	UNK	UNK	.804	.804	.080	UNK	UNK	UNK	317
.950 JDJ	C	.950	UNK	UNK	UNK	UNK	UNK	4.00	UNK	UNK	318

Case Type: A = Rimmed, bottleneck. B = Rimmed, straight. C = Rimless, bottleneck. D = Rimless, straight. E = Belted, bottleneck. F = Belted, straight. G = Semi-rimmed, bottleneck. H = Semi-rimmed, straight. I = Rebated, bottleneck. J = Rebated, straight. K = Rebated, belted bottleneck L = Rebated, belted straight.

Primer Type: S = Small rifle (.175"). SP = Small pistol (.175"). L = Large rifle (.210"). LP = Large pistol (.210"). B-1 = Berdan #1. B-2 = Berdan #2.

Other codes: V = OAL depends upon bullet used. V = Rifling twist varies, depending upon bullet and application. ∂ = Belt/Rim Diameter. Unless otherwise noted, all dimensions in inches.

Handgun Cartridges of the World

(Current & Obsolete—Blackpowder and Smokeless)

It can be stated unequivocally that the United States is the only country where the handgun has developed fully as a sporting arm, used for hunting, as well as various kinds of match and silhouette shooting. This has had a profound effect on the development of handguns and handgun cartridges in America. Shortly after World War II, for instance, there was renewed interest in the single-action revolver. This resulted in the introduction of new single-action models by Sturm, Ruger & Co. In turn, it became profitable for Colt's to reintroduce its single-action revolver, which had been considered obsolete. Now, Ruger and several other manufacturers and importers continue the single-action tradition.

Handgun hunting was responsible for new cartridges designed primarily for field use, such as the .22 Remington Jet, .221 Remington Fireball, .44 Magnum, .454 Casull, .475 Linebaugh, and .500 Linebaugh. The increasing popularity of silhouette pistol competition has given rise to specialized types of handguns designed particularly for this sport, such as the Thompson/Center Contender, Wichita Silhouette Pistol, Merrill Sportsman (now the RPM XL), and a number of custom handguns based on the Remington XP-100 action and the 7mm BR Remington cartridge. Some of these silhouette pistols chamber cartridges that are suitable for varmint and big-game hunting.

The sporting handgun is a uniquely American innovation. Using a handgun for hunting reduces the effective range to about 100 yards, depending on the skill of the shooter. However, handguns offer the advantages of lightness and easy portability, decided advantages in rough terrain or heavy brush.

Handguns are divided into several types, depending on intended use. Military and police handguns are designed for defensive use at short range. Typical bore sizes vary from 9mm to .45-caliber. The semi-automatic pistol is preferred by the world's military establishments, although the revolver is still used by some military police agencies. In recent years, police organizations in the United States have switched to the 9mm or .40 Auto and, in some instances, the .45 Automatic. Military and police handguns are usually of medium weight and have three- to five-inch barrels. Caliber is represented by the 9mm Luger, .40 S&W, and .45 Automatic (ACP). Off-duty or special assignment police arms are usually lighter and have shorter barrels than standard arms.

Pocket-type self-defense handguns have generally been small, lightweight, and of relatively small caliber, varying from .22 to .38. Today, the trend is toward pocket-type handguns chambered for cartridges that are more substantial. These high-end models are often of superior quality and capable of surprising accuracy and dependability.

Well-made pocket or self-defense handguns can be good small-game and plinking guns. Target pistols are characterized by adjustable target sights and usually a barrel of six inches or so in length. Match pistols often are so specialized as to be of little practical use for anything else.

Hunting handguns also tend to be specialized, due to their long barrels and heavy frames. Because most also have adjustable sights, these can be used for target shooting, too. Any handgun can be used for hunting small game at short ranges, provided its user can hit with it. Serious hunting handguns vary in caliber from .22 to .50, depending on the game to be hunted. Magnum cartridges are preferred for big game. Some single-shot pistols, such as the Thompson/Center Contender, are chambered for rifle cartridges like the .30-30 and the .223 Remington.

Because handgun cartridges are limited in velocity, an important consideration is the type of bullet used. The semi-wadcutter, as designed by the late Elmer Keith, is probably the best type of cast-lead bullet. Some modern jacketed handgun bullets with a large area of exposed lead at the nose have also proven highly effective on lighter species. In competent and practiced hands, the .357 Magnum has given a good account of itself on deer-size animals and, in some cases, even larger quarry. One must realize that handgun cartridges used for big game deliver marginal ballistics for that purpose, compared to high-powered rifle cartridges. Thus, shooter skill is critical.

Some handgun cartridges have also become popular as rifle cartridges. This includes the .357 and .44 Magnums, as well as the venerable .44-40 Winchester and .45 Colt. These make a good combination for owners of handguns in these chamberings, because standard factory ammunition can then be used interchangeably in rifles and pistols. However, some rifles can withstand much higher pressures than most handguns, and handloads that are safe in a rifle may wreck a handgun. Use caution and common sense when handloading.

Handgun cartridges are divided into three major types, those intended for semi-automatic pistols, those to be used in revolvers, and those for single-shot pistols. Those designed for semi-automatic pistols are either rimless or semi-rimmed to facilitate feeding from the magazine. Revolver cartridges are, in general, of rimmed construction, although some revolvers have been made to handle semi-rimmed or rimless cartridges, such as the .32 Automatic, .30 Carbine, 9mm Luger, .380 Automatic, and the .45 Automatic. Single-shot pistol cartridges are often bottlenecked and rimmed or rimless. At one time, bullets intended for revolver cartridges were of lead, while those for auto-pistol cartridges were jacketed to facilitate feeding. At present, it is common practice to use jacketed bullets in revolvers, particularly for hunting, although match shooters prefer light loads and lead bullets. Lead bullets are also used for target loads in pistols. Jacketed bullets have been used in some military revolvers since before World War I because of international agreements.

Owing to limitations in the design strength of typical revolvers and pistols, smokeless powder did not improve the performance of handgun cartridges to the extent it did rifle cartridges. Consequently, blackpowder cartridges of medium to large caliber are almost as effective as modern non-magnum handgun cartridges. In fact, many modern handgun cartridges originated as blackpowder numbers, and their performances with smokeless powder is about the same as it was with their original blackpowder loadings.

When selecting a handgun or handgun cartridge, give careful consideration to the gun's intended use. Most individuals have a tendency to overdo it, regarding power, following the idea that bigger is better. While a few experts can achieve long-range hits, most handgun hunting is for small game or varmints at ranges of 50 yards or less. It takes a great deal of practice before one can hit a target with any consistency at 100 yards and beyond. Power will not compensate for poor marksmanship, so it is best to start with something you can handle and move up to a larger chambering after proficiency has improved. Remember, the average person must expend hundreds of rounds to develop proficiency with a .22 rimfire pistol, and it takes even more practice with larger chamberings.

The .22 Long Rifle rimfire is probably the most popular handgun cartridge, followed by the .38 Special and 9mm Luger among the centerfires. The .22 rimfire is adequate for small game at close ranges and can serve as a house gun for home protection. The .38 Special has the advantage of reloadability, and it is possible to regulate the power to cover shooting situations from very light target loads to full-power self-defense or field loads. For serious self-defense, the .38 Special and the .380 Automatic are considered minimum. The .38 Special and the .357 Magnum are probably the most widely used revolver cartridges, while the 9mm, .40 S&W, and .45 Automatic are the most popular pistol cartridges. For match competition, the .22 rimfire, .38 Special, and 45 Automatic may still lead the pack, although other centerfire numbers have recently made gains.—*F.C.B.*

13th Edition Update

This chapter was previously arranged so that the so-called "current" cartridges of the day were listed first, then those opined to be "obsolete." Not only did we remove several of the really oddball cartridges for inclusion of the CD, we reorganized this chapter so that the cartridges are listed in the order they appear in the Dimensional Table, just like they are in other chapters and regardless of whether they're current or obsolete. Can't find what you're looking for? Those cartridges removed from this chapter to the CD included with this book include: 2.7 Kolibri Auto; 3mm Kolibri; 4.25 Liliput Auto (4.25 Erika Auto); 5mm Clement Auto; 5mm Bergmann; 6.5mm Bergmann; .32 Protector; 7.5mm Roth-Sauer; .30 (7.76mm) Borchardt; 9.8mm Automatic Colt (9.65 Browning Automatic Colt; .401 Herter Powermag; .44 Merwin & Hulbert; .44 Smith & Wesson American; .44 Webley/.442 RIC/.442 Revolver Center Fire/.442 Kurz/10.5x17Rmm; .44 Colt; 11.75mm Montenegrin Revolver/11mm Austrian Gasser/11.25x36 Montenegrin; 11mm French Ordnance Revolver; 11mm German Service Revolver; .450 Revolver/.450 Adams/.450 Short/.450 Colt; .476 Eley/.476 Enfield MkIII/.476 Revolver (.455/476); .50 Remington.

—*J.L.S.P.*

5.45x18mm Soviet

Historical Notes:	This modern pistol cartridge was developed in the Soviet Union, in the 1970s, for the PSM compact semi-automatic pistol. Its design follows Soviet tradition, in that the case is bottlenecked and bullet caliber is the same as for the service rifle (the 5.45mm AK-74). Case length and overall loaded length are similar to the 9mm Makarov cartridge, although the base and rim diameter of the 5.45x18mm Soviet is smaller. Thus far, Russia is the only country to have adopted this cartridge and the PSM pistol for it.
General Comments:	The concept behind this cartridge is unknown. By Western standards, this cartridge is a very poor choice for self-defense. Muzzle energy is about the same as the .22 Long Rifle. However, a key to its purpose may be bullet construction, which consists of a gilding metal jacket around a two-piece core consisting of a steel front and lead rear halves. If penetration is the purpose, then this bullet should prove effective against body armor. Beyond this, it seems to have little value. It is one of the few new cartridges to enter production in Russia for many years. Manufactured only in the Commonwealth of Independent States, cases are normally lacquered steel with a Berdan primer. Bullet diameter is about .210-inch.

5.45x18mm Soviet Factory Ballistics

Bullet (grains/type)	Powder	Grains	Velocity	Energy	Source/Comments
40 FMJ	FL		1034	95	Factory load

.22 Remington Jet Magnum
.22 Center Fire Magnum

Historical Notes:	The .22 Remington Jet, also known as the .22 Center Fire Magnum, was introduced jointly by Remington and Smith & Wesson. The former developed the cartridge, the latter the revolver. The first news of this cartridge leaked out in 1959, but production revolvers and ammunition were not available until 1961. The S&W Model 53 revolver is the only revolver ever to chamber this cartridge, and it was discontinued in 1971. The .22 Jet grew out of popular wildcat handgun cartridges, such as the Harvey .22 Kay-Chuk and others based on the altered .22 Hornet case. However, the .22 Jet is actually based on a necked-down .357 Magnum case. Marlin once offered the Model 62 lever-action rifle for the .22 Jet, H&R offered it in the Topper, and Thompson/Center offered it in the Contender, for a time.
General Comments:	The .22 Jet is strictly a hunting number, intended to provide high velocity and flat trajectory in the field. The M53 revolver will also fire regular .22 Long Rifle ammunition by use of supplemental steel chamber inserts and an adjustable firing pin. This cartridge has ample performance for small game at ranges out to 100 yards, for those who can shoot a revolver that well.

When first announced, most gun writers praised the fantastic performance of this round. A muzzle velocity of 2460 fps was supposed to be developed in an 8½-inch barrel. Chronographed tests by various individuals, including the book's original author, indicated an actual velocity of only around 2000 fps in this barrel length. Quite a letdown, but it is still a good cartridge. The S&W Model 53 in .22 Jet was discontinued because of problems with the cylinder locking up when firing full-powered loads. This ammunition is no longer manufactured commercially.

.22 Remington Jet Magnum Loading Data and Factory Ballistics

Bullet (grains/type)	Powder	Grains	Velocity	Energy	Source/Comments
40 HP	2400	10.5	1800	288	Hornady, Sierra
45 SP	2400	12.8	1700	288	Hornady, Sierra
40 HP	FL		2460	535	Factory load

Cartridges and cylinder must be free of grease or oil to prevent setback of cases when fired.

.221 Remington Fireball

Historical Notes: This cartridge was introduced, early in 1963, for the Remington XP-100 bolt-action, a single-shot pistol based on a shortened, lightened 700 series rifle action. The pistol had a streamlined nylon-plastic stock, ventilated barrel rib, and adjustable sights. This was the first handgun made by Remington since its pocket automatics were discontinued, back in 1935. The Thompson/Center Contender was also available in .221 Remington for a time, but no longer. Remington was the only source for .221 Fireball ammunition. It is still available.

General Comments: The .221 Fireball follows the modern design in .22-caliber high-velocity pistol cartridges for small-game and varmint hunting at long range. The rimless case is a shortened version of the .222 Remington. The cartridge is well adapted to rifles, as well as pistols. The bullet is designed for quick expansion on small animals and is very deadly at all practical ranges. The XP-100 pistol has a 10-inch barrel and is intended for use with a scope. It is capable of sub-MOA 100-yard groups, when fitted with a scope and fired from a rest. It is much more powerful than the older .22 Remington Jet used in the S&W .22 WMR revolver. Muzzle energy of the .221 Fireball is greater than the .357 Magnum. Despite the caliber designation, .224-inch is the proper bullet diameter. The .221 Fireball was chambered in the Remington Model 700 Classic rifle on a limited-run basis in the late 2000s.

.221 Remington Fireball Loading Data and Factory Ballistics

Bullet (grains/type)	Powder	Grains	Velocity	Energy	Source/Comments
50 SP	IMR 4198	17.0	2610	755	Speer, Hornady, Sierra, Nosler
50 SP	IMR 4227	15.5	2600	750	Speer, Hornady, Sierra, Nosler
55 SP	IMR 4198	16.0	2400	704	Speer, Hornady, Nosler
50 SP	FL		2650	780	Remington factory load

5.5mm Velo Dog Revolver *

Historical Notes: This round was introduced, in 1894, for the Velo Dog revolver, manufactured by Galand, of Paris. It derives its name from the French word velocycle, meaning, roughly, "bicycle." Later, a number of Belgian and German revolvers also chambered this round. The cartridge was loaded in the United States by Peters, Remington, and Winchester, up until about 1940. However, no American company made a gun for it. Fiocchi of Italy still loads this cartridge.

General Comments: The 5.5mm Velo Dog is a centerfire .22 of slightly less power than the .22 Long Rifle rimfire. It bears some resemblance to the obsolete .22 Extra Long Maynard centerfire rifle cartridge. However, it is easy to distinguish between these by the head markings, and because the 5.5mm has a metal-cased bullet. The Velo Dog revolver was designed for cyclists to shoot pursuing dogs. This was a unique period in history—can you imagine what would happen today if some cyclist shot a dog! The cartridge became obsolete because it is ballistically inferior to the popular .22 Long Rifle.

Editor's note: Others might argue that the present period is historically unique. Try to fathom the logic that suggests it's OK for an unrestricted dog to attack a harmless cyclist or pedestrian, but that it is not OK for that person to effectively defend himself!

*There is some uncertainty as to the proper designation for this cartridge. There is also a loading called the "5.75 Velo Dog," which could be the correct name for this cartridge—it would seem that we should have been able to resolve this, but that is not yet the case. Maybe we will solve the mystery next edition.

5.5mm Velo Dog Revolver Factory Ballistics

Bullet (grains/type)	Powder	Grains	Velocity	Energy	Source/Comments
45 FMJ	FL		750	55	Fiocchi factory load

.25 (6.35mm) Automatic (.25 ACP)

Historical Notes: This cartridge was introduced in the United States, in 1908, with the Browning-designed Colt's-manufactured .25 Vest Pocket Automatic pistol. It had been introduced in Europe a few years earlier in the F.N. Baby Browning, which is practically identical to the Colt's. The design of these two pistols has been copied by manufacturers all over the world. Dozens of different pistols have used this cartridge. The original Browning is still made (for European consumption), but Colt's did not resume manufacture of its Vest Pocket model after World War II. American Arms, Beretta, Iver Johnson, Jennings, Lorcin, Phoenix Arms, Sundance, Taurus, Ortgies, Astra, Star, Kelt-Tech, Rohrbaugh,and Walther have all made pistols in this chambering.

General Comments: The .25 Automatic offers surprising velocity for such a small cartridge. However, delivered energy is quite modest. This, combined with the full metal jacketed bullet of the conventional load, adds up to very poor stopping or killing power on anything. Lighter, expanding bullets lack adequate penetration or delivered energy to suggest any significant improvement. The .25 Auto is not powerful enough for hunting anything but pests, nor is it adequate for serious self-defense. However, .25 Automatic pistols are popular because of their small size and low cost. Their principal usefulness might be as a threat, because no sane person wants to be shot if that can be avoided, not even with the little .25. Winchester and Hornady recently have offered hollowpoint loads in an effort to improve terminal ballistics.

Editor's Note: Three important facts are often overlooked when discussing the value of this cartridge. First, compared to any rimfire chambering, the .25 Automatic provides superior functioning in typical concealable pistols. Despite being very underpowered, well-placed shots from a .25 Auto do beat throwing rocks and will certainly disable or kill. Second, owing to a properly designed case and bullet, this cartridge is dramatically more dependable in a pocket pistol than any rimfire round. Finally, any functional gun that a person can and will carry and use correctly has significant defensive value.

.25 (6.35mm) Automatic (.25 ACP) Loading Data and Factory Ballistics

Bullet (grains/type)	Powder	Grains	Velocity	Energy	Source/Comments
50 FMJ	Bullseye	1.2	810	73	Hornady, Sierra
45 JHP	FL		815	66	Factory load, Winchester new
50 FMJ			760	64	NA

.25 North American Arms (NAA)

Historical Notes: First developed in 1999, by Kentucky firearms writer J.B. Wood, the .25 NAA cartridge is a .32 ACP case necked to .25-caliber. Mr. Wood's goal was to increase reliable expansion of .25-caliber bullets when fired from a short-barreled handgun. The concept of bottleneck cases to drive smaller-diameter bullets to greater speeds is more than a century old.

General Comments: Fired in a re-barreled Savage model 1908 self-loading pistol with Hornady test ammo, bullet expansion ranged from .360- to .412-inch. With perceived recoil in the .22 Long Rifle range, the improved feeding of a bottleneck cartridge and consistent hollowpoint bullet expansion, the North American Arms corporation decided to offer this chambering in its Guardian mini-pistol product line in 2002 or 2003. CorBon produces the ammo, which bears a CorBon .25 NAA headstamp and claims a muzzle velocity of 1200 fps with a 35-grain JHP bullet for 121 ft-lbs from a two-inch barrel.

.25 North American Arms Loading Data

Bullet (grains/type)	Powder	Grains	Velocity	Energy	Source/Comments
35 Hornady XTP	Herco	2.6	1050	85	Test Load by Hornady

.256 Winchester Magnum

Historical Notes: The .256 Winchester Magnum handgun cartridge was announced, in 1960. However, no arms were available until late in 1962, and most of these were not on the market in quantity before 1963. The Marlin Model 62 lever-action rifle was the first rifle officially announced for this cartridge. This was followed by a new Ruger single-shot pistol named the Hawkeye, which made the scene ahead of the Marlin. The Ruger Hawkeye was discontinued in 1966, and the Marlin 62 was dropped a few years later. The .256 Magnum is based on the .357 Magnum case necked-down to accept .257-inch diameter bullets. Some difficulty developed trying to design a revolver for this cartridge due to the cylinder gap and high pressure. The Ruger Hawkeye has a completely enclosed breech. Thompson/Center single-shot pistols were also available in this chambering.

General Comments: Fired in the Ruger Hawkeye, with its enclosed breech and 8½-inch barrel, the .256 Magnum develops an average muzzle velocity of about 2360 fps. From a 24-inch rifle barrel, muzzle velocity is over 2800 fps—this with the 60-grain SP bullet originally loaded by Winchester. When first announced, the velocity was listed as 2200 fps, as the factory used a test barrel shorter than 8½ inches. Although similar to the old .25-20 cartridge, the .256 has greater powder capacity, is loaded to higher pressures and, therefore, gives superior performance. When used in a rifle, many shooters prefer 75- or 85-grain bullets. The .256 Magnum should be an excellent varmint and small-game round at close ranges. In a rifle, it would be effective out to 200 or 225 yards. See the 18th Edition of Gun Digest for an excellent report by Yard and Helbig on shooting the .256. Winchester was the only source of this ammunition. Though Winchester ceased production of this cartridge in the early 1990s, cases are easily formed from .357 Magnums, so the handloader has no problem.

.256 Winchester Magnum Handgun Loading Data and Factory Ballistics

Bullet (grains/type)	Powder	Grains	Velocity	Energy	Source/Comments
60 SP	2400	14.6	2300	705	Hornady
60 SP	H4227	16.0	2300	705	Hornady
75 SP	2400	13.0	2000	668	Hornady
60 SP	FL		2200	650	Winchester factory load

7mm Nambu

Historical Notes: This unusual pistol cartridge was manufactured only in Japan for the Japanese "Baby" Nambu semi-auto pistol, which was introduced about 1920. It was not an official Japanese military cartridge, but was specially made for high-ranking officers who were required to purchase their own sidearms. The 7mm Nambu pistol is a scaled-down version of the original model Nambu, which was developed about 1904. The 7mm Nambu pistol was something of a mystery, until after World War II, when quantities were brought back by returning GIs. The 7mm Nambu cartridge is a collector's item, and the pistols are scarce.

General Comments: By Western standards, the 7mm Nambu would not be considered an adequate self-defense cartridge. For sporting use, it would be effective only on small game or birds. The pistol has a seven-shot magazine, 3¼-inch barrel, weighs only 16 ounces, and is extremely well made and of good material and finish. The 1963 17th Edition of Gun Digest includes an article by Roy D. Strengholt, which covers the 7mm Nambu pistol and cartridge in considerable detail. The 7mm Nambu is unusual in that it is one of the very few pistol cartridges to use a 7mm (.283-inch)-diameter bullet.

7mm Nambu Factory Ballistics

Bullet (grains/type)	Powder	Grains	Velocity	Energy	Source/Comments
56 FMJ	FL		1250	196	Factory load *

*Approximate

7mm Bench Rest Remington

Historical Notes: Originally not a commercial cartridge, but a chambering only for the Remington Model XP-100 Silhouette target pistol, the 7mm BR has graduated to a full-fledged commercial cartridge. It has also become a rifle as well as a pistol round. It is based on the 308x1½-inch Barnes case necked-down to 7mm. Originally the cartridge was made by shortening and necking-down the Remington BR case, a special .308 Winchester case with a Small Rifle primer pocket made especially for this purpose. Remington's Mike Walker was instrumental in developing the 7mm BR.

This idea isn't new, because the British had developed a similar, although slightly longer, cartridge as an experimental military round, as early as 1945. In addition, more than one person has necked the .308x1½-inch case down to 7mm. Elgin Gates worked with a similar cartridge, in 1952. The Remington BR line of cartridges originated, according to company literature, in 1978. There is also a .22 BR and a 6mm BR covered elsewhere in this book. This cartridge was designed to provide an out-of-the-box silhouette cartridge, with ballistics calculated to strike the best balance for accuracy, velocity, and bullet weight to hit and knock down the metal targets.

General Comments: External dimensions of the Remington .308 BR case are identical to the .308 Winchester. However, the walls are thinner and are annealed to facilitate reforming, and the primer pocket is sized for the Small Rifle primer. Ballistics of the factory cartridge showed a 140-grain bullet at a muzzle velocity of 2215 fps and 1525 ft-lbs of energy, as registered from a 15-inch barrel. It would do better in a slightly longer barrel. These short 1½-inch cartridges often develop maximum velocity in a relatively short barrel, usually about 16 to 18 inches.

The 7mm BR would be a good medium-range varmint and short-range deer cartridge. It cannot be improved to any extent by handloading, since the standard factory load is about tops for the 140-grain bullet. Remington no longer catalogs this cartridge.

7mm Bench Rest Loading Data and Factory Ballistics

Bullet (grains)	Powder	Grains	Velocity	Energy	Source/Comments
100	W748	34.0	2400	1279	Sierra, Hornady
120	748	32.0	2300	1410	Sierra, Hornady
130	H322	27.0	2100	1277	Sierra, Speer, Nosler
140	748	30.0	2150	1450	Sierra, Hornady, Speer
150	H335	28.0	2000	1333	Sierra, Speer, Nosler
160	748	28.0	2000	1421	Sierra, Hornady, Speer
140	FL		2215	1525	Remington factory load

7.62mm Russian Nagant Revolver

Historical Notes: This military revolver cartridge was adopted by Russia, in 1895, and used in the Nagant and Pieper revolvers, which were both seven-shot designs, as opposed to the usual six. The Nagant design is unique in that, when the hammer is cocked, the cylinder moves forward over the barrel shank to form a gas seal. The velocity gain from this arrangement is significant. No other revolver has ever used this ingenious, though complicated, system.

General Comments: Russian Nagant revolvers have been sold in moderate quantities in the United States, but are more of a collector's item than a practical gun. Ammunition in shooting quantities is difficult to find, but can be made from .32-20 Winchester cases, which are very similar. Power and effectiveness are about the same as the .32 S&W Long. Most versions of the cartridge have the bullet seated completely inside the case. Velocity of the 108-grain FMJ flat-nose bullet in the Nagant revolver is about 1100 fps, but the conventional Pieper revolver delivers only 725 fps. Bullet diameter is .295-inch. Both guns and ammunition were recently in production in Russia. Fiocchi manufactured this cartridge quite recently.

7.62 Russian Nagant Revolver Loading Data and Factory Ballistics

Bullet (grains/type)	Powder	Grains	Velocity	Energy	Source/Comments
115 Cast	Bullseye	3.0	800	165	Lyman No. 311008
98 FMJ	FL		750	122	Fiocchi factory load
108 FMJ	FL		725	125	Factory load – Pieper revolver
108 FMJ	FL		1100	290	Factory load – Nagant revolver

7.62x25mm Russian Tokarev

Historical Notes: The 7.62x25mm Tokarev was the official Soviet pistol cartridge, adopted in 1930 for the Tokarev Model TT-30 and modified Model TT-33 automatic pistols. The pistols are a basic Browning-type design similar to the Colt's .45 Auto pistol. However, these incorporate many original features to simplify manufacturing processes, and must be considered an advance over Browning's original patented design. These pistols often have a crude finish, but are well made and of excellent design. These have a 4½-inch barrel and a magazine capacity of eight rounds. Large quantities have been sold as military surplus. Some were made in Communist China and Hungary, as well as Russia. The Hungarian-made Tokarev, in a modified form called the "Tokagypt," is chambered for the 9mm Parabellum cartridge. The Chinese began exporting both pistols and ammunition to the United States in 1987, at very reasonable prices.

General Comments: The cartridge is very similar in dimension to the 7.63mm (.30) Mauser, and most brands of Mauser ammunition can be fired in the Tokarev pistol. The 7.62mm Tokarev is a fair field cartridge for small game, with good velocity and flat trajectory, but needs soft-point bullets for maximum effectiveness. The handloader can use loading data for the 7.63 Mauser. The Speer .30-caliber plinker bullet of 100 grains makes a good hunting bullet, but, because it is slightly heavier than the standard weight, it must be loaded to lower velocity.

Chinese and Russian ammunition are steel-cased and Berdan-primed with corrosive primers. Such ammunition is not reloadable. Hansen Cartridge has imported quantities of 7.62x25mm ammunition with reloadable cases and non-corrosive Boxer primers.

7.62x25 Russian Tokarev Loading Data and Factory Ballistics

Bullet (grains/type)	Powder	Grains	Velocity	Energy	Source/Comments
86	Bullseye	5.0	1390	365	Duplicate factory ball
87 FMJ	FL		1390	365	Factory load

7.63mm (7.65) Mannlicher

Historical Notes: This straight-walled rimless cartridge was used in the Models 1900, 1901, and 1905 Mannlicher military automatic pistols. These were manufactured in Austria (Steyr) and in Spain. Austrian guns are well-made and finished, but the Spanish types are sometimes of doubtful quality. These pistols were common military surplus items, in the 1950s. Some dealers also had ammunition.

General Comments: The 1900 and slightly-modified 1901 and 1905 Mannlicher pistols operate on the delayed blowback system. The non-detachable magazine is in the grip and holds eight rounds, the 1905 with 10. These guns are loaded from the top by means of a special charger, after retracting the slide. The 7.63 cartridge is only slightly more powerful than the .32 Automatic, and its use in the field would have to be confined to small game. There is also a locked-breech Model 1903 Mannlicher auto pistol that fires a lower-powered cartridge that is otherwise similar to the bottlenecked 7.63 Mauser. The standard Mauser cartridge must not be fired in these Model 1903 pistols, as that will quickly damage the action.

7.63 (7.65) Mannlicher Loading Data and Factory Ballistics

Bullet (grains/type)	Powder	Grains	Velocity	Energy	Source/Comments
86	Unique	3.2	1000	193	Mauser bullet
85 FMJ	FL		1025	201	Factory load

.30 (7.65x21mm) Luger

Historical Notes: Introduced, in 1900, by Deutsche Waffen u. Munitions Fabriken, in Germany, the 7.65mm was designed by Georg Luger for the Luger automatic pistol. The cartridge is still used chiefly in the Luger pistol, although some SIG, Beretta M951, Browning Hi-Power, Ruger P89, and Walther P-38 pistols are chambered for this round. It was adopted as standard issue by the Swiss, Brazilian, Bulgarian, and Portuguese armies, but none of them currently issue it for front-line service.

General Comments: This is another bottlenecked rimless cartridge similar to the .30 Mauser, but shorter and not quite as powerful. It is not noted for great stopping power because of the small-diameter, lightweight, full jacketed bullet. It is used occasionally for small-game hunting and will do a fair job on rabbits and the like, provided the bullets are properly placed. The only manufacturer still offering this cartridge is Winchester. Bullet diameter is .308-inch.

.30 (7.65x21mm, 7.65mm) Luger Loading Data and Factory Ballistics

Bullet (grains/type)	Powder	Grains	Velocity	Energy	Source/Comments
93	Unique	5.0	1115	257	Lyman duplication of factory ball loading
100	Unique	4.8	1210	325	Speer plinker
93 FMJ	FL		1220	305	Factory load

.30 (7.63x25mm) Mauser

Historical Notes: The .30 Mauser cartridge was developed by American gun designer Hugo Borchardt for the first successful commercial, automatic pistol of the same name. The Borchardt pistol was made by Ludwig Loewe & Co. (later DWM) of Berlin, Germany. Both the pistol and cartridge were introduced in 1893. The Borchardt automatic pistol was later redesigned, emerging as the well-known Luger pistol. This cartridge was adopted by Paul Mauser for his famous Model 1896 pistol, though with increased power for his more rugged design. It has been used mainly in the Mauser M1896 military automatic pistol and various imitations or copies manufactured in Spain and China.

General Comments: Until the .357 Magnum cartridge came along, the .30 Mauser was the high-velocity champion of the pistol world. It has a flat trajectory that makes long-range hits possible, but lacks stopping power because of the light, full jacketed bullet. However, it has been used successfully for hunting small game and varmints at moderate ranges. Handloading with soft-point or hollowpoint hunting bullets improves performance considerably. At one time, both Remington and Winchester loaded this cartridge, but it has been dropped.

.30 (7.63x25mm) Mauser Loading Data and Factory Ballistics

Bullet (grains/type)	Powder	Grains	Velocity	Energy	Source/Comments
86 FMJ	Bullseye	4.5	1160	257	Lyman
86 FMJ	Unique	6.0	1230	289	Lyman
86 FMJ	FL		1410	375	Factory load

.32 Automatic Colt Pistol (.32 ACP)/7.65mm Browning

Historical Notes: Designed by John Browning for his first successful automatic pistol, this cartridge was first manufactured by FN, in Belgium, and introduced in 1899. It was marketed in the United States when Colt's turned out a pocket automatic on another Browning patent, in 1903. The .32 Automatic Colt Pistol (ACP) is one of the more popular pistol cartridges ever developed. In the United States, Colt's, Remington, Harrington & Richardson, Smith & Wesson, and Savage chambered pistols for this cartridge. In Europe, every company that made automatic pistols chambered the .32 ACP. It was also used in the German Pickert revolver. In Europe, it is known as the 7.65mm Browning.

General Comments: This cartridge uses a semi-rimmed cartridge case and a .308-inch diameter bullet. The .32 Automatic is the minimum cartridge that should really be seriously considered for self-defense. In the United States, it is used exclusively for small pocket-type guns and is not considered adequate for police or military use. However, in Europe it is often used in police pistols and as an alternative, but unofficial, chambering for military sidearms. As a hunting cartridge, it is not powerful enough for anything larger than small game.

Loading tables generally give bullet diameter of the .32 Automatic as .312-inch or .314-inch. It is actually closer to .308-inch, and this is important if you handload. Effective small-game loads can be made by using 100-grain .30-caliber rifle bullets intended for light loads and plinking, such as the Speer .30-caliber Plinker. All major ammunition makers offer this cartridge. Winchester recently introduced a load with a jacketed hollowpoint bullet. Other makers have followed suit.

.32 (7.65mm) Automatic/.32 ACP Loading Data and Factory Ballistics

Bullet (grains/type)	Powder	Grains	Velocity	Energy	Source/Comments
71 FMJ	Bullseye	2.2	800	100	Sierra, Hornady
71 FMJ	700X	2.0	850	114	Sierra, Hornady
60 JHP	FL		970	125	Winchester factory load
71 FMJ	FL		905	129	Factory load
74 FMJ/JSP	FL				Factory load, early

.32 Smith & Wesson

Historical Notes: Designed for the Smith & Wesson Model 1½, hinged-frame, single-action revolver introduced in 1878, the .32 S&W is an old and very popular cartridge, widely used in the United States and Europe for low-priced, pocket-type revolvers. Originally a blackpowder cartridge, it has been loaded with smokeless powder exclusively since 1940. In the United States, Colt's, Harrington & Richardson, Hopkins & Allen, Iver Johnson, Smith & Wesson, and others have made revolvers for this cartridge. In England, Webley & Scott made revolvers for it. Elsewhere in Europe, the Bayard and Pickert revolvers chambered it. The original loading used nine grains of blackpowder.

General Comments: The .32 Smith & Wesson formerly ranked with the .32 Automatic in general popularity, and for the same reasons. It is low-powered and adaptable to small, light, inexpensive, pocket-type handguns. Ballistically, it is not quite as good as the .32 Automatic. It is very similar to the .32 Short Colt, but the two are not interchangeable, because of a difference in bullet and case diameter. Like the .32 Automatic, the .32 S&W is about the minimum cartridge for self-defense. It is considered inadequate for police work. It is used occasionally for hunting small game at very short ranges, but is too underpowered for consideration as a sporting cartridge. This ammunition is still available.

.32 Smith & Wesson Loading Data and Factory Ballistics

Bullet (grains/type)	Powder	Grains	Velocity	Energy	Source/Comments
85 Lead	Bullseye	1.1	705	93	NA
85 Lead	Blackpowder (Fg)	9.0	680	90	Factory load
98 Lead	Smokeless powder		705	115	Factory load

.32 Smith & Wesson Long
.32 Colt New Police

Historical Notes: This cartridge was developed for the Smith & Wesson First Model, solid-frame, hand-ejector revolver, introduced in 1903. The same cartridge, loaded with a flat-nose bullet, is called the .32 Colt New Police. Colt's, Harrington & Richardson, Iver Johnson, and Smith & Wesson were the principal companies making revolvers in this chambering in the United States. Many Spanish and other European revolvers, such as the Bayard and Pickert, chambered the round. In Europe, it had not been as widely used as the shorter .32 S&W until some ISU centerfire target shooters discovered the .32 S&W Long, and now there are several high-class European target autoloaders for the wadcutter loading of this cartridge.

General Comments: The .32 S&W Long is the smallest revolver cartridge deemed adequate for police use in the United States, and it has been fairly popular with detectives or plainclothes officers. It has always been available in a variety of short, light, small-frame revolvers, some of which are very well made. It has a reputation for excellent accuracy and has been used for target and match shooting in the past, as well as in ISU shooting. It is as accurate as the .38 S&W Special, but not as versatile. It is the minimum size for sporting use and with handloaded, hunting-type bullets it is quite effective on small game. It is not as popular or widely used for self-defense as it once was, because of the development of compact .38-caliber revolvers. Its range and effectiveness can be increased by handloading. The original load was 13 grains of blackpowder and a 98-grain bullet.

Note: Previous editions of this book incorrectly listed the .32-44 Target as being interchangeable with the .32 Smith & Wesson Long. Not so. The .32-44 was a chambering for the S&W No. 3 Target revolver and will not chamber in .32 S&W Long revolvers. The .32-44 designation translates as "a .32 on a .44 frame." Like its larger sibling, the original .38-44 S&W Target, the .32-44 S&W Target featured an elongated case with a bullet that was loaded flush with the case mouth, somewhat in the spirit of the 7.62mm Russian Nagant Revolver cartridge.

Bullet (grains/type)	Powder	Grains	Velocity	Energy	Source/Comments
90 Lead	700X	1.8	700	98	Hornady
98 Lead	Unique	1.8	665	96	Speer
98 Lead	Blackpowder (Fg)	13.0	780	132	Factory load
98 Wadcutter	Smokeless powder		705	115	Factory load

.32 H&R Magnum

Historical Notes: The .32 H&R Magnum was the result of a joint project between Harrington & Richardson and Federal Cartridge Co. It was introduced, in 1984, for the five-shot H&R Model 504, 532, and 586 revolvers. This was followed later in the same year by Charter Arms and its six-shot .32 H&R Magnum Police Undercover revolver, and, in 1985, by the Ruger New Model .32 Magnum Single-Six and SP101 revolvers.

The .32 H&R Magnum is simply the older .32 Smith & Wesson Long case lengthened by .155-inch. Therefore, any .32 Magnum revolver will also accept and fire both the .32 S&W and the .32 S&W Long. This makes for a convenient situation, because the shooter has a choice of three different cartridges that will work in one handgun. Two loadings of the cartridge were offered, a lead semi-wadcutter bullet of 95 grains, or an 85-grain jacketed hollowpoint.

General Comments: According to factory ballistics, the .32 Magnum delivers double the energy of the .32 S&W Long and 13-percent more energy than the standard .38 Special load. However, chronograph tests demonstrated that actual velocity at the muzzle ranges 60 to 100 fps below factory-advertised figures. Nevertheless, the cartridge performance level is well above that of any other .32-caliber handgun cartridge currently available. The .32-20 can be handloaded to equal the .32 Magnum in a revolver, but new .32-20 revolvers have not been available since before World War II.

What kept H&R from chambering its revolvers for the .32-20? To do so would have required extensive design changes in its revolvers, because the .32-20 is too long. In fact, .32-20 case length is nearly the same as .32 Magnum overall cartridge length. By the late 1980s, both H&R and Charter Arms had gone out of business (both are again producing firearms), leaving Ruger and Dan Wesson as the sole supplier of revolvers in this chambering. Federal was the only ammunition maker to undertake production.

13th Edition Update: H&R no longer manufacturers handguns and was acquired by The Freedom Group through Marlin Firearms. Charter Arms is back in business and offers four revolvers for the .32 H&R. Dan Wesson has been acquired by CZ-USA, but offers no .32-caliber revolvers. Smith & Wesson and Ruger do manufacturer revolvers for the .32 H&R, and any revolver chambered for the newer .327 Federal Magnum can also safely fire .32 H&R Magnum cartridges. Currently a modest, but serviceable, selection of .32 H&R Magnum loads are available from Federal, Black Hills, Buffalo Bore, and DoubleTap ammunition.

.32 H&R Magnum Loading Data and Factory Ballistics

Bullet (grains/type)	Powder	Grains	Velocity	Energy	Source/Comments
85 JHP	Unique	4.0	900	153	Hornady
90 Lead	Unique	3.4	815	145	Hornady
98 Lead	Unique	3.0	815	145	Speer
85 JHP	FL		1100	230	Factory load
85 JHP	FL		1300	318	Buffalo Bore Factory Load
90 Sierra JHC	True Blue	6.5	1150	264	Sierra
130 Keith Style Hard Cast	FL		1125	365	Buffalo Bore Factory Load

.32 North American Arms (NAA)

Historical Notes: Culminating from a joint development effort between North American Arms and writer Ed Sanow, the .32 NAA uses an ordinary .380 ACP case necked-down to house a .32-caliber bullet. In 2002, North American Arms decided to offer this chambering in its Guardian mini-pistol product line.

General Comments: Behind the neck, all case dimensions and configurations, including the extractor groove, rimless case, cartridge diameter, and bolt face engagement are identical to the .380 ACP. CorBon produces the ammo, which will bear a CorBon .32 NAA headstamp. The cartridge uses a proprietary bullet designed by Hornady.

.32 North American Arms Factory Ballistics

Bullet (grains/type)	Powder	Grains	Velocity	Energy	Source/Comments
60 JHP	FL		1222	199	CorBon factory load (2.5"bbl)

.32 Short Colt/.32 Long Colt/ .32 S&W Gallery

Historical Notes: Introduced by Colt's, in 1875, along with the New Line model revolvers, this was originally a black-powder cartridge using a 90-grain outside-lubricated bullet. There is also a .32 Short Colt, which is identical, except for a shorter case length. In England and Europe, this is known as the .320 caliber revolver. The .32 Short and Long Colt cartridges are actually obsolete, having been displaced by the .32 S&W and .32 S&W Long. Colt's is the only company that used this cartridge in the United States. It was more popular in Europe, where a number of blackpowder .320 revolvers were made.

General Comments: The .32 Colt cartridge was originally of the outside-lubricated type, which used a bullet of .313-inch diameter. Later, this was changed to an inside-lubricated type, which necessitated a bullet of .299-inch diameter, so that the lubricating grooves would fit inside the case. Bullet weight was reduced from 90 to 80 or 82 grains in the inside-lubricated type, and this shortened overall length a little. In power and usefulness, the Colt cartridges are nearly the same as the .32 S&W Short and Long, but not nearly as accurate. Winchester only recently discontinued this loading.

.32 Short Colt/.32 Long Colt Loading Data and Factory Ballistics

Bullet (grains/type)	Powder	Grains	Velocity	Energy	Source/Comments
55 Lead	Blackpowder	4.5			Wadcutter lead in 32 Short Colt
80 Lead	Bullseye	1.8	732	94	Approximate Factory Equivalent 32 Short Colt
80 Lead	FL		745	100	Factory Load - Short Colt
82 Lead	FL		755	104	Factory Load - Long Colt

.32 Colt

Historical Notes: This cartridge was Colt's attempt at solving the problems associated with outside-lubricated cartridges. The .32 Colt utilized a longer case to fully cover the lubricated portion of the bullet and carried a hollow-based bullet to help obturation in the bore. This was necessary, because the bullets had to be undersized to fit in the case. Reports were that the effort was not very successful. Loading was an 82-grain lead bullet with 12 grains of blackpowder.

.320 Revolver

Historical Notes: The .320 Revolver cartridge originated, in England, about 1870. It was the first used in the Webley revolver, but later, a number of other British and European pocket-type guns chambered it. The .320 served as the inspiration for the .32 Short Colt. It is no longer loaded by European ammunition manufacturers. At one time, it was also manufactured in the United States, but was discontinued in the late 1920s.

General Comments: The .320 Revolver is nearly identical to the .32 Short Colt in ballistic performance. The 320 is a short-range small-game number only. Use the same loading data as given for the .32 Short Colt. Recently, .320 Revolver ammunition was offered by Fiocchi.

.320 Revolver Factory Ballistics

Bullet (grains/type)	Powder	Grains	Velocity	Energy	Source/Comments
80 Lead	FL		550	54	Factory load

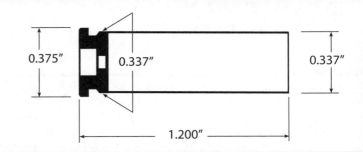

NEW
.327 Federal Magnum

Historical Notes: Introduced, in 2008, by the Federal Cartridge Company, the .327 Federal Magnum is an attempt to improve the performance of the .32 H&R Magnum. Factory .32 H&R Magnum ammunition, as per SAAMI specifications, is not loaded to the cartridge's full potential. This is due to the weaker H&R revolvers chambered for this cartridge. Cartridge performance for the .32 H&R Magnum can be substantially improved with handloads, when fired in Ruger or S&W revolvers. The .327 Federal Magnum takes this performance to a new level. This was accomplished by increasing the case capacity and loading the cartridge to a substantially higher pressure (45,000 psi) than the .32 H&R Magnum has at 21,000 CUP. In fact, the .327 Federal Magnum is loaded to a higher pressure than any other commercially loaded defensive handgun cartridge. Since .327 Federal Magnum cartridges cannot be chambered in any other .32-caliber revolver, there is no concern of over-pressure issues. Ruger worked with Federal during the development of this cartridge and initially offered a three-inch version of its SP 101 six-shot revolver in this chambering. With factory loads, a 100-grain bullet will leave the barrel of the SP 101 at about 1400 fps.

General Comments: Many who had never fired this cartridge initially considered it similar to its predecessor—the .32 H&R Magnum—as suitable for ladies or other recoil-conscious shooters. That's not the case. The .327 Federal Magnum is a handful in a 28-ounce SP 101 with full power loads. Federal does offer an 85-grain, low-recoil load that is much more controllable, but it is still markedly more powerful than any factory .32 H&R Magnum load. The terminal performance of this cartridge with both the 100- and 115-grain Speer Gold Dot loads approaches that of the .357 Magnum with similar bullets. Penetration in 10-percent gelatin is in excess of 14 inches, and bullets exhibit wide expansion. The design of these two Gold Dot bullets is very important to this cartridge, because prior to them, there were no .312-diameter bullets that could withstand the velocity this cartridge is capable of producing.
Over the last three years, I have spent a great deal of time shooting, testing, and handloading this cartridge for three revolvers and a Marlin 1894 re-chambered from .32 H&R Magnum. I was always a fan of the .32 H&R Magnum, and the .327 Federal has become my favorite revolver cartridge. If you can manage the recoil from a handgun, it is a viable self-defense option, and, from a rifle, it is capable of taking deer-sized game out to 100 yards. From the 16-inch barreled Marlin, the 110-grain bullet speeds along at over 2000 fps. One thing that sets the .327 Federal Magnum apart from all other revolver cartridges is the fact that any revolver so chambered will also fire .32 Short, .32 Long, and .32 H&R Magnum ammunition. This cartridge's versatility is unmatched.—R.A.M.

327 Federal Magnum Loading Data and Factory Ballistics

Bullet (grains/type)	Powder	Grains	Velocity	Energy	Source/Comments
85 JHP	True Blue	8.7	1644	510	Ramshot
90 Lead SWC	True Blue	7.9	1536	471	Ramshot
100 JHP	True Blue	7.7	1441	461	Ramshot
85 JHP	FL		1400	370	Federal Factory load
100 Gold Dot HP	FL		1500	500	Speer Factory load
100 JSP	FL		1500	500	Federal Factory load
100 Keith Hard Cast	FL		1300	375	Buffalo Bore Factory load
100 JHP	FL		1450	466	Buffalo Bore Factory load
115 Gold Dot HP	FL		1300	375	Speer Factory load

7.5mm Swiss Army Revolver

Historical Notes: This cartridge was adopted by the Swiss Army, in 1882, and officially used until 1903. The Swiss Army revolver is based on a modified Nagant system. In the early 1960s, quantities of these revolvers were sold on the American market by surplus dealers. These are quite well made and finished. Both blackpowder and smokeless powder ammunition is encountered.

General Comments: The 7.5mm Swiss revolver cartridge is identical to and fully interchangeable with the 7.5mm Swedish and Norwegian rounds. Modern smokeless powder ammunition was loaded by Norma for the Swedish Nagant, and this can be used in the Swiss revolver. The two cartridges differ only in bullet type. Most Swedish cartridges use an outside-lubricated bullet, whereas the Swiss also used an inside-lubricated type. Ballistics are about the same as the .32 S&W Long. For additional information, see the 7.5mm Swedish Nagant Revolver. Fiocchi now produces this ammunition.

7.5mm Swiss Army Factory Ballistics

Bullet (grains/type)	Powder	Grains	Velocity	Energy	Source/Comments
102 to 110 Lead	ML		700	115	Military load

8mm Rast-Gasser

Historical Notes: The 8mm Rast-Gasser military cartridge was introduced, in 1898, for the solid-frame Rast-Gasser military revolver patented in 1873. A number of different revolvers manufactured in Belgium and Germany chambered the round. Although popular in Europe, the 8mm Rast-Gasser was never manufactured in the United States. The round is obsolete and ammunition difficult to obtain.

General Comments: The Gasser solid-frame revolver design is noted for its simplicity of disassembly. It also has a rebounding hammer and a spring-mounted, separate firing pin. These are usually well made and rather sturdy. Quantities have been sold at various times in surplus stores.

The cartridge resembles the 8mm French Lebel Revolver round quite closely. Bullet diameter is .320-inch. Rim and body diameter are nearly identical to the .32 S&W Long. The .32 S&W case is shorter, but both cartridges are of approximately the same power. Lyman cast bullet No. 313445 (95 grains) can be adapted for handloading. Loading data for the .32 S&W can be used as a guide in working up loads. This ammunition is now offered by Fiocchi.

8mm Rast-Gasser Factory Ballistics

Bullet (grains/type)	Powder	Grains	Velocity	Energy	Source/Comments
115 to 126 Lead	FL		750 - 785	140 - 170	Factory load
125	FL		787	170	1914-1918 factory load
126 Lead	FL		770	166	Fiocchi factory load

8mm Nambu

Historical Notes: This was the official Japanese military pistol cartridge introduced, in 1904, for the Nambu auto pistol. It was also used in the modified 1925 model and the odd-looking 1934 model. This was the official Japanese pistol cartridge in World War II, although other pistols and cartridges were used. It was used only by Japan.

General Comments: Quite a few 8mm Nambu pistols were brought back from the Pacific battle areas by returning GIs at war's end. Ammunition has been a problem, because most captured stores were destroyed. Externally, the cartridge resembles the 7.65mm Luger, but uses a larger diameter bullet and a semi-rimmed case. In power, it is slightly superior to the .32 Automatic. Most Nambu cartridges are collector's items.

Bullet diameter is .320-inch. Cast .32-caliber revolver bullets sized as close to this as possible would undoubtedly work in weights of 83 to 100 grains. Use only light charges of powder. In the 1980s, Brass Extrusion Laboratories, Ltd. of Bensenville, Illinois (now MAST Technology, Inc.; www.mast-technology.com), manufactured 8mm Nambu cases for Midway (www.midwayusa.com), though Midway no longer sells this ammunition. Today this cartridge is commercially loaded by the Old Western Scrounger (www.ows-ammo.com) and the Buffalo Arms Co (www.buffaloarms.com).

8mm Nambu Loading Data and Factory Ballistics

Bullet (grains/type)	Powder	Grains	Velocity	Energy	Source/Comments
83 Lead	Unique	3.0	950	165	Estimated velocity
102 FMJ	ML		960	202	Military load

8mm Lebel Revolver

Historical Notes: This cartridge is for the French 1892 Ordnance Revolver, commonly called the Lebel. This is a six-shot, solid-frame, double-action gun. Bayard and Pieper also made revolvers in this chambering. Small lots have shown up in surplus stores, but these are of interest mostly to military collectors.

General Comments: The 8mm Lebel revolver cartridge closely resembles the .32-20 WCF, and ammunition can be made by sizing .32-20 cases. This is not a common item, but surplus stores have occasionally offered this ammunition. The .32 Smith & Wesson Long can be fired in these revolvers, but the cases bulge badly and accuracy is poor. When cooking up your own loads, stick to moderate charges and velocity, as the Lebel revolver is not designed for high pressures. For field use, this is another .32 S&W Long-class cartridge suitable only for small game. Bullet diameter is .330-inch, and one can use the Lyman No. 32359 cast bullet. Fiocchi currently offers this ammunition.

8mm Lebel Revolver Loading Data and Factory Ballistics

Bullet (grains/type)	Powder	Grains	Velocity	Energy	Source/Comments
115 Lead	Bullseye	2.8	700	126	Lyman No. 32359
102 Lead	ML		625	104	Military load

7.5mm Swedish Nagant Revolver

Historical Notes: The cartridge listed here is the 7.5mm Swedish, designed for the 1887 Swedish Nagant military revolver manufactured by Husqvarna. Since the end of World War II, large quantities of these revolvers have been sold as surplus in the United States. This has a short, rimmed case with an outside-lubricated bullet and is usually loaded with blackpowder. The revolver is long obsolete, but Norma of Sweden loaded this cartridge with Berdan-primed cases and smokeless propellants.

General Comments: The 7.5mm Swedish Nagant Revolver cartridge was practically unknown in the United States, prior to 1948. It is listed here, because of the large number of these revolvers imported. Many Nagant revolvers were altered to use the .22 Long Rifle, by lining the barrel and bushing the cylinder. The .32 Short or Long Colt can be fired in these revolvers, but they fit loosely and accuracy is terrible. Cartridge cases can be made from empty .32-20 cases trimmed back to .895-inch in length. The Australian .310 Martini cartridge will also work, if cut to the proper length. The Swedish Nagant revolver was intended for blackpowder, and only low-pressure smokeless powder loads are safe. Ballistically, the 7.5mm cartridge is in the same class as the .32 S&W Long. Fiocchi loads the 7.5mm Swiss, which is essentially the same case with a different loading and which can be used in these guns.

7.5mm Swedish Nagant Revolver Loading Data and Factory Ballistics

Bullet (grains/type)	Powder	Grains	Velocity	Energy	Source/Comments
105 Lead	Bullseye	2.0	720	120	Duplicates factory load
105 Lead	Blackpowder (FFFg)	11.5	725	121	Duplicates factory load
104 Lead	FL		725	121	Factory load
107 Lead	FL		710	108	Fiocchi factory load

8mm Roth-Steyr

Historical Notes: The 8mm Roth-Steyr cartridge and auto pistol were adopted by the Austro-Hungarian cavalry, in 1907. No other country or gun employed this cartridge. It was a popular post-World War II surplus item, all but unknown on the American market prior to the war. It is a recoil-operated pistol of rather odd appearance, resembling some modern air pistols.

General Comments: The 8mm Roth-Steyr cartridge is similar to the .32 Automatic, but longer and more powerful. It would make a fair field cartridge for small game if loaded with hunting-type bullets. The Roth-Steyr pistol has a non-detachable magazine in the grip that holds 10 shots. As with most Austrian-designed auto pistols of the period, it is loaded by retracting the slide (bolt) and inserting a special charger from the top. It can be loaded without the charger, but this is rather slow and hard on the fingers. Fiocchi still manufactures this cartridge.

8mm Roth-Steyr Loading Data and Factory Ballistics

Bullet (grains/type)	Powder	Grains	Velocity	Energy	Source/Comments
116 Lead	Unique	3.3	1050	283	Lyman No. 313226
113 FMJ	FL		1070	287	Fiocchi factory load
116 FMJ	ML		1090	309	Military load

.35 Smith & Wesson Auto/.35 Automatic

Historical Notes: Smith & Wesson introduced this cartridge and a new auto pistol, in 1913. The S&W pistol is the only one that ever chambered this cartridge. It was discontinued (in .35 S&W chambering), in 1921. The pistol was based on designs of the Belgian C.P. Clement. Commercial ammunition was loaded until about 1940.

General Comments: The .35 S&W Auto is actually a .32-caliber cartridge and is similar to the .32 Automatic. In fact, it is possible to fire .32 Automatic ammo in some .35 semi-auto pistols. The cartridge designation was probably to prevent confusion with the .32 Automatic. However, it has created more confusion than it prevented. The .32 Automatic is a better cartridge, and Smith & Wesson eventually chambered its pistol for that more popular round.

.35 Smith & Wesson Auto Loading Data and Factory Ballistics

Bullet (grains/type)	Powder	Grains	Velocity	Energy	Source/Comments
76 FMJ	Bullseye	1.6	809	110	Duplicate factory load
76 FMJ	FL		809	110	Factory load

9mm Ultra

Historical Notes: This cartridge was designed for the Walther PP Super semi-auto pistol, introduced in 1972-'73. This seven-shot autoloader was designed particularly for the West German police. It was not available to the civilian market until 1975, and then only in small numbers. Quite a few guns in this chambering have shown up in the United States, as the West German police discontinued using this chambering. In recent years, the SIG Sauer P230 and the Benelli B76 auto pistols have also been chambered for the 9mm Ultra. The cartridge was actually developed, in 1936, for the German Air Force, but was never officially adopted.

The 9mm Ultra is one millimeter longer than the .380 Auto and one millimeter shorter than the 9mm Luger, with the same general case dimensions. In terms of inches, the .380 case length is .680-inch, the 9mm Ultra is .720-inch, and the 9mm Luger is .760-inch.

Original loading of the 9mm Ultra (by Hirtenberger, of Austria) used a 100-grain full-jacketed bullet at a muzzle velocity of 1060 fps. GECO (Dynamit-Nobel) loads a 94-grain full-jacketed bullet at an initial velocity of 1054 fps. Both bullets are of truncated cone shape. Ammunition is hard to find in the United States, and American companies do not load it. The case has a slightly rebated rim .02-inch smaller than the base.

General Comments: European police have traditionally carried small .32 Automatic and .380 Automatic pistols. However, with the increase in crime and attacks by terrorist groups, they found themselves outgunned by those on the other side of the law. There was some reluctance to adopt the full-powered 9mm military auto-pistol, which is heavier and bulkier than the more convenient .32 and .380 autos. The 9mm Ultra was an effort to provide greater stopping power, while retaining the small, handy pistols police were used to carrying. This was not successful, and most German police now carry 9mm Luger-chambered pistols.

The best that can be said about the 9mm Ultra is that it is as good as, and probably more effective than, the .380 Automatic. Handloaded with 9mm jacketed hollowpoint bullets, it would certainly be satisfactory for small-game hunting. Hirtenberger, Fiocchi, and Dynamit Nobel still offer this cartridge. It is sometimes called the 9mm Police.

9mm Ultra Loading Data and Factory Ballistics

Bullet (grains/type)	Powder	Grains	Velocity	Energy	Source/Comments
100	W231	3.6	1010	225	NA
123 FMJ	FL		1070	350	Fiocchi factory load
124 FMJ	ML		1050	308	Military load

9mm Browning Long

Historical Notes: This Browning-designed pistol cartridge was popular in Europe, but never adopted by American manufacturers. It was introduced with the FN Browning 1903 Model pistol. Sweden used the pistol and cartridge as an official military sidearm, starting in 1907, and sold most of these pistols as surplus after World War II. Most were altered to use the standard .380 Automatic for the American market. In addition to the Browning, Le Francais and Webley & Scott pistols used this cartridge.

General Comments: The 9mm Browning Long has been used only to a very limited extent in the United States. In size, it is a shortened .38 Automatic, and, in power, is between the .380 and .38 Colt Automatic. For field use, it would be strictly a small-game number. Bullet diameter is the same as the 9mm Luger. Bullets for reloading are easy to obtain. Like all auto pistol cartridges, killing power can be improved with soft-point or half-jacketed hunting bullets. Even in Europe, this cartridge is essentially obsolete.

9mm Browning Long Loading Data and Factory Ballistics

Bullet (grains/type)	Powder	Grains	Velocity	Energy	Source/Comments
75 Lead	Unique	5.0	1078	192	Lyman No. 358101
95 FMJ	Unique	5.0	1050	230	Estimated Velocity
116 FMJ	Unique	4.8	1000	255	Estimated Velocity
110 FMJ	FL		1100	300	Factory load

9mm Glisenti

Historical Notes: Adopted for the Italian military Model 1910 Glisenti auto pistol, the 9mm Glisenti was also used in other pistols and submachine guns. It was the official Italian pistol cartridge, during World War I and II. It is similar in physical measurement to the 9mm Luger (Parabellum), but is not loaded as heavily. Regular 9mm Luger ammunition should not be fired in pistols intended for the Glisenti cartridge or loading.

General Comments: The 9mm Glisenti is in about the same class as the .38 Automatic and is not quite as powerful as the standard 9mm Luger. Quite a few Glisenti pistols have been sold on the American market through military surplus dealers. Ammunition can be made by loading 9mm Luger cases down to the proper velocity and pressure levels. Bullet diameter is .355-inch, so standard 9mm Luger bullets can be used. This cartridge is now obsolete, but Fiocchi has recently manufactured it.

9mm Glisenti Loading Data and Factory Ballistics

Bullet (grains/type)	Powder	Grains	Velocity	Energy	Source/Comments
116 FMJ	Bullseye	4.0	1070	294	
123 FMJ	FL		1070	350	Fiocchi factory load
124 FMJ	ML		1050	308	Military load

9x21mm

Historical Notes: In many countries, such as Italy, Mexico, and France, it is illegal for private citizens to own semi-automatic pistols in military chamberings, such as 9x19mm Parabellum (9mm Luger). Faced with a strong demand for a powerful, semi-automatic pistol in a non-military chambering, the 9x21mm cartridge was developed, in the mid-1980s. It is a 9x19mm Parabellum case lengthened two millimeters. However, a blunt, truncated-cone bullet seated deeply in the case mouth is used. Overall loaded length is, therefore, the same as the 9mm Luger cartridge. Thus, magazines, breech faces, and feed ramps that are suitable for one cartridge work fine with the other with little or no modification.

General Comments: Ballistically, the 9x21mm offers the same performance as the 9mm Luger, so those barrels and recoil springs can be used. Firearms manufacturers find it easy to transition from 9mm to 9x21 to produce this chambering as needed for specialized markets.

For self-defense, the 9x21mm is fully the ballistic equal of the 9mm Luger. It is suitable for small-game hunting with expanding bullets. For handloading, 9mm Luger data can be used. Despite its similarity, these two cartridges are not interchangeable.

With the Western European Union consolidating firearms laws, the prohibition against private ownership of pistols in military chamberings will be ended. The purpose for which the 9x21mm was developed will no longer exist. Therefore, the 9x21mm will probably become history. Fiocchi recently offered this ammunition.

9x21mm Loading Data and Factory Ballistics

Bullet (grains/type)	Powder	Grains	Velocity	Energy	Source/Comments
90 JHTP	Blue Dot	10.2	1482	437	Lyman
124 FMJ	AA No. 7	9.8	1335	490	Lyman
147 Lead	AA No. 7	8.0	1089	385	Lyman No. 356637
123 FMJ	FL		1181	380	Patronen factory load (Hungarian)
124 FMJ	FL		1110	340	Fiocchi factory load

9mm Bayard Long (9mm Bergmann-Bayard Long)

Historical Notes: This cartridge is for the 1910 Model Bergmann-Bayard automatic pistol, which was the official Danish military sidearm for many years. The Spanish also used both pistol and cartridge and, consequently, many Spanish-made pistols were made for this round. The Astra and various Colt's-Browning copies or modifications are found in the 9mm Bayard chambering.

General Comments: The 9mm Bayard has never been manufactured in the United States. Pistols in this chambering are mostly military surplus, which were imported and sold after World War II. The cartridge is quite similar to the .38 Automatic, but longer. The Astra Model 400 is designed for the 9mm Bayard and will handle the .38 Automatic without any adjustment, but most other pistols will not. It is a potent round and makes a good field cartridge if loaded with hunting-type bullets. Bullet diameter is .355-inch, and any 9mm Luger bullet can be used, cast or jacketed. Standard loads for the 9mm Luger or the .38 Colt Automatic will work fine in these pistols.

9mm Bergmann-Bayard Long Loading Data and Factory Ballistics

Bullet (grains/type)	Powder	Grains	Velocity	Energy	Source/Comments
116 JSP	Unique	7.0	1280	420	NA
125 FMJ	FL		1120	352	Factory load

9mm Steyr

Historical Notes: The standard Austrian military pistol cartridge for the Steyr Model 1912 auto pistol, the case is approximately 23 millimeters long, as compared to the 9mm Luger, which is 19 millimeters. Apparently, the only other countries besides Austria to use this as a military round were Romania and Chile, which adopted both the Steyr pistol and cartridge, in 1912. This cartridge is very similar to the 9mm Bergmann-Bayard, and these two are often confused. However, 9mm Steyr ammunition is usually found with a nickel-jacketed bullet. The 9mm Bayard case is slightly longer. Quantities of 9mm Steyr pistols have appeared on the United States surplus military market and, for awhile, ammunition was readily available.

General Comments: The 9mm Steyr is quite similar to the 9mm Bayard. The Astra Model 400 will sometimes handle both, but other pistols will not. The 9mm Steyr is a good field cartridge, similar to the .38 Colt Automatic in performance. Bullet diameter is the same as the 9mm Luger, and one can use Luger bullets for reloading. Any standard load for the 9mm Luger or .38 Automatic will work in the Steyr pistol. Fiocchi of Italy still loads this round.

9mm Steyr Loading Data and Factory Ballistics

Bullet (grains/type)	Powder	Grains	Velocity	Energy	Source/Comments
119 Lead	Unique	6.5	1200	379	Lyman No. 356402
115 FMJ	FL		1200	360	Factory load
116 FMJ	ML		1200	370	Military load

9mm Federal

Historical Notes: The 9mm Federal was developed by Federal Cartridge Co. and first appeared in its 1989 ammunition catalog. It is a rimmed version of the 9mm Luger, intended for use in revolvers. The first handgun specifically chambered for it was the Charter Arms Pit Bull revolver, also introduced in 1989. This was a five-shot double-action revolver with a 2½-inch barrel similar to the older Police Bulldog model. The use of any rimless cartridge in double-action revolvers has never been entirely satisfactory, because of extraction difficulties. The 9mm Federal was designed to eliminate this problem in the same way that the .45 Auto Rim removed the need for the half-moon clips in .45 Automatic revolvers. However, the 9mm Federal lacks the very thick rim characteristic of the .45 Auto Rim. Shortly after this round's introduction, Charter Arms went out of business, though that company has since been resurrected. No other manufacturer chambered this cartridge.

General Comments: Initial loading of the 9mm Federal was a 115-grain jacketed hollowpoint bullet at 1280 fps muzzle velocity from a four-inch test barrel. Ballistically, this equals or exceeds most +P .38 Special loads and is pushing close to .357 Magnum performance. The principal advantage of the 9mm Federal was the short case length, which would allow shortening the length of the cylinder and frame of revolvers designed for it, thus reducing weight and bulk. However, no gun manufacturer ever did this; Charter Arms merely chambered it in a .38 Special-sized cylinder. As a self-defense or field cartridge, this would be equal to the 9mm Luger.

Unfortunately, the 9mm Federal will chamber in most .38 S&W revolvers. Firing such a combination, particularly in the old top-break type, would almost certainly result in destruction of the revolver and injury or death to the shooter and bystanders. Also, some lots or makes of .38 S&W ammunition will fit the 9mm Federal chamber, but it might not be safe to fire these in 9mm Federal guns, because of the grossly oversize bullet. Last, but not least, 9mm Luger cartridges will chamber and fire in 9mm Federal revolvers, but this can create extraction and other mechanical problems. In all cases, stick to the ammunition for which the gun is chambered. Reloading data for the 9mm Luger can be used as a guide in working up reloads. In 1992, Federal ceased manufacture of this exceedingly ill-conceived cartridge.

9mm Federal Loading Data and Factory Ballistics

Bullet (grains/type)	Powder	Grains	Velocity	Energy	Source/Comments
115	HS 6	7.7	1270	410	NA
115 JHP	FL		1280	420	Factory load

9mm Luger (9x19mm Parabellum)
9mm Luger +P

Historical Notes: The 9mm Luger, or 9mm Parabellum, was introduced, in 1902, with the Luger automatic pistol. It was adopted first by the German Navy, in 1904, and then by the German Army, in 1908. Since that time, it has been adopted by the military of practically every non-Communist power. It has become the world's most popular and widely used military handgun and submachine gun cartridge. In the United States, Colt's, Smith & Wesson, Ruger, and many others chamber the 9mm, as do many foreign-made pistols. In 1985, the 9mm Luger was adopted as the official military cartridge by U.S. Armed Forces, along with the Beretta Model 92-F (M-9) 15-shot semi-auto pistol.

General Comments: Although the 9mm Luger delivers good performance for police, military, or sporting use, it was not popular in the United States until fairly recently. The principal reason was that no American-made arms were chambered for it initially. In 1954, Smith & Wesson brought out its Model 39 semi-automatic in this chambering, and Colt's chambered its lightweight Commander for the 9mm Luger, in 1951. This plus the influx of military pistols chambered for the 9mm greatly increased both popularity and acceptance in this country. Currently the 9mm Luger is the most widely used cartridge in the United States, though a principal complaint has always been that the 9mm Luger lacks stopping power as a defensive cartridge. However, the only automatic pistol cartridge with proven stopping power is the .45 Automatic. For hunting use, the 9mm Luger is adequate for most small game, if hollowpoint bullets are used. Modern, premium jacketed hollow point loads can dramatically improve performance. A variety of 9mm loadings are offered by every major U.S. ammunition maker.

13th Edition Update: The term "stopping power" as referred to in the above text is really nothing more than words used to describe something that gun writers have never been able to quantify like they do with velocity and group size. Since the 1980s, when the 9mm became a very popular cartridge for use by law enforcement officers, those who have conducted research into the ability of a handgun cartridge to actually "stop" a bad guy have learned a great deal. Additionally, modern bullet engineering, combined with the moderately high velocities obtainable with a 9mm Luger, 9mm Luger +P, and 9mm Luger +P+ loads has changed not only the outlook on, but the performance of, the 9mm Luger. Extensive tests in 10-percent ordnance gelatin have shown that many defensive loads for the 9mm expand to a wider diameter and penetrate as deeply as many .45 Auto loads—and they do this with a higher impact velocity, which translates to more tissue destruction. Anyone armed with a 9mm and good defensive ammo should feel just as safe as if they were carrying a .45 Auto.—R.A.M.

9mm Luger (9x19mm Parabellum, 9mm Luger +P) Loading Data and Factory Ballistics

Bullet (grains/type)	Powder	Grains	Velocity	Energy	Source/Comments
100	Unique	5.1	1150	294	Hornady
115	Herco	6.0	1200	368	Speer
115	Bullseye	4.8	1250	399	Speer, Hornady, Sierra
115	231	5.2	1150	338	Speer, Hornady, Sierra
124/125	Unique	5.5	1150	364	Speer, Sierra
124/125	700X	4.3	1150	364	Speer, Sierra
80 TAC-XP JHP	FL		1560	433	DoubleTap Factory Load
115 FMJ	FL		1160	345	Factory load
124 JHP	FL		1300	465	Buffalo Bore Factory Load
124 FMJ	ML		1299	465	Military load, U.S.
124 FMJ	FL		1120	345	Factory load
147 JHP	FL		975	310	Factory load

9mm Mauser

Historical Notes: Introduced in 1908, this cartridge was developed for the Export Model Mauser auto pistol. Both cartridge and pistol had a relatively short life and were discontinued, in 1914, with the outbreak of World War I. Production was not resumed after the war. The 9mm Mauser was designed as a more powerful round than the 7.63mm Mauser, in an effort to capture sales in Africa and South America. It failed in this effort and never became popular, although it is potentially a good field cartridge. The 9mm Mauser was revived, in 1933-'34, when the Swiss-designed Neuhausen submachine gun and, later, the Austrian Steyr-Solothurn were chambered for this round. Manufacture of this cartridge then resumed in several European countries. Today, the 9mm Mauser (DWM No. 487) is a collector's item.

General Comments: The 9mm Mauser is more powerful than the 9mm Luger and has an edge on the .38 Colt Super Automatic. It develops 534 ft-lbs of energy at the muzzle, compared to 465 and 430 for top factory loadings of the 9mm Luger and .38 Colt Super, respectively. According to the DWM catalog, the 9mm Mauser is loaded with a 123- or 128-grain full-jacketed bullet at an initial velocity of 1362 fps. With modern bullets, this would make a good small- to medium-game hunting cartridge. The case is approximately .23-inch longer than the 9mm Luger and is rimless and Berdan-primed. Empty cases are easily reloaded with any standard 9mm (.355-inch) 100- to 130-grain bullet.

9mm Mauser Loading Data and Factory Ballistics

Bullet (grains/type)	Powder	Grains	Velocity	Energy	Source/Comments
125	BlueDot	10.6	1300	467	Estimated Velocity
128 FMJ	FL		1362	534	Factory load

9x23 Winchester

Historical Notes: Winchester introduced this cartridge early in 1996, announcing it at the annual NRA convention. This chambering was designed to meet a specific requirement of the International Practical Shooting Confederation (IPSC) competition, and is not well known outside that discipline.

IPSC competitors have struggled for years to concoct the lowest recoiling load that will qualify for Major Power Factor designation. IPSC Power Factor (PF) is bullet weight in grains, times muzzle velocity in feet per second, divided by 1,000. To qualify as a "Major Cartridge," a load must generate at least 175 PF units. To qualify as a "Minor," it must produce 125 PF units (new rules are now under consideration). Scoring includes a bonus for competitors using a Major power factor cartridge. Owing to magazine capacity and grip size considerations, the 9mm-bore size is highly preferred. Because of the muzzle braking devices used, combining a heavy charge of powder with a light bullet to achieve a given PF results in a load that generates less disruption to the shooter's hold, compared to a heavier bullet loaded at lower velocity but generating the same PF. This allows the shooter to get back on target faster. Therefore, the standard approach has been to load unusually light bullets at unusually high velocities. The trouble is that, for any given PF, the lighter the bullet, the greater the muzzle energy. Since we have found no free lunches in the world of kinetics, it follows that, to achieve more muzzle energy, the load must also generate more chamber pressure. Therefore, IPSC loads tend to generate unusually high chamber pressures—many loads commonly used by top competitors have approached the pressure levels of magnum rifle proof loads! When firing such loads in a conventional pistol, one thing is certain, eventually, something will give. Winchester's solution to this significant problem was to design a new case.

General Comments: While the 9x23 looks like a stretched 9mm Luger, there are significant internal differences. The 9x23 has an unusually thick web section. This prevents the dangerous case wall blowout that can occur with any conventional pistol cartridge when an unusually high-pressure loading is fired in a gun with a feed ramp in the bottom of the chamber that extends further forward than the "solid" portion of the case (the web). The 9x23mm case has sufficient capacity to allow IPSC shooters to achieve Major Power Factor using relatively light bullets and without generating gun-wrecking pressures. Nevertheless, IPSC shooters who insist upon using ever-lighter bullets will eventually run into trouble. Ballistics are quite impressive. Given proper loads, this cartridge would seem to qualify as a serious self-defense number.

9x23mm Winchester Factory Ballistics

Bullet (grains/type)	Powder	Grains	Velocity	Energy	Source/Comments
124	FL		1450	577	Winchester factory load
124	FL		1460	585	Winchester factory load

9mm Winchester Magnum

Historical Notes: Reports on the 9mm Winchester Magnum were circulating as early as 1977, but, 11 years later, in late 1988, it was still not exactly an over-the-counter item, although a few individuals were using it in Thompson/Center pistols. This cartridge was listed in the 1988 Winchester-Western Sporting Arms and Ammunition Catalog. In any event, the 9mm Magnum is one of two cartridges developed by Winchester for the stainless steel Wildey gas-operated semi-automatic pistol. This is a rather large handgun (weighing more than three pounds unloaded), and holding 14 of these 9mm Magnum rounds. That gun was advertised as available in five-, six-, seven-, eight-, or 10-inch barrel lengths. It had a ventilated, raised rib over the barrel and an adjustable, target-type rear sight. This pistol and cartridge are intended primarily for silhouette competition, but have an obvious field application for hunting small to medium game or even big game in the hands of an expert.

General Comments: The 9mm Winchester Magnum bears some resemblance to the older 9mm Mauser cartridge and develops roughly comparable ballistics. The Mauser 9mm fires a 128-grain bullet at 1362 fps, whereas the Winchester version has a 115-grain bullet that starts out at 1475 fps. The energies developed are 534 and 556 ft-lbs, respectively, so these are not very far apart. A 115-grain bullet with a muzzle velocity of 1475 fps (five-inch barrel) is impressive, but less than top handloads in the .357 Magnum, which can develop over 1550 fps with 125-grain bullets. The 9mm Magnum is certainly more powerful than either the 9mm Luger or the .38 Colt Super and, if loaded with hunting-type bullets, should prove to be very effective for a broad range of hunting situations.

9mm Winchester Magnum Factory Ballistics

Bullet (grains/type)	Powder	Grains	Velocity	Energy	Source/Comments
115 FMJ	FL		1475	556	Factory load

.380 Automatic Colt Pistol
(9mm Kurz/9x17mm/.380 ACP)

Historical Notes: This cartridge was designed by John Browning and introduced in Europe by FN of Belgium, in 1912, as the 9mm Browning Short. It had previously been added to the Colt Pocket Automatic line, in 1908. Several governments have adopted it as the official military pistol cartridge. These include Czechoslovakia, Italy, and Sweden. It is also much used by European police. Colt's, High Standard, Remington, and Savage have made pistols in this chambering, in the United States. In Europe, Browning, Beretta, Bayard, CZ, Frommer, Astra, Star, Llama, Walther and others made or make .380 Automatic-chambered pistols. This cartridge is also called 9x17mm.

General Comments: This is another cartridge that has been very popular, because of the light, handy pistols that are chambered for it. The .380 Auto has more stopping power and is a far better cartridge for almost any purpose than the .32 Auto. It is about the minimum pistol cartridge considered adequate for police or military use. For self-defense, it is not as powerful as the 9mm Luger, .38 Auto, and a few others, but this is offset, to a certain extent, by the reduced size and weight of the arms it is used in. For hunting or field use, it will do a good job on rabbits, birds, or other small game. It offers high velocity, which is an advantage for field use. With cast or swaged half-jacketed bullets of hunting type, it will do a good job on small game, but not many shooters want to bother handloading it.

13th Edition Update: Shortly after the 2008 election, there was a renewed nationwide interest in super-compact concealed carry handguns. All of a sudden, .380 Autos became the most popular handguns of all time. Sales sky-rocketed for itty bitty pistols like the Ruger LCP, and it was almost impossible to find .380 Auto ammunition on any shelf. The renewed interest in this cartridge has driven ammo manufacturers to engineer some very effective .380 ammunition for defensive handguns. Those from Buffalo Bore, DoubleTap, and Winchester are perfect examples and take the .380 Auto into .38 Special performance range. The Buffalo Bore load is indeed a +P load, but it should be noted that +P .380 Auto ammunition is not recognized by SAAMI and should only be fired in handguns designed for it or in those specified to be safe for its use by the ammunition manufacturer.—R.A.M.

.380 Automatic Colt Pistol (9mm Kurz/9x17mm/.380 ACP) Loading Data and Factory Ballistics

Bullet (grains/type)	Powder	Grains	Velocity	Energy	Source/Comments
90 JHP	Bullseye	3.0	900	162	Sierra, Hornady, Speer
95 FMJ	Bullseye	3.2	900	171	Speer, Sierra
95 FMJ	Unique	3.7	900	171	Speer, Sierra
80 Barnes TAC-XP	FL		1050	196	DoubleTap Factory Load
85 JHP	FL		1000	189	Factory load
88 JHP	FL		990	191	Factory load
90 JHP +P	FL		1200	288	Buffalo Bore Factory Load
90 JHP	FL		1000	200	Factory load
95 FMJ	FL		955	192	Factory load
95 Bonded PDX1	FL		1000	211	Winchester Factory Load
100 Hard Cast Lead FN	FL		1150	294	Buffalo Bore Factory Load

.38 Short & Long Colt

Historical Notes: The .38 Long Colt was once the official United States Army revolver cartridge (1892 to 1911). The short version was used mainly in the Colt Army & Navy Model revolver with swing-out cylinder, developed in 1887. The .38 Long Colt was introduced, in 1875, as one of several chamberings for Colt's New Line, New Police and New House revolvers.

General Comments: Since this was once a military cartridge, a number of Colt's and S&W revolvers in this chambering are still around. The .38 Long Colt cartridge can be fired in a .38 Special revolver, but not vice versa. During the Spanish-American War and the Philippine insurrection, the Army found that the .38 Long Colt had insufficient stopping power for combat use. The cartridge was therefore dropped, in 1911, in favor of the .45 Automatic. This was the experience that made the U.S. Army reluctant to adopt the 9mm Luger. It was forced to do so, in 1985, largely as a NATO-inspired political decision. Advocates of a smaller caliber admit the superior stopping power of the .45, but point out that extra weight and reduced magazine capacity are detrimental factors that should also be considered. The .38 Long Colt is in about the same class as the standard .38 Special loading, but it is not nearly as accurate or as versatile. Some of the old .38 Long Colt revolvers will accept .38 Special or .357 Magnum ammunition, but never fire these in the old .38s. Firing the .357 Magnum would be particularly dangerous, probably wrecking the gun and possibly injuring the shooter or bystanders. Remington has recently manufactured .38 Short Colt ammunition. Black Hills Ammunition has recently reintroduced .38 Long Colt ammunition in response to demands from the cowboy action shooting fraternity.

.38 Short & Long Colt Factory Ballistics

Bullet (grains/type)	Powder	Grains	Velocity	Energy	Source/Comments
150 Lead	FL		770	195	Factory load

.38 Special (.38 Special +P/.38-44 High Velocity/.38 Smith & Wesson Special)

Historical Notes: Also known as the .38 Colt Special and, more generally, as simply the .38 Special, this cartridge was developed by S&W and introduced with its Military & Police Model revolver, in 1902. This was originally a military cartridge meant to replace the unsatisfactory .38 Long Colt then in use by the Army. Colt's brought out its version, in 1909, which differs from the original only in bullet shape, the Colt's being a flat-point style. Colt's, Smith & Wesson, and others make revolvers specifically for this cartridge. Several Belgian, Brazilian, German, and Spanish firms also make .38 Special revolvers. The S&W 52 Target Auto, available until 1993, was made for the mid-range wadcutter load. A number of good quality, lever-action Winchester clones (1866, 1873, 1892) are chambered for the .38 Special.

General Comments: The .38 Special is considered one of the best-balanced, all-round handgun cartridges ever designed. It is also one of the most accurate and is very widely used for match shooting. Any .357 Magnum revolver will also shoot the .38 Special. At one time, it was the standard police cartridge here and largely in Mexico and Canada. It is also usable in lightweight pocket revolvers. Several companies make over/under, two-shot, derringer-type pistols in this chambering that are compact and relatively powerful for close-in self-defense. The .38 Special is also a very popular sporting cartridge for hunting small to medium game and varmint-type animals. With modern hunting bullets, it is effective for this purpose. Because of its moderate recoil, the average person can learn to shoot well with it in a short time, something not true of the .357 or .44 Magnums. The .38 Special is loaded by all major commercial ammunition manufacturers. Bullet weights from 95 to 200 grains have been available.

Note: Previous editions of this book incorrectly listed the .38-44 Target as being interchangeable with the .38 Special. Not so. The .38-44 was a chambering for the top-break S&W No. 3 Target revolver and is not to be confused with the later .38-44 High Velocity chambered in the N-frame Hand Ejector Outdoorsman. (In both cases, the .38-44 designation translates as "a .38 on a .44 frame.") The .38-44 for the No. 3 revolver featured a bullet loaded flush with the case mouth, which will not chamber in revolvers intended for the .38 Special.

.38 Smith & Wesson Special Loading Data and Factory Ballistics

Bullet (grains/type)	Powder	Grains	Velocity	Energy	Source/Comments
110 JHP	Bullseye	4.7	1000	244	Hornady, Speer, Sierra
125 JHP	231	5.5	1000	278	Sierra, Speer, Nosler
140 JHP	2400	10.4	950	281	Speer, Sierra
158 JHP	Herco	5.0	900	284	Speer, Nosler, Sierra
148 WC	Bullseye	3.1	800	210	Speer, Hornady
95 JHP	FL		1175	291	Factory load
110 JHP	FL		995	242	Factory load
125 JHP	FL		945	248	Factory load
130 FMS	ML		950	260	Military load
148 WC	FL		710	132	Factory load
150 LRN	FL		890	270	Factory load
158 Hard Core Cast +P	FL		1250	548	Buffalo Bore Factory Load
200 LRN	FL		730	236	Factory load

.357 Magnum (.357 S&W Magnum)

Historical Notes: This chambering was introduced, in 1935, by Smith & Wesson for its heavy-frame revolver. Ammunition was developed by Winchester, in cooperation with Smith & Wesson. Major Douglas B. Wesson (of S&W) and Philip B. Sharpe are credited with much of the final development work. The .357 Magnum is based on the .38 Special case lengthened about 1/10-inch, so it will not chamber in standard .38 Special revolvers. This was the most powerful handgun cartridge in the world, until the .44 Magnum was introduced, in 1955. Colt's, Ruger, Smith & Wesson, and many others manufacture revolvers for this cartridge. There has also been a proliferation of imported single- and double-action revolvers, and several single-shot pistols chamber it. There is even a semi-auto pistol in this chambering. American .357 Magnum revolvers have been used in Canada, Mexico, and other countries.

General Comments: This is probably the most popular high-velocity handgun cartridge in the United States for police, hunting, and target work. The .357 Magnum provides nearly double the velocity and more than three times the energy of standard .38 Special loads. It is noted for its flat trajectory, deep penetration, and great knockdown power. It has been used successfully on deer, black bear, elk, and even grizzly bear. However, it is not fully adequate for these larger animals, unless used by an excellent marksman. It is also used in repeating and single-shot rifles as matched arms to go along with a revolver. In a 20- to 24-inch rifle barrel, standard factory 158-grain loads develop about 1650 fps muzzle velocity, and special (rifle only) handloads will develop over 2000 fps. It is considered the best all-round handgun-hunting cartridge for small and medium game and, under proper conditions, for deer at short range. During the Korean conflict, it was very effective against the body armor used by the Communist forces. Nearly every major commercial ammunition manufacturer offers .357 Magnum ammunition.

.357 Magnum Loading Data and Factory Ballistics

Bullet (grains/type)	Powder	Grains	Velocity	Energy	Source/Comments
110 JHP	2400	19.0	1500	550	Sierra, Speer
125 JHP	2400	16.0	1200	400	Nosler, Speer, Hornady
140 JHP	W296	16.0	1200	448	Speer, Hornady, Sierra
158 JHP	2400	13.5	1200	505	Hornady, Speer, Sierra, Nosler
110 JHP	FL		1295	410	Factory load
125 JHP	FL		1450	583	Factory load
140 JHP	FL		1360	575	Factory load

Bullet (grains/type)	Powder	Grains	Velocity	Energy	Source/Comments
158 JHP, Lead	FL		1235	535	Factory load
180 JHP	FL		1090	475	Factory load
140 FTX	FL		1440	644	Hornady Factory Load

.357 Remington Maximum

Historical Notes: The .357 Maximum was announced as a joint venture between Remington Arms Co. and Sturm, Ruger and Co. This cartridge is a 3/10-inch elongation of the .357 Magnum case. The first handgun to chamber the round was the Ruger Blackhawk .357 Maximum single-action revolver, introduced in 1983. This was followed, in 1984, by the Dan Wesson double-action, stainless-steel revolver, the Seville single-action stainless-steel revolver, and the Thompson/Center Contender single-shot pistol. During the same year, Harrington & Richardson chambered its Model 258 single-shot rifle for the round, as did Savage in its Model 24V and Model 24VS Camper over/under rifle shotgun combination guns. Although Remington developed the commercial .357 Maximum, a similar wildcat cartridge was actually developed by Elgin Gates at an earlier time.

Unfortunately, the .357 Maximum revolvers all developed excessive gas-cutting on the top strap, just forward of the cylinder, within 1,000 rounds or so, when fired with full factory loads. Ruger withdrew its Blackhawk .357 Maximum revolver from production, pending additional research and possible engineering changes. Dan Wesson, when its revolvers were still in production, prior to that company's purchase by CZ, eliminated the problem by establishing a .002-inch barrel/cylinder gap for its .357 Maximum revolvers. (The Dan Wesson revolvers have interchangeable barrels that are easily replaced and fine-tuned by the customer, using a furnished gap tool.) Top strap erosion, of course, is not a problem with the single-shot Thompson/Center Contender or the rifles chambering the .357 Maximum.

General Comments: Efforts to develop ultra high-velocity revolvers have not been crowned with unbridled success. The .22 Remington Jet in the Model 53 Smith & Wesson revolver is another example of a combination that was discontinued because of mechanical troubles. In the case of the .357 Maximum, the cartridge differs from the standard .357 Magnum only in case length, so one can drop back to shooting the .357 Magnum in any Maximum revolver, or simply handload to lower velocity levels using the Maximum case. Factory ballistics were taken in a 10½-inch vented test barrel, and actual muzzle velocity from a revolver with the same-length barrel is about 200 fps lower than the advertised figure.

The .357 Maximum was conceived primarily as an ultra-velocity, flat-trajectory silhouette cartridge. That it would also make a good field cartridge for hunting small and medium game is obvious. Many would consider it a good deer cartridge, but, when used in a handgun, it would be rather marginal for that purpose. Of course, a good deal depends on the skill of the person using it and, as noted elsewhere, the older, less powerful .357 Magnum has killed its share of big game. Certainly, the .357 Maximum has been used as a big-game handgun cartridge, but the measure of success has reflected more upon the person behind the gun than the cartridge.

.357 Remington Maximum Loading Data and Factory Ballistics

Bullet (grains/type)	Powder	Grains	Velocity	Energy	Source/Comments
125 JHP	W296	25.0	1800	900	Hornady, Speer
140 JHP	W296	23.5	1700	899	Hornady, Speer
158 JHP	W296	21.0	1550	843	Hornady, Speer
180 FMJ	H4227	18.4	1300	676	Sierra, Nosler, Speer, Hornady
158 JHP	FL		1825	1168	Factory load
180 JHP	FL		1550	960	Factory load

.357 SIG

Historical Notes:	This cartridge is based upon the .40 S&W case, simply necked down with a short neck and a sharp shoulder. The design purpose was to achieve .357 Magnum revolver ballistics from typical semi-automatic pistols. This cartridge design offers several potential advantages. First, its compact nature allows use of a smaller (shorter) grip frame in pistols so chambered. For shooters with smaller hands, this is significant; many find guns chambered for the .45 Automatic and 10mm cartridges entirely too big for proper handling and accurate shooting. Second, compared to the parent cartridge, the .357 SIG can effectively launch lighter bullets at greater velocity to achieve similar muzzle energy with less recoil. All of these considerations figured in the development of this cartridge.				
General Comments:	The .357 SIG is loaded to a comparatively high pressure level—the same as top factory .357 Magnum loads and 14-percent higher than the .40 S&W or the 9mm Luger. The combination of high pressure, reasonable case capacity, and no barrel venting (as seen in .357 Magnum revolvers) allows this petite cartridge to generate significant ballistics—fully the equal of the .40 S&W in terms of muzzle energy. However, in the typical short pistol barrels used, there is a price to pay for this level of performance—muzzle blast is significant. Compared to the .40 S&W, the .357 SIG has only one advantage, that being a slight reduction in recoil. Time will tell if that will prove sufficient cause to popularize this cartridge.				

.357 SIG Loading Data and Factory Ballistics

Bullet (grains/type)	Powder	Grains	Velocity	Energy	Source/Comments
88 JHP	AA No. 5	11.1	1616	510	Accurate/1.13" OAL
95 FMJ	AA No. 5	11.0	1572	520	Accurate/1.135" OAL
115 XTP	AA No. 9	13.5	1434	525	Accurate/1.14" OAL
124 XTP	AA No. 9	13.0	1387	530	Accurate/1.14" OAL
147 XTP	Vit N350	6.9	1170	445	VihtaVuori/1.135" OAL
95 FMJ	AA No. 5	11.0	1572	520	Accurate/1.135" OAL
125 JHP	FL		1350	505	Speer & Federal factory load

.38 Automatic (.38 ACP)

Historical Notes:	This is another cartridge designed by John Browning and introduced by Colt's, in 1900, for its .38 Automatic. In its original form, this pistol was designed as a military gun. From this evolved the seven-shot sporting and eight-shot military models of 1902. This cartridge was stepped up in power, in 1929, and the improved round called the .38 Super Auto. In the United States, only Colt's chambered it. In England, Webley & Scott chambered it in one version of its military automatic. In Spain, a number of automatics have been made for the .38 ACP.				
General Comments:	Although developed for military and self-defense uses, the .38 Colt Auto achieved a degree of popularity for sporting use through its relatively high velocity. The military turned it down, because of previous poor results with the .38 Long Colt. No guns designed for this cartridge have been made since 1928, but plenty of the older model Colt pistols are still used. In power, it is about the same as the 9mm Luger, but it has a longer semi-rimmed case. This cartridge is now obsolete and is no longer loaded by any major ammunition maker.				

.38 Automatic/.38 Automatic Colt Pistol (ACP) Loading Data and Factory Ballistics

Bullet (grains/type)	Powder	Grains	Velocity	Energy	Source/Comments
115 FMJ	Bullseye	5.0	1150	338	Hornady
125 JHP	Bullseye	4.7	1100	336	Hornady
130 FMJ	FL		1040	312	Factory load

.38 Super Automatic
.38 Super Automatic +P

Historical Notes: Introduced by Colt's, in 1929, as an improved version of the older .38 Auto, the Super Auto is identical to the original cartridge, except that it uses a more powerful loading. This is a fine high-speed sporting cartridge for the improved Government Model automatic pistol, but it should not be used in the older Colt pocket models. The Thompson submachine gun was once available in a .38 Super chambering. In Spain, Llama has made pistols for it. It is not popular in Europe, but is very popular in Canada, Mexico, and South America, where pistols in military chamberings have been prohibited.

General Comments: This was, for many years, the most powerful automatic pistol cartridge made in the United States, from the standpoint of both velocity and energy. It makes a good sporting cartridge for hunting small to medium game, because the flat trajectory permits accurate long-range shots. However, the original metal-cased bullet did not bring out the full potential. With good expanding-type bullets, it is one of our better hunting cartridges for a pistol. It is more powerful than the 9mm Luger, but both are adequate for about the same range of game. It can give greater penetration than the .45 Automatic, but is inferior in stopping power for defensive use. For handloading, any 9mm bullet can be used. However, unless proper round-nosed or conical shapes are used, it will be necessary to single load most rounds. This chambering has been extremely popular among IPSC competitors. Both Remington and Winchester offer this cartridge.

.38 Super Automatic +P Loading Data and Factory Ballistics

Bullet (grains/type)	Powder	Grains	Velocity	Energy	Source/Comments
115 FMJ	Bullseye	5.0	1200	368	Hornady, Sierra, Speer
125 JHP	231	5.4	1150	500	Sierra, Hornady, Speer
115 JHP	FL		1300	431	Factory load
125 JHP	FL		1240	427	Factory load
130 FMJ	FL		1215	426	Factory load

.38 Smith & Wesson/.38 Colt New Police/
.38 Super Police/.380/200 (British)

Historical Notes: Designed by Smith & Wesson for its hinged-frame revolvers introduced about 1877, the .38 S&W is one of the more widely adopted American revolver cartridges; it has been used all over the world. England began using it as an official service cartridge prior to World War II, and it is well-distributed through the British Commonwealth. Large numbers of Spanish-made revolvers in this chambering are used in Mexico and South America, but it has never been very popular in Europe outside the UK. It is also known as the .38 Colt New Police and, with a 200-grain bullet, as the .38 Super Police. Colt's, H&R, Hopkins & Allen, Iver Johnson, Ruger, and S&W have made revolvers in this chambering, in the United States. Webley & Scott made many of the British service arms. The British service load is called the .380/200.

General Comments: The .38 S&W is another cartridge that owes most of its popularity to the fact that it is well-suited to lightweight pocket guns. It is also a good short-range cartridge for defense use and has better stopping power than any of the .32s and even some of the larger automatic pistol cartridges. The British military figured out that the shocking power of this cartridge with a 200-grain bullet was about the same as its older .455 military cartridge. In actual combat, this proved correct, thus permitting the use of lighter guns. The .38 S&W is not a particularly satisfactory hunting cartridge, because the curved trajectory limits its use to short ranges. However, it can be improved for hunting through judicious handloading. Remington still offers .38 S&W ammunition.

.38 Smith & Wesson Loading Data and Factory Ballistics

Bullet (grains/type)	Powder	Grains	Velocity	Energy	Source/Comments
148 Lead	Bullseye	2.5	700	161	Speer
158 Lead	Unique	3.0	700	172	Speer
145 Lead	FL		685	150	Factory load
200 Lead	ML		630	176	Military load, British

9mm Russian Makarov

Historical Notes: This is the current Russian military cartridge used in the Makarov and Stechkin auto-pistols. It was adopted shortly after the end of World War II, and its design may have been inspired by an experimental German cartridge called the 9mm Ultra. Other countries from the former Warsaw Pact also use the round. Chinese-made Makarov pistols have recently appeared on surplus shelves, along with 9mm Makarov ammunition.

General Comments: The Soviet 9mm pistol cartridge is intermediate in size and power between the .380 Automatic and the 9mm Luger. Technically, it can be described as a 9x18mm, although it differs dimensionally from the 9x18 Ultra and is not interchangeable with that cartridge. It is a well-designed cartridge for its purpose, although a little underpowered by Western standards. It is satisfactory for small game, when loaded with hunting-type bullets, which are now available. Loading data and components are available from various manufacturers. The Makarov pistol is of medium size and is similar to the German Walther. The Stechkin is a selective-fire type that can be used with the holster stock as a sub-machine gun. Both pistols are well made. Cases are easily formed by passing 9mm Luger cases over an expander ball and then trimming to length.

9mm Russian Makarov Loading Data and Factory Ballistics

Bullet (grains/type)	Powder	Grains	Velocity	Energy	Source/Comments
90 JHP	Unique	4.3	966	185	Lyman
95 FMJ	AA No. 5	5.0	909	173	Lyman
95 Lead	Unique	4.0	1016	215	Lyman No. 364653
100 JHP	Unique	4.1	887	173	Lyman
95 FMJ	ML		1060	237	Military load

.380 Short & Long Revolver

Historical Notes: The .380 Revolver cartridge is a British innovation for the Webley revolver and originated somewhere between 1868 and '70. It was loaded in the United States, until shortly after World War I. The .38 Short Colt was copied from it, and most .380 revolvers will accept the Colt version. It has been largely replaced by the inside-lubricated .38 S&W.

General Comments: The .380 is in the same class as the .38 Short Colt or .38 S&W. Use the same loading data. This ammunition recently has been available from Fiocchi.

.380 Revolver Factory Ballistics

Bullet (grains/type)	Powder	Grains	Velocity	Energy	Source/Comments
124 Lead	FL		625	110	Factory load

.40 Smith & Wesson

Historical Notes: This cartridge was developed as an in-house joint venture between Winchester and Smith & Wesson within six months from the time it was first discussed, in June 1989. Mr. Bersett at Winchester, and Mr. Melvin at S&W, were primarily responsible for this cartridge's development and standardization.

At that time, the FBI had been working with the 10mm Automatic, developing a load that met its criteria for bullet diameter, weight, and velocity. The folks at Winchester and Smith & Wesson realized that the power level the FBI had settled on could easily be achieved using a much shorter cartridge. This would facilitate accuracy and allow use of a smaller, more comfortable grip frame.

General Comments: Until quite recently, none of the factory loads available actually took full advantage of this cartridge's potential. Several now offered actually generate about 500 ft-lbs of energy in typical guns. This is serious power for such a small package and rivals the best the .45 Automatic can offer. However, such a powerful and compact package requires comparatively high pressures. High peak pressure and a short barrel equate to high noise and muzzle blast. Nevertheless, for its purpose, this has to be considered a superior cartridge design. It has already completely eclipsed the similar .41 Action Express.

.40 S&W Auto Loading Data and Factory Ballistics

Bullet (grains/type)	Powder	Grains	Velocity	Energy	Source/Comments
135 JHP	Universal	7.5	1324	524	Hodgdon
155 JHP	Universal	6.6	1186	482	Hodgdon
180 JHP	Universal	5.8	1046	435	Hodgdon
200 JHP	HS 7	7.4	907	363	Hodgdon
155 JHP	FL		1140	447	Factory load
155 JHP	FL		1205	500	Factory load
155 FMJ-SWC	FL		1125	436	Factory load
180 JHP	FL		990	392	Factory load
180 JHP	FL		1015	412	Factory load

10mm Automatic

Historical Notes: The 10mm Auto was introduced, in 1983, as the cartridge for the Bren Ten semi-auto pistol, made by the now-defunct Dornaus & Dixon Enterprises, Inc., of Huntington Beach, California. Ammunition was loaded by Norma, with a 200-grain full-jacketed truncated cone bullet, similar to some 9mm Luger and .45 Automatic loads of some years back. According to data furnished by Norma, the ammunition is loaded to a mean working pressure of 37,000 psi, with a maximum pressure of 44,400 psi. This is getting up in the area of some rifle loads and makes this a rather hot handgun cartridge. Muzzle velocity is listed as 1200 fps, and energy at the muzzle as 635 ft-lbs. This makes this cartridge more powerful than the .357 Magnum or the obsolete lead bullet .41 Magnum police load. Muzzle energy is about double that of the .45 Automatic. Gun and cartridge are the creation of Jeff Cooper and associates, who were trying to develop the ideal combat weapon. Colt's and several others have offered the 10mm chambering.

General Comments: The Bren Ten semi-auto pistol was based on a modification of the much-praised Czech CZ-75 pistol design. It had a five-inch barrel, 11-shot magazine, and weighed 39 ounces. It was a full-size combat-type pistol intended primarily for law enforcement/self-defense use, but it had many design problems.

The 10mm cartridge is an ideal combat round with good stopping power, particularly with an expanding-type bullet. However, recoil is quite heavy. It would also be a good field cartridge for small to medium game or larger animals, in the hands of a good shot and skilled hunter. In the late 1980s, the FBI adopted this cartridge in a slightly reduced loading, along with a matching S&W pistol, as standard issue. Problems with the guns delayed general issue. Ammunition was initially quite expensive. This discouraged non-handloaders from doing much shooting with the round. Overall, the Bren Ten pistol and cartridge represent an excellent concept for a combat handgun, and it reflects the extensive background and experience of Cooper.

Hornady, Speer, Sierra, and Nosler offer suitable bullets. The 10mm Auto cartridge has been loaded by Federal, Winchester, Remington, CCI, and other U.S. ammunition manufacturers. Actual ballistics are generally about 100 fps slower than early factory claims, so actual 10mm Automatic factory loads do not significantly exceed .45 Automatic +P ballistics.

10mm Automatic Loading Data and Factory Ballistics

Bullet (grains/type)	Powder	Grains	Velocity	Energy	Source/Comments
155 JHP	BlueDot	12.0	1250	538	Hornady, Sierra
180 JHP	BlueDot	10.0	1150	529	Hornady, Sierra
200 FMJ	BlueDot	8.5	1100	537	Hornady
170 JHP	FL		1340	680	Norma factory load
180 JHP	FL		1030	425	Factory load
180 JHP	FL		950	361	FBI factory loading
200 FMC	FL		1200	635	Factory load

.41 Short Colt

Historical Notes: The .41 (Short) Colt uses a heel-base bullet of about .401-inch maximum diameter. One of an entire line of cartridges designed for application in various revolvers with cylindrical (i.e., non-shouldered) chambers, this was never a very successful cartridge. The chief complaints involved limited case support for the bullet, as well as the problems associated with the necessary external grease grooves, which tended to attract dirt. In fact, it was said that this type of cartridge was among the deadliest on the frontier, not because of its ballistic effect, but because the dirt and grime it carried into even a minor wound was almost certain to lead to a fatal infection.

The historical reason for the invention of heel-based cartridges stemmed from the era of the conversion cap-and-ball revolver. It was a simple matter to bore a hole of cylinder-mouth diameter full-length through the cylinder. The heel-base bulleted cartridge was invented for use in guns so converted. The original loading used a 160-grain lead bullet and 14 grains of blackpowder.

General Comments: The .41 Short Colt was never a popular chambering and offered limited ballistics. It was also very difficult to handload properly. Lyman once offered moulds that cast hollow-base bullets of inside case diameter. These were easier to load and removed the problem of the external-lube groove but were not sufficiently accurate to engender any following.

.41 Long Colt

Historical Notes: Introduced by Colt's, with its double-action or Lightning Model revolver, in 1877, it was later used in the New Army, New Navy, Army Special, Single Action Army, and the Bisley. No revolvers have chambered this cartridge since about the early 1930s. The .41 Short Colt is identical to this cartridge, except for case length (.65-inch) and the 160-grain bullet used. Both rounds were originally blackpowder cartridges using outside-lubricated bullets with a diameter of .401-inch. Smokeless powder, inside-lubricated cartridges have hollow-base bullets of .387-inch diameter intended to expand into the bore upon exiting the case.

General Comments: Although obsolete for a long time, the .41 Long Colt was, for some years, quite popular. It is largely a short-range number, with its slow, heavy bullet, but it has good stopping power. Its performance can be duplicated by using the 200-grain bullet in the .38 Special. It actually is no more powerful than the .38 Special and, in addition, is neither as accurate nor as versatile. It was never popular for hunting, although it would certainly be adequate for small to medium game. These cartridges are now collector's items, as there has been no commercial manufacture for many years until recently; Midway USA (www.midwayusa.com)is currently carrying the round, manufactured by Ultramax, intended for cowboy action shooters. Brass is available from Starline (www.starlinebrass.com).

.41 Long Colt Loading Data and Factory Ballistics

Bullet (grains/type)	Powder	Grains	Velocity	Energy	Source/Comments
200 Lead	Bullseye	3.4	730	235	Duplicate factory load
200 Lead	FL		730	235	Factory load

.41 Action Express

Historical Notes: The .41 Action Express (.41 AE) was designed, in 1986, by Evan Whildin, vice president of Action Arms. The cartridge is unique among modern handgun cartridges, in that it has a rebated rim that will fit 9mm bolt faces and can be used in guns originally designed for the 9mm without the need for extensive changes. The .41 AE is chambered in the Action Arms AT-88, which is a beefed-up copy of the Czech CZ-75 auto pistol. The cartridge was originally developed with a 170-grain JHP bullet at 1130 fps initial velocity. However, the first commercial ammunition, loaded by Samson, in Israel, and imported into the United States, has a 200-grain flat-nose bullet with a muzzle velocity of 1000 fps, and a 180-grain JHP bullet, also at 1000 fps.

General Comments: The .41 AE cannot be readily formed from any other case, although it is possible to make cases from .41 Magnum cases by trimming to .866-inch and turning down the rim on a lathe. This is, in fact, how the first experimental cartridges were made by Whildin. According to Bob Olsen, of Action Arms, the cross-sectional area of the bullet is 33-percent greater than the 9mm, and the bullets are one-third heavier. He also says that the Samson cases have been strengthened to prevent any bulging in blowback guns. Bullet diameter is the same as the .41 Magnum, .410-inch.

The .41 AE delivers practically the same ballistics as the .41 Magnum police load, which should make it an effective police or self-defense cartridge. The AT-88 pistol is based on a well-proven design and is accurate and pleasant to shoot. Recoil of the .41 AE is quite noticeably less than the .45 Automatic. The 180-grain load should be a good field load. However, one can handload cases with lighter jacketed or cast bullets. Israel Military Industries (Samson) is the only commercial manufacturer of this round. This concept is so good and performance so nearly ideal for this type of gun that it is quite surprising that this innovative round did not catch on.

.41 Action Express Loading Data and Factory Ballistics

Bullet (grains/type)	Powder	Grains	Velocity	Energy	Source/Comments
170 JHP	Unique	6.9	1100	457	Sierra
170 JHP	Herco	7.1	1100	457	Sierra
210 JHP	Unique	5.5	900	378	Sierra, Hornady
180 JHP	FL		1000	400	Factory load
200 FMJ	FL		1000	448	Factory load

.41 Remington Magnum

Historical Notes: The .41 Remington Magnum revolver cartridge was introduced, in June 1964, along with the S&W Model 57 revolver. This is a heavy-frame gun, essentially the same as the older .44 Magnum, but of smaller caliber. The .41 Magnum is very similar to an old, but little-known wildcat cartridge called the .400 Eimer. Bore diameter of the .41 Magnum is a true .410-inch, rather than the .401-inch of the .41 Long Colt. Both a police load and a more powerful soft-point hunting round were originally introduced.

Like most new cartridges, a number of individuals claim to have originated or influenced the design of the .41 Magnum. It might be well to mention that the .400 Eimer appeared around 1924. Possibly, a number of persons working over a span of time convinced Remington that it would be a good idea to bring out such a round. Probably Elmer Keith deserves the major credit.

General Comments: There has been much argument, as to the need for a police cartridge with greater stopping power than the .357 Magnum. Few understand why a blunt, 200-grain bullet for the .357 would not have served this purpose. In addition, a lighter 210-grain police load could have been worked up for the .44 Magnum. However, someone wanted a new cartridge, and the .41 Magnum was the result.

Actually, the new round was a more practical all-round hunting cartridge for the average individual than was the .44 Magnum. The .357 is not entirely adequate for big game, except in the hands of a good shot and experienced handgun hunter. The .44 Magnum is overpowered for anything but big game, and most people do not shoot very well with it. The .41 Magnum covers the small-game, medium-game, and varmint-through-deer classes quite adequately. Its effectiveness on anything heavier than deer would depend upon who was using it and under what conditions.

Recoil and muzzle blast of the .41 Magnum are slightly less than the .44 Magnum, but still heavy. For the average shooter, mastering either will require about the same amount of training and practice. The 210-grain lead police load, with its 1150 fps velocity, is relatively pleasant to shoot and quite adequate for small game or varmints at average handgun ranges. Factory-claimed velocities are for an 83/8-inch barrel. Velocities developed from the six-inch barrel is about 1000 fps for the police load, and 1360 to 1400 fps for the soft-point hunting load. In summation, the .41 Magnum is not quite as powerful as the .44 Magnum, but it is all the gun the average handgun hunter needs. A number of police departments have adopted the .41 Magnum, but most have since dropped it in favor of 9mm Luger or .40 S&W semi-automatic pistols. All major domestic commercial ammunition makers have offered this cartridge, but, as of this writing, it has yet to find truly widespread popularity.

.41 Remington Magnum Loading Data and Factory Ballistics

Bullet (grains/type)	Powder	Grains	Velocity	Energy	Source/Comments
170 JHP	2400	21.0	1400	740	Sierra
210 JHP	W296	20.0	1200	672	Speer, Nosler, Sierra, Hornady
210 JHP	H110	20.0	1200	672	Speer, Nosler, Sierra, Hornady
170 JHP	FL		1420	761	Factory load
175 JHP	FL		1250	607	Factory load
210 Lead	FL		965	434	Factory load
210 JHP	FL		1300	788	Factory load

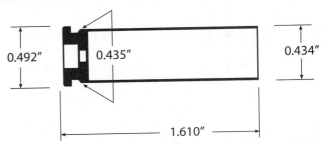

NEW
.414 Super Mag

Historical Notes: In the mid-1970s, handgun silhouette shooter Elgin Gates began developing a line of powerful magnum revolver cartridges for the purpose of IHMSA handgun silhouette shooting competitions. His work on the .357 Super Mag led to that cartridge's adoption by Remington as the .357 Maximum. The .414 Super Mag is Elgin's .41-caliber entry into the long-range revolver competition shooting and hunting arena. It is essentially a lengthened version of the .41 Remington Magnum case.

General Comments: Gates developed a full line of Super Mag revolver cartridges covering calibers from 7mm to .61. The three most popular were the .357, .414, and .445. The .357 Super Mag become the .357 Maximum, and the .414 and .445 were offered in limited numbers by Wesson Arms. Though all of these cartridges have mostly faded into the obscure category, they retain a limited but cult-like following by some who enjoy shooting at excessive long ranges with revolvers. However, it is doubtful that the .414 will ever see resurgence. For the hunter, the .414 offers the same performance as the .44 Magnum.—R.A.M.

.414 Super Mag Loading Data

Bullet (grains/type)	Powder	Grains	Velocity	Energy	Source/Comments
210 Sierra JHP	H 110	27.4	1500	1049	Sierra
210 Sierra JHP	AA 1680	30.6	1450	980	Sierra

10.4mm Italian Revolver

Historical Notes: This cartridge was developed for the Italian Model 1874 service revolver, but was also used in the Glisenti Model 1889 revolver. It is sometimes listed as the 10.35 Italian Revolver or 10.35 Glisenti. Blackpowder and smokeless powder ammunition is encountered. Both of the above revolvers have been sold from time to time in surplus stores.

General Comments: The 10.4 Italian cartridge is similar to the .44 S&W Russian. It would be an effective short-range self-defense or small-game hunting number. This ammunition is still commercially available from Fiocchi.

10.4mm Italian Revolver Factory Ballistics

Bullet (grains/type)	Powder	Grains	Velocity	Energy	Source/Comments
177 Lead	Blackpowder		735	212	Military load
177 Lead	Smokeless powder		800	240	Factory load

.44 Smith & Wesson Russian

Historical Notes: This cartridge was designed by S&W for its Russian Model military revolver, in 1870, the first models of which were made for the Imperial Russian Army. A civilian or commercial model was also manufactured, beginning in 1878. Colt's Bisley Target Model and its regular single-action were available in this chambering. The German firm of Ludwig Loewe made copies of the S&W Russian Model revolver in the same chambering.

General Comments: Originally loaded with blackpowder, the .44 S&W Russian was one of the most accurate and popular cartridges of its day. It was the favorite of Buffalo Bill Cody and many other western characters. Good accuracy to 200 yards was reported, and some of the first precision handgun shooting was accomplished with this cartridge. It was made obsolete by the .44 S&W Special, which was better suited to early smokeless powders. Any gun chambered for the .44 Special or the .44 Magnum will also shoot the .44 Russian. This makes a good field cartridge, but it is not as good as the .44 Special, due to the old blackpowder revolvers it was used in and the fact that it cannot be handloaded to the same level. Cases can be made by trimming .44 Special cases to a length of .97-inch. Fiocchi and Black Hills offer .44 Russian ammunition, and others may soon offer it for use in cowboy action shooting.

.44 Smith & Wesson Russian Factory Ballistics

Bullet (grains/type)	Powder	Grains	Velocity	Energy	Source/Comments
246 Lead	Bullseye	3.6	700	265	NA
246 Lead	Blackpowder (FFFg)	20.0(?)	770	324	Factory load

.44 Smith & Wesson Special

Historical Notes: With the coming of bulkier smokeless powders, the .44 Russian cartridge case proved too small to permit efficient use of full charges of the new propellants. Though originally a blackpowder cartridge, the .44 Special—which is about .2-inch longer than the Russian—eliminated this problem and provided more power, while using the same bullets as the older .44 Russian. This cartridge was introduced about 1907. Both Colt's and S&W made revolvers in this chambering, and a few Spanish and other European revolvers were also made to handle it. There has been a rebirth of interest in the .44 Special in the past few decades.

General Comments: The .44 S&W Special is one of the most accurate and powerful big-bore revolver cartridges. However, it was never factory loaded to its full potential. It was left to the handloader to develop truly effective hunting loads. Experiments to maximize .44 Special's big game hunting potential, by men like Elmer Keith, culminated in the .44 Magnum. The .44 S&W Special is still popular for target or field use. Revolvers for the .44 Special are not strong enough to handle loads as heavy as those used in Magnum guns. Winchester, Remington, Federal, Black Hills, CorBon, and others load this ammunition.

.44 Smith & Wesson Special Loading Data and Factory Ballistics

Bullet (grains/type)	Powder	Grains	Velocity	Energy	Source/Comments
180 JHP	231	6.8	900	324	Sierra, Hornady
200 JHP	231	6.0	800	284	Speer, Nosler, Hornady
240 JHP	HS-6	7.5	750	300	Hornady, Speer
200 JHP	FL		900	360	Factory load
200 L-SWC	FL		1035	476	Factory load (very optimistic data)
246 Lead	Smokeless powder		755	310	Factory load

.44 Auto Mag

Historical Notes: Introduced late in 1971, this cartridge was developed for the Auto Mag pistol designed by the late Harry Sanford of Pasadena, California. The gun was also made and marketed for a few years by High Standard. The cartridge is made by simply cutting off .30-06 or .308 Winchester cases to a length of 1.30 inches, inside reaming the case neck to accept .429-inch diameter bullets, and trimming to a length of 1.298 inches. The newly formed case is then loaded with standard .429-inch jacketed bullets of 200 to 240 grains. For a time, .44 Auto Mag cases were made in Mexico, by Cartuchos Deportivos Mexico, and headstamped CDM. Loaded ammunition was later offered by Norma of Sweden. A few custom loaders furnished loaded rounds. Loading and trim dies are made by RCBS (www.rcbs.com). The .44 Auto Mag cartridge was used only in the Auto Mag semi-auto pistol, which is no longer in production.

General Comments: The Auto Mag semi-auto pistol operates on the short recoil principle, with a six-lug, front-locking rotary bolt. Made almost entirely of stainless steel, it has a 6½-inch barrel, an overall length of 11½ inches, and weighs about 3½ pounds. This was the most powerful commercial semi-auto pistol manufactured at that time. When loaded to maximum, a 200-grain bullet can be pushed at over 1500 fps, and the 240-grain to 1400 fps. Unfortunately, the Auto Mag pistol had a rather short and stormy career marked by more than its share of manufacturing, marketing, and mechanical troubles. The .44 Auto Mag pistol was developed primarily as a sporting gun. It has been used to take all kinds of big game, including deer, elk, moose, and Kodiak bear. It is in the same class as the .44 Magnum.

44 Auto Mag Loading Data

Bullet (grains/type)	Powder	Grains	Velocity	Energy	Source/Comments
180 JHP	2400	25.0	1600	1024	Sierra
200 JHP	W296	26.5	1500	999	Hornady
240 JHP	W296	24.0	1350	972	Sierra, Hornady
240 JHP	H110	23.0	1400	1045	Hornady

.44 Remington Magnum

Historical Notes: This cartridge was developed by Smith & Wesson and Remington and introduced, in 1955, for a new, heavy-frame .44 Magnum revolver. Ruger, Colt's, Smith & Wesson, and others make revolvers for this cartridge. Its development was inspired and much preliminary work done by Elmer Keith and that era's group of hand-cannon fanatics, who insisted on the ultimate in handgun accuracy, range, and power. Ruger introduced a semi-auto carbine in .44 Magnum chambering, in 1961, and Marlin introduced its Model 94 lever-action, in 1967.

General Comments: In addition to having been the world's most powerful commercial handgun cartridge for many years, the .44 Magnum also has a well-deserved reputation for superb accuracy. It is used more as a field or hunting round than anything else, but a few police officers favored it because of its ability to penetrate an automobile body. It takes a seasoned handgunner to shoot it well, as both recoil and muzzle blast are considerable. This is one of the few commercial handgun cartridges that can be considered fully adequate for big-game hunting. It has been used to take deer, black bear, elk, moose, and the big Alaskan brown bears. It has often been chambered in rifles, with the Model 1894 Winchester or the Remington rolling-block action generally used. In a 20- or 24-inch rifle barrel, the standard factory load will develop about 1720 fps at the muzzle and 1580 ft-lbs of energy. This equals the energy of the .30-30 rifle cartridge. It is a very flexible cartridge when handloaded and can be made to cover any situation within the scope of the modern revolver. Very few, if any, police departments use it, because it is simply too much for the average police officer to handle. Its use in police work is largely a personal thing. All major manufacturers of commercial ammunition offer this cartridge in a variety of bullet weights.

.44 Remington Magnum Loading Data and Factory Ballistics

Bullet (grains/type)	Powder	Grains	Velocity	Energy	Source/Comments
180 JHP	Unique	14.0	1500	900	Hornady, Sierra
200 JHP	W296	26.0	1450	934	Hornady, Speer
240 JHP	H110	23.0	1350	971	Speer, Hornady, Sierra, Nosler
250 FMJ	2400	21.0	1250	868	Sierra
180 JHP	FL		1610	1035	Factory load
210 JHP	FL		1495	1042	Factory load
210 JHP	FL		1250	729	Factory load
240 Lead	FL		1350	971	Factory load
240 JHP	FL		1180	741	Factory load
240 Lead	FL		1000	533	Factory load
240 Lead	FL		1350	971	Factory load
250 FMJ	FL		1180	775	Factory load
255 FTX	FL		1410	993	Hornady Factory Load

.44 Bull Dog

Historical Notes: The .44 Bull Dog appears to have originated about 1880, perhaps a year or two prior to that. The first reference the original author of this book could locate was in the 1880 Homer Fisher gun catalog, reproduced in L.D. Satterlee's Ten Old Gun Catalogs; British Webley Bull Dog revolvers were advertised therein. American companies loaded the round up to about 1938-'39. The 1933 Winchester catalog lists it as for "Webley, British Bull Dog and H&R revolvers."

General Comments: The Bull Dog-type pocket revolver was quite popular through the late 1800s. The .44 Bull Dog cartridge was much superior to some of the rimfire cartridges of that period. It provided reasonably good short-range stopping power in a compact gun. However, it is solely a short-range, self-defense round and of little value for anything else. It is in the same general class as the .41 Short Colt. The cartridge has been obsolete for a good many years. Both blackpowder and smokeless powder loadings are encountered.

Bullet (grains/type)	Powder	Grains	Velocity	Energy	Source/Comments
168 to 170 Lead	FL		460	80	Factory load

.45 Winchester Magnum

Historical Notes: The .45 Magnum was first listed in the 1979 Winchester gun and ammunition catalog, although reports of its impending release had circulated some two years earlier. The cartridge was chambered in the on-again, off-again Wildey gas-operated semi-automatic pistol and has been adopted as a standard chambering for the Thompson/Center Contender single-shot pistol. The cartridge is, essentially, an elongated version of the .45 Automatic. Both gun and cartridge were developed, initially, for silhouette competition, but with the ballistics developed (a 230-grain bullet at a muzzle velocity of 1400 fps), the cartridge should prove an effective hunting round.

General Comments: The .45 Winchester Magnum develops 72-percent higher velocity and 200-percent greater muzzle energy than the standard .45 Automatic, and it's in the same class as the .44 Magnum revolver cartridge. With its rimless case, it is a natural for use in a semi-automatic rifle, if one were ever developed. The Wildey .45 Magnum, along with the .44 Auto Mag, the Desert Eagle, and the LAR Grizzly, are the only automatic pistols that truly qualify as big-game handguns. The potential is there for a fine combination silhouette and hunting pistol. The price is high, and for strictly silhouette shooting, the much lower-priced Thompson/Center Contender in the same chambering might appeal to many potential buyers. The availability of commercial ammunition with hunting-type bullets would also be a factor, although there is a good variety of such bullets available to the handloader.

.45 Winchester Magnum Loading Data and Factory Ballistics

Bullet (grains/type)	Powder	Grains	Velocity	Energy	Source/Comments
185 JHP	BlueDot	20.0	1850	1406	Hornady
200 JHP	2400	22.5	1500	999	Speer
225 JHP	H110	26.0	1500	1124	Speer
230 FMJ	BlueDot	17.0	1550	1227	Hornady
260 JHP	W296	25.0	1500	1300	Speer
230 FMJ	FL		1400	1001	Factory load, Winchester

All of the above loads were developed in a Thompson/Center Contender pistol with a 10-inch barrel. These loads are not recommended for any other handgun.

NEW

.460 Rowland

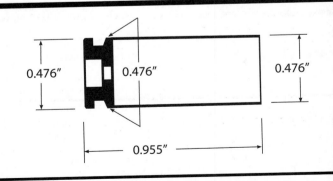

Historical Notes: This cartridge was developed by northwest Louisiana native Johnny Rowland, who grew up on a farm shooting guns and enjoying the outdoors. Rowland has developed a number of gun-related products, including the .460 Rowland. The idea with this round was to develop a handgun hunting cartridge for the 1911 pistol that would offer .44 Magnum levels of power. To do this, Rowland increased the .45 Auto case by 1/16-inch, to ensure .460 Rowland cartridges could not be loaded in

.45 Auto handguns. The other main difference between the .460 Rowland and the .45 Auto is that the Rowland round is loaded to a much higher pressures, 40,000 psi as compared to 19,000 psi. Despite the .460 designation, the .460 Rowland uses .451-diameter bullets just like a .45 Auto.

General Comments: The .460 Rowland is indeed a powerhouse cartridge, something you will realize the first time you fire one. Most 1911s in .460 Rowland are built with a compensator to combat the intense recoil. Currently, Buffalo Bore, CorBon, and Wilson Combat all offer factory loaded ammunition for the .460 Rowland in various bullets weights from 185- to 255-grain. External ballistics are very similar to that of the .44 Magnum, as is terminal performance, when similar bullets are compared. As of now, a .460 Rowland handgun is a custom option, and Wilson Combat offers its Hunter 1911 in this cartridge.—R.A.M.

.460 Rowland Loading Data and Factory Ballistics

Bullet (grains/type)	Powder	Grains	Velocity	Energy	Source/Comments
185 JSWC	Longshot	13.5	1503	927	Hodgdon
200 JHP	Longshot	13.8	1456	941	Hodgdon
230 XTP	Longshot	12.0	1336	911	Hodgdon
185 JHP	FL		1425	834	CorBon Factory load
230 JHP	FL		1250	798	CorBon Factory load
230 XTP	FL		1200	735	Wilson Combat Factory load
255 HC FN (Lead)	FL		1300	957	Buffalo Bore Factory load

.45 Webley

Historical Notes: The earliest reference that could be located, regarding the .45 Webley, was in the 1876 James Brown & Son gun catalog.* However, it may have originated a year or two earlier than that. American companies manufactured it up to about 1939. The 1933 Winchester catalog says it is for "Webley and Bull Dog double-action revolvers." It is obsolete.

General Comments: The .45 Webley is similar to the .450 Revolver cartridge, but has a slightly longer case. The two will interchange in most revolvers. Originally a blackpowder cartridge, the .45 Webley was loaded with 20 grains of powder and a 230-grain bullet. Smokeless powder was also used in late loadings. In power, it is in the same class as the .41 Short Colt, but probably has superior stopping power, because of the larger, heavier bullet. Ammunition could probably be made by cutting off .455 Webley cases.

*L.D. Satterlee op. cit.

.45 Webley Factory Ballistics

Bullet (grains/type)	Powder	Grains	Velocity	Energy	Source/Comments
230 Lead	FL		550	150	Factory load, U.S.

.45 Automatic Rimmed (.45 Auto Rim)

Historical Notes: During World War I, both Colt's and Smith & Wesson manufactured revolvers for the .45 Automatic cartridge. This required use of a half-moon clip to support and then eject the rimless .45 Automatic. Thousands of these revolvers were sold on the civilian market, after the war ended. In 1920, the Peters Cartridge Co. introduced a rimmed version of the .45 Automatic, which eliminated the need for half-moon clips in the revolver. The round was also loaded with a lead bullet, to reduce rifling wear inherent with use of the jacketed .45 Automatic bullets in the unusually soft barrels used.

General Comments: Cylinder throats in these revolvers were considerably oversized. Bill Falin, chief ballistician at Accurate Arms, has suggested that this might have been done by design as a simple means of mitigating chamber pressure when standard .45 Automatic military rounds were used. Bill's testing demonstrated that heavily jacketed full metal jacket bullets do not obturate until the rifling is contacted and, so, a significant amount of gas escapes before peak chamber pressure occurs. Considering the significant pressure of original .45 Automatic loads, which launched 230-grain bullets from the 1911 at an honest 930 fps with powders such as Unique, this might well have been necessary to keep these somewhat fragile revolvers in one piece. In any case, this is certainly an interesting conjecture.

The .45 Auto-Rim (.45 Automatic Rimmed), while similar in performance to the .45 Automatic, is probably a better field or hunting cartridge, because it can be handloaded with semi-wadcutter, hollowpoint, and other lead hunting bullets. When using such bullets at slightly increased velocities, it is every bit as good as the .45 Colt revolver cartridge for small through medium game. Many war-surplus .455 Webley revolvers have been altered to shoot the .45 Auto-Rim, and many of these are used in the field. The cartridge is probably more widely used than at anytime since it was introduced. This cartridge is no longer offered by commercial ammunition makers.

.45 Automatic Rimmed Loading Data and Factory Ballistics

Bullet (grains/type)	Powder	Grains	Velocity	Energy	Source/Comments
185 JHP	Bullseye	5.5	850	297	Hornady
200	Bullseye	4.90	750	250	Hornady, Sierra
230	Unique	6.6	800	327	Speer, Sierra
230 Lead	FL		805	331	Factory load

.45 Automatic Short/.45 HP

Historical Notes: In many countries, such as Italy, France, and Mexico, it has been illegal for private citizens to own semi-automatic pistols in military chamberings such as .45 Automatic. Gun owners in these countries created a strong demand for a powerful, semi-auto pistol in a non-military chambering. The .45 Automatic Short was developed in response to that demand. It is sometimes called the .45 HP.

This cartridge uses a .45 Automatic case shortened by one millimeter. All other case dimensions remain the same. A standard 230-grain FMJ bullet is used, but is seated out so that cartridge overall length and muzzle velocity are identical to the .45 Automatic using the same loads. Pistols originally designed for the .45 Automatic can quickly be converted to the Short by installing a new barrel. All other parts remain the same.

General Comments: Because the chamber of the .45 Automatic Short is shorter than the .45 Automatic, the latter round will not chamber in a .45 Short barrel. The letter of the law in the appropriate countries is, therefore, preserved, while shooters can still obtain .45 Automatic performance. The .45 Automatic is famous for its stopping power, and the Short offers identical ballistics. Loading data for the two is interchangeable. With the Western European Union consolidating firearm laws, the prohibition against private ownership of pistols in military chamberings will soon end. Therefore, the purpose for which the .45 Automatic Short exists will end, and this cartridge will become obsolete. Only Hirtenberger AG, of Austria, has commercially loaded this ammunition.

.45 Automatic Short Factory Ballistics

Bullet (grains/type)	Powder	Grains	Velocity	Energy	Source/Comments
230 FMJ	FL		835	356	Hirtenberger factory load

.45 Glock Auto Pistol (.45 GAP)

Historical Notes: In 2003, Winchester announced ammunition for a new Glock auto pistol. The .45 GAP (Glock Auto Pistol) cartridge is 1/8-inch shorter than the timeless .45 ACP cartridge, but delivers similar performance. The shorter cartridge case allows a trimmer, more-ergonomic shape in the Glock Model 37 pistol.

Many knowledgeable pistol shooters consider the 230-grain bullet to be about the best available for .45-caliber autoloading pistols. For law enforcement use, the frontal area of a .45-caliber bullet offers a stopping power advantage, given correct bullet design. During load development, Winchester engineers achieved .45 ACP velocities in the shorter .45 GAP case using 230-grain bullets. Winchester also developed Law Enforcement-Only loads for this cartridge for duty use, with its proprietary T-Series bullets, and for training with frangible bullets. Speer offers ammunition in a variety of loads.

.45 Glock Auto Pistol (.45 GAP) Loading Data and Factory Ballistics

Bullet (grains/type)	Powder	Grains	Velocity	Energy	Source/Comments
175 Frangible	FL		1000		Winchester
185 TMJ FN	FL		1020		Speer
185 SilverTip	FL		1000		Winchester
200 GDHP	FL		950		Speer
230 FMJ	FL		850		Winchester
230 JHP	FL		880		Winchester
185 Hdy XTP	Longshot	7.5	1075		Hodgdon
200 Speer GDHP	Longshot	6.8	1000		Hodgdon

.45 Automatic Colt Pistol (.45 Automatic +P/.45 ACP)

Historical Notes: This cartridge was developed by John Browning, in 1905, and adopted by the United States Ordnance Department, with the Colt-Browning automatic pistol, in 1911. It has also been made the official military handgun chambering by several other governments, notably Argentina, Mexico, and Norway. The .45 Automatic is the most powerful military handgun cartridge in use today. It is also one of the most difficult to master. The Colt Government Model auto-pistol and its copies, as well as the Colt's and Smith & Wesson Army Model 1917 revolvers, are the principal arms chambered for the .45 Automatic in the United States. Ruger, S&W, Springfield Armory, Glock, Numrich, and many other companies now also offer guns in this chambering. Several submachine guns have used it. About 1943, a number of Re-ising semi-automatic rifles were marketed in this chambering. Imitations of the Colt's auto pistol have been made in Argentina, China, Korea, Norway, Spain, and the United States. It was replaced, in 1985, as the official U.S. military handgun cartridge by the 9mm Parabellum. However, it remains in U.S. Marine Corps service and has proven increasingly popular with police agencies in the United States.

General Comments: The .45 Automatic has been proven in combat all over the world as having excellent stopping power. It has also developed into a first-class match cartridge, with accuracy equal to the best. It requires practice for the average person to develop skill with this cartridge, particularly when fired in some untuned semi-automatics. It is used far more for target shooting than hunting, its curved trajectory limiting its effective range. Despite this, it is quite adequate for any small or medium game. Like all the other semi-auto pistol cartridges, it is a better hunting round with soft-point and hollow-point bullets. At one time, a number of police departments switched from the .38 Special to the .45 Automatic. All major and minor commercial ammunition manufacturers offer this cartridge. After several years of declining sales, it is enjoying a resurgence of popularity, especially after its centennial celebration, in 2011.

.45 Automatic (.45 ACP/.45 Auto) Loading Data and Factory Ballistics

Bullet (grains/type)	Powder	Grains	Velocity	Energy	Source/Comments
185 JHP	Bullseye	5.0	900	333	Hornady, Sierra, Nosler
200 JHP	BlueDot	10.0	900	360	Speer, Sierra
230 FMJ	Bullseye	5.0	800	327	Nosler, Speer, Sierra
230 FMJ	Unique	6.0	800	327	Speer, Nosler, Hornady, Sierra
185 FMJ SWC	FL		770	244	Factory load
185 JHP	FL		1000	411	Factory load
185 JHP	FL		1140	534	Factory load (+P)

.45 Automatic (.45 ACP/.45 Auto) Loading Data and Factory Ballistics

Bullet (grains/type)	Powder	Grains	Velocity	Energy	Source/Comments
230 FMJ	FL		835	356	Factory load
230 JHP	FL		875	391	Factory load
230 FMJ	ML		855	405	Military load

.454 Casull

Historical Notes: The .454 Casull, originally called the .454 Magnum Revolver, was developed by Dick Casull and Jack Fulmer, in 1957. The first public announcement was made by P.O. Ackley, in the November 1959 issue of Guns & Ammo magazine. Solid-head .45 Colt cases and specially altered Colt's and Ruger single-action revolvers were used for initial development. The .454 Casull employs a special case, originally offered only by Federal, that is .1-inch longer than the .45 Colt case, to prevent this round from chambering in .45 Colt revolvers. A five-shot single-action revolver, designed by Dick Casull and manufactured by Freedom Arms Co., is chambered for this cartridge. The revolver is made of stainless steel throughout, has a 7½-inch barrel and weighs 50 ounces in standard configuration. Ammunition is now loaded and marketed by Winchester, Hornady, Buffalo Bore, CorBon, and Black Hills Ammunition.

General Comments: The .454 Casull is primarily a hunting cartridge, although it will probably find acceptance among metallic silhouette shooters. The .454 Casull is one of the most powerful revolver cartridges available. Anyone who contemplates hunting dangerous game with a handgun should seriously consider the .454 Casull and the Freedom Arms revolver. For those wishing a reduced load, standard .45 Colt ammunition can be fired in the .454 revolver. There has been a persistent call for a magnum .45 revolver ever since the .44 Magnum was introduced, and the .454 certainly provides all that could be desired in .45-caliber. Firing lead-bullet .45 Colt loads in a .454 can leave a lead ring deposit in the front of the chamber. If this deposit is not removed before chambering and firing full-power .454 loads with the unusually hard bullets used in such rounds, the cylinder can be damaged beyond repair. This is not conjecture—it has happened.

.454 Casull Loading Data and Factory Ballistics

Bullet (grains/type)	Powder	Grains	Velocity	Energy	Source/Comments
240 FA JHP	AA No. 9	31.0	1916	1955	Accurate
260 FA JFP	AA No. 9	30.0	1835	1945	Accurate
300 H XTP	AA No. 9	26.0	1623	1755	Accurate
260 JHP	FL		1723	1730	Factory load
300 JHP	FL		1353	1220	Factory load
300 Spr UniCore	FL		1500	1500	Buffalo Bore factory load
325 LBT LFN	FL		1525	1675	Buffalo Bore factory load
360 LBT LWN	FL		1425	1630	Buffalo Bore factory load

.460 Smith & Wesson

Historical Notes: Announced, in 2005, as a joint Hornady-Smith & Wesson development, the .460 Smith and Wesson (S&W) is the fastest revolver cartridge ever produced, reaching velocities of about 2200 fps with 200-grain bullets. It is chambered in the S&W M460 Extreme Velocity Revolver for long-range handgun hunting. Used by a skilled pistol shooter, the .460 S&W cartridge can achieve MOA accuracy at 100 yards.

General Comments: The .460 S&W uses the .454 Casull case lengthened to 1.8 inches as its parent case. It is the first commercial revolver cartridge to use tipped bullets. Hornady and CorBon offer loaded ammunition for the .460 S&W. Hornady and Starline supply reloading components and data for this cartridge. It is well suited for whitetail deer hunting at 150 yard-plus ranges.

.460 Smith & Wesson

Bullet (grains/type)	Powder	Grains	Velocity	Energy	Source/Comments
220 Hornady SST	FL		2200	2149	Hornady
225 Barnes X	H110	42.0	2243	2513	Hodgdon
240 Hdy XTP	H4227	45.0	2198	2574	Hodgdon
250 Barnes X	Li'l Gun	42.0	2044	2319	Hodgdon

.455 Revolver MkII
.455 Webley Revolver MkII

Historical Notes: This is a British military revolver cartridge, adopted in 1897 and designated the .455 Revolver MkII. It is a modification of an earlier round originally designed for blackpowder, the .455 Revolver MkI. Modern revolvers will chamber and fire either the old or the new cartridge. The .455 Webley was used officially in both World War I and II, although it was partly replaced by the .380/200 (.38 S&W), which was adopted in the mid-1930s. In addition to the Webley revolver, both Colt's and Smith & Wesson chambered arms for this cartridge. Ammunition was loaded by American companies up to about 1940.

General Comments: The .455 Webley Revolver cartridge was never very popular or widely used in the United States, because standard American sporting and military arms in .45 Automatic were more easily obtainable. However, after World War II, many obsolete .455 revolvers were sold at low prices in the United States, and this changed the situation somewhat. It is better known and more widely used than previously, but most .455 revolvers have been altered to shoot the .45 Automatic through the use of half-moon clips or the rimmed .45 Auto-Rim cartridge. The .455 Revolver is not a very satisfactory field cartridge, because of the low velocity and curved trajectory. On the other hand, it has excellent short-range stopping power. It can be improved by handloading and with the use of semi-wadcutter, hunting-type bullets. It is now essentially obsolete. However, Fiocchi of Italy still produces commercial ammunition labeled .455 Webley (MKI).

.455 Revolver MkII Loading Data and Factory Ballistics

Bullet (grains/type)	Powder	Grains	Velocity	Energy	Source/Comments
260 Lead	Unique	5.0	610	213	NA
262 FMJ	FL		700	285	Fiocchi factory load
265 FMJ	ML		600	220	Military load

.45 Colt Government

Historical Notes: This was something of a bastardized cartridge, combining the length of the S&W Schofield revolver round with the rim of the Colt SAA round. Army ordnance described at least one version of this cartridge officially as Revolver Ball Cartridge, Caliber .45. The Remington-UMC version was labeled (on the box and case heads) as .45 Colt. The evident military incentive for such a loading seems obvious: With both S&W and Colt .45-caliber revolvers (similar, but differently chambered) in use, supplying the correct ammunition to far-flung outposts must have been something of a logistical nightmare. One has to wonder how often troopers found themselves in possession of ammunition that would not work in the gun they had been issued. The .45 Colt ammunition is longer than the Schofield cylinder; chambering Schofield ammunition in the Colt leaves precious little room for rim clearance. It seems likely that some early .45 Colt SAAs would not have chambered some Schofield ammunition, even when the gun was clean. Conversely, the .45 Colt Government, combining the shorter case and smaller rim, worked (after a fashion) in either gun. Ballistically, it differed little from the standard .45 Colt ordnance loading, which was significantly lighter than the original commercial loading. Available information suggests that this cartridge was available between the late 1870s and the 1930s.

General Comments: When the chips are down, having any ammunition that will fit and work in the gun at hand is much better than throwing rocks. However, the Schofield does not function as dependably using the smaller-rimmed .45 Colt Government cases; incautious manipulation or a somewhat worn gun can result in the extractor slipping past the rim of one or more partially extracted cases. The gun cannot, then, be closed. Worse, if the cylinder is the slightest bit dirty (blackpowder, remember), removing the offending case can require a dowel, a hammer, and at least three hands!

.45 Colt Government Factory Ballistics

Bullet (grains/type)	Powder	Grains	Velocity	Energy	Source/Comments
255 LRNFP	Blackpowder (FFFg)	28.0	800	360	Factory load, 1.10-inch case *

*QuickLOAD estimated data. Semi-balloon head sample, headstamped "REM-UMC" over ".45 COLT;" slightly rounded primer stamped "U;" 255-grain RNFP bullet appears to match bullets used in original .45 (Long) Colt loads.

.45 Smith & Wesson (.45 S&W Schofield)

Historical Notes: This cartridge was introduced, in 1875, for the Smith & Wesson Schofield revolver. This revolver was adopted by the U.S. Army in that year and used until 1892, when it and the .45 Colt Army revolver were replaced by the Colt Army & Navy Model in .38-caliber. Commercial .45 S&W ammunition was loaded continuously until about 1940 and was reintroduced about 1997 by Black Hills Ammunition, in response to demands from cowboy action shooters for a superior, reduced-power, .45-caliber cartridge. Some authorities believe Gen. George A. Custer used a Schofield revolver at the Battle of the Little Big Horn.

General Comments: The Smith & Wesson Schofield revolver was a single-action, hinged-frame type. It employed a special heavy barrel latch designed by Gen. Schofield, hence the name. The cylinder of this revolver was not long enough to accept the .45 Colt cartridge, so a shorter round was designed. In addition, to improve extraction, rim diameter was enlarged slightly. Later, to simplify supply contingencies, a .45-caliber cartridge designed with a rim to fit both .45 Colt-chambered revolvers and .45 S&W-chambered revolvers was loaded by government arsenals. A similar commercial loading, eventually called the .45 Colt Government, followed. This cartridge was used in both the Schofield Model and the Colt Army Model. Ammunition for the .45 S&W can be used in most .45 Colt revolvers, but the reverse is not true. Although the Colt Single Action Army revolver is the one always depicted as the universal sidearm of the Old West, the S&W was also quite popular. These old guns were made for blackpowder, so heavy smokeless powder charges should never be used. This cartridge and handgun are again in production, with Black Hills Ammunition supplying loads that duplicate the original, and Navy Arms and others marketing the replica revolver.

.45 Smith & Wesson (.45 S&W Schofield) Loading Data and Factory Ballistics

Bullet (grains/type)	Powder	Grains	Velocity	Energy	Source/Comments
230 Lead	Bullseye	4.6	740	277	NA
230 Lead	Blackpowder (FFFg)	28.0	730	276	NA
250 Lead	Blackpowder (FFFg)	28.0	710	283	Factory load
230 Lead	Smokeless powder		730	276	Factory load
250 Lead	Smokeless powder		710	283	Factory load

.45 Colt

Historical Notes: This was introduced, in 1873, by Colt's as one of the cartridges for its famous Peacemaker single-action revolver. Both the cartridge and the revolver were adopted by the U.S. Army, in 1875. This served as the official handgun cartridge of the Army, until 1892 (some 17 years), when it was replaced by the .38 Long Colt. The .45 Colt is one of the cartridges that helped civilize and settle the American West. It was originally a blackpowder number, loaded with 40 grains of FFg powder and a 255-grain lead bullet. Testing has demonstrated that muzzle velocity of the original loading almost certainly exceeded 900 fps in the original revolvers. Various importers offer excellent Italian-made replicas of the original Colt's model, and Ruger and several other makes of more modern single-action revolvers are currently chambered in .45 Colt.

General Comments: This is one of the most famous American handgun cartridges and still a favorite with big-bore advocates. It is extremely accurate and has more knockdown and stopping power than nearly any common handgun cartridge, except the .44 Magnum. It is a popular field cartridge and can be safely handloaded to velocities in excess of 1000 fps with 250-grain cast bullets. Blackpowder revolvers should not be used with any load developing more than about 800 fps muzzle velocity. Although the .45 Colt has a larger case than the .45 Automatic or the .45 Auto-Rim, it is not quite as efficient with factory-duplicating loads using smokeless powder. Using special revolvers, some very heavy loads have been established for the .45 Colt case. These put it in almost the same class as the .44 Magnum. Such loads should not be attempted except by an experienced person who fully understands what he is doing and who will ensure that those loads are only used in a revolver that will withstand the pressures generated. This is another cartridge that has developed a rebirth of interest. Federal, Remington, Winchester, Black Hills Ammunition, CorBon, and others all offer .45 Colt loads.

.45 Colt Loading Data and Factory Ballistics

Bullet (grains/type)	Powder	Grains	Velocity	Energy	Source/Comments
185 JHP	700X	9.0	1100	497	Sierra
225 JHP	Unique	9.0	950	451	Speer
240 JHP	Unique	8.7	850	385	Sierra
250 JHP	IMR 4227	17.0	800	355	Hornady, Nosler
250 JHP	Unique	7.5	800	355	Hornady
260 JHP	IMR 4227	16.0	850	417	Speer
255 Lead	Blackpowder (FFg)	40.0	930	490	Factory load
225 JHP	Smokeless powder		920	423	Factory load
255 Lead	Smokeless powder		860	420	Factory load

.455 Revolver MkI
.455 Colt/.455 Enfield

Historical Notes: The .455 Revolver MkI was adopted by the British Army, in 1892, to replace the .476 MkIII and the .455 Enfield MkI ammunition. Despite the different designations, these two cartridges actually have the same case dimensions; they differ only in bullet diameter, type, and construction. The .476 was a blackpowder cartridge, and so was the 455 MkI at its inception. However, in 1894, the propellant was changed to the new cordite, and, after a few years, it was found that the smokeless powder burned more efficiently in a shorter case. Consequently, a shorter case was adopted, in 1897, and this altered round was designated the .455 Revolver MkII. This is the .455 Webley familiar to American shooters. It has a case .11-inch to .14-inch shorter than the original round.

The .455 Colt is nothing more than Colt's commercial designation of the .455 Revolver MkI, in a somewhat improved loading. It is listed in various publications and was loaded by American companies under this name, but was discontinued in the late 1930s. This is not a Colt-designed cartridge, but it does have different ballistics than the British MkI. Later, new cartridge dimensions were adopted, and this round was called the .455 Colt MkII.

General Comments: The .455 MkI, .455 MkII, .455 Colt, and the original .476 Revolver rounds are all interchangeable and can be fired in early British service arms. The .450 Revolver cartridge can also be fired in .455 revolvers. However, the .455 Webley is the only one still commercially loaded. Use the same bullet and .455 Webley loading data for any of the .455 cartridges listed here. Power and performance are the same. Fiocchi has recently offered this ammunition.

Editor's note: Those not at least slightly confused by the profusion of large-caliber British cartridge designations are a rare breed.

.455 Revolver MkI, .455 Colt Factory Ballistics

Bullet (grains/type)	Powder	Grains	Velocity	Energy	Source/Comments
265 Lead	Blackpowder		700	289	Kynoch factory load
265 Lead	Cordite powder		600	212	Kynoch factory load
265 Lead	Smokeless powder		757	337	Factory load, U.S.
262 Lead	FL		850	420	Fiocchi factory load

.455 Webley Automatic

Historical Notes: The .455 Webley semi-rimmed pistol cartridge was adopted by the British Navy, in 1912, for use in the 455 Webley self-loading pistol. The pistol was not entirely satisfactory and was replaced by the end of World War I. The cartridge resembles the .45 Automatic, but uses a very blunt pointed bullet.

General Comments: This cartridge has seen very little use in the United States, although a number of Webley pistols in this chambering were sold in military surplus stores after World War II. In performance, it is inferior to the .45 Automatic. Because of the relatively low velocity, it is not as good a field cartridge as the .45 Automatic.

.455 Webley Automatic Loading Data and Factory Ballistics

Bullet (grains/type)	Powder	Grains	Velocity	Energy	Source/Comments
200 Lead	Unique	6.2	775	265	Lyman No. 452460
224 FMJ	Smokeless powder		700	247	Military load

.480 Ruger

Historical Notes: After a half-century of production, millions of shooters use Bill Ruger's firearms—but only one very special pistol cartridge bears the man's name. The .480 Ruger was never intended to be the biggest and heaviest-recoiling handgun cartridge on the block. It splits the difference between the .44 Remington Magnum and .454 Casull cartridges.

General Comments: Using a Hornady 325-grain XTP Magnum bullet (diameter .475-inch) and Hornady brass, the .480 Ruger offers a significant velocity and energy increase over the .44 Remington Magnum cartridge, but without the recoil disadvantage of other super-powered handgun cartridges. The key to delivering the two-thirds of a ton of muzzle energy is a well-reasoned balance between bullet weight, velocity, and operating pressure, in a cartridge derived from the venerable .45-70 case. The cartridge is chambered in Ruger's rugged double-action six-shooter, the Super Redhawk, which wears an integral scope mounting system on the top strap. It should serve big-game handgun hunters and metallic silhouette target shooters with distinction.

.480 Ruger Factory Ballistics

Bullet (grains/type)	Powder	Grains	Velocity	Energy	Source/Comments
325 Hornady XTP	FL		1350	1315	Hornady

.500 JRH

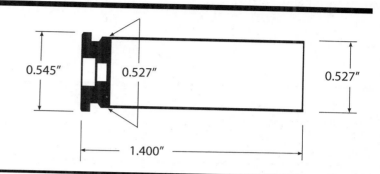

0.545" 0.527" 0.527"

1.400"

Historical Notes: The .500 JRH is the brainchild of Jack Huntington, a gunsmith out of Northern California. Jack wanted a full-power, no-compromise, .50-caliber cartridge that would fit in a standard-frame revolver, like the Freedom Arms Model 83, with a maximum case length of 1.4 inches. Huntington turned a dummy case in his lathe in 1993, and the .500 JRH became an honest to goodness commercially loaded reality, when Starline began producing brass and Buffalo Bore began offering loaded ammunition.

General Comments: The very first .500 JRH revolver was a Model 83 from Freedom Arms and, today, Magnum Research is offering its BFR chambered for the .500 JRH. Brass for the round, which is manufactured by Starline, is available from JRH Advanced Gunsmithing, though .500 Smith & Wesson brass can be easily cut down to form .500 JRH brass. The specifications call for turning down the rim, but Magnum Research BFR revolvers will accept the larger rim of the .500 Smith & Wesson case. The .500 JRH has a reputation for fine accuracy, and is should be very effective for hunting large and even dangerous game.—R.A.M.

.500 JRH Loading Data and Factory Ballistics

Bullet (grains/type)	Powder	Grains	Velocity	Energy	Source/Comments
350 JFP	FL		1350	1416	Grizzly Cartridge Factory Load
400 WFN - Cast	FL		1300	1501	Grizzly Cartridge Factory Load
425 TCFN - Cast	FL		1380	1797	Buffalo Bore Factory Load
440 LFN - Cast	FL		950	882	Buffalo Bore Factory Load
440 LFN - Cast	W 231	10	950	882	Jack Huntington
440 TC	W 296	29.5	1350	1780	Jack Huntington

.50 Action Express

Historical Notes: The .50 Action Express (.50 AE) was developed, in 1988, for the IMI Desert Eagle semi-auto pistol, imported by Magnum Research, Inc. It is another development by Evan Whildin, then of Action Arms. It was part of a program to upgrade performance of the semi-auto pistol through new cartridge design. The .50 AE has the same rim diameter, case length, and overall length as the .44 Magnum. However, base diameter is .547-inch, so, like the .41 AE, the .50 AE has a rebated rim. This allows simple adaptation to the Desert Eagle pistol, which was designed for use with the .44 Magnum. Since the rim is the same, it is possible to change chamberings by the simple process of installing a new barrel, a very practical design.

General Comments: The .50 AE uses a .500-inch bullet * weighing 325 grains at a muzzle velocity of 1400 fps. This load develops 1414 ft-lbs of muzzle energy, which makes the .50 AE one of the world's most powerful pistol cartridges. This is an excellent field cartridge for deer-size animals or as a backup when hunting dangerous game. Speer now offers factory ammunition.

* The original design featured a standard .50-caliber .510-inch bullet, but when a polygonally-rifled bore was adopted, the gauge plug defining the limit of "Sporting Devices" fell through the barrel. This rendered the .50 AE a "destructive device," so bore size was reduced and the case was tapered to accommodate the smaller bullet.

.50 Action Express Loading Data and Factory Ballistics

Bullet (grains/type)	Powder	Grains	Velocity	Energy	Source/Comments
300 JHP	AA No. 7	27.5	1579	1568	Accurate Arms
325 Speer Uni-Core	AA 1680	37.8	1305	1227	Accurate
325 JHP	FL		1400	1414	Factory load

.500 Smith & Wesson

Historical Notes: Introduced by Smith and Wesson, in 2003, for big-game hunting in the first commercial .50-caliber revolver, the .500 S&W became the most powerful factory production cartridge in history. The M500 revolver and .500 S&W cartridge constitute an effective combination for big-game hunting at reasonable ranges.

General Comments: The .500 S&W uses a rimmed case 1.625 inches long, with a rim diameter of .560-inch. To fit in the M500 revolver's cylinder, the overall length for a loaded cartridge cannot exceed 2¼ inches. The .500 S&W cartridge is best suited to heavy-duty hunting revolvers or modern single-shot pistols and rifles. Factory ammunition is available from Hornady, CorBon, and Winchester. Hornady and Starline offer reloading components.

.500 Smith & Wesson Loading Data and Factory Ballistics

Bullet (grains/type)	Powder	Grains	Velocity	Energy	Source/Comments
350 Hornady XTP	FL		1900	2805	Hornady
500 Hornady SP	FL		1425	2254	Hornady
275 Barnes XPB	Li'lGun	44.0	2137	2788	Hodgdon
350 Hdy XTP	H110	43.0	1877	2737	Hodgdon
400 Sierra JSP	Li'l Gun	37.0	1725	2642	Hodgdon
500 Hdy SP	H110	32.2	1436	2286	Hodgdon

Cartridge	Case	Bullet Dia.	Neck Dia.	Shoulder Dia.	Base Dia.	Rim Dia.	Rim Thick.	Case Length	Ctge. Length	Primer	Page
5.45X18mm Soviet	C	.210	.220	UNK	.300	.300	UNK	.7	.98	SB	323
.22 Remington Jet (.22 CF Magnum)	A	.223	.247	.350	.376	.440	.055	1.28	1.58	SP	323
.221 Remington Fireball	C	.224	.251	.355	.375	.375	.040	1.40	1.82	SP	324
5.5mm Velo Dog Revolver	B	.225	.248	UNK/NA	.253	.308	UNK	1.12	1.35	SP-B	324
.25 Automatic Colt Pistol (.25 ACP)	D	.251	.276	UNK/NA	.277	.298	.038	.62	.91	SP	325
.25 North American Arms (NAA)	C	.251	.276	.330	.337	.337	.046	.745	.960	UNK	325
.256 Winchester Magnum	A	.257	.277	.378	.378	.440	.055	1.30	1.53	SP	326
7mm Nambu	C	.280	.296	.337	.351	.359	UNK	.78	1.06	B	326
7mm Bench Rest Remington				Based on Rem. 308 BR case shortened to 1.50						SP	327
7.62mm Russian Nagant Revolver	B	.295	.286	–	.335	.388		1.53	1.53	B	328
7.62X25mm Russian Tokarev	C	.307	.330	.370	.380	.390	UNK	.97	1.35	B	328
7.63mm (7.65) Mannlicher	D	.308	.331	UNK/NA	.332	.334	.030	.84	1.12	B	329
.30 (7.65X21mm) Luger	C	.308	.322	.374	.388	.391	.045	.75	1.15	SP-B	329
.30 (7.63X25mm) Mauser	C	.308	.332	.370	.381	.390	.045	.99	1.36	SP-B	329
.32 Automatic Colt Pistol (ACP)	H	.309	.336	UNK/NA	.336	.354	.040	.68	1.03	SP	330
.32 S&W	B	.312	.334	UNK/NA	.335	.375	.045	.61	.92	SP	331
.32 S&W Long/.32 Colt New Police	B	.312	.335	UNK/NA	.335	.375	.048	.93	1.27	SP	331
.32 H&R Magnum	B	.312	.333	UNK/NA	.333	.371	.050	1.08	1.35	SP	332
.32 North American Arms (NAA)	C	.312	.337	.373	.374	.374	.045	.680	.984	UNK	333
.32 Short Colt	B	.313	.313	UNK/NA	.318	.374	.045	.63	1.00	SP	333
.32 Long Colt	B	.313	.313	UNK/NA	.318	.374	.045	.92	1.26	SP	333
.32 Colt	B	?	.313	UNK/NA	.318	.374	.052	.755	1.26	SP	333
.320 Revolver	B	.317	.320	UNK/NA	.322	.350	UNK	.62	.90	B	334
.327 Federal Magnum	B	.312	.337	UNK/NA	.337	.371	.050	1.20	1.46	S	334
7.5mm Swiss Army	B	.317	.335	UNK/NA	.345	.407	UNK	.89	1.29	B	335
8mm Rast-Gasser	B	.320	.332	UNK/NA	.334	.376	UNK	1.037	1.391	?	335
8mm Nambu	G	.320	.338	.388	.408	.413	UNK	.86	1.25	B	336
8mm Lebel Revolver	B	.323	.350	UNK/NA	.384	.400	UNK	1.07	1.44	B	336
7.5mm Swedish Nagant Revolvr	B	.325	.328	UNK/NA	.350	.406	UNK	.89	1.35	B	337
8mm Roth-Steyr	D	.329	.353	UNK/NA	.355	.356	UNK	.74	1.14	B	337
.35 S&W Auto/.35 Automatic	D	.32?	UNK	UNK	UNK	UNK	UNK	UNK	UNK	UNK	337
9mm Ultra	D	.355	.374	UNK/NA	.386	.366	UNK	.72	1.03	SP-B	338
9mm Browning Long	D	.355	.376	UNK/NA	.384	.404	UNK	.80	1.10	B	339
9mm Glisenti	D	.355	.380	UNK/NA	.392	.393	UNK	.75	1.15	B	339
9x21mm	D	.355	.380	UNK/NA	.392	.393	UNK	.830	1.16	SP	339
9mm Bayard Long	D	.355	.375	UNK/NA	.390	.392	UNK	.91	1.32	B	340
9mm Steyr	D	.355	.380	UNK/NA	.380	.381	UNK	.90	1.30	B	340
9mm Federal	B	.355	.382	UNK/NA	.386	.435	UNK	.754	1.163	SP	341
9mm Luger (9x19mm Parabellum)	D	.355	.380	UNK/NA	.392	.393	.042	.754	1.16	SP-B	341
9mm Mauser	D	.355	.376	UNK/NA	.389	.390	.050	.981	1.38	B	342
9x23mm Winchester	D	.355	.380	UNK/NA	.390	.392	.042	.900	1.245	LP	343
9mm Winchester Magnum	D	.355	.379	UNK/NA	.392	.394	.046	1.16	1.545	SP	343
.380 Automatic Colt Pistol (ACP)/ 9mm Browning Short/9mm Kurz	D	.356	.373	UNK/NA	.373	.374	.040	.68	.98	SP	344
.38 Short Colt	D	.357	.357	UNK/NA	.378	.433	.055	.76	1.10	SP	345
.38 Long Colt	B	.357	.377	UNK/NA	.378	.433	.055	1.03	1.32	SP	345
.38 Special (.38 S&W Special)	B	.357	.379	UNK/NA	.379	.440	.054	1.16	1.55	SP	345
.357 Magnum S&W	B	.357	.379	UNK/NA	.379	.440	.055	1.29	1.51	SP	346
.357 Remington Maximum	B	.357	.375	UNK/NA	.375	.433	.055	1.59	1.97	SP	347
.357 SIG	C	.357	.381	.424	.425	.424	UNK	.865	1.140	SP	348
.38 Automatic/.38 Super Automatic	H	.358	.382	UNK/NA	.383	.405	.045	.90	1.28	SP	348
.38 S&W/.38 Colt New Police	B	.359	.386	UNK/NA	.386	.433	.055	.78	1.20	SP	349
9mm Russian Makarov	D	.363	.384	UNK/NA	.389	.396	UNK	.71	.97	B	350
.380 Short & Long Revolver	B	.375	.377	UNK/NA	.380	.426	.046	.70	1.10	SP-B	350
.40 S&W Auto	D	.400	.423	UNK/NA	.423	.424	.050	.850	1.135	SP	351

Dimensional Data

Cartridge	Case	Bullet Dia.	Neck Dia.	Shoulder Dia.	Base Dia.	Rim Dia.	Rim Thick.	Case Length	Ctge. Length	Primer	Page
10mm Automatic	D	.400	.423	UNK/NA	.423	.424	.050	.99	1.26	LP	351
.41 Short Colt	B	.401	.404	UNK/NA	.405	.430	.052	?	?	SP	352
.41 Long Colt	B	.386/401	.404	UNK/NA	.405	.430	.052	1.13	1.39	SP	352
.41 Action Express	J	.410	.434	UNK/NA	.435	.394	.045	.866	1.17	SP	353
.41 Remington Magnum	B	.410	.432	UNK/NA	.433	.488	.054	1.28	1.58	LP	353
.414 Super Mag	B	.410	.434	UNK/NA	.435	.492	.059	1.610	1.965	L	354
10.4mm Italian Revolver	B	.422	.444	UNK/NA	.451	.505		.89	1.25	B	355
.44 S&W Russian	B	.429	.457	UNK/NA	.457	.515	.050	.97	1.43	LP	355
.44 S&W Special	B	.429	.457	UNK/NA	.457	.514	.055	1.16	1.62	LP	355
.44 Auto Mag	D	.429	.457	UNK/NA	.470	.473	.048	1.298	1.620	LP	356
.44 Remington Magnum	B	.429	.457	UNK/NA	.457	.514	.055	1.29	1.61	LP	357
.44 Bull Dog	B	.440	.470	UNK/NA	.473	.503		.57	.95	SP-B	357
.45 Winchester Magnum	D	.451	.475	UNK/NA	.477	.481	.045	1.198	1.55	LP	358
.460 Rowland	D	.451	.476	UNK/NA	.476	.476	.044	.955	1.27	LP	358
.45 Webley	B	.452	.471	UNK/NA	.471	.504		.82	1.15	LP-B	359
.45 Auto-Rim	B	.452	.472	UNK/NA	.476	.516	.085	.898	1.28	LP	359
.45 Automatic Short/.45 HP	D	.452	.476	UNK/NA	.476	.476	.044	.860	1.17	LP	360
.45 Glock Auto Pistol (GAP)	D	.452	.473	UNK/NA	.476	.470	.049	.760	1.137	LP	360
.45 Automatic Colt Pistol (ACP)	D	.452	.476	UNK/NA	.476	.476	.044	.898	1.17	LP	361
.454 Casull	B	.452	.476	UNK/NA	.480	.512	.055	1.39	1.70	S*	362
.460 Smith & Wesson	B	.452	.478	UNK/NA	.478	.520	.059	.1.80	2.290	LP	362
.455 Webley Revolver Mk-II	B	.454	.476	UNK/NA	.480	.535		.77	1.23	LP-B	363
.45 Colt Government	B	.454	.478	UNK/NA	.478	.506	.055	1.10	1.44	LP	363
.45 S&W Schofield	B	.454	.478	UNK/NA	.478	.522	.055	1.10	1.43	LP	364
.45 Colt	B	.454	.476	UNK/NA	.480	.512	.055	1.29	1.60	LP	365
.455 Enfield (.455 Colt)	B	.455	.473	UNK/NA	.478	.530	.035	.87	1.35	LP-B	365
.455 Webley Automatic	H	.455	.473	UNK/NA	.474	.500		.93	1.23	B	366
.480 Ruger	B	.475	.504	UNK/NA	.540	.540	.065	1.285	1.650	UNK	366
.500 JRH	B	.500	.527	UNK/NA	.527	.545	.055	1.40	1.80	L	367
.50 Action Express	J	.500	.540	UNK/NA	.547	.514	.055	1.285	1.610	LP	367
.500 Smith & Wesson	B	.500	.530	UNK/NA	.530	.560	.059	2.250		LP	368

Notes on handgun primers: Magnum pistol cartridges are usually loaded with Magnum pistol primers and the ..22 Remington Jet and 2.56 Winchester are sometimes loaded with Small Rifle primers. During WWI, Frankford Arsenal made .45 Automatic cases with special No. 70 primers of .204" diameter instead of the standard .210"

Case Type: A = Rimmed, bottleneck. B = Rimmed, straight. C = Rimless, bottleneck. D = Rimless, straight. E = Belted, bottleneck. F = Belted, straight. G = Semi-rimmed, bottleneck. H = Semi-rimmed, straight. I = Rebated, bottleneck. J = Rebated, straight. K = Rebated, belted bottleneck. L = Rebated, belted straight.

Primer Type: S = Small rifle (.175"). SP = Small pistol (.175"). L = Large rifle (.210"). LP = Large pistol (.210"). B = Berdan type. B-1 = Berdan #1. B-2 = Berdan #2.

Other codes: V = OAL depends upon bullet used V – Rifling twist varies, depending upon bullet and application. ∂ = Belt/Rim Diameter. Unless otherwise noted, all dimensions in inches. Twist (factory) is given as inches of barrel length per complete revolution, e.g., 12 = 1 turn in 12", etc.

*Full-power loads always use small rifle primers.

Military Rifle Cartridges of the World

(Current & Obsolete—Blackpowder and Smokeless)

The sale and use of surplus military firearms in the United States goes back to at least the Civil War, and probably earlier. During World War I, American companies manufactured rifles for the British, French, and Russian governments. At war's end, when military orders were canceled, they found themselves stuck with undelivered quantities. As a result, a lot of new Enfields, Lebels, and Mosin-Nagant rifles showed up in the civilian market and, for a time, 7.62mm Russian and 8mm Lebel sporting ammunition was loaded by American companies. However, nothing in previous history matched the variety and quantity of military arms marketed in the United States after World War II. The first influx occurred about 1947-'48 and were mostly captured enemy guns. However, in the 1950s, practically all the world powers were in the process of adopting new and more modern military small arms. They sold their older models to surplus dealers, who immediately offered those guns in the United States. This period offered unprecedented opportunities to shoot, experiment with, and remodel military rifles. Dealers sold many fine and brand new military rifles and handguns at very low prices. Few of these arms sold at prices over $35 to $40, and many sold at $10 to $25. Some of these same guns will bring upward of $300 on today's market. Not a single issue or model ever went down in value.

The Gun Control Act of 1968 ended the importation of surplus guns on such a scale. It is doubtful we will ever again see anything comparable to the war surplus phenomenon during the period between 1948 and 1968, although recently the surplus market did loosen up again. Consequently, a variety of military rifles are used for target practice, plinking, and small- and big-game hunting in America. Tinkers and gunsmiths can convert most military rifles into first-class sporting arms, and tens of thousands were so altered. Naturally, the cartridges used by these various rifles are of interest to those shooting the guns because, after all, the gun is of no use without the ammunition. That era exposed the American sportsman to chamberings all but unknown prior to World War II, which influenced subsequent cartridge development in this country.

Military ammunition represents one of the most highly developed categories of the metallic cartridge. Military ballisticians have spent untold millions of dollars in research to determine the best and most efficient combination of primer, case, powder, and bullet. The resulting degree of perfection explains why military cartridges are so popular for sporting use and why any cartridge adopted as a nation's official military chambering is so likely to become popular in civilian applications. American military cartridges have been highly esteemed in sporting circles, and all but the old 6mm Lee and .50-70 are still loaded and used. (Manufacturers have recently reintroduced .50-70 components, and sportsmen are again using this cartridge for sports like cowboy action shooting, for example). Foreign military chamberings do not offer the American sportsman anything new or different, although most are quite good in basic design and performance. These cartridges largely parallel what we already have available. The exceptions are the various 6.5mm and 7mm chamberings, which represent an area that was formerly neglected here.

Middle European, Mediterranean, Scandinavian, and Asian countries have favored 6.5mm cartridges for their military rifles. These cartridges are all quite similar in performance and power and offer little to choose from for sporting use. From the American viewpoint, the 6.5mm Mannlicher-Schoenauer and the 6.5x55mm Swedish are the best choices. However, any of these are good deer and antelope cartridges, superior to anything in the .30-30 class for this purpose. Most are appropriate for use against larger game, when loaded with heavier bullets. The 7x57mm Mauser is another cartridge well known in sporting circles and is well adapted to North American game and hunting conditions. It is listed along with the 8x57mm Mauser and the .303 British under American sporting cartridges, because all three are loaded in this country and have been for many years. An interesting recent development has been the widespread availability of the 7.62x53R Russian and 7.62x39mm Soviet cartridges and guns to shoot them.

A surprising number of obsolete single-shot and repeating blackpowder military rifles have shown up, since 1948. Many of these rifles are brand new or in first-class condition. This has spurred shooting interest. The centerfire blackpowder cartridges listed include those that an average neophyte might encounter, along with a few comparatively rare, albeit interesting, examples. Calibers vary from .32 to .60, with bullet weights from 250 to over 500 grains. The original powder used was coarse granulation blackpowder similar to what we know as Fg. The charge ranged from 40 grains to more than 80 grains. There was also variation of the powder charge within the same cartridge, owing to use of different bullets and lot-to-lot variations in powder density and performance. Most countries also had a carbine loading, which was lighter than standard. In power, all these old cartridges are similar to our own .45-70 and are adequate for most North American big game at short to moderate range. Standard loadings from these rounds all have a very curved trajectory, which makes it difficult to hit anything beyond 200 yards, although these will kill much further away. At known ranges, these are typically quite accurate and will turn in good scores out to 500 or even 1,000 yards.

Continued use of blackpowder military rifles will eventually require reloading of fired cases. All but the American cartridges use Berdan primers, usually of 6.37mm (.251-inch), 6.46mm (.254-inch) or 6.5mm (.256-inch) size. These sizes are available from RWS. Lyman, Hornady, RCBS, and others make loading dies for the more popular blackpowder cartridges. It is often possible to make reloadable cases from similar modern cases by trimming and reforming. To produce good ballistics and proper burning, blackpowder charges should fill the case to the base of the bullet; while seating the bullet, it should slightly compress the charge. When using smokeless powder to load blackpowder cartridges, *never* exceed original velocities or pressures, as few rifles are strong enough to safely withstand such treatment. Accurate Arms offers simple instructions for loading AA 5744, so as to duplicate the pressure and velocity of the original blackpowder load in any typical rifle cartridge. In brief, begin with a charge that fills 45 percent of the available powder space in the case (room left over with bullet seated normally). Increase the charge as needed, until the load duplicates the velocity of the original blackpowder loading. After firing with blackpowder, cases must be soaked and scrubbed in soap or detergent to remove the fouling, then dried before reloading. A bullet alloy of one part tin to 16 or 20 parts lead is about right for blackpowder, but a mixture of one-to-10 is more satisfactory with smokeless charges. Use of hard, jacketed bullets in blackpowder rifles is not good practice, as these will often rapidly wear the bore, sometimes destroying accuracy within only 100 rounds or so. If you use common sense and exercise reasonable caution, shooting obsolete military rifles is a lot of fun and is perfectly safe, if the gun is in good condition.

The subject of military rifles is too broad and involved to be covered adequately in a book devoted primarily to cartridges. However, we have included tables listing the more common smokeless and blackpowder military rifles and their characteristics. In passing, it might be well to at least mention two badly abused phases of the military rifle subject—safety and value. Some authors who should know better have bluntly stated, and without qualification, that all surplus military arms are unsafe, worthless pieces of junk. This simply is not true. The idea that any military power would arm its troops with guns inherently dangerous to fire is too silly to merit serious discussion. Toward the end of World War II, Germany and Japan turned out some shoddy, makeshift arms for drill, guard, or civilian use, and some used castings that were definitely not safe to fire. Others looked like hell, but were actually quite stout. In any event, these were not standard military issue, and the surplus gun market handled very few of these. For marketers to have sold dangerous and unsafe guns would have ended the big surplus military boom long before the Gun Control Act of 1968. That is just a matter of common sense.

I believe it is entirely correct to state that no standard military rifle is any more dangerous than any other if it is in good condition and fired with the cartridge and load for which it was designed. Use the correct ammunition and exercise common sense in handloading, and you will not get in trouble. Alteration of military rifles to other than the original chambering is alright, too, if you know what you're doing. On the other hand, this can be dangerous if mishandled, for it requires knowledge of the relative strength, mechanics, and metallurgy of military rifle actions.

Value? Only you can determine the value a certain gun has for you. "Value," as such, has really been beaten to death. Such terms as "good," "bad," "worthless," or a "good buy" are all relative, for their meaning will vary with the buyer and his individual ideas. As late as 1940, one could buy U.S. 1873 .45-70 Springfield rifles for $6.50 used and $11 brand new. I owned several and wish I'd had both the money and the foresight to have purchased a whole garage full, because these rifles are currently worth quite a bit in good condition. One must understand, though, that alteration of a military rifle destroys its value as a collector's item.

American-made sporting ammunition included the more popular foreign military chamberings up until about the mid-1930s. The 6.5mm Mannlicher-Schoenauer, 7x57mm Mauser, 7.65mm Mauser, 7.62mm Russian, 8mm Mauser, and 8mm Lebel were all made in the United States, along with the .303 British. At present, few American sporting rifles chamber foreign military cartridges, and only the 6.5x55mm Swedish, 7mm and 8mm Mauser, and .303 British are loaded here. However, Norma and RWS have recently loaded some of these cartridges in sporting versions. Most of these are imported through U.S. dealers.

Hunters should not use military ammunition loaded with full metal jacket bullets. These bullets are designed to wound, not necessarily kill. Also, bear in mind that full jacketed bullets will not break up on contact; more often than not, these will ricochet badly. This is also true of the big, low-velocity bullets fired by blackpowder rifles.

Handloading will improve the performance of most military cartridges to varying degrees. Most European ammunition is loaded with corrosive Berdan-type primers which (without special tools) are not as quick or easy to decap and re-prime as the Boxer-primed cases used by American manufacturers. Many others use steel cases that are not routinely reloadable. Norma continues to import ammunition and cases made for American primers in a number of military chamberings. Availability of reloadable cases is an important consideration, because the supply of surplus ammunition is not inexhaustible. The ultimate use of your rifle may depend on just such a small item as this.

Some military cartridges have never been loaded as sporting ammunition, but the handloader can correct this deficiency. Some of the old blackpowder military rifles have been relegated as wall hangers, because of lack of ammunition, but this situation is changing, as small manufacturers now offer these cases to the handloader. Buffalo Arms (www.buffaloarms.com) offers many such cases. Many cartridges listed in Chapter 6 are obsolete, from the military viewpoint. The United States, the United Kingdom, and all NATO countries have adopted the 7.62x51mm NATO round, as have Japan, Australia, and many Asian countries. In addition, practically all these countries now use the 5.56x45mm (.223 Remington) for their military rifles. The U.S. used this smaller round almost exclusively in Vietnam. Russia and most former satellite countries have adopted the Russian M43 or 7.62x39mm cartridge. In 1974, the Soviet Union adopted a new .22-caliber round designated the 5.45x39mm.

Recent development in military cartridges has been in the realm of caseless cartridges, something that hasn't been fully successful to date. The word from ordnance circles is, "Happiness is still a cartridge case." — *F.C.B.*

13th Edition Update

As with several of the chapter that came before this one, we've taken a handful of the oddest and most difficult to find rounds and relocated to them to the CD included with this book. As the original author stated above, many included in this chapter have long been obsolete, so we certainly attempted to be judicious with our cull, making a decided effort to leave here in the paper pages those that consumers are more likely to encounter at a gun show or chambered for firearms in a retail store's well-stocked used gun rack, or rounds that, though obsolete, still had most if not all of their components (brass, primers, powder, and bullets), still available from at least a source or two. To that end, the list of cartridges removed from this chapter include: 6.5x53.5mm Daudeteau; 6.5x58mm Portuguese Vergueiro; 6.8x57mm Chinese; .280 British; .276 Enfield; .276 Pedersen; 7.62x45mm Czech M52; 8x58Rmm Danish Krag; 8x53Rmm Japanese Murata; 8x60Rmm Guedes M85 Portuguese; 9.5x60Rmm Turkish Mauser; 10.15x61Rmm Jarmann; 10.15x63Rmm Serbian Mauser; 11x60Rmm Japanese Murata; 11x50Rmm Belgian Albini M67/72; 11x53Rmm Belgian Comblain M71; 11.15x58Rmm (.43) Spanish Remington (11x53mm Spanish); 11.15x58Rmm Austrian Werndl M77; 11.43x50Rmm (.43) Egyptian Remington; 11.4x50Rmm Austrian Werndl M73; 11.4x50Rmm Brazilian Comblain M74; 11.3x50Rmm Beaumont M71; 11.63x33mm Belted (.458x1-inch Barnes); 11x52Rmm Netherlands Beaumont M71/78.— *J.L.S.P.*

4.85mm British

Historical Notes: This was an experimental British military cartridge of less than .22-caliber that more or less parallels similar developments by Germany. Although entered in the NATO trials of 1977, none of these small-caliber cartridges were ever adopted, even though some of these cartridges developed initial velocities in excess of 4000 fps. The problem with these small, lightweight, high-velocity bullets is that all lose velocity and energy rapidly and, from a military viewpoint, are not very effective beyond moderate range. A gilding, metal-clad, steel jacketed bullet of .192-inch diameter with lead alloy core and flat base was used. Both Ball and tracer types were made. Further development ended after the 1977 NATO trials.

General Comments: The dimensions of the 4.85mm British are practically identical to the wildcat 5mm/223 except that the case is about a 1/5-inch longer, due to a longer neck. Muzzle velocity would be similar.

4.85mm British Factory Ballistics

Bullet (grains/type)	Powder	Grains	Velocity	Energy	Source/Comments
56	ML		3117	1210	Military load (L1E1 Ball)

5.7x28mm FN P90 (Belgium)

Historical Notes: Developed, in the late 1980s, by FN for its then new P90 personal-defense gun, this cartridge is intended to replace the 9x19mm Parabellum pistol cartridge. Claimed ballistic performance is much superior to the 9mm cartridge. As yet, no major country has adopted this new chambering.

General Comments: The 5.7x28mm cartridge is somewhat similar in shape to the commercial .221 Fireball cartridge. However, the two are not interchangeable. A sharply pointed ball bullet weighing only 23 grains is used, as intended range is limited. Despite this, this bullet has been designed to penetrate helmets and body armor at 50 meters without breaking up.

13th Edition Update: FNH USA now produces the Five-seveN series of pistols and PS90 carbines that chamber this round. Numerous law enforcement agencies and military personnel around the world, including, it is reported, the U.S. Secret Service, are regularly employing this round and numerous firearms chambered for it, such as the AR-57.

5.7x28mm FN P90 Factory Ballistics

Bullet (grains/type)	Powder	Grains	Velocity	Energy	Source/Comments
23 FMJ-BT Ball	ML		2790	400	Military Load

5.45x39mm Soviet

Historical Notes: This is a Russian cartridge, introduced about 1974 for use in the new AK-74 assault rifle. There are both fixed-stock and folding-stock versions, and the 5.45mm rifle has a redesigned flash reducer/muzzle brake that distinguishes it from the earlier AK-47. This cartridge has a more slender case and a thicker rim than the 7.62x39mm (M43) cartridge. The bullet is .221- to .222-inch in diameter and weighs from 53 to 54 grains. This bullet is almost one-inch long and has a very sharp spitzer point, a boat-tail base, a mild steel core, a short lead filler on top, and an air space in the nose. The bullet is designed to be unstable in tissue, thus producing a more severe wound. The British used somewhat the same idea in the design of their MKVII .303 bullet, used in World War II. Casualty reports from Afghanistan, where the new 5.45mm cartridge and rifle first appeared, tend to confirm the lethality of the bullet. Muzzle velocity is approximately 2950 fps.

The first 5.45mm Soviet cartridges publicly available to western military intelligence were brought out of Afghanistan by writer Galen Greer, while on assignment for Soldier of Fortune magazine, in 1980, and the first information made public was in the October 1980 issue of that magazine. Until that time, the existence of a new Russian military cartridge had mostly been rumor. Later, the round was withdrawn from service in Afghanistan. Cases are lacquered steel with Berdan primers.

General Comments: The Russians apparently designed this cartridge as a result of experience on the receiving end of the U.S. M-16 rifle and 5.56mm round, in Vietnam. The 5.45mm Russian is a well-designed cartridge, for its intended purpose. The long, thin, boat-tail bullet reduces aerodynamic drag to the minimum and results in a higher retained velocity at long range. The bullet is designed to be stable in flight and provide good accuracy at all ranges out to maximum, but unstable on contact, so as to tumble easily, which enhances lethality. It is a better designed military bullet than the original used in the United States M193 5.56mm cartridge. However, the new 5.56mm SS109 (M855) NATO standard round, with its heavier bullet and improved shape, probably has an edge over the Soviet bullet.

5.45x39mm Russian Factory Ballistics

Bullet (grains)	Powder	Grains	Velocity	Energy	Source/Comments
54	ML		2950	1045	Military load (SBT Ball)

5.56x45mm NATO

Historical Notes: The 5.56x45mm cartridge was originally developed for the Armalite AR-15 rifle. It was first tested by the U.S. Air Force as a possible replacement for the M-1 Carbine, in 1960-'61. The AR-15 later evolved into the selective-fire M-16 adopted by the U.S. military, in 1964, after several years of testing by the U.S. Continental Army Command at Fort Monroe, Virginia. The rifle and cartridge were first combat tested in Vietnam, in the early 1960s.

General Comments: As initially loaded, the 5.56x45mm Ball cartridge had a 55-grain spitzer boat-tail bullet at a muzzle velocity of 3250 fps. It was the standard U.S. military loading, until 1984. In 1980, the 5.56mm, FN-designed, 62-grain SS109 bullet was adopted by NATO. Designated the M855 in the United States, the new load uses a spitzer boat-tail bullet with a mild steel penetrator in front of the lead base. Muzzle velocity is 3100 fps. Adoption also involved changes in 5.56mm rifles to a quicker rifling twist of 1:7, to stabilize the longer, heavier bullet. This much improved bullet resulted in higher retained velocity and greater accuracy at long range. It also has much improved penetration characteristics over the old M193 55-grain projectile at all ranges.

The 5.56mm case is similar in configuration to and interchangeable with the commercial .223 Remington, although SAAMI warns that dimensional differences between military chambers and commercial chambers may make it unsafe to fire military ammunition in sporting rifles. Additional information and loading data can be found under that listing in Chapter 2.

5.56x45mm NATO Factory Ballistics

Bullet (grains/type)	Powder	Grains	Velocity	Energy	Source/Comments
55 FMJ-BT M193 Ball	ML		3250	1325	U.S. Military load, old
62 FMJ-BT M855 Ball			3100	1325	NATO load, new

5.8x42mm Chinese

Historical Notes: Surprisingly, in the mid-1990s, the Chinese military introduced a new, indigenous, 5.8x42mm Small-Caliber High-Velocity (SCHV) assault rifle round and a new family of small arms to use it. This was the result of research spanning more than two decades. Like the Russians, the advantages of SCHV assault rifle ammo observed in Vietnam War battle reports did not go unnoticed by the Chinese military. So, in March, 1971, the Chinese military logistic department commenced a small arms research project, in Beijing, known as the "713 Conference," in order to develop the design criteria for an indigenous SCHV assault rifle cartridge.

The design criteria called for a cartridge of approximately 6mm-caliber at 1,000 meters per second muzzle velocity, with the goals of reducing recoil and ammo weight, while improving accuracy and terminal ballistics over the Type 56/M43 7.62x39mm full-caliber intermediate round. The following "744 Conference" narrowed down the calibers under consideration to 5.8mm and 6mm. The project completed its development in 1987, and the new SCHV assault rifle cartridge was officially designated as the DBP87.

The Chinese military has since developed a variety of small arms chambered for the new 5.8mm cartridge. The first was the QBZ87 assault rifle primarily used as the test bed for further 5.8mm ammo development. The QBZ87 was an undated 7.62mm Type 81 assault rifle chambered for the new 5.8mm round. The QBZ87 has now been largely withdrawn from frontline services and handed over to paramilitary, military academies, and reservists.

Next came the QBZ95 assault rifle family, comprised of the QBZ95 assault rifle, QBB95 squad automatic rifle/light machine gun, and the QBZ95B carbine. The QBZ95 (Qing, Bu-Qiang, Zi-Dong, 1995 Si, or Infantry Rifle Automatic, Model 1995), is a modern looking 7.1-pound (3.25-kilogram) assault rifle in a bullpup configuration. Like other bullpup rifles, such as French FAMAS, Austrian AUG, and the British SA80, the QBZ has its magazine and action located behind its trigger and pistol grip.

General Comments: The 5.8mm ammo is much more conventional than the weapons chambered for it. The 5.8mm standard rifle load has a 64-grain (4.15g) bullet, with a full metal jacket made of steel and wearing a copper-washed coating. The 24.3mm long projectile has a very streamlined external shape, with a sharp bullet ogive and a sizeable boat-tail. The 5.8mm bullet has a composite core that consists of a pin-shaped hardened steel penetrator located near the base of the bullet, with lead as the filling material between the penetrator and the jacket, as well as in the tip cavity.

The 5.8mm cartridge has a 42mm long case, with a one-degree taper in the body from its 10.5mm-diameter base. The bottleneck shoulder and the neck are both 4 millimeters long. The shorter but wider 5.8mm case is more space efficient than the long and slim case of the 5.56mm. The tapered case design also helps with both ammo feeding and extraction. However, the straight-wall case design of the 5.56mm has better accuracy.

5.8x42mm Chinese Factory Ballistics

Bullet (grains/type)	Powder	Grains	Velocity	Energy	Source/Comments
64 gr FMJ BT	Corrosive	approx 28.0	3050	1325	Timothy G. Yan

6mm SAW (U.S.)

Historical Notes: In the early 1970s, the U.S. Army began studies to develop a new infantry squad machine gun called the Squad Automatic Weapon (SAW). Frankford Arsenal began computerized parametric design analyses, in July 1971, to design a cartridge to meet user requirements. After several experimental designs based on the 5.56x45mm case proved unsuccessful, a new case having a larger .410-inch diameter head and a length of 1.779 inches was adopted. A 6mm diameter (.243-inch) 105-grain full metal jacket boat-tail bullet was used.

General Comments: Cartridge cases for the 6mm SAW will be found in both steel (with a phenolic varnish finish) and in aluminum (with an anodized finish). The aluminum case is longer than the steel case. The 6mm SAW was never adopted, although considerable quantities of ammunition were loaded experimentally by Frankford Arsenal. This cartridge is frequently encountered in collections. It is historically significant as the first cartridge designed using computerized parametric design analysis. Interestingly, ballistics are quite similar to the circa-1895 Lee Navy cartridge.

6mm SAW Factory Ballistics

Bullet (grains/type)	Powder	Grains	Velocity	Energy	Source/Comments
105 FMJ-BT	ML		2520	1480	Military load, XM732 Ball

6mm Lee Navy
.236 Navy

Historical Notes: The 6mm Lee cartridge, also known as the .236 Navy, was used in the 1895 Lee Straight Pull bolt-action military rifle manufactured by Winchester for the United States Navy. About 15,000 of these rifles were made and used by the Navy on a trial basis. Winchester, Remington, and Blake also chambered sporting rifles for this cartridge. No factory loaded ammunition has been available since 1935.

General Comments: The .244, or 6mm, was revived in two cartridges introduced by Remington and Winchester in 1955, those being the .244 (now the 6mm Remington), and .243. The 6mm Lee cartridge died out, mainly because it was too far ahead of its time; the powders available in 1895 were not suitable to this cartridge. A few shooters who have old rifles for this round handload and use it for hunting. It is a good varmint, medium-game, deer, black bear, and antelope cartridge at moderate ranges. It is not as powerful as the 6mm Remington or the .243 Winchester. By increasing the rim to fit the standard Mauser bolt face and necking the case to accept .224-inch bullets, Winchester created the .220 Swift. See Chapter 3 for data.

6.5x50mm Japanese Arisaka

Historical Notes: This cartridge, best known for its use in the modified Mauser-type Model 38 Japanese bolt-action rifle of 1905, was actually introduced in 1897, intended for a discontinued rifle found to be unsafe in service. It was introduced in the United States after World War II, as the result of captured rifles brought back by returning GIs and, later, by the surplus arms dealers who sold large numbers of the Model 38 rifles and carbines. Sporting ammunition in 6.5x50mm has recently been loaded by Norma, using the American-type Boxer primer. Military ammunition has a Berdan-type primer, usually of .199-inch or .217-inch size. Military ball ammunition of recent production, with steel cases and Berdan primers, has recently been imported from China.

General Comments: The 6.5x50mm has a semi-rimmed case, but is otherwise not radically different from other 6.5mm military cartridges. It has the shortest case and shortest powder capacity of any of the military 6.5mms, but is, nonetheless, an efficient design with smokeless powder. The Japanese Model 38 rifle has an unusually strong action, which allows the cartridge to be loaded to its full potential. Because commercial sporting ammunition and reloadable cases are available, this is one of the more useful military cartridges. In power, it is on a par with any of the other 6.5 military rounds and is fine for antelope, deer, sheep, and black bear. It makes a far more effective deer cartridge than the .30-30. To solve the ammunition availability problem, some 6.5mm Arisaka rifles have been re-chambered to the wildcat 6.5-257 Roberts, which makes a fine conversion.

6.5x50mm Japanese Arisaka Loading Data and Factory Ballistics

Bullet (grains/type)	Powder	Grains	Velocity	Energy	Source/Comments
120 SP	IMR 4350	43	3000	2400	Maximum load
120 SP	H380	36	2680	1918	NA
120 SP	IMR 4895	34	2650	1870	NA
140 SP	IMR 4350	40	2680	2240	NA
140 SP	H380	34	2360	1735	NA
156 SP	IMR 4064	28	2060	1460	Duplicates factory loading
160 SP	IMR 4320	34	2500	2408	NA
139 Ball	ML		2500	1930	Military load
139 SP	FL		2430	1815	Norma factory load
156 SP	FL		2070	1475	Norma factory load

6.5x54mm Mannlicher-Schoenauer (Greek)

Historical Notes: This original Greek military cartridge was designed in 1900 and used in the 1903 Mannlicher bolt-action rifle. It is also a popular sporting number in Europe and the United States. All major American ammunition companies loaded the 6.5mm Mannlicher, until about 1940. The Austrian-made Mannlicher-Schoenauer sporting rifle was the only rifle routinely available in this chambering. Sporting ammunition is loaded in Europe, and RWS has imported Boxer-primed, reloadable cases and a good variety of sporting loads. European ammunition uses the Berdan primer, usually the 5.5mm or .217-inch size.

General Comments: The 6.5mm M-S has always had a certain following in the United States, even though American rifle makers do not chamber it as a standard option. It is a very fine cartridge for North American hunting, with far better killing power than the .30-30 or anything in that class. In fact, every species of big game on earth has been taken with this cartridge. A great many elephants were killed by ivory hunters using this little 6.5mm and heavy, solid bullets. It did not make enough noise to bother a herd and gave deep penetration for well-placed brain shots. In the hands of an experienced hunter, it will do for any North American big game. However, by today's standards, it is considered primarily a deer, sheep, antelope, and black bear cartridge. In power, it is often compared to the .257 Roberts, and there is some validity for this. On the other hand, the 6.5mm M-S is loaded with bullets of around 160 grains in weight, compared to the 120-grain top weight of the .257. It is the long, heavy bullet that makes this a good killer on the tougher varieties of game.

6.5x54mm Mannlicher-Schoenauer (Greek) Loading Data and Factory Ballistics

Bullet (grains/type)	Powder	Grains	Velocity	Energy	Source/Comments
139-140 SP	IMR 3031	35	2510	1950	Antelope, deer
139-140 SP	IMR 4895	36	2400	1790	NA
156 SP	IMR 4350	38	2510	2182	NA
156 SP	IMR 3031	34	2460	2100	Duplicates original military load
160 SP	IMR 4064	38	2450	2140	Heavy game
140 SP	FL		2250	1575	Hirtenberger factory load
159 SP	FL		2330	1740	RWS factory load
159 Ball	ML		2223	1740	Military load

6.5x53Rmm Mannlicher (Dutch & Romanian)

Historical Notes: This is an earlier rimmed version of the 6.5x54mm Greek cartridge. It was designed by Mannlicher and used in the bolt-action Dutch Models 1892 and 1895 and Romanian Models 1892 and 1893. The cartridge was dropped by both countries after World War II.

General Comments: This cartridge delivers ballistics practically identical to the regular 6.5x54mm Mannlicher-Schoenauer known for many years in the United States and, at one time, loaded by most cartridge companies. The rimmed version is used in a few single-shot and combination European sporting rifles. Commercial hunting ammunition for rifles so chambered was once loaded in both England and Europe.

This cartridge was introduced in the United States after World War II, when quantities of the Dutch and Romanian military rifles and carbines were sold in surplus stores. Only imported sporting ammunition is available, but some dealers have furnished hunting loads based on the military round with the bullet replaced. Rifles in this chambering are suitable for deer, antelope, black bear, and the like. The British listed this cartridge as the .256 Mannlicher, and many bolt-action rifles were turned out for it by Jeffery and others. It has been popular in parts of Africa. No commercial manufacturer currently offers this ammunition. Brass can be made from .303 British cases.

6.5x53Rmm Mannlicher Loading Data and Factory Ballistics

Bullet (grains/type)	Powder	Grains	Velocity	Energy	Source/Comments
120 SP	IMR 4895	33	2440	1590	NA
120 SP	IMR 4064	35	2650	1875	NA
140 SP	IMR 3031	35	2550	2360	NA
156 SP	IMR 3031	34	2445	2095	Duplicates military ball load
156 SP	IMR 4350	38	2510	2192	NA
160 SP	IMR 3031	34	2250	1810	NA
156 – 159 Ball	ML		2433	2085	Military load
160 SP	FL		2350	1960	Factory load

6.5x55mm Swedish Mauser

Historical Notes: A Mauser- and Swedish-designed military cartridge adopted in 1894, the 6.5x55mm was used in the Swedish Models 94, 96, and 38 rifles and carbines. These are based on a modification of the Spanish Mauser 1893 bolt-action. Norway also adopted this cartridge for its 1894 and 1912 Krag-Jorgensen rifles. Ammunition for sporting use is loaded by Norma and others. Military ammunition uses the Berdan primer, usually of .199-inch or .216-inch diameter. Sporting rifles are currently available on the American market in this chambering. Federal and PMC produce 6.5x55mm ammunition. Remington apparently produced a few rifles in 6.5x55mm some years ago, and one version of the Model 70 Winchester was also so chambered. The military ball is a spitzer boat-tail of very advanced design. Both copper and clad-steel jacket types exist.

General Comments: The 6.5x55 Swedish cartridge is another surplus, post-war immigrant that has become quite popular in the United States. For North American hunting, it is one of the best of the foreign military cartridges. It has been highly developed as a match and hunting round in the Scandinavian countries and has a reputation for superb accuracy. With lighter bullets (77- to 100-grain), it will do very well for varmint shooting of all kinds. The 120-grain bullet is fine for antelope or deer, and heavier (140- to 160-grain) bullets make it suitable for most types of big game. The Swedish Mauser and the Norwegian Krag are intended for working pressures of only about 45,000 psi, and this must be considered when handloading. With a stronger action, maximum loads and performance could be notably increased. Except for a slightly larger rim and base diameter and a shorter neck, this cartridge is very similar to the 6.5x57mm Mauser cartridge. It is not known exactly who designed it, but, undoubtedly, its design was influenced by Mauser developments. Chapter 2 contains more information on this round.

6.5x55mm Swedish Mauser Loading Data and Factory Ballistics

Bullet (grains/type)	Powder	Grains	Velocity	Energy	Source/Comments
100 HP	IMR 3031	44	3100	2140	Varmint load
120 SP	IMR 4350	50	2780	2062	Deer, antelope
129 SP	IMR 4895	41	2625	1990	NA
140 SP	IMR 4350	45	2520	1980	NA
140 SP	IMR 4831	50	2590	2090	NA
156 SP	IMR 4350	43	2500	2168	NA
160 SP	IMR 4350	42	2430	2100	Heavy game
77 FMJ	FL		3120	1660	Norma bird factory load
139 SP	FL		2790	2395	Norma factory load
156 SP	FL		2490	2150	Norma factory load
139 Ball	ML		2625	2126	Military load

6.5x52mm Italian (Mannlicher-Carcano)

Historical Notes: This was the official Italian military cartridge adopted in 1891 for the bolt-action Mannlicher-Carcano rifle. This rifle was a Mannlicher-inspired design in every respect except the bolt, which is a Mauser-type with double locking lugs at the front. It is also the only military rifle of smokeless powder design to use gain-twist rifling. This Italian 6.5mm cartridge is very similar to the 6.5mm Mannlicher-Schoenauer in size, shape, and performance. Both unprimed cases and loaded ammunition have been made by Norma.

General Comments: The Italian 6.5mm military cartridge was unfamiliar to American shooters, until after World War II. Large quantities of Italian Model 91 rifles and carbines have been sold at very low prices, and because we are a great nation of bargain hunters, this is now a fairly widely used cartridge. Many surplus arms dealers furnished hunting ammunition that consisted of the military round with the full-jacketed bullet replaced by a soft-point. Reloadable cases can be made very easily from 6.5x54mm Mannlicher cases. This is a good deer, antelope, or black bear cartridge, but the low working pressure limit of the Carcano rifle prevents loading it as heavily as similar military 6.5mms.

6.5x52mm Italian Mannlicher-Carcano Loading Data and Factory Ballistics

Bullet (grains/type)	Powder	Grains	Velocity	Energy	Source/Comments
140 SP	IMR 4895	33	2250	1570	Maximum for Carcano rifle
140 SP	IMR 3031	34	2320	1730	NA
156 SP	IMR 4064	37	2280	1806	NA
156 SP	IMR 4350	35	2340	1898	NA
160 SP	IMR 4350	35	2320	1919	NA
139 SP	FL		2580	2045	Norma factory load
156 SP	FL		2430	2045	Norma factory load
162 Ball	ML		2296	1902	Military load

7x57mm Mauser

Historical Notes: The 7x57mm Mauser is another cartridge that, although designed as a military round, was widely adapted for sporting purposes. Contrary to what most cartridge books say, it was not introduced in 1893. It was actually developed in 1892 and used in a limited number of Model 1892 Mauser rifles, a modification of the Belgian-Mauser pattern of 1889. In 1893, Mauser introduced an improved bolt-action rifle in 7x57mm that was officially adopted by the Spanish military. Subsequently, with minor modifications, the 7mm-chambered rifle was adopted by other European and many Latin-American governments. The Remington Model 1902 rolling block rifle was also manufactured in 7x57mm Mauser, as was the Model 70 Winchester. More recently, several U.S. gun makers have chambered it in their finest guns.

The original 7mm military round employed a 173-grain bullet with a muzzle velocity of 2296 fps and an energy of 2025 ft-lbs. Other loadings were used by various countries, with bullets ranging in weight from 139 grains up to the original 173 grains. Those loads on which data is available are listed below.

Model 93 Mauser rifles in 7mm were used by Spanish troops in Cuba, during the Spanish-American War. The effectiveness of this combination against American forces was responsible for the eventual adoption of the Mauser-system 1903 Springfield rifle. San Juan Hill was defended by only about 700 Spaniards armed with the new Mauser 7mm rifles, but they inflicted some 1,400 casualties on the 15,000 Americans who attacked their position.

General Comments: The United States saw a large influx of surplus 7mm military rifles, after World War II. Many who purchased those fine rifles immediately wanted the gun altered to use a more familiar American sporting cartridge. This was foolish, because the 7x57mm is one of the best all-round cartridges available for North American big-game hunting. With the proper bullet for the job at hand, the 7mm will handle any big game here. It might not be the choice for grizzly bear in heavy brush, but, in the hands of an experienced hunter, it will be far superior to the .30-30 for any purpose. If the barrel is in good shape, it is best to leave a 7mm military rifle in its original chambering. Loading data is in Chapter 2. All major manufacturers offer 7x57mm sporting ammunition.

Bullet (grains/type)	Powder	Grains	Velocity	Energy	Source/Comments
139 Ball	ML		2950	2580	Military load, Brazil & Colombia
142 Ball	ML		2740	2365	Military load, Uruguay
155 Ball	ML		2300	1820	Military load, Mexico
162 Ball	ML		2295	1890	Military load, Mexico
173 Ball	ML		2296	2025	Original military loading used by Spain & others

7.35mm Italian Carcano

Historical Notes: The 7.35mm cartridge was adopted by Italy, in 1938, to replace the 6.5x52mm round that had been used since 1891. Experience in Ethiopia and other places had demonstrated the desirability for a larger caliber in combat use. The Model 91 Carcano rifle was modified slightly for the new cartridge, but retained the same basic action. That happened about the time Italy became involved in various military actions, and the new cartridge created a critical supply problem, causing it to be withdrawn from service. Quantities of 7.35mm rifles were used against the Russians by Finnish troops and reportedly gave good service. No sporting ammunition is currently loaded for this chambering, although Norma offered it for many years.

General Comments: Many thousands of the Italian Model 38 service rifles and carbines were sold here as surplus. These rifles were sold at extremely low prices and are now in rather widespread use all over the country. In power, the 7.35mm is between the .30-30 and the .300 Savage, making it a good deer and black bear cartridge, if the proper hunting bullet is used. It is actually a better cartridge than the .30-30, in many respects. Reloadable cases can be made from empty 6.5x54mm Mannlicher cases as imported by RWS. This is done by expanding the neck, running the shell through a full length sizing die, and then trimming back to proper length. The Carcano action is designed for working pressures of only about 38,000 psi, and the loads given below should not be exceeded. In a strong, modern action, it would be possible to equal the .300 Savage in performance, but this cannot be done safely in the military Carcano.

7.35mm Italian Carcano Loading Data and Factory Ballistics

Bullet (grains/type)	Powder	Grains	Velocity	Energy	Source/Comments
128 SP	IMR 3031	38	2495	1776	Approximates military load ballistics
128 SP	IMR 4895	40	2500	1782	NA
150 SP	IMR 4320	40	2550	2175	NA
150 SP	IMR 4895	38	2450	2005	NA
150 SP	H380	41	2490	2070	NA
128 Ball	ML		2483	1749	Military load

.30 Carbine (.30 M-1 Carbine)

Historical Notes: In 1940, the U.S. Ordnance Department concluded that a light carbine might have certain advantages over the .45-caliber semi-auto pistol in many combat situations. Various designs were submitted by a number of private manufacturers and, in the end, Winchester's offering was selected. The semi-auto .30 M-1 Carbine was officially adopted, in 1941. This cartridge, a modification of the .32 Winchester self-loading round of 1906, was hardly a revolutionary new design, but it served the purpose. About the same time, the Germans developed their assault rifle and the 7.92mm Kurz (short) cartridge. The M-1 Carbine is not an assault rifle, and the military insists it was designed to fulfill a different purpose. A few sporting rifles and handguns have chambered the .30 Carbine (See Chapter 2).

General Comments: In mid-1963, the government released .30 M-1 Carbines for sale to civilians, through the National Rifle Association, at the very moderate price of around $20. Thousands of these rifles, as a result, have been used for sporting purposes. Federal, Winchester, and Remington load soft-point sporting ammunition and, so, the M-l Carbine must be considered from other than a strictly military viewpoint. The .30 Carbine cartridge is in the same class as the .32-20 WCF, but slightly more powerful. It is wholly a small-game and varmint number, despite contrary claims by those who love the short, light, and handy M-1 Carbine. The modest accuracy of the Carbine, combined with the ballistics of this cartridge, limit the effective sporting accuracy range to about 150 yards. The original author of this book used an M-1 Carbine to hunt small game and deer as early as 1943, before most people could get their hands on one of these guns, so he had a pretty good idea of the capability of this cartridge. Remember that the .32 Winchester self-loading round became obsolete in 1920, because it was ineffective and more or less useless for sporting purposes. The .30 Carbine was derived from that round and shares the same shortcomings. However, the .30 Carbine can shoot relatively cheaper military ammunition, and this allows use of the gun in many situations not economically feasible with the .32 SL. However, don't kid yourself about the so-called "terrific power" of the .30 Carbine cartridge, because it's just not there. Despite this, it can be a very useful cartridge within its limitations, and its use and popularity have increased considerably over the years.

Editor's note: Had the military adopted a normal, modern rifle pressure standard, instead of the inexplicably modest 40,000 psi specified, we might have a somewhat different opinion of this cartridge. Loading to normal .30-06 pressures provides about 400 fps more velocity, which seems significant.

.30 Carbine Loading Data and Factory Ballistics

Bullet (grains/type)	Powder	Grains	Velocity	Energy	Source/Comments
100 Plinker	2400	15.5	2170	1045	Speer
110 SP	IMR 4227	15.0	2010	985	NA
125 Lead RN	AA 1680	15.0	1756	855	Accurate Arms
110 Ball	ML		1975	955	Military load, M-1
110 SP	FL		1990	965	Factory load

7.5x54mm French MAS

Historical Notes: In 1924, the French army adopted a new cartridge, the 7.5x58mm MLE 1924C, for a new automatic rifle. In 1929, to avoid ammunition mix-ups with the 7.92x57mm, the French changed to a 4mm shorter cartridge of slightly larger diameter, creating the 7.5x54mm MLF 1929C. This cartridge was originally used in light machine guns and other automatic arms, but, in 1934, the Berthier Model-07/15 bolt-action rifle was also modified for this round. In 1936, a newly designed bolt-action rifle (MAS 36) in the new 7.5mm was adopted. This rimless cartridge replaced the rimmed 8mm Lebel, which the French army had used since 1886.

General Comments: Fair quantities of French military rifles in this chambering have appeared on the surplus market from time to time, as the French are noted for hanging on to their obsolete military hardware long after it's of any real value. Sporting ammunition for this chambering has never been manufactured. However, A.L.M. Arsenal, in France, recently produced this cartridge with a Boxer primer. Some of the surplus dealers made up hunting ammunition by replacing the military bullet with a similar soft-point type. The 7.5mm MAS is in the same class as the .30-40 Krag or the .303 British and can be used for the same range of game. Performance can be improved a little in handloading, but only Berdan-primed military cases have formerly been available. The military load develops about 40,000 psi breech pressure. The initials "MAS" represent the French arsenal that developed this cartridge and rifle, Manufacture d'Armes de Saint Etienne.

7.5x54mm French MAS Loading Data and Factory Ballistics

Bullet (grains/type)	Powder	Grains	Velocity	Energy	Source/Comments
150 SP	IMR 4831	54	2680	2400	Duplicates military ball
150 SP	IMR 4895	48	2800	2620	NA
180 SP	IMR 4895	44	2590	2692	NA
140 Ball	ML		2600	2100	Military load, MLE 1929C

.30 Army (.30-40 Krag)

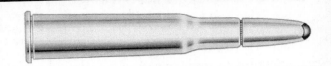

Historical Notes: The .30 U.S. Army, or .30-40 Krag, was the first small-bore military cartridge adopted by the U.S. Army. It was adopted, in 1892, for the Norwegian-invented, American-modified, Krag-Jorgensen bolt-action rifle. Original loads used 40 grains of smokeless powder with a 220-grain full metal jacket round-nose bullet. The .30-40 Krag cartridge remained in service only a few years, before being replaced, in 1903, by the rimless .30-03 cartridge, predecessor to the .30-06.

General Comments: In 1893, Winchester began offering its High Wall single-shot rifle chambered for the .30-40 Krag, thus becoming the first commercial producer in the United States to offer a small-bore, smokeless-powder sporting cartridge. This was nearly two years before the smokeless powder .30-30 loading was offered.

Editor's note: A glance at the following ballistics might suggest, to the astute reader, that original loads used pressures that would today seem excessive for the Krag rifle. Indeed, this seems to have been the case, as the rated velocity was routinely achieved in production rifles and, considering the limited case capacity and characteristics of contemporary domestic smokeless powders, pressures had to have been rather brisk, perhaps exceeding 55,000 psi. It seems at least possible that use of such unusually high-pressure loads contributed to the subsequent problems that earned the single locking lug Krag action a reputation, perhaps undeserved, for weakness.

.30-40 Krag Factory Ballistics

Bullet (grains/type)	Powder	Grains	Velocity	Energy	Source/Comments
220 FMJ-RN Ball	ML		2200	2365	Military load, special

7.62x51mm NATO (.308 Win.)

Historical Notes: For the NATO small arms trials, in the early 1950s, the U.S. submitted its new T-65 cartridge. This was basically a shortened .30-06 case using the same caliber bullet and similar case head dimensions. Case length was reduced from 63 millimeters in the .30-06 to 51 millimeters for the 7.62mm T-65. This allowed a lighter, more compact cartridge and rifle. Some of the other NATO Allies submitted entries that were far more advanced than the T-65 cartridge. However, the U.S. used its considerable influence to override all Allied objections, in order to have the 7.62x51mm NATO cartridge adopted; it remains a NATO standard to this day. In 1957, the U.S. Army adopted the M-14 rifle in 7.62x51mm. The M60 machine gun is also chambered for this cartridge, as are various sniper rifles.

General Comments: During the Vietnam War, the U.S. military adopted the 5.56x45mm cartridge for the new M-16 rifle, which greatly upset the other NATO Allies. A new series of NATO tests was begun in the late 1970s, which resulted in the 5.56x45mm cartridge being standardized, in 1980. Both 7.62x51mm and 5.56x45mm remain NATO standard rounds. Recent tendencies have been to chamber infantry assault rifles for the 5.56x45mm, leaving the 7.62x51mm cartridge for machine guns. Nearly all NATO Allies manufacture the 7.62x51mm cartridge. Many non-NATO countries, such as Japan, Australia, Brazil, Taiwan, South Africa, and others also use this cartridge. Ball, tracer, match, armor piercing, and frangible types exist.

7.62x51mm NATO Factory Ballistics

Bullet (grains/type)	Powder	Grains	Velocity	Energy	Source/Comments
150 FMJ-BT Ball	ML		2750	2520	Military load, M80
168 HP-BT Match	ML		2680	2680	Military load, M852

7.5x55mm Swiss Schmidt-Rubin

Historical Notes:
The first Swiss 7.5mm cartridge was adopted, in 1889, for the Schmidt-Rubin straight-pull rifle of the same year. The original loading used a .299-inch diameter, 213-grain paper-patched lead bullet and a charge of 29 grains of semi-smokeless powder. Muzzle velocity was 1970 fps. Later, a steel-capped hollow-base lead bullet was used, followed by a 190-grain copper or iron-jacketed round-nose bullet with a smokeless powder loading (Model 90/03). In 1911, the 174-grain spitzer boat-tail bullet was adopted and the diameter increased to .308-inch. Golden State Arms Corp. once imported Japanese-made cases with Boxer primer pockets for loading sporting ammunition. Both unprimed cases and loaded rounds are available from Norma.

General Comments:
The 7.5mm Swiss military cartridge is another of the surplus items that has become well known to American shooters only since the end of the war. The Swiss army made a number of improvements in the straight-pull Schmidt-Rubin rifle, and the older, less desirable models were sold off as obsolete surplus. The original Model 89, with rear locking lugs, a very long receiver, and a protruding box magazine, was one of those. The improved Model 1911, with its shorter receiver, forward-located locking lugs, and a less conspicuous magazine, is another.

The 190-grain load develops about 37,000 psi breech pressure, and the 174-grain load about 45,500 psi, (the latter also uses a slightly larger diameter bullet. The 1911 cartridge, considerably more powerful than the older loading, should not be used in the Model 89 rifle. In a suitable action, the 7.5mm Swiss cartridge can be loaded to deliver performance equal to the .308 Winchester and is suitable for the same range of applications. Reloadable cases can be readily made by necking up .284 Winchester brass. The .284's rebated rim works just fine in the Schmidt-Rubin rifle.

7.5x55mm Swiss Schmidt-Rubin Loading Data and Factory Ballistics
(Model-1911 rifle, or later models, using .308-inch diameter bullets)

Bullet (grains/type)	Powder	Grains	Velocity	Energy	Source/Comments
130 SP	IMR 3031	46	3000	2608	Varmint load
150 SP	IMR 3031	45	2820	2658	NA
165 SP	IMR 4895	42	2570	2430	NA
180 SP	IMR 4064	45	2570	2642	NA
200 SP	IMR 4350	49	2460	2700	NA
174 Ball	ML		2560	2540	Military load
180	FL		2650	2805	Factory load

.30-06 Springfield (7.62x63mm U.S./.30-06 Government/.30-06 U.S.)

Historical Notes:
The .30-06 Springfield is a United States military cartridge, adopted in 1906 for the Model 1903 Springfield service rifle, which was based on the Mauser bolt-action system. The .30-06 is actually a slightly modified version of the original 1903 cartridge, which was loaded with a 220-grain round-nose bullet at a muzzle velocity of 2300 fps. Because of cartridge developments in Europe, it was considered advisable to change to a lighter weight, pointed 150-grain bullet at an increased velocity (2700 fps). At the same time, the case neck was shortened by .07-inch. This improved round was designated the "Ball Cartridge, caliber .30, Model of 1906," but, in practice, this cumbersome nomenclature was shortened to .30-06. The .30-06 version can be chambered and fired in any rifle made for the original 1903 round, but the reverse is not true, because of the difference in case neck length. For many years, both the 1903 and 1906 configurations were loaded by sporting ammunition manufacturers. Shooting the '06 in the '03 chamber reportedly gave poor accuracy. Old catalogs list both rounds. Occasionally, the 1903 version is called the .30-45, because the original loading used 45 grains of smokeless powder. For additional discussion, see the .30-03 listing in Chapter 3.

Again, because of military developments in Europe, the Army switched to a 172-grain bullet with a nine-degree boat-tail, in 1926. This new round was designated the "Ball, caliber .30, M1." Muzzle velocity, originally the same as the 150-grain load of 2700 fps, was later reduced to 2640 fps, because of difficulty maintaining pressure specifications at the higher velocity. In 1940, the 150-grain flat-base bullet was re-adopted as the "Cartridge, Ball, caliber .30, M2," and that was the load used in World War II. The return to the lighter bullet came about, at least in part, because of difficulties adapting the new Garand semi-automatic rifle to handle the 172-grain load. The heavier boat-tail bullet was superior for machine gun use, because of its greater maximum range of nearly 6,000 yards, compared to about 3,500 yards for the 150-grain loading.

The rimless .30-03 and 3.0-06 replaced the older rimmed .30-40 Krag as the official U.S. military round. The .30-06 has, in turn, been superseded by the 7.62x51mm, also known as the 7.62mm NATO or, in its commercial version, the .308 Winchester. In Europe, the .30-06 is known as the 7.62x63mm and is widely used.

General Comments: During World War II, the U.S. government supplied .30-06 arms and ammunition to many Allied nations, including Great Britain, Netherlands, France, China, Australia, New Zealand, and Brazil. To keep their inventory of guns ready, many countries undertook manufacture of .30-06 ammunition after the war.

In the 1950s and 1960s, vast quantities of surplus .30-06 ammunition were sold on the U.S. market; shooters will often encounter ball, armor-piercing, and tracer types. Ammunition loaded before and during World War II is corrosively primed. Practically all U.S. military ammunition loaded after 1952 has non-corrosive primers. The principal exception is Frankford Arsenal Match ammunition marked FA 53, 54 or 56, which used the old-style corrosive priming, because it provided superior accuracy.

.30-06 Springfield Factory Ballistics

Bullet (grains/type)	Powder	Grains	Velocity	Energy	Source/Comments
150 FMJ Ball	ML		2740	2500	Military load, M2
172 FMJ-BT Ball	ML		2640	2660	Military load, M1
220 FMJ-RN Ball	ML		2300	2585	Military load, M-1903

Note: Myriad other M-1906 military loadings were adopted for various applications, with differing bullet weights and muzzle velocities.

7.62x39mm (7.62x39mm Soviet M43)

Historical Notes: This "assault rifle" cartridge was adopted by Russia, in 1943. It did not come into general use until after World War II, but the Russians now use it as their principal infantry small-arms cartridge. Original use was in the SKS semi-automatic carbine, later replaced by the AK-47 selective-fire assault rifle. The RPD light machine gun also uses the M43 cartridge. Finland, and those ex-satellite countries in the Soviet bloc, use the M43 cartridge in arms furnished by Russia or of their own design. This cartridge was adopted as the result of Russian military experience against German assault rifles chambered for the 7.92mm Kurz. Ruger introduced its Mini-30 semi-automatic rifle chambered for the 7.62x39mm, in 1987, and the bolt-action M77 Mark II rifle, in 1991. Most military ammunition has a steel case and corrosive Berdan primer, but reloadable cases are now readily available.

General Comments: The M43 is a ¼-inch longer than the German 7.92mm Kurz and will give substantially better performance with newer powders. This cartridge has been loaded commercially by Federal, Winchester, Remington, and Black Hills with Boxer-primed reloadable cases. Better handloads and factory ammunition using soft-point bullets up to about 150 grains place this cartridge far ahead of any reasonable .30-30 load, in terms of delivered energy beyond 100 yards.

7.62x39mm Loading Data and Factory Ballistics

Bullet (grains/type)	Powder	Grains	Velocity	Energy	Source/Comments
110 Sierra HP	AA 1680	27.5	2547	1580	Accurate Arms, Maximum load (.308")
125 Sierra SP	AA 1680	25.5	2368	1555	Accurate Arms, Maximum load (.311")
150 Sierra SP	AA 2015	26.0	2072	1430	Accurate Arms, Maximum load (.311")
122 Ball	ML		2329	1470	Military load
123 SP	FL		2300	1440	Black Hills factory load
150 SP	FL		2200	1610	Black Hills factory load

7.62x53Rmm Russian

Historical Notes: Sometimes called the 7.62x54Rmm Russian, this cartridge was adopted, in 1891, with the Model 1891 Mosin-Nagant bolt-action rifle. Its 150-grain spitzer bullet was adopted in 1909. This cartridge was standard issue in the Russian army, during World War II. It is still standard issue for medium machine guns and the SVD sniper rifle. It was also adopted by Finland, China, and most ex-satellite nations. It remains one of the few rimmed military cartridges still in standard issue. Early in World War I, Winchester made M95 lever-action muskets, and Remington made rolling block rifles for Imperial Russia. Later, Russian Nagant rifles were manufactured in the United States by New England Westinghouse Co., Remington, and Winchester. After the war, a large number of surplus rifles were sold commercially, and Remington loaded a 150-grain bronze-point hunting round. Additional Russian Nagant rifles and carbines have been sold in surplus stores, since the end of World War II. Many of these rifles were captured during the Korean conflict. Surplus Mosin rifles are being imported from China, Finland, Hungary, Poland, Romania, and Russia.

General Comments: The 7.62x54Rmm Russian cartridge has been kicked around since about 1919 and is fairly well known to American shooters. Remington discontinued loading this round, about 1950. It was recently offered by Norma and Lapua. Various surplus military ammunition (corrosive Berdan primed and steel cased) has recently been imported into the United States. Russian military cartridges use Berdan primers, usually of 6.45 mm (.254-inch) diameter.

With the 150-grain bullet, the 7.62mm Russian is in the same class as the .30-06. However, since the rifle has a shorter magazine, it will not do as well as the .30-06 when loaded with heavier bullets. Although military bullets measure .309- to .311-inch in diameter, rifles with tighter bores will shoot .308-inch bullets just fine. However, many rifles have grossly oversized bores. In such rifles, .308-inch jacketed bullets are hopelessly inaccurate, though .311-inch bullets will shoot with a modicum of accuracy. Properly sized cast bullets will shoot with impressive accuracy (minute-of-angle groups are no problem). Unfortunately, there is no ready source of appropriate commercial jacketed or cast bullets sized large enough for specimens with bores running larger than about .313-inch. Standard working pressure is about 45,000 psi.

7.62x53Rmm Russian Loading Data and Factory Ballistics

Bullet (grains/type)	Powder	Grains	Velocity	Energy	Source/Comments
150 SP	IMR 3031	49	2800	2620	Approximates military ball load
180 SP	IMR 4320	48	2630	2772	NA
220 SP	IMR 4350	45	2350	2705	NA
147 Ball	ML		2886	2727	Military load, Type LPS bullet
150 SP	FL		2950	2820	Norma factory load
180 SP	FL		2580	2650	Norma factory load
185 Ball	ML		2660	2910	Military load, Type O bullet

.303 British

Historical Notes: As a military cartridge, the .303 British must be considered one of the most successful of its type. Developed during 1887 and adopted in 1888, it was the official military cartridge of the British Commonwealth in World War I and II. In 1957, the 7.62x51mm NATO cartridge replaced it.

Originally, the .303 cartridge was loaded with a 215-grain round-nose bullet encased in a cupro-nickel jacket. This bullet, backed by 70 grains of compressed blackpowder, developed a muzzle velocity of 1850 fps. Muzzle energy was 1630 ft-lbs. In the 1890s, in response to reports from the frontier that the jacketed round-nose solid bullet was ineffective against tribesmen, Capt. Bertie Clay, at the arsenal at Dum Dum, India, perfected an expanding bullet, with the jacket open at the nose to expose the lead core. This bullet mushroomed on impact. Such projectiles became known as Dum Dum bullets, which has led to much confusion and nonsense through the common parlance and lay misunderstanding of what expanding bullets are, how they work, and why they are beneficial.

In 1892, propellant charging was changed to use the new Cordite smokeless powder. Muzzle velocity of the new loading was 1970 fps, which produced 1850 ft-lbs of energy. Owing to the efficiency of the new powder, this worthwhile ballistic improvement was accompanied by a significant reduction in peak chamber pressure. In 1910, a load using a 174-grain pointed flat-base bullet was adopted; velocity for that loading was 2440 fps, which produces 2310 ft-lbs of energy. This was the MkVII round, still in use when the .303 was discontinued.

Bullets for the MkVII cartridge had an aluminum- or fiber-filled tip, with a base of conventional lead alloy. This made the bullet longer than normal for its weight. It also produced a stable projectile in flight that would tumble easily on contact, thus increasing wounding potential.

The .303 cartridge was designed for the Lee-Metford MkI magazine rifle, a turn-bolt type invented by James Paris Lee, an American. (In studying these things, it is surprising how often significant firearms and cartridge inventors were forced to travel beyond their own shores to find acceptance.) In 1895, the segmental and shallow Metford-type rifling was discontinued in favor of the deeper Enfield-type. (Interestingly, Metford had also patented the so-called Enfield rifling, prior to his segmental form.) From this point on, the rifle was known as the Lee-Enfield. Many variations and types exist.

General Comments: The .303 British cartridge has been used extensively in Africa, Canada, and India by settlers and government workers. It gained a bad reputation, because the full jacketed military bullets tended to tumble on impact. However, with proper sporting bullets, it does quite well on the lighter, non-dangerous game varieties. Norma offers one loading, a 150-grain soft-nose. U.S. companies now load it with a 180-grain soft-point.

Although usually classed with the .30-40 Krag, the .303 actually has a worthwhile edge over the Krag. For one thing, it has a nominal operating pressure of 45,000 to 48,000 psi, compared to 40,000 to 42,000 psi for the .30-40. In addition, late model Enfield rifles are much stronger than the Krag. Enfield No. 4 MkI rifles have been successfully converted to use the 7.62mm NATO, which has a nominal maximum pressure of 62,000 psi. Finally, the modest increase in bore area gives the edge to the .303.

Ammunition for the .303 loaded in Britain had the Berdan primer and, in older lots, usually Cordite powder. Military ammunition loaded by American companies has the Boxer primer and American-type nitrocellulose powder.

Proper jacketed bullet diameter for the .303 is .311-inch. Cast bullets may run to .312-inch or even .313-inch. Loading data will be found in Chapter 2.

.303 British Factory Ballistics

Bullet (grains/type)	Powder	Grains	Velocity	Energy	Source/Comments
215 Ball	FFg	70.0	1850	1630	Original blackpowder load
215 Ball			1970	1850	Original Cordite load
175 Ball	ML		2440	2310	Military load, MkVII Ball
215 Ball	ML		2050	2010	Military load, MkVI Ball

7.7x58mm Japanese Arisaka

Historical Notes: The 7.7mm cartridge was adopted by the Japanese, in 1939, to replace the older 6.5mm, but they ended up using both cartridges during World War II. They also adopted a new rifle, the Model 99 Arisaka, which was a modification of the earlier 1905 gun. Norma has offered empty cases and sporting ammunition for this chambering with American Boxer-type primer pockets. No sporting rifles have ever been manufactured in this chambering.

General Comments: The 7.7mm, or .31 Jap, as it is sometimes called, is ballistically very similar to the .303 British cartridge and uses the same .311-inch diameter bullets. However, it is a rimless type, whereas the British case is rimmed. There is also a semi-rimmed Japanese version for machine gun use. The 7.7mm Japanese can be used for the same kinds and sizes of game as the .303 British. With good Norma sporting ammunition available, this has become one of the more useful military cartridges for North American hunting. Military loads develop about 42,000 psi, which, as with the 6.5mm Arisaka, seems unusually mild for a modern military chambering, particularly when one considers the unusual strength of these rifles.

7.7x58mm Japanese Arisaka Loading Data and Factory Ballistics

Bullet (grains/type)	Powder	Grains	Velocity	Energy	Source/Comments
130 SP	IMR 3031	46	2950	2510	Duplicates factory loading
150 SP	IMR 3031	41	2680	2400	NA
180 SP	IMR 4064	45	2490	2470	Duplicates factory loading
215 SP	IMR 4064	42	2240	2405	NA
130 SP	FL		2950	2510	Norma factory load
175 Ball	ML		2400	2237	Military load
180 SP	FL		2490	2470	Norma factory load

7.65x53mm Mauser (Argentine)

Historical Notes: Mauser-designed for the 1889 Belgian pattern rifle, the 7.65mm was also adopted by Argentina, Bolivia, Columbia, Ecuador, Peru, and Turkey. In the United States, Remington and Winchester loaded sporting ammunition and furnished rifles in this chambering, until about 1936. It has been obsolete in the United States since that time, but sporting ammunition has always been loaded in Europe. The Remington Model 30 and Winchester Model 54 bolt-action rifles were chambered for the 7.65mm, and it enjoyed a limited popularity for a few years. With the influx of 1891 Argentine Mauser military rifles, it is having another go-around on the American market. Evidently, a very similar but unique Belgian Mauser cartridge also exists. The catalog drawing suggests that it has slightly smaller case head, probably less body taper and, perhaps, a slightly shorter case neck (the sketch is insufficiently dimensionally denoted to establish facts).

General Comments: The 7.65mm is among the best designed of all Mauser cartridges. This number gives excellent performance for North American hunting. In power, its slightly larger usable case capacity and slight bore-size increase place it ahead of the .308 Winchester and quite close to factory .30-06 loads, particularly with bullets up to about 165 grains, which makes it adequate for all medium game.

Arsenal primers are Berdan 5.5mm or .217-inch, a size available in several European makes. Occasionally one encounters discontinued American-made cases or ammunition, and these use conventional Boxer Large Rifle primers. Cases can be made from empty .30-06 cases through the use of case-forming dies available from several American manufacturers. Bullet size is .313-inch, but .311-inch or .312-inch diameter bullets will give satisfactory accuracy. Norma-made cases and loaded ammunition use Boxer primers.

7.65x53mm Mauser Loading Data and Factory Ballistics

Bullet (grains/type)	Powder	Grains	Velocity	Energy	Source/Comments
150 SP	IMR 4895	47	2810	2638	
150 SP	IMR 4895	42	2550	2172	
174 SP	IMR 4895	45	2590	2600	
175 SP	IMR 4350	49	2560	2550	
175 SP	IMR 4831	53	2456	2346	
180 SP	FL		2590	2685	Norma factory load
150 SP	FL		2920	2841	Norma factory load
155 FMJ-BT Ball	ML		2710	2530	Military load, Type S
174 FMJ-BT Ball	ML		2460	2340	Military load, Type SS
211 FMJ Ball	ML		2130	2150	Military load, Original

8x50Rmm Siamese Mauser (Type 45)

Historical Notes: Originally adopted in 1902, this cartridge actually derives its name from the Thai year of adoption—1945. It was a standard Siamese military cartridge from 1902 until World War II. It is historically significant for two reasons. First, the 8x50Rmm Siamese is the first rimmed military cartridge adapted to a unique variation of the popular Mauser rifle. Second, it was the first cartridge to be manufactured in quantity in Thailand (National Arsenal, Bangkok). During World War II, the production machinery was moved to the hills to escape Japanese seizure. The machinery served to supply the guerrilla movement. When the war ended, it was moved back to Bangkok.

General Comments: The 8x50Rmm cartridge was loaded with a .321-inch-diameter, round-nose bullet with a copper-nickel jacket, in a brass cartridge case with Berdan priming. Some manufacture of this cartridge was also contracted out to Japan and Germany. In 1923, a new cartridge was adopted, the 8x52Rmm, and existing rifles for the older round were re-chambered and rear sights modified. During the late 1970s, thousands of these surplus rifles were sold in the United States. It is hard to avoid noticing the similarity between this circa-1895 cartridge and the circa-1955 7.62x51mm NATO round.

8x50Rmm Siamese Mauser Factory Ballistics

Bullet (grains/type)	Powder	Grains	Velocity	Energy	Source/Comments
237 Ball	FL		2050 (est.)	2210	NA

8x52Rmm Siamese (Type 66)

Historical Notes: In 1923, the Siamese army adopted a new cartridge with a pointed bullet. Case length was two millimeters longer than the older 8x50Rmm Siamese cartridge, so the two are not interchangeable. The new round was adapted to a new Mannlicher infantry rifle and carbine, as well as to Madsen, Browning, and Vickers machine guns. Older rifles for the 8x50Rmm cartridge were re-chambered. The 8x52Rmm cartridge remained in production in Thailand, until 1953, after which ball ammunition was contracted out (chiefly to Kynoch, in England), until finally discontinued, in the late 1960s.

General Comments: The pointed, flat-base ball bullet of the 8x52Rmm cartridge will be found with both cupro-nickel-clad steel and gilding metal jackets. Cases are of brass with Berdan primers. Boxer-primed cases will also be encountered. In addition to ball loadings, there were tracer, armor-piercing, and armor-piercing incendiary types. This cartridge was also made by Kynoch (U.K.), in Japan and Denmark, and by Sako of Finland. Surplus rifles in this chambering are often encountered in the United States.

8x52Rmm Siamese Factory Ballistics

Bullet (grains/type)	Powder	Grains	Velocity	Energy	Source/Comments
181 Ball	ML		2250	2615	Military load *

*Estimated ballistics

7.92x33mm Kurz

Historical Notes: This cartridge was developed, during 1940-'41, for use in the newly conceived German MKB42 assault rifle. It first was tested in combat against the Russian army at Cholm, Russia, in late 1942. Several changes and modifications culminated in the Sturmgewehr rifle, or Stg-44. This was the first successful assault rifle cartridge and, as such, marks an important milestone in military history that has had a profound effect on small arms development.

The 7.92mm Kurz is a short version of the standard 7.92mm (8mm) Mauser cartridge. No commercial sporting rifle has ever been made for this round. Ammunition was manufactured in East Germany for some years for export customers.

General Comments: This is a medium-range cartridge designed to increase infantry firepower by permitting more accurate and controlled full-automatic fire. That is not possible with lightweight shoulder guns using full-powered cartridges, such as the .30-06 or the German 8x57mm Mauser. This combination must have been quite effective, because it was used against the Russians, who almost immediately copied it and brought out a similar assault rifle and cartridge. It has been demonstrated that, in close combat in cities, jungles, or similar areas, these reduced-power cartridges have all the range and penetration necessary.

The German Sturmgewehr, or assault rifle, had a 16-inch barrel, weighed 10 to 11 pounds loaded and used a 30-shot magazine. As a sporting cartridge, the 7.92mm Kurz would be less powerful than the .30-30 and not very well suited for anything but small to medium game. Because guns for this cartridge are capable of full-automatic fire, none have been sold in fireable condition, because these come under the National Firearms Act and require a special license to own. This ammunition has never been commercially manufactured. Military ammunition is not reloadable, as it is steel cased and Berdan primed.

7.92x33mm Kurz Loading Data and Factory Ballistics

Bullet (grains/type)	Powder	Grains	Velocity	Energy	Source/Comments
125	4198	20	2070	1193	NA
125	4198	23	2310	1485	Maximum load
125 Ball	ML		2247	1408	Military load

8x50Rmm Austrian Mannlicher

Historical Notes: This was an Austrian military cartridge adopted, in 1888, for the Mannlicher Model 88 straight-pull rifle, and also used in the later improved Model 95. This cartridge was also used by Bulgaria, Greece, and Hungary. It remains fairly popular as a sporting cartridge in Europe, and many Mannlicher rifles have been chambered for it. Sporting ammunition is still loaded in Europe by Hirtenberger, and this cartridge was recently imported to the United States. This was originally a blackpowder design. A smokeless powder loading was adopted about 1890.

General Comments: During the 1920s and '30s, a few European sporting rifles chambered for the 8x50Rmm cartridge were imported into the United States and used, to a limited extent, for big-game hunting. This is another cartridge in the .30-40 Krag class, which is adequate for most North American big game. It uses .323-inch bullets, of which there is a good variety available for handloading. Berdan-primed cases appear to use the 5.1mm or .199-inch primer, although this is variable. Hirtenberger ammunition is Boxer primed and loaded at 40,000 to 42,000 psi.

The Model 88 Mannlicher straight-pull rifle uses a hinged block on the underside of the bolt to lock the action. This design is not noted for great strength, and pressures must be kept quite low for safety. The Model 95 has a revolving bolt head and forward locking lugs, which provide greater strength. Many 95s were altered to shoot the standard German 8mm Mauser service cartridge.

8x50Rmm Austrian Mannlicher Loading Data and Factory Ballistics

Bullet (grains/type)	Powder	Grains	Velocity	Energy	Source/Comments
159 SP	IMR 3031	48	2460	2142	NA
227 SP	IMR 3031	45	2040	2102	NA
244 SP	IMR 3031	45	2010	2200	Approximates military load
196 SP	FL		2310	2320	Hirtenberger factory load
244 Ball	ML		2030	2240	Military load, smokeless powder

Above loads are for the Model 88 action, provided it is in good condition.

8x50Rmm Lebel

Historical Notes: The 8mm Lebel was the first smallbore, smokeless powder military cartridge developed by any world power. The cartridge and the Lebel bolt-action rifle were both adopted, in 1886. The original loading used a 232-grain, jacketed flat-nose flat-base bullet called the Balle M. In 1898, a solid bronze, spitzer boat-tail, 198-grain bullet was adopted, the famous Balle D. The cartridge was further updated, in 1932, with the adoption of the Balle 32M, which had a cupro-nickel-clad steel jacket over a lead core. This spitzer boat-tail bullet weighed 190 grains. Its rimmed case was not well adapted to automatic arms, so it was replaced by the rimless 7.5x54mm MAS round, in 1929. Remington manufactured rolling blocks and Mannlicher-Berthier chambered in 8x50Rmm Lebel for the French government during World War I. When the war ended, all the surplus was sold commercially, and Remington turned out sporting ammunition with a 170-grain, bronze-pointed bullet. Few rifles have been made in this chambering. Military production of this cartridge in France continued, even under German occupation.

General Comments: Probably more 8mm Lebel rifles were sold during the 1920s and '30s than after World War II. The Remington factory products were all brand new and in perfect condition, which is more than can be said for the more recent war surplus models that have shown up. The 8mm Lebel cartridge is in the .308 Winchester-class and makes a fine cartridge for deer or elk hunting. Modern 8mm Lebel sporting ammunition is difficult to find. Plenty of good .323-inch bullets are available, and American cases can easily be reloaded. Military cases have Berdan primers of .199-inch or .216-inch size and are less practical to reload.

8x50Rmm Lebel Loading Data and Factory Ballistics

Bullet (grains/type)	Powder	Grains	Velocity	Energy	Source/Comments
170 SP	IMR 4895	49	2570	2500	NA
198 SP	IMR 3031	46	2380	2481	Duplicates military ball
198 SP	IMR 4895	45	2450	2645	NA
170	FL		2640	2630	Remington factory load
198	ML		2380	2481	Military load, Balle D, Balle 32M

7.9x57mmJ and 7.9x57mm JS (8mm German Mauser)

Historical Notes: The 8mm Mauser is one of the world's truly great military cartridges. It was the official German military cartridge in both World Wars and was also adopted by Czechoslovakia, Poland, China, and other countries. It is also a popular sporting round in many parts of the world.

Although designated the 8mm "Mauser," the original military round was designed for the German Model 88 commission rifle, which was a modified Mannlicher-type, not a Mauser design. This rifle was known officially as the Gewehr 88, or German Infantry Model 1888. It was designed by the German Infantry Board or Commission at Spandau Arsenal. It was replaced, in 1898, by the superior Mauser model of that year.

The original J Patrone cartridge used a round-nose 226-grain bullet of .318-inch diameter. Muzzle velocity was 2093 fps. In 1905, the Germans adopted an improved cartridge that retained the original 8x57mm case, but employed a larger-diameter bullet (.323-inch). The new S Patrone bullet was lighter (154 grains) and was pointed or spitzer-type. Muzzle velocity was upped to 2880 fps. Although the rifle had a significantly longer barrel than the '03 Springfield, the 17-percent muzzle energy advantage that the 7.9x57mmJS load had over the .30-06 ball loading is quite surprising. There is evidence that German smokeless powder of that era was vastly superior to anything available in this country and, perhaps, anywhere else. This no doubt accommodated the above noted ballistic potential of the 7.9x57mmJS loading. External ballistic calculations prove that the German military loading was a significantly superior battlefield cartridge, compared to the U.S. military loading. All German military rifles manufactured since 1905 originated with the .323-inch bore. All earlier military and many civilian arms were re-rifled to accommodate .323-inch bullets.

The original German 8mm military cartridge was designated by a "J" for "Infanterie." (The story is that U.S. military intelligence officers who were tasked to discover the secret of the superior performance of the German cartridge captured classified German documents toward the end of World War I and then mistook the ornate German script "I" for a "J." If true, it is indeed ironic that, worldwide, including Germany, the designation has been bastardized to "J.") The later bullet, for the .323-inch diameter groove, is indicated by an "S," for spitzer-type. Sporting ammunition in 8mm is labeled by the same system. The 8x57mmJ or 1888 cartridge can be fired safely in the 1905 or "S"-bore rifles, though accuracy is poor. However, it is not safe to fire the larger "S" (.323-inch) bullet in the smaller "J" (.318-inch) bore.

General Comments: Thousands of 8mm military rifles have been sold through surplus dealers, since the end of World War II. Most were bought to obtain the 98 Mauser action, which served as the basis for building a sporting rifle for some U.S. cartridges. In many instances, the cost of making up a custom rifle on a military action wasn't justified. However, if the original chambering was retained and modifications held to the minimum, many of these rifles were a good buy.

The 8x57mmJS Mauser is an outstanding sporting cartridge in its own right, being in the same class as our .30-06. U.S. ammunition companies load only the "S" version of the 8mm, but hold it to a very mild pressure level, so the round could safely be fired in a "J"-bored rifle. This has a 170-grain bullet at 2360 fps, which about duplicates the .30-40 Krag in power. Norma makes both 165- and 196-grain sporting loads that bring out the full potential of this cartridge. Sporting loads and handloading data will be found in Chapter 2.

7.9x57mmJ and 7.9mmJS Factory Ballistics

Bullet (grains/type)	Powder	Grains	Velocity	Energy	Source/Comments
154 Ball	ML		2880	2835	Military load, S Patrone
226 Ball	ML		2095	2200	Military load, J Patrone

WARNING! Many "J"-bore (.318-inch) rifles still exist and will fire "S"-bore (.323-inch) cartridges, potentially creating dangerous pressures. When in doubt, check the bore diameter CAREFULLY!

8x63mm Swedish

Historical Notes: This is a Swedish round, introduced, in 1932, for use in various Browning air- or water-cooled machine guns and for the m/40 rifle (note that the lower-case "m" and the slash between it and the numeral "40" is the frequently encountered representation of the designation for this particular Swedish rifle. It is, of course, not the same as the U.S. M40 rifle). Swedish military rifles and light machine guns are chambered for the standard 6.5x55mm cartridge. Its use is confined to Sweden, and it is practically unknown outside there. It was never actually loaded as a sporting cartridge.

General Comments: The 8x63mm nearly duplicates the wildcat 8mm-06 cartridge, which is the .30-06 necked up to accept .323-inch bullets. However, the 8x63mm has a larger-diameter case and should be capable of delivering about 15-percent more energy if loaded to the same pressure. The 8x63mm Swedish is significantly more powerful than the .30-06 Springfield.

8x63mm Swedish Loading Data and Factory Ballistics

Bullet (grains/type)	Powder	Grains	Velocity	Energy	Source/Comments
150 SP	4895	60	3050	3100	NA
170 SP	4320	57	2820	3020	NA
225 SP	4350	57	2450	2960	NA
218 Ball	ML		2493	3025	Military load

8x59mm Breda

Historical Notes:
This cartridge was for the Italian Breda Model 1937 and 1938 machine guns. Insofar as can be established, it has never been used as a sporting cartridge.

General Comments:
Different bullet weights and muzzle velocities are listed for the 8mm Breda, and this may reflect the various military loadings. Bullet diameter varies from .322-inch to .326-inch. The cartridge case is fatter and 1/10-inch longer than the 8mm Mauser. The original purpose of the 8mm Breda was to replace the 6.5mm Italian cartridge as a more effective machine gun round. Since case capacity and published ballistics both suggest that this cartridge came close to matching modern .300 Magnum energy levels, it would seem that it was indeed a significant step up from the 6.5mm Italian Carcano.

8x59mm Breda Loading Data

Bullet (grains/type)	Powder	Grains	Velocity	Energy	Source/Comments
210 Ball	ML		2600	3160	Military load

8x56Rmm Austrian-Hungarian Mannlicher (8mm Hungarian M31)

Historical Notes:
This cartridge was developed, in 1930, for the Solothurn machine gun. It was subsequently adopted by Hungary, about 1931. Design goes back to the mid-1920s, when it was developed to replace the 8x50Rmm Austrian round. It was designated the M30 in Austria, and the M31 in Hungary. It differs from the older Austrian 8x50Rmm, having a longer tapered shoulder, plus a bullet of slightly larger diameter. It was used in the Hungarian Model 35 Mannlicher bolt-action rifle, and also the modified Model 95 straight-pull Mannlicher. In 1940, Hungary adopted the standard German 8mm military round, and many of its rifles were then altered to that chambering. As far as we know, no sporting rifles were turned out in the 8mm Hungarian chambering.

General Comments:
This cartridge is often confused with the 8x56mm Mannlicher-Schoenauer, which is a rimless sporting cartridge, whereas the Hungarian military round is rimmed. The two are not interchangeable, as there is considerable difference in case dimensions, as well as bullet diameter.

Rifles in this chambering are common on the American market, and ammunition is also readily available. The .329-inch diameter bullet makes handloading a problem, because bullets of this size are not normally available. It is possible to use .323-inch bullets, but accuracy is poor. Military rifles in this chambering should be considered primarily collector's items, because of the ammunition supply problem. In power, the 8x56Rmm Hungarian and the 8x50Rmm Austrian cartridge are in the .30-40 Krag class.

8x56Rmm Hungarian Mannlicher Loading Data and Factory Ballistics

Bullet (grains/type)	Powder	Grains	Velocity	Energy	Source/Comments
198 SP	IMR 3031	46	2310	2358	.323-inch bullet
206 Ball	IMR 3031	45	2300	2420	Military load

10.4x38Rmm Swiss Vetterli M69/81

Historical Notes:
This Swiss cartridge was adopted, in 1869, for use in the Vetterli turn-bolt rifle. The official military round is a rimfire, but a centerfire version was also loaded in Europe. The cartridge and rifle were discontinued, in 1889.

General Comments: The 10.4mm, or .41 Swiss, cartridge is quite well known in the United States, and most American companies loaded it, until about 1942. Thousands of surplus Swiss Vetterli rifles have been sold in this country, and a surprising number have been used for hunting deer. For a time, there was a good supply of both rifles and cartridges on dealers' shelves. American ammunition was loaded with smokeless powder. The .41 Swiss would be a barely adequate short-range cartridge for deer-class animals. The rimfire military version cannot be reloaded. This cartridge is unusual, in that it is one of the few rimfire military rounds.

10.4x38Rmm Swiss Vetterli M69/81 Factory Ballistics

Bullet (grains/type)	Powder	Grains	Velocity	Energy	Source/Comments
334 Lead	ML		1345 *	1330	Military load

*Some sources list MV as 1427 fps, and this, perhaps, refers to a later smokeless loading.

10.4x47Rmm Italian Vetterli M70

Historical Notes: This Italian cartridge was adopted in 1870. It was used in the Vetterli single-shot turn-bolt rifle and, later, a modified box-magazine repeater (Vitali system). Many of these cartridges were loaded with a brass-coated bullet.

General Comments: The 10.4 Italian service cartridge has not been produced for many years, but occasional lots of surplus ammunition have appeared in stores. In performance, it is practically identical to the 10.4mm Swiss Vetterli. Italian Vetterli rifles are fairly common in the United States.

10.4x47Rmm Italian Vetterli M70 Loading Data and Factory Ballistics

Bullet (grains/type)	Powder	Grains	Velocity	Energy	Source/Comments
250 Lead	IMR 4198	27	1300	935	Lyman #429251
313	Blackpowder (Fg)	62	1345	1255	Military load

10.75x58Rmm Russian Berdan
(.43 Russian Berdan)

Historical Notes: The 10.75x58Rmm was adopted by Russia, in 1868, and used in the Berdan I and the Krnka M69 rifles. After 1871, it was used in the Berdan II rifle. These were all single-shot arms. This was the first military cartridge with the outside centerfire Berdan primer and a bottleneck case. Large quantities of these cartridges were manufactured in the United States by Remington and Winchester, for the Russian government. Most of the Berdan rifles were made by Colt's, but the Russians also manufactured these guns at their Tula arsenal.

General Comments: This was primarily a military cartridge and was not used to any great extent for sporting purposes. During the 1950s and '60s, a fair number of the old Colt's-made Berdan I and II rifles showed up in various surplus stores, along with suitable blackpowder ammunition. In the United States, this was known as the .43 Russian Berdan cartridge.

The Berdan I rifle is a forward-hinged, lift-block type (striker-fired), and the Berdan II is a turn-bolt single-shot, somewhat similar to the Model 71 Mauser. The Krnka is a breech-loading conversion of the Russian muzzleloading rifle. In 1867, the Berdan I-type action was tested by an American military board, as a possible means of converting the muzzleloading Springfield to breech-loading.

10.75x58Rmm Russian Berdan Loading Data and Factory Ballistics

Bullet (grains/type)	Powder	Grains	Velocity	Energy	Source/Comments
250 Lead	IMR 4198	33	1400	1085	Lyman #429251
370 Lead	IMR 4198	31	1410	1630	NA
370 Lead	Blackpowder (Fg)	77	1450	1725	Military load, paper-patched bullet

11x59Rmm French Gras
11x59mm Vickers

Historical Notes: This French cartridge was adopted, in 1874, for the Gras single-shot rifle, a metallic cartridge breech-loaded conversion of the Chassepot needle gun. This was the first modern French military cartridge. It was replaced, in 1886, by the then-revolutionary 8mm Lebel. Many Remington rolling block rifles were chambered for the 11mm Gras, and these, along with the Gras rifle, were used extensively in the Balkans and French colonial areas. Remington loaded this cartridge at one time. The Japanese purchased and used many of the Gras-modified rifles and the 11mm Gras cartridge.

The 11mm Vickers was used by both the British and French, during World War I, in the Vickers aircraft machine gun, to shoot down German artillery observation balloons; the cartridge is also referred to as the 11mm Vickers Balloon Gun cartridge. It uses the same case as the 1874 French Gras rifle cartridge and was actually developed by the French for their Hotchkiss anti-balloon gun. The more reliable Vickers machine gun was later modified to shoot the same cartridge. By 1917, it was found that the standard rifle cartridge was not as satisfactory for shooting down observation balloons as a larger caliber carrying a heavier tracer/incendiary bullet. This was the reason for the development of a special-purpose cartridge. Rather than waste time, the French simply used what was immediately available and adopted the Gras rifle case. Some of these cartridges are headstamped WESTERN 2-17, indicating that these cartridges were manufactured in the United States by Western Cartridge Co., in February 1917.

General Comments: Neither this rifle nor this cartridge have ever been used to any degree in the United States. It would be suitable for North American big-game hunting at short range, like most of the other blackpowder military cartridges. It is very similar in performance to the 11mm Mauser.

The 11mm Vickers appears to have a longer, heavier bullet than the original Gras cartridge. It is also of the full jacketed type, and some are brass covered. One should be careful working with these rounds, because many have tracer/incendiary bullets.

11x59Rmm French Gras Loading Data and Factory Ballistics

Bullet (grains/type)	Powder	Grains	Velocity	Energy	Source/Comments
365 Lead	IMR 4198	36	1420	1635	Lyman #446109
385 Lead	IMR 4198	33	1400	1675	NA
385 Lead	Blackpowder (Fg)	78	1493	1903	Military load

11.15x60Rmm (.43) Mauser
(11x60Rmm Mauser)

Historical Notes: This was the first of a long line of military cartridges designed by Paul Mauser. The 11mm Mauser was adopted by the German military, in 1871, with the M71 bolt-action single-shot Mauser rifle. Later, this rifle was converted to a tubular magazine repeater in the Model 71/84. This cartridge became a popular sporting cartridge in Europe and East Africa, but it is no longer loaded in Europe. Canadian Industries Limited (Dominion Brand) once offered a smokeless powder version that was imported into the United States.

General Comments: A popular military and sporting round through the 1870s and '80s, the 11mm Mauser was loaded in the United States by Remington and Winchester. It enjoyed only limited popularity here, because our own .45-70 military load was easier to obtain. A modernized version using smokeless powder was produced for H. Krieghoff, of Suhl, Germany, and chambered in Mauser bolt-action rifles, in the 1920s. A few were imported into the United States. The 11mm Mauser is still a potent short-range cartridge for North American big game. Most military ammunition uses the Berdan primer, usually of 6.5mm (.254-inch) size. Correct bullet diameter is .446-inch.

11.15x60Rmm (43) Mauser Loading Data and Factory Ballistics

Bullet (grains/type)	Powder	Grains	Velocity	Energy	Source/Comments
370 Lead	Blackpowder (Fg)	77	1430	1680	Duplicates military load, paper-patched bullet
387 Lead	IMR 4198	32	1335	1530	NA
387 Lead	IMR 4198	35	1510	1955	Maximum load
385	FL		1360	1580	CIL factory load
386 Lead	ML		1425	1740	Military load

11.43x55Rmm Turkish/ .45 Peabody-Martini/ .450 Turkish Peabody-Martini

Historical Notes: This cartridge was used by Turkey, from 1874 until 1887. It was replaced by the 9.5mm Mauser. This round was used primarily in the Peabody-Martini single-shot rifle, many of which were made in the United States. This cartridge was loaded in England and called the .450 Turkish Peabody-Martini and the .45 Peabody-Martini in the United States. It was popular in the Balkans and on occasion is still used there.

General Comments: This is another cartridge that was not distributed very extensively in the United States. A few of the old, single-shot under-lever Peabody-Martini rifles have been sold at various times, but 11.43mm ammunition is hard to come by. A Lyman #446187 cast lead bullet weighing 465 grains can be used for handloading.

11.43x55Rmm Turkish Loading Data and Factory Ballistics

Bullet (grains/type)	Powder	Grains	Velocity	Energy	Source/Comments
465 Lead	Blackpowder (Fg)	80	1280	1690	Approximates military load
465 Lead	IMR 4198	36	1410	2050	Lyman #446187
486 Lead	ML		1263	1720	Military load

11.5x57Rmm (.43) Spanish Reformado

Historical Notes: This was the original centerfire, Berdan-primed Spanish military cartridge. It was adopted about 1867 and used in early rolling block rifles manufactured by Remington for the Spanish government. It was also used in some Berdan and Snider conversions of the Spanish muzzleloader. Over a million rounds of this ammunition and many rolling block rifles were captured by American troops in Cuba, during the Spanish-American War. It was replaced by the 11.15mm Spanish Remington cartridge, in 1871.

General Comments: Although this cartridge is listed as .43-caliber, the bullet has a base band that is actually .454-inch in diameter. The bullet is brass covered and has a 10-degree beveled base.

In the tropical climate of Cuba, the brass-covered bullets often turned green with verdigris and were thought to be "poisoned" bullets by American troops. In terms of bacterial count and infectious wounds, these probably were poisoned, for all practical purposes. Rim and base diameter and case length are almost identical to the 11.15mm Spanish Remington, and cases could be made by expanding and trimming 11.15mm cases.

11.5x57Rmm (.43) Spanish Reformado Loading Data and Factory Ballistics

Bullet (grains/type)	Powder	Grains	Velocity	Energy	Source/Comments
250 Lead	IMR 4198	32	1220	825	Lyman #454485
395 Ball	Blackpowder (Fg)	74	1280	1435	Military load

.577/450 Martini-Henry

Historical Notes: This cartridge was adopted by Great Britain, in 1871, for use in the famous Martini-Henry falling-block, single-shot rifle. Originally a rolled-type cartridge case, it was later changed to a drawn case. To some extent, it still is a popular sporting cartridge in England, other parts of the British Commonwealth, and Africa. It was loaded, in England, with both black and smokeless powders having nearly identical ballistics.

The .577/450 cartridge entered history with the B Company, 24th Regiment of the British Army, on January 22-23, 1879. On that day, Lieutenants John Chard and Gonville Bromhead, with some 140 men, defended Rork's Drift, in Natal, South Africa, from more than 4,000 Zulu warriors. When the battle was over, more than 20,000 rounds of .577/450 ammunition had been fired by the defenders.

General Comments: Many Martini-Henry rifles were imported into the United States, which created a mild interest in this cartridge. With its large diameter and heavy lead bullet, it is a good killer on most game at close range. It has been used in Africa and India on all kinds of animals, including the dangerous varieties. It would be adequate for anything in North America out to 100 to 150 yards or so.

.577/450 Martini-Henry Loading Data and Factory Ballistics

Bullet (grains/type)	Powder	Grains	Velocity	Energy	Source/Comments
400 Lead	IMR 4198	38	1450	1865	Lyman #457124
500 Lead	Blackpowder (Fg)	80	1320	1935	Lyman #457125
325 Lead	FL		1600	1845	Kynoch factory load
370 Lead	FL		1450	1725	Kynoch factory load
480 Lead	ML		1350	1940	Military load

11.7x51Rmm Danish Remington/ .45 Danish Remington

Historical Notes: This cartridge was adopted by Denmark, in 1896. It was used in the Remington rolling block rifle. This cartridge and guns chambered for it were available as early as 1878. Some were made by Remington, and some by the Danes. Remington also loaded this cartridge for many years.

General Comments: The 11.7mm, or .45 Danish Remington, has seen considerable use as a target and hunting loading in Scandinavian countries. It is less known in the United States, only because of the few Danish rolling block rifles that have trickled in. It is similar to the .45-70, but the case is a little (.09-inch) shorter. Performance is practically identical. Any load used in the .45-70 will give almost the same results in the 11.7mm. However, such loads should be reduced by at least one grain, to compensate for the slightly smaller case of the Danish cartridge. It would be adequate for any North American game at short range.

11.7x51Rmm Danish Remington Loading Data and Factory Ballistics

Bullet (grains/type)	Powder	Grains	Velocity	Energy	Source/Comments
300 Lead	IMR 4198	34	1480	1460	Lyman #457191
405 Lead	IMR 4198	29	1340	1615	Lyman #457124
380 Lead	Blackpowder (Fg)	50	1350	1535	Remington factory load
387 Lead	ML		1345	1550	Military load

.45 Remington Thompson

Historical Notes: This cartridge was developed for use in the Thompson M-1923 "Military Model" submachine gun. While this cartridge has been described as a stretched .45 Automatic, this is not precisely correct. Both case and bullet diameter are smaller than in the .45 Automatic (.472- versus .476-inch, and .447- versus .451-inch, respectively). The sample cartridge is headstamped "REM-UMC" over ".45 ACP." Development was in 1923, as a joint venture of Remington Arms and Auto Ordnance Corp. Intended application was a long-barreled version of the Thompson that could provide significantly improved ballistics over the standard .45 Automatic-chambered versions.

General Comments: When one considers that this number generated ballistics exceeding any standard .44 Magnum factory loading fired from a pistol, this was, indeed, a significant ballistic improvement, compared to the .45 Automatic. However, it seems likely that the Thompson, despite its significant weight and good design, must have been something of a handful when firing such loads fully automatic.

.45 Remington Thompson

Bullet (grains/type)	Powder	Grains	Velocity	Energy	Source/Comments
250	FL		1450	1165	Factory load

.50 Browning 12.7x99mm

Historical Notes: The German 13mm TUF anti-tank rifle of World War I made quite an impression on U.S. Army higher-ups, who began developing a similar cartridge before the end of the war. Design genius John M. Browning undertook the project, completing his new heavy machine gun and cartridge work, in 1921. Both gun and cartridge were adopted by the U.S. Army, in 1923. It has remained the standard ever since. The cartridge has been adopted and made by at least 30 countries, including the United States, Britain, Canada, France, Belgium, Israel, Netherlands, Japan, Singapore, and Taiwan. Many bullet types will be encountered, including ball, armor-piercing, tracer, incendiary, sabot hyper-velocity, and others.

General Comments: This cartridge is normally found with a Boxer-primed brass case, although steel cases will occasionally be encountered. There are two FMJ-BT ball bullet types, both with mild steel cores. The M2 ball weighs 720 grains and has a muzzle velocity of 2810 fps, while the M33 Ball weighs 668 grains and has a muzzle velocity of 2910 fps. Recently, long-range target rifles from McMillan, Barrett, and others have chambered this round. It has, thus, moved down from exclusive use in heavy machine guns. The Fifty Caliber Shooters Association (FCSA) holds 1,000-yard (and longer) competitive events. In modern rifles, five-shot groups at 1,000 yards often fall within a six-inch circle, and many groups under three inches have been recorded. With known wind conditions, it is routine to hit a 55-gallon drum at ranges of about a mile.

.50 Browning Factory Ballistics

Bullet (grains/type)	Powder	Grains	Velocity	Energy	Source/Comments
668 FMJ-BT Ball			2910	12,550	Military load, M33
720 FMJ-BT Ball			2810	12,600	Military load, M2

.50-70 Musket (.50 Gov't.)

Historical Notes: The .50-70 was the United States military rifle cartridge from 1866 to 1873. It was the first centerfire cartridge in general use by the U.S. military. The design was derived from the .50-60-400 Joslyn rimfire. It was used in various models and modifications of the single-shot Springfield rifle, until replaced by the .45-70, in 1873. It was also chambered in the Remington single-shot military rifle and in a variety of sporting rifles, both single-shot and repeating. The original cartridge had the inside, Benet-type primer. It has been obsolete since the turn of the century.

General Comments: The .50-70, or .50 Government, was a popular cartridge through the 1870s and '80s. It was said to be very effective on buffalo and other heavy game. It was the popularity of this cartridge that induced Winchester to bring out the .50-110, which was, in effect, an improved and more powerful version of the .50-70. Very few rifles in this chambering remain in use, and ammunition is almost non-existent. However, it would be adequate for any North American big game at short range. Cases with the later Boxer-type priming can be reloaded. Most .50-70 rifles were intended for blackpowder; only very light charges of smokeless powder can be considered safe. In 1934, Francis Bannerman & Sons, of New York City, advertised both .50-70 Springfield rifles and ammunition. Rifles were still available as late as 1940. Until recently, no sporting rifles chambered this round since the early 1900s. The rise of cowboy action shooting and blackpowder metallic cartridge silhouette competition has renewed interest in this round. Cases and guns have recently been produced. There was also a carbine version with a shorter case (1.35 inches instead of 1.94 inches).

.50-70 Musket (.50 Gov't.) Loading Data and Factory Ballistics

Bullet (grains/type)	Powder	Grains	Velocity	Energy	Source/Comments
350 Lead	IMR 3031	38.0	1310	1333	Lyman No. 518145
422 Cast	IMR 4198	25.5	1129	1194	Lyman No. 515141
425 Lead	AA 5744	30.0	1419	1900	Accurate Arms
550 Lead	AA 5744	25.0	1208	1780	Accurate Arms
450 Lead	IMR 3031	36.0	1270	1611	Lyman No. 515141
450 Lead	IMR 4198	26.0	1410	1987	NA
425 Lead	FL		1275	1535	Factory load
450 Lead	FL		1260	1488	Factory load

.50-70 Government (.50 Gov't.)

Historical Notes: The .50-70 was the United States military rifle cartridge from 1866 to 1873. It was the first centerfire cartridge in general use by the U.S. military. The design was derived from the .50-60-400 Joslyn rimfire. It was used in various models and modifications of the single-shot Springfield rifle, until replaced by the .45-70, in 1873. It was also chambered in the Remington single-shot military rifle and in a wide variety of sporting rifles, both single-shot and repeating. The original cartridge had the inside, Benet-type primer. It has been obsolete since the turn of the century.

General Comments: The .50-70, or .50 Government, was a popular cartridge through the 1870s and '80s. It was said to be very effective on buffalo and other heavy game. It was the popularity of this cartridge that induced Winchester to bring out the .50-110, which was, in some sense, an improved and more powerful version of the .50-70. Until recently, very few rifles in this chambering were in use. The recent rise of popularity of the cowboy action game has changed that, and now both cartridge and gun are once again available. The .50-70 is adequate for any North American big game at short range. Cases with the later Boxer-type priming can be reloaded. Most .50-70 rifles were intended for blackpowder; only very light charges of smokeless powder can be considered safe in these firearms. In 1934, Francis Bannerman & Sons, of New York City, advertised both .50-70 Springfield rifles and the ammunition. Rifles were still available as late as 1940. No sporting rifles have chambered this round, since the early 1900s. There was also a carbine version with a shorter case (1.35 inches instead of 1.94 inches).

Blackpowder metallic cartridge silhouette rifle competition continues to be a popular, if niche sport, and this round is often encountered on the firing line. Cowboy action shooting participants also use this round. Shiloh Sharps (ww.shilohrifle.com) continues to make very fine guns of the applicable era in this round for competition, hunting, and other sporting use.

.50-70 Government Loading Data

Bullet (grains/type)	Powder	Grains	Velocity	Energy	Source/Comments
300 Lead	Blackpowder (Fg)		1323	1165	QuickLOAD *
450 Lead	Blackpowder (Fg)		1113	1235	QuickLOAD *

*Estimated ballistics

.577 Snider (14.7mm)

Historical Notes: This British cartridge was adopted in 1867. It was used in the Snider breech-loading conversion of the Enfield Musket. The Snider system was invented by Joseph Snider, an American, who first offered it to his home country, but was turned down. The converted rifle was usually referred to as the "Snider Enfield." The original cartridge had a cardboard body with a metal base—essentially identical to more recent "paper" shotgun shells. Later, this was improved by using a coiled brass case designed by Colonel Boxer, the man who invented the Boxer-type primer. Modern .577 ammunition has a drawn brass case. Some Martini-Henry single-shot rifles were also chambered for this cartridge. This cartridge was replaced in British military service by the .577/450, in 1871.

General Comments: A large number of Snider Enfield rifles were sold in the United States by Francis Bannerman & Sons, of New York City. Small numbers were also imported, during the 1950s, by various surplus military arms dealers. The .577 cartridge was loaded in England with either a solid lead bullet or a lead-base, copper-tube type. The case appears to be straight, at first glance, but it has a slight taper and shoulder similar to some American blackpowder cartridges of the same period. The dimensions of the .577 case are very similar to those of the 24-gauge shotgun shell. Brass 24-gauge shells can be used to make ammunition for .577 Snider rifles by trimming about a half-inch from the length. Neither the Snider rifle nor the .577 cartridge are very practical for American hunting, but these guns are a lot of fun to shoot. The big bullet has ample power for hunting, but the curved trajectory makes it a short-range proposition.

.577 Snider Loading Data and Factory Ballistics

Bullet (grains/type)	Powder	Grains	Velocity	Energy	Source/Comments
350 Lead	Blackpowder (Fg)	73	1310	1330	NA
350 Lead	IMR 4198	31	1380	1480	NA
450 Lead	Blackpowder (Fg)	73	1270	1610	NA
450 Lead	IMR 4198	30	1300	1690	NA
476 Lead	IMR 4198	30	1250	1650	Lyman #575213
480 Lead	Blackpowder (Fg)	70-73	1250	1665	Military load

Dimensional Data

Cartridge	Case	Bullet Dia.	Neck Dia.	Shoulder Dia.	Base Dia.	Rim Dia.	Rim Thick.	Case Length	Ctge. Length	Primer	Page
4.85mm British	C	.197	.220	.353	.375	.376	.041	1.925	2.455	B	373
5.7x28mm FN P90 (Belgium)	C	.220	.249	.309	.310	.310	UNK	1.13	1.71	B	373
5.45x39mm Soviet	C	.221	.246	.387	.395	.394	.053	1.56	2.22	B	373
5.56x45mm NATO	C	.224	.249	.349	.373	.375	.041	1.76	2.26	Bx	374
5.8x42mm Chinese	C	.224	UNK	UNK	UNK	UNK	UNK	1.660	2.30	UNK	374
6mm SAW (U.S.)	C	.243	.273	.382	.410	.410		1.779	2.58	Bx	375
6mm Lee Navy/.236 Navy	C	.244	.278	.402	.445	.448	.050	2.35	3.11	Bx	376
6.5mm Japanese Arisaka	G	.263	.293	.425	.455	.471	.045	2.00	2.98	B	376

Dimensional Data

Cartridge	Case	Bullet Dia.	Neck Dia.	Shoulder Dia.	Base Dia.	Rim Dia.	Rim Thick.	Case Length	Ctge. Length	Primer	Page
6.5x45mm Mannlicher-Schoenauer (Greek)	C	.263	.287	.424	.447	.450	UNK	2.09	3.02	B	377
6.5x53Rmm Mannlicher (Dutch & Romanian)	A	.263	.297	.423	.450	.526	.066	2.10	3.03	B	377
6.5x55mm Swedish Mauser	C	.264	.297	.435	.480	.480	UNK	2.16	3.15	B	378
6.5x52mm Italian (Mannlicher-Carcano)	C	.265	.295	.430	.445	.448	.045	2.05	3.02	B	379
7x57mm Mauser	C	.284	.320	.420	.470	.474	.055	2.23	3.06	B	379
7.35mm Italian Carcano	C	.298	.323	.420	.445	.449	UNK	2.01	2.98	B	380
.30 Carbine (.30 M-1 Carbine)	D	.308	.335	UNK	.355	.360	UNK	1.29	1.65	Bx	380
7.5x54mm French MAS	C	.308	.340	.441	.480	.482	.054	2.11	2.99	B	381
.30 Army (.30-40 Krag)	A	.308	.338	.415 (.419)	.457 (.4577)	.540	UNK	2.31	3.10 (3.089)	Bx	382
7.62x51mm NATO (.308 Win.)	C	.308	.338	.447	.466	.470	UNK	2.01	2.75	Bx	382
7.5x55mm Swiss Schmidt-Rubin	C	.308	.334	.452	.494	.496	.058	2.18	3.05	B	383
7.62x63mm U.S. (.30-06 Springfield))	C	.308	.340	.441	.470	.473	UNK	2.49	3.34	Bx	383
7.62x39mm Soviet (M43)	C	.311	.340 (,337)	.344 (.396)	.438 (.433)	.440	.053	1.52 (1.528)	2.20	S	384
7.62x53Rmm Russian	C	.310	.340	.394	.443	.445	UNK	1.52	2.20	B	385
.303 British	A	.311	.337	.402	.458	.530	UNK	2.21	3.05	B	385
7.7x58mm Japanese Arisaka	C	.311	.338	.431	.472	.474	.042	2.28	3.13	B	386
7.65x53mm Mauser (Argentine)	C	.313	.338	.429	.468	.470	.040	2.09	2.95	B	387
8x50Rmm Siamese Mauser (Type 45)	A	.321	.347	.450	.480	.550	UNK	1.98	2.97	B	388
8x52Rmm Siamese (Type 66)	A	.321	.347	.460	.500	.550	UNK	2.04	2.96	B, Bx	388
7.92x33mm Kurz	C	.323	.352	.440	.470	.470	UNK	1.3	1.88	B	388
8x50Rmm Austrian Mannlicher	A	.323	.351	.462	.501	.553	.040	1.98	3.00	B	389
8x50Rmm Lebel	A	.323	.347	.483	.536	.621	.068	1.98	2.75	B	390
7.9x57mm J&JS (8mm Mauser JS)	C	.323	.353	.443	.469	.473	UNK	2.24	3.17	B	390
8x63mm Swedish	C	.323	.356	.456	.488	.479	UNK	2.48	3.36	B	391
8x59mm Breda	C	.326	.357	.433	.491	.469	UNK	2.33	3.17	B	392
8x56Rmm Austrian-Hungarian Mannlicher (M31)	A	.329	UNK	UNK	UNK	UNK	UNK	UNK	UNK	UNK	392
10.4x38Rmm Swiss Vetterli	A	.415	.437	.518	.540	.630	.055	1.60	2.20	B-RF	392
10.4x47Rmm Italian Vetterli M/70	A	.430	.437	.517	.540	.634	.058	1.87	2.46	B	393
10.75x58Rmm Russian Berdan (43 Russian Berdan)	A	.430	.449	.506	.567	.637	.080	2.24	2.95	B	393
11x59Rmm French Gras/ 11x59mm Vickers	A	.445	.468	.531	.544	.667	.075	2.34	3.00	B	394
11.15x60Rmm (43) Mauser/ 11x60Rmm Mauser	A	.446	.465	.510	.516	.586	.075	2.37	3.00	B	394
11.43x55Rmm Turkish/ .45 Peabody-Martini	A	.447	.474	.560	.582	.668	UNK	2.30	3.12	B	395
11.5x57Rmm Spanish Reformado	B	.454	.466	UNK	.525	.631	UNK	2.26	3.06	B	395
.577/450 Martini Henry	A	.455	.487	.628	.668	.746	.050	2.34	3.12	B	396
11.7x51Rmm Danish Remington/ .45 Danish Remington	B	.462	.486	UNK	.514	.579	UNK	2.01	2.45	B	396
.45 Remington Thompson	D	.447	.470	UNK	.472	.471	.044	1.12	1.45	LP	397
.50 Browning/12.7x99mm	C	.510- (.511)	.555- (.560)	.708- (.714)	.800- (.804)	.800- (.804)	.080	3.90 (3.91)	5.43- (5.545)	Bx	397
.50-70 Govt. Musket	B	.515	.535	UNK	.565	.660	.060	1.75	2.25	L	398
.50-70 Gov't.	B	.515	.535	UNK/NA	.565	.660	.060	1.75	2.25	Bx	398
.577 Snider (14.7mm)	B	.570	.602	UNK/NA	.660	.747	.052	2.00	2.45	B	399

Case Type: A = Rimmed, bottleneck. B = Rimmed, straight. C = Rimless, bottleneck. D = Rimless, straight. E = Belted, bottleneck. F = Belted, straight. G = Semi-rimmed, bottleneck. H = Semi-rimmed, straight. I = Rebated, bottleneck. J = Rebated, straight. K = Rebated, belted bottleneck. L = Rebated, belted straight.

Primer Type: B = Berdan. Bx = Boxer. RF = Rimfire.

Other codes: Unless otherwise noted, all dimensions in inches. Twist (factory) is given as inches of barrel length per complete revolution, e.g., 12 = 1 turn in 12", etc. * = Gain twist. Dimensions shown in some instances do not exactly coincide with dimensions found in The Book of Rifles (W.H.B. Smith, Harrisburg, Pa., 1960). Differences amount to only a few thousandths of an inch, doubtless attributable to specimen variations. Parentheses indicate maximum cartridge specifications.

British Sporting Rifle Cartridges

(Current & Obsolete – Blackpowder and Smokeless)

Over the past four or five decades, there has appeared a tremendous volume of writing about British cartridges. Much of these writings are concerned with the very biggest and most fascinating of these, the elephant cartridges. However, at best, many of the authors were misinformed (and some of their information appeared in these pages).

Part of the reason for the lack of knowledge about the big British cartridges in years past was the great cost and relative scarcity of rifles chambered for these cartridges. Without the gun in hand, it is difficult to discover the truth about these cartridges, much less generate the interest in digging for the truth. If one cannot shoot one's .577 BPE, for example, not much can be learned about its performance. Few writers ever had the chance to examine—and fewer still to shoot—a big British rifle. Therefore, much of their reportage was second-hand.

In recent years, the resurrection of the manufacture of cases and bullets for the great rifles of old Africa has helped bridge the knowledge gap and generate enthusiasm. There has never been a lack of firearms to study, stored by collectors who could not shoot the gun. With cases, bullets, and even loaded ammunition again available, it is again feasible to shoot these rifles. We have all learned a lot from those who have done so.

A very few writers and gun collectors have come along over the years with enough intense interest in the old British rifles and cartridges to actually make those guns shoot. This required, in times past, a knowledge of what could be expected of the gun, so that one did not blow up a good deer rifle trying to make it into an elephant stopper. One had to know how to get bullets of the right weight and composition, how to modify or manufacture cases to fit, and something of the loading techniques involved, as well. Without someone to first make a given gun shoot, to prove that it could be done, there would not be enough interest in shooting it to justify the commercial manufacture of appropriate components.

Perhaps every lover of English rifles owes a large debt of gratitude to Ross Seyfried, who did much of the early testing and research with his own rifles. He proved that these guns could be made to shoot, just like new. Seyfried was not alone in those endeavors, but he is unique in that he had the drive, luck, persistence, and patience to get his results published.

Seyfried and I experimented together decades ago, with paper-patch bullets for Cordite-cartridge, double barrel rifles. (We published our results in the *American Rifleman*.) There was no other way to get bullets of the correct size, though it was possible to obtain a few types of cases and Berdan primers with difficulty. We both know how pleasant it is today to be able to buy top-quality, Boxer-primed cases or bullets of the correct size and weight for what were, a few years ago, totally obscure British firearms. Such component production and availability were beyond our fondest dreams two decades ago. Today's availability of cases and components would not exist, but for the work of early experimenters who helped re-establish a demand for British cartridge cases and bullets.

I have had a very long-term interest in British cartridges and the rifles that shoot them, and have been fortunate enough to have acquired a few British double-barrel rifles, which I shoot

as often as possible. That interest and involvement has led me to revise this chapter. While I make no claim to knowing everything about British cartridges, I have attempted here to correct the most grievous errors.

A short time ago, no British producer was loading metallic cartridges. Existing supplies of loaded cartridges were eventually exhausted and, ultimately, the metallic cartridge portion of the English ammunition industry ceased to exist. This forced those who wanted to shoot their English rifles into becoming handloaders.

There were a few exceptions. Federal Cartridge Co. came out with .470 Nitro and .416 Rigby rounds. Before that, Jim Bell offered loaded ammunition for some of the more common British numbers. However, for the most part, it was impossible to buy loaded ammunition.

Today, we again see the grand old name of Kynoch on new cartridges loaded in England. The company of Kynamco has begun development and loading of ammunition to match double-barrel rifles made in the golden era of British rifle manufacture, specifically those rifles made between World War I and II. This is indeed a happy state of affairs.

In previous editions, this author claimed that many, if not most, of the British cartridges were obsolete. I received a nice letter from Ronald Sichel, one of the directors of John Rigby & Co. He kindly informed me that the .275 Rigby (essentially a rather lively loading of the old 7x57) is alive and well and always has been, no matter that we had declared otherwise. He mentioned that Rigby & Co. also offers rifles in a variety of chamberings, including the .450 Rigby, and still makes double-barrel rifles for the .470, as well as for the .577 Nitro and .600 Nitro. We had stated that only Holland & Holland built English-made double-barrel .470s, but that was also incorrect, and several other companies are still in this business.

For many decades, uninformed writers have mistakenly compared many of the big double-barrel rifle cartridges, from the .400 Jeffery on up to the .458 Winchester Magnum. However, the big English double-barrel rifle cartridges worked at relatively low chamber pressure, so the rifles would work perfectly under the blazing hot sun of Africa, when one was faced with an unhappy elephant. The .458 was always (until very recently) loaded with a bullet that was too heavy for its small case, and its attendant high pressure led many to curse it in that hot sun in front of that angry elephant. In some cases, those hunters are no longer with us; perhaps if they had used a cartridge designed for the conditions encountered, they would be.

Early British blackpowder cartridges were loaded with lead bullets that were either grooved and lubricated, or without grooves and paper patched. Paper-patching is simply wrapping the bullet with two layers of paper moistened for the application, then allowing it to dry and, finally, lubing with a waxy substance before loading it into the case. This provided a non-leading bullet of soft lead that was one of the most deadly projectiles ever devised. These are extremely accurate, expand easily, and do not break up. Consequently, these bullets perform very well in the hunting field.

The British went hunting in Africa at a time when no suitable rifles or cartridges existed anywhere in the world. Their desperate need for proper dangerous-game rifles and cartridges was unique, because they were just about the only ones hunting in Africa. Incidentally, their development of the double-barrel rifle as the best of the best for hunting dangerous game came out of that need.

The first elephant rifles were muzzleloaders, and the first cartridge-firing elephant guns used blackpowder and lead bullets. These cartridges were so big as to be nearly unbelievable by today's standards. These were the gauge-rifles, ponderous 4-, 6-, or 8-bore guns that weighed up to 25 pounds. A 4-bore rifle, nominally four balls to the pound, has a bore diameter of about one inch. Some of these were smoothbores, a holdover from the muzzleloader days, but most were rifled.

These big lead bullets were not very effective against elephant, as is so well recorded by early African hunter and writer Frederick Courtenay Selous. To improve performance, manufacturers and handloaders alike often hollowed out these bullets and filled the cavity with explosive compounds; such projectiles are, technically, shells. These bullets still did not work all that well, as many a severely flattened hunter could attest to.

Gauge-rifles for dangerous game were usually 10-bores and larger. Experienced hunters considered the 12-bore a bit small for safe use against the biggest game. The .450s and .500s and even the .577 BPEs (Black-Powder Express) of the latter days of the nineteenth century were essentially deer and medium-game rifles, not the elephant stompers these numbers became when loaded with cordite.

Along the way came the Paradoxes (a name copyrighted by Holland & Holland) and their ilk, which were light smoothbores (usually 8-, 10-, or 12-bores) with a bit of rifling in what would be termed the choke area of the bore. These fired shotshells quite well, and also gave enough spin to round balls or bullets to give adequate accuracy and performance on medium to large game at reasonable ranges.

The coming of smokeless or nitro powder (cordite, in England) brought bullet designers many headaches, as they attempted to design bullets to work at the higher velocities provided by the new propellants. Historians have written much on the success or failure of all different types of jacketed bullets that have been, and are still being, developed. The English directed much research toward answering the call from Africa for good bullets to use against dangerous game. It was discovered that "full-patch," or "solid" bullets (the bullet nose fully covered or protected with gilding metal or, with Rigby's bullets, mild steel), would reach the brain of an elephant or Cape buffalo or rhino quite easily and, therefore, adequate elephant rifles could be built much lighter than ever before, and of smaller bore size.

Because there were no precedents, the British made some big mistakes in early smokeless cartridge and rifle production. Common among those were building rifles either too heavy or too light for the new smokeless powder loads, and using soft brass cartridges that worked okay with blackpowder, but poorly with smokeless. The .450/400x3¼-inch Nitro Express (NE) was one of these blackpowder rounds given a new lease on life through cordite. It preceded the .375 H&H Magnum, as one of the best all-around cartridges for Africa.

Unfortunately, early rifles for the 4.50/400x3¼-inch NE often weighed 11 pounds or more, far too much for the performance level of the cartridge. A quarter-century later, gun makers commonly made lighter .465 & .470 Nitro Expresses. Early cases for the .450/400x3¼-inch were not hard enough for cordite usage. The cartridge design featured a rather long neck. In addition, the chambers of hunting rifles were commonly pitted from neglect or fouling. The frequent result of this combination was a case stuck in the chamber, with the case rim broken or torn off by the extractor. This tied up the rifle until the problem could be resolved. The solution eventually came in the form of better cartridge designs and better-quality brass cases.

The main problem in cartridge development was in determining how small the bore could be for any given game size—a problem that is still with us. Many hunters today believe that the biggest gun is the best, while others try to make the smallest work for everything. Clearly, the biggest guns will be adequate for the smallest game, but the converse has never been true. This, though, is the main reason behind the myriad early British cartridges. The British were hunting worldwide and were among the very few hunting dangerous game at a time when nothing was known about the new cordite loads and their jacketed bullets.

Many British cartridges were decades ahead of their time, good ideas that needed better powders and better steels to achieve fruition. The .275 H&H Belted Rimless Magnum, for instance, came out around 1912 and is a ringer for the 7mm Remington Magnum. Too often, our sense of provincialism restricts us into making comparisons within our immediate sphere of knowledge, with the result being that we often overlook originators. Westley Richards, for instance, claims to have been the first to draw brass into cartridges, a fact seldom mentioned in American or German gun journals.

Rigby's .450 Nitro Express cartridge design eventually became the king of the cordite elephant slayers. It threw a 480-grain jacketed bullet at just over 2100 fps. Every maker offered rifles in that chambering, and most of the world's hunters of dangerous game were happy. Then, for political reasons, the British government prohibited the importation of .450-bore rifles into India and the Sudan, so the British gunmakers invented variations on the .450 NE theme. The new elephant rifles were designated .465, .470, .476, and a few others. All these cartridges worked just about like the .450 NE had, and you paid your money and took your choice. Each maker had his specialty.

If you wanted somewhat more power than these standard Nitro-powered elephant cartridges offered, there were three choices. The .500 NE was just a bit more powerful than all of the .470 class, but the .577 NE and the .600 NE were tops. These chamberings were the ultimate life-insurance policies, for those who were involved in frequent close encounters with elephants. The .700 Nitro did not exist during the golden age of African hunting, which ran from roughly 1900 to the early 1940s.

Today's gun collectors and knowledgeable shooters are no strangers to many British cartridges, as perhaps they were a quarter-century ago. While it was then extremely difficult to get cases or bullets for the British cartridges, today there are several good sources. Bertram, of Australia, offers good, new cases that the handloader can form into most of the cartridges needed to feed British firearms. HDS, A-Square, Bell, and Buffalo Bore offer a bewildering selection of cases. Woodleigh, another Australian Company, makes bullets. These are as close as you can get to original shapes and weights and are of outstanding quality. Bullets are also made for some of the British numbers by Barnes, Ballard, DKT, Hawk, Star, Liberty, and a few others.

To add flavor to today's user of British cartridges, Federal Cartridge Co. offers loaded ammunition in .416 Rigby and .470 NE. Ruger chambers its single-shot No. 1 and Express Model 77 in .416 Rigby and, recently, .404 Jeffery. American gunsmith Butch Searcy will make you a double-barrel rifle in .470 or in a variety of chamberings at a reasonably affordable price. Several Italian, French, German, and Dutch companies make good double-barrel rifles in classic English chamberings. In England, Holland & Holland, Purdey, Westley Richards, Powell, and a few others still make good rifles in a variety of chamberings, and John Rigby & Co., now with headquarters here in the U.S., even has a newer elephant stopper in its .450 Rimless Magnum.

Older rifles chambered for some of the more obscure cartridges pop up from time to time and, because of the happy state of affairs in today's market, are again permitted to sing their old songs through the loving ministrations of their new owners. Cases and loading components are available through Huntington Die Specialties or the Old Western Scrounger (now owned by Navy Arms Co.). Handloaders can often rework these cases into what they need using custom dies, which are available from RCBS. The *Double Gun Journal* occasionally publishes handloading data. It is no great effort to get just about any oddball British rifle shooting today.

Two books have appeared to help shooters and collectors of English cartridges. One is by George Hoyem, *The History and Development of Small Arms Ammunition, Volume Three*, and the other by Bill Fleming, *British Sporting Rifle Cartridges*. John "Pondoro" Taylor's classic *African Rifles and Cartridges* has been reprinted many times and is still the best book ever written on the hunting of African game with most of the British cartridges. Today, there are many good reference books on British rifles and cartridges, and the collector or shooter has a much easier time finding information on these than ever before.

The .458 Winchester Magnum made its debut after World War II, when folks like John Taylor recommended something similar to it that would be inexpensive, American, and work alright in Africa. In spite of its pressure problems, the .458 took care of business in Africa well enough for many years, and it is still widely used there.

Today, with makers like Ruger offering affordable rifles for the .416 Rigby, and with the advent of the .416 Remington, there is a swing away from the .458, as more shooters realize its limitations. There has not been too great a swing back toward the British cartridges yet, except for the .416 and the .470. Those two have remained popular because of ammunition availability, and because these are two of the very best big-game cartridges ever loaded anywhere, fully capable of keeping the spirit of British cartridges going for another century or so. We may see some of the other old-timers become popular with Kynoch ammunition again available.

For many of the reasons given here, there exists, at least in collections, a great wealth of oddball and never very popular British cartridges. Hoyem and Fleming depict many that have popped up, but firearms for some of these cartridges are exceedingly scarce. Here we tell the story of what we feel are the most successful British cartridges.

Many people take their British rifles hunting or target shooting today. If you would do so, please make sure yours is safe to shoot. Be certain to check the size of the bore in your rifle and verify the correct chambering before you attempt to shoot it. We know of some rifles more than 120 years old, yet their owners shoot these guns frequently, and even take these guns hunting. These guns are in perfect condition. The owners shoot loads that are very conservative and thoroughly safe. Because we cannot personally inspect your firearms and advise you on the wisdom of shooting each (and for other reasons), we give very limited loading data.

Another caution might be in order. It is the opinion of David Winks, the now-retired chief barrel maker for Holland & Holland, that no one should ever fire homogeneous bullets of any type through fine rifle barrels, specifically those on British double-barrel rifles. Because of extremely tough construction, these bullets are too hard on the bore, in his expert opinion.

Winks also said he used *Cartridges of the World* nearly every day at the H&H shop, a philosophy echoed by the folks at John Rigby & Co. We sincerely hope this revised chapter will be of some added value to them, and to the many lovers of British rifles and their cartridges worldwide.

We welcome your input to correct any misinformation found here. Please let us know of your ideas for future inclusions or omissions for the next edition of *Cartridges of the World*. We wish you good shooting with your British firearms.

—*Ray Ordorica, British Cartridge Editor*

13th Edition Update

As with many of the chapter that came before this one, we've taken a handful of the oddest and most difficult to find rounds and relocated to them to the CD included with this book. The list of cartridges removed from this chapter includes: .246 Purdey; .255 Jeffery Rook; .26 BSA (.26 Rimless Belted Nitro Express); .256 Fraser Flanged/.256 Fraser Rimless/.256 Swift Flanged/.256 Swift Rimless; .256 Gibbs Magnum; .300 (.295) Rook; .300 Sherwood; .380 Short and Long (Rifle); .400 Purdey (3-inch) Light Express/.400 Straight 3-inch.

.297/230 Morris Short, Long, Extra Long & Lancaster Sporting

Historical Notes: These cartridges are listed together because all are very similar. The Morris Long has a long neck, the Extra Long has a really long neck (11/8-inch case length), and the Lancaster Sporting resembles the Short, but its shoulder is farther forward. These first appeared in an Eley ad, in 1882. These cartridges are target or practice rounds to be fired from a barrel insert for the British .577/450 Martini-Henry service rifle. The idea originated with Richard Morris and was adopted by the British army. Some models of the .303 Enfield rifle used an insert for the Morris cartridges. In addition, barrel and chamber inserts were available for the Webley & Scott .450 and .455 revolvers. European-made single-shot pistols and rifles are occasionally found chambered for the Morris cartridges. These cartridges were listed in Eley-Kynoch catalogs as late as 1962. The company B.S.A. made Martini-action rifles for these cartridges.

General Comments: The .297/230 cartridges were used for target practice and small-game shooting. Power is about the same as the standard .22 rimfire. These cartridges lost adherents, because .22 rimfire ammunition is cheaper, and even though the centerfire Morris cartridges can be reloaded. The Morris numbers were originally blackpowder loadings, but late-issue ammunition used smokeless powder. Bullets were of lead in solid or hollowpoint types.

.297/230 Morris Short, Long, and Extra Long Loading Data and Factory Ballistics

Bullet (grains/type)	Powder	Grains	Velocity	Energy	Source/Comments
43 lead	Unique	3.0	900	75	Lyman #225438
43 lead	2400	4.0	1200	137	Lyman #225438
37 lead	Blackpowder	3.25	875	62	Eley factory load
37 lead	Blackpowder	5.5	1200	118	Eley factory load

.244 H&H Magnum

Historical Notes: This, the last belted magnum developed by Holland & Holland, was introduced, in 1955, for the maker's Mauser-type bolt-action sporting rifles. Custom-made rifles in this chambering are seen occasionally. American loading handbooks have listed it in the past.

General Comments: The high-velocity .244 Holland & Holland Magnum is based on the .375 H&H Magnum case necked down to 6mm. This is a very large-capacity case for the caliber. Only very slow-burning powders will develop maximum velocity in a case this big, so the British were forced to use something other than cordite for this cartridge. American powders such as IMR-4350, IMR-4831, and similar powders give good results with bullets of 100 grains. Holland & Holland advertised a muzzle velocity of 3500 fps with the 100-grain bullet. The .244 H&H Magnum is a long-range, light-game cartridge. It would also be an excellent varmint and small-game number under any conditions. Barrel life was extremely limited.

.244 H&H Magnum Factory Ballistics

Bullet (grains/type)	Powder	Grains	Velocity	Energy	Source/Comments
100 SP	FL		3500	2720	Factory load

.240 Magnum Flanged & .240 Magnum Rimless H&H .240 Apex (.240 Super Express)

Historical Notes: This pair of 6mm cartridges was introduced by Holland & Holland, in the early 1920s. The rimmed cartridge was, of course, designed for double-barrel rifles, and the belted rimless version for magazine rifles. H&H also called this the .240 Super Express, but original ammunition boxes from the maker give the names in the header here.

General Comments: Performance of these two .240s is similar to that of the .243 Winchester. Holland data gives a velocity of 2900 fps with a 100-grain bullet for the belted version. In a strong, modern single-shot or bolt-action rifle using modern powders, performance could be increased significantly. However, this usually does not work for double-barrel rifles, because those guns are sighted and regulated for a specific loading. If you change things, the rifle may not shoot your loads to the same point of impact as the original load. That is why most rimmed British cartridges have a limited selection of bullet weights and velocities. The British were well ahead of the United States in the development of good 6mm cartridges. Either of these cartridges would do anything that could be done by the .243 or 6mm Remington.

.240 Magnum Flanged and Rimless H&H (.240 Apex) Factory Ballistics

Bullet (grains/type)	Powder	Grains	Velocity	Energy	Source/Comments
100 SP	FL		2900	1865	Factory load

.297/250 Rook

Historical Notes: Introduced by Holland & Holland for its semi-smoothbore rifles, this load dates back prior to 1880. It is a target and small-game cartridge, usually used in single-shot rifles based on the small Martini action, though occasionally seen in very fine break-action single- and double-barrel rifles. Incidentally, the rook is a bird similar to our crow.

General Comments: In performance, the .297/250 is similar to the old .25 Stevens rimfire. However, it is a centerfire bottlenecked cartridge and can be reloaded. There were a half-dozen or more of these so-called "rook" cartridges. None were very widely used outside Britain. Like the others, this is entirely a small-game cartridge. Bullet diameter is .250-inch.

.297/250 Rook Factory Ballistics

Bullet (grains/type)	Powder	Grains	Velocity	Energy	Source/Comments
56 lead	Blackpowder	6.5	1150	164	Factory load

.242 Rimless Nitro Express

Historical Notes: Developed in 1923, by Kynoch, for J. Manton & Co. (Calcutta), this cartridge was first called the .242 Manton. It was listed in late, post-war Kynoch catalogs.

General Comments: The .242 Rimless is very similar to the .243 Winchester and 6mm Remington in power and capacity. The case is a little longer than the American 6mms, but not quite as large in diameter. When loaded with American powders and used in a strong, modern bolt-action, it will deliver performance very similar to the .243 Winchester. This would be an effective cartridge for the same general range of game and shooting conditions as the .243 Winchester. Bullets are .249- to .253-inch diameter, so .243-inch bullets would not give satisfactory accuracy. One might be able to swage down .25-caliber bullets to fit, but be sure to slug your bore before attempting to handload for this cartridge.

.242 Rimless Nitro Express Factory Ballistics

Bullet (grains/type)	Powder	Grains	Velocity	Energy	Source/Comments
100 SP	FL		2800	1740	Factory load, Kynoch

.275 Rigby (7x57mm)

Historical Notes: This round, identical to the 7x57mm Mauser, was adopted by John Rigby & Co., in 1907, for Rigby bolt-action magazine rifles. Rigby was, at that time, the British outlet for Mauser. Rigby's original rifle featured the 175-grain bullet. In its 1924 catalog, Rigby lists three versions of the Mauser, its No. 1 rifle for the 175-grain bullet, and its No. 2 and 3 rifles for the 140-grain bullet, all designed for deer stalking. The No. 1 and 2 rifles weighed 7½ pounds, and the No. 3 was built to weigh 6¾ pounds.

General Comments: This cartridge was made famous by Walter D.M. Bell, the British hunter who killed nearly one thousand elephants with it, in the early years of the twentieth century. He killed every one using solid bullets of 175-grain weight, usually with one shot. Bell was one of the finest marksmen the world has seen, and you can read about his successes in his The Wanderings of an Elephant Hunter. Unfortunately, many men who read Bell's books and tried to emulate his success with this little cartridge—but without Bell's skill or luck—have gotten themselves killed. The .275 Rigby is a fine deer and medium-game cartridge. A light No. 3 Rigby, stoked with the 140-grain Nosler Partition, is one of the finest all-around rifles available for thin-skinned game in the 200-pound-and-under class.

.275 Rigby (7x57) Factory Ballistics

Bullet (grains/type)	Powder	Grains	Velocity	Energy	Source/Comments
140 Solid or LT Capped SN-SP	FL		3000	2800	Factory load
175 Solid or SN	FL		2300	2066	Factory load

.275 Belted Magnum (H&H)
.275 Flanged Magnum (H&H)

Historical Notes: Introduced in England, in 1911-'12, the belted version for bolt-actions and the flanged for single-shot and double-barrel rifles, these are the first 7mm Magnums. These cartridges came out shortly after the .280 Ross created quite a stir in the smallbore high-velocity field. A fair number of American custom rifles have been made for this round, but no factory rifles. The belted version, known in the United States as the .275 H&H Magnum, was loaded by the Western Cartridge Co., until 1939. The rimmed load was slightly reduced from the belted. It was developed by F.W. Jones, as an improvement of the .280 Ross. Eley and Kynoch loaded bullets of 105, 140, 143, 150, 160, and 180 grains.

General Comments: The .275 H&H Magnum is similar to the 7mm Remington Magnum. With modern powders in a good rifle, this ancient British number will do anything that can be done by the 7mm Magnum. Be sure to slug your rifle to get the correct bore size, and fit your bullets accordingly. This pair is a good long-range duo for mountain or plains hunting of light to medium game.

.275 Belted Magnum & Flanged Magnum (H&H) Factory Ballistics

Bullet (grains/type)	Powder	Grains	Velocity	Energy	Source/Comments
140 SP	FL		2650	2184	Factory load, British
160 SP	FL		2700	2600	Factory load, British
175 SP	FL		2680	2800	Western factory load

.275 No. 2 Magnum
(7mm Rigby Magnum Flanged)

Historical Notes: This is a rimmed necked cartridge designed for Rigby double-barrel rifles. It was introduced in 1927 and was still available in the early 1960s. It is advertised for "deer-stalking and all classes of non-dangerous game." It is another cartridge in about the same class as the 7x57mm Mauser.

.275 No. 2 Magnum Factory Ballistics

Bullet (grains/type)	Powder	Grains	Velocity	Energy	Source/Comments
140 SP	FL		2675	2230	Factory load

.280 Flanged (.280 Lancaster)

Historical Notes: Developed by Lancaster, this rimmed .280 cartridge is similar to the rimless .280 Ross and used in single-shot and double-barrel rifles. It was introduced shortly after the Ross cartridge appeared, in 1906. It is said to have been a favorite with King George V.

General Comments: The rimmed .280 is loaded to slightly lower velocities than the .280 Ross. When the rimless Ross cartridge was introduced, in 1906, it created considerable interest all over the world. It was only natural to bring out a rimmed version for the man who preferred the double-barrel rifle. Both cartridges have practically the same power and effectiveness. These high-speed .280 cartridges lost popularity, after a few big-game hunters were killed while using them on heavy or dangerous game under adverse conditions. One of the most famous of these was Sir George Grey, killed by a lion in Africa.

Bullet (grains/type)	Powder	Grains	Velocity	Energy	Source/Comments
140 SP	FL		2800	2440	Factory load
160 SP	FL		2600	2400	Factory load
180 SP	FL		2400	2300	Factory load

.280 Ross (.280 Rimless)

Historical Notes: This timeless cartridge was designed by F.W. Jones, a consultant to Eley and Sir Charles Ross, and introduced, in 1906, for the Canadian straight-pull Ross rifle. This was one of the first modern, high-velocity small-bore cartridges. It was originally a military design, but quickly caught the fancy of sportsmen, because of its high velocity, flat trajectory, and excellent killing power. The German .280 Halger Magnum is based on the Ross case. At one time, Remington and Winchester loaded .280 Ross ammunition. American companies discontinued it, in 1935. It is actually a semi-rimmed case.

General Comments: The .280 Ross is an example of what happens when hunters get overly enthusiastic about something new. It proved to have fantastic killing power on thin-skinned game. Even dangerous species were dispatched, occasionally, as if struck by lightning. However, there is a big difference between killing dangerous game under ideal conditions and stopping those critters cold when conditions get rough. Some men gave their lives to find this out, and the .280 Ross hit the skids. The original Ross bullet was made to expand quickly on medium-sized game. But, since no one bullet weight or type will do all things, this and other cartridges have been maligned because someone used them on game or under conditions for which they were not designed. The .280 Ross is adequate for most North American game and non-dangerous African plains varieties, if you select the proper bullet. The early straight-pull Ross rifles gained a bad reputation, because the bolt on those rifles could be assembled incorrectly, in which case, firing would likely result in a potentially fatal action failure.

.280 Ross Factory Ballistics

Bullet (grains/type)	Powder	Grains	Velocity	Energy	Source/Comments
140 SP	FL		2900	2620	Factory load
150 SP	FL		2800	2610	Factory load
160 SP	FL		2700	2600	Factory load
180 SP	FL		2550	2600	Factory load

.280 Jeffery (.33/280 Jeffery)

Historical Notes: The .280 Jeffery is another of the series of .28-caliber cartridges designed as answers to the .280 Ross. The exact date of introduction is not established, but was about 1915. The firm of Jeffery built Mauser-type bolt-action magazine rifles for this cartridge.

General Comments: This cartridge is based on the .333 Jeffery case necked-down to accept .288-inch diameter bullets. It has a larger case than the .280 Ross and holds more powder, but is not loaded to a much higher velocity. With modern powders, it could be handloaded to deliver a good deal higher velocity within safe pressure limits. However, today there are better and more modern 7mm cartridges available. The .280 Jeffery is a good cartridge for non-dangerous game at moderate to long ranges, with good bullets. Still, locating bullets of the correct diameter is no difficult task.

Bullet (grains/type)	Powder	Grains	Velocity	Energy	Source/Comments
140 SP	FL		3000	2800	Factory load

.300 Belted Rimless Magnum (H&H)/.30 Flanged Magnum (H&H Super .30)

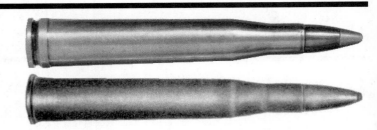

Historical Notes: The belted version here is the .300 Holland & Holland Magnum familiar to most of the world. The flanged version is for double-barrel rifles and is loaded a bit lighter. These cartridges originated in 1925. Additional data on the belted version is located in Chapter 2.

General Comments: Performance of this pair with original factory loads is on a par with that of the .30-06, perhaps a bit better. The flanged version must be loaded to give proper regulation in the double-barrel rifle, but the belted version, in a good bolt rifle, easily surpasses .30-06 performance.

.300 Belted Rimless Magnum (H&H Super .30) Factory Ballistics

Bullet (grains/type)	Powder	Grains	Velocity	Energy	Source/Comments
150 SP	FL		3000	3000	Factory load, British
180 SP	FL		2750	3020	Factory load, British
220 SP	FL		2300	2115	Factory load, British

.30 Flanged Magnum Factory Ballistics

Bullet (grains/type)	Powder	Grains	Velocity	Energy	Source/Comments
150 SP	FL		2875	2755	Factory load
180 SP	FL		2575	2653	Factory load
220 SP	FL		2250	2475	Factory load

.375/303 Westley Richards
.375/303 Axite

Historical Notes: This cartridge was introduced by Westley Richards, in 1905, and was listed in its catalogs for several years thereafter. It was also listed in the 1909 Charles Lancaster & Co. catalog. It was used in high-velocity double-barrel rifles by Westley, with Lancaster oval-bore rifling, in single-shot falling-block rifles, and in Lee-action magazine rifles.

General Comments: Power is about the same as the .300 H&H Magnum. It was loaded with Axite, a new Kynoch powder said by the makers to be "comparatively free from erosive and corrosive effects."

.375/303 Westley Richards Factory Ballistics

Bullet (grains/type)	Powder	Grains	Velocity	Energy	Source/Comments
215 SP	FL		2500	2981	Factory load
200 SP	FL		2726	2980	Factory load

.303 British

General Comments: The .303 British military cartridge is also a popular sporting round throughout the British Commonwealth and much of the world. It is covered in detail under military cartridges (Chapter 7), and also listed with American sporting cartridges (Chapter 2). English and Canadian loads offer greater variety and performance than those loaded in the United States.

.303 British Factory Ballistics

Bullet (grains/type)	Powder	Grains	Velocity	Energy	Source/Comments
150 SP	FL		2700	2440	Factory load, British
174 SP	FL		2450	2315	Factory load, British
180 SP	FL		2540	2580	Factory load, Canadian
192 SP	FL		2200	2070	Factory load, British
210 SP	FL		2050	1960	Factory load, British
215 SP	FL		2050	2010	Factory load, British

.303 Magnum

Historical Notes: This cartridge was introduced by Jeffery, in 1919, and subsequently adopted by the British Match Rifle Committee. It had a short life, being listed by Kynoch only until 1930. Case configuration is the same as the experimental .276 military round, and case capacity is the same as the .30-06.

General Comments: This cartridge was designed for target shooting at long ranges. Performance is identical to top .30-06 handloads.

.303 Magnum Factory Ballistics

Bullet (grains/type)	Powder	Grains	Velocity	Energy	Source/Comments
174 FMJ	FL		2850	3050	Factory load

.310 Cadet (.310 Greener)

Historical Notes: This cartridge was introduced by Greener, in 1900, as a target round for the small Martini sporting and training rifles. Many were made for the Australian government as cadet rifles. It also became a popular sporting cartridge for small-game shooting. Thousands of the Australian Martini cadet rifles were imported into the United States, after World War II. The .310 cartridge is rather well known in the United States, as a result.

General Comments: The .310 Cadet cartridge is similar in size and performance to the .32-20. In fact, .310 ammunition can be made from .32-20 cases. Back in the '50s, Winfield Arms Co. and Klein's Sporting Goods, of Chicago, sold several hundred .310 Martini rifles and actions. According to a 1955 data circular, these Martini actions were tested with proof loads of up to 60,000 psi, in order to determine what range of cartridges those guns would safely chamber. Some were re-chambered for the .32 Winchester Special, others were re-bored to .357 Magnum. Quite a few have been rebarreled to .22 Hornet or 218 Bee. Ken Warner has one for the .44 Magnum. The .310 Cadet cartridge is a good small-game and pest number at moderate ranges, and it also is a good target round.

.310 Cadet Factory Ballistics

Bullet (grains/type)	Powder	Grains	Velocity	Energy	Source/Comments
84 lead	FL		UNK	UNK	Factory load
120 lead	Blackpowder	6.0	1200	385	Factory load
125 lead	FL		UNK	UNK	Factory load

.318 Rimless Nitro Express (.318 Westley Richards/ .318 Accelerated Express)

Historical Notes: This cartridge was developed by Westley Richards, in 1910, for its bolt-action, Mauser-type magazine rifles. It was intended for use in Africa, and it made a fine name for itself there. It was one of the most popular medium-bore cartridges in Africa, even after the advent of the .375 H&H Magnum. Many gunmakers have chambered bolt-action rifles for this round. It is very similar to Elmer Keith's .333 OKH and the very popular wildcat, the .338-06. There was a square-shouldered version of this cartridge, as well, designed to improve headspace control. Because this was not a major problem, the square-shouldered version did not last. It was fired in the standard chamber.

General Comments: The .318 can be used in standard-length bolt-actions of fairly light weight. This cartridge threw bullets of good weight at respectable velocities that proved very deadly on all sorts of game and, as a result, it became very popular. It worked so well on all African medium game, that it got some hunters in trouble when they tried to extend its usefulness to dangerous game, sometimes at the cost of their lives. The .318 W-R has been used with great success on all North American big game, though it is not recommended for use against the biggest bears or any kind of dangerous game in a tight spot.

The .318 case is very similar to the .30-06 in size, shape, and capacity. The 180-grain bullet was used on the lighter animals, while the 250-grain was preferred for all medium to heavy game. Bullet types were solid, soft-point, and the Westley Richards copper-capped. Fraser had a "ratchet" bullet load for this cartridge. Bullets of the necessary .330-inch diameter for the .318 W-R can be obtained by swaging existing .33-caliber bullets. In addition, Woodleigh makes best-quality bullets in soft-nose or solid persuasion of the exact size. Cases can be made from .30-06 cases.

.318 Rimless Nitro Express Factory Ballistics

Bullet (grains/type)	Powder	Grains	Velocity	Energy	Source/Comments
180 SP	FL		2700	2920	Factory load
250 SP	FL		2400	3200	Factory load

.333 Jeffery Flanged & Rimless

Historical Notes: These are the two versions of the .333 Jeffery, introduced in 1908. The rimmed cartridge was intended for double-barrel rifles. The rimless-type, intended for magazine rifles, became more popular. The rimmed .333 was discontinued, after World War II. Both have about the same power. German-made Mauser rifles were also chambered for the rimless version.

General Comments: The .333 Jeffery earned a fine reputation on all varieties of African big game, including picked shots at elephants. Of course, most professional ivory hunters knew it was on the light side for such animals and used their heavy rifles when in close cover or when they needed to drop dangerous game quickly. On soft-skinned game, it gave excellent penetration, particularly with the 300-grain bullet. This cartridge was the inspiration for the domestic wildcat .333 OKH, designed by Elmer Keith, et al.

.333 Jeffery Flanged and Rimless Factory Ballistics

Bullet (grains/type)	Powder	Grains	Velocity	Energy	Source/Comments
250 SP	FL		2500	3480	Factory load, Rimless
300 SP	FL		2200	3230	Factory load, Rimless
250 SP	Cordite	67.0	2400	3200	Factory load, Flanged
300 SP	Cordite	63.0	2150	3090	Factory load, Flanged

.33 BSA
(.33 Belted Rimless/.330 BSA)

Historical Notes: A belted cartridge, this was introduced by Birmingham Small Arms, in 1921, for its bolt-action sporting rifles based on the military Enfield. It was never very popular and was discontinued many years ago.

General Comments: Like the rimless .26 BSA, the .33 was an effort to furnish a high-velocity cartridge in a popular caliber. Neither effort was a commercial success. The 165-grain bullet starts out at 3000 fps, but its blunt shape and relatively light weight cause it to slow down quite rapidly. At 100 yards, velocity is down to about 2650. The .33 BSA offered good killing power on light game, but failed to penetrate properly on heavy game. For this reason, it was not a successful general-purpose cartridge for African game. Why the manufacturer did not offer a choice of bullets with weights up to about 250 grains is a mystery. Basically, this is a good case design for modern rifles. The handloader can improve this one and put it in the same class as the .338-06 or the .318 Westley Richards. Properly handloaded, the .33 BSA would do well on most North American big game. This cartridge uses .338-inch diameter bullets. In fact, if you lengthen the case an 1/8-inch and move the shoulder forward a bit, you have the .338 Winchester Magnum. When handloading this cartridge, remember that the British Enfield action will not stand the same high working pressure as will the Mauser 98.

.33 BSA Factory Ballistics

Bullet (grains/type)	Powder	Grains	Velocity	Energy	Source/Comments
165 SP	FL		3000	3290	Factory load
175 SP	FL		2900	3265	Factory load *
*Estimated ballistics					

.400/350 Rigby

Historical Notes: The first of John Rigby & Co.'s .350s, this cartridge was introduced in November 1899. This is the old .400 Purdey case necked down to .35-caliber. Rigby provided single-shot, double-barrel, and bolt-action rifles in this chambering. The cartridge utilized outstanding soft-points and solids of 310 grains at about 2100 fps. The .400/350 was, at one time, the most popular and widely used medium-bore cartridge for African hunting. It was succeeded by the .350 No. 2, which is identical in case dimensions, but has a bullet of only 225 grains at somewhat higher velocity. That cartridge was also loaded in a rimless version, but this—the original and, some say, the best of the .350 Rigbys—was only available as a rimmed case. The magazine boxes of Rigby's bolt rifles were slanted to accommodate the rim.

General Comments: The .400/350 is a rimmed case that resembles the old .35 Winchester in general appearance. However, it is longer and uses heavier .358-inch diameter bullets. Popularity of the .400/350 was due, in a large part, to the excellent bullet design, which gave uniform and dependable results. The incomparable John "Pondoro" Taylor had a single-loader in this chambering, and that rifle was a great favorite of his. He used it on lion and other big game. Penetration and overall performance were excellent. The .400/350 would be a good cartridge for most North American big game, particularly where ranges are short.

Bullet (grains/type)	Powder	Grains	Velocity	Energy	Source/Comments
310 SP	FL		2100	3035	Factory load

.350 Rigby Magnum & .350 No. 2 Rigby

Historical Notes: The rimmed version of this cartridge, the .350 No. 2, was the successor to the .400/350 Rigby. Cases are identical. The only difference from the .400/350 is bullet weight and velocity. The rimless .350 Rigby Magnum was designed for bolt-action magazine rifles. Both of these came out in 1908, and both used a bullet of only 225 grains in order to increase the velocity of what was already a fully successful cartridge. This, it was felt, was necessary to compete with speedier cartridges that were all the rage at the time.

General Comments: The .350 Rigby Magnum and the No. 2 were popular with many African and Asian hunters. Their performance is similar to that of the .35 Whelen. Many hunters preferred the .350 Rigby Magnum over the .375 H&H Magnum, because the Rigby had less recoil. Either of these would be a fine cartridge for any North American big game short of big bear, although some hunters who can put up with the poorer trajectory prefer the heavier bullet of the original .400/350. Recently, Rigby chambered its medium-bore double-barrel rifles for the 9.3x74Rmm. Barnes and Speer make bullets of the correct diameter.

.350 No. 2 & .350 Rigby Magnum Factory Ballistics

Bullet (grains/type)	Powder	Grains	Velocity	Energy	Source/Comments
225 SP	FL		2625	3440	Factory load, Rimless
225 SP	FL		2575	3312	Factory load, No. 2

.400/360 Nitro Express (2¾-inch) Westley Richards/ Fraser/Evans/Purdey

Historical Notes: Although these cartridges have similar names, these are not interchangeable. The Purdey version uses a bigger bullet than the others—.367-inch diameter. The other versions have bullets from .358- to .360-inch diameter. The Purdey is usually marked .400/360P or .400/360B. There are significant variations in bullet weight and in rim thickness, as well. In addition, Westley Richards had a rimless version of the .400/360, loaded with a 314-grain bullet.

General Comments: These cartridges all generate about the same power. All are fine for use against medium-size game, particularly for close-range hunting. All appeared about 1900. The Purdey and Evans versions use a 300-grain bullet at 1950 fps, while the Westley Richards version threw a 314-grain bullet at 1900 fps. The Fraser used a 289-grain bullet. Often the correct load is engraved on the rifle in question. Information leading to the correct loading is sometimes given in the proof marks on British firearms. These rifles are quite common today, and correct chambering is often quite difficult to determine. The best way to determine what you have is to make a chamber cast and measure it precisely. Be sure to slug your bore.

.400/360 NE (2¾-inch) Factory Ballistics

Bullet (grains/type)	Powder	Grains	Velocity	Energy	Source/Comments
289 SP	FL		UNK	UNK	Fraser factory load
300 SP	FL		1950	2537	Purdey factory load
300 SP	FL		1950	2537	Evans factory load
314 SP	FL		1900	2520	Westley Richards factory load

.360 No. 5 Rook

Historical Notes: Introduced between 1875 and 1880, this cartridge was loaded until World War II. It was used in handguns and rifles. The 1909 Charles Lancaster & Co. catalog illustrates it for its underlever single-shot rifle and the Webley New "Express" revolver. Many other arms chambered the .360 No. 5.

General Comments: In addition to the versions listed below, shot and blank cartridges were also offered. Although ammunition catalogs separate rifle and revolver loadings, in actual practice, any version could be used in rifles or in late-model revolvers. The .360 No. 5 cartridge is very similar to the .380 Long and the .38 Long Colt. This is a small-game and target load.

.360 No. 5 Factory Ballistics

Bullet (grains/type)	Powder	Grains	Velocity	Energy	Source/Comments
82 lead	Blackpowder		UNK	UNK	Factory load
125 lead	Blackpowder		1050	310	Factory load
134 lead	Blackpowder		1025	312	Factory load
134 lead	Smokeless powder		1025	312	Factory load
145 lead	Smokeless powder		1075	373	Factory load

.360 Express (2¼-inch)
.360 Nitro For Black Powder
.360 Nitro Express

Historical Notes: The .360 (2¼-inch) is a blackpowder cartridge that first appeared before 1873. It was loaded with a great variety of bullet weights as a blackpowder cartridge, from 71 to 215 grains. Cartridge case length also varied considerably. The 2¼-inch version was the most common, but a length of 27/16 inches was also common and a favorite length of Alexander Henry, who was arguably the best craftsman of the nineteenth century. Some cases were as long as 2¾ inches.

Nitro loadings were with bullet weights of 190, 200, 250, and 300 grains (at least). Nitro versions date from around 1900-1902. Some blackpowder loads were paper patched, others of bare lead.

General Comments: This cartridge would be useful for small, thin-skinned game. In power, it is about the same as the .38-55 and would not be a bad short-range woods cartridge for deer-size animals. It was used mostly in single-shot and double-barrel rifles. If you have a rifle in this bore size, be sure to make a chamber cast to find out the true dimensions, before you attempt to handload for it. Bertram of Australia makes cases for the .360 that are long enough to produce suitable loads for any version of this basic case.

.360 Express (2¼-inch)/.360 Nitro For Black Powder Factory Ballistics

Bullet (grains/type)	Powder	Grains	Velocity	Energy	Source/Comments
134 lead	Blackpowder		1025	312	Factory load
134 lead	Smokeless powder		1025	312	Factory load
190 (360 NBP)	Smokeless powder		1700	1222	Factory load
300 (360 NE)	Smokeless powder		1650	1820	Factory load

.360 No. 2 Nitro Express

Historical Notes: This cartridge was introduced by Eley Brothers, in 1905, as a cartridge for single-shot and double-barrel rifles. The .360 No. 2 was moderately popular, but could not compete with the .375 H&H Magnum, which appeared on the market only a few years later.

General Comments: This is a large, rimmed, bottlenecked case noted for the low pressure it develops. In its day, it was considered a good all-around cartridge for thin-skinned African or Indian game. It would be adequate for any North American big game at moderate ranges and would make a good woods cartridge.

.360 No. 2 Nitro Express Factory Ballistics

Bullet (grains/type)	Powder	Grains	Velocity	Energy	Source/Comments
320 SP	FL		2200	3442	Factory load

.375 Flanged Nitro Express (2½-inch) (.370 Flanged)

Historical Notes: Introduced in 1899, this is a straight rimmed case not to be confused with the .375 Flanged Magnum, which has a larger necked case. It was used in single-shot and double-barrel rifles, although BSA made a bolt-action Lee magazine rifle in this chambering.

General Comments: The straight .375 rimmed cartridge is suitable for much hunting use and would be adequate for almost any North American big game, particularly for hunting in woods or brush. Bullets are no problem. This one is very similar in concept to the .375 Winchester, but the two are not interchangeable. This cartridge lends itself to some improvement by handloading, which is okay in a single-shot or magazine rifle. One can make cases from .405 Winchester cases. Elmer Keith had a Lancaster oval-bore double-barrel rifle in this chambering, which he used for elk on occasion. The grand old master liked the rifle and chambering very much, once he got it regulated properly, which he said was quite a chore.

.375 Flanged Nitro Express (2½-inch) Factory Ballistics

Bullet (grains/type)	Powder	Grains	Velocity	Energy	Source/Comments
270 SP	FL		2000	2400	Factory load
300 SP	FL		1900	2405	Factory load *

*Estimated ballistics

.400/375 Belted Nitro Express (H&H)

Historical Notes: This was the world's first belted case. It was introduced, in 1905, by Holland & Holland, to compete with the rising popularity of the 9.5mm Mannlicher-Schoenauer. The .400/375 was used mainly in bolt-action rifles, but some double-barrel and single-shot rifles also chambered it. It was listed in British ammunition catalogs until 1936-'38. Many of Holland & Holland's rifles in this chambering were apparently take-downs on Mannlicher actions and, later, on Mauser 98 actions.

General Comments: The power of the .400/375 is nearly identical to that of the 9.5mm Mannlicher, or in the same class as the .358 Winchester. It would be adequate for most North American big game at moderate ranges. Cases can be made from .240 Weatherby cases. Bullets designed for .375 Magnum velocities will perform poorly at these low velocities, but one might have good luck with cast bullets or with those designed for the .375 Winchester rifle.

.400/375 Belted Nitro Express (H&H) Factory Ballistics

Bullet (grains/type)	Powder	Grains	Velocity	Energy	Source/Comments
270 SP/FMJ	FL		2175	2840	Factory load
320	Cordite	43.0	2000	2840	Factory load *
*Estimated ballistics					

.375 Rimless Nitro Express (2¼-inch) 9.5x57mm MS

General Comments: This is the British designation for the 9.5mm Mannlicher-Schoenauer, and it may be listed either or both ways. There is a very slight difference in loading between the two listings, but these cartridges are interchangeable. This cartridge takes bullets of .375-inch diameter, and performance is similar to that of the .400/375. The 9.5mm M-S is not listed in late European catalogs. Additional data is in the section on European cartridges.

.375 Rimless Nitro Express (2¼-inch) (9.5x57mm MS) Factory Ballistics

Bullet (grains/type)	Powder	Grains	Velocity	Energy	Source/Comments
270 SP	FL		2150	2771	Factory load, European
270 SP	FL		2100	2643	Factory load, British

.369 Nitro Express (Purdey)

Historical Notes: This cartridge was brought out, in 1922, by Purdey, for double-barrel rifles of its manufacture.

General Comments: The .369 Purdey was loaded with only one bullet weight (270 grains) and offers ballistics practically identical to the .375 H&H Flanged Magnum with the same bullet. The .369 uses bullets of .375-inch diameter. It is a good cartridge suitable for any of the heavier varieties of North American big game. It could be improved by handloading, but, because it was only used in double-barrel rifles, it is not normally practical to change performance of the load.

.369 Nitro Express (Purdey) Factory Ballistics

Bullet (grains/type)	Powder	Grains	Velocity	Energy	Source/Comments
270 SP	FL		2500	3760	Factory load

.375 Flanged Magnum
.375 Belted Rimless Magnum
.375 H&H Magnum

Historical Notes: In 1912, Holland & Holland brought out perhaps the most famous pair of cartridges ever devised, the .375 Magnum in belted and flanged versions. The belted version was for magazine rifles, and the rimmed for doubles and single-loaders. When these cartridges came out, nothing else similar was available. Their only competitors were the .450/400 in doubles, the .404 Jeffery in magazine rifles, and the smaller .350 Rigby Magnum and No. 2. The .375 offered very flat trajectory, adequate bullet weight, and outstanding performance in handy rifles of top quality. The belted version has always been with us, and Kynoch again loads the rimmed version today.

General Comments: This cartridge has been very successful and, hence, very popular in Africa, India, and, of course, Alaska. Nearly every manufacturer in the world makes or has made rifles in the belted version of this cartridge. Double-barrel rifles are still occasionally made for the flanged version.

The .375 rimmed is loaded to slightly less velocity than the belted case, but not enough to make any real difference. One can use the same loading data as the .375 belted magnum. However, you cannot change ballistics without causing the barrels of a double-barrel rifle to shoot to different points of impact; you have to regulate your load to the individual rifle by trial and error. A rifle in either version of this cartridge makes a fine all-around hunting rifle for anything on the face of the earth.

.375 H&H Flanged Magnum Loading Data and Factory Ballistics

Bullet (grains/type)	Powder	Grains	Velocity	Energy	Source/Comments
270 SP	IMR 4350	83.0	2620	4115	N/A
300 SP	IMR 4350	80.0	2500	4160	N/A
235 SP	FL		2750	3945	Factory load
270 SP	FL		2600	4050	Factory load
300 SP	FL		2400	3835	Factory load

.375 Belted Magnum Factory Ballistics

Bullet (grains/type)	Powder	Grains	Velocity	Energy	Source/Comments
235 SP	FL		2800	4090	Factory load
270 SP	FL		2650	4200	Factory load
300 SP	FL		2500	4160	Factory load

.400 H&H Magnum

Historical Notes: When Holland & Holland began receiving inquiries asking them to develop a cartridge that would increase in power over its legendary .375 H&H Magnum, Technical Director Russell Wilkin began working on the problem. The requests were for a cartridge that could produce 6000 ft-lbs of energy at the muzzle, which is an enormous leap over the .375's 4160 ft-lbs, so Wilkin decided to create two cartridges, a .465, and a more manageable .411-caliber cartridge that could be called the ".400 Holland & Holland Magnum." This bore diameter fit neatly between the .375 and the .465 calibers and would be legal in those African countries that require a minimum .40-caliber rifle to hunt dangerous game.

General Comments: Holland retained the belted case head of the .375 H&H, mostly for aesthetic reasons. The shoulder has been moved back to lengthen the neck, providing plenty of grip on the bullet to withstand inertia under recoil in the magazine of a bolt-action rifle. A shallow shoulder angle ensures a smooth feed from magazine to chamber. Field-testing shows the .400 has a very similar trajectory to the .375 at normal hunting ranges.

.400 H&H Magnum Factory Ballistics

Bullet (grains/type)	Powder	Grains	Velocity	Energy	Source/Comments
400 Woodleigh	FL		2400	5115	Holland & Holland

.450/400 3¼-inch
BPE (Nitro For Black)/
Nitro Express

Historical Notes: The .450/400 3¼-inch uses a necked-down .450 3¼-inch case. In blackpowder form, it was loaded with about 110 grains of powder. Bullet weight varied from 230 to 300 grains. The Nitro for Black version was stoked with 45 to 48 grains of cordite and with bullets from 270 to 316 grains. The Nitro Express version was loaded with 400-grain soft-points or solid bullets over 56 to 60 grains of cordite. Nitro versions of these cartridges were available with rims in two thicknesses. The later, thicker version is .042-inch and exists because of the great length of the case neck. In blackpowder versions it extracted easily, but, on the Nitro version, any slight bit of corrosion in the chamber caused the case to stick, and the rim would pull off. Hence the change. Jeffery eliminated the long neck in his version, a good idea, indeed!

General Comments: The blackpowder version was considered appropriate for deer hunting and was usually chambered in a lightweight rifle. The Nitro version is the smallest of the British cartridges that can be considered as an appropriate dangerous game cartridge. It is practical for all-around use on African game. Before the advent of the .375 H&H Magnum, it was one of the most popular cartridges worldwide. If one is a cool and good shot, he can take this one against the biggest elephant, which is just what John "Pondoro" Taylor did many times. He speaks quite highly of it in his African Rifles and Cartridges. Many double-barrel rifles are encountered today for both blackpowder and Nitro versions of this cartridge. The Nitro rifles tend to be quite heavy for the chambering, probably because rifle makers did not know that such weight was not necessary for this chambering. Jeffery designed a similar three-inch .40-caliber Nitro round, the .400 Jeffery, that is not interchangeable with this one. Some of his rifles were quite light, but a great many were built on ponderous actions and weighed more than 11 pounds, when 9½ would have been adequate.

.450/400 3¼-inch BPE Nitro for Black and Nitro Express Factory Ballistics

Bullet (grains/type)	Powder	Grains	Velocity	Energy	Source/Comments
230 to 300 lead	Blackpowder (FFg)	110.0	UNK	UNK	Factory load
270 to 316 SP	Cordite	45.0 – 48.0			Factory load, Nitro for Black
400 SP	Cordite	56.0 – 60.0	2150	4110	Factory load, Nitro Express

.450/400 2⅜-inch BPE
.450/400 2⅜-inch Nitro For Black
.450/400 2⅜-inch Nitro Express

Historical Notes: These are different loadings of the same cartridge, a blackpowder load that originated circa 1880. The Nitro For Black and Nitro Express versions originated circa 1899. These are based on the old .450-bore base-diameter case shortened and necked down to .40-caliber, and loaded with 80 grains of blackpowder and a 210- to 270-grain lead bullet. The Nitro For Black version, made for use in blackpowder rifles, was loaded with 270-grain bullets and developed very low pressure. The full Nitro version featured 300- to 400-grain bullets over 40 to 43 grains of cordite. There was a similar BP Express cartridge of 2 7/8 -inch length and some other rather rare variations on this theme.

General Comments: The British worked up smokeless loads for many of their old blackpowder cartridges. For single-shot rifles, this was not difficult. However, with a double-barrel rifle, the load had to be balanced to shoot to the same point of impact as the original blackpowder load. Just working up the same velocity for the same bullet did not always work. Various bullets and velocities had to be tried to arrive at the right combination. Once that load was found, it provides fine short-range deer hunting performance. The Nitro Express version with 43 grains of cordite and the 400-grain bullet would be quite a bit more powerful and generally more useful.

Bullet (grains/type)	Powder	Grains	Velocity	Energy	Source/Comments
210 - 270 lead	Blackpowder (FFg)	79.0 - 84.0			NA
270 RN copper-tubed lead	Cordite	38.0	1650	1630	Factory load, Nitro for blackpowder
300 RN HP	Cordite	40.0			Factory load, Nitro Express
400 RN HP	Cordite	42.0-43.0			Factory load, Nitro Express

.400 Jeffery Nitro Express
.450/400 3-inch

Historical Notes: This cartridge was designed by Jeffery, in 1902. According to John "Pondoro" Taylor*, the short case was brought out because the longer blackpowder cartridge had a tendency to stick in the chamber after firing. Overall length is shorter, but the shoulder is farther forward. The .400 Jeffery was designed exclusively for cordite; it was never available with blackpowder. As with the 3¼-inch version, this was very popular before the .375 H&H Magnum appeared. It is still one of the most effective all-around cartridges for Africa.

General Comments: The .400 Jeffery throws a 400-grain bullet at adequate velocity, and hence is more effective on the largest game than is the 300-grain .375 H&H Magnum loading. However, it is less versatile as to available guns and loads, and that is where the .375 shines. Taylor wrote that he considered either of the .450/400s, the 3- or 3¼-inch versions, adequate for any African game under almost any conditions, if used by an experienced hunter. Taylor killed about 1,500 elephant. In the process, he used just about every available cartridge, so his opinion is something to consider. Elmer Keith wrote that a double-barrel rifle for this cartridge would be his first choice for crawling through an Alaskan alder thicket after big bear. Bullets of proper diameter may be obtained from Barnes or Woodleigh or from many smaller custom makers. Bertram makes cases that can be formed into either of these two grand .40s. The availability of good bullets in this size (.411-inch diameter) has made this cartridge newly popular. Good, reasonably light double-barrel rifles for it are becoming hard to find. A-Square used to offer factory .400 NE ammunition.

* Op. cit.

.400 Jeffery (.450/400 Nitro Express 3-inch) Factory Ballistics

Bullet (grains/type)	Powder	Grains	Velocity	Energy	Source/Comments
400 SP	Cordite	60.0	2100	3920	Factory load, standard

Loads using 55 or 57 grains of cordite were offered for use in extremely hot climates. A 300-grain loading was also offered. It was not particularly popular.

.416 Rigby

Historical Notes: A proprietary cartridge introduced by John Rigby, in 1911, for his magnum Mauser-actioned rifles, both cartridge and rifle established a record for reliability on dangerous game that endures to this day. Magazine rifles were initially offered for this round, but, until recently, Rigby made only one double-barrel rifle for it—by special order, and with lots of monetary persuasion. Today, it is chambered by Ruger in single-shot and magazine rifles, and by several other manufacturers. Federal Cartridge Co. offers premium .416 Rigby ammunition. The .416 Rigby is probably the best magazine cartridge for big game ever offered. Recently, two "copies" have appeared, the .416 Remington Magnum and .416 Weatherby Magnum. Both use a belted case, which is a mistake. The clean line of the non-belted case makes for better feeding through a magazine, which adds an extra margin of reliability.

General Comments: The .416 Rigby delivers greater striking energy than the .404 Jeffery. For those who prefer the bolt-action rifle, it is a great favorite for use against dangerous game in almost any situation. Because the .416 Remington and Weatherby are now standard items, many great bullets are available in this caliber. This cartridge is a handloader's dream. Numerous moulds are available for those who would shoot cast bullets.

.416 Rigby Factory Ballistics

Bullet (grains/type)	Powder	Grains	Velocity	Energy	Source/Comments
410 SP	FL		2370	5100	Factory load
400 SP	FL		2430	5245	Federal factory load

.404 Jeffery/ .404 Rimless Nitro Express 10.75x73mm

Historical Notes: Introduced by W.J. Jeffery, in 1909, the .404 Jeffery was vastly popular for many years, then died slowly over many decades. It now has a new lease on life. In 1993, Dynamit Nobel announced it would restart production of .404 Jeffery ammunition, and Ruger announced that the M77 rifle would be chambered for that cartridge. A Canadian company, NASS, recently announced a line of proprietary cartridges ranging from 7mm to .458, based on the 404 case. In the United States, Dakota Arms, of Sturgis, South Dakota (and now part of the Freedom Group that includes Remington and Marlin, among others), has introduced its own line of proprietary cartridges based on the .404 case, these ranging from 7mm to .416. Bullets of .423-inch diameter are now available for the .404. Norma, RWS, and Bertram make cases. The .404 was designed to be a bolt-action cartridge that would duplicate the ballistics of the rimmed .400 Jeffery and the .450/400 3¼-inch. The .404 is also popular on the Continent, where it is metrically named the 10.75x73mm. Today, it is loaded a bit hotter than originally.

General Comments: The .404 made a great name for itself in Africa, where inexpensive bolt rifles let its performance be experienced by those who could not afford a double-barrel rifle for one of the .400 Nitro Express rounds. At one time, a higher-velocity 300-grain load was available for the .404. It gave good results on thin-skinned game, but proved rather unreliable on the heavier species. With the standard 400-grain bullet, the .404 was a very popular, general-purpose cartridge in Africa and India. Properly used, it is adequate for any game found there. It is somewhat overpowered for North American game and lacks the flat trajectory and long-range potential necessary for much of our hunting. The .404 is a good cartridge for hunting bear or other big game at close quarters. The .404 uses .423-inch diameter bullets, which are available from Barnes, Woodleigh, and RWS.

.404 Jeffery Factory Ballistics

Bullet (grains/type)	Powder	Grains	Velocity	Energy	Source/Comments
300 SP	FL		2600	4500	Factory load
400 SP	FL		2125	4020	Factory load
400 SP	FL		2300	4700	Factory load, modern

.425 Westley Richards Magnum/ .425 Westley Richards Semi-Rimmed Magnum

Historical Notes: Westley Richards introduced this cartridge, in 1909. The most common and quite successful version has a rebated rim that fits the standard-diameter Mauser bolt face. Westley made double-barrel rifles, as well as bolt-actions, for the .425. It is a very good cartridge, and several unsuccessful attempts have been made to resurrect it.

The .425 is a sort of poor-man's magnum. Its rebated rim is .30-06 size, so any .30-06 or 8mm Mauser action can be made to accept it with minimal gunsmithing. The result is a very good and powerful big-game rifle at reasonable cost. Bullet diameter is .428- to .435-inch. Barnes and Woodleigh make such bullets.

General Comments: The .425 was designed for use against dangerous game. It was intended to take the place of the .450-bore in India, though W-R offered its .476 for Africa. The .425 proved to be a fine cartridge and was offered with solids and with the Leslie Taylor-designed, capped soft-nose bullets. Taylor was the general manager of W-R at the turn of the century, and he was personally involved in bullet design, among many other things. The so-called LT-capped bullets worked very well and were incorporated into most other W-R cartridges, including the .318 and .476.

.425 Westley Richards Magnum Factory Ballistics

Bullet (grains/type)	Powder	Grains	Velocity	Energy	Source/Comments
410 SP	FL		2350	5010	Factory load

.500/450 No. 1 Carbine
.500/450 No. 1 Express
.500/450 No. 1 Musket
.500/450 No. 2 Musket

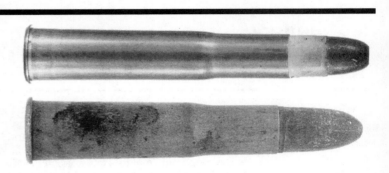

Historical Notes: Perhaps no cartridges in the world are more abundant or more confusing than those of British origin labeled .500/450 and followed by one or another designator. There are no less than 19 listings of individually identified cartridges in Bill Fleming's British Sporting Rifle Cartridges. Many of these cartridges were loaded with a great variety of bullet weights. All of these were bottleneck cartridges, and all originated with blackpowder loadings. The No. 1 Carbine was Westley Richards' first drawn-brass case, which appeared just before 1880. W-R was also responsible for the Musket and the 2¾-inch No. 1 Express, and possibly others of this lot. The oldest of the .500/450s used a coiled-brass case of 2½-inch length, dating to 1871. Some of these cartridges were loaded well into the twentieth century.

General Comments: All of the .500/450s are in the same class as the .45-70 and would be fairly effective short-range cartridges for North American game. Because of the great variation in designs, the handloader should be careful to determine exactly which of the many variants he has before attempting to build cartridges for it. The company CH4D (www.ch4d.com) has a large selection of .500/450 die types in stock.

.500/450 No. 1 Express Factory Ballistics

Bullet (grains/type)	Powder	Grains	Velocity	Energy	Source/Comments
270 lead	Blackpowder		1900	2160	Factory load

.500/450 No. 2 Musket Factory Ballistics

Bullet (grains/type)	Powder	Grains	Velocity	Energy	Source/Comments
480 lead	Blackpowder		1300	1805	Factory load
480 lead	Smokeless powder		1300	1805	Factory load
500 lead	Smokeless powder		1350	2025	Factory load

.450 3¼-inch BPE

Historical Notes: There were a great many "straight" British cartridges of nominal .450 designation, ranging from the .450 No. 1—barely longer than the .45 Colt—up to the .450 3¼-inch. In Bill Fleming's British Sporting Rifle Cartridges, there is a progression of no less than nine different lengths illustrated, in coiled paper, coiled brass, and drawn brass. The 3¼-inch drawn-brass version originated prior to 1877, and coiled-brass versions were in existence before 1871. Bullet weights ran from about 270 grains up to 365 in the Nitro For Black versions. Powder charges were from 105 to at least 120 grains of blackpowder (Greener indicates 150 grains). Nitro loadings for blackpowder rifles used up to 55 grains of cordite. The .450 3¼-inch was loaded in France, Germany, Austria, and Canada, and most likely elsewhere. It was one of the best blackpowder cartridges in the world.

General Comments: The 3¼-inch BPE version became one of the most popular cartridges ever devised. It was a deer cartridge or for medium-size game, at best. Selous and Taylor both used this cartridge to take elephant, but they both knew this was something of a stunt. The .450 BP and Nitro For Black versions lasted until well into the twentieth century, and many rifles that chamber them are still in use. The editor of this chapter once owned a plain-grade Watson hammer double-barrel that would regulate perfectly with bullets from 300 to 400 grains and shot to its sights at more than a half-mile.

.450 3¼-inch Nitro Express

Historical Notes: When cordite and suitable full-patch bullets were loaded into what had been one of the world's most popular deer cartridges, the result was the new standard-of-the-world in elephant cartridges. This replaced the ponderous 8-, 6-, and 4-bore blackpowder rifles. John Rigby and Co. introduced this cartridge, in 1898. For many years, it was considered the standard elephant or dangerous-game cartridge and enjoyed great popularity. It utilizes 480-grain bullets of .458-inch diameter.

General Comments: The .450 Nitro is considered adequate for dangerous African game—or any other game, for that matter—under almost any conditions. It would most likely have been the only British cartridge used for big-game hunting, except for a British law that prohibited importation of .45-caliber rifles or cartridges into India. British rifle makers had to come up with something new, so the .425, .470, .476, and others came into being. Nevertheless, the .450 NE was, and still is, a winner, and a great many double-barrel rifles for this cartridge are still in service.

13th Edition Update: A-Square (www.a-squareco.com) was offering this cartridge for a time, but its website now states the following:

The .450 N.E. (3¼") has been discontinued and can no longer be supported. This cartridge started out as a black powder cartridge in the 1870's. It has gone from there to Black Powder Express, to Nitro for Black Powder, and thence to Nitro Express. Cartridge, chamber and throat dimensions have gone all over the map in the ensuing 130 years. Further, we have seen barrels with grooves as tight as .450" and bores as tight as .438" to grooves as loose as .461". Though these dimensional variations may work with black powder and cast lead bullets, they are totally unsafe with smokeless powder and jacketed bullets. For smokeless powder and modern .458" bullets to safely work, the groove diameter must be .458" with a bore diameter of .450". There are too many rifles in .450 N.E. (3¼") that do not have barrels of such dimensions and therefore we cannot safely support this cartridge.

.450 3¼-inch Nitro Express Factory Ballistics

Bullet (grains/type)	Powder	Grains	Velocity	Energy	Source/Comments
465 (various)			2150	4770	A-Square
480 lead	Smokeless powder		2150	4930	Factory load

.500/450 3¼-inch Magnum Express (BPE)

Historical Notes: This cartridge originated with a coiled-brass case in the 1870s. Loaded with about 140 grains of blackpowder in the drawn-brass version, it was once very popular in Africa. Typical express-bullet weight was 325 grains.

General Comments: This was popular enough that it was loaded in both black and smokeless (Nitro for Black) versions, until the start of World War II. This must have caused some problems with owners of Nitro versions of this cartridge, which was an extremely powerful elephant cartridge, and surely some orders of ammunition arrived in the heart of Africa that would fit the rifle, but did not give the needed performance.

.500/450 3¼-inch Magnum BPE Factory Ballistics

Bullet (grains/type)	Powder	Grains	Velocity	Energy	Source/Comments
325 SP	Blackpowder		1950	2745	Factory load
325 SP	Smokeless powder		1950	2745	Factory load
365 SP	Smokeless powder		1875	2850	Factory load

.500/450 3¼-inch Nitro Express

Historical Notes: This is a rimmed necked case introduced (probably by Holland & Holland) around the turn of the century. It is based on the blackpowder .500/450 Magnum Express shell. It was used in single-shot and double-barrel rifles and made a great name for itself in Africa. It was usually loaded with 480-grain soft-point or solid bullets, but other slightly lighter loadings sometimes appear. It is a fine performer. Theodore Roosevelt had a double-barrel rifle in this chambering. H&H opened this up to become the .500/465 after the ban on .450-bore rifles in India and the Sudan.

General Comments: This was a prime competitor of the .450 3¼-inch Nitro Express. Performance of the two is practically identical. The British developed several .45-caliber large bores, all of which produced about 5000 ft-lbs of muzzle energy. These cartridges have about the same killing power, and the choice becomes more or less a matter of individual preference. All are large cartridges that develop quite low pressures and are therefore suitable for hot climates where dangerous game abounds. Younger African guides have, in many instances, switched to bolt-action rifles in contemporary chamberings, because those rifles are less expensive than the classic English doubles, if not as quick for the second shot. The bullet used in British .45-caliber cartridges varies from .454- to .458-inch in diameter, so there are plenty of jacketed or cast bullets available to fit almost any of these cartridges.

.500/450 Magnum Nitro-Express (3¼-inch) Factory Ballistics

Bullet (grains/type)	Powder	Grains	Velocity	Energy	Source/Comments
480 SP	FL		2175	5080	Factory load

.450 No. 2 Nitro Express (3½-inch)

Historical Notes: This cartridge uses a longer case than the .500/450 Magnum, but uses the same bullet weight loaded to the same velocity. It was introduced about 1900-'02 by Eley. It was designed to give very low pressures in single-shot and double-barrel rifles and has a thick rim to aid extraction. It was loaded with 480-grain bullets, 70 to 80 grains of cordite, and with a great variety of bullet types. It later was opened up to become the .475 No. 2 for importation into India.

General Comments: The only logical reason for designing a larger capacity case to deliver the identical ballistics of a smaller cartridge is to reduce breech pressure. It appears that some British cartridges gave extraction difficulties during the era of transition from blackpowder to smokeless powder. At first, this was believed to be the result of the higher pressures developed by smokeless powder. Later, the manufacturers discovered that most of the trouble could be eliminated by making the case walls thicker. Many rifles in this chambering are still around.

.450 No. 2 Nitro-Express (3½-inch) Factory Ballistics

Bullet (grains/type)	Powder	Grains	Velocity	Energy	Source/Comments
480 SP	FL		2175	5050	Factory load

.450 Rigby

Historical Notes: Introduced in 1995, Rigby's newest cartridge is just one more feather in the hat of this very old but still progressive and always innovative company. John "Pondoro" Taylor said that Rigby always had Africa in mind when it brought out a new cartridge. That tradition continues today, with the company under the direction of Paul Roberts. Roberts actually went to Africa himself to test and see the results of the .450 Rigby in the field. The cartridge has already made a good name for itself there and will surely become another of the all-time great classics.

General Comments: Rigby offers the .450 Rigby in bolt-action or double-barrel rifle versions. In its standard factory loading, this cartridge throws a 480-grain Woodleigh soft-nose or solid bullet at 2350 fps. This gives it quite a trajectory and terminal-performance edge on the .450-470 group, and it far surpasses the somewhat overstrained .458. The case is basically the same one that the .416 Rigby uses, with a sharp shoulder for good and consistent resistance to the striker blow, and with a .458-inch bullet. Similar in size to the .460 Weatherby, this improved design is unhampered by a belt and, thus, gives smooth, quiet, and sure feeding from the magazine. This will be a good choice for the person wanting to take only one rifle to Africa. It will also be right at home with anyone who appreciates a good, powerful rifle.

13 Edition Update: Paul Roberts was one of the secondary owners of the now nearly 300-year-old John Rigby & Co. It first passed out of family hands in 1951, when it was purchased by the firm's accountant, Vernon Harris. Harris later sold the company to David Marx and Michael Shea, who subsequently partnered with Roberts. The company was sold again, in 1997, and operated in California for a time, before its assets were sold out of bankruptcy, in 2006. Today it is a privately held company, with its corporate offices in Dallas, Texas, while production of the guns has returned to London, England.

.465 H&H Magnum

Historical Notes: When Holland & Holland began receiving inquiries asking it to develop a cartridge that would feature an increase in power over its legendary .375 H&H Magnum, Technical Director Russell Wilkin began working on the problem. The requests were for a cartridge that could produce 6000 ft-lbs of energy at the muzzle, which is an enormous leap over the .375's 4160 ft-lbs. To achieve this performance goal, it was decided to go to a belted cartridge with a larger head diameter than that of the .375 H&H Magnum. Holland is still fine-tuning this cartridge, but it appears that the stated performance goal will be reached. If so, the .465 H&H Magnum with a 480-grain Woodleigh bullet will have as much energy at 200 yards as the .375 H&H does at the muzzle.

General Comments: The .465 has a head diameter of .580-inch, measured just in front of the belt. The case is 2.89 inches long and has the sloping profile characteristic of Holland offerings. At hunting ranges, the .465's trajectory will be very similar to both the .400 H&H and its predecessor, the .375 H&H Magnum.

13th Edition Update: No amount of Googling or other web research has turned up any more information on this cartridge. Holland & Holland's website declares the cartridge was introduced in 2003, but other web resources say that this cartridge still lacks SAAMI and CIP recognition as recently as 2010. We see no indication that anyone is loading what should be a proprietary round, not even Holland & Holland.

.465 H&H Magnum Factory Ballistics

Bullet (grains/type)	Powder	Grains	Velocity	Energy	Source/Comments
480 Woodleigh	FL		2375	6012	Holland & Holland

.500/465 Nitro Express

Historical Notes: This cartridge dates back to 1907 and was intended for use in Holland & Holland's single-shot and double rifles.

General Comments: The .500/465 Nitro Express launches 480-grain solids or soft-point bullets out of a 28-inch barrel at roughly 2150 fps with 4930 ft-lbs of energy at the muzzle. Kynoch (www.kynochammunition.co.uk/) currently produces this round, as does A-Square (www.a-squareco.com). Midway USA (www.midwayusa.com) can provide Bertram brass.

.500/465 Nitro Express Factory Ballistics

Bullet (grains/type)	Powder	Grains	Velocity	Energy	Source/Comments
480 SP	Cordite	73	2150	4930	Factory load
480 (various)	FL		2150	4930	A-Square factory load

.470 Nitro Express

Historical Notes: The .470 was introduced in 1900 and, according to John Taylor, was designed by Joseph Lang. It is another extremely popular cartridge of the British gun trade and was adopted by most rifle makers. It was used mostly in double-barrel rifles and was a favorite of elephant hunters. Like most cartridges in this group, it originated as a replacement for the .450 Nitro Express, which was banned in India and the Sudan for a number of years. Holland & Holland, Purdey, and others still make guns in this chambering, in England. It was (and still is) Rigby's choice, when it gave up the .450 NE.

General Comments: The .470 Nitro was probably the most popular and widely used of the various .47-caliber cartridges. It is certainly the most enduring. It had plenty of killing power for any of the heavy or dangerous varieties of game, and it is potent lion or tiger medicine in a tight spot. It can, like any powerful cartridge, be used for smaller game than that for which it was designed, and that, in fact, is how most of the big double-barrel rifles are still used today. Federal Cartridge Co. began making loaded ammunition, in 1989, using best-quality 500-grain solids and soft-points at 2150 fps. Handloading components are today widely available, and many makers still offer double-barrel rifles in this chambering. It is one of the best choices in any new double-barrel rifle, because of ammunition and component availability. Federal does not offer components to the handloader, but bullets are available from A-Square, Barnes, Trophy Bonded Bullets, and Woodleigh, and from many smaller custom shops. HDS, Bertram, and Norma make cases, and Kynoch again offers loaded ammunition.

Bullet (grains/type)	Powder	Grains	Velocity	Energy	Source/Comments
500 SP/FMJ	FL		2150	5130	Factory load, British
500 SP/FMJ	FL		2150	5130	Federal factory load

.476 Nitro Express
.476 Westley Richards

Historical Notes: This cartridge was a Westley Richards development, introduced in 1907. It was used in single- and double-barrel rifles, but was not as popular as others of the same class. The 520-grain bullets were of .476-inch diameter, and the impressive LT-capped bullets were available as soft-points.

General Comments: Nothing much can be said about the .476 Nitro Express that has not already been mentioned about other cartridges in the same class. These cartridges are all nearly identical in power. The .476 is considered adequate for any and all African or Indian big game. It was a favorite of Elmer Keith's. Barnes and others offer bullets of this size.

.476 Nitro Express Factory Ballistics

Bullet (grains/type)	Powder	Grains	Velocity	Energy	Source/Comments
520 SP	FL		2100	5085	Factory load

.475 3¼-inch Nitro Express

Historical Notes: This cartridge, like the .470, was designed to replace .45-caliber British cartridges used in India and the Sudan. Most were introduced between 1905 and 1910. This one came out about 1900. It is a straight rimmed shell intended for single-shot or double-barrel rifles and took a 480-grain bullet of apparently varying diameter. Cartridges with bullets as small as .474-inch and as large as .483-inch have been encountered.

General Comments: The .475 Nitro has about the same performance as the .470, .465, etc., and was considered a good, general-purpose round for heavy and dangerous game of all types. Barnes and others offer bullets for loading this cartridge.

.475 3¼-inch Nitro Express Factory Ballistics

Bullet (grains/type)	Powder	Grains	Velocity	Energy	Source/Comments
480 SP	FL		2175	5040	Factory load, British

.475 No. 2 Nitro Express
.475 No. 2 Jeffery

Historical Notes: This round was developed to replace the .450 No. 2, when the British government prohibited .45-caliber cartridges in India and the Sudan. The .475 No. 2 Nitro Express was used, of course, in double-barrel rifles. The standard version used a 480-grain bullet with 80 or 85 grains of Cordite.

Jeffrey's load was with a 500-grain bullet and three different powder charges, 75, 80, and 85 grains of Cordite. The various cartridges would interchange, but, unless the load matched the rifle, it would not regulate properly. There were some bullet variations, but the most common was of .489-inch diameter.

General Comments: The .475 is a very large, impressive-looking cartridge, with an overall length of almost 4½ inches. It undoubtedly gave its user some added bravado or confidence that might have been well needed in a tight spot, in spite of the fact that performance was about the same as that of shorter cartridges. It has ample power for any African or Indian game and would also take care of anything in North America. The .475 case is made unusually heavy, to reduce expansion and facilitate extraction. Pressures are quite low. A-Square (http://a-squareco.com/) and Barnes (www.barnesbullets.com) offer bullets that are suitable for handloading this cartridge. A-Square also offers ammunition.

.475 No. 2 Nitro Express Factory Ballistics

Bullet (grains/type)	Powder	Grains	Velocity	Energy	Source/Comments
480 SP	FL		2200	5170	Factory load, standard
480 (various)	FL		2200	5170	A-Square factory load
500 SP	FL		2150	5140	Jeffery factory load

.505 Gibbs (.505 Rimless)

Historical Notes: The .505 Gibbs was introduced, in 1911, as a proprietary cartridge by Gibbs for use in Mauser-type bolt-action magazine rifles. Rifles in .505 Gibbs were imported by American dealers and used to a limited extent here. A few custom-built rifles chambered for the .505 were also turned out by American gunmakers. Most of these big-bore Nitro cartridges were developed around 1910, and this one was still available until quite recently. Bullets and cases are still available, and a few Ruger M77 Expresses have been rebarreled to this round.

General Comments: When the first of the .505 rifles showed up in the United States, there were all kinds of stories floating around about the horrendous recoil; several individuals were alleged to have suffered broken shoulders or collarbones, as a result of firing these cartridges. This sort of nonsense made "heroes" out of those who fired these guns and "survived," but hardly contributed to the popularity of the cartridge. The English must have more sturdy frames than we Americans, because none of them appear to have fractured anything.

The .505 is slightly less powerful than the .500 Jeffery, but both have an edge over the .458 Winchester. The .505 Gibbs is considered adequate for anything in Africa and has a good reputation against elephant, buffalo, and lion. Barnes makes bullets specifically designed for this cartridge.

.505 Gibbs (.505 Rimless) Factory Ballistics

Bullet (grains/type)	Powder	Grains	Velocity	Energy	Source/Comments
525 SP	FL		2300	6190	Factory load
525 (various)	FL		2300	6190	A-Square factory load

.577/500 No. 2 BP Express
12.7mm British No. 2

Historical Notes: The .577/500 No. 2 Express is another blackpowder cartridge. It was introduced sometime before 1879. It resembles the .577/500 Magnum Nitro Express, but has a shorter case and is not interchangeable. There were a number of different cartridges bearing the .577/500 designation, though, thankfully, not as many as with the .500/450. This one has a three-inch case, and there was a version an 1/8-inch longer. Both were loaded with blackpowder and Nitro For Black, and the longer version became a full Nitro load. Bullet weight in this caliber varied from 300 grains up to 570, with corresponding variances in the blackpowder charge, that ranging from 130 to about 160 grains. At one time, it was loaded in Germany as the 12.7mm British No. 2.

General Comments: The .577/500 No. 2 Express was popular in India for shooting thin-skinned game such as tiger. The blackpowder and Nitro For Black versions were not popular in Africa, as these cartridges were not powerful enough for general use there. Bullet diameter is nearly the same as the old .50-caliber Sharps cartridges, and Lyman moulds in various weights will work for cast bullets. Keep smokeless loads on the light side, as these old rifles do not take kindly to high pressures. Dave Davidson of 4-D Tool & Die (now CH4D) explains that some versions of the .577/500 are unique from the .500 No. 2 Express. These .577/500s are bigger than the No. 2 at the case head and rim. In those versions, case-head dimensions match the .577 Nitro.

.577/500 No. 2 BP Express Factory Ballistics

Bullet (grains/type)	Powder	Grains	Velocity	Energy	Source/Comments
300 lead	FL		1870	2340	Factory load
340 lead	Blackpowder		1925	2800	Factory load

.577/500 3⅛-inch Nitro Express

Historical Notes: This number evolved from a blackpowder cartridge based on the .577 case necked to .50-caliber. It looks like, but is not the same as, the shorter .577/500 No. 2 Express, being about 1/8-inch longer. It enjoyed moderate popularity. The full Nitro load utilized cordite with an 570-grain cupro-nickel bullet.

General Comments: This cartridge was more popular in India than Africa. It would be more useful for general big-game hunting than any of the more powerful "elephant" cartridges of the same caliber. It would be adequate for deer, bear, elk, or moose at moderate ranges and would be fine for woods hunting. The old .45-70 military round is considered capable of killing any American game at short range, and it only develops 2000 ft-lbs of muzzle energy. The .577/500 is a good deal more potent.

.577/500 3⅛-inch Nitro Express Factory Ballistics

Bullet (grains/type)	Powder	Grains	Velocity	Energy	Source/Comments
440 lead	Axite	58.0	UNK	UNK	Factory load, Nitro for blackpowder
570 FMJ	Cordite	UNK	UNK	UNK	Factory load, Nitro Express

.500 Express (BPE) Nitro For Black

Historical Notes: The straight .500 was offered in a great variety of lengths, including 1½-, 2-, 2¼-, 2½-, 25/8-, 3-, and 3¼-inch. All were blackpowder cartridges. Some were quite successful and lasted, while others faded long before the turn of the century. This cartridge size originated in about the mid- to late 1860s and, over time, a great many lengths were tried. They are, of course, chambered in rifles that are still around. The most successful of these was the three-inch version. Bullet weights run from 340 to 440 grains, and the charge is from 123 to 142 grains of blackpowder. Around the beginning of the smokeless era, Westley Richards came out with two versions of this cartridge, one three-inch, the other in a shorter case, both called the Long Range cartridge. These cartridges utilized heavier bullets and either light charges of cordite or heavy blackpowder loads.

Bullet (grains/type)	Powder	Grains	Velocity	Energy	Source/Comments
400 SP	FL		1900	3530	Factory load

General Comments: The blackpowder .500 was popular in India as a good general-purpose firearm, but was not highly regarded in Africa. This cartridge is similar to the .50-140 Sharps. It would be adequate for any North American big game. Late loads used smokeless powder, but delivered the same ballistics as the original blackpowder load. There is a variety of bullet moulds available today that will make just about any of the .500 BP cartridges work. To prevent rapid bore damage, only cast or swaged-lead bullets should be used in these guns.

.500 Nitro For Blackpowder Express Factory Ballistics

.500 Nitro Express (3-inch and 3¼-inch)

Historical Notes: The .500 Nitro Expresses were derived from what were originally blackpowder cartridges. The smokeless versions were introduced in the 1890s. A 570-grain bullet is used in both case lengths, and ballistics are about identical. The longer case works at a bit lower pressure. There were also loadings utilizing a 480-grain bullet and slightly reduced charges of cordite.

General Comments: The .500 NE was considered a real killer on practically anything. John A. Hunter, a game-control hunter with the Kenya Game Department for 26 years, considered it his favorite. His book Hunter is recommended for those who enjoy reading good, firsthand experiences of a guide and African shooting. The .500 Nitro resembles the .50-140 Sharps. A-Square (http://a-squareco.com/) and Barnes (www.barnesbullets.com) make appropriate bullets. A-Square also now offers the 3-inch loading.

500 Nitro Express (3-inch, 3¼-inch) Factory Ballistics

Bullet (grains/type)	Powder	Grains	Velocity	Energy	Source/Comments
570 SP	Smokeless powder		2150	5850	Factory load
570 (various)			2150	5850	A-Square

.500 Jeffery

Historical Notes: The .500 Jeffery was a proprietary cartridge developed by Schuler, in Germany, for bolt-action rifles. It was also adopted by Jeffery for its bolt-action magazine rifles based on the Mauser action. It has a rebated, or undercut, rim of smaller diameter than the base, so as to fit the standard-diameter Mauser bolt face. Earlier editions of this book stated that this cartridge is interchangeable with the German 12.5x70 Schuler, but, according to custom gunsmith James Tucker, this is not the case.

General Comments: The .500 Jeffery is similar to the .505 Gibbs, but it has a shorter case and is loaded to higher velocities and energies. The .500 Jeffery was designed to provide the man who preferred the repeating rifle with the same killing power as some of the popular, rimmed, double-barrel rifle cartridges. The .500 Jeffery is the most powerful cartridge used in any of the British magazine rifles. The .500 Jeffery is considered adequate for large or dangerous African game under any conditions. It is also quite accurate, and a good shot who can handle the recoil can get 100-yard groups of two inches. Most shooters claim the apparent recoil of .500 Jeffery magazine rifles is less than that of similarly chambered double-barrel rifles. (http://a-squareco.com/) and Barnes (www.barnesbullets.com) make appropriate bullets, and A-Square offers factory ammunition.

Bullet (grains/type)	Powder	Grains	Velocity	Energy	Source/Comments
535 SP	FL		2400	6800	Factory load, British
570 (various)			2300	6695	A-Square factory load

.577 BPE 2½-, 2¾-, 3-, and 3¼-inch

Historical Notes: The .577 Express series began about 1870, with the 2½-inch version. Its predecessors were, of course, the .577 Snider variants, which date from 1866. Numerous shorter coiled-brass and drawn-brass .577-bore cartridges were developed, but the best were the Expresses, specifically those that lasted long enough to become Nitro cartridges. The shortest of these is the 2¾-inch version. Bore size evolved into .585-inch diameter, and the best Express bullets weighed about 520 to 650 grains. The charge was 135 to 190 grains of blackpowder.

General Comments: All of these were for use on the heavier non-dangerous game, though, as happens, some hunters used these cartridges against tigers and lions with varying success. There was a great variety of bullets available, and success was directly tied to utilizing the proper bullet. To prevent rapid damage to the bore, only cast or swaged-lead bullets should be used in these rifles.

.577 Nitro Express 2¾-, 3-, and 3¼-inch

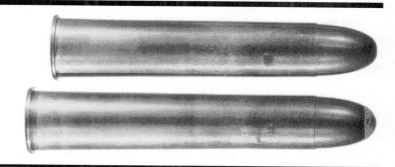

Historical Notes: These were all originally blackpowder cartridges, but, when loaded with Cordite and proper bullets, became some of the best real stoppers for dangerous game. All three originated around the turn of the century. The short case and the 3¼-inch shell were overshadowed by the 3-inch version.

General Comments: The .577 enjoyed a great reputation as an elephant killer and was a standard chambering found in any battery of African rifles. It was popular with professional ivory hunters for close-cover work. Many claim it is superior to the .600 Nitro, because it gave greater penetration. Rifles for the .577 could be made a few pounds lighter than the .62-caliber guns, which also contributed to the round's popularity.

Cartridges of this size were usually for emergency use under difficult conditions. Most hunters used lighter rifles of smaller calibers for ordinary shooting, but had the big .577 as a backup. Rifles for the .577 weighed 13 pounds or more, and that's a lot of weight if you have to carry it very far at the ready. Gunbearers usually carried the heavy guns until needed, but not because the British were lazy; an exhausted man just cannot handle a rifle of such heft and weight in a pinch. A-Square (http://a-squareco.com/) and Barnes (www.barnesbullets.com) make appropriate bullets.

.577 Nitro Express Factory Ballistics

Bullet (grains/type)	Powder	Grains	Velocity	Energy	Source/Comments
750 SP/FMJ	FL		2050	7010	Factory load
750 (various)	FL		2050	7010	A-Square factory load

.600 Nitro Express
(2⁸/₁₀-inch & 3-inch)

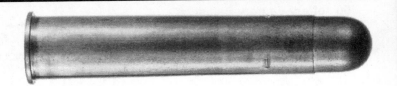

Historical Notes: The .600 in either length was the largest and most powerful of the English cordite elephant cartridges, until 1988. These were introduced by Jeffery, before 1901. The 28/10-inch version came out in 1899. The .600 is of original design and is not based on any earlier blackpowder cartridge. It was used in single-shot and double-barrel rifles. Despite its reputation, only a small number of guns have been made in this chambering. In the early 1990s, Heym, of Germany, introduced the Magnum Express bolt-action rifle in this chambering. Components for handloading are available from A-Square (http://a-squareco.com/), Barnes (www.barnesbullets.com), Huntington (www.huntingtons.com), Old Western Scrounger (www.ows-ammo.com), Bertram (carried through Buffalo Arms, www. buffaloarms.com), and Woodleigh (www.woodleighbullets.com.au/).

General Comments: At one time, the .600 Nitro Express was the most powerful commercial rifle cartridge in the world, but now the .700 Nitro Express overshadows it. The .600 was designed to deliver the maximum possible stopping power against elephants under the most difficult and dangerous conditions. Even professional ivory hunters considered it overpowered for anything but emergency use. It is said that a head shot that missed the brain of an elephant would still knock it down for a considerable length of time—according to John Taylor, up to 30 minutes. Rifles for the .600 usually weighed 16 pounds or more.

There were at least three loadings for the cartridge— at 2050, 1950, and 1850 fps. It is necessary to use the rifle's designated load, or the two barrels will not shoot to the same point of impact. The 2.8-inch version of 1899 may have only been a developmental stage of this outstanding big cartridge. A-Square and Barnes offer appropriate bullets and A-Square loads factory .600 NE ammunition.

.600 Nitro Express Factory Ballistics

Bullet (grains/type)	Powder	Grains	Velocity	Energy	Source/Comments
900 SP/FMJ	Cordite	120.0	2050	8400	Factory load
900 SP/FMJ	Cordite	110.0	1950	7600	Factory load
900 SP/FMJ	Cordite	100.0	1850	6840	Factory load
900	(various)		1950	7600	A-Square factory load *

*A-Square will custom-load this ammunition to match the velocity of the load for which the rifle was originally regulated.

.700 Nitro Express

Historical Notes: The .700 Nitro Express is a new cartridge, an original design not based on altering the caliber or configuration of an existing cartridge. It was developed, in 1988, by Jim Bell, of Bell Basic Brass (formerly Brass Extrusion Laboratories, Ltd., and now MAST Technology, Inc.; www.masttechnology. com), and William Feldstein, of Beverly Hills, California. It was chambered in a limited number of double-barrel rifles made by Holland & Holland.

The round came about, because Feldstein wanted H&H to build him a .600 Nitro Express. The company refused, because it had already completed its official last .600 NE some years before and wasn't interested in reviving the chambering. Bell and Feldstein then decided to approach H&H on the possibility of building a series of rifles in a new chambering, something completely different from anything previously made. Since H&H was actually looking for a big-bore cartridge, there was really only one way to go, and that was up. Thus, the .700 Nitro Express was born.

According to Jim Bell, the .700 is based on scaling up the old .600 Nitro using a totally new case, not only of larger diameter, but also a full ½-inch longer. This bullet is a true .700-inch diameter and

weighs 1,000 grains. (The originators planned to sell cased cartridges to collectors.) Although these rifles are very, very expensive, H&H has a continual backorder amounting to millions of dollars worth of .700 Nitro Expresses! On top of that, several years after the first .700 NE was built, in response to an unending din of protest from potential customers, H&H, after coming to terms with the owner of the "official last" .600 NE H&H rifle, went back into the business of building .600 NE-chambered double-barrel rifles.)

General Comments: A .70-caliber bullet weighing 1,000 grains with a muzzle velocity of 2000 fps generates a muzzle energy of 8900 ft-lbs of energy—this is certainly the most powerful sporting cartridge in the world. The Taylor Knockout Value is 200. It will, of course, be more than adequate for any game animal found anywhere on this planet. For those who insist on the biggest, this is it. The .700 H&H double-barrel rifles for this cartridge are very lively and handy, not at all cumbersome. These are fully usable, if costly, tools. However, keeping the weight of such a rifle down to a level that will allow the average hunter to use it properly guarantees that recoil will be quite heavy. A-Square (www.huntingtons.com) offers bullets, cases, and ammunition.

700 Nitro Express Factory Ballistics

Bullet (grains/type)	Powder	Grains	Velocity	Energy	Source/Comments
1,000 SP/FMJ	FL		2000	8900	A-Square factory load

Dimensional Data

Cartridge	Case	Bullet Dia.	Neck Dia.	Shoulder Dia.	Base Dia.	Rim Dia.	Rim Thick	Case Length	Ctge. Length	Berdan Primer Size/Kynoch #	Page
.297/230 Morris Extra Long	A	.223	.240	.274	.296	.248	UNK/NA	1.125	1.45	UNK/NA	403
.297/230 Morris Short	A	.225	.240	.274	.294	.347	UNK/NA	.58	.89	.177/69	403
.297/230 Morris Long	A	.225	.240	.274	.295	.345	UNK/NA	.80	1.1	.177/69	403
.244 H&H Magnum	E	.244	.263	.445	.508	.532	UNK/NA	2.78	3.58	.217/60	404
.240 Magnum Flanged	A	.245	.274	.402	.448	.513	UNK/NA	2.50	3.25	.217/81	404
.240 Magnum Rimless H&H (.240 Apex)	E	.245	.274	.403	.450	467	.035	2.49	3.21	.217/81	404
.297/250 Rook	A	.250	.267	.294	.295	.343	UNK/NA	.82	1.1	.177/69	404
.242 Rimless Nitro Express	C	.253	.281	.405	.465	.465	UNK/NA	2.38	3.20	.217/59	405
.275 Rigby (7x57mm)	C	.284	.324	.428	.474	.475	UNK/NA	2.24	3.07	.217	405
.275 Belted Magnum	E	.284	.325	.454	.513	.532	UNK/NA	2.50	3.42	.217/81	406
.275 Flanged Magnum	A	.284	UNK/NA	UNK/NA	UNK/NA	UNK/NA	UNK/NA	UNK/NA	UNK/NA	UNK/NA	406
.275 No. 2 Magnum	A	.284	.318	.450	.510	.582	UNK/NA	2.50	3.26	217	406
7mm Rigby Flanged Magnum	A	.284	.315	.406	.456	.524	UNK/NA	2.49	3.24	.243/34	406
.280 Flanged (.280 Lancaster)	A	.287	.316	.423	.535	.607	UNK/NA	2.60	3.62	.217/60	406
.280 Ross (.280 Rimless)	G	.287	.317	.404	.534	.556	UNK/NA	2.59	3.50	.217/59	407
.280 Jeffery (.33/280 Jeffery)	C	.288	.317	.504	.542	.538	UNK/NA	2.50	3.45	.217/59	407
.300 Belted Rimless Magnum	E	.308	.338	.447	.513	.530	UNK/NA	2.85	3.60	.217/60	408
.30 Flanged Magnum (H&H Super .30)	A	.308	.338	.450	.517	.572	UNK/NA	2.93	3.69	UNK/NA	408
.375/303 Westley Richards (Axite)	A	.311	.343	.390	.457	.505	UNK/NA	2.50	3.36	UNK/NA	408
.303 British	A	.312	.340	.401	.460	.540	UNK/NA	2.21	3.05	UNK/NA	409
.303 Magnum	C	.312	.345	.462	.530	.557	UNK/NA	2.35	3.25	UNK/NA	409
.310 Cadet (.310 Greener)	B	.324	.320	UNK/NA	.353	.405	.035	1.12	1.72	.177/69	409
.318 Rimless Nitro Express	C	.330	.358	.445	.465	.465	UNK/NA	2.39	3.40	.217/81	410
.333 Jeffery Rimless	C	.333	.359	.496	.540	.538	UNK/NA	2.48	3.48	.217/59	410
.333 Jeffery Flanged	A	.333	.356	.484	.544	.625	UNK/NA	2.50	3.49	.317	410
.33 BSA	E	.338	.369	.453	.534	.534	UNK/NA	2.40	3.10	.217/59	411
.400/350 Rigby	A	.358	.380	.415	.470	.520	UNK/NA	2.75	3.60	.241/34	411
.350 Rigby Magnum	C	.358	.380	.443	.519	.525	UNK/NA	2.75	3.60	.241/34	412
.350 No. 2 Rigby	A	.358	.380	.415	.470	.520	.050	2.75	3.60	.241/34	412
.400/360 Nitro Express (2¾-inch)	A	.358	.375	.437	.470	.590	UNK/NA	2.75	3.59	.241	412
.360 No. 5 Rook	B	.362	.375	UNK/NA	.380	.432	UNK/NA	1.05	1.45	UNK/NA	413
.360 Express (2¼-inch)	B	.365	.384	UNK/NA	.430	.480	.040	2.25	3.00	.241/34	413
.360 Nitro (2¼-inch)	B	.365	.384	UNK/NA	.430	.480	.040	2.25	2.80	.241/34	413

Dimensional Data

Cartridge	Case	Bullet Dia.	Neck Dia.	Shoulder Dia.	Base Dia.	Rim Dia.	Rim Thick	Case Length	Ctge. Length	Berdan Primer Size/Kynoch #	Page
.360 No. 2 Nitro Express	A	.367	.393	.517	.539	.631	.045	3.00	3.85	.254/40	414
.375 Flanged Nitro Express (2½-inch)	B	.375	.397	–	.456	.523	UNK/NA	2.50	3.10	.217/34	414
.400/375 Belted Nitro Express (H&H)	E	.375	.397	.435	.470	.466	UNK/NA	2.50	3.00	.217	414
.375 Rimless Nitro Express 2¼ (9.5x57mm)	C	.375	.400	.460	.471	.473	.40	2.25	2.94	.217	415
.369 Nitro Express (Purdey)	A	.375	.398	.475	.543	.616	UNK/NA	2.69	3.60	.254/40	415
.375 Flanged Magnum	A	.375	.404	.450	.515	.572	UNK/NA	2.94	3.80	.217/40	415
.375 Rimless Belted Magnum	E	.375	.404	.440	.464	.530	UNK/NA	2.85	3.60	.217/60	415
.400 H&H Magnum	C/E	.411	.441	.492	.513	.532	.050	2.846	3.55	L	416
.450/400 Nitro Express (3¼-inch) & BPE	A	.405	.432	.502	.544	.615	.040	3.25	3.85	.254/40	417
.450/400 (2⅜-inch)	A	.407	.427	.456	.545	.616	.035	2.38	2.95	UNK/NA	417
.400 Jeffery Nitro Express (.450/400 3-inch)	A	.410	.434	.518	.545	.613	UNK/NA	3.00	3.75	.254/40	418
.416 Rigby	C	.416	.445	.539	.589	.589	.062	2.90	3.72	Bx	418
.404 Jeffery (.404 Rimless Nitro Express)	C	.422	.450	.520	.544	.537	.045	2.87	3.53	.217/81	419
.425 Westley Richards Magnum	I	.435	.456	.540	.543	.467	UNK/NA	2.64	3.30	UNK/NA	419
.500/450 No. 2 Musket	A	.458	.486	.535	.576	.658	UNK/NA	2.36	2.90	UNK/NA	420
.500/450 No. 1 Express	A	.458	.485	.530	.577	.660	UNK/NA	2.75	3.38	.241/31A	420
.450 3¼-inch BPE	A	.405	.432	UNK/NA	UNK/NA	UNK/NA	UNK/NA	UNK/NA	UNK/NA	.254/inch	421
.450 Nitro Express (3¼-inch)	B	.458	.479		.545	.624	.040	3.25	4.11	.254/40	421
.500/450 Magnum Express BPE (3¼-inch)	A	.458	.479	.500	.570	.644	UNK/NA	3.25	3.91	.254/40	422
.500/450 Nitro Express (3¼-inch)	A	.458	.479	.500	.570	.644	UNK/NA	3.25	3.91	.254/40	422
.450 No. 2 Nitro Express (3½-inch)	A	.458	.477	.518	.564	.650	UNK/NA	3.50	4.42	.254/40	423
.450 Rigby	B	.458	.475	.539	.589	.589	UNK/NA	2.90	3.80	Bx	423
.465 H&H Magnum	F	.468	.494	.531	.582	.579	UNK/NA	UNK/NA	UNK/NA	UNK/NA	423
.500/465 Nitro Express	A	.466	.488	.524	.573	.650	UNK/NA	3.25	3.89	.254/40	424
.470 Nitro Express	A	.475	.500	.528	.572	.646	.035	3.25	4.00	.254/40	424
.476 Nitro Express/Westley Richards	A	.476	.508	.530	.570	.643	UNK/NA	3.00	3.77	.254/40	425
.475 Nitro Express (3¼-inch)	B	.483	.502	UNK/NA	.545	.621	UNK/NA	3.25	4.00	.254/40	425
.475 No. 2 Nitro Express/Jeffery	A	.489	.510	.547	.576	.666	UNK/NA	3.50	4.33	.254/40	425
.505 Gibbs	C	.505	.530	.588	.635	.635	UNK/NA	3.15	3.85	.254/40	426
.577/500 No. 2 BPE	A	.507	.538	.560	.641	.726	.055	2.83	3.40	.251/31A	426
.577/500 Nitro Express (3⅛-inch)	A	.508	.526	.585	.645	.717	.055	3.13	3.74	.251/31A	427
.500 Express Nitro For Black (3-inch)	B	.510	.535	UNK/NA	.580	.660	.055	3.01	3.39	.251/31A	427
.500 Nitro Express (3¼-inch)	B	.510	.535	UNK/NA	.580	.660	.040	3.25	3.63	.251/31A	428
.500 Nitro Express (3-inch)	B	.510	.535	UNK/NA	.580	.660	UNK/NA	3.00	3.80	.251/31A	428
.500 Jeffery	I	.510	.535	.615	.620	.575	UNK/NA	2.75	3.47	.254/40	428
.577 BPE	B	.584	.608	UNK/NA	.660	.748	.052	3.25	UNK/NA	.254/40	429
.577 Nitro Express	B	.584	.608	UNK/NA	.660	.748	.052	3.00	3.70	.254/40	429
.600 Nitro Express	B	.620	.648	UNK/NA	.697	.805	UNK/NA	3.00	3.68	.254/40	430
.700 Nitro Express	B	.700	.728	UNK/NA	.780	.890	UNK/NA	3.50	4.20	Bx	430

Case Type: A = Rimmed, bottleneck. B = Rimmed, straight. C = Rimless, bottleneck. D = Rimless, straight. E = Belted, bottleneck. F = Belted, straight. G = Semi-rimmed, bottleneck. H = Semi-rimmed, straight. I = Rebated, bottleneck. J = Rebated, straight. K = Rebated, belted bottleneck. L = Rebated, belted straight.

Primer Type: B = Berdan. Bx = Boxer. RF = Rimfire.

Other codes: Unless otherwise noted, all dimensions in inches. Dimensions shown in some instances do not exactly coincide with dimensions found in *The Book of Rifles* (W.H.B. Smith, Harrisburg, Pa., 1960). Differences amount to only a few thousandths of an inch, doubtless attributable to specimen variations. Parentheses indicate maximum cartridge specifications. UNK/NA = Unknown/Not Available

AR-15 Cartridges
CONTINUALLY EVOLVING BY J. GUTHRIE

More often than not, in the world of new cartridges, someone who has a fanciful idea to reach a new ballistic plateau comes up with a cartridge, and then gunmakers respond in kind with firearms adapted or designed around the new round. Quite often, the evolution is parallel. The .500 Smith & Wesson and the X-frame revolver are good examples; the pair was conceived and born together. But the AR-15, more than any other rifle in history, has broken that mold and reversed the development path of norm. In the last decade especially, a plethora of new cartridges have appeared that were designed just for the AR-15.

Quite a lot of the rounds came from military ballisticians and ammunition companies trying to improve on the 5.56X45mm NATO's battlefield lethality—or lack thereof. Long-range shooters and competitors also sought to improve on the much-maligned 5.56, those marksmen seeking a projectile fired from that particular rifle that had enough gas to stay supersonic longer and slip the wind better. Hunters, too, are using the AR-15 to tackle any and all of North America's small and big game, and still another set of developmental talent wanted to give shooters the option to tackle big game or stop a vehicle or boat in its tracks via big-bore hunting and interdiction rounds.

The AR-15 platform as become the most popular rifle in the world, and even though most are chambered for the .223 Remington/5.56 NATO cartridge, many other cartridges are now available for this versatile rifle.

AR-15 Cartridges

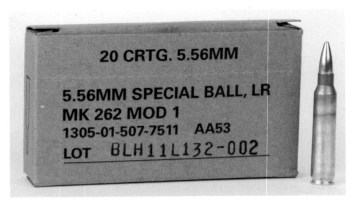

The .5.56 X 45mm/.223 Remington. This is the cartridge that started it all, when it comes to the AR 15. It is still the most popular, but its stablemates are ever increasing.

There are two basic limiting factors when it comes to cartridges for the AR 15; they have to fit into the AR's magazine and the rim diameter needs to be less than about .495-inch in diameter.

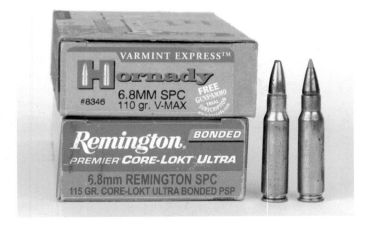

The first cartridge to really spark modern AR 15 cartridge development was the 6.8 Remington SPC. Not only is it a practical cartridge, it has provided another case for wildcatters to work with.

It seems the only limit for engineers, ballisticians, wildcatters, hunters, and shooters has ben making a new round fit in the rifle's magazine—and it is *amazing* what will fit in an AR magazine.

One of the reasons the AR-15 has proven so popular with shooters and spawned this new crop of purpose-built cartridges is the gun's inherent ability to easily adapt to just about any military or police, hunting, shooting, or competition mission. With a steady trickle of improvements since the rifle's adoption by the U.S. military in the early 1960s, the AR-15 has evolved into a rifle that is extremely reliable, accurate and, most importantly, adaptable. The rifle's relatively simple design also made it a natural platform for experimentation.

5.56X45mm NATO

It might seem odd to include the 5.56 NATO here, since it is the most popular AR-15 cartridge and the current military chambering, but the round has undergone considerable changes since its adoption. There are essentially two classes of this cartridge. The first and original class features light bullets like the 55-grain found in the M193 round. The second, epitomized by the Mk 262, Mod 0, and Mod 1 rounds developed by Black Hills, uses heavier bullets for long-range, precision shooting.

Built for the U.S. Navy's Mk 12 SPR and now coveted by snipers and designated marksmen using similar rifles, the Mk 262's 77-grain Sierra MatchKing projectile has a listed effective range of 600 yards, though it has certainly been put to use at longer ranges. It achieves velocities around 2,750 feet per second (fps) from 18-inch barrels and benefits from advanced propellants. Hornady loads a 75-grain hollowpoint boat-tail bullet in its .223 TAP line with similar specs.

These four popular AR-15 cartridges show the versatility the platform offers. From left to right - .223 Remington, 6.5 Grendel, 6.8 Remington SPC and .450 Bushmaster.

Slower 1:7 twist rates are required to stabilize the heavier/longer bullets. Once they strike soft tissue, the bullets yaw and usually fragment to some degree, greatly increasing lethality over that of the more widely issued rounds like the M855 62-grain Penetrator or Green Tip. Serendipitously, the bigger bullets also perform quite well at close-quarters distances, when fired from short-barreled rifles like the Mk 18 (10.3-inch barrel) fielded by entry teams.

Shooters of all types have benefited from the military's extensive efforts to improve on the 5.56mm NATO round, and now we have ammo options that extend the range and increase accuracy and lethality.

Intermediate Cartridges

The most obvious way to improve lethality or increase a rifle's maximum effective range is to use a larger cartridge, but that usually calls for a bigger rifle. It's easy enough to lengthen a commercial rifle's receiver a fraction of an inch, but, with several million M-16 and M-4

Though the 6.5 Grendel (right) offers a substantial ballistic improvement over the .223 Remington (left), its fat case does drastically limit magazine capacity.

rifles on hand, those hoping to get into the military supply chain needed to do so with a round that fit in a standard Mil-Spec magazine. That set a lot of talented designers and ballisticians to work and produced a whole gaggle of really clever, useful cartridges.

Probably the most successful and popular round is the 6.8mm Special Purpose Cartridge. After the 5.56's lackluster performance in Afghanistan, in 2001, U.S. Special Operations Command shooters worked to come up with something better that still worked in an M4. They did some experimentation with PPC cartridges, but designers finally settled on the obsolete .30 Remington case, because of its smaller rim diameter. There was enough case capacity to push 110- and 115-grain bullets to velocities substantially beyond what the 7.62X39mm could produce with 123-grain FMJ bullets. Swapping calibers was an armorer-level job that required only a barrel, bolt, and magazine change.

The 6.8mm SPC worked like a charm for close- and long-range engagements, producing far better results than that experienced with the 5.56 mm. Why the round was not adopted by units outside of SOCOM is anyone's guess. Several U.S. manufacturers started producing commercial ammunition with open-tipped match, polymer-tipped, and hunting bullets, and nearly every AR manufacturer soon had a 6.8 in their catalog. Hunters have found the round perfect for whitetails and other medium-sized game, when the shots fall inside 300 yards. And, while the 6.8 mm SPC is

The .264 LBC-AR and the 6.5 Grendel cartridges are interchangeable. It's very likely the Grendel will, however, make the .264 LBC-AR extinct, due to the Grendel's recent standardization by SAAMI.

not the U.S. Military's next service round, it is now firmly entrenched in the AR-15 shooting community. The round is now the second-most popular AR-15 chambering. One of the more versatile intermediate rounds is the 6.5 mm Grendel developed by Bill Alexander, of Alexander Arms. He took a 6mm PPC case, shortened the neck, moved the shoulder forward, and increased the diameter to take advantage of all those 6.5mm bullets with their superb ballistic coefficients. The end result is a cartridge that can better the 5.56 NATO—or 7.62 NATO for that matter—in just about every category. The Grendel is also a capable competition round, one with the reach to compete at the 1,000-yard line, something the 6.8 mm SPC cannot do. With properly constructed bullets, it is a great varmint or medium-game hunting round.

Factory ammunition runs from 90 to 130 grains and is loaded by Hornady, Alexander Arms, Wolf, and Black Hills, though the latter is headstamped .264 LBC-AR. Alexander Arms recently relinquished the trademark claim, which recently lead to the Grendel's SAMMI standardization, which should open the doors for more companies to produce ammunition.

Americans have an affinity for anything .30-caliber, so it was a foregone conclusion a .30-caliber cartridge for ARs would

AR-15 Cartridges

The AR 15, mostly when matched with the .223 Remington, has become the most-used rifle in the ever growing sport of 3-gun competition.

hunting rounds, with minimal recoil and reasonable trajectories out to 200 yards.

A cartridge originally built for SOCOM/JSOC units, the Blackout is also loaded with 208- and 220-grain bullets that never break the sound barrier. The two vastly different bullet weights allow operators to initiate ambushes or handle sentry duty quietly, before swapping magazines to go head-to-head with AK-47s at ranges beyond 300 yards—with a rifle that has a nine-inch barrel.

In the world of AR cartridges, the .30 Remington AR is one of the few not conceived with martial aspirations. It was designed from the start by Remington engineers as a hunting cartridge, a way to fit .308 Winchester performance into an AR-15 and avoid the less svelte AR-10. This round essentially picks up where the 6.8mm SPC left off, able to achieve around 2,750 fps with 123- and 125-grain bullets from 22-inch barrels. The cartridge is a handloader's dream and a favorite of this edition's editor. In fact, Richard Mann puts the .30 RAR in a class by itself, deeming it one of the best AR hunting cartridges extant.

With its inherent modularity, combined with a wide array of cartridges, the AR 15 is the most versatile rifle on the planet. Suitable for law enforcement, military, sport shooting, and hunting, it excels at all of them.

eventually make an appearance. Actually, several .30-caliber AR cartridges have burst onto the scene recently, including the .300 Blackout, 7.62X40mm Wilson Tactical, and .30 Remington AR.

The .300 Blackout and 7.62X40mm WT both are based on 5.56 NATO brass and are loaded with a variety of bullets suited to a variety of tasks. The concept is an old one and was standardized to a degree by J.D. Jones, of SSK Industries, who used .221 Fireball brass and trademarked the .300 Whisper. The Blackout and Whisper are interchangeable to a degree, with Blackout rounds firing safely in Whisper chambers. In short-barreled PDWs (personal defense weapons) the .30-caliber bullet is much more effective than either 5.56 or 9 mm bullets. When fired through 16-inch barrels, the cartridges make fine

good, solid bullets and a lightweight AR carbine fed from a high-capacity detachable magazine. Pair the rifle with a weapons light and a 1X-optic like an Aimpoint, Trijicon, or EOTech, and you might have the perfect guide's gun for backing up hunters or tracking wounded bears in Alaska. It weighs less, provides more firepower, and permits faster follow-up shots than most other rifle actions.

The Future

This chapter honestly just scratches the surface of AR cartridges and has covered some of the more common factory chamberings specifically designed around the AR-15. Nearly anything that could squeeze its way through the magazine well has been tried, including the Winchester Super Short Magnums. *The 13th Edition of Cartridges of the World* has several new AR-15 cartridges like the .358 Gremlin, which are designed specifically to meet the state of Indiana's centerfire rifle deer hunting restrictions. And you can bet the *14th Edition* will have even more. Heck, bolt-action up-

Some doubt that an AR-15 can be used for game as large as this 200-plus pound black bear. However, Remington's .30 AR cartridge has taken the AR-15 to the next level, with ballistics that match that of the legendary .300 Savage cartridge.

Big-Bore ARs

At varying points in the last decade, several enterprising souls looked into an AR magazine and thought to fill it up completely with one massive cartridge instead of a couple little ones. The resulting cartridges—the .450 Bushmaster, .458 SOCOM, and .50 Beowulf, among others—are big league heavy hitters. They all use a rebated rim to fit inside a standard AR bolt head and generally run at pressures well below that of the 5.56mm. The only real concern with fitting cartridges of this size in an AR resides in the bolt thrust and making sure the gas port is both the right size and sits in the right place for reliable function. All three rounds obviously produce substantially more recoil than 5.56mm rifles, but the rifle seems up to the task. (Scope mounts are another matter.)

Rifle manufacturers seem to have divvied up the calibers between themselves, with Rock River Arms building .458 SOCOM rifles, Bushmaster producing the .450 Bushmaster, and Alexander Arms building rifles chambered for the cartridge it invented.

Ammunition is a little hard to find and, in some cases, expensive, but available. Reloaders usually prefer the SOCOM over the Bushmaster and Beowulf, because the wider selection of available bullets.

The .458 and .50 were envisioned as interdiction and barrier-beating rounds for stopping cars at roadblocks and ventilating two-legged predators hiding behind cinderblock walls and the like. It seems most shooters use these big-boress to turn mobile pork into stationary pork. The rounds are also ideal for close-range bear hunting or hitting anything with bullets weighing in excess of 250 grains and moving over 2,000 fps. Most Beowulf loads produce over 2,900 foot-pounds (ft-lbs) of muzzle energy.

Imagine the possibilities of combining one of these big-bore cartridges loaded with

As of now, the .30 Remington AR cartridge offers the best balance of power and external ballistics of any AR-15 cartridge. With bullets between 110 and 150 grains, it is suitable for big game to around 300 yards.

pers chambered for .50 BMG are available for the truly adventurous AR-15 owner. Who knows what else is to come?

As propellant and bullet technologies advance, expect to see has-been cartridges revisited and revamped. Somewhere, someoner will need a round tailored to a very specific purpose, and it is very likely an AR-15, M-16, or M-4 will be able to chamber that round and get the job done better than any other rifle around. All that is needed is for some enterprising wildcatter to step up and design the next best thing. ∎

SAAMI

SPORTING ARMS AND AMMUNITION MANUFACTURERS INSTITUTE BY JOHN HAVILAND

American shooters and hunters can buy a box of .30-06 cartridges produced by Federal, Hornady, or other ammunition manufacturers and fire them confidently and safely in rifles produced by Remington, Ruger, or other firearm makers. That reliable interchangeability of ammunition is entirely the result of the work of the Sporting Arms and Ammunition Manufacturers' Institute, Inc. (SAAMI), which is an association of the nation's leading manufacturers of firearms, ammunition, and components.

Decades ago, that wasn't the case. At the turn of the last century and into the 1920s, the American firearms and ammunition industry was shifting from an era of cartridges loaded with blackpowder to an increasing number of new cartridges loaded with smokeless propellants. Confusion with cartridge names was common. For example, the .40-60 Winchester and the .40-60 Marlin are different cartridges. However, the .40-*65* Winchester and .40-*60* Marlin *are* interchangeable and both can be fired in the same rifle. Perhaps the low pressures generated by blackpowder were a bit more forgiving of firing a cartridge that failed to conform to a rifle chamber, but the higher pressures generated by smokeless powders were not.

"Back then, there were really no safety or reliability standards," said

Factory-loaded cartridges of the same cartridge designation, suchas these .458 Winchester rounds, are within SAAMI specifications and are therefore interchangeable in a variety of firearms for that given cartridge, no matter which American company produces the cartridges.

Rick Patterson, the managing director of SAAMI. "One company's cartridges might work in their firearms, but not even fit in another company's gun chambered for the same cartridge! Essentially, everyone was wildcatting."

To rectify the problem, SAAMI was founded, in 1926, at the request of the Federal Government, its mission to create and coordinate firearm and ammunition industry standards for cartridge interchangeability, safety, reliability, and quality. Because firearms and ammunition are not regulated by the U.S. Consumer Product Safety Commission, SAAMI is a voluntary safety association comprised of the nation's leading manufacturers of sporting firearms, ammunition, and cartridge components. SAAMI members include firearms companies like Browning, Colt's, Marlin, Mossberg, Remington, Ruger, Savage, and Smith & Wesson, and ammunition manufacturers like Federal, Hornady, and Olin-Winchester.

When a company submits a new cartridge for SAAMI approval, it must provide quite a bit of data about the cartridge to start the acceptance process. Data includes cartridge and chamber dimensions, bullet diameter, and maximum average pressure limits, among other information.

"All members of the SAMMI Technical Committee go through the information with a fine-toothed comb, to make sure there are no errors," Patterson said. "From there, the information goes to Ammunition Committee for review to make sure, among other things, the cartridge differs from other established cartridges, and

ABOVE: Although .223 Remington cartridges are manufactured by a variety companies, they all fit and fire safely in firearms chambered for the .223. American shooters can thank SAAMI for that.

CENTER: American ammunition companies make dozens and dozens of different styles of .22 Long Rifle cartridges. All of them, though, will fit and fire in a variety of .22 LR firearms from full-sized rifles on down to handguns like this Colt Woodsman.

BOTTOM: When a shooter chambers a factory cartridge like this 7mm Remington Magnum in his rifle he can thank SAAMI that it will chamber and fire safely.

SAAMI specifications require factory-loaded cartridges to meet specific case and bullet dimensions (left). SAAMI specifications also helped standardize such old cartridges as the .220 Swift (bottom).

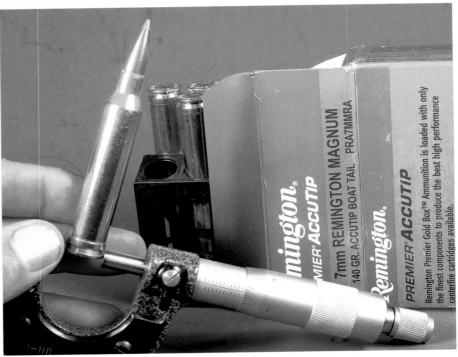

then it goes on to the Firearms Committee to make sure the cartridge works in firearms." Finally, a Joint Committee of the three sub-committees gives final approval to the cartridge. All this review may take up to six months.

"Once approved, the sponsoring company provides ammunition for the approved cartridge for use in our reference ammunition program," Patterson explained. "That ammunition is then fired in the test labs of different companies to calibrate their testing equipment, so that everyone's testing equipment is calibrated the same." (SAAMI recognizes two pressure measuring systems. The preferred is the piezoelectric transducer system, where pressure is measured in pounds per square inch (psi). The other and older system is the copper crusher method, where pressure is expressed in copper units of pressure (CUP).

These cartridge approval committees, and other SAAMI committees, are made up of volunteers from SAAMI member employees.

"We have only three full-time employees," Patterson said, "but, we have 150 volunteers from member companies, and many consultants."

SAAMI does not test propellants used by handloaders to reload cartridges and shotshells.

"Really, our only guidelines for propellants are that they do not exceed the maximum average pressure for a particular cartridge," Patterson said. "That leaves a lot of innovative room to come up with a better cartridge design."

Nor does SAMMI test firearms.

"We only proof ammunition, as in 'here are the dimensions and the maximum average pressure at which it is loaded.' That provides lots of room for innovation on the part of the firearm manufacturer to come up with any firearm that will handle the cartridge and work safely within its pressure limits."

That lack of firearm testing is one of many differences between SAAMI and its European counterpart, the Permanent International Commission for Firearm Testing (CIP). CIP is an international

LEFT: This device measures pressure via the copper crusher system. A pressure barrel is inserted and a small cylinder of copper is positioned over the cartridge case. The pressure generated in the chamber then crushes the copper cylinder.

BELOW: These itty bitty copper cylinders are used in the copper crusher pressure measuring system. The shorter cylinder on the left has been crushed during the testing process and will be measured to determine the amount of pressure that compressed it.

organization comprised of 14 mainly European countries made up of a gathering of national proof houses sponsored by those countries' governments.

"How should I say this in a politically correct way?" Patterson posed to me when we spoke. "Europe has socialized medicine, so those governments figure they will end up footing the bill for the mistakes people make with all products, including firearms, so they figure they might as well have a hand in safeguarding firearms and ammunition."

Before a civilian firearm is sold in any of the CIP member countries, it is tested for safety in one of the proof houses by firing higher than normal pressure, or "proof," loads. Firearms that pass the test are stamped with a proof mark specific to that proof house. Ammunition is also tested at regular intervals, to ensure it meet pressure guidelines.

"In the United States system, the government doesn't have such a stake in such things as they do in Europe. But we do have a legal system that assesses high punitive penalties and financial awards." said Patterson. "SAAMI approval of a cartridge provides consumers with a measure of confidence that, not only will the cartridge fit firearms chambered for it, but will fire safely.

SAAMI endorsement of a cartridge also provides manufacturers with some legal and liability protection, because they can point to the fact it was loaded to SAMMI specifications."

Several of SAMMI's committees also have their hats in the political ring. The Legal and Legislative Affairs Committee tracks the development of state and federal product liability laws and legislation that may impact the design, manufacture, and sale of firearms, ammunition, and propellants by SAAMI member companies. The Committee actively represents SAAMI members in Washington, D.C., before Congress, the Executive Branch, the Bureau of Alcohol, Tobacco, Firearms, and Explosives, the Federal Bureau of Investigation's National Instant Criminal Background Check System, and other federal regulatory agencies.

"We're always willing to provide technical information, because we wouldn't want any politician to make decisions in a void of accurate technical information," Patterson said.

According to SAAMI's website, the Legal and Legislative Affairs Committee also monitors state legislative proposals. For example, the Committee played a leading role in defeating sever-

al California bills, including bullet serialization and firearms micro-stamping legislation that, while well-intentioned, were neither realistic nor workable. Had these bills passed, they would have had disastrous consequence for law enforcement, citizens, and SAAMI member companies alike.

The Committee is proactive, too, working to advance legislation consistent with SAAMI's mission. For example, the Committee worked together with a strong coalition of business groups, shooting sports organizations, and the conservation community to win passage in Congress of the Protection of Lawful Commerce in Arms, a law that blocks "junk" lawsuits that would blame firearm manufactures for the actions of criminals.

The Environmental Committee, meanwhile, examines environmental issues affecting the shooting sports by analyzing and collecting data and offering policy proposals to regulatory agencies and the shooting public. Responding to concerns about lead and lead mobility at shooting ranges, for example, SAAMI commissioned E.A. Engineering, Science and Technology, Inc., to prepare a literature search on the issue.

The SAAMI Logistics and Regula-

RIGHT and FAR RIGHT: The ballistic lab at Western Powders is equipped with a piezoelectric transducer system. It is a higher tech version of the copper crusher system.

BELOW: Pressure testing requires a properly chambered pressure barrel for every cartridge tested. Here are just a few of the pressure test barrels at the Western Powders laboratory.

tory Affairs Committee (SLARAC) works to shape the constantly evolving transportation and storage regulations, both international and domestic, so that SAAMI products can be distributed economically, securely, and safely throughout the world. SLARAC works closely with domestic and international regulatory bodies. Nationally, this involves the Federal Departments of Commerce, State, Transportation, Labor, Homeland Security, and Justice.

The SLARC produces much information that is readily available to any shooter, range, shooting club, or law enforcement agency that is interested. SLARAC brochures include "Lead Mobility, Small Arms Ammunition (Properties & Recommendations for Storage & Handling)," "Smokeless Powder (Properties & Storage)," "Sporting Ammunition Primers (Properties, Handling & Storage for Handloading)," and "Sporting Firearms (Safe Handling Considerations and Shipping Guidelines for Interstate Transportation)." SAAMI also publishes informational and firearms safety pamphlets like "A Century of Success in Reducing Firearms Accidents," "A Responsible Approach to Firearms Safety," and "Unsafe Firearm-Ammunition Combinations."

Of most interest to shooters and hunters are SAAMI's books that detail industry standards for centerfire pistol and revolver and rifle cartridges, rimfire cartridges, and shotshells. These books, such as *Centerfire Pistol & Revolver* and

Rimfire, include explanations of pressure measuring systems, velocity versus barrel length data, cartridge maximum average pressure, and detailed cartridge and chamber drawings with minimum and maximum dimensions.

For example, the .357 Magnum has a maximum average pressure of 35,000 pounds per square inch firing 125-grain jacketed soft-point bullets at 1,475 fps from a four-inch ventilated barrel. Conversely, the .22 Long Rifle standard velocity load shooting a 40-grain solid lead bullet has a velocity of 1,135 fps with a maximum average pressure of 24,000 psi. Interestingly, the chamber drawings in the *Rimfire* book show a .22 LR match chamber is .1875-inch shorter than the .22 Long Rifle sporting chamber. No matter, though, because all .22 LR cartridges will fit and fire safely in all .22 LR chambers. Shooters can thank SAAMI for that positive interchangeability of all brands of .22 rimfires and, for that matter, all other cartridges in their appropriate chambers. Not only

that, SAAMI safeguards shooters' rights by keeping an eye on the political climate and backdoor attempts to limit the sale of firearms and ammunition.

In short, SAAMI is the organization that dictates the standards for ammunition manufacture. Conformity to SAAMI specifications, however, is not mandatory. A lot of small, custom ammunition manufacturers do not verify there ammunition meets SAAMI standards. This does not mean the ammunition they produce *isn't* safe, just that it has not been verified to meet SAAMI specs.

An example would be companies like Buffalo Bore, which offers "Heavy" loads for the .45-70, .35 Remington, and other cartridges (their creation a response, in part, to the ongoing popularity of cowboy action shooting and the modern guns of the sport that can handle the increased pressures of these rounds). Generally, these companies post warnings on their ammunition boxes to keep these higher pressure loads from being fired in the weaker firearms (such as first

and second generation Colt SAAs and other older and antique firearms), that cause SAAMI to limit maximum operating pressures in the first place.

Some shooters will actually complain that SAAMI limits the performance of cartridges with these lower pressure limits. The .257 Roberts and the 7mm Mauser are perfect examples. With maximum average operating pressures of 54,000 and 51,000, respectively, both cartridges are indeed hindered. However, there are so many older rifles of questionable integrity chambered for either one of these cartridges that these limits are what keep shooters safe. (In modern bolt-action rifles, both the .257 Roberts and the 7mm Mauser can be safely loaded to pressures equivalent to more modern sporting cartridges like the .243 Winchester and the 7mm-08 Remington.) Taken in that light, it should be easy to see that SAAMI is indeed on the side of shooters, and it is an organization imperative to all, hobbiests, competitors, hunters, and all other shooters, that this book is about. ■

These cartridge and chamber schematics found on the following four pages are for the .22 LR, .357 Magnum, .30-06, and 12-gauge 2 ¾-inch are actual SAAMI drawings. These are the schematics used by ammunition and firearms manufacturers when they create ammunition or cut chambers in firearms for these cartridges. Note the minimum and maximum measurements. This explains some of the variance between listed cartridge dimensions in this volume and those that might be obtained when measuring actual cartridges. SAAMI has drawings like this for every SAAMI-approved cartridge. These drawings contain a great deal more information than is presented for each cartridge in this volume, which is intended to offer a basic guide to cartridge identification and history. You can visit the SAAMI web site, www.saami.org, to view drawings for all SAAMI-approved cartridges. (*Schematics Courtesy of SAAMI.*)

Click HERE to return to the Table of Contents

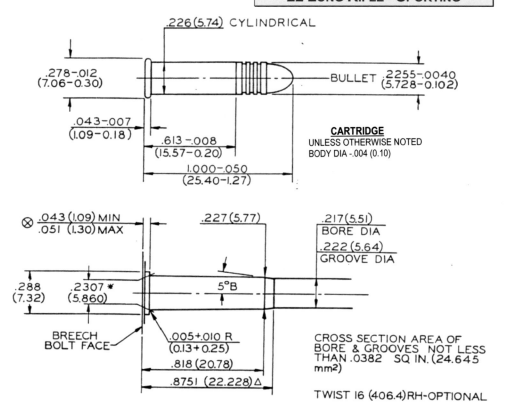

SPORTING ARMS AND AMMUNITION MANUFACTURERS' INSTITUTE, INC.
Since 1926

MAXIMUM CARTRIDGE / MINIMUM CHAMBER

22 LONG RIFLE - SPORTING

.226 (5.74) CYLINDRICAL

.278 -.012
(7.06 - 0.30)

BULLET .2255 -.0040
(5.728 - 0.102)

.043 -.007
(1.09 - 0.18)

.613 -.008
(15.57 - 0.20)

1.000 -.050
(25.40 - 1.27)

CARTRIDGE
UNLESS OTHERWISE NOTED
BODY DIA -.004 (0.10)

⊗ .043 (1.09) MIN
.051 (1.30) MAX

.227 (5.77)

.217 (5.51)
BORE DIA
.222 (5.64)
GROOVE DIA

.288
(7.32)

.2307 *
(5.860)

5°B

BREECH
BOLT FACE

.005 +.010 R
(0.13 +0.25)

.818 (20.78)

.8751 (22.228) Δ

CROSS SECTION AREA OF
BORE & GROOVES NOT LESS
THAN .0382 SQ IN. (24.645
mm2)

TWIST 16 (406.4) RH-OPTIONAL

CHAMBER
UNLESS OTHERWISE NOTED
ALL DIA +.002 (0.05)
LENGTH TOL +.015 (0.38)

NOTE
B = BASIC
(XX.XX) = MILLIMETERS   ⊗ = HEADSPACE DIMENSION
* DIMENSIONS ARE TO INTERSECTION OF LINES   Δ = REFERENCE DIMENSION
ALL CALCULATIONS APPLY AT MAXIMUM MATERIAL CONDITION (MMC)

Click HERE to return to the Table of Contents

S A A M I®

SPORTING ARMS AND AMMUNITION MANUFACTURERS' INSTITUTE, INC.
Since 1926

MAXIMUM CARTRIDGE / MINIMUM CHAMBER

357 MAGNUM

CARTRIDGE
UNLESS OTHERWISE NOTED
BODY DIA -.006 (0.15)

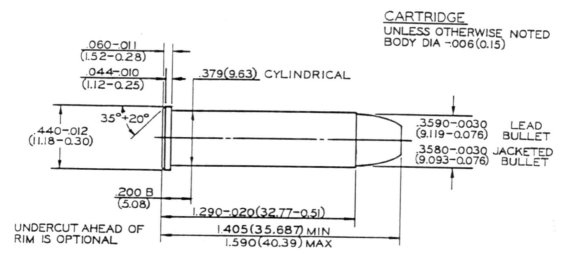

.060-.011 (1.52-0.28)

.044-.010 (1.12-0.25)

.379 (9.63) CYLINDRICAL

35°+20°

.440-.012 (11.18-0.30)

.3590-.0030 (9.119-0.076) LEAD BULLET

.3580-.0030 (9.093-0.076) JACKETED BULLET

.200 B (5.08)

UNDERCUT AHEAD OF RIM IS OPTIONAL

1.290-.020 (32.77-0.51)

1.405 (35.687) MIN
1.590 (40.39) MAX

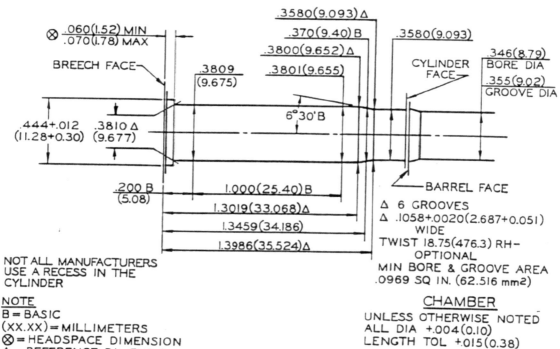

⊗ .060 (1.52) MIN
.070 (1.78) MAX

.3580 (9.093) △
.370 (9.40) B
.3800 (9.652) △
.3801 (9.655)

.3580 (9.093)

.346 (8.79) BORE DIA
.355 (9.02) GROOVE DIA

BREECH FACE

.3809 (9.675)

CYLINDER FACE

.444+.012 (11.28+0.30)

.3810 △ (9.677)

6°30'B

.200 B (5.08)

1.000 (25.40) B

BARREL FACE

1.3019 (33.068) △

△ 6 GROOVES

1.3459 (34.186)

△ .1058+.0020 (2.687+0.051) WIDE

1.3986 (35.524) △

TWIST 18.75 (476.3) RH-OPTIONAL

NOT ALL MANUFACTURERS USE A RECESS IN THE CYLINDER

MIN BORE & GROOVE AREA
.0969 SQ IN. (62.516 mm2)

NOTE
B = BASIC
(XX.XX) = MILLIMETERS
⊗ = HEADSPACE DIMENSION
△ = REFERENCE DIMENSION
* = DIMENSIONS ARE TO INTERSECTION OF LINES
ALL CALCULATIONS APPLY AT MAXIMUM MATERIAL CONDITION (MMC)

CHAMBER
UNLESS OTHERWISE NOTED
ALL DIA +.004 (0.10)
LENGTH TOL +.015 (0.38)

Click HERE to return to the
Table of Contents

SAAMI
SPORTING ARMS AND AMMUNITION MANUFACTURERS' INSTITUTE, INC.
Since 1926

MAXIMUM CARTRIDGE / MINIMUM CHAMBER

30-06 SPRINGFIELD

CARTRIDGE
UNLESS OTHERWISE NOTED
BODY DIA -.008 (0.20)

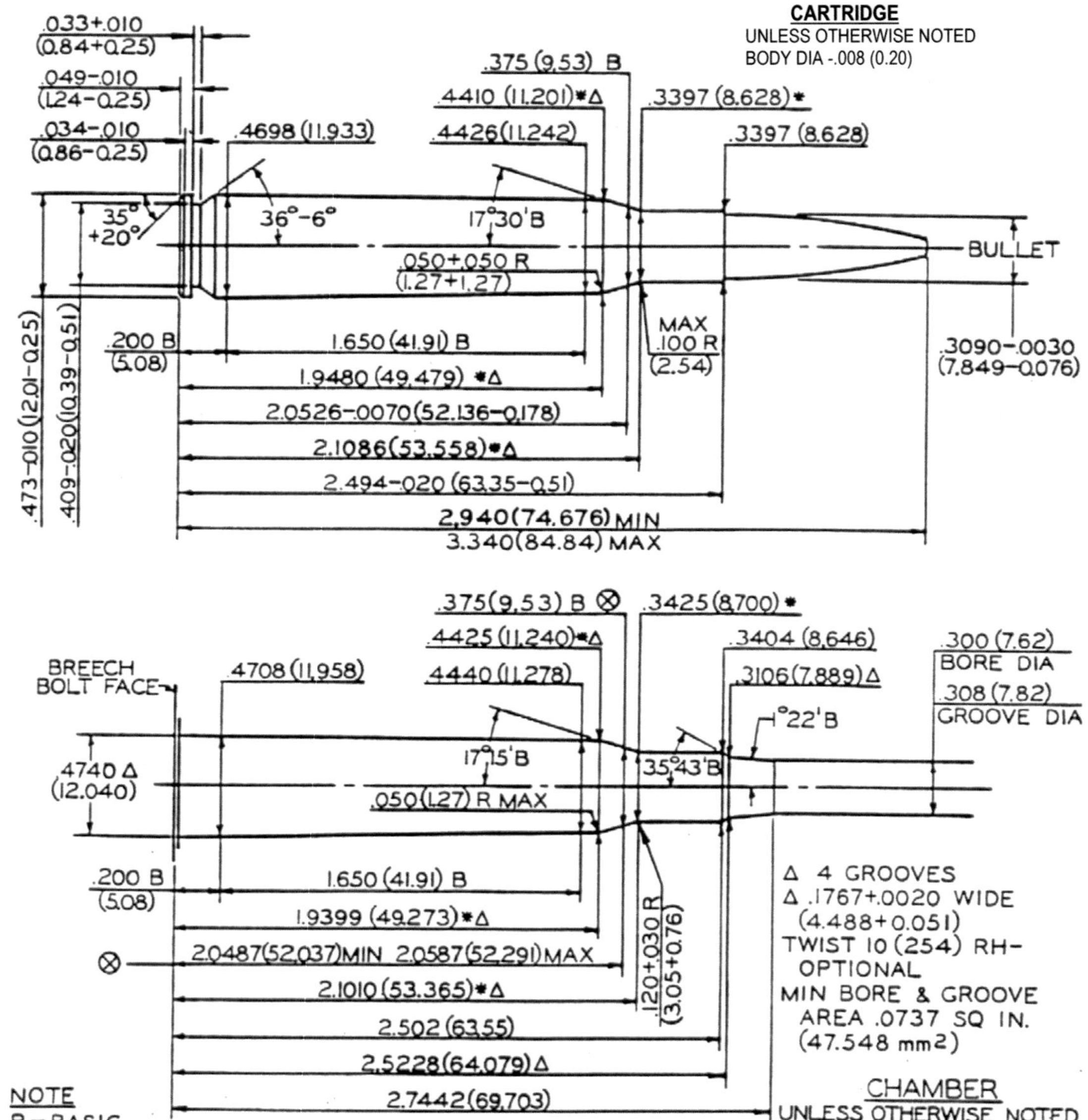

.033+.010 (0.84+0.25)
.049-.010 (1.24-0.25)
.034-.010 (0.86-0.25)
.4698 (11.933)
.375 (9.53) B
.4410 (11.201) *Δ
.4426 (11.242)
.3397 (8.628) *
.3397 (8.628)
35° +20°
36°-6°
17°30' B
BULLET
.050+.050 R (1.27+1.27)
.473-.010 (12.01-0.25)
.409-.020 (10.39-0.51)
.200 B (5.08)
1.650 (41.91) B
1.9480 (49.479) *Δ
2.0526-.0070 (52.136-0.178)
2.1086 (53.558) *Δ
2.494-.020 (63.35-0.51)
MAX .100 R (2.54)
.3090-.0030 (7.849-0.076)
2.940 (74.676) MIN
3.340 (84.84) MAX

.375 (9.53) B ⊗
.3425 (8700) *
.4425 (11.240) *Δ
.4440 (11.278)
.3404 (8.646)
.3106 (7.889) Δ
.300 (7.62) BORE DIA
.308 (7.82) GROOVE DIA
BREECH BOLT FACE
.4708 (11.958)
1°22' B
.4740 Δ (12.040)
17°15' B
35°43' B
.050 (1.27) R MAX
.200 B (5.08)
1.650 (41.91) B
1.9399 (49.273) *Δ
2.0487 (52.037) MIN 2.0587 (52.291) MAX
.120+.030 R (3.05+0.76)
2.1010 (53.365) *Δ
2.502 (63.55)
2.5228 (64.079) Δ
2.7442 (69.703)

Δ 4 GROOVES
Δ .1767+.0020 WIDE (4.488+0.051)
TWIST 10 (254) RH-OPTIONAL
MIN BORE & GROOVE AREA .0737 SQ IN. (47.548 mm2)

CHAMBER
UNLESS OTHERWISE NOTED
ALL DIA +.002 (0.05)
LENGTH TOL +.015 (0.38)

NOTE
B = BASIC
(XX.XX) = MILLIMETERS
⊗ = HEADSPACE DIMENSION
* DIMENSIONS ARE TO INTERSECTION OF LINES   Δ = REFERENCE DIMENSION
ALL CALCULATIONS APPLY AT MAXIMUM MATERIAL CONDITION (MMC)

Click HERE to return to the
Table of Contents

SAAMI¹
SPORTING ARMS AND AMMUNITION MANUFACTURERS' INSTITUTE, INC.
Since 1926

MAXIMUM CARTRIDGE / MINIMUM CHAMBER

12-GAUGE – 2¾"

CARTRIDGE
UNLESS OTHERWISE NOTED
LENGTH TOL -.250 (6.35)

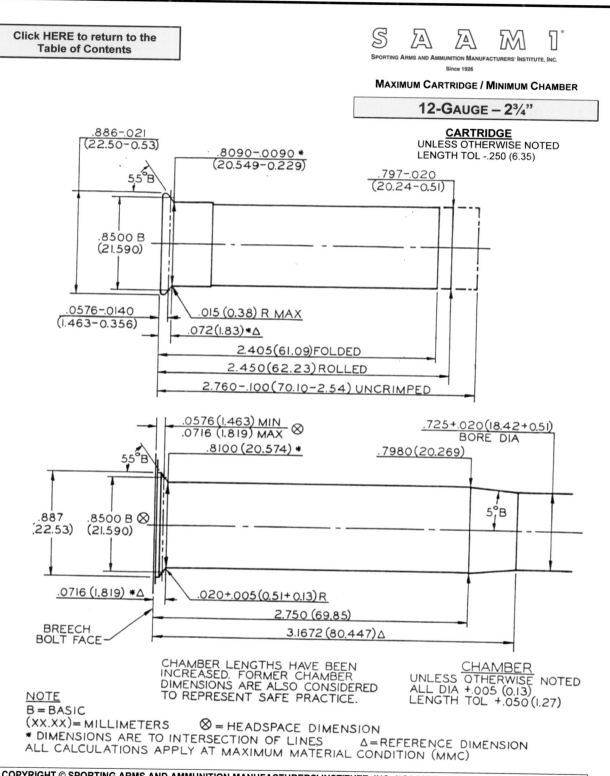

CHAMBER LENGTHS HAVE BEEN
INCREASED. FORMER CHAMBER
DIMENSIONS ARE ALSO CONSIDERED
TO REPRESENT SAFE PRACTICE.

CHAMBER
UNLESS OTHERWISE NOTED
ALL DIA +.005 (0.13)
LENGTH TOL +.050 (1.27)

NOTE
B = BASIC
(XX.XX)= MILLIMETERS   ⊗ = HEADSPACE DIMENSION
* DIMENSIONS ARE TO INTERSECTION OF LINES   Δ=REFERENCE DIMENSION
ALL CALCULATIONS APPLY AT MAXIMUM MATERIAL CONDITION (MMC)

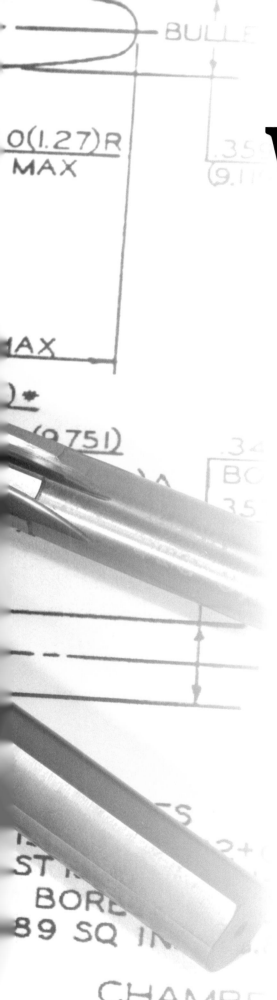

Wildcats

ANSWERING "WHAT IF?"

BY CHUB EASTMAN

Anyone who's spent much time sitting at their loading bench or at the range when there's no hunting season in the immediate future has, at one time or another, had passing thoughts about a magic cartridge that will fit a specific need or perform better than whatever rounds they already have. It's also about the time when the word "wildcat" comes into the conversation, with avid shooters sitting around the campfire or over a cup of coffee at the gun shop. It doesn't seem to make any difference if they are hunters, plinkers, or serious competitive shooters who punch holes in paper or aimed at shoot steel plates or balloons.

Being one that fits into a couple of these categories, curiosity got the best of me, and I started digging through the back shelves of my man cave to see what could be found that pointed to when and where this obsession started. No one seems to know where the term "wildcat" came from. Truthfully, though, there hadn't been much activity in developing different cartridges beyond those offered by ammunition manufacturers until after WWI, when some of the soldiers came home with souvenirs like the German '98 Mauser and other bolt-action rifles. These were stronger and more versatile than the lever-action and single-shot rifles that were in use by most hunters at the time. Indeed, reloading was something only the buffalo hunters did.

Through the 1920s and '30s, reloading was in its infancy, but a few individuals got serious about developing cartridges that could fill the performance gap seen in the offerings from ammunition manufacturers of the day. Quite a number of these "wildcat" cartridges were eventually adopted as standard cartridges. An example of this is found in Remington's 1992 catalog, which lists 28 different rifle cartridges that were not offered in any manufacturer's catalog in 1950. Half of those listed cartridges were derived from wildcats developed years before.

Another example of wildcat innovation surfaced when I thumbed through *Volume I* of P. O. Ackley's *Handbook For Shooters and Reloaders*, which was published in 1962. Out of 567 pages of print, there are 316 pages devoted to specific cartridges and the load data for each. Of all the cartridges listed from .17-caliber to the .505 Gibbs, less than a third are commercial cartridges, while the rest are wildcats of one configuration or another. *Handbook For Shooters and Reloaders, Volume II,* which was printed in 1966, has even more wildcats listed and about the same percentage of data for commercial cartridges as for wildcats.

As a note, the most interesting cartridge I found was developed by Ackley for Bob Hutton, who was the technical writer for *Guns & Ammo* magazine. It was called the ".22 Eargesplitten Loudenboomer" and was a .378 Weatherby case necked down to .22 with a sharp 40-degree shoulder. Practical for any use? I don't think so, but Hutton wanted to set the world record for velocity for the .22-caliber cartridge. Ackley's test firing of the cartridge reached 4,600 fps with a 50-grain bullet. In his remarks, Ackley was sure that these velocities would be higher as loads

In addition to a reamer for the chamber and reloading dies, you will also need GO and NO-GO gauges to insure the barrel is chambered properly.

were developed. It would be interesting to locate the final results and see what bullet was used that could withstand that kind of velocity.

Up until the late 1940s and early '50s, reloading was becoming more popular, as advancements in reloading tools and related items became more available to the average shooter. It's ironic that nearly all commercial ammunition manufacturers considered reloading to be a passing fad. In their minds, the products they offered to the shooting consumer were good enough, having enough variation in calibers and bullet construction that everyone should be happy.

Little did they know at the time that a very enthusiastic and growing industry was gaining ground rapidly. Names like Speer, Hornady, RCBS, Nosler, Pacific, Redding, Sierra, and Barnes began to appear on dealer shelves. By the time the decision makers in the ivory towers of commercial ammunition manufacturing plants realized the demand and interest in reloading was real and not going to go away, they were forced to look at the component business to keep shooters happy.

When a shooter/hunter became an active reloader, they generally did so to save money to start with, or that was the excuse

used to justify the expense, time, and floor space it took to brew your own ammunition. However, I know from my own experience some 40 years ago that I didn't spend any less money, because I just got to shoot more. Also, I found out that, if done correctly, the reloads were more accurate than factory ammunition, and I liked that specialty bullets designed for different applications could be used.

In a lot of cases, as expertise and proficiency increased, one's mind would start to question the potential of a specific bullet type or diameter, maybe a more efficient case design to burn the powder more effectivly, etc. When this starts to happen, it's called the "What if?" scenario, and that's how wildcats are born. Every time one of the ammunition manufacturers presents a new cartridge, there are an uncountable number of reloaders who start asking, "What if?"

The best example of this phenomenon goes clear back to when the .30-06 was developed as the military cartridge for the 1903 Springfield. The number of different wildcat cartridges that have been developed using .30-06 brass as a starting point would amaze you. It has been necked up and necked down, the case straightened, shoulder moved forward and backward

Wildcatting on Your Own

By Richard Mann

Wildcatting will continue until the brass cartridge case is obsolete. Even then, serious shooters will be working to come up with a way to improve on whatever handheld, projectile-launching device is at their disposal. Back in the days Eastman talks about, there were just a select few gun guys tinkering with wildcats. Today, anyone can create their own cartridge with the help of smart guys like Dave Kiff at Pacific Tool & Gauge. Dave can advise on case shape and fashion reamers for chambers and reloading dies.

If building a wildcat is something you want to do, you really don't need a good reason. For avid handloaders and what friend and fellow writer John Barsness calls "rifle loonies," the entire process is fun. On the other hand, sometimes very good reasons do exist for new cartridge creation, and sometimes the answer is simple.

A perfect example came about when Scott Jones, a reader from Indiana, contacted me about wanting to try a current wildcat cartridge. You see, Indiana has long been a state that's prohibited deer hunting with rifles. However, a few years ago, Indiana

legalized rifle hunting if the rifle cartridge case was less than 1.625 inches long and if it held a .35-caliber bullet. For 2012, the state extended the allowable case length to 1.8 inches. Jones wanted to hunt deer with a rifle, but the only way to get there was with a wildcat or a rifle that fired a .35-caliber or larger pistol cartridge.

Jones and I discussed the .358 Hoosier wildcat, which uses a shortened .358 Winchester case; the .358 BFG, which uses the Winchester WSSM case; and the .35 Gremlin, which is fashioned from a 7.62X39 Russian case. All of these require excessive

modification, so I suggested that Jones just trim a .35 Remington case back by .12-inch to 1.80 inches and forget all the complicated case forming. Heck, he could still use standard .35 Remington dies for loading and, in a bolt-action rifle, amp up the cartridge's performance, since SAAMI limits the .35 Remington to just 33,500 psi.

Jones agreed and is working on the project now, but has not decided what to call the cartridge. He suggested the .35 Mann/Jones. I have no interest in the cartridge being named after me and thought something catchier like the .358 Indiana sounded much better.

Other cartridge conversions can be more complicat-

and shortened, shoulder angle changed, and neck length made shorter or longer. Some of the different wildcats developed from the basic .30-06 case that have made it all the way to being an accepted standard cartridge with factory rifles chambered for them are the .25-06, .270 Win, .280 Rem, .35 Whelen, and .338-06 A-Square. The shortened versions are the .308 Win, 7mm-08 Rem, .260 Rem, and .243 Win.

Let your imagination go when you look at the .375 H&H or .300 H&H brass. Almost all belted magnum cartridges that are popular standard factory cartridges today came from this brass. The .300 Win. Mag., 7mm Rem. Mag., .338 Win. Mag., and some of the first Weatherby cartridges can all be traced back to the H&H brass.

The list goes on and is longer than one would initially think. Wildcatters have been busy for quite a while. In a conversation with Kent Sakamoto, Marketing Manager for RCBS, the subject of wildcats came up. After scratching his head, he said that, in the company's specialty dies catalog, there are more than 700 non-SAAMI (Small Arms Ammunition Manufacture Institute) cartridges listed. He also said he gets requests for more than 100 non-cataloged die sets a year for wildcats being developed.

I will be one to admit to having been bitten by the wildcat bug a couple times over the years. Both times the "What if?" question kept knawing at the back of my head until I had to do something about it.

The first time was more than 30 years ago, with my old reliable, put-together custom rifle built on a Sako action chambered for .280 Rem. This was the big-game rifle I used to put meat on the table. It worked great on everything from antelope to moose, as long as the bullet was put in the right spot. Only problem I had was that the load I had painstakingly worked up and used for everything I shot was a little on the warm side. After a couple firings, the primer pockets weren't doing their job. (Please realize this was in the days before chronographs, pressure barrels, experience, and common sense.) If I could only get this performance without a pressure problem, that would cure all that was wrong and save a lot of wear and tear on my Sako action. After a lot of research in *Rifle* and *Handloading* magazines, along with counsel from a few older, more experienced shooters and a gunsmith or two, I decided to re-chamber the gun for the .280 Ackley Improved.

Fire-forming was a necessary and simple matter of firing a standard .280 Rem. car-

Wildcat cartridges do not have to be overly complicated. The wildcat on the left was derived from the .35 Remington. The middle cartridge is sort of an Improved .35 Remington called the .35 SuperMann and was developed by the Richard Mann, the lead editor of this *13th Edition*. The cartridge on the right is nothing more than a .35 Remington that has had the case shortened to meet the Indiana 1.8-inch maximum for use in rifles intended for deer hunting.

ed, and that's where a smart guy like Kiff can help. Dave well understands the mechanics of how a cartridge case and chamber need to interface. Additionally, he has worked with so many wildcat reamers, he also knows where problems can surface. After all, a lot of things need to be considered, like feeding and brass availability. To work and work well, dimensions have to be exact.

This book can help a great deal with the initial stages of wildcat design. You can use the cartridge measurement table in the back of this book to identify potential parent cases for your new creation, and you might even discover that someone else has already been there and

done that. A call to Hornady, RCBS, or Redding isn't a bad idea, either. All these companies have put together hundreds of dies sets for wildcat cartridges and may already have what you're looking for. This was the case when Charlie Sisk and I put together the 416 SM² cartridge. (SM stands for Short/Mag and Sisk/Mann, hence the "squared" moniker. Redding already had a die set for the .416/300 WSM it had put together for some other wildcatter.

Maybe the most complicated part of creating a wildcat is speculating on its ballistic performance and developing loads that are safe. Experienced handloaders can make an educated guess by

comparing cases of a similar design with a similar capacity—but this method isn't just a guess, it's more of a WAG (wild-ass-guess). Computer programs like Quick-Load can help, but nothing is a substitute for actual laboratory pressure testing.

A few companies like Recreational Software and Oehler Research make pressure testing equipment for the hobbyist. I've some experience with these, and they can provide meaningful and useful data. The best option is to send your cartridge and a pressure barrel to a ballistics lab (along with a sizeable check to cover their time), and let them work up safe handloading data for you. Of course, you can wing it on

your own using standardized handloading practices while watching for pressure signs. The problem with this approach is that you will never know for sure.

Wildcatting is an interesting endeavor and can be very rewarding. It can also get expensive and be quite frustrating. But you never know, you just might come up with the next best thing. Of course, you may not live to relish in all the glory. It's unlikely that either Ned Roberts or Townsend Whelen ever expected the cartridges that carry their names would become such iconic American hunting cartridges. Then again, they both had the experience to know a good thing when they saw it.

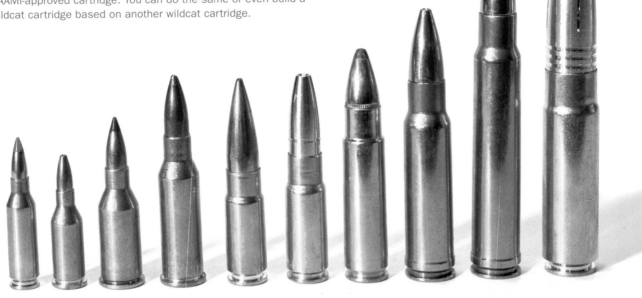

Wildcatters are only limited by their imagination. These 10 wildcat cartridges from .17- to .510-caliber were all based on a factory, SAAMI-approved cartridge. You can do the same or even build a wildcat cartridge based on another wildcat cartridge.

tridge in the Improved chamber. Trim the case to square up the mouth, and it was ready to go. Now I had the performance and velocity (estimated) as before, bolt lift was with the little finger, and cases never wore out. A great cartridge, and others must have thought the same thing, as the .280 Ackley Improved was accepted by SAAMI a couple years ago and the chamber pressures were set equal to the .270 Win so that handloaders could take full advantage of the case capacity; original .280 Rem. pressures were quite a bit lower, because

Some avid wildcatters like Gary Reeder, who have worked on numerous cartridge conversions, have put together their own handloading/conversion manual. Data like this is invaluable to the handloader working with a specific wildcat cartridge.

of the rifles originally chambered for this cartridge. With the new pressure limit, the performance is very near equal to the 7mm Rem. Mag. using less powder and cheaper brass. (Check the new Nosler reloading manual for comparison.)

Like a lot of hunters, I went through the belted magnum stage when I thought I needed a .338 Win. Mag. for elk and moose. The concerns that presented themselves were that it kicked like hell, ammo and brass were expensive, and you could only load three in the magazine. Other than that, it was or is a great cartridge.

A good friend and fellow writer Steve Timm and I had a long discussion on the merits of the .338-06 he'd used for a few years. It was also a cartridge he had written a couple articles on. I started looking at my notes kept from hunts of the past, where elk and moose had been the main goal. I realized I had not shot any of the larger critters at a range that exceeded 250 yards.

When comparing the .338-06 to the .338 Win. Mag., you'll find the .338-06 is less than 100 yards behind the .338 Win Mag, i.e., whatever the .338 Win. Mag. did at 300 yards, the .338-06 could do at 200 yards. Besides it's more important where the bullet goes than how much horsepower it has. Best of all, recoil was very tolerable.

I was convinced and committed to give it a go. This is an easy gun conversion, as the only thing needed is a .30-06 or .270 Win. action. Screw in the .338 barrel, chamber it, and you are ready to go. Simply run a .30-06 case through a .338-06 sizing die, trim to even the case mouth, load, and head for the range.

Does it work? So far it has accounted for a mountain grizzly in British Columbia at very close quarters, three trips to Africa for plains game, and numerous trips afield for elk. The only times the second shot was needed were when the first shot didn't go where it should have.

Some wildcats are this easy to convert to, others take a bit of work to form the cases. If the "What if?" question keeps coming up in the back of your mind, do a little research and see if you can make a good thing better. If nothing else, it makes for good campfire conversation when your shooting buddies ask, "What caliber is that thing?" ∎

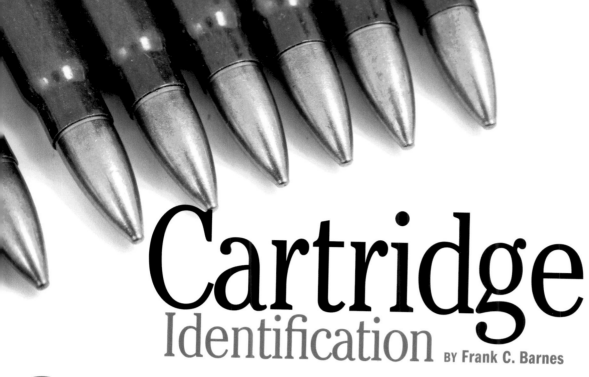

Cartridge
Identification
BY Frank C. Barnes

artridge identification is important to anyone who works with cartridges, whatever the reason. It is of particular consequence to those involved in forensic firearms identification, military intelligence, or serious collecting. In addition to the information presented here, the collector of old, obsolete cartridges has special problems involving ignition systems and types not manufactured for 100 years or more. Much of this is beyond the scope of this book, but the basic procedures are still the same.

In teaching classes in firearms identification, I always tell my students that the easiest way to identify a cartridge is to look at the headstamp, if there is one, because in many instances that will tell you exactly what it is. Unfortunately, it isn't always that simple, since some cartridges don't have headstamps, or if it is a military or foreign round, the headstamp may not be readily decipherable. Additionally, the headstamp may be misleading. You might be dealing with a wildcat cartridge, something made by necking an original case up or down or otherwise changing the configuration. For example, the .30-06 case is used as the basis for a variety of wildcats using both military and commercial cases, so the headstamp would only indicate the original case, not the actual cartridge. Cartridge identification may range from a simple determination of caliber to the more complex ascertainment of the country of origin, date of origin, place of manufacture, and type of gun involved.

The various factors and problems involved in cartridge identification can be summarized as follows:

1. What is the caliber and/or other designation of the cartridge? For example, .38 Special, 9mm Luger, .250 Savage, 7.62x39mm (M43) Russian, .303 British, etc.
2. What type of cartridge is it, handgun, rifle, sporting, or military? Is it modern or obsolete?
3. What is the country of origin, who made it, and when was it made? The headstamp is usually the clue to these answers, but it may not do for all of them.
4. What is the functional character of the cartridge—ball, tracer, incendiary, explosive, sporting, match, etc.?
5. Is the cartridge functional? This usually requires actual testing and is important primarily to those in the forensic field. Obviously, one does not test-fire rare and valuable collectors cartridges.

Cartridges are classified on the basis of ignition type, case shape, and rim type. Combustion of the propellant charge is initiated by the primer. If the priming compound is distributed around the rim of the cartridge, it is a rimfire. If the priming compound is contained in a separate cup in the center of the case head, it is a centerfire. Until the advent of Remington"s EtronX® ammunition and rifle system featuring electronic ignition in the year 2000, all small arms cartridges are percussion-fired, that is, the primer is detonated by the blow or impact of a hammer or firing pin. However, some military ammunition, usually of a size 20mm or greater, is electrically fired. There are two types of centerfire primers currently in general use, Boxer and Berdan. The Boxer primer is entirely self-contained with the anvil as a part of the primer. The Berdan type lacks the anvil that is produced as a small "teat" or protrusion in the primer pocket. Boxer-primed cases have a single flash hole in the center of the primer pocket, whereas Berdan-primed cases have two or more flash holes surrounding the anvil. The Boxer-type primer is used almost exclusively in the United States at the present time, although some Berdan-primed cartridges were manufactured here in the 1800s and early 1900s. The Berdan type is preferred by many European manufacturers and is usually an indication of such origin.

The cartridge base and rim type are important identifying features. These also serve an important functional purpose in feeding and extraction of the cartridge within the gun mechanism. There are five rim types: rimmed, semi-rimmed, rimless, belted and rebated.

Rimmed cartridges have a rim or extractor flange of larger diameter than the case base, often with a grooved or undercut area immediately ahead of the rim. Semi-rimmed cartridges have a rim that is only slightly larger in diameter than the base, and usually also a distinct undercut area between the rim and case base. It is sometimes difficult to recognize a semi-rimmed cartridge without actually measuring rim and base diameter, and these can easily be mistaken for a rimless case. Rimless cartridges have a rim and base of the same diameter although the rim may actually be .001- or .002-inch larger than the base. These are the most common type of military cartridges. Belted cartridges have a distinct belt or flange at the base, just forward of the rim, and an extractor groove between the rim and the belt. Rebated cartridges have a rim of significantly smaller diameter than the case body at the base, plus a definite extractor groove between rim and base or belt. Only a few rebated cartridges have been com-mercialized with success, and those are usually easy to identify. In several rebated rim designs, the rim is only very slightly smaller than the case head. The .404 Jeffery and its derivatives (chiefly the Imperial and Canadian Magnums) are the best examples. These can be difficult to identify without taking careful measurements. Also, note that naming a case design "semi-rimmed" versus "rimmed" is strictly a subjective call—there is no specified difference in base diameter and rim diameter that automatically separates these two styles. However, cases described as semi-rimmed are usually visually distinguishable from similar rimless cases.

The shape or configuration of the cartridge case is also an important identifying characteristic. Cartridges can be divided into the following 12 case types, with their corresponding letter designation used in the cartridge dimensional tables at the end of each chapter:

A. Rimmed bottleneck
B. Rimmed straight
C. Rimless bottleneck
D. Rimless straight
E. Belted bottleneck
F. Belted straight
G. Semi-rimmed bottleneck
H. Semi-rimmed straight
I. Rebated bottleneck
J. Rebated straight
K. Rebated belted bottleneck
L. Rebated belted straight

It will be important to note when referencing these letter designations that some cases described and lettered as straight are atually often tapered; case diameter can be considerably larger at the base, compared to the neck.

The bullet or projectile also provides a clue to the identity of a cartridge, its functional use, and the gun it is fired in. Based on the material or construction, bullets are divided into two major types, lead and jacketed. Lead bullets are used for low-velocity guns, such as handguns or black-powder arms. However, these may also be used for target practice in more powerful guns. Training cartridges may have wooden, fiber, composition or plastic bullets. The shape of the projectile is also important and can be round-nose, flat-nose, conical or spitzer (sharp pointed). Because of the Hague Convention, military bullets do not have lead exposed at the point and are restricted to full-metal-jacket types. Sporting ammunition or that intended for civilian use can have a variety of bullet tips with varying degrees of lead exposed, hollow-point, plastic tips and bronze or other metal tips, to control expansion in the target.

Bullets for military use can also be classified in terms of special functional design, such as ball; tracer (T); armor-piercing (AP); incendiary (I); high explosive (HE); and observation/ranging, or spotter-tracer types. There can also be two or more of these combined in the same bullet, such as APT, API-T, HEI, or HE-T. Not all types are made in every cartridge, since their function is developed to fulfill a specific military requirement. In addition, makeup depends, to

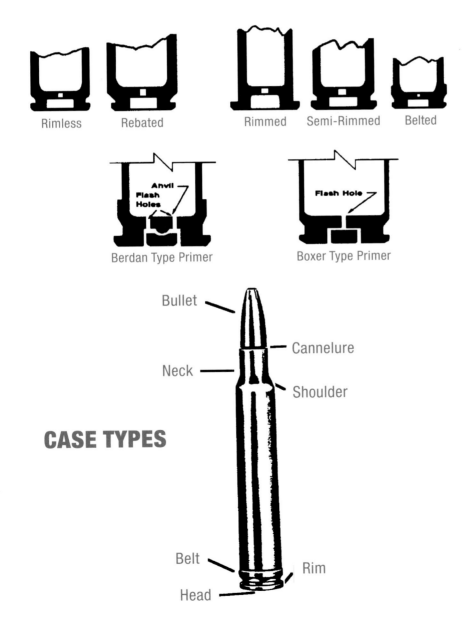

Rimless   Rebated   Rimmed   Semi-Rimmed   Belted

Anvil
Flash
Holes

Berdan Type Primer

Flash Hole

Boxer Type Primer

Bullet

Cannelure

Neck

Shoulder

CASE TYPES

Belt

Rim

Head

some extent, on the gun for which each is loaded. In general, ball or full metal jacket (FMJ) bullets are intended for use against personnel or unarmored vehicles. These usually have a lead core covered by a cupro-nickel jacket, or a mild steel jacket plated with some copper alloy. These can be easily identified with a magnet. At one time, the French 8mm Lebel military bullet was made of solid bronze. Tracer bullets are used for fire correction or target designation. These cannot be distinguished from ball, unless some identifying marking, such as a colored tip (usually, but not always, red), is included. Armor-piercing bullets are also similar to ball except they have a hardened steel or tungsten alloy core. They may or may not have a colored tip. Incendiary bullets contain an incendiary mixture that ignites on impact; visual identification depends on the color-coding system used. High-explosive bullets are uncommon, but do exist. These are made to explode on impact and can only be recognized by the color-coding. Observation and ranging bullets are intended to produce a flash and/or a puff of smoke to mark the point of impact. Again, these are recognizable only when color-coded. One should handle any ammunition with a colored bullet tip with great care, as appropriate.

The headstamp is the stamped markings on the head of the cartridge. Information that can be obtained from the headstamp is extremely varied and depends on the intended purpose or use of the cartridge and who manufactured it.

Headstamps consist of one or more parts or information elements. Cartridges intended for sporting or civilian use usually have two elements. One identifies the specific chambering, the other identifies the manufacturer. Military cartridges can have from one to five elements, including cartridge, date and place of manufacture, plus other identifying markings. Some headstamps are segmented, that is, these have one or more segment lines that divide the head into two to four equal parts. This usually indicates an older cartridge, since most countries discontinued segment lines shortly after World War I. The location of the elements is most conveniently indicated by its clock-face orientation, with 12 o'clock at the top, three o'clock at the right, six o'clock at the bottom, and nine o'clock at the left. The basic U.S. military headstamp prior to World War II had two elements, with the factory code at 12 o'clock and the date at six o'clock. Rapid expansion of ammunition manufacturing facilities as the result of the war introduced many new designs without any effort at standardization. Some used three elements spaced equidistant from each other while others adopted a four-element system located at 12, three, six, and nine o'clock. Also, the location of the factory code was changed, in some instances, to six o'clock or another location.

Worldwide, there are more than 800 military headstamps in existence plus some 400 or more commercial headstamps that have existed at various times. Obviously, this is a complex and highly specialized field. Several volumes have been published on headstamps, including at least three by various U.S. governmental agencies. In addition, some books for cartridge collectors include headstamp data on obsolete cartridges. Since it would require another whole book to adequately cover the subject, it is quite impossible to include more than a few basics here. However, we have listed several sources for such data to assist those readers who find a need for it.

The procedure for identifying a cartridge, using the tables in *Cartridges of the World*, are as follows:

1. First look at the headstamp and see what, if any, information is provided there.
2. Look at the cartridge and determine what type it is: straight, necked, rimmed, rimless, etc.
3. Measure the dimensions of the cartridge and make up a table as follows:

   Type (A, B, C, D, etc., as shown in the tables)
   Bullet Diameter
   Neck Diameter
   Shoulder Diameter (if there is one)
   Base Diameter
   Rim Diameter
   Case Length
   Cartridge Length

Now go to the cartridge measurement tables in Chapter 13 or at the end of each group chapter and compare your data with the dimensional data. Check bullet diameters under the proper type, then compare case length and, finally, other dimensions with your measurements. The type of cartridge case, caliber, and case length are the key elements to start with. For practice, two examples are shown below. See if you can identify the cartridges.

Example #1
Type: C

Bullet Diameter:	.308"
Neck Diameter:	.340"
Shoulder Diameter:	.441"
Base Diameter:	.470"
Rim Diameter:	.473"
Case Length:	2.490"
Cartridge Length:	3.340"

Example #2
Type: B

Bullet Diameter:	.410"
Neck Diameter:	.432"
Shoulder Diameter:	n/a
Base Diameter:	.433"
Rim Diameter:	.488"
Case Length:	1.280"
Cartridge Length:	1.580"

Bear in mind that there is a certain amount of manufacturing tolerance to be allowed for and your measurements may vary .001- to .002-inch plus or minus from some dimensions in the table. The cartridge in Example 1 will be found in the chapter on modern rifle cartridges; Example 2 is in the chapter on handgun cartridges. Not every known cartridge is listed in *Cartridges of the World*, particularly the more obscure blackpowder types. However, practically all modern sporting and military are included, so most readers will not have any difficulty. The idea here is to help you to determine what the cartridge is rather than where it originated or when.

In trying to identify cartridges, there are a couple things the reader should know. For one thing, the major ammunition manufacturers have, from time to time, made up batches of ammunition on special order with the purchaser's headstamp. Anyone can do this if your order is large enough and you have the money. Then there is the matter of commercial reloading firms that turn out ammunition for police departments and others using recycled cases of varying make and loaded with powder and bullets never used by the original company. Last, but not least, you have the individual handloader whose imagination is unbounded and who may turn out a few wondrous and non-standard products.

Cartridge Identification

Headstamp Markings of the Principal American Ammunition Manufacturers

Federal Cartridge Co.
Rimfire, AL EP, G or G, HP, F, XL, XR and WM
Centerfire, FC

General Electric Co.
GE plus date (military)

Newton Arms Co.
NA plus caliber (Made by Rem.)

Peters Cartridge Co.
Rimfire, P or PETERSHV Centerfire, P, PC, P.C.,
PCCO,

PETERS E. Remington & Sons
E REMINGTON & SONS (1870-1890)

Remington Arms Co.
U, UMC, REM, REM*, UMC, R-P, RAH

Robin Hood Ammunition Co.
R, RHA, R.H.A. Co.

Savage Arms Co.
S.A. Co. (made by U.S. Cartridge Co.)

Savage Repeating Arms Co.
S.A. Co., S.R.A.CO.

Richard Speer Manufacturing Co.
SPEER WEATHERBY

Union Metallic Cartridge Co.
U, UMC or R B (Purchased by Remington in
1911)

United States Cartridge Co.
US, U.S., *U.S CARTRIDGE CO*,U.S.C. CO. or
RL (1869 to 1936)

Western Cartridge Co.
SUPER X, SUPER-X, W, WCC, W.C. Co. WEST-
ERN

Winchester
W, H, SUPER SPEED, W.C. Co.

Winchester-Western
W-W, super speed

There were about 15 other companies that manufactured ammunition at various times, particularly during the 1860-1900 period. Also a number of private firms manufactured military ammunition during World War I and II.

United States Arsenal Headstamp Markings

Alleghany Ordnance Plant	KS plus date
Denver Ordnance Plant	DEN plus date
Des Moines Ordnance Plant	DM plus date
Eau Claire Ordnance Plant	EW plus date
Evansville Ordnance Plant	ECS plus date
Frankford Arsenal	CF plus date (45-70) F plus date FA plus date
Lake City Arsenal	LC plus date
Lowell Ordnance Plant	LM plus date
Milwaukee Ordnance Plant	M plus date
Saint Louis Ordnance Plant	SL plus date
Twin Cities Ordnance Plant	TW plus date
Utah Ordnance Plant	U plus date UT plus date

U.S. Small Arms Ammunition Color Codes

Bullet Tip Marking	Functional Type
Black	Armor piercing (AP)
Red	Tracer
White	Tracer, aircraft type
Blue	Incendiary

Bibliography of Cartridge Identification Publications

Jane's Directory of Military Small Arms Ammunition, by Ian V. Hogg. Jane's Publications, Inc., N.Y., N.Y., 1988.

Cartridges For Collectors, by Fred A. Datig. The Fadco Publishing Co., Vol. I, 1956 and Vol. 2, 1958.

Cartridges For Collectors, by Fred A. Datig. Borden Publishing Co., Los Angeles, Calif., Vol. 3, 1967.

Handbuch der Pistolen und Revolver Patronen, Vol. 1, by Hans A. Erlmeier und Jakob H. Brandt. E. Schwend GmbH, West Germany, 1967.

History of Modern U.S. Military Small Arms and Ammunition, by F.W. Hackley, W.H. Woodin, and E.L. Scranton. The Macmillan Co., N.Y., N.Y., 1967.

Cartridges, by Herschel C. Logan. The Stackpole Co., Harrisburg, PA, 1959.

Cartridge Guide 11/71, by Dr. Manfred R. Rosenberger, and Lilla E. Rosenberger. Sporting Goods GmbH, Bremen, West Germany, 1971.

The American Cartridge, by Charles R. Suydam. G. Robert Lawrence, Santa Ana, CA, 1960.

Centerfire Metric Pistol and Revolver Cartridges, Volume 1 of Cartridge Identification, H.P. White and B.D. Mundhall. The Infantry Journal Press, Washington, DC, 1948.

Centerfire American and British Pistol and Revolver Cartridges, Volume 2 of Cartridge Identification, by H.P. White and B.D. Munhall. The Combat Force Press, Washington, DC, 1950.

Cartridge Headstamp Guide, by H.P. White and B.D. Munhall. H.P. White Laboratory, Bel Air, MD, 1963.

Small-Caliber Ammunition Identification Guide, Volume 1 & 2; Army Material Development and Readiness Command, DST-1160G-514-78-Vol. I & II.

Recognition Guide of Ammunition Available to, or Used by, The Viet Cong; Dept. of the Army Pamphlet #381-12, 1966.

Small Arms Ammunition Identification Guide; U.S. Army Foreign Science Technology Center, FSTC-CW-7-68, Washington, DC 20315.

EXAMPLES OF HEADSTAMP STYLES

SINGLE ELEMENT
6 O'CLOCK

DOUBLE ELEMENT
6 & 12 O'CLOCK

TRIPLE ELEMENT
2,10 & 6 O'CLOCK

RIMFIRE
FEDERAL CART. CO.

QUADRUPLE ELEMENT
3,6,9 & 12 O'CLOCK

DOUBLE SEGMENTED
3 & 9 O'CLOCK

QUADRANGLE SEGMENTED
FOUR ELEMENTS
2,4,8 & 10 O'CLOCK

MILITARY
DENVER ORDNANCE
PLANT 1943

COMMERCIAL
REMINGTON

COMMERCIAL
WESTERN CART. CO.

European Sporting Rifle Cartridges

(Current & Obsolete – Blackpowder and Smokeless)

European sporting cartridges are, at least nowadays, better known than those of British origin. European arms makers are well represented by a world-wide distributing system and they advertise what they make. They also manufacture products for a mass market at prices that place them within economic reach for those who could not possibly afford a fine British double-barrel gun.

The Mauser and Mannlicher turn-bolt systems have been the backbone of European sporting rifle manufacture since the 1890s, long before American companies adopted the type. Because the designers intended these cartridges for the same type of rifle, there is great similarity between many modern European and American cartridge designs. We have borrowed freely from each other, and it is often difficult to tell who originated what. Continental gunmakers have also produced very fine, handcrafted double-barrel rifles and combination guns as good as anything turned out by the British. Unfortunately, there has always been a certain prejudice against double-barrel rifles not made in Britain. This resulted because some cheap rifles of this type were turned out on the continent and simply didn't measure up to the required high standards. The Austrians and Germans, on the other hand, developed the drilling or combination gun—the over/under rifle-shotgun—to a greater extent than anyone else did. These multi-purpose firearms feature various combinations of rifled tubes and shot barrels. When it comes to an all-around gun, nothing is superior to a good combination gun.

Gun makers have produced sporting arms all over Europe, including Russia. Today, guns from that latter country are seeing more use outside the Soviet bloc. For decades, the Japanese have made superb firearms. Many of these are now being sold by their own marketing branches here in the United States. Of course, some of our old-line companies with a tradition as American as Yankee Doodle have been, for years, selling guns under their own names that are actually made in Europe or Japan.

European sporting ammunition originates mostly in Italy, Austria, Germany, Finland, Sweden, and Britain. The French chemist Vieille developed the first commercially successful smokeless powder, in 1885. The French adapted this to the 8mm Lebel military cartridge. Commercial manufacture of ammunition started in Germany, during 1856, when Heinrich Utendoerffer founded a plant to make percussion caps and, later, primers. By 1871, he was turning out Berdan-primed centerfire cases for the Bavarian Werder rifle. This enterprise later grew into the great Rheinisch-Westfäfllishe-Sprengstoff-AG, or RWS, as we know it today. Early cartridges or cases made by the firm have "H. Utendoerffer" stamped into the head, sometimes with raised letters.

RWS developed the non-mercuric, non-corrosive primer, in the 1920s, and began to market this significantly improved product under the trade name Sinoxid. Deutsche Waffen und Munitionsfabriken (DWM) is another important German firm that is, unfortunately, no longer in the commercial ammunition business. Hirtenberger-Patronenfabrik, located near Vienna, Austria, was one of the world's largest munitions makers, until destroyed during World War II; organized, in 1860, by the Mandl brothers, both industrial fires and acts of war have razed it several times. The company has started production again and has once more become an important source of sporting ammunition. Norma Precision (formerly Norma Projektilfabrik), manufactures sporting ammunition and components in Sweden. Norma has exported products to the United States since shortly after the end of World War II. It makes the Weatherby line of cases and ammunition and also offers cases for many of the more popular American and European cartridges. The firm of G. Roth manufactured a large variety of sporting ammunition, but did not survive World War II. Lapua of Finland exports to the United States, as does Fiocchi of Italy, and Eley of Britain.

European cartridges, with few exceptions, have metric designations, usually expressed in millimeters. By international agreement, one millimeter equals .03937-inch, or one inch equals 2.54 centimeters (which equals 25.4 millimeters). Metric cartridge designation is quite simple, once you understand it. The first figure represents bore diameter, the second figure represents case length. An "R" indicates a rimmed case, and its absence a rimless one. The designer or manufacturer can tack a name on the end of the numeric designation. Europeans used single-shot and combination guns that extract better with a rimmed case, so they have an "R," or rimmed, version of almost all popular rimless cartridges. Ballistics and case dimensions are usually, though not always, identical.

Some confusion surrounds two different 8mm cartridges. The original 8mm German military cartridge, adopted in 1888, used a .318-inch diameter bullet designed to work in a 7.92mm bore. So did 8mm sporting rounds of the same period. However, in 1905, the German army altered the cartridge and bore design to use a .323-inch diameter bullet—bore diameter was unchanged, but the grooves were deepened to improve accurate barrel life. Shortly thereafter, 8mm sporting cartridges also reflected this change. The old diameter is indicated by a "J" (actually the old German letter form for "I," standing for "Infanterie"), and the new one by an "S." For example, the 8x57mmJ has a .318-inch bullet, and the 8x57mmS (or 8x57mmJS) the .323-inch bullet. It will not hurt anything but accuracy to use the .318-inch bullet in a .323-inch bore—but it might blow up the gun to do the opposite! The proper designation is always on the box, and it is usually stamped on the cartridge head. Read the label! Modern rifles are practically all chambered for the "S" (.323-inch) bullet. European arms and ammunition firms seized upon many American and British cartridges over the years, but they never took to the British belted-type case as we here in the U.S. did. The .22 WCF (5.6x35Rmm), .22 Savage HP (5.6x52Rmm), .25-35 (6.5x52Rmm), and .30-06 (7.62x63) are popular in Europe and listed in late catalogs. The .30-30 WCF is also popular, but Europeans firms don't currently load it. Cartridges of 6mm and 7mm were highly developed in Europe, long before these cartridges became popular here. The 8mm is to Europeans what the .30-caliber is to Americans and, consequently, they have a large variety of cartridges in this caliber, some of advanced design. The 8x68mmS, for example, is a magnum round more powerful than the .300 Weatherby or the .300 Winchester Magnum.

German Mauser-system bolt-action rifles once competed with the more expensive British rifles for use in African hunting. The Germans developed some unusually potent cartridges for dangerous game, but currently use American or British magnum cartridges. They have revived few of their African cartridges since the war.

European centerfire ammunition of modern production by RWS, Norma, Hirtenberger, IMI, Fiocchi, Lapua, and Sako use Boxer primers. RWS still offers nine different types of Berdan primers, as well as Boxer types to satisfy the needs of handloaders. Ammunition for obsolete cartridge rifles is a problem, but, in some instances, handloaders can easily re-form available metric or American cases to work satisfactorily. (Buffalo Arms—www.buffaloarms.com—offers commercially reformed cases that accommodate loading of practically any cartridge you might encounter. These cases, along with a set of custom dies from RCBS, will get you shooting in no time.)

European hunting is quite different from that found in the United States. Differences include both game and methods of taking. Europeans have no large, predatory dangerous game, although the wild boar can be a rough customer, under certain conditions. Conservation is highly developed, and the shooting of game very selective; weeding out old or undesirable animals is as important as collecting a trophy. In most countries, one must pass a rigid course in gun handling and hunting knowledge before being eligible for a permit or license. The German test is especially difficult. Also, in Europe, there is no wide-open hunting. One must get permission or make advance arrangements, and a guide of some sort is usually required. Hunters stalk several varieties of deer, ranging in size from the 40-pound class roebuck to the hirsch or red stag, which is almost as large as an American elk. The chamois, a prime trophy, is present in the higher mountainous areas. Hunters also pursue small game, mostly hare, and they have good bird shooting opportunities. They do not indulge in formal varmint hunting, although I understand pest shooting has developed some following. Along open fields, long shots are not unusual, but great velocity and flat trajectory are not as important as in some areas of North America. Great knockdown and killing power is not required for European hunting, and their cartridges reflect this. The more popular hunting cartridges develop from around 2000 ft-lbs of energy to not much over 2500 ft-lbs of energy, while the trend in the United States is toward energy in excess of 3000 ft-lbs.

The Germans once did a great deal of social target shooting, and many older cartridges originated for this. The Schuetzen, or free rifle, arrived here with German immigrants and was highly popular, off and on, from about 1850 to 1920—its heyday the 1890-1910 period. Many of our cartridges and bolt-action rifles reflect European ideas and design.

Although more information is available on European cartridges than British, the same problem exists in attempting to establish the exact dates of introduction. I sent letters to the principal European manufacturers requesting such information, but, in many instances, records no longer existed. Old catalogs and books were of considerable assistance. If nothing else, these provided sufficient information to establish the period of introduction within a few years. We know that most blackpowder cartridges originated in the 1870s and 1880s, and early smokeless numbers after 1885. Sometimes a cartridge was designed for a specific rifle. The rifle's introduction date then provides a good estimate of cartridge origination date. Individual gunmakers or small companies operated during fixed dates, and their designs can often be approximately dated on that basis. Again, if the reader has specific information of this nature and finds what he believes to be an error in dating, let us know. This way, corrections or new data can be included at a future time.—F.C.B.

13th Edition Update

As with several of the chapters before this one, we have removed sev cartridges in the most-unlikely-to-encounter or can't-find-reloading supplies categories for inclusion on the CD of arcane and obsolete cartridges. The list of relocated cartridges here includes: 5.6x33mm Rook & Tesching/5.6x33Rmm Rook & Tesching; 6x29.5R Stahl; 6x58mm Forster/6x58Rmm Forster; 6.5x40Rmm; 6.5x27Rmm/6.5Rmm Ronezewski; 6.5x48Rmm Sauer; 6.5x53.5mm Daudeteau; 8x51mm Mauer/8x51Rmm Mauser; 8x42Rmm - M-88; 8x71mm Peterlongo; 8x54mm Krag-Jorgensen; 8x72Rmm Sauer/8x72Rmm Jugdewehr/8x72R .360-inch; 9x71mm Peterlongo; 9x63mm; 9x70Rmm Mauser; 9.3x53mm Swiss/9.2x53Rmm Swiss; 9.3x72mm Sauer; 9.3x65R Collath; 9.1x40Rmm; 9.5x47Rmm; 9.5x73mm Miller-Greiss Magnum; 10.25x69Rmm Hunting-Express/10.25x68mm Express;10.5x47Rmm; 10.75x57mm (Mannlicher); 10.75x63mm Mauser; 10.75x65Rmm Col-lath; 11.2x60mm Schüler/11.2x60mm Mauser; 11.2x72mm Schüler/-11.2x72mm Mauser; 10.8x47Rmm Martini (Tar-get); and 12.17x44Rmm Remington M67 (Norway & Swe-den)/12x42Rmm Swedish Remington CF.

5.6x35Rmm Vierling
.22 Winchester Centerfire

Historical Notes: This is the European, or metric designation, for the .22 Winchester Centerfire, which was introduced in 1885 and picked up by European gunmakers a year or so later. It was loaded to much higher velocity there than in the United States, thus providing the inspiration for the .22 Hornet, which is based on the same case. Single-shot, combination, and repeating rifles of European manufacture have been chambered for the 5.6x35Rmm Vierling.

General Comments: The 5.6x35Rmm (.22 WCF) is a popular small-game and target round in Europe. Although originally a blackpowder number, the Germans adapted it to smokeless powder and stepped up the velocity long before wildcatters created the .22 Hornet in the United States. As loaded in Europe, it is a good 100- to 150-yard small-game or target cartridge. The 5.6x35Rmm Vierling can easily be formed from .22 Hornet cases.

5.6x35Rmm Vierling (22 Winchester Centerfire) Loading Data and Factory Ballistics

Bullet (grains/type)	Powder	Grains	Velocity	Energy	Source/Comments
48 SP	2400	8.0	2120	480	Lyman #225414
39 SP	FL		1940	325	RWS factory load
39 SP	FL		2630	600	RWS factory load
46 SP	FL		2030	418	RWS factory load

5.6x50mm Magnum
5.6x50Rmm Magnum

Historical Notes: Most authorities agree that the 5.6x50mm Magnum was developed by DWM in cooperation with Friedrich W. Heym, a noted German gunmaker, and was introduced in 1968 or 1969. It is an offshoot of the 5.6x47Rmm (basically a rimmed version of the .222 Remington Magnum), dating back to about 1967. However, the 5.6x50mm case is .118-inch longer than the .222 Remington Magnum and has greater powder capacity, resulting in a higher muzzle velocity. The rimmed version was intended for use in single-shots, combination guns, and drillings, with the rimless cartridge for bolt-action rifles. Neither is very well known or used to any extent in the United States.

General Comments: In Germany, the 5.6x50mm was used for deer hunting and was loaded with a bullet designed for that purpose. In the United States, it would be primarily a varmint cartridge. Where more power than the .222 or .223 Remington is desired, most Americans would opt for the .22-250 Remington or the .220 Swift, because both rifles and ammunition are available here on an over-the-counter basis. Loading dies for the 5.6x50mm are available from RCBS, Forster/Bonanza, and Lyman. RWS and Hirtenberger have recently offered 5.6x50mm Magnum ammunition.

13th Edition Update: Hirtenberger as its own entity is no longer in business, having been taken over by Swedish conglomerate RUAG Ammotec (www.ruag.com/en/Ammotec/Ammotec_Home). Original Hirtenberger ammo is occasionally found in the surplus marketplace. RUAG is also the parent company of the European brands RWS, Rottweil, GECO, and Norma, and markets ammo for both civilian and law enforcement use under those original names, as well as the Hitenberger brand. Also, Forster/Bonanza is now simly Forster Products, www.forsterproducts.com.

5.6x50mm Magnum, 5.6x50Rmm Magnum Loading Data and Factory Ballistics

Bullet (grains/type)	Powder	Grains	Velocity	Energy	Source/Comments
50 SP	IMR 3031	28.5	3400	1284	Hornady
50 SP	W748	29.5	3500	1360	Hornady
55 SP	IMR 4064	27.5	3300	1330	Hornady
55 SP	W748	28.5	3300	1330	Hornady
60 SP	IMR 4064	27.0	3200	1360	Hornady
50 SP	FL		3590	1430	Factory load – 5.6x50mm
50 SP	FL		3510	1365	Factory load – 5.6x50mm
55 SP	FL		3280	1310	Factory load – 5.6x50Rmm

5.6x57mm RWS
5.6x57Rmm RWS

Historical Notes: The 5.6x57mm was introduced by RWS, about 1964, as a cartridge for hunting deer and chamois. Germany has a law that requires a minimum remaining energy level at 200 meters in order for a cartridge to be legal for taking these animals. The 5.6x57mm was designed with this in mind. It is also loaded with a properly designed bullet for these larger animals, and there is a rimmed version.

General Comments: The 5.6x57mm is in about the same class as the .220 Swift and, as loaded in Europe, would probably do very well for American deer or antelope. However, it would be classed as a varmint cartridge here in the U.S. It is a good cartridge, but the difficulty of finding ammunition would rule out any great popularity in this country. Twist used in rifles of this chambering is 1:10, as opposed to what used to be conventional for .22-caliber centerfires in the U.S., 1:12 to 1:14 inches (newer .22-centerfires often have 1:10 twists; rifles designed for long-range target shooting often have 1:8 twist). The cartridge also has an unusually thick neck, which allows the use of .22 rimfire adapter units, but it presents problems to the handloader. It is manufactured by RWS and by Hirtenberger. Factory ballistics of both versions are identical.

13th Edition Update: Hirtenberger, as a standalone entity, is no longer in business, having been taken over by Swedish conglomerate RUAG Ammotec (www.ruag.com/en/Ammotec/Ammotec_Home). Original Hirtenberger ammo is occasionally found in the surplus marketplace. RUAG is also the parent company of the European brands RWS, Rottweil, GECO, and Norma, and RUAG markets ammo for both civilian and law enforcement use under those original names, as well as the Hitenberger brand.

5.6x57mm, 5.6x57Rmm RWS Loading Data and Factory Ballistics

Bullet (grains/type)	Powder	Grains	Velocity	Energy	Source/Comments
50 SP	IMR 4320	40.0	3900	1689	Hornady
55 SP	W760	42.5	3800	1764	Hornady
55 SP	IMR 4350	41.0	3700	1672	Hornady
55 SP	IMR 4320	39.0	3790	1758	Hornady
60 SP	IMR 4320	38.5	3700	1824	Hornady
74 SP	RI-22	43.0	3400	1890	NA
55 SP	FL		3510	1505	Hirtenberger factory load
74 SP	FL		3410	1910	RWS factory load

5.6x61mm & 5.6x61Rmm Vom Hofe Super Express

Historical Notes: These two cartridges were introduced, in 1937, by E.A. Vom Hofe for his line of German-made Mauser-action express rifles. Some were exported to the United States between the wars. These chamberings were reintroduced by Stoeger Arms Corp., in 1962. The new rifles were based on the Swedish Husqvarna-Mauser action. Both the rimless and rimmed versions were listed in late DWM catalogs. Dimensions and ballistics are identical; these cartridges differ only in the rim.

General Comments: The 5.6x61mm Vom Hofe came out two years after the Winchester .220 Swift. It is one of the very few ultra-velocity .22 cartridges developed in Europe. Bullet diameter is identical to the .22 Savage Hi-Power, but the standard bullet is 10-percent heavier. The .22 Savage has remained popular in Europe, and is still loaded there. Velocity is close to the .220 Swift and, with its 77-grain bullet, the 5.6 is much more effective on deer-size animals. By American standards, it would be considered a long-range varmint cartridge. In Europe, it is looked on as a proper cartridge for deer or boar. If the bullet is designed for the job, there is no reason why it would not be entirely effective for use in open country. The heavier bullet should also have superior wind-bucking ability at long range. The 5.6 bears some resemblance to the .228 Ackley Magnum, which is made from the necked-down and shortened .30-06 case. Although neither cartridge is now loaded in Europe, new empty cases are available from Old Western Scrounger (www.ows-ammo.com)/Gibbs Rifle Co. (www.gibbsrifle.com) and from Huntington's Sportsman's Store (www.huntingtonsports.com). Bullets are available from both sources and from Hornady (www.hornady.com).

5.6x61mm & 5.6x61Rmm Vom Hofe Super Express Loading Data and Factory Ballistics

Bullet (grains/type)	Powder	Grains	Velocity	Energy	Source/Comments
70 SP	IMR 4895	37.0	2800	1215	RWS
77 SP	H870	61.0	3460	2050	RWS
87 SP	IMR 4350	52.0	3310	2110	RWS
77 SP	FL		3708	2350	RWS factory load (obsolete, very optimistic)
77 SP	FL		3480	2070	RWS factory load (obsolete)

6x57mm Mauser
6.2x57mm RWS

Historical Notes: This is a little-known German cartridge that dates back to around 1895. Physical measurements indicate it is the 6.5x57mm Mauser necked down to 6mm. The 6.5mm, in turn, was based on the 1893 7x57mm Mauser necked down. This is a very interesting situation, because it means the 6x57mm is practically identical to the modern .244/6mm Remington. The two differ only by a minor variation in the shoulder angle. The .244 Remington is the .257 Roberts necked down to 6mm (.244) with the shoulder angle increased from 20 degrees/45 minutes to 26 degrees. The commercial .257 Roberts was originated by necking down the original 7x57mm Mauser without other notable changes.

By a long and devious process, different individuals and companies arrived at practically the same point, but at different times. It just goes to prove that there is very little new under the sun. For all practical purposes, the .244 Remington originated, or at least existed, before the turn of the century—it's just that it took 60 years before Remington finally got around to offering the ammunition!

General Comments: Records of ballistics or the specific rifle that the 6x57mm was used in are lacking. However, two bullet weights were available, a 120-grain soft-point and a 123-grain hollowpoint. Considering the time and powders available, muzzle velocity was probably near 2600 fps. This would be a fine deer, antelope, or black bear cartridge. Standard ballistics are not known, and no loading data duplicating the original loads has been developed.

.244 Halger Magnum

Historical Notes: Although this cartridge has an English cartridge designation, it is a 6mm magnum that originated in Germany. It was introduced, in the 1920s, by Halger Arms Co., of Hamburg*. The originators were named Halbe and Gerlich, and the Halger was formed by combining the first three letters of each name. The case is rimless (actually no more than the 6.5x57mm case), intended for use in Mauser bolt rifles, but there were some rimmed cases also made.

General Comments: The velocity of the .244 Halger is impressive, at least on paper. However, the Halger line of cartridges turned out to be somewhat overrated, when tested here. Regardless, this would still be a highly effective cartridge, even if velocity was a couple hundred feet per second below claims. An 87-grain bullet would be mostly for varmint shooting, but heavier bullets could be handloaded for deer or larger animals. In size and general performance, it is very similar to the 6mm Remington. Bullet diameter is .243-inch, so any 6mm bullet would be suitable for handloading with proper data.

* See "Halger and His Rifles" by Phil Sharpe (Gun Digest, 7th ed.).

.244 Halger Magnum Loading Data and Factory Ballistics

Bullet (grains/type)	Powder	Grains	Velocity	Energy	Source/Comments
90 SP	IMR 4350	47.0	3270	2142	NA
105 SP	IMR 4350	44.0	3020	2130	NA
87 SP	FL		3770	2745	DWM factory load (optimistic)

6x62mm Freres
6x62Rmm Freres

Historical Notes: This is a recent German development by Metallwerk Elisenhutte GmBH (MEN). While it appears to be based on the .30-06, case-head diameter is greater, and the 6x62mm should not be made from .30-06 cases. Instead, use 9.3x62mm cases, which was undoubtedly what was used as a basis for this new number and which should be available from Norma and others. The 6x62mm is the first new 6mm cartridge developed in Europe in many years. This number is almost unknown in the United States.

General Comments: What we have here is a super, or magnum, 6mm suitable for all types of small and medium game at long range. The 6x62mm offers more performance than the .243 Winchester or 6mm Remington and requires a long action to accommodate its length. For U.S. hunting conditions, the 100-grain SP bullet load should be selected.

6x62mm Freres Factory Ballistics

Bullet (grains/type)	Powder	Grains	Velocity	Energy	Source/Comments
85 SP	FL		3460	2260	MEN factory load
100 SP	FL		3313	2442	MEN factory load

6.5x52Rmm (.25-35 Winchester)

General Comments: This is the metric version of the .25-35 WCF. This load was used in European single-shot and combination guns. It is not listed in the latest RWS catalogs, although it has been popular in Germany for many years. European loading was practically identical to that used by U.S. ammunition companies.

6.5x52Rmm (.25-35 Winchester) Factory Ballistics

Bullet (grains/type)	Powder	Grains	Velocity	Energy	Source/Comments
117 SP	FL		2230	1285	RWS factory load

6.5x58Rmm Sauer

General Comments: This is the longest of the rimmed, tapered, 6.5mm cartridges developed for the Sauer-made single-shot and combination guns, as well as some Mauser repeating rifles. The others were the 6.5x40Rmm and the 6.5x48Rmm. All have the same type of tapered case. The 6.5x58Rmm, the most popular, is not listed in recent RWS catalogs. It is less powerful than the .25-35 WCF and, by American standards, would be underpowered for deer-sized animals.

6.5x58Rmm Sauer Loading Data and Factory Ballistics

Bullet (grains/type)	Powder	Grains	Velocity	Energy	Source/Comments
120 Lead	4198	15.0	1480	588	Lyman #266455GC
120 Lead	4895	21.0	1650	730	Lyman #266455GC
127 SP	3031	24.0	2100	1288	RWS bullet
127 SP	FL		2020	1140	Factory load

6.5x54mm Mauser

Historical Notes: This is one of the shortest of the Mauser rimless necked cases and was introduced around 1900. It was chambered mostly in the K Model (Kurz) or short-action carbine. The deluxe type M sporter was also available in 6.5x54. This Mauser cartridge was gradually displaced by the more universally popular 6.5x54mm Mannlicher-Schoenauer. It was once listed in DWM catalogs.

General Comments: In both appearance and performance, the 6.5x54mm Mauser is similar to the Mannlicher round. These cartridges are suitable for the same general size and type of big game. Mauser rifles in this chambering were imported into the United States, until World War II. The case has a shorter body of slightly larger diameter than the 6.5 Mannlicher. Ammunition can be made by reforming and trimming .308 Winchester or .300 Savage cases. One can use the same loading data as for 6.5 Mannlicher with very similar results. However, when using home-swaged cases, reduce maximum loads by three or four grains to account for the reduced capacity, compared to original cases.

6.5x54mm Mauser Loading Data and Factory Ballistics

Bullet (grains/type)	Powder	Grains	Velocity	Energy	Source/Comments
120 SP	IMR 4895	36.0	2500	1665	
119 SP	FL		2362	1468	DWM factory load

6.5x57mm Mauser & RWS
6.5x57Rmm Mauser & RWS

Historical Notes: The 6.5x57mm Mauser was developed, about 1893-'94, as a necked-down version of the 7x57mm Mauser. Listed as a hunting cartridge, it was never adopted as an official military cartridge by any power. However, it undoubtedly influenced the design of many of the 6.5mm military cartridges, such as the 6.5x55mm Swedish and 6.5x68mm Portuguese. The three have similar dimensions and performance, but are not the same and can not be interchanged. The rimmed version is used mostly in combination guns. Both are listed in late RWS and Hirtenberger catalogs.

General Comments: As a commercial cartridge, the 6.5x57mm has not been widely used in the United States, although German-made rifles in this chambering have been imported. On the other hand, several virtually identical wildcat numbers have enjoyed limited popularity. These are based on either necking down the 7x57mm case or necking up the .257 Roberts case. The two cases are similar, except for shoulder angle and length. The funny thing is that several individuals claim to have "invented" the wildcat version, not knowing that Paul Mauser beat them to it by 100 years. There are a number of chamber configurations used in making up wildcat versions of the 6.5x57, and few, if any, will interchange. Immediately after World War II, a number of Japanese 6.5mm Arisaka military rifles were re-chambered to handle various 6.5/.257 or 6.5/7mm wildcat cartridges. However, this is a tricky thing that should be checked out by a gunsmith before actually doing any shooting—better safe than sorry. It should be noted that reforming 6mm Remington, .257 Roberts or 7x57mm cases into 6.5x57mm cases by simply neck sizing the case will not necessarily accommodate proper headspace control. To solve this problem, neck the case up to at least .30-caliber before forming it in the 6.5x57mm full-length sizing die.

6.5x57mm Mauser & RWS, 6.5x57Rmm Mauser & RWS Loading Data and Factory Ballistics

Bullet (grains/type)	Powder	Grains	Velocity	Energy	Source/Comments
129 SP	IMR 4350	44.5	2800	2246	Hornady
140 SP	IMR 4350	43.5	2700	2267	Hornady
160 SP	IMR 4350	41.5	2500	2221	Hornady
93 FMJ	FL		3320	2255	RWS factory load
96 FMJ	FL		3290	2290	Factory load
119 SP	FL		2821	2097	Factory load
123 SP	FL		2683	1967	Factory load
127 SP	FL		2850	2290	RWS factory load
154 SP	FL		2670	2435	RWS factory load
157 SP	FL		2450	2080	DWM factory load

6.5x58mm Portuguese

See also Chapter 7

General Comments: The 6.5x58mm Portuguese (used in the Portuguese Mauser-Vergueiro rifle) is often confused with the 6.5x57mm Mauser. Performance is about the same, but these cartridges are not interchangeable. The 6.5x57mm was never adopted as a military round. There is also a 6.5x58Rmm Sauer and a 6.5x58Rmm Krag-Jorgensen, which are distinct cartridges.

6.5x58Rmm Krag-Jorgensen

Historical Notes: This Danish target cartridge was developed, in 1933, by necking-down the 8mm Model 89 military round. It is used in single-shot match rifles based on the Krag-Jorgensen action. Its use is confined almost entirely to Denmark.

General Comments: The 6.5mm is popular in the Scandinavian countries for target and hunting use. This particular round was designed to adapt the local military rifle to that caliber without altering the action in any way. By retaining the same rimmed case, only a new barrel is required. Rifles for this cartridge are quite rare in the United States. However, if you can find the now-obsolete Norma 8x58Rmm Danish Krag cases with Boxer primers, you can neck these down to make ammunition. This would make a good deer cartridge.

6.5x58Rmm Krag-Jorgensen Loading Data and Factory Ballistics

Bullet (grains/type)	Powder	Grains	Velocity	Energy	Source/Comments
140 SP	IMR 4350	46.0	2500	1935 *	
139 SP	FL		2500	1930 *	Factory load

*Approximate ballistics only.

6.5x61mm Mauser
6.5x61Rmm Mauser

Historical Notes: Developed by DWM for various German-made Mauser action rifles, the 6.5x61mm was introduced in the 1930s. There is also a rimmed version for single-shot and combination guns. This cartridge was only moderately popular and has not been revived.

General Comments: The 6.5x61mm is very similar to the .256 Newton. According to the late Phil Sharpe*, it was developed after RWS had imported and tested a .256 Newton rifle. Performance is similar, and .256 loading data could be used as a starting point for working up handloads. The 6.5x61mm would be adequate for most North American game, under proper conditions.

* Op cit.

6.5x61mm, 6.5x51Rmm Mauser

Bullet (grains/type)	Powder	Grains	Velocity	Energy	Source/Comments
120 SP	4831	55.0	2860	2180	NA
140 SP	4350	50.0	2640	2170	NA
119 SP	FL		3090	2510	NA
139 SP	FL		2906	2596	NA
157 SP	FL		2749	2617	NA

6.5x65mm RWS
6.5x65Rmm RWS

Historical Notes: Developed by RWS, about 1988, this is the first new European 6.5mm cartridge in many years. Case-head diameter matches the 9.3x62mm (which is about .004-inch larger than the .30-06), but this case is, as indicated, three millimeters longer than the 9.3x62mm. A rimmed version is offered for single-shot and combination guns. RWS is the only manufacturer.

General Comments: Ballistic performance of this modern 6.5mm is superior to most European 6.5mm cartridges. It is in the same class as the 6.5mm Remington Magnum. This would be a good choice for small and medium game at long range. While the lighter-weight bullets are popular for European hunting, American shooters should select the heavier bullet.

6.5x65mm, 6.5x65Rmm RWS Factory Ballistics

Bullet (grains/type)	Powder	Grains	Velocity	Energy	Source/Comments
108 SP	FL		3460	2260	RWS factory load
127 SP	FL		3313	2442	RWS factory load

6.5x68mm RWS
6.5x68Rmm RWS

Historical Notes: This cartridge was developed by RWS about 1938-'39 and marketed in the spring of 1940. While this has been called the 6.5x68mm Schuler, such a name is erroneous, because that particular gunmaker had nothing to do with its development. It was originally chambered in German-made, Mauser-action rifles. However, the Mannlicher-Schoenauer bolt-action was imported by Stoeger in 6.5x68mm, and Charles Leavell, of Sumpter, South Carolina, also brought in 6.5x68mm and 8x68mm rifles. At one time, the German-made Vom Hofe rifles were available for this round, and it is occasionally referred to as the 6.5mm Vom Hofe Express. It is listed in late RWS and Hirtenberger catalogs, and a few American-made custom rifles have been made for it.

General Comments: The 6.5x68mm is the most powerful of the many European 6.5mm cartridges. In dimensions and performance, it is similar to the .264 Winchester Magnum, except that the .264 has a belted case. On paper, the 6.5x68mm boasts a higher velocity with the 93-grain bullet than the .264 does with the 100-grain. It has an extremely flat trajectory. With the light bullet, this would be important mostly for long-range varmint shooting. Arguments as to which of the two is more powerful are rather academic because, with the same bullet weight, chamber pressure, and barrel length, there really isn't much difference. It is largely a matter of personal choice and which rifle you prefer. Regardless, the 6.5x68mm is a terrific ultra-velocity small-bore cartridge and would be a good all-round cartridge for North American hunting. It is capable of cleanly killing anything from varmint to grizzly bear, if the hunter does his part and uses the proper bullet.

6.5x68mm RWS, 6.5x68Rmm RWS Loading Data and Factory Ballistics

Bullet (grains/type)	Powder	Grains	Velocity	Energy	Source/Comments
87 SP	H4831	73.0	3700	2710	Hodgdon
120 SP	H4831	68.0	3300	2980	Hodgdon
140 SP	H4831	63.0	3000	2800	Hodgdon
93 SP	FL		3950	3180	RWS factory load (optimistic)
123 SP	FL		3450	3255	RWS factory load (optimistic)
140 SP	FL		2920	2651	Hirtenberger factory load

7x33mm Sako
7x33mm Finnish

Historical Notes: This cartridge originated, in 1942, when Sako was producing 9mm Parabellum cartridges in large quantities. The base of the 7x33mm is the same size as the 9mm, but the case was lengthened to the maximum possible for the available case-making equipment. It was then necked down to 7mm. The original bullet weight was 92.6 grains, but was soon changed to 78 grains, which has been standard ever since. Both soft-point and full metal jacket bullets are available.

This caliber was originally developed for capercaillie and black grouse hunting. These birds were widely hunted and were the most important hunting species in Finland, following WWII. For bird hunting, full metal jacket bullets were standard.

General Comments: The ballistics of the 7x33mm are similar to the .30 Carbine, and velocity at 200 yards is only 1500 fps. Post-WWII hunting in Finland was mostly for food, and the slow, round-nose bullet is a good killer that does not destroy much meat. The 7x33mm is considered effective for bird hunting to about 150 yards. The first rifles chambered for the 7x33mm were the Sako L42 and later L46 models, and about 6,000 guns were produced, before this caliber was dropped from production, in the 1960s. The popularity of the .222 Remington was the principal reason for the demise of the 7x33mm.

7x33mm Sako (7x33mm Finnish) Loading Data and Factory Ballistics

Bullet (grains/type)	Powder	Grains	Velocity	Energy	Source/Comments
78 SP	N110 (Vihta Vuori)	16.5	2430	1030	Sako
78 SP or FMJ	FL		2400	998	Sako factory load

7x57mm Mauser
7x57Rmm Mauser

General Comments: An extremely popular sporting round over much of the world. European loads are much more diverse and useful than those generally provided by American companies. RWS ammunition is available in the larger cities of the United States and many parts of the world.

See Chapter 2 for United States and other load data; see Chapter 7 for military load information, and consult the RWS/DWM ballistic tables for data.

7x57mm, 7x57Rmm Mauser Factory Ballistics

Bullet (grains/type)	Powder	Grains	Velocity	Energy	Source/Comments
123 SP	FL		2955	2390	RWS factory load
139 SP	FL		2625	2125	RWS factory load
154 SP	FL		2690	2473	RWS factory load
177 SP	FL		2460	2385	RWS factory load

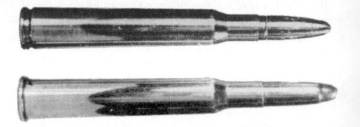

7x64mm Brenneke
7x65Rmm Brenneke

Historical Notes: This cartridge was developed by Wilhelm Brenneke, in 1917, and used in various Mauser-action sporting rifles. Ammunition is listed in the current RWS, Norma, Federal, and Remington catalogs. Brenneke never fabricated ammunition, because he was a designer and gunmaker, and this task was left to the companies equipped to turn out commercial ammunition. There is a near-identical rimmed version, listed as the 7x65Rmm, used in single-shot or combination firearms.

General Comments: Those who think everything new and worthwhile always originates as the result of good old Yankee ingenuity better take a close look at this cartridge. The 7x64mm Brenneke is virtually identical to the .280 Remington and the wildcat 7mm-06, and has been around for more than 75 years. The base diameter of the 7x64mm is a little smaller than the .280, so these cartridges will not actually interchange, but differences are slight. Visibly, the only way an expert can tell these cartridges apart without reading the head markings is by the brass texture or the German-type bullet.

The 7x64mm Brenneke is adequate for any North American big game with the proper bullet. In its original form, it was loaded with a special bullet designed by Brenneke, called the Brenneke Torpedo. Quite a large variety of bullet types are offered in each weight, to adapt the cartridge to practically any game or shooting situation.

7x64mm Brenneke, 7x65Rmm Brenneke Loading Data and Factory Ballistics

Bullet (grains/type)	Powder	Grains	Velocity	Energy	Source/Comments
139 SP	IMR 4350	54.5	3000	2810	Hornady (7x65Rmm)
154 SP	IMR 4350	52.5	2900	2877	Hornady (7x65Rmm)
175 SP	IMR 4350	50.5	2700	2833	Hornady (7x65Rmm)
139 SP	FL		2955	2690	Factory load
139			2806	2430	Patronen (Hungarian)
154 SP	FL		2822	2772	Norma factory load
162 SP	FL		2890	3000	RWS factory load
170			2625	2600	Patronen (Hungarian)
173 SP	FL		2790	2990	Factory load

NEW

7mm Blaser Magnum

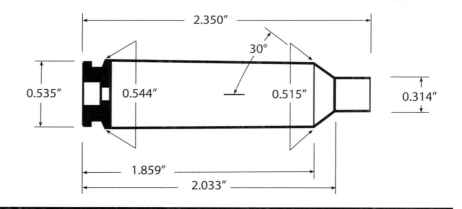

Historical Notes: The idea for four new Blaser cartridges originated in a Las Vegas hotel. Bernhard Knöbel, who was relatively new at Blaser, wanted something fresh to add to the brand. Working with Christer Larsson of Norma, a man who is a very savvy ballistics engineer, they decided on a new line of cartridges based on the .404 Jeffery case, but without a magnum belt. The plan was to develop four cartridges—a 7mm, .30, .338, and .375—that would have a ballistic advantage over the 7mm Remington Magnum, .300 Winchester Magnum, .338 Winchester Magnum, and the famed .375 H&H. An additional requirement was that all four of these cartridges would operate at a maximum average pressure of 58,000 psi. Norma engineers, after extensive testing and evaluation, decided on barrels with four grooves, a case with more taper than the Winchester Short Magnums, a neck length that was 1.1-caliber in length, and a shoulder angle of 30 degrees.

General Comments: The 7mm Blaser Magnum cartridge is currently available only in rifles from Blaser currently sold in Europe. Therefore, it is listed as a European Sporting Rifle cartridge. In the near future, Blaser expects to offer its rifles chambered for all four of its new magnum cartridges in the United States. Norma currently catalogs one 7mm Blaser load; a 156-grain Norma Oryx bullet at 3035 fps, but ballistic reports from Norma show load development work with a 140-grain Nosler Accubond being driven to 3150 fps. These ballistics almost exactly mirror the performance of the 7mm Remington Magnum. But remember, the 7mm Blaser is a beltless magnum. Whether this cartridge will gain a following in the States remains to be seen, but that prospect seems doubtful, unless American sporting arms manufacturers start chambering it in more affordable rifles.—R.A.M.

7mm Blaser Magnum Factory Ballistics

Bullet (grains/type)	Powder	Grains	Velocity	Energy	Source
140 Nosler Accubond	FL		3150	3085	Norma
156 Norma Oryx	FL		3035	3192	Norma

7x66mm Vom Hofe Super Express

Historical Notes: This is a rimless 7mm magnum, developed for the post-World War II Vom Hofe rifles built on the Swedish Husqvarna-Mauser action. These rifles were first advertised in the United States by Stoeger, in 1962, but the 7mm Super Express cartridge was introduced in Germany about 1956. What is apparently the same cartridge has also been listed as the 7x66mm Vom Hofe, and also as the 7.6x66mm Vom Hofe. It was once loaded by DWM. E.A. Vom Hofe has been dead for some years, and the operation was reactivated by Walter Gehmann, once a world-champion rifle shot, although the Vom Hofe name was retained. Gehmann operates a large gun and sport shop in Karlsruhe, with a branch in Stuttgart (www.gehmann.com). The cartridge he offered differed ballistically and in form from the pre-war type. The case is 66 millimeters long, the rim measures .507-inch, the head is .544-inch, and the shoulder measures .504-inch. Thus, it will be seen that the rim diameter is of the type smaller than the head, a lá the .284 Winchester. The shoulder form is unusual, being of modified venturi style.

General Comments: Ballistics claimed for the 7mm Super Express are quite impressive. With the 170-grain bullet, it beats out the 175-grain load of the 7mm Remington Magnum by almost 300 fps, and the 7mm Weatherby Magnum by 164. Not even some of the oversized wildcat 7mm magnum cartridges claim such performance. This makes one wonder what barrel length was used for the velocity tests. American cartridges are usually chronographed from 24- or 26-inch barrels, but Europe ballisticians often use a 30-inch barrel. Regardless, the 7mm Vom Hofe Super Express is as good as any of the other 7mm magnums. It would be an excellent all-round cartridge for North American hunting. It would also do for most non-dangerous African game. It would be at its best for plains or mountain hunting, or anytime long shots entered the picture. Case capacity significantly exceeds the 7mm Remington and Weatherby Magnums.

7x66mm Vom Hofe Super Express Loading Data and Factory Ballistics

Bullet (grains/type)	Powder	Grains	Velocity	Energy	Source/Comments
130 SP	IMR 4350	68.0	3350	3250	
175 SP	IMR 4350	60.0	2900	3280	
120 SP	FL		3520	3340	Gehmann factory load
123 SP	FL		3640	3630	Factory load
140 SP	FL		3356	3540	Gehmann factory load
169 SP	FL		3300	4090	Factory load (very optimistic)
170 SP	FL		3052	3540	Gehmann factory load

7x72Rmm

Historical Notes: A popular, straight, tapered case for single-shot and combination guns, this load was last listed in the 1960 RWS catalog, but it is not currently available. Date of origin is not determined, but it is also shown in RWS manuals of circa 1934. This is seldom used in the United States, except for an occasional combination gun brought back from Europe. In terms of energy or power, it is in the .30-30 class and would not be satisfactory for anything larger than deer at short to moderate range. Bullet diameter is standard, and one can use any American-made .284-inch bullets for handloading. This round has occasionally been loaded, as demand dictates.

7x72Rmm Loading Data and Factory Ballistics

Bullet (grains/type)	Powder	Grains	Velocity	Energy	Source/Comments
139 SP	IMR 4198	23.0	1850		NA
139 SP	IMR 4198	28.0	2300	1640	
160 SP	IMR 4895	27.0	1810	1168	
139 SP	FL		2440	1835	Factory load

7x73mm Vom Hofe (Belted)

Historical Notes: Developed by E.A. Vom Hofe and his partner Schnienmann, in 1931, this cartridge is unusual in that it has a belted case, something German designers normally avoided. Original rifles were based on the Mauser 98 action and made by the firm of Hoffmann, in Berlin. After 1936, Vom Hofe made rifles in his own name. The 7x73mm was not as popular as other Vom Hofe cartridges and manufacture of it was not resumed after World War II.

General Comments: The 7x73mm belted delivered the same ballistics as the smaller and shorter 7mm Super Express rimless introduced later. Dimensions of the 7x73mm case are close to the .300 H&H Magnum, but the Vom Hofe has a larger base and belt diameter (about .013-inch greater). It is at least possible that the 7x73mm was originally developed by necking down the full-length .300 H&H case. Some American wildcats, such as the 7mm Mashburn (Long) were made much the same way. Velocity must have been taken in a 30-inch barrel, because similar United States cartridges (usually chronographed in 24- to 26-inch barrels) do not achieve such velocities with the same weight bullet.

The 7x73mm is scarce and practically unknown in the United States. It would be entirely adequate for North American big game. In power, it has a slight edge over the 7mm Weatherby Magnum.

7x73mm Vom Hofe (Belted) Factory Ballistics

Bullet (grains/type)	Powder	Grains	Velocity	Energy	Source/Comments
170 SP	FL		3290	4120	Factory load (very optimistic)

7x75Rmm Vom Hofe Super Express

Historical Notes: This big cartridge was introduced by Vom Hofe about 1939 and is currently loaded by the Walter Gehmann Co. in Germany (www.gehmann.com). The 7x75Rmm is quite potent, in the same general class as the 7mm Remington Magnum. It is more than adequate for North American game. Cases are imported by Old Western Scrounger. (www.ows-ammo.com). Loading data and factory ballistics are not available.

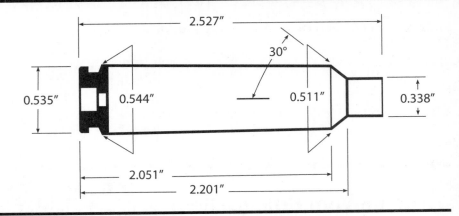

NEW
.300 Blaser Magnum

Historical Notes: The idea for four new Blaser cartridges originated in a Las Vegas hotel. Bernhard Knöbel, who was relatively new at Blaser, wanted something fresh for the brand. Working with Christer Larsson of Norma, a man who is a very savvy ballistics engineer, they decided on a new line of cartridges based on the .404 Jeffery case, but without a magnum belt. The plan was to develop four cartridges—a 7mm, .30, .338, and .375—that would have a ballistic advantage over the 7mm Remington Magnum, .300 Winchester Magnum, .338 Winchester Magnum, and the famed .375 H&H. An additional requirement was that all four of these cartridges would operate at a maximum average pressure of 58,000 psi. Norma engineers, after extensive testing and evaluation, decided on barrels with four grooves, a case with more taper than the Winchester Short Magnums, a neck length that was 1.1-caliber in length, and a shoulder angle of 30 degrees.

General Comments: The .300 Blaser Magnum cartridge is currently available only in rifles from Blaser currently sold in Europe. Therefore, it is listed as a European Sporting Rifle cartridge. In the near future, Blaser expects to offer its rifles chambered for all four of its new magnum cartridges in the United States. Norma currently catalogs one .300 Blaser load; a 200-grain Norma Oryx bullet at 2822 fps, but ballistic reports from Norma show load development work with a 180-grain Barnes Tipped Triple Shock being driven to 3050 fps. This level of performance exceeds that of the .300 Winchester Magnum by about 100 fps. Whether this cartridge will gain a following in the States remains to be seen, but that seems doubtful, unless American sporting arms manufacturers start chambering it in more affordable rifles.—R.A.M.

.300 Blaser Magnum Factory Ballistics

Bullet (grains/type)	Powder	Grains	Velocity	Energy	Source
180 Barnes Tipped TSX	FL		3050	3719	Norma
200 Norma Oryx	FL		2822	3538	Norma

.308 Norma Magnum

Historical Notes: The .308 Norma Magnum was introduced, in 1960, by Å.B. Norma Projektilfabrik, of Åmotfors, Sweden. In its original form, this cartridge was something of a semi-wildcat, because only unprimed brass cases were available and no commercial rifles were chambered for it. However, about 18 months after it was introduced, Norma began producing factory ammunition. Several European manufacturers chamber the round as standard or on order.

General Comments: The .308 Norma Magnum is practically identical to the wildcat .30-338, which is the .338 Winchester Magnum necked-down to .30-caliber. However, the two cases are not interchangeable because of a difference in body length. Almost any standard-length .30-06 rifle can be rechambered to take the .308 Norma cartridge. This cartridge is also similar to a number of .30-caliber wildcat magnums, based on the blown-out and shortened .300 H&H case, and known collectively as the .300 "short magnum" group; the .30 Luft, .300 Apex, and Ackley Short .30 Magnum are representative of this class. The .308 Norma Magnum is adequate for any North American big game and should do well on African plains game. Powder capacity is only a hair greater than the .300 H&H, but the shape of the case is radically different. This is a proprietary cartridge of European origin designed specifically for the American market. It has previously been placed with the American cartridges because most U.S. readers will look for it here. Technically, it belongs in the chapter covering European cartridges.

.308 Norma Magnum Loading Data and Factory Ballistics

Bullet (grains/type)	Powder	Grains	Velocity	Energy	Source/Comments
100 SP	H380	70.0	3500	2721	Speer
110 SP	IMR 4350	75.5	3400	2824	Sierra, Hornady
125 SP	IMR 4350	76.0	3400	3209	Sierra, Hornady
150 SP	IMR 4350	72.0	3200	3420	Hornady, Nosler, Sierra, Speer
150 SP	IMR 4831	73.0	3150	3306	Nosler, Speer
165 SP	IMR 4350	71.0	3100	3522	Sierra, Speer, Nosler
180 SP	IMR 4831	73.0	3000	3598	Sierra
220 SP	IMR 4350	68.0	2800	3831	Hornady
180 SP	FL		3100	3842	Norma factory load

NEW
.300 Norma Magnum

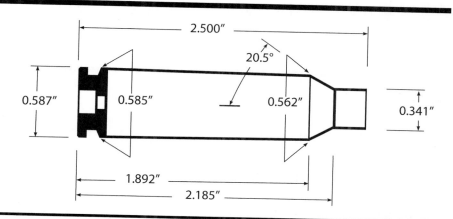

Historical Notes: In early 2007, a ballistician by the name of Jimmie Sloan began looking into long-range shooting and what it took to achieve success at 1,000 and 1,500 yards with a portable individual weapon system. Sloan was unsatisfied with the cartridges available at the time. He wanted a rifle cartridge capable of shooting a bullet with a very high ballistic coefficient, one that weighed 300 grains and traveled at velocities around 2800 fps. A wildcat cartridge known as the .338R was the result. In 2009, Norma AB Precision legitimized the cartridge as the .338 Norma Magnum. The .300 Norma Magnum is nothing more than the .338 Norma Magnum necked down to .308-caliber. Aside from that, the case dimensions are almost identical.

General Comments: The .300 Norma Magnum generates .30-378 Weatherby ballistics from a non-belted case with a standard, radius-free shoulder. Though yet to be offered as a factory loading by any American ammunition manufacturers, wildcatters have already gone to work by Ackley Improving the case so that it has a 40-degree shoulder. Brass for the .300 Norma Magnum is available from MidwayUSA (www.midwayusa.com). Though similar in name and caliber to the .308 Norma Magnum, these cartridges are not the same; the .300 Norma Magnum will push a 200-grain bullet to the same velocities the .308 Norma Magnum will push a 180-grain bullet. It's too early to predict with any certainty the future of this cartridge, but long-range shooters are showing a real interest—R.A.M.

.300 Norma Magnum Loading Data and Ballistics

Bullet (grains/type)	Powder	Grains	Velocity	Energy	Source/Comments
208 Hornady A-Max	H-1000	89.3	3089	4406	Jimmie Sloan
220 Sierra Matchking	H-1000	86.3	3003	4404	Jimmie Sloan
240 Sierra Matchking	Ramshot Magnum	85.0	2943	4615	Jimmie Sloan

.30R Blaser

Historical Notes: Blaser (www.blaser-usa.com) and RWS (www.rws-munition.de/en.html) cooperated in developing this round, in 1990. Being rimmed, it is intended for use in single-shot and combination guns. RWS is the only manufacturer. Note the nomenclature is a combination of European and United States practices.

General Comments: Ballistically, this newer cartridge fills the slot between the .30-06 and the .300 H&H Magnum. It is suitable for all types of large North American game. Bullet diameter is .308-inch. Bullets of 150 to 180 grains work best for most applications.

.30R Blaser Loading Data and Factory Ballistics

Bullet (grains/type)	Powder	Grains	Velocity	Energy	Source/Comments
150 SP	RI-22	68.0	3069	3110	RWS
180 SP	RI-22	64.0	2870	3290	RWS
220 SP	RI-22	58.0	2481	3008	RWS
250 SP	RI-22	57.0	2335	3026	RWS
150 SP	FL		3085	3165	RWS factory load
180 SP	FL		2820	3190	RWS factory load

8x48Rmm Sauer

General Comments: This obsolete blackpowder cartridge was used in single-shot and combination guns. It is shown in post-World War II RWS catalogs as a discontinued number. It was popular in its day, and rifles in this chambering are common. In power, it is similar to the .32-40 WCF and would qualify as a deer cartridge for short-range shooting.

13th Edition Update: Quality Cartridge (www.qual-cart.com) currently lists brass for this round.

8x48Rmm Sauer Factory Ballistics

Bullet (grains/type)	Powder	Grains	Velocity	Energy	Source/Comments
155 Lead	IMR 4198	18.0	1500	780	Lyman #316475GC
196 SP	FL		1665	1215	DWM factory load

8.15x46Rmm

Historical Notes: This is an old, popular target cartridge that was sometimes used for hunting. The exact date of introduction has not established, but it dates back to the period between 1890 and 1900. Single-shots, combination guns, and repeating rifles were chambered for the round. It is listed in current RWS catalogs. Modern loads have jacketed bullets, usually flat-nose soft-points, but, at one time, lead bullets were commonly used. A variety of diameters were factory offered, designed to fit different rifles. According to Fred Datig, this cartridge was developed by Frohn, of Suhl, Germany. For many years, it was the cartridge for 200-meter off-hand target shooting, in Germany and Austria.

General Comments: The 8.15x46Rmm was practically unknown in the United States, until after World War II, when returning GIs brought back various rifles in this chambering (mostly single-shots). Older rifles are intended for low pressure, so one should be careful when handloading and stick to moderate loads, if there is any doubt. Ammunition can be made from resized or fire-formed .32-40 cases. In power, the 8.15x46Rmm is comparable to the .32-40. Thus, it is a little underpowered for deer-sized animals, but would be fine for any small to medium game. Cases are available from RWS (http://rws-munition/de/en.html) and are imported by Old Western Scrounger (www.ows-ammo.com). Quality Cartridge (www.qual-cart.com) also lists brass for this round.

8.15x46Rmm Loading Data and Factory Ballistics

Bullet (grains/type)	Powder	Grains	Velocity	Energy	Source/Comments
151 SP	IMR 4895	30.0	1900	1240	NA
190 Lead	IMR 3031	23.0	1500	956	Lyman #338237
151 SP	FL		1805	1090	RWS factory load

8x57Rmm 360

Historical Notes: Based on the 9.3x72Rmm case, this old German cartridge is a copy of the British .360 Nitro Express No. 2. Loaded first with blackpowder and, later, with smokeless, a fair number of combination guns will be found chambered for this round. Bore diameter is .318-inch.

General Comments: Due to low breech pressure, ballistic performance of the 8x57Rmm is only moderate. It is suitable for all types of small and medium game at close range, but falls off badly at longer ranges. This cartridge is now obsolete. For handloading, use only .318 diameter bullets.

13th Edition Update: Quality Cartridge (www.qual-cart.com) currently lists brass for this round.

8x57Rmm 360 Loading Data and Factory Ballistics

Bullet (grains/type)	Powder	Grains	Velocity	Energy	Source/Comments
196 SP	RI-19	37.5	1893	1561	RWS
196 SP	IMR 3031	26.0	1560	1059	RWS
196 SP	IMR 4350	37.0	1820	1441	RWS
196 SP	FL		1800	1410 *	

* Estimated ballistics.

8x57mmJ Mauser

Historical Notes: This original 8x57mm cartridge was adopted, in 1888, along with the Model-88 Commission rifle, by the German Army. Many sporting rifles were subsequently chambered for this cartridge. Ammunition is still being manufactured by RWS in Germany. Bullet diameter is .318-inch.

General Comments: The later 8x57mmJS uses a .323-inch diameter bullet and is loaded to higher pressures. Never fire 8x57mmJS ammunition in rifles chambered for 8x57mmJ ammunition. American manufacturers offer only the 8x57mmJS load, but it is deliberately loaded down to be safe to fire in 8x57mmJ chambers. The 8x57mmJ would be adequate for any large North American game at medium ranges. Use only .318-inch diameter bullets.

This cartridge is now universally called the 8x57mmJ Mauser or, simply, the 8mm Mauser, and has caused considerable historical confusion. The story goes that the fancy German script capital "I" in the German word "Infanterie" (Infantry) was mistaken by interpreters as a capital "J." If true, this represents an interesting bit of irony, since even the Germans now routinely refer to this cartridge using the bastardized "J" designation.

13th Edition Update: Quality Cartridge (www.qual-cart.com) currently lists brass for this round.

8x57mmJ Mauser Loading Data and Factory Ballistics

Bullet (grains/type)	Powder	Grains	Velocity	Energy	Source/Comments
150 SP	IMR 3031	47.0	2800	2611	RWS
170 SP	IMR 3031	45.0	2600	2552	RWS
196 SP	RI-1550	46.0	2225	2145	RWS
196 SP	FL		2391	2488	Factory load
198 SP	FL		2647	3075	Factory load

8x75mm
8x75Rmm

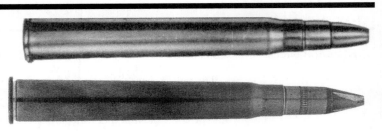

Historical Notes: These two cartridges are listed together, because one is a rimmed version of the other. These cartridges were introduced around 1910 and are based on the older 9.3x74Rmm case necked-down. These cartridges were intended to provide a powerful 8mm for African use. The rimless version was for bolt-action express rifles, the rimmed for combination guns or single-shots.

General Comments: At the turn of the century, and until start of World War I, there was considerable competition between German and British gunmakers for the African gun trade. The Germans made good repeating rifles at moderate prices and gained sales by underselling the British. However, the British seemed to always keep one jump ahead, in the matter of popular cartridge design. The Germans were constantly trying to come up with something that would compete with the British offerings. The 8x75mm is one of a number of German efforts to produce an express 8mm cartridge. Two bullet diameters were used, the earlier .318-inch, and the later .323-inch, or "S," size. The large-diameter bullet should not be used in the smaller bore. Many 8mm cartridges come in two different bullet diameters. One must be very careful about this, because the large-diameter "S" round is often loaded to higher velocity and pressure. The 8x75mm is in about the same class as the .300 H&H Magnum and is powerful enough for any North American big game.

8x75mm, 8x75Rmm Factory Ballistics

Bullet (grains/type)	Powder	Grains	Velocity	Energy	Source/Comments
180 SP	RI-22	71.0	2791	3115	RWS
200 SP	RI-22	68.0	2713	3270	RWS
196 SP	FL		2715	3230	Factory loading for .318-inch bore rifles
198 SP	FL		3050	4120	Factory loading for S-bore rifles

WARNING! Many J-bore (.318-inch) rifles still exist and, depending upon throat and cartridge neck dimension, it can be possible to chamber "S" bore (.323-inch) cartridges. Firing such a combination can create dangerous pressures. When in doubt, check bore diameter CAREFULLY!

8x58Rmm Sauer

General Comments: This blackpowder cartridge was once used in single-shot and combination guns. A popular schüetzen cartridge in its day, it is long obsolete. It differs from the 8x48Rmm only in length. This cartridge is based on the 9.3x72Rmm case and offers similar performance to the 8x57Rmm 360. Power is about the same as the .32-40 WCF, and it could be used for deer at short range. For handloading, use only .318-inch diameter bullets.

13th Edition Update: Quality Cartridge (www.qual-cart.com) currently lists brass for this round.

8x58Rmm Sauer Loading Data and Factory Ballistics

Bullet (grains/type)	Powder	Grains	Velocity	Energy	Source/Comments
196 SP	IMR 4064	34.0	1942	1642	
196 SP	RI-19	39.0	1877	1533	RWS
196 SP	FL		1690	1248	Factory load

8x56mm Mannlicher-Schoenauer

Historical Notes: Introduced about 1908 for various Mannlicher-Schoenauer rifles and carbines, the 8x56mm became quite popular and was picked up by other European gunmakers. It was also manufactured for a short time by American ammunition companies, but no U.S. commercial sporting rifles were chambered for it.

General Comments: The 8x56mm Mannlicher has seen only limited use in the United States, although it is popular in Europe. Ballistically, it is a little more powerful than the .35 Remington. Both shoot approximately the same weight bullet at similar velocity. By American standards, this would be a good short-range cartridge for deer or black bear. While it is a good cartridge, performance is no better than what is available in American chamberings. Western Cartridge Co. discontinued it, about 1938. Bullets of .323-inch diameter are used for handloading. This cartridge should not be confused with the 8x56mm Hungarian.

13th Edition Update: Quality Cartridge (www.qual-cart.com) currently lists brass for this round.

8x56mm Mannlicher-Schoenauer Loading Data and Factory Ballistics

Bullet (grains/type)	Powder	Grains	Velocity	Energy	Source/Comments
170 SP	IMR 4895	44.0	2260	1935	NA
200 SP	IMR 3031	40.0	2050	1875	NA
200 SP	FL		2165	1920	Western factory load
200 SP	FL		2200	2150	Eley-Kynoch factory load
202 SP	FL		2170	2105	RWS factory load

8x57RmmJS Mauser

Historical Notes: This is the rimmed version of the 8x57mmJS German military round, for use in single-shot and combination guns. Introduced, in 1888, with the .318-inch "J" bullet, it was adapted, in 1905, to the larger "S"-type, or .323-inch diameter bullet, corresponding to a similar change in the military round. Popular in Europe and listed in the latest RWS and Hirtenberger catalog, it is seldom seen in the United States.

General Comments: The 8x57RmmJS gives the same performance as the Rimless 8x57mmJS Mauser familiar to American shooters. It is in the same class as the .30-06 and would do for any North American big game. RWS and Hirtenberger cases and ammunition with American Boxer primers are available, but other European brand cases are made for the Berdan primer. Be sure you use the proper bullet diameter for your particular gun. RWS cartridges for the .323-inch, or "S," bore size have a blackened primer and a cannelured bullet. Bullet diameters are clearly marked on the box. The "S" is available in heavier loadings and higher velocities than the "J" (.318-inch) loading.

13th Edition Update: Hirtenberger, as its own entity, is no longer in business, having been taken over by Swedish conglomerate RUAG Ammotec (www.ruag.com/en/Ammotec/Ammotec_Home). Original

Hirtenberger ammo is occasionally found in the surplus marketplace. RUAG is also the parent company of the European brands RWS, Rottweil, GECO, and Norma and markets ammo for both civilian and law enforcement use under those original names, as well as the Hitenberger brand.

8x57RmmJS Mauser Loading Data and Factory Ballistics

Bullet (grains/type)	Powder	Grains	Velocity	Energy	Source/Comments
170 SP	IMR 4895	49.0	2650	2660	8x57mmJR (.318-inch bullet)
196 SP	IMR 4064	45.0	2440	2600	NA
225 SP	IMR 4350	50.0	2230	2498	NA
170 SP	FL		2591	2535	Hirtenberger factory load, 8x57RmmJS (.323-inch bullet)
178 SP	FL		2380	2230	Factory load, 8x57RmmJ (.318-inch bullet)
196 SP	FL		2312	2327	Hirtenberger factory load, 8x57RmmJS (.323-inch bullet)
227 SP	FL		2130	2290	Factory load, 8x57RmmJ (.318-inch bullet)

8x57mmJS Mauser

Historical Notes: Information on the 8x57mm is given in Chapters 2 and 7. As a military round, the 8mm Mauser is another casualty of World War II, replaced by the .30-06 and the 7.62x51mm NATO round in the West and by the Russian M-43 or 7.62x39mm in the East. As a sporting round, the 8mm Mauser is still popular, and many rifles in this chambering are in use. European sporting loads put it in the same class as the .30-06, fully capable of handling any game or situation the .30-06 can. American manufacturers load this cartridge to lower velocity and pressure than European makers. The "S" bullet diameter is .323-inch.

8x57mmJS Mauser Loading Data and Factory Ballistics

Bullet (grains/type)	Powder	Grains	Velocity	Energy	Source/Comments
150 SP	IMR 4064	50.0	2800	2612	Sierra, Hornady
170 SP	H380	49.0	2500	2360	Hodgdon, Hornady
200 SP	H205	55.0	2500	2776	Speer
220 SP	IMR 4064	39.0	2200	2365	Sierra, Barnes
250 SP	RI-15	42.0	2250	2811	Barnes
165 SP	FL		2854	2985	Norma factory load
170 SP	FL		2657	2666	Hirtenberger factory load
198 SP	FL		2732	3282	RWS factory load

8x60mmJ Mauser & RWS
8x60mmS Mauser & RWS
8x60RmmJ Mauser & RWS
8x60RmmS Mauser & RWS

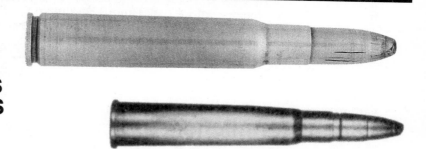

Historical Notes: The 8x60mmS and 8x60RmmS were introduced, soon after World War I, to replace the 8x57mmJS in sporting rifles. After the war, German civilians were forbidden to own rifles in the military chambering, yet many did! Converting these to 8x60mmS was a simple chamber lengthening job, not costly, and many were so altered, in order to be legally licensed. A few years later, the 8x60mm was offered in the old bullet diameter (.318-inch) as well, probably to add performance to older 8x57mmJ sporting rifles, via the same easy conversion.

General Comments: The 8x60mm comes in a confusing variety of types and loads. Both rimless and rimmed case are available for the .318-inch and "S" (.323-inch) diameter bullets. There is a standard and a magnum loading, as well as one called the Magnum-Bombe. Case dimensions are the same, but there is a difference in bullet weight and velocity. In the standard load, the 8x60mm is almost identical to the .30-06 in power, but the magnum loading brings it up to the .300 H&H Magnum performance level. It has sufficient power for North American big game and could be used for anything the .30-06 can handle. On heavy game, such as moose, elk, or grizzly bear, it would have an edge over the .30-06, if one used maximum loads. It is a popular round in Europe and has been used to some extent in Africa, although most African hunters do not consider it any better than the .300 H&H. It is still loaded by RWS (http://rws-munition/de/en.html).

13th Edition Update: Quality Cartridge (www.qual-cart.com) currently lists brass for the 8x60mmS Mauser round.

8x60mmJ Mauser & RWS, 8x60mmS Mauser & RWS, 8x60RmmJ Mauser & RWS, 8x60RmmS Mauser & RWS Loading Data and Factory Ballistics

Bullet (grains/type)	Powder	Grains	Velocity	Energy	Source/Comments
159 SP	IMR 3031	48.0	2820	2805	NA
196 SP	IMR 4895	49.0	2570	2875	NA
159 SP	FL		2820	2805	Norma factory load ("S" bore)
187 SP	FL		2810	3275	RWS factory load ("S" bore)
196 SP	FL		2580	2890	RWS factory load

8x64mmJ Brenneke
8x64mmS Brenneke
8x65RmmJ Brenneke
8x65RmmS Brenneke

Historical Notes: These two cartridges were developed by Wilhelm Brenneke, about 1912, for Mauser rifles and combination guns. Originally, loaded ammunition was furnished only by DWM, but RWS made empty cases for Brenneke. Mauser-system Brenneke rifles are again available for the 8x64mmS cartridge, made in Berlin by the original W. Brenneke firm. The 8x64mm cartridge is based on the 9.3x62mm case, while the 8x65Rmm is based on the 9.3x74Rmm case.

General Comments: Like most other 8mm cartridges, the 8x64mm and 8x65Rmm are loaded with both .318-inch "J" and .323-inch "S" bullets. Modern rifles are always chambered for the "S"-type bullet. This is a constant source of confusion to Americans who own or are interested in 8mm rifles. It is also the principal reason 8mm cartridges are not popular here, because even the sporting goods dealers do not want to bother with two bullet diameters and the difficulty they can cause typical customers. The 8x64mmS is very similar to the wildcat 8mm-06 and has plenty of punch for North American big game.

Bullet (grains/type)	Powder	Grains	Velocity	Energy	Source/Comments
150 SP	IMR 4350	60.0	2770	2560	NA
170 SP	IMR 4064	52.0	2710	2760	NA
225 SP	IMR 4831	61.0	2400	2900	NA
225 SP	IMR 4350	57.0	2450	2955	NA
154 SP	FL		2952	2986	Factory load
185 SP	FL		2890	3420	Factory load
227 SP	FL		2578	3347	Factory load

8x68mmS RWS

Historical Notes: First loaded by RWS, in 1938-'39, for marketing in the spring of 1939, this cartridge is still listed in its latest catalogs, as well as in Hirtenberger catalogs. This is one of the most modern and powerful of the 8mm cartridges. After the 1:9½ twist of the standard 8mm barrel was found to be unnecessarily fast, a 1:11 twist was adopted.

General Comments: The 8x68mmS is in the same class as the .338 Winchester Magnum, although it has a slightly smaller-diameter bullet of less weight. It is powerful enough for the largest and toughest North American big game and would be superior to the .300 H&H Magnum for African hunting. Some authorities compare it to the .300 Weatherby or the .300 Winchester Magnum, but the 8x68mmS has an edge over both.

This is one 8mm furnished only in a single bullet size, .323-inch. Case dimensions are similar to the belted .300 Magnums, but the 8x68mmS is a rimless cartridge with no belt. It has not been used in the United States very widely to date, but would be popular if more hunters were familiar with it. It is one of the best European cartridges for all-round use in North America. Performance is almost identical to the 8mm Remington Magnum.

13th Edition Update: Hirtenberger, as its own entity, is no longer in business, having been taken over by Swedish conglomerate RUAG Ammotec (www.ruag.com/en/Ammotec/Ammotec_Home). Original Hirtenberger ammo is occasionally found in the surplus marketplace. RUAG is also the parent company of the European brands RWS, Rottweil, GECO, and Norma, and markets ammo for both civilian and law enforcement use under those original names, as well as the Hitenberger brand.

8x68mmS RWS Loading Data and Factory Ballistics

Bullet (grains/type)	Powder	Grains	Velocity	Energy	Source/Comments
125 SP	W760	81.0	3500	3401	Hornady
150 SP	W760	76.0	3300	3628	Hornady
150 SP	IMR 4350	73.5	3200	3412	Hornady
170 SP	IMR 4831	75.5	3100	3629	Hornady
170 SP	IMR 4350	72.0	3100	3629	Hornady
200 SP	RI-22	78.0	2971	3920	RWS (optimistic)
220 SP	IMR 4831	67.0	2700	3562	Hornady
187 SP	FL		3180	4195	Factory load (optimistic)
196 SP	FL		2985	3879	Hirtenberger factory load (optimistic)
200 SP	FL		2985	3958	Hirtenberger factory load (optimistic)

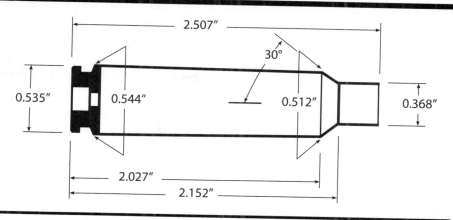

NEW
.338 Blaser Magnum

Historical Notes: The idea for four new Blaser cartridges originated in a Las Vegas hotel. Bernhard Knöbel, who was relatively new at Blaser ,wanted something fresh for the brand. Working with Christer Larsson of Norma, a man who is a very savvy ballistics engineer, they decided on a new line of cartridges based on the .404 Jeffery case without a magnum belt. The plan was to develop four cartridges—a 7mm, .30, .338, and .375—that would have a ballistic advantage over the 7mm Remington Magnum, .300 Winchester Magnum, .338 Winchester Magnum, and the famed .375 H&H. An additional requirement was that all four of these cartridges would operate at a maximum average pressure of 58,000 psi. Norma engineers, after extensive testing and evaluation, decided on barrels with four grooves, a case with more taper than the Winchester Short Magnums, a neck length that was 1.1-caliber, and a shoulder angle of 30 degrees.

General Comments: The .338 Blaser Magnum cartridge is currently available only in rifles from Blaser currently sold in Europe. Therefore, it is listed as a European Sporting Rifle cartridge. In the near future, Blaser expects to offer its rifles chambered for all four of its new magnum cartridges in the United States. Norma currently catalogs one .338 Blaser load, a 230-grain Norma Oryx bullet at 2822 fps, but ballistic reports from Norma show load development work with a 210-grain Barnes Tipped Triple Shock being driven to 2950 fps, demonstrating about a 100 fps advantage over the .338 Winchester Magnum, but from a beltless case. Whether this cartridge will gain a following in the States remains to be seen, but that seems doubtful, unless American sporting arms manufacturers start chambering it in more affordable rifles.—R.A.M.

.338 Blaser Magnum Factory Ballistics

Bullet (grains/type)	Powder	Grains	Velocity	Energy	Source
210 Barnes Tipped TSX	FL		2950	4059	Norma
230 Norma Oryx	FL		2822	4068	Norma

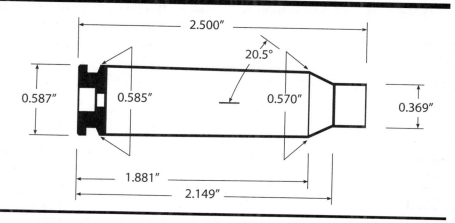

NEW
.338 Norma Magnum

Historical Notes: In early 2007, a ballistician by the name of Jimmie Sloan began looking into long-range shooting and what it took to achieve success at 1,000 and 1,500 yards with a portable individual weapon system. Sloan was unsatisfied with the cartridges available at the time. He wanted a rifle cartridge capable of shooting a bullet with a very high ballistic coefficient, one that also weighed 300 grains and traveled at velocities around 2800 fps. A wildcat cartridge known as the .338R was the result, and the first reamers for the cartridge were manufactured by Dave Kiff at Pacific Tool & Gauge. Norma AB Precision showed interest in the cartridge, and the .338 Norma Magnum was born. The U.S. Military has also shown interest in this cartridge, since its legitimization by Norma. The cartridge case for the .338 Norma Magnum is very similar to the .338 Lapua Magnum, however, the .338 Norma Magnum has a slightly larger diameter shoulder and is about a quarter-inch shorter.

General Comments: Many that are in the know, when it comes to long-range shooting, consider the .338 Norma Magnum superior to the .338 Lapua Magnum. Balistically, the .338 Norma Magnum is very similar to the .338 Lapua Magnum. However, with the .338 Norma Magnum, a 300-grain Sierra Matchking can be loaded so that it does not intrude into the case where gases could flow over the heel of the boat-tail of the bullet. The cartridge is gaining a solid following and is a perfect example of how wildcatters like Jimmie Sloan can positively influence cartridge development. Currently, Black Hills (www.black-hills.com) is offering loaded ammunition.—R.A.M.

.338 Norma Magnum Loading Data and Factory Ballistics

Bullet (grains/type)	Powder	Grains	Velocity	Energy	Source/Comments
200 Nosler Accubond	MRP	95.0	3211	4578	Norma
230 Norma Oryx	MRP	90.5	2956	4462	Norma
300 Sierra Matchking	MRP 2	85.0	2644	4656	Norma

9x56mm Mannlicher-Schoenauer

Historical Notes: The 9x56mm Mannlicher-Schoenauer was one of the early cartridges for the Austrian-made Mannlicher-Schoenauer sporting rifle. The rifle was introduced in 1900, and most of the original cartridges for it were developed between 1900 and 1910. Catalog references indicate that the 9x56mm was added to the line of available chamberings about 1905. Remington loaded this round until the late 1930s. Modern Mannlicher-Schoenauer sporting rifles were once chambered for the 9x56. The 9x56mm is no longer loaded in Europe.

General Comments: The 9x56mm developed a moderate following, but most hunters preferred the more powerful 9x57mm Mauser. The 8x56mm Mannlicher is still loaded, and one can make 9x56mm ammunition by expanding the neck of the smaller caliber case. The 9x56mm is a notch or two above the .35 Remington, but is largely a short-range woods cartridge for deer or possibly elk. It was never very popular in the United States, because it had little to offer beyond available American cartridges. However, it is a perfectly good cartridge if you do not hunt anything larger than deer and are willing to put up with the difficulty of trying to find the now-obsolete ammunition. For handloading, use .356-inch diameter bullets.

13th Edition Update: Quality Cartridge (www.qual-cart.com) currently lists brass for this round.

9x56mm Mannlicher-Schoenauer Loading Data and Factory Ballistics

Bullet (grains/type)	Powder	Grains	Velocity	Energy	Source/Comments
200 SP	IMR 3031	40.0	2110	1980	NA
205 SP	FL		2114	2234	Factory load
245 SP	FL		2100	2400	Eley-Kynoch factory load
280 SP	FL		1850	2128	Remington factory load

9x57mm Mauser
9x57Rmm Mauser

Historical Notes: Shortly after the 8x57mm Mauser military round was introduced, in 1888, an entire family of cartridges was developed on this case length by necking it both up and down. The rimless cases were used in bolt-action repeating rifles and a rimmed version was usually made available for combination or single-shot guns. The 9x57Rmm is the rimmed twin of the pictured cartridge. This was a popular round used all over the world, and the old Remington Model 30 and Winchester Model 54 bolt-action rifles were available in 9x57mm. Most American ammunition companies loaded it, until 1936-'38. It is now obsolete both in Europe and the U.S.

The 9x57mm Mauser is in the same class as the .358 Winchester and would be suitable for all North American big game under most hunting conditions, although it is not a long-range cartridge. African hunters liked it as a meat-getter, but considered it too light for dangerous game. Velocity is moderate, but, with the proper bullet, it penetrates well on thin-skinned animals. Bullet diameter is .356-inch, but .357- to .358-inch bullets can be swaged down and used.

13th Edition Update: Quality Cartridge (www.qual-cart.com) currently lists brass for both versions of this round.

9x57mm, 9x57Rmm Mauser Loading Data and Factory Ballistics

Bullet (grains/type)	Powder	Grains	Velocity	Energy	Source/Comments
245 Lead	IMR 3031	38.0	1950	2075	Lyman #358318GC
250 SP	IMR 3031	44.0	2260	2980	
280 SP	IMR 3031	43.0	2030	2570	
280 SP	IMR 4064	46.0	2045	2610	
205 SP	FL		2423	2682	Factory load
245 SP	FL		2150	2520	Eley-Kynoch factory load
275 SP	FL		1850	2090	Remington factory load
281 SP	FL		1920	2285	RWS factory load

.358 Norma Magnum

Historical Notes: This cartridge was developed by Norma and introduced in the United States, in 1959. At the start, no rifles were chambered for the .358 Norma Magnum. However, empty cases and loaded ammunition were available. The Schultz & Larsen Model 65 and the Husqvarna bolt-action were made available in this chambering, early in 1960. No mainstream American gun manufacturer ever chambered this cartridge. Like the .308 Norma Magnum, it is a proprietary cartridge and perhaps should be listed under European cartridges. However, it was designed for the American market and is listed here because many custom rifles were made here.

General Comments: The .358 Norma Magnum is a short, magnum-type cartridge intended to work through standard-length actions. It is nearly identical to the wildcat .35 Ackley belted, short magnum. It is also nearly identical to the wildcat .35-338, which is the .338 Winchester necked-up to .35-caliber.

The .358 Norma Magnum delivers the same performance as the slightly larger .375 H&H Magnum and would be suitable for the same range of game. It is overpowered for most North American big game, but would be an excellent choice for the big Kodiak bears. It is another good all-around number for the person who wants to be prepared for hunting anything, anywhere, at any time. A-Square has reintroduced this ammunition.

.358 Norma Magnum Loading Data and Factory Ballistics

Bullet (grains/type)	Powder	Grains	Velocity	Energy	Source/Comments
180 SP	IMR 4895	69.0	3100	3842	Speer
200 SP	IMR 3031	66.5	2900	3736	Hornady
225 SP	IMR 4350	75.0	2900	4203	Nosler
250 SP	IMR 4320	68.0	2800	4353	Hornady
250 SP	IMR 4350	76.0	2700	4048	Speer
250 SP	Norma MRP	78.0	2500	3470	Speer
300 SP	IMR 4350	71.0	2600	4504	Barnes
250 SP	FL		2790	4322	Norma factory load

9.3x57mm Mauser

Historical Notes: This is a rimless necked case and is another of the cartridges based on the 8x57mm Mauser expanded to take larger diameter bullets. It dates back to 1900 or earlier, and was used in both Mauser and Mannlicher sporting rifles. Except for the larger diameter bullet, it is nearly identical to the 9x57mm. The 9.3x57mm is not listed in the current RWS catalog, but Norma (www.norma-usa.com) makes cases and loaded ammunition. Apparently, no rifles are currently made for this round. A cartridge designated as the 9.3x57Rmm is not the rimmed version of this cartridge, rather that number has a straight case.

General Comments: The 9.3x57mm is in the same class as the old .35 WCF or the newer .358 Winchester. It would do for any North American big game at short to moderate ranges. It would be good for hunting in brush or heavily-wooded areas. It may also be listed as the 9.2mm Mauser, and is often confused with the 9x57mm Mauser, because these cartridges differ only in bullet diameter. To further complicate matters, there is a 9.5x57mm Mannlicher, which looks similar, but is not interchangeable. Barnes (www.barnesbullets.com) and Speer (www.speer-bullets.com) make appropriate bullets for handloading this number.

9.3x57mm Mauser Loading Data and Factory Ballistics

Bullet (grains/type)	Powder	Grains	Velocity	Energy	Source/Comments
232 SP	IMR 3031	47.0	2330	2785	NA
286 SP	IMR 3031	43.0	2070	2705	NA
286 SP	FL		2065	2714	Norma factory load

9.3x64mm Brenneke

Historical Notes: This is the largest and most powerful of the various Brenneke cartridges. Wilhelm Brenneke was one of the best known of the German cartridge designers, and many of his ideas were commercial successes. He developed the popular and effective Brenneke-Torpedo bullets.* His career began in the late 1890s, but most of his modern cartridges were perfected in the period around 1910. He was a contemporary of Charles Newton, in the development of high-velocity cartridges. There are marked similarities between the Brenneke and Newton cartridges, but it is probably a case of parallel development, rather than any influence of one by the other. Brenneke was born in 1864 and died in 1951. The 9.3x64mm is still loaded by RWS. German-made, Mauser-system bolt-action rifles are still available for the 7.8mm and 9.3mm Brenneke cartridges.

General Comments: Except in name, the 9.3x64mm has "Magnum" written all over it. This .375 H&H Magnum-class number is certainly adequate for any North American big game and most game worldwide. The estimable John Taylor rated it right along with the .375 H&H Magnum as an excellent all-round cartridge for African hunting. Rifles and ammunition were unavailable for a number of years, because of World War II. Now that this cartridge is in production again, its use may increase. Not well known in the United States, it would probably be more of a success here if better publicized. Barnes (www.barnesbullets.com) and Speer (www.speer-bullets.com) make appropriate bullets. A-Square (www.a-squareco.com) offers ammunition and components. Quality Cartridge (www.qual-cart.com) lists this brass.

* For an account of Brenneke's life and developments, see the 14th Edition of Gun Digest.

9.3x64mm Brenneke Loading Data and Factory Ballistics

Bullet (grains/type)	Powder	Grains	Velocity	Energy	Source/Comments
286 SP	IMR 4350	76.0	2725	4716	RWS
270 SP	RI-15	67.0	2820	4768	RWS
293 SP	IMR 4350	65.0	2629	4563	RWS
247 SP	FL		2760	4178	RWS factory load

Bullet (grains/type)	Powder	Grains	Velocity	Energy	Source/Comments
285 SP	FL		2690	4580	RWS factory load
286 Lion	FL		2650	4460	A-Square factory load
293 SP	FL		2570	4298	RWS factory load

9.3x74Rmm

Historical Notes: The 9.3x74Rmm is a popular German cartridge for single-shot, double-barrel, and combination guns. It originated, in the early 1900s, in answer to the .400/360 Nitro Express, which British gunmakers developed in various versions. It is quite similar to, but slightly longer than, the .400/360 Westley Richards, also loaded and chambered in various rifles by the Germans. The 9.3x74Rmm is listed in the current RWS and Norma catalog. Austrian and German combination guns are still available in this chambering, as are barrels for Thompson/Center rifles from SSK Industries.

General Comments: A popular round for heavy game, the 9.3x74Rmm is on par with the .375 Flanged Magnum Nitro Express. It gained a good reputation in Africa for general use against most game, including elephant. It would be more than adequate for North American big game. An over/under combination gun, in 9.3x74Rmm chambering and with a 12- or 16-gauge shot barrel, would be a terrific outfit for the world-wide, one-gun hunter. There is not much of anything, large or small, that such a gun could not handle. For handloading, .365-inch diameter bullets should be used. Barnes (www.barnesbullets.com) and Speer (www.speer-bullets.com) make such bullets, which should work well in most rifles. A-Square (www.a-squareco.com) and Norma (www.norma.cc; www.ruag.com/ammotec) offer ammunition and components.

9.3x74Rmm Loading Data and Factory Ballistics

Bullet (grains/type)	Powder	Grains	Velocity	Energy	Source/Comments
250 SP	H380	60.0	2400	3198	Barnes
270 SP	IMR 4895	55.0	2300	3172	Speer
286 SP	IMR 4064	55.0	2300	3360	Barnes
232 SP	FL		2630	3535	Norma factory load
258 SP	FL		2460	3465	RWS factory load
285 SP	FL		2280	3290	RWS factory load
286 SP	FL		2360	3530	Norma/A-Square factory load

9.5x57mm Mannlicher-Schoenauer/9.5x56mm MS

Historical Notes: Introduced, in 1910, for the Mannlicher-Schoenauer rifle and carbine, this cartridge is also listed as the 9.5x56mm, 9.5x56.7mm, and the .375 Nitro Express Rimless. Old Eley-Kynoch catalogs listed it as the 9.5mm Mannlicher-Schoenauer. It is not listed in current RWS catalogs, and no modern European rifles are being chambered for it, partly because it lacked sufficient headspace control, indicating that incautious chambering or case annealing could lead to dangerous case stretching and, potentially, case head separations.

General Comments: The 9.5 Mannlicher was popular for a number of years with those who liked the light, handy Mannlicher sporting rifles. It did not have a good reputation in Africa for heavy or dangerous game, but was liked by many as a meat-getter and performed well on thin-skinned, non-dangerous game.

It is seldom seen in the United States. This is a good short-range cartridge for almost any North American big game. It is in the same general class as the .358 Winchester, but uses a larger diameter bullet that is typically heavier.

13th Edition Update: Quality Cartridge (www.qual-cart.com) currently lists brass for this round.

9.5x57mm Mannlicher-Schoenauer Loading Data and Factory Ballistics

Bullet (grains/type)	Powder	Grains	Velocity	Energy	Source/Comments
270 SP	IMR 3031	44.0	2150	2780	NA
286 SP	IMR 3031	42.0	2040	2638	NA
270 SP	FL		2150	2780	Eley-Kynoch factory load
272 SP	FL		2148	2791	Factory load

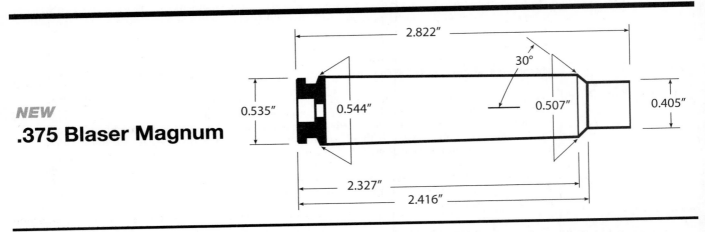

NEW
.375 Blaser Magnum

Historical Notes: The idea for four new Blaser cartridges originated in a Las Vegas hotel. Bernhard Knöbel, who was relatively new at Blaser, wanted something fresh for the brand. Working with Christer Larsson of Norma, a man who is a very savvy ballistics engineer, they decided on a new line of cartridges based on the .404 Jeffery case without a magnum belt. The plan was to develop four cartridges—a 7mm, .30, .338, and .375—that would have a ballistic advantage over the 7mm Remington Magnum, .300 Winchester Magnum, .338 Winchester Magnum, and the famed .375 H&H. An additional requirement was that all four of these cartridges would operate at a maximum average pressure of 58,000 psi. Norma engineers, after extensive testing and evaluation, decided on barrels with four grooves, a case with more taper than the Winchester Short Magnums, a neck length that was 1.1-caliber, and a shoulder angle of 30 degrees.

General Comments: The .375 Blaser Magnum cartridge is currently available only in rifles from Blaser currently sold in Europe. Therefore, it is listed as a European Sporting Rifle cartridge. In the near future, Blaser expects to offer its rifles chambered for all four of its new magnum cartridges in the United States. Norma currently catalogs one .375 Blaser load, a 300-grain Norma Oryx bullet at 2690 fps, but ballistic reports from Norma show load development work with a 270-grain Barnes Triple Shock being driven to 2755 fps. These velocities exceed that of the most famous .375-caliber rifle cartridge of all time, the .375 H&H, by about 100 fps. Whether this cartridge will gain a following in the States remains to be seen, but that seems doubtful, unless American sporting arms manufacturers start chambering it in more affordable rifles.—R.A.M.

.375 Blaser Magnum Factory Ballistics

Bullet (grains/type)	Powder	Grains	Velocity	Energy	Source
270 Barnes TSX	FL		2755	4552	Norma
300 Norma Oryx	FL		2690	4821	Norma

9.3x48Rmm/9.3x57Rmm/
9.3x70Rmm/9.3x72Rmm/
9.3x80Rmm

Historical Notes: These five cartridges are lumped together, because the only real difference is case length. These cartridges all date back to the 1890s, and all were originally blackpowder cartridges. Most of these cartridges were still loaded until the start of World War II, but only the 9.3x72Rmm survived the war and is listed in late RWS catalogs. All are of the straight, rimmed type and were used in single-shot and combination guns.

General Comments: Old catalogs show the same bullet as suitable for all or most of these cartridges. Despite the difference in case length, there really is not much difference in ballistics or power. All are primarily medium-game cartridges fully adequate only for deer or similar animals. These cartridges can best be compared to the .38-55, although that old American cartridge has a slight edge over most of the various straight-cased 9.3s. Few modern guns are being made for any of these chamberings. Barnes (www.barnesbullets.com) makes one style of jacketed flat-point bullet for the .38-55 WCF that should work well in any of these numbers.

Various 9.3x48Rmm, 9.3x57Rmm, 9.3x70Rmm, 9.3x72Rmm, 9.3x80Rmm, 9.3x82Rmm Factory Ballistics

Bullet (grains/type)	Powder	Grains	Velocity	Energy	Source/Comments
160 SP	FL		1650	973	Factory load
190 SP	FL		1700	1225	Factory load
300 SP	FL		1650	1820	Factory load
193 SP	FL		2020	1750	RWS factory load
193 SP	FL		1640	1155	Factory load

10.3x60Rmm Swiss

Historical Notes: A Swiss target cartridge originally developed for single-shot Martini-action rifles, the 10.3x60Rmm is nothing more than the Swiss version of the obsolete British .450/400 (23/8-inch) Blackpowder Express. Some Swiss-loaded ammunition is so marked on the box. Some modern bolt-action rifles have been made in Switzerland in this chambering. The British loaded a 255-grain lead bullet, but the Swiss use heavier bullets of soft-point or full jacketed type with smokeless powder. The Swiss loading is in the same class as the .405 Winchester and would do for any North American big game at short to medium range. This chambering is still popular in Switzerland, and guns and ammunition are still manufactured in Switzerland and in Germany by RWS. In at least one Swiss canton, the 10.3x60Rmm is the only lawful cartridge for big-game hunting. Bullet diameter is .415-inch.

10.3x60Rmm Swiss Factory Ballistics

Bullet (grains/type)	Powder	Grains	Velocity	Energy	Source/Comments
253 SP	RI-15	66.0	2432	3324	RWS
330 SP	FL		2070	3143	RWS and Swiss factory loading

10.75x73mm (.404 Rimless Nitro Express/.404 Jeffery)

Historical Notes: This is the metric designation for the .404 Jeffery or .404 Rimless Nitro Express. One of the most popular rounds used in Africa, the .404/10.75x73mm is now back in production at RWS. The new RWS loads are assembled with Australian-made Woodleigh bullets having bonded cores and clad-steel jackets. Ruger now offers the bolt-action M77 and the No. 1 single-shot in this chambering.

General Comments: Overall length is the same as the popular .375 H&H Magnum, so rifles with magnum-length actions are suitable for this cartridge. Some say it is too powerful for North American game, but, as Elmer Keith used to say, "Too much gun always beats the alternative." Bullets for handloading are offered by Barnes (www.barnesbullets.com) and Woodleigh (www.woodleighbullets.com).

10.75x73mm (.404 Rimless Nitro Express/.404 Jeffery) Loading Data and Factory Ballistics

Bullet (grains/type)	Powder	Grains	Velocity	Energy	Source/Comments
347 SP	RI-15	80.0	2335	4200	RWS
400 SP	RI-15	75.5	2220	4379	RWS
400 SP/FMJ	FL		2315	4761	RWS factory load

10.3x65Rmm Baenziger

Historical Notes: This was, at one time, a popular European target cartridge, particularly in Switzerland. It is now obsolete, but the Swiss manufactured it until after the end of World War II. Swiss Martini-action single-shot rifles were made for the 10.3x65Rmm. This cartridge is actually the brass 2.5-inch .410 (10.35mm, or 36-gauge) shotgun shell loaded with a lead or soft-point bullet. However, the rim is a bit thicker than the average .410 shotshell's. DWM case No. 164 is listed, in the 1904 catalog, under schrotflinten, or shotguns. Ammunition can be made from brass .410 cases, although the rim usually has to be built up to the proper thickness. A brass washer is the easiest solution to this. The equally hard-to-find .405 Winchester case can also be used, if trimmed to the right length and the rim turned down. New brass cases from Bertram Bullet Co. are being imported. Lyman #412263 (290-grain) cast bullets can be sized and used. Power is about the same as the 44 Magnum revolver cartridge fired in a rifle, so it would make a fairly satisfactory short-range deer number.

There is also a 10.3x65Rmm Swiss target cartridge (old DWM case No. 237A) that is practically identical to the above except for a thin rim. This one has been obsolete for a good many years. Cases are currently made by Bertram Bullet Co. and sold through Buffalo Arms Co. (www.buffaloarms.com).

10.3x65Rmm Baenziger Loading Data and Factory Ballistics

Bullet (grains/type)	Powder	Grains	Velocity	Energy	Source/Comments
290 Lead	3031	43.0	1625	1705	Lyman #412263
285 SP	FL		1785	1940	Factory load

10.75x68mm Mauser

Historical Notes: The 10.75x68mm was a Mauser development and is so listed in German ammunition catalogs. It was introduced in the early 1920s. Pre-World War II Mauser magnum-action Type A sporting rifles were chambered for this round and exported to the United States. Post-war Browning and Dumoulin bolt-action rifles were available for this cartridge in Europe. Kynoch, of England, once made the 10.75x68mm cartridge.

General Comments: This was a popular big-game cartridge with many African and Indian hunters. The 10.75x68mm has been used on all kinds of dangerous game, including elephant. However, professional ivory hunters did not consider it satisfactory for elephant. This was apparently due to bullet design. The soft-point bullet could not be depended on to hold together and, so, did not always penetrate properly. In power, it falls short of the British .404 Rimless Nitro Express. With top loads, it approaches .375 H&H Magnum energy levels—no faint praise. However, it is not considered as good a general-purpose cartridge as the .375 H&H. There is no question of it being perfectly adequate for North American big game. Bullet diameter is .424-inch. Ammunition is available from Old Western Scrounger (www.ows-ammo.com), and Barnes (www.barnesbullets.com) offers bullets. Buffalo Arms Co. also sells die sets (www.buffaloarms.com).

Bullet (grains/type)	Powder	Grains	Velocity	Energy	Source/Comments
347 SP	IMR 3031	59.0	2250	3900	NA
347 SP	FL		2200	3740	Eley-Kynoch factory load
347 SP	FL		2230	3830	RWS factory load

NEW
.45 Blaser

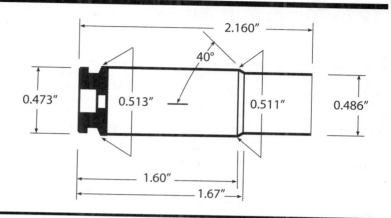

Historical Notes: Europeans have different ideas about a lot of things. For instance, while Blaser plans on eventually offering its new line of magnum cartridges in the United States, it has no intention of doing so with what might be the most marketable off all its new cartridges.

The .45 Blaser was specifically designed for driven wild boar hunts. This cartridge has a .513-inch base diameter, like the .458 Winchester Magnum, but a rim diameter of .473, like the .308 Winchester. This, in conjunction with its short overall length, makes it readily adaptable to short-action bolt rifles. Currently, it is only available in Blaser rifles, and the .45 Blaser ammunition manufactured by W. Romney isn't sold in the U.S. The round also possesses an unusually shaped case by modern standards, one having an excessively long .49-inch neck. This long case neck allows the use of heavy .458-caliber bullets, but prevents them from protruding into the powder column behind the shoulder.

General Comments: With the capability of launching a 350-grain bullet at just over 2000 fps, the .45 Blaser has very similar ballistics to .45-70 loads designed for modern rifles. However, the rimless design of the .45 Blaser makes it much more suitable to bolt and/or semi-auto rifles. It would be a great cartridge to use when hunting wild hogs or a variety of other medium and large game at short to moderate ranges.—R.A.M.

.45 Blaser Factory Ballistics

Bullet (grains/type)	Powder	Grains	Velocity	Energy	Source
349 SJSP	FL		2034	3205	Blaser

.460 Steyr (11.64mm)

Historical Notes: Certain European countries restrict the sale of military-caliber firearms, including those chambering cartridges of .50-caliber. Around 2004, Steyr Mannlicher GmbH developed a proprietary cartridge for the European large-caliber market by shortening the .50-caliber Browning Machine Gun cartridge case and sizing it to accept 11.64mm (.458-inch) bullets.

General Comments: This cartridge is not currently available in the United States. In the European market, it closely duplicates the performance of the .50 BMG cartridge for non-military applications. The .460 Steyr is well-suited for heavy, single-shot bolt-action target rifles that offer long range, terminal ballistic, and other performance advantages, such as the Steyr HS 50 Long Range rifle. Barrel twists used by Steyr are 1:12 and 1:14. Steyr (www.steyrarms.com) also supplies loaded ammunition.

Bullet (grains/type)	Powder	Grains	Velocity	Energy	Source/Comments
600 Steyr Brass Solid	FL		3000	11989	Steyr

12.5x70mm Schüler

Historical Notes: Some authorities say this cartridge was an original Schüler development; others claim Jeffery introduced it. John Taylor said the ammunition was loaded only in Europe, and that would indicate Schüler originated it. Krieghoff-Schüler Magnum rifles were chambered for this round and were exported from the 1920s until World War II. The exact date of introduction is obscure. Earlier editions of this book stated that this cartridge is interchangeable with the .500 Jeffrey but, according to custom gunsmith James Tucker, this is not the case.

General Comments: Until the introduction of the .460 Weatherby Magnum, this was the most powerful magazine-rifle cartridge in existence. It was used very successfully in Africa on some game. Bullet diameter is .510-inch. Factory loads were made in both soft-point and full metal jacket types. German full metal jacket bullets had weak jackets and did not perform well against heavy animals. In earlier editions of this text, this cartridge was erroneously listed as the 12.7x70mm. Barnes (www.barnesbullets.com) makes an appropriate bullet.

12.5x70mm Schüler Factory Ballistics

Bullet (grains/type)	Powder	Grains	Velocity	Energy	Source/Comments
535 SP	FL		2400	6800	Factory load

Dimensional Data

Cartridge	Case Type	Bullet Dia.	Neck Dia.	Shoulder Dia.	Base Dia.	Rim Dia.	Rim Thck.	Case Length	Ctge. Length	Primer: Berdan Dia.	RWS Primer No.	Old DWM Case No.	Page
5.6x35Rmm Vierling (.22 WCF)	A	.222	.241	.278	.300	.297	UNK	1.40	1.62	.177	1584	539	458
5.6x50mm/5.6x50Rmm Magnum	C/A	.224	.254	.355	.375	.376	.038	1 97	2.21	UNK/NA	UNK	UNK/NA	459
5.6x57mm/5.6x57Rmm RWS	C/A	.224	.281	.436	.469	.470	UNK	2.24	2.54	UNK/NA	UNK	UNK/NA	459
5.6x61mm & 5.6x61Rmm Vom Hofe Super Express	C/A	.227	.259/ .260	.468/ .479	.476/ .470	.480/ .533	.062	2.39	3.13	.217	5603	431M	460
6x57mm Mauser/6x57mm RWS	C	.243	.284	.420	.475	.476	.045	2.23	2.95	.217	5603	494	461
.244 (6mm) Halger Magnum	A	.243	.287	.435	.467	.470	UNK	2.25	3.04	.217	5603	UNK/NA	461
6x62mm/6x62Rmm Freres	C/A	.243	.271	.451	.474	.470	UNK	2.42	3.13	.217	UNK	UNK/NA	461
6.5x52Rmm (.25-35 Winchester)	A	.257	.280	.355	.420	.500	UNK	2.04	2.53	.217	5603	519	462
6.5x58Rmm Sauer	B	.264	.291	UNK	.433	.501	UNK	2.30	3.08	.217	5603	463	462
6.5x54mm Mauser	C	.264	.289	.432	.468	.463	UNK	2.12	2.67	.217	5603	457A	462
6.5x57mm/6.5x57Rmm Mauser & RWS	C/A	.264	.292	.430	.470/ .471	.474/ .521	UNK	2.24	3.16/ 3.18	.217	5603	404A	463
6.5x58mm Portuguese	C	.264	.293	.426	.468	.465	UNK	2.28	3.22	.217	5603	457	464
6.5x58Rmm Krag-Jorgensen	A	.264	.300	.460	.500	.575	UNK	2.29	3.25	.217	5603	UNK/NA	464
6.5x61mm/6.5x61Rmm Mauser	C/A	.264	.296/ .297	.452	.477	.479/ .532	UNK	2.40	3.55	.217	5603	431L-431M	464
6.5x65mm/ 6.5x65Rmm RWS	C/A	.264	.296	.430	.474/ .475	.470/ .531	UNK	2.56	3.15	UNK/NA	UNK/NA	UNK/NA	465
6.5x68mm/6.5x68Rmm RWS	C/A	.265	.295	.481	.520	.510	UNK	2.66	3.27	.238	1698	UNK/NA	465
7x33mm Sako/Finnish	C	.284	.307	.365	.388	.390	UNK	1.30	1.73	UNK/NA	UNK/NA	UNK/NA	466
7x57mm/7x57Rmm Mauser	C/A	.284	.320	.420	.470	.474/ .521	.035/ .056	2.24	3.06/ 3.07	.217	5603	380D-M93A	466
7x64mm/7x65Rmm Brenneke	C/A	.284	.305/ .308	.422	.463	.468/ .521	.055	2.51/ 2.53	3.21	.217	5603	557-557A	466

Dimensional Data

Cartridge	Case Type	Bullet Dia.	Neck Dia.	Shoulder Dia.	Base Dia.	Rim Dia.	Rim Thck.	Case Length	Ctge. Length	Primer: Berdan Dia.	RWS Primer No.	Old DWM Case No.	Page
7mm Blaser Magnum	I	.284	.314	.515	.544	.535	.054	2.35	3.14	UNK/NA	L	UNK/NA	467
7x66mm Vom Hofe Super Express	C	.284	.316	.485	.543	.510	.048	2.58	3.25	.217	UNK	603	468
7x72Rmm	B	.284	.311	UNK/NA	.425	.482	UNK	2.84	3.48	.217	5603	573	468
7x73mm Vom Hofe (Belted)	E	.284	.315	.483	.527	.533	UNK	2.87	3.88	.217	5603	575	469
7x75Rmm Vom Hofe Super Express	A	.284	.318	.416	.468	.519	.050	2.95	3.68	.217	UNK	UNK	469
.300 Blaser Magnum	I	.308	.338	.511	.544	.535	.054	2.56	3.30		L		470
.308 Norma Magnum	E	.308	.340	.489	.514	.529	.048	2.56	3.30	UNK	UNK	UNK	470
.300 Norma Magnum	C	.308	.341	.562	.585	.587	.059	2.50	3.68		L		471
.30R Blaser	I	.308	.343	.441	.480	.531	UNK	2.68	3.80	UNK	UNK	UNK	472
8x48Rmm Sauer	B	.316	.344	UNK	.432	.500	.040	1.88	2.58	.254	1775	462A	472
8.15x46Rmm	A	.316	.346	.378	.421	.484	UNK	1.82	2.28	.250	1794	455	472
8x57Rmm 360	A	.318	.333	.375	.427	.485	UNK	2.24	2.96	UNK	UNK	UNK	473
8x57Jmm Mauser	C	.318	.350	.435	.470	.473	UNK	2.24	3.17	UNK	UNK	UNK	473
8x57mm/8x57Rmm		.318	UNK	UNK	UNK	UNK	UNK	UNK	UNK	UNK	UNK	UNK	474
8x58Rmm Sauer	B	.318	.345	UNK	.438	.499	UNK	2.28	3.00	.254	1775	462	474
8x56mm Mannlicher-Schoenauer	C	.323	.347	.424	.465	.470	.045	2.21	3.04	.217	5603	528	475
8x57mmJS/8x57RmmJS Mauser	C/A	.323	.350	.435	.470	.473/ .526	.043/ .048	2.24/ 2.25	3.17/ 3.55	.217	5603	366D1	475-476
8x60mmJ or S/8x60RmmJ or S Mauser & RWS	C	.323	.350	.431	.470	.468/ .526	.050	2.365	3.11	.217	5603	542	477
8x64mmJ or S/8x65RmmJ or S Brenneke	C/A	.323	.348	.421/ .424	.464/ .468	.469/ .520	UNK/NA	2.51/ 2.56	3.32/ 3.65	.217	5603	558-558A	477
8x68mmS RWS	C	.323	.354	.473	.522	.510	UNK/NA	2.65	3.38	.238	1698	UNK/NA	478
.338 Blaser Magnum	I	.338	.368	.512	.544	.535	.054	2.507	3.34	UNK/NA	L	UNK/NA	479
.338 Norma Magnum	C	.338	.369	.570	.585	.587	.059	2.50	3.68	UNK/NA	L	UNK/NA	479
9x56mm Mannlicher-Schoenauer	C	.356	.378	.408	.464	.464		2.22	3.56	.217	5603	491E	480
9x57mm/9x57Rmm Mauser	C/A	.356	.380	.424/ .428	.467	.468/ .515	.045/ .050	2.24	3.10/ 3.08	.217	5603	491A-491B	480
.358 Norma Magnum	E	.358	.384	.489	.508	.526	.048	2.52	3.22	UNK/NA	L	UNK/NA	481
9.3x80Rmm	B	.365	.386	UNK/NA	.430	.485	UNK/NA	3.14	3.50	.254	1775	77B	485
9.3x57mm Mauser	C	.365	.389	.428	.468	.469		2.24	3.23	.217	5603	491	482
9.3x64mm Brenneke	A	.366	.395	.474	.507	.496	.051	2.520	3.37	UNK/NA	UNK/NA	UNK/NA	482
9.3x74Rmm	A	.366	.387	.414	.465	524	052	2.93	3.74	.217	5603	474A	483
9.5x57mm Mannlicher-Schoenauer (9.5x56mm)	C	.375	.400	.460	.471	.473	.040	2.25	2.94	.217	5603	531	483
9.3x64mm Brenneke	C	.366	.395	.474	.507	.496	.051	2.52	3.37	UNK/NA	L	UNK/NA	482
.375 Blaser Magnum	I	.375	.405	.507	.544	.535	.054	2.822	3.622	UNK/NA	L	UNK/NA	484
9.3x48Rmm	B	.376	.382	UNK/NA	.433	.492	UNK/NA	1.89	2.35	.254	1775	246	485
9.3x57Rmm	B	.376	.389	UNK/NA	.428	.486	UNK/NA	2.24	2.80	.254	1775	77E	485
9.3x70Rmm	B	.376	.387	UNK/NA	.427	.482	UNK/NA	2.75	3.45	.254	1775	77F	485
9.3x72Rmm	B	.376	.385	UNK/NA	.427	.482	UNK/NA	2.84	3.27	.254	1775	77D	485
10.3x60Rmm Swiss	A	.415	.440	.498	.547	.619	UNK/NA	2.36	3.08	UNK	UNK/NA	UNK/NA	485
10.75x73mm/.404 Rimless Nitro/ .404 Jeffery	C	.421	.450	.520	.544	.537	.045	2.86	3.53	.217	UNK/NA	555	485
10.3x65Rmm Baenziger	B	.423	.431	UNK/NA	.462	.505	UNK/NA	2.56	3.15	UNK/NA	UNK/NA	164	486
10.75x68mm Mauser	C	.424	.445	.470	.492	.488	UNK/NA	2.67	3.16	.217	5603	515A	486
.45 Blaser	I	.458	.486	.511	.513	.473	.054	2.16	2.70	UNK/NA	L		487
.460 Steyr (11.64mm)	C	.458	.501	.719	.805	.805	.089	3.64	4.80	UNK/NA	Bx	UNK	487
12.50x70mm Schüler	I	.510	.535	.615	.620	.578	UNK/NA	2.94	3.50	.254	2703	UNK	488

Case Type: A = Rimmed, bottleneck. B = Rimmed, straight. C = Rimless, bottleneck. D = Rimless, straight. E = Belted, bottleneck. F = Belted, straight. G = Semi-rimmed, bottleneck. H = Semi-rimmed, straight. I = Rebated, bottleneck. J = Rebated, straight. K = Rebated, belted bottleneck. L = Rebated, belted straight.

Other codes: Unless otherwise noted, all dimensions in inches. Primer L = Large rifle (0.210-inch) UNK/NA = Unknown/Not Applicable
Dimensions shown in some instances do not exactly coincide with dimensions found in *The Book of Rifles* (W.H.B. Smith, Harrisburg, Pa., 1960). Differences amount to only a few thousandths of an inch, doubtless attributable to specimen variations. Parentheses indicate maximum cartridge specifications.

American Rimfire Cartridges

(Current & Obsolete – Blackpowder and Smokeless)

Rimfire cartridges differ from centerfire cartridges in that the priming compound is contained in the rim. Ignition occurs when the firing pin crushes the rim. Rimfire cartridges are of historical as well as practical interest. Although only one of a number of ignition systems leading to the modern centerfire, the rimfire was the first truly *successful* system and is still alive and well, more than 150 years later.

The common .22 rimfire had its origin with the Flobert BB Cap, in 1845, which led to the Smith & Wesson-developed .22 Short of 1857. The idea of rimfire ignition goes back to Roberts' French patent of 1831. This provided for the priming compound covering the entire head interior. The rimfire evolved by leaving the primer mix out of the center. After Smith & Wesson introduced its First Model revolver—a .22 Short chambering, in 1857—development of rimfire arms and cartridges bloomed. The New Haven Arms Co. began manufacturing .44 Henry ammunition in 1861, and .56-56 Spencer ammunition was made in quantity beginning about 1862, (although the Spencer rifle design dates back to 1860). Both of these cartridges were used by Federal troops in the Civil War. Chambering of the first successful metallic cartridge repeating arms was for rimfire cartridges. By the end of the Civil War, numerous rimfire cartridges in various calibers were available.

A great many rimfire cartridges have been developed for rifles and handguns here and in Europe. In the late 1800s, something like 75 different rimfire cartridges had been loaded by American companies, but only about 42 were still around by 1900. The decline in the number of rimfire cartridges occurred, because many early types put on the market were really experimental and, so, had a very short life. These are of academic interest primarily to collectors. Space limitations rule out any effort to list all of these here. The criteria for inclusion of a cartridge is that it was loaded by American companies and survived to the turn of the century. The more obscure numbers, and those of British or Continental origin, have been covered fairly well elsewhere. The more popular rimfires lasted well past the turn of the century, and a few are still in use. The .22 Short rimfire is, in fact, the *oldest* American cartridge, having survived since 1857. It will probably still be around as long as we own and shoot firearms.

The decline in the number of rimfire cartridge types can be illustrated by a review of old catalogs. Forty-two U.S. types were in common production in 1900; by 1918, that number had dwindled to 32 and, by the 1930s, the number was down to a mere 17. After World War II, the count was less than 10. Some older rimfires are still loaded in Europe and, from time to time when available, these are imported here. Many of the cartridges listed here were available on an over-the-counter basis up through the 1920s. One or two of the obsolete rimfires would probably be useful to modern shooters, but it is unlikely ammunition manufacturers will revive these cartridges. While many shooters would welcome a return of the .25 Stevens Long, it seems unlikely this will ever happen.

Rimfire cartridges have advantages, as well as weaknesses, when compared to centerfire cartridges. In smaller calibers, the rimfire is cheaper to manufacture and, within equivalent pressures, is just as good as the centerfire. One important disadvantage of the rimfire is that it is not practical to reload. This was a big consideration with early buffalo hunters and pioneers of the Old West. It was also no small consideration among match shooters,

who developed top accuracy by loading their own. The rimfire will not stand up under the pressures of modern high-velocity centerfire loads, but solid-head centerfires can be made much stronger. Large-caliber rimfire cartridges cost nearly as much as similar centerfire rounds, so there is an economic point beyond which the rimfire just is not worthwhile.

If any statements made before this give the impression that the rimfire cartridge is about to become extinct, don't worry. Nothing could be further from the truth. As recently as 1959, Winchester introduced the .22 Magnum Rimfire and, in 1970, Remington introduced the 5mm Remington Rimfire Magnum. The .22 Magnum caught on immediately and is well into its fifth decade of popularity. The 5mm Magnum did not fare so well, despite ballistics that were somewhat superior to the .22 Magnum. It was discontinued after only a few years.

Despite the failure of the 5mm Magnum in the 1970s, Hornady introduced the .17 Hornady Magnum Rimfire, in 2002. It is similar in appearance to the earlier 5mm Magnum, but, with a 17-grain V-Max bullet at 2550 fps, its trajectory is more nearly similar to the centerfire .22 Hornet. More than a dozen rifle makers are chambering for the .17 HMR, and it seems destined for a long life.

The .22 Long Rifle has become the most accurate and highly developed sporting cartridge in existence. Its popularity for match shooting and small-game or varmint hunting remains not only undiminished, but is increasing, if anything. There are dozens of makes, models, and types of .22 rimfire arms currently manufactured, and new models appear in a steady stream. The .22 Long Rifle has established a place so secure, it will be with us as long as guns are made.

Modern rimfire cartridges are intended for target, plinking, or small-game hunting. The .22 Long Rifle does very well out to 75 yards on rabbit-sized animals, and on coyote or fox with a well-placed bullet. The .17 Hornady Magnum will extend this range to nearly 200 yards. The .22 Short is a good plinking round and is used in Olympic pistol competition. The high-velocity Long Rifle is a useful self-defense round; it will penetrate better than the .32 Smith & Wesson, when fired from a handgun. The .22 WMR develops handgun energies nearly equal to some .38 Special loads.

It would surprise many to know how many deer are killed each year by poachers using the .22 Long Rifle. However, it is *not* to be considered a deer cartridge. There is, reportedly, a case of an elephant that was killed with a .22 Long Rifle, but that hardly qualifies it as an elephant cartridge, either. Still, within their capabilities and limitations, modern rimfire cartridges are among the most useful we have.— *F.C.B., with additional text by S.S.*

13th Edition Update

This is one chapter we didn't cut anything from, regarding obsolete cartridges. First, the majority were originally marked "obsolete" in the last Edition, and we didn't want to eliminate the entire chapter. Second, there are lots of rimfires out there, old and new, and it's often hard to tell the difference between similar cartridges. Couple this last with the fact that so many are not interchangeable with one another, and we felt it best to leave this chapter intact so that the best possible attempt can be made at identifying a cartridge and the gun/s it goes with before one attempts to fire either.—*J.L.S.P.*

.17 Mach 2

Historical Notes: A 2004 joint rimfire cartridge development between Hornady and CCI, the .17 Mach 2 cartridge delivers higher velocities and flatter trajectories than the .22 Long Rifle cartridge. Hornady designed the .17 Mach 2 for plinking, varminting, and small-game hunting. In quality firearms, the .17 Mach 2 is capable of MOA or better accuracy.

General Comments: The .17 Mach 2 cartridge is not reloadable. It uses the rimfire .22 Stinger case as its parent. Exactly .100-inch longer that the .22 Long Rifle case, the Stinger case is necked down to accept .172-inch diameter bullets weighing 17 grains. The .17 Mach 2 is well-suited to 18/22-inch barrels with a 1:9 rifling twist. Ruger, Marlin, Thompson/Center, and other manufacturers offer rifles chambered for the .17 Mach 2. Hornady, CCI, Remington, and Eley supply loaded ammunition.

.17 Hornady Magnum Rimfire (.17 HMR)

Historical Notes: In 2002, Hornady provided shooters with serious reasons to consider a rimfire cartridge for medium-range (200-yard) varmint hunting. Its new .17 HMR is the fastest rimfire commercially available. It pushes a 17-grain bullet on trajectories very similar to the larger .22 Hornet centerfire cartridge.

General Comments: Launching a 17-grain V-Max bullet at 2550 fps, Hornady's bottleneck rimfire cartridge printed five-shot groups measuring .460-inch at 100 yards, and 1.005 inches at 200 yards, using a Wiseman-barreled Marlin rifle in factory tests. Flattening the .22 WMR's trajectory by more than 10 inches at 200 yards, the flat-shooting .17 HMR also drifts 15 inches less in a 10 mph wind. Contributing to this fine performance is the boat-tail V-Max bullet with a polymer tip engineered for dramatic expansion. Hornady achieves this performance at pressures slightly greater than the .22 WMR, which suggests existing .22 WMR rifle designs can be readily adapted to the .17 HMR. As a measure of the popularity of the new .17 HMR cartridge, rifles and pistols are available from Anschütz, Cooper, H&R 1871, Marlin, New England Arms, Remington, Ruger, Rogue River, Savage, and Thompson/Center.

5mm Remington Rimfire Magnum

Historical Notes: The 5mm Remington Rimfire Magnum was announced in 1969, but not actually introduced until 1970. Only the Remington bolt-action Model 591 clip-loading and Model 592 tubular magazine repeating rifles were available for the round. It was not adopted by other ammunition manufacturers. For a time, Thompson/Center furnished barrels in 5mm Remington for the Contender pistol. This was the only modern bottlenecked rimfire case. However, a number of the obsolete blackpowder rimfires were necked, so it is not an entirely new development. Bullet diameter is .2045-inch with a weight of 38 grains and a muzzle velocity of 2100 fps. This round developed the highest velocity of any rimfire at the time (newer, 30-grain .22 WMR loads offer greater muzzle velocity).

General Comments: The 5mm Remington represented an interesting development, one that exceeds the performance of some of the early .22 centerfires. Its effective killing range on small, varmint-type animals is 25 to 50 yards greater than the .22 Winchester Magnum Rimfire. This is due to the better sectional density of the smaller diameter bullet combined with 150 fps higher initial velocity. Both are essentially varmint cartridges. In both, the hollowpoint-type bullets ruin too much edible meat for small-game shooting. However, the .22 WMR is available with a non-expanding full jacketed bullet, or one could switch to the interchangeable .22 WRF for small-game hunting. In summary, the 5mm Remington has the edge for varmint shooting, but the .22 WMR is more versatile for small game. On the other hand, a good full metal jacket small-game bullet for the 5mm Remington might have changed that analysis. The choice would be largely a matter of use and personal preference. Remington has long since discontinued the Model 591 and 592, and no rifles are currently made in 5mm RFM. Ammunition, likewise, is no longer made by Remington. The 5mm RFM is another good idea that didn't catch on, although it had a lot to recommend it. Ammunition is available on a limited basis from Aguila (www.aguilaammo.com).

.22 BB Cap

Historical Notes: The rimfire .22 BB Cap, or Bulleted Breech Cap, is one of the oldest successful self-contained cartridges. It originated, in 1845, for the Flobert indoor target rifle. These guns were also known as saloon (salon) or parlor rifles and were quite popular through the turn of the century. A great many individuals and companies have made both rifles and pistols for the .22 BB Cap. This type of social, indoor shooting has become virtually extinct. American companies loaded the .22 BB Cap up to World War II, but discontinued it after the war. The original cartridge had only a priming charge and a .22-caliber lead round ball, but American ammunition contained a small charge of powder and a conical bullet in many makes. The original case was a tapered percussion cap without a well-defined rim.

General Comments: Many insist the .22 BB Cap is completely worthless, but the original author of this book did not agree. Rainy afternoons of target practice in the basement or garage will create a certain appreciation for this little pipsqueak. These cartridges are also handy for a preliminary sighting-in of .22 rimfire rifles or pistols. Modern loads have sufficient power to kill rats, mice, sparrows, or other pests out to 40 yards or so. At close range, RWS BB Caps will penetrate an inch of soft pine board. These could seriously injure or even kill a human, so one should always be careful—these are not toys.

There is considerable variation in case length and dimensions between different makes. The CCI "Mini-Cap," loaded in .22 Short and Long Rifle cases, duplicated performance of the older .22 BB and CB cap for indoor target practice.

.22 CB Cap

Historical Notes: The .22 CB Cap, or Conical Bullet Cap, is something of a cross between the .22 BB Cap and .22 Short. It has been manufactured in various sizes. In original form, it was supposed to combine the 29-grain .22 Short bullet with the .22 BB Cap case and a light charge of blackpowder. In actual manufacture, some CB Cap cases have a length about halfway between the BB Cap and Short. It is not a transitional design leading to the .22 Short, but, rather, a more powerful version of the BB Cap. The earliest catalog reference appears to be about 1888, although it probably originated prior to this. American companies loaded it up to 1942, but most discontinued it after World War II. CCI occasionally catalogs this load, and RWS has offered these rounds.

General Comments: The .22 CB Cap managed to combine about all the disadvantages of the .22 BB Cap and Short into one generally useless cartridge. It was no more accurate than either of the other two and made enough noise to nullify the indoor virtues of the BB Cap. It also required a backstop almost as heavy as did the Short and was just as dangerous indoors. In killing power, it wasn't that much better than the BB Cap to make any real difference, although it might provide an additional 10 or 15 yards of effective range. In recognition of this, almost everyone quit making it, and there were few laments from the shooting public. The original charge was 1½ grains of blackpowder, but, after 1920, smokeless powder was used exclusively. CCI has produced loads with the 29-grain CB Cap bullet in the .22 Short case at a velocity of 710 fps. Remington offers its CBee, which is a low-velocity round based on the .22 Long case, with a 33-grain hollowpoint bullet at a muzzle velocity of 700 fps. These loads are intended for indoor target practice, gallery, or pest shooting.

.22 Winchester Automatic

Historical Notes: Used only in the Winchester Model 1903 semi-auto rifle, the .22 Winchester Automatic round was dropped from standard Winchester production, in the 1970s. The rifle has been obsolete, since 1932. This cartridge has a 45-grain inside-lubricated bullet and will not chamber in any standard .22 Long Rifle gun. It was designed at a time when blackpowder and semi-smokeless-powder .22 rimfires were still loaded and popular. The purpose was to prevent use of anything but smokeless powder ammunition in the semi-auto rifle, so as not to foul the action. Blackpowder will gum up such actions and render them inoperable in short order. Remington later brought out a similar cartridge for the same reason. The two are not interchangeable.

General Comments: The .22 Winchester Automatic had little to offer over the standard Long Rifle, except smokeless powder and the semi-auto rifle in which it was fired. In killing power and range, it was on a par with the .22 Long Rifle. This cartridge is now a collector's item.

.22 Short

Historical Notes: The .22 Short is the oldest American, commercial, self-contained metallic cartridge—it has been in continuous production for more than 143 years! It was introduced, in 1857, for the Smith & Wesson First Model revolver and is still widely used all over the world.

Although now popular as a short-range gallery or plinking round, the .22 Short was originally intended for self-defense. It is still used for Olympic match shooting, and heavy target pistols are built specifically for it. The initial loading was a 29-grain bullet and four grains of a fine-granulation blackpowder (probably similar to what we would now call FFFFg). After 1887, it was available with semi-smokeless powder and, within a short time, smokeless powder. Remington introduced non-corrosive (Kleanbore) priming for its rimfire line in 1927, and the first high-velocity type in 1930. The .22 Short can be fired in any arm chambered for the Long Rifle, but most semi-auto guns will not function properly with the .22 Short. Since the end of World War II, a number of small .22 Short pocket-automatic pistols and revolvers have appeared on the market.

General Comments: In the high-velocity loading, the Short is quite adequate for small-game or bird hunting. However, killing power declines rapidly beyond 50 yards. Hunting should be confined to animals not more than two pounds in weight.

The .22 Short can be deceiving, because it looks small and relatively harmless. When fired from a rifle, it can penetrate two inches of soft pine board and has an extreme range of almost one full mile. It can seriously wound or kill a person right up to the limit of its range—be careful! Make sure of your backstop before shooting any .22 rimfire.

The hollowpoint bullet weighs 27 grains and has about 25 fps higher velocity than the solid; this is a particularly effective squirrel load. CCI is the only remaining manufacturer of the hollowpoint load. Although sales today are vastly overshadowed by the less expensive .22 Long Rifle, the .22 Short cartridge was king during its first century of production.

.22 Short/40-grain

Historical Notes: We have almost no information on this interesting variation. The sample is labeled as an RWS .22 Short case loaded with a .22 Long Rifle bullet. The case appears to be pure copper, which suggests that this round is quite old. Headstamp is an RWS crest with a centered uppercase "R."

General Comments: We have included this number, because it will serve to demonstrate that rimfire ammunition is as varied and numerous in design as any other type. As we gain further information, we hope to improve the historical details included with this entry.

.22 Long

Historical Notes: The .22 Long is usually referred to as a combination of the Long Rifle case and the Short bullet. This is not true for several reasons. Foremost, the .22 Long happens to be 16 years older than the Long Rifle. It is listed in the 1871 Great Western Gun Works catalog for the seven-shot Standard revolver. A few years later, it was also listed in Remington and Stevens catalogs as a rifle cartridge. The .22 Long Rifle was not on the market until 1887. The Long was originally a blackpowder number loaded with a 29-grain bullet and five grains of a fine granulation blackpowder (probably similar to what we now call FFFFg). Smokeless powder was available, for a time, in standard and high-velocity loads. At present, only the high-velocity load is available. A shot load was also offered.

General Comments: The original blackpowder loading of the .22 Long had a slightly higher velocity than did the .22 Short or Long Rifle, but this was not true of later smokeless loads. The present high-velocity Long has a velocity between the Short and Long Rifle. The .22 Long is not as accurate as the Short or Long Rifle and has outlived any useful purpose it might have once had. We think the reason it hangs on is that a great many people still think it has a higher velocity and greater killing power than the Long Rifle.

Editor's note: Others believe that firing enough .22 Short rounds in a .22 Long Rifle-chambered gun will damage the chamber, and that the .22 Long gives similar performance to the .22 Short, but without the potential for chamber damage. Old ideas, true or not, are tenacious, because people will not readily accept concepts in opposition to what they believe. In any event, the .22 Long is strictly a small-game, short-range cartridge ballistically just a notch above the .22 Short. Only CCI still offers the .22 Long.

.22 Long Rifle

Historical Notes: Information available indicates that the .22 Long Rifle was developed by the J. Stevens Arms & Tool Co., in 1887. It is the .22 Long case with a five-grain blackpowder charge (likely with a granulation similar to what we would now call FFFFg), and a 40-grain bullet instead of the original 29-grain. The Peters Cartridge Co. is supposed to have first manufactured it, specifically for Stevens. If this is true, then why does the 1888 Stevens catalog refer to a UMC .22-caliber Long rimfire rifle cartridge? This would be a gross ingratitude, at best. This 1888 catalog lists the Nos. 1, 2, 9, and 10 model break-open rifles as available in the new chambering with increased rifling twist. The New Model Pocket or Bicycle rifle also chambered it. The 1888 Marlin-Ballard catalog recommends the new .22 Long "Rifle" cartridge for its No. 3 Gallery rifle as being more accurate than the common .22 Long or Extra Long.

At one time, the .22 Long Rifle was available in blackpowder, semi-smokeless, and smokeless powder loads. Remington introduced the first high-velocity type, in 1930. The 40-grain solid and 36- and 38-grain hollowpoint bullet have been available for many years. The original case was not crimped, a feature that finally appeared in 1900. Space does not permit a full discussion of the different loads and types of .22 Long Rifle cartridges or the rifles and handguns that chamber it. Suffice to say, it is the most accurate and highly developed of any rimfire cartridge ever.

General Comments: The .22 Long Rifle is the most popular match cartridge in existence, and also the most widely used small-game and varmint cartridge. The high-velocity hollowpoint is the best field load and will do a good job on rabbit-sized animals out to 75 yards. Beyond that, it is unreliable. The Long Rifle is a great favorite of poachers for killing game out of season with close-up head shots. The modest report does not alarm or alert passersby or officials. At close range, the high-velocity load with the solid-lead bullet will penetrate six inches of soft pine board and has a maximum range of nearly two miles. Maximum range is achieved at the relatively low angle of between 25 and 30 degrees, so one must be very careful. Humans shot with the .22 Long Rifle often show little immediate distress, survive without complications for several days, then die very suddenly. This is mentioned because many individuals regard .22 rimfires as play things not powerful enough to be dangerous. Careless shooting with the .22 rimfire has probably led to the closure of more areas to hunting and caused more trouble than any other cartridge. Use your head and be careful! There is also a .22 Long Rifle shot cartridge, loaded by most companies and useful mostly for rat and other pest control.

.22 Stinger, Spitfire, Viper, Yellow Jacket, Super-Max, Xpediter, etc.

Historical Notes: The .22 Stinger was the first in a series of developments aimed at improving the performance of the .22 Long Rifle. Introduced by CCI, early in 1977, the concept was an immediate success and quickly copied by Winchester with its Xpediter, by Remington in its Yellow Jacket, and by Federal with the Spitfire. All of these cartridges are much the same and are based on reducing the weight of the hollowpoint bullet from 36 to around 30 grains and loading it into a case full of relatively slow-burning powder. The result is a 30-percent increase in muzzle velocity and a 25-percent increase in muzzle energy, as compared to the standard .22 Long Rifle hollowpoint high-velocity loading. The overall loaded length of these rounds is the same as the regular .22 Long Rifle, and so are all other dimensions, with the exception of the case length. Some use a standard-length .22 Long Rifle case and settle for a somewhat lower muzzle velocity, while others use a longer case to achieve maximum velocity. As a group, these are referred to as hyper-velocity .22s. Only Stinger, Yellow Jacket, and Viper brands are still in production.

General Comments: The original author fired all of the increased velocity .22 Long Rifle cartridges available at the time, in both rifles and handguns, comparing the performance with the standard line of .22 rimfires, as well as the .22 WMR. When fired into paraffin blocks and soap bars, the hyper-velocity hollowpoints demonstrated superior expansion and energy transfer, compared to the regular high-velocity hollowpoints.

Malfunctions can occur when firing the hyper-velocity Long Rifles in auto pistols, and Barnes didn't think they are well suited to those types of handguns. They worked fine in revolvers.

Field-testing didn't demonstrate any great advantage of one over the other in shooting jackrabbits, nor any great superiority over the .22 WMR or the standard Long Rifle high-velocity hollowpoint. The hyper-velocity cartridges do inflict greater tissue damage than does the .22 Long Rifle hollowpoint. However, dead is dead, and you can't accomplish anything beyond that.

These cartridges do provide increased velocity and energy for .22 rimfire rifles. They probably extend the effective range on varmints or small game by a few yards. These cartridges cost some 65-percent more than regular .22 Long Rifle high-velocity hollowpoint, which is a negative factor. They certainly have a place in the .22 rimfire lineup, but their increased performance is most pronounced when they are fired from a rifle, rather than a handgun. In some instances, particularly in short-barreled pistols and revolvers or any revolver with a large barrel-to-cylinder gap, these loads can generate much less energy than standard .22 Long Rifle high-velocity loads. The bullets actually exit the muzzle more slowly.

.22 Hyper-Velocities Factory Ballistics

Bullet (grains)	Powder	Grains	Velocity	Energy	Source/Comments
29	FL, Win.		1680	182	Xpediter (obsolete)
32	FL, CCl		1640	191	Stinger
33	FL, Fed.		1500	164	Spitfire (obsolete)
33	FL, Rem.		1500	164	Yellowjacket
34	FL, Win.		1500	169	Super-Max. (obsolete)
36	FL, Fed.		1410	158	Spitfire (obsolete)
36	FL, Rem.		1410	158	Viper
36	FL, CCI		1425	162	CCI, HP+V

.22 Extra Long

Historical Notes: Introduced about 1880, the .22 Extra Long was used in Ballard, Remington, Stevens, Wesson, and late (1916) versions of the 1902 and 1904 Winchester bolt-action rifles, as well as S&W revolvers. It was listed in ammunition catalogs as late as 1935. It used the same 40-grain, outside-lubricated bullet that was later adapted to the .22 Long Rifle, but the longer case held more (six grains) blackpowder. It was more powerful than the Long Rifle, but not noted for great accuracy. Smokeless powder loads had nearly the same velocity as the modern Long Rifle loadings.

General Comments: The .22 Extra Long will not chamber in arms made for the Long Rifle, but, since the only dimensional difference is case length, the Short, Long, or Long Rifle can be fired in the Extra Long chamber. In terms of killing power, the Extra Long is in the same class as the standard velocity Long Rifle. At one time, the .22 Extra Long was advertised as a 200-yard target cartridge, but it certainly would not qualify for this by today's standards. Case length and overall cartridge length made the Extra Long unsuitable to most repeating actions, which is another reason it became obsolete. Never fire any high-velocity or hyper-velocity .22 cartridge in any blackpowder gun.

.22 Remington Automatic

Historical Notes: This cartridge was developed for the Remington Model 16 autoloading rifle (actually introduced in 1914), and was discontinued in 1928. Ammunition has not been loaded since the end of World War II. The purpose of the cartridge was the same as the Winchester .22 Automatic, to prevent use of action-gumming blackpowder ammunition in a semi-auto rifle. No other gun used this round, and it is not interchangeable with the 2.2 Winchester. This is an example of senseless, jealous rivalry, if ever there was one.

General Comments: This was another .22 Long Rifle-class cartridge. It had an inside-lubricated 45-grain bullet in solid or hollowpoint type, both with the same ballistics. It was neither as accurate nor as effective (generally) as the Long Rifle.

.22 Winchester Rimfire (WRF)
.22 Remington Special

Historical Notes: Introduced for the Winchester Model 1890 pump-action rifle, the original Winchester loading had a flat-nose bullet, while Remington used a round-nose type and called it the .22 Remington Special. The two are identical and interchangeable. Bullet can be either a 45-grain solid or a 40-grain hollowpoint in standard or high-velocity loading. This cartridge uses a flat-base inside-lubricated bullet, rather than the "heel" type of outside-lubricated bullet of the Short, Long, Long Rifle, and Extra Long. The .22 WRF was chambered in various Remington, Stevens, and Winchester single-shot and repeating rifles and Colt's revolvers. It is no longer routinely loaded by the ammunition manufacturers, and no one makes rifles for it. However, in late 1986, Winchester made a special run of .22 WRF ammunition. This must have been aimed more at collectors than shooters. It has since been produced in limited amounts.

General Comments: The .22 WRF was the first notable improvement in the killing power of the various .22 rimfires. It is not as accurate as the Long Rifle, but in field use, this is of no consequence. Out to 75 yards, it will kill small animals more reliably than the Long Rifle. Although there is little difference in bullet diameter between the WRF and the standard .22 rimfires, the WRF has a larger case diameter to accept the bullet's full diameter. It is much too large to fit the standard .22 Long Rifle chamber. The .22 Short or Long Rifle fits the WRF chamber quite loosely and will not fire or extract in many guns. When these do fire, the case often splits, which allows particles to escape the action with possible danger to the shooter and bystanders; accuracy is extremely poor. The .22 WRF can be safely fired in any gun chambered for the .22 Winchester Magnum Rimfire. Winchester produced one batch of these cartridges in 1995.

13th Edition Update: Previous editions of this book listed this cartridge as obsolete. However, there seems to be a bit of renewed interest in the cartridge. CCI is currently loading this round as a 45-grain jacketed hollowpoint with a muzzle velocity of 1300 fps and energy of 169 ft-lbs. CCI does not recommend this round for use in revolvers, noting that most revolvers have undersized bores that resist the use of copper-jacketed bullets.

.22 Winchester Magnum Rimfire (WMR)

Historical Notes: The .22 Magnum Rimfire was introduced, in 1959, by Winchester, but the company didn't market a gun to shoot it until well into the following year. Ruger and Smith & Wesson, on the other hand, advertised revolvers for the new round before the end of 1959, and Savage chambered its Model 24, a .22/.410-bore over/under combination gun, for the Magnum Rimfire shortly thereafter. The discontinued slide-action Winchester Model 61 was the first rifle of that manufacture available for the new round. At present, there is a wide variety of single-shot and repeating rifles, as well as pistols and revolvers of American and European manufacture available in .22 Magnum Rimfire caliber. The standard bullet is a jacketed 40-grain type, although Federal introduced a 50-grain bullet, in 1988. CCI recently introduced a hyper-velocity loading with a 30-grain bullet, and Federal soon joined the "hyper-velocity" fray with a similar loading.

General Comments: The .22 Winchester Magnum Rimfire is an elongated and more powerful version of the older .22 WRF. Case dimensions are the same except for length, and the WRF can be fired in any gun chambered for the Magnum Rimfire. It is not a safe practice to re-chamber older guns for the new round. The .22 WRF is loaded with outside-lubricated lead bullets, while the .22 WMR is loaded with jacketed bullets. With a thin-jacketed 40-grain bullet at about 1900 fps, this is the most potent rimfire cartridge currently available. It is more powerful than the .22 Winchester Centerfire, forerunner of the .22 Hornet. Claimed ballistics in a six-inch pistol barrel exceed any other rimfire fired from a rifle, thus, it is a very effective 125-yard varmint or small-game cartridge, although overly destructive on animals intended for the pot, unless solid bullets are used. CCI also loads a shot version.

.22 ILARCO/.22 WMR Short

Historical Notes: The .22 ILARCO Rimfire originated in 1987 and was manufactured in experimental quantities by Winchester for the Illinois Arms Co. It is the .22 Winchester Magnum Rimfire shortened to the same loaded length as the .22 Long Rifle. It was chambered in the Illinois Arms Co.'s Model 180 auto/semi-auto rifle that features a 165-round drum-type magazine. The full-auto version was available only to law-enforcement agencies. The reason for the shorter cartridge was that the Model 180 was designed for the .22 Long Rifle and the action wouldn't handle the longer .22 WMR. The Illinois Arms Co. was bought by Feather Industries, of Boulder, Colorado, and the .22 ILARCO was discontinued. The cartridge is sometimes referred to as the .22 WMR Short.

General Comments: Shortening the .22 WMR made sense, even though there was some velocity loss. For one thing, the short case used the same jacketed bullet as the parent cartridge and didn't pick up dirt and debris the way sticky, outside-lubricated .22 Long Rifle cartridges can. With a 165-round magazine and full-auto fire, this was a matter of some importance. Also, the .22 WMR is too long to function in practically any .22 semi-automatic pistol, but many of these could be adapted to fire the .22 ILARCO. Unfortunately, this cartridge never went into production, and existing specimens are now collector's items.

.22 ILARCO/.22 Short WMR Short Factory Ballistics

Bullet (grains/type)	Powder	Grains	Velocity	Energy	Source/Comments
40 FMJ	FL		1350	160	Winchester factory load

.25 Short

Historical Notes: Originally, this pistol cartridge was developed for the F.D. Bliss revolver, also known as the .25 Bacon & Bliss. It was chambered in other cheap handguns of the period. Date of introduction was around 1860, and both Remington and Winchester listed it in catalogs up to 1920. It is a collector's item now.

General Comments: The .25 Short had a 43-grain, outside-lubricated bullet and five grains of powder. Bullet diameter is actually .245- to .246-inch, and it closely resembles the .22 Short. In power, it is similar to the blackpowder .22 Long Rifle fired from a short pistol barrel. There is no record of any rifle having been chambered for the .25 Short. It should not be confused with the .25 Stevens Short.

.25 Stevens Short

Historical Notes: Introduced in 1902, this cartridge was intended as a shorter, cheaper, and less powerful version of the .25 Stevens. The original loading used 4½ to five grains of blackpowder, but only smokeless powder was in use, when it was discontinued in 1942. Remington, Winchester, and Stevens rifles chambered this round. It could be fired in any rifle chambered for the .25 Stevens.

General Comments: The .25 Stevens Short was not nearly as effective a field cartridge as the longer version. However, it was somewhat cheaper and certainly as good or better than the .22 Short for small game at close range. More expensive than the .22 Long Rifle and no better for hunting purposes, it was never popular.

.25 Stevens

Historical Notes: Various dates can be found for the introduction of the .25 Stevens, with most authorities agreeing on 1900. References in old books and catalogs would indicate an actual date of 1890, but this is uncertain. In any event, this cartridge was developed jointly by the J. Stevens Arms & Tool Co. and the Peters Cartridge Co. The Stevens Crack Shot No. 15 rifle came out in 1900, and one of its original chamberings was the .25 Stevens. However, the Stevens Favorite rifle, manufactured from 1894 to 1935, may have been the first model available in this chambering. Both of these are under-lever single-shots. Remington and Winchester also chambered rifles for the .25 Stevens. The original load was a 67-grain bullet and 10 to 11 grains of blackpowder. Semi-smokeless powder was also used, but smokeless was the only propellant offered when the round was discontinued, in 1942. Remington did preliminary work on an improved, high-velocity loading prior to World War II, but the project was dropped after the war. The improved round, called the .267 Remington Rimfire, was rumored to have had a muzzle velocity of 1400 fps with the 67-grain bullet.

General Comments: The .25 Stevens had an excellent reputation on small game, especially for not ruining edible meat. Most complaints centered around the high cost, as compared to the .22 Long Rifle, as well as the high trajectory, which made hits beyond 60 to 70 yards difficult. For years, gun writers called for a high-velocity version, but the ammunition companies failed to respond. With modern powder and a longer case, a velocity of 1600 to 1800 fps might be possible.

Rifles are no longer chambered for this round and ammunition is no longer manufactured, so it appears to be a dead number. Many who used the .25 Stevens were sorry to see it go, but, with the .22 Magnum Rimfire, there isn't much need for it. It had an inside-lubricated bullet and was available with solid and hollowpoint bullets.

.30 Short

Historical Notes: This old-timer originated in the early 1860s and was used mostly in low-priced handguns, such as the Sharps four-barrel, the Standard revolver, and various single-shots. Colt's New Line revolvers were also made in .30 Short and .30 Long chamberings. The .30 Short was listed in ammunition catalogs as late as 1919.

General Comments: The .30 Short had a 50- to 58-grain lead bullet and five to six grains of blackpowder. Not a powerful round by any standard, its use was confined to pocket or house guns. It was not as good of a cartridge as the .32 Short rimfire, and one wonders why it survived for so long. It is now a collector's item.

.30 Long

Historical Notes: This rimfire was cataloged as early as 1873, but may have originated earlier. Adapted to Colt's, Standard X.L., and Sharps handguns, it was also used in some single-shot rifles. The .30 Short survived until 1920; the .30 Long disappeared before WWI.

General Comments: The .30 Short and .30 Long were interchangeable in most guns. The bullet was actually .290- to .295-inch and of outside-lubricated type. Power of the .30 Long was about the same as the .32 Short rimfire.

.32 Long Rifle

Historical Notes: This cartridge has an inside-lubricated bullet and a longer case than the regular .32 Long rimfire. It appears on cartridge lists from 1900 into the early 1920s. Both Remington and Winchester loaded it. Some say it was a smokeless powder improvement over the older .32 Long, but the 1918-'19 Remington catalog lists it as available in the blackpowder loading only. It has been obsolete for many years and is a collector's item.

General Comments: Case length of the .32 Long Rifle is between that of the .32 Long and Extra Long rimfires; other dimensions are practically identical. It could be fired in any rifle chambered for the Extra Long, and most rifles or revolvers made to handle the Long. The outside-lubricated bullet was messy to carry in the pocket or loose in a container. These bullets picked up lint and dirt, stained the pocket, etc. Inside-lubricated bullets are much cleaner to handle under any conditions, which is the reason efforts were made to produce such versions. However, this required a smaller diameter bullet, which gave unacceptable accuracy in the original barrel. That may have been why the .32 Long Rifle had a short life. No one seems to have made a gun specifically for it, or at least the author found no reference to such. The original load was an 81- or 82-grain lead bullet with 13 grains of blackpowder.

.32 Extra Short/.32 Protector

Historical Notes: This cartridge was made for the Remington magazine pistol and the Chicago Firearms Co.'s Protector palm pistol. The Remington pistol was manufactured from 1871 until 1888, and the odd palm pistol originated sometime in the 1880s. This fixes the date of introduction for the .32 Extra Short at 1871, though some authorities indicate a later date. The cartridge was listed in Remington catalogs until 1920. It was also known as the .32 Protector.

General Comments: The .32 was a popular chambering for both handguns and rifles for many years. The .32 Extra Short was probably designed to increase the magazine capacity of the Remington-Rider magazine pistol. Since it held five short rounds, it would have held only three of the standard .32 Short rimfires. A longer pistol would have been unhandy. Likewise, a reduced magazine capacity would not have been competitive with the five- and seven-shot revolvers of the day. Sales departments have to consider all these angles. The Remington magazine pistol had a tubular magazine below the barrel and a "lever" that protruded slightly above the hammer. Lever and hammer were drawn back together, which cocked the gun and extracted the empty shell. Release of the lever chambered a new round as it returned to the forward position. It was of limited popularity. The original load was five to 5½ grains of blackpowder with a 54- to 60-grain lead bullet.

.32 Short

Historical Notes: The .32 Short rimfire originated under a Smith & Wesson patent of 1860, and early cartridge boxes were so marked. It was first used in the Smith & Wesson New Model 1½ and Model 2 revolvers. It was later adapted to Colt's revolvers and others with names such as Allen, Blue Jacket, Enterprise, Favorite, Whitney, X.L., and many, many others. It was also used in a variety of rifles, including models from Remington, Stevens, and Winchester. It was loaded and listed in some ammunition catalogs as late as 1972. Navy Arms had .32 rimfire ammunition made in Brazil, in 1990. Until recently, .32 Short ammunition has been available from that source.

General Comments: Rifles and pistols using the .32 Short rimfire were popular up to the early 1900s. Stevens single-shot rifles were available in this chambering, until 1936. There are tens of thousands of guns around for this cartridge. It actually was a good small-game cartridge out to 50 yards, as it would kill cleanly with hits in the forward body area and not spoil meat. Accuracy wasn't outstanding, but adequate for field use. However, ammunition costs more than .22 Long Rifle loads, which is a consideration in choosing a rimfire gun. The .32 rimfire is obsolete. The original load had an 80-grain bullet and nine grains of blackpowder.

.32 Long

Historical Notes: The .32 Long was originally a revolver cartridge and was later used extensively in various rifles. It was introduced for the Smith & Wesson New Model 2 revolver, in 1861. It was quickly picked up by other manufacturers and offered in such makes as the Allen, Enterprise, Favorite, Forehand & Wadsworth, Harrington & Richardson, Pioneer, Webley, X.L., and many others. Colt's New Line revolvers were available in this chambering, also. Stevens single-shot pistols and rifles featured it, as did Marlin, Ballard, Maynard, Remington, and Winchester single-shot rifles. It is no longer produced in the United States. Navy Arms had .32 Long ammunition made in Brazil, in 1990. Until recently, this ammunition was available from that source.

General Comments: The .32 Long rimfire has a heavier bullet and delivers more energy than the .32 Short, although velocity is about the same. The original load had an outside-lubricated 90-grain lead bullet with 12 to 13 grains of blackpowder. It was a good short-range small-game number because, like other cartridges in the same class, it killed cleanly without ruining edible meat. However, it was not effective beyond 50 yards, because of the relatively high trajectory, which made bullet placement difficult at long range. Single-shot Stevens rifles in this chambering were made until 1936.

.32 Extra Long

Historical Notes: The exact date of introduction of this cartridge is obscure. It is listed in various catalogs of 1876, so it probably originated in the mid-1870s. Ballard, Remington, Stevens, and Wesson single-shot rifles chambered it. It does not appear in post-World War I catalogs. Many gun companies charged extra for rifles chambered to shoot any of the extra-long rim- or centerfire cartridges. Some authorities place the date of introduction as 1866.

General Comments: The original load for the .32 Extra Long rimfire was a 90-grain outside-lubricated lead bullet and 18 to 20 grains of blackpowder. The bullet is the same as that used in the ordinary .32 Long, but there were variations, depending on who manufactured the ammunition. The .32 Extra Long was not a very accurate cartridge and never established itself as a match round. It extends the effective hunting range of the rimfire .32 out to perhaps 65 to 75 yards, but doesn't possess appreciably greater killing power than the .32 Long.

.38 Short

Historical Notes: When the Civil War ended, in 1865, a number of rimfire cartridges had been developed and used successfully in battle; most were large-caliber rifle cartridges. After the war, there was demand for smaller-caliber metallic cartridges for revolvers and sporting rifles. Both the .38 Short and Long rimfires date from this period. These are listed in the 1869 Folsom Bros. & Co. gun catalog. The Remington Model 1866 revolving rifle was available in .38 rimfire. In 1871, the Remington New Model revolver was advertised as available with an extra .38 rimfire cylinder. The .38 Short rimfire was listed in the 1876 J. Brown & Son catalog for use in Ballard, Remington, and Wesson rifles and Allen, Colt's, Enterprise, Whitney, X.L., and other pistols. This is now an obsolete cartridge, but it was manufactured until 1940.

General Comments: The .38 Short rimfire is in the same class as the centerfire .38 Short Colt. The original loading was a 130-grain lead bullet and 18 grains of blackpowder. Like most older rimfires, the bullet is outside-lubricated. Bullet diameter is .375-inch, the same as the ball fired in .36-caliber cap-and-ball revolvers. The .38 Short probably originated as a cartridge for breech-loading conversions of these old revolvers. Many catalogs listed the .38 Short for use in pistols and revolvers, whereas the .38 Long is shown as a rifle round. The Rollin White patent covering the bored-through cylinder, held by Smith & Wesson, did not expire until 1869. This undoubtedly had an effect on the use of the rimfire .38 Short for revolvers.

.38 Long

Historical Notes: The rimfire .38 Long is another old-timer dating to before 1865 and the end of the Civil War. The Remington-Beals single-shot rifle was available in .38 Long, from 1867 until it was discontinued in 1875. The Remington revolving rifle of 1866 was also made for it. It was used in Allen, Ballard, Remington, Stevens, and Wesson rifles of later date, and in Enterprise, Favorite, Forehand & Wadsworth, and Colt's revolvers. It was a popular rifle and pistol chambering up to the turn of the century. It was replaced by similar centerfire rounds. American companies stopped loading it, in the late 1920s.

General Comments: The rimfire .38 Long is in the same general class as the centerfire .38 Long Colt. The original load was a 150-grain outside-lubricated bullet and 18 grains of blackpowder. However, loads varied with different manufacturers, ranging from a 140- to 150-grain bullet and up to 21 grains of powder with the light bullet. In a rifle, it was a good short-range small-game load, but accuracy was only fair. No one has made rifles in this chambering since the end of World War I.

.38 Extra Long

Historical Notes:
The rimfire .38 Extra Long appeared about 1870 and was chambered in Ballard, Howard, Remington, Robinson, and F. Wesson single-shot rifles. It was not a standard Ballard chambering, but a special-order item that cost 50 cents extra. It was strictly a rifle chambering, being too long for most revolvers. Because of mediocre accuracy, plus the development of similar centerfire cartridges, the .38 Extra Long rimfire did not have a long life. It was not carried in the 1918-'19 Remington catalog, but was listed in the 1916 Winchester catalog.

General Comments:
The .38 Extra Long is in a class well below the centerfire .38-40 WCF blackpowder loading. The original load was a 150-grain outside-lubricated bullet and 30 to 31 grains of blackpowder. However, some companies loaded lighter bullets down to 140 grains and with slightly more powder. It was not a bad small- to medium-game cartridge out to about 80 yards or so. It was introduced at a time when the centerfire was emerging as the dominant type, so it did not build up a following. The centerfire .38 Extra Long was developed by Ballard, in 1855-'56, and was preferred because it was reloadable.

.41 Short (Derringer)

Historical Notes:
This is an old and once very popular rimfire, because of the light, handy arms that chambered it. The .41 Short was introduced with the National Arms Co. breech-loading derringer, in 1863. It was originally called the .41-100 rimfire. The National derringer was patented by Daniel Moore, in 1861 and 1863. It was made by National from its introduction until 1870, when the company was purchased by Colt's. From 1872 to 1890, this rotating-barrel derringer was manufactured by Colt's. Colt's also adapted the .41 Short to the Thuer-patented or Third Model derringer, as well as the House pistol, or Cloverleaf cylinder model, of 1871. Derringers made by Allen, Enterprise, Williamson, X.L., and others were also of .41 Short chambering. The Remington over/under or double-barrel derringer, manufactured from 1866 to 1935, was the most famous and popular of the lot. Several low-priced pocket revolvers were also chambered for the .41 Short. It has been obsolete since World War II, but special lots of ammunition have been loaded since the war.

General Comments:
The .41 Short rimfire is so underpowered as to be worthless for anything but rats, mice, or sparrows at short range. Fired from the average derringer at a tree or hard object 15 to 25 yards away, the bullet will often bounce back and land at your feet. Nevertheless, it was a popular self-defense cartridge and, at point-blank range, could inflict a severe wound or kill a human being. These .41 derringer pistols were more of a threat or morale builder than anything else. The original load was a 130-grain outside-lubricated lead bullet and 13 grains of blackpowder. Late loads used smokeless powder.

.41 Long

Historical Notes:
This is a longer and slightly more powerful version of the .41 Short. It originated in 1873, and the Colt's New Line revolvers appear to be the first to chamber it. The Enterprise No. 4, Favorite No. 4, Forehand & Wadsworth, Webley, and other revolvers were available in this chambering. A few cheap single-shot rifles also chambered it. It has been obsolete since the 1920s.

General Comments:
The rimfire .41 Long is a better cartridge than the Short, but not by much. There was some variation in bullet weight and powder charge, but the original load used a 163-grain bullet and 13 to 15 grains of blackpowder. The centerfire .41 Short is an outgrowth of this cartridge. Guns chambered for the Long could also shoot the .41 Short rimfire. In power, this cartridge is in about the same class as the .38 S&W centerfire in the blackpowder loading.

.44 Short

Historical Notes: The .44 Short was a handgun cartridge, although it could be fired in arms chambered for the .44 Long rimfire. It is well-established in old catalogs dating from 1870 and chambered in popular pistols and revolvers, including those made by Allen, Forehand & Wadsworth, and Remington. It is best noted as being the cartridge for the single-shot Hammond Bulldog pistol made by the Connecticut Arms & Mfg. Co., of Naubuc, Connecticut. This pistol is believed to have been marketed before the end of the Civil War, which would place the date of origin of the .44 Short about 1864-'65. It has been obsolete since the 1920s.

General Comments: The rimfire .44 Short is a better handgun cartridge than the .41 Short or Long, but wasn't generally as popular. The type and variety of guns that chambered it was rather limited. The original load was a 200- or 210-grain outside-lubricated bullet and 15 to 17 grains of blackpowder. While velocity was low, with the 200-grain bullet, short-range stopping power was fairly good. Performance was similar to the centerfire British .44 Webley cartridge.

.44 Henry Flat

Historical Notes: This old and particularly historic cartridge is one of the milestones in the development of modern arms and ammunition. It was developed by B. Tyler Henry for the lever-action repeating rifle bearing his name, the forerunner of the original Winchester lever-action rifle and conceptually and functionally similar to all models up to the 1876. The Henry rifle was manufactured by the New Haven Arms Co., from 1860 to 1866, at which time it was reorganized as the Winchester Repeating Arms Co.

The .44 Henry cartridge was manufactured from 1860-'61 to 1934. Two versions of the cartridge were offered. The early case was .815-inch long. Bullet and powder charge were the same. Colt's revolvers were also made in .44 Henry chambering. The Henry rifle and cartridge saw limited use in the Civil War.

General Comments: The .44 Henry, although quite successful, was not a powerful round. Barely adequate for deer and certainly no match for buffalo or grizzly bear, its principal advantage was in the 15-shot repeating rifle. This provided undreamed-of firepower, something that could be decisive in combat. In recognition of this fact, Winchester brought out an improved rifle chambered for the .44-40 cartridge, in 1873. From that date on, Winchester was in continuing competition with the makers of single-shot rifles and their big, powerful buffalo cartridges. The .44 Henry used a 200-grain bullet and 26 to 28 grains of blackpowder.

.44 Extra Long

Historical Notes: This Ballard-developed cartridge is a longer, more powerful version of the rimfire .44 Long. Unfortunately, it was introduced about 1869, and soon the .44-40 Winchester Center Fire was establishing a reputation in the West. This number had a very short life, becoming obsolete by the 1880s. The exact date of introduction is vague, but probably between 1870-'75. It is listed in the 1876 catalogs as adapted to Ballard, Remington, and F. Wesson rifles.

General Comments: The .44 Extra Long isn't as good a general-purpose cartridge as the .44-40 Winchester. For one thing, it used an outside-lubricated bullet and, in addition, overall length was too long for many repeating actions. It was loaded with a 218-grain bullet and 46 grains of blackpowder. It was not noted for great accuracy. In power, it would be primarily a small-game number. Effective range was not much over 75 yards or so.

.44 Long

Historical Notes: The rimfire .44 Long originated with the Ethan Allen carbine, patented in 1860 and manufactured by Allen & Wheelock, of Worcester, Massachusetts. It was later adapted to rifles made by Ballard, Howard, Remington, Robinson, and F. Wesson. It was fairly popular, but was replaced by similar centerfire types. It became obsolete, in the early 1920s.

General Comments: With a 220-grain bullet and 28 grains of blackpowder, the .44 Long was a potent short-range cartridge for small game. The .44-40 WCF rapidly became the dominant .44-caliber cartridge after it was introduced, in 1873. It could be reloaded and was available in repeating rifles and revolvers, important factors on the western frontier. Other .44 cartridges, particularly the rimfire, gradually declined in use and popularity. The .44 Long was neither as powerful nor as accurate as the .44-40.

.46 Long

Historical Notes: The .46 Long rimfire was listed in an advertisement by Schuler, Hartley & Graham's, in 1864. It is listed in the 1887 Remington catalog as a short-range chambering for the Remington rolling block single-shot Sporting Rifle No. 1, and also for Ballard rifles. The cartridge was loaded by Remington, Winchester, and others and carried in ammunition catalogs up to World War I, but did not survive the war. It originated in the early 1870s.

General Comments: The .46 Long was loaded by Remington, with a 305-grain bullet and 35 grains of blackpowder. Winchester listed a 300-grain bullet and 40 grains of powder. There may have been other loadings by other companies. It was a marginal short-range deer cartridge.

.46 Short

Historical Notes: The .46 Short rimfire is usually listed for the Remington Single Action Army revolver. However, the 1878 and 1891 Winchester catalogs both describe this cartridge as, "For Remington, Smith & Wesson, and other Army revolvers." Both Remington and Winchester loaded this cartridge. It was carried in their catalogs up to World War I, but did not appear after the war. Date of introduction was circa 1870.

General Comments: The .46 Short rimfire was listed in Remington catalogs as having a 227-grain bullet and 20 grains of blackpowder. Winchester's loading was a 230-grain bullet and 26 grains of powder. As a revolver cartridge, it would have been less powerful than the .44-40 WCF.

.46 Extra Long

Historical Notes: The .46 Extra Long rimfire was a Ballard cartridge for its single-shot rifle and may also have been used by others. It does not appear in the Remington 1871 catalog, so it originated sometime after that date. Remington appears to have been the only one that loaded this cartridge, and it was carried in later catalogs up to World War I, but did not reappear after that war.

General Comments: Remington listed the .46 Extra Long as being loaded with a 305-grain bullet and 57 grains of blackpowder. There was never a smokeless loading. It would have been somewhat more powerful than the .46 Long and a better short-range deer cartridge. None of the .46-caliber rifle cartridges enjoyed a reputation for great accuracy. However, since these cartridges survived for quite a few years, these evidently did have a fair following.

.56-46 Spencer

Historical Notes: This post-Civil War sporting cartridge was introduced by Spencer, in 1866, for his repeating small carbine and sporting rifle. It was also listed as the No. 46 or .46/100 caliber. Spencer lever-action sporting arms were manufactured from 1866 until the firm failed, in 1868-'69. Winchester bought up the surplus guns and Spencer patents, but did not manufacture those rifles. However, the company sold off surplus rifles through its agents, from 1869 to 1872. The cartridge has been obsolete since before World War I, but was cataloged until 1919.

General Comments: The .56-46 Spencer is actually a .44-caliber, bottlenecked cartridge. It was considerably more powerful than the .44-40 WCF. A 320- to 330-grain bullet and 45 grains of blackpowder was the standard load. It was a fairly good short-range deer cartridge, but not satisfactory for larger game. The actions of early repeating rifles weren't suited to large or long cartridges. This lack of power caused many hunters and the military to adopt the single-shot rifle, even though the repeater was well-proven. Full-powered repeating rifles, able to compete with the single-shot rifle on any basis, did not appear until 1880.

.50 Remington Navy

Historical Notes: Developed for the single-shot, rolling block, Remington Navy pistol of 1865, this load was replaced within a year by an identical, inside-primed centerfire type. The final commercial version, Boxer primed, was manufactured until World War I. The Remington Navy pistol has been obsolete since the early 1870s.

General Comments: The .50-caliber rimfire was a rather potent handgun round. Velocity was low, but the big heavy bullet would have had considerable effectiveness. However, .44- or .45-caliber handguns are more efficient, and the military eventually standardized on .45-caliber cartridge arms. The original load was a 290-grain bullet and 23 grains of blackpowder.

.56-50 Spencer

Historical Notes: This cartridge was actually designed by Springfield Armory, late in 1861. It was used in the 1865 model Spencer repeating carbine, a seven-shot, lever-action arm with a 20- or 22-inch barrel. The magazine was in the buttstock and was loaded through a trap, as with modern .22 rimfire rifles. This particular rifle and cartridge was manufactured too late for use in the Civil War, but was issued to troops fighting Indians on the western frontier. The .56-50 cartridge was listed in ammunition catalogs until 1920. The 1918-'19 Remington catalog illustrated it as "adapted to Spencer, Remington UMC, Sharps, Peabody and other rifles and carbines." The 1865 Spencer incorporated the Stabler magazine cutoff not present on earlier models. Spencer didn't like the .56-50 cartridge, because he thought it had an excessive crimp; it is not advertised in Spencer catalogs. He designed a slightly different version, which became known as the .56-52.

General Comments: The .56-50 cartridge was loaded with a 350-grain bullet and 45 grains of blackpowder. It could penetrate almost a foot of soft pine at a range of 15 feet and was a potent short-range cartridge. It was adequate for deer-sized animals, but not satisfactory against larger game. Most western hunters preferred the more powerful single-shot rifles and their big, long-range cartridges. The Spencer action was not adaptable to the long centerfire cartridges that were developed in the years immediately after the Civil War.

.56-52 Spencer/.56-52 Spencer Necked

Historical Notes: Dating from 1866, this is an alteration of the Army-designed .56-50, which Spencer believed had too much crimp. His approach was to incorporate a slight bottleneck, but many manufacturers omitted this, so it is difficult to distinguish between these two rounds. However, these cartridges are interchangeable, and any arm chambered for one will fire the other. Spencer .56-52 ammunition was listed in ammunition catalogs, up until 1920.

The .56-52 is more a sporting than a military round. Power is the same as the .56-50, but some companies loaded a heavier bullet. Remington produced a cartridge with 45 grains of powder and a two-groove, flat-point, 400-grain bullet. The .56-50 was always loaded with a 350-grain bullet. By modern standards, the .56-52 would barely qualify as a short-range deer cartridge. It was more powerful than modern smokeless factory .44-40 WCF loads.

.56-56 Spencer

Historical Notes:

This is the original cartridge for the first Spencer rifle and carbine, patented March 6, 1860, and manufactured in quantity, beginning in 1862. Despite great opposition from the U.S. Army Ordnance Department, these guns were finally adopted and used during the Civil War. These first appeared at the Battle of Antietam, in September 1862, and later played a decisive role in other important engagements. The Spencer is credited as having provided the Union armies with an advantage in firepower that gave them a critical edge in turning back the Confederate forces at Gettysburg. President Lincoln tested the Spencer rifle, in 1863, and insisted that the Army place substantial orders with Christopher M. Spencer. Many authorities insist that, if the Spencer rifle had been adopted at the onset of the war and issued in quantity, it would have shortened the Civil War by a year or more and greatly reduced the ultimate number of casualties. (Since more combatants died from dysentery than from battlefield wounds and injuries, it would seem that last contention probably has even more merit than the originators might have realized.) The .56-56 cartridge was loaded by ammunition manufacturers, until 1920.

General Comments:

The Spencer rifle was a seven-shot repeater of lever-action type, with the magazine located in the buttstock and loaded through a trap in the buttplate. It could be fired at the rate of seven shots in 12 seconds, faster in the hands of a real expert. Parts were interchangeable, and the gun could be disassembled with only a screwdriver. The .56-56 cartridge was loaded with a 350- to 360-grain bullet and 42 to 45 grains of blackpowder. Bullet diameter varies from .540- to .555-inch between various makes of ammunition. Ballard and Joslyn carbines also used this cartridge. It was a short-range number, not very effective on anything larger than deer.

.58 Miller/.58 Allin

Historical Notes:

This cartridge was used in the 1867 Miller breech-loading conversion system of the muzzleloading Springfield rifled musket. It was listed in an advertisement by Schuyler, Hartley & Graham's, in 1864. It came in two case lengths, 13/16 inches and 17/16 inches, and was used chiefly in first-model Allin conversions. The Miller swinging-block conversion was one of a number of experimental alterations used by the military, in an effort to salvage the million-plus .58-caliber muskets left over from the Civil War. The idea was to convert those guns to some viable breech-loading system rather than into scrap. Although some of the conversion units worked quite well, the effort was not entirely successful, and most of these guns were eventually sold off as surplus or scrap metal. There must have been a fair number of the Miller conversions around, though, because the cartridge was listed in ammunition catalogs at least as late as 1910. This cartridge is also called the .585 Springfield, .58 Musket, .58 Allen, and .58 Ball.

General Comments:

The .58 Miller rimfire featured a 500-grain bullet backed by 60 grains of blackpowder for a muzzle velocity of approximately 1150 fps. It would have been a pretty good short-range deer cartridge. Some specimens have a heavy crimp, which affects the measurable length of the unfired case and results in variations in published figures for the case length. Remington, Winchester, and others listed this round.

Dimensional Data

Cartridge	Case	Bullet Dia.	Neck Dia.	Shoulder Dia.	Base Dia.	Rim Dia.	Rim Thick.	Case Length	Ctge. Length	Page
.17 Mach 2	A	.172	.195	.224	.225	.275	.040	.594	UNK/NA	491
.17 Mach 2	A	.172	.1900	.2046	.2260	.2780	.007	.7140	1.000	491
.17 Hornady Magnum Rimfire	A	.172	.195	.240	.241	.291	.046	1.052	UNK/NA	491
5mm Remington Magnum	A	.205	.225	.259	.259	.325	.050	1.020	UNK/NA	491
.22 BB Cap	B	.223	.224	UNK/NA	.224	.270	.040	.284	.343	492
.22 CB Cap	B	.222	.225	UNK/NA	.225	.271	.040	.420	.520	492
.22 Winchester Automatic	B	.222	.250	UNK/NA	.250	.310	.040	.665	.915	492
.22 Short	B	.223	.224	UNK/NA	.225	.273	.040	.423	.686	493
.22 Short/40-grain (RWS load)	B	.223	.224	UNK/NA	.225	.272	.042	.415	.798	493
.22 Long	B	.223	.224	UNK/NA	.225	.275	.040	.595	.880	493
.22 Long Rifle	B	.223	.224	UNK/NA	.225	.275	.040	.595	.975	494
.22 Stinger, etc. (hyper-velocities)	B	.223	.24	UNK/NA	.225	.275	.040	.694	.975	494
.22 Extra Long	B	.223	.225	UNK/NA	.225	.275	.040	.750	1.16	495
.22 Remington Automatic	B	.223	.245	UNK/NA	.245	.290	UNK/NA	.663	.920	495
.22 WRF & Remington Special	B	.224	.242	UNK/NA	.243	.295	.046	.960	1.17	496
.22 Winchester Magnum Rimfire	B	.224	.240	UNK/NA	.241	.291	.046	1.052	1.35	496
.22 ILARCO/.22 WMR Short	UNK/NA	UNK/NA	UNK/NA	UNK/NA	UNK/NA	UNK/NA	UNK/NA	UNK/NA	UNK/NA	497
.25 Short	B	.246	.245	UNK/NA	.245	.290	UNK/NA	.468	.780	497
.25 Stevens Short	B	.251	.275	UNK/NA	.276	.333	UNK/NA	.599	.877	497
.25 Stevens	B	.251	.276	UNK/NA	.276	.333	UNK/NA	1.125	1.395	497
.30 Short	B	.286	.292	UNK/NA	.292	.346	UNK/NA	.515	.822	498
.30 Long	B	.288	.288	UNK/NA	.288	.340	UNK/NA	.613	1.020	498
.32 Long Rifle	B	.312	.318	UNK/NA	.318	.377	UNK/NA	.937	1.223	498
.32 Extra Short/.32 Protector	B	.316	.318	UNK/NA	.317	.367	UNK/NA	.398	.645	499
.32 Short	B	.316	.318	UNK/NA	.318	.377	UNK/NA	.575	.948	499
.32 Long	B	.316	.318	UNK/NA	.318	.377	UNK/NA	.791	1.215	499
.32 Extra Long	B	.316	.317	UNK/NA	.318	.378	UNK/NA	1.150	1.570	500
.38 Short	B	.375	.376	UNK/NA	.376	.436	UNK/NA	.768	1.185	500
.38 Long	B	.375	.376	UNK/NA	.376	.435	UNK/NA	.873	1.380	500
.38 Extra Long	B	.375	.378	UNK/NA	.378	.435	UNK/NA	1.480	2.025	501
.41 Short	B	.405	.406	UNK/NA	.406	.468	UNK/NA	.467	.913	501
.41 Long	B	.405	.407	UNK/NA	.407	.468	UNK/NA	.635	.985	501
.44 Short	B	.446	.445	UNK/NA	.445	.519	.066	.688	1.190	502
.44 Henry Flat	B	.446	.445	UNK/NA	.446	.519	.066	.875	1.345	502
.44 Extra Long	B	.446	.456	UNK/NA	.457	.524	UNK/NA	1.250	1.843	502
.44 Long	B	.451	.455	UNK/NA	.458	.525	UNK/NA	1.094	1.842	503
.46 Long	B	.454	.456	UNK/NA	.456	.523	UNK/NA	1.25	1.876	503
.46 Short	B	.456	.458	UNK/NA	.458	.530	UNK/NA	.836	1.336	503
.46 Extra Long	B	.459	.457	UNK/NA	.457	.525	UNK/NA	1.534	2.285	503
.56-46 Spencer	A	.465	.478	.555	.558	.641	UNK/NA	1.035	1.595	504
.50 Remington Navy	B	.510	.535	UNK/NA	.562	.642	UNK/NA	.860	1.280	504
.56-50 Spencer	B	.512	.543	UNK/NA	.556	.639	.065	1.156	1.632	504
.56-52 Spencer	B	.512	.540	UNK/NA	.559	.639	.065	1.035	1.500	504
.56-52 Spencer Necked	A	.525	.547	.558	.560	.642	.065	1.020	1.660	504
.56-56 Spencer	B	.550	.560	UNK/NA	.560	.645	.065	.875	1.545	505
.58 Miller	B	.585	.620	UNK/NA	.628	.709	UNK/NA	1.193	1.701	505

A = Rim, bottleneck. B = Rim, straight. Unless otherwise noted, all dimensions are in inches. These cases have slight taper at case mouth-to-neck juncture, neck diameter measurement is taken at case mouth. UNK/NA = Unknown/Not Applicable

Note: Rimfire cartridges dimensions show considerable variation, depending upon manufacturer, specific production lot and production era.

Current Rimfire Factory Ballistics

Load	Bullet Weight (grains)	Muzzle Velocity (fps)	Velocity 50 yards (fps)	Velocity 100 yards (fps)	Muzzle Energy (ft. lbs.)	Energy 50 yards (ft. lbs.)	Energy 100 yards (ft. lbs.)	Trajectory 50 yards (inches)	Trajectory 100 yards (inches)
.17 Mach II Hornady NTX	15.5	2050	UNK	1450	149	UNK	75	UNK	ZERO
.17 Mach II Hornady V-Max	17	2100	1884	1677	166	134	106	ZERO	-3.0
.17 HMR CCI TNT-HP Lead Free	16	2500	2176	1867	222	168	124	ZERO	-0.1
.17 HMR Federal Speer TNT	17	2530	2150	1804	242	173	123	ZERO	-0.2
.17 HMR Remington Accutip-V	17	2550	2212	1901	245	185	136	ZERO	-0.1
.17 HMR CCI FMJ	20	2375	2155	1940	250	206	157	ZERO	-0.2
.17 HMR Hornady HP XTP	20	2375	2143	1918	250	204	163	ZERO	-0.2
.22 LR Remington Golden Bullet RN	29	1095	982	903	72	62	52	ZERO	-7.4
.22 LR CCI LRN (Long)	29	710	673	637	32	29	26	ZERO	-17.4
.22 LR Winchester Tin RN	30	1650	1393	1184	181	129	93	ZERO	-8.1
.22 LR Federal Copper Plated HP	31	1430	1197	1046	141	99	75	ZERO	-4.6
.22 LR CCI Stinger HP	32	1640	1386	1182	191	137	99	ZERO	-2.8
.22 LR CCI Segmented SLHP	32	1640	1388	1182	191	137	99	ZERO	-8.2
.22 LR Remington CBee HP	33	740	687	638	40	35	30	ZERO	-16.9
.22 LR Remington Yellow Jacket TCHP	33	1500	1247	1075	165	114	85	ZERO	-4.1
.22 LR Federal Copper Plated HP	36	1260	1104	1003	127	97	80	ZERO	-5.6
.22 LR Winchester Tin RN	37	1280	1162	1071	135	111	94	ZERO	-4.7
.22 LR Federal Copper Plated HP	38	1260	1110	1010	134	104	86	ZERO	-5.5
.22 LR Remington Subsonic HP	38	1050	965	901	93	79	69	ZERO	-7.7
.22 LR Federal Solid	40	1240	1103	1011	137	108	91	ZERO	-5.6
.22 LR CCI Segmented SLHP	40	1050	987	935	98	86	78	ZERO	-7.2
.22 LR CCI Velocitor CPHP	40	1435	1286	1161	183	147	120	ZERO	-3.6
.22 Magnum Winchester JHP Tin	28	2200	2047	1896	301	261	223	ZERO	-1.0
.22 Magnum Federal Speer TNT	30	2200	1777	1419	322	210	144	ZERO	-1.3
.22 Magnum CCI Maxi- Mag TNT HP	30	2050	1762	1487	280	247	149	ZERO	-1.1
.22 Magnum Hornady V-Max	30	2200	1911	1639	322	243	179	ZERo	-3.0
.22 Magnum Remington Accutip-V	33	2000	1730	1495	293	219	164	ZERO	-4.5
.22 Magnum Winchester JHP	34	2120	1861	1617	339	251	197	ZERO	-3.0
.22 Magnum CCI Gamepoint	40	1875	1692	1519	312	254	206	ZERO	-1.3
.22 Magnum Federal FMJ	40	1880	1570	1311	314	219	153	ZERO	-2.1
.22 Magnum Remington PSP	40	1910	1610	1340	324	227	159	ZERO	-2.0
.22 Magnum Winchester JHP	40	1910	1685	1478	324	252	193	ZERO	-1.4
.22 Magnum Wildcat Dyna-Point JHP	45	1550	1387	1243	240	192	154	ZERO	-2.8
.22 Magnum Federal JHP	50	1530	1347	1197	260	201	159	ZERO	-3.3

Rimfire Cartridges – Factory Ballistics

Cartridge	Bullet (grs.)	Mid Range Trajectory Muzzle Velocity	Mid Range Trajectory Muzzle Energy	100 yards (inches)	Remarks
25 Short	43	750	53	6.10	Handgun ballistics
25 Stevens Short	65	950	130	5.4	Smokeless loading
25 Stevens	65-67	1180	208	5.1	Smokeless loading
30 Long	75	750	81		8 grains blackpowder
30 Short	58	700	62		Approximate handgun ballistics
32 Extra Short	54	650	51		Approximate ballistics
32 Short	80	950	160	5.6	Late smokeless load, rifle ballistics
32 Long	90	180	5.2		Modern smokeless load
32 Long Rifle	81-82	960	186	4.9	Approximate rifle ballistics
32 Extra Long	90	1050	221	4.7	Approximate ballistics
38 Short	125-130	725	150		Handgun ballistics
38 Long	150	750	190		Handgun ballistics
	150	980	320	4.5	Rifle ballistics
38 Extra Long	150	1250	526	3.8	3-inch barrel ballistics
41 Short	130	425	52		3-inch barrel ballistics
41 Long	163	700	180		Handgun ballistics
41 Swiss	300	1325	1175	4.7	Blackpowder
	334	1345	1330	4.3	Smokeless load
44 Short	200-210	500	112		Approximate handgun ballistics
44 Long	220	825	332	4.5	Approximate rifle ballistics
44 Extra Long	218	1250	763	3.5	Approximate rifle ballistics
44 Henry Flat	200	1125	568	3.9	Approximate rifle ballistics
50 Remington Navy	290	600	234		Approximate ballistics
56-46 Spencer	330	1210	1080		Approximate ballistics
56-50 Spencer	350	1230	1175		Approximate ballistics
56-52 Spencer	340, 386, 400	1200	1300		Approximate ballistics
56-56 Spencer	350	1200	1125		Approximate ballistics
58 Miller/Allin	500	1150	1468		Approximate ballistics

The following rimfire cartridges are not included above because ballistic data could not be located; the same group, (except the 61 and 69 rimfires) is, however, listed in the Dimensional Data table: 35 Alcan, 9mm Ball, 42 Forehand & Wadsworth, 46 Ex. Short, 46 Short, 46 Remington-Carbine, 56-46 Ex. Long, 46 Hammond Carbine, 50 Ball Carbine, 50 Remington Navy, 50 Remington Pistol, 50 Warner Carbine, 50-60 Peabody, 61 rimfire and 69 rimfire.

Shotgun Shells
(Current & Obsolete – Blackpowder and Smokeless)

Shotguns, or "fowling pieces," as these guns were originally called, were among the earliest firearms to achieve sporting status. Of course, the use of a number of small pellets of varying sizes for military and hunting purposes predates what we would consider true sporting firearms made primarily for that pursuit. Originally, all guns were smoothbored, because rifling was unknown, until around 1500. American colonists used shot in their flintlock muskets, because it was easier to hit small moving targets, such as birds or rabbits. Single-barrel and side-by-side double-barrel flintlock shotguns reached a high state of development in the late eighteenth and early nineteenth centuries.

In England, Joseph Manton and others turned out high-quality flintlock shotguns that were the equal of any made today. When percussion replaced the flintlock, fine shotguns of this type were also manufactured. As a matter of fact, single- and double-barrel muzzleloading percussion shotguns were still popular until the early twentieth century. This wasn't due to reluctance by hunters to accept the new breechloaders, but, rather, because muzzleloaders were cheaper and didn't require expensive shotgun shells. For a largely rural population, it was simple economics.

The first breechloading shotguns appeared in the late 1840s, although some experimental types go back much earlier. The Lefaucheaux pinfire shotshell was patented in France, in 1836. In 1852, Charles Lancaster marketed an improved breechloading shotgun, which was followed by others and gradually led to our modern break-open type. The 1864 Schuyler, Hartley, and Graham catalog illustrated several breechloading shotguns.

The general acceptance of the breechloading shotgun depended on the development of a gun that was affordable to middle-class hunters, rather than only the wealthy. One disadvantage of the flintlock, percussion lock, and the pinfire designs is that these guns all require external hammers. As soon as breechloaders firing self-contained centerfire ammunition became available, a number of internal-lock shotguns began to appear, starting in the 1870s. The first modern hammerless, breechloading double-barrel gun was the Anson and Deeley, introduced in England, in 1875. This shotgun incorporated the self-cocking principle, which operated when the breech was opened, and is the design typical of all present-day doubles.

The pump-action shotgun was mostly developed in the United States in the late 1800s (though the first and not terribly functional design was actually created in England), and is, today, the most popular type in this country; this is also a matter of economics, because one usually can purchase a good pump-action shotgun for less than half the price of a double. The principal of choke-boring was long recognized by 1871, but wasn't widely known or used prior to that time. In that year, it was further developed and publicized by the American Fred Kimble. Shortly thereafter, choke-boring became standard on practically all shotguns. Walter Roper, also an American, was issued the first patent for choke-boring, in 1866. However, his screw-on device was for single-barrel guns only and did not become popular. By 1990, screw-in chokes had become the practice on nearly all shotguns.

The type of shotgun used is largely a matter of personal preference, and one has no great advantage over another as a practical matter. As to gauge, the 12- will cover the widest variety of game and hunting conditions, and, for the man on a limited budget, the repeating 12-gauge with an adjustable or interchangeable choke system is the way to go. The 16-gauge is almost as good, but very few guns are still made in this gauge. Actually, the best shotgun is the one in which you have the most confidence and can shoot the best. There is nothing wrong with the 20- or 28-gauge, or even the .410-bore, except that these relatively small bore sizes impose limits on what game and ranges you can hunt effectively. At one time, smaller-gauge shells were less expensive, but today those shells cost the same or even more than the larger gauges, so economy is no reason to pick one over the other, unless you are a handloader.

Bore and Gauge Defined

The gauge or bore diameter of a shotgun is designated differently from that of a rifle or pistol. The system used goes back to earliest muzzleloading days. It was the custom, then, to give the "gauge" of muskets in terms of how many lead balls of the bore diameter weighed one pound. A 12-gauge, thus, had a bore of such diameter that a round lead ball weighing $1/12$-pound would just enter the barrel. Sometimes gauge was given as a "12th-pounder" or "20th of a pounder" (20-gauge). In England, modern terminology often uses 12-"bore" or 20-"bore," rather than "gauge," although the two mean the same thing.

The gauge system has persisted to the present. However, there are exceptions, such as with the .410-bore, which is always referred to as .410-bore, and never .410-gauge. This shell is actually a 68-gauge or .410-inch (.41-caliber). Then there's the 9mm rimfire shotshell, which is also a bore-size designation, rather than a gauge. At one time, shotguns were made in every gauge from about 1-gauge down to 32-gauge. Shotguns above 4-gauge were usually punt guns mounted on some type of support or swivel and used in boats for the market hunting of waterfowl. In addition, "gauge designations" larger than 10-gauge were often misrepresented, e.g., the bore of a 4-gauge gun would not accept a ¼-pound pure lead sphere. American manufacturers no longer load shotshells larger than 10-gauge for sporting use, but some European companies still turn out 8-gauge shells.

Shotgunning Myths

There are all sorts of odd ideas regarding shotguns. It is at least worth some effort to stamp out a few of these. For example, there is the idea that some shotguns shoot "harder" than others of the same gauge. The idea may arise in part from the fact that some shotguns have stocks poorly fitted to the user. Since apparent recoil is more severe than with other guns, the owner decides he has a harder-shooting gun. On the other hand, a shooter who has a gun that fits and handles exceptionally well may conclude he has a "hard shooter" because he does such good work with it.

Another outdated belief is that the longer the barrel, the longer the effective range. Modern smokeless powder shotshells develop maximum velocity in about 20 to 22 inches of barrel. Anything

Modern Shotshells

Shotgun shells were originally made from wound paper or drawn brass, although some have also been made from drawn aluminum, cast zinc, and molded or drawn plastic, the latter two of which are currently the most popular design. Paper shotshells (Federal Cartridge Company still makes paper-hulled shotshells), consisted of a laminated paper tube made by winding glue-impregnated paper sheets around a mandrel. The tube was then coated with paraffin wax to make it moisture-resistant, cut to proper length, and one end plugged with a tightly rolled paper or composition base wad. The final step was to add a crimped-on brass (or other metal) head, which incorporated the rim and primer pocket. Inside the shell, the height of the internal base wad determined the volumetric capacity of the hull and, therefore, loading density. Cases were divided into high-brass and low-brass types, depending upon intended loading.

In general, the low brass wad was used with blackpowder or bulk smokeless powder, because these powders required more volume to function correctly. The high brass wad was used with dense smokeless powders that required less volume. So, you can see, this dispels another myth, i.e., the terms "high-brass" or low-brass do not refer to the heights of the brass head. Over the years, shells with a high-brass head have become associated with high-velocity or magnum loads, and shotshells with low metal heads with target or light field loads.

Almost all modern shotgun shells are made from some variety of polyethylene plastic. Such shells were first introduced by Remington, in 1958. Most plastic shells have metal heads of brass, brass-plated steel, or anodized aluminum. A few makers have marketed all-plastic shells without metal heads

Smokeless powder has completely replaced blackpowder for loading shotshells. Early smokeless powders were termed "bulk" powders, because these could be loaded bulk-for-bulk with blackpowder. However, these powders didn't all weigh the same, even though ballistics were similar with equal volume, and, so, a system of nomenclature evolved to accommodate this. Regardless the powder type, the charge is given in "drams equivalent." Thus, a shotshell marked "3¼-1¼" means the ballistics are the same as 3¼ drams of blackpowder and 1¼ ounces of lead shot.

Shotgun shell primers differ from rifle primers in size and type. The three- or four-piece No. 209 battery-cup primer is used in most modern shells. Until recently, some European shotshells used Gevelot-type primers, and all-brass shotshells usually take Large Rifle primers. Brass shells are shorter, but have the same volume as those of paper or plastic. These cases require larger wad diameters, as well.

There has been more meaningful development of high-performance shotshells in the past couple decades than there has been previously in the history of arms. Shotshells now shoot payloads farther, hit game harder, and are manufactured more precisely than ever. But it has come at a price: It's not uncommon to pay $1, $2, or even more per round.

Considering what one gets in the deal, the new high-performance shotshells are well worth their prices. Yet, there is a dichotomy. Concurrently, low-tech "shootin' shells" are comparatively cheaper than ever in the history of shotshells. That's because of the global "dumping" of low-grade ammo from countries where their manufacture is subsidized. That's right, some shells sell for less in the U.S. than they can be manufactured for, even in their countries of origin. Global economy—most interesting.

The Lead Toxicity Issue

It has been recognized, since the late 1800s, that the ingestion of lead shot pellets by bottom-feeding waterfowl can cause a toxic reaction and lead to the death of the bird. In 1959, a wildlife biologist named Frank Bellrose completed a 15-year study on the possible affects of lead shot ingestion and the resultant lead poisoning (called "plumbism"), on North American waterfowl.

over that is just for balance and looks. If the barrel is too long, it will actually reduce velocity slightly through friction or drag. A shotgun with a 26-inch barrel will kill just as far away as one with a 40-inch barrel. In addition, the short barrel will be much faster in getting on target. In deference to those who refuse to accept this, some shotgun manufacturers provide at least one model available with extra-long tubes! If it takes a 36-inch barrel to make you happy or build your confidence, by all means, use one. However, beyond placing the muzzle 10 inches closer to the target, it does not give you any ballistic advantage over the fellow using a much shorter barrel.

The effective range of shotguns is another matter usually subject to much argument and misunderstanding. Some people believe the larger the gauge, the higher the velocity. Others believe that the smaller the gauge, the higher the velocity. Obviously, there is room for all sorts of confusion here, but both claims are wrong. The average muzzle velocity of a similar 10-, 12-, 16-, or 20-gauge load is nearly the same. Why, then, does a larger gauge have a greater effective range? It is a matter of pattern density. For example, if you fire a .410-bore at a dove flying 40 or 50 yards away, the chances are he will fly right through the pattern without being touched. If he is hit, the pellet or pellets will do as much damage as if fired from a 12-gauge. On the other hand, if you fired at this same bird with a 20-gauge, your chances of bringing him down would be greater, because you have thrown more pellets in his path. With a 12-gauge at this same range, the pattern density is great enough that the chances of the bird slipping through are even more reduced. We are, of course, assuming here the same degree of choke for all guns, because choke controls pattern size and density at a given range. There isn't much difference in the actual diameter of the pattern thrown by different gauges at the same range, if all other factors are equal. However, pattern *density* (the number of pellets in the pattern) will absolutely vary according to gauge, with the advantage going to the larger bore. This is also contrary to common belief, so, if you disagree, go out and pattern a number of guns of different gauges but similar choke (and be sure you use the same size shot and type of load in all guns.

The results of this study were released in a bulletin known as the *Bellrose Report*. One of the conclusions in this report was that between two and three percent of the population in each waterfowl species in North America was lost each year through lead poisoning.

Truthfully, this was actually only a very rough estimate and one based upon incomplete data. The Bellrose study was based on the examination of bird gizzards furnished by hunters who had removed these from formerly live, healthy birds they had shot. In other words, *none of the wildfowl in the study were suffering from or had died from lead poisoning.*

The Bellrose Report wasn't intended to be a final conclusion on the subject, but rather an effort to point out a potential problem in a limited area and, at that, one possibly requiring further study. Unfortunately, this report was seized on by the U.S. Fish and Wildlife Service and the National Wildlife Federation as a *cause célèbre*, something that would demonstrate their deep concern for wildfowl and the ecology. The original study had encompassed a relatively small area in the Midwest, but this didn't stop the extrapolation of the data to cover all of North America, although there was no valid basis for such a conclusion. Whatever the merits of the argument, the fact is that Federal law now bans lead shot for virtually all waterfowl hunting (the one exception tends to be in some late-season snow goose hunting regulations, which have been instituted for some much-needed population control over the last decade or so). Furthermore, the outlook for the future has leaned towards an extension of the lead shot ban to encompass other kinds of hunting, as well, such as can now be seen on some public hunting lands frequently used for upland bird and small-game hunting.

Waterfowl Loads

To be classified as a "waterfowl" load these days, ammo must contain non-toxic shot. This means that, rather than the traditional lead, waterfowl cartridges now contain other metals such as bismuth, iron/steel, tungsten, the brands of non-toxic shot pellets known as Hevi-Shot/Hevi-Metal and NICE SHOT, and the new proprietary steel shot from Federal Cartridge Company known as FLITESTOPPER. Steel shot was the first widely used substitute for lead shot in shotshells intended for waterfowl hunting, but, as it turns out, steel shot has (or at least had, given the super-high-performance loadings available at the 2012 SHOT show), a lot of bad features, not the least of which is the ability to ruin the bores of older shotguns. It is as hard as the barrel steel of many high-grade shotguns and can dig grooves in the bores if allowed unprotected contact. Also, steel shot won't compress the way lead shot does as it passes through the choke and, so, will eventually bulge the choke area.

Steel shot also has (or again, had) poor ballistic properties, compared to lead shot of the same diameter. Lead shot of equal size is 44-percent denser. This means that steel shot doesn't carry over distance as well as lead shot, and it loses velocity and energy at a faster rate.

In descending order of actual use, today's shot payloads typically contain steel, tungsten and iron, or tungsten and polymer (in a matrix), bismuth, Hevi-Shot, or the other proprietary materials just mentioned above.

There has been relatively little, if any, actual development of late on the bismuth front. And there is good reason. Bismuth works great just as it is. It offers two major advantages. First, it acts almost exactly like traditional lead. This means it works great, since lead was/is the single finest material for shot (not withstanding the controversy over toxicity). Also, bismuth lends itself superbly to use in the older, finer shotguns that cannot handle steel or hard tungsten loads. Thanks for this product availability goes to Bob Petersen, the former publisher and general gun guru. (Incidentally, Bob's affinity for the .410-bore also has resulted in the availability of these diminutive cartridges in the Bismuth line for the waterfowler.)

Tungsten is a very heavy (heavier than lead) and extremely hard metal. This means that, to match a lead load, tungsten must be "watered down" with something else. This dilution is usually accomplished by mixing the tungsten with iron, steel, or some kind of plastic (polymer). In the tungsten/polymer shot, powdered tungsten is suspended in a plastic matrix and then formed into round pellets.

LEAD SHOT
1. TUBE
2. SHOT
3. WAD
4. POWDER

STEEL SHOT
5. PRIMER
6. BASE WAD
7. HEAD
8. CUSHION
(lead only)

Although the Brits generally are credited with brainstorming tungsten/polymer shot, there have been a couple North American companies that have offered such ammunition to the general trade. One was Federal, but the sales numbers and sales velocity of Federal's tungsten/polymer loading were not enough to keep that superb offering in the line. Without question, Federal's tungsten/polymer load was a great performer, and while it's not as popular as it was when it was initially introduced, the company conitnues to be an innovator in waterfowl loads, with high-performance choices like those in its Black Cloud lineup. Meanwhile, Kent Cartridge Co., headquartered in Canada, continues to offer tungsten/polymer ammunition, which work great, but this company has also recently made improvements to its steel shot loadings, with the relatively new line of super-high-velocity rounds known as SilverSteeel.

As you can see by even just the mention of the loads from Federal and Kent, most recent developments in non-toxic waterfowling ammunition has been with regular steel shot and with tungsten/other-metal combinations. The metal combo-shot used by the various companies comes in a variety of proprietary names such as Hevi-Shot (formerly a Remington product, but one now marketed independently), and the smaller company known as NICE SHOT, which offers its non-toxic pellets for handloaders. The trend for the metal combo loads has been for companies to offer payloads per volume that are heavier than lead, which, in theory, means they are ballistically superior. This trend is so evident with the heavier metal combos that, in addition to waterfowl loads, companies now are offering this kind of shot in high-density turkey hunting ammunition and upland bird loads (though this last is mostly to satisfy recent laws restricting the use of lead shot on certain public

lands altogether, waterfowl habitat or not). On the steel front, most development has been a form of fine-tuning, in which velocities are increased while pattern uniformity is improved. Without question, velocity is the prime determinant in the success of steel shot load, and it doesn't hurt with the combo metal loads, either.

There are several reasons why velocity is so crucial for loads that contain super-hard payloads. With respect to steel, the higher velocity stretches the effective distance a bit. But, with all super-hard pellets, it is the way they take game that makes velocity so crucial. Because the pellets are so hard, they do not deform as lead does (even plated, hardened lead deforms a bit). This means that each individual pellet acts similarly to a full metal jacket rifle bullet; it puts a small hole in its wake, but does little other damage on the way. This was the characteristic that caused many birds hit with steel shot in the early days of steel introduction to be hit hard, yet limp off through the air, only to fall dead a mile or so away after they had bled out. Higher velocity helps preclude this kind of problem.

Years ago, really high velocities (over 1300 fps) were achieved with non-toxic loads only when the payload was relatively light for the bore diameter. In 12-gauge, this generally meant one-ounce payloads. Since then, companies have offered many heavier payloads at the higher velocities, thus removing one more negative variable from the equation. To make things even better, changes in wads and manufacturing techniques have taken waterfowling loads to new highs in every respect. And not insignificantly, virtually all commercial non-toxic waterfowling ammunition these days is as close to being waterproof as is possible.

Turkey Loads

Developments in wild turkey hunting loads have continually focused on ways to deliver the densest patterns at ever increasing distances. This means developing ammunition that patterns superbly at high velocity. In the long ago, muzzle velocities of 1200 to 1300 fps were typical for shotshells. Now it's common to find loads, some even with quite heavy payloads, that send the shot out of the barrel at 1400 fps or faster.

Most turkey loads continue to keep muzzle velocities in the 1300 to 1400 fps range, but now deliver that speed with heavier shot charges. And what shot charges they are! Although Federal and Mossberg originally developed the 3½-inch 12-gauge shell as a way to put more of the lighter steel shot into waterfowl ammunition, the 3½-inch 12-gauge shell has found a welcome home among many turkey hunters who don't mind the recoil of a gun that shoots 2½ ounces or more of shot out of the barrel at high velocity.

Federal Cartridge Co. upped the ante a bit, in recent times, with the development of what it calls the FLITECONTROL wad. By its very design, this wad keeps the shot swarm together longer, which extends the density of the pattern downrange. This wad is used in both turkey loads and those for waterfowl.

Major breakthroughs in ammunition seem to be happening with regularity these days, and Federal's new Mag-Shok turkey hunting load, with its all-new wad design, takes patterning for big toms to a whole new level. Initial tests resulted in roughly twice as many pellets in the head/neck kill zone as was common with more traditional ammunition from the same gun/choke combination. At the heart of Federal's new turkey ammunition is an ingenious wad that keeps the pellet swarm tighter. The new wad is thick and made of a plastic that is about the same hardness as that used for steel shot loads for waterfowling. However, that's about where any similarity to most wads ends. A cross-section of the wad itself would remind one of the Nosler Partition bullet's jacket design, with the front partition area being about twice the length of the back divider. The front partition holds the buffered shot, while the rear encapsulates the top of the powder charge. Truly, it is quite different from the typical wad.

The front section of the wad, literally, is a cup that holds the shot all the way out the barrel and then some. There are no petals, slices, or slots in the front part of the wad, as is normal in most modern wad designs. Yet, at the bottom of the front part of the wad, there are three partial cutouts that, upon firing, merely relieve the bottom area of the front, shot-containing cup. These cutouts flare out, though almost not at all, during the firing process. It looks like they are there more to relieve some kind of pressure effect on the wad itself than anything else.

Most intriguing is the base, or skirt, of the long, orangish, one-piece wad. The skirt has six major petals that, upon exiting the barrel, flare out, causing major wind drag that, in turn, pulls the wad away from the shot that then continues on at normal velocity. This means the shot doesn't leave the wad until it is long gone from the barrel, and that means the pattern begins to open up much later, making it much tighter at any distance. Couple that wad with hard, copper-plated shot, and the world of turkey hunting just got a lot easier.

Upland Game Loads

There hasn't been a dramatic development in upland game loads that there has been in other arenas. About the biggest news in the past few years is that where 1300 fps was common for upland loads a decade or longer ago, 1400 fps, or even a little more, is now in vogue with the latest offerings.

Although the higher speeds work well, their primary advantage, if any, is that they mitigate, at least a bit, the amount of lead ahead of a moving target necessary to effect a hit. This probably translates into a few more pattern-edge hits for those whose timing is a little rusty. Other than that, there is an increase in felt recoil that naturally goes with the higher velocity.

Also recently, there has been a slight level of advancement in upland game loads for the smaller gauges. One must consider that, in the general shotgunning world, there are the 12- and 20-gauge, and then there's everything else, in which everything else doesn't add up to the volume of either of the top two. Nonetheless, there still is "everything else." Generally speaking, companies are now offering comparatively heavy shot charges for the 28-gauge and .410-bore guns. For example, there are 28-gauge loads with one ounce of shot (the classic shot charge weight of the 16-gauge), and Winchester, at least, now offers a three-inch .410-bore with ¾-ounce of shot (classically the shot charge weight of the 28-gauge). Although the heavier 28-gauge loading maintains velocity at slightly above 1200 fps, which is classic, the heavier .410-bore load does not. For example, the classic ½-ounce target loading for the .410-bore has a muzzle velocity of 1200 fps. The traditional three-inch .410-bore loading with 11/16-ounce of shot has a muzzle velocity of around 1135 fps, and the ¾-ounce loading goes out at 1100 fps. This data suggests that hitting relatively tough targets at relatively close ranges is where the heavier payloads shine.

Deer Hunting Loads

It was common practice with muzzleloading shotguns to load a solid roundball for big-game hunting. This worked fine, if the range was short, but accuracy beyond 40 yards was poor. It could be improved upon by using a patched ball, but the lack of proper sights limited what can be accomplished with a smooth-bored gun. When self-contained shotshells arrived, those were furnished in all gauges with a roundball loading. However, when choke-boring became common, it was necessary to use an undersized ball to prevent possible choke damage and, so, it became common practice to load a ball sized one or two gauges smaller than the bore. Thus, a 13-gauge ball was loaded in 12-gauge shells, a 17- or 18-gauge ball in the 16-gauge, and so on. These undersized lead balls usually were deformed when passing through the choke, so were even less accurate than bore-sized balls. Roundball loads in 12- and 16-gauge were useful in heavy cover, where they offered good short-range power on deer-size animals. In addition, 4-, 8-, and 10-gauge balls were used on dangerous game in Africa and India. Roundball loads were discontinued, in 1941.

The rifled slug has an accuracy potential that will allow one to hit deer at ranges of 100 yards (and now more), provided your shotgun is equipped with a set of rifle sights or a scope and is properly sighted in. Rifled slugs were introduced by RWS in Germany, in 1898. This slug, known as the Brenneke, is still available under the Rottweil label. The American, or Foster-type, slug, was introduced by Winchester, in 1936. The two differ in that the Brenneke is solid lead with a series of felt and card wads screwed to the base, whereas the Foster type has a deep, hollow base similar to the old Minié ball projectile used during the Civil War. Both have a series of angular grooves swaged into the outer circumference, and both work on the same principal as the badminton shuttlecock, in that most of the weight is forward of the center of air pressure, which causes these projectiles to fly point forward.

The newest slug design is a saboted copper solid designed to work in rifled shotgun bores, which have become common in specialized shotguns intended only for use with slugs. When fired from these rifled barrels, these slugs (made by Remington and others), can provide rifle-like accuracy and terminal performance.

Without question, effective range for shotgun ammunition in the deer/big-game hunting world took a giant step forward with the use of rifled barrels in conjunction with saboted slugs. Briefly, this move alone doubled (even more in some instances), the effective range of the shotgun slug. Where credible distance for the more traditional shotgun slugs was somewhere around 50 yards, now 100 yards or more are common distances for successful shots.

Rifling the barrels of shotguns spins the projectile, allowing it to fly more truly to the target—as is the case with bullets in

SABOT SLUG

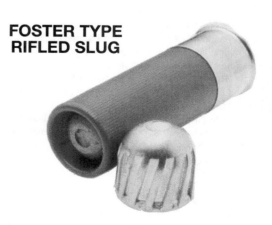

FOSTER TYPE RIFLED SLUG

rifles and handguns. But, with modern shotgun ammunition, the maximum in accuracy and velocity for shotgun slugs has been achieved by using a sub-bore-diameter slug (bullet) cradled in a sabot (French for "shoe"). The plastic sabot engages the rifling, transferring the spin to the slug. After exiting the barrel, the sabot, due to air resistance, falls away from the slug, and the slug continues at high velocity to the target.

Advances in plastics and manufacturing techniques have allowed ammo makers to offer loads that are extremely accurate for shotguns and up the velocity several notches in the process. Some modern slug loads deliver a projectile weight and velocity similar, if not, in some cases, superior, to the blackpowder express rifle cartridges used against dangerous game in Africa and India at the end of the nineteenth century.

Depending upon the gun/ammo combination, it is relatively easy to achieve groups of four inches or less at 100 yards with a projectile that delivers above the traditional minimum of 1000 ft-lbs of energy for deer-killing performance. In some combinations, groups of two inches or less at 100 yards are achievable. This was considered to be good delivered *rifle* accuracy several decades ago. This means that today's deer hunter in the woods now can use a shotgun as effectively as their ancestor did the venerable Winchester Model 1894 rifle in .30 WCF.

Fortunately, development hasn't been limited only to the saboted slug loads for rifled barrels (saboted slug loads typically do not work very well in smoothbores). There also has been some advancement in ammunition for shotgun slug hunters who continue to use smoothbore guns. Nothing smaller than the 12-gauge slug can be considered adequate for any North American big game, and the .410-bore slug is useless for anything but small game at short range. The 12-gauge Brenneke slugs have proven effective on thin-skinned African game, including some dangerous species, such as lion and leopard. Shotgun slugs can be compared to the old large-bore blackpowder cartridges such as the big .45- and .50-caliber numbers. If you could only own one gun, consider a 12-gauge shotgun with an extra slug barrel. It will cover a greater range of game and hunting conditions than any other single gun.

Gauge Rifles

What we call the "gauge rifles" are from 12- to 4-bores, though a few 2-bores have appeared (see the 2010 edition of *Gun Digest*). These are rifles of full weight and power, rifled through and through, and originally were blackpowder cartridge guns intended for use against large and dangerous game. Bore- or gauge-designated cartridges larger than 8-gauge are seldom of true implied bore size. We include the gauge rifles here so that the reader may better differentiate them from shotguns with the same bore or gauge designations.

4-Bore: The bore designation indicates the number of bore-size lead balls to the pound, hence the 4-bore would nominally accept a round ball that weighed ¼-pound, or 1,750 grains. In actuality, the brass-cased 4-bore was loaded with a round ball of about 1,250 grains, or with a blunt or conical bullet that weighed about 1,880 grains. The usual propellant charge was 12 to 14 drams (325 to 380 grains) of blackpowder. Muzzle velocity was from 1300 to 1500 fps. Some 4-bore cartridges were loaded with up to 70 grains of cordite.

The 4-bore saw some use in Africa before the turn of the century, and in India for tiger shooting as recently as 1920. Typical 4-bore rifles weigh from 20 to 25 pounds. There is still quite a bit of interest in these, and at least one outfit is making new double-barrel and single-shot 4-bore rifles today. Variances in cases length were from about 3½ inches up to a 4¼-inch version.

8-Bore: The 8-bore was more popular than the 4-bore, because rifles for it could be built lighter. Typical 8-bores weighed about 15 to 16 pounds, hence were much handier and easier to use. Performance was not far behind that of the 4-bore, either. Typical loads are a 1,250-grain conical bullet at about 1500 fps, or a spherical ball of 860 grains at 1650 fps. Case length is from three to 3½ inches. Powder charge was about 10 to 12 drams (270 to 325 grains) of blackpowder.

A Paradox-type 8-bore cartridge with lighter loadings was also common. The Paradox was a Holland & Holland invention, which featured rifling in the choke area of its otherwise smoothbore barrels. These were also sometimes known as "ball-and-shot" guns, though some makers also used that name for smoothbores that had no rifling in the chokes. Numerous makers turned out variations on this theme and gave their creations highly individual names. Paradoxe 8-bores were a bit lighter than fully rifled guns and were, thus, handier still. The 8-bore Paradox was more of a big-game gun, while the 10- and 12-bore Paradoxes were more like heavily loaded shotguns, used only occasionally for big game.

10-Bore: Ten-bore rifles were also used against dangerous game and were, like the bigger bores, also loaded with detonating shells and/or lead-covered steel bullets for maximum penetration and performance. Here again, the Paradoxes were popular and efficient, and a common load used a 700-grain ball in front of a five-dram charge for 1300 fps. The full rifle load would give more than 1600 fps to the same round ball, or about 1500 fps to a somewhat heavier conical ball.

12-Bore: The 12-bore rifle saw lots of service against big game, but this size cartridge was probably most commonly seen as a Paradox load, either round ball or conical ball. In this guise, it was quite popular. The 12-bore Paradox worked well on medium-size game and was useful with shot loads for filling the pot with birds and small game. Most 12-bore Paradox-types weighed from seven to eight pounds. In a fully rifled arm, the weight would be more than 10 pounds and the load significantly more powerful. Case length for fully rifled arms varies from 18/10-inch up to 2¾ inches.

Gauge rifles were either single-shot or double-barrels. These evolved from muzzleloading firearms of similar bore size and, while the rapid-fire capability of these early breechloaders must have been a boon to the early explorers and hunters, it was no panacea.

The usual lead bullet's performance was such that it wasn't a good idea to take head shots on elephant. The skull of that beast consists of honeycombed cellular bone, and a lead ball could not be counted on to penetrate that, much less stay on course and find the brain. Shots to the head that missed the brain had little or no immediate effect on the animal, so the usual and much surer target was the body. A 4-bore ball through the heart would kill the elephant, but apparently not very quickly, as may be determined from the writings of many early African hunters.

The gauge rifles have a fascination matched by few other British or other sporting firearms. The cartridges are interesting and greatly varied, well worthy of study, collecting, or, if we are lucky enough to find a suitable rifle, shooting.

—F.C.B., with additional text by Steve Comus and Jennifer L.S. Pearsall

1- to 4-Gauge

Historical Notes: In most instances, gauges larger than 8-gauge were somewhat misnamed. Two-gauge shells are actually 4-gauge, and 4-gauge shells actually 5- or 6-gauge. Guns chambered for such cartridges were generally either punt guns, permanently or semi-permanently mounted on movable platforms, or very heavy smoothbore or fully rifled arms used by African hunters for taking the biggest and most dangerous species. In the former instance, the guns were used by market hunters, who were an important part of the expanding U.S. economy, as they provided much-needed protein for those who came to occupy new communities. The theory behind these large-bore punt guns was to launch a vast charge of shot against large flocks of birds that were on the water. In this way, the market gunner killed scores of birds with only one shot. Those used in Africa against dangerous game were also quite effective, more so when the cartridge was filled with a charge of shot. These are interesting cartridges that are well worth collecting and studying.

4-Gauge

Historical Notes: The 4-gauge was popular as a long-range waterfowl chambering in unusually heavy shotguns. Toward the latter part of the nineteenth century, the 4-gauge saw significant application in market hunting, but it saw very little use in any other application in the United States. However, both smoothbore and rifled versions were made for African hunting in that same era.

General Comments: New guns in this bore size have been produced recently, in both England and Belgium. It seems unlikely that any significant hunting need exists for such a gun, which suggests that the "magnum syndrome" is not limited to North America. Guns chambered for the paper-cased version are actually bored between 5- and 6-gauge size, while those chambered for the brass version can have a full 1.052-inch bore, which is truly 4-gauge. Pictured is a 3.93-inch long never-loaded casing featuring a steel head and paper body. This type of shell has no important length limitation—cutting the paper tube an inch longer adds very little cost. Therefore, in all the larger gauges (12-gauge on up), very long cases and matching chamberings were quite common. One is intrigued to speculate just how much shot might safely be fired at what velocity from such artillery-class combinations.

8-Gauge

Historical Notes: This was a very popular chambering, from the late 1880s through 1917. In 1918, U.S. legislation prohibited waterfowl hunting with this or any larger gauge. In the U.S. and elsewhere, this was prized as a long-range duck and goose gun. While "8-gauge" sounds impressively huge, performance of factory loads was quite similar to that of modern 10- and 12-gauge Magnums, to wit, 1¾ to 2¼ ounces of shot launched at about 1200 fps. Since those original 8-gauge loads lacked any system to protect the shot from bore abrasion, and because propellant gas sealing was not particularly effective, it is quite unlikely that the best 8-gauge loads of 100 years ago were anywhere nearly as effective as the best modern 12-gauge offerings.

General Comments: Although prohibited for waterfowl hunting in the United States, there is no prohibition against other applications. Therefore, the 8-gauge is making a significant comeback for other purposes, particularly turkey hunting, where it excels. The 8-gauge shells came in three-, 3¼-, 3¾-,and even four-inch lengths. Bore diameter is .835-inch. Gamebore Cartridge Co. of England (www.gamebore.com) currently offers 3¼-inch cased loads.

10-Gauge

Historical Notes:
This is the only shotshell larger than the 12-gauge still commercially produced in the United States. Larger gauges were outlawed for sporting use, in 1918. American-made single- and double-barrel guns in 10-gauge were manufactured until World War II. Then, after a short hiatus, several arms companies reintroduced the big 10- and, for a while, these guns gained popularity. However, two things have worked to nearly eliminate any sporting benefit offered by the 10-gauge for migratory bird hunting. First was the introduction of the 3½-inch 12-gauge shell, which has a higher pressure standard than the 10-gauge. Second was the adoption of mandatory non-toxic loads (originally, only steel was available) for hunting migratory species. There is nothing the 10 can do with steel shot that the higher-pressure 12-gauge loading cannot do better. However, the 10-gauge still has an advantage for turkey hunting, where large doses of lead shot are the preferred medicine and velocity isn't so important as it is with steel shot loads. The most commonly seen shell sizes are 29/16-, 25/8-, 27/8-, and 3½-inch. In England, Gamebore (www.gamebore.com) recently produced both the 27/8- and 3½-inch shells. Bore diameter is .775-inch.

11-Gauge

Historical Notes:
There is very little information on this oddball shotshell. Both Parker Brothers and UMC Co. headstamps were known producers, both listed as being in West Meridan, Connecticut, long ago. The Parker shell featured a large, American-type Berdan primer with three holes inside the case. The UMC loading evidently featured an internal primer, as it had no external opening to accept a primer. Best information is that two double-barrel guns and about 200 shells were made, in the 1890s. Dimensions for the 11-gauge are: Rim, .835-inch; base, .790-inch; mouth, .782-inch; length, 2½ inches. 11-gauge bore diameter is .751-inch.

12/14-Gauge Martini Shotgun

Historical Notes:
Our sample of this interesting shotshell is labeled as Caliber 12/14 Martini Shotgun, for Police. The headstamp has lightly etched Arabic markings. The case head includes a .85-inch-wide by .95-inch-deep, square-bottomed annular groove located around the approximately .3-inch diameter primer. Outside diameter of this groove is about .540 inches.

General Comments:
Previous editions of this book contained little background information on this shotshell. However, according to a gracious letter received by Mr. Glyn Jones of the Firearms Licensing Department of the Wiltshire Constabulary (UK), the 12/14-gauge Martini shotgun cartridge was made by W.W. Greener for a version of the Greener GP shotgun (a single-shot built on a Martini-type action), that was supplied to the Egyptian Police. In Mr. Jones' words:

Greeners had supplied a large number of GPs to the Egyptian Police authorities, in 1922, in 14-bore (gauge) ... . The cartridge as supplied had a conventional base, but was of a fairly unusual bore size. Some years later, (1935) the authorities became concerned about widespread criminal use of the guns by corrupt policemen. The unusual ammunition for this gun was not available outside of police sources, and the authorities were easily able to keep a check on what policemen had been issued with, and make them account for any used. However, it transpired that criminals were padding out commonly available 16-bore cartridges with adhesive tape to fit the 12/14 chamber. This became apparent after an incident in which a gun was lent by a policeman to a relative to murder his mother-in-law. The gun exploded, severely injuring the would-be murderer, and the method was thus exposed when the crime scene was investigated with perpetrator and remains of gun still present.

Greener's solution was to modify the guns so that three pins attached to each other internally flew forward from the face of the block when the trigger was pulled. One of these was the central firing pin, as normal. The other two, located just each side of the central firing pin, were slightly longer, so they would strike the base of a conventional cartridge on either side of the primer and stop the central firing pin from coming into contact with the primer.

The next step was to manufacture the special cartridge with the annular base groove; the two longer pins would fall into this groove and, thus, allow the firing pin to strike the primer. The modified gun was designated Greener GP Mk III, and the first deliveries were made in 1938.

Mr. Jones adds that Leyton Greener (1903-1983) invented and designed the modification, although the patent for it was actually filed by his cousin, Jasper Hutton Howlett.

12-Gauge

Historical Notes: If there is one shotshell that holds all titles as most versatile, most popular, and most varied in loading, the 12-gauge is it. Except for the .22 rimfire, by almost any measure the 12-gauge is the most popular sporting chambering ever offered. It is commonly available loaded with shot made of lead, steel, tungston/iron, tungston/polymer, or bismuth. Current shot charges range from about 7/8-ounce to 2½ ounces. Common shot sizes range from No. 9 through 000 Buck. Slugs are typically one-ounce or 1¼-ounce, but other weights are available. Further, it is relatively simple to have a moderately sized batch of custom loaded 12-gauge ammunition (with either an odd-sized shot or reduced velocity), produced by a major manufacturer.

To gain a true perspective, just consider that, at one time in this country, there were literally thousands of distinct 12-gauge loadings offered. In 1995, 12-gauge commercial offerings from only the big three shotshell manufacturers totaled 435 unique manufacturer and component combinations. Further, other significant commercial manufacturers offer hundreds more loadings, especially in the various non-toxic shot offerings. In fact, commercially available, unique 12-gauge loadings exceed the total of all currently available high-powered rifle loadings for all cartridges by a significant margin.

The 12-gauge has been and is still used for police and military applications and, as recently as the Vietnam conflict, was the preferred gun of front-line troops for jungle combat. No gun is more intimidating or more effective for home-defense situations. The 12-gauge is also at home, given proper loads, hunting big-game up through whitetail deer at ranges to about 100 yards, with some shotguns and loads stretching useful range further. For sporting use, the 12-gauge performs admirably on clay pigeons. The key word here is "versatility." If any chambering offers that characteristic, this is the one.

In 1866, a rebated-rim, reloadable steel 12-gauge shell was patented by Thomas L. Sturtevant. Revolving magazine four-shot guns chambered for this shell were offered by the Roper Sporting Arms Co., until the early 1880s. Eley, in England (www.eley.co.uk/) currently produces two- and 2½-inch shells, while here in the United States, the 2¾-, three-, and 3½-inch lengths are most common and available from a variety of sources. Longer and shorter versions exist, and a rebated rim 2 3/8-inch steel case is known to have been produced. Bore diameter for the 12-gauge is .729-inch.

14-Gauge

Historical Notes: This chambering was generally available between 1880 and the early 1900s. Shells were domestically available until sometime after World War I, and generally available, in Europe, until the 1970s. Original loads included a three-dram (powder), one-ounce (shot charge) load. The 14-gauge was experimented with, in the 1950s, by Winchester, which used an aluminum casing with both roll and modified-roll crimps. There was also a modified version, using a 12-gauge case head and lower body. Both brass and plastic versions of the latter are known. Most commonly seen shell lengths are two, 2½ and 29/16 inches. The French still produce empty hulls for the 29/16-inch version. Bore diameter for the 14-gauge is .693-inch.

15-Gauge

Historical Notes: Winchester's 1877 catalog listed brass shells in this gauge, the only year these were listed. Obviously, the 15-gauge is extremely rare. Examples are found only in the best collections. The 15-gauge would have a bore diameter of .677-inch.

16-Gauge

Historical Notes: The 16-gauge lingers on in what seems to be a nearly perpetual state of surprising continued existence. Introduction of three-inch 20-gauge loadings should have sounded the 16's death knell, since the 20-gauge can launch the same shot charge at just about the same velocity and, with modern plastic shot cups, patterning is substantially equivalent. However, there are just too many perfectly good 16-gauge guns still in use, and the shells, in surprising variety, are still commonly stocked at the retail level. The 16-gauge is even available in steel shot loadings.

In 1866, a rebated-rim, reloadable-steel, 16-gauge shell was patented by Thomas L. Sturtevant. Revolving magazine four-shot guns chambered for this shell were offered by the Roper Sporting Arms Company, until the early 1880s. The most common shell lengths in this gauge are 2½- and 2¾-inch, both currently produced by various European manufacturers, and the latter in U.S. production. The bore diameter for 16-gauge is .662-inch.

.64 Maynard

Historical Notes: Brass shells of this description were loaded for various models of Maynard sporting guns. The Model 1865 used a 25/16-inch shell with a Boxer primer. The Model 1873, adapted to both the No. 3 and No. 4 breechloading shotguns, used a 27/16-inch case featuring a modified Berdan primer. The Model 1882 was adapted to a reloadable case of 27/16-inch length. This gun, when equipped with interchangeable barrels, also fired the .40-40 Maynard cartridge. All Maynard shotshells were made with brass cases. This bore diameter corresponds to about 18-gauge.

18-Gauge

Historical Notes: This European gauge was loaded for use in custom shotguns. This ammunition was manufactured by Braun & Bloem, Kynoch, and Gustave Genschow. United Metallic Cartridge Co. produced a small batch for use in an experimental Browning shotgun. These UMC shells were 17/8 inches long and sometimes featured a 20-gauge headstamp. European pinfire versions of the 18-gauge in 29/16-inch length also exist. This gauge has a .637-inch bore.

20-Gauge

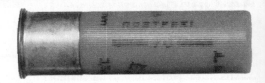

Historical Notes: Very much alive and well, the 20-gauge has always been popular, because it can be chambered in a smaller, lighter gun than the 12-gauge and offers sufficient punch for use against most sporting fowl. It is also completely at home breaking clay pigeons. Usefulness of the 20-gauge has improved dramatically, since the blackpowder era, when the top loading was 2¾ drams with 7/8-ounce of shot. The comparatively recent standardization of the three-inch loading brings 20-gauge performance into a new class, with shot charges up to 1¼ ounces at higher velocity. Loaded with modern shot-protect-ing cups, the 20-gauge three-inch Magnum practically duplicates the performance of top 16-gauge loads. Current loadings range from one to 1¼ ounces of shot and include several buckshot combi-nations and the 5/8-ounce slug. Steel shot loadings up to one ounce are also gaining in utility and popularity. By a wide margin, the 20-gauge is the second most popular U.S. chambering. The 2½-inch version is currently available from various European manufacturers. Bore size is .615-inch.

24-Gauge

Historical Notes: Single-shot shotguns in this bore size were produced in the United States, until the late 1930s, by Stevens and Harrington & Richardson. The standard load was two-drams equivalent and ¾-ounce of shot. Shells in this gauge, and the double-barrel guns that shoot these rounds, are still manufactured in Europe. These have recently been available in the United States through American Arms Company and Beretta. Both CBC and Fiocchi have made this ammunition available domestically. Current loads launch 11/16-ounce of shot. The most common shell lengths in this gauge are two and 2½ inches. The 2½-inch version is still produced by Fiocchi. Midway USA (www.midwayusa.com) carries the Fiocchi fully loaded shells, as well as brass cases produced by Magtech. Bore size is .580-inch.

.55 Maynard

Historical Notes: Brass shells of this description were loaded for the various models of Maynard sporting guns. The Model 1865 used a 2¼-inch shell with a Boxer primer. The Model 1873, adapted to both the No. 1 and No. 2 breechloading shotguns, used a 23/8-inch case featuring a modified Berdan primer. The 1882 loading used a reloadable case of 25/16-inch length and was adapted to the No. 1 and No. 2 breech-loading guns. This bore size corresponds to the 28-gauge.

28-Gauge

Historical Notes: The 28-gauge 2¾-inch is currently manufactured in the United States. The original blackpowder loading used a 2½-inch shell with 1¾ drams of powder and 5/8-ounce of shot. Federal Cartridge now lists a 2¾-inch, 2¼-dram, ¾-ounce load with either Nos. 6, 7½, or 8 shot at a velocity of 1295 fps. The 28-gauge is perfectly adequate for use in hunting upland birds and is at home breaking clay pigeons. However, recent innovations in shotshell technology have limited the 28-gauge's popularity since three-inch .410-bore loadings can practically duplicate 28-gauge performance. Nevertheless, light, easy handling and graceful guns still attract shotgunners, and the 28-gauge hangs on to a small but dedicated following, chiefly for these reasons. Bore size is .550-inch.

32-Gauge

Historical Notes: American manufacturers offered 32-gauge guns well into the 1930s. The Winchester Model 1886 rifle was routinely offered on a custom basis thusly chambered and barreled for the 32-gauge shotshell, which is essentially a .52-caliber bore. The standard loading was ½-ounce of shot, but a 5/8-ounce shot load and a 158-grain roundball loading were also offered. Loads in this gauge have been con-tinuously available in Europe, and shells are domestically available through Fiocchi loaded with either No. 6 or No. 8 shot. Guns in this chambering have recently been imported through the American Arms Co. Even before World War II, the .410-bore practically duplicated 32-gauge performance. Nevertheless, light, easy-handling guns with graceful lines still attract European shotgunners, and the 32-gauge hangs on to a small but dedicated following there, chiefly for these reasons. Currently, Fiocchi offers the 2½-inch shell (available through Midway USA, www.midwayusa.com). Actual 32-gauge bore size is .526-inch.

11.15x52mm

Historical Notes: This European brass shotshell was popular in the early 1900s. It was generally loaded with shot, but was also available in a ball loading for use in rifled barrels. Performance of this loading would be quite similar to the modern .44 Magnum shot loadings offered by CCI/Speer (CCI still offers this load in the slightly shorter .44 Special configuration). The intended purpose was small-game hunting. For targets the size of rabbits and hares, the 11.15x52mm was reasonably effective. This bore size corresponds to .439-inch and would be called a 55-gauge.

.44 XL (1⁹⁄₁₆-inch)

Historical Notes: Made in the early 1900s, shotguns in this bore size were intended solely for use in hunting small game. This could be considered a forerunner to the .410-bore shotshell. Brass cases and paper shot containers were used. Overall length was 21/32-inch with a case length of 19/32-inch. The standard loading used No. 8 shot in a folded paper container, which protruded substantially from the brass case. Both single-barrel and double-barrel shotguns were offered in this chambering. Actual bore diameter was similar to the .44-caliber rifle cartridges (.425-inch) and would be called 61-gauge.

.410-Bore

Historical Notes: Though gun and load selection are somewhat limited, the .410-bore (12mm) is a perfectly good dove and quail chambering and can be argued to be the ideal small-game shell. A light, handy, .410-bore breech-break shotgun is a pleasure to carry on long hunts, and top three-inch loads deliver all the punch necessary to cleanly anchor rabbits and smaller species. Many use this diminutive chambering for breaking clay pigeons. Interestingly, it is possible to fire .410-bore shells in .45/70-chambered rifles. There are also a slug loading and one in 000 Buck (a three-pellet load in the three-inch shell), but their value for anything beyond their current rage as an alternate home-defense round is certainly moot. The .410-bore follows the 12- and 20-gauge in popularity. Many young shooters have learned to shoot with a .410-bore, and that tradition continues. The .410-inch bore would be called 68-gauge.

.360 Centerfire

Historical Notes: Similar to the more popular 9mm rimfire, this chiefly European chambering is strictly in the small-game and pest-control genre. Shells are found in both paper and brass and are 1¾ inches long. While it might be possible to dispatch smaller species of small game with this and others of the various diminutive shotshell chamberings, such use is ethically questionable. Nevertheless, none of these are toy cartridges. All high-velocity shot pellets are equally dangerous, regardless of source. The chief problem with these various diminutive shotshells is the lack of sufficient shot volume to achieve useful hunting pattern densit, and with shot of sufficient size, to get the job done. A.360-inch bore would be called a 99-gauge.

9.1x40mm

Historical Notes:
The 9.1x40mm (.358-inch x 1.575-inch) was an early European shotshell intended for small-game hunting. It was also offered in a ball loading, for use in rifles. While it might be possible to dispatch smaller species of small game with this and others of the various diminutive shotshell chamberings, such use is ethically questionable. The chief problem with these various diminutive shotshells is lack of sufficient shot volume to achieve useful hunting pattern density, and with shot of sufficient size, to get the job done. This corresponds to a .358-inch bore and would be called a 101-gauge.

9mm Rimfire

Historical Notes:
This cartridge was offered by Winchester for use in the Model 36 shotgun, which was introduced in 1920 and discontinued in 1927. Only 20,306 such shotguns were made. While that is a very small production total for a mainline arms manufacturer, this actually represents a surprising number of guns, considering the limited usefulness and market.

The only viable use for such a chambering is pest control. While it might be possible to dispatch smaller species of small game with this and others of the various diminutive shotshell chamberings, such use is ethically questionable. The chief problem with this and other diminutive shotshells is the lack of sufficient shot volume to achieve useful hunting pattern densities, and with shot of sufficient size, to get the job done. The shotshell length was 19/16-inch. This corresponds to a .354-inch bore and would be called a 105-gauge. Fiocchi again offers 9mm rimfire shotshells, available through Midway USA (www.midwayusa.com).

9mm Centerfire

Historical Notes:
Recently available in Europe (by Spanish manufacture), these are found with plastic bodies and a metal head. The only viable use for such a chambering is pest control. While it might be possible to dispatch smaller species of small game with this and others of the various diminutive shotshell chamberings, such use is ethically questionable. The chief problem is the lack of sufficient shot volume to achieve useful hunting pattern densities and with shot of sufficient size, to get the job done. This corresponds to a .354-inch bore and would be called a 105-gauge.

.32 Rimfire

Historical Notes:
Stevens offered its No. 20 Favorite shotgun in this chambering. Shell casings were copper or brass and shot containers were wood or paper. Case length was 7/8-inch for copper rolled rim or 25/32-inch for those with wooden shot containers. Overall length for the wooden container shotshells was 17/32-inch. Remington UMC and WRA manufactured these shells. The only viable use for such a chambering is pest control. While it might be possible to dispatch smaller species of small game with this and others of the various diminutive shotshell chamberings, such use is ethically questionable. The chief

problem is lack of sufficient shot volume to achieve useful hunting pattern densities, and with shot of sufficient size, to get the job done. A .320-inch bore would be called a 142-gauge.

Note: All case length and diameter measurements include surprisingly generous tolerances, typically about .010-inch for length and about .020-inch for diameter. Numbers given for case base diameter are representative of a value somewhere near the middle of the radius of the fold where the case body blends into the rim. Generally, diameter of the cylindrical portion of the case head is somewhat smaller.

.310 Remington

Historical Notes: This brass-cased, rimfire shotshell was made by Remington for a mini-skeet shooting game. The shotgun was a bolt-action used to shoot miniature clay pigeons. Shell length was 11/16-inch.

7mm

Historical Notes: This is a European shotshell and long obsolete. It was also available in a ball loading. Shells are usually copper-based with a paper body. The only potential value of such a chambering is pest control. The 7mm shotshell corresponds to a .276-inch bore and would be called a 223-gauge. The most commonly seen length is 1¼-inch.

6mm

Historical Notes: Little is known about this diminutive chambering. The example seen here has a metal case head and paper body. The only potential value of such a chambering is pest control. The 6mm corresponds to a .236-inch bore and would be called a 353-gauge.

.20-Caliber Wingo

Historical Notes: These straight-walled rimfire shells were loaded by Winchester, in the 1970s, for chambering in unique, single-shot lever-action shotguns used in special indoor Wingo skeet-shooting galleries. The shells feature a .22 rimfire rim size, but have a smaller case body to prevent chambering of standard .22 rimfire ammunition in these guns. Wingo ammunition was assembled with 2.1 grains of ball powder and approximately 113 No. 12 shot pellets. Winchester-Western was the sole manufacturer of this cartridge. The .20-caliber Wingo corresponds to a .200-inch bore and would be called a 582-gauge.

Collath Gauges

Historical Notes: Available in 0-, 1-, 3-, 4-, 5-, 6-, 7-, and 8-gauge, these were an early 1900s European development. The shells used a unique gauging system. The 1-gauge is somewhat smaller than the common 12-gauge. Pinfire versions also existed. Collath ammunition was cataloged as late as 1911. The 5-gauge shell in Frank Napoli's collection has a metal band around the outer brass and paper joint. The empty shells were made in Frankfurt, Germany, and available in the Alfa Arms Catalog of 1911. Although never very popular, specimens are sometimes seen in collections and at gun shows. The unusual sizings and headstamps can cause significant confusion.

Shotshell Cartridges Dimensional Data

The following table is not exhaustive. It does not include many of the rarer, though known, case lengths and types. It should, however, provide sufficient information to help the reader identify 99 percent of those shotshells or casings he might come upon. If the example does not fit any of these data, likely it is sufficiently rare to merit advisement from a serious collector.

In many instances, data in this table represents approximations or estimates. In addition, you will note a significant number of "?" entries. We anxiously await reader input toward improving the provided dimensional data and filling in the remaining blanks. The purpose of including estimates is to help the reader make a preliminary identification of either a loaded shell or a fired casing. We believe the included estimated dimensional data will be sufficiently close to accommodate that end.

Note that loaded shell lengths can vary dramatically, especially in those shells using a folded or roll crimp. However, such variance is always toward the shorter side. In the larger gauges, current SAAMI specifications provide for a "minus" variance as great as ¼-inch.

Gauge or Bore	Possible Sep. Shot Container	Crimp Types	Likely Case Body Material Types (not including case head)	Diameter (inch) Rim	Base	Mouth	Length (inches) Closed Fold	Roll	Open	Normal Bore Diameter (inches)	Priming Type	Comments
Collath 3-gauge	None	Roll w/Card	Paper	?	?	?		?	2.91	?	Pinfire	Rare
Collath 5-gauge	None	Roll w/Card	Paper	.803	.731	.666			2.56	?	Centerfire	Rare
.20-Caliber Wingo	None	Star(?)	Brass	.270	.21	.21	?	?	?	.200	Rimfire	
6mm	None	Roll w/ Card	Paper	?		?	?	?	?	.236	?	Rare
7mm	None	Roll w/ Card	Paper	?	?	?	?	1.20	1.25	.276	?	
.310 Remington	None	Taper w/Card	Brass	.378	.320	.315		1.05	1.06	.310	Rimfire	
.32 Centerfire	Wood or Paper	Tape w/Card	Copper or Brass	?	?	?	?	.85	.88	.320	Rimfire	
.32 Centerfire	Wood or Paper	Taper w/Card	Copper or Brass	?	?	?	?	.78	1.22	.320	Rimfire	
9mm Centerfire	None	Roll or Taper	Paper, Plastic or Brass	.436	.391	.370		1.67	1.75	.354	Centerfire	
9mm Rimfire	None	Taper w/Card	Brass	.385	.323	.320		1.65	1.66	.354	Rimfire	
9mm Rimfire	None	Taper	Paper or Brass	.410	.344	.326		.40	.40	.354	Rimfire	Single Ball Load
9mm Rimfire	None	Roll or Taper	Paper or Brass	.410	.344	.326		1.44	1.45	.354	Rimfire	
9.1x40mm	None	Taper w/Card	Brass	?	?	?		1.55	1.58	.358	Centerfire	
9.1mm Long	None	Taper w/Card	Brass	?	?	?		?	?	.358	Centerfire	
.360 Centerfire	None	Roll or Taper	Paper, Plastic or Brass	.474	.422	.417		1.70	1.75	.360	Centerfire	
.410-Bore	?	Star	Paper, Brass or Aluminum	.525	.470	.465	1.84	1.90	2.00	.410	Centerfire	
.410-Bore	Plastic	Star	Paper, Plastic or Brass	.525	.470	.465	2.36	2.40	2.50	.410	Centerfire	
.410-Bore	Plastic	Taper w/Card	Brass	.525	.470	.465		2.85	2.88	.410	Centerfire	
.410-Bore	Plastic	Roll or Star	Paper or Plastic	.525	.470	.465	2.84	2.90	3.00	.410	Centerfire	
44 XL	Paper or Wood	Taper w/Card	Brass	.525	.471	.443		1.57	2.03	.425	Centerfire	
11.15x 52mm	None	Taper w/Card	Brass	?	?	?		2.00	2.05	.439	Centerfire	
32-Gauge	Plastic	Roll or Taper	Paper, Plastic or Brass	.640	.580	.575	2.30	2.35	2.50	.526	Centerfire	Pinfire also
28-Gauge	None	Taper/Roll/ Star	Paper or Brass	.680	.620	.615	2.25	2.31	2.50	.550	Centerfire	Pinfire also
28-Gauge	Plastic	Roll or Star	Paper or Plastic	.680	.620	.615	2.50	2.56	2.75	.550	Centerfire	
.55 Manard '65	None	Taper w/Card	Brass	?	?	?		2¼	2¼	.550	Boxer	
.55 Manard '73	None	Taper w/Card	Brass	?	?	?		2 3/8	2 3/8	.550	Berdan	
.55 Manard '73	None	Taper w/Card	Brass	?	?	?		2 5/16	2 5/16	.550	Berdan	Reloadable
24-Gauge	None	Roll or Star	Paper or Plastic	.725	.655	.640	1.70	1.80	2.00	.580	Centerfire	
24-Gauge	None	Taper/Roll/ Star	Paper, Plastic or Brass	.725	.655	.640	2.20	2.30	2.50	.580	Centerfire	Pinfire also
20-Gauge	Plastic	Roll or Star	Paper or Plastic	.760	.690	.675	2.20	2.30	2.50	.615	Centerfire	Pinfire also
20-Gauge	Plastic	Taper w/Card	Brass	.760	.690	.675		2.60	2.63	.615	Centerfire	
20-Gauge	Plastic	Roll or Star	Paper or Plastic	.760	.690	.675	2.45	2.55	2.75	.615	Centerfire	

Gauge or Bore	Possible Sep. Shot Container	Crimp Types	Likely Case Body Material Types (not including case head)	Diameter (inch)			Length (inches) Closed		Open	Normal Bore Diameter (inches)	Priming Type	Comments
				Rim	Base	Mouth	Fold	Roll				
20-Gauge	Plastic	Taper w/Card	Brass	.760	.690	.675		2.85	2.88	.615	Centerfire	
20-Gauge	Plastic	Roll or Star	Paper or Plastic	.760	.690	.675	2.71	2.80	3.00	.615	Centerfire	
18-Gauge	None	Roll w/Card	Paper	.782	.712	.697		?	1.88	.637	Centerfire	Cases only, factory loads never seen
18-Gauge	None	Roll or Taper	Paper or Brass	.782	.712	.697		?	2.56	.637	Pinfire	
18-Gauge	None	Roll or Taper	Paper or Brass	.782	.712	.697		?	2.56	.637	Centerfire	
.64 Manard '65	None	Taper w/Card	Brass	?	?	?		2 5/16	2 5/16	.640	Boxer	
.64 Manard '73	None	Taper w/Card	Brass	?	?	?		2 7/16	2 7/16	.640	Berdan	
.64 Manard '82	None	Taper w/Card	Brass	?	?	?		2 7/16	2 7/16	.640	Berdan	Reloadable
16-Gauge		Taper/Roll/ Star	Paper or Brass	.810	.740	.720	2.19	2.23	2.50	.662	Centerfire	
16-Gauge		Roll w/Card	Paper	.810	.740	.720	2.25		2.56	.662	Centerfire	Pinfire also
16-Gauge	Plastic	Roll or Star	Paper or Plastic	.810	.740	.720	2.44	2.48	2.75	.662	Centerfire	
16-Gauge	None	Roll w/Card	Paper	.810	.740	.720		2.73	3.00	.662	Centerfire	
15-Gauge	None	Roll w/Card	Paper	.813	.743	.728	?	?	?	.678	Pinfire	Very Rare
15-Gauge	None	Taper w/Card	Brass	.813	.743	.728	?	?	?	.678	Centerfire	Very Rare
14-Gauge	None	Roll or Star	Paper	.839	.769	.754	1.70	1.75	2.00	.693	Centerfire	
14-Gauge	None	Taper/Roll/ Star	Paper or Brass	.839	.769	.754	2.20	2.25	2.50	.693	Centerfire	
14-Gauge	None	Roll w/Card	Paper	.839	.769	.754		2.31	2.56	.693	Centerfire	Pinfire also
14-Gauge	Plastic (?)	Taper w/Card	Aluminum	?	?	?		?	?	.693	Centerfire	Experimental
14-Gauge	Plastic (?)	Roll or Taper	Plastic or Brass	.875	.805	.754		?	?	.693	Centerfire	Experimental
12/14 Martini	None	Partial Star	Brass	.892	.792	.735	2.86		2.88	?	Berdan	Police Load
12-Gauge	Plastic	Roll w/Card	Plastic	.875	.805	.790		1.25	1.50	.729	Centerfire	
12-Gauge	Plastic	Roll w/Card	Plastic	.875	.805	.790		1.64	1.88	.729	Centerfire	Pinfire also
12-Gauge	Plastic	Roll w/Card	Paper, Plastic	.875	.805	.790		1.76	2.00	.729	Centerfire	Pinfire also
12-Gauge	None	Taper w/Card	Steel	?	?	?		2.35	2.38	.729	Centerfire	Pinfire also
12-Gauge	Plastic	Taper/Roll/ Star	Paper, Plastic or Brass	.875	.805	.790	2.16	2.26	2.50	.729	Centerfire	Pinfire also
12-Gauge		Taper w/Card	Brass	.875	.805	.790		2.60	2.63	.729	Centerfire	Pinfire also
12-Gauge *	Plastic	Taper/Roll/ Star	Paper, Plastic or Brass	.875	.805	.790	2.41	2.45	2.75	.729	Centerfire	Pinfire also
12-Gauge		Taper w/Card	Brass	.875	.805	.790		2.85	2.88	.729	Centerfire	Pinfire also
12-Gauge *	Plastic	Taper/Roll/ Star	Paper, Plastic or Brass	.875	.805	.790	2.66	2.76	3.00	.729	Centerfire	Pinfire also
12-Gauge *	Plastic	Roll or Star	Paper or Plastic	.875	.805	.790	3.16		3.50	.729	Centerfire	
12-Gauge	None	Roll w/Card	Paper	0.875	.805	.790		3.76	4.00	.729	Centerfire	
12-Gauge	None	Roll w/Card	Paper	.875	.805	.790		4.76	5.00	.729	Centerfire	
11-Gauge	None	Roll w/Card	Paper ?	.835	.790	.782		2.36	2.50 ?	.751	?	Very Rare
11-Gauge	None	Taper w/Card	Brass	.835	.790	.782		2.48	2.50	.751	Berdan	Very Rare
11-Gauge	None	Taper w/Card	Brass	.835	.790	.782		2.48	2.50	.751	Inside	Very Rare
10-Gauge	None	Roll w/Card	Paper	.925	.850	.830		2.36	2.57	.775	Centerfire	Pinfire also
10-Gauge	None	Roll w/Card	Paper	.925	.850	.830		2.42	2.63	.775	Centerfire	Pinfire also
10-Gauge *	Plastic	Taper/Roll/ Star	Paper, Plastic or Brass	.925	.850	.830	2.49	2.67	2.89	.775	Centerfire	Pinfire also
10-Gauge *	Plastic	Taper/Roll/ Star	Paper, Plastic or Brass	.925	.850	.830	3.11	3.29	3.50	.775	Centerfire	Pinfire priming is also seen
8-Gauge *	None	Roll or Taper	Paper or Brass	.998	.913	.902		2.75	3.00	.835	Centerfire	
8-Gauge *	Plastic	Roll or Taper	Paper or Brass	.998	.913	.902		3.00	3.25	.835	Centerfire	
8-Gauge *	None	Roll or Taper	Paper or Brass	.998	.913	.902		3.13	3.38	.835	Centerfire	
8-Gauge *	None	Taper/Roll/ Star	Paper, Plastic or Brass	.998	.913	.902		3.25	3.50	.835	Centerfire	
8-Gauge *	None	Roll w/Card	Paper	.998	.913	.902		3.75	3.93	.835	Centerfire	
8-Gauge *	None	Roll w/Card	Paper	.998	.913	.902		4.00	4.25	.835	Centerfire	
4-Gauge *	None	Roll w/Card	Paper or Plastic	1.127	1.041	1.114	2.0-4.2	Various 2.5-4.25	.918 .975 **	Berdan & Pinfire	Often a Slug	

Gauge or Bore	Possible Sep. Shot Container	Crimp Types	Likely Case Body Material Types (not including case head)	Approximate Case Dimensions Length (inches)						Normal Bore Diameter (inches)	Priming Type	Comments
				Diameter (inch)			Closed		Open			
				Rim	Base	Mouth	Fold	Roll				
4-Gauge *	None	Roll w/Card	Paper or Plastic	1.127	1.041	1.114	2.0-4.2	Various 2.5-4.25	.918 .975 **	Berdan & Pinfire	Often a Slug	
3-Gauge	None	Taper or Roll	Paper or Brass	1.515	1.388	1.350	4.12	3.875	4.125	1.157	Centerfire	
2-Gauge *	None	Taper or Roll	Paper or Brass	1.888	1.735	1.715		4.500	4.875	1.325 **	Berdan	Usually a Slug

Collath/Gauge Comparisons (Collath #/Gauge #): 0 = 10; 1 = 12; 2 (not used); 3 = 14; 4 = 16; 5 = 18; 6 = 20; 7 = 24; 8 = 28
Brass shotgun shells often use Berdan primers.

* These were also used for dangerous game hunting in Africa. The larger sizes were also used for market hunting in various places. See Chapter 8 for a more complete discussion. Guns were also built with both fully rifled and "paradox" (smooth, excepting the very end, which was rifled) bores. Choking was not used.

** Bore diameters are estimates. These "gauges" were never properly described or standardized. Bore diameter measurements indicate that what various manufacturers described as a 4-gauge (bore) was closer to 5- or 6-gauge (at least three bore diameters are known). Similarly, the "2-gauge (bore)" was actually a 4-gauge (bore).

NOTE: 6 drams = 1 ounce = 437.5 grs.

Downrange Velocities and Energies
Lead and Steel Shot
12-Gauge, 2³/₄-Inch Loads

Load	Velocity @ 3 ft. Nominal ft/sec.	Measured ft/sec.	Downrange Velocity, Measured at 40 yd. ft/sec.	Energy p/Pellet at 40 yd. ft-lb.
11/8-oz. #2 Steel	1365	1350	773	4.84
11/4-oz. #2 Steel	1300	1305	761	4.69
11/4-oz. #4 Lead	1330	1319	803	4.64
11/2-oz. #4 Lead	1260	1252	778	4.35
11/2-oz. #4 Lead*	1260	1240	793	4.52

*Buffered load

40-Yard Penetration
20 Percent Ordnance Gelatin
Lead and Steel Shot
12-Gauge, 2³/₄-Inch Loads

Load	Velocity At 3 ft. ft/sec.	Energy Per Pellet At 40 yd. ft-lb.	Energy Density At 40 yd. ft-lb/sq. in.	Penetration in Gelatin inches
11/8-oz. #2 Steel	1350	4.84	274	2.0
11/4-oz. #2 Steel	1305	4.69	265	1.9
11/4-oz. #4 Lead	1319	4.64	350	2.5
11/2-oz. #4 Lead	1252	4.35	328	2.4
11/2-oz. #4 Lead*	1240	4.52	341	2.5

*Buffered load

Pellet Count and Distribution in Patterns
Full, Modified and Improved Cylinder Chokes
Lead and Steel Shot
12-Gauge, 2³/₄-Inch Loads, 1979

Load	Choke	Approx. Number Pellets in Load	Pattern Percent 40 Yards			Pellets in Pattern 40 Yards		
			30" Circle	20" Circle	Annular Area, 30"-20" Circle	30" Circle	20" Circle	Annular Area, 30"-20" Circle
11/8-oz. #2 Steel	Full	135	76	47	29	103	64	39
11/8-oz. #2 Steel	Mod.	135	68	40	28	92	54	38
11/8-oz. #2 Steel	Imp. Cyl.	135	44	22	22	60	30	30
11/4-oz. #2 Steel	Full	150	76	47	29	114	71	43
11/4-oz. #2 Steel	Mod.	150	68	40	28	102	60	42
11/4-oz. #2 Steel	Imp. Cyl.	150	44	22	22	66	33	33
11/4-oz. #4 Lead*	Full	169	72	43	29	122	73	49
11/4-oz. #4 Lead*	Mod.	169	56	29	27	95	49	46
11/2-oz. #4 Lead*	Full	202	73	44	29	147	89	58
11/2-oz. #4 Lead"XX"	Full	202	87	59	28	176	119	57

*This is a standard, non-buffered load

Notes: Area of 30" Circle:707 sq. in.
Area of 20" Circle:314 sq. in.
Annular area:707 - 314:393 sq. in.

COMPARATIVE SHOTGUN SLUG PERFORMANCE

Gauge	Shell Length ins./mm	Slug Weight oz./grs.	Slug Type	Velocity (fps)			Energy (fpe)		
				MV	50 yds	100 yds	MV	50 yds	100 yds
10	31/2/89	13/4/766	Foster	1280	1080	970	2785	1980	1605
12	3/76	11/4/547	Foster	1600	1320	1130	3110	2120	1785
12	3/76	13/8/600	Brenneke	1502	1144	936	3017	1749	1240
12	3/76	1/437.5	Foster	1760	1345	1075	3009	1396	891
12	3/76	1/437.5	Sabot	1550	1410	1190	2400	1665	1220
12	23/4/70	11/4/547	Foster	1520	1260	1090	2805	1930	1450
12	23/4/70	11/10/490	Brenneke	1590	1190	975	2745	1540	1035
12	23/4/70	1/437.5	Foster	1680	1285	1045	2741	1605	1061
12	23/4/70	1/437.5	Foster	1610	1330	1140	2520	1725	1255
12	23/4/70	1/437.5	Sabot	1450	1320	1130	2100	1475	1120
12	23/4/70	1/437.5	Foster	1560	1175	977	2364	1342	927
16	23/4/70	4/5/350	Foster	1600	1180	990	1990	1075	755
16	23/4/70	9/10/415	Brenneke	1590	1190	975	2320	1300	875
20	23/4/70	3/4/328	Foster	1600	1270	1070	1865	1175	835
20	23/4/70	7/8/370	Brenneke	1590	1190	975	2080	1165	780
410	21/2/63.5	1/5/88	Foster	1830	1340	1060	650	345	215
410	3/76	1/4/110	Brenneke	1755	1162	917	780	342	213

U.S. Military Ammunition (5.56 to 20mm)

(Description and Identification)

Much of this information was originally published in our 3rd Edition. Since then, we have had requests for a reprint of the data *covering U.S. military cartridges. The information was compiled to* provide a quick and easy to use reference source for the identification of the more modern U.S. military ammunition—that is, the post-World War II period. Many of the cartridges listed here are no longer in use, but have become collectors' items of increasing scarcity and value over time.

The identification of armor-piercing, incendiary, or explosive-type munitions is a matter of concern to collectors, to shooters of surplus military weapons, and also to police, firemen, and others. The data provided here will enable the reader to identify the various types of U.S. military ammunition likely to be encountered on the surplus market or in use by the military. Insofar as the original author and subsequent editors are aware, this is the only popular publication that has published most of the information contained in this chapter, particularly the identifying color codes.

In addition to the standard military cartridges listed here, the various branches of the service also use a number of commercial cartridges such as the .22 Short and .22 Long Rifle; .22 Hornet; .32 ACP; .38 S&W; .38 S&W Special; 9mm Parabellum (now the official U.S. Military handgun cartridge); .45-70 blank; and the .410-bore, 12-, and 10-gauge shotgun shells. Details of all these are not provided in this chapter, but are covered elsewhere in this book. There are a number of new ammunition developments in the U.S.

military not listed here, but most of these are experimental or in the developmental stage and have not been officially adopted. The cartridges listed here are those that have been standardized and are—or were—in official use.

This material was, to a large extent, abstracted from two out-of-print government publications: *Small Arms and Small Arms Ammunition, Vol. 2,* Office of the Chief of Ordnance, Washington D.C., and *Small Arms Ammunition Pamphlet 23-1,* Dept. of the Army Frankford Arsenal, Philadelphia, Pennsylvania. Don't write to the author or publisher of this book asking where you can get copies of these—we don't know! Such things as industrial or manufacturing codes and drawing numbers have also been omitted, because they would not be of interest to the great majority of readers of *Cartridges of the World.*

Note: The second figure that appears with some of the data, particularly the weights and pressures, is a manufacturing tolerance and was left in so that the reader will understand that some variations can be expected between different lots and manufacture of ammunition. Also, it should be understood that, in some instances, the powder type given has been changed from tubular to ball powder in recent years. As an example, 56-2 grs. means a standard weight of 56 grains with no more than a 2-grain variation (+/-1 grain) being acceptable. The rest of the data is more or less self-explanatory.

5.56x45mm

Cartridge, Caliber 5.56mm, Ball, M193

Weapon:	Rifle, 5.56mm, M16; M16E1
Ballistic Perf.:	
Velocity:	3250 ±40 fps at 15 feet; Std. Dev.40 fps max.
Pressure:	52,000 psi max. avg.; avg. pressure plus 3 Std. Dev. 58,000 psi max.
Port Pres.:	15,000 psi 2,000 psi
Accuracy:	2.00" mean radius max. avg. at 200 yards
Cartridge:	182 - 14 grs.
Case:	94 - 5 grs.
Bullet:	56 - 2 grs.
Primer, Perc.:	
Prim. Wt:	4.0 grs. approx.
Compos.:	Lead Styphnate
Propellant:	
Brand:	IMR8208M WC846
Type:	Single Base Double Base Tubular Spheroidal
Weight:	25.5 grs. 28.5 grs.
Ident.:	Plain tip

Cartridge, Caliber 5.56mm, Ball, M855A1

Weapon:	Rifle, 5.56mm, M16A2, M249
Ballistic Perf.:	
Velocity:	3020 ±40 fps
Pressure:	52,000 psi max. avg.; avg. pressure plus 3 Std.
Dev.:	58,000 psi max.
Port Pres.:	15,000 psi 2,000 psi
Accuracy:	2.00" mean radius max. avg. at 200 yards
Cartridge:	187 - 14 grs.
Case:	94 - 5 grs.
Bullet:	62 - 2 grs.
Primer, Perc.:	
Prim. Wt:	4.0 grs. approx.
Compos.:	Lead styphnate
Propellant:	
Brand:	IMR8208M WC846
Type:	Single Base Spheroidal Tubular
Weight:	
Ident.:	Green tip

Cartridge, Caliber 5.56mm, Grenade Rifle, M195

Weapon:	Rifle, 5.56mm, XM16E1; M16
Ballistic Perf.:	
Velocity:	140 ± 165 fps at 5.5 ft. (Grenade 1.56 lbs). No individual shot below 140 fps
Cartridge:	127.5 - 4 grs.
Case:	98 - 3 grs.
Primer, Perc.:	
Prim. Wt:	4.0 grs. approx.
Compos.:	Lead Styphnate
Propellant:	
Brand:	IMR4475
Type:	Single Base, Tubular
Weight:	25.0 grs.
Wad:	.5 grs. max., Cardboard, Royal Satin coated (both sides) Booklined Yellow
Ident.:	Case mouth closed with 7 petal rose crimp red tip

Cartridge, Caliber 5.56mm, Tracer, M196

Weapon:	Rifle, 5.56mm, M16; XM16E1
Ballistic Perf.:	
Velocity:	3200 ±40 fps at 15 feet; Std. Dev. 40 fps max.
Pressure:	52,000 psi max. avg./avg. pressure plus 3 Std. Dev. 58,000 psi max.
Port Pres.:	15,000 psi 2,000 psi
Accuracy:	5.00" mean radius max. avg. at 200 yards
Trace:	The trace shall be visible from a point not greater than 75 yards from the the muzzle of weapon to a point not less than 500 yards from the muzzle.
Cartridge:	177 - 11 grs.
Case:	94 - 5 grs.
Bullet:	54 - 2 grs.
Point Filler:	28 - .5 grs. - lead-antimony

Base Clos.:	Vinyl
Tracer:	2.7 grs. approx.
Ign.:	1.0 gr.
Sub Ign.:	.05 gr.
Primer, Perc.:	
Prim. Wt:	4.0 grs. approx.
Compos.:	Lead Styphnate
Propellant	
Brand:	IMR 8208M
Type:	Single Base Tubular
Weight:	25.3 grs.
Ident.:	Red Tip

Cartridge, Caliber 5.56mm, Test, High Pressure, M197

Weapon:	Used to proof test barrels and weapons (not a service cartridge)
Ballistic Perf.:	
Pressure:	70,000 3,000 psi, max. Std. Dev. 3500 psi
Cartridge:	174 - 11 grs.
Case:	94 - 5 grs.
Bullet:	C10524197 - 56 - 2 grs.
Primer:	4.0 grs. approx.
Propellant	
Brand:	HPC 3
Type:	Double Base Flake
Weight:	20.0 grs.
Ident.:	Case Stannic Stained or Nickel Plated

Cartridge, Caliber 5.56mm, Tracer, M856A1

Weapon:	Rifle, 5.56mm, M16A2, M249
Ballistic Perf.:	
Velocity:	2795 ±40 fps
Pressure:	52,000 psi max. avg./ avg. pressure plus 3 Std. Dev. 58,000 psi max.
Port Pres.:	15,000 psi 2,000 psi
Accuracy:	5.00" mean radius max. avg. at 200 yards
Trace:	The trace shall be visible from a point not greater than 75 yards from the muzzle of the weapon to a point not less than 500 yards from the muzzle.
Cartridge:	177 - 11 grs.
Case:	94 - 5 grs.
Bullet:	63.8 grs.
Primer, Perc.:	
Prim. Wt:	4.0 grs. approx.
Compos.:	Lead Styphnate
Propellant:	
Brand:	
Type:	
Weight:	
Ident.:	Orange tip

Dummy Cartridge, Caliber 5.56mm, M199

Weapon:	Rifle, 5.56mm, XM16E1; M16 - Training
Cartridge:	150 - 7 grs.
Case:	94 - 7 grs.
Bullet:	56 - 2 grs.
Primer:	None
Propellant:	None
Ident.:	Impressed upon the case, 6 corrugations, approx. .030-inch deep equally spaced about the periphery.

Cartridge, Caliber 5.56mm, Blank, XM200

Weapon:	Rifle, 5.56mm, M16; XM16E1 with blank firing attachment, M13
Ballistic Perf.:	
Screen pert:	No perforations in paper screen at 15 ft.
Cyclic Rate: per minute	Min. 550 rds. per minute, max. 800 rds.
Cartridge:	109.5 - 4 grs.
Case:	98 - 3 grs.
Bullet:	None, Case Mouth closed with 7-petal rose crimp
Primer, Perc.:	
Prim. Wt:	4.0 grs. approx.
Compos.:	Lead Styphnate
Propellant:	HPC 13
Type:	Double Base, Flake
Weight:	7.0 grs.

Wad:	None
Ident.:	Cannelure approx 1/22 from head and mouth closed with 7-petal rose crimp

Dummy Cartridge, Caliber 5.56mm, Inert Loaded, M232

Weapon:	Rifle, 5.56mm, XM16E1, M16
Cartridge:	181.5 - 7.0 grs.
Case:	94 - 5 grs.
Bullet:	56 - 2 grs.
Primer:	None
Propellant:	31 grs. Sodium Carbonate Monohydrate
Ident.:	Cartridge, chemical black

Dummy Cartridge, Caliber 5.56mm, Inert Loaded, M857

Weapon:	Rifle, 5.56mm, M16A2, M249
Cartridge:	187.5 - 7.0 grs.
Case:	94 - 5 grs.
Bullet:	61 - 2 grs.
Primer:	None
Propellant:	31 grs. Sodium Carbonate Monohydrate
Ident.:	Cartridge, chemical black

.30-CALIBER CARBINE

Cartridge, Caliber .30, Carbine, Ball, M1

Weapon:	Carbine, Caliber .30, M1; Carbine., Caliber .30, M2
Ballistic Perf.:	
Velocity:	1900 ±30 fps
Pressure:	40,000 psi, max. avg.
Accuracy:	1.5" mean radius max. avg. at 100 yards
Cartridge:	146 - 13 grs. (with gilding metal jacketed bullet) 193 - 13 grs. (with gilding metal clad steel jacketed bullet)
Case:	71 - 6 grs.
Bullet:	111 - 3 grs. (with gilding metal jacket) 108 - 3 grs. (with gilding metal clad steel jacket)
Primer, Perc.:	Lead Styphnate
Propellant:	
Brand:	WC820 HPC5
Type:	Double Base Double Base Spheroidal Flake
Weight:	13 grs. 13 grs.
Point Ident.:	Plain Tip

Cartridge, Caliber .30, Carbine, M13

Weapon:	Carbine Cal .30, M1; Carbine, Caliber .30, M2
Ballistic Perf.:	None
Cartridge:	177 grs.
Case:	66 grs.
Bullet:	111 - 3 grs. - 108 - 3 grs.
Ident.:	Drilled case, no primer

Cartridge, Caliber .30, Carbine, Rifle Grenade, M6

Weapon:	Carbine, Caliber .30, M1; Carbine, Caliber .30, M2
Ballistic Perf.:	
Velocity:	Shall propel grenade (AT, Practice, M11A3) with velocity of 145 ±15 fps at 5 feet
Cartridge:	103 grs.
Case:	77 grs.
Wad:	Pressed Paper, Commercial
Primer, Perc.:	
Propellant:	
Brand:	IMR 4809 and Black Powder
Weight:	21 grs.
Ident.:	Case Mouth closed with 5-petal rose crimp

Cartridge, Caliber .30, Carbine, Test, High Pressure, M18

Weapon:	Carbine, Caliber .30 M1; Carbine, Caliber .30, M2
Ballistic Perf.:	
Pressure:	47,500 2,500 psi max. avg.
Cartridge:	233 grs. approx.
Case:	71 - 6grs.
Bullet:	152 - 3 grs.
Primer, Perc.:	
Propellant:	

Brand: HPC-5
Type: Double Base, Flake
Weight: 14 grs.
Ident.: Case is stannic stained

Cartridge, Caliber .30, Carbine, Tracer, M27

Weapon: Carbine, Caliber .30, M1; Carbine, Caliber .30, M2
Ballistic Perf.:
Velocity: 1800 ±30 fps
Pressure: 40,000 psi, max. avg.
Trace: Bright Trace from 100 to 400 yards
Accuracy: 3.5" mean radius max. avg. at 100 yards
Cartridge: 191 - 13 grs.
Case: B6200957, 71 - 6 grs.
Bullet: 103 - 4 grs.
Tracer: 5.5 grs. approx.
Igniter: .5 gr. approx.
Primer, Perc.:
Propellant:

Brand:	HPC-5	WC 820
Type:	Double Base Flake	Double Base Spheroidal
Weight:	13 grs.	13 grs.
Point Ident.:	Orange Tip	

7.62mm, NATO (.308 WIN.)

Cartridge, Caliber 7.62mm, NATO, Ball, M59

Weapon: Gun, Machine, 7.62mm, M60; M73 Rifle, 7.62mm, M14
Ballistic Perf.:
Velocity: 2750 ±30 fps at 78 feet
Pressure: 50,000 psi, max. avg.
Accuracy: Carton or Clip Pack - 5" mean radius at 600 yards; Link Pack - 7½" mean radius at 600 yards
Cartridge: 393 - 27 grs.
Case: 190 - 20 grs.
Bullet: 150.5 - 6.5 grs. (cut cannelure)
150.5 - 5.5 grs. (knurled cannelure)
Core: 55 - 2 grs. - steel
Fill., Pt.: 24 - 1 grs. - lead-antimony
Fill., Base: 14.5 - 1 grs. - lead-antimony
Primer, Perc.:
Prim. Wt: 5.430 - .520 grs.
Pellet Wt: .600 - .120 grs.
Compos.: Lead Styphnate
Propellant:

Brand:	WC 846	IMR 4475
Type:	Double Base Spheroidal	Single Base Tubular
Weight:	46 grs.	41 grs.
Point Ident.:	Plain tip	

Cartridge, Caliber 7.62mm, NATO, Test, High Pressure, M60

Weapon: Used to proof test barrels and weapons (Not a service cartridge)
Ballistic Perf.:
Pressure: 67,500 2,500 psi, avg.
Cartridge: 412.0 - 23.5 grs.
Case: 190 - 20 grs.
Bullet: 174.5 - 3.0 grs.
Primer, Perc.:
Prim. Wt: 5.43 - .52 grs.
Pellet Wt: .60 - .12 grs.
Compos.: FA-956, Lead Styphnate
Propellant:
Brand: IMR 4475
Type: Single Base Tubular
Weight: 41 grs.
Ident.: Stannic Stained Case

Cartridge, 7.62mm, NATO, AP, M61

Weapon: Gun, Machine, 7.62mm, M60; M73 Rifle, 7.62mm, M14
Ballistic Perf.:
Velocity: 2750 fps ±30 fps at 78 feet
Pressure: 50,000 psi, max. avg.

Accuracy: 7.5" mean radius at 600 yards
Cartridge: 393 - 27 grs.
Case: 190 - 20 grs.
Bullet: C7553740 - 150.5 - 6.5 grs. (cut cannelure);
150.5 - 5.5 grs. (knurled cannelure)
Core: 55 - 2 grs. - steel
Fill., Pt: 24 - 1 grs. - Lead Antimony
Primer, Perc.:
Prim. Wt: 5.430 - .520 grs.
Pellet Wt: .600 - .120 grs.
Compos.: FA-956, Lead Styphnate
Propellant:

Brand:	IMR 4475	WC 846
Type:	Single Base Tubular	Double Base Spheroidal
Weight:	41 grs.	46 grs.
Point Ident.:	Black Lacquer	

Cartridge, Caliber 7.62mm, NATO, Tracer, M62

Weapon: Gun, Machine, 7.62mm, M60; M73 Rifle, 7.62mm, M14
Ballistic Perf.:
Velocity: 2750 ±30 fps at 78 feet
Pressure: 50,000 psi, max. avg.
Accuracy: 15" mean radius, max. avg., at 600 yards
Trace: Visible trace between 100 and 850 yards, min.
Cartridge: 383 - 29 grs.
Case: 190 - 20 grs.
Bullet: 142 - 4 grs.
Fill., Pt: 72.0 - 1.5 grs. - Lead Antimony
Tracer: 6.5 grs. approx.
Ign.: 1.0 grs. approx.
Sub-ign.: 1.0 grs. approx.
Primer, Perc.:
Prim. Wt: 5.43 - .52 grs.
Pellet Wt: .60 - .12 grs.
Compos.: FA-956, Lead Styphnate
Propellant:
Type: Double Base Spheroidal
Weight: 46 grs.
Point Ident.: Orange Lacquer

Cartridge, Caliber 7.62mm, NATO, Tracer, M62

(Overhead Fire Application)
Weapon: Gun, Machine, 7.62mm, M60; M73 Rifle, 7.62mm, M14
Ballistic Perf.:
Velocity: 2680 ±30 fps at 78 feet
Pressure: 50,000 psi, max. avg.
Accuracy: 9" mean radius, max. avg. at 600 yards
Extreme Spread, Max. per target: 45 inches
Trace: Visible trace between 100 and 850 yards, min.
Cartridge: 387 - 29 grs.
Case: 190 - 20 grs.
Bullet: 146 - 4 grs.
Fill., Pt: 72 - 1.5 grs. - Lead Antimony
Base Seal: None
Tracer: 6.5 grs. approx.
Igniter: 1.0 grs. approx.
Sub-ign.: 1.0 grs. approx.
Primer Perc.:
Prim. Wt: 5.43 - .52 grs.
Pellet Wt: .60 - .12 grs.
Compos.: FA-956, Lead Styphnate
Propellant:
Type: Double Base Spherical
Weight: 46 grs.
Ident.: Red Lacquer

Dummy Cartridge, Caliber 7.62mm, NATO, M63

Weapon: Gun, Machine, 7.62mm, M60; M73 Rifle, 7.62mm, M14
Requirements: Training and Gun Functioning
Bullet Pull: 175 lb. min.
Cartridge: 258 - 21.5 grs.
Case: 190 - 20 grs.
Bullet: 68 - 1.5 grs.
Ident.: 6 corrugations spaced equally around periphery of case

---

Cartridge, Caliber 7.62mm, NATO, Grenade Rifle, M64

Weapon: Rifle, 7.62mm, M14
Ballistic Perf.:
Velocity: Cartridge shall propel a grenade weighing 1.56lbs. 160 ±5 fps at 5.6 feet beyond the forward end of the grenade when fully positioned for launching.
Cartridge: 233 - 21 grs. (HPS 4 Propellant)
236 - 21 grs. (IMR8097 Propellant)
241 - 21 grs. (WC830 Propellant)
Case: 190 - 20 grs. - Copper Alloy
Primer, Perc.:
Prim. Wt: 5.430 - .520 grs.
Pellet Wt: .600 - .120 grs.
Compos.: FA-956, Lead Styphnate
Propellant:

Brand:	HPC4	1MR8097	WC830
Type:	Double Base Tubular	Single Base Tubular	DoubleBase Spherical
Weight:	37 grs.	40 grs.	45 grs.
Wad:	Pressed Paper		
Ident.:	Rosette Crimp		

Cartridge, Caliber 7.62mm, NATO, Ball, M80

Weapon: Gun, Machine, 7.62mm, M60; M73 Rifle, 7.62mm, M14
Ballistic Perf.:
Velocity: 2750 ±30 fps at 78 feet
Pressure: 50,000 psi, max. avg.
Accuracy: Carton or Clip Pack - 5" mean radius, max. avg. at 600 yards; Link Pack - 7.52" mean radius, max. avg. at 600 yards
Cartridge: 392 - 31 grs.
Case: 190 - 20 grs.
Bullet: 149 - 3 grs.
Primer, Perc.:
Prim. Wt: 5.43 - .52 grs.
Pellet Wt: .60 - .12 grs.
Compos.: FA-956, Lead Styphnate
Propellant:

Type:	Double Base Spheroidal	Single Base Tubular	Single Base Tubular
Weight:	46 grs.	41.5 grs.	41 grs.
Ident.:	Plain Tip		

Cartridge, Caliber 7.62mm, NATO, Ball, M80

(Overhead Fire Application)
Weapon: Gun, Machine, 7.62mm, M60; M73 Rifle, 7.62mm, M14
Ballistic Perf.:
Velocity: 2750 ±30 fps at 78 feet
Pressure: 50,000 psi, max. avg.
Accuracy: 5" mean radius, max. avg. at 600 yards; Extreme Spread, max. per target - 25 inches
Cartridge: 393 - 31 grs.
Case: 190 - 20 grs.
Bullet:
Primer, Perc.:
Prim. Wt: 5.43 - .52 grs.
Pellet Wt: .60 - .12 grs.
Compos.: FA-956, Lead Styphnate
Propellant:

Brand:	WC 846	IMR 8138M	IMR4475
Type:	Double Base	Single Base Tubular	Single Base Tubular
Spheroidal			
Weight:	46 grs.	41.5 grs.	41 grs.
Point Ident.:	Plain Tip		

Cartridge, Caliber 7.62mm, NATO, Blank, M82

Weapon: Rifle, 7.62mm, M14, Machine Gun, M60; M73 with blank-firing attachment
Ballistic Perf.:
Screen Perf.: Perforations in paper screen shall be less than .1-inch in diameter at 15 ft. from muzzle of gun
Cartridge: 222 - 225 grs. approx.
Case: 201 grs. approx.
Wad: .030-inch tagboard or chipboard
Primer, Perc.:
Prim. Wt: 5.430 - .520 grs., 5 grs. approx.
Compos.: Lead Styphnate - FA-956; FA-1023
Propellant:

Brand:	SR4759	HPC-2	WC818
Type:	Single Base Tubular	Double Base Flake	Double Base Spheroidal
Weight:	17.5 grs.	14.5 grs.	14.5 grs.
Ident.:	No bullet, crimped mouth, double tapered neck and orifice sealed with red lacquer		

Cartridge, Caliber 7.62mm, Match, M118

Weapon:	Rifle, 7.62mm, M14 (National Match)
Ballistic Perf.:	
Velocity:	2550 ±30 fps at 78 feet
Pressure:	50,000 psi, max. avg.
Accuracy:	3.5" mean radius, max. avg. at 600 yards
Cartridge:	390 grs. approx.
Case:	190 - 20 grs.
Bullet:	175.5 - 3.0 grs.
Primer, Perc.:	
Prim. Wt:	5.43 - .52 grs.; 5.3 grs. approx.; 5 grs. approx.
Pellet Wt:	.60 - .12 grs.; .7 - .2 grs.; .58 -.08 grs.
Compos.:	FA-956, FA-961, FA-1023
Type:	Lead Styphnate
Propellant:	
Brand:	WC 846	IMR 4895
Type:	Double Base Spherical	Single Base Tubular
Weight:	44 grs.	42 grs.
Ident.:	Special head stamping-Match stamped on head of case or NM stamped on head of case of cartridges for National Matches	

Cartridge, Caliber 7.62mm, Match, M852

Weapon:	Rifle, 7.62mm, M14 (National Match)
Ballistic Perf.:	
Velocity:	2550 ±30 fps at 78 feet
Pressure:	50,000 psi, max. avg.
Accuracy:	3.5" mean radius, max. avg. at 600 yards
Cartridge:	383 grs. approx.
Case:	190 - 20 grs.
Bullet:	168 grs. Hollow point boattail
Primer, Perc.:	
Prim. Wt:	5.43 - .52 grs.; 5.3 grs. approx.; 5 grs.approx.
Pellet Wt:	.60 - .12 grs.; .7 - .2 grs.; .58 -.08 grs.
Compos.:	FA-956 FA-961 FA-1023
Type:	Lead Styphnate
Propellant:	
Brand:	IMR 4895
Type:	Single Base Tubular
Weight:	42 grs.
Ident.:	Special head stamping-Match stamped on head of case or NM stamped on head of case of cartridges for National Matches

Cartridge, Caliber 7.62mm, Ball, Frangible, M160

Weapon:	Gun, Machine, 7.62mm, M73
Ballistic Perf.:	
Velocity:	1320 ±50 fps
Accuracy:	4.0" mean radius max. avg. at 100 yards
Perf.:	The bullet of the cartridge shall not perforate a 3/162 thick plate Dural .2024 T4 (or equal) with a Brinell hardness of 105 to 125 under a 500 kilogram load at a range of 25 yards.
Cartridge:	315 - 24 grs.
Case:	190 - 20 grs.
Bullet:	108.5 - 3 grs., Bakelite, Natural and powdered lead
Primer, Perc.:	
Prim. Wt:	5.43 - .52 grs.
Compos.:	FA-956
Propellant:	
Brand:	SR8074	HPC-8	WC140
Type:	Single Base Tubular	Double Base Flake	Single Base Spheroidal
Weight:	10.5 grs.	8.3 grs.	11.4 grs.
Ident.:	Green tip; White annulus		

Dummy Cartridge, Caliber 7.62mm, Inert Loaded, M172

Weapon:	Gun, Machine, M60, Testing Metallic Link Belts and Gun Function

---

Requirements:	Bullet Extr.: The force required to extract the bullet from the cartridge case shall not be less than 173 lbs.
Cartridge:	385 - 23 grs.
Case:	190 - 20 grs.
Bullet:	149 - 3 grs.
Filler:	Sodium Carbonate Monohydrate or equal
Ident.:	Cartridge, black oxide, no primer or primer vent hole

Cartridge, Caliber 7.62mm, NATO, Ball, Duplex, M198

Weapon:	Rifle, 7.62mm, M14
Ballistic Perf.:	
Velocity:	Front Bullet - 2750 ±30 fps at 78 feet Rear Bullet - 2200 fps min. indiv. at 78 feet
Pressure:	52,000 psi, max. avg.
Accuracy:	(Front Bullet) 2" mean radius, max. avg. at 100 yards
Dispersion:	(Rear Bullet) between 5 and 10 inches CEP at 100 yards
Cartridge:	411 - 31 grs.
Case:	190 - 20 grs.
Bullet:	(Front) 84 - 4 grs. (Rear) 85 - 4grs.
Primer, Perc.:	
Prim. Wt:	5.43 - .52 grs.
Compos.:	FA-956, Lead Styphnate
Propellant:	
Type:	Double Base Spheroidal
Weight:	45.5 grs.
Point Ident.:	Green Lacquer

.30 (.30-06)

Cartridge, Caliber .30, Tracer M1

Weapon:	Gun, Machine, Cal .30, M37; Gun, Machine, Cal .30 Browning M1919A4; Gun, Machine, Cal .30, M1919A6; Rifle, U.S. Cal .30, M1
Ballistic Perf.:	
Velocity:	2700 ±30 fps at 78 feet GM Bullet 2665 ±30 fps for GMCS Bullet
Pressure:	52,000 psi, max. avg.
Accuracy:	18" mean radius max. avg. at 600 yards
Tracer:	Visible Light from Muzzle to 900 yards
Cartridge:	408 - 27 grs. (GM Bullet) 399 - 27 grs. (GMCS Bullet)
Case:	200 − 20 grs.
Bullet:	152.5 - 3.5 grs. 143.5 - 3.5 grs.
Tracer:	13 grs. approx.
Igniter:	3 grs. approx.
Primer, Perc.:	
Prim. Wt:	5.43 - .520 grs. - Lead Styphnate
Propellant:	
Type:	Double Base, Spheroidal - IMR4895
Weight:	50 grs.
Point Ident.:	Red tip

Cartridge, Caliber .30, Test, High Pressure, M1

Weapon:	(For Proof Testing all Caliber .30 Weapons)
Ballistic Perf.:	
Pressure:	67,500 psi, max. avg.
Cartridge:	432 - 24 grs.
Bullet:	173 - 3 grs.
Primer, Perc.:	
Prim. Wt:	5.5 grs.
Compos.:	FA961 - Lead Styphnate
Propellant:	
Brand:	IMR 4198
Type:	Single Base, Tubular
Weight:	52 grs.
Ident.:	Stannic Stained (tinned) Case

Cartridge, Caliber .30, Ball, M2

Weapon:	Gun, Machine, Cal .30, M37; Gun, Machine, Cal .30 Browning M1919A4; Gun, Machine, Cal .30, M1919A6; Rifle, U.S. Cal .30, M1
Ballistic Perf.:	
Velocity:	2740 ±30 fps at 78 ft
Pressure:	50,000 psi, max. avg.

Accuracy:	7.5" mean radius max. avg. at 600 yards
Cartridge:	408 - 23 grs.
Case:	200 - 20 grs.
Bullet:	152 - 3 grs.
Primer, Perc.:	
Prim. Wt:	5.43
Compos.:	Lead Styphnate
Propellant:	
Brand:	IMR4895	WC852	CMR-100
Type:	Single Base Tubular	Double Base Spheroidal	Single Base Tubular
Weight:	50 grs.	50 grs.	45 grs.
Point Ident.:	Plain Tip		

Cartridge, Caliber .30, Ball, M2

(Overhead Fire Application)

Weapon:	Guns, Machine, Caliber .30; M37, Browning M1919A4 and M1919A6
Ballistic Perf.:	
Velocity:	2740 ±30 fps at 78 feet
Pressure:	50,000 psi maximum average
Accuracy:	5.0" mean radius maximum average at 600 yards
Cartridge:	408 - 23 grs.
Case:	200 - 20 grs.
Bullet:	152 - 3 grs.
Primer, Perc.:	
Prim. Wt:	5.43
Compos.:	FA956 - Lead Styphnate
Propellant:	
Brand:	IMR4895	WC852	CMR-100
Type:	Single Base Tubular	Double Base Spheroidal	Single Base Tubular
Weight:	50 grs.	50 grs.	45 grs.
Point Ident.:	Plain Tip		

Cartridge, Caliber .30, Armor Piercing, M2

Weapon:	Gun, Machine, Cal .30, M37; Gun, Machine, Cal .30 Browning M1919A4; Gun, Machine, Cal .30, M1919A6; Rifle, U.S. Cal .30, M1
Ballistic Perf.:	
Velocity:	2715 ±30 fps at 78 feet
Pressure:	54,000 psi, max. avg.
Accuracy:	10" mean radius max. avg. at 600 yards
Cartridge:	424 - 28 grs.
Case:	200 - 28 grs.
Bullet:	166 - 7.5 grs.
Primer, Perc.:	
Prim. Wt:	5.43
Compos.:	Lead Styphnate
Propellant:	
Brand:	WC852	IMR 4895
Type:	Double Base Spheroidal	Single Base Tubular
Weight:	55 grs.	55 grs.
Point Ident.:	Black tip	

Cartridge, Caliber .30, Grenade Rifle, M3

Weapon:	Rifle, U.S. Caliber .30, M1
Ballistic Perf.:	
Velocity:	Shall propel Grenade (Practice, M11A2) with a velocity of 180 ±15 fps at 5.5ft
Cartridge:	246 - 20 grs.
Case:	200 - 20 grs.
Wad:	Paper
Primer, Perc.:	
Prim. Wt:	5.43 - .520 grs.
Compos.:	Lead Styphnate
Propellant:	
Type:	Single Base, IMR 4895
Weight:	40 grs. + 5.0 1.0 gr. Black powder
Ident.:	Case mouth closed with 5-petal rose crimp and sealed with red lacquered disc

Cartridge, Caliber .30, API, M14

Weapon:	Gun, Machine, Cal .30, M37 (Tank) Gun, Machine, Cal .30, Browning, M1919A4; Gun, Machine, Cal .30, 1919A6; Rifle, U.S. Cal .30, M1
Ballistic Perf.:	
Velocity:	2780 ±30 fps at 78 feet

Pressure:	54,000 psi, max. avg.
Accuracy:	15" mean radius max. avg. at 600 yards
Incend:	Shall produce flash when fired against steel target at 175 yards
Penetra:	Avg. penetration depth of .422-in. when fired against steel plate at 100 yards

Cartridge:	407 - 30 grs.	
Case:	200 - 20 grs.	
Bullet:	151 - 6 grs.	
Primer, Perc.:		
Compos.:	Lead Styphnate	
Propellant		
Brand:	WC 852	IMR 4895
Type:	Double Base	Single Base
	Spheroidal	Tubular
Weight:	50 grs.	50 grs.
Point Ident.:	Aluminum	

Cartridge, Caliber .30, Frangible, Ball, M22

| Weapon: | Gun, Machine, Cal .30, M37; Gun, Machine, Cal .30, Browning, M1919A4; Rifle, U.S. Cal .30, M1 |

Ballistic Perf.:

Velocity:	1320 ±30 fps at 53 feet 1500 fps, max. individual at 53 feet
Accuracy:	2.0" mean radius max. avg. at 100 yards
Perf.:	Shall not perforate aluminum plate at 25 yards 3/162 Dural 2024 T4 with Brinell Hardness of 105 to 125 under 500 Kilogram load
Cartridge:	320 - 24 grs.
Case:	220 - 20 grs.
Bullet:	108.3 grs. Bakelite
Primer, Perc.:	
Prim. Wt:	5.5 grs.
Compos.:	Lead Styphnate
Propellant	
Brand:	SR 4759
Type:	Single Base, Tubular
Weight:	11 grs.
Point Ident.:	Green and white tip

Cartridge, Caliber .30, Tracer, M25

| Weapon: | Gun, Machine, Cal .30 Browning, M1917A1 Gun, Machine, Cal .30, M37 (Tank) Gun, Machine, Cal .30 Browning, M1919A4 Gun, Machine, Cal .30 Browning, M1919A6 Rifle, U.S. Cal .30 M1 |

Ballistic Perf.:

Velocity:	2665 ±30 fps at 78 feet	
Pressure:	50,000 psi, max. avg.	
Trace:	Bright Trace, 75 to 900 yards	
Cartridge:	401 - 25 grs.	
Case:	200 - 20 grs.	
Bullet:	145.5 - 4 grs.	
Primer, Perc.:		
Prim. Wt:	5.430 - .520 grs.	
Compos.:	Lead Styphnate - FA956	
Propellant		
Brand:	WC 852	IMR 4895
Type:	Double Base	Single Base
	Spheroidal	Tubular
Weight:	50 grs.	50 grs.
Point Ident.:	Orange tip	

Cartridge, Caliber .30, Tracer, M25 (Steel Case)

Same as Cartridge, Tracer, Cal .30, M25, except:
| Case: | Steel, 180 - 20 grs. |

Cartridge, Caliber .30, Dummy, M40

Weapon:	For training purposes in all caliber .30 weapons
Ballistic Perf.:	None
Cartridge:	268 - 21.5 grs.
Case:	200 - 20 grs.
Bullet:	68 - 1.5 grs.
Ident.:	Corrugated case - no primer

Cartridge, Caliber .30, Match, M72

Weapon:	Rifle, U.S. Caliber .30, M1 National Match
Ballistic Perf.:	
Velocity:	2640 ±30 fps at 78 feet

Pressure:	50,000 psi, max. avg.
Accuracy:	3.5" mean radius max. avg. at 600 yards
Cartridge:	425 grs. approx.
Case:	200 - 20 grs.
Bullet:	175.5 - 3 grs.
Primer Perc.:	
Prim. Wt:	5 to 5.6 grs.
Compos.:	FA961 or FA1023 - Lead Styphnate
Propellant	
Brand:	IMR 4895
Type:	Single Base, Tubular
Weight:	50 grs.
Ident.:	MATCH stamped on head of case, and NM stamped on head of case of cartridges for National Matches

Cartridge, Caliber 30, Blank, M1909

Weapon:	Gun, Machine, Cal .30, Browning M1919A4; Gun, Machine, Cal .30 M1919A6; Rifle, U.S. Cal .30, M1
Ballistic Perf.:	None	
Cartridge:	218 - 20 grs.	
Case:	200 - 20 grs.	
Primer Perc.:		
Propellant		
Brand:	WC Blank	SR 4990
Type:	Double Base	Single Base
	Spheroidal	Flake
Weight:	12 grs.	12 grs.
Wad:	Paper 25 grs.	
Ident.:	No bullet, mouth sealed with red lacquered disc

Cartridge, Caliber .30, Blank, M1909 (Steel Case)

Same as Cartridge, Blank, Cal .30, M1909 except:
| Case: | Steel, 180 - 20 grs. |

9mm

Cartridge, Caliber 9mm, Ball, NATO, M882

Weapon:	Pistol, Automatic, Cal 9mm, M9, M11
Ballistic Perf.:	
Velocity:	1251 ±25 fps at 16 meters
Pressure:	27,000 psi, max. avg.
Accuracy:	
Cartridge:	179 grs.
Case:	42 grs.
Bullet:	124 grs. Copper Alloy
Primer, Perc.:	
Propellant	
Brand:	HPC 26
Type:	Double Base	Flake
Weight:	5 grs.	6 grs.
Point Ident.:	Plain tip

Cartridge, Caliber 9mm, Test, High Pressure, M905

Weapon:	Used to proof test barrels and weapons (Not a service cartridge)
Ballistic Perf.:	
Pressure:	50,000 psi, max. avg.
Cartridge:	179 grs.
Case:	42 grs.
Bullet:	124 grs.
Primer, Perc.:	Lead Styphnate
Propellant	
Brand:	WC 370
Type:	Double Base Ball
Weight:	7.5 grs.
Ident.:	Tinned Case, HPT headstamp

Cartridge, Caliber 9mm, Practice Tracer, M939

Weapon:	AT-4 Subcaliber Trainer
Ballistic Perf.:	
Velocity:	885 ±25 fps at 25.5 feet
Pressure:	27,000 psi, max. avg.
Trace:	Visible trace to match AT-4 rocket trajectory
Cartridge:	
Case:	Aluminum
Bullet:	Brass
Tracer:	
Ignit.:	

Primer, Perc.:	Lead Styphnate
Propellant	
Brand:	
Type:	
Weight:	
Point Ident.:	Red Lacquer over Blue Tip

Cartridge, Caliber 9mm, Dummy, M917

Weapon:	Pistol, Automatic, Cal 9mm, M9, M11
Ballistic Perf.:	Not applicable
Cartridge:	179 grs. approx.
Bullet:	124 grs.
Ident.:	Hole in side wall of case

.45

Cartridge, Caliber .45, Ball, M1911

Weapon:	Pistol, Automatic, Cal .45, M1911A1 Gun, Submachine, Cal. 45, M3A1
Ballistic Perf.:	
Velocity:	855 ±25 fps at 25.5 feet
Pressure:	19,000 psi, max. avg.
Accuracy:	7.46" diagonal (max. avg.) at 50 yards
Cartridge:	331 - 17 grs.
Case:	87 - 10 grs.
Bullet:	234 - 6 grs. Copper Alloy .231 grs. Gilding Metal Clad Steel
Primer, Perc.:	
Propellant	
Brand:	SR 7970	HPC 1
Type:	Single Base	Double Base
	Flake	Flake
Weight:	5 grs.	5 grs.
Point Ident.:	Plain tip

Cartridge, Caliber .45, Ball, M1911, (Steel Case)

Weapon:	Pistol, Automatic, Cal .45, M1911A1 Gun, Submachine, Cal .45, M3A1
Ballistic Perf.:	
Velocity:	855 ±25 fps at 25.5 feet
Pressure:	19,000 psi, max. avg.
Accuracy:	7.46" diagonal (max. avg.) at 50 yards
Cartridge:	321 - 20 grs.

Cartridge, Caliber .45, Ball, M1911, Match Grade

Weapon:	Pistol, Automatic, Cal .45, M1911A1 National Match
Ballistic Perf:	
Velocity:	855 ±25 fps at 25.5 feet
Pressure:	19,000 psi, max. avg.
Accuracy:	3" diagonal (max. avg.) at 50 yards
Cartridge:	334 - 17 grs.
Case:	87 - 10 grs.
Bullet:	234 - 6 grs.
Primer, Perc.:	
Propellant	
Brand:	SR 7970	HPC 1
Type:	Single Base	Double Base
	Flake	Flake
Weight:	5 grs.	5grs.
Ident.:	Special head stamping - Match - stamped on head of case, and NM stamped on head of case of cartridges for National Matches

Cartridge, Caliber .45, Test, High Pressure, M1

Weapon:	Used to proof test barrels and weapons (Not a service cartridge)
Ballistic Perf.:	
Pressure:	22,000 psi, max. avg.
Cartridge:	332-16 grs.
Case:	87 - 10 grs.
Bullet:	234 - 6 grs.
Primer, Perc.:	Lead Styphnate
Propellant	
Brand:	SR 7970	HPC 1
Type:	Single Base	Double Base
	Flake	Flake
Weight:	7 grs.
Ident.:	Stannic Stained Case

Cartridge, Caliber .45, Blank, M9

Weapon:	Pistol, Automatic, Cal .45, M1911A1

Ballistic Perf.:

Screen Perf.:	.12 dia. max. perforations in paper screen at 15 feet

Cartridge:	104 grs. approx.
Propellant:	7 grs.

Cartridge, Caliber .45, Tracer, M26

Weapon:	Pistol, Automatic, Cal .45, M1911A1 Gun, Submachine, Cal .45, M3A1

Ballistic Perf.:

Velocity:	885 ±25 fps at 25.5 feet
Pressure:	19,000 psi, max. avg.
Trace:	Visible trace between 15 and 150 yards, min.

Cartridge:	331 - 17 grs.	
Bullet:	203 grs. approx.	
Tracer:	3 grs. approx.	
Ignit.:	2.5 grs. approx.	
Primer, Perc.:	Lead Styphnate	
Propellant:		
Brand:	SR 7970	HPC 1
Type:	Single Base Flake	Double Base Flake
Weight:	5 grs.	5 grs.
Point Ident.:	Red Lacquer	

Cartridge, Caliber .45, Tracer, M26 (Steel Case)

Same as Cartridge, Cal .45, M26, except:	
Case:	Steel, 82 - 10 grs.

Cartridge, Caliber .45, Blank, Line Throwing M32

Case:	Brass
Primer:	Non-mercuric, non-corrosive
Propellant:	Commercial
Ballistics:	
Pressure:	20,000 psi
Ident.:	No bullet, rimmed long case, ".45 M32" stamped on head of case
Note:	This cartridge used with Lyle life-saving gun, Cal 45/70.

Cartridge, Caliber .45, Match, Wad Cutter

(Commercial)

Weapon:	Pistol Automatic Cal .45, M1911A1, National Match

Ballistics:

Velocity:	The mean velocity of 10 rds. at 15 ft. from the muzzle of the gun shall be 765 ±45 fps
Pressure:	The mean pressure of 10 rds. shall not exceed 18,000 psi. The extreme variation shall not exceed 6200 psi.
Accuracy:	Average extreme spread of 5-5 shot targets at 50 yards shall not exceed 3.0 inches

Cartridge:	
Case:	Brass
Bullet:	185 grains Gilding Metal
Propellant:	Commercial
Primer:	Commercial Lead Styphnate
Ident.:	Head stamp in accordance with commercial practice

Cartridge, Caliber .45, Dummy, M1921

Weapon:	Pistol, Automatic, Cal .45, M1911A1 Gun, Submachine, Cal .45, M3A1
Ballistic Perf.:	Not applicable
Cartridge:	313 grs. approx.
Bullet:	234 - 6 grs.
Ident.:	Hole in side wall of case

Cartridge, Caliber .45, Dummy, M1921 (Steel Case)

Same as Cartridge, Dummy, Cal .45, M1921, except:	
Ctg. weight:	301 grs. approx.
Case:	Steel, 82 - 10 grs.

Cartridge, Caliber .50, Tracer, M1

Weapon:	Gun, Machine, Caliber .50, Browning, M2 Heavy Barrel (Turret Type); Gun, Machine, Caliber .50, Browning, M2, Heavy Barrel (Flexible); Gun, Machine, Caliber .50, Tank, M85

Ballistic Perf.:

Velocity:	2700 ±40 fps at 78 feet
Pressure:	52,000 psi, max. avg.
Trace:	Bright trace from 250 to 1600 yards

Cartridge:	1785 - 68 grs.
Case:	850 - 50 grs.
Bullet:	676 - 17 grs.
Tracer:	65 grs.
Ignit. Comp.:	10 grs.
Primer, Perc.:	
Prim. Wt.:	18.5 grs. approx.
Propellant:	
Brand:	IMR 5010
Type:	Single Base, Tubular
Weight:	240 grs.
Point Ident.:	Red tip

Cartridge, Caliber .50, Test, High-Pressure, M1

Weapon:	For proof testing all caliber .50 weapons

Ballistic Perf.:

Pressure:	65,000 psi, max. avg.

Cartridge:	2108 - 62 grs.
Bullet:	999 - 11 grs.
Primer, Perc.:	
Prim. Wt.:	18.5 grs. - Styphnate Cloride
Propellant:	WC 860
Type:	Double Base, Spheroidal
Weight:	240 grs.
Ident.:	Stannic stained case

Cartridge, Caliber .50, Incendiary, M1

Weapon:	Gun, Machine, Caliber .50, Browning, M2 Heavy Barrel (Turret Type); Gun, Machine, Caliber .50, Browning, M2, Heavy Barrel (Flexible); Gun, Machine, Caliber .50, Tank, M85

Ballistic Perf.:

Velocity:	2950 ±30 fps at 78 feet
Pressure:	54,000 psi, max. avg.

Cartridge:	1704 grs. approx.
Bullet:	633 - 26 grs.
Incend.:	34 - 2 grs.
Primer, Perc.:	
Prim. Wt.:	18.5 grs.
Propellant:	
Brand:	WC860
Type:	Double Base Spheroidal
Weight:	240 grs.
Point Ident.:	Blue tip

Cartridge, Caliber .50, Blank, M1

Weapon:	Gun, Machine, Caliber .50, Browning, M2, Heavy Barrel (Flexible)
Ballistic Perf.:	None
Cartridge:	891 grs. approx.
Propellant:	
Brand:	WC-150
Weight:	46 grs.
Type:	Double Base, Spheroidal
Wad:	1.5 grs. approx.-Fiberlic No. 2 Kraftboard, or equal (commercial); 256 grs. approx. - Strawboard covered with thin red paper (commercial)
Primer, Perc.:	
Prim. Wt.:	18.5 grs. approx.
Ident.:	No bullet-mouth sealed with vermilion lacquered wad

Cartridge, Caliber .50, Armor Piercing, M2

Weapon:	Gun, Machine, Caliber .50, Browning, M2, Heavy Barrel (Turret Type); Gun, Machine, Caliber .50, Browning, M2, Heavy Barrel (Flexible); Gun, Machine, Caliber .50, Tank, M85

Ballistic Perf.:

Velocity:	2810 ±fps at 78 feet
Pressure:	53,000 psi, max. avg.
Accuracy:	10.0" mean radius max. avg. at 600 yards

Cartridge:	1812 - 73 grs.	
Case:	850 - 80 grs.	
Bullet:	708 - 22 grs.	
Primer Perc.:		
Prim. Wt.:	18.5 grs. approx.	
Propellant:		
Brand:	WC 860	IMR 5010
Type:	Double Base Spheroidal	Single Base Tubular
Weight:	235 grs.	235 grs.
Point Ident.:	Black tip	

Cartridge, Caliber .50, Dummy, M2

Weapon:	All Caliber .50 Weapons - for training personnel and testing weapon mechanism
Cartridge:	1215 - 60 grs. (GMCS Bullet Jacket); 1248 - 60 grs. (GM Bullet Jacket)
Ident.:	Three holes in case, no primer

Cartridge, Caliber .50, Ball, M2

Weapon:	Gun, Machine, Caliber .50, Browning, M2, Heavy Barrel (Turret Type); Gun, Machine, Caliber .50, Browning, M2, Heavy Barrel (Flexible)

Ballistic Perf.:

Velocity:	2810 ±0 fps at 78 feet
Pressure:	55,000 psi, max. avg.
Accuracy:	9" mean radius max. avg. at 600 yards

Cartridge:	1813 - 73 grs.
Case:	850 - 50 grs.
Bullet:	709.5 - 22 grs.
Primer Perc.:	
Prim. Wt.:	18.5 grs.
Propellant:	
Brand:	WC 860
Type:	Double Base, Spheroidal
Weight:	235 grs.
Ident.:	Plain tip

Cartridge, Caliber .50, Armor Piercing Incendiary, M8

Weapon:	Gun, Machine, Caliber .50, Browning, M2 Heavy Barrel (Turret Type); Gun, Machine, Caliber .50, Browning, M2, Heavy Barrel (Flexible); Gun, Machine, Caliber .50, Tank, M85

Ballistic Perf.:

Velocity:	2910 ±30 fps at 78 feet
Pressure:	55,000 psi, max. avg.
Accuracy:	12" mean radius max. avg. at 600 yards
Incen. Fl.:	Incendiary flash must be capable of initiating combustion of flammable liquids
Penetrat.:	Bullet or core must completely perforate armor plate at 100 yards

Cartridge:	1764.5 - 78.5 grs.	
Bullet:	662.5 - 27 grs.	
Primer Perc.:		
Prim. Wt.:	18.5 grs. approx.	
Propellant:		
Brand:	WC 860	IMR 5010
Type:	Double Base Spheroidal	Single Base Tubular
Weight:	233 grs.	233 grs.
Point Ident.:	Aluminum	

Cartridge, Caliber .50, Armor Piercing Incendiary (Same as Cartridge, Caliber .50, Armor-Piercing), M8

Cal .50, M8, Steel Case, Incendiary, M8 except:	
Case:	Steel, 800 - 50 grs.

Cartridge, Caliber .50, Tracer, M10

Weapon:	Gun, Machine, Caliber .50, Browning, M2 Heavy Barrel (Turret Type); Gun, Machine, Caliber .50, Browning, M2, Heavy Barrel (Flexible); Gun, Machine, Caliber .50, Tank, M85

Ballistic Perf.:

Velocity:	2860 ±40 fps at 78 feet
Pressure:	54,000 psi, max. avg.
Trace:	Bright trace from 225 to 1600 yards

Cartridge: 1752 - 68 grs.
Bullet: 643 - 17 grs.
Tracer: 65 grs.
Ignit.: 11 grs.
Primer Perc.:
Prim. Wt: 18.5 grs.
Propellant
Brand: IMR 5010
Type: Single Base, Tubular
Weight: 240 grs.
Point Ident.: Orange tip

Cartridge, Caliber .50, Tracer, M17

Weapon: Gun, Machine, Caliber .50, Browning, M2 Heavy Barrel (Turret Type); Gun, Machine, Caliber .50, Browning, M2, Heavy Barrel (Flexible); Gun, Machine, Caliber .50, Tank, M85

Ballistic Perf.:
Velocity: 2860 ±40 fps at 78 feet
Pressure: 54,000 psi, max. avg.
Trace: Bright trace from 100 to 1600 yards
Cartridge: 1737 - 68 grs.
Bullet: 643 - 17 grs.
Ignit.: 11 grs.
Tracer: 40 grs.
Primer Perc.:
Prim. Wt: 18.5 grs.
Propellant
Brand: IMR 5010
Type: Single Base, Tubular
Weight: 225 grs.
Point Ident.: Brown tip

Cartridge, Caliber .50, Armor-Piercing, M2/M85 Incendiary, Tracer, M20

Weapon: Gun, Machine, Caliber .50, Browning, M2 Heavy Barrel (Turret Type); Gun, Machine, Caliber .50, Browning, M2, Heavy Barrel (Flexible); Gun, Machine, Caliber .50, Tank, M85

Ballistic Perf.:
Pressure: 55,000 psi
Incend. Fl.: Incendiary flash must be capable of initiating combustion of flammable liquids
Penetra.: Bullet or core must completely penetrate 7/8" armor plate at 100 yards
Trace: Must exhibit visible trace from 100 to 1600 yards
Cartridge: 1718 - 76.5 grs.
Bullet: 619 - 25 grs.
Primer Perc.:
Prim. Wt: 18.5 grs.
Propellant
Brand: IMR 5010
Type: Single Base, Tubular
Weight: 230 grs.
Point Ident.: Red tip, aluminum

Cartridge, Caliber .50, Armor Piercing Incendiary, (Same as Cartridge, Caliber .50, Armor-Piercing), M20

Tracer Cal .50, M20, Steel Case, Incindiary, Tracer, M20 except:
Case: Steel, 800 - 50 grs.

Cartridge, Caliber.50, Tracer, Headlight, M21

Weapon: Gun, Machine, Caliber .50, Browning, M2 Heavy Barrel (Turret Type); Gun, Machine, Caliber .50, Browning, M2, Heavy Barrel (Flexible); Gun, Machine, Caliber .50, Tank, M85

Ballistic Perf.:
Velocity: 2840 ±40 fps at 78 feet
Pressure: 55,000 psi, max. avg.
Trace: Bright trace from 200 to 500 yards
Cartridge: 1808 - 68 grs. (with gilding metal jacket bullet) 1775 - 68 grs. (with gilding metal clad steel jacket bullet)
Case: 850-50grs.
Bullet: 699 - 17 grs. (with gilding metal jacket); 666 - 17 grs. (with gilding metal clad steel jacket)
Primer Perc.:
Prim. Wt: 18.5 grs. approx.
Propellant:
Brand: IMR 5010

Type: Single Base, Tubular
Weight: 240 grs.
Point Ident.: Red tip

Cartridge, Caliber .50, Incendiary, M23

Weapon: Gun, Machine, Caliber .50, Browning, M2 Heavy Barrel (Turret Type); Gun, Machine, Caliber .50, Browning, M2, Heavy Barrel (Flexible); Gun, Machine, Caliber .50, Tank, M85

Ballistic Perf.:
Velocity: 3400 ±30 fps at 78 feet
Pressure: 58,000 psi, max. avg.
Incend. Fl.: Incendiary flash must be capable of initiating combustion of flammable liquids
Cartridge: 1581 grs. approx.
Case: 850 - 50 grs.
Bullet: 512 - 24 grs.
Incen.: 90 grs. Max.
Primer Perc.:
Prim. Wt: 18.5 grs. approx.
Propellant
Brand: IMR 4831
Type: Single Base, Tubular
Weight: 237 grs. approx.
Point Ident.: Medium blue tip, slight blue annulus

Cartridge, Caliber .50, Ball, M33

Weapon: Gun, Machine, Caliber .50, Browning, M2 Heavy Barrel (Turret Type); Gun, Machine, Caliber .50, Browning, M2, Heavy Barrel (Flexible); Gun, Machine, Caliber .50, Tank, M85

Ballistic Perf.:
Velocity: 2910 ±30 fps at 78 feet
Pressure: 55,000 psi, max. avg.
Cartridge: 1762.5 - 76.5 grs.
Case: 850 – 50 grs.
Bullet: 661.5 - 25 grs.
Primer Perc.:
Prim. Wt: 18.5 grs.
Propellant

Brand:	WC860	IMR5010
Type:	Double Base Spheroidal	Single Base Tubular
Weight:	235 grs.	235 grs.
Ident.:	Plain tip	

Cartridge, Caliber .50, Spotter-Tracer, M48

Weapon: Rifle, Spotting, Caliber .50, M8C
Ballistic Perf.:
Velocity: 1850 ±20 fps at 78 feet
Accuracy: 10" mean radius at 600 yards
Trace: Bright trace from 100 to 1500 yards
Pressure: 35,000 psi max. avg.
Spotting: Must flash and produce smoke upon impact
Cartridge: 1651 grs.
Bullet: 827 - 18 grs.
Primer M26:
Primer Perc.:
Prim. Wt: 18.5 grs. approx.
Propellant:
Brand: IMR 4831
Type: Single Base, Tubular
Weight: 120 grs.
Point Ident.: Yellow tip, red annulus

Cartridge, Caliber .50, Spotter-Tracer, M48A1

Weapon: Rifle, Spotting, Caliber .50, M8C
Ballistic Perf.:
Velocity: 1745 ±20 fps at 78 feet
Trace: Bright trace from 100 to 1500 yards
Pressure: 38,000 psi max. avg.
Impact: Must flash and produce smoke upon impact against steel plate at 175 yards
Cartridge: 1744 - 71 grs. (with GMCS flash tube or steel flash tube), 1714 - 71 grs. (with Al - alloy flash tube)
Case: 740 - 50 grs.
Bullet: 827 - 18 grs.
Primer Perc.:
Primer Wt.: 18.5 grs. approx.
Propellant

Type: Single Base, Tubular
Weight: 110 grs.
Point Ident.: Yellow tip, red annulus

Cartridge, Caliber .50, Spotter-Tracer, M48A2

Weapon: Rifle, Spotting, Caliber .50, M8C
Ballistic Perf.:
Velocity: 1745 ±20 fps at 78 feet
Pressure: 38,000 psi max. avg.
Cartridge: 1744 - 71 grs. (with GMCS flash tube or steel flash tube); 1714 - 71 grs. (with Al - alloy flash tube)
Case: 740 - 50 grs.
Bullet: 828 - 18 grs.
Primer Perc.:
Prim. Wt: 18.5 grs. approx.
Propellant: 110 grs. approx.
Type: Single Base, Tubular
Point Ident.: Yellow tip, red annulus

Dummy Cartridge, Caliber .50, Inert Loaded, XM176

Weapon: All caliber .50 weapons
Ballistic Perf.: None
Cartridge: 1752 - 82 grs.
Bullet: 661.5 - 27 grs.
Primer: No primer
Inert Prop.: Sodium Carbonate - Monohydrate, 5 grs.
Ident.: Cartridge coated with black chemical finish

Cartridge, Caliber .50, Target Practice, T249E2

Weapon: Rifle, Spotting, Caliber .50, M8C
Ballistic Perf.:
Velocity: 1745 ±20 fps at 78 feet
Pressure: 38,000 max. avg.
Accuracy: 5" mean radius at 600 yards
Cartridge: 1738 - 61 grs. (with GMCS or steel flash tube); 1708 - 61 grs. (with Alalloy Flash Tube)
Bullet: 817 4 grs.
Primer Perc.:
Prim. Wt: 18.5 grs. approx.
Propellant:
Brand: IMR 7383
Type: Single Base, Tubular
Weight: 110 grs. approx.
Point Ident.: Green tip

Cartridge, Caliber .50, Armor Piercing Incendiary, T49

Weapon: Gun, Machine, Caliber .50, Browning, M2 Heavy Barrel (Turret Type); Gun, Machine, Caliber .50, Browning, M2, Heavy Barrel (Flexible); Gun, Machine, Caliber .50, Tank, M85

Ballistic Perf.:
Velocity: 3400 ±30 fps at 78 feet
Pressure: 58,000 psi, max. avg.
Accuracy: 10" mean radius at 600 yards
Cartridge: 1597 grs. approx.
Bullet: 501 grs.
Primer Perc.:
Prim. Wt.: 18.5 grs.
Propellant
Brand: WC 860
Weight: 252 grs.
Type: Double Base, Spheroidal
Point Ident.: Blue tip, silver annulus

Cartridge, Caliber .50, Test, High Pressure, T251

Weapon: Rifle, Spotting, Caliber .50, M8C
Ballistic Perf.:
Pressure 55,000 psi, max. avg.
Cartridge: 1902 - 50 grs.
Case: 740 - 50 grs.
Bullet: 999-11 grs.
Primer Perc.:
Primer Wt.: 18.5 grs. approx.
Propellant
Brand: IMR 4831
Type: Single Base Tubular
Weight: 142 grs.
Ident.: Stannic Stained Case

Dummy Cartridge, Caliber 20mm, M51A1B1

Weapon:	Guns, Automatic, 20mm, M39, M61, XM168 and GAU-4 (XM130)
Requirements:	Projectile extraction: The cartridge assembly shall withstand a 3900 pound tension force without separation of the projectile from the cartridge case
Cartridge:	3850 grains, min.
Bullet:	Steel, 1520 30 grains
Ident.:	Cartridge chromate finish, marking opaque, color black

Cartridge, Caliber 20mm, Armor Piercing Incendiary Tracer, M52E1 (USAF)

Weapon:	Gun, Automatic, 20mm, M39, M61 and GAU-4 (XM130)
Ballistic Perf.:	(Single shot - test barrel)
Velocity:	3380 ±50 fps at 78 feet
Pressure:	Not to exceed 60,500 psi
Accuracy:	15-in. mean radius - 600 yards
Cartridge:	3900 grains approx.
Case:	M103, Brass
Prim. Elec.	22 grs.
Propellant:	WC 870, weight to meet ballistic requirements
Projectile:	1530 grains approx. Rotating
Blank:	133 grains approx. Gilding Metal
Ident.:	Projectile black and red - marking opaque; color orange

Cartridge, Caliber 20mm, Armor Piercing Incendiary, M53 (USAF)

Weapon:	Guns, Automatic, 20mm, M39, M61 and GAU-4 (XM 130)
Ballistic Perf.:	Single shot - test barrel
Velocity:	3380 ±250 fps at 78 feet
Pressure:	Not to exceed 60,500 psi
Accuracy:	15-in. mean radius max. avg. at 600 yards
Cartridge:	3980 grains approx.
Case:	2150 grs.
Prim. Elec.:	22 grs.
Propellant:	WC 870, weight to meet ballistic requirements
Projectile:	1540 35 grs. Rotating
Blank:	133 grains approx., Gilding Metal
Nose:	100 grains approx., Aluminum Alloy
Ident.:	Projectile black and band, red marking, opaque color red

Cartridge, Caliber 20mm, Test, High Pressure, M54A1 (USAF)

Weapon:	For use in Proofing Guns, Automatic, 20mm, M39, M61, XM168 and GAU-4 (XM130)
Ballistic Perf.:	
Pressure:	Shall equal or exceed 62,500 psi and shall not exceed 72,500 psi
Cartridge:	4392 grains approx.
Case:	M103, Brass, 2150 grs.
Prim. Elec.:	22 grs.
Propellant:	WC 870 or IMR 7013. Weight to meet ballistic requirements
Projectile:	1965 10 grains
Ident.:	Projectile, Purple marking, black opaque

Cartridge, Caliber 20mm, Target Practice, M55A2 (USAF)

Weapon:	Guns, Automatic, 20mm, M39, M61, and XM168 and GAU-4 (XM130)
Ballistic Perf.:	(Single shot-test barrel)
Velocity:	3380 ±50 fps at 78 feet
Pressure:	Not to exceed 60,500 psi
Accuracy:	15-in. mean radius, max. avg. at 600 yards
Cartridge:	3935 grains approx.
Case:	2150 grs.
Prim. Elec.:	22 grs.
Propellant:	WC 870, weight to meet ballistic requirements
Projectile:	1521 30 grs.
Ident.:	Projectile blue, opaque black marking

Cartridge, Caliber 20mm, High Explosive Incendiary, M6A3 (USAF)

Weapon:	Guns, Automatic, 20mm, M39, M61, and GAU-4 (XM130)
Ballistic Perf.:	(Single shot - test barrel)
Velocity:	3380 ±250 fps at 78 feet
Pressure:	Not to exceed 60,500 psi
Accuracy:	15-in. mean radius at 600 yards
Function:	The projectile shall function with high order detonation upon impact.
Cartridge:	2965 grs. approx.
Case:	Brass, 2150 grs.
Prim. Elec.:	22 grs.
Propellant:	WC 870, weight to meet ballistic requirements
Projectile:	1565 grains approx.
Charged Proj.:	1230 grs.approx.
Charge:	165 grs. min.
Rotating Blank:	133 grs. approx. (Gilding Metal)
Ident.:	Projectile yellow, black opaque marking

Cartridge, Caliber 20mm, High Explosive Incendiary, M97A2 (USAF)

Weapon:	Guns, Automatic, 20mm, M24 and M24A1
Ballistic Perf.:	(Single shot - test barrel)
Velocity:	2680 ±50 fps at 78 feet
Pressure:	Shall not exceed 51,000 psi
Accuracy:	15-in. mean radius at 600 yards
Function:	Projectile shall detonate high order on impact with the target plate.
Cartridge:	4000 grs. approx.
Case:	Brass, 1520 grs.
Prim. Elec.:	22 grs.
Propellant:	IMR 7013, WC 875; Weight to meet ballistic requirements
Projectile:	HEI-2000 40 grs.
Fuze:	Point Detonating
Ident.:	Projectile yellow, marking black opaque

Cartridge, Caliber 20mm, Target Practice, M99A1 (USAF)

Weapon:	Guns, Automatic, 20mm, M24 and M24A1
Ballistic Perf.:	(Single shot - test barrel)
Velocity:	2680 ±50 fps at 78 feet
Pressure:	Shall not exceed 51,000 psi
Accuracy:	15-in. mean radius at 600 yards
Cartridge:	4000 grs. approx.
Case:	Brass, 1520 grs.
Prim. Elec.:	22 grs.
Projectile:	2000 35 grs.
Ident.:	Projectile blue, marking black opaque

Cartridge, Caliber 20mm, Target Practice, M204

Weapon:	Gun, Automatic, 20mm, M3
Ballistic Perf.:	(Single shot - test barrel)
Velocity:	2680 ±50 fps at 78 feet
Pressure:	Shall not exceed 51,000 psi
Accuracy:	15-in. mean radius at 600 yards
Cartridge:	4000 grs. approx.
Case:	Brass, 1520 grs.
Prim. Perc.:	26 grs.
Propellant:	4814, IMR 7013 or WC 875 - Weight to meet ballistic requirements
Projectile:	TP, M99A1 - 2000 - 35 grs.
Ident.:	Projectile blue, marking black opaque

Cartridge, Caliber 20mm, Target Practice - Tracer, M206

Weapon:	Gun, 20mm, Automatic Gas Operated, Manual or Electric Fired, M139
Ballistic Perf.:	
Velocity:	3460 ±50 fps at muzzle
Pressure:	49,500 psi max. avg.
Cartridge:	317 Grams approx.
Case:	134 5.8 Grams, Steel
Primed:	145 Grams
Primer Perc.:	10 Grams
Propellant:	50 Grams, approx.
Projectile:	120 2 Grams
Ident.:	Projectile blue, red T's, black letters

Cartridge, Caliber 20mm, Target Practice - Tracer, M206E1

Weapon:	Gun, 20mm, Automatic Gas Operated, Manual or Electric Fired, M139
Ballistic Perf.:	
Velocity:	3460 ±50 fps
Pressure:	49,500 psi max. avg.
Cartridge:	
Primer Perc.:	29 grs.
Ident.:	Projectile blue, red T's, black letters

Cartridge, Caliber 20mm, High Explosive Incendiary M210

Weapon:	Gun, Automatic, 20mm, M3
Ballistic Perf.:	
Velocity:	2680 ±50 fps at 78 ft.
Pressure:	Shall not exceed 51,000 psi
Cartridge:	4000 grains approx.
Case:	Brass - 1520 grs.
Primer Perc.:	26 grs.
Propellant:	IMR 7013, 4815 or WC 875; Weight to meet ballistic requirements
Projectile:	2000 40 grains

Cartridge, Caliber 20mm, Armor Piercing Incendiary - Tracer, M601

Weapon:	Gun, 20mm, Automatic, Gas operated, Manual or Electric Fired, M139
Ballistic Perf.:	
Velocity:	3610 ±50 fps
Pressure:	49,500 psi max. avg.
Cartridge:	310 grains
Case:	134 5.8 Grams, Steel
Primed:	145 Grams
Primer Perc.	10 Grams
Propellant:	53 Grams, approx.
Projectile:	111 2 Grams
Ident.:	Projectile black, orange T's, red tip and white letters

Cartridge, Caliber 20mm, Armor Piercing Incendiary - Tracer, M601E1

Weapon:	Gun, 20mm, Automatic, Gas operated, Manual or Electric Fired, M139
Ballistic Perf.:	
Velocity:	3610 ±50 fps
Pressure:	49,500 psi max. avg.
Cartridge:	
Primer Perc.:	29 grs.
Propellant:	To meet ballistic requirements
Projectile:	112.5 Grams
Ident.:	Projectile black, orange T's, red tip and white letters

Cartridge, Caliber 20mm, Test, High Pressure, MK101 Mod 0 (USN)

Weapon:	Gun, 20mm, chambered to fire MK100 series 20mm ammunition
Ballistic Perf.:	
Pressure:	Not to exceed 72,500 psi
Cartridge:	4285 50 grs.
Case:	1880 grs. (Steel)
Prim. Elec.:	22 grs.
Propellant:	Tubular or ball, nitrocellulose, weight to meet ballistic requirements
Projectile:	1700 grs., inert
Ident.:	Green or blue projectile with brown nose and ¼" black letters reading "High Pressure Test Round"

Cartridge, Caliber 20mm, Test, Low Pressure, MK102 Mod 0 (USN)

Weapon:	Gun, 20mm, chambered to fire MK100 series ammunition
Ballistic Perf.:	
Pressure:	
Cartridge:	4285 50 grs.
Case:	1880 grs. (Steel)
Prim. Elec.:	22 grs.
Propellant:	Tubular or ball, nitrocellulose, weight

	to meet ballistic requirements
Projectile:	1700 grs., inert
Ident.:	Blue or green projectile with brown nose and ¼" black letters reading "Low Pressure Test Round"

Dummy Cartridge, Caliber 20mm, MK103 Mod 0 (USN)

Inert round. Has empty primer pocket and holes in case; or when made up from rejected service case, has primer pocket plugged with brass or empty primer cup staked with three equally spaced crimps. Case may be empty or loaded with inert material. Projectile is usually brass or bronze plated.

Cartridge, Caliber 20mm, Target Practice, MK105 Mod 0 (USN)

Weapon:	Guns, Automatic, 20mm, MK11 and MK12
Ballistic Perf.:	(Single shot - test barrel)
Velocity:	3350 fps at muzzle
Pressure:	60,000 psi
Accuracy:	15-in. mean radius at 600 yards
Cartridge:	4285 50 grs.
Case:	1880 grs. (Steel) 20mm, MK5 Mod 0
Prim. Elec.:	22 grs., MK47 Mod 0
Propellant:	Tubular or ball, nitrocellulose, 650 grs. approx.
Projectile:	1700 grs., inert
Ident.:	Green or blue projectile with black lettering or blue projectile with brown nose and black lettering

Cartridge, Caliber 20mm,High Explosive Incendiary MK106 Mod 0 and 1 (USN)

Weapon:	Guns, Automatic, 20mm, MK11 and MK12
Ballistic Perf.:	(Single shot - test barrel)
Velocity:	3350 fps at muzzle
Pressure:	60,000 psi
Accuracy:	15-in. mean radius at 600 yards
Cartridge:	4285 50 grs.
Case:	1880 grs. (Steel) 20mm, MK5 Mod 0
Prim. Elec.:	22 grs., MK47 Mod 0
Propellant:	Tubular or ball, nitrocellulose, 650 grs. approx.
Projectile:	1700 50 grs., Impact detonating
Ident.:	Unpainted fuze, red and yellow projectile

Cartridge, Caliber 20mm, Armor Piercing-Incendiary, MK107 Mod 0 (USN)

Weapon:	Guns, Automatic, 20mm, MK11 and MK12
Ballistic Perf.:	(Single shot - test barrel)
Velocity:	3350 fps at muzzle
Pressure:	60,000 psi
Accuracy:	15-in. mean radius at 600 yards
Cartridge:	4285 50 grs.
Case:	1880 grs. (Steel) 20mm, MK5 Mod 0
Prim. Elec.:	22 grs., MK47 Mod 0
Projectile:	1700 50 grs.
Ident.:	No fuze. Nose of projectile blue or brown with red band. Body of projectile black with white lettering

Cartridge, Caliber 20mm, Armor Piercing -Tracer, MK108 Mod 0 (USN)

Weapon:	Guns, Automatic, 20mm, MK11 and MK12
Ballistic Perf.:	(Single shot - test barrel)
Velocity:	3350 fps at muzzle
Pressure:	60,000 psi
Accuracy:	15 inch mean radius at 600 yards
Cartridge:	4285 50 grs.
Case:	1880 grs. (Steel) 20mm, MK5 Mod 0
Projectile:	1700 50 grs.
Ident.:	No fuze. Hollow windshield. Brown or yellow nose, black projectile body with white lettering

Designation	Description
M1	Cartridge, Ball, Carbine, Caliber .30
M1	Cartridge, Blank, Caliber .50 (T40)
M1	Cartridge, Incendiary, Caliber .50
M1	Cartridge, Test, High Pressure, Caliber .50
M1	Cartridge, Test, High Pressure, Caliber .45
M1	Cartridge, Test, High Pressure, Caliber .30
M1	Cartridge, Tracer, Caliber .30
M1	Cartridge, Tracer, Caliber .50 (AN-MI)
M1E1	Cartridge, Incendiary, Caliber .50 (M1 loaded to 3100 f/s)
M1911	Cartridge, Ball, Caliber .45
M1911	Cartridge, Ball, Match Grade, Caliber .45
M1909	Cartridge, Blank, Caliber .30
M1921	Cartridge, Dummy, Caliber .45
M2	Cartridge, AP, Caliber .50
M2	Cartridge, AP, Caliber .30
M2	Cartridge, Ball, Caliber .50 (AN-M2)
M2	Cartridge, Ball, Caliber .30
M2	Cartridge Dummy, Caliber .50
M2	Cartridge, 12 Gage
M3	Cartridge, Grenade, Rifle, Caliber .30
M3	Cartridge, Igniter, Caliber .38 (for Igniter, Grenade, Frangible M3
M6	Cartridge, Grenade Carbine, Caliber .30 (T6)
M7	Cartridge, Grenade, Auxiliary (T18)
M8	Cartridge, Armor-Piercing-Incendiary, Caliber .50 (T16)
M8E1	Cartridge, Armor-Piercing Incendiary, Caliber .50, Loaded with Double Base Powder to a Higher Velocity
M9	Cartridge, Blank, Caliber .45 (T31)
M10	Cartridge, Tracer, Caliber .50 (T12)
M10E1	Cartridge, Tracer, Caliber .50, Loaded to an Increased Velocity with Double Base Powder
M12	Cartridge, Shot, Caliber .45 (T23)
M13	Cartridge, Dummy, Carbine, Caliber .30
M14	Cartridge, Armor-Piercing-Incendiary, Caliber .30 (T15)
M14A1	Cartridge, Armor-Piercing-Incendiary, Caliber .30 (T15 with T1E48 Bullet)
M15	Cartridge, Shot, Caliber .45 (T29)
M16	Cartridge, Tracer, Carbine, Caliber .30 (T24)
M17	Cartridge, Tracer, Caliber .50 (T9)
M18	Cartridge, High Pressure Test, Carbine, Caliber .30 (T27)
M19	Shell, Shot Gun (All Brass), 12 Gage - 00 Buck
M20	Cartridge, Armor-Piercing-Incendiary-Tracer, Caliber .50 (T28)
M21	Cartridge, Tracer, Headlight, Caliber .50 (T1E1)
M22	Cartridge, Ball, Frangible, Caliber .30 (T44)
M23	Cartridge, Incendiary, Caliber .50 (T48)
M24	Cartridge, Ball, Caliber .22, Long Rifle (T42)
M25	Cartridge, Tracer, Caliber .30 (T10)
M26	Cartridge, Tracer, Caliber .45 (T30)
M27	Cartridge, Tracer, Carbine, Caliber .30 (T43)
M32	Cartridge, Blank, Line Throwing, Caliber .45 (T124)
M33	Cartridge, Ball, Caliber .50 (T122)
M33E1	Cartridge, Ball, Caliber .50
M33E2	Cartridge, Ball, Caliber .50
M35	Shell, Shot Gun .410 (T135)

Designation	Description
M39	Cartridge, Ball, Caliber .22 (Hornet) (T200)
M40	Cartridge, Dummy, Caliber .30
M41	Cartridge, Ball, Caliber .38, Special
M48	Cartridge, Spotter-Tracer, Caliber .50 (T189E1)
M48A1	Cartridge, Spotter-Tracer, Caliber .50 (T189E3)
M48A1E1	Cartridge, Spotter-Tracer
M51	Cartridge, Dummy, 20mm
M51E3	Cartridge, Dummy, 20mm
M51E5	Cartridge, Dummy, 20mm (T272E4)
M51E6	Cartridge, Dummy, 20mm
M52	Cartridge, Armor-Piercing, Incendiary Tracer, 20mm (T230)
M53	Cartridge, Armor-Piercing Incendiary, 20mm (T221E3)
M54	Cartridge, High Pressure Test, 20mm
M55	Cartridge, Ball, 20mm (T199E1)
M56	Cartridge, High Explosive Incendiary, 20mm (T198E1)
M58	Cartridge, High Explosive Incendiary, 20mm (T241)
M59	Cartridge, 7.62mm, NATO, Ball (T104E2)
M60	Cartridge, 7.62mm, NATO, High Pressure Test(T17E1)
M61	Cartridge, 7.62mm, NATO, Armor-Piercing (T93E2)
M62	Cartridge, 7.62mm, NATO, Tracer (T102E2)
M62	Cartridge, 7.62mm, NATO, Tracer (Overhead Fire Application)
M63	Cartridge, 7.62mm, NATO, Dummy (T70E5)
M64	Cartridge, 7.62mm, NATO, Grenade, Rifle (T116E1)
M65	Cartridge, Ball, Caliber .22 Hornet (T200E1)
M72	Cartridge, Match, Caliber .30 (T291)
M80	Cartridge, 7.62mm, NATO, Ball, (T233)
M80	Cartridge, 7.62mm, NATO, Ball, Overhead Fire Application)
M80E1	Cartridge, 7.62mm, NATO, Ball (Canadian C1)
M82	Cartridge, 7.62mm, NATO, Blank
M95	Cartridge, Armor-Piercing Tracer, 20mm
M96	Cartridge, Incendiary, 20mm
M97E2	Cartridge, High Explosive Incendiary, 20mm
M97A1	Cartridge, High Explosive Incendiary, 20mm
M99A1	Cartridge, Target Practice, 20mm
M118	Cartridge, 7.62 Match
M160	Cartridge, 7.62mm, Ball, Frangible
M172	Cartridge, Dummy, 7.62mm (Inert Loaded)
M181	Cartridge, 14.5mm (with fuze sec) Tracer Low Charge
M182	Cartridge, 14.5mm (with fuze 6 sec) Used with M3l Field
M183	Cartridge, 14.5mm (with fuze PD) Used with M31 Field
M193	Cartridge, 5.56mm Ball
M196	Cartridge, 5.56mm Tracer
M197	Cartridge, 5.56mm High Pressure Test
M198	Cartridge, 7.62mm Ball Duplex
M199	Cartridge, Dummy 5.56mm
M200	Cartridge, 5.56mm Blank
M204	Cartridge, 20mm Target Practice
M206E1	Cartridge, 20mm Target Practice Tracer
M210	Cartridge, 20mm High Explosive Incendiary
M274	Cartridge, 12 Gage Shotgun, No. 4, Hard Chilled Shot
M601EI	Cartridge, 20mm Armor Piercing Incendiary Tracer

Designation	Description
M855A1	Cartridge, 5.56mm, Ball
M856A1	Cartridge, 5.56mm, Tracer
M857	Cartridge, 5.56mm, Dummy
M882	Cartridge, 9mm, Ball
M905	Cartridge, 9mm, High Pressure Test
M917	Cartridge, 9mm, Dummy
M939	Cartridge, 9mm, Practice Tracer
M852	Cartridge, 7.62mm, Match

EXPERIMENTAL (XM) SERIES
U.S. MILITARY CARTRIDGES

Designation	Description
XM75	Cartridge, Spotter, 10mm
XM101	Cartridge, Spotting, 20mm
XM106	Cartridge, Practice, 20mm
XM107	Cartridge, High Pressure, 20mm
XM108	Cartridge, Spotter, 15mm
XM108E1	Cartridge, Spotter, 15mm
XM115	Cartridge, 7.62mm, Ball
XM142	Cartridge, Caliber .38 Special, Ball
XM147	Dummy Cartridge, 20mm
XM156	Cartridge, Caliber .50 Spotter-Tracer
XM157	Cartridge, Spotter-Tracer, 15mm
XM162	Cartridge, 12 Gage Shotgun; Plastic #00 Buckshot
XM170	Cartridge, Ball, 15mm
XM171	Cartridge, High Presure Test, 15mm
XM176	Dummy Cartridge, Cal. .50, Inert Loaded
XM177	Dummy Cartridge, 15mm
XM178	Cartridge, 7.62mm, Ball, Overhead Fire
XM179	Cartridge, 7.62mm, Tracer, Overhead Fire
XM180	Cartridge, 7.62mm, Tracer, Overhead Fire
XM192	Cartridge, 7.62mm Blank (Short Case)
XM195	Cartridge, 5.56mm, Grenade
XM202	Cartridge, 8.94mm Select
XM205	Cartridge, 20mm High Explosive Incendiary
XM207	Cartridge, 20mm Armor Piercing
XM220	Cartridge, 20mm Target Practice Tracer
XM232	Dummy Cartridge, 5.56mm Inert Loaded
XM239	Cartridge, 20mm High Pressure Test
XM240	Dummy Cartridge, 20mm
XM242	Cartridge, 20mm High Explosive Incendiary Tracer
XM243	Cartridge, 20mm High Explosive Incendiary Tracer
XM244	Cartridge, 20mm High Explosive Incendiary Tracer
XM246E3	Cartridge, 20mm High Explosive Incendiary Tracer
XM254	Dummy Cartridge, 20mm, Plastic
XM257	Cartridge, Shotshell, 12 Gage No. 4B Special
XM552	Cartridge, 20mm Heat Dual Purpose
XM554	Cartridge, 30mm Practice
XM599	Cartridge, 20mm High Explosive Incendiary Tracer

EXPERIMENTAL (T) SERIES
U.S. MILITARY CARTRIDGES

Designation	Description
T1	Cartridge, Explosive, Caliber .50
T1	Cartridge, Armor-Piercing, Caliber .276
T1	Cartridge, Tracer, Caliber .30
T1E1	Cartridge, Tracer, Headlight, Caliber .50 (M21)
T1E2	Cartridge, Tracer, Headlight, Caliber .50

Designation	Description
T5	Cartridge, Armor-Piercing, Anti-Tank, Caliber .30
T6	Cartridge, Grenade, Carbine, Caliber .30 (M6)
T7	Cartridge, Grenade, Carbine, Caliber .30 (Long Case)
T8	Cartridge, Tracer, Caliber .50 - 1000 yds.
T9	Cartridge, Tracer, Caliber .50 - 2500 yds. (M17)
T10	Cartridge, Tracer, Night, Caliber .30 (Dim Igniter) (M25)
T12	Cartridge, Tracer, Caliber .50 (M10)
T13	Cartridge, Tracer, Caliber .30 Delay
T14	Cartridge, Tracer, Caliber .50
T15	Cartridge, Armor-Piercing-Incendiary, Caliber .30 (M14)
T15E1	Cartridge, Armor-Piercing-Incendiary Caliber .30
T16	Cartridge, Armor-Piercing-Incendiary, Caliber .50 (M8)
TI7	Cartridge, Tracer, Caliber .30 (Clad Steel Jacketed for Improved Accuracy)
T18	Cartridge, Auxiliary, Grenade (M7)
T19	Cartridge, Explosive, Caliber .60
T19E1	Cartridge, Explosive, Caliber .60
T19E2	Cartridge, Explosive, Caliber .60
T19E3	Cartridge, Explosive, Caliber. 60
T19E4	Cartridge, Explosive, Caliber .60
T20	Cartridge, Tracer, Caliber .50 (Spot) 500 yds.
T21	Cartridge, Tracer, Caliber .50 (Spot) 1000 yds.
T22	Cartridge, Ball, Caliber .30 with Steel Case (M2 Alternate)
T23	Cartridge, Shot, Caliber .45 (M12)
T24	Cartridge, Tracer, Carbine, Caliber .30 (M16)
T25	Cartridge, Ball, Caliber .50 with Steel Case (M2 Alternate)
T26	Cartridge, Igniter, Caliber .38 (Component for Igniter, Grenade, Frangible, M3)
T27	Cartridge, Carbine, High Pressure Test, Caliber .30 (M18)
T28	Cartridge, Armor-Piercing-Incendiary-Tracer, Caliber .50 (M20)
T28E1	Cartridge, Armor-Piercing-Incendiary-Tracer, Caliber .50 (Dim Igniter)
T29	Cartridge, Shot, Caliber .45 (M15)
T30	Cartridge, Tracer, Caliber .45 (M26)
T31	Cartridge, Blank, Caliber .45 (M9)
T32	Cartridge, Ball, Caliber .60-1196 grain bullet
T32E1	Cartridge, Ball, Caliber .60-1137 grain bullet
T32E2	Cartridge, Ball, Caliber .60
T33	Cartridge, High Pressure Test, Caliber .60
T33E1	Cartridge, High Pressure Test, Caliber .60 (T33 with M36A1 Primer)
T34	Cartridge, High Explosive Incendiary, Caliber .50
T35	Cartridge, Dummy, Caliber .60
T35E1	Cartridge, Dummy, Caliber .60
T36	Cartridge, Incendiary, Caliber .60
T36E1	Cartridge, Incendiary, Caliber .60
T36E2	Cartridge, Incendiary, Caliber .60 (With #28 Primer)
T36E3	Cartridge, Incendiary, Caliber .60 (T36E2 with M36A1 Percussion Primer)
T37	Cartridge, Tracer, Caliber .50 with trajectory to match 3.5-inch Forward Firing Rocket
T38	Cartridge, Armor-Piercing-Tracer, Caliber .50
T38E1	Cartridge, Armor-Piercing-Incendiary, Caliber .50
T39	Cartridge, Armor-Piercing-Incendiary, Caliber .60

Designation	Description
T39E1	Cartridge, Armor-Piercing-Incendiary, Caliber .60 (T39 with M36A1 Percussion Primer)
T39E2	Cartridge, Armor-Piercing-Incendiary, Caliber .60
T39E3	Cartridge, Armor-Piercing-Incendiary, Caliber .60
T39E4	Cartridge, Armor-Piercing-Incendiary, Caliber .60
T39E5	Cartridge, Armor-Piercing-Incendiary, Caliber .60
T39E6	Cartridge, Armor-Piercing-Incendiary, Caliber .60
T40	Cartridge, Blank, Caliber .50 (M1)
T41	Cartridge, Incendiary, High Velocity, Caliber .60
T41E1	Cartridge, Incendiary, High Velocity, Caliber .60
T42	Cartridge, Ball, Caliber .22, Long Rifle Jacketed Bullet (M24)
T43	Cartridge, Tracer, Carbine, Caliber .30 (M27)
T44	Cartridge, Ball, Frangible, Caliber .30 (M22)
T44E1	Cartridge, Ball, Frangible, Caliber .30
T45	Cartridge, Armor-Piercing, Caliber .60
T45E1	Cartridge, Armor-Piercing, Caliber .60
T46	Cartridge, Armor-Piercing-Tracer, Caliber .60
T46E1	Cartridge, Armor-Piercing-Tracer, Caliber .60
T47	Cartridge, High Explosive, Incendiary, Caliber .60
T48	Cartridge, Incendiary, Caliber .50 (500 grain bullet) M23
T48E1	Cartridge, Incendiary, Caliber .50 (500 grain bullet)
T48E2	Cartridge, Incendiary, Caliber .50 (500 grain bullet)
T49	Cartridge, Armor-Piercing-Incendiary, Caliber .50 (500 grain bullet)
T50	Cartridge, Incendiary, Caliber .60 - .50
T51	Cartridge, Armor-Piercing-Incendiary, Caliber .60-.50
T52	Cartridge, Tracer, Caliber .60 - .50
T53	Cartridge, Tracer, Caliber .30
T54	Cartridge, Tracer, Caliber .50
T55	Cartridge, Tracer, Caliber .60
T56	Cartridge, Blank, Caliber .50 with Electric Primer
T57	Cartridge, Grenade, Auxiliary, High Pressure Test
T58	Cartridge, Incendiary, Caliber .50 (White Phosphorus Loading)
T59	Cartridge, Carbine, Spotting, Caliber .30
T60	Cartridge, Armor-Piercing-Incendiary-Tracer, Caliber .60
T60E1	Cartridge, Armor-Piercing-Incendiary-Tracer, Caliber .60 (T60 with M36A1 Percussion Primer)
T61	Cartridge, Antenna Erecting
T62	Cartridge, Armor-Piercing, Carbine, Caliber .30
T63	Cartridge, Armor-Piercing-Incendiary-Tracer, Caliber .50 (500 grain) R. V.
T64	Cartridge, Tracer, Caliber .50 (Rocket Fire Control, 2000 100 yds; Dim 500 yds bright)
T65	Cartridge, Ball, Caliber .30, Short Case (7.62mm NATO)
T65E1	Cartridge, Ball, Caliber .30, Short Case
T65E2	Cartridge, Ball, Caliber .30 (for Light Rifle)
T65E3	Cartridge, Ball, Caliber .30 (for Light Rifle)
T65E4	Cartridge, Ball, Caliber .30, Short Case, 10 Caliber, 145 grain, Minimum Boattail

Designation	Description
T66	Cartridge, Incendiary-Tracer, Caliber .60, Light Weight Bullet, High Velocity
T67	Cartridge, Grenade, Caliber .45
T68	Cartridge, High Explosive Incendiary, Caliber .60, Light Weight Bullet
T69	Cartridge, Ball, Frangible, Caliber .30 (Carbine Case, Ball Frangible Bullet) (Velocity 1300 30f/s at 78ft)
T70	Cartridge, Dummy, Caliber .30, Short Case (to match Cartridge, Ball, Caliber .30, T65)
T70E1	Cartridge, Dummy, Caliber .30 (FAT1EI Case, .030 Wall Ball Bullet)
T70E2	Cartridge, Dummy, Caliber .30 (FAT1EI Case, .020 Wall Ball Bullet)
T70E3	Cartridge, Dummy, Caliber .30 (FAT1EI Case and Based Tracer Jacket)
T70E4	Cartridge, Dummy, Caliber .30 (FAT1E3 Case, 20 Wall Ball Bullet)
T70E5	Cartridge, Dummy, Caliber .30 (M63)
T71	Cartridge, Test, High Pressure, Caliber .30, Short Case (To match Cartridge, Ball, Caliber .30, T65)
T71EI	Cartridge, Test, High Pressure, Caliber .30 (T71 with case, brass, FAT1E3; 183 grains approx.) (M60)
M72	Cartridge, Tracer, Caliber .30 (25 yds dim igniter trace)
M72E1	Cartridge, Tracer, Caliber .30
T73	Cartridge, Signal, Caliber .45
T73E1	Cartridge, Signal, Caliber .45
T73E2	Cartridge, Signal, Caliber .45
T74	Cartridge, Frangible, Caliber .30, Loaded with SR-4990 Powder (Point Identification is Green with Tan Tip)
T75	Cartridge, Armor-Piercing-Incendiary, Caliber .50/.60 Assembled w/Bullet, Armor-Piercing-Incendiary, Caliber .50, T49
T76	Cartridge, Armor-Piercing-Incendiary-Tracer, Caliber .60 with Bright Igniter
T76E1	Cartridge, Armor-Piercing-Incendiary-Tracer, Caliber .60 (T60 with Primer, Percussion, M36A1)
T77	Cartridge, Ball, Caliber .60
T77E1	Cartridge, Ball, Caliber .60 (T77 w/Primer, Percussion, M36A1)
T78	Cartridge, Incendiary, Caliber .30, Assembled with Bullet, Incendiary, Caliber .30
T79	Cartridge, Blank, Carbine, Caliber .30
T80	Cartridge, Ball, Caliber .60 (T77 Assembled with M52A3 Electric Primer)
T80E1	Cartridge, Ball, Caliber .60 (T77 Assembled with FAT38 Electric Primer)
T80E2	Cartridge, Ball, Caliber .60 (T77E1 with Cut Cannelure in Sabot)
T81	Cartridge, Incendiary, Caliber .60 (T36E2 Assembled w/Remington T41 Electric Primer)
T81EI	Cartridge, Incendiary, Caliber .60 (T36E2 with Electric Primer, M52A3 and Double Crimp)
T82	Cartridge, Armor-Piercing-Incendiary, Caliber .60 (T39 Assembled with Remington T41 Electric Primer)
T82E1	Cartridge, Armor-Piercing-Incendiary, Caliber .60 (T39E1 with Electric Primer, M52A3 and Double Crimp)
T83	Cartridge, Armor-Piercing-Incendiary-Tracer, Caliber .60 (T60 Assembled with Remington T41 Electric Primer)
T83E1	Cartridge, Armor-Piercing-Incendiary-Tracer, Caliber .60 (T60 Assembled with M52A3 Primer)
T84	Cartridge, Armor-Piercing-Incendiary-Tracer, Caliber .60 (T76 Assembled with Remington T41 Electric Primer)

Designation	Description
T84E1	Cartridge, Armor-Piercing-Incendiary-Tracer, Caliber .60 (T76 Assembled with Remington T41 Electric Primer)
T85	Cartridge, High Pressure Test, Caliber .60 (T33 Assembled with Remington T41 Electric Primer)
T85E1	Cartridge, High Pressure Test, Caliber .60 (T33 Assembled with Remington T41 Electric Primer)
T86	Cartridge, Lachrymatory, Caliber .50 (T78 Bullet Charged with LI#2)
T87	Cartridge, Incendiary, Caliber .50 (T78 Bullet Charged with White Phosphorus)
T88	Cartridge, Incendiary, Caliber .30 (Prototype of T87 Charged with White Phosphorus)
T89	Cartridge, Tracer, Caliber .30 (Headlight)
T90	Cartridge, Armor-Piercing, Caliber .30 (Short Case)
T91	Cartridge, High Explosive-Incendiary, Caliber .60
T92	Cartridge, Signal, Caliber .45 (National Fireworks)
T92E1	Cartridge, Signal, Caliber .45 (National Fireworks)
T93	Cartridge, Armor-Piercing, Caliber .30 (140-5 grains AP Bullet for Light Rifle)
T93E1	Cartridge, Armor-Piercing, Caliber .30 (T93 with Case, Brass, 183 grains approx.)
T93E2	Cartridge, Armor-Piercing, Caliber .30 (T93E1 with Bullet, AP, Caliber .30) (M61)
T94	Cartridge, Ball, Caliber .50 (Ball M2 w/aluminum case)
T96	Cartridge, Signal, Carbine, Caliber .30 (National Fireworks)
T97	Cartridge, Armor-Piercing-Incendiary, Caliber .60 (5.25 radius Ogive)
T98	Cartridge, Tracer, Smoke, Caliber .50
T99	Cartridge, Observing, Caliber .30
T100	Cartridge, Release, Life Vest
T101	Cartridge, Armor-Piercing-Incendiary, Caliber .30 (Light Rifle)
T101E1	Cartridge, Armor-Piercing-Incendiary, Caliber .30 (T101 w/Case, Brass, 183 grains approx)
T101E2	Cartridge, Armor-Piercing-Incendiary, Caliber .30 (T101E1 with 10 Caliber Ogive Bullet)
T102	Cartridge, Tracer, Caliber .30 (Light Rifle)
T102E1	Cartridge, Tracer, Caliber .30 (T102 with Case, Brass, 183 grains approx)
T102E2	Cartridge, Tracer, Caliber .30 (T102E1 with with10 Caliber Ogive Bullet) (M62)
T103	Cartridge, Observing, Caliber .30 (Light Rifle)
T103E1	Cartridge, Observing, Caliber .30 (T103 with Case, Brass, 183 grains approx)
T103E2	Cartridge, Observing, Caliber .30 (T103 with Case, Brass, 183 grains approx)
T104	Cartridge, Ball, Caliber .30 (Light Rifle)
T104E1	Cartridge, Ball, Caliber .30 (T104 with Case, Brass, 183 grains approx)
T104E2	Cartridge, Ball, Caliber .30 (T104E1 with 10 Caliber Ogive Bullet) (M59)
T106	Cartridge, Ball, Caliber .60 (High Velocity)
T107	Cartridge, Multiple Bullet, Caliber .30
T116	Cartridge, Grenade, Rifle, Caliber .30
T116E1	Cartridge, Grenade, Rifle, Caliber .30
T116E2	Cartridge, Grenade, Rifle, Caliber .30
T117	Cartridge, Ball, Caliber .35 Pistol
T117E1	Cartridge, Ball, Caliber .35 Pistol
T118	Cartridge, Tracer, Caliber .50 (Short Dim Igniter)

Designation	Description
T119	Cartridge, Armor-Piercing-Incendiary, Caliber .30 (Tungsten Carbide Core)
T119E1	Cartridge, Armor-Piercing-Incendiary, Caliber .30 (T119 w/Cast, Brass, FAT 1E2, 183 gr. approx)
T120	Cartridge, Ball, Caliber .60
T122	Cartridge, Ball, Caliber .50 (M33)
T124	Cartridge, Blank, Line Throwing, Caliber .45
T128	Cartridge, Guard, Caliber .30
T130	Cartridge, Practice, 20mm (T118 Gun)
T131	Cartridge, High Pressure Test, 20mm, (T118 Gun)
T132	Cartridge, Dummy, 20mm, Inert Loaded
T133	Cartridge, Armor-Piercing-Incendiary, 20mm (T118 Gun)
T134	Cartridge, High Explosive, 20mm (T118 Gun)
T135	Shell, Shot Gun, .410 Aluminum Case #6 Shot (M35)
T136	Shell, Shot Gun Slug, .410, 220 Grain Slug
T137	Cartridge, Spotting. Caliber .50 (Winchester Centrifugal Armed)
T138	Cartridge, Spotting, Caliber .50 (Winchester Inertia Armed)
T139	Cartridge, Tracer, Caliber .50 (BAT Rifle)
T140	Cartridge, Spotting, Caliber .30 (BAT Rifle)
T142	Cartridge, Practice, 27mm
T143	Cartridge, Dummy, 27mm
T144	Cartridge, High Explosive, 27mm
T145	Cartridge, High Pressure Test, 27mm
T147	Cartridge, Incendiary, 27mm
T148	Cartridge, High Explosive-Incendiary, 20mm (Percussion Primer; 1600 grain shell)
T148E1	Cartridge, High Explosive-Incendiary, 20mm (Percussion Primer; 1600 grain shell)
T149	Cartridge, High Explosive-Incendiary, 20mm (Electric Primer; 1600 grain shell)
T150	Cartridge, Armor-Piercing-Incendiary, 20mm (Percussion Primer; 1600 grain shell)
T150E1	Cartridge, Armor-Piercing-Incendiary, 20mm (Percussion Primer; 1600 grain shell)
T151	Cartridge, Armor-Piercing-Incendiary, 20mm (Electric Primer; 1600 grain shell)
T152	Cartridge, Dummy, 20mm (1600 grain shell)
T53	Cartridge, Practice, 20mm (Percussion Primer; 1600 grain Projectile)
T153E1	Cartridge, Practice, 20mm (Percussion Primer; 1600 grain Projectile)
T154	Cartridge, Practice, 20mm (Electric Primer; 1600 grain shell)
T155	Cartridge, High Pressure Test, 20mm (Percussion Primer; Modified M99 Projectile)
T155E1	Cartridge, High Pressure Test, 20mm (Percussion Primer; Modified M99 Projectile)
T156	Cartridge, High Pressure Test, 20mm (Electric Primer; Modified M99 Projectile)
T158	Cartridge, Practice, 30mm (Velocity 2000 f/s; 4220 grains; HF1070 grains; pressure 40,000 psi - T121 Gun)
T159	Cartridge, Dummy, 30mm
T160	Cartridge, High Explosive-Incendiary, 30mm w/Shell, T239E6
T160E1	Cartridge, High Explosive-Incendiary, 30mm with Shell, T239E7
T161	Cartridge, High Pressure Test, 30mm
T162	Cartridge, Incendiary, 30mm
T163	Cartridge, High Explosive-Incendiary, 20mm (Length 7.190 in.; T39E3 Projectile)
T164	Cartridge, Armor-Piercing-Incendiary, 20mm
T165	Cartridge, Practice, 20mm

Designation	Description
T166	Cartridge, Ball, 20mm using T114 Projectile
T167	Cartridge, Test, High Pressure, 20mm
T168	Cartridge, Dummy, 20mm
T169	Cartridge, Test, Low Pressure, 20mm
T170	Cartridge, Warning Flash
T170	Cartridge, Warning Flash
T170E1	Cartridge, Photoflash
T172	Cartridge, Ball, Caliber .30 (T65E3 with 172 grain M1 Bullet)
T173	Cartridge, Ball, Caliber .30 (T65E3 with all-steel serrated bullet)
T174	Cartridge, Ball, Caliber .30 (Standard Caliber .30 Round with all-steel serrated bullet)
T175	Cartridge, Spotting, Caliber .50 (Used with BAT weapon)
T176	Cartridge, Spotting Caliber .50 (Used with BAT weapon)
T177	Cartridge, Tracer, Caliber .50 (Used with BAT weapon)
T178	Cartridge, Practice, Caliber .50 (Used with BAT weapon)
T185	Cartridge, Bomb Release
T188	Cartridge, Tracer, Caliber .50
T189	Cartridge, Spotter-Tracer, Caliber .50
T189E1	Cartridge, Spotter-Tracer, Caliber .50 (M48)
T189E2	Cartridge, Spotter-Tracer, Caliber .50
T189E3	Cartridge, Spotter-Tracer Caliber .50 (M48A1)
T190	Cartridge, Spotting, Caliber .50
T191	Cartridge, Spotting, Caliber .50
T192	Cartridge, Tracer, Caliber .50
T193	Cartridge, Tracer, Caliber .50
T194	Cartridge, Practice, Caliber .50
T195	Cartridge, Spotter-Tracer, Caliber .50
T196	Cartridge, Spotter-Tracer, Caliber. 50
T197	Cartridge, Spotter-Tracer, Caliber .50
T198	Cartridge, High Explosive-Incendiary, 20mm
T198E1	Cartridge, High Explosive-Incendiary, 20mm (M56)
T199	Cartridge, Practice, 20mm
T199E1	Cartridge, Practice, 20mm (M55)
T200	Cartridge, Ball, Caliber .22 (M39)
T200E1	Cartridge, Ball, Caliber .22 (M65)
T201	Cartridge, Ball, Caliber .60
T202	Cartridge, Armor-Piercing-Incendiary, Caliber .60
T203	Cartridge, Incendiary, Caliber .60
T204	Cartridge, Practice, 30mm
T205	Cartridge, Dummy, 30mm
T206	Cartridge, High Explosive-Incendiary, 30mm
T206E10	Cartridge, High Explosive-Incendiary, 30mm
T206E11	Cartridge, High Explosive-Incendiary, 30mm
T206E12	Cartridge, High Explosive-Incendiary, 30mm
T206E13	Cartridge, High Explosive-Incendiary, 30mm
T206E14	Cartridge, High Explosive-Incendiary, 30mm
T207	Cartridge, Test, High Pressure, 30mm
T208	Cartridge, Incendiary, 30mm
T221	Cartridge, Armor-Piercing-Incendiary, 20mm (with anvil)
T221E1	Cartridge, Armor-Piercing-Incendiary, 20mm (without anvil)
21E2	Cartridge, Armor-Piercing-Incendiary, 20mm
T221E3	Cartridge, Armor-Piercing-Incendiary, 20mm (M53)
T222	Cartridge, High Explosive-Incendiary, 30mm
T223	Cartridge, Test, High Pressure, 30mm
T224	Cartridge, Target Practice, 30mm

Designation	Description
T225	Cartridge, Dummy, 30mm
T228	Cartridge, Dummy, 20mm (M51)
T230	Cartridge, Armor-Piercing-Incendiary-Tracer, 20mm (M52)
T232	Cartridge, Armor-Piercing-Incendiary-Tracer, 20mm
T233	Cartridge, Ball, Caliber .30 (Light Rifle) (M80)
T239	Cartridge, Ball, 30mm
T239E1	Cartridge, Ball, 30mm
T240	Cartridge, High Explosive-Incendiary, 30mm
T241	Cartridge, High Explosive-Incendiary, 20mm (M58)
T249	Cartridge, Practice, Caliber .50 (Used w/BAT weapon)
T249E1	Cartridge, Practice, Caliber .50 (Used w/BAT weapon)
T249E2	Cartridge, Practice, Caliber .50 (Used w/BAT weapon)
T251	Cartridge, High Pressure Test, Caliber .50 (Used w/BAT weapon)
T252	Cartridge, Dummy, Caliber .50 (Used w/BAT weapon)
T252E1	Cartridge, Dummy, Caliber .50 (Used w/BAT weapon)
T252E2	Cartridge, Dummy, Caliber .50 (Used w/BAT weapon)
T253	Cartridge, Test, High Pressure, 30mm
T266	Cartridge, High Explosive-Incendiary, 30mm
T267	Cartridge, Test, High Pressure, 30mm
T268	Cartridge, Ball, 30mm
T269	Cartridge, Dummy, 30mm
T270	Cartridge, High Explosive-Incendiary, 30mm
T271	Cartridge, Ball, 9mm
T272	Cartridge, 20mm, Dummy
T272E1	Cartridge, 20mm, Dummy
T272E2	Cartridge, 20mm, Dummy
T272E3	Cartridge, 20mm, Dummy
T272E4	Cartridge, 20mm, Dummy
T275	Cartridge, 7.62mm, Ball, NATO
T275E1	Cartridge, 7.62mm, Ball, NATO
T275E2	Cartridge, 7.62mm, Ball, NATO
T276	Cartridge, Caliber .38, Special
T283	Cartridge, 20mm, Armor-Piercing-Incendiary-Tracer
T291	Cartridge, Caliber .30, Match (M72)
T334	Cartridge, Practice, 30mm
MK101 Mod 0	Cartridge, 20mm, High Pressure Test
MK102 Mod 0	Cartridge, 20mm, Low Pressure Test
MK103 Mod 0	Cartridge, 20mm, Dummy
MK105 Mod 0	Cartridge, 20mm, Target Practice
MK106, Mod 0, and Mod 1	Cartridge, 20mm. High Explosive-Incendiary
MK107 Mod 0	Cartridge, 20mm, Armor Piercing-Incendiary
MK108 Mod 0	Cartridge, 20mm, Armor Piercing-Tracer

Cartridge Identification by Measurement

The purpose of this table is to assist the cartridge collector and other interested persons in the identification of unknown cartridges or cartridge cases based upon dimensional information. The following chart contains all cartridges found in this book and its accompanying CD, organized in order of increasing bullet diameter, then increasing case length. With only minor variations, these dimensions are constant within any specific cartridge type. Once these dimensions are known, other details will allow identification of the unknown cartridge or case. Those details—rim type, neck diameter, base diameter, shoulder diameter, and cartridge length—are listed in separate columns of this table. By measuring and eliminating options, the interested party can rapidly learn the proper name of the cartridge or case in hand.

Consider a hypothetical identification:

We take the case or cartridge in hand and measure bullet diameter or case neck internal diameter (assuming a fired case that is not damaged, this will usually be no more than about .004-inch larger than bullet diameter). This measurement is easily accomplished to about .001-inch accuracy with a dial caliper. We look in the third column of this table and find the approximate bullet diameter. This limits our search to a reasonable number of cartridges.

Next, we note case length, again measured with sufficient accuracy using a dial caliper. In most instances, this will narrow our search to one or, at most, a few choices. We will then review rim type and other aspects of the cartridge in order to eliminate options. Eventually only one cartridge will remain.

As a specific example of this process, consider the following: We have a loaded cartridge, which has a military headstamp that is meaningless to us. The exposed bullet measures about .244-inch. We cannot be certain of exact bullet diameter. Nevertheless, we can narrow our search to those listings with bullets of .243-inch, .244-inch, and .245-inch diameter, and see the bullet is clearly larger than .228-inch and smaller than .249-inch. The case measures about 2.35-inch in length. This narrows our search to only two possibilities (within the specified range of bullet diameters), the 6x62mm Freres and 6mm Lee Navy. The base of the case measures about .445-inch. This eliminates the 6x62mm Freres (.474-inch). Further, the rim is about the same diameter as the base (rimless, case type C). We are satisfied with our identification, the 6mm Lee Navy.

CARTRIDGE	CASE TYPE	BULLET DIAMETER	NECK DIAMETER	SHOULDER DIAMETER	BASE DIAMETER	RIM DIAMETER	RIM THICKNESS	CASE LENGTH	CARTRIDGE LENGTH	PRIMER	PAGE
.10 Eichelberger Long Rifle	A	.1030	.122	.223	.225	.275	.043	.568	UNK/NA	RF	167
.10 Eichelberger Pup	A	.1030	.122	.247	.249	.308	.050	.767	UNK/NA	SR	167
.10 Eichelberger Squirrel	A	.1030	.122	.291	.294	.350	.065	.613	UNK/NA	SR	168
.12 Eichelberger Long Rifle	A	.1230	.140	.224	.225	.275	.043	.568	UNK/NA	RF	168
.12 Eichelberger Win Mag RF	A	.1230	.140	.238	.241	.293	.050	1.064	UNK/NA	RF	169
.12 Cooper	A	.123	.145	.247	.249	.308	.050	1.106	UNK/NA	SR	169
.12 Eichelberger Carbine	C	.123	.147	.356	.356	.360	.050	1.240	UNK/NA	SR	169
.14 Eichelberger Dart	C	.144	.164	.274	.278	.301	.043	.640	UNK/NA	SP	170
.14 Cooper	A	.144	.166	.247	.249	.3085	.051	1.104	UNK/NA	SR	171
.14 Walker Hornet	A	.144	.170	.285	.294	.350	.065	1.350	UNK/NA	SR	171

CARTRIDGE	CASE TYPE	BULLET DIAMETER	NECK DIAMETER	SHOULDER DIAMETER	BASE DIAMETER	RIM DIAMETER	RIM THICKNESS	CASE LENGTH	CARTRIDGE LENGTH	PRIMER	PAGE
.14 Jet Junior	A	.144	.177	.366	.378	.440	.059	1.260	UNK/NA	SP	172
.14 Eichelberger Bee	A	.144	.162	.329	.349	.408	.065	1.310	UNK/NA	SR	170
.14/222	C	.144	.165	.356	.375	.375	.041	1.70	1.92	S	172
14/222 Eichelberger Mag	C	.144	.170	.356	.376	.378	.045	1.850	UNK/NA	SR	173
.17 Hornet	A	.172	.194	.294	.298	.345	.050	1.35	1.72	S	14
.17 Ackley Hornet	A	.172	.195	.290	.295	.345	.060	1.39	1.47	S	174
.17-32 Magnum	A	.172	.196	.335	.335	.375	.055	.900	1.45	S	173
.17 VHA (Varmint Hunters Assn.)	C	.172	.196	.305	.316	.315	.043	1.201	1.60	S	174
.17 Remington	C	.172	.198	.355	.374	.377	.041	1.79	1.86	S	15
.17/222	C	.172	.199	.355	.375	.375	.041	1.69	1.82	S	176
.17 Mach IV/Mach III	C	.172	.199	.361	.375	.378	.041	1.40	UNK/NA	S	175
.17 Ackley Improved Bee	A	.172	.201	.341	.350	.408	.060	1.35	1.78	S	175
.17 Remington Fireball	C	.172	.204	.3655	.3759	.332	.045	1.41	1.83	S	14
4.6x30 HK	C	.183	.209	.305	.316	.315	.043	1.201	1.516	S	16
4.85mm British	C	.197	.220	.353	.375	.376	.041	1.925	2.455	B	373
.19 Badger	C	.198	UNK/NA	UNK/NA	UNK/NA	UNK/NA	UNK/NA	UNK/NA	1.3	S	176
.19 Calhoon	A	.198	.215	.286	.294	.350	.063	1.39	1.47	S	177
.19-223 Calhoon	C	.198	.224	.364	.373	.373	.041	1.76	2.0	S	177
.204 Ruger	C	.204	.231	.360	.375	.378	.045	1.850	2.260	SR	16
.20 Vartarg	C	.204	.232	.360	.374	.375	.048	1.40	1.90	S	178
.20 Tactical	C	.204	.233	.360	.373	.375	.041	1.755	2.1	S	178
.20 PDK	C	.204	.247	.400	.421	.417	.049	1.683	2.236	S	179
5mm Remington Magnum	A	.205	.225	.259	.259	.325	.050	1.020	UNK/NA	UNK/NA	491
5.45x18mm Soviet	C	.210	.220	UNK/NA	.300	.300	UNK/NA	.70	.98	SB	323
5.7x28mm FN P90 (Belgium)	C	.220	.249	.309	.310	.310	UNK/NA	1.13	1.71	B	373
5.45x39mm Soviet	C	.221	.246	.387	.395	.394	.053	1.56	2.22	B	373
.22 BB Cap	B	.222	.224	UNK/NA	.224	.270	.040	.284	.343	UNK/NA	492
.22 CB Cap	B	.222	.225	UNK/NA	.225	.271	.040	.420	.520	UNK/NA	492
5.6x35Rmm Vierling (.22 WCF)	A	.222	.241	.278	.300	.297	UNK/NA	1.40	1.62	.177/1584/539	458
.22 Winchester Automatic	B	.222	.250	UNK/NA	.250	.310	.040	.665	.915	UNK/NA	492
.22 Short	B	.223	.224	UNK/NA	.225	.273	.040	.423	.686	UNK/NA	493

CARTRIDGE	CASE TYPE	BULLET DIAMETER	NECK DIAMETER	SHOULDER DIAMETER	BASE DIAMETER	RIM DIAMETER	RIM THICKNESS	CASE LENGTH	CARTRIDGE LENGTH	PRIMER	PAGE
.22 Short/40-grain RWS load	B	.223	.224	UNK/NA	.225	.272	.042	.415	.798	UNK/NA	493
.22 Long	B	.223	.224	UNK/NA	.225	.275	.040	.595	.880	UNK/NA	493
.22 Long Rifle	B	.223	.224	UNK/NA	.225	.275	.040	.595	.975	UNK/NA	494
.22 Stinger, etc. (hyper velocities)	B	.223	.224	UNK/NA	.225	.275	.040	.694	.975	UNK/NA	494
.22 Extra Long	B	.223	.225	UNK/NA	.225	.275	.040	.750	1.16	UNK/NA	495
.297/230 Morris Extra Long	A	.223	.240	.274	.296	.248	UNK/NA	1.125	1.45	UNK/NA	403
.22 Hornet	A	.223	.242	.274	.294	.345	.060	1.40	1.72	S	17
.22 Remington Automatic	B	.223	.245	UNK/NA	.245	.290	UNK/NA	.663	.920	UNK/NA	495
.22 Remington Jet	A	.223	.247	.350	.376	.440	.055	1.28	1.58	SP	323
.22 Winchester Magnum RF	B	.224	.240	UNK/NA	.241	.291	.046	1.052	1.35	UNK/NA	496
.218 Bee	A	.224	.241	.331	.349	.408	.060	1.35	1.68	S	17
.218 Mashburn Bee	A	.224	.241	.340	.349	.408	.060	1.34	1.75	S	181
.22 Reed Express	C	.224	UNK/NA	UNK/NA	UNK/NA	UNK/NA	UNK/NA	UNK/NA	UNK/NA	UNK/NA	182
.22 WRF & Remington Special	B	.224	.242	UNK/NA	.243	.295	.046	.960	1.17	UNK/NA	496
.22 K-Hornet	A	.224	.242	.286	.294	.345	.060	1.39	1.70	S	181
.22 PPC	C	.224	.245	.430	.440	.441	.050	1.52	1.96	S	21
.22 Waldog	C	.224	.245	.431	.440	.441	.053	1.375	1.820	S	182
.22 BR Remington	C	.224	.245	.450	.466	.468	.045	1.502	2.00	S	183
.224 Weatherby Magnum	E	.224	.247	.405	.413	.425	.045	1.92	2.44	L	22
.223 Remington	C	.224	.249	.349	.373	.375	.041	1.76	2.10	S	19
5.56x45mm NATO	C	.224	.249	.349	.373	.375	.041	1.76	2.26	Bx	374
5.8x42mm Chinese	C	.224	UNK/NA	UNK/NA	UNK/NA	UNK/NA	UNK/NA	1.66	2.30	UNK/NA	374
.223 Ackley Improved	C	.224	.250	.365	.375	.378	.041	1.76	V	S	185
.221 Remington Fireball	C	.224	.251	.355	.375	.375	.040	1.40	1.82	SP	324
.219 Donaldson Wasp	A	.224	.251	.402	.418	.497	.058	1.71	2.10	L	183
.219 Zipper	A	.224	.252	.364	.421	.497	.058	1.94	2.26	L	108
.222 Remington Rimmed	A	.224	.253	.357	.375	.440	.049	1.70	2.13	S	249
.222 Remington	C	.224	.253	.355	.375	.375	.041	1.70	2.15	S	18
.222 Remington Magnum	C	.224	.253	.355	.375	.375	.041	1.85	2.21	S	109
5.6x50mm Magnum/ 5.6x50Rmm Magnum	C/A	.224	.254	.355	.375	.376/(?)	.038	1.97	2.21	UNK/NA	459
.22-250 Remington	C	.224	.254	.412	.466	.470	.045	1.91	2.33	L	22

CARTRIDGE	CASE TYPE	BULLET DIAMETER	NECK DIAMETER	SHOULDER DIAMETER	BASE DIAMETER	RIM DIAMETER	RIM THICKNESS	CASE LENGTH	CARTRIDGE LENGTH	PRIMER	PAGE
.22 Fawn	A	.224	.255	.430	.435	.492	.060	1.30	1.90	S	179
.226 JDJ	A	.224	.256	.410	.419	.467	.045	1.93	V	L	24/249
.22 PDK	C	.224	.256	.400	.421	.417	.049	1.75	2.25	S	180
.22 Taranah Hornet	A	.224	UNK/NA	UNK/NA	.294	.350	.063	UNK/NA	UNK/NA	UNK/NA	180
.225 Winchester	A	.224	.260	.406	.422	.473	.045	1.93	2.50	L	21
.220 Wotkyns-Wilson Arrow	G	.224	.261	.402	.443	.472	.045	2.205	2.70	L	185
.223 WSSM	I	.244	.272	.544	.555	.535	.054	1.67	2.175 (2.360)	L	25
6mm Dasher	C	.224	.271	.462	.470	.470	.050	1.54	V	S	187
.224 Clark	C	.224 (.2249)	.275	.455	.471	.473	.045	2.237	3.075	L	184
.224 Texas Trophy Hunter	C	.224	UNK/NA	UNK/NA	UNK/NA	UNK/NA	UNK/NA	UNK/NA	UNK/NA	UNK/NA	184
5.6x57mm RWS/5.6x57Rmm RWS	C/A	.224	.281	.436	.469	.470/(?)	UNK/NA	2.24	2.54	UNK/NA	459
.25-222 Copperhead	C	.224	.285	.357	.375	.378	.045	1.850	2.485	L	190
.297/230 Morris Short	A	.225	.240	.274	.294	.347	UNK/NA	.58	.89	.177/69	403
.297/230 Morris Long	A	.225	.240	.274	.295	.345	UNK/NA	.80	1.1	.177/69	403
5.5mm Velo Dog Revolver	B	.225	.248	UNK/NA	.253	.308	UNK/NA	1.12	1.35	SPB	324
5.6x61mm & 5.6x61Rmm Vom Hofe Super Express	C/A	.227	.259/ .260	.468/ .470	.476/ .479	.480/ .533	?/.062	2.39	3.13	.217/5603/ 431M	460
.22 Winchester CF (WCF)	A	.228	.241	.278	.295	.342	.058	1.39	1.61	S	110
.22 Savage High Power	A	.228	.252	.360	.416	.500	.056	2.05	2.51	L	111
.228 Ackley Magnum	C	.228	.265	.445	.470	.473	.045	2.25	2.55	L	186
6 Whisper	C	.243	UNK/NA	UNK/NA	.370	.375	.040	UNK/NA	UNK/NA	UNK/NA	250
6mm PPC	C	.243	.260	.430	.441	.442	.50	1.50	2.12	S	25
6mm Bench Rest Remington	C	.243	.263	.457	.466	.468	.045	1.52	2.19	S	111
6x45mm (6mm/223)	C	.243	.266	.354	.376	.378	.041	1.76	2.26	S	186
6x47mm	C	.243	.266	.357	.375	.378	.045	1.85	2.485	S	190
6mm CHeetah	C	.243	.260	.456	.470	.473	.049	2.00	UNK/NA	LR	188
.240 Weatherby	E	.243	.271	.432	.453	.473	.045	2.50	3.06	L	30
6x62mm Freres/ 6x62Rmm Freres	C/A	.243	.271	.451	.474	.470/(?)	UNK/NA	2.42	3.13	.217	461
6mm Norma BR	C	.243	.271	.458	.469	.470	.051	1.56	2.44	S	26
6XC Tubb	C	.243	.271	.450	.466	.468	.049	1.898	2.808	L	27
6mm JDJ	A	.243	.272	.415	.421	.470	.045	1.905	2.65	L	250

CARTRIDGE	CASE TYPE	BULLET DIAMETER	NECK DIAMETER	SHOULDER DIAMETER	BASE DIAMETER	RIM DIAMETER	RIM THICKNESS	CASE LENGTH	CARTRIDGE LENGTH	PRIMER	PAGE
6mm SAW (U.S.)	C	.243	.273	.382	.410	.410		1.779	2.58	L	375
6mm-250 Walker	C	.243	.274	.420	.468	.470	.045	1.91	2.21	L	187
6mm/30-30 Ackley Improved	A	.243	.275	.392	.422	.502	.058	2.03	2.55	L	189
6.17 Spitfire	C	.243	.275	.510	.530	.530	.050	2.05	2.8	L	251
6.17 Flash	C	.243	.275	.510	.530	.530	.050	2.80	3.55	L	251
.240 Hawk	C	.243	.276	.454	.4712	.473	.049	2.485	UNK/NA	L	191
.244 Remington	C	.243	.276	.429	.470	.472	.045	2.23	2.90	L	112
6mm Remington /.244 Remington	C	.243	.276	.429	.470	.472	.045	2.23	2.91 2.825	L	29
.243 Winchester	C	.243	.276	.454	.470	.470	.49	2.05	2.71	L	27
6mm-284	I	.243	.276	.475	.500	.473	.049	2.165	2.80	L	191
Spitzer 6mm-06	C	.243	.276	.441	.470	.473	.049	2.494	3.35	L	188
6x57mm Mauser/6x57mm RWS	C	.243	.284	.420	.475	.476	.045	2.23	2.95	.217/5603 494	461
.244 (6mm) Halger Magnum	A	.243	.287	.435	.467	.470	UNK/NA	2.25	3.04	.2175603	461
.244 H&H Magnum	E	.244	.263	.445	.508	.532	UNK/NA	2.78	3.58	.217/60	404
6mm Lee Navy (.236 Navy)	C	.244	.278	.402	.445	.448	.050	2.35	3.11	L	113/376
.240 Magnum Flanged	A	.245	.274	.402	.448	.513	UNK/NA	2.50	3.25	.217/81	404
.240 Magnum Rimless (.240 Apex)	E	.245	.274	.403	.450	467	.035	2.49	3.21	.217/81	404
.243 WSSM	I	.243	.287	.544	.555	.535	.054	1.67	2.060 (2.360)	L	28
.25 Short	B	.246	.245	UNK/NA	.245	.290	UNK/NA	.468	.780	UNK/NA	497
.297/250 Rook	A	.250	.267	.294	.295	.343	UNK/NA	.82	1.1	.177/69	404
.25 Stevens Short	B	.251	.275	UNK/NA	.276	.333	UNK/NA	.599	.877	UNK/NA	497
.25 Automatic Colt Pistol (ACP)	D	.251	.276	UNK/NA	.277	.298	.038	.62	.91	SP	325
.25 NAA (North American Arms)	C	.251	.276	.330	.337	.337	.046	.745	.960	UNK/NA	325
.25 Stevens	B	.251	.276	UNK/NA	.276	.333	UNK/NA	1.125	1.395	UNK/NA	497
.242 Rimless Nitro Express	C	.253	.281	.405	.465	.465	UNK/NA	2.38	3.20	.217/59	405
.25-20 Marlin	A	.257	.274	.329	.349	.405	UNK/NA	1.33	UNK/NA	S	114
.25-20 Winchester	A	.257	.274	.329	.349	.405	.060	1.33	1.60	S	31
.255 Banshee	A	.257	.278	.297	.298	.345	.050	1.335	1.80	S	252
.256 Winchester Magnum (handgun)	A	.257	.277	.378	.378	.440	.055	1.30	1.53	SP	326
.257 Kimber	C	.257	.279	.365	.376	.378	.041	1.82	2.485	UNK/NA	195

CARTRIDGE	CASE TYPE	BULLET DIAMETER	NECK DIAMETER	SHOULDER DIAMETER	BASE DIAMETER	RIM DIAMETER	RIM THICKNESS	CASE LENGTH	CARTRIDGE LENGTH	PRIMER	PAGE
.25-21 Stevens	B	.257	.280	UNK/NA	.300	.376	UNK/NA	2.05	2.30	S	114
.25-35 Winchester (WCF)/ 6.5x52Rmm	A	.257	.280	.355	.420	.500 (.506)	.059	2.04	2.53	L	31/462
.25 Remington	C	.257	.280	.355	.420	.421	.045	2.04	2.54	L	116
.25-36 Marlin	A	.257	.281	.358	.416	.499	.056	2.12	2.50	S	115
.25-25 Stevens	B	.257	.282	UNK/NA	.323	.376	UNK/NA	2.37	2.63	S	114
.257 Raptor	C	.257	.283	.370	.376	.378	.045	1.86	2.135	S	252
.25-45 Sharps	C	.257	.284	.353	.376	.378	.045	1.76	2.135	S	32
.250/3000 Ackley Improved	C	.257	.284	.445	.467	.473	.045	1.91	2.52	L	193
.256 Winchester Magnum (rifle)	A	.257	.285	.368	.381	.440	.060	1.281	1.59	S	145
.257 Weatherby Magnum	E	.257	.285	.490	.511	.530	.048	2.55	3.25	L	36
.25-284	I	.257	.285	.495	.500	.473	.049	2.17	2.80	L	195
.257 STW (Shooting Times Westerner)	E	.257	.285	.487	.511	.532	.050	2.85	3.60	L	196
.25 Gibbs	C	.257	UNK/NA	UNK/NA	.440	.468	.045	UNK/NA	UNK/NA	UNK/NA	196
.250 Savage	C	.257	.286	.413	.468	.470	.045	1.91	2.52 (2.515)	L	33
.25-06 Remington	C	.257	.287	.441	.470	.471	.045	2.49	3.00	L	35
.257 JDJ	A	.257	.288	.415	.421	.473	.045	1.905	2.81	L	253
.250-06 JDJ	C	.257	UNK/NA	UNK/NA	.440	.468	.045	UNK/NA	UNK/NA	UNK/NA	253
.257 Ackley Improved	C	.257	.288	.457	.471	.474	.045	2.23	2.78	L	194
6.53 Scramjet	C	.257	.289	.510	.530	.530	.055	2.80	3.575	L	254
.257 Mini Dreadnaught	G	.257	.290	.425	.445	.467	.045	2.145	V	L	253
.257 Roberts (.257 Roberts +P)	C	.257	.290	.430	.468	.473	.045	2.23	2.74	L	34
.25 Hunter	A	.257	.293	.430	.435	.492	.046	1.625	2.30	L	192
.25 Ackley Krag	A	.257	.293	.442	.457	.540	.059	2.31	UNK/NA	L	193
.25 Ackley Krag Short	A	.257	.293	.442	.457	.540	.059	2.24-2.31	V	L	193
6.5mm Mannlicher-Schonauer (Greek)	C	.263	.287	.424	.447	.450	UNK/NA	2.09	3.02	B	377
6.5mm Japanese Arisaka	G	.263	.293	.425	.455	.471	.045	2.00	2.98	B	376
6.5 Mini Dreadnaught	G	.263	.296	.425	.445	.467	.045	2.150	V	L	257
6.5x53R Mannlicher (Dutch & Romanian)	A	.263	.297	.423	.450	.526	.066	2.10	3.03	B	377
6.5mm JDJx30	A	.264	.285	.409	.419	.497	.058	2.03	V	L	256
6.5mm Whisper	C	.264	.286	.357	.372	.375	.041	1.36	V	S	254

CARTRIDGE	CASE TYPE	BULLET DIAMETER	NECK DIAMETER	SHOULDER DIAMETER	BASE DIAMETER	RIM DIAMETER	RIM THICKNESS	CASE LENGTH	CARTRIDGE LENGTH	PRIMER	PAGE
6.5x25 CCBJ	C	.257	.287	.379	.390	.393	.049	.984	1.169	S	225
6.5x54mm Mauser	C	.264	.289	.432	.468	.463	UNK/NA	2.12	2.67	.217/5603/ 457A	462
.264 (6.5mm) Win. Magnum	E	.264	.289	.490	.515 (.5127)	.532	.047	2.52	3.29	L	40
.256 (6.5mm) Newton	C	.264	.290	.430	.469	.473	.045	2.44	3.40	L	116
6.5x58Rmm Sauer	B	.264	.291	UNK/NA	.433	.501	UNK/NA	2.30	3.08	.217/5603/ 463	462
6.5x57mm/6.5x57Rmm Mauser & RWS	C/A	.264	.292	.430	.471/ .470	.474/ .521	UNK/NA	2.23/ 2.24	3.16/ 3.18	.217/5603/ 404A	463
6.5mm JDJ No. 2	A	.264	.292	.450	.466	.502	.059	2.00	V	L	258
6.5mm JDJ	A	.264	.293	.410	.419	.467	.045	1.93	V	L	256
6.5/270 JDJ	C	.264	UNK/NA	UNK/NA	.440	.468	.045	UNK/NA	UNK/NA	UNK/NA	258
.264 LBC-AR	C	.264	.293	.428	.439	.441	.059	1.526	2.20	S	199
6.5mm Grendel	C	.264	.293	.428	.439	.441	.059	1.526	2.26	SR	38
6.5x58mm Portuguese	C	.264	.293	.426	.468	.465	UNK/NA	2.28	3.22	.217/5603 457	464
6.508 A-Square/.260 Rem	C	.264	.294	.452	.468	.467	.045	.025	2.80	LR	37
6.5mm Leopard	C	.264	.295	.539	.551	.533	.049	2.093	UNK/NA	LR	201
6.5x65mm/6.5x65Rmm RWS	C/A	.264	.296	.430	.474/ .475	.470/ .531	UNK/NA	2.56	3.15	UNK/NA	465
.264 Hawk	C	.264	.296	.454	.471	.473	.049	2.485	UNK/NA	L	199
6.5x61mm/6.5x61Rmm Mauser	C/A	.264	.296/.297	.452	.477	.479/.532	UNK/NA	2.40	3.55	.217/5603 431L-431M	464
6.5 Creedmoor	C	.264	.297	.458	.467	.468	.054	1.915	2.72	L	39
6.5x52mm American	C	.264	.297	.465	.470	.473	.054	2.024	2.735	L	197
EABCO 6.5mm BRM	A	.264	UNK/NA	UNK/NA	UNK/NA	UNK/NA	UNK/NA	UNK/NA	UNK/NA	UNK/NA	198
6.71 Phantom	C	.264	.297	.510	.530	.530	.055	2.05	2.8	L	258
6.5x55 Swedish Mauser	C	.264	.297	.435	.480 (.477)	.480 (.479)	.050	2.16	3.15	L	37/378
6.5-284 Norma	I	.264	.297	.475	.500	.470	.051	2.17	3.23	SR	39
6.71 Blackbird	C	.264	.297	.524	.544	.544	.055	2.80	3.575	L	259
6.5 STW (Shooting Times Westerner)	E	.264	.298	.487	.511	.532	.050	2.85	3.60	L	197
6.5x58R Krag-Jorgensen	A.	.264	.300	.460	.500	.575	UNK/NA	2.29	3.25	.217/5603 431L-431M	464
6.5-06 Ackley Improved	C	.264	.300	.455	.471	.473	.045	2.50	3.30	L	200
6.5 Remington Magnum	E	.264	.300	.490	.512	.532	.047	2.17	2.80	L	117

CARTRIDGE	CASE TYPE	BULLET DIAMETER	NECK DIAMETER	SHOULDER DIAMETER	BASE DIAMETER	RIM DIAMETER	RIM THICKNESS	CASE LENGTH	CARTRIDGE LENGTH	PRIMER	PAGE
6.5x52mm Italian Mannlicher-Carcano	C	.265	.295	.430	.445	.448	.045	2.05	3.02	B	379
6.5x68mm/6.5x68Rmm RWS	C/A	.265	.295	.481	.520	.510	UNK/NA	2.66	3.27	.238/1698	465
.270 REN	B	.277	.295	UNK/NA	.298	.350	.060	1.29	UNK/NA	S	201
.270 JDJ	A	.277	.305	.415	.419	.467	.045	1.905	2.875	L	259
.270 JDJ No. 2	C	.277	UNK/NA	UNK/NA	.440	.468	.045	UNK/NA	UNK/NA	UNK/NA	260
.270 IHMSA	C	.277	.305	.448	.471	.473	.045	1.866	2.60	L	202
.270 Gibbs	C	.277	UNK/NA	UNK/NA	.440	.468	.045	UNK/NA	UNK/NA	UNK/NA	202
.270 Weatherby Magnum	E	.277	.305	.490	.511	.530	.048	2.55	3.25	L	43
6.8 SPC (Special Purpose Cartridge)	C	.277	.306	.401	.421	.417	.049	.1.686	2.26	LR	41
.270 Winchester	C	.277	.307	.440	.468	.470	.045	2.54	3.28	L	41
.270 Hawk	C	.277	.308	.453	.471	.473	.049	2.486	UNK/NA	LR	202
.270 Savage	C	.277	.308	.413	.470	.470	.045	1.88	2.62	L	203
.270 Ackley Improved	C	.277	.308	.450	.470	.470	.045	1.88	2.62	L	203
.270 WSM	I	.277	.314	.538	.555	.535	.054	2.10	2.56 (2.860)	L	42
7mm Nambu	C	.280	.296	.337	.351	.359	UNK/NA	.78	1.06	B	326
7mm TCU	C	.284	.302	.350	.373	.375	.041	1.74	2.28	S	203
7mm Whisper	C	.284	.306	.357	.372	.375	.041	1.36	V	S	260
7mm-30 JDJ	A	.284	.306	.409	.419	.497	.058	2.03	V	L	261
7-30 Waters	A	.284	.306	.399	.422 (.4215)	.506	.058	2.04	2.52	L	44
7x33mm Sako/Finnish	C	.284	.307	.365	.388	.390	UNK/NA	1.30	1.73	UNK/NA	466
7mm GNR	A	.284	.312	.400	.420	.502	.058	2.055	2.65	L	263
.280 Ackley Improved	C	.284	.311	.454	.470	.472	.049	2.525	3.33	L	48
7x72Rmm	B	.284	.311	UNK/NA	.425	.482	UNK/NA	2.84	3.48	.217/5603 573	468
7mm JDJ	A	.284	.312	.415	.421	.473	.045	1.905	V	L	261
7mm JRS	C	.284	.312	.454	.470	.467	.045	2.525	3.455	L	204
7mm Gibbs	C	.284	UNK/NA	UNK/NA	.440	.468	.045	UNK/NA	UNK/NA	UNK/NA	205
.280 JDJ	C	.284	.312	.455	.470	.467	.045	2.505	V	L	363
7mm Weatherby Magnum	E	.284	.312	.490	.511	.530	.048	2.55	3.25	L	51
7mm JDJ No. 2	A	.284	.313	.450	.466	.502	.059	2.00	V	L	261
7mm Blaser Magnum	I	.284	.314	.515	.544	.535	.054	2.35	3.14	L	467

CARTRIDGE	CASE TYPE	BULLET DIAMETER	NECK DIAMETER	SHOULDER DIAMETER	BASE DIAMETER	RIM DIAMETER	RIM THICKNESS	CASE LENGTH	CARTRIDGE LENGTH	PRIMER	PAGE
7mm Dakota	C	.284	.314	.531	.544	.544	.042	2.50	3.33	L	265
7 STE (Shooting Tmes Easterner)	A	.284	.315	.454	.467	.502	.059	2.1	2.54	L	206
7mm SGLC (Simpson's Good Little Cartridge)	C	.284	.315	.465	.470	.473	.054	2.024	2.735	L	205
7mm-08 Remington	C	.284	.315	.454	.470	.473	.050	2.04 (2.035)	2.80	L	45
7mm Rigby Flanged Magnum	A	.284	.315	.406	.456	.524	UNK/NA	2.49	3.24	.243/34	406
.280 Hawk (7mm Hawk)	C	.284	.315	.454	.471	.473	.049	2.485	UNK/NA	LR	204
.280 Remington/7mm Express Remington	C	.284	.315	.441	.470	.472	.045	2.54	3.33	L	47
.285 OKH/7mm-06	C	.284	.315	.442	.470	.472	.045	2.55	3.35	L	207
7x73mm Vom Hofe Belted	E	.284	.315	.483	.527	.533	UNK/NA	2.87	3.88	.217/5603/575	469
7mm Remington Magnum	E	.284	.315	.490	.511	.525	.047	2.50	3.24	L	48
.280 GNR	A	.284	.316	.448	.463	.543	.075	2.525	3.0	L	262
7x66mm Vom Hofe Super Express	C	.284	.316	.485	.543	.510	.048	2.58	3.25	.217/603	468
7mm STW (Shooting Times Western)	E	.284	.316	.487	.513	.532	.048	2.85	3.65	L	51
7.21 Tomahawk	C	.284	.318	.557	.577	.577	.060	2.05	2.80	L	264
7x75Rmm Vom Hofe Super Express	A	.284	.318	.416	.468	.519	.050	2.95	3.68	.217	469
.275 Flanged Magnum .275 No. 2 Magnum	A	.284	.318	.450	.510	.582	UNK/NA	2.50	3.26	.217	406
7.21 Firehawk	C	.284	.318	.524	.544	.544	.055	2.80	3.55	L	266
7.21 Firebird	C	.284	.318	.557	.577	.577	.060	2.80	3.6	L	267
.284 Winchester	I	.284	.320	.465 (.4748)	.495 (.500)	.470	.049	2.17	2.75	L	46
7x57mm/7x57mmR Mauser	C	.284	.320	.420 (.4294)	.470	.474	.046	2.24 (2.235)	3.06	L	466
7x57mm Mauser	C	.284	.320	.420	.470	.474	.055	2.23	3.06	B	379
7x57mm Mauser/7x57Rmm Mauser	C/A	.284	.320	.420	.470	.474/.521	.035/.056	2.24	3.06/3.07	.217/5603/380DM93A	44
7x61 Sharpe & Hart Super	E	.284	.320	.478	.515	.532	.048	2.40	3.27	L	118
7mm Canadian Magnum	I	.284	.322	.530	.544	.532	.046	2.83	3.60	L	265
.275 Rigby (7x57)	C	.284	.324	.428	.474	.475	UNK/NA	2.24	3.07	.217	405
.275 Belted Magnum	E	.284	.325	.454	.513	.532	UNK/NA	2.50	3.42	.217/81	406
.275 H&H Magnum	E	.284	.375	.375	.513	.532	.048	2.50	3.30	L	118
7x64mm Brenneke 7x65Rmm Brenneke	C/A	.284	.305/.308	.422	.463	.468/.521	.055	2.51, 2.53	3.21	.217/5603/557/557A	466

CARTRIDGE	CASE TYPE	BULLET DIAMETER	NECK DIAMETER	SHOULDER DIAMETER	BASE DIAMETER	RIM DIAMETER	RIM THICKNESS	CASE LENGTH	CARTRIDGE LENGTH	PRIMER	PAGE
7mm Bench Rest (based on Rem. 308 BR case shortened to 1.50-inch)	C	.284	UNK/NA	SP	UNK/NA	UNK/NA	UNK/NA	1.5	UNK/NA	UNK/NA	327
.28-30-120 Stevens	B	.285	.309	UNK/NA	.357	.412	UNK/NA	2.51	2.82	L	119
.30 Short	B	.286	.292	UNK/NA	.292	.346	UNK/NA	.515	.822	UNK/NA	498
.280 Flanged (.280 Lancaster)	A	.287	.316	.423	.535	.607	UNK/NA	2.60	3.62	.217/60	406
.280 Ross (.280 Rimless)	G	.287	.317	.404	.534	.556	UNK/NA	2.59	3.50	.217/59	407
7mmRem. SAUM	I	.284	.320	.534	.550	.534	.050	2.035	2.450 (2.825)	L	49
7mm WSM	I	.284	.321	.538	.555	.535	.054	2.10	2.560 (2.860)	L	50
7mm Rem. Ultra Mag	I	.284	.322	.525	.550	.534	.050	2.85	3.450 (3.600)	L	52
.30 Long	B	.288	.288	UNK/NA	.288	.340	UNK/NA	.613	1.020	UNK/NA	498
.280 Jeffery (.33/280 Jeffery)	C	.288	.317	.504	.542	.538	UNK/NA	2.50	3.45	.217/59	407
7.62mm Russian Nagant Revolver	B	.295	.286	UNK/NA	.335	.388	UNK/NA	1.53	1.53	B	328
7.35mm Italian Carcano	C	.298	.323	.420	.445	.449	UNK/NA	2.01	2.98	B	380
.30 Remington	C	.307	.328	.402	.420	.421	.045	2.03	2.525	L	120
7.62mm Russian Tokarev	C	.307	.330	.370	.380	.390	UNK/NA	.97	1.35	B	328
.30 (7.65x21mm) Luger	C	.308	.322	.374	.388	.391	.045	.75	1.15	SPB	329
7.62 Micro-Whisper	C	.308	.328	.382	.389	.392	.045	.846	V	SP/SR	267
.30-30 Winchester	A	.308	.328	.402	.422 (.4215)	.502	.058	2.03 (2.039)	2.53	L	54
.30-30 Ackley Improved	A	.308	.328	.405	.422	.502	.058	2.04	2.54	L	210
.30-30 Wesson	A	.308	.329	.330	.380	.440	UNK/NA	1.66	2.50	L	119
7.63 Mini-Whisper	C	.308	.329	.375	.381	.385	.045	.985	V	SP/SR	268
.30 Herrett	A	.308	.329	.405	.421	.505	.058	1.61	2.01	L	209
.300 Whisper	C	.308	.330	.369	.375	.375	.041	1.50	2.575	S	268
.30-378 Weatherby Magnum	K	.308	.330	.560	.589	.603/.580	.060	2.90	3.865	L	69
7.63 (7.65) Mannlicher	D	.308	.331	UNK/NA	.332	.334	.030	.84	1.12	B	329
.30 (7.63mm) Mauser	C	.308	.332	.370	.381	.390	.045	.99	1.36	SPB	329
.30 USA Rimless	C	.308	.333	.417	.454	.456	.054	2.31	3.10	L	120
.308 CorBon	C	.308	.333	.532	.545	.532	.050	2.08	2.80	L	271
.303 Savage/.301 Savage	A	.308 (.311)	.334 (.3322)	.408 (.4135)	.439	.501	.058	2.0 (2.015)	2.52	L	122

CARTRIDGE	CASE TYPE	BULLET DIAMETER	NECK DIAMETER	SHOULDER DIAMETER	BASE DIAMETER	RIM DIAMETER	RIM THICKNESS	CASE LENGTH	CARTRIDGE LENGTH	PRIMER	PAGE
.30 Kurz	C	.308	.334	.443	.470	.473	.045	1.29	1.65	L	207
.300 AAC Blackout	C	.308	.334	.361	.375	.375	.045	1.368	1.78	S	55
7.5mm Schmidt-Rubin	C	.308	.334	.452	.494	.496	.058	2.18	3.05	B	383
.300 Winchester Magnum	E	.308	.334	.4891	.5126	.530	.046	2.60 (2.62)	3.30	L	68
.30 Carbine	D	.308	.335		.355	.360	.046	1.29	1.65	Bx/S	53/380
.309 JDJ	A	.308	.335	.453	.470	.514	.058	2.20	3.16	L	270
.30-06 JDJ	C	.308	.335	.455	.470	.467	.045	2.455	V	L	270
.307 GNR	A	.308	.336	.379	.380	.433	.055	1.55	2.0	S	269
.30-8mm Remington	E	.308	.337	.487	.511	.532	.047	2.85	3.65	L	67
.300 Weatherby Magnum	E	.308	.337	.495	.513 (.5117)	.530	.048	2.82 (2.825)	3.56	L	382
.30 Army (.30-40 Krag)	A	.308	.338	.415 (.419)	.457 (.4577)	.540	.059	2.31	3.10 (3.089)	Bx/L	58/382
7.62x51mm NATO (.308 Winchester)	C	.308	.338	.447	.466	.470	UNK/NA	2.01	2.75	Bx	382
.300 Blaser Magnum	I	.308	.338	.511	.544	.535	.054	2.56	3.30	L	470
.300 Belted Rimless Magnum	E	.308	.338	.447	.513	.530	UNK/NA	2.85	3.60	.217/60	408
.300 H&H Magnum	E	.308	.338	.447	.513	.530	.048	2.85	3.60	L	63
.308x1.5Inch	C	.308	.338	.450	.466	.470	.048	1.50	2.05	L	208
.30 Flanged Magnum (H&H Super .30)	A	.308	.338	.450	.517	.572	UNK/NA	2.93	3.69	UNK/NA	408
.300 Dakota	C	.308	.338	.531	.544	.544	.046	2.55	3.33	L	272
.300 Savage	C	.308	.339	.443 (.4466)	.470	.470	.045	1.87	2.62	L	55
.300 Pegasus	C	.308	.339	.566	.580	.580	.058	2.99	3.75	L	273
7.5x54mm French MAS	C	.308	.340	.441	.480	.482	.054	2.11	2.99	B	381
7.62x63mm U.S. (.30-06)	C	.308	.340	.441	.470	.473		2.49	3.34	Bx	383
.30-06 Springfield	C	.308	.340	.441	.470	.473	.045	2.49	3.34	L	62
.30-03 Government	C	.308	.340	.441	.470	.473	.045	2.54	3.34	L	120
.30-06 Ackley Improved	C	.308	.340	.454	.470	.473	.045	2.49	3.35	L	210
.30 Gibbs	C	.308	UNK/NA	UNK/NA	.440	.468	.045	UNK/NA	UNK/NA	UNK/NA	211
.308 Norma Magnum	E/C	.308	.340	.489	.514	.529	.048	2.56	3.30	L	470
.30-338 Winchester Magnum	E	.308	.340	.491	.513	.532	.048	2.50		L	211
.30 Remington AR	I	.308	.341	.488	.500	.492	.054	1.525	2.260	S	56
.300 Norma Magnum	C	.308	.341	.562	.585	.587	.059	2.50	3.68	L	471

CARTRIDGE	CASE TYPE	BULLET DIAMETER	NECK DIAMETER	SHOULDER DIAMETER	BASE DIAMETER	RIM DIAMETER	RIM THICKNESS	CASE LENGTH	CARTRIDGE LENGTH	PRIMER	PAGE
.300 Remington SAUM	I	.308	.344	.534	.550	.534	.050	2.015	2.450 (2.825)	L	64
.300 WSM	I	.308	.344	.538	.555	.535	.054 (2.860)	2.10	2.560	L	64
.30 Newton	C	.308	.340	.491	.523	.525	UNK/NA	2.52	3.35	L	121
7.82 Patriot	C	.308	.340	.557	.577	.577	.060	2.05	2.8	L	271
7.82 Warbird	C	.308	.340	.557	.577	.577	.060	2.80	3.60	L	274
.300 Canadian Magnum	I	.308	.342	.530	.544	.532	.046	2.83	3.60	L	273
.30R Blaser	A	.308	.343	.441	.480	.531	UNK/NA	2.68	3.80	UNK/NA	472
.30 TC (Thompson/Center)	C	.308	.344	.464	.470	.473	.054	1.92	2.645	L	61
.308 Marlin Express	A	.308	.344	.448	.463	.502	.049	1.910	2.585	L	60
.307 Winchester	G	.308	.344	.454	.470	.506	.059	2.02 (2.015)	2.60 (2.56)	L	59
.308 Winchester	C	.308	.344	.454	.470	.470	.049	2.01 (2.015)	2.75	L	61
.300 Ruger Compact Magnum (RCM)	C	.308	.344	.515	.532	.532	.040	2.1	2.825	L	65
.300 Remington Ultra Mag	I	.308	.344	.525	.550	.534	.050	2.085 (3.600)	3.450	L	68
.32-40 Remington	A	.309	.330	.358	.453	.535	UNK/NA	2.13	3.25	S	121
.32 Automatic Colt Pistol (ACP)	H	.309	.336	UNK/NA	.336	.354	.040	.68	1.03	SP	330
7.62X53Rmm (M43) Russian	C	.310	.340	.394	.443	.445	UNK/NA	1.52	2.20	B	385
7.62x39mm Soviet	C	.311	.340 (.337)	.344 (.396)	.438 (.433)	.440	.053	1.52 (1.528)	2.20	S	57/284
.303 British	A	.311	.337	.402	.458	.530	.062	2.21	3.05	B	69/385
.303 British	A	.311	.338	.401	.458	.530	.062	2.21 (2.222)	3.05 (3.075)	L	409
7.7mm Japanese Arisaka	C	.311	.338	.431	.472	.474	.042	2.28	3.13	B	386
.375/303 Westley Richards	A	.311	.343	.390	.457	.505	UNK/NA	2.50	3.36	UNK/NA	408
.32 Long Rifle	B	.312	.318	UNK/NA	.318	.377	UNK/NA	.937	1.223	UNK/NA	498
.32-20 Winchester	A	.312	.326	.338 (.3424)	.353	.405	.058	1.32 (1.315)	1 59	S	70
.32-20 Marlin	A	.312	.326	.338	.353	.405	UNK/NA	1.32	UNK/NA	S	122
.32-30 Remington	A	.312	.332	.357	.378	.437	UNK/NA	1.64	2.01	S	123
.32 H&R Magnum	B	.312	.333	UNK/NA	.333	.371	.050	1.08	1.35	SP	332
.32 S&W	B	.312	.334	UNK/NA	.335	.375	.045	.61	.92	SP	331
.32 S&W Long	B	.312	.335	UNK/NA	.335	.375	.048	.93	1.27	SP	331

CARTRIDGE	CASE TYPE	BULLET DIAMETER	NECK DIAMETER	SHOULDER DIAMETER	BASE DIAMETER	RIM DIAMETER	RIM THICKNESS	CASE LENGTH	CARTRIDGE LENGTH	PRIMER	PAGE
.32 NAA (North American Arms)	C	.312	.337	.373	.374	.374	.045	.680	.984	UNK/NA	333
.327 Federal Magnum	B	.312	.337	UNK/NA	.337	.371	.050	1.20	1.46	S	334
.327 Martin Meteor	A	.312	.396	.379	.379	.440	.060	1.50	1.77	S	212
.32-35 Stevens & Maynard	B	.312	.339	UNK/NA	.402	.503	UNK/NA	1.88	2.29	S	123
.303 Magnum	C	.312	.345	.462	.530	.557	UNK/NA	2.35	3.25	UNK/NA	409
.32 Short Colt	B	.313	.313	UNK/NA	.318	.374	.045	.63	1.00	SP	333
.32 Long Colt	B	.313	.313	UNK/NA	.318	.374	.045	.92	1.26	SP	333
.32 Colt	B	UNK/NA	.313	UNK/NA	.318	.374	.052	.755	1.26	SP	333
7.65x53mm Argentine Mauser	C	.313	.338	.429	.468	.470	.040	2.09	2.95	B	387
.32-40 Bullard	A	.315	.332	.413	.453	.510	UNK/NA	1.85	2.26	S	124
.32 Extra Long	B	.316	.317	UNK/NA	.318	.378	UNK/NA	1.150	1.570	UNK/NA	500
.32 Extra Short	B	.316	.318	UNK/NA	.317	.367	UNK/NA	.398	.645	UNK/NA	499
.32 Short	B	.316	.318	UNK/NA	.318	.377	UNK/NA	.575	.948	UNK/NA	4999
.32 Long	B	.316	.318	UNK/NA	.318	.377	UNK/NA	.791	1.215	UNK/NA	499
8x48Rmm Sauer	B	.316	.344	UNK/NA	.432	.500	.040	1.88	2.58	.254/1775/462A	472
8.15x46Rmm	A	.316	.346	.378	.421	.484	UNK/NA	1.82	2.28	.250/1794/455	472
.32 Long, CF*	B	.317	.318	UNK/NA	.321	.369	UNK/NA	.82	1.35	S	124
.32 Ballard Extra Long*	B	.317	.318	UNK/NA	.321	.369	UNK/NA	1.24	1.80	S	124
.320 Revolver	B	.317	.320	UNK/NA	.322	.350	UNK/NA	.62	.90	B	334
7.5mm Swiss Army Revolver	B	.317	.335	UNK/NA	.345	.407	UNK/NA	.89	1.29	B	335
8x57Rmm 360	A	.318	.333	.375	.427	.485	UNK/NA	2.24	2.96	UNK/NA	473
8x75mm/8x75Rmm	C/A	.318	.345	.411	.466	.467/.522	UNK/NA	2.94	3.50/3.51	.217/5603/514/ A514	474
8x57Jmm Mauser	C	.318	.350	.435	.470	.473	UNK/NA	2.24	3.17	L	473
.35 S&W Auto/.35 Automatic	D	.320	UNK/NA	UNK/NA	UNK/NA	UNK/NA	UNK/NA	UNK/NA	UNK/NA	UNK/NA	337
8mm Rast-Gasser	B	.320	.332	UNK/NA	.334	.376	UNK/NA	1.037	1.391	UNK/NA	335
.32-40 Ballard & Winchester	B	.320	.338	UNK/NA	.424	.506	.058	2.13	2.59	L	125
8mm Nambu	G	.320	.338	.388	.408	.413	UNK/NA	.86	1.25	B	336
.32 Winchester Self Loading (WSL)	H	.320	.343	UNK/NA	.346	.388	UNK/NA	1.28	1.88	S	125
.32 Remington	C	.320	.344	.396	.420	.421	.045	2.04	2.57	L	126
.32 Winchester Special	A	.321	.343	.396 (.4014)	.422 (.4219)	.506	.058	2.04	2.55 (2.565)	L	71

CARTRIDGE	CASE TYPE	BULLET DIAMETER	NECK DIAMETER	SHOULDER DIAMETER	BASE DIAMETER	RIM DIAMETER	RIM THICKNESS	CASE LENGTH	CARTRIDGE LENGTH	PRIMER	PAGE
8x50Rmm Siamese (Type 45)	A	.321	.347	.450	.480	.550	UNK/NA	1.98	2.97	B	388
8x52Rmm Siamese (Type 66)	A	.321	.347	.460	.500	.550	UNK/NA	2.04	2.96	B, Bx	388
8x58Rmm Sauer	B	.322	.345	UNK/NA	.438	.499	UNK/NA	2.28	3.00	.254/1775/462	474
.325 WSM	I	.323	.358	35381	.555	.535	.054	2.10	2.560	LR	73
8mm Remington Magnum	E	.323	.351 (.3541)	.485 (.4868)	.509 (.5126)	.530	.047	2.85	3.57 (3.600)	L	73
.32 Ideal	B	.323	.344	UNK/NA	.348	.411	UNK/NA	1.77	2.25	S	126
8x56mm Mannlicher-Schoenauer	C	.323	.347	.424	.465	.470	.045	2.21	3.04	.217/5603/528	475
8x50Rmm Lebel	A	.323	.347	.483	.536	.621	.068	1.98	2.75	B	390
8x64mmS Brenneke 8x65RmmS Brenneke	C/A	.323	.348	.424/.421	.468/.464	.469/.520	UNK/NA	2.51, 2.56	3.32/3.65	.217/5603/558/ 558A	477
8mm Lebel Revolver	B	.323	.350	UNK/NA	.384	.400	UNK/NA	1.07	1.44	B	336
8x60mmS Mauser & RWS /8x60RmmS Mauser & RWS	C	.323	.350	.431	.470	.468/.526	.050	2.365	3.11	.217/5603/542	477
8x57mmJS Mauser/ 8x57RmmJS Mauser	C/A	.323	.350	.435	.470	.473/.526	.043/.04 8	2.24/2.25	3.17/3.55	.217/5603/366D1	72/475
8mm-06	C	.323	.351	.441	.470	.473	.045	2.47	3.25	L	213
8x50Rmm Austrian Mannlicher	A	.323	.351	.462	.501	.553	.040	1.98	3.00	B	389
7.92x33mm Kurz	C	.323	.352	.440	.470	.470	UNK/NA	1.30	1.88	B	388
7.9x57mmJS (8mm Mauser JS)	C	.323	.353	.443	.469	.473	UNK/NA	2.24	3.17	B	390
8x68mmS RWS	C	.323	.354	.473	.522	.510	UNK/NA	2.65	3.38	.238/1698	478
8mm JDJ	A	.323	.356	.455	.470	.514	.058	2.22	V	L	275
8x63mm Swedish	C	.323	.356	.456	.488	.479	UNK/NA	2.48	3.36	B	391
.310 Cadet	B	.324	.320	UNK/NA	.353	.405	.035	1.12	1.72	.177/69	409
7.5mm Swedish Nagant Revolver	B	.325	.328	UNK/NA	.350	.406	UNK/NA	.89	1.35	B	337
8x59mm Breda	C	.326	.357	.433	.491	.469	UNK/NA	2.33	3.17	B	392
8x56Rmm Austrian-Hungarian Mannlicher (M31)	A	.329	UNK/NA	UNK/NA	UNK/NA	UNK/NA	UNK/NA	UNK/NA	UNK/NA	UNK/NA	392
8mm Roth Steyr	D	.329	.353	UNK/NA	.355	.356	UNK/NA	.74	1.14	B	337
.318 Rimless Nitro Express	C	.330	.358	.445	.465	.465	UNK/NA	2.39	3.40	.217/81	410
.333 Jeffery Flanged	A	.333	.356	.484	.544	.625	UNK/NA	2.50	3.49	.317	410
.333 Jeffery Rimless	C	.333	.359	.496	.540	.538	UNK/NA	2.48	3.48	.217/59	410
.338 Spectre	C	.338	.361	.415	.425	.420	.049	1.25	2.10	L	276

CARTRIDGE	CASE TYPE	BULLET DIAMETER	NECK DIAMETER	SHOULDER DIAMETER	BASE DIAMETER	RIM DIAMETER	RIM THICKNESS	CASE LENGTH	CARTRIDGE LENGTH	PRIMER	PAGE
.33 Winchester	A	.333	.365	.443	.508	.610	.065	2.11	2.80	L	127
.338 Whisper	C	.338	.360	.457	.463	.466	.048	1.47	V	S	275
.338 Woodswalker	A	.338	.360	.410	.420	.482	.060	1.86	2.51	L	281
.338-223 Straight	D	.338	.362	UNK/NA	.376	.378	.041	1.41	2.25	S	214
.338 JDJ	A	.338	.365	.453	.470	.514	.058	2.20	V	L	277
.340 Weatherby Magnum	E	.338	.366	.495	.513	.530	.048	2.82	3.60	L	77
.338 A-Square	K	.338	.367	.553	.582	.603/.580	.060	2.85	3.67	L	281
8.59 Galaxy	C	.338	.368	.557	.577	.577	.060	2.05	2.80	L	279
.338 Blaser Magnum	I	.338	.368	.512	.544	.535	.054	2.507	3.34	L	479
.338 Federal	C	.338	.369	.454	.470	.473	.049	2.01	2.75	LR	75
.33-08	C	.338	.369	.454	.470	.470	.049	2.015	2.82	L	213
.338 Winchester Magnum	E	.338	.369	.480 (.491)	.515 (.5127)	.530	.047	2.49 (2.50)	3.30 (3.34)	L	77
.338 Norma Magnum	C	.338	.369	.570	.585	.587	.059	2.50	3.68	.238/1698	479
.338-06 A-Square	C	.338	.370	.441	.470	.473	.049	2.494	3.240 (3.440)	L	76
.338 Lehigh	C	.338	.369	.4268	.439	.441	.053	1.40	2.26	S	276
.33 BSA (.33 Belted Rimless)	E	.338	.369	.453	.534	.534	UNK/NA	2.40	3.10	.217/59	411
.338 Canadian Magnum	I	.338	.369	.530	.544	.532	.046	2.83	3.60	L	380
8.59 Titan	C	.338	.369	.557	.577	.577	.060	2.80	3.60	L	382
.338-378 Weatherby Magnum	E	.338	.369	.561	.581	.579	.063	2.193	3.638	L	79
.338-06 JDJ	C	.338	.370	.455	.470	.467	.045	2.465	V	L	278
.338 Marlin Express	A	.338	.370	.493	.506	.553	.055	1.890	2.585	L	74
.338 Ruger Compact Magnum (RCM)	C	.338	.370	.515	.532	.532	.040	2.10	2.825	L	75
.338 GNR	A	.338	.370	.435	.463	.543	.075	2.545	3.20	L	278
.338 Lapua Magnum	C	.338	.370	.540	.590	.590	.060	2.72	3.60	L	78
.338 Remington Ultra Mag	I	.338	.371	.526	.550	.534	.050	2.76 (3.600)	3.450	L	78
.330 Dakota	C	.338	.371	.530	.544	.544	.045	2.57	3.32	L	279
.338 Excaliber	C	.338	.371	.566	.580	.580	.058	2.99	3.75	L	282
.338/50 Talbot	C	.338	.380	.748	.774	.782	.080	3.76	4.25	50 BMG	214
.348 Winchester	A	.348	.379 (.3757)	.485	.553	.610	.062	2.26 (2.255)	2.80 (2.795)	L	79
.35 Winchester Self Loading (WSL)	H	.351	.374	UNK/NA	.378	.405	.045	1.14	1.64	S	127

CARTRIDGE	CASE TYPE	BULLET DIAMETER	NECK DIAMETER	SHOULDER DIAMETER	BASE DIAMETER	RIM DIAMETER	RIM THICKNESS	CASE LENGTH	CARTRIDGE LENGTH	PRIMER	PAGE
.351 Winchester Self Loading (WSL)	H	.351	.374	.378	.407	1.38	.045	1.91	16	UNK/NA	128
9mm Ultra	D	.355	.374	UNK/NA	.386	.366	UNK/NA	.72	1.03	SPB	338
9mm Bayard Long	D	.355	.375	UNK/NA	.390	.392	UNK/NA	.91	1.32	B	340
9mm Browning Long	D	.355	.376	UNK/NA	.384	.404	UNK/NA	.80	1.10	B	339
9mm Mauser	D	.355	.376	UNK/NA	.389	.390	.050	.981	1.38	B	342
9mm Winchester Magnum	D	.355	.379	UNK/NA	.392	.394	.046	1.16	1.545	SP	343
9mm Glisenti	D	.355	.380	UNK/NA	.392	.393	UNK/NA	.75	1.15	B	339
9mm Luger (9x19mm Parabellum)	D	.355	.380	UNK/NA	.392	.393	.042	.754	1.16	SPB	341
9x21mm	D	.355	.380	UNK/NA	.392	.393	UNK/NA	.830	1.16	SP	339
9x23mm Winchester	D	.355	.380	UNK/NA	.390	.392	.042	.900	1.245	LP	343
9mm Steyr	D	.355	.380	UNK/NA	.380	.381	UNK/NA	.90	1.30	B	340
9mm Federal	B	.355	.382	UNK/NA	.386	.435	UNK/NA	.754	1.163	SP	341
9x25 Dillon	C	.355	.382	.423	.423	.424	.050	.99	1.26	SP	215
9mm Action Express	I	.355	.390	.433	.435	.394	.045	.866	1.152	S	215
.380 Automatic (9mm Browning Short)	D	.356	.373	UNK/NA	.373	.374	.040	.68	.98	SP	344
9x56mm Mannlicher-Schoenauer	C	.356	.378	.408	.464	.464	UNK/NA	2.22	3.56	.217/5603/491E	480
9x57mm Mauser/ 9x57Rmm Mauser	C/A	.356	.380	.428/.424	.467	.468/.515	.045/.05 0	2.24	3.10/3.08	.217/5603/491/A491B	480
.38 Short Colt	D	.357	.357	UNK/NA	.378	.433	.055	.76	1.10	SP	345
.38 Casull	C	.357	UNK/NA	UNK/NA	.476	.476	.044	UNK/NA	1.17	UNK/NA	283
.357 Remington Maximum	B	.357	.375	UNK/NA	.375	.433	.055	1.59	1.97	SP	347
.38 Long Colt	B	.357	.377	UNK/NA	.378	.433	.055	1.03	1.32	SP	345
.357 S&W Magnum	B	.357	.379	UNK/NA	.379	.440	.055	1.29	1.51	SP	346
.38 Special	B	.357	.379	UNK/NA	.379	.440	.054	1.16	1.55	SP	345
.357 SIG	C	.357	.381	.424	.425	.424	UNK/NA	.865	1.140	SP	348
.357 Auto Magnum	C	.357	.382	.461	.470	.473	.048	1.298	1.60	LP	216
.356 GNR	A	.358	.360	.433	.434	.498	.054	1.250	UNK/NA	UNK/NA	284
.358 JDJ	A	.358	.362	.453	.470	.514	.058	.220	3.065	L	284
.357 Herrett	A	.358	.375	.405	.420	.505	.058	1.75	2.10	L	217
.400/360 Nitro Exp. (2¾-inch)	A	.358	.375	.437	.470	.590	UNK/NA	2.75	3.59	.241	412
.35/30-30 (.35-30)	A	.358	.378	.401	.422	.506	.058	2.04	2.55	L	217

CARTRIDGE	CASE TYPE	BULLET DIAMETER	NECK DIAMETER	SHOULDER DIAMETER	BASE DIAMETER	RIM DIAMETER	RIM THICKNESS	CASE LENGTH	CARTRIDGE LENGTH	PRIMER	PAGE
.35 Winchester	A	.358	.378	.412	.457	.539	UNK/NA	2.41	3.16	L	128
.400/350 Rigby	A	.358	.380	.415	.470	.520	UNK/NA	2.75	3.60	.241/34	411
.350 No. 2 Rigby	A	.358	.380	.415	.470	.520	.050	2.75	3.60	.241/34	412
.350 Rigby Magnum	C	.358	.380	.443	.519	.525	UNK/NA	2.75	3.60	.241/34	412
.38 Automatic & .38 Super Automatic	H	.358	.382	UNK/NA	.383	.405	.045	.90	1.28	SP	348
.358 BFG (1.625 Inch)	I	.358	.382	.539	.555	.535	.054	1.625	2.37	L	218
.35 Newton	C	.358	.383	.498	.523	.525	UNK/NA	2.52	3.35	L	129
.35 Gremlin	C	.358	.384	.427	.438	.440	.059	1.495	2.25	S	222
.35 Remington	C	.358	.384	.419 (.4259)	.458 (.4574)	.460	.046	1.92	2.52	L	80
.35 Indiana	C	.358	.384	.437	.458	.460	.046	1.80	2.70	L	219
.25 SuperMann	C	.358	.384	.437	.458	.460	.046	1.91	2.78	L	220
.358 Norma Magnum	E	.358	.384	.489	.508	.526	.048	2.52	3.22	L	481
.35-06 JDJ	C	.358	.385	.455	.470	.467	.045	2.445	V	L	285
.358 STA (Shooting Times Alaskan)	E	.358	.386	.502	.513	.532	.048	2.85	3.65	L	286
9.09 Eagle	C	.358	.387	.557	.577	.577	.060	2.05	2.80	L	286
.35 Whelen	C	.358	.388	.441	.470	.473	.045	2.50 (2.494)	3.34	L	83
.356 Winchester	G	.358	.388	.454	.4703	.508	.058	2.02 (2.015)	2.56	L	81
.358 Hoosier	C	.358	.388	.454	.470	.473	.048	1.80	2.70	L	221
.358 Winchester	C	.358	.388	.454	.4703	.473	.048	2.01 (2.015)	2.78	L	82
.350 Remington Magnum	E	.358	.388	.495	.5126	.532	.046	2.17	2.80	L	83
.35 Sambar	I	.358	UNK/NA	.538	.555	.535	.054	2.10	2.86	UNK/NA	221
.358/300 WSM	I	.358	.390	.538	.550	.534	.054	2.10	2.56	L	223
.358 UMT (Ultra Mag Towsley)	E	.358	.390	.525	.550	.534	.054	2.85	3.50	UNK/NA	223
.38 S&W/.38 Colt New Police	B	.359	.386	UNK/NA	.386	.433	.055	.78	1.20	SP	349
.35-30 Maynard (1882)	B	.359	.395	UNK/NA	.400	.494	UNK/NA	1.63	2.03	S	129
.35-40 Maynard (1873)	B	.360	.390		.400	.492		2.06	2.53	S	130
.35-40 Maynard (1882)	B	.360	.390	UNK/NA	.400	.492	UNK/NA	2.06	2.53	S	130
.360 No. 5 Rook	B	.362	.375	UNK/NA	.380	.432	UNK/NA	1.05	1.45	UNK/NA	413
9mm Russian Makarov	D	.363	.384	UNK/NA	.389	.396	UNK/NA	.71	.97	B	350

CARTRIDGE	CASE TYPE	BULLET DIAMETER	NECK DIAMETER	SHOULDER DIAMETER	BASE DIAMETER	RIM DIAMETER	RIM THICKNESS	CASE LENGTH	CARTRIDGE LENGTH	PRIMER	PAGE
.360 Nitro (2¼-inch)	B	.365	.384	UNK/NA	.430	.480	.040	2.25	2.80	.241/34	413
.360 Express (2¼-inch)	B	.365	.384	UNK/NA	.430	.480	.040	2.25	3.00	.241/34	413
9.3x80Rmm	B	.365	.386	UNK/NA	.430	.485	UNK/NA	3.14	3.50	.254/1775/ 77B	485
9.3x74Rmm	A	.365	.387	.414	.465	.524	.052	2.93	3.74	.217/5603/ 474A	483
9.3x62mm Mauser	C	.365	.388	.447	.473	.470	.044	2.42	3.29	.217/5603/ 474	84
9.3x57mm Mauser	C	.365	.389	.428	.468	.469	UNK/NA	2.24	3.23	.217/5603/ 491	482
9.3 Sisk	C	.366	.388	.486	.512	.532	.047	2.85	3.57	L	224
9.3mm JDJ	A	.366	.389	.455	.465	.506	.058	2.22	V	L	287
9.3 BS	E	.366	.390	.495	.5126	.532	.046	2.165	2.80	L	225
.366 DGW (David G. Walker)	C	.366	UNK/NA	UNK/NA	.589	.586	.058	UNK/NA	UNK/NA	UNK/NA	225
.370 Sako Magnum/7.3x66mm Sako	C	.366	.405	.450	.477	.470	.047	2.598	3.346	L	85
9.3x64mm Brenneke	C	.366	.395	.474	.507	.496	.051	2.52	3.37	L	482
.360 No. 2 Nitro Express	A	.367	.393	.517	.539	.631	.045	3.00	3.85	.254/40	414
.35-30 Maynard (1865)	B	.370	.397	UNK/NA	.408	.771/1.07	.037	1.53	1.98	Externally primed	130
.38-40 Remington Hepburn	B	.372	.395	UNK/NA	.454	.537	UNK/NA	1.77	2.32	S	131
.38 Short	B	.375	.376	UNK/NA	.376	.436	UNK/NA	.768	1.185	UNK/NA	500
.38 Long	B	.375	.376	UNK/NA	.376	.435	UNK/NA	.873	1.380	UNK/NA	500
.380 Short & Long Revolver	B	.375	.377	UNK/NA	.380	.426	.046	.70	1.10	SPB	350
.38 Long, CF*	B	.375	.378	UNK/NA	.379	.441	UNK/NA	1.03	1.45	S	131
.38 Ballard Extra Long*	B	.375	.378	UNK/NA	.379	.441	UNK/NA	1.63	2.06	S	131
.38 Extra Long	B	.375	.378	UNK/NA	.378	.435	UNK/NA	1.480	2.025	UNK/NA	500
.375 Whisper	C	.375	UNK/NA	UNK/NA	UNK/NA	UNK/NA	UNK/NA	UNK/NA	UNK/NA	UNK/NA	287
.375/454 JDJ Woodswalker	B	.375	UNK/NA	UNK/NA	UNK/NA	UNK/NA	UNK/NA	UNK/NA	UNK/NA	UNK/NA	288
.375 JDJ	A	.375	.396	.453	.470	.514	.058	2.20	3.13	L	288
.375 Flanged Nitro Express (2½-inch)	B	.375	.397	UNK/NA	.456	.523	UNK/NA	2.50	3.10	.217/34	414
.400/375 Belted Nitro Express (H&H)	E	.375	.397	.435	.470	.466	UNK/NA	2.50	3.00	.217	414
.376 Steyr	I	.375	.398	.472	.501	.494	.048	2.35	3.075	L	87
.369 Nitro Express (Purdey)	A	.375	.398	.475	.543	.616	UNK/NA	2.69	3.60	.254/40	415
.378 Weatherby Magnum	E	.375	.399	.560	.582	.579	.063	2.913	3.65	L	90

CARTRIDGE	CASE TYPE	BULLET DIAMETER	NECK DIAMETER	SHOULDER DIAMETER	BASE DIAMETER	RIM DIAMETER	RIM THICKNESS	CASE LENGTH	CARTRIDGE LENGTH	PRIMER	PAGE
.375 Winchester	B	.375	.400	UNK/NA	.415 (.4198)	.502	.063	2.02	2.56	L	86
.375 Rimless NE (9.5x57mm)	C	.375	.400	.460	.471	.473	.40	2.25	2.94	.217	415
9.5x57mm Mannlicher-Schoenauer/ 9.5x56mm Mannlicher-Schoenauer	C	.375	.400	.460	.471	.473	.040	2.25	2.94	.217/5603/ 531	483
.38-35 Stevens	B	.375	.402	UNK/NA	.403	.492	UNK/NA	1.62	2.43	S	132
.375 H&H Magnum	E	.375	.402	.440 (.4478)	.521	.530	.046	2.85	3.60	L	88
.375 Dakota	C	.375	.402	.529	.544	.544	.046	2.57	3.32	L	290
.375 Canadian Magnum	I	.375	.402	.530	.544	.532	.046	2.83	3.60	L	291
.375 Weatherby Magnum	E	.375	.402	.492	.512	.531	.051	2.85	3.540 (3.800)	L	89
.375 Whelen & Ackley Improved Whelen	C	.375	.403	.442/.455	.470	.473	.045	2.50	3.42	L	226
.375 Remington Ultra Mag	I	.375	.405	.525	.550	.534	.050	2.85	3.540 (3.600)	L	89
.378 Weatherby Magnum	K	.375	.399	.560	.582	.603/.579	.063	2.913	3.65	L	90
.375 Rimless Belted Magnum	E	.375	.404	.440	.464	.530	UNK/NA	2.85	3.60	.217/60	415
.375 Flanged Magnum	A	.375	.404	.450	.515	.572	UNK/NA	2.94	3.80	.217/40	415
9.53 Hellcat	C	.375	.404	.557	.577	.577	.060	2.05	2.80	L	289
9.53 Saturn	C	.375	.404	.557	.577	.577	.060	2.80	3.60	L	292
.375-06 JDJ	C	.375	.405	.457	.470	.467	.045	2.435	V	L	289
.375 Ruger	C	.375	.405	.515	.532	.532	.050	2.58	3.34	L	86
.375 Blaser Magnum	I	.375	.405	.507	.544	.535	.054	2.822	3.622	L	482
.375 A-Square	K	.375	.405	.551	.582	.603/.580	.060	2.85	3.65	L	292
.38-50 Maynard (1882)	B	.375	.415	UNK/NA	.421	.500	.069	1.97	2.38	S	132
.375 JRS Magnum	E	.375	.498	.485	.535	UNK/NA	.048	2.84	3.69	L	290
9.3x48Rmm	B	.376	.382	UNK/NA	.433	.492	UNK/NA	1.89	2.35	.254/1775/ 246	485
9.3x72Rmm	B	.376	.385	UNK/NA	.427	.482	UNK/NA	2.84	3.27	.254/1775/ 77D	485
9.3x70Rmm	B	.376	.387	UNK/NA	.427	.482	UNK/NA	2.75	3.45	.254/1775/ 77F	485
9.3x57Rmm	B	.376	.389	UNK/NA	.428	.486	UNK/NA	2.24	2.80	.254/1775/ 77E	485
.38-50 Remington Hepburn	B	.376	.392	UNK/NA	.454	.535	UNK/NA	2.23	3.07	S	133
.38-50 Ballard Everlasting	B	.376	.395	UNK/NA	.425	.502	UNK/NA	2.00	2.72	S	133

CARTRIDGE	CASE TYPE	BULLET DIAMETER	NECK DIAMETER	SHOULDER DIAMETER	BASE DIAMETER	RIM DIAMETER	RIM THICKNESS	CASE LENGTH	CARTRIDGE LENGTH	PRIMER	PAGE
.38-90 Winchester Express	A	.376	.395	.470	.477	.558	UNK/NA	3.25	3.70	L	134
.38-56 Winchester	A	.376	.403	.447	.506	.606	.065	2.10	2.50	L	133
.38-72 Winchester	A	.378	.397	.427	.461	.519	UNK/NA	2.58	3.16	L	134
.38-55 Winchester/.38-55 Ballard	B	.379	.392	.3938	.422	.506	.058	2.12 (2.085)	2.51	L	90
.41 Long Colt	B	.386/4 01	.404	UNK/NA	.405	.430	.052	1.13	1.39	SP	352
.40 S&W Auto	D	.400	.423	UNK/NA	.423	.424	.050	.850	1.135	SP	351
10mm Auto	D	.400	.423	UNK/NA	.423	.424	.050	.99	1.26	LP	351
.41 Short Colt	B	.401	.404	UNK/NA	.405	.430	.052	UNK/NA	UNK/NA	SP	352
.38-40 Winchester	A	.401	.416	.438 (.4543)	.465	.520	.058	1.30	1.59	LP	91
.400 CorBon	C	.401	.423	.469	.470	.471	.050	.898	1.20	LP	293
.40-44 Woodswalker	A	.401	.428	.455	.455	.510	.055	1.295	V	LP	293
.40-454 JDJ	A	.401	.428	.470	.470	.510	.055	1.395	V	LP	294
.40-70 Sharps (Straight)	B	.403	.420	UNK/NA	.453	.533	.078	2.50	3.18	L	137
.40-50 Sharps (Straight)	B	.403	.421	UNK/NA	.454	.554	.078	1 88	2.63	B1	135
.40-50 Sharps (Necked)	A	.403	.424	.489	.501	.580	UNK/NA	1.72	2.37	B1	135
.40-60 Marlin	B	.403	.425	UNK/NA	.504	.604	UNK/NA	2.11	2.55	S	136
.40-85 (.40-90) Ballard	B	.403	.425	UNK/NA	.477	.545	UNK/NA	2.94	3.81	S	138
.40-90 Sharps (Straight)	B	.403	.425	UNK/NA	.477	.546	UNK/NA	3.25	4.06	B1	138
.40-70 Sharps (Necked)	A	.403	.426	.500	.503	.595	UNK/NA	2.25	3.02	L	137
.40-110 Winchester Express	A	.403	.428	.485	.565	.651	UNK/NA	3.25	3.63	L	139
.40-63/.40-70 Ballard Everlasting	B	.403	.430	UNK/NA	.471	.555	UNK/NA	2.38	2.55	S	136
.40-90 Sharps (Necked)	A	.403	.435	.500	.506	.602	UNK/NA	2.63	3.44	B1	139
.40-60 Winchester	A	.404	.425	.445	.506	.630	UNK/NA	1.87	2.10	S	140
.41 Short	B	.405	.406	UNK/NA	.406	.468	UNK/NA	.467	.913	UNK/NA	501
.41 Long	B	.405	.407	UNK/NA	.407	.468	UNK/NA	.635	.985	UNK/NA	501
.40-70 Winchester	A	.405	.430	.496	.504	.604	UNK/NA	2.40	2.85	L	140
.450/400 Nitro Express (3¼-inch)	A	.405	.432	.502	.544	.615	.040	3.25	3.85	.254/40	417
.450 3¼-inch BPE	A	.405	.432	UNK/NA	UNK/NA	UNK/NA	UNK/NA	UNK/NA	UNK/NA	.254/40	421
.40-70 Remington	A	.405	.434	.500	.503	.595	UNK/NA	2.25	3.00	L	140
.400 Whelen	C	.405	.436	.462	.470	.473	.048	2.49	3.10	L	226

CARTRIDGE	CASE TYPE	BULLET DIAMETER	NECK DIAMETER	SHOULDER DIAMETER	BASE DIAMETER	RIM DIAMETER	RIM THICKNESS	CASE LENGTH	CARTRIDGE LENGTH	PRIMER	PAGE
.40-65 Winchester	B	.406	.423	UNK/NA	.504	.604	UNK/NA	2.10	2.48	L	141
.401 Winchester Self Loading (WSL)	H	.406	.428	UNK/NA	.429	.457	.055	1.50	2.00	L	142
.40-82 Winchester Center Fire (WCF)	A	.406	.428	.448	.502	.604	.060	2.40	2.77	L	141
.40-72 Winchester	B	.406	.431	UNK/NA	.460	.518	UNK/NA	2.60	3.15	L	141
.450/400 (2³/₈-inch)	A	.407	.427	.456	.545	.616	.035	2.38	2.95	UNK/NA	417
.40-90 Peabody "What Cheer"	A	.408	.433	.546	.586	.659	UNK/NA	2.00	3.37	B1	142
.41 Remington Magnum	B	.410	.432	UNK/NA	.433	.488	.054	1.28	1.58	LP	355
.41 Special	B	.410	.432	UNK/NA	.433	.488	.056	1.16	1.60	LP	227
.41 Action Express	J	.410	.434	UNK/NA	.435	.394	.045	.866	1.17	SP	353
.414 Super mag	B	.410	.434	UNK/NA	.435	.492	.059	1.61	1.965	L	354
.41 GNR	A	.410	.436	.458	.461	.514	.055	1.24	1.60	L	295
.410 GNR	A	.410	.439	.477	.480	.512	.055	1.349	1.69	L	295
.400 Jeffery Nitro Express (.450/400 3-inch)	A	.410	.434	.518	.545	.613	UNK/NA	3.00	3.75	.254/40	418
.408 Cheytac	C	.408	.438	.601	.637	.640	.065	3.04	4.307	LR	294
.411 Express	C	.411	UNK/NA	UNK/NA	.440	.468	.045	UNK/NA	UNK/NA	UNK/NA	296
.411 JDJ	A	.411	.425	.455	.465	.506	.058	2.235	V	L	296
.411 Hawk	C	.411	UNK/NA	UNK/NA	.440	.468	.045	UNK/NA	UNK/NA	UNK/NA	297
.405 Winchester	B	.412	.436	UNK/NA	.461	.543	.075	2.58	3.18	L	143
.40-90 Bullard	A	.413	.430	.551	.569	.622	UNK/NA	2.04	2.55	L	144
.40-75 Bullard	B	.413	.432	UNK/NA	.505	.606	UNK/NA	2.09	2.54	S	143
10.4mm Swiss Vetterli	A	.415	.437	.518	.540	.630	.055	1.60	2.20	B-RF	392
10.3x60Rmm Swiss	A	.415	.440	.498	.547	.619	UNK/NA	2.36	3.08	UNK/NA	485
.40-40 Maynard (1882)	B	.415	.450	UNK/NA	.456	.532	UNK/NA	1.78	2.32	S	144
.416 Aargaard	C	.416	.441	.492	.506	.496	.049	2.35	UNK/NA	LR	228
.416 Rigby	C	.416	.445 (.4461)	.539 (.5402)	.589	.586	.058	2.90	3.75	L	418
.416 JDJ	A	.416	.430	.455	.465	.506	.058	2.22	V	L	298
.416 Barnes	A	.416	.432	.484	.505	.608	.065	2.112	2.95	L	227
.416 UMT (Ultra Mag Towsley)	C	.416	.440	.525	.550	.534	.050	2.85	3.54	L	229
.416 Dakota	C	.416	.441	.527	.544	.544	.042	2.85	3.645	L	301
.416-06 JDJ	C	.416	.443	.455	.470	.467	.045	2.415	V	L	298

CARTRIDGE	CASE TYPE	BULLET DIAMETER	NECK DIAMETER	SHOULDER DIAMETER	BASE DIAMETER	RIM DIAMETER	RIM THICKNESS	CASE LENGTH	CARTRIDGE LENGTH	PRIMER	PAGE
.416 Weatherby Magnum	K	.416	.444	.561	.584	.603/.580	.062	2.915	3.75	L	93
.416 Ruger	C	.416	.445	.515	.532	.532	.050	2.58	3.24	L	92
.416 Rigby	C	.416	.445	.539	.589	.589	.062	2.90	3.72	Bx	94
10.57 Maverick	C	.416	.445	.557	.577	.577	.060	2.05	2.80	L	299
10.57 Meteor	C	.416	.445	.557	.577	.577	.060	2.80	3.62	L	302
.416 Rimmed	A	.416	.446	.549	.573	.665	.060	3.300	4.100	L	300
.416 BGA	C	.416	UNK/NA	UNK/NA	.504	.492	UNK/NA	UNK/NA	UNK/NA	UNK/NA	301
.416 Remington Magnum	E	.416	.447	.487	.509	.530	.046	2.85	3.60	L	93
.416 Taylor	E	.416	.447	.491	.513	.532	.048	2.50	3.34	L	299
.416 Hoffman	E	.416	.447	.491	.513	.532	.048	2.85	3.60	L	300
.416 SM²	B	.416	.447	.538	.555	.535	.054	2.072	3.75	L	229
.40-60 Maynard (1882)	B	.417	.448	UNK/NA	.454	.533	UNK/NA	2.20	2.75	S	145
.40-70 Maynard (1882)	B	.417	.450	UNK/NA	.451	.535	UNK/NA	2.42	2.88	B1	145
.44 Evans Long (.44-40 Straight)	B	.419	.434	UNK/NA	.449	.509	UNK/NA	1.54	2.00	L	146
.44 Evans Short	B	.419	.439	UNK/NA	.440	.513	UNK/NA	.99	1.44	S	145
10.75x73mm/.404 Rimless Nitro Express/.404 Jeffery	C	.421	.450	.520	.544	.537	.045	2.86	3.53	.217/555	485
10.4mm Italian Revolver	B	.422	.444	UNK/NA	.451	.505	UNK/NA	.89	1.25	B	355
.404 Jeffery (.404 Rimless Nitro Express)	C	.422	.450	.520	.544	.537	.045	2.87	3.53	.217/81	419
.425 Express	E	.423	.429	.490	.513	.532	.048	2.552	3.34	L	303
10.3x65Rmm Baenziger	B	.423	.431	UNK/NA	.462	.505	UNK/NA	2.56	3.15	UNK/NA	486
.44 Henry Center Fire Flat	B	.423	.443	UNK/NA	.445	.523	UNK/NA	.88	1.36	S	146
10.75x68mm Mauser	C	.424	.445	.470	.492	.488	UNK/NA	2.67	3.16	.217/5603/515A	486
.44 Game Getter/.44-40 Marlin/.44 Colt Lightning	A	.427	.443	.458	.471	.520	.065	1.31	Varies	L	147
.44-40 Winchester (.44 WCF)	A	.427/.429	.443	.4568	.471	.525	.058	1.31	1.92	LP	95
.44-40 Extra Long	A	.428	.442	.463	.468	.515	UNK/NA	1.58	1.96	S	147
.444 Marlin	B	.429	.453	.4549	.469	.514	.058	2.16 (2.225)	2.57	L	95
.44 S&W Russian	B	.429	.457	UNK/NA	.457	.515	.050	.97	1.43	LP	355
.44 Remington Magnum	B	.429	.457	UNK/NA	.457	.514	.055	1.29	1.61	LP	357
.44 S&W Special	B	.429	.457	UNK/NA	.457	.514	.055	1.16	1.62	LP	355

CARTRIDGE	CASE TYPE	BULLET DIAMETER	NECK DIAMETER	SHOULDER DIAMETER	BASE DIAMETER	RIM DIAMETER	RIM THICKNESS	CASE LENGTH	CARTRIDGE LENGTH	PRIMER	PAGE
.44 Auto Mag	D	.429	.457	UNK/NA	.470	.473	.048	1.298	1.620	LP	356
.440 CorBon	I	.429	.461	.529	.538	.510	.055	1.280	1.59	LP	303
.44/454 JDJ Woodswalker	B	.429	UNK/NA	UNK/NA	.480	.515	.055	UNK/NA	UNK/NA	UNK/NA	304
.458 SOCOM	I	.458	.452	.530	.538	.473	.048	1.575	2.015	UNK/NA	304
10.447mm Italian M/70	A	.430	.437	.517	.540	.634	.058	1.87	2.46	B	393
10.75x58Rmm Russian Berdan	A	.430	.449	.506	.567	.637	.080	2.24	2.95	B	393
.445 Super Magnum	B	.432	.456	UNK/NA	.457	.514	.055	1.60	1.985	LP	230
.425 Westley Richards	I	.435	.456	.540	.543	.467	UNK/NA	2.64	3.30	UNK/NA	419
.416 Barrett	C	.416	.460	.730	.803	.804	.083	3.273	4.563	Bx	302
.44 Long Center Fire (Ballard)*	B	.439	.440	UNK/NA	.441	.506	UNK/NA	1.09	1.65	S	147
.44 Extra Long Center Fire (Ballard)*	B	.439	.441	UNK/NA	.441	.506	UNK/NA	1.63	2.10	S	148
.44 Wesson Extra Long*	B	.440	.441	UNK/NA	.441	.510	UNK/NA	1.63	2.19	S	148
.44 Bull Dog	B	.440	.470	UNK/NA	.473	.503	UNK/NA	.57	.95	SPB	357
.44-90 Remington Special (Necked)	A	.442	.466	.504	.520	.628	.075	2.44	3.08	L	148
.44-95/.44-100 Peabody "What Cheer"	A	.443	.465	.550	.580	.670	UNK/NA	2.31	3.32	B1	149
.44-100 Wesson	B	.445	UNK/NA	UNK/NA	.515.520	.605.610	UNK/NA	3.38	3.85	L	151
.44-70 Maynard (1882)	B	.445	.466	UNK/NA	.499	.601	UNK/NA	2.21	2.87	B1	149
11mm French Gras 11x59Rmm Vickers	A	.445	.468	.531	.544	.667	.075	2.34	3.00	B	394
.44-100 Ballard	B	.445	.485	UNK/NA	.498	.605	.080	2.81	3.25	L	150
.44-75 Ballard Everlasting	B	.445	.487	UNK/NA	.497	.603	UNK/NA	2.50	3.00	B2	150
.44 Short	B	.446	.445	UNK/NA	.445	.519	.066	.688	1.190	UNK/NA	502
.44 Henry Flat	B	.446	.445	UNK/NA	.446	.519	.066	.875	1.345	UNK/NA	502
.44 Extra Long	B	.446	.456	UNK/NA	.457	.524	UNK/NA	1.250	1.843	UNK/NA	502
11.15x60Rmm (.43) Mauser	A	.446	.465	.510	.516	.586	.075	2.37	3.00	B	394
.44-77 Sharps & Remington	A	.446	.467	.502	.516	.625	UNK/NA	2.25	3.05	LB1	151
.44-90 Sharps Necked	A	.446	.468	.504	.517	.625	.065	2.63	3.30	B1	152
.44-60 Sharps & Remington (Necked)	A	.447	.464	.502	.515	.630	UNK/NA	1.88	2.55	LB1	152
.44-60 Winchester & Peabody "Creedmoor"	A	.447	.464	.502	.518	.628	UNK/NA	1.89	2.56	B1	153
.45 Remington Thompson	D	.447	.470	UNK/NA	.472	.471	.044	1.12	1.45	LP	397

CARTRIDGE	CASE TYPE	BULLET DIAMETER	NECK DIAMETER	SHOULDER DIAMETER	BASE DIAMETER	RIM DIAMETER	RIM THICKNESS	CASE LENGTH	CARTRIDGE LENGTH	PRIMER	PAGE
11.43mm Turkish/ .45 Peabody-Martini	A	.447	.474	.560	.582	.668	UNK/NA	2.30	3.12	B	395
.45 Wildey Magnum	C	.450	UNK/NA	UNK/NA	.500	.473	.048	1.295	1.58	L	232
.44 Long	B	.451	.455	UNK/NA	.458	.525	UNK/NA	1.094	1.842	UNK/NA	503
.45 Winchester Magnum	D	.451	.475	UNK/NA	.477	.481	.045	1.198	1.55	LP	358
.460 Rowland	D	.451	.476	UNK/NA	.476	.476	.044	.955	1.27	LP	258
.45 GAP (Glock Automatic Pistol)	D	.452	.473	UNK/NA	.476	.470	.049	.760	1.137	LP	360
.45 Webley	B	.452	.471	UNK/NA	.471	.504	UNK/NA	.82	1.15	LPB	359
.45 Auto-Rim	B	.452	.472	UNK/NA	.476	.516	.085	.898	1.28	LP	359
.45 Automatic Short/.45 HP	D	.452	.476	UNK/NA	.476	.476	.044	.860	1.17	LP	360
.45 Automatic Colt Pistol (ACP)	D	.452	.476	UNK/NA	.476	.476	.044	.898	1.17	LP	361
.454 Casull	B	.452	.476	UNK/NA	.480	.512	.055	1.39	1.70	S	362
.460 S&W	B	.452	.478	UNK/NA	.478	.520	.059	1.80	2.290	LP	362
11.5x57Rmm (.43) Spanish Reformado	B	.454	.466	UNK/NA	.525	.631	UNK/NA	2.26	3.06	B	395
.455 Webley Revolver MkII	B	.454	.476	UNK/NA	.480	.535	UNK/NA	.77	1.23	LPB	363
.45 Colt	B	.454	.476	UNK/NA	.480	.512	.055	1.29	1.60	LP	365
.45 S&W Schofield	B	.454	.478	UNK/NA	.478	.522	.055	1.10	1.43	LP	364
.45 Colt Government	B	.454	.478	UNK/NA	.478	.506	.055	1.10	1.44	LP	363
.45-50 Peabody (Sporting)	A	.454	.478	.508	.516	.634	UNK/NA	1.54	2.08	UNK/NA	152
.45-75 Winchester (Centennial)	A	.454	.478	.547	.559	.616	UNK/NA	1.89	2.25	L	154
.45-60 Winchester	B	.454	.479	UNK/NA	.508	.629	UNK/NA	1.89	2.15(?)	L	153
.45-100 Ballard	B	.454	.487	UNK/NA	.498	.597	UNK/NA	2.81	3.25	L	154
.455 Webley Automatic	H	.455	.473	UNK/NA	.474	.500	UNK/NA	.93	1.23	B	366
.455 Enfield (.455 Colt)	B	.455	.473	UNK/NA	.478	.530	.035	.87	1.35	LPB	365
.577/450 Martini Henry	A	.455	.487	.628	.668	.746	.050	2.34	3.12	B	396
.46 Short	B	.456	.458	UNK/NA	.458	.530	UNK/NA	.836	1.336	UNK/NA	503
.45-75/.45-70 Sharps 2¹/₁₀-inch	B	.457	UNK/NA	UNK/NA	UNK/NA	UNK/NA	UNK/NA	2.10	2.90	L	155
.45-82/.45-85/.45-90 Winchester & .45-90 Winchester High Velocity	B	.457	.477	UNK/NA	.501	.597	.065	2.40	2.88	L	156
.45-70 Van Choate	B	.457	Same as .45-70	UNK/NA	UNK/NA	UNK/NA	UNK/NA	2.25	2.91	L	155
.45-70 Government	B	.458	.475 (.480)	.4813	.500	.600 (.608)	.065	2.105	2.55	L	96

CARTRIDGE	CASE TYPE	BULLET DIAMETER	NECK DIAMETER	SHOULDER DIAMETER	BASE DIAMETER	RIM DIAMETER	RIM THICKNESS	CASE LENGTH	CARTRIDGE LENGTH	PRIMER	PAGE
.450 Rigby	B	.458	.475	.539	.589	.589	UNK/NA	2.90	3.80	Bx	423
.45 Silhouette	B	.458	.477	UNK/NA	.501	.600	.065	1.51	1.97	L	231
.450 No. 2 Nitro Express (3½-inch)	A	.458	.477	.518	.564	.650	UNK/NA	3.50	4.42	.254/40	423
.458x2-inch American	F	.458	.478	UNK/NA	.508	.532	.048	2.00	2.60	L	233
.458 Winchester Magnum	F	.458	.478 (.4811)	.4825	.513	.532	.046	2.50	3.34	L	99
.450 Nitro Express (3¼-inch)	B	.458	.479	UNK/NA	.545	.624	.040	3.25	4.11	.254/40	421
.500/450 Nitro Express (3")	A	.458	.479	.500	.570	.644	UNK/NA	3.25	3.91	.254/40	422
.500/450 Magnum Express	A	.458	.479	.500	.570	.644	UNK/NA	3.25	3.91	.254/40	422
.450 Bushmaster	J	.458	.480	UNK/NA	.500	.473	.050	1.70	2.26	L	97
.457 WWG (Wild West Guns)	B	.458	.480	UNK/NA	.5039	.605	.070	2.21	2.49	L	99
.450 Marlin	F	.458	.480	UNK/NA	.511	.532	.047	2.09	2.55	L	98
.450 Alaskan	A	.458	.480	.515	.547	.605	.062	2.25	2.79	L	235
.450 Howell	C	.458	.480	.515	.545	.534	.045	2.5	3.25	L	235
.460 G&A Special	C	.458	.480	.530	.545	.545	.049	2.86	UNK/NA	L	237
.458 Lott	F	.458	.481	UNK/NA	.513	.532	.050	2.80	3.400 (3.600)	L	100
.450 Watts Magnum	F	.458	.481	UNK/NA	.513	.530	.048	2.85	3.65	L	236
.450 KNR	A	.458	UNK/NA	UNK/NA	UNK/NA	UNK/NA	UNK/NA	UNK/NA	UNK/NA	UNK/NA	236
.460 A-Square Short	K	.458	.484	.560	.582	.603/.580	.060	2.50	3.50	L	307
.458 Whisper	F	.458	.485	UNK/NA	.506	.525	.048	1.75	V	L	305
.460 Alliance	I	.458	.485	.530	.550	.534	.045	1.575	2.015	L	234
.458 Canadian Magnum	I	.458	.485	.530	.544	.532	.046	2.83	3.60	L	306
.450 Dakota	C	.458	.485	.560	.582	.580	.058	2.90	3.74	L	307
.460 Weatherby Magnum	K	.458	.485	.560	.584	.603/.580	.062	2.91	3.75	L	100
.450 Ackley Magnum	E	.458	.487	.503	.512	.532	.048	2.85	3.65	L	306
.450 Assegai	A	.458	.487	.549	.573	.665	.060	3.300	4.100	L	305
.450 Bonecrusher	A	.458	.488	.530	.535	.610	.060	1.40	1.77	L	234
.45-90/.45-100/.45-110 Sharps (2⁴/₁₀-inch, 2⁶/₁₀-inch, 2¾-inch)	B	.458	.489	UNK/NA	.500	.597	.065	2.40, 2.60, 2.75, 2.87	2.85, 3.00	B1	156
.45-120/.45-125 (3-inch) Sharps	B	.458	.490	UNK/NA	.506	.597	.065	3.25	4.16	L	157
.458x1½-inch Barnes	F	.458	.493	UNK/NA	.509	.530	UNK/NA	1.50	2.19	Bx	231
.460 Steyr (11.64mm)	C	.458	.501	.719	.805	.805	.089	3.64	4.80	Bx	487

CARTRIDGE	CASE TYPE	BULLET DIAMETER	NECK DIAMETER	SHOULDER DIAMETER	BASE DIAMETER	RIM DIAMETER	RIM THICKNESS	CASE LENGTH	CARTRIDGE LENGTH	PRIMER	PAGE
.46 Extra Long	B	.459	.457	UNK/NA	.457	.525	UNK/NA	1.534	2.285	UNK/NA	503
11.751Rmm Danish Remington	B	.462	.486	UNK/NA	.514	.579	UNK/NA	2.01	2.45	B	396
.56-46 Spencer	A	.465	.478	.555	.558	.641	UNK/NA	1.035	1.595	UNK/NA	504
.500/465 Nitro Express	A	.466	.488	.524	.573	.650	UNK/NA	3.25	3.89	.254/40	424
.465 H&H Magnum	E/C	.468	.494	.531	.582	.579	.063	2.894	3.55	L	423
.475 Ackley & OKH Magnum	F	.474	.496	UNK/NA	.508	.528	.048	2.739	3.518	L	238
.475 Linebaugh	B	.475	.495	UNK/NA	.501	.600	.065	1.50	1.77	L	308
.475 JDJ	B	.475	.497	UNK/NA	.502	.604	.065	2.10	V	L	309
.475 Wildey Magnum	I	.475	.497	UNK/NA	.500	.473	.048	1.295	1.58	L	238
.470 Capstick	F	.475	.499	UNK/NA	.513	.532	.048	2.85	3.65	L	309
.470 Nitro Express	A	.475	.500	.528	.572	.646	.035	3.25	4.00	.254/40	424
12.04 Bibamufu	C	.475	.500	.557	.577	.577	.060	2.80	3.62	L	310
.475 Lehigh	J	.475	.504	UNK/NA	.504	.480	.044	.950	1.17	LP	237
.480 Ruger	B	.475	.504	UNK/NA	.540	.540	.065	1.285	1.65	UNK/NA	366
.470 Nitro Express	A	.475	.504	.528 (.5322)	.5728	.655	.037	3.25	3.98	L	101
.476 Nitro Express (Westley Richards)	A	.476	.508	.530	.570	.643	UNK/NA	3.00	3.77	.254/40	425
.475 Nitro Express (3¼-inch)	B	.483	.502	UNK/NA	.545	.621	UNK/NA	3.25	4.00	.254/40	425
.475 No. 2 Nitro and Jeffery	A	.489	.510	.547	.576	.666	UNK/NA	3.50	4.33	.254/40	425
.500 Cyrus	L	.500	.528	.580	.582	.531	.058	2.333	2.90	L	239
.500 S&W	B	.500	.530	UNK/NA	.530	.560	.059	1.625	2.250	LP	368
.50 Action Express	J	.500	.540	UNK/NA	.547	.514	.055	1.285	1.610	LP	367
.500 Wyoming Express	F	.500	UNK/NA	UNK/NA	UNK/NA	UNK/NA	UNK/NA	1.37	1.765	LR	310
.510 GNR	B	.500	.514	.548	.550	.614	.070	1.19	UNK/NA	UNK/NA	311
.50 Beowulf	J	.500	.525	UNK/NA	.535	.445	.055	1.65	2.125	UNK/NA	311
.50 GI	J	.500	.526	UNK/NA	.526	.480	.048	.899	1.221	UNK/NA	312
.500 JRH	B	.500	.527	UNK/NA	.527	.545	.055	1.40	1.80	L	367
.505 Gibbs	C	.505	.530	.588	.635	.635	UNK/NA	3.15	3.85	.254/40	426
.577/500 No. 2 Express	A	.507	.538	.560	.641	.726	.055	2.83	3.40	.251/31A	426
.577/500 Nitro Express (3¹/₈-inch)	A	.508	.526	.585	.645	.717	.055	3.13	3.74	.251/31A	427
.50-90 Sharps	B	.509	.528	UNK/NA	.565	.663	.060	2.50	3.20	L	157
.50-140 (3¼") Sharps & Winchester	B	.509/.512	.528	UNK/NA	.565	.665	.060	3.25	3.94	L	158

CARTRIDGE	CASE TYPE	BULLET DIAMETER	NECK DIAMETER	SHOULDER DIAMETER	BASE DIAMETER	RIM DIAMETER	RIM THICKNESS	CASE LENGTH	CARTRIDGE LENGTH	PRIMER	PAGE
.500 Phantom	I	.500	.535	UNK/NA	.620	.532	UNK/NA	1.525	2.28	UNK/NA	312
.500 Express Nitro for Black (3-inch)	B	.510	.535	UNK/NA	.580	.660	.055	3.01	3.39	.251/31A	427
.500 Nitro Express (3¼-inch)	B	.510	.535	UNK/NA	.580	.660	.040	3.25	3.63	.251/31A	428
.500 Nitro (3")	B	.510	.535	UNK/NA	.580	.660	UNK/NA	3.00	3.80	.251/31A	428
.50 Remington Navy	B	.510	.535	UNK/NA	.562	.642	UNK/NA	.860	1.280	UNK/NA	504
.500 Jeffery	I	.510	.535	.615	.620	.575	UNK/NA	2.75	3.47	.254/40	428
12.50x70mm Schüler (.500 Jeffery)	I	.510	.535	.615	.620	.578	UNK/NA	2.94	3.50	.254/2703	488
.510 Nitro Express	B	.510	.535	UNK/NA	.565	.665	UNK/NA	3.245	4.185	L	241
.500 A-Square	K	.510	.536	.568	.582	.603/.580	.060	2.90	3.74	L	315
.50 Peacekeeper	K	.510	.538	.565	.586	.603/.580	.058	2.882	V	L	315
.50 TAC	I	.510	.538	.580	.582	.531	.058	2.333	3.75	L	239
.500 Linebaugh	B	.510	.540	UNK/NA	.553	.610	.062	1.405	1.755	L	313
.500 Belted Magnum	L	.510	.540	UNK/NA	.584	.603/.580	.062	2.50	3.25	L	240
.495 A-Square	L	.510	.542	UNK/NA	.582	.603/.580	.060	2.80	3.60	L	314
.500 Whisper	K	.510	.549	.563	.580	.603/.580	.060	2.90	V	L	313
.50 McMillan FatMac	C	.510	.550	1.111	1.152	1.158	.090	2.645	V	50 BMG	242
.50 McMurdo	C	.510	.554	.725	.800	.802	.078	3.70	5.722	50 BMG	241
.50 BMG (Browning Machine Gun)	C	.510 (.511)	.555 (.560)	.708 (.714)	.800 (.804)	.800 (.804)	.080	3.90 (3.91)	5.43 (5.545)	Bx/50 BMG	102/397
.50 American Eagle	I	.510	.560	.714	.804	.440	.053	UNK/NA	UNK/NA	UNK/NA	316
.50-100/.50-105/.50-110 Winchester/.50-110 Winchester High Velocity	B	.512	.534	UNK/NA	.551	.607	.063	2.40	2.75	L	159
.56-52 Spencer Rifle	B	.512	.540	UNK/NA	.559	.639	.065	1.035	1.500	UNK/NA	504
.56-50 Spencer	B	.512	.543	UNK/NA	.556	.639	.065	1.156	1.632	UNK/NA	504
.50-115 Bullard	G	.512	.547	.577	.585	.619	UNK/NA	2.19	2.56	L	158
.50-95 Winchester/Winchester Express	A	.513	.533	.553	.562	.627	UNK/NA	1.94	2.26	L	160
.50 U.S. Carbine	B	.515	.535	UNK/NA	.560	.660	UNK/NA	UNK/NA	UNK/NA	B1	160
.50-70 Government Musket	B	.515	.535	UNK/NA	.565	.660	.060	1.75	2.25	L	398
.50-70 Government	B	.515	.535	UNK/NA	.565	.660	.060	1.75	2.25	Bx	398
.56-52 Spencer (Necked)	A	.525	.547	.558	.560	.642	.065	1.020	1.660	UNK/NA	504
.505/530 Woodleigh	C	.530	UNK/NA	UNK/NA	UNK/NA	UNK/NA	UNK/NA	UNK/NA	UNK/NA	UNK/NA	242
.56-56 Spencer	B	.550	.560	UNK/NA	.560	.645	.065	.875	1.545	UNK/NA	505
.577 Snider (14.7mm)	B	.570	.602	UNK/NA	.660	.747	.052	2.00	2.45	B	399

CARTRIDGE	CASE TYPE	BULLET DIAMETER	NECK DIAMETER	SHOULDER DIAMETER	BASE DIAMETER	RIM DIAMETER	RIM THICKNESS	CASE LENGTH	CARTRIDGE LENGTH	PRIMER	PAGE
.577 Blackpowder Express (3¼-inch)	B	.584	.608	UNK/NA	.660	.748	.052	3.25	UNK/NA	.254/40	429
.577 Nitro Express (3-inch)	B	.584	.608	UNK/NA	.660	.748	.052	3.00	3.70	.254/40	429
.585 Nyati	I	.585	.605	.650	.660	.532/.586	UNK/NA	2.79	3.525	L	243
.577 Tyrannosaur	C	.585	.614	.673	.688	.688	.060	2.99	3.71	L	316
14.5 JDJ	C	.585	UNK/NA	UNK/NA	.804	.804	.080	UNK/NA	UNK/NA	UNK/NA	317
.58 Miller	B	.585	.620	UNK/NA	.628	.709	UNK/NA	1.193	1.701	UNK/NA	505
.58 Carbine (Berdan)	B	.589	.625	UNK/NA	.640	.740	UNK/NA	UNK/NA	UNK/NA	B2	161
.58 U.S. Musket (Berdan)	B	.589	.625	UNK/NA	.646	.740	.062	1.75	2.15	B1	161
.600/577 JDJ	B	.620	UNK/NA	UNK/NA	.660	.748	.052	UNK/NA	UNK/NA	UNK/NA	317
.600 Nitro Express	B	.620	.648	UNK/NA	.697	.805	UNK/NA	3.00	3.68	.254/40	430
.700 Nitro Express	B	.700	.728	UNK/NA	.780	.890	UNK/NA	3.50	4.20	Bx	430
.729 Jongmans	C	.727	UNK/NA	UNK/NA	.804	.804	.080	UNK/NA	UNK/NA	UNK/NA	244
.700 JDJ	C	.727	UNK/NA	UNK/NA	.804	.804	.080	UNK/NA	UNK/NA	UNK/NA	317
.950 JDJ	C	.950	UNK/NA	UNK/NA	UNK/NA	UNK/NA	UNK/NA	UNK/NA	4.0	UNK/NA	318

Key To Abbreviations

Notes: Bullet diameter can vary by several thousandths. The sizes listed are those that are most commonly encountered or are as specified in appropriate standards.

Cartridge length is not a particularly useful measure for identifying cartridges: This often varies widely, depending upon load type and bullet weight; it can vary between manufacturers; and it can vary with time, standard length from one era might not hold in another. An example is the 45-70 cartridge: 405gr. loads from the 1870s are about 2.625" long while current standards call for a maximum length of 2.55". Similar examples abound.

Case type: (For simplicity the various common rimmed/rimless pairs are listed together but with separate dimension, where variation occurs): A = Rimmed, bottleneck. B = Rimmed, straight. C = Rimless, bottleneck. D = Rimless, straight. E = Belted, bottleneck. F = Belted, straight. G = Semi-rimmed, bottleneck. H = Semi-rimmed, straight. I = Rebated, bottleneck. J = Rebated, straight. K = Rebated, belted bottleneck. L = Rebated, belted straight.

Primer type: S = Small rifle (.175"). SP = Small pistol. (.175"). L = Large rifle (.210"). LP = Large pistol (.210"). Bx = Boxer. B = Berdan type. B-1 = Berdan #1. B-2 = Berdan #2. 50 BMG = CCI-35/VihtaVuori-110/RWS-8212.

Note on blackpowder primers: Not all companies used the same primer type or size in the same caliber or length case. For example, the 45-70 or its equivalent was usually loaded with the standard Large Rifle-diameter primers. However, Marlin's version used Small Rifle-diameter primer and Sharps Co., ammunition used Berdan primers. Primer type and size listed is what appears to have been the most general (common?) size and type used.

Finally, earliest loadings for the military and possibly other cartridges used an internal primer and were not reloadable. This practice continued until about 1877, perhaps later with some manufacturers. In some instances the earliest outside primers were .250" in diameter. Some early 30-06 military loading also used a .250" primer. It is possible other oddball primer sizes might be encountered, for example, both the 38-40 and the 45 Automatic have sometimes been loaded with small-diameter Boxer primers. Likely this is true of the 44-40 and perhaps many other chamberings, too.

Notes on handgun primers: Magnum pistol cartridges are usually loaded with special Magnum primers and the 22 Remington Jet and 256 Winchester are sometimes loaded with Small Rifle primers. The 454 Casull is always loaded with Small Rifle primers. During WWI, Frankford Arsenal made 45 Automatic cases with special #70 primers of .204" diameter instead of the standard .210". Recently, at least one foreign manufacturer produced 45 Automatic ammunition using Small Pistol primers.

* Cartridges so marked used an outside lubricated bullet when originally introduced; these bullets were heel-based. The front was about the same diameter as the outside of the case neck (shell mouth) just like a modern 22 rim fire cartridge. Later, inside-lubricated loadings used an inside case mouth diameter bullet: these bullets usually had a long, hollow base intended to expand to fill the rifling while providing a cleaner-to-handle load. (This system was never particularly successful.)

V** Various versions exist, these differ chiefly in length of the case and loaded cartridges.

** Original 22-10-45 Maynard case length was 1.25".

*** This is a blackpowder primer smaller than standard Small Rifle or Pistol size. It has not been used or available for decades.

**** The 8x60mm, 8x60Rmm (dimensionally similar to the 8x60mm Mauser, except for the rim) and 8x64mm Brenneke, are dimensionally the same as "S" designated series, shown, excepting use of bullets of .318" diameter.

Other codes: Belt/Rim Diameter. Twist (standard factory) is given as inches per complete revolution, e.g., 12 means 1 turn in 12 inches of barrel, etc. 25.4mm, exactly, equals 1 inch. Unless otherwise noted, all dimensions are in inches. Data in parenthesis represents SAAMI maximum specifications. UNK/NA = Unknown/Not Applicable

ENTER TO WIN
NEW PRIZES BEING ADDED ALL THE TIME!

HIGH CALIBER
SWEEPSTAKES
www.GunDigest.com

ENTER ONLINE TO WIN! CHECK BACK OFTEN!

NO PURCHASE NECESSARY TO ENTER OR WIN.
Open only to legal residents of the United States and the District of Columbia age 18 years or older.
However, because of state regulations, this sweepstakes is not open to residents of Rhode Island.
All firearm transfers will be conducted in strict compliance with all applicable federal, state and local laws.
Limit: One online entry per person.